HUMAN DEVELOPMENT

EIGHTH EDITION

Grace J. Craig
University of Massachusetts

with

Don Baucum
University of Alabama at Birmingham

Prentice Hall ■ Upper Saddle River, New Jersey 07458

Library of Congress Cataloging-in-Publication Data

Craig, Grace J.
 Human development / Grace J. Craig with Don Baucum. —8th ed.
  p. cm.
 Includes bibliographical references and indexes.
 ISBN 0–13–922774–1
  1. Developmental psychology. I. Baucum, Don. II. Title.
 BF713.C7 1999
 155—dc21   98–28291
                                                                CIP

Editorial director: Charlyce Jones-Owen
Editor-in-chief: Nancy Roberts
Executive editor: Bill Webber
Acquisitions editor: Jennifer Gilliland
Editor-in-chief of development: Susanna Lesan
Development editor: Carolyn Smith
Assistant editor: Anita Castro
Editorial assistant: Kate Ramunda
AVP, Director of manufacturing and production:
Barbara Kittle
Senior managing editor: Bonnie Biller
Production liaison: Fran Russello
Editorial/production supervision: Bruce Hobart
(Pine Tree Composition)
Manufacturing manager: Nick Sklitsis
Prepress and manufacturing buyer: Tricia Kenny

Permissions editor: Jill Dougan
Copyeditor: Carolyn Ingalls
Creative design director: Leslie Osher
Interior designer: Diana McKnight, Joseph Rattan Design
Cover designer: Ximena Tamvakopoulos
Cover photos: Jonathan Levine/Tony Stone Images,
Laurence Monneret/Tony Stone Images,
Patrisha Thomson/Tony Stone Images, Chris Shinn/Tony
Stone Images, Ron Krisel/Tony Stone Images
Director, Image Resource Center: Lori Morris-Nantz
Photo research supervisor: Melinda Lee Reo
Image permission supervisor: Kay Dellosa
Photo researcher: Kathy Ringrose
Line art coordinator: Guy Ruggiero/Margret Van Arsdale
Illustrator: Asterisk Group, Inc.
Marketing manager: Michael Alread

This book was set in 10/12.5 Palatino by Pine Tree Composition, Inc. and was printed and bound by Courier Companies, Inc. The cover was printed by Phoenix Color Corp.

Quoted material on pp. 202–203 is from *Winnie-the-Pooh* by A. A. Milne, illustrated by E. H. Shepard. Copyright 1926 by E. P. Dutton, renewed 1954 by A. A. Milne. Used by permission of Dutton Children's Books, a division of Penguin Putnam Inc.
For permission to use copyrighted photos, grateful acknowledgment is made to the copyright holders on pages 673–674, which is hereby made part of this copyright page.

 ©1999, 1996, 1992, 1989, 1986, 1983, 1980, 1976 by Prentice-Hall, Inc.
Simon & Schuster/A Viacom Company
Upper Saddle River, New Jersey 07458

Printed in the United States of America
10 9 8 7 6 5 4 3 2 1

ISBN 0-13-922774-1

Prentice-Hall International (UK) Limited, *London*
Prentice-Hall of Australia Pty. Limited, *Sydney*
Prentice-Hall Canada Inc., *Toronto*
Prentice-Hall Hispanoamericana, S.A., *Mexico*
Prentice-Hall of India Private Limited, *New Delhi*
Prentice-Hall of Japan, Inc., *Tokyo*
Simon & Schuster Asia Pte. Ltd., *Singapore*
Editora Prentice-Hall do Brasil, Ltda., *Rio de Janeiro*

■■■■■■ Brief Contents

■■■■ Contents

PART TWO

CHILDHOOD

4 ■ INFANTS AND TODDLERS: PHYSICAL, COGNITIVE, AND LANGUAGE DEVELOPMENT

5 ■ INFANTS AND TODDLERS: PERSONALITY DEVELOPMENT AND SOCIALIZATION

6 ■ PRESCHOOL CHILDREN: PHYSICAL, COGNITIVE, AND LANGUAGE DEVELOPMENT

7 ■ PRESCHOOL CHILDREN: PERSONALITY DEVELOPMENT AND SOCIALIZATION

8 ■ MIDDLE CHILDHOOD AND ELEMENTARY SCHOOL CHILDREN: PHYSICAL AND COGNITIVE DEVELOPMENT

PART THREE

ADOLESCENCE

11 ■ ADOLESCENCE: PERSONALITY DEVELOPMENT AND SOCIALIZATION

PART FOUR

ADULTHOOD

---

13 ■ Young Adults: Personality Development and Socialization

14 ■ MIDDLE-AGED ADULTS: PHYSICAL AND COGNITIVE DEVELOPMENT

16 ■ OLDER ADULTS: PHYSICAL AND COGNITIVE DEVELOPMENT

18 ■ DEATH AND DYING

■

■■■■■ Preface

The story of a human life—in any cultural context—is a rich and compelling drama. The systematic study of human development in context is a challenge for students and researchers alike. *Human Development, Eighth Edition,* draws from many fields (developmental psychology, sociology, anthropology, history, nursing, medicine, and public health, to name a few), to provide an up-to-date presentation of the key topics, issues, and controversies in the study of lifespan development.

In this edition of *Human Development,* I have been joined by Don Baucum, writer and psychology professor, who draws on his own observations, his extensive teaching experience, and an engaging writing style to breathe life and voice into the narrative. Together, we have attempted to provide a sound, often thought-provoking survey of contemporary developmental research and theory as well as applications to everyday life. Because this field is so challenging, open-ended, and controversial, ample opportunities are included for students to consider a wide variety of perspectives and kinds of evidence. Students are encouraged to weigh the evidence against personal experience, and to develop an informed, critical perspective on how we come to be who and what we are as human beings and what each of us can expect in our years to come.

STUDENT DIVERSITY

Today's college students are more diverse than ever. Any single classroom may have a cross-section of students varying widely in age, ethnic background, personal experiences, and outlook. They also vary in academic background, career interests, and exposure to the social sciences. Each of these factors, and more, create "filters" through which they perceive human development and life in general. Many students of human development will pursue a future in fields related to human service, including social work, education, nursing, counseling, various areas of psychology, and program administration. Some are already coaches, counselors, tutors, or parents. Many will become parents at some future time. Most have some curiosity about their own childhood, adolescence, and current circumstances.

This text speaks to that diversity. *Human Development* presents people as they are in many cultural settings around the world. Rather than generalize from any one group of people, it makes a special effort to explain how developmental phenomena apply or relate to a wide range of peoples. The contemporary case studies and research efforts incorporated in the text reflect this variety. Hopefully, students will be able to find themselves in the pages of the text, regardless of their background; yet, at the same time, escape the confines of parochialism.

CHRONOLOGICAL ORGANIZATION

In the field of human development there is always the question of whether to organize developmental research and theory by topics, such as cognition, genetics, and moral development, or to present child and adult development as it happens, chronologically, emphasizing the holistic interrelationships. In *Human Development*, we have chosen to present child and adult development in each of the classic age divisions: the prenatal period, infancy, early childhood, middle childhood, adolescence, and early, middle, and later adulthood. With the exception of prenatal development, each age range includes two chapters: one on physical and cognitive development, one on social and personality development. Additional chapters focus on essential topics such as background and research methods in human development and death and dying. A central theme throughout is the complex interplay of biological and environmental factors in shaping human development. Consequently, there is a full chapter on heredity and environment near the beginning of the text. Here we define the contemporary issues around the processes of development in today's multicultural contexts.

SPECIAL FEATURES AND STUDY AIDS

Throughout this text, we have woven cultural diversity and personal relevance into the ongoing narrative. There are also special features to highlight this emphasis. There are three kinds of specialized boxes. *A Matter for Debate* explores controversies about human development and encourages thought and discussion. *Eye on Diversity* examines ethnic, racial, gender, and cross-cultural issues in development. Finally, *In Theory, In Fact* focuses on popular concepts about development that are sometimes supported by research and sometimes not.

In addition, each chapter begins with objectives for study, and each chapter section includes *Review & Apply* questions to firm up those objectives. Near the end of each chapter is a section called *Using What You've Learned*, which encourages students to apply the text material through exercises such as observing and interviewing people or researching an important topic. Each chapter also includes a detailed summary and an up-to-date list of suggested readings to further enhance learning. Finally, throughout each chapter, key issues are summarized in tables, figures, and study charts, and key terms are defined in the margins.

SUPPLEMENTS

In today's academic world, even the most comprehensive textbook is only one element in a larger teaching and learning package. The support materials for instructors and students are stronger than ever for the Eighth Edition.

Instructor's Resource Manual. The extensive Instructor's Resource Manual contains chapter outlines, lecture suggestions, and video cases linked to the new ABC News/Prentice Hall Video Libraries accompanying *Human Development*. The new IRM also boasts more student activities for both inside and outside the classroom, detailed teaching suggestions for using the rest of the ancillary package, and an updated list of video and film suggestions from outside suppliers.

Test Item File. The Test Item File for the Eighth Edition has been extensively revised and rewritten. The new edition contains multiple choice, fill in, short answer, and essay tests, and contains a greater number of conceptual and applied items.

Prentice Hall Computerized Testing. For Windows, Macintosh and DOS platforms. The questions in the Test Item File are available on all three platforms and allow instructors complete flexibility in building and editing their own customized tests. Advances in the most recent version of this software now allow instructors to load their tests onto the World Wide Web or a Local Area Network in an on-line testing format.

Study Guide. The Study Guide is designed with an attractive visual format that incorporates line drawings and illustrations from the textbook. Each chapter includes an outline, thought-provoking chapter-opening questions, learning objectives, detailed guided reviews, and multiple-choice tests with explanations of correct answers.

Color Transparencies for Lifespan Development, Series II. A set of more than 100 full-color transparencies has been created to accompany *Human Development*, featuring illustrations from within the text as well as from outside sources.

ABCNEWS

ABC News/Prentice Hall Video Libraries

Lifespan Development, 1996
Human Development, 1998
Two video libraries consisting of feature segments from award-winning programs such as *Nightline, 20/20, PrimeTime Live,* and *The Health Show* are available to qualified adopters of *Human Development, Eighth Edition.*

ACKNOWLEDGMENTS

As was true of previous editions, the Eighth Edition of *Human Development* reflects the contributions of many individuals: People of all ages that Don and I have met in classrooms, clinical encounters, and interviews; students and research assistants; colleagues, teachers, and mentors; family members and friends. Their experiences, ideas and insights are reflected in this text.

I would like to thank reviewers who read earlier drafts of the chapters of this text: Dorothy J. Shedlock, State University of New York, Oswego; Bradley J. Caskey, University of Wisconsin, River Falls; John S. Klein, Castleton State University, Frank R. Asbury, Valdosta State University; Rick Caulfield, University of Hawaii at Manoa; Sander M. Latts, University of Minnesota; Pamela Manners, Troy State University; Jack Thomas, Harding University.

Special thanks also go to my primary researcher, Albertina Navarro-Rios, for her steadfast and conscientious search for basic and applied research. She was consistently juggling several topics at once to keep pace with a demanding schedule. Thanks in no small part to her diligence, together with her insight and thoughtful suggestions, this edition reflects the newer research trends and the contemporary topics of debate.

At Prentice Hall, I would like to thank our principal editor, Jennifer Gilliland, who led the general planning and maintained faith in the final product. Our development editor, Carolyn Smith, performed minor miracles in the early stages of this edition, working with Don on forging a new, more accessible reading style. Her ideas, sense of humor, suggestions, and careful editing got this project off the ground and flowing. Our production editor, Bruce Hobart, deserves special thanks for his long hours of coordinating, juggling, and managing manuscript, artwork, photos, and page proofs, and keeping us all on schedule. For the attractive and student-friendly design and appearance of the text I am grateful to Diana McKnight and Leslie Osher, who created and managed the design, and Kathy Ringrose, who researched the photos. Finally, Fran Russello deserves special credit for untangling problems, smoothing rough spots, and pulling together the final stages of this project.

GJC

Perspectives and Research Methods

CHAPTER

1

CHAPTER OBJECTIVES

By the time you have finished this chapter, you should be able to do the following:

1. Define biological and experiential processes of development and explain how they interact.
2. Explain how historical, socioeconomic, and cultural factors influence our understanding of human development.
3. Use a historical perspective to discuss how attitudes toward children and adolescents have changed.
4. List and explain descriptive methods for gathering developmental data.
5. Contrast the personality theories of Freud and Erikson.
6. Contrast early behaviorism with contemporary cognitive psychology.
7. List and explain important considerations in developmental research.
8. Give the basic thinking behind Piaget's cognitive-developmental theory.
9. Discuss the ethical principles that researchers should follow when conducting developmental research.

Complex and rich, full of quest and challenge, human development is the product of many strands—the blending of the biological and the cultural, the intertwining of thought and feeling, the synthesis of inner stirrings and external pressures. By way of introduction, consider the following characterization of the human lifespan:

- A newborn child gasps to fill its lungs and then cries (or perhaps gurgles and sputters) to announce its arrival. Birth marks the beginning of an independent, individual life, although the journey actually began much earlier—at conception.
- Normally, infants form attachment bonds with those who care for them, and as their needs are met, they learn to trust the world.
- Toddlers touch, pull, push, and climb over, under, and through to discover how the world works and what their place is in it.
- A kindergartner uses the intricacies of language to command, inquire, persuade, tease, and attack—all in an effort to learn more about the world and the many different people in it.
- A group of neighborhood schoolchildren create rituals, customs, and rules for themselves—practices that mirror and sometimes mock adults.
- Adolescents struggle with choice and decision; they examine and assert what is important and meaningful in life.
- A young adult dreams and plans a lifestyle that he or she hopes will include a bold career, clever children, and a rewarding life both at work and at home.
- Middle-aged men and women reassess their life and try to juggle the demands of work with the often conflicting needs of their nearly grown children and their own aging parents.
- Older adults review the meaning of their experiences and accomplishments, wondering whether they have made the most of what came their way.
- Finally, for better or for worse, the life cycle ends.

Development begins with conception and continues throughout life; for reference, we somewhat arbitrarily assign stages to it (see Table 1–1). However, lifespan development takes as many different courses as there are people in the world. Every human being develops in a unique way, embedded in the **context** of his or her environment. We will reiterate the theme of context many times in the chapters to follow—family context, social context, cultural context, and others. Context emphasizes that development does not take place in a vacuum; in addition to being determined by biological processes basic to all normal humans, development is profoundly affected by the different worlds that the child and later the adult experience all along the way. That is, developmental changes over the lifespan "arise from a mixture of biological, psychological, social, historical, and evolutionary influences and their timing across the lives of individuals" (Featherman, 1983).

The goal of this text is to examine developmental trends, principles, and processes throughout the human lifespan and across many disciplines. We'll look at the human organism at each age and stage, with attention to the biological, anthropological, sociological, and psychological forces that influence development. We will pay special attention to human relationships, for they help define who we are and how we relate to the world around us. Whether sensitive and fragile, sturdy and supportive, stormy and anxious, or quietly comfortable and comforting, relationships exert a profound influence on development. We are, first and foremost, *social* creatures, and the complex developmental changes that occur over an individual's lifespan cannot be understood without viewing them in the context of historical events, individual experiences, and the social and cultural forces that define the times (Stoller & Gibson, 1994). At the same time, we must consider how each individual interprets and reacts to those forces, with a perspective that people actively participate in how their own development proceeds. People are not simply pawns in a game; we are the game itself. That's the basic framework we will use in considering human development. For practical reasons, we divide human growth and change during each stage into three major areas or domains: (1) physical growth and development, (2) cognitive development, including language, and (3) personality development and socialization. Also for practical reasons, beginning with Part Two we somewhat arbitrarily group physical and cognitive development together and discuss personality development and socialization

TABLE 1–1   THE HUMAN LIFESPAN

STAGE	AGES COVERED
Prenatal period	Conception to birth
Infancy	Birth to 18–24 months of age
Toddlerhood	12–15 months to 2–3 years of age
Preschool period	2 years to 6 years of age
Middle childhood	6 years to about 12 years of age
Adolescence	12 years to 18–21 years of age
Young adulthood	18–21 years to 40 years of age
Middle adulthood	40 years to 60–65 years of age
Older adulthood	60–65 years of age to death

context   The particular setting or situation in which development occurs; the "back drop" for development.

separately. Always bear in mind, however, in accordance with the **holistic approach** to development, that people are "whole" creatures, not at all compartmentalized.

KEY ISSUES IN HUMAN DEVELOPMENT

Development refers to the changes over time in the body and in the thinking or other behavior of a person that are due both to biology and to experience. That description sounds simple enough, but the questions that arise are virtually endless. What makes us tick? What causes us to change and become unique individuals? How much of who and what we are is "built in," and how much is a result of the things that happen to us along the way? How do those forces interact and help mold us? Also, how do we as individuals help determine our own development? And how do our relationships with **significant others,** the people who are important to us, influence what we become?

Perhaps even prehistoric members of the species Homo sapiens asked such questions in trying to understand themselves and their children. But as far as we know, they didn't *study* development, at least not scientifically. Stated simply, the scientific approach stresses that research must be conducted as objectively and systematically as possible and that theories must be both testable and verifiable. That approach also specifies procedures for achieving those goals. An understanding of the scientific approach is essential as a starting point in thinking critically about development.

In applying the scientific approach to human development or to any other aspect of human behavior, we identify two possible causes: Either human behavior is biological and essentially automatic (given the necessary conditions for it to occur), or it is a result of each individual's unique experiences. Everything we are, everything we think, feel, and do can be reduced to these two basic causes—which almost always interact to determine development.

This is not to say that science is the only way to look at things; it's simply what science *is*. Nor is science necessarily the best way to look at everything. But the scientific approach does have certain advantages, as we'll see.

HOW DEVELOPMENT WORKS

Some developmental processes, such as growth during the prenatal period or the onset of puberty, are primarily biological. Others depend mainly on experience. Acquiring the speech patterns and accents of the neighborhood you grow up in or learning a new language while in another country are examples of development influenced primarily by personal experience.

However, most development throughout the lifespan is a result of *interactions* between biology and experience. Most development cannot be neatly categorized as either biological or experiential; instead, it involves an ongoing, dynamic interplay between the two basic sets of causes. For example, perhaps you were born with a certain intellectual potential based on the specific nature of your central nervous system; that is, your biological makeup established a range within which your intelligence could fall. But how intelligent you actually are today is also a function of your childhood experiences at home and at school, along with many other experiential factors. Perhaps you were born with certain personality tendencies such as shyness or gregariousness. Your present personality, however, is also a function of your interactions with other

The first stage in the lifespan is prenatal development.

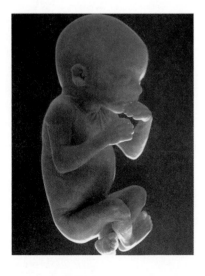

holistic approach   People are "whole" creatures, not at all compartmentalized.

development   The changes over time in the structure, thought, or behavior of a person as a result of both biological and environmental influences.

significant others   Anyone whose opinions an individual values highly.

people, the self-concept you began to develop in infancy, the social and cultural contexts you grew up in, and much more.

Thus, gone are the days when theorists focused on single aspects of development to the exclusion of everything else. Gone too are the days when arguments raged over whether aspects of cognition and personality are *either* a function of biology *or* a function of experience. Language, for example, clearly develops as a function of built-in capabilities interacting with experience: All normal human infants are "prewired" with the capacity for speech, and they spontaneously go through a sequence that includes making simple speech sounds and eventually babbling nonsense syllables. However, infants obviously must experience a particular language in order to produce their first words and simple sentences. Infants also spontaneously show emotions such as anger or distress, but they must eventually learn how to handle their emotions within their particular culture (Hebb, 1966).

The second stage in the lifespan is infancy.

We also see interaction in the relationship between inherited physical characteristics such as body type, skin color, or height, and a person's self-concept and social acceptance. Behavior may also be influenced by expectations based on stereotypes, such as that fat people are jolly, that adolescents are awkward, that tall people are leaders.

Theorists still disagree about *how much* a given characteristic or behavior is a result of biology versus experience. As we'll see, again using intelligence as an example, some theorists attribute intellectual ability to biology to the tune of as much as 75–80%. At the other extreme, some theorists believe that only 25% is biologically based. So the controversies of the past aren't entirely dead. Three closely related contexts in which debate continues are nature and nurture, heredity and environment, and maturation and learning.

NATURE AND NURTURE   The oldest way of contrasting what is built into people with what is acquired through experience is "nature" versus "nurture." In this context, *nature* means biology in a global and typically immutable sense, as in expressions like "human nature" or "it's in his or her nature." *Nurture* means experience, with emphasis on caregiving, socialization, and especially acculturation (acquiring and adapting to characteristics of the culture you live in). For example, a controversy once raged over whether children are born basically "good" or basically "evil." If children are born with tendencies to behave positively toward self and others, to share and cooperate and work for the common good, and so on, we must then explain aggressive, criminal, and other undesirable behaviors of some individuals as having somehow been acquired as a result of their experiences in childhood or beyond. Otherwise, we simply label those individuals as having been born "abnormal," an assertion that is circular and says nothing: Why are some children antisocial and bad? Because they're abnormal. How do we know they're abnormal? Because they're bad. Alternately, if we assume that children are born basically bad, socially acceptable behavior must somehow be a result of experience. The implications of either position are profound. We'll return to this topic later in the chapter.

The third stage in the lifespan is toddlerhood.

HEREDITY AND ENVIRONMENT   Nowadays the issue of biology versus experience is more often cast in the context of *heredity* and *environment*. The focus shifts: We look more specifically at genetic factors that might underlie and predispose and therefore set the stage for development, in interaction with specific effects of the individual's physical and social environment. Heredity-oriented theorists assume that there are underlying biological structures, citing evidence from experiments with animals and statistical procedures with

The fourth stage in the lifespan is the preschool period.

humans to support their case. They also point out that specific genes underlying development and behavior have been identified, emphasizing those that are known to cause defects such as mental retardation. On the other hand, environmental explanations focus on an individual's experiences pertaining to thinking and reasoning, plus environmental factors such as nutrition and health—each of which can also contribute to mental retardation. As noted earlier, nowadays each view acknowledges the other: Heredity and environment interact, but theorists still disagree over the relative contributions of each. The position that they take on this question determines the direction and nature of their research.

The intricate details of how heredity and environment determine development are the subject of Chapter 3.

MATURATION AND LEARNING When development is considered in terms of maturation and learning, the emphasis often shifts to *timing*. For example, how does skeletal/muscular development, which is biologically based, interact with practice, which is experiential? In particular, what kinds of practice, when they are practiced, and how often they are practiced result in optimal development of musculature and motor abilities? Similar questions arise in considering cognitive and personality development, in which neurological and hormonal maturation interact with experience. How might the onset of puberty, a biological process, be affected by the individual's experiences during childhood? Down the line, how is the biological event of menopause (cessation of menstrual periods due to hormonal changes) affected by a woman's lifestyle, if at all? What are the relative contributions of maturation and learning? Also, are there "critical" periods during which maturation and learning must interact to produce optimal development? Questions like these will arise at many points in later chapters.

ADDITIONAL QUESTIONS ABOUT DEVELOPMENT

Three other issues are important to gaining an overall perspective on development. In some respects, they overlap with those just discussed. The issues are stages versus continuity, critical versus sensitive periods, and active versus passive development.

STAGES VERSUS CONTINUITY IN DEVELOPMENT As development proceeds, do behaviors and capabilities build continually on each other, so that we gradually accumulate behaviors and skills and knowledge about the world around us? Or does development occur "stepwise" in **stages** that are qualitatively different, so that we achieve new ways of understanding our world abruptly?

Some developmental changes are clearly gradual and cumulative, resulting in steadily increasing organization and function. For example, an infant's motor development progresses from the random waving of arms and legs to purposeful reaching and grasping. Somewhat later, the ability to use symbols—especially words—develops gradually and progresses steadily toward reading, manipulation of number concepts, and eventually higher-level thinking.

In general, continuity in development throughout the lifespan is the prevailing view nowadays. However, some theorists stress stages of development, as we'll see later in this chapter and elsewhere. Notable among them are cognitive-developmental theorists, who view cognitive abilities as developing in discrete stages during which children see the world in qualitatively

stages Discrete periods often with abrupt transitions from one to the next.

different ways when compared with adults. To put it simply, children *think* differently than adults do, and there is good evidence for that observation.

In general, though, the truth seems to lie somewhere in between the extremes of gradual continuity and abrupt stages. There is little evidence that people make rapid, abrupt transitions from one stage to the next, even in theories that emphasize stages. Instead, to the extent that stages of development are meaningful, we move gradually from each stage to the next and often go back and forth between them.

CRITICAL VERSUS SENSITIVE PERIODS The question of how maturation interacts with learning naturally leads to a related question: Are there **critical periods** during which certain types of development *must* occur or else will *never* occur? Consider the effects of certain diseases during pregnancy (Chapter 2). If a pregnant woman who lacks immunity for rubella (German measles) is exposed to the virus about 2 months after conception, severe birth defects such as deafness or even miscarriage are likely. If, however, the same woman is exposed to rubella 6 months after conception, the virus won't affect her developing baby.

The fifth stage in the lifespan is middle childhood.

Another example comes from the animal world. There is a critical time span that occurs several hours after birth during which goslings become "bonded" to the mother goose simply by being in her presence; this process is known as *imprinting* (see Chapter 3). The goslings will not imprint before or after that critical period. Might there be a similar critical period during which human infants become emotionally attached to their caregivers? More generally, are there critical periods for acquiring certain types of skills and behaviors?

Theorists disagree. Whereas recent evidence indicates that early experiences have a decisive and permanent impact on the architecture of the brain and directly affect how the brain is "wired" (Shore, 1997; see also Ramey & Ramey, 1998), it's often more accurate to think in terms of **sensitive** or **optimal periods** during which certain types of learning and development occur best and most efficiently, but not exclusively. For example, if you acquire a second language during childhood, you have a much better chance of using it like a native speaker than if you acquire it after adolescence. Also, you will learn some aspects of the language more quickly and easily as a child than you will later in life. You *can* learn a second language at any time in your life, however; and with enough effort, you can learn to speak it almost like a native.

There clearly is such a thing as *readiness*, though, which refers to reaching a maturational point at which a specific behavior can be learned; before that maturational level is achieved, the behavior cannot be learned. Using walking as an example, no amount of special training will get a 3-month-old to walk without support; at that level of maturation, the infant simply lacks the necessary musculature and coordination.

The precise nature of the timing of human development is still not known. Just what periods are optimal for particular behaviors remain a major focus of research.

ACTIVE VERSUS PASSIVE DEVELOPMENT This last question is derived from philosophy, but it turns out to be a very practical issue in education as well as in everyday life. Especially while we're children, do we *actively* seek knowledge and understanding of our world, of morality, of values, or do we *passively* react to what we experience and what we are "taught"? Do we mold ourselves, or are we molded by others and by the physical environment?

Theorists who emphasize active development—often referred to as "organismic" theorists—argue that we are active participants in our own

critical period The only point in time when a particular environmental factor can have an effect.

sensitive or **optimal periods** The times during which certain types of learning and development occur best and most efficiently, but not exclusively.

development. Individuals seek to interact with other individuals as well as with events, and they are changed in the process. In turn, they act on those objects and events, and change them too, all while thinking about what they experience and trying to figure it out and understand it for themselves. Curiosity and the desire to acquire knowledge and understanding are central to development.

Theorists who view development more as a passive process—often referred to as "mechanistic" theorists—see humans as passively reacting to events in their environment. From this perspective, we are driven primarily by our internal drives and motivations in conjunction with the external incentives provided by others and the environment in general. Development is determined largely by rewards and punishments, which shape and mold us. Note that the use of the word *determine* here also implies that everything we know or do is a function of past or present conditions.

So which view is correct?

The best answer is that both are. Much of the time we actively approach the world in all its complexity, and we construct our own view of it to guide us, yet we often have little choice except to react to what the physical and social world serves up for us. In other words, our active human minds *interact* with the forces of society and nature, and that interaction determines what we do and what we become.

REVIEW & APPLY

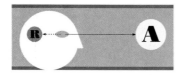

1. What is meant by the term *development*, and what roles do biological processes and experiential influences play in development?
2. Specifically, how do heredity and environment interact to influence development? And are heredity and environment all there are?
3. Which of the major developmental issues have been resolved, and which ones haven't? Why?

HISTORICAL AND CONTEMPORARY PERSPECTIVES ON DEVELOPMENT

As noted at the beginning of the chapter, in Western civilization, childhood is considered to last until about age 12. Then comes adolescence, which lasts to at least age 18, and then we become adults.

That arrangement wasn't always the case, however.

WHAT IS CHILDHOOD?

Historically, attitudes toward childhood have varied considerably. In the Middle Ages, children were viewed as infants until age 6 or 7. Children above age 7 or so were considered small adults and were treated to adult conversation, jokes, music, food, and other entertainment (Aries, 1962; Plumb, 1971). Medieval painters typically didn't distinguish between children and adults except for physical size. Clothing, hair styles, and activities were much the same for individuals of all ages.

By 1600, however, childhood was beginning to be considered a period of innocence, much as it is today, and parents began trying to protect children from the excesses and sins of the adult world. Children were seen less as

STUDY CHART ‣ KEY ISSUES IN HUMAN DEVELOPMENT

TOPIC	QUESTION
Nature and nurture	To what extent is development a result of inborn biological factors ("nature"), and to what extent is it a product of the individual's socialization ("nurture")?
Heredity and environment	To what extent do specific genetic factors set the stage for development, and to what extent do specific factors in the individual's environment such as conditioning and learning affect development?
Maturation and learning	How does maturation, which is biologically based, interact with learning, which is experiential, to shape development?
Stages versus continuity	Does development occur in stages that are qualitatively different, or does the individual gradually accumulate behaviors, skills, and knowledge in a continual process?
Critical versus sensitive periods	Are there critical periods during which certain types of development must occur or else will never occur?
Active versus passive development	Do individuals actively seek knowledge and self-understanding, or do they passively react to what they experience and are taught?

anonymous members of the clan or community and more as individuals within a family. By the eighteenth century, this attitude had gained broad support in the upper-middle classes, and children were given a status of their own (Aries, 1989; Gelis, 1989).

Although it appears that at least some accounts of children as "miniature adults" were exaggerated (Pollock, 1983, 1987; Elkind, 1986; Hanawalt, 1993), there is still no doubt that children were treated differently in the Middle Ages than they are now. This difference is especially clear when we note the advent of child labor laws and compulsory schooling in the late nineteenth century (Kett, 1977). No longer could children be sent into the adult world as soon as they were physically capable of working.

CHANGES IN CHILD-REARING PRACTICES As attitudes toward children changed, so did child-rearing practices. As a result, methods of discipline have varied throughout history. Harsh physical punishment was the rule in parts of ancient Greece, just as it was in nineteenth-century Europe and America. Terrorizing children with stories of ghosts and monsters was long a popular form of control (DeMause, 1974).

The twentieth century brought not only a shift toward more humane child-rearing practices, with legal protection for children's rights, but also the increased questioning of preconceptions about children and development. Child behaviors that were once viewed as dangerous or otherwise undesirable, such as thumb sucking and masturbation, are now generally accepted as normal. Rigid schedules for feeding, toilet training, and play have given way to concerns about the child's readiness (Wolfenstein, 1955).

Attitudes toward children vary across cultures as well. For example, researchers found that Japanese children up to 3 years of age sleep with their parents, grandparents, or siblings—never alone. This sleeping arrangement appears to have evolved as part of a socialization process that attempts to foster a close relationship between children and their parents, and reflects a culture that values collective harmony. In contrast, by age 3, American children

By the 18th century, children were seen as persons in their own right, with their own interests, as illustrated in John Singleton Copley's painting *Boy with Bow and Arrow.*

are likely to sleep alone in a separate room—a sleeping arrangement that promotes individuality and helps children adapt to a society that values independence (Nugent, 1994).

Attitudes toward childhood in different cultures may also vary according to the percentage of children (and adolescents) in the culture. Societies with more children, for example, might experience pressures to put children in the workforce early rather than to keep them in school. Figure 1–1 shows the percentages of the population under age 15 for selected countries.

WHAT IS ADOLESCENCE?

Although ancient documents, including those of the Greeks, Romans, and Chinese, refer to an intermediate period between childhood and adulthood, prolonged adolescence as a separate period of development is much more recent and is largely limited to industrialized nations. In the eighteenth, nineteenth,

FIGURE 1–1   PERCENT OF POPULATION UNDER AGE 15, SELECTED COUNTRIES

Source: Britannica Book of the Year, 1997.

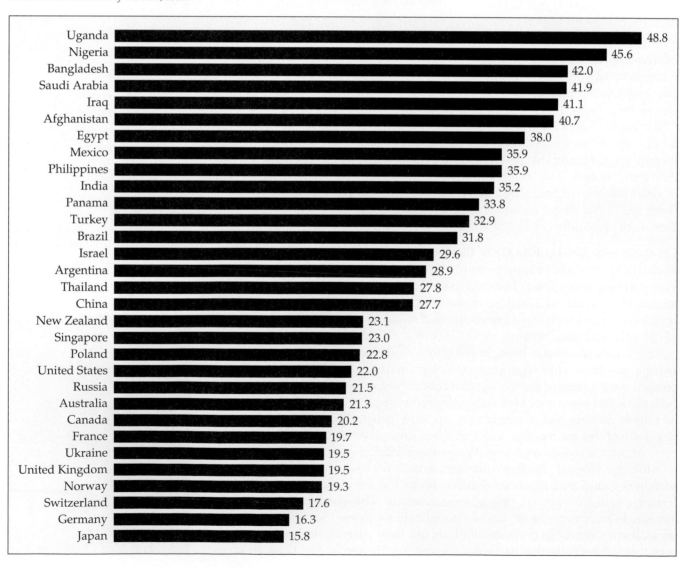

and early twentieth centuries, when unskilled labor was in great demand, youths who were capable of working became adults and quickly blended into adult life. After World War I, however, advancing technology and rapid social change made it necessary for young people to stay in school longer, thereby remaining financially and psychologically dependent on their parents. Thus, industrialization created adolescence as we know it today.

The modern view of adolescence as a separate period of dependence, rather than self-sufficiency, was noted by G. Stanley Hall as early as 1904. By midcentury, other theorists were drawing attention to this period (e.g., see Clark, 1957).

Adolescents are highly sensitive to the society around them—its unwritten rules, its values, its political and economic tensions. They form plans and expectations about their own future, and these expectations depend in part on the cultural and historical setting in which they live. For example, adolescents who spend their childhood in a period of economic expansion, when jobs are plentiful and family incomes high, expect to find similar conditions when they enter the job market. They expect their standard of living to be at least as high as that of their parents, and they may be unprepared to accept a lower standard of living if economic conditions worsen when they enter adulthood (Greene, 1990).

The sixth stage in the lifespan is adolescence.

Economic and cultural conditions can make adolescence a brutally short prelude to independence, or they can result in prolonged dependence on the family. In nineteenth-century Ireland, for example, potato famines caused widespread poverty and suffering. Young men stayed home because their labor was needed to help the family survive, and their progress toward adult independence was delayed. By contrast, in the United States, the Great Depression of the 1930s conferred unexpected responsibilities on young people—adolescents had to grow up as quickly as possible. Many young people took on adult tasks and entered the job market sooner than they would have otherwise.

Cultural and historical factors can be a major source of psychological stress during adolescence (see "Eye on Diversity," page 14). In the 1950s, for example, adolescents were likely to look to adults for answers to many of their questions about life and living. But when adolescents of the 1960s looked to authority figures, they found uncertainty and conflicting values, along with what they perceived as hypocrisy and self-interest. Many felt that the social order was breaking down, a situation that provided an impetus for drug use, sexual promiscuity, and "dropping out." Some never recovered even as adults, although many at least managed to profit from the experience and come through adolescence with a deeper understanding of themselves and their values.

Kenneth Keniston (1975) saw the problems of adolescents as arising from "tension between self and society"—a lack of correspondence between feelings about who they are and what society wants them to be. According to Keniston, adolescents feel ambivalent not only toward the social order but also toward themselves. They may feel that society is too rigid and confining and therefore try to break away by assuming temporary identities and roles.

In sum, researchers now realize that the social and historical context of development is as important to the outcome of adolescence as are individual differences (Jessor, 1993). Just as children do, adolescents come of age in a particular *cultural niche* that affects every aspect of their lives, from fads and fashion to economics and educational opportunity, leisure time, health, and nutrition. The cultural niche defines what adolescence is.

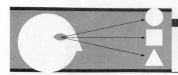

EYE ON DIVERSITY

WHEN WAR INTERRUPTS CHILDHOOD

What happens to a child's development when her life is interrupted by war? The published diaries of Zlata Filipovic, a Bosnian girl caught in the horror of her country's civil war, provide a painful glimpse of what it's like to grow up in the midst of bombings, death, and destruction (Filipovic, 1994). Despite Zlata's suffering, her diaries bear witness to the strength of her personality, spirit, and family unit. Indeed, research has shown that five factors interact to determine the amount of suffering a child experiences during war: the child's psychobiological makeup; the disruption of the family unit; the breakdown of the community; positive influences exerted by the culture; and the intensity, suddenness, and duration of the war experience (Elbedour et al., 1993).

Before the conflict among the Bosnians, Serbs, and Croatians catapulted her country into a wrenching civil war, Zlata lived the life of a normal preteenager in Sarajevo. She had good friends, loved popular music, excelled in school, and lived with her parents in a spacious apartment that was always filled with friends and relatives. Zlata's life changed in the spring of 1992, when Sarajevo became the target of an intense Serb attack. Over the next 2 years, Zlata witnessed the horrors of war at first hand and was transformed from an innocent child into a teenager who longed for peace. That transfor-

mation is chronicled on the pages of her diary—"Mimmy"—which is excerpted here:

Thursday, 5/7/92. Dear Mimmy, I was almost positive the war would stop, but today.... Today a shell fell on the park in front of my house, the park where I used to play and sit with my girlfriends. A lot of people were hurt. AND NINA IS DEAD. A piece of shrapnel lodged in her brain and she died. She was such a sweet, nice little girl. We went to kindergarten together, and we used to play together in the park. Is it possible I'll never see Nina again? Nina, an innocent 11-year-old little girl—the victim of a stupid war. I feel sad. I cry and wonder why? She didn't do anything. A disgusting war has destroyed a young child's life....

Monday, 6/29/92. Dear Mimmy, Boredom!!! Shooting!!! Shelling!!! People being killed!!! Despair!!! Hunger!!! Misery!!! Fear!!! That's my life! The life of an innocent 11-year-old schoolgirl!! A schoolgirl without a school, without the fun and excitement of school. A child without games, without friends, without the sun, without birds, without nature, without fruit, without chocolate or sweets, with just a little powdered milk. In short, a child without a childhood.

Monday, 8/2/93. Dear Mimmy, Some people compare me with Anne

Frank [the Dutch Jewish girl who was killed by the Nazis during World War II and who left a diary]. That frightens me, Mimmy. I don't want to suffer her fate.

Sunday, 10/17/93. Dear Mimmy, Yesterday our friends in the hills reminded us of their presence and that they are now in control and can kill, wound, destroy ... yesterday was a truly horrible day. Five hundred and ninety shells. From 4:30 in the morning on, throughout the day. Six dead and 56 wounded. That is yesterday's toll....

Sometimes I think it would be better if they kept shooting, so that we wouldn't find it so hard when it starts up again. This way, just as you relax, it starts up AGAIN. I am convinced now that it will never end. Because some people don't want it to, some evil people who hate children and ordinary folk. We haven't done anything. We're innocent. But helpless!

Although Zlata's childhood was scarred by war, the closeness of her parents may have contributed to her will to endure. Indeed, research has pointed to the importance of the adults in helping children process and cope with the horrors of war and in influencing their moral development during difficult periods (Garbarino, et al., 1991).

WHAT IS ADULTHOOD?

In industrialized nations, the adult years account for approximately three-quarters of the life span. We distinguish among three age periods: young adulthood (the 20s and 30s), middle adulthood (the 40s and 50s), and later adulthood (age 60 or 65 and up). Age guidelines, however, do not always reflect how a particular person sees herself or himself with respect to adulthood. Socioeconomic status, rural or urban setting, ethnic background, historical periods, wars, financial depression, and other life events strongly influence the definitions, expectations, and pressures of adulthood as well as those of childhood and adolescence.

For example, adults who do hard physical labor for their livelihood may reach their prime at age 30 and enter "old age" by the time they're 50. In contrast, professional people need to develop both mature analytic ability and self-confidence to reach their prime. Recognition and financial success may not come to them until they are in their 40s or early 50s, and their productivity may continue into their late 60s and beyond. Periods or stages in adulthood are also determined in part by socioeconomic status; the higher the person's social class, the more likely the person is to delay in moving from earlier stages to later ones (Neugarten & Moore, 1968).

Thus, the periods of young and middle adulthood are the most variable of any in the lifespan. In contrast, in later adulthood, most people will encounter the same social milestones such as retirement and the physical changes associated with advanced age.

DEVELOPMENT AND CHANGING FAMILIES

Attitudes about family size, structure, and function have also changed over the years. Until the 1920s, American families were large, usually including members from three or more generations. Grandparents, parents, and children frequently lived under the same roof and did the same kind of work. Children were expected to stay close to home because their parents needed help in running the family farm or store. Parents had many children, not only because they needed to provide more helping hands but also because so many children were killed by infectious diseases like strep throat and measles.

Today most children remain financially dependent on their parents until their mid-20s. The high cost of raising children to maturity, the widespread use of contraception, and the growing number of working women have resulted in smaller families. Children receive a great deal of individual attention in small families. Parents, in turn, make greater and more extended psychological investments in their children. To illustrate the latter point, Table 1–2 gives the percentages of young adults living at home or in college dormitories in the United States from 1960 to 1995.

The attitudes, values, and expectations of children are linked to how they are reared. Even in the same culture, different families can have very different approaches. For example, the child-rearing practices of dual-income families are clearly affected by their social circumstances and their beliefs and values

The seventh stage in the lifespan is young adulthood.

With the birth of a new baby, the roles of some of the siblings may change.

TABLE 1–2   YOUNG ADULTS LIVING AT HOME OR IN COLLEGE DORMITORIES, UNITED STATES, 1960–1995

| YEAR | MALE | | FEMALE | |
	NUMBER	PERCENT OF POPULATION	NUMBER	PERCENT OF POPULATION
1960	1,185,000	11	853,000	7
1970	1,129,000	9	829,000	7
1980	1,894,000	10	1,300,000	7
1985	2,685,000	13	1,661,000	8
1990	3,213,000	15	1,774,000	8
1995	3,166,000	15	1,759,000	8

Source: U.S. Census Bureau, 1997.

(Jordanova, 1989). If the mother of a large family works outside the home, older children often take care of their younger siblings. In such families children may learn many of their social roles, values, and competencies from other children rather than from their parents. The older children learn nurturant, responsible behavior, and the younger children tend to develop strong ties to their siblings and a sense of competence among their peers. Family bonds and affiliation usually become stronger (Werner, 1979). In contrast, children of wealthy parents are often cared for by nannies. Since these children have less contact with their parents and siblings, they may not develop strong family bonds (Coles, 1980).

Families develop their own identity and child-rearing patterns as a result of the historical period in which they exist, the cultural norms that shape them, and the developmental stages of their members. The function of the family changes to meet changes in social requirements—as does the family itself.

REVIEW & APPLY

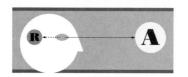

1. How have attitudes toward childhood changed over time?
2. How did attitudes toward adolescence change in the twentieth century?
3. How have attitudes toward families changed?

STUDYING HUMAN DEVELOPMENT: DESCRIPTIVE APPROACHES

Having taken a brief look at the nature of development and the major periods of human development, we now turn to *how* developmentalists know what they know, with emphasis on how they go about their work. Discussed first are approaches that primarily involve describing development, which is sometimes the goal in itself. At other times, descriptive approaches merge with experimental approaches, as discussed later. Along the way we'll also begin our coverage of major developmental theorists.

THE CASE-STUDY APPROACH AND PERSONALITY THEORIES

The now-legendary personality theorists of the early and mid-twentieth century used an approach known as the *case study*. A case study depends on much more than simple observations of development. Through a combination of interviews, observations, formal testing, and whatever other information can be obtained (such as interviews with parents and siblings), the researcher tries to obtain a complete picture of the individual. Often the individuals studied are famous people such as Nobel prizewinners or infamous people such as serial killers. Sometimes, too, case studies are used in studying uncommon psychiatric disorders; because of the small numbers of people who suffer from some disorders, other research approaches aren't feasible.

A good case study can be useful because of the intricate detail it provides. But that detail is also a shortcoming; the task of sorting out the detail and making sense of it can be very time-consuming. It is also difficult to determine what causes what. For example, physical or sexual abuse or other emotional trauma during early childhood is almost always found in the case histories of adults with multiple personality disorder (Frischholz, 1985). Does this finding necessarily mean that child abuse *causes* multiple personality? If a case can be made for one individual, does that instance necessarily generalize to all such individuals?

Case studies are infrequently used in modern developmental research. They do, however, remain important in clinical diagnosis and treatment, because they can provide a rich, descriptive picture of the changing and *whole* individual in an environmental context. Primarily using case studies, theorists have also formulated elaborate theories of human personality development and functioning. Two of the best known of those theories are outlined next.

An elderly Sigmund Freud with his daughter Anna. Anna Freud carried on the psychoanalytic tradition while broadening its emphasis upon the ego and defense mechanisms.

FREUD'S PSYCHOANALYTIC THEORY Sigmund Freud (1856–1939) used clinical case studies of his adult patients—along with recollections of his own childhood—in developing what came to be known as **psychoanalytic theory.** Over a period of more than 40 years, he refined his theory, which evolved into an extremely intricate view of human development and human nature. The basics of Freud's theory are covered here; we will consider the implications of psychoanalytic theory in later chapters.

In classic psychoanalytic theory, there are two developmental sequences, which overlap at points. The first sequence deals with the structure of personality and its basic components; the second involves stages during which personality development is affected in various ways.

From birth, according to Freud, the infant is dominated by the **id**—the primitive, selfish component of personality. That is, the id represents the "animal" within us, and it generates biologically based impulses or "instinctual wishes" that *must* be dealt with one way or another. The impulses have to do with things like obtaining food and water and other necessities of survival, as well as with sex and aggression (Freud viewed the latter as central forces around which most of personality is dynamically structured). The id operates according to the *pleasure principle*: It seeks immediate gratification and avoids pain. The id is also part of the much larger *unconscious mind* that Freud saw as governing most of our behavior without our direct awareness. For example, as toddlers (if not sooner), we are already accumulating unconscious fears, guilts, and conflicts that must be reckoned with throughout life.

As development proceeds, the **ego** gradually evolves from the id and eventually becomes a separate component of the personality. It serves as the id's "executive agent" for impulses. The ego is *conscious mind*, consisting of what we're aware of and thinking about at any given time, and it serves to negotiate between the id's impulses and external reality. If the id sends up an impulse for sex, for example, the ego must deal with it somehow—either by satisfying the impulse or by diverting it through *defense mechanisms* (discussed later in this chapter and in Chapter 7). The ego thus operates according to the *reality principle* and must continually reconcile impulses and other unconscious forces with the demands and constraints of society.

The **superego** begins to evolve from the ego during the preschool period. It consists of what we call *conscience*, in addition to what Freud called *ego ideal*: our images and beliefs regarding what we should be as persons. The superego can be said to operate according to the *morality principle*. It interacts dynamically with the id and the ego: If, for example, the id produces an impulse for sex and if the ego devises a way to gratify the impulse, the superego may intervene if it disapproves of what the ego proposes to do. How might the super-

psychoanalytic theory A theory based on the theories of Freud, whose view of human nature was deterministic. He believed that personality is motivated by innate biological drives.

id The primitive, hedonistic component of personality.

ego The conscious, reality-oriented component of personality.

superego The conscience component, which includes the ego ideal.

ego intervene? It might threaten and perhaps deliver liberal doses of shame and guilt.

With regard to personality as a whole, Freud's three components may develop with differing strengths: A person with a "strong" id and a "weak" superego, for example, has little in the way of moral and ethical controls on behavior. A person with an "overdeveloped" superego is constantly guilt-ridden and tentative about everything.

From a different perspective, development progresses through the **psychosexual stages** listed and described in Table 1–3. Here, however, the focus is on *erogenous zones* that shift over the first several years of development. An erogenous zone is an area of the body that produces intense gratification when stimulated. In the first stage—which corresponds to much of infancy—that area centers on the lips and mouth; hence, Freud called it the *oral stage*. Next comes the *anal stage*, in which the erogenous zone shifts to the region around the anus, and during which toilet training typically occurs. Then comes the *phallic stage*, in which the erogenous zone shifts to the genitals, where it remains for life. After that stage, according to Freud, there is a *latency period* during middle childhood when sexual urges become dormant; and finally the true *genital stage arrives*, which begins at puberty when sexual feelings again become prominent.

Freud had much less to say about the latter two stages; he spent most of his career working on the first three. Casual observation of children's behaviors during the oral, anal, and phallic stages do seem to correspond to what Freud emphasized. Infants do interact primarily by "mouthing" objects; toddlers do become concerned with eliminatory functions; and preschoolers do have at least a primitive sexuality in that they can become sexually aroused. Freud was the first theorist to draw attention to such aspects of behavior, although his explanations differed markedly from those that are widely accepted today.

Freud also proposed that *fixations* can occur during the psychosexual stages and can affect the personality for life. Fixations are "arrestments" in development that cause the adult to continue to seek gratifications in ways that are

psychosexual stages Freud's stages of personality development used on erogenous zones.

TABLE 1–3 FREUD'S PSYCHOSEXUAL STAGES

Oral: Birth to age 1 or $1\frac{1}{2}$. Infant derives pleasure and gratification primarily from stimulation of the mouth and lips.

> EXAMPLE FIXATION: *oral-incorporative*, in which the individual continues to derive important gratification from activities such as eating, drinking, and smoking.

Anal: Age 1 to 3. Child derives pleasure and gratification primarily from eliminatory functions.

> EXAMPLE FIXATIONS: *anal-retentive*, in which the individual's personality is characterized by stinginess and stubbornness, as well as by "emotional constipation" and difficulty expressing feelings; *anal-expulsive*, in which the individual has "emotional diarrhea" and can't keep thoughts and feelings in.

Phallic: Age 3 to 5 or 6. The erogenous zone shifts to the genitals and becomes sexual.

> MAJOR ISSUE TO BE RESOLVED: Oedipus or Electra complex.

Latency: Age 5 or 6 to 12. Sexual impulses are dormant.

Genital: Age 12 on. Primacy of sexual impulses returns with adolescence and puberty.

appropriate only for children. If, for example, a child is either overfed or underfed during infancy, the child might develop into an adult who excessively chews gum, smokes, drinks, or talks. However, although no one denies that early experiences can profoundly affect later personality, research over the many years since Freud formulated his theory has provided little, if any, support for the influence of fixations. You will still hear some of the terms in Table 1–3 used in everyday conversation, however.

Freud's dynamics of psychosexual development have been especially controversial, but they are worth exploring because they underscore some of the problems of the case-study method. On the basis of his patients' reports and his own childhood, Freud argued that all boys experience what he called the *Oedipus complex*—so named after the legendary Thebian king who killed his father, Laius, and unwittingly married his mother, Jocasta. Freud believed that during the phallic stage, the boy develops lustful desires for his mother, but then becomes afraid that his father will castrate him for those desires (*castration anxiety*). Eventually, however, he *identifies* with his father and tries to be as similar to him as possible, particularly with regard to moral principles. The idea is that the father won't castrate the boy if the boy is just like the father. The boy's superego thus develops as a result of the Oedipus complex.

The eighth stage in the lifespan is middle adulthood.

Girls, Freud proposed, experience the *Electra complex* during the phallic stage. This term also derives from Greek mythology: Electra plotted to kill her mother, Clytemnestra, for having killed her father, Agamemnon. In the Electra complex, the girl develops lustful desires for her father in conjunction with *penis envy*, which causes her to wish to possess her father's penis. Eventually she resolves the conflict symbolically either by identifying with the mother or through hoping to have a male child. But, according to Freud, penis envy isn't nearly the driving force that castration anxiety is, so that girls acquire much less in the way of moral principles and a personal ethic. In effect, women wind up with a weaker superego.

As you might imagine, subsequent research has not borne out the idea of Oedipus or Electra conflicts for preschoolers. But we'll defer the evidence to Chapter 7, where it will be discussed in the context of gender development.

In spite of its subjectivity and overemphasis on sexuality, classic psychoanalytic theory revolutionized the way we look at personality and motivation, thus setting the stage for more objective and accurate theories. Freud's lasting contributions include his idea of the unconscious mind, which—although not emphasized today—remains important. We aren't always aware of why we do things, and at least some of what we do is a result of needs and desires like those that Freud attributed to the id. Freud also originated the idea of ego defense mechanisms such as *denial* (refusing to face reality) and *rationalization* (talking yourself out of things you want when you can't have them), which are still accepted as ways in which our egos go about dealing with frustration and other unpleasant aspects of daily life.

Thus, Freud's theory is an excellent example of the need to be *eclectic* in studying theories of development and behavior in general: Take the good, take what works; don't throw out a theory in its entirety because some of the theory doesn't hold up.

As for Freud's view that our basic motives are exclusively selfish and in a sense "bad," see "A Matter for Debate" (page 20) for more on that view and on opposing views of human nature.

ERIKSON'S PSYCHOSOCIAL THEORY Erik Erikson (1904–1994) is called a *neo-Freudian* because his theory of personality development was derived from

A MATTER FOR DEBATE

ARE PEOPLE INHERENTLY GOOD, BAD, OR NEITHER?

The ultimate nature of man (and woman) is an age-old issue that appears in classic philosophical and religious writings alike, and it remains very much alive in modern times. Are people inherently good at the "core" of personality, with positive motives toward self and others? Are we inherently bad at the core, in the sense of being exclusively selfish and with propensities toward aggression and conquest? Or are we born essentially neutral in this respect? Think about your opinion of people in general, based on those whom you know and those whom you've read or heard about in the media, good and bad. How did these people come to be that way? Are the altruistic, humanity-oriented, good people in our world behaving that way naturally, or is their behavior a means to selfish ends? Are the bad people—the child molesters, the rapists, the serial killers—inherently good people who were severely warped by society somewhere along the way? Or are people the way they are entirely as a result of their rearing and life experiences, having started out neither good nor bad?

John Locke (1632–1704) was an English philosopher who argued that each person is born a tabula rasa, a Latin term meaning a "blank slate." This argument follows logically from the *empiricist* position that everything we know and everything we are comes about through experience via the senses. Therefore, nothing could be "built-in," beyond the basic biological processes that allow us to develop and function. Locke's view was elaborated in the twentieth century by John B. Watson (1878–1958). Watson was a strict behaviorist who repeatedly made statements to the effect that he could take any normal child and, given complete control over the child's environment, could turn that child into any kind of person he wished—skilled or unskilled, good or bad (e.g., see Watson, 1925). Thus, society is entirely responsible for who and what we will become. In accordance with the mechanistic position that we are passive and molded by the environment (page 10), we also don't have much say in the matter.

Meanwhile, another English empiricist, Thomas Hobbes (1588–1679), proposed that people are inherently selfish and in need of strict molding and ongoing control if they are to become cooperative members of society. A very similar position underlies Freud's psychoanlytic theory: At the core are selfish motives for survival, sex, and aggression; there is nothing positive or altruistic. These views are also highly consistent with the Christian doctrine of *original sin*, which holds that people have inherent tendencies to be self-serving and to trangress against others in the process. Daily functioning, then, requires that we work at keeping our dark inner drives and desires in check.

Finally, Jean Jacques Rousseau (1712–1778) took the opposing view, holding that people are born inherently good but are often corrupted by the "evils" of society. In a very similar vein, Abraham Maslow and Carl Rogers, the twentieth-century founders of *humanistic psychology* (discussed in Chapter 13), argued that our inner self is basically good, with positive motives toward both self and others. We actively seek personal growth and fulfillment, at the same time that we are concerned with love, belongingness, and the welfare of those around us.

Which view is correct? There is as yet no clear answer. While there is evidence that very young infants sense the distress of others and are disturbed by it (Hoffman, 1981), suggesting that empathy is inborn, it is evident that very young infants are keenly oriented toward gaining pleasure and avoiding pain first and foremost. It is also obvious that children must *learn* the specific morals and values of their social environment. Thus, whether we learn to be good members of society after starting out essentially bad, good, or neutral remains a matter for debate.

Freud's, but with a quite different emphasis. Erikson, who studied under Freud, devised a theory that didn't directly contradict psychoanalytic theory but placed much less emphasis on unconscious forces and much more on ego functions. Erikson focused mainly on the effects of social interactions in shaping personality; his approach is therefore termed **psychosocial theory.** Based on case studies and thoughtful observations of people in various cultures, Erikson's theory also differs from Freud's in that it covers the entire human lifespan instead of being limited to the early years.

psychosocial theory In Erikson's theory, the phases of development during which the individual's capacity for experience dictates major adjustments to the social environment and the self.

Erikson became disenchanted with psychoanalytic theory because he felt that it dealt only with extremes of behavior. Although he believed that development occurs in stages, the earlier ones corresponding to those Freud proposed, he emphasized the manner in which social "crises" or conflicts are resolved in each stage (see Table 1–4). This emphasis differs markedly from Freud's emphasis on psychosexual maturation as the primary determinant of personality development. Although Erikson agreed with Freud that early experiences are extremely significant, he saw personality development as a dynamic process that continues throughout life. Also, although he at least tacitly agreed with Freud that gratification of impulses and drives is a key force in life, he saw ego "synthesis" and the ordering and integration of experience as equally important.

The core concept of Erikson's theory is *ego identity*, a basic sense of who we are as individuals in terms of self-concept and self-image. A distinct part of each of us is based on the culture we grow up in, beginning with our interactions with caregivers during infancy and continuing with interactions with others outside the home as we grow and mature. Although Erikson's theory remains descriptive, it is less subjective than Freud's. In its emphasis on social interactions, it also suggests what parents and others might actually do in fostering good development—as well as what we might do for ourselves.

Regarding the eight stages in Table 1–4, Erikson proposed that each stage builds on what went before. Although the adjustments a person makes at each stage can be altered or reversed later, the preferable course of development is "positive" resolution at each stage. For example, children who are denied affection and attention in infancy can make up for that lack if they are given extra attention at later stages. But development proceeds more smoothly if children get what they need in infancy and start out with a good sense of trust in others and in the world around them. In addition, although each conflict is "critical" at only one stage, it is present throughout life. For example, autonomy needs are especially important to toddlers, but throughout life, people must continually test the degree of autonomy they can express in each new relationship.

OBJECTIVE METHODS OF GATHERING DEVELOPMENTAL DATA

Next we turn to more objective ways of studying development and behavior. Among these are systematic observation, questionnaires and surveys, and psychological testing. Correlation as a descriptive tool is also discussed.

SYSTEMATIC OBSERVATION   Depending on the setting in which the research takes place, there are two general approaches to observing and describing behavior: **naturalistic** or **field observation,** in which researchers go into everyday settings and observe and record behavior while being as unobtrusive as possible; and **laboratory observation,** in which researchers set up controlled situations designed to elicit the behavior of interest. One example of field observation is presented in "Eye on Diversity" on page 23. Here's another example, a hypothetical one. Suppose that researchers are interested in how children play together and share (or don't share) toys. After having videotaped the child at play and having carefully defined the behaviors of interest, observers would then independently record instances of the behaviors and check their results against those of their colleagues to eliminate any errors or subjectivity. In the end, the researchers would have an objective record of the target behavior as it naturally occurs, rather than of the behavior occurring under "artificial" conditions such as in a lab.

Or would they? Aside from practical problems (such as that the behaviors of interest might not always occur), there's the real possibility that the mere presence of an observer—especially one with a camera—changes things.

naturalistic or **field observation** The method in which researchers go into everyday settings and observe and record behavior while being as unobtrusive as possible.

laboratory observation   The method in which researchers set up controlled situations designed to elicit the behavior of interest.

TABLE 1–4 ERIKSON'S PSYCHOSOCIAL STAGES

1. *Trust versus mistrust* (birth to age 1 year): From their early caregiving, infants learn about the basic trustworthiness of their environment. If their needs are consistently met and if they receive attention and affection, they form a global impression of the world as a safe place. If, on the other hand, their world is inconsistent, painful, stressful, and threatening, they learn to expect more of the same and come to believe that life is unpredictable and untrustworthy.

2. *Autonomy versus shame and doubt* (age 1 to 3 years): Toddlers discover their own body and the way to control it. They explore feeding and dressing, toileting, and new ways of moving about. When they begin to succeed in doing things for themselves, they gain a sense of self-confidence and self-control. But if they continually fail and are punished or labeled as messy, sloppy, inadequate, or bad, they learn to feel shame and self-doubt.

3. *Initiative versus guilt* (age 3 to 6): Children explore the world beyond themselves. They discover how the world works and how they can affect it. For them, the world consists of both real and imaginary people and things. If their explorations and activities are generally effective, they learn to deal with things and people in a constructive way and to gain a sense of initiative. However, if they are severely criticized or overpunished, they instead learn to feel guilty for many of their own actions.

4. *Industry versus inferiority* (age 6 to 12): Children develop numerous skills and competencies in school, at home, and in the outside world. According to Erikson, a sense of self is enriched by the realistic development of such competencies. Comparison with peers is increasingly important. A negative evaluation of self compared with others is especially disruptive at this time.

5. *Ego identity versus ego diffusion* (age 12 to 18 or so): Before adolescence, children learn a number of different roles—student or friend, older sibling, athlete, musician, and the like. During adolescence, it becomes important to sort out and integrate those roles into a single, consistent identity. Adolescents seek basic values and attitudes that cut across their various roles. If they fail to form a central identity or cannot resolve a major conflict between two major roles with opposing value systems, the result is what Erikson calls *ego diffusion*.

6. *Intimacy versus isolation* (age 18 or so to 40): In late adolescence and young adulthood, the central developmental conflict is intimacy versus isolation. Intimacy involves more than sexual intimacy. It is an ability to share oneself with another person of either sex without fear of losing personal identity. Success in establishing intimacy is affected by the extent to which the five earlier conflicts have been resolved.

7. *Generativity versus self-absorption* (age 40 to 65): In adulthood, after the earlier conflicts have been partly resolved, men and women are free to direct their attention more fully to the assistance of others. Parents sometimes "find themselves" by helping their children. Individuals can direct their energies without conflict to the solution of social issues. But failure to resolve earlier conflicts often leads to a preoccupation with self in terms of health, psychological needs, comfort, and the like.

8. *Integrity versus despair* (age 65 and older): In the last stages of life, it is normal for individuals to look back over their lives and judge themselves. If, when looking back, we find that we're satisfied that our life has had meaning and involvement, the result is a sense of integrity. But if our life seems to have consisted of a series of misdirected efforts and lost chances, the result is a sense of despair.

Source: Adapted from Erikson's *Childhood and Society* (1963).

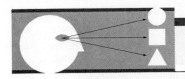

EYE ON DIVERSITY

A NATURALISTIC STUDY OF CHILDREN'S SOCIAL BEHAVIOR

David Day and colleagues (1979) used a naturalistic study of children's social behavior to evaluate what happens when children with special needs due to physical or mental disabilities are integrated with typical children in preschool classes. The children were observed while the teacher and teacher's aides were involved with them in activities such as block building, art, and story time.

The evaluation procedure began with the completion of a profile on each child. The profile included the number of siblings, birth order, and prior preschool experiences; the child's medical history; the child's family structure, including the parents' reasons for enrolling the child in the program; and the child's special needs, based on physical and/or intellectual disability, recorded or threatened abuse, and emotional stress. Various

developmental indexes, such as the results of developmental tests and psychologists' assessments, were also included.

Once the profiles were completed, the observation of the children started. Each child was observed several times during a 5-to-10-day period, during intervals of 30 seconds and at various points during the school day. After each set of observations, the children's behavior was coded on data sheets under the headings Task Involvement, Cooperation, Autonomy, Verbal Interaction, Use of Materials, Maintenance of Activity, and Consideration. Observations of staff members' behavior were noted as well.

The resulting data could be used to answer questions such as these: Do typical children pay attention to their task, or are they distracted by the children with special needs? Do the typical children finish the task? Do they show consideration for other children, both typical ones and those with special

needs? What is their verbal interaction like? Which disabilities interfere most with normal interactions?

The data from preliminary studies using this procedure contained some interesting findings. Some children with severe physical disabilities communicated fairly normally with other children, but children with minor speech problems often had considerable difficulty communicating. And typical children who had severely disabled classmates frequently showed increased consideration for others, with no reduction in verbal interaction and learning (Day, et al., 1979).

Much more remains to be assessed, but it seems that special-needs children benefit from the examples and help of their typical peers. Typical children also benefit from improved social skills and positive attitudes, with no loss of language and learning achievements (Turnbull & Turnbull, 1990).

Perhaps even young children will play differently when an adult is watching, and it isn't always possible or ethical to observe them without their knowledge. This situation becomes even more of a problem with older children and adults. There are additional problems with regard to ethics: What if one child starts hitting another child in a conflict over a toy? Can the observer intervene? If such difficulties can be resolved, however, naturalistic observation can be a very useful method that provides a rich body of information about what people do in real life.

In a laboratory setting, various techniques are used to elicit the behaviors under study, which can then be observed under highly controlled conditions. An example is the "strange situation" test devised by Mary Ainsworth (1973) to study the quality of infant-mother attachment (see Chapter 5). Each of several infants experiences the same events and in the same order: A stranger enters the room, the mother leaves and and returns, and the stranger leaves and returns. The observers record the infants' reactions from behind a one-way mirror. Contrast those conditions with what might happen if you tried to study such behaviors in haphazard field settings such as people's homes, where you might have to wait for quite some time to see what the infant does when a stranger happens along.

But do infants necessarily behave the same way in a laboratory setting as they do in their "natural" homes? They probably do in research environments such as the strange situation test, but this may not be the case with all

The ninth stage in the lifespan is older adulthood.

behaviors and across all age ranges. There is no way to be absolutely sure. Thus, there's always a trade-off between field and laboratory research, and each type has its advantages and disadvantages. When interpreting developmental research, the researcher always needs to consider the setting in which the research was conducted and to evaluate the findings accordingly.

QUESTIONNAIRES AND SURVEYS The "paper and pencil" method asks questions about past and present behavior. Obvious limitations are that the researcher gets only the information that the respondents are willing or able to report. On the positive side, however, surveys can include large numbers of people and can be scored by computer. Even with their limitations, surveys can therefore be very useful.

An example is the National Household Survey on Drug Abuse (NHSDA), discussed in Chapter 11. The NHSDA is a confidential questionnaire administered annually by a division of the U.S. Department of Health and Human Services to thousands of people (over 18,000 in 1996) age 12 and over, who live at home or in other noninstitutional settings. It is by far the best survey of its kind, providing much detail about drug users according to age, sex, race/ethnicity, educational level, and employment status with regard to commonly abused drugs. Yet the numbers tend to be on the low side. Because drug abuse is generally undesirable and largely illegal, some respondents who use or abuse drugs won't tell the truth no matter what assurances they're given as to confidentiality. A related problem, also characteristic of surveys in general, is that not all of the people who are selected to fill out the questionnaire agree to participate (typically about 20% refuse on the NHSDA), and as a consequence, more "nonusers" may be included in the results.

PSYCHOLOGICAL TESTING Intelligence testing is frequently used in developmental research. As we'll see later in more detail, the testing basically involves administering questions and problems that assess an individual's intelligence quotient (IQ)—an approximate measure of current intellectual functioning. Personality tests are also sometimes used in developmental contexts. Personality-related testing with children often takes the form of checklists filled out by parents or other caregivers. Word-association exercises and sentence-completion tests can be used directly with children. For example, children might be asked to complete a thought, such as "My father always. . . ."

"Projective" tests are sometimes employed as well: Children might be shown a series of ambiguous pictures and asked to interpret, react to, analyze, or arrange them so as to construct a story. It is assumed that the children will project their thoughts, attitudes, and feelings as they respond. For example, in one study, 4-year-olds participated in a game called the bears' picnic. The experimenter told a series of stories involving a family of teddy bears. The child was then handed one of the bears and invited to complete the story (Mueller & Tingley, 1990).

Three considerations should be kept in mind in interpreting findings based on psychological testing. First, tests should be *reliable*, meaning that they yield similar scores from one testing occasion to the next. Second, tests should have good *validity*, meaning that they actually measure what they are supposed to measure. And third, the best psychological tests are *standardized*, meaning that they have been administered to representative samples of people to establish *norms* to which an individual's responses can be compared. Standardization also includes the provision of instructions and procedures that allow the tests to be administered in the same way every time.

If a test isn't reliable, valid, and standardized, there is no good way to know what the resulting data mean. For that reason, the American Psychological Association requires that such information be included with standardized tests. Developmental researchers, in turn, tend to use tests that have been shown to be highly reliable and valid.

DEVELOPMENTAL RESEARCH DESIGNS

Because development is a dynamic and continuous process, developmental studies—in contrast to other types of research—often focus on change over time. How do researchers gather data about developmental change? There are three general approaches: The longitudinal design, the cross-sectional design, and the hybrid sequential-cohort design; these are illustrated in Figure 1–2.

THE LONGITUDINAL DESIGN   In a **longitudinal design,** one group of individuals is studied repeatedly at different points in the lifespan. For example, researchers track development in areas such as language acquisition, cognitive development, and physical skills. Or children can be followed into adulthood to see whether early personality characteristics persist.

Some developmental processes can be looked at very closely by studying individuals every week or even every day. For example, a group of 2- and 3-year-old children might be tested weekly to create a detailed picture of their language development. Longitudinal designs have also been applied to change over a period of many years. A prominent example is the classic study of "gifted" children that was initiated in 1921 by Lewis Terman and was still

longitudinal design   A study in which the same objects are observed continuously over a period of time.

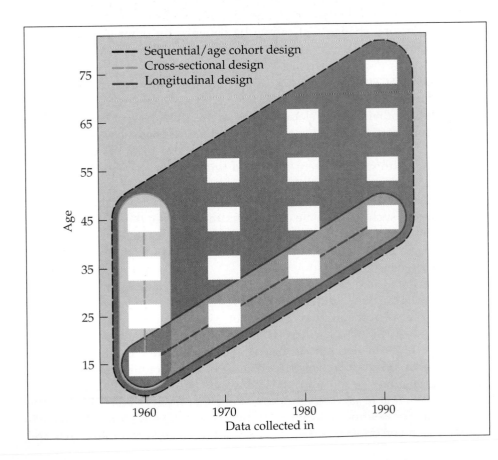

FIGURE 1–2

The longitudinal, cross-sectional, and sequential/age cohort research designs. The diagonal rows (see bottom row circled in red) represent longitudinal studies, and the vertical columns (see left column circled in green) represent cross-sectional studies. The complete illustration is of the sequential/age cohort design, and it shows four age cohorts that are being studied at four different times.

going on in 1987 (Shneidman, 1989). It is projected to continue past the year 2000.

Longitudinal studies have some serious drawbacks, though. In studies of intelligence, for example, subjects can become practiced and familiar with the tests and can appear to show progressive gains quite apart from those associated with development. Also, in practical terms there's a limit to how many such studies a researcher can conduct in a lifetime. In general, longitudinal research requires a great deal of time from both researchers and subjects.

Another problem with longitudinal studies is the possibility of *bias*. Researchers initially select subjects who are representative of the population of interest. As the study continues, some subjects become ill, go on vacation, move away, or simply stop participating in the research project, with the effect that the remaining subjects may no longer be representative of the original target population. For example, a study of personality change might become biased because the remaining subjects tend to be the more cooperative and emotionally stable ones, leading researchers to believe that people generally become more cooperative and stable as they age. Similarly, subjects who participate in longitudinal studies may be healthier, wealthier, and wiser than their peers (Friedrich & Van Horn, 1976).

Researchers, too, may move away, lose interest, or even die if the study continues long enough. Terman, for example, died in 1956, though his study lives on. Another example is the Berkeley Guidance Study of personality change (see Casper et al., 1987, 1988), which began in 1928 and has had numerous principal researchers in its sixty-year history. The original purposes and methods of such studies may become outdated, since it is difficult to incorporate new approaches and still obtain data that can be compared with earlier findings.

Nevertheless, since longitudinal studies yield detailed data about individual developmental change that cannot be obtained by other means, the approach continues to be used when the necessary resources are available.

THE CROSS-SECTIONAL DESIGN **Cross-sectional designs** compare individuals of different ages at a particular time. Although cross-sectional research cannot assess individual development, it has the advantage of being quicker, cheaper, and more manageable than longitudinal research. An example is a study of change in children's understanding of sarcasm, in which third graders and sixth graders were compared with adults (Capelli et al., 1990). From differences in what the children attend to, the researchers concluded that younger children tend to miss cues during an occasion in which someone is being sarcastic, such as when the context contradicts what the speaker has said or when the speaker simply uses a different tone of voice. In other words, understanding sarcasm depends in part on a child's level of thinking and language comprehension.

Cross-sectional designs require careful selection of participants to ensure that the results are due to differences in development and not to other kinds of differences between the groups. That is not usually a hard requirement with children, but with adults of widely differing ages, it is difficult and sometimes impossible. In particular, studies of changes in adult intelligence associated with aging have been plagued by problems of comparability. Other factors, such as public health and education, have changed substantially in recent decades, so that at any given time, adults of differing ages aren't likely to be comparable. For example, education strongly affects IQ test scores, but the education that a person who is now 70 years old received back in the 1930s and

cross-sectional designs A method of studying development in which a sample of individuals of one age are observed and compared with one or more samples of individuals of other ages.

1940s differs in many ways from the education that a current 30-year-old received in the 1970s and 1980s. Such differences are called *cohort effects*—we would say that the 30-year-old cohort differs in important ways from the 70-year-old cohort. Early research on intellectual change indicated a decline in later adulthood that was greatly exaggerated for just that reason. We'll take a closer look at that research in Chapter 16.

THE SEQUENTIAL-COHORT DESIGN Because of problems with each of the approaches just described, researchers are now more inclined toward a mix of the two, which is called the **sequential-cohort design.** Thus, a researcher might start with a group of 4-year-olds, a group of 6-year-olds, and a group of 8-year-olds and then study each cohort for several years. Comparisons could then be made both longitudinally and cross-sectionally.

CORRELATION AS A DESCRIPTIVE TOOL

Does watching violence on television make children more violent and aggressive? Indeed it can, though in ways that researchers are still trying to unscramble through experimental research.

Does height cause weight or weight cause height, or are they each the result of some combination of genetic and environmental factors? To measure the relationship between these two variables, researchers use the technique of correlation.

Before that research began to be conducted, however, tests of a possible relationship between televised violence and children's aggression went essentially like this: Measure the number of hours that selected children spend watching violent TV shows; then apply a second measure, such as a scale for aggressiveness; finally, compare the two. If children who watch a lot of violent TV are more aggressive, and if children who watch little violent TV are less aggressive, there's clearly a relationship of some kind.

The statistical technique that researchers use to measure such relationships is **correlation,** which yields a number that ranges either from 0 to +1.00 or from 0 to −1.00. The former is called *positive correlation*. In our example, as one variable (watching violent TV) increases, the other variable (aggressiveness) also increases. That is, the two variables "change" in the same direction: Children who spend more hours watching violent TV are also more aggressive on the scale, and vice versa.

To illustrate *negative correlation*, suppose that we found that children who watch more violent TV turn out to be *less* aggressive (a result that a Freudian might predict on the grounds that watching violent TV could provide an acceptable outlet for aggressive impulses that might otherwise be expressed in reality). If so, then more hours of watching TV violence would correspond to *lower* scores on the aggressiveness scale, and fewer hours of watching TV violence would correspond to *higher* scores. In other words, the measures would be reversed: As one increases, the other decreases, and vice versa. The measures change in opposite directions, yielding a negative number.

As a general frame of reference, correlations between 0 and .20 or 0 and −.20 are viewed as *weak* or nonexistent; correlations between about .20 and about .60, whether positive or negative, are *moderate*; and correlations exceeding .60, in either a positive or a negative direction, are *strong*.

It is important to bear in mind that correlation tells us absolutely nothing about causation, meaning what causes what. Although there is now a large body of experimental evidence that suggests that watching violence on television makes children more aggressive than they otherwise would be, we can't know that result from positive correlation alone. All that correlation tells us is that there's a pattern, nothing more. On the basis of correlation alone, it *might* be true that watching TV violence increases aggressiveness. But the reverse might also be true: Maybe children who are inherently more aggressive prefer

sequential-cohort design A mix of the longitudinal and cross-sectional designs.

correlation A mathematical statement of the relationship or correspondence between two variables.

to watch violent TV programs. In that case, aggressiveness causes such children to watch TV violence. There are many other possibilities: Maybe the more aggressive children are that way because their parents are violent and punish them harshly (behavior that tends to make children more aggressive) and because the parents also select violent TV programs for the family to watch.

In sum, although correlation is not an indicator of what causes what, it is an excellent research tool when used and interpreted appropriately.

REVIEW & APPLY

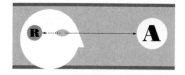

1. In developing his theory, Freud relied on case studies of his patients; how might this reliance have biased his theory?
2. Name two objective observation techniques, and give the advantages and disadvantages of each.
3. Describe problems with questionnaires and surveys.
4. Discuss why reliability, validity, and standardization are important in psychological testing.
5. Describe the basic procedures, advantages, and limitations of each of the three developmental research designs.
6. Discuss why correlation isn't the same as causation, and give an original example.

STUDYING HUMAN DEVELOPMENT: EXPERIMENTAL APPROACHES

The preceding section implied that only experiments can yield trustworthy information about cause-and-effect relationships. In this section we consider experimentation in detail, in the context of several theoretical perspectives that are important in studying and understanding development.

THE SEARCH FOR CAUSE AND EFFECT

Humans have always been curious about how things work. Early humans undoubtedly manipulated and poked and prodded things to see what would happen. Build a raft out of rocks; it sinks. Build a raft out of branches and limbs; it floats. Let the raft get waterlogged, though, and it too sinks. Startle a wildebeest; it runs away. Sneak up on a wildebeest and poke it with a spear, though, and it doesn't run far. Such simple tests, often driven by the need to survive, would have been among the first experiments.

Throughout the ages, humans have continued to perform experiments, and those experiments have become progressively more intricate and complex. True experimentation, however, was not applied to aspects of human development until the early twentieth century, beginning primarily with the **strict behaviorists.** In strict (or "radical" or "stimulus-response" or simply "S-R") behaviorism, only what is directly observable is considered worthy of study. Thinking, feeling, knowing, and the like are *covert behaviors* that can't be seen or measured with instruments. The premise of strict behaviorists was that researchers must limit themselves to *overt behavior*, meaning that which can be observed and measured objectively.

From that perspective, as well as from contemporary ones to be discussed later, psychological experiments take two basic forms: those that focus on

strict behaviorism The view that only observable, measurable behavior can be studied scientifically.

individuals, whose behavior is studied and assessed one subject at a time; and those in which the focus is on groups of individuals assessed collectively by averaging. *Experimental design*, which is a broad term that refers to the many considerations necessary in conducting meaningful experiments, depends on which approach is selected.

EXPERIMENTS FOCUSING ON INDIVIDUALS

Single-subject designs are exemplified by the work of B. F. Skinner, whose research is discussed in detail in Chapter 3. One subject at a time—rat, pigeon, chimpanzee, or human—is exposed to **contingencies** that are expected to alter or otherwise affect behavior. A contingency is a relationship between behavior and its consequences. Single-subject designs are most often cast in the context of *conditioning*, which is the application of contingencies to behavior. A demonstration of conditioning typically begins by recording specific behaviors as they naturally occur, to obtain what is called a baseline. It then proceeds to manipulate contingencies to see how those behaviors change. *Behavior modification*, which can be an effective method of eliminating problem behaviors and establishing desirable ones, generally takes this approach: First identify and carefully define instances of the behavior, and record the baseline rate at which they occur, and then provide contingencies such as rewards or punishments to see whether the behavior changes for the better.

CONDITIONING AND LEARNING **Learning** refers to a relatively permanent change in behavior potential as a result of practice or experience. The definition has three key elements: (1) The change is permanent and normally endures throughout the subject's life; (2) what actually changes is the *potential* for behavior (the subject may learn something that doesn't affect behavior until later, if ever); and (3) learning requires some kind of experience (learning does not result from growth or maturation). In contrast to conditioning experiments, experiments on learning and cognitive processes more often involve groups of subjects.

contingency A relationship between behavior and its consequences.

learning The basic developmental process of change in the individual as a result of experience or practice.

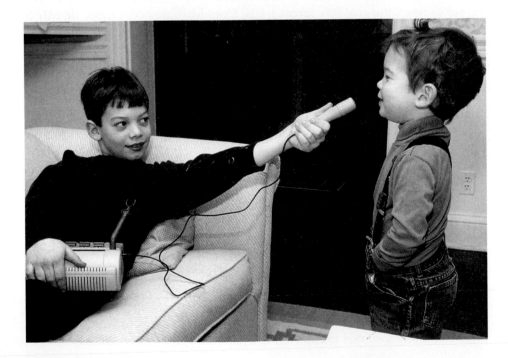

Because they assume that people are reactive beings, behaviorists study how individuals respond to their environment rather than investigating what they think or feel about these responses.

EXPERIMENTS FOCUSING ON GROUPS

Experimental psychologists who study development are inclined to conduct group experiments to get at general principles that might apply to all humans. From that perspective, individual differences become a nuisance. For example, it is assumed that human memory basically works the same way for everyone. Yet some people find it easier to memorize information than others do—a difference that may be related to neurological differences or early learning experiences and practice. Such differences get in the way when you're trying to develop general theories. How do researchers deal with individual differences? Essentially by averaging. Conduct the memory research by using groups of people, and then average their performance scores.

As we'll see, there are many considerations in conducting group experiments that provide definitive information about development and behavior. Let's look at these in context, starting with learning theory, the school of thought and research that laid the groundwork for group experimentation.

LEARNING THEORY AND BEHAVIORISM   The early **learning theorists** studied what they called *instrumental* behaviors, meaning behaviors that are instrumental in producing consequences. They studied behaviors such as a rat's running a maze to reach a "goal box" and obtain food, using measures such as how much time it takes the rat to reach the goal box across repeated *trials*. A trial consists of placing the rat at the beginning of the maze and then measuring its progress toward the goal box. How many trials it takes the rat to run the maze without making errors (such as going into dead-end corridors) was a major focus of the analysis.

The learning theorists used concepts such as learning, motivation, drives, incentives, and inhibitions, which are covert behaviors. As Clark Hull (1884–1952) argued, such terms are scientific to the extent that they can be defined in terms of observable operations (e.g., see Hull, 1943). An **operational definition** of "hunger drive," for example, is stated as the number of hours of food deprivation that a rat experiences before an experiment, or perhaps as the percent of reduction in the rat's body weight below normal. Learning can be operationally defined in terms of the progressive reduction in time that it takes the rat to reach the goal box across trials. Does learning occur more rapidly if motivation in the form of hunger drive is increased? Up to a point. After that, the rat is too weak to run the maze.

The learning theorists devised formulas for learning and behavior by averaging the behavior of individual subjects, and they eventually produced general "laws" of learning. An example is the *classic learning curve* illustrated in Figure 1–3. Learning a skill, such as playing a musical instrument, is characterized by rapid improvement in performance at first, then by progressively slower improvement. Suppose a child is learning to play the guitar. At first the child improves rapidly in fingering and plucking strings and making chords; but it will be many years before the child becomes a virtuoso, if ever. The learning curve holds up fairly well for complex human skills, even though it originated in observations about how rats' performance in running mazes improves over time.

ELEMENTS OF GROUP EXPERIMENTAL DESIGN   In such early experiments, we can see the basic elements of experimental design that are generally applicable today. Here's an example that illustrates elements of modern experimental design. In now-classic research on children's learning of aggressive behavior through observation and imitation (Bandura, 1965; see also Bandura, 1969), three randomly assigned groups of preschool boys and girls watched a film in

learning theorists   A term that usually refers to strict behaviorists who focused on learning.

operational definitions   The actual procedures researchers use in conducting experiments.

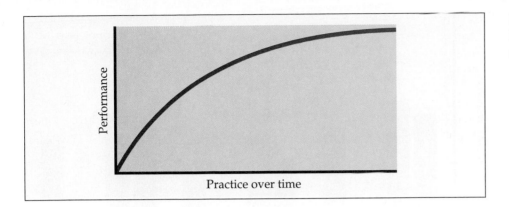

FIGURE 1–3 THE CLASSIC LEARNING CURVE

Source: Adapted from Hull, 1943.

which an adult model "beat up" an inflated Bobo doll in specific ways. One group saw the model "rewarded" at the end of the film with praise from another adult. A second group saw the model "punished," and a third group saw the model experience no consequences either way. Thus, there were three different experimental treatments that constituted the **independent variable**—that which is manipulated by the experimenter to see what effects it will have on behavior.

The researchers next allowed each child to play with a Bobo and counted the number of aggressive acts the children displayed—specific acts that they had seen the model perform. That was the **dependent variable**—what the experiment measures to determine whether the independent variable had an effect. The results are presented in Figure 1–4, where the blue bars represent the average number of imitated acts for each group at this point in the experiment, which was called the *performance test*. As you can see, the consequences that the model received had a marked impact on the children's imitation: For both boys and girls, those who saw the model punished imitated significantly fewer aggressive behaviors. Note, however, that the overall levels for boys and girls were quite different on the performance test.

In the next phase of the experiment, called the *learning test*, the researchers offered all of the children rewards for reproducing as much of the model's behavior as they could. Now things changed considerably. Look at the green bars: *All* of the children reproduced high levels of aggressive behavior regardless of what they had seen happen to the model, and the previously large differences between boys and girls became minimal. The implication was that children readily learn how to commit aggressive acts when they watch such acts in films and on TV, whether or not the children actually display those behaviors at the time.

In contrast to our hypothetical rat research discussed earlier, Bandura's experiment had good **ecological validity:** What was done in the lab corresponded nicely to what might happen in the real world. Although Urie Bronfenbrenner (see Chapter 3) has characterized American developmental psychology as "the science of the strange behavior of the child in a strange situation with a strange adult for the shortest period of time" (1979), this isn't always the case.

On the basis of a single experiment such as Bandura's, however, researchers would not make a sweeping generalization such as saying that watching adults being aggressive increases children's aggressiveness. Instead, they would want to repeat or **replicate** the experiment using different children,

independent variable The variable in an experiment that is manipulated in order to observe its effects on the dependent variable.

dependent variable The variable in an experiment that changes as a result of manipulating the independent variable.

ecological validity The extent to which research applies to what happens in the real world.

replication Systematic repetitions of experiments to determine if findings are valid and generalizable.

FIGURE 1–4

Children's imitation of an adult model whom they saw be rewarded, be punished, or experience no consequences for aggressive behavior toward a Bobo doll.

Source: Adapted from Bandura, 1969.

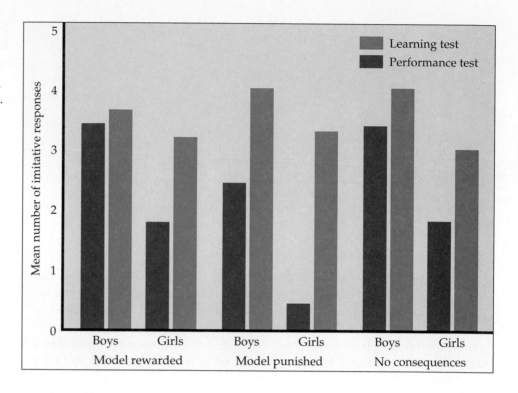

different kinds of filmed or televised aggression, along with differing measures of the children's behavior.

In sum, group experimental research consists of the following steps:

1. Define the problem, and formulate hypotheses about what causes what.
2. Define independent and dependent variables.
3. Perform the experiment, and collect data.
4. Interpret what happened, and draw whatever conclusions are warranted.

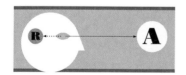

REVIEW & APPLY

1. Why is it important to understand cause and effect in human development?
2. What lasting contributions did the early behaviorists make?
3. How could you go about devising an experiment on children's TV watching and *prosocial* behavior such as helping and sharing? Specify your operational definitions and your independent and dependent variables.

COGNITION IN DEVELOPMENTAL THEORIES

Experimental psychology has come a long way away from the narrow view espoused by the strict behaviorists; developmentalists now often *prefer* to deal with covert processes such as thinking and feeling. But they still emphasize the need to verify those processes via observable or otherwise measurable behavior. What some call the "cognitive behaviorism" of today deals with how we process information, how our interactions with others affect us and our concept of self, how cognition develops, and many other topics related to the

STUDY CHART ‣ RESEARCH METHODS

METHOD	DESCRIPTION
Case study	Through a combination of interviews, observations, formal testing, and other information, the researcher tries to obtain a complete picture of a particular individual.
Naturalistic observation	Researchers go into everyday settings and observe and record behavior while being as unobtrusive as possible.
Laboratory observation	Researchers set up controlled situations that will predictably elicit the behavior of interest.
Survey	Using questionnaires or interviews, researchers ask questions about past and present behavior.
Psychological testing	An individual is presented with a set of questions and problems designed to assess his or her intelligence or personality.
Correlation	Statistical methods are used to determine the extent to which two variables increase or decrease relative to each other.
Single-subject experiment	One subject at a time is exposed to contingencies that are expected to alter or otherwise affect behavior.
Group experiment	Two or more groups of subjects are exposed to treatments that differ in terms of a single variable, known as the independent variable. If the behavior of the two groups differs, researchers can conclude that the difference was caused by the independent variable.

mind and how it works—always with an eye toward evidence based on objective research. Traditional behaviorism is still very much alive, however, with regard to basic learning processes.

Cognitive theories take various forms. Three general approaches are introduced here, each with themes that we'll return to repeatedly in the chapters that follow: information-processing theory, social-cognitive theory, and cognitive-developmental theory.

INFORMATION-PROCESSING THEORY
Since the 1960s, developmental psychologists have turned their attention to covert, cognitive processes. By far the most popular approach to studying human cognition is **information-processing theory.**

As humans, we constantly process information. You're carrying out that process right now as you attend to the letters and words on this page and as you filter out irrelevant sights and sounds around you. As you read, you translate words and sentences into facts and ideas, thinking about them and (ideally) storing them for later reference, such as when you take an exam on this material.

Many information-processing theorists use computer analogies in developing models of how memory and other aspects of human cognition work. A computer has hardware—the machine itself—and it has software—the programs that instruct its operations. By analogy, we also have hardware—our central nervous system—and software—our natural and learned strategies for processing information. Information is input into computers, which then perform certain operations on the information, store it, and generate output. We selectively attend to information and perceive, associate, compute, or otherwise operate on it. The information is then stored in memory and retrieved

information-processing theory
A theory of human development that uses the computer as an analogy for the way the human mind receives, analyzes, and stores information.

later as necessary. Finally, "output" may be generated in the form of responses—words and actions.

This is not to say, however, that computers and humans learn and remember things in exactly the same way. For one thing, the electronic hardware of a computer is quite different from the organic human brain; we do not store information in the form of bits (0s or 1s) the way a computer does. For another, computer processing is *serial*, meaning that only one one piece of information is processed at a time, even though modern computers run so fast that it's easy to overlook that fact. Humans, in contrast, can attend to and think about more than one thing at time, using *parallel* processing. If, for example, you're an experienced driver on an open stretch of freeway, you can readily attend to what's necessary to keep the car going down the road while thinking about something else, such as the wonderful time you're going to have with the person you're driving to see.

In general, however, the computer model works well and has generated volumes of important research questions. For example, some researchers study how informational processes develop in children, with emphasis on *encoding*: the process of identifying key aspects of an object or event to form an internal representation of it (Siegler, 1986). Compared with adults, do children of differing ages select different aspects, or perhaps fewer aspects, of an object to store as a mental image? Do children of differing ages use different strategies for encoding or retrieving information from memory? Only in recent years have information theorists designed experiments to answer such questions, or, in the words of some, to discover how the human "computer" reprograms itself to work with new material (Klahr et al., 1987).

SOCIAL-COGNITIVE THEORY

We'll also see numerous examples of a somewhat different approach to studying cognition, which is derived primarily from social psychology instead of the world of computers. Generally referred to as **social cognition,** this approach emphasizes beliefs and attitudes and other "units" of knowledge—along with where they come from. Social-cognitive theories employ concepts such as *self*: the individual's sense of who he or she is. Also, social cognitive theorists often focus on how social situations—as opposed to characteristics of the person— affect development and behavior. They study how behavior differs from one situation to another, noting, for example, that a person who is normally honest might behave quite differently if the stakes are high enough.

Social-cognitive theorists recognize that children and adults observe their own behavior, the behavior of others, and also the consequences of those behaviors, as in Bandura's observational-learning experiment discussed earlier. Even young children can anticipate consequences on the basis of the observations of past events. Also, people form opinions about themselves and others and then behave in a fashion that is consistent with those opinions (Miller, 1989). Thus, social-cognitive theorists also depart considerably from the strict behaviorism that went before them.

COGNITIVE-DEVELOPMENTAL THEORY

Cognitive-developmental theory focuses on thinking, reasoning, and problem solving, with emphasis upon how such processes develop, beginning in infancy. Jean Piaget (1896–1980) exemplifies this line of research, although there is currently considerable interest in the more culture-specific approach of Lev Vygotsky as discussed in Chapter 4.

social cognition Thought, knowledge, and understanding that involve the social world.

cognitive-developmental theory An approach that focuses on the development of thinking, reasoning, and problem solving.

Throughout his life, Jean Piaget retained his interest in the thoughts and behavior of children.

Piaget believed that the mind does not simply respond to stimuli but instead grows, changes, and adapts to the world. Piaget and other cognitive psychologists, including Jerome Bruner and Heinz Werner, have been called *structuralists* because they are concerned with the structure of thought and the way in which the mind operates on information (Gardner, 1973b).

Piaget's investigations grew out of his early work on IQ tests (see Chapter 8), which he was hired to help standardize. He soon became much more interested in children's wrong answers than their correct ones, because the wrong answers gave him clues to how children think. He saw consistent patterns in the wrong answers, patterns suggesting that children think in qualitatively different ways than adults do. In other words, differences between children and adults are not confined to how much children know but also include the *way* they know.

As we'll see in more detail in later chapters, Piaget and his associates devised tests to assess children's development and find out how children at different cognitive levels think. On the basis of their findings, Piaget proposed the stages of cognitive development summarized in Table 1–5.

A key feature of Piaget's theory is that the mind is an active participant in the learning process. If information or an experience that the person encounters fits within an existing mental framework, it is **assimilated.** If it does not fit, the mind may simply reject it, or the mind may **accommodate** the new information or experience. Assimilation thus consists of interpreting new experiences in terms of existing mental structures—called **schemes** or **schemas**—without changing them. Accommodation, on the other hand, means changing existing schemes to integrate new experiences. Most learning situations involve an interaction between both processes: We interpret what we experience in terms of what we already know, and since new experiences are rarely exactly like older ones, we notice and process differences as well. Consider learning to drive a car with a five-speed transmission if all you've driven before is

assimilation In Piaget's theory, the process of making new information part of existing schemas.

accommodation Piaget's term for the act of changing our thought processes when a new object or event does not fit existing schemas.

schemes or schemas Piaget's term for mental structures that process information, perceptions, and experiences; the schemes of individuals change as they grow.

Table 1–5 Piaget's Stages of Cognitive Development

1. *Sensorimotor* (birth to about age 2 years): Infants learn about the world through looking, grasping, mouthing, and other actions. Intelligence relies on the senses and bodily motion, beginning with simple reflexes that give rise to more complex, voluntary behaviors.

2. *Preoperational* (age 2 to about 7): Children form concepts and use symbols such as language to help them communicate. Such concepts are limited to their personal, immediate experience. Preoperational children have very limited, sometimes "magical" notions of cause and effect and have difficulty classifying objects or events. They do not hold broad, general theories, but use their daily experiences to build specific knowledge. Preoperational children don't make generalizations about classes of objects (e.g., all grandmothers), nor can they think through the consequences of a particular chain of events.

3. *Concrete operational* (age 7 to 11 or 12): Children begin to think logically, classify on more than one dimension at a time, and understand mathematical concepts, provided that they can apply these operations to concrete or at least concretely imaginable objects or events. Concrete operational children begin to use logic in their thinking, but they may have difficulty understanding that a particular animal can be both a "dog" and a "terrier," and they can deal with only one classification at a time. Yet 7-year-olds understand that terriers are a smaller group within the larger group, dogs. They can also see other subgroups such as terriers and poodles as "small dogs," and golden retrievers and St. Bernards as "large dogs." This kind of thinking shows an understanding of *hierarchy* in classification.

4. *Formal operational* (age 11 or 12 years on): Individuals can explore logical solutions to both concrete and abstract concepts. They can think systematically about all possibilities and can come up with logical solutions; they can project into the future or recall the past in solving problems; and they can reason by analogy and metaphor. Formal operational thinking no longer needs to be tied to physical objects or events. It allows the individual to ask and answer "what if" questions ("What if I were to say this to that person?"); and it also allows them to "get inside the heads" of other people and take on their roles or ideals.

an automatic. You'll assimilate things like manipulating the steering wheel and gas and brake pedals, and at the same time, you'll be accommodating the clutch and gearshift.

As we'll also see, other researchers have applied Piaget's theorizing beyond its emphasis on understanding the physical world to areas such as moral reasoning and the way in which we acquire a sense of self. Although Piaget's theory is not without its critics, it is a highly influential theory that continues to be extended.

Review & Apply

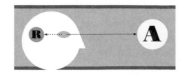

1. What are the differences between information-processing theory and social-cognitive theory? What do they have in common?
2. How does Piaget's theory differ from information-processing theory and social-learning theory?

According to Piaget, children learn by actively exploring what is in their environment.

ETHICS IN DEVELOPMENTAL RESEARCH

Obviously, researchers must follow ethical principles when conducting research with humans. They should never knowingly harm anyone or violate basic human rights, nor should they want to. This principle is especially important when conducting research on "dependent" groups such as children or extremely old people. But ethical issues in developmental research are often more complex than they may appear, as the following hypothetical situation illustrates.

> Three-year-old Emma, who is newly separated from her mother in her first preschool class, sits in a room with an unfamiliar adult in a white lab coat. The researcher asks her to sit on a high chair and place her head in a helmet-like device through which she will look at pictures. To hold her head still, she must bite a hard rubber bar. Emma balks, frowns, and begins to tremble. Despite the urging of her teacher's aide to do what the "doctor" says, she seems unable to follow the instructions. Soon tears appear on her cheeks.

Such a scenario could happen in research on children's eye movements and visual processing. It sounds harmless, but the anxiety created by any test situation may be problematic for a child. Researchers must always ask questions like the following: Are the results of the research potentially important enough to justify putting vulnerable individuals under stress? Is it ethical to test people without giving them information that they can understand about the purposes of the research?

GUIDELINES FOR ETHICAL RESEARCH

Most people agree that experiments using humans are necessary, especially if we are to understand and control the impact of potentially harmful environ-

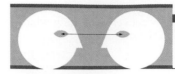

A MATTER FOR DEBATE

WATSON'S "LITTLE ALBERT" EXPERIMENT

Initially reported in 1920, J. B. Watson and Rosalie Rayner's "Little Albert" experiment has long been a classic in the annals of psychology—it is one of the most widely cited studies ever. It is discussed in nearly every introductory psychology and developmental textbook, typically in the context of conditioning and learning. Here we'll consider the study from a different vantage point: that of ethics in psychological research.

The basic experiment went like this: An 11-month-old infant known as Albert B. was taught to fear a white laboratory rat through *classical conditioning* (see Chapter 3). The child initially had no fear of the rat. Then came repeated "trials" in which one experimenter presented the rat to Albert and another experimenter—behind Albert's back—made a loud, frightening noise by striking a steel bar with a claw hammer. As a result, Albert acquired a pronounced fear of the rat and (to a lesser extent) of any white, furry, or fluffy objects. Although the actual conditions of the experiment were more complex and at times haphazard, and although Albert's fear response wasn't always as predictable or profound as many textbooks suggest, he did acquire reactions consistent with those of a *phobia*—an extreme, unreasoning fear of an object or a situation.

Was Watson and Rayner's experiment ethical by contemporary standards? Today we're inclined to answer

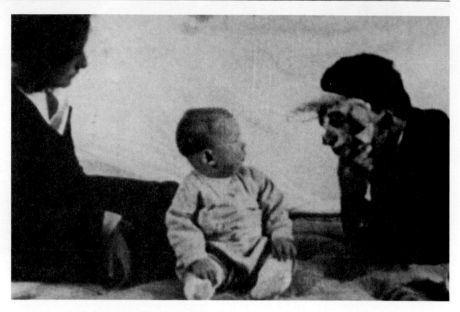

J. B. Watson, Rosalie Rayner, and Albert.

with an immediate "No!" on a number of grounds. For example, it hardly seems ethical to repeatedly expose a helpless infant to an extremely frightening situation. Moreover, there was considerable potential for lasting psychological harm—once phobias have been acquired, they tend to persist. In addition, it is not clear whether Albert's mother even knew what was going on, much less that she gave informed consent for her child to be subjected to such procedures.

On the other hand, modern ethical standards for psychological research didn't exist at the time, so, at least technically, Watson and Rayner aren't cul-

pable. More to the point, relatively little was known about how children acquire phobias and other fears. Thus, it *might* be argued that the potential benefits in understanding the origins of children's fears outweighed the risks to Albert. There was also no way for Watson and Rayner to know that Albert's fear might persist—indeed, that was one of their research questions.

One thing is clear, however: The Little Albert experiment could not and would not be conducted today.

Primary source on the details of the experiment: Harris, 1979.

---

mental events. A recurring case in point is research on the effects of televised violence on children; another case would be research on the effects of televised inducements for unhealthy behaviors such as smoking, noting the recent controversy over (and elimination of) the character "Joe Camel" because of his appeal to children.

However, any potential benefits must be weighed against the rights of research participants. To achieve balance, researchers must consider whether a research project might have "a negative effect upon the dignity and welfare of the participants" (American Psychological Association, 1973), one that cannot be justified by the possible findings of the research study. Would the research on Emma warrant the potential harm to her? What about J. B. Watson's experiment with a young child, discussed in "A Matter for Debate" on facing page?

The following basic principles have been proposed by the Society for Research in Child Development (1990) to guide reputable and honest researchers.

PROTECTION FROM HARM   No treatment or experimental condition should be mentally or physically harmful. But although physical injury is easily avoided, it is often difficult to determine what is psychologically harmful. For example, in studies of obedience, is it reasonable to give children orders to see whether they will follow them? Another example concerns failure on tests. Suppose that a researcher wants to demonstrate that a 9-year-old can understand a particular concept but that a 5-year-old cannot. All the 5-year-old children, knowingly or unknowingly, will experience repeated failure. Is it ethical to have children (or anyone) go through the confusion of trying to solve what for them are unsolvable problems? Do we "debrief" such children truthfully, or do we lie and make them feel that they did well regardless of the actual results?

Most research organizations have screening committees to make sure that research projects aren't likely to be harmful to the participants. Federal guidelines for social and psychological research with humans specify that the study should involve minimal risk—that is, the risk of harm should be no greater than that experienced in daily life or in the performance of routine psychological tests (U.S. Department of Health and Human Services, 1983). Screening committees are becoming more stringent. Many committees, for example, feel that they have a responsibility to protect people's right to self-esteem and to expose them only to test situations that will enhance their self-concept (Thompson, 1990).

INFORMED CONSENT   All major professional organizations believe that people should participate in experiments only voluntarily, be fully informed of the nature and possible consequences of the experiment, and not be coerced in any way. Each of these conditions is an aspect of *informed consent*. Since infants and young children cannot provide informed consent, their parents do so on their behalf. Researchers should also be sensitive to other forms of inducement. How easily, for example, can a 9-year-old in school or a 70-year-old in a nursing home say "no" to someone who looks like a teacher or an administrator (Thompson, 1990)? In addition, adults and children must be free to discontinue their participation in the research at any point, for whatever reason and without attempts being made to prevent them from doing so.

There is potential conflict, however, between informed consent and the "deception" that is often necessary in research with humans. The general rule is that subjects cannot be deceived in ways that might affect their decision to participate, although they can be deceived about the purposes of the research. In the latter case, however, subjects must be debriefed afterward and in a timely fashion and must be told the true nature of the research.

PRIVACY   Information obtained in a research project must remain confidential. Most researchers publish their "numbers," but names and information about individual participants cannot be disclosed without their written permission. No agencies or individuals except the researchers should have access to participants' records, including information about their private lives, thoughts, and fantasies. Also, test scores must be protected from inappropriate use by individuals or groups outside the research project.

KNOWLEDGE OF RESULTS Individuals have the right to be informed of the results of research in terms that are understandable to them. When children are involved, these results may be shared with their parents.

BENEFICIAL TREATMENTS Each child who participates in the study has the right to profit from any beneficial treatments provided to other participants in the study. For example, if a child is assigned to a comparison group in a study of a new vaccine and does not receive it, the child is entitled to receive the vaccine at a later time. In general, researchers should supply any positive benefits of research to all subjects in return for their participation.

REVIEW & APPLY

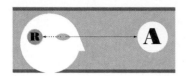

1. Discuss how researchers reconcile conflicts between the principle of informed consent and the need for deception.
2. Why are privacy and confidentiality important in developmental research?

SUMMARY

Key Issues in Human Development

■ Development refers to the changes over time in the body and in the thinking or other behavior of a person that are due both to biology and to experience.

■ The nature-nurture debate involves the degree to which particular traits are biologically based ("nature") or gained through experience ("nurture"). (See the study chart on page 11.)

■ Today the debate usually focuses on the specific genetic factors underlying development and the way in which they interact with factors in the individual's environment.

■ A related issue is how much development depends on maturation and how much it is affected by learning.

■ Other questions about development are whether development unfolds gradually or in stages, whether there are critical periods during which certain types of development must occur, and whether people actively seek knowledge or passively react to what they experience.

Historical and Contemporary Perspectives on Development

■ Until the late nineteenth century, children were sent into the adult world as soon as they were physically capable of working.

■ After about 1600, childhood became recognized as a period of innocence, and attitudes toward children began to change.

■ The twentieth century brought a shift toward more humane child-rearing practices.

■ Prolonged adolescence as a separate period of development is a recent concept that is largely limited to industrialized nations. The experience of adolescence is strongly affected by economic, cultural, and historical factors.

■ Adulthood is generally divided into three age periods: young adulthood, middle adulthood, and later adulthood. Individuals experience these periods differently, depending on such factors as socioeconomic status, ethnic background, and historical events.

■ Families also develop their own identity and child-rearing patterns, which are affected by historical and cultural conditions.

Studying Human Development: Descriptive Approaches

■ In the case study approach, the researcher tries to obtain a complete picture of an individual through interviews, observations, formal testing, and other information. (See the study chart on page 33.)

■ Freud based his psychoanalytic theory on case studies of his adult patients.

■ Freud believed that the infant is dominated by the id, which generates instinctual wishes that must be dealt with. The id operates according to the pleasure principle.

■ According to Freud, the ego develops from the id and serves as its "executive agent." The ego operates according to the reality principle.

■ In Freud's theory the superego develops from the ego and consists of what we call conscience; the superego operates according to the morality principle.

■ Freud also proposed that development proceeds in a series of psychosexual stages on the basis of specific erogenous zones.

■ Freud believed that boys experience the Oedipus complex, developing lustful desires for the mother but eventually identifying with the father and trying to be as similar to him as possible; girls, he believed, experience a similar complex, which he called the Electra complex.

■ Erik Erikson developed a psychosocial theory of development in which social "crises" or conflicts are resolved in each of several stages.

■ The core concept of Erikson's theory is ego identity, a basic sense of who we are as individuals.

Objective Methods of Gathering Developmental Data

■ In naturalistic or field observation, researchers go into everyday settings and observe and record behavior while being as unobtrusive as possible; in laboratory observation, researchers set up controlled situations that will predictably elicit the behavior of interest.

■ Questionnaires and surveys ask questions about past and present behavior.

■ Intelligence and personality tests are sometimes used in developmental contexts. Such tests should be reliable, meaning that they yield similar scores from one testing occasion to the next, and should have high validity, meaning that they actually measure what they are supposed to measure. The tests

are standardized so that scores can be compared with established norms.

■ In a longitudinal research design, one group of individuals is studied repeatedly at different points in the lifespan. Cross-sectional designs compare individuals of different ages at a particular time. A mix of these two designs is referred to as a sequential-cohort design.

■ Statistical correlation can be used to establish a relationship between two variables. Correlation is not the same as causation.

Studying Human Development: Experimental Approaches

■ In single-subject experimental designs, one subject at a time is exposed to contingencies that are expected to alter or otherwise affect behavior.

■ Learning refers to a relatively permanent change in behavior potential as a result of practice or experience.

■ The early learning theorists studied instrumental behaviors, which are behaviors that are instrumental in producing consequences.

■ In a group experiment, subjects are randomly assigned to different groups, which are treated in exactly the same way in all respects except one. The difference in treatment is the independent variable, and the behavior of the subjects is the dependent variable.

Cognition in Developmental Theories

■ A popular approach to studying human cognition is information-processing theory. In this approach, human mental processes are often compared with the workings of a computer.

■ In social-cognitive theory, the emphasis is on beliefs, attitudes, and other units of knowledge. An important concept is the self, the individual's sense of who he or she is.

■ Cognitive-developmental theory focuses on thinking, reasoning, and problem solving, with emphasis on how such processes develop.

■ Jean Piaget investigated how the individual grows, changes, and adapts to the world. A key feature of his theory is that the mind is an active participant in the learning process.

■ In Piaget's theory, if information presented to a person fits within an existing mental structure (scheme or schema), it is assimilated. If the information does not fit, the mind may reject it or may accommodate it by changing existing schemes. Most learning situations involve an interaction between both processes.

Ethics in Developmental Research

■ The Society for Research in Child Development has proposed the following basic principles to guide researchers: (1) No treatment or experimental condition should be mentally or physically harmful; (2) people should participate in experiments voluntarily and be fully informed of the nature and possible consequences of the experiment; (3) information obtained in a research project must remain confidential; (4) participants should be informed of the results of research; (5) all participants in a study have the right to profit from any beneficial treatments provided to other participants.

KEY TERMS

context	psychosocial theory	operational definition
holistic approach	naturalistic or field observation	independent variable
development	laboratory observation	dependent variable
significant others	longitudinal design	ecological validity
stages	cross-sectional design	replication
critical periods	sequential-cohort design	information-processing theory
sensitive or optimal periods	correlation	social cognition
psychoanalytic theory	strict behaviorism	cognitive-developmental theory
id	contingency	assimilation
ego	learning	accommodation
superego	learning theorists	schemes or schemas
psychosexual stages		

USING WHAT YOU'VE LEARNED

Imagine that you've just hired a research firm to study the influence of computers on different age cohorts in the United States. You suspect that the "computer revolution" is having a more pervasive effect on society than is generally believed and that this effect is probably different for children, young adults, and older adults. Your job is to help define what you want to learn from the research and to help the research firm design the study. Accomplishing these goals requires that you ask yourself the following questions:

■ What are some important research issues?
■ What are some of your hunches that might be framed as hypotheses?
■ What age groups will you study?
■ Do you want to conduct a simple survey of attitudes and practices, or do you want to do an experiment?
■ What kinds of problems might make this research difficult?

SUGGESTED READINGS

BELL-SCOTT, P., GUY-SHEFTALL, B., JOYSTER, J., SIMS-WOOD, J., DECOSTA-WILLIS, M., & FULTZ, L. (1991). *Double stitch: Black women write about mothers and daughters.* Boston: Beacon. An anthology of stories, poems and essays by African American women. The metaphor of quilting helps set the stage for rich images of effective networks of mothers, daughters, and extended kin.

BOWLBY, J. (1990). *Charles Darwin: A new life.* New York: Norton. A powerful psychological analysis of Darwin's internal struggles and family life, as well as his achievements as a naturalist.

COLES, R. (1990). *The spiritual life of children.* Boston: Houghton Mifflin. Through the words and pictures of children, this noted teacher and child psychiatrist shares with the reader some surprisingly profound child understandings of the meaning of life and of human experience.

FILIPOVIC, Z. (1994). *Zlata's diary: A child's life in Sarajevo.* New York: Viking. This book contains the personal diaries of a young girl caught in the struggle to capture Sarajevo during the Bosnian/Serbian war.

GIES, F., & GIES, J. (1990). *Life in a medieval village.* New York: Harper & Row. Two skilled historians reconstruct the customs, practices, and social conditions in rural medieval England.

HEWETT, S. (1991). *When the bough breaks: The cost of neglecting our children.* New York: Basic Books. A compelling social commentary on the plight of children in the United States today.

KAGAN, J. (1984). *The nature of the child.* New York: Basic Books. A noted developmental psychologist highlights the research of the last few decades. He editorializes on the effects of early experiences, yet suggests that there are also numerous opportunities for transformations in later childhood and adolescence.

MILLER, P. (1989). *Theories of developmental psychology* (2nd ed.). New York: W. H. Freeman. Miller provides an excellent overview of the major developmental theories, as well as a useful discussion of the role of theories in developmental psychology.

STOLLER, E. P., & GIBSON, R. C. (1994). *Worlds of difference: Inequality in the aging experience.* Thousand Oaks, CA: Pine Forge Press. The authors present readings, drawn from social science and literature, describing the diversity of forces that shape the lives of people as they age. The book emphasizes the important influence of historical and social forces on lifespan development.

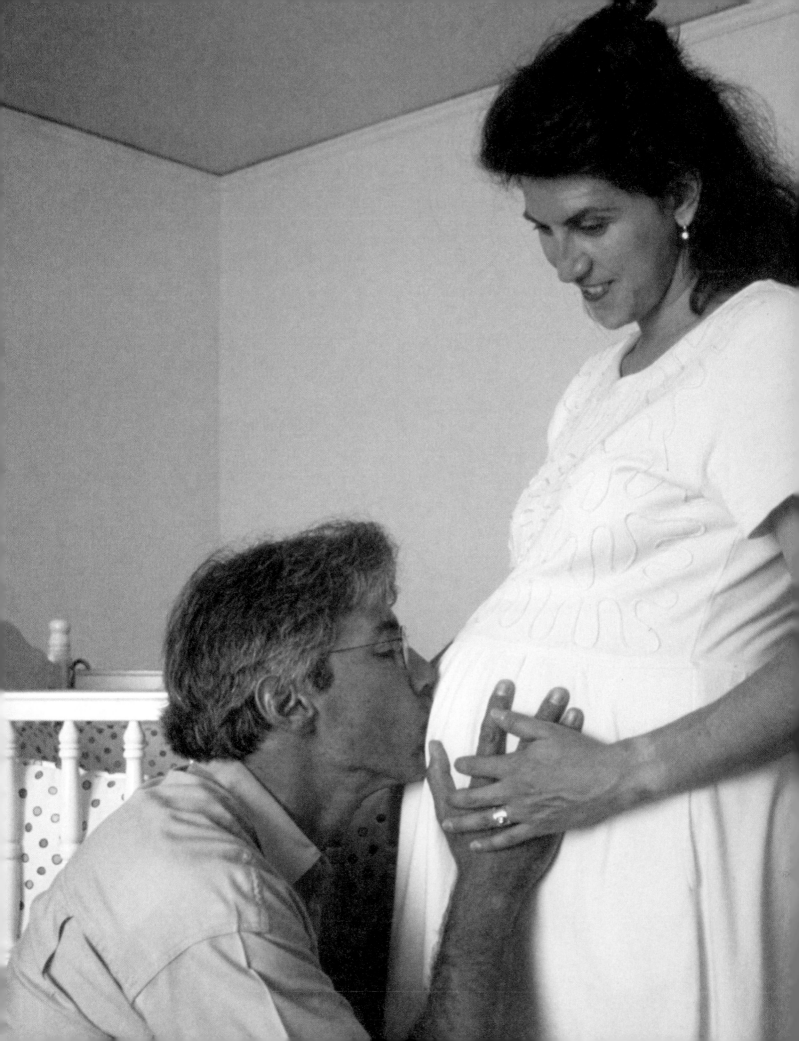

Prenatal Development and Childbirth

CHAPTER

2

CHAPTER OUTLINE

- **Prenatal Growth and Development**
  Periods and Trimesters
  Conception and the Germinal Period
  The Embryonic Period
  The Fetal Period
  Developmental Trends

- **Prenatal Environmental Influences**
  Maternal Age
  Maternal Health and Nutrition
  Prenatal Health Care
  Critical Periods in Prenatal Development
  Teratogens and Their Effects

- **Childbirth**
  Stages of Childbirth
  First Impressions
  Approaches to Childbirth
  Complications in Childbirth

- **The Evolving Family**
  The Transition to Parenthood
  The Beginnings of Attachment

CHAPTER OBJECTIVES

By the time you have finished this chapter, you should be able to do the following:

1. Describe the three prenatal developmental periods and the major characteristics of each.
2. Discuss general trends that occur in prenatal growth and development.
3. Explain the importance of critical periods in prenatal development, especially with regard to teratogens.
4. Summarize environmental factors that influence prenatal development.
5. List and describe the three stages of childbirth.
6. Discuss the benefits and liabilities of medical advances in childbirth.
7. Describe natural or prepared childbirth.
8. Summarize the changes involved in making the transition to parenthood.
9. Discuss factors in parent-to-infant attachment.

 human life is conceived, and in about a week the mother and father of that life may know it exists. Not everyone is ready for the experience of parenthood. But for those who are, the news that conception has occurred can be a wondrous moment indeed. The tests are positive: "We're having a baby!"

Aside from the shopping and borrowing spree to get ready for the baby, which will characterize much of the next nine months, the prospective parents start deliberating a multitude of issues—especially if it's their first baby. "Life won't be the same around here. . . ." "What kind of parent will I be?" "Will it be a girl or a boy?" "Should we find out or just wait and see?" "We're *actually* going through with it—we're having a baby! Gee. . . ." "What will he or she be like?" "And what about a name. . . ."

And joy abounds. But the months before a baby's birth can be stressful as well. First-time parents in particular tend to do a lot of worrying. The mother may imagine having a baby who will be attractive, easy, and smart and who will one day fulfill her dreams, but she may also imagine a baby who is malformed, weak, or ugly, or who may someday wreak havoc on the family (Bruschweiler-Stern, 1997). Fathers are subject to such imaginings too. Prospective parents also wonder whether childbirth will be an ordeal and whether it will be painful or dangerous. Perhaps it's a good thing that they usually don't fully realize what's in store for them after their baby arrives and immediately starts making demands on their time and energy.

In this chapter we'll focus on the biologically programmed sequence of events leading up to the birth of a baby, with emphasis on what goes right but also with some attention to what can go wrong—a theme we'll return to in Chapter 3 in the context of heredity. Prenatal development normally occurs within a highly controlled and safe environment—the uterus—and follows an orderly sequence. But even in the uterus there are environmental influences that affect development. Thus, even a newborn baby can display individual characteristics that aren't necessarily **congenital** (inborn or hereditary). The expectations and anxieties, advantages and deprivations, stability and disruptions, health and illnesses of a family into which a child is born affect not only

congenital Inborn or hereditary.

Ritual preparations for childbirth include the baby shower.

the child's life after birth but also the child's prenatal development. The childbirth process, too, is a biologically programmed sequence, but the reality of a particular child's birth is strongly defined by the cultural, historical, and family contexts within which it takes place.

PRENATAL GROWTH AND DEVELOPMENT

The development of a unique human individual begins with fertilization. A one-celled, fertilized egg that can be seen only under a microscope carries all of the genetic information needed to create an entire new organism. But often that organism does not develop further. An estimated 50% to 70% of all fertilized eggs are lost within the first 2 weeks (Beller & Zlatnik, 1994; Grobestein et al., 1983). And of the survivors, perhaps 25% will be lost through miscarriage later in the pregnancy.

A living human ovum at the moment of conception. Although some sperm cells have begun to penetrate the outer covering of the ovum, only one will actually fertilize it.

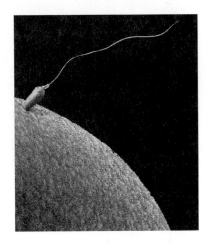

PERIODS AND TRIMESTERS

Prenatal development can be viewed in terms of **trimesters** or in terms of **periods** or stages with regard to the developing child. Trimesters simply break the 9 months of the mother's pregnancy into three 3-month segments. The first trimester is from conception to about 13 weeks, the second from 13 weeks to just over 25 weeks, and the third from 25 weeks to birth, which normally occurs around 38 weeks (266 days) after conception. Periods are more specific than trimesters and reflect developmental milestones. These are described in the study chart on page 48.

CONCEPTION AND THE GERMINAL PERIOD

Women are born with all the **ova,** or egg cells, they'll ever have (about 400,000), which "ripen," typically one at a time, throughout a woman's reproductive years. About the 10th day after the beginning of a regular menstrual period, an ovum is stimulated by hormones and enters a sudden period of

trimesters   The three equal time segments that comprise the gestation period.

periods   Stages.

ova   Egg cells.

STUDY CHART ▸ MAJOR MILESTONES OF PRENATAL DEVELOPMENT

TRIMESTER	PERIOD	WEEKS	LENGTH AND WEIGHT	MAJOR EVENTS
First	Germinal	1		The one-celled zygote multiplies and forms a blastocyst.
		2		The blastocyst burrows into the uterine lining. Structures that feed and protect the developing organism begin to form—amnion, chorion, yolk sac, placenta, and umbilical cord.
	Embryonic	3–4	1/4 inch	A primitive brain and spinal cord appear. Heart, muscles, backbone, ribs, and digestive tract begin to develop.
		5–8	1 inch	Many external body structures (e.g., face, arms, legs, toes, fingers) and internal organs form. The sense of touch begins to develop, and the embryo can move.
	Fetal	9–13	3 inches; less than 1 ounce	A rapid increase in size begins. The nervous system, organs, and muscles become organized and connected, and new behavioral capacities (kicking, thumb sucking, mouth opening, and rehearsal of breathing) appear. External genitals are well formed, and the fetus's sex is evident.
Second		13–25 or 26	12 inches; 1.8 pounds	The fetus continues to enlarge rapidly. In the middle of this period, fetal movements can be felt by the mother. Vernix and lanugo appear to keep the fetus's skin from chapping in the amniotic fluid. All of the neurons that will ever be produced in the brain are present by 24 weeks. The eyes are sensitive to light, and the baby reacts to sound.
Third		25 or 26–38	20 inches; 7.5 pounds	The fetus has a chance of survival if born at around this time. It continues to increase in size. The lungs gradually mature. Rapid brain development causes sensory and behavioral capacities to expand. In the middle of this period, a layer of fat is added under the skin. Antibodies are transmitted from mother to fetus to protect against disease. Most fetuses rotate into an upside-down position in preparation for birth.

growth that continues for 3 or 4 days. By the end of the 13th or 14th day of growth, the follicle (sac) surrounding the ovum, breaks and the ovum is released. It then begins its journey down one of the two **fallopian tubes** (see Figure 2–1). The release of the ovum is called **ovulation**.

Most of the time, ovulation occurs around the 14th day after the onset of menstruation. A mature ovum survives for about 3 days. A man's **sperm** cells—which in a normal adult male are produced at a rate of about one billion per day—survive for as long as 2 or 3 days after being ejaculated into a woman's vagina. This timing means that there's a "window" of several days before and after ovulation during which sexual intercourse might result in conception. If the ovum is not fertilized, it simply continues down the fallopian tube and disintegrates in the *uterus*, also illustrated in Figure 2–1.

Sperm and ova are single cells, each normally containing exactly half of the new individual's genetic makeup, as we'll see in Chapter 3. The events leading up to the union of these two cells are remarkable. During a male's period of peak fertility in young adulthood, some 300 million sperm are deposited in the vagina during each instance of sexual intercourse. Yet only one of them may penetrate and fertilize an ovum and determine the sex and genetic traits of the child.

For the tiny sperm cells, the trip to a potential rendezvous with an ovum in a Fallopian tube is long and difficult. The sperm must work their way upward through a foot-long passageway containing acidic fluids that can be lethal, as well as obstacles such as mucus. But finally one sperm arrives at the right place at the right time and penetrates the cell membrane of the ovum to begin fertilization. Over the next 24 hours, the genetic material of two individuals "fuses" and is translated into a new living entity (Beller & Zlatnik, 1994) called a **zygote** (from the Greek root for "yoke or join together").

The **germinal period** thus begins with conception and fertilization, and it continues until the developing organism makes its journey down to the uterus

fallopian tubes Two passages that open out of the upper part of the uterus and carry the ova from the ovary to the uterus.

ovulation The release of the ovum into one of the two fallopian tubes; occurs approximately 14 days after menstruation.

sperm The male reproductive cell (or gamete).

zygote The first cell of a human being that occurs as a result of fertilization; a fertilized ovum.

germinal period After conception, the period of very rapid cell division and initial cell differentiation, lasting for approximately two weeks.

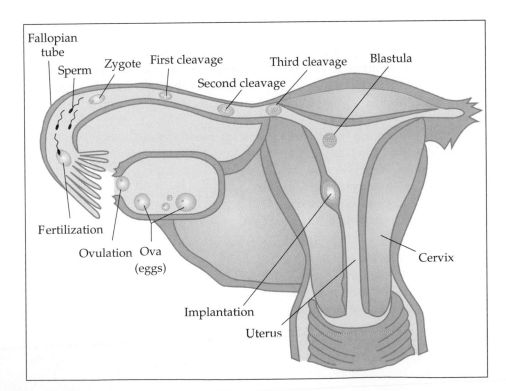

FIGURE 2–1

The journey of the fertilized egg is shown as it moves from the ovary to the uterus. Fetal development begins with the union of sperm and egg high in the fallopian tube. During the next few days, the fertilized egg, or zygote, travels down the fallopian tube and begins to divide. Cell divisions continue for a week until a blastula is formed. By this time, the blastula has arrived in the uterus. Within the next few days it will implant itself in the uterine wall.

Identical twins (top) have the same genes and physical characteristics, including sex; fraternal twins (bottom) can be as similar or different as siblings born at different times.

monozygotic (identical) twins Twins resulting from the division of a single fertilized ovum.

dizygotic (fraternal) twins Twins resulting from the fertilization of two separate ova by two separate sperm.

blastula The hollow, fluid-filled sphere of cells that forms several days after conception.

embryonic period The second prenatal period, which lasts from the end of the second week to the end of the second month after conception. All the major structures and organs of the individual are formed during this time.

embryo From the Greek term "swell."

and achieves *implantation* as discussed later. Implantation is complete at about 2 weeks after conception.

The germinal period is a time of very rapid cell division and organization. About 48 hours after conception, the one-celled zygote divides to produce two cells. Then a second division takes place in each cell, yielding four cells. And so on. The rate of cell division increases, so that by the 6th day, more than 100 cells (each one smaller, but containing exact copies of the original zygote's genetic material) have been produced.

WHAT CAUSES TWINS?   Sometimes the first division of the zygote produces two identical cells that then separate and develop into two individuals. The result is **monozygotic (identical) twins.** Because they develop from the same cell, identical twins are always the same sex and share the same physical traits.

In other cases, two ova are released at the same time and *each* unites with a different sperm, producing **dizygotic (fraternal) twins.** The genetic traits inherited by fraternal twins can be as similar as or as different from those of any other two siblings. Fraternal twins may also be of the same sex or different sexes. Certain fertility drugs, which increase the number of ova that ripen in a given month, also increase the chance of conceiving fraternal twins or triplets, even sextuplets.

DIFFERENTIATION   Toward the end of the first week, the dividing cells have become a **blastula**—a ball of cells around a fluid-filled center—that has made its way to the uterus. Now the cells begin the process of *differentiation*—that is, they begin separating into groups according to their future function. Some of the cells move to one side of the hollow sphere and form the embryonic disc, from which the child itself will develop. The other group of cells begins to develop into the supportive structures that will nourish and protect the embryo. This is also the point at which home urine tests can assess pregnancy: The cells of the supportive structures begin secreting a detectable hormone called *human chorionic gonadotropin (HCG)*, which shuts down further ovulation and prevents the next menstrual period (Nilsson & Hamberger, 1990).

IMPLANTATION   At the same time, the blastula, now floating in the uterus, begins to burrow into the uterine lining, breaking tiny blood vessels to obtain nutrients. That process triggers hormonal changes that signal the beginning of pregnancy. Within a few days, if all goes well, the blastula is implanted in the uterine wall.

The crucial process of implantation is far from automatic, however. Over 50% of blastulas don't implant successfully—some because they are incompletely formed, others because the uterine environment is inhospitable (Beller & Zlatnik, 1994). An unsuccessful implantation may yield what resembles a heavy menstrual period that arrives a bit late, so that the woman may not even realize that she was temporarily pregnant.

THE EMBRYONIC PERIOD

The **embryonic period** begins when implantation is complete. It is a time of major structural development and growth that continues until 2 months after conception (the term **embryo** comes from the Greek word for "swell").

Two crucial processes occur simultaneously during the embryonic period: (1) The outer layer of cells produces all the tissues and structures that will house, nurture, and protect the developing child for the remainder of the prenatal period; and (2) the cells of the inner, embryonic disc differentiate into the embryo itself.

THE SUPPORTING STRUCTURES The outer layer of cells produces three structures: the **amniotic sac,** a membrane filled with watery **amniotic fluid** that helps cushion the embryo and otherwise protect it; the **placenta,** a disc-shaped mass of tissue growing from the wall of the uterus that serves as a partial filter; and the **umbilical cord,** a rope of tissue containing two arteries and a vein that connect mother to child.

The placenta is also formed partly from the tissues of the uterine wall, and it continues to grow until about the seventh month of pregnancy. The placenta provides for the exchange of materials between mother and embryo, keeping out larger particles of foreign matter but allowing nutrients to pass through. Thus, enzymes, vitamins, and even antibodies to protect against disease pass in to the embryo, while the resulting waste products in the embryo's blood pass out to the mother for elimination. Sugars, fats, and proteins also pass through to the embryo, but some bacteria and some salts do not. Note that the mother and the embryo do not actually share the same blood system. The placenta allows for the exchange of nutritive and waste materials by diffusion across cell membranes, normally without any exchange of blood cells.

Unfortunately, viruses contracted by the mother during pregnancy can also pass the placental barrier, as can potentially harmful drugs and other substances that find their way into the mother's bloodstream. These are discussed at length later in the chapter.

THE EMBRYO During the 6 weeks of the embryonic period, the embryo develops arms, legs, fingers, toes, a face, a heart that beats, a brain, lungs, and all the other major organs. By the end of the period, the embryo is recognizably human, as illustrated in Figure 2–2.

The embryo grows rapidly and changes daily. Immediately after implantation it develops into three distinct layers: the *ectoderm,* or outer layer, will become the skin, the sense organs, and the nervous system; the *mesoderm,* or middle layer, will become muscles, blood, and the excretory system; and the *endoderm,* or inner layer, will become the digestive system, lungs, thyroid, thymus, and other organs. Simultaneously, the *neural tube* (the beginning of the nervous system and the brain) and the heart start to develop. By the end of the fourth week after conception (and therefore only 2 weeks into the embryonic period), the heart is beating and the primitive nervous system is functioning. Yet at 4 weeks, the embryo is still only 6 millimeters (about 1/4 inch) long.

During the second month, all of the structures that we recognize as human develop rapidly. The arms and legs unfold from small buds on the sides of the trunk. The eyes become visible, seemingly on the sides of the head, at about 1 month, and the full face changes almost daily. The internal organs—the lungs, digestive system, and excretory system—are also forming, although they aren't yet functional.

SPONTANEOUS ABORTIONS Many *miscarriages,* or **spontaneous abortions,** occur during the embryonic period. They're usually caused by inadequate development of the placenta, the umbilical cord, or the embryo itself (Beck, 1988), or by unsuccessful implantation. Again, however, many toxic substances can pass through the placenta, including some that can cause spontaneous abortion. Poor health and nutrition on the mother's part can be a risk factor too, as

amniotic sac A fluid-filled membrane that encloses the developing embryo or fetus.

amniotic fluid Fluid that cushions and protects the embryo or fetus.

placenta A disk-shaped mass of tissue that forms along the wall of the uterus through which the embryo receives nutrients and discharges waste.

umbilical cord The "rope" of tissue connecting the placenta to the embryo; this rope contains two fetal arteries and one fetal vein.

spontaneous abortions Miscarriages; expulsion of the prenatal organism before it is viable.

FIGURE 2–2
THE EMBRYONIC PERIOD

This is a lifesize illustration of the growth of the human embryo and fetus from 14 days to 15 weeks.

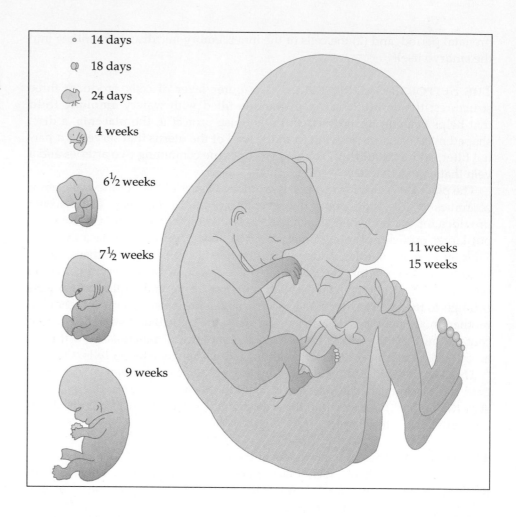

○ 14 days

◎ 18 days

24 days

4 weeks

6½ weeks

7½ weeks

9 weeks

11 weeks
15 weeks

we'll see. On average, almost 90% of spontaneous abortions occur by 12 or 13 weeks, and such abortions beyond 20 weeks are rare.

THE FETAL PERIOD

The **fetal period** lasts from the beginning of the third month until birth—or for about 7 months of the average 266-day prenatal period. During this period, the organs and systems mature and become functional. The **fetus** (French for "pregnant" or "fruitful") begins to kick, squirm, turn its head, and eventually turn its body. Even with its eyes still sealed shut, the fetus starts to squint. It can also frown, open its mouth, practice breathing with the thin amniotic fluid, and make sucking motions—maybe even suck its thumb.

During the third month, physical structures become more complete. The eyes, still set toward the sides of the head, develop their irises, and all of the nerves needed to connect the eye to the brain are formed. Teeth develop under the gums; ears begin to appear on the sides of the head; fingernails and toenails begin to form. The fetus develops a thyroid gland, a thymus gland, a pancreas, and kidneys. The sexual organs become complete in both the male and the female. The liver starts to function, and the stomach begins to move.

By the 12th week, the vocal cords have developed, the taste buds have formed, and the ribs and vertebrae have begun to ossify (harden into bone). The fetus, though unable to survive on its own, has acquired almost all of its body systems. At this point it is still only about 3 inches (7½ centimeters) long and weighs around half an ounce (14 grams).

fetal period The final period of prenatal development, lasting from the beginning of the second month after conception until birth. During this period, all organs mature and become functional.

fetus French for "pregnant" or "fruitful."

Structural details such as lips, toenails, and buds for adult teeth are added during the next several months. Basic organs like the heart, lungs, and the brain mature to the level that is essential for survival.

In the fourth month, the body becomes longer, so that the head doesn't look quite as out of proportion as it did previously. The heart muscle strengthens and starts beating fast—120 to 160 times a minute.

In the fifth month, the fetus acquires a strong hand grip and increases the amount and force of its movements. The mother can feel its elbows, knees, and head as it moves around during its wakeful periods.

In the sixth month, the fetus grows to about 12 inches in length and weighs approximately $1\frac{1}{2}$ pounds. The eyes are completely formed, and the eyelids can open. Bone formation progresses; hair on the head continues to grow; and the fetus begins to straighten its posture so that the internal organs can shift to their proper positions.

Brain development is particularly noteworthy during this time. The size of the brain increases sixfold (Moore, 1988). Going into the second trimester, brain waves are virtually absent, with electrical patterns similar to those of brain death in adults. But before about 24 weeks, bursts of electrical activity begin to occur, indicating that the brain is becoming functional. The foundation is laid for sensing pain and making cortical associations (Kuljis, 1994). Brain development also allows for regulation of other body functions, such as breathing and sleeping.

At the end of the second trimester (i.e., after 24 weeks), a healthy fetus reaches the **age of viability.** It now has about a 50–50 chance of surviving outside the uterus if given high-quality intensive care. However, over half of all fetuses born at 24 weeks have serious defects. In contrast, at 25 weeks nearly 80% percent survive (69% with no major handicap); and at 29 weeks over 90% survive with a good outcome, provided that they receive top-quality care (Allen et al., 1993; Kantrowitz, 1988).

In spite of modern medical advances and highly specialized care, however, infants who are born at earlier periods don't fare as well. At 23 weeks, for example, only 15% survive, and five out of six of them have serious medical problems or defects (Allen et al., 1993). Moreover, specialized care for the very small infant is extremely expensive.

THE THIRD TRIMESTER   Think of the first trimester as the time when basic structures are formed and the second trimester as a period of maturation of organs, particularly the brain, in preparation for basic survival. The third trimester is a time of extensive brain maturation and system "rehearsal." During this trimester the fragile fetus is transformed into a vigorous, adaptive baby.

At 7 months the fetus weighs about 3 pounds. Its nervous system is mature enough to control breathing and swallowing. During the seventh month the brain develops rapidly, forming the tissues that become localized centers for the various senses and motor activities. The fetus is sensitive to touch and can feel pain, and it may even have a sense of balance.

Can the fetus hear at 7 months? Sure. It has long been known that a fetus can be startled by very loud sounds occurring close to the mother, though hardly at all by moderate sounds. That's partly because sounds from outside the mother are muffled, but also because the fetus is surrounded by a variety of sounds occurring *within* the mother. There are digestive sounds from the mother's drinking, eating, and swallowing. There are breathing sounds. There are circulatory system sounds that correspond to the rhythm of the mother's

age of viability   The age (at about 24 weeks) at which the fetus has a 50–50 chance of surviving outside the womb.

Stages of prenatal development: (A) A two-celled organism showing the first cleavage a few hours after fertilization. (B) The germinal period at 2 days—no cell differentiation exists yet. (C) An embryo at 21 days. Note the primitive spinal cord. (D) A 4-week-old embryo. One can now distinguish the head, trunk, and tail. The heart and nervous system have started to function by this time. (E) A 5-week-old embryo. The arms and legs are beginning to unfold from the sides of the trunk. (F) A 9-week-old fetus showing the umbilical cord connection with the placenta. (G) A 160-week-old fetus showing the umbilical cord connection with the placenta. All internal organs have formed but are not yet fully functional. (H) A 20-week-old fetus. At this stage, most internal organs have begun to function, and the fetus is able to kick, turn its head, and make facial expressions.

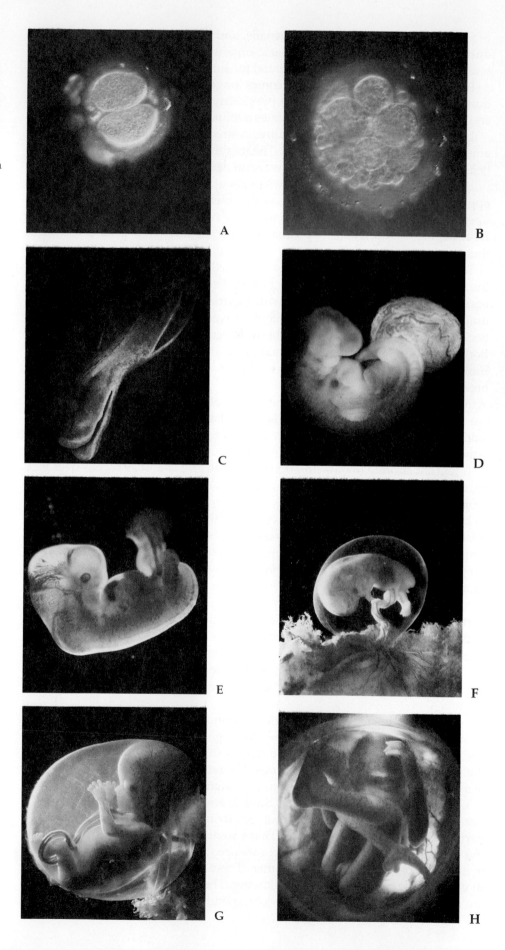

heartbeat. In fact, the internal noise level in the uterus has been characterized as being as high as that in a small factory (Aslin et al., 1983; Restak, 1986).

With regard to overall sensory development, fetuses can grasp and grimace as early as 15 weeks, near the beginning of the second trimester, and reflex movements are elicited when the soles of the feet or the eyelids are touched. By 20 weeks, the senses of taste and smell are formed. By 24 weeks, the sense of touch is more fully developed. Going past 25 weeks, responses to sound become more consistent. At 27 weeks, a light shone on the mother's abdomen can cause the fetus to turn its head, and brain scans verify that the fetus reacts. Such reactions—facial expressions, turning, kicking, ducking—may also be purposeful movements that make the fetus more comfortable (Fedor-Freybergh & Vogel, 1988).

In the eighth month, the fetus may gain as much as half a pound per week. It now begins to prepare for life in the outside world. Fat layers form under the skin to protect the fetus from the temperature changes that it will encounter at birth. The survival rate for infants born at 8 months is greater than 90% in well-equipped hospitals, but the babies still face risks. Breathing may be difficult; initial weight loss may be greater than that of full-term babies; and because their fat layers have not fully formed, temperature control may be a problem. For that reason, babies born at this developmental stage are usually placed in incubators and given the same type of care as babies born earlier.

Fetal sensitivity and behavior also develop rapidly in the eighth month. Around the middle of the month, the eyes open, and the fetus may be able to see its hands (although the uterus is quite dark). It is possible that *awareness* starts at about 32 weeks, since many of the fetus's neural circuits are quite advanced. Brain scans also show periods of rest that look like dream sleep.

During the ninth month, the fetus develops daily cycles of activity and sleep. Its hearing capacity is thought to be quite mature (Shatz, 1992). Throughout the ninth month, the fetus continues to grow. It also shifts to a head-down position in preparation for the trip through the birth canal. The *vernix caseosa* (a cheeselike protective coating) starts to fall away, and the fine body hair that some babies are born with—called *lanugo*—normally dissolves. Antibodies to protect against disease pass from the mother to the fetus and supplement the fetus's own developing immune reactions. Approximately 1 to 2 weeks before birth, the baby often "drops" as the uterus settles lower into the pelvic area. The fetus gains weight at a slower rate; the mother's muscles and uterus begin sporadic, painless contractions; and the cells of the placenta start to degenerate.

Thus, in about nine months, the intially one-celled zygote has developed into perhaps 10 trillion cells organized into organs and systems. It is a child ready to be born. But before we get to that, there's more to consider about the prenatal period.

DEVELOPMENTAL TRENDS

During the prenatal period (and throughout childhood), physical growth and motor development exhibit three general trends. Although there are individual differences in the timing of various aspects of development and the trends are just that (not laws or principles), children tend to follow the same sequences as their bodies grow and their motor skills become refined.

First, development proceeds from the top of the body down, or from "head to tail"; this is termed the **cephalocaudal trend.** During the prenatal period, the fetus's head is disproportionately larger than the rest of its body, and it will be years before the rest of the body catches up. (Incidentally, the cephalo-

cephalocaudal trend The sequence of growth that occurs first in the head and progresses toward the feet.

caudal trend in physical growth is part of the reason that toddlers "toddle": They're top-heavy.) A similar trend can be seen in motor development: Infants control eye and head movements first, then arm and hand movements, and finally movement of their legs and feet.

Second, development usually proceeds from the middle of the body outward, or from "near to far"; this is the **proximodistal trend.** The inner arms and upper legs develop earlier, and infants reach and grab with their full hand long before they can pick up something like peas and bits of carrot with their finger and thumb.

Finally, there's the **gross-to-specific trend:** A fetus initially reacts to a poke on the skin with gross, generalized, whole-body movements, but after birth and in early childhood, the movements become more localized and specific. Note, however, that even young children, when learning to write, still often move their whole bodies, perhaps including their tongues. Only later do they confine the action to the fingers, the hand, and wrist motions.

REVIEW & APPLY

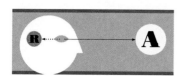

1. Why is the union of a sperm and an ovum to produce a human being a remarkable achievement?
2. What special difficulties may occur during prenatal development?
3. Discuss the three prenatal stages and the advances that occur during each stage.
4. Describe the three general growth trends, and give an example of each.

PRENATAL ENVIRONMENTAL INFLUENCES

Up to this point, we have focused mainly on normal developmental processes. But the sequence we have outlined occurs only under normal environmental conditions. Ideal conditions include a well-developed amniotic sac with a cushion of amniotic fluid; a fully functional placenta and umbilical cord; an adequate supply of oxygen and nutrients; and—just as important—freedom from invading disease organisms and toxic chemicals.

Most pregnancies in the United States (92–95%) result in full-term, healthy babies. However, every year some 150,000 or more babies (5–8% of live births) are born with birth defects. These range from minimal physical or mental defects that may have little impact on the future development of the child to gross anomalies that spell certain and almost immediate death. Although we often assume that birth defects happen only in families with defective genetic makeup (as discussed in Chapter 3), in reality they can happen to anyone, and only a small proportion are the result of inherited factors. The majority of birth defects are caused by environmental influences during the prenatal period or during childbirth. Thus, heredity and environment can interact to produce birth defects.

In this section we begin by considering maternal age and health in general. Then we turn to a discussion of the many harmful things a mother can ingest or otherwise be exposed to and how they affect the child developing inside her body.

MATERNAL AGE
The age of the mother interacts with the prenatal development of the child in ways that aren't fully understood. Very young mothers are at greater risk for having miscarriages or having children with birth defects, possibly because

proximodistal trend The sequence of growth that occurs from the midline of the body outward.

gross-to-specific trend The tendency to react to stimuli with generalized, whole-body movements at first, with these responses becoming more local and specific later.

their bodies aren't yet mature. The greatest success rate is for mothers in their twenties. With regard to mothers past their twenties, one theory simply states that older mothers have older ova (remember that all of a woman's ova were formed before she was born). Through aging alone, ova might be more likely to be defective in ways that affect development. Or there could be a greater risk of damage to the eggs, because aging allows more time for exposure to harmful agents (Baird & Sadornick, 1987). Of course, older mothers' bodies are older too, and this characteristic could cause imperfect implantation. The differing hormonal balance of older mothers could also be a factor.

Whatever the cause, the incidence of some prenatal defects or abnormalities increases steadily with age, especially for first-time mothers. For instance, the incidence of Down syndrome—which includes marked physical malformations and mental retardation—increases steadily for mothers over age 35. For women age 45 and older, the risk goes up to 1 in 25 births, compared with 1 in 800 for women under age 35. While such statistics don't necessarily mean that older women shouldn't have children (1 in 25 is still only a 4% chance), older women should consider these statistics in deciding whether to have a child. Advanced age in pregnancy is one of the first issues that comes up in prenatal counseling for prospective parents, as discussed in Chapter 3.

The hormonal balance and tissue development in older first-time mothers may be a factor in the higher incidence of prenatal defects or abnormalities reported for this population.

MATERNAL HEALTH AND NUTRITION

Mothers who begin pregnancy in good health and fitness, eat a balanced diet rich in protein and calcium, and gain about 25 pounds (11⅓ kilograms) are more likely to give birth to healthy babies. But in some parts of the world—including parts of the United States—mothers are undernourished or malnourished and don't gain enough weight during pregnancy.

Fetal malnutrition can be caused by the mother's imbalanced diet and vitamin or protein or other deficiencies, as well as by deficiencies in the mother's digestive processes and overall metabolism. The most noticeable symptoms of fetal malnutrition are low birth weight, smaller head size, and smaller overall size compared with newborns who have been in the uterus for the same amount of time (Metcoff et al., 1981; Simopoulos, 1983). Malnourished pregnant women also more often have spontaneous abortions, give birth prematurely, or lose their babies shortly after birth.

In countries that have been ravaged by famine or war, the effects of malnutrition on child development are clear. There are high rates of miscarriage and stillbirth, and children born to malnourished mothers may quickly develop diseases and fail to thrive unless immediate dietary adjustments are made. Another unfortunate outcome is that malnutrition can cause reduced brain development both in the late fetal period and in early infancy; this difficulty is probably never overcome, even with good later nutrition. Even in our own relatively developed society, it is estimated that 3–10% of infants show signs of fetal malnutrition (Simopoulos, 1983). Predictably, as noted by Zeskind and Ramey (1981), most cases of fetal malnutrition occur in poverty-stricken families.

Food supplement programs begun at birth can have major benefits, however. In a large long-term study in Guatemala, the health of children who received food supplements in infancy and early childhood improved almost immediately. Even more striking were the long-term gains produced by a special program of protein-rich supplements. Years later adolescents and young adults who had received the special supplements from birth performed significantly better in tests of knowledge, arithmetic, reading, vocabulary, and speed of information processing than peers who had received no supplements before

The effects of malnutrition on child development are painfully apparent in countries ravaged by famine or war.

they were 2 years old. The difference was particularly dramatic for individuals in poorer families and those with good primary education (Pollitt et al., 1993).

How does the *duration* of a period of illness malnutrition affect the fetus? Research with animals has shown that the mother can protect the fetus from the effects of short-term malnutrition by drawing on her own stored reserves. She can also protect her own tissues from serious long-term effects. Both mother and fetus thus appear to be capable of recovering from limited malnutrition (Jones & Crnic, 1986). Therefore, if previously well-nourished mothers go through a temporary period of malnutrition during pregnancy but the baby has a good diet and responsive caregivers after birth, there may be no long-lasting effects (Stein & Susser, 1976). Also, if the period of fetal malnourishment has been relatively short, it can sometimes be compensated for by infant nutrition programs or by combined health, nutrition, and child-care programs.

PRENATAL HEALTH CARE

One of the single best predictors of healthy, full-term babies is five or more prenatal visits to a doctor or health-care facility beginning in the first trimester of pregnancy. Good prenatal care usually includes a careful health history, a full medical examination, and counseling about potential risks. It also includes assessment and recommendations regarding good nutrition during pregnancy. Public-health outreach programs to provide prenatal health care to expectant mothers who might not otherwise receive it have been shown to be effective in reducing infant-mortality and premature-birth rates (Murphy, 1993).

CRITICAL PERIODS IN PRENATAL DEVELOPMENT

The effects of many environmental influences depend on the point in the developmental sequence when the influence occurs. Tragically, many damaging effects on prenatal development can occur before the woman is even aware that she is pregnant.

Figure 2–3 indicates *critical periods* of prenatal development, meaning periods during which the developing child is at greatest risk for different kinds of

FIGURE 2–3

Critical periods in prenatal development. Green represents highly sensitive periods; blue represents less sensitive periods.

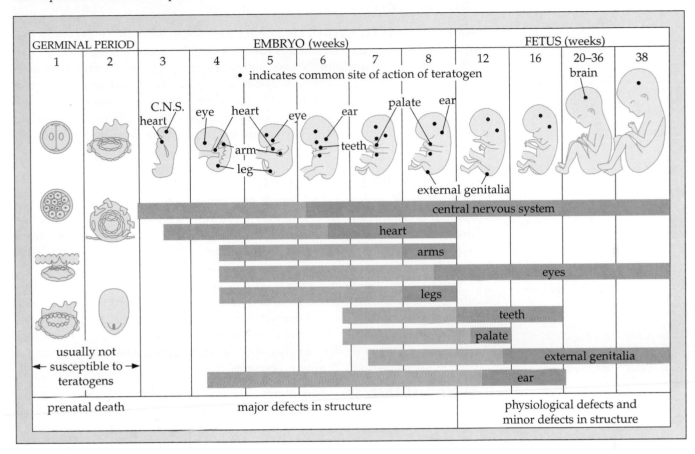

defects as a result of **teratogens**—diseases, chemical substances, or anything else that can harm the child. (The term comes from the ancient Greek word for "monster.") Note in particular that major defects in the central nervous system and the heart may occur as a result of diseases that the mother contracts or substances that she ingests during the early embryonic period. (Prior to implantation, the developing child usually is not susceptible to teratogens because it is not yet connected to the mother's body.)

Sometimes exposure of the mother to a particular teratogen inevitably causes damage to the embryo or fetus. Accidentally ingested poisons act that way. More often, however, the teratogen results in *increased risk* of damage, which may or may not occur. Whether there is damage depends on a complex interaction of factors, including the amount and duration of exposure, the developmental stage of the fetus, the overall health of the mother, and genetic factors.

An extreme example involved thalidomide, a mild tranquilizer that was taken by pregnant women in 1959 and 1960 to relieve nausea and other symptoms of morning sickness. The drug was thought to be harmless. But within the next 2 years as many as 10,000 babies were born with severe deformities as a result of thalidomide use. A careful study of the pregnancies showed that the nature of the deformity was determined by the timing of the drug use. If the mother took the drug between the 34th and 38th days after her last menstrual

teratogens Toxic agents of any kind that cause abnormalities or birth defects.

period, the child had no ears. If she took the drug between the 38th and 47th days, the child had missing or stunted arms; and if she took the drug during the latter part of that time range, the child also had missing or stunted legs (Schardein, 1976).

AMOUNT AND DURATION OF EXPOSURE   Small amounts of exposure to a toxic agent may have no effect because a healthy mother's metabolism can often break down or eliminate toxic substances quickly. Often a drug or chemical agent must reach a certain concentration, or *threshold* level, in a fetal organ or tissue layer to have an impact. On the other hand, sometimes even a small amount of a drug can move through the mother's body quickly and with no permanent damage to her, yet be caught in the immature fetal tissue (Hutchinson, 1991).

TERATOGENS AND THEIR EFFECTS

The variety of environmental factors that can adversely affect prenatal development is staggering. Drugs, diseases, hormones, blood factors, radiation—along with maternal age, nutrition, stress, and type of prenatal care—all play a part in the development of the embryo or fetus. There may be still other drugs or environmental agents whose influences have not yet been determined.

Some drugs and other chemicals can be turned into waste products and be eliminated by the mother's mature body but not by the embryo or fetus. Thus, drugs that cross the placental barrier and are "trapped" and accumulate in the developing child to the threshold level can cause severe damage. From that perspective, almost no drug or chemical—even a normally harmless substance such as aspirin—is safe during pregnancy.

MATERNAL DISEASES   Not all diseases affect a developing embryro or fetus. For example, most kinds of **bacteria** do not cross a normal placental barrier, so that even a severe bacterial infection in the mother may have little or no effect on the fetus, provided that it is treated and does not markedly affect the mother's overall health. However, smaller organisms such as many **viruses**—particularly rubella (German measles), herpes simplex, and many varieties of cold and flu viruses—do cross the placental barrier and can inflict harm. Rubella, for example, can cause blindness, heart defects, deafness, brain damage, or limb deformity in the embryo or fetus, depending on the specific period during which the mother contracts it. Some of the maternal diseases and other maternal conditions that can affect an embryo or a fetus are summarized in Table 2–1.

In general, diseases may enter the child by one of three routes: directly through the placenta, as occurs with rubella and the human immunodeficiency virus (HIV); indirectly through the amniotic fluid, as sometimes occurs with syphilis and gonorrhea; and during labor and delivery, when there is interchange of blood and other bodily fluids. HIV can also be contracted after birth, through breast feeding.

Maternal infections may affect the embryo or fetus in a variety of ways. They may produce miscarriage or stillbirth. They may produce defective or malformed tissues and organs, and sometimes they cause death. Or they may produce no effect at all—especially when the mother has antibodies for the diseases.

One of the most devastating viruses that can be transmitted to the embryo or fetus is HIV, which causes **acquired immune deficiency syndrome (AIDS)**. Although the number of babies with AIDS is still low, it is increasing rapidly. In 1989, 547 infants died of AIDS; in 1993, approximately 1800 babies were

bacteria   Microscopic creatures that cause infections but can't pass the placental barrier.

viruses   Ultra microscopic organisms that reproduce only within living cells and can pass the placental barrier.

acquired immune deficiency syndrome (AIDS)   A fatal disease caused by HIV. Anyone can be infected through sexual contact or through exposure to infected blood or needles.

TABLE 2–1   EFFECTS OF MATERNAL DISEASES DURING PREGNANCY

Acquired Immune Deficiency Syndrome (AIDS): AIDS is an incurable, largely untreatable, and usually fatal disease caused by the human immunodeficiency virus (HIV), in which the immune system breaks down and the person dies from what would normally be minor bacterial and viral infections. (See the text discussion on how babies can contract HIV from their mothers.)

Diabetes: Maternal diabetes can cause numerous physical malformations; it also sometimes causes stillbirth. The fetus may grow larger than normal, increasing the chance of birth difficulties. Diabetes is normally controlled through a special diet.

Gonorrhea: Many people carry the bacterial infection gonorrhea but display no symptoms of the disease. Gonorrhea can cause blindness if contracted from the mother during delivery. For that reason, newborns are routinely given silver nitrate eye drops immediately after birth. Gonorrhea can be treated by antibiotics, although increasingly antibiotic-resistant strains of gonorrhea continue to evolve.

Herpes simplex: The virus that causes genital herpes can cross the placental barrier, but infection is much more common during birth. Risks for the newborn include blindness, neurological problems, mental retardation, and death in a significant number of cases. Cesarian section is recommended if the mother has active herpes at the time that the baby is due to be born. Herpes simplex is currently incurable.

High blood pressure: Chronic high blood pressure can be treated with drugs, but if it is not controlled during pregnancy, it can cause miscarriage.

Influenza: The many strains of influenza virus can cross the placental barrier. The most common effects are spontaneous abortion early in pregnancy or premature labor later. Maternal fever, if uncontrolled, can also be fatal to the fetus.

Rh factor: Rh incompatibility between the mother and the developing child is a disease in the sense that a protein component of the mother's blood can cause severe birth defects or death in the fetus. Most women are Rh-positive, but some lack the blood component and are Rh-negative. If an Rh-negative mother has an Rh-positive child and their blood comes into contact through placental seepage or during birth, the mother's bloodstream begins building up antibodies that attack and destroy fetal red blood cells. Whereas there is usually no danger for a first-born child (and none for the mother), later-born children are highly at risk if they're also Rh-positive. Rh-negative mothers can be treated to prevent the buildup of the antibodies (Kiester, 1977; Queenan, 1975).

Rubella: If the rubella virus is contracted during the first 16 weeks of pregnancy (but after implantation), a frequent recommendation is to terminate the pregnancy because the risks of damage to the embryo or fetus are so great. Nonetheless, parents sometimes choose to continue the pregnancy, and some have normal children.

Syphilis: Syphilis is a bacterial infection that normally doesn't pass the placental barrier during the first half of the pregnancy. It is most likely to be transmitted near or during birth. Syphilis can cause premature labor and miscarriage, deafness, and skin sores and lesions. Although syphilis can be treated by antibiotics, the drugs themselves can affect the embryo or fetus. C-section 1 to 2 weeks early is often recommended.

Toxemia of pregnancy: The causes of *preeclampsia* and the more severe *eclampsia* experienced by some pregnant women during the third trimester aren't known. Maternal symptoms of the disorders include elevated blood pressure, blurred vision, and puffy swelling of the face and hands. Eclampsia can cause fetal brain damage or death. Both forms of toxemia can usually be controlled, however, with bed rest and a special diet.

Source: The Columbia University College of Physicians and Surgeons *Complete Home Medical Guide,* 1985.

born with the disease (Nozyce, M., et al. 1994). It still isn't understood why some babies born to HIV-positive mothers get the virus but many more don't. Some surveys indicate an average of about 24% (Gabiano et al., 1994); others cite from 15–40%, including those infected *in utero*, during labor and delivery, or by breast-feeding (Conner et al., 1994).

LEGAL AND ILLEGAL DRUGS Studies indicate that many women consume a wide range of drugs during pregnancy. A Michigan study of nearly 19,000 women found that they consumed an average of three prescription drugs during their pregnancies (Piper et al., 1987). Prescription drugs such as tetracycline, an antibiotic, have been shown to have adverse effects on fetal teeth and bones and contribute to other congenital defects. Some anticonvulsant medications given to mothers with epilepsy can cause structural malformations, growth delays, heart defects, mild mental retardation, or speech irregularities in babies (Vorhees & Mollnow, 1987). Oral contraceptives, which may cause malformation of the fetal sexual organs, provide another tragic example. Mothers who took the hormone diethylstilbestrol (DES) to help prevent miscarriages had daughters with a higher than normal incidence of vaginal cancer or cervical abnormalities, and sons who were sterile or prone to develop testicular cancer.

In addition to prescription drugs, many over-the-counter (OTC) medications can harm the embryo or fetus. Some of these are listed in Table 2–2 along with other substances that can cause harm. Many drugs can harm the developing child when ingested by the mother. There are also industrial chemical pollutants that might find their way into the mother's system and cause damage.

ALCOHOL The most widely used "recreational" drug in our society is alcohol, and it has the potential to cause severe and permanent birth defects. How much alcohol can be safely consumed during pregnancy—if any—is still unclear, and it also isn't known for sure what prenatal periods are most critical in this respect. But it is known that heavy drinking, defined as 4 ounces (120 milliliters) or more per day, can cause extensive damage. One study found that one-third of all infants born to mothers who drink heavily have congenital abnormalities (Ouellette et al., 1977). Another study found that as little as 2 ounces (60 milliliters) of alcohol daily taken early in pregnancy is sufficient to produce facial deformities (Astley et al., 1992). And in a carefully conducted study of drug-free women in Ireland, noticeable effects on the newborn were found for women who drank as little as three glasses of beer per week (Nugent et al., 1990).

Children of mothers who drink heavily during pregnancy may be born with **fetal alcohol syndrome (FAS).** The symptoms of this condition include low birth weight and general physical and neurological abnormalities such as a small brain and malformation of heart and limbs. FAS children also have distinctive facial characteristics such as a thin upper lip, a poorly developed indentation above the upper lip, a wide space between the margins of the eyelids, and flat cheekbones (Rosett et al., 1981). Similar though milder abnormalities due to drinking during pregnancy are termed **fetal alcohol effects (FAE)** (Vorhees & Mollnow, 1987).

FAS occurs as often as once per thousand births and has been identified as the third leading cause of mental retardation in our society (Streissguth, 1997; Streissguth et al., 1983). FAS is ten times higher in lower-income African-American and Native American families than in the general population (Abel, 1995).

fetal alcohol syndrome (FAS) Congenital abnormalities, including small size, low birth weight, certain facial characteristics, and possible mental retardation, resulting from maternal alcohol consumption during pregnancy.

fetal alcohol effects (FAE) Similar though milder abnormalities due to drinking during pregnancy.

TABLE 2–2   SELECTED DRUGS AND CHEMICALS AND THEIR EFFECTS DURING PREGNANCY

Alcohol: Drinking can cause fetal alcohol syndrome (FAS) and the less severe fetal alcohol effects (FAE). The effects are the same regardless of which alcohol-containing beverage is consumed: beer, wine, liqueur, or liquor.

Amphetamines: Drugs in the amphetamine family were once widely prescribed as an aid to dieting because they suppress appetite. Today they're prescribed only rarely, but forms such as *methamphetamine* are widely available on the illegal market. Amphetamine use during pregnancy can cause stillbirth and prematurity, as well as many of the same effects as those caused by cocaine.

Cocaine: Cocaine ingestion during pregnancy, whether in powder or crack form, can have numerous lasting physical and psychological effects on the child.

Marijuana: The effects on the embryo or fetus when mothers smoke marijuana (or other forms of the drug such as hashish) still are not fully understood.

Mercury, lead, and other pollutants: Poisoning by mercury, lead, and other industrial byproducts can occur through pollution of the water supply. The pollutants then find their way up the food chain into fish (Reuhl & Chang, 1979) and other food sources. Dangerous chemicals can also be ingested through direct consumption of tainted water or air (Vorhees & Mollnow, 1987) and can cause profound mental retardation and neurological impairment in the developing child. Other potentially harmful chemicals include polychlorinated biphenyls (PCBs), found in electrical transformers and paint (Jacobson, Jacobson, Schwartz, Fein, & Dowler, 1984), as well as food preservatives, insecticides, and even some cosmetics and hair dyes.

Narcotics: In general, narcotics such as codeine, morphine, heroin, dilaudid, and even methadone (a maintenance drug that supresses narcotics withdrawal symptoms) depress fetal respiration and can cause behavioral disturbances in the infant. Babies born to women who use such drugs regularly are smaller than normal and are less responsive as newborns. The babies show drug withdrawal symptoms—extreme irritability, shrill crying, vomiting, shaking, and poor temperature control. They tend to have low appetite and difficulty sucking, and their sleep patterns are disturbed, at least for the first several weeks. At 4 months, they are more tense and rigid and less well coordinated than normal babies. Up to 12 months, they may have difficulty maintaining attention, and researchers suspect that attention and language deficits may persist well into childhood (Vorhees & Mollnow, 1987).

Over-the-counter (OTC) drugs: Many OTC medications such as analgesics, cough medicines, laxatives, and allergy pills are—at best—unsafe. Aspirin in large doses can lead to excessive bleeding and other problems (Briggs et al., 1986). Large doses of antacid tablets or cough syrups, especially those containing codeine, may not be entirely safe (Brackbill et al., 1985). Even vitamins are risky if taken in excess. Moreover, such substances don't clear from the fetus's system as easily as they do from the mother's.

Tobacco: Smoking, whether cigarettes, cigars, or pipes, and also dipping or chewing tobacco, can cause serious birth problems and birth defects.

Tranquilizers and sleeping pills: Like alcohol, tranquilizers and sleeping pills are central nervous system depressants. Although their effects aren't generally thought to be severe (except in the case of thalidomide), they cause the baby to be born sedated, and they increase the risk of respiratory distress and anoxia.

The more alcohol that is consumed during pregnancy, the greater the risk of damage to the embryo or fetus. Even when alcohol is consumed in moderate amounts such as an ounce or two daily, researchers have found higher rates of respiratory and heart-rate abnormalities in the newborn, difficulty in adapting to normal sounds and lights, and lower mental development scores later in infancy (Streissguth et al., 1984). Other effects include less attentiveness and compliance with adults during the preschool years, and increased chances of learning disabilities, attention problems, and hyperactivity (Briggs et al., 1986; Streissguth et al., 1989; Barr et al., 1990; Newman & Buka, 1991).

Also note that even moderate alcohol use may interact with stress (which might lead to alcohol use in the first place). A recent study of alcohol-consuming mother monkeys found that their infants later displayed significant impairments in attention and neuromotor functioning (Schneider et al., 1997). The effects were greater for infants whose mothers had been experimentally exposed to "mild" psychological stress. That outcome might help explain why babies born to mothers in stress-ridden lower-income neighborhoods have higher rates of alcohol-related birth defects.

So the conclusion about alcohol is easy: *Any* level of drinking during pregnancy is risky.

TOBACCO Tobacco, with its chief ingredient, nicotine, has been clearly linked to fetal abnormalities. Among mothers who smoke heavily, rates of spontaneous abortion, stillbirth, and prematurity are much higher than in the nonsmoking population. Babies born to heavy smokers tend to weigh less at birth than those born to nonsmokers and have delayed growth that can continue for years (Naeye, 1979, 1980, 1981; Streissguth et al., 1989; Vorhees & Mollnow, 1987). Children of mothers who smoke regularly may do more poorly in school and have a shorter attention span than children of nonsmokers (Naeye & Peters, 1984; Vorhees & Mollnow, 1987).

How does smoking damage or even kill fetuses? Research points to the placenta—the site of nutrient exchange between the bloodstream of the mother and that of the fetus. Some forms of damage to the placenta that interfere with nutrient exchange occur only among women who smoke, and other forms occur more often among women who smoke than among those who don't (Naeye, 1981). Researchers also suggest that smoking can constrict blood vessels in the uterus, reducing the flow of nutrients (Fried & Oxorn, 1980). Both effects can also reduce the flow of oxygen, with potential harm to brain tissue.

MARIJUANA Smoking marijuana during pregnancy is also inadvisable, although the effects of marijuana use have been less thoroughly studied than those of alcohol and tobacco. The results of a series of studies in Jamaica are noteworthy. In Jamaica, marijuana is used in much higher doses among some segments of the population than in the United States. Newborn infants who were exposed to marijuana before birth have relatively high-pitched cries and behave in a fashion similar to that of infants experiencing mild narcotics withdrawal (see Table 2–2). Thus, it appears that high doses of marijuana affect the central nervous system and, hence, the infant's neurological control (Lester & Dreher, 1989).

COCAINE The 1970s and 1980s saw a dramatic increase in the use of cocaine powder and later crack cocaine as recreational drugs. There was a corresponding increase in cocaine-related birth problems. Although cocaine powder and crack cocaine may have equal potency (depending on the extent to which they are diluted by sellers to increase profits), smoking crack causes the drug to

Smoking has been clearly linked to fetal abnormalities.

enter the user's system and to reach the brain and other parts of the body much faster than does inhaling or injecting the powder. Crack therefore produces higher concentrations of cocaine and is potentially more harmful to the embryo or fetus (or to the newborn child via breast milk).

Early studies of prenatal exposure to cocaine found few negative effects (Madden et al., 1986), and some pregnant mothers, lulled into a false sense of security, used cocaine to ease labor. But more extensive research has demonstrated that the risk of severe damage to the unborn child is considerable. Mothers who use cocaine experience more labor complications, and their infants have a high risk of prematurity, growth retardation, mental retardation, and even death by cerebral hemorrhage (Bateman et al., 1993). The infants also tend to smile less, are harder to console, and suck and root less intensely than normal infants (Phillips et al., 1996). Many infants born to cocaine-using mothers have difficulty establishing motor control, orienting to visual objects or sounds, and achieving normal regulation of waking and sleeping.

The majority of cocaine-exposed infants can be classified as "fragile." They are easily overloaded by normal environmental stimulation, have great difficulty controlling their nervous system, and often cry frantically and seem unable to sleep. Even after a month, they still have difficulty attending to normal stimulation without losing control and lapsing into urgent, high-pitched cries (Chasnoff, 1989). Even years later, after the most obvious symptoms have subsided, children of cocaine-using mothers have much higher rates of attention-deficit disorder, language delays, and learning disabilities (Hutchinson, 1991).

Clearly, mothers should avoid even the slightest cocaine use during pregnancy. Moreover, since cocaine use is illegal, some people believe that there should be criminal penalties for mothers who knowingly use it during pregnancy. (See "A Matter for Debate," page 66.)

Finally, note that the majority of expectant mothers who abuse drugs are *polydrug* users: They consume drugs in combinations that can compound the effects on the developing child. Since drug-using mothers often suffer malnutrition and health problems as well, it can be very difficult to identify the effects of specific teratogens (Newman & Buka, 1991). Nevertheless, it seems clear that the more drugs are consumed during pregnancy, the worse off the child will be.

---

1. Summarize aspects of the mother's age, health, and nutrition that can help or harm the developing child.
2. Discuss the kinds of damage that occur during each critical period of prenatal development.
3. Of the drugs cited in this section, what are the worst ones to use during pregnancy, and why?

REVIEW & APPLY

CHILDBIRTH

Although attitudes toward pregnancy and approaches to childbirth vary from one culture to another, the birth of every normal human child follows the same biological timetable. In this section we'll look closely at the stages of childbirth and characteristics of the newborn.

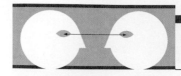

A MATTER FOR DEBATE

PROSECUTING VERSUS TREATING CRACK MOTHERS

Crack cocaine use by pregnant mothers can have severe and lasting effects on the developing child. It was the crack "epidemic," which began in the early 1980s, that played a major role in focusing the attention of state criminal justice systems, social services agencies, and especially the medical community on drug use during pregnancy.

Drug-using mothers are often prosecuted under existing child-abuse laws, which can result in felony convictions. Such convictions are hard to obtain, however; they often become bogged down in legal details. For example, in a 1997 case, a major point at issue was whether an existing law regarding child abuse also applies to a fetus. Convictions in several states have been overturned by rulings that such laws do not apply.

In a 1996 survey, the National Court Appointed Special Advocate Association (CASA) studied thirty-five criminal cases in twenty states, most involving charges of child abuse or delivery of drugs to a minor. The researchers found that in most of the cases, the charges were dismissed or later overturned. Civil prosecutions for abuse and neglect—based on a mother's testing positive for drugs when her baby is born—have been more successful, at least in removing the babies from the mother and placing them in foster care. However, even successful criminal or civil prosecutions address the problem of prenatal effects only to the extent that they serve as a possible future deterrent.

Can we instead treat mothers during pregnancy? The first problem is detection: Expectant mothers are not routinely screened for drug use, partly because such screening would cause many to avoid prenatal care rather than risk detection. When prenatal-care professionals do detect drug use during pregnancy, mothers don't necessarily always submit to treatment voluntarily. Mandatory, court-enforced treatment for pregnant mothers may work, although there is a need for further research on its efficacy. Moreover, in many cases, treatment is not a practi-

cal approach. Drug-abusing mothers-to-be typically lack the resources to pay for treatment, and publicly or privately funded treatment programs for such mothers are scarce. Thus, convicted or civilly committed pregnant addicts are often sent to prison while awaiting treatment. While in prison, they often receive no prenatal care. Finally, when they do receive prenatal treatment and abruptly cease drug use, there are increased risks to the embryo or fetus as a result of *in utero* withdrawal—risks that include abortion and premature delivery.

The solution? Since criminal prosecution and incarceration have no proven benefits, the Committee on Substance Abuse of the American Academy of Pediatrics recommends preventive education programs for *all* women of childbearing age before they become pregnant.

Primary sources: The National Center on Addiction and Substance Abuse at Columbia University (1996); American Academy of Pediatrics (1996).

STAGES OF CHILDBIRTH

The process of childbirth can be divided into three stages: initial labor, labor and delivery, and afterbirth.

INITIAL LABOR The first stage is the period during which the cervical opening of the uterus begins to dilate to allow for passage of the baby. Although **initial labor** can last from a few minutes to over 30 hours, the norms are 12 to 15 hours for the first child and 6 to 8 hours for later children. Labor begins with mild uterine contractions, usually spaced 15 to 20 minutes apart. As labor progresses, the contractions increase in frequency and intensity until they occur only 3 to 5 minutes apart. The muscular contractions of labor are involuntary, and it's best if the mother tries to relax during this period.

Some mothers experience *false labor* (called *Braxton-Hicks contractions*), especially with the first child. False labor can be hard to distinguish from real labor, but one test that usually works is to have the expectant mother walk around. The pains of false labor tend to diminish, whereas those of real labor become more uncomfortable.

Two other events occur during initial labor. First, a mucus plug that covers the cervix is released. This process is called *showing*, and it may include some

initial labor The first stage is the period during which the cervical opening of the uterus begins to dilate to allow for passage of the baby.

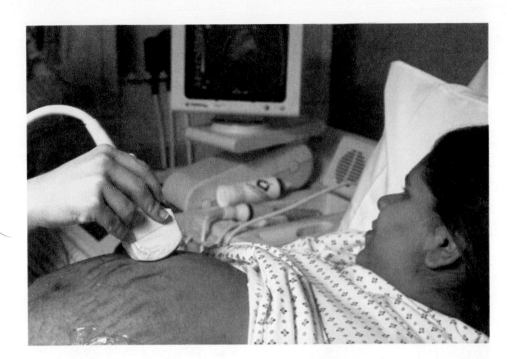

The safety and reliability of ultrasound imagery used to inspect the fetus makes this technique popular among the medical professional.

bleeding. Second, the amniotic sac may break, and some amniotic fluid may rush forth, as when a mother's "water breaks."

LABOR AND DELIVERY   The second stage of childbirth begins with stronger and more regular contractions and ends with the actual birth of the baby. Once the cervix is fully dilated, contractions begin to push the baby through the birth canal. **Labor and delivery** usually takes from 10 to 40 minutes, and like initial labor, it tends to be shorter with succeeding births. Contractions come every 2 to 3 minutes and are longer and more intense than those that occur during initial labor. If she is fully conscious, the mother can assist in the delivery by controlling her breathing and "pushing" or bearing down with her abdominal muscles during each contraction.

Normally, the first part of the baby to emerge from the birth canal is the head. First it "crowns," or becomes visible, and then it emerges farther with each contraction. The tissue of the mother's *perineum* (the region between the vagina and the rectum) must stretch considerably to allow the baby's head to emerge. In U.S. hospitals, the attending physician often makes an incision called an **episiotomy** to enlarge the vaginal opening. It is believed that an incision will heal more neatly than the jagged tear that might otherwise occur. Episiotomies are much less common in Western Europe.

Finally, in most normal births, the baby is born in a facedown position. After the head is clear, the baby's face twists to the side so that its body emerges with the least resistance.

AFTERBIRTH   The expulsion of the placenta, the umbilical cord, and related tissues marks the third stage of childbirth, called **afterbirth.** This stage is virtually painless and typically occurs within 20 minutes after the delivery. Again, the mother can help by bearing down. The afterbirth is checked for imperfections that might indicate damage to the newborn.

labor and delivery   The second stage of childbirth, which begins with stronger and more regular contractions and ends with the actual birth of the baby. Once the cervix is fully dilated, contractions begin to push the baby through the birth canal.

episiotomy   An incision to enlarge the vaginal opening.

afterbirth   The third and last stage of childbirth, typically occurring within 20 minutes after delivery, during which the placenta and umbilical cord are expelled from the uterus.

The sequence of childbirth.

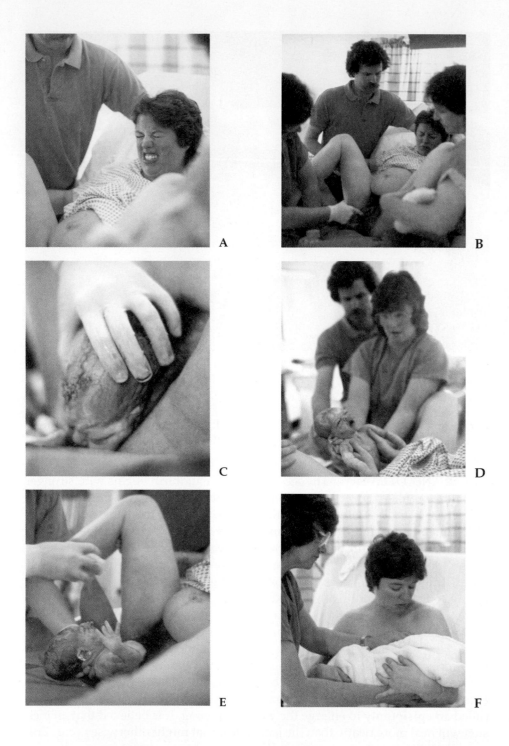

A   B

C   D

E   F

FIRST IMPRESSIONS

The new baby has arrived, and everyone wants to know how much it weighs and whom it looks like. What do **neonates** (newborns) look like, and how do they react to being born?

SIZE AND APPEARANCE   At birth the average full-term infant weighs between $5\frac{1}{2}$ and $9\frac{1}{2}$ pounds (2.5 and 4.3 kilograms) and is between 19 and 22 inches (about 48 and 56 centimeters) long. The skin may still be partly covered with the vernix caseosa and the lanugo hair (which drops off sometime during the first month).

neonates   Babies in the first month of life.

The newborn's head looks misshapen and elongated because of a process called *molding*. The soft, bony plates of the skull, connected only by cartilage areas called **fontanelles,** are squeezed together in the birth canal to allow the baby's head to pass through. Because fontanelles don't fully harden and fuse the skull until late in infancy, infants' heads should never be bumped or thumped. Also, a neonate's external genitalia may appear enlarged because of the presence of hormones that passed to the baby prior to birth.

The new parents may initially be shocked by their baby's appearance. It will take several months for the neonate to become a smooth, plump infant like those shown on TV and in magazine ads.

IS BIRTH TRAUMATIC?   Whether or not birth is "traumatic" and whether, as Freud proposed, it is related to adult anxiety, birth *is* a radical transition from the protected, supporting environment of the uterus to a much less certain, even harsh, external environment. No longer will oxygen and nutrients be provided as needed. Newborns must breathe for themselves and learn to communicate their needs and wants in a social world that may or may not be responsive to them.

Childbirth is remarkably stressful for the newborn. But the full-term baby is well prepared to cope with the stress (Gunnar, 1989). In the last few moments of birth, the infant experiences a major surge of adrenalin and noradrenalin, the hormones that counter stress. The adrenalin also helps counteract any initial oxygen deficiency and prepares the baby for breathing through the lungs. The first breaths may be difficult because the amniotic fluid that was in the lungs must be expelled and millions of tiny air sacs in the lungs must be filled. Yet within minutes most infants are breathing regularly.

What about pain? The newborn also has relatively high levels of a natural painkiller called beta-endorphin circulating in its blood. That, along with the stimulating hormones, causes most infants to be unusually alert and receptive shortly after birth. Many experts have suggested that this period of extended alertness, which may last for an hour or more, is an ideal time for the parents and the infant to get acquainted (Nilsson, 1990).

A PERIOD OF ADJUSTMENT   Despite their helpless appearance, full-term newborns are sturdy little beings who are already making a profound adjustment to their new life—from having the mother's body do everything for them to functioning on their own as separate individuals. There are four critical areas of physical adjustment: respiration, blood circulation, digestion, and temperature regulation.

With the first breaths of air, the lungs are inflated and begin to work as the basic organ of the child's own respiratory system. During the first few days after birth, neonates experience periods of coughing and sneezing. These often alarm new parents, but they serve to clear mucus and amniotic fluid from the infant's air passages. The onset of breathing marks a significant change in the neonate's circulatory system, too. The baby's heart no longer needs to pump blood to the placenta for oxygen. Instead, a valve in the baby's heart closes and redirects the flow of blood to the the lungs. The shift from fetal to independent circulatory and respiratory systems begins immediately after birth but is not completed for several days. **Anoxia** (lack of oxygen) for more than a few minutes at birth or during the first few days of adjustment may cause permanent brain damage.

Before birth the placenta provided nourishment, but now the infant's own digestive system must begin to function. This change is longer and slower than the dramatic changes in respiration and circulation that occur immediately

fontanelles   The soft, bony plates of the skull, connected only by cartilage.

anoxia   Lack of oxygen that can cause brain damage.

after birth. The neonate's temperature regulation system also adjusts gradually to its new environment. Within the uterus, the baby's skin was maintained at a constant temperature. After birth, the baby's own metabolism must protect it from even minor changes in external temperature. For that reason—unless they're in incubators—babies must be carefully covered to keep them warm during the first few days and weeks of life. Gradually they become able to maintain a constant body temperature, aided by a layer of fat that accumulates during the early weeks.

THE APGAR TEST   Not all neonates are equally well equipped to adjust to the changes that occur at birth, and it is essential to detect any problems or weaknesses as early as possible. In 1953 Virginia Apgar devised a standard scoring system that allows hospitals to evaluate an infant's condition quickly and objectively. The **Apgar Scale** is presented in Table 2–3. One minute and again at 5 minutes after birth, the scorer observes the neonate's pulse, breathing, muscle tone, general reflex response, and general skin tone. A perfect Apgar score is 10 points, with a score of 7 or more considered normal. Scores below 7 indicate that some bodily processes are not functioning fully and may require special procedures. A score of 4 or less requires immediate emergency measures. Later, during the first few days of life, the neonate will also typically be assessed on the more detailed Brazelton Neurobehavioral Assessment Scale discussed in Chapter 4.

APPROACHES TO CHILDBIRTH

Although the biology of childbirth is universal, the precise ways in which babies are delivered and cared for vary considerably across generations, across cultures, and from one family to another. Some cultures, for example, view childbirth as similar to an illness. Among the Cuna Indians of Panama, pregnant women visit the medicine man daily for drugs and are sedated throughout labor and delivery. Among the !Kung-San, a tribal society in northwestern Botswana, women tell no one about their initial labor pains and go out into the bush alone to give birth. They deliver the baby, cut the cord, and stabilize the newborn—all without assistance (Komner & Shostak, 1987).

In some cultures, home birthing is still the norm. But in most Western industrialized nations, most births occur in hospitals (although home births are

TABLE 2–3   APGAR SCORING SYSTEM FOR INFANTS

	SCORES		
	0	1	2
Pulse:	Absent	Less than 100	More than 100
Breathing:	Absent	Slow, irregular	Strong cry
Muscle tone:	Limp	Some flexion of extremities	Active motion
Reflex response:	No response	Grimace	Vigorous cry
Color*:	Blue, pale	Body pink, extremities blue	Completely pink

Apgar Scale   A standard scoring system that allows hospitals to evaluate an infant's condition quickly and objectively.

*For nonwhites, alternative tests of mucous membranes, palms, and soles are used.
Source: "Proposal for a New Method of Evaluating the Newborn Infant" by V. Apgar, *Anesthesia and Analgesia,* 1953, 32, 260. Used by permission of the International Anesthesia Research Society.

again on the rise in the United States). The extent to which the father is involved during childbirth also varies considerably both across and within cultures.

"TRADITIONAL" CHILDBIRTH A hundred and fifty years ago, "traditional" childbirth meant home delivery with the assistance of a family doctor or a *midwife*—a woman experienced in childbirth, with or without formal training and in those days more often without. With the advent of modern medicine, birthing shifted to hospitals, where the mother could be assisted by specialized medical staff and emergency equipment in case of complications. Infant and maternal mortality decreased significantly as a result. Therefore, today when we speak of **traditional childbirth** we're actually talking about hospital labor and delivery.

Until recent decades the father was excluded from the labor and delivery rooms. (Think about those old movies in which the father paces up and down outside the delivery room and finally sees his baby for the first time through the nursery window.) And because childbirth was assumed to be highly painful, the mother was usually anesthetized and sedated. Since such medications easily pass the placental barrier, the baby was also anesthetized and sedated. And although this practice doesn't necessarily have harmful long-term effects, it does produce babies who are groggy and less alert at birth and therefore are less responsive to parents and others. Although no one disputes the importance of easing the mother's pain, it is clear that medications should be used with caution (Broman, 1986).

CONTEMPORARY PRACTICES In general, the mother's experience of childbirth depends on her experience and mental set and her knowledge about what to expect. That view is the basis for what is now known as **"natural" or prepared childbirth** that can take various forms but is based on procedures primarily developed by Fernand Lamaze (1958), a French obstetrician. Whether or not prepared childbirth is practiced in its entirety, the approach has had a major impact on the procedures hospitals use during childbirth.

In prepared childbirth the expectant mother and her coach (father, family member, or friend) attend a short series of classes. They learn about the biology of childbirth, and the mother practices relaxation exercises and control of her breathing, with the coach assisting her. (The relaxation exercises help reduce the pain of labor and delivery; the breathing and other techniques help distract the mother from any discomfort she may be feeling.) When the day arrives, the coach is present throughout childbirth to provide support and to help the mother stay as relaxed as possible. Medication can be kept to a minimum or perhaps not used at all, so that the mother is conscious and alert and actively assists in the birthing process.

Generally, labor is shorter and less stressful for both mother and infant if the mother and coach have accurate knowledge about what is happening in each stage (Slade et al., 1993; Mackey, 1995). It is also helpful if only limited medication is used and the mother is able to participate. There is also less fear and muscle tension when the mother knows what to expect, especially if the delivery is her first. As a result, both parents feel more in control of the birth process (Leventhal et al., 1989).

Today most U.S. hospitals allow the father or other coach to be present during labor and delivery. Some hospitals also provide more homelike delivery and recovery rooms, or entire **birthing centers** either within or near the hospital. Birthing centers are designed to accommodate the entire process, from labor through delivery and recovery (Parker, 1980). They combine the privacy,

Pregnant women and their coaches exercise and practice for prepared (natural) childbirth while their teacher looks on.

traditional childbirth Hospital labor and delivery.

"natural" or prepared childbirth This can take various forms but is based on procedures primarily developed by Fernand Lamaze, a French obstetrician.

birthing centers Designed to accommodate the entire process, from labor through delivery and recovery.

serenity, and intimacy of a home birth with the safety and backup of medical technology, viewing the parents' social, psychological, and aesthetic needs as just as important as medical considerations (Allgaier, 1978). The delivery is most often performed by a licensed nurse-midwife rather than by a physician.

Most birthing centers encourage prepared childbirth and an early return home, generally within 24 hours. They also encourage mothers to spend as much time as possible with the newborns to help promote attachment (Allgaier, 1978; Parker, 1980). That practice is also the norm in modern hospitals, in contrast to earlier practices in which the baby was whisked away after birth and kept in a nursery.

Most parents find birthing centers deeply satisfying. The centers keep the focus on the family and give the parents the maximum possible independence and control (Eakins, 1986). In all, the philosophy of childbirth has changed. It is now much more likely to be viewed as a natural, nonpathological event during which technological intervention should be kept to a minimum.

Birthing centers are not equipped to handle everyone, though. They screen out women with high-risk factors or complications. Typical guidelines exclude women over 35 having their first baby, women bearing twins, women suffering from diseases like diabetes or cardiac problems, and women who have had previous Cesarean deliveries (Lubic & Ernst, 1978). A hospital delivery is also recommended if there are signs of potential problems with the baby or the birth.

HIGH TECHNOLOGY FOR HIGH-RISK PREGNANCIES   The branch of medicine known as **perinatology** considers childbirth not as a single point in time but as a span of time that begins with conception and continues through the first several months of life. Perinatologists, who specialize in the management of high-risk pregnancies and deliveries, are usually associated with major hospitals that have the resources to support such pregnancies. They monitor the mother and her baby through pregnancy and delivery, using prenatal screening procedures such as amniocentesis and fetoscopy (described in Chapter 3) to identify potential problems requiring prompt medical treatment (see "Eye on Diversity," page 73).

In the past quarter-century, obstetrical medicine has progressed dramatically. Infants who would not have survived in the 1970s are now thriving in record numbers. For example, today over 80% of premature infants weighing 750 to 1000 grams (1.6 to 2.2 pounds) will survive in a well-equipped intensive care unit for newborns (Ohlsson et al.,). In 1972, only one out of five survived.

The new medical advances include drugs, microsurgery, diagnostic tools, and preventive measures. For example, many hospitals routinely use **fetal monitors,** which can be applied either externally or internally. The external monitor records the intensity of uterine contractions and the baby's heartbeat by means of two belts placed around the mother's abdomen. The internal monitor consists of a plastic tube containing electrodes, which is inserted into the vagina and attached to the baby's head. It is used to measure uterine pressure, fetal breathing, and head compression (Goodlin, 1979). The monitor can signal compression of the umbilical cord, poor fetal oxygen intake, and other kinds of fetal distress (*Pediatrics*, 1979). Typically, the internal-monitoring device is used only in high-risk situations. The use of fetal monitors in low-risk pregnancies, formerly a common practice, is now discouraged by the American College of Obstetrics and Gynecology (BIRTH, 1988), partly on the

perinatology   A branch of medicine that deals with childbirth as a span of time including conception, the prenatal period, delivery, and the first few months of life.

fetal monitor   The external monitor records the intensity of uterine contractions and the baby's heartbeat by means of two belts placed around the mother's abdomen. The internal monitor consists of a plastic tube containing electrodes, which is inserted into the vagina and attached to the baby's head.

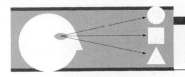

EYE ON DIVERSITY

NEWBORNS AT RISK

In the United States, about 90% of babies are born on time and healthy, scoring a 9 or 10 on the Apgar Scale. Only about 10% are born preterm; only 7% weigh less than 5½ pounds; and less than 1% die in their first year. Because of medical advances and health education, infant mortality rates in most of the developed nations have fallen steadily in the last five decades, from 47 deaths per 1000 births in 1940 to an all-time low of 8.1 in 1995 (Children's Defense Fund, 1991; National Center for Health Statistics, 1993a; 1993b; 1995).

Despite these optimistic statistics, some infants still face serious risks at birth. Let's take a closer look at the statistics on the roughly 10% of American babies who come into the world struggling to survive. Who are these infants? Can some of their problems be prevented?

Black infants and those in poor families are more than twice as likely to die in their first year, compared with white infants and those in families above the poverty line. Premature babies or babies with low Apgar scores are far more likely to be born when the mother is under age 15 or over age 44, poor, or unmarried (National Center

for Health Statistics, 1993a). Are there any common threads in this pattern?

One of the best predictors of low birth weight is the absence of prenatal care starting in the first 3 months of pregnancy. Teenage mothers, minority mothers, unmarried mothers, and women living in poverty are far more likely to delay prenatal care than are married, more affluent women over age 20 (National Center for Health Statistics, 1993a). Some places lack basic health services for poor families, services that can often remedy maternal health problems like high blood pressure, anemia, or poor nutrition before they become risk factors for the infant; nor are there educational programs to address potentially harmful behaviors like smoking, alcohol use, and drug use, as well as the basics of child care.

Young mothers are particularly at risk. Usually they are physically and emotionally immature and lack the stamina, patience, and understanding to care even for a healthy child. Often a lack of basic education, along with isolation from peers and family, makes it even more difficult for them to cope with motherhood. As one social worker reported:

I will never forget the look of fatigue which I saw on the face of a

14-year-old girl who had given birth to twins four months previously. She looked old beyond her years as she sat on the stoop of her parents' house in rural South Carolina. Her mother and brother were away at work, her younger siblings in school, while she remained home to care for her babies and her youngest brother. Her father had tried to be supportive, but now, he had moved several hundred miles away to find work, so the bulk of the child care fell on her. At an age when her peers were starting high school, dreaming of their futures and beginning to date, it seemed her future had arrived. She was at home, lonely, chasing a toddler, changing diapers, and soothing two restless babies.

In spite of improved medical technology, the death rate for low-birth-weight babies has actually risen in the 1990s (National Center for Health Statistics, 1993b), especially where poverty has increased and drug use and AIDS are widespread (Wiener & Engel, 1991). Faced with such statistics, Marian Wright Edelman of the Children's Defense Fund asks (1992), "Is this the best America can do?"

---

grounds that fetal monitors are linked to an increase in potentially unnecesary Cesarian sections as discussed later.

In all, the new technology of childbirth is a blessing for many families, especially those facing premature or high-risk deliveries. But some critics argue that it is too frequently applied to deliveries that should be routine. For example, some consumer advocates argue that the high rate of Cesarean births is a result of increased technology in the delivery room.

COMPLICATIONS IN CHILDBIRTH

BREECH PRESENTATION   More difficult births occur when the baby is positioned in a **breech presentation** (buttocks first) or a posterior presentation (facing toward the mother's abdomen instead of toward her back). In each of these cases, there is potential injury to the mother or anoxia for the infant due to

breech presentation   The baby's position in the uterus such that the buttocks will emerge first; assistance is usually needed in such cases to prevent injury to the infant, producing anoxia.

FIGURE 2–4
Two types of breech presentation. Delivery in this position is difficult for both mother and baby.

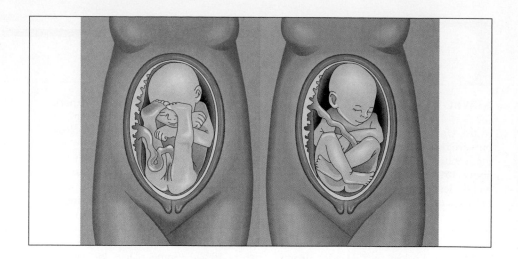

strangling. Figure 2–4 shows two types of breech presentation. Attempts are made to turn the baby to the proper birth position; if they are unsuccessful, the infant may be delivered by Cesarian section.

CESAREAN SECTION   Various other complications may occur during childbirth. In addition to breech presentation, these include early breaking of the amniotic sac without labor (thus leaving the fetus unprotected), failure to begin labor or to respond to attempts to induce labor postterm, and serious fetal emergency. In such cases the childbirth team may resort to **Cesarean section** surgery, in which the baby is removed through the mother's abdominal wall. This procedure, often called "C-section," is frequently performed under regional anesthesia so that the mother is awake and aware. Because the procedure is quick, very little of the anesthesia reaches the infant. The outcome for both mother and infant is excellent in most cases.

Nevertheless, many believe that the rate of Cesarian births is far too high (LoCicero, 1993). The percentage of C-sections performed in the United States was 5.5% in 1970. By 1980, it had risen to 18%, and it was 24.4% in 1987 (Cohen & Estner, 1983; Marieskind, 1989). Though C-sections have recently declined somewhat, they are still the most common form of major surgery. Nearly a million are performed each year, with some hospitals performing over 40% of childbirths by this method.

Why is the high rate of C-sections a problem, given that the procedure is relatively safe? For one thing, it is major abdominal surgery, which requires a much longer recovery period than normal childbirth. For another, it is expensive and puts a greater strain on parents and their health insurance providers. Third, some consumer advocates argue that the sharp rise in the rate of C-sections is a consequence of increased use of certain medical procedures that seem to interrupt the natural process of labor. They argue that the use of fetal monitors and the regular administration of four or five different kinds of drugs, such as painkillers or drugs to induce labor, actually create situations that lead to the need for surgical childbirth.

Finally, and perhaps most important, the psychological reaction to Cesarean childbirth can be quite negative. Many mothers report feeling disappointed and disillusioned, particularly those who had general instead of regional anesthesia and "missed the event." Repeated studies report that some mothers who have

Cesarean section   Surgical procedure used to remove the baby and the placenta from the uterus by cutting through the abdominal wall.

had a C-section are disappointed or even angry, are slow to choose a name for the baby, test lower on self-esteem shortly after giving birth, and have more difficulty feeding their infants (Oakley & Richards, 1990). And there appears to be more intense postpartum depression following C-sections than following normal vaginal deliveries (Cohen & Estner, 1983; Kitzinger, 1981).

Premature Infants   The most common indicator of prematurity is low birth weight. As specified by the World Health Organization, a newborn who weighs less than $5\frac{1}{2}$ pounds (2.5 kilograms) is usually classified as having low birth weight and being in need of special attention.

Two indicators of low birth weight are frequently confused, however. The first is **preterm status.** An infant born before a gestation period of 35 weeks (or 37 weeks from the mother's last menstrual period) is preterm. Most preterm infants weigh less than $5\frac{1}{2}$ pounds (2.5 kilograms). The second indicator is **small-for-date.** A full-term newborn who weighs less than $5\frac{1}{2}$ pounds is considered small-for-date. Fetal malnutrition, for example, can produce small-for-date babies.

Prematurity can occur for a number of reasons. The most common cause is a multiple birth, in which two or more infants are born at the same time. Other causes include diseases or disabilities of the fetus, maternal smoking or other drug use, and malnutrition. In addition, maternal diseases such as diabetes or polio may lead to delivery of a baby before full term.

Immediately after birth, premature infants usually have greater difficulty adjusting to the external world than full-term babies do. Temperature control is a common problem: Premature infants have even fewer fat cells than normal infants and have a harder time maintaining body heat. For that reason, newborns weighing less than $5\frac{1}{2}$ pounds are usually placed in incubators immediately after birth. Another common problem is the difficulty of matching the nutritional environment of the late fetal period. In their first few months, premature infants seem unable to catch up to full-term infants in weight and height.

Many researchers believe that the effects of prematurity can last long after infancy. Historically, studies indicated that premature infants suffer more illnesses in their first 3 years of life, score lower on IQ tests, and are slightly more prone to behavioral problems than full-term babies (Knobloch et al., 1959). However, more recent research has found that such difficulties are experienced by less than one-quarter of premature infants (Bennett et al., 1983; Klein et al., 1985). Still, researchers have also found a high prior rate of prematurity among children who were later diagnosed as being learning disabled, having reading problems, or being distractible or hyperactive.

All such reports must be interpreted very carefully. It cannot be concluded, for example, that prematurity *causes* such defects. Although premature babies may be less able to adjust to the shock of birth, the relationship between prematurity and later problems is more complex than that. For example, conditions like malnutrition, faulty development of the placenta, or crowding in the uterus may result in a number of symptoms, only one of which is low birth weight. So prematurity is often a *symptom* of a disability or malfunction rather than a cause.

Some of the later problems of premature infants may also arise from the way they're treated during the first few weeks of life. Because of the need to keep them in incubators, they receive less of the normal caregiver contact experienced by most newborns. Few premature infants are breast-fed; few are

preterm status   An infant born before a gestation period of 35 weeks.

small-for-date   A full-term newborn who weighs less than $5\frac{1}{2}$ pounds.

held even while being bottle-fed; and some are unable to suck at all for the first several weeks. As a result, they miss the social experiences of feeding, which normally establish an early bond between the caregiver and the full-term infant. And caregivers may be less responsive to "preemies" because they are unattractive or sickly, or display their characteristic high-pitched, grating cry.

The consequences of limited early contact due to prematurity can be seen throughout infancy (Goldberg, 1979). On average, preterm infants are held farther from the parent's body, touched less, and cooed at less. Later, they tend to play less actively than full-term babies and have difficulty absorbing external stimuli. Even so, many of the differences between premature and full-term babies disappear by the end of the first year, especially when parents actively compensate by spending extra time with the premature babies and making extra efforts to get them to respond. In many hospitals parents are encouraged to become involved in the care of premature infants. The parents put on masks and gowns, and they enter the intensive care unit to help with feeding, diaper changes, and other care. They stimulate the baby by gently stroking and talking to it, and the result is better attachment and caregiving when the baby is sent home.

There have been several follow-up studies of premature infants whose parents helped care for them in the hospital. The parents learned to be especially responsive to the often subtle behaviors of their infants that might indicate needs and discomforts, and the children improved at each developmental stage. As infants, these babies developed more appropriately in performing social and intellectual tasks (compared with premature infants whose parents did not care for them in the hospital.) At age 12, the children showed higher intellectual and social competence (Beckwith & Cohen, 1989; Goldberg et al., 1988).

Some of the detrimental effects of prematurity may be offset by an enriched environment during the first year of life. In a pilot program for infants who had been born prematurely because of fetal malnutrition (Zeskind & Ramey, 1978), the infants were given high-quality day care in addition to the necessary medical and nutritional services. Most of them reached normal performance levels by 18 months. A matched group of fetally malnourished infants received the same medical and nutritional services but were cared for at home. Those infants reached normal levels more slowly, and deficits in their performance were still apparent at age 2.

HIGH-RISK INFANTS High-risk infants, meaning those born with physical disabilities, present similar problems to those of preterm infants with regard to early experience. Ill or handicapped infants are likely to be separated from their parents for medical reasons and often have developmental problems that interfere with their ability to signal their parents and give them positive feedback for good caregiving. The result is often a fussy, unresponsive baby and confused, perhaps overattentive caregivers.

It can be extremely difficult for parents to become attached to a handicapped infant. In addition to problems such as early separation and hospitalization, deficiencies such as visual or auditory impairment may severely restrict the baby's ability to respond. Moreover, parents frequently need to go through a period of mourning over the "perfect" child who didn't arrive before they can accept, nurture, and become emotionally attached to the less-than-perfect baby who did. Support groups consisting of other parents with handicapped infants can be very constructive. Such groups help parents realize that they are not alone, and members who are going through similar experiences can often suggest helpful techniques.

1. Describe the three stages of childbirth. What can the mother do during each stage to assist in the process?
2. Why is birth stressful for the newborn? How is the full-term baby equipped to handle the process?
3. Contrast "traditional" childbirth with contemporary practices.
4. Why are Cesarean births controversial?
5. Discuss short- and long-term effects of prematurity.
6. What have researchers learned about the effects of an enriched environment for premature infants?

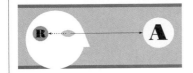

REVIEW & APPLY

THE EVOLVING FAMILY

As we've seen, childbirth is not just a medical event but is also a psychological and social milestone full of meaning for the family. The family system will no longer be the same. The neonate immediately starts signaling his or her presence, needs, health status, and personal style; and the parents, grandparents, and siblings respond in ways that reflect their personal and cultural beliefs. In this section we consider several aspects of the family's adjustment to its new member.

THE TRANSITION TO PARENTHOOD

The phrase "we're expecting" carries with it the understanding that expectant parents are making changes in their lives that may involve new roles and relationships. Aside from finding a place for baby in the home, adjusting to parenthood is a major life change for adults—especially with a first child. And major life changes are often accompanied by stress and the need to communicate and solve problems. The new parents must also make economic and social adjustments, and they often need to reevaluate and modify existing relationships. Related factors are the cultural attitudes of the family toward childbearing and child rearing.

Motivations for childbearing vary considerably from one culture to another. In some societies—including ours in times past—children are valued as financial assets or as providers for the parents in their old age. In other societies, children represent those who will maintain the family traditions or fulfill the parents' personal needs and goals. Or children may be regarded simply as a duty or a necessary burden. Certain cultures accept children as inevitable, a natural part of life for which conscious decision-making simply isn't necessary. In India, for example, traditional Hindu women want to have children in order to guarantee themselves a good life and afterlife (LeVine, 1989).

In all cultures, of course, pregnant women must adjust to the physical, psychological, and social changes that come with motherhood. Profound bodily changes occur that can hardly be ignored. Even before the fetus is large enough to cause changes in a woman's appearance, she may feel nauseated or experience fullness or a tingling sensation in her breasts. Often she may suffer fatigue and emotional hypersensitivity during the early weeks of pregnancy—with direct effects on other family members. In contrast, in the middle stage of pregnancy she may experience a sense of heightened well-being. In fact, some of her bodily systems, such as the circulatory system, may show increased ca-

Motivations for having children vary from culture to culture.

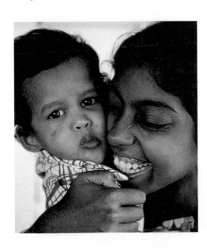

pacity and functioning. Finally, in the last stages of pregnancy some physical discomfort is usual, along with, at times, a feeling of emotional burden. Increased weight, reduced mobility, altered balance, and pressure on internal organs from the growing fetus are among the changes experienced by all pregnant women. Other symptoms, such as varicose veins, heartburn, frequent urination, and shortness of breath, contribute to the discomfort that women feel. There are wide individual differences in the *amount* of discomfort, fatigue, or burden that women experience during the last few weeks, however. Some women find the last stages of pregnancy to be much easier than do others.

The physical changes of pregnancy affect the mother's psychological state. She must come to terms with a new body image and an altered self-concept, and she must deal with the reactions of people around her. Some women experience a feeling of uniqueness or "distance" from friends, whereas others desire friendship and protection. Pregnancy may also be accompanied by considerable uncertainty about the future. In particular, the mother may be unsure about career plans following childbirth, anxious about her ability to care for a child, fearful of the possibility of birth defects, concerned about finances, or uncomfortable with the idea of being a mother. Ambivalence is common: A woman may be eager to have a child, yet disappointed that she will have to share her time, energy, and husband with that child (Osofsky & Osofsky, 1984). And women sometimes wonder whether they will be able to fulfill the expectations of everyone who will need them—the new baby, any older children, the husband, aging parents, close friends, and perhaps also job supervisors and coworkers.

THE FATHER'S CHANGING ROLE At first glance, the father's role seems easy compared with the major physical and emotional changes that the mother undergoes. Yet that perception usually isn't the case. Fathers report feeling excitement and pride, but some report feelings of rivalry with the coming child. And most men report an increased sense of responsibility that can seem overwhelming at times. Some report envy of their wife's ability to reproduce, and some report feeling like a mere bystander (Osofsky & Osofsky, 1984). Fathers worry about the future as much as mothers do. They feel concern about their ability to support the new family and about the role of parent. Fathers also tend to be concerned about whether the child will like and respect them and whether they will be able to meet the child's emotional needs (Ditzion & Wolf, 1978; Parke, 1981). Some fathers take the opportunity to learn more about children and parenting. Others make new financial arrangements. Many attempt to give their wife more emotional support. When there are other children in the family, fathers often spend more time with them and help them prepare for the new arrival (Parke, 1981).

Expectant fathers may also sometimes go through a phase in which they identify with their wife and actually display symptoms of their wife's pregnancy (Pruett, 1987). A somewhat extreme example occurs among the natives of the Yucatán in Mexico, where pregnancy is "confirmed" when the woman's *mate* experiences nausea, diarrhea, vomiting, or cramps (Pruett, 1987). Closer to home, expectant fathers sometimes crave the proverbial dill pickles with ice cream, and they also experience troubling dreams and disturbing changes in sexual desires, just as women sometimes do.

CULTURAL PRESCRIPTIONS It's easy to see that *both* parents' attitudes toward pregnancy and childbirth are often shaped by their culture. In the United States, for example, pregnancy was formerly treated as an abnormal condition. A pregnant woman was not seen in public or in school or in an office pursuing

Mother and father share the joy of admiring their newborn child.

a career. But beginning some 150 years ago, massive changes in family structure, roles, and perceptions of pregnancy took place; further changes have occurred in this century, particularly during World War II and in the years that followed. There were a rapid increase in the number of mothers working outside the home and a rise in mother-only families (Hernandez, 1997) that continues today—placing more pregnant as well as nonpregnant women in the workforce. Today women are encouraged to work until close to delivery. Women take the discomfort and fatigue of pregnancy in stride and go on with their normal lives.

In sum, social attitudes, coupled with the expectant parents' needs and emotions, can make pregnancy a period of stress, change, and adjustment. Such conflicts may be more intense in young parents, particularly those who lack the support of family and friends (Osofsky & Osofsky, 1984). None of these feelings will harm the fetus directly, of course, unless the mother suffers severe or prolonged emotional stress. Nevertheless, parental attitudes and stress do affect maternal diet, hormonal levels, rest, exercise, drug use, and resistance to disease, any of which can affect the developing child. Such attitudes and stress also help create the social environment that the child enters at birth.

THE BEGINNINGS OF ATTACHMENT

Attachment is an emotional bond between parents and children. It includes elements like feeling close and loving. Attachment, of course, works in both directions: The parents ideally become strongly attached to the baby and the baby to them. This reciprocal relationship begins at birth and continues to unfold and change in subtle ways throughout childhood, as we'll see in detail in Chapter 5.

After the initial birth cry or gurgle and the filling of the lungs, an alert newborn calms down and has time to relax on its mother's chest, if given the opportunity. After a little rest, the infant may struggle to focus on the mother's or father's face. The infant seems to listen as the parents watch in fascination and begin talking to it. They examine everything—the fingers and toes, the wrinkled but perhaps smiling face, the funny little ears. There is close physical contact, cradling, and stroking. Many infants find the breast and almost immediately start to nurse, with pauses to look about. Infants who have experienced little or no anesthesia may display adrenalin-heightened alertness and exploration for half an hour or more as their parents hold them close, establish eye contact, and talk to them.

It is now clear that babies are capable of limited imitation. They move their heads, open and close their mouths, and even stick out their tongues in response to the facial gestures of their parents (Meltzoff & Moore, 1989). Moreover, a baby's physical responses trigger physical processes within the mother's body. When babies lick or suck on the mother's nipples, secretion of prolactin (a hormone important in nursing) and of oxytocin (a hormone that causes the uterus to contract and reduces bleeding) increases. The infant also benefits from early breast-feeding: Although milk often is not yet available, the mother produces a substance called *colostrum* that appears to help clear the infant's digestive system and can confer many of the mother's immunities to the newborn (breast- versus bottle-feeding is discussed in Chapter 4).

Some researchers have proposed that early interactions between infants and their parents are also psychologically significant. In one study of 28 first-time, low-income, and therefore high-risk mothers (Klaus & Kennell, 1976), the hospital staff gave half of the mothers 16 extra hours of contact with their infants during the first 3 days after birth. The two groups of mothers and infants were

attachment The emotional bond that develops between a child and another individual. The infant's first bond is usually characterized by strong interdepence, intense mutual feelings, and vital emotional ties. ■

later examined at 1 month, 1 year, and 2 years. Over the 2-year period, the mothers with extra contact consistently showed significantly greater attachment to their babies. Subsequent research has deemphasized the importance of early bonding as defined by Klaus and Kennell (e.g., Field, 1979). For example, parents who adopt children long after the first few hours, days, or weeks after birth can become just as strongly attached to them. However, early contact is helpful in getting off to a good start, especially for teenage mothers or those who have had little or no experience with newborns, and for mothers of premature and high-risk infants.

Fathers who participate in their child's birth report an almost immediate attraction to the infant, with feelings of elation, pride, and heightened self-esteem (Greenberg & Morris, 1974). Some studies report that such fathers are more deeply involved with and attached to their infants than those who do not participate in their infant's birth and early care (Pruett, 1987). New fathers who don't participate in childbirth and do not have early contact with their infants frequently feel more distant from their wives and somewhat ignored when the baby arrives. Often the companionship between husband and wife is sharply reduced (Galinsky, 1980). Altogether, many studies report that fathers who begin a relationship with their newborns early continue to provide more direct care to their infants and play with them more.

Greater involvement by the father has many benefits. In one study, infants whose fathers were actively involved in caregiving scored higher on motor and mental development tests (Pederson et al., 1979). In another study, such infants were found to be more socially responsive than average (Parke, 1979). Remember, though, that fathers who choose to have early contact with their infants may differ in many other ways from those who do not choose to have such contact (Palkovitz, 1985), so we cannot always be sure that the early contact itself is the cause of the later developmental benefits.

We'll see evidence for the importance of attachment again and again in later chapters. We'll also see the effects of the family environment on many aspects of development. In the next chapter, however, we take a closer look at the biological side of things—heredity—and how it interacts with environment in producing the unique traits of the new person.

REVIEW & APPLY

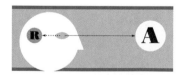

1. What are some of the changes that family members must make to accommodate a first child?
2. Describe some of the physical, psychological, and social changes that affect a woman's experiences during pregnancy.
3. How might extra early contact be important to the formation of attachment bonds between infants and their caregivers?

SUMMARY

Prenatal Growth and Development

■ Prenatal development is often viewed in terms of trimesters. The first trimester is from conception to 13 weeks; the second, from 13 weeks to 25 weeks; and the third, 25 weeks to birth.

■ Each month a woman's ovaries release one egg cell, or ovum, which journeys down one of the Fallopian tubes. There it may be fertilized by a man's sperm. (See study chart on page 48.)

- After fertilization, the genetic material of ovum and sperm merge to form a zygote, which migrates to the uterus and implants itself in the uterine wall.
- If the division of the zygote produces two cells that develop into two separate individuals, the result is monozygotic (identical) twins. If two ova are released at the same time and each unites with a different sperm, the result is dizygotic (fraternal) twins.
- The embryonic period begins with implantation and continues for two months. During this period the outer layer of cells produces the amniotic sac, amniotic fluid, the placenta, and the umbilical cord. The cells of the inner layer differentiate to form the embryo itself.
- During the second month, all the structures of the embryo develop rapidly, including the arms and legs, the eyes, and the internal organs.
- During the fetal period, the organs and systems mature and become functional, and the fetus begins to move. Physical structures become more complete.
- Structural details such as lips, toenails, and buds for adult teeth are added during the second trimester. The body becomes longer, and the heart starts beating. Brain development is particularly noteworthy.
- At the end of the second trimester a healthy fetus reaches the age of viability, meaning that it has a 50–50 chance of surviving outside the womb if given intensive care.
- During the third trimester, the brain matures, and the fetus grows rapidly. Fetal sensitivity and behavior develop, and the fetus goes through daily cycles of activity and sleep.
- Development proceeds from the top of the body down; this process is termed the cephalocaudal trend. It also proceeds from the middle of the body outward; this is the proximodistal trend.

Prenatal Environmental Influences

- Although most pregnancies in the United States result in full-term, healthy babies, sometimes birth defects occur. The majority of these are caused by environmental influences during the prenatal period or during childbirth.
- The incidence of prenatal defects or abnormalities increases steadily with age, especially for first-time mothers.
- Fetal malnutrition can be caused by a mother's imbalanced diet and vitamin or protein or other deficiencies, as well as by deficiencies in the mothers' digestive processes and overall metabolism.
- The single best predictor of healthy, full-term babies is prenatal visits to a doctor or health-care facility beginning in the first trimester of pregnancy.

- There are critical periods during which the developing child is at greatest risk for different kinds of defects as a result of teratogens—diseases, chemical substances, and the like.
- Many viruses—particularly rubella (German measles), herpes simplex, and HIV—can cross the placental barrier and cause defects such as blindness, deafness, brain damage, or limb deformity.
- Certain prescription drugs and many over-the-counter medications can harm the fetus.
- Heavy drinking can cause extensive damage to the fetus. The symptoms of fetal alcohol syndrome include low birth weight and physical and neurological abnormalities.
- Smoking has been clearly linked to fetal abnormalities as well as higher rates of spontaneous abortion, stillbirth, and prematurity.
- High doses of marijuana affect the central nervous system.
- Infants who have been exposed to cocaine before birth have great difficulty controlling their nervous system and often cry frantically and seem unable to sleep. Later in childhood they have higher rates of attention-deficit disorder and learning disabilities.

Childbirth

- Childbirth occurs in three stages: initial labor, in which the cervix begins to dilate; labor and delivery, in which the cervix becomes fully dilated and the baby is pushed through the birth canal; and afterbirth, in which the placenta and umbilical cord are expelled.
- The average full-term infant weighs between $5\frac{1}{2}$ and $9\frac{1}{2}$ pounds, and is between 19 and 22 inches long.
- Although childbirth is stressful for the newborn, the baby immediately begins to adjust to its new environment. Respiration, blood circulation, digestion, and temperature regulation begin.
- With the use of the Apgar Scale, newborns are evaluated 1 minute and 5 minutes after birth to detect any problems or weaknesses.
- With the advent of modern medicine, birthing shifted from the home to the hospital, where the mother could be assisted by specialized medical staff rather than by a midwife.
- Today many expectant parents choose natural or prepared childbirth. They attend classes where they learn about the biology of childbirth, and the mother practices relaxation exercises. The father or a friend serves as a "coach" during labor and delivery.
- Perinatologists specialize in the management of high-risk pregnancies and deliveries, using advanced technologies such as fetal monitors.

- Complications in childbirth include breech presentation, early breaking of the amniotic sac without labor, failure to begin labor, and serious fetal emergency. In such cases the baby may be removed through the mother's abdominal wall in a procedure known as a Caesarian section.
- An infant born before a gestation period of 35 weeks is preterm; a full-term newborn who weighs less than 5½ pounds is considered small-for-date. Premature infants usually have greater difficulty adjusting to the external world, and the effects can last long after infancy.
- Because premature infants must be kept in incubators, it is more difficult for caregivers to form a bond with them. This is an even greater problem in the case of disabled infants.

The Evolving Family

- Adjusting to parenthood is a major life change for adults, especially with a first child. The parents must make economic and social adjustments and must modify existing relationships.
- Pregnant women must adjust to numerous physical, psychological, and social changes.
- Fathers also react emotionally to their wife's pregnancy.
- Both parents' attitudes toward pregnancy and childbirth are shaped by their culture.
- Attachment is an emotional bond between parents and children. It is a reciprocal relationship that begins at birth. It is strongest when parents have a great deal of contact with the baby immediately after birth.

KEY TERMS

congenital
trimesters
periods
ova
fallopian tubes
ovulation
sperm
uterus
zygote
germinal period
monozygotic (identical) twins
dizygotic (fraternal) twins
blastula
embryonic period
embryo
amniotic sac
amniotic fluid

placenta
umbilical cord
spontaneous abortions
fetal period
fetus
age of viability
cephalocaudal trend
proximodistal trend
gross-to-specific trend
teratogens
bacteria
viruses
acquired immune deficiency
    syndrome (AIDS)
fetal alcohol syndrome (FAS)
fetal alcohol effects (FAE)
initial labor

labor and delivery
episiotomy
afterbirth
neonates
fontanelles
anoxia
Apgar Scale
traditional childbirth
"natural" or prepared childbirth
birthing centers
perinatology
fetal monitor
breech presentation
Cesarean section
preterm status
small-for-date
attachment

USING WHAT YOU'VE LEARNED

How have birthing practices changed since you were born? Interview a friend who recently gave birth. Next, interview your mother, your grandmother, or the mother of a friend about her birthing experiences. Have her describe the setting, expectations, medical practices, and customs. What medical staff were present? Who else attended? Were medications given?

Were there critical moments as she experienced the birth? What were some of the meanings of this event—for example, as a medical-surgical event, a personal challenge, or a family milestone? What are some of the advantages or disadvantages of today's practices compared with those of earlier decades?

SUGGESTED READINGS

DAVIS, E. (1997). *Heart & hands: A Midwife's guide to pregnancy and birth* (3rd ed.). Berkeley, CA: Celestial Arts. A comprehensive resource for parents who want to understand midwife care, including detailed answers to questions about pregnancy, birth, and postpartum.

DORRIS, M. (1989). *The broken cord.* New York: Harper & Row. A sensitive and compelling account of a single father's struggle in raising a child who had fetal alcohol syndrome. Expanded discussion of this complex problem among the Native American population.

EISENBERG, A., MURKOFF, H. E., & HATHAWAY, S. E. (1996). *What to expect when you're expecting.* New York: Workman Publishing. A popular, practical guide that addresses concerns of mothers- and fathers-to-be from the planning stage through the postpartum period.

KITZINGER, S. (1996). *The complete book of pregnancy and childbirth* (rev. ed.). New York: Knopf. One of the better guides for health and well-being for expectant parents, full of useful pictures and diagrams.

NILSSON, L. (1990) *A child is born.* New York: Delacorte Press. Vivid full-color photography of the course of prenatal development with up-to-date text on the psychological as well as the medical facts of prenatal development and childbirth.

SILBER, S. J. (1991). *How to get pregnant with the new technology.* New York: A Time-Warner Book. This very-well-written book combines an excellent review of current research with a readable format. It addresses the normal process of conception and the respective male and female causes of infertility in detail, with a positive and upbeat approach.

STREISSGUTH, A. P., & KANTOR, J. (Eds.). *The challenge of fetal alcohol syndrome: Overcoming secondary disabilities.* Seattle: University of Washington Press. In this collection of readings the authors summarize recent findings and explore educational and treatment options for children with fetal alcohol syndrome.

Heredity and Environment

CHAPTER OUTLINE

CHAPTER 3

CHAPTER OBJECTIVES

By the time you have finished this chapter, you should be able to do the following:

1. Explain the principles and processes of genetic reproduction.
2. Describe the causes and characteristics of genetic abnormalities.
3. Discuss the application of genetic counseling and research, including methods of prenatal screening.
4. Describe contributions and controversies in the fields of ethology, sociobiology, and behavioral genetics.
5. Discuss and contrast classical and operant conditioning.
6. Explain how social-learning theory and self-concept pertain to development.
7. Discuss environment in terms of the ecological systems model.
8. Discuss the family as a primary transmitter of culture.
9. Explain how historical social conditions affect development.

Shortly after Leonardo da Vinci died in 1519 at the age of 67, his younger half-brother Bartolommeo set out to reproduce a living duplicate of the great painter, sculptor, engineer, and author. Since he and Leonardo were related, the father that Bartolommeo chose was himself. He chose as his wife a woman whose background was similar to that of Leonardo's mother. She was young and came of peasant stock, and had also grown up in the village of Vinci. The couple produced a son, Piero, who was then carefully reared in the same region of the Tuscan countryside, between Florence and Pisa, that had nurtured Leonardo. Little Piero soon displayed artistic talent, and at the age of 12 he was taken to Florence, where he served as an apprentice to several leading artists, at least one of whom had worked with Leonardo. According to Giorgio Vasari, the leading art historian of the period, the young Piero "made everyone marvel . . . and had made in five years of study that proficiency in art which others do not achieve save after length of life and great experience of many things." In fact, Piero was often referred to as the second Leonardo.

At the age of 23, however, Piero died of a fever, and so it is impossible to predict with certainty what he might have gone on to achieve—though there is some indication in that Piero's works have often been attributed to the great Michelangelo. Nor is it possible to say positively how much of Piero's genius was due to heredity and how much to environment. Full brothers share, on the average, 50% of their genes, but Bartolommeo and Leonardo were half-brothers and so would have had only about a quarter of their genes in common. Piero's mother and Leonardo's mother do not appear to have been related, but in the closely knit peasant village of Vinci it is quite possible that they had ancestors in common and thus shared genes. On the other hand, a strong environmental influence cannot be ruled out. The young Piero was undoubtedly aware of his acclaimed uncle; and certainly his father, Bartolommeo, provided every opportunity that money could buy for the boy to emulate him. But Bartolommeo's efforts to give the world a second Leonardo by providing a particular heredity and environment might, after all, have had little influence. Piero possibly was just another of the numerous talented Florentines of his time. (Excerpt from *Humankind.* Copyright © 1978 by Peter Farb. Reprinted by permission of Houghton Mifflin Co. and Jonathan Cape. All rights reserved.)

Nature versus nurture, heredity versus environment: This age-old debate has generated volumes of theory and research and continues to do so. In this chapter we take a detailed look at heredity and environment and how each works, beginning with genetic mechanisms that set the stage for conception and prenatal development and continue to influence development throughout the lifespan. Then we look in more detail at how the different *levels* of environment work, beginning with basic conditioning and learning processes and continuing through family systems and culture and society at large—always bearing in mind that the influences of heredity and environment are intricately intertwined.

Human development, in other words, does not take place in a vacuum. It "is an outgrowth of cultural life and thus inextricably bound to particular contexts" (Goodnow, Miller, and Ressel, 1995). Thus, a central theme in the study of development is the dynamic, *reciprocal* manner in which nature and environmental contexts interact—the child affects the family, the family affects the child.

A FRAMEWORK FOR STUDYING HEREDITY AND ENVIRONMENT

Heredity can be divided into two areas of study: (1) what we inherit as a species, meaning what all normal humans have in common; and (2) what differs from one person to the next, meaning the specific and unique gene combinations inherited by each individual. Similarly, environment can be divided into two areas: (1) what all humans necessarily experience and (2) what differs from one person to the next.

Species heredity, then, includes needs we all have for oxygen and food, plus behaviors we all engage in, such as breathing and eating. It is also true that we all must have a biological mother. Therefore, it is plausible to consider other things as common to virtually all normal humans; examples include the beginnings of language development and the formation of attachment bonds between infants and caregivers.

Individual heredity, on the other hand, sets the stage for differences that are biologically based and that make each person unique. Perhaps one person inherits a need for more oxygen or food than another person, based on differences in basic metabolism. Or perhaps one child has a longer prenatal period and another child a shorter one because of genetic differences. Perhaps one child acquires language more easily than another. It is therefore plausible to consider inheritance when studying behavior that clearly differs from one individual to another.

Species environmental influences include experiences that we all *must* have in order to develop. A human baby is a helpless creature, so all living humans must be fed and cared for during infancy—the ones who aren't will perish. Some of who and what we are as adults is therefore shared with all other living people with regard to experience as well as biology. Also, people normally are exposed to some form of language, grow up in some form of culture, and so on, and this experience clearly results in certain commonalities in development and behavior.

STUDY CHART ▸ HEREDITY AND ENVIRONMENT IN INTERACTION

HEREDITY:

Species—Built-in needs and functions pertaining to survival

Individual—Built-in needs and functions that are unique to each individual

ENVIRONMENT:

Species—Experiences that all people normally have in common

Individual—Experiences that are unique to each individual

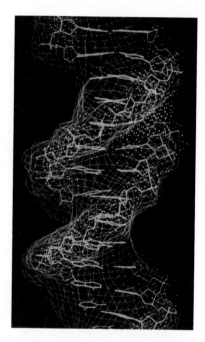

DNA contains the genetic code that regulates the functioning and development of the organism. It is a large molecule composed of carbon, hydrogen, oxygen, nitrogen, and phosphorus atoms.

genes The basic units of inheritance.

deoxyribonucleic acid (DNA) A large, complex molecule composed of carbon, hydrogen, oxygen, nitrogen, and phosphorus. It contains the genetic code that regulates the functioning and development of an organism.

Finally, *individual environmental influences* are those that vary from one person to another. Eating, for example, takes many different forms: People in different cultures eat with knives and forks, spoons, chopsticks, a hollowed-out branch, or their fingers. Similarly, and largely as a result of the particular environment we live in, we eat many different kinds of foods—some of which would make people in other cultures gag. We also learn quite different languages. All such differences clearly affect each individual's development.

In sum, when we're assessing development in terms of what people have in common, it is usually necessary to unscramble the effects *both* of heredity and of environment. In assessing individual differences, it is again necessary to unscramble the effects of both. Add to that factor the complexity that arises when we consider the reciprocal interaction of heredity and environment—as when, for example, an infant's innate temperament and related behaviors influence the parents and in turn help *determine* the family environment in which the child will develop (Saudino & Plomin, 1997). People affect their environments in ways that affect them in return. And people *think* about what's happening and often act so as to shape their environments and select their experiences (Rutter, 1997; Rutter et al., 1997).

HOW HEREDITY WORKS

GENES

Genes "organize nonliving material into living systems" (Scott, 1990). They direct cells to form the brain, the heart, the tongue, the toenails. They give one person dimples and another red hair. Genes are made up of **deoxyribonucleic acid (DNA),** which is composed of carbon, hydrogen, oxygen, nitrogen, and phosphorus atoms. It has been observed that "the human body contains enough DNA to reach the moon and return 20,000 times if all of it were laid out in a line" (Rugh & Shettles, 1971).

The structure of DNA resembles a long spiral staircase. Two long chains are made up of alternating phosphates and sugars, with cross-links of four different nitrogen bases that pair together. The order in which those paired nitrogen bases appear varies, and it is that variation that makes one gene different from another. A single gene might be a chunk of the DNA stairway perhaps 2000 steps long (Kelly, 1986). Thus, relatively minor variations in the structure of DNA produce dramatic differences in individuals.

When a cell is ready to divide and reproduce, the DNA staircase unwinds, and the two long chains separate. Each chain then attracts new material from the cell to synthesize a second chain and form new DNA. Occasionally there is a mutation, an alteration, in these long strips of nucleic acid. In most cases, mutation is maladaptive and the cell dies, but a small number of mutations survive and perhaps even benefit the organism.

DNA contains the genetic code, or blueprint, that regulates the development and functioning of the organism. It is the *what* and *when* of development. DNA is confined to the nucleus of the cell. **Ribonucleic acid (RNA),** a substance formed from DNA, acts as a messenger to other parts of the cell. It is the *how* of development. Short chains of RNA move through the cell and act as catalysts for the formation of new tissue.

CHROMOSOMES

Each gene is a tiny biochemical *locus* on a **chromosome.** A chromosome can consist of tens of thousands of such chained-together loci, yielding close to 1 million genes in all (Kelly, 1986).

In normal humans, each cell contains exactly 46 chromosomes arranged in 23 pairs. They can be photographed under a light microscope when a cell is preparing to divide, producing illustrations called **karyotypes.** Twenty-two of the pairs are called **autosomes** and are numbered from largest to smallest—the distinction is simply that they are not involved in determining sex. The 23rd pair are the **sex chromosomes:** XX in females and XY in males. Thus, the upper illustration is female, and the lower one male.

CELL DIVISION AND REPRODUCTION

In the process termed **mitosis,** each cell normally divides and duplicates itself exactly. First, the DNA of each gene replicates itself. Each chromosome then splits and reproduces the former chromosomal arrangement of the original cell. Thus, two new cells are formed, each containing 46 chromosomes in 23 pairs just like those in the original cell, as shown on the left side of Figure 3–1.

Also shown in Figure 3–1 is **meiosis,** which is how reproductive cells (ova and sperm) are formed. This process results in **gametes,** cells that contain only 23 chromosomes (as opposed to 46 in 23 pairs). In males, meiosis takes place in the testes and involves two divisions, resulting in four fertile sperm cells. Meiosis in females, which takes place in the ovaries and is completed before birth, is also a two-stage process. But the end result is one relatively large functional ovum and three smaller *polar bodies* that are not capable of being fertilized.

Meiosis is the reason that children are not exactly like their parents. Individual variation occurs in several ways. First, when the parents' chromosomes separate at the beginning of meiotic division, genetic material often randomly *crosses over* and is exchanged between the chromosomes, resulting in unique new ones. To that, add the possibility of viable mutations in genetic material, noted earlier. Next, in the final stage of meiotic division, which chromosomes go into which sperm or ovum is determined by chance. (This process is called *independent assortment.*) Similarly, at the time of fertilization and conception, which sperm and which ovum unite is also determined by chance. Because of all these possibilities for variation, it has been estimated that the same two parents could produce hundreds of trillions of unique children—many times the number of humans who have ever lived. Thus, we can safely assume that no two people (other than monozygotic twins) are genetically identical.

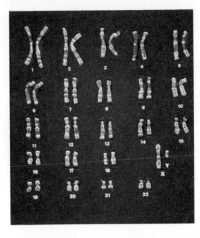

To develop a normal human baby, the zygote must have 23 pairs of chromosomes, or 46 chromosomes.

ribonucleic acid (RNA) A substance formed from, and similar to, DNA. It acts as a messenger in a cell and serves as a catalyst for the information of new tissue.

chromosome Chains of genes, visible under a microscope.

karyotype A photograph of a cell's chromosomes arranged in pairs according to size.

autosomes All chromosomes except those that determine sex.

sex chromosomes The 23rd chromosome pair that determines sex.

mitosis The process of ordinary cell division that results in two cells identical to the parent.

meiosis The process of cell division in reproductive cells that result in an infinite number of different chromosomal arrangements.

gametes reproductive cells (sperm and ova).

FIGURE 3–1 COMPARISON OF MITOSIS AND MEIOSIS

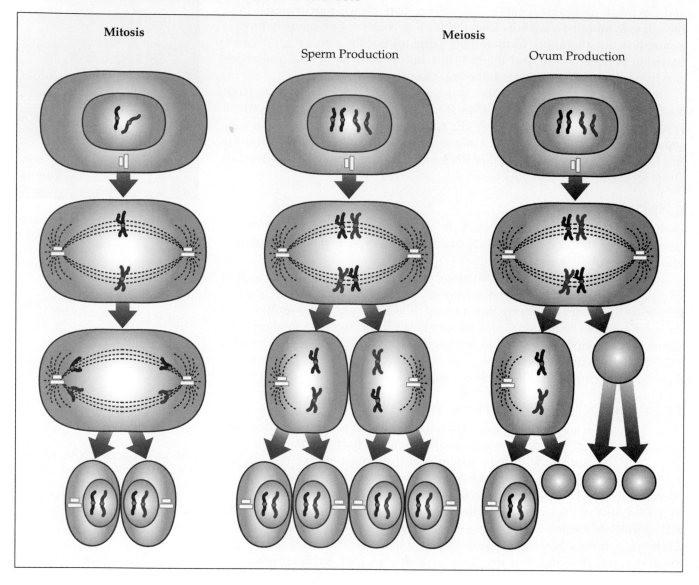

alleles A pair of genes, found on corresponding chromosomes, that affect the same trait.

genotype The genetic makeup of a given individual or group.

phenotype In genetics, those traits that are expressed in the individual.

dominant In genetics, one gene of a gene pair that will cause a particular trait to be expressed.

recessive In genetics, one of a gene pair that determines a trait in an individual only if the other member of that pair is also recessive.

HOW GENES COMBINE

All of the tens of thousands of genes in each of the 22 pairs of autosomes are matched. Alternate forms of the same gene are called **alleles;** one allele is inherited from the mother, and the other from the father. All of the pairs of alleles in a cell constitute the person's **genotype,** or biochemical makeup. In females, since the sex chromosomes are XX, genes all exist as matched allele pairs. But in males (XY), there are many genes on the X chromosome for which there is no counterpart on the Y chromosome.

SIMPLE DOMINANCE AND RECESSIVENESS Some inherited traits, such as eye color, are determined by a single gene pair. A child might inherit an allele for brown eyes *(B)* from the father and an allele for blue eyes *(b)* from the mother. The child's genotype for eye color would therefore be *Bb*. But what **phenotype**—actual eye color in this case—will the child display? As it happens, the allele for brown eyes *(B)* is **dominant,** and the allele for blue eyes *(b)* is **recessive.** When an allele is dominant, its presence in a gene pair will

Heredity and environment in interaction. The child resembles her mother (heredity) and is learning how her mother puts on her makeup (environment).

cause that trait to be expressed as the phenotype. Thus, an individual with the genotype *BB* or *Bb* will have the phenotype brown eyes.

If the two alleles for a simple dominant-recessive trait are the same, the individual is said to be **homozygous** for that trait. With regard to eye color, a homozygous individual could be either *BB* or *bb*. If the alleles differ, the individual is **heterozygous**—*bB* or *Bb*. So, for example, a recessive trait such as blue eyes can be displayed by a child of parents who both have brown eyes if *both* parents are heterozygous for that trait. What are the chances that heterozygous brown-eyed parents would produce a blue-eyed child? Four combinations are possible: *BB*, *bB*, *Bb*, and *bb*. Since only *bb* can produce a child with blue eyes, the chance is 1 out of 4, or 25%. Note that if either brown-eyed parent is homozygous, there is no chance of having a blue-eyed child.

Other traits determined by simple dominance-recessiveness include hair color, hair type, skin pigmentation, nose shape, and dimples, plus numerous genetic defects and disorders discussed later in the chapter.

INCOMPLETE DOMINANCE AND CODOMINANCE   Dominant alleles can be only partially dominant, and recessive ones only partially recessive. The *sickle-cell* trait that often occurs in individuals of African descent is an example of *incomplete dominance*: People with a single recessive gene for the trait have a marked percentage of abnormal, "sickle-shaped" red blood cells that interfere with oxygen transport throughout the body, but such individuals have normal (dominant) red blood cells as well. Sickle-cell carriers tend to experience pain in the joints, blood clotting, swelling, and infections under conditions of oxygen shortage, such as at high altitudes. *Sickle-cell anemia*, however, occurs when an individual inherits both recessive alleles. The symptoms are much more severe, and without blood transfusions many such individuals do not survive past their teens.

Codominance is related but works a bit differently. Neither allele is dominant, and the resulting phenotype is an equal blend of the two. The A and B blood types are an example: If an individual gets an allele for each, the result is type AB blood.

homozygous   Referring to the arrangement in which the two alleles for a simple dominant-recessive trait are the same.

heterozygous   Referring to the arrangement in which the two alleles for a simple dominant-recessive trait differ.

POLYGENIC INHERITANCE   More complex traits do not result from the alleles of a single gene pair but rather from a combination of many gene pairs. In determining height, for example, several gene pairs combine to create taller or shorter phenotypes—though environmental factors such as nutrition also play an important role in determining actual height. The overall system of interactions among genes and gene pairs is called *polygenic inheritance*. Such interactions frequently give rise to phenotypes that differ markedly from those of either parent.

SEX-LINKED INHERITANCE   *Sex-linked inheritance* involves the 23rd chromosome pair. Because the X chromosome contains more genes than the Y chromosome, males are much more likely than females to display recessive traits. If a normally recessive allele appears on the male's X chromosome, there often is no allele on the Y chromosome to offset it, and the recessive trait will be expressed as the individual's phenotype. In contrast, in females the recessive trait will be expressed only if it occurs on both X chromosomes.

REVIEW & APPLY

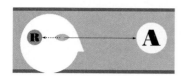

1. Contrast species heredity and individual heredity.
2. Contrast species environmental influences and individual environmental influences.
3. What is the difference between mitosis and meiosis, and what purpose does each serve?
4. Discuss how dominance and recessiveness, codominance, and polygenetic inheritance work.

CHROMOSOMAL AND GENETIC ABNORMALITIES

In each human cell there are some 100,000 genes, containing an estimated 3 *billion* codes. Yet mishaps are rare. Most of the mishaps that do occur are minor ones that do not affect normal development. Some do, however, as we will see in this section.

Ninety-four percent of all babies born in the United States are healthy and normal. Babies born with birth defects account for approximately 6% of all births and 25% of deaths in the first year of life (Wegman, 1990). In turn, about 70% of the birth defects are thought to be due to teratogens and prenatal or birth complications, as discussed in Chapter 2. That proportion still leaves about 2% that may be attributable to chromosomal or genetic anomalies. Many of these defects are lethal, resulting in early spontaneous abortion. Many others produce serious malformations.

SEX-LINKED ABNORMALITIES

Sex-linked abnormalities can involve defects in the number of sex chromosomes or in the genes contained in them. They can also involve simple dominant-recessive patterns.

EXTRA OR MISSING CHROMOSOMES   Males are sometimes born with extra X chromosomes (XXY or XXXY) or extra Y chromosomes (XYY or XYYY). These extra chromosomes result in the impairments summarized in Table 3–1. Similarly, females can have extra chromosomes (XXX, XXXX, or more), or only one (XO). These conditions also cause impairments or abnormalities.

TABLE 3–1 SELECTED SEX-LINKED ABNORMALITIES

Hemophilia: A genetic disorder that prevents normal blood clotting (see text).

Klinefelter's syndrome (XXY, XXXY, XXXXY): Occurs in about 1 in every 1000 live-born males. The phenotype includes sterility, small external genitalia, undescended testicles, and breast enlargement. Symptoms are more pronounced with more X's. About 25% of men with Klinefelter's are mentally retarded. Physical manifestations can be eased by hormone replacement therapy in adolescence. The testosterone injections must be continued for life, however, to maintain male secondary sexual characteristics.

"Supermale" syndrome (XYY, XYYY, XYYYY): Also occurs at a rate of about 1 in 1000 males. These men tend to be taller than average, with a greater incidence of acne and minor skeletal abnormalities. While not mentally retarded, supermales tend to be slightly below average in intelligence. In the past it was hypothesized that men with this genotype are more aggressive and develop differently from males with a normal genotype. However, that conclusion turned out to be exaggerated. Although, on average, XYY males have less impulse control than XY males, and some are more aggressive with their wives or sexual partners, there is little or no difference between XYY males and XY males on a broad range of aggression measurements (Theilgaard, 1983). Thus, the National Academy of Sciences recently concluded that there is no evidence to support a relationship between an extra Y chromosome and aggressive, violent behavior (Horgan, 1993).

"Superfemale" syndrome (XXX, XXXX, XXXXX): Occurs in about 1 in 1000 females. Although these women appear normally female and are fertile and capable of bearing children with normal sex chromosome counts, the women tend to score slightly below average in intelligence. The deficits become more pronounced with more X's.

Turner's syndrome (XO): Occurs in about 1 in 10,000 live-born females. One of the X chromosomes is either missing or inactive. Individuals with Turner's syndrome usually have an immature female appearance (because they do not develop secondary sex characteristics) and lack internal reproductive organs. They may be abnormally short and sometimes are mentally retarded. Once the disorder is discovered, usually at puberty when the girl fails to develop normal secondary sex characteristics, hormone replacement therapy may be initiated to help her appear more normal. However, she will remain sterile.

CHROMOSOMAL BREAKAGE   Both males and females can be affected by an inherited genetic disorder called *fragile-X syndrome*, which occurs once in about 1200 live-born males and about 2500 live-born females. (The ratios are different because females have two X chromosomes, whereas males have one, so in females a normal X chromosome *may* offset a fragile one.) The term refers to potential breakage of a small portion of the tip of the X chromosome, which can have profound effects. Resulting growth abnormalities include a large head, higher than normal weight at birth, large protruding ears, and a long face. Some babies with this condition also display atypical behavioral patterns such as hand clapping, hand biting, and hyperactivity. Fragile-X syndrome is the second most common chromosomal defect associated with mental retardation.

Because fragile-X syndrome involves a recessive gene on the X chromosome, it affects males and females differently. Males tend to be more severely affected because they lack a second X chromosome that might counter the effects. However, almost 20% of males with a fragile X chromosome do not experience the syndrome (Barnes, 1989). Recent research suggests that unstable gene mutation is the culprit: One of the subunits of the recessive gene repeats itself up to several thousand times. The more it repeats itself, the more severe the symptoms (Sutherland & Richards, 1994).

DOMINANT-RECESSIVE SEX-LINKED DEFECTS Recessive genes on the X chromosome are much more likely to be expressed as the phenotype in males. Pattern baldness is a common example. Beginning as early as in their twenties, many men display receding hairlines and thinning hair, whereas few women do. Several variations of recessive color blindness are also much more common in males, for the same reason.

Hemophilia is the most dramatic example of a sex-linked abnormality that is more likely to occur in males than in females. It results from a relatively rare recessive gene on the X chromosome for which there is no Y counterpart. Hemophiliacs are deficient in an element of blood plasma needed for normal blood clotting. They may bleed indefinitely from a small wound that would normally seal itself within moments. Internal bleeding is especially dangerous, since it may go unnoticed and cause death. Although hemophilia is quite rare, occurring only once in every 4000 to 7000 male births, it assumed considerable media prominence in the 1980s because of its association with AIDS. Many hemophiliacs who received blood transfusions contracted HIV because donated blood was not routinely screened for the virus.

AUTOSOMAL ABNORMALITIES

Like sex-linked disorders and defects, abnormalities involving the other 22 pairs of chromosomes can result from extra chromosomes, defective genes, or dominant-recessive patterns. Selected autosomal abnormalities are described in Table 3–2.

Down syndrome is the most common autosomal defect. It is the leading cause of genetically based mental retardation. The most common version is *trisomy-21*, in which an extra chromosome is attached to the 21st pair. Down syndrome occurs once in every 800 births for mothers under age 35 and becomes progressively more likely as the age of the mother increases (see Chapter 2). Individuals with Down syndrome usually have distinctive physical characteristics such as a round face and slanted eyes without eyefolds (the reason for the former pejorative label "mongoloid idiot"). Heart abnormalities, hearing problems, and respiratory problems are also common.

There is broad individual variation among people with Down syndrome, especially with regard to degree of mental retardation. It is a myth, for example, that no one with Down syndrome is able to function in society. The notions that children with Down syndrome are happy and carefree and that adults with Down syndrome are stubborn and uncooperative are also erroneous.

Historically, researchers often painted a grim picture of the expected life-span and adult functioning for individuals with Down syndrome, but those conclusions were based primarily on adults whose education and health had been neglected or who had spent many years "warehoused" in institutional environments. Today special education can make a major difference in the lives of people with this syndrome. Some young adults with Down syndrome have been able to achieve a great deal in work, independent living, and even the arts (Turnbull & Turnbull, 1990).

GENETIC COUNSELING

Most recessive and non-sex-linked genes are not expressed. As a result, many of us never know what kinds of defective genes we carry—yet we all probably harbor at least five to eight potentially lethal recessive genes in addition to many less harmful ones.

You can obtain valuable information about your genetic makeup, and that of a potential partner, through **genetic counseling.** This is a widely available

genetic counseling Counseling that helps potential parents evaluate their risk factors for having a baby with genetic disorders.

TABLE 3–2   SELECTED AUTOSOMAL ABNORMALITIES

Cystic fibrosis: Cystic fibrosis is the most common recessive genetic disease of childhood among Caucasian-Americans, occurring in about 1 in 1000 births. The symptoms involve the exocrine glands, which produce mucus throughout the body, including the lungs and digestive tract, and are also responsible for sweat production to aid in cooling the body. Because of the severity of this defect, sufferers often die by early adulthood. Persons with cystic fibrosis must undergo extensive physical therapy to loosen the mucus several times a day—a fatiguing, time-consuming process. Most males are sterile; women, though fertile, have continuing respiratory problems throughout pregnancy that affect fetal health.

Down syndrome: Occurs in about 1 in 1000 live births. Risk increases with maternal age: Pregnancies in women over age 35 (5–8% of all pregnancies) account for 20% of all Down syndrome births (also see text).

Huntington's chorea: Unlike the other defects discussed here, Huntington's chorea is carried by a *dominant* gene—meaning that the gene need be inherited from only one parent. It occurs in 5–10 people per 100,000 and is characterized by progressive dementia, random jerking movements, and a lopsided, staggering walk, symptoms that do not appear until about 38 years of age on average. Thus, many people who eventually develop the disease are unaware that they are carrying the defective gene and may therefore have children who inherit the gene. Huntington's chorea is believed to be caused by an unstable or repeating gene; hence, in some individuals the condition is far more severe than in others (Sutherland & Richards, 1994).

Phenylketonuria (PKU): Phenylketonuria (PKU) is a recessive defect in amino acid metabolism caused by inability to remove the amino acid phenylalanine from the body. Phenylalanine builds up in the brain, causing cells to become damaged and die. This condition causes severe neurological symptoms such as irritability, athetoid motion (uncontrollable muscle twitches and movements), hyperactivity, convulsive seizures, and severe-to-profound mental retardation. The disorder is detected through a mandatory blood test given to all newborns in the United States. If the test is positive, the child is immediately started on a rigid diet to control phenylalanine consumption. The diet controls the worst symptoms of the disorder—especially retarda-

tion. Treated phenylketonurics have normal life expectancies and can reproduce. However, fertile females with PKU have a very high risk of miscarriage or birth defects because the fetus grows in an abnormal uterine environment. Since Nutrasweet, the artificial sweetener, contains phenylalanine, diet sodas and other Nutrasweet-containing products include a warning label informing phenylketonurics of the risks associated with consumption.

Sickle-cell disease and sickle-cell anemia: In the United States this disorder is more common among African-Americans—about 1 in 12 are heterozygous for the recessive gene that causes abnormal sickling of red blood cells. In approximately 1 out of every 100 African-American couples, both partners are carriers of the recessive gene, creating a 25% risk of having an afflicted child. Only 1 in 650 African Americans actually has sickle-cell anemia, however. The symptoms of the disorder include oxygen deprivation, pain and swelling in the joints, blood clots, infections, and tissue damage to the cells. Medical treatment of sickle-cell anemia has improved, and the condition need not be fatal in most cases.

Tay-Sachs disease: A recessive gene known as *hex a enzyme,* which controls the production of a single enzyme, appears to cause Tay-Sachs disease. When this gene is faulty, the body fails to break down the fatty substances in brain cells (called sphingolipids), causing lethal concentrations and cell death. Tay-Sachs is very rare in the general population, occurring in 1 of 200,000 to 500,000 births. However, among Ashkenazi Jews, 1 out of 30 are carriers, so 1 in every 5,000 births produces a baby with Tay-Sachs disease. The child, who appears normal at birth, begins to show slight but noticeable weakness by 6 months. By 10 months the disorder is obvious. Children who were happy, recognized their parents, and appeared physically normal become too weak to move their heads, are irritated by sound, and cannot control their eye movements. After the first year there is a steady physical decline. Convulsive seizures usually begin at 14 months, and by 18 months children with the disorder must be tube fed. Their tiny bodies lie limp and frog-legged, and their heads start to enlarge. They usually die of pneumonia between the ages of 2 and 4.

The boy in the center has Down Syndrome, a chromosomal disorder. He is participaing in an inclusive classroom.

ultrasound A technique that uses sound waves to produce a picture of the fetus in the uterus.

amniocentesis A test for chromosomal abnormalities that is performed during the second trimester of pregnancy; it involves the withdrawal and analysis of amniotic fluid with a syringe.

resource that can help potential parents evaluate genetic risk factors in childbearing and enable them to make intelligent decisions (Garber & Marchese, 1986; Behrman, 1992). It includes analysis of parental medical records and family histories, parental blood screening, and prenatal screening of the fetus. Prenatal screening can detect chromosomal or genetic accidents that occur randomly or through mutation. For example, a couple who are both in their early twenties and have no family history of Down syndrome may still have a child with Down syndrome because of the random occurrence of trisomy.

If genetic counseling reveals the presence of a heritable genetic abnormality, the counselor evaluates the couple's risk of having a baby with the disorder, puts the risk in perspective, and suggests reproductive alternatives (such as adoption or artificial insemination of donor ovum or sperm) if the couple de-

TABLE 3–3 CHARACTERISTICS OF CANDIDATES FOR GENETIC COUNSELING

- Anyone who is aware of a family history of inherited genetic disorders or has a genetic disorder or defect.
- The parents of a child who has a serious congenital abnormality or defect.
- A couple who has experienced more than three miscarriages or a miscarriage in which fetal tissue analysis indicated chromosomal abnormality.
- A pregnant woman over age 35 or a father over age 44 who because of age has an increased risk of chromosomal damage.
- Prospective parents belonging to certain ethnic groups that are at high risk for certain disorders, such as Tay-Sachs disease, sickle-cell anemia, or thalassemia.
- A couple who are aware of prenatal exposure to an excessive dose of radiation, drugs, or other environmental agents that can result in birth defects.

Source: Adapted from Lauersen (1983).

cides that the risk is too great. Table 3–3 summarizes characteristics of individuals for whom genetic counseling is recommended.

PRENATAL SCREENING Prenatal screening is used to determine whether genetic (or other) defects are actually present in the developing child. Three popular procedures are discussed here; additional procedures are presented in Table 3–4.

Ultrasound is the least invasive and most widely used method of providing information about the growth and health of the fetus. Harmless high-frequency sound waves produce a picture called a *sonogram*. Sonograms can detect structural problems such as body malformations, especially cranial anomalies such as *microcephaly* (extremely small upper head) that are invariably associated with severe mental retardation. Though it is normally done around the 15th week, ultrasound can be done earlier in high-risk pregnancies. For example, if doctors suspect an ectopic (tubal) pregnancy, which is extremely hazardous for the mother, they may use ultrasound as early as 3 to 4 weeks after conception to get a picture of the gestational sac.

In **amniocentesis,** amniotic fluid is withdrawn from the amniotic sac with a syringe inserted through the mother's abdominal wall. The fluid contains

TABLE 3–4 PRENATAL ASSESSMENT METHODS

Amniocentesis: A procedure for obtaining discarded fetal cells by using a syringe. The cells which can be karyotyped and analyzed for major chromosomal and some genetic disorders (see text).

Chorionic villus sampling (CVS): In this procedure, fetal cells for karyotyping are drawn from membranes surrounding the fetus, either with a syringe or with a catheter (see text).

Fetoscopy: Fetoscopy is used to inspect the fetus for limb and facial defects. In this method, a needle containing a light source is inserted into the uterus to view the fetus directly and withdraw a sample of fetal blood or tissue for the prenatal diagnosis of genetic disorders. Fetoscopy is not usually done until 15 to 18 weeks after conception. The risk of miscarriage and infection is greater than that associated with amniocentesis.

Maternal blood analysis: Since some fetal cells enter the maternal bloodstream early in pregnancy, maternal blood analysis can be a helpful diagnostic tool around 8 weeks after conception. A blood sample is obtained and tested for alpha fetoprotein, which is elevated in the presence of kidney disease, abnormal esophageal closure, or severe central nervous system defects.

Preimplantation genetic diagnosis: This procedure is associated with in vitro fertilization, in which sperm and ova are mixed together outside the mother's body and implanted in either the uterus or the fallopian tubes. Cells are removed from the embryo and analyzed for defects before the embryo is implanted in the mother's body. Recently a healthy baby girl was born to parents carrying the cystic fibrosis gene after the procedure was performed (Handyside et al., 1992). The British researchers responsible for her birth suggest that this costly procedure may help in the prenatal diagnosis of such disorders as Duchenne's muscular dystrophy, sickle-cell anemia, and Tay-Sachs disease.

Ultrasound: A procedure in which high-frequency sound waves produce a picture of the fetus called a sonogram. Sonograms can detect structural problems (see text).

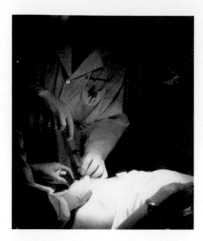

In amniocentesis, a needle is inserted into the mother's abdominal wall to obtain a sample of amniotic fluid. The cells in the fluid are then examined for genetic abnormalities.

discarded fetal cells, which can be karyotyped and analyzed for major chromosomal and some genetic abnormalities. This procedure, too, is usually not done until the 15th week of pregnancy, and the results are not available for 2 weeks because the fetal cells must be cultured. Amniocentesis may increase the risk of miscarriage, but only slightly. Obstetricians routinely recommend this procedure for women over 35 because of the increased risk of birth defects, especially Down syndrome, when the mother is older.

A newer procedure called **chorionic villus sampling (CVS)** can be conducted much earlier than amniocentesis, at around 8 to 12 weeks after conception. In this procedure, cells are drawn from the membranes surrounding the fetus, either with a syringe or with a catheter. Because more cells are collected in this procedure than in amniocentesis, the test can be completed more quickly. However, the procedure involves slightly more risk than amniocentesis, with a small percentage of fetuses aborting spontaneously (Wyatt, 1985). Recent research has also linked CVS with limb abnormalities and fetal death.

Because of the added risk, about half of all high-risk mothers wait and use amniocentesis together with ultrasound (Reid, 1990). Those who choose CVS often do so because there is a strong chance that they are carrying a baby with a serious genetic defect. Abortion early in the pregnancy (before 12 weeks) is safer and has less serious psychological effects than abortion later in the pregnancy. In general, hospitals that perform CVS frequently have greater success in avoiding fetal damage (Kuliev et al., 1992).

PARENTAL DECISION MAKING The genetic counselor's primary function is to help prospective parents make an informed decision before or during pregnancy. The counselor's advice, of course, depends on the specific disorder involved. For example, when genetic assessment shows that both parents have the recessive gene for Tay-Sachs disease (see Table 3–2), which is fatal, the counselor explains that there is a 25% chance that their child will have the disease. Couples who want to have children may then decide to use prenatal screening to determine whether the fetus has Tay-Sachs disease; if it does, they typically will decide to terminate the pregnancy.

In contrast, the counselor's role in advising carriers of sickle-cell anemia is less straightforward. As noted earlier, in its worst form this disorder causes severe pain and perhaps early death. Yet many sufferers lead relatively normal lives, and it is not yet possible to determine through prenatal testing how seriously the child will be affected.

ADVANCES IN GENETIC RESEARCH AND TREATMENT

Both the technology of genetic research and our understanding of genetic determinants are advancing rapidly. Nearly 5000 types of genetic defects have been identified and cataloged (McKusick, 1994). **Corrective gene therapy**—the repair or substitution of individual genes to correct defects—is also advancing, though somewhat more slowly and with many obstacles to achieving its full potential remaining (Friedmann, 1997; Felgner, 1997; Blaese, 1997; Ho & Sapolsky, 1997).

Remarkable advances have been made in the genetic engineering of plants, bacteria, and even animals. For example, it is now possible to transplant genetic material from one species into another, a process called **gene splicing.** The result is a hybrid with characteristics of both donors. Gene splicing has been used to create a strain of bacteria that produces a medically useful human growth hormone (Garber & Marchese, 1986). Another process, **cloning,** is more controversial. It enables scientists to duplicate an animal from a single

chorionic villus sampling (CVS) In this procedure, cells are drawn from the membranes surrounding the fetus, either with a syringe or with a catheter. Because more cells are collected in this procedure than in amniocentesis, the test can be completed more quickly.

corrective gene therapy The repair or substitution of individual genes to correct defects.

gene splicing Transplantation of genetic material from one species into another, with the result being a hybrid with characteristics of both donors.

cloning Technique in which scientists can duplicate an animal from a single somatic cell.

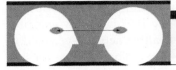

A MATTER FOR DEBATE

HUMAN CLONING

In February of 1997, Ian Wilmut and colleagues at the Roslin Institute in Scotland announced the first successful cloning of an adult mammal: a sheep named Dolly. Since then, researchers at the University of Massachusetts have refined the procedure and successfully produced a small herd of genetically identical cattle, and more mammal clonings are under way.

Wilmut's success immediately stimulated a debate over the cloning of humans-to-be—a topic that has long been popular in science fiction but previously thought to be impossible in real life. The cloning of Dolly also prompted policy statements and attempts at legislation to ban all research on human cloning on moral, ethical, and religious grounds. As a result of the bans, scientific researchers fear that genetic research in general will be impeded.

Let's examine some of the issues in cloning humans. The readiest observation is that there are already far too many people on the earth and that their numbers are increasing geometrically. Do we need clones in addition to all those people? Another point is that Wilmut's successful cloning was preceded by hundreds of failed attempts; attempts to clone humans would probably follow a similar pattern. This point raises serious ethical questions, such as what would happen if a "partially" successful procedure produced badly malformed human clones: Wouldn't they have the same right to life as other humans do? There is also the possibility that humans would be

Dolly makes a media appearance at the Roslin Institute.

cloned to provide perfect replacement organs and tissues, then sacrificed. Would this sacrifice be ethically unacceptable? Most by far would say yes, but it is not hard to imagine a booming underground industry in human "spare parts" for those who can afford them.

Some people argue that cloning might be acceptable in certain cases. A couple could replace a dying child (assuming the child isn't dying from a genetic disorder), infertile couples could clone a child from either partner, a gay or lesbian couple could have their own children. Perhaps specific human organs for replacement could eventually

be cloned without producing an entire human, thereby eliminating ethical concerns. And if there ever is a war or a plague or other catastrophe that wipes out most of humanity, the technology of cloning might save us as a species.

One thing appears certain: Now that cloning humans is a distinct possibility, efforts to do so *will* take place—with or without government approval and funding. Thus, perhaps the real issue for debate is how we will handle human cloning when and if it becomes a reality.

Source: *Scientific American* (1997).

---

somatic cell. In 1997 the scientific world was stunned by the announcement of the successful cloning of a sheep, giving rise to widespread debate over the possibility of cloning human beings (see "A Matter for Debate," above).

Gene therapy has been used on humans in a few cases. In the 1970s a boy was forced to live in a sterile bubble because of a genetic immune-system disorder that placed him at risk of dying from even the slightest infection. This rare condition, called severe combined immunodeficiency (SCID), which ultimately claimed his life, has become the target of the first federally approved clinical trials of human gene therapy. In September 1990, for example, a 4-year-old girl with SCID began receiving, via intravenous saline solution, approximately 1 billion gene-altered immune system cells. By 1993 her body was producing its own immunities, and she had become a healthy, active 7-year-old.

Other diseases are also candidates for gene therapy. The most promising ones are caused by a single gene that can be isolated early and then replaced, deactivated, or repaired. In the case of cystic fibrosis, for example, the gene treatment may be delivered by an aerosol spray applied to the lungs. The cure for sickle-cell anemia would be more complicated, since the healthy gene must be delivered to the blood cells along with another gene that can deactivate the damaged versions. Ultimately, the goal is to remove the damaged cells, alter them, and return them to the patient. In each case, the genes must reach the right target—for example, the bone marrow, liver, or cells in the skin—and the process is extremely complex (Verma, 1990).

Other diseases being treated in clinical trials of gene therapy include cancers, hemophilia, and rheumatoid arthritis. Progress is also being made in the search for AIDS-resistant genes that might account for the fact that many carriers of HIV do not develop AIDS (O'Brien & Dean, 1997).

Advances are being made in other areas as well. One promising strategy is to develop synthetic strands of DNA that can attack viruses and cancers without harming healthy tissue. The goal is to make strands that seek out the target gene and inhibit its ability to produce disease-related proteins (Cohen & Hogan, 1994; Friedmann, 1997). Another strategy is to synthesize some of the proteins that regulate or trigger the genes (Tjian, 1995).

The Human Genome Project (Wertz, 1992), a 15-year, $3-billion-or-more research effort, is attempting to map all human genes and identify those that cause disorders as well as normal characteristics. It has made such rapid progress that it may be completed as early as 2003. But as we gain this knowledge, what will we do with it? We will certainly try to prevent severe disorders, but will couples also decide to abort children who are normal but simply lack specific characteristics and traits that the parents view as desirable? Will insurance companies use karyotypes to deny coverage to individuals who are at risk for developing expensive disorders and diseases? Already large numbers of children are being genetically tested. Some people seek testing under false names to avoid having their genetic codes revealed. Clearly, many ethical issues must be resolved before human genetic engineering becomes routine.

REVIEW & APPLY

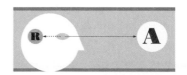

1. Contrast chromosomal and genetic abnormality.
2. Why are males more susceptible to recessive defects than females?
3. Describe the three primary methods of prenatal screening.
4. What are the ethical implications of recent advances in genetic research and treatment?

HERITABILITY OF COMPLEX BEHAVIORS AND TRAITS

Up to this point, we've focused on inheritance of fairly specific characteristics. In this section we turn to inheritance of more global characteristics, such as behavioral tendencies, intelligence, and personality. First we take a look at what some theorists have proposed with regard to species heredity and what we as humans might have in common. Then we consider individual differences.

EVOLUTIONARY VIEWPOINTS

Evolution refers to the process through which species *change* across generations, acquiring adaptive characteristics and losing characteristics that have become maladaptive or useless. Evolution is a *fact*: You can see evidence of evolution if you take a tour through the paleoanthropology exhibits at a natural history museum. Look at how humanoid anatomy—especially skull sizes and shapes—has changed or evolved over the past couple of million years. For generations, beginning with the work of Charles Darwin (1809–1882), theorists and researchers have sought to understand how evolution works. While this research still continues, one *theory*—that of **natural selection**—has become well established because it provides plausible explanations for some kinds of evolutionary change.

Natural selection works like this: Individuals' genetic makeup changes more or less randomly during meiosis. Characteristics that turn out to be adaptive—that is, contribute to survival and eventual reproduction—are passed along to the next generation. Characteristics that are maladaptive may lead to death or may make the individual unable to reproduce, and therefore are not transmitted to offspring.

Most theorists now take natural selection for granted, at least where physical characteristics are concerned. But what about psychological characteristics? For example, do humans have instincts like those observed in other animals? Short of that, do humans have universal, genetically determined behavioral tendencies that we might call *predispositions*? If so, to what extent do such predispositions vary from one individual to the next?

ETHOLOGY AND SOCIOBIOLOGY **Ethologists** study patterns of animal behavior, including behavior that is guided by **instinct.** For a behavior to be considered instinctive, it must meet three criteria: (1) It must occur in all normal members of a species; (2) it must always occur under the same conditions; and (3) it must occur in essentially the same way every time. Dogs, cats, birds, rats, and other animals have evolved behaviors that meet these criteria. Have humans?

Not in the strictest sense. As noted earlier, we all eat, but we eat so many different foods, prepared and consumed in so many different ways, that human eating behavior cannot be viewed as instinctive in ethological terms. We could also view the universal sequence of early language development—crying, cooing, and then babbling—as instinctive, but *preprogrammed* is a better term for these behaviors because infants quickly learn to modify them and to perform them in many different situations.

Another possibility is that infants are biologically preprogrammed to become emotionally attached to caregivers and vice versa, as proposed by Mary Ainsworth and John Bowlby (1991) (see also Chapter 5). That programming could be physical as well as psychological: Most adults are attracted to a baby's doll-like appearance and other cute features, and most adults are distressed by the sounds of a baby's crying; this appearance and behavior promotes approach and contact and thus enhances attachment.

Perhaps flirting behavior is part of a preprogrammed courtship pattern in humans. Perhaps aggressive behavior is part of a preprogrammed territorial defense pattern (Bowlby, 1982; Eibl-Eibesfeldt, 1989). Just because human behavior doesn't strictly qualify as instinctive doesn't mean that it isn't built-in in

evolution Process through which species change across generations, acquiring adaptive characteristics and losing characteristics that have become maladaptive or useless.

natural selection Darwin's theory of how evolution works.

ethology The study of patterns of animal behavior, especially behavior that is guided by instinct.

instinct Behavior that occurs in all normal members of a species, under the same conditions, and in the same way.

Puberty unfolds according to a genetically determined maturational sequence.

some way. It is possible that complex patterns of human social behavior are genetically determined, at least in part (Hess, 1970; Wilson, 1975). Generalizing from research on lower animals, **sociobiologists** contend that human behavior patterns that express dominance, territoriality, nurturance, mating, and aggression show a thin veneer of learned culture on top of a genetically inherited and therefore biological pattern of behavior. There is as yet no good way to prove such contentions, however, so the debate continues.

BEHAVIORAL GENETICS Researchers in the field of **behavioral genetics** take a somewhat different tack. They look at direct connections between behavior and physical characteristics such as growth, hormone changes, and brain structures. The hormone changes associated with pubescence and sexual maturation, for example, produce new behavioral tendencies—such as sexual advances—that vary somewhat across cultures but have a distinctive underlying pattern (Scarr & Kidd, 1983).

Researchers in this area also study individual differences that may be attributable to genetic factors, such as inherited differences in personality, interests, or even learning style (Plomin, 1983; Scarr & Kidd, 1983). An example is a child's tendency to approach or to avoid the unfamiliar, which may be partly genetically determined (Kagan & Snidman, 1991). Researchers are exploring possible genetic predispositions for mental disorders, alcoholism, aggressive behavior, and even crime. Table 3–5 summarizes some current, often conflicting, scientific views on the degree to which certain traits are heritable.

RESEARCH ON HERITABILITY OF TRAITS

As Table 3–5 shows, one common strategy for identifying and clarifying genetic influences on behavior is to study adopted children. Another is to compare identical and fraternal twins.

ADOPTION STUDIES In the extensive Minnesota Adoption Studies, adopted children were compared with their biological parents, their adoptive parents, and the biological children of their adoptive parents (Scarr & Weinberg, 1983).

sociobiology A branch of ethology that maintains that social behavior is largely determined by an organism's biological inheritance.

behavioral genetics The study of relationships between behavior and physical/genetic characteristics.

TABLE 3–5 BEHAVIORAL GENETICS: WHAT THE CURRENT RESEARCH SAYS

Crime: Family, twin, and adoption studies suggest heritability of 0% to more than 50% for the predisposition to crime.

Manic depression: Twin and family studies indicate heritability of 60–80% for susceptibility to manic depression. In 1987 two groups reported locating different genes linked to manic depression, one in Amish families and the other in Israeli families. Both reports have been retracted.

Schizophrenia: Twin studies show heritability of 40–90%. In 1988 a group reported finding a gene linked to schizophrenia in British and Icelandic families. Other studies documented no linkage, and the initial claim has been retracted.

Alcoholism: Twin and adoption studies suggest heritability ranging from 0% to 60%. In 1990 a group claimed to have linked a gene with alcoholism. A recent review of the evidence concluded that it does not support a link.

Intelligence: Twin and adoption studies show a heritability of performance on intelligence tests of 20–80%.

Source: Adapted from Horgan, J. (June 1993). Eugenics revisited. *Scientific American*, p. 124.

In addition, the adoptive parents were compared with their biological children. When test scores of adopted children were compared with those of nonadopted peers, the results indicated that adoptive families influenced the children's intellectual abilities; *as a group*, the adopted children had higher IQs than their nonadopted peers and achieved more in school. But when individual differences *within* the group were analyzed, children's test scores were closer to those of their biological parents than to those of their adoptive parents.

Adoption studies also focus on similarities and differences in attitudes, interests, personality, and behavior patterns such as addiction (Fuller & Simmel, 1986). According to several studies, some attitudes, vocational interests, and personality traits are highly resistant to the adoptive family environment and therefore may be genetic (Scarr & Weinberg, 1983). That tendency is particularly true if the child's genetic predisposition is at odds with that of the adopted parents: The expression of genetically based interests and habits may simply be delayed until the child matures and is less influenced by parental restrictions and behaviors.

TWIN STUDIES Twin studies have repeatedly shown that identical twins are more alike in intelligence than fraternal twins, suggesting that the development of intelligence has a strong genetic component.

Twin studies have also found that a wide range of personality traits are at least partially inherited. Three such characteristics are emotionality, sociability, and activity level—sometimes called the *EAS traits* (Goldsmith, 1983; Plomin, 1990). Emotionality is the tendency to be aroused easily to a state of fear or anger. Sociability is the extent to which individuals prefer to do things with others rather than alone. Activity level is simply the frequency and degree to which the person is active as opposed to docile and relaxed. Similarity in twins' emotionality seems to last a lifetime, but similarity in their activity levels and sociability diminishes somewhat in later adulthood, probably because of the different life events that twins experience when they are apart (McCartney et al., 1990).

Some studies suggest that identical twins are more similar than fraternal twins in personality traits like sociability, emotionality, and activity level. But how much of this similarity can be attributed to genetic influence and how much to the environment?

In sum, although twin studies offer considerable evidence for a genetic influence on different temperaments and personality styles, they are unable to tell us how genes interact with the environment. A quiet, easygoing child experiences a different environment than an impulsive, angry, assertive child, and other people will respond differently to a quiet child than they would to an assertive one. Thus, the child helps shape his or her environment, which, in turn, limits and molds how the child expresses feelings. In this way a child's personality has a tremendous impact on the environment in which he or she lives (Kagan et al., 1993).

REVIEW & APPLY

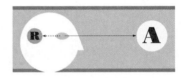

1. Is evolution a theory or a fact? Why?
2. What are the criteria for instinctive behavior? Do humans have instincts?
3. What information do adoption studies and twin studies provide with regard to heritability of traits?

HOW ENVIRONMENT WORKS— FROM SIMPLE TO COMPLEX

The other side of the coin is environment. In this section we turn to environmental factors, starting with basic learning and conditioning processes that directly affect development and proceeding to environmental influences at the level of the family and society at large.

Environmental factors cannot be neatly categorized. The developing child's environment consists of multiple settings that interact and change over time. By adolescence, for example, environment has moved well beyond the home, to the neighborhood, the school, and an ever-expanding world of influences beyond those, all peopled with changing friends and acquaintances. The environment also consists of books, television, movies, and increasingly, the Internet.

BASIC LEARNING PROCESSES

As we saw in Chapter 1, two basic kinds of learning occur in the environment that the person experiences literally from birth (and perhaps during the late fetal period). These are *classical conditioning* and *operant conditioning*, which often work together. Another important kind of learning is *observational learning*.

Although the basic principles of learning are usually presented in terms of controlled laboratory procedures, these principles apply to many situations we encounter in everyday life, whether deliberately contrived by others or occurring naturally in our interactions with the physical and social environment. Also note that although classical and operant conditioning approaches were developed primarily through research with laboratory animals, they have since been demonstrated extensively in human studies as well. While the current view is that conditioning can't explain all of human behavior, it is nonetheless true that it applies to some human behavior quite well.

CLASSICAL CONDITIONING   In **classical conditioning,** which originated in the work of Ivan Pavlov (1849–1936; see Pavlov, 1928), two or more stimuli are paired and become associated with each other in the subject's brain. In Pavlov's lab, dogs were conditioned to salivate and otherwise to prepare to receive food in response to sounds such as a bell tone or the click of a metronome. The sound was repeatedly paired with the food until eventually the sound alone produced salivation. Then the experimenters varied things like the timing of the two stimuli and recorded the effects in terms of how quickly the association was learned, how permanent it was, and so on.

Experiments on conditioning are carried out according to the following procedure. Start with an *unconditioned stimulus (UCS)* that elicits an *unconditioned response (UCR)*. In Pavlov's early research, the UCS was food and the UCR was salivation, but virtually any "automatic" stimulus-response relationship will do—all that's necessary is that the subject respond immediately and consistently to the UCS. Then repeatedly pair the UCS with a novel stimulus such as a sound, a flash of light, or anything that doesn't produce the response in question. Eventually that novel stimulus alone will produce the response. At that point, the novel stimulus has become a *conditioned stimulus (CS)*, which produces a *conditioned response (CR)*. Pavlov's bell, for example, became a CS that when presented *alone* would produce the CR of salivation. The UCR and the CR aren't exactly the same, however; a dog will never salivate as much to the bell as it will to actual food.

Figure 3–2 illustrates this procedure. Note that classical conditioning works best if the bell CS slightly *precedes* the food UCS. In cognitive terms, the CS comes to serve as a *cue* that the UCS is on the way, so that the dog begins salivating in anticipation of the arrival of food.

Classical conditioning is a powerful force in our lives, beginning in early infancy. This point is illustrated by a classic experiment conducted by Lipsitt and Kaye (1964). Ten 3-day-old infants were given 20 trials in which a tone CS was paired with a pacifier UCS. The UCR was sucking (a natural response to a pacifier). After the 20 trials, the tone alone consistently elicited a sucking CR.

classical conditioning   A type of learning in which a neutral stimulus, such as a bell, comes to elicit a response, such as salivation, by repeated pairings with an unconditioned stimulus, such as food.

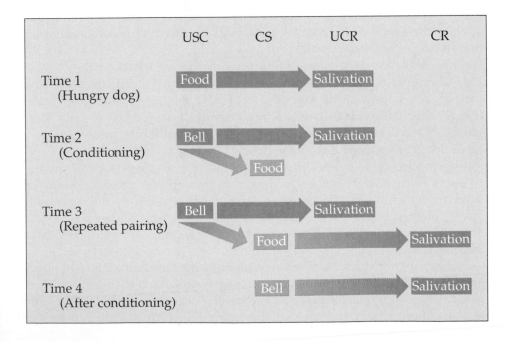

FIGURE 3–2
THE CLASSICAL
CONDITIONING PROCEDURE

B. F. Skinner in his prime, observing the operant behavior of a rat in one of his Skinner boxes. Modern operant conditioning research uses computers instead of the rack of electronic equipment shown in the background and the cumulative recorder shown in the foreground, but Skinner boxes remain the same.

In everyday life a cat learns that the sound of an electric can opener might be followed by a tasty treat, a dog learns that the sound of a car in the driveway might be followed by the arrival of its beloved owner, a toddler learns that the word "No!" might be followed by a pop on the bottom. In each case the subject learns that one stimulus follows the other and that it has an emotional reaction—positive or negative. Although emotional reactions aren't always involved in classical conditioning, in many cases they are. As an example, the learning-theory explanation of **phobias** is that they are acquired by classical conditioning: If you have an unreasoning, horrified fear of bees, for example, it could be because you were badly stung more than once as a child; thus, the sight of a bee alone elicits fear before the bee actually stings you. Similar reasoning applies to phobias for snakes, spiders, heights, tightly enclosed places, and the many other things people sometimes fear to the extent of irrationality.

Positive emotional reactions can be conditioned too, of course, in the same way that negative ones are. Reactions of relaxation or pleasure are often associated with previously neutral stimuli, like an old song that brings back memories of a sunny day at the beach or the excitement of a high school dance. Also, many behaviors associated with eating display elements of classical conditioning, in the sense that we derive a sense of pleasure just from smelling good foods while they're being prepared, or perhaps even from merely thinking about eating them.

OPERANT CONDITIONING **Operant conditioning** was so named by B. F. Skinner (1904–1990; see especially Skinner, 1953). He believed that a subject's behavior "operates" on the environment and is repeated—or not—because of its consequences. Those consequences can take various forms, such as receiving rewards for performing certain behaviors or avoiding unpleasant outcomes by performing certain behaviors. Many kinds of stimuli can serve as rewards (food, praise, social interactions, and so on) or as unpleasant outcomes (pain, discomfort). In Skinner's rather extreme view, *all* of what we do (and don't do) occurs because of the consequences.

The idea of manipulating consequences in order to change behavior is the basis of the procedure known as **behavior modification.** Behavior modification programs have been used to change undesirable behaviors of children and adolescents, as well as individuals in criminal and psychiatric institutional settings (Baker & Brightman, 1989).

Some of the basic elements of Skinner's view were based on the work of E. L. Thorndike (1874–1949), who was highly respected as an educator but is perhaps best known for his **law of effect** (1911). Simplified, this "law" states that (1) when behavior is followed by satisfying consequences, it tends to be repeated, and (2) when behavior is followed by unsatisfying consequences, it tends not to be repeated. Thorndike defined "satisfying" simply as what a subject freely seeks or does, and "unsatisfying" as what a subject normally avoids or doesn't do. Subjects eat certain foods, so those foods are satisfying. And subjects such as the cats Thorndike worked with in his early research normally avoid confined places such as cages, so that situation must be unsatisfying. Thorndike's cats would learn whatever behavior was necessary (in the form of tripping latches or pulling strings) to escape.

Skinner used different terminology in applying Thorndike's law of effect. The first part of the "law," in which behavior is performed in order to achieve a satisfying effect, translates into *reinforcement*. The second part, in which subjects avoid outcomes that are unsatisfying, translates into *punishment*. Each of

phobia Unreasonable fear of an object or situation.

operant conditioning A type of conditioning that occurs when an organism is reinforced or punished for voluntarily emitting a response.

behavior modification A method that uses conditioning procedures such as reinforcement, reward, and shaping, to change behavior.

law of effect A principle of learning theory stating that a behavior's consequences determine the probability of its being repeated.

STUDY CHART ▸ POSITIVE AND NEGATIVE REINFORCEMENT AND PUNISHMENT		
	PRESENT STIMULUS	TAKE STIMULUS AWAY
Stumulus is Appetitive (A "Goody")	Positive Reinforcement	Negative Punishment
Stimulus is Aversive	Positive Punishment	Negative Reinforcement

these effects can be further subdivided according to whether they're accomplished by *presenting* or *removing* a stimulus when the behavior occurs. This process results in four possible sequences: positive reinforcement, negative reinforcement, positive punishment, and negative punishment.

In *positive reinforcement,* which is also called *reward training,* the subject receives rewards for each instance of the behavior, and the behavior predictably increases (becomes more likely). Example: a child is praised for sharing toys with another child.

In *negative reinforcement,* also called *escape training* or *active avoidance training,* behavior results in something unpleasant or aversive being taken away or simply not occurring; again the behavior predictably increases. Phobias are maintained by negative reinforcement: The person approaches the object or situation, becomes fearful, and then avoids the object—in effect making it go away. That's why phobias are self-perpetuating if untreated: The person never sticks around long enough to find out that the fear is disproportionate—that dogs don't *always* bite, that bees don't *always* sting, and so on.

In *positive punishment,* also called *passive avoidance,* behavior results in something aversive being presented or happening. Example: A child is scolded for misbehavior, and—ideally—the misbehavior stops.

Finally, in *negative punishment,* or *omission training,* the behavior results in something desirable or pleasant being taken away; this training should also make the behavior stop or become less likely. In the case of the child who misbehaves, privileges such as TV time are taken away. Some schools use a version of negative punishment called the *time-out procedure.* A child who misbehaves is removed to a quiet room and left alone there for a short period. The logic behind this technique is that children misbehave in order to get attention from other children or from the teacher, so that the attention is in effect "removed."

Two other operant conditioning procedures are important. The first is **shaping,** which is how behaviors are established in the first place. This training is accomplished by means of *successive approximations,* as follows. The procedure can be used in toilet-training a child: First praise the child for going toward the bathroom, then for actually going inside, and eventually for climbing on the potty and completing the act successfully. Shaping can also be therapeutically effective, as with autistic children who don't speak at all and therefore can't be reinforced for communicating: First reward the child for making *any* vocal sounds, then for making sounds resembling speech, and eventually only for actual words (see Lovaas, 1977).

The second procedure is **partial reinforcement,** which is more typical of what happens in everyday life than the "continuous" reinforcement discussed so far. In partial reinforcement, only some instances of a behavior are rein-

shaping Systematically reinforcing successive approximates to a desired act.

partial reinforcement A procedure in which only some responses are reinforced; produces much stronger habits than continuous reinforcement.

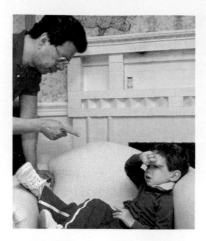

To avoid the unpleasant stimulus of being scolded, this child may behave differently from now on.

forced—not every instance. Partial reinforcement can take various forms, but the most powerful version is the *variable-ratio schedule*. Some instances of behavior are reinforced, some not—and unpredictably. The result is that the behavior persists much longer if reinforcement is later discontinued.

The effects of a variable-ratio schedule can be seen in children who throw tantrums in stores in an attempt to get toys or candy. Sometimes the parents give in and buy the toy in order to stop the embarrassing and annoying behavior that the child is displaying. The child therefore learns to keep trying, even when the parents don't give in—just because it didn't work this time doesn't mean it won't work next time. The parents may also unwittingly shape longer and louder tantrum behavior by trying to hold out before occasionally giving in.

SOCIAL LEARNING

Social-learning theorists enlarged the scope of learning theory to explain complex social behaviors and patterns. Albert Bandura (1977), for example, points out that in daily life people attend to the consequences of their own actions— that is, they notice which actions succeed and which fail or produce no result—and adjust their behavior accordingly. In this way they receive *conscious* reinforcement in addition to external rewards or punishments. They think about what behaviors would be appropriate in specific circumstances and anticipate what may happen as a result of certain actions.

As we saw in Chapter 1, observational learning and conscious imitation of what we see in our social environment play a major role in learning and development. Just as people learn directly by experiencing the consequences of their own behavior, they also learn by watching another person's behavior and its consequences (Bandura, 1977; Bandura & Walters, 1963). In their early years, for example, children learn through observation the many aspects of sex-appropriate behavior and also the moral expectations of their culture. They also learn how to express aggression or dependency or how to engage in prosocial behaviors like sharing. As they grow to adulthood, they learn career-appropriate attitudes and values, social-class and ethnic attitudes, and moral values.

THE EVOLVING SELF-CONCEPT Socialization also includes learning key concepts about the social world and about *self* as distinct from others. This occurs as a result of individual thought processes in conjunction with the social environment. Self-concept begins with self-awareness. Infants initially are unable to differentiate between themselves and the world around them. Gradually, however, they realize that their bodies are separate and uniquely their own; in fact, much of infancy is devoted to making that distinction. Later, young children compare themselves with their parents, peers, and relatives, realizing that they are smaller than their older brothers and sisters, darker or fairer, fatter or thinner.

In expressing their self-concept, children demonstrate their capabilities. They also identify their preferences and possessions (Harter, 1988). In middle childhood, self-knowledge expands to include a range of trait labels. A fifth grader may describe himself or herself as popular, nice, helpful, smart in school, and good at sports. Self-attributes become logical, organized, and generally consistent.

During adolescence, self-knowledge becomes more abstract, and we often display considerable concern about how others regard us. This is when the intellect becomes capable of formulating philosophies and theories about the way things are and the way they ought to be. With this new mental ability, adolescents develop a sense of ego identity—a coherent, unified idea of the self. Throughout adulthood there is both continuity and change in the self-concept. Major life events, new jobs, marriage, birth of children or grandchildren, divorce, unemployment, war, and personal tragedy cause us to reexamine who we are with respect to our life circumstances.

SOCIALIZATION AND ACCULTURATION

Socialization is the general process by which the individual becomes a member of a social group—a family, a community, a tribe. It includes learning all the attitudes, beliefs, customs, values, roles, and expectations of the social group. Socialization is a lifelong process that helps individuals live comfortably and participate fully in their culture or cultural group within the larger society (Goslin, 1969).

During childhood we are socialized into some roles immediately and into others later. A young girl may play many roles every day: pupil, neighbor, big sister, daughter, church member, team member, best friend, and so forth. When she reaches her teens she will acquire several more roles. Each new role will require her to adjust to the behavior, attitudes, expectations, and values of the surrounding social groups.

In the past, researchers saw children's behavior as almost entirely the result of how parents and teachers behaved. For example, children were believed to identify passively with and then imitate certain influential adults in their life. More recently, socialization has come to be viewed as a two-way process. Many studies have focused on how parents and children influence each other's behavior (Hetherington & Baltes, 1988). Infants are socialized by their experience within the family, but their very presence forces family members to learn new roles.

In sum, socialization occurs in all stages of life, not just during childhood and adolescence. Adults learn new roles to prepare for expected life changes. A middle-aged man who wants to change jobs may take a course to expand his

Young children are able to identify their most prized possessions.

Through the process of socialization, children everywhere learn the attitudes, beliefs, customs, values, and expectations of their society.

In Bronfenbrenner's ecological model, we study this child's learning as it relates to 4 levels of the environmental context.

vocational skills. A recently divorced woman may have to change her lifestyle to match her reduced income or to seek a job to support herself. However, during childhood the processes of socialization produce behaviors that persist later in life. Socialization helps create a core of values, attitudes, skills, and expectations that shape the person the child becomes.

AN ECOLOGICAL MODEL　Perhaps the most influential model of human development in the context of the social environment was proposed by the American psychologist Urie Bronfenbrenner. According to Bronfenbrenner's **ecological systems model** (1979, 1989), human development is a dynamic, reciprocal process. In essence, the growing person actively restructures the multiple settings in which he or she lives, and at the same time is influenced by those settings, the interrelationships among them, and external influences from the larger environment. Bronfenbrenner pictures the social environment as a *nested* arrangement of four concentric systems, as illustrated in Figure 3–3. A key feature of the model is the fluid, back-and-forth interactions among the four systems.

The **microsystem,** or first level, refers to the activities, roles, and interactions of an individual and his or her immediate setting, such as the home, day-care center, or school. For example, in the home, development may be encouraged by the mother's sensitivity to the child's moves toward independence. In turn, the child's moves toward independence may encourage the mother to think of new ways to promote this kind of behavior. Because of its immediacy, the microsystem is the environmental level that is most frequently studied by psychologists.

The **mesosystem,** or second level, is formed by the interrelationships among two or more microsystems. Thus, development is affected by the formal and informal connections between the home and school or among the home, school, and peer group. For example, a child's progress at a day-care center may be affected positively by his or her parents' close communication with the teachers. Similarly, the attentiveness of the teachers is likely to benefit the child's interactions at home.

ecological systems model
A model of child development in which the growing child actively restructures aspects of the four environmental levels in which he or she lives while simultaneously being influenced by these environments and their interrelationships.

microsystem　The first level, which refers to the activities, roles, and interactions of an individual and his or her immediate setting, such as the home, day-care center, or school.

mesosystem　The second level, which is formed by the interrelationships among two or more microsystems.

FIGURE 3–3 ECOLOGICAL SYSTEMS MODEL OF CHILD DEVELOPMENT

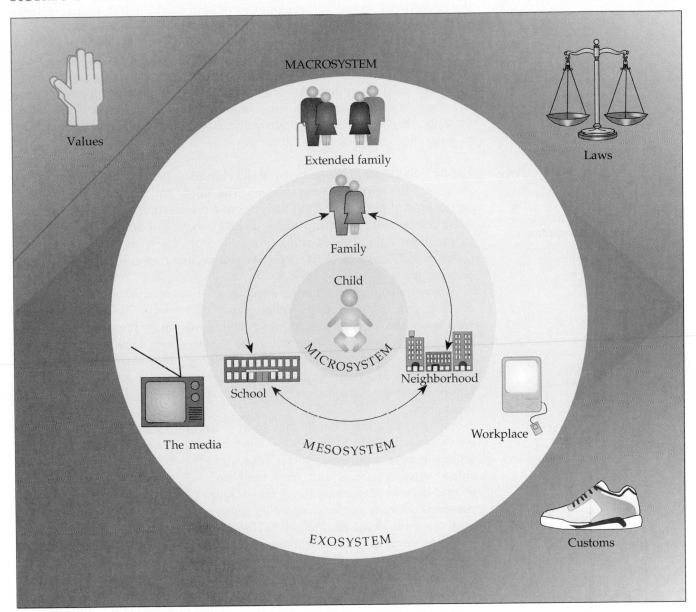

The **exosystem,** or third level, refers to social settings or organizations beyond the child's immediate experience that affect the child. Examples range from formal settings, such as a parent's workplace and the community health and welfare systems, to less formal organizations like the child's extended family or the parents' network of friends. For example, the child's mother may be employed by a company that allows her to work at home two or three days a week. That flexibility may enable the mother to spend more time with her child; thus, it may also indirectly promote the child's development. At the same time, the increased time that the mother spends with her child may make her less tense and therefore more productive on the job.

Unlike the other levels, the **macrosystem,** or outermost level, does not refer to a specific setting. It consists of the values, laws, and customs of the society in which the individual lives. For example, laws providing for *mainstreaming—*

exosystem The third level, which refers to social settings or organizations beyond the child's immediate experience that affect the child.

macrosystem Unlike the other levels, this, the outermost level, does not refer to a specific setting. It consists of the values, laws, and customs of the society in which the individual lives.

Similarity of interests may cause more intimacy between certain family members.

inclusion of handicapped children in regular school classes—profoundly affect the educational and social development of both disabled and normal children in these classes. In turn, the success or failure of mainstreaming may encourage or discourage other governmental efforts to integrate the two groups.

Although actions designed to encourage development can occur at all levels, Bronfenbrenner (1989) suggests that those occurring at the macrosystem level are especially important. For that reason, the macrosystem has the power to influence every other level. For example, government programs like Head Start have had an enormous impact on the educational and social development of generations of American children.

FAMILY SYSTEMS At the heart of development, however, is the family, especially with regard to young children. The family has a tremendous influence on the kind of person the child becomes and on the child's place in society. Indeed, the type of family into which a child is born can dramatically affect the expectations, roles, beliefs, and interrelationships experienced throughout life (Hartup, 1989), as well as the child's cognitive, emotional, social, and physical development.

The way people interact in families has an intricate and dynamic impact on development. Each family member may play a specific role in interactions with other family members. An older sibling may be responsible for younger siblings. Each family member may have alliances with some family members but not with others. Two sisters, for example, may frequently gang up against their brother. The network of interrelationships and expectations within the family is a major influence on the child's social, emotional, and cognitive development.

Siblings in the same family may share many similar experiences, such as an overly strict mother or middle-class suburban family values. Yet there is also a set of *nonshared* experiences and relationships. In one series of studies, relationships between parents and their firstborn and between parents and their second-born were compared over time (Dunn, 1986). As we might expect, relationships between mothers and firstborns were often close and intense, at least until the birth of the second child. Things then became more complicated. If the firstborn child had an affectionate relationship with the father, the affection tended to increase, as did the amount of conflict between the mother and the firstborn. If the mother gave a good deal of attention to the second child, the conflict between the mother and the first child escalated. In fact, the more the mother played with the second baby at age 1, the more the siblings quarreled with each other a year later.

Clearly, members of the same family do not necessarily experience the same environment. When adolescents are asked to compare their experiences with those of their siblings, they often note more differences than similarities. Although they may see some similarities in family rules and expectations, there are many differences in the timing and impact of events such as divorce. Even larger differences occur in how each sibling is treated by the other siblings (Plomin, 1990).

In a recent study, parents and adolescents were asked to rate their family environment. There was some agreement on whether or not the family was well organized, had a strong religious orientation, or was often in conflict. But there was considerable disagreement between parents and their adolescent children on how cohesive the family was, how much expressiveness or independence was allowed, and whether or not the family had an intellectual orientation (Carlson et al., 1991). It seems clear that as each child enters the family, the nature of the family and interactions within it change, and therefore the general social environment that the child experiences changes as well.

THE FAMILY AS TRANSMITTER OF CULTURE   Besides integrating the individual child into the family unit, parents interpret the society and its culture. Religious and ethnic traditions and moral values are conveyed to children from an early age. In a cohesive, homogeneous society like the Israeli *kibbutz*, people outside the family reinforce and expand parental teachings. There is little contradiction between the family's way of doing things and the customs of the community. But in a more complex, multiethnic society such as ours, cultural traditions often oppose each other. Some parents struggle to instill their own values so that their children will not become assimilated into the culture of the majority. Parents express cultural values to their children in their attitudes toward aspects of daily life such as food, clothing, friends, education, and play.

Transmission of culture is not a simple matter. The more diverse the social fabric, the more pressure is felt by the family system. It also becomes more difficult to transmit values when they are unfocused and in transition, and this difficulty may be the main challenge American families face today. It is important to keep in mind that although we speak of a family unit, a social environment, and a culture, none of these is a single, fixed entity. An individual's social environment, already complex at the moment of birth, changes constantly and dynamically.

Although some cultural characteristics, such as incest taboos, are nearly universal (Farb, 1978), many others are not. Cultural differences may lead to **ethnocentrism**—the tendency to assume that your culture's beliefs, perceptions, and values are true, correct, and factual, and that other culture's are false, unusual, or downright bizarre. It may be especially hard to suspend judgment on cultural differences that are close at hand. For example, it is often assumed that single-parent families are less representative of "family values" than families in which both parents are present. Yet a poor single mother living in the inner city who turns to her own mother for child care may transmit as clear a message about the importance of family as an intact nuclear family living in the suburbs.

Parental influences are just one element in the larger process of socialization. Socialization is a lifelong process through which individuals learn to function as members of social groups—families, communities, work and friendship groups, and many others. Becoming a member of a group involves recognizing and dealing with the expectations of others—family members, peers, teachers, and bosses, to name just a few. Whether they are tense and anxiety-producing or smooth and secure, our relationships with others determine what we learn and how well we learn it.

Socialization also forces people to deal with new situations. Infants are born into families; children go to school; families move to new neighborhoods; adolescents begin to date; people marry and raise their own families; older people retire from jobs; friends and relatives become ill or die. Adapting to such changes throughout life is an essential part of socialization. Throughout the socialization process, the individual's evolving self-concept acts as a filter to moderate the impact of the environment. Unlike a camera, which captures every light image and imprints it on film, the self-concept captures only

ethnocentrism The tendency to assume that our own beliefs, perceptions, customs, and values are correct or normal, and that those of others are inferior or abnormal.

selected images. As a result, each person experiences the social environment in different ways.

SOCIAL INFLUENCES ON DEVELOPMENT THROUGH THE LIFESPAN

Finally, it's important to consider how each individual's development interacts with changing cultural and historical factors, producing what we call generations and cohorts.

Several investigators have studied the generation that was born during the Great Depression and experienced World War II as adolescents. Those individuals entered college or the labor market during the postwar boom of the late 1940s and early 1950s, and many served in the armed forces during the Korean War. That war was followed by a period of economic well-being and relatively low unemployment. Thus, the period during which that generation entered adulthood was significantly marked by specific historical factors (Featherman et al., 1984). Compare that cohort with the the "baby boomers" born in the post-World War II period of 1946–1960. That large group enjoyed the benefits of a growing economy in childhood and adolescence, and experienced adolescence and adulthood in the turbulent 1960s. Are members of those two cohorts similar? In some ways yes, but in other ways definitely not.

Baltes (1987; Hetherington & Baltes, 1988) suggests that lifespan development involves more than the interaction of developmental and historical change. He suggests that three factors interact. **Normative age-graded influences** are the biological and social changes that normally happen at predictable ages—a combination of species heredity and species environmental factors, as discussed at the beginning of the chapter. Included in this category are puberty, menopause, and some physical aspects of aging, as well as predictable social events such as entering first grade, marrying, or retiring, which often occur at particular times. **Normative history-graded influences** (also species environmental factors) are historical events, such as wars, depression, and epidemics, that affect large numbers of individuals at about the same time.

Nonnormative influences are individual environmental factors that do not occur at any predictable time in a person's life. Examples include divorce, unemployment, illness, moving to a new community, sudden economic losses or gains, career changes, even a chance encounter with an influential individual—critical events that may define turning points in an individual's life (Bandura, 1982). Development therefore is more than just a product of age or history; it includes the timing and influence of certain events that affect us as a group or uniquely as individuals.

Baltes believes that factors like race, sex, and social class *mediate* both the type and the effects of these influences. For example, girls experience puberty (an age-graded effect) earlier than boys. African-American men are more likely to experience unemployment (a nonnormative influence) than white men. The effects of divorce may be different in an African-American family than in a white family (Harrison et al., 1990).

The impact of these influences also differs according to age. Children and older adults are often more strongly affected by age-graded influences. Adolescents and young adults are often most affected by history-graded influences; trying to find a first job during a depression or fighting in a war is more likely to occur at these ages. Nonnormative events can happen at any time, but

normative age-graded influences The biological and social changes that normally happen at predictable ages—a combination of species heredity and species environmental factors.

normative history-graded influences (also species environmental factors) The historical events, such as wars, depressions, and epidemics, that affect large numbers of individuals at about the same time.

nonnormative influences Individual environmental factors that do not occur at any predictable time in a person's life.

their effects can be mediated by family or friends. The cumulative effect of these events can be particularly important for older adults. Figure 3–4 and Table 3–6 show how these influences interact at different ages for people in different generations.

Glen Elder and colleagues (Elder et al., 1988) provide an interesting example of how history-graded and age-graded factors, mediated by sex, might interact to produce different outcomes. Using an extensive longitudinal design, they studied two groups of people. Members of the first group were infants when the Great Depression began. Members of the second group were of school age (about 10 years old) at that time. Since it took approximately 9 years for real recovery from the Depression to occur, members of the first group were 1 to 10 years old during the period of economic hardship, whereas members of the second group were 10 to 18 years old. Elder found that boys who were younger during those years showed more negative effects of the stress and deprivation experienced by their families than boys who were older at the time. Indeed, the older boys often worked to help the family survive, thereby further limiting their exposure to the family problems that often accompanied unemployment and poverty.

The girls in the study showed a different pattern. The younger girls apparently formed an unusually strong mother-daughter bond while the family was suffering economic hardship. Thus, the girls who were younger during the Depression were actually more goal-oriented, competent, and assertive than those who were adolescents at the time (Elder et al., 1988).

FIGURE 3–4   A LIFESPAN PROFILE OF INFLUENCES

Age-graded, history-graded, and nonnormative influences affect people more directly at different times in their lifespans.

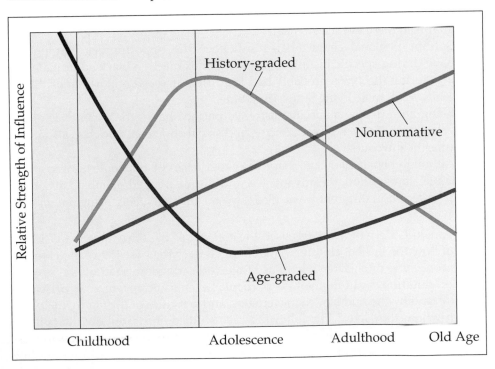

TABLE 3–6 HOW HISTORICAL EVENTS AFFECT DIFFERENT AGE COHORTS

HISTORICAL EVENT	YEAR BORN					
	1912	1924	1936	1948	1960	1972
1932 (the Depression)	20 years old (starting out)	8 years old (schoolchild)				
1944 (World War II)	32 (parenting/career)	20 (starting out)	8 (schoolchild)			
1956 (Postwar boom)	44 (middle age)	32 (parenting/career)	20 (starting out)	8 (schoolchild)		
1968 (Vietnam War era)	56 (preretirement)	44 (middle age)	32 (parenting/career)	20 (starting out)	8 (schoolchild)	
1980	68 (retired)	56 (preretirement)	44 (middle age)	32 parenting/career)	20 (starting out)	8 (schoolchild)

Note: Those who started out during the Depression were more affected than schoolchildren, whereas those who established a career during the postwar boom were more affected than those nearing retirement.

Several conclusions can be drawn from these findings (Stoller & Gibson, 1994):

1. Development is influenced by an individual's personal characteristics, the life events to which that person is exposed, and the ways in which he or she adapts to these events.
2. Specific personal characteristics influence the opportunities that people have during specific historical periods. For example, a black adult male living during the 1950s probably had far different social opportunities than a white adult male living at the same time.
3. Being born during a specific historical period shapes the experience of development. Gender, race, ethnicity, and social and economic class also influence the life course.
4. Although historical events shape the experiences of all people born in a particular time period, the advantaged and disadvantaged members of society are affected in different ways. (See "Eye on Diversity," on facing page.)

Donald J. Hernandez (1994) used the concept of the life course in his analysis of how the lives of children have changed over the past 150 years. Hernandez conceived of children's lives as "trajectories distinguished by the specific order, duration, and timing of the particular events and resources experienced in life, and by the number, characteristics, and activities of the family members with whom they live." The following case studies illustrate how the cultural and historical experiences individuals are exposed to at various times in their lives affect their attitudes, values, and abilities:

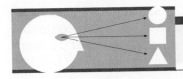

EYE ON DIVERSITY

CHILDREN WHO SURVIVE

Throughout history, children have been forced to grow up in terrible social environments. Perhaps the major caregiver is mentally ill or a drug abuser. Perhaps the child is exposed to oppressive poverty, overcrowding, or criminality. Some children experience repeated losses through war and disasters; others are physically abused or seriously neglected. Usually these unfortunate children develop lifelong personality scars. They may feel insecure, lonely, and helpless. As adults, they are more likely to become child abusers, criminals, or drug addicts themselves. Some may suffer mental illness; others may be unable to sustain meaningful relationships.

Yet some children survive devastating childhood experiences without serious scars—they succeed despite their negative environment. What factors help make these children *resilient*? How do they learn strategies for coping with enormous stress?

Norman Garmezy tells of a preadolescent boy growing up in the slums of Minneapolis (Pines, 1979). He lives in a rundown apartment building with his father, an ex-convict who is dying of cancer; an illiterate mother; and seven brothers and sisters, two of whom are mentally retarded. Despite this environment, the boy's teachers report that he is unusually competent, performs well academically, and is liked by most of his classmates. How does he manage?

After studying hundreds of resilient children, researchers have identified five characteristics that they all share:

1. They are socially competent and at ease with both peers and adults. Adults often describe them as appealing or charming and willing to learn.
2. They are self-confident. They look at problems as challenges, and they believe that they have the ability to master new situations. Garmezy offers an example: A young girl wanted to bring her lunch to school as other children did, but there was nothing at home to put between the slices of bread. Not discouraged, she made bread sandwiches. After that, whenever she was forced to "make do" or encountered a difficult situation, she would tell herself to "make bread sandwiches."
3. They often are very independent. They think for themselves and listen to adults, but they are not necessarily dominated by them.
4. They usually have a few good relationships that provide security (Pines, 1984; Rutter, 1984)—relationships with peers, a teacher, an aunt, or a neighbor.
5. Finally, they are achievers. Some do well academically; others become good athletes, artists, or musicians. They enjoy the positive experiences of achievement; they learn that they can succeed and that they can affect their environment.

Emmy E. Werner (1989b) and her colleagues have conducted a longitudinal study of resilient children who live in Kauai, Hawaii. The study, which has continued for more than 30 years, reaffirms that it is possible to triumph over a deprived childhood and that certain factors consistently contribute to the triumph. Of the 201 children identified by the researchers as high risk because of their stressful home environments, 72 grew into competent, caring people who were able to handle the demands of adult life. Among the factors that contributed to the long-term resiliency of these individuals was a supportive network of family members, teachers, and other key adults who acted as backups when parents were unavailable. Of most importance, these children had at least one person in their lives who gave them unconditional love.

There is still a great deal that we don't know about resilient children, however. The interplay between these children's temperament and talents and their life circumstances is complex (for a review of the issues, see Basic Behavioral Science Task Force, 1996). Nevertheless, research on resilient children may help us understand children in more normal situations as they learn strategies for coping with the stresses of everyday life (Anthony & Cohler, 1987).

Ruth was born in Russia in 1913. One of five children in an orthodox Jewish family, she experienced persecution firsthand as soldiers repeatedly tried to kill her and her family because of their religious beliefs. When Ruth was 12, she came to the United States and settled in Kansas City, Missouri, where she started school. After 4 years, her father, a poor tailor, insisted that Ruth quit school and help support the family, which now had seven children. Despite her lack of education, Ruth was able to earn enough money after several years to move to New York City, where she met and married her husband. They had two children, both of whom graduated from college and became successful professionals. Because of the scarring experiences she had as a child, Ruth spent her married life protected by the cocoon of her family. As she grew older, her husband made all the real-world decisions for the family, and she became increasingly fearful and unable to function outside the home.

Judy was born in 1948, the youngest of three children. Her father was a lawyer and her mother was a homemaker. Judy attended private schools and, like her father, became a lawyer. Asked about her childhood and youth, she remembers fearing the atomic bomb and hiding under the desk during air raid drills in grade school; Judy also recalls the Korean War, the space race, the start of the civil rights movement, the assassination of John F. Kennedy, Vietnam, and Watergate. During the 1960s, she became a student activist, registering voters in the South and protesting the Vietnam War. While attending law school, she married a fellow activist. Both now have government careers and perform extensive volunteer work. Sometimes Judy wonders whether she made the right decision in choosing not to have children.

These two women's values and life experiences were strongly shaped by the historical events of the times in which they lived. The differences between them force us to take a closer look at the relationships between developmental and historical changes over the lifespan, and at how the timing and influence of events affect each person differently.

REVIEW & APPLY

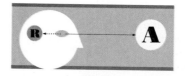

1. Define and contrast classical and operant conditioning.
2. Discuss Bronfenbrenner's ecological systems model at each level.
3. How do different patterns of family interaction influence development?
4. How do families transmit culture, and what role do they play in the process of socialization?
5. Discuss Baltes's model of lifespan influences.

SUMMARY

A Framework for Studying Heredity and Environment

- Species heredity refers to what all normal humans have in common, whereas individual heredity refers to the specific and unique gene combinations inherited by each individual.
- Species environmental influences include experiences that all humans must have in order to develop, while individual environmental influences are those that vary from one person to another. (See the study chart on page 88.)

How Heredity Works

- Deoxyribonucleic acid (DNA) contains the genetic code that regulates the development and functioning of the organism.

- Genes are located on chromosomes. Every human cell contains 46 chromosomes arranged in 23 pairs; the 23rd pair are the sex chromosomes—XX in females and XY in males.
- In mitosis, each cell divides and duplicates itself exactly, forming two new cells that each contain 46 chromosomes arranged in 23 pairs.
- Reproductive cells (ova and sperm) are formed by meiosis. This process results in gametes, cells that contain only 23 chromosomes and, therefore, only half the genetic code of the parent.
- Alternate forms of the same gene are called alleles; one allele is inherited from the mother and the other from the father. All of the pairs of alleles in a cell constitute the person's genotype.

- The actual expression of a person's genotype is the phenotype. The expression of simple traits such as eye color depends on the combination of dominant and recessive alleles for those traits in the genotype.
- More complex traits result from a combination of many gene pairs. The overall system of interactions among genes and gene pairs is called polygenic inheritance.

Chromosomal and Genetic Abnormalities

- Sex-linked abnormalities can be caused by extra or missing chromosomes or chromosomal breakage (fragile-X syndrome). Some sex-linked defects, such as hemophilia, are caused by recessive genes on the X chromosome and therefore are more likely to occur in males than in females.
- Autosomal abnormalities can also result from extra chromosomes, defective genes, or dominant-recessive patterns. The most common autosomal defect is Down syndrome, the leading cause of genetically based mental retardation.
- Genetic counseling is available to help potential parents evaluate genetic risk factors in childbearing and make intelligent decisions.
- The most common forms of prenatal screening are ultrasound, amniocentesis (withdrawal of amniotic fluid for testing), and chorionic villus sampling (withdrawal of fetal cells for testing).
- Significant advances have been made in genetic research and treatment. Gene therapy has been used on humans in a few cases.

Heritability of Complex Behaviors and Traits

- Evolution is the process through which all species change across generations. A generally accepted theory of how evolution occurs is Darwin's theory of natural selection, in which traits that enable an organism to survive and reproduce are passed along to the next generation.
- Ethologists study patterns of animal behavior, especially behavior that is guided by instinct. Human behaviors are not instinctive, but some appear to be biologically preprogrammed. Sociobiologists believe that certain complex patterns of human social behavior have a genetic component, but this argument has not been proved.
- Behavioral geneticists study direct connections between behavior and physical characteristics, including individual differences that may be attributable to genetic factors.

- Research on heritability of traits makes use of adoption studies and studies of identical and fraternal twins.

How Environment Works—From Simple to Complex

- There are two basic kinds of learning: classical conditioning and operant conditioning. Another important kind of learning is observational learning.
- In classical conditioning, two or more stimuli are paired and become associated with each other. Many everyday behaviors, including some emotional reactions, are acquired in this way.
- In operant conditioning, behaviors are acquired as a response to their consequences. Consequences can be of four kinds: positive reinforcement, negative reinforcement, positive punishment, and negative punishment. (See the study chart on page 107.)
- Operant conditioning can be carried out through shaping, in which a desired behavior is shaped through successive approximations. Everyday behaviors are typically shaped through partial reinforcement, in which only some instances of the behavior are reinforced.
- Observational learning and conscious imitation play a major role in learning and development. Social concepts—particularly concepts of self—also influence what is learned.
- Socialization is the general process by which the individual becomes a member of a social group. It is a two-way process that occurs in all stages of life.
- Bronfenbrenner's ecological systems model of human development contains four levels: the microsystem, the mesosystem, the exosystem, and the macrosystem.
- The family has a tremendous influence on the kind of person the child becomes and on the child's place in society. Besides integrating the child into the family unit, parents interpret the society and its culture.
- According to Baltes, lifespan development involves three basic types of factors: normative age-graded influences, normative history-graded influences, and non-normative influences. The effects of these factors are mediated by others, such as race, sex, and social class.
- Longitudinal research has shown that development is influenced by an individual's personal characteristics, the life events to which that person is exposed, and the ways in which he or she adapts to these events.

KEY TERMS

genes
deoxyribonucleic acid (DNA)
ribonucleic acid (RNA)
chromosome
karyotype
autosomes
sex chromosomes
mitosis
meiosis
gametes
alleles
genotype
phenotype
dominant
recessive
homozygous

heterozygous
genetic counseling
ultrasound
amniocentesis
chorionic villus sampling (CVS)
corrective gene therapy
gene splicing
cloning
evolution
natural selection
ethology
instinct
sociobiology
behavioral genetics
classical conditioning
phobia

operant conditioning
behavior modification
law of effect
time-out procedure
shaping
partial reinforcement
ecological systems model
microsystem
mesosystem
exosystem
macrosystem
ethnocentrism
normative age-graded influences
normative history-graded
   influences
nonnormative influences

USING WHAT YOU'VE LEARNED

Take a close look at your parents and yourself. *Physically*, how much are you alike? Can you identify features that you share with your mother or your father, such as your father's nose or your mother's eyes? What about differences? In each case, what's your best guess about where those come from?

Now consider yourself and your parents *psychologically*. Are there behaviors, habits, or attitudes that you share with one or both of your parents? Consider little things, such as how you handle eating utensils, what foods you like, what condiments you prefer, whether you like to get up early in the morning or sleep late, and so on. Then consider more global things like personality traits, temperament, intelligence, and problem-solving approaches. In each case, you'll find similarities and differences. Why? What's your best guess about what's more important in each case, heredity or environment?

Finally, which is more clear-cut, the physical or the psychological?

SUGGESTED READINGS

CART, C. S., METRESS, E. K., & METRESS, S. P. (1992). *Biological bases of human aging and disease.* Boston: Jones and Bartlett. A highly readable and informative source on age-related biological and physiological changes in adulthood.

FOUTS, R., WITH MILLS, S. T. (1997). *Next of kin: What chimpanzees have taught me about who we are.* New York: William Morrow. Roger Fouts provides an engaging personal saga of his pioneering communication with chimpanzees, using sign language. The narrative spans his 30-year friendship with the famous Washoe.

GOULD, S. J. (1993). *Eight little piggies: Reflections in natural history.* New York: W. W. Norton. Before dismissing the claims of behavioral genetics, the reader may want to consider these short essays on animal behavior in this entertaining collection by a noted natural historian.

LYNCH, E. W., & HANSON, M. J. (Eds.) (1992). *Developing cross-cultural competence: A guide for working with young children and their families.* Baltimore: Paul Brookes. Insightful contributions from authors representing several ethnic, cultural, and language groups, illustrating family patterns and values in contemporary American communities.

PLOMIN, R. (1990). *Nature and nurture: An introduction to human behavioral genetics.* Pacific Grove, CA: Brooks/Cole. This brief, accessible book translates the technical genetic research for the lay reader without losing the intriguing challenges of the field.

TOBIN, J. J., WU, D. Y. H., & DAVIDSON, D. H. (1989). *Preschool in three cultures: Japan, China, and the United States.* New Haven: Yale University Press. In detailed, case-study fashion, these authors present a vivid and persuasive picture of cultural variation in the way three preschools nurture, educate, and socialize students.

Infants and Toddlers: Physical, Cognitive, and Language Development

CHAPTER

4

123

CHAPTER OBJECTIVES

By the time you have finished this chapter, you should be able to do the following:

1. Describe what neonates can do.
2. Summarize physical and motor development during infancy.
3. Explain the effects of infant malnutrition.
4. Summarize perceptual development during infancy.
5. Explain and critique Piaget's theory of cognitive development during the sensorimotor stage.
6. Describe the role of perceptual organization in infant cognition.
7. Summarize language development during infancy.
8. Discuss the roles of imitation, conditioning, innate language structure, and cognitive development in language learning.

Neonates enter the world quite capable of sensing their environment and responding to it. They can see and hear, taste and smell, feel pressure and pain. They're selective in what they look at. They learn, although their abilities are limited. During their first 2 years, infants change more rapidly and more dramatically than during any other 2-year period. Some changes are obvious. Infants crawl, sit, walk, and talk. Other changes are harder to assess. It's difficult indeed to know exactly what an infant sees, hears, and thinks.

Neonates communicate their needs with a cry, a yawn, or an alert squint, but they are born profoundly ignorant. They have no real knowledge of life, of day and night, self and other, mine and yours, boy and girl, mothers and fathers and sons and daughters. Yet just 2 short years later, children are thinking, reasoning, and expressing their thoughts and feelings through language. At the same time, language helps them structure what they know and understand. Because of the enormous power that language provides, it is considered a bridge out of infancy and a key aspect of cognitive development.

In this chapter we begin with a close look at the competencies of the neonate and then discuss what is known about physical, motor, and perceptual development during the first 2 years of life. After that we focus on cognitive and language development.

NEONATES

The first month is a very special period because the baby must adjust to life outside the protected environment of the mother's womb. As we saw in Chapter 2, the first month is a time of recovery from the birth process and adjustment of vital functions such as respiration, circulation, digestion, and regulation of body temperature. It is also a time for developing a balance between overstimulation and understimulation in a challenging physical and social environment. How well equipped is a normal neonate for such tasks?

Child development researchers now know that infants are capable of more complex responses and mental activities than was previously believed.

INFANT COMPETENCIES AND STATES

Until the 1960s it was thought that neonates are incapable of organized, self-directed behavior. In fact, it was not uncommon to view the infant's world as a "blooming, buzzing confusion," as William James described it in 1890. Developmental literature stated that infants do not use higher brain centers until they are almost a year old and that newborns see light and shadow but do not perceive objects or patterns. Behavior in the first weeks of life was considered to be almost entirely reflexive.

Subsequent research showed that newborns' capabilities had been grossly underestimated. We now know that neonates are capable of organized, predictable responses and of more complex cognitive activity than was once thought. They have definite preferences and a striking ability to learn. Moreover, they deliberately attract attention to their needs.

The key to the new understanding of infants is in the development of more accurate and effective ways of observing their behavior. Early studies often put infants at a disadvantage. Even adults who are placed flat on their backs to stare at a ceiling while covered up to their necks with blankets are not their most perceptive or responsive selves. When neonates are placed stomach down on the mother's skin in a warm room, they display an engaging repertoire of behaviors that wouldn't otherwise be seen.

In this section we'll discuss infant states of arousal, reflexes, and early learning abilities. Later we'll consider neonatal sensory and perceptual capabilities and the beginnings of active cognition.

INFANT STATES OF AROUSAL   If you watch sleeping newborns, you'll notice that they sometimes lie calmly and quietly and at other times twitch and grimace. Similarly, when they are awake, babies may either be calm or thrash about wildly and cry. Through extensive observation of infants' activity, P. H. Wolff (1966) identified six newborn behavioral states: *waking activity, crying, alert inactivity, drowsiness, regular sleep,* and *irregular sleep.* These states are described in Table 4–1. They are regular and follow a predictable daily cycle.

TABLE 4–1 INFANT STATES OF AROUSAL

Waking activity: The baby frequently engages in motor activity involving the whole body. The eyes are open, and breathing is highly irregular.

Crying: The baby cries and engages in vigorous, disorganized motor activity. Crying may take different forms, such as "hunger" cries, "anger" cries, and "pain" or "discomfort" cries (Wolff, 1969).

Alert inactivity: The eyes are open, bright, and shining. They follow moving objects. The baby is fairly inactive, with a quiet face.

Drowsiness: The baby is fairly inactive. The eyes open and close. Breathing is regular, but faster than in regular sleep. When the eyes are open, they may have a dull, glazed quality.

Regular sleep: The eyes are closed and the body is completely relaxed. Breathing is slow and regular. The face looks relaxed, and the eyelids are still.

Irregular sleep: The eyes are closed, but there are gentle limb movements such as writhing, stirring, and stretching. Grimaces and other facial expressions occur. Breathing is irregular and faster than in regular sleep. Rapid eye movements (REMs) occasionally occur; these may indicate dreaming.

An infant's responsiveness to others and to the environment depends on his or her behavioral state. In a state of alert inactivity, infants are easily stimulated and react to a sound or sight with increased activity. Infants who are already in an active state tend to calm down when stimulated. At first, newborns spend most of the day in either regular or irregular sleep. As an infant matures and the higher brain centers "wake up," the percentages shift. For example, by 4 to 8 weeks a typical baby is sleeping more during the night and less during the day. There are longer periods of alert inactivity and waking activity, and the baby is more responsive to caregivers—as well as to researchers.

Much to the delight of parents and caregivers, by 4 months the average baby is usually sleeping through the night. Gradually the baby settles into the family routine, in the daytime as well as at night.

REFLEXES Infants enter the world with biologically based behaviors that can be classified as **survival reflexes** and **primitive reflexes.** Survival reflexes are just that: reflexes necessary for adaptation and survival, especially during the first few weeks, before the higher brain centers begin to take control (see Table 4–2). Breathing, for example, is reflexive although it is also subject to voluntary control after the first few months. Coughing, sneezing, gagging, hiccupping, yawning, and many other reflexes not included in Table 4–2 are also present at birth and throughout life. In contrast, rooting and sucking, highly adaptive reflexes for finding the nipple and obtaining milk, are reflexive at first but become entirely voluntary after a few months.

Primitive reflexes do not have apparent survival value but may have been important at some point in our evolutionary history. The Moro reflex, for example, is the newborn's startle reaction. When newborns are startled by a loud sound or by being dropped, they react first by extending both arms to the side, with fingers outstretched as if to catch onto someone or something. The arms then gradually come back to the midline. Thus, the Moro reflex might have had survival value in the distant past: In case of a fall, infants who grasped their mother's body hair would be most likely to survive. A related reflex is the palmar grasp. When the palm of an infant's hand is stimulated by an object such as a finger or a pencil, the infant's fingers will close tightly in a grasp.

survival reflexes Reflexes necessary for adaptation and survival, especially during the first few weeks before the higher brain centers begin to take control.

primitive reflexes These reflexes do not have apparent survival value but may have been important at some point in our evolutionary history.

Table 4–2   Reflexes of the Neonate

Survival Reflexes

Breathing: Infants reflexively inhale to obtain oxygen and exhale to expel carbon dioxide. Breathing is permanently reflexive in that it doesn't require conscious effort, although after the first few months of life, we can voluntarily control our breathing—up to a point.

Rooting: If you touch an infant's cheek, the infant will turn its head toward the stimulus and open its mouth as if expecting a nipple. This reflex normally disappears after 3 or 4 months.

Sucking: If you touch or otherwise stimulate an infant's mouth, the infant will respond by sucking and making rhythmic movements with the mouth and tongue. This reflex gradually becomes voluntary over the first few months.

Pupillary: The pupils of infants' eyes narrow when in bright light and when going to sleep, and widen when in dim light and when waking up. This is a permanent reflex.

Eye-blink: Infants blink in response to an object's moving quickly toward their eyes or to a puff of air. This is a permanent reflex.

Primitive Reflexes

Moro (startle): When infants are startled by loud sounds or by being suddenly dropped a few inches, they will first spread their arms and stretch out their fingers, then bring their arms back to their body and clench their fingers. This reflex disappears after about 4 months.

Palmar: When an infant's palm is stimulated, the infant will grasp tightly and increase the strength of the grasp if the stimulus is pulled away. This reflex disappears after about 5 months.

Plantar: When an object or a finger is placed on the sole of an infant's foot near the toes, the infant responds by trying to flex the foot. This reflex is similar to the palmar reflex, but it disappears after about 9 months.

Babinski: If you stroke the sole of an infant's foot from heel to toes, the infant will spread the small toes and raise the large one. This reflex disappears after about 6 months.

Stepping: When infants are held upright with their feet against a flat surface and are moved forward, they appear to walk in a coordinated way. This reflex disappears after 2 or 3 months.

Swimming: Infants will *attempt* to swim in a coordinated way if placed in water in a prone position. This reflex disappears after about 6 months.

Tonic neck: When infants' heads are turned to one side, they will extend the arm and leg on that side and flex the arm and leg on the opposite side, as in a fencing position. This reflex disappears after about 4 months.

Indeed, some neonates can grasp with enough strength to support their full weight for up to a minute (Taft & Cohen, 1967).

Primitive reflexes normally disappear during the first several months of life and therefore have diagnostic value: If they do *not* disappear more or less on schedule, it may be a sign of neurological problems.

LEARNING AND HABITUATION

Learning is readily observable from birth. Neonates quiet down in response to familiar sounds, songs, or lullabies. The neonate's early ability to imitate facial expressions demonstrates learning. Improved methods of observation have yielded useful information about the infants' ability to learn fairly complex

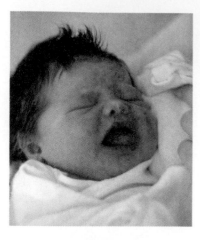  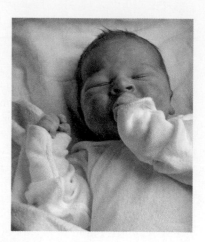

Some reflexes of the newborn: (left) rooting reflex, (middle) stepping reflex, and (right) sucking reflex.

responses. Newborns' ability to turn their heads has been used in many learning experiments. In pioneering conditioning studies (Papousek, 1961), newborns were taught to turn their heads to the left to obtain milk whenever a bell was rung. For the same reward, they learned to turn their heads to the right at the sound of a buzzer. Then the bell and the buzzer were reversed, and the infants quickly learned to turn their heads in the appropriate direction.

CLASSIC EXPERIMENTS ON INFANT LEARNING Because sucking comes under voluntary control early, it has been used extensively in studies of neonatal learning and visual preferences. Jerome Bruner and colleagues (Kalnins & Bruner, 1973) assessed whether infants could control sucking when it was linked to rewards other than feeding. Pacifiers were wired to a slide projector. If the infants sucked, the slide came into focus; if they did not, the picture blurred. The researchers found that the infants—some as young as 3 weeks—quickly learned to focus the picture and also adapted quickly if conditions were reversed. That is, they learned to stop sucking in order to get the picture into focus.

There were also experiments in which infants learned to turn on a light by turning their heads to the left (Papousek, 1961). But then an interesting thing happened, revealing a key facet of infant learning called **habituation.** After a while, the infants lost interest in turning on the light, as if they were bored with the game. Their interest could be revived by reversing the problem, but they soon became bored again.

Habituation is a form of learning that involves becoming accustomed to stimuli and then no longer responding to them, and it serves an important adaptive function throughout the lifespan. Infants, for example, need to adapt to or ignore nonmeaningful stimuli like the light touch of their clothing or any repetitive noises in their environment (radiator poppings, noises from the street). Habituation also gives rise to an important research technique. In the **habituation method,** researchers habituate infants to certain stimuli in order to study their perceptual capabilities. For example, a newborn's response at the onset of a moderately loud tone is a faster heartbeat, a change in breathing, and sometimes crying or generally increased activity. As the tone continues, however, the infant soon habituates, or stops responding. Then the frequency of the tone is changed slightly. If responding resumes, it is clear that the infant perceived the difference.

habituation The process of becoming accustomed to certain kinds of stimuli and no longer responding to them.

habituation method To study infant perceptual capabilities, researchers habituate infants to certain stimuli and then change the stimuli.

ASSESSMENT   During the first few days of a baby's life, hospitals perform evaluations that may include a neurological examination and a behavioral assessment. Brazelton's (1973) Neonatal Behavioral Assessment Scale is used by many hospitals. The 44 separate measures on the test are grouped into seven behavioral clusters. The clusters include habituation, orientation, motor tone and activity, range of state, regulation of state, autonomic stability, and reflexes. (See Table 4–3.) Thus, although the scale includes the usual neurological tests, it also assesses the newborn's behavioral capabilities and social responsiveness.

Newborns differ in their responses to new, prolonged, or slightly annoying stimuli. Some can easily detect, attend to, and habituate to changes in their environment. Others may be less responsive, still others overly responsive and too easily irritated—behaviors that decrease attention span and adaptability. By assessing the newborn's competencies and patterns of responding, the Brazelton scale supplies early information about a child's potential personality and social development. Parents who observe a physician's administering the Brazelton scale become much more sensitive to the capabilities and individuality of their neonate (Parke & Tinsley, 1987). With "difficult" babies in particular, parents can also receive special training that teaches them what to expect and methods of coping with their baby's behavior.

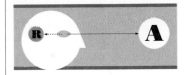

REVIEW & APPLY

1. Discuss infant states of arousal and how they change during the first few months of life.
2. Which reflexes of the newborn are necessary for survival and which apparently are not? Explain why.
3. How do researchers know that infants learn? How do researchers apply their knowledge of infant habituation to learn about the perceptual capacities of neonates?

TABLE 4–3   CLUSTERS IN THE NEONATAL BEHAVIORAL ASSESSMENT SCALE

Habituation: How quickly does the infant habituate to a light, bell, rattle, or pin prick?

Orientation: How readily does the infant quiet and turn toward a light, bell, voice, or face?

Motor tone and activity: How strong and steady is the motor activity?

Range of state: How quickly and easily does the infant shift from sleeping to alertness? To crying?

Regulation of state: How does the infant calm or quiet down? How easily is the infant soothed?

Autonomic stability: Does the infant react to noises with tremors or unusual startles?

Reflexes: Are there regular and strong responses to each of 17 reflexes?

Source: Adapted from Lester, Als, and Brazelton (1982).

Every day in an infant's life brings new opportunities for discovery.

PHYSICAL AND MOTOR DEVELOPMENT

Infancy is a time of perceptual and motor discovery. Infants learn to recognize faces, foods, and familiar routines. They explore flowers, insects, toys, and their own bodies. Every day brings opportunities for discovery of the people, objects, and events in their environment. Such discovery is not only exciting but also helpful in learning to adapt.

MATURATION OR A DYNAMIC SYSTEM?

For decades, developmental psychologists carefully studied maturational characteristics. Arnold Gesell (1940), a pioneer in the field, observed hundreds of infants and children. He recorded the details of when and how certain behaviors emerged, such as crawling, walking, running, picking up a small pellet, cutting with scissors, managing a pencil, or drawing human figures. On the basis of the resulting data, he compiled detailed reports of the capabilities of *average* children at different ages.

In the healthy, well-nourished children whom Gesell observed, the behaviors under study emerged in an orderly and predictable sequence. By knowing the age of a child, Gesell could predict not only what the child's approximate height and weight was but also what the child knew or was able to do. He concluded that development does not depend primarily on the environment. Instead, he believed—given a normal environment—that most of a child's achievements result from an internal biological timetable. Behavior emerges as a function of maturation.

Gesell's theory and method had a major shortcoming, however. The children he studied came from the same socioeconomic class and community, so that their shared environment may have caused them to develop in similar ways. We now know that children raised in widely different social or historical contexts develop quite differently from those described in Gesell's schedules. For example, contemporary American infants normally begin "free" walking between 11 and 13 months of age instead of at 15 months as Gesell observed, presumably because baby care customs have changed. In the 1930s, infants spent more time resting and lying flat on their backs than they do now, so that they did not get as much early practice with the skills leading up to walking.

There are also cultural differences in the onset of walking. On average, African-American infants walk a few weeks earlier than Caucasian-American infants. West Indian infants, whether in Jamaica or East London, normally walk a month earlier than other London infants. That is the case because their mothers use massage and encourage vigorous exercise (Hopkins, 1991). Infants raised in some Guatemalan villages—where they spend their first year confined to a small, dark hut, are not played with, are rarely spoken to, and are poorly nourished—walk months later (Kagan, 1978).

Despite the shortcomings of his research, Gesell's contribution remains substantial. If we use his findings carefully and don't overinterpret them, we at least have a baseline of developmental milestones to which we can compare individual infants' development. Bear in mind, however, that Gesell's milestones are averages and only that; quite normal children vary widely in the ages at which they develop maturationally based behaviors. Children develop at their own pace and in the context of their social and cultural environment.

Contemporary developmental psychologists have gone well beyond Gesell's studies in analyzing the form and processes of infants' developing

Gesell observed that many infant behaviors emerged in an orderly and predictable sequence in healthy, well-nourished children.

competencies. Perceptual, motor, cognitive, and emotional development go hand in hand in a particular social context. The infant reaches out for an attractive object and pulls it in for closer inspection. The baby who has just begun to walk, toddles precariously toward the outstretched arms of an eager, encouraging parent. And the toddler explores the world from a new perspective. Motor development is intimately related to the infant's perceptual, cognitive, and social development. Body, brain, and experience influence each other (Thelen, 1987, 1989). Physical and motor developments occur not simply through maturation but in a dynamic system of evolving competencies that augment and complement each other (Bushnell & Boudreau, 1993; Lockman & Thelen, 1993).

AN OVERVIEW OF THE FIRST 2 YEARS

THE FIRST 4 MONTHS   By about 4 months, most infants have nearly doubled in weight. (Figure 4–1 illustrates growth rates for height and weight over the first two years of life.) Their skin has lost the newborn look, and their fine birth hair is being replaced by permanent hair. Their eyes have begun to focus. When awake, they babble contentedly and smile in response to pleasant stimuli.

At birth, the size of an infant's head represents about one-quarter of its total body length. Around age 4 months, however, the body starts to grow and lengthen much more rapidly than the head, and the proportions change markedly (see Figure 4–2). By young adulthood, the head accounts for only one-tenth of total body length.

The infant's teeth and bones are also changing. In some children the first tooth erupts at 4 or 5 months. Many bones are still soft cartilage. They tend to be pliable under stress and rarely break. Muscles, however, may pull easily and be injured, for example, when infants are hoisted by the arms and swung about in play (Stone et al., 1973).

STUDY CHART ▸ A SUMMARY OF INFANT COMPETENCIES

AGE (IN MONTHS)	PERCEPTION	MOTOR BEHAVIOR	LANGUAGE	COGNITION
4 Active looking	Visually tracks objects; perceives colors, discriminates between shapes, and focuses almost as well as an adult; responds to sounds as low as 43 dB; turns toward sounds (bells, voices)	Holds up head, chest; grasps objects; rolls from stomach to back	Babbles; coos; imitates own sounds	Remembers objects, sounds; discovers and examines own hands and fingers; begins to play social interaction games (mimics caregivers' imitation of his or her own sounds)
8 On the move	Responds to sounds at 34 dB; has integrated vision and hearing; has mastered visually guided reach	Sits up without support; stands with support; crawls, creeps, "bear walks," or "scoots"; passes objects from hand to hand	Imitates some repeated speech sounds ("mama," "dada"); babbles more complex sounds	Discriminates between familiar and unfamiliar faces; exhibits stranger anxiety; hunts for hidden objects; plays more advanced social games; imitates some adult gestures and actions
12 First words, first steps		Walks with support; masters pincer grasp; starts to feed himself or herself	Understands and uses a few words, including "no"	Looks for a hidden object in its usual hiding place, but not in the place he or she last saw it; is aware of separation between self and caregiver, and exercises choice; begins to pretend by symbolically representing familiar activities (eating, drinking, sleeping)
18 Pretend play		Walks without support; attains a better mastery of feeding himself or herself; can stack two or more blocks; can scribble	Combines two words to form a sentence; names body parts, familiar pictures	Understands the concept of object permanence; attempts to use objects for their intended purposes; includes a second person in pretend play; pretending includes imitative games ("reading")
24 End of Infancy		Walks, runs, climbs stairs; can pedal a tricycle; can throw overhand	Follows simple verbal directions; uses three or more words in combination	Uses objects to represent other objects (a broom for a horse, a sack for a hat)

FIGURE 4–1

The weight and height of about 50% of the infants at a given age will fall in the purple regions; about 15% will fall in each of the white regions. Thus, on the average, 80% of all infants will have weights and heights somewhere in the purple and white regions of the graphs. Note that as the infants age, greater differences occur in weight and height within the normal range of growth.

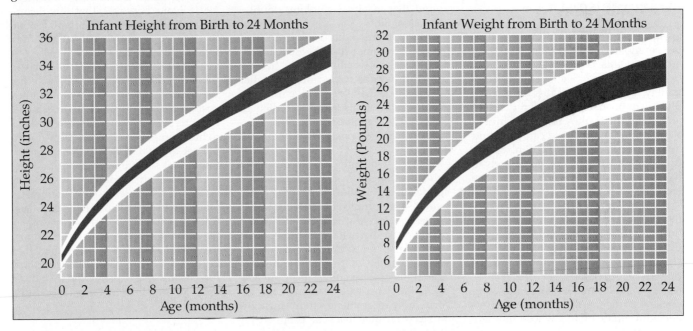

Most of the newborn's reflexes normally disappear in the second and third months, gradually being replaced by voluntary actions. The well-coordinated stepping reflex, for example, is replaced by more random, less well-coordinated kicking (Thelen, 1989). The transition from reflexes to higher brain center control is also the time when sudden infant death syndrome is most common. (See "A Matter for Debate," page 134.)

Self-discovery also usually begins at this time. Infants discover their own hands and fingers, and they spend minutes at a time watching them, studying

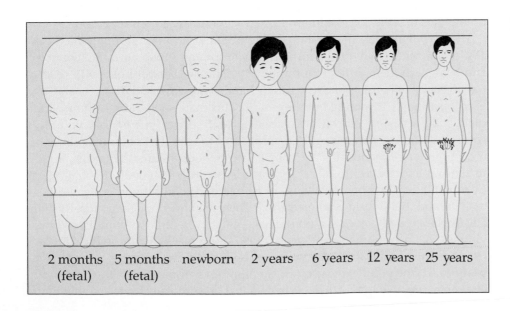

FIGURE 4–2

The cephalocaudal (head-downward) and proximodistal (center-outward) development that we saw in prenatal growth continues after birth, and the proportions of the baby's body change dramatically during infancy.

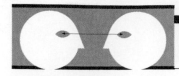

A MATTER FOR DEBATE

SUDDEN INFANT DEATH SYNDROME (SIDS)

Sudden infant death syndrome (SIDS) is the most common cause of death among infants between 2 weeks and 6 months in age. There are approximately 10,000 such deaths each year. SIDS is defined as the sudden death of an apparently healthy infant or child in whom no medical cause can be found in a postmortem examination. Sometimes called "crib death," SIDS tends to happen without warning, while the child is asleep.

Researchers have been unsuccessful in finding the precise cause of SIDS, but they have identified circumstances in which it is more likely to occur. The risk is increased if the mother was ill during her pregnancy or did not receive prenatal care. Smoking and drug abuse by the mother are often connected to SIDS. Infants whose mothers smoke and are also anemic are at high

risk (Bulterys et al., 1990). It has been found that maternal smoking doubles the risk of SIDS.

Many infants who die of SIDS had severe breathing and digestive problems in the preceding week. Second and third children also are at higher risk for SIDS than the average firstborn child. Also, infants who later died of SIDS have been observed to be less active and less responsive than their siblings.

Death frequently occurs at night when the infant is asleep, regardless of its position (Shannon et al., 1987). Recent research indicates, however, that babies who are put to sleep in a prone position (on their stomachs) may be at greater risk for SIDS (Dwyer et al., 1991). Because of this and other research linking sleeping position and SIDS, the American Academy of Pediatrics now recommends putting babies to sleep on their back or propped on their side against pillows (AAP Task

Force on Infant Positioning and SIDS, 1992). Note, however, that this recommendation is more important for babies for whom the risk of SIDS is high than for healthy babies.

SIDS seems to occur most often in winter. Although researchers have not yet found a physiological cause, they suspect irregularities in the autonomic nervous system, especially as it relates to breathing and heart functions (Shannon et al., 1987). Recent research has found that some infants apparently are born with an immature respiratory center. This defect, combined with other problems such as illness, head colds, or exposure to cold air or smoke, may result in cessation of breathing. Vestibular stimulation by rocking has been shown to be beneficial for premature babies in reducing *apnea* (halting of breathing), which is often associated with SIDS.

---

their movements, bringing them together, and grasping one hand with the other.

FIVE TO 8 MONTHS By 8 months, although babies have gradually gained weight, their general appearance doesn't differ dramatically from that of 4-month-olds. Their hair is thicker and longer. By this time, too, their legs are oriented so that the soles of their feet no longer face each other.

By about 5 months, most infants achieve an important milestone called *visually guided reach*: They can accurately reach out and grasp an attractive object and bring it to them, often mouthing it. In contrast, 1-month-olds will react to the object by opening and closing their hands and waving their arms and perhaps opening their mouth, but they can't coordinate such motions into a complete act. Successful reaching requires accurate depth perception, voluntary control of arm movements and grasping, and the ability to organize these behaviors into a sequence (Bruner, 1973). Throughout the first 5 months, infants use visual information to direct exploration with their fingers (Rochat, 1989). Eventually they combine reaching, grasping, and mouthing into a smooth sequence, and their world is transformed: They can now engage in more systematic exploration of objects—with the hands, the eyes, and the mouth used individually or in combination (Rochat, 1989). **Fine motor skills,** which involve use of the hands and fingers, continue to be refined. By 5 months the infant has progressed from a reflexive grasp to a voluntary scooping grab. Most 8-month-old babies are able to pass objects from hand to hand, and some are able to use

fine motor skills Competence in using the hands.

Many 8-month-olds start to play social games like peekaboo.

the thumb and finger to grasp. They are usually able to bang two objects together—often joyfully and endlessly.

Gross motor skills—those involving the larger muscles or the whole body—show refinement as well. Most 8-month-olds can get themselves into a sitting position, and nearly all can sit without support if placed in a sitting position. If they are placed on their feet, many 8-month-olds can stand while holding on to a support. Some may be walking, using furniture for support. By now, all valuables and any small objects that could be swallowed should be placed beyond the infant's reach. Infants learn to crawl (with the body on the ground) or creep (on hands and knees). Other infants develop a method called "bear walking," which employs both hands and feet. Still others "scoot" in a sitting position.

Especially interesting with regard to infant crawling at 8 months and older is a series of studies by Karen Adolph and colleagues (1997), which demonstate infants' capabilities when confronted with crawling up and down "slopes" at varying angles. For example, without training, 8½-month-olds "charged up" steep slopes with no hesitation, then—perhaps after surveying the downward side—continued head first and required rescue by the experimenters. In contrast, older infants (walking 14-month-olds) were more discriminating. They walked up the steep slopes and then carefully slid down.

Many 8-month-olds begin to play social games, such as peekaboo, bye-bye, and patty-cake, and most enjoy handing an item back and forth with an adult. Another quickly learned game is dropping an object and watching someone pick it up and hand it back—another source of endless pleasure for some infants.

NINE TO 12 MONTHS   By 12 months most infants are about three times heavier than they were at birth. Girls tend to weigh slightly less than boys.

On average, about half of infants 12 months old are standing alone and taking their first tentative steps toward becoming toddlers. As noted earlier,

gross motor skills   Those skills that involve the larger muscles or the whole body and that show refinement as well.

By 12 months, many infants are actively exploring their environment.

At 18 months, most toddlers are able to walk alone, and they like to carry or pull toys with them.

pincer grasp The method of holding objects, developed at around the age of 12 months, in which the thumb opposes the forefinger.

however, the age at which walking begins varies widely, depending both on individual development and on cultural factors.

The ability to stand and walk gives the toddler a new visual perspective. Locomotion allows for more active exploration. Infants can now get into, over, and under things. Their world has broadened once again. The child's motor development is spurred on by new and exciting things to be approached and seen. Exploring at new levels and with new skills promotes cognitive and perceptual development (Bushnell & Boudreau, 1993; Thelen, 1989). Twelve-month-olds actively manipulate their environment. They undo latches, open cabinets, pull toys, and twist lamp cords. Their newly developed **pincer grasp,** with thumb opposing forefinger, allows them to pick up grass, hairs, matches, dead insects, you name it. Because they can turn on the TV, open windows, and poke things into electrical outlets, relatively constant supervision and a "child-proofed" house are necessary.

Now babies can play games and "hide" by covering their eyes. They can roll a ball back and forth with an adult and throw small objects, making up in persistence for what they lack in skill. Many children begin to feed themselves at this age, using a spoon and holding their own drinking cup. It isn't yet the neatest behavior, but it is a beginning of independent self-care.

EIGHTEEN MONTHS An 18-month-old weighs up to four times its birth weight, but by this age the rate of increase in weight has slowed. Almost all children are walking alone at this age. Some are not yet able to climb stairs, however, and most have considerable difficulty kicking a ball because they can't free one foot. They also find pedaling tricycles or jumping nearly impossible.

At 18 months children may be stacking two to four cubes or blocks to build a tower, and they often manage to scribble with a crayon or a pencil. Their ability to feed themselves has improved considerably, and they may be able to undress themselves partly. Many of their actions imitate what they see others doing—"reading" a magazine, sweeping the floor, or "chatting" on a toy telephone.

TWENTY-FOUR MONTHS By their second birthday, toddlers typically weigh just over four times as much as they did at birth, and their rate of growth is continuing to taper off.

Two-year-olds can usually pedal a tricycle, jump in place on both feet, balance briefly on one foot, and throw a ball. They climb up steps. They crawl into, under, and over objects and furniture; they manipulate, carry, handle, push, or pull anything within reach. They pour water, mold clay, stretch the stretchable, bend the bendable. They transport items in carts and wagons. In every way imaginable they explore, test, and probe their physical world. Two-year-olds can also dress and undress with assistance.

If they are given a crayon or pencil, 2-year-olds may scribble and be fascinated with the magical marks that appear. They may stack six to eight blocks or cubes to build towers, and they can construct a three-block "bridge." Their spontaneous block play shows matching of shapes and symmetry.

In sum, physical and motor development during the first 2 years is a complex, dynamic process. For infants to thrive, their basic needs must be met. They must get enough sleep, feel safe, receive consistent care, and have appropriate, stimulating experiences. Each developing system—perceptual and motor skills, for example—supports the others. Brain development, too, depends on the information the child receives from actions and sensory explorations (Lockman & Thelen, 1993). These interacting systems are helped or hindered by the social context in which the infant develops (Hazen & Lockman, 1989; Thelen & Fogel, 1989). Much remains to be learned about how brain maturation and experience interact, however, in terms of the myriad ways in which experience modifies brain structures (e.g., see Nelson & Bloom, 1997).

INFANT NUTRITION AND MALNUTRITION

The United States may be the best-fed nation in the world, but many Americans still suffer from nutritional deficiencies. For example, in 1992 a national program serving low-income families reported that 20–24% of poor infants suffered from iron deficiency anemia (Pollitt, 1994). Similar figures have been reported for other nutritional deficiencies.

Serious deficiencies in the first 30 months of life have effects that are rarely eliminated later. Physical growth may be permanently stunted, resulting in shorter children and adults, as well as delays in maturation and learning (Waterlow, 1994). Long-term deficits in brain size, together with deficits in attention and information processing, also occur.

Around the world, especially in the developing nations, the situation is generally worse (see Figure 4–3. It is estimated that 86% of the world's babies are born in developing nations, where over 40% of them experience periods of at least moderate malnutrition (Lozoff, 1989).

There are two basic types of malnutrition: insufficient total quantity of food and inadequate quantities of certain kinds of food. With regard to the former, starvation or severe lack of food produces deficiencies in protein and total caloric intake, and results in a condition called *marasmus*. Muscles waste away, and stored fat is depleted, although there are no long-term negative effects if

FIGURE 4–3 WORLDWIDE CALORIE CONSUMPTION AND AREAS OF FAMINE

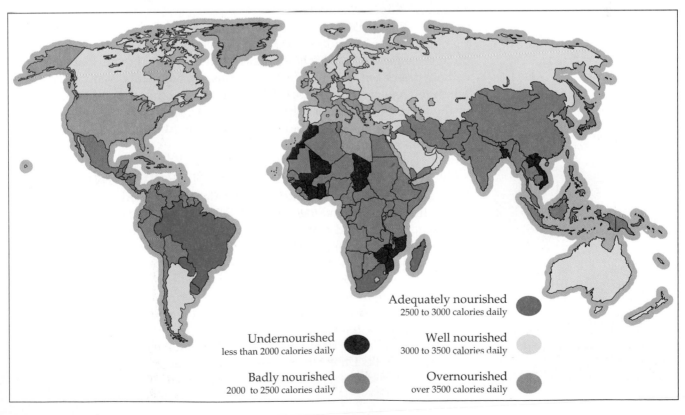

Adequately nourished
2500 to 3000 calories daily

Undernourished
less than 2000 calories daily

Well nourished
3000 to 3500 calories daily

Badly nourished
2000 to 2500 calories daily

Overnourished
over 3500 calories daily

the period of starvation is relatively short. Another type of severe malnutrition, called *kwashiorkor*, is caused by insufficient protein. The term, Swahili for "deposed child," refers to an African practice of placing a nursing child in the home of relatives for weaning if the mother becomes pregnant again. Once removed from the mother's protein-rich breast milk, such children often suffer protein deficiency. The effects of kwashiorkor in the first 3 years of life can be highly damaging in the long run because brain development is directly affected.

For many children, lack of sufficient protein in infancy starts a downward cycle that seriously limits their potential. In Barbados, 129 children who were healthy at birth but malnourished during the first year of life were studied through age 11. With a vigorous public health and nutrition program, the children eventually caught up in most aspects of physical growth, but in academic tests at age 11 they showed an average 12-point deficit compared with matched pairs (Galler, 1984). What went wrong? In a careful follow-up study using parent interviews, teacher reports, and observation of the children, two facts emerged. First, the children's behavior was characterized by impulsiveness and attention deficit. Second, their parents, most of whom had also been through periods of protein malnutrition, had low energy and depressive symptoms. They were not able to provide a stimulating, focused, or consistent environment for their children (Salt et al., 1988). Parental depression and hopelessness, together with impulsive and inattentive children, are commonly found in studies of protein malnutrition (Lozoff, 1989).

Even in cases of severe malnutrition during infancy, food supplement programs combined with education can produce dramatic results. In a study in Bogotá, Colombia, poor children who were given food supplements for the first 3 years of life showed much less growth retardation and all-around better functioning than comparison groups that did not participate in the program. The improvement was still evident 3 years after the supplements had been discontinued (Super et al., 1990).

In the United States, severe forms of malnutrition are rare, but protein and iron deficiencies are quite common. Many people who can afford a good diet often consume too many "empty calories" in the form of foods that are high in carbohydrates but low in protein, vitamins, and minerals. Many people who ingest too few calories cannot afford protein-rich foods. In addition, the diets of the poor most often lack vitamins A and C, riboflavin, and iron (Eichorn, 1979), all of which are required for healthy body functioning, immune system action, and brain development.

BREAST-FEEDING VERSUS BOTTLE-FEEDING

Milk is the major source of nutrients for infants. It is used almost exclusively for the first 6 months and together with solid foods for the next 6 to 12 months. Throughout the world many women choose to breast-feed their infants. The breast milk of a well-fed mother contains a remarkably well-balanced combination of nutrients, as well as antibodies that help protect the infant from diseases. Even a malnourished mother's milk provides almost adequate nutrients, often at a cost to her own health.

Breast milk suits most babies, and breast-fed babies tend to have fewer digestive problems than bottle-fed babies. In addition, breast milk is always fresh and ready at the right temperature, does not have to be refrigerated, and is normally sterile. Unless the mother is very ill, has an inadequate diet, or uses alcohol or other drugs, breast milk is better for a baby's health.

Although breast-feeding is more nutritious than bottle-feeding, many other factors influence a mother's choice.

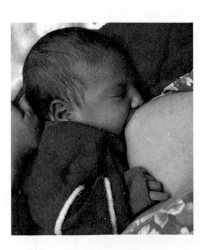

Despite these advantages, many mothers choose bottle-feeding. Bottle-feeding causes no hardship or nutritional problems for the great majority of infants in developed countries, but the shift to commercial infant formula has resulted in widespread malnutrition in poorer countries. There, bottle-fed babies have a much higher mortality rate than breast-fed babies (Latham, 1977). Malnutrition occurs when people lack the money to buy expensive milk substitutes. In addition, many babies die when commercial formula is diluted with contaminated water, thereby transmitting intestinal diseases to the infant.

Why do some mothers breast-feed and others bottle-feed? It appears that good nutrition is only one of many factors influencing the choice. Obviously, cultural factors, personal factors (such as allocating time for work and child care, social obligations, and the availability of a peer group that accepts breast-feeding), and even national policies may have an effect. For example, until recently the United States lacked a family-leave policy. Many women who returned to work a few weeks after the birth of their child found it difficult to combine full-time employment with breast-feeding.

WEANING AND INTRODUCTION OF SOLID FOODS   Some mothers in developed countries begin weaning their babies from the breast at 3 or 4 months or even earlier; others continue breast-feeding for as long as 2 or 3 years. Although extended breast-feeding is rare among middle- and upper-class mothers in the United States, 2 or 3 years is not unusual in certain American subcultures and some other cultures.

Normally, sometime between 3 and 5 months, infants gradually start accepting strained foods. Usually they begin with simple cereals, such as rice, and expand to a variety of cereals and pureed fruits, followed later by strained vegetables and meats. Some infants are allergic to specific foods; others respond well to almost everything that is offered to them. By 8 months most infants are eating a broad range of specially prepared foods, and milk consumption is usually reduced.

Weaning is a crucial time because of the possibility of malnutrition, as we saw earlier. Particularly vulnerable are 1-year-olds who have already been weaned from the breast in families that cannot afford nutritious foods. Such children may survive on diets composed of potato chips, dry cereals, and cookies—foods that typically provide calories but few nutrients. Even if enough milk or a variety of nutritious foods is available, however, 1-year-olds may be unwilling to drink a sufficient amount of milk from a cup or eat to protein-rich foods.

1. Why do researchers believe that physical and motor development constitute a dynamic system?
2. What are the milestones of motor development during the first 2 years?
3. Give an example of how the infant's motor development is shaped in a particular social context. How can caregivers apply that knowledge so as to encourage motor development?
4. What are the short-term and long-term effects of the two kinds of malnutrition? How can we apply what we have learned about the usefulness of food supplements?
5. Why is breast milk generally better for a baby's health? Under what circumstances might breast milk *not* be better?

REVIEW & APPLY

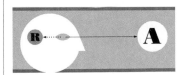

SENSORY AND PERCEPTUAL DEVELOPMENT

Can newborn babies see patterns and the details of objects? Can they see color and depth? Can they hear a low whisper? How sensitive are they to touch? Research indicates that all of the senses are operating at birth. Thus, **sensation**—the translation of external stimulation into neural impulses—is highly developed. But **perception**—the active process of interpreting information from the senses—is limited and selective at birth. Perception is a cognitive process that gives organization and meaning to sensory information. It develops rapidly over the first 6 months, followed by fine-tuning over the first several years of life.

STUDYING INFANT PERCEPTUAL CAPABILITIES

Basic physiological measures provide information about infants' reactions to environmental stimulation. Heart activity, brain-wave activity, and the electrical response of the skin provide indirect information about what infants perceive and understand. Researchers also use highly refined pictures of an infant's movements—for example, eye movement or hand manipulation. But technology is only part of the answer. A good research *paradigm* (method or model) is just as important.

Classical and operant conditioning, as discussed in Chapter 3, can be used to assess infant sensory and memory capabilities. Simply put, an infant can't be conditioned to respond to stimuli that the infant can't perceive.

An especially useful strategy in measuring infant competencies is the **novelty paradigm,** which is closely related to the habituation method discussed earlier. Babies quickly tire of looking at the same image or playing with the same toy. They habituate to repeated sights and often show their lack of interest by looking away. If given a choice between a familiar toy and a new one, most infants will choose the new one, provided that they can perceive the difference. Researchers use this approach in setting up experiments to determine how small a difference in sound, pattern, or color young infants are capable of detecting.

Another popular approach is the **preference method,** in which infants are given a choice between stimuli to look at or listen to. Researchers record which stimulus the infant attends to more. If an infant consistently spends more time attending to one of the two stimuli, the preference indicates that the infant can both perceive a difference and deliberately respond to it. The preference method can also be combined with behaviors such as sucking.

The **surprise paradigm** is a useful way of studying infants' understanding of the world around them. Humans tend to register surprise—through facial expression, physical reaction, or vocal response—when something happens that they don't expect, or conversely, when something doesn't happen that they do expect. Infants' surprise reactions can be assessed by measuring changes in their breathing and heart rate as well as simply observing their facial expressions or bodily movements.

VISION

From anatomical research we know that infants are born with a full, intact set of visual structures. Although most of these structures must develop further over the next few months, neonates do have some visual skills. Newborns' eyes are sensitive to brightness; their pupils contract in bright light and dilate

---

sensation The simple registration of stimulus by a sense organ.

perception The complex process by which the mind interprets and gives meaning to sensory information.

novelty paradigm A research plan that uses infants' preferences for new stimuli over familiar ones to investigate their ability to detect small differences in sounds, patterns, or colors.

preference method Infants are given a choice between stimuli to look at or listen to. Researchers record which stimulus the infant attends to more. If an infant consistently spends more time attending to one of the two stimuli, the preference indicates that the infant can both perceive a difference and deliberately respond to it.

surprise paradigm A research technique used to test infants' memory and expectations. Infants cannot report what they remember or expect, but if their expectations are violated they respond with surprise.

in darkness. They have some control over eye movements, and they can visually track (follow) an object such as a face or a doctor's penlight as it moves across their field of vision. Newborns focus optimally on objects at a range of 7 to 10 inches (17.8 to 25.4 centimeters), with objects beyond this distance appearing blurred. Thus, they are nearly blind to details of objects on the far side of a room (Banks & Salapatek, 1983). Newborns also lack fine convergence of the eyes, indicating that they can't focus both eyes on a single point. They are not able to focus effectively until the end of the second month (Fantz, 1961).

It is clear that newborns can visually perceive their environment, within limits, because they are selective about what they look at. Newborns prefer to look at moderately complex patterns. They look primarily at the edges and contours of objects, especially curves (Roskinski, 1977). Newborn babies are therefore highly responsive to the human face (Fantz, 1958). It is not surprising, then, that they normally develop the ability to recognize their mothers' faces quite early. An experiment by Carpenter (1974) showed that newborns can recognize the mother's face as early as 2 weeks after birth. Using the preference method, Carpenter presented each infant with pictures of its familiar mother and an unfamiliar woman; 2-week-olds preferred to look at the mother. In some cases infants turn their heads completely away from an unfamiliar face (MacFarlane, 1978).

The coordination of vision with reaching—the visually guided reach—is one of the milestones in development.

One of the more remarkable examples of visual perception in neonates is their seeming ability to imitate facial expressions. Imitation has been demonstrated with infants no more than 2 or 3 days old. Researchers wait for a time when the neonate is alert, calm, and not too hungry, and therefore is most receptive (Gardner & Karmel, 1984). The infant and adult look at each other, and the adult goes through a random series of scripted expressions such as pursing the lips, sticking out the tongue, and opening the mouth. In between, the adult presents a neutral facial expression. Analysis of videotapes reveals remarkable consistency in infants' matching of the adult's expressions (Meltzoff & Moore, 1989). Although it has been argued that newborns perform such behaviors in response to a variety of stimuli and might not strictly be imitating, it does appear that they see the stimuli and respond to them in a selective way that at least resembles imitation.

How relevant are infant visual preferences? Early behavioral competencies such as gazing at familiar objects (like the mother's or father's face) and imitating facial expressions are important factors in developing and sustaining early attachment between infant and parents. The baby who alertly explores the mother's face or who is soothed when held by a familiar father, helps the parents feel competent, too.

EARLY DEVELOPMENT OF VISUAL PERCEPTION   By the first 4 to 6 months, infants' visual abilities improve rapidly. Even before they can grasp or crawl, they explore their world visually. Focusing ability improves rapidly; 3- to 4-month-olds focus almost as well as adults (Aslin, 1987). Infants' visual acuity also sharpens dramatically (Banks & Dannemiller, 1987; Fantz et al., 1962).

Color discrimination improves steadily during the first year. Although newborns can see bright colors, they prefer black-and-white patterns over colored ones for the first 1 to 2 months, probably because of the greater contrast. By 2 months, infants pick out more subtle colors like blue, purple, or chartreuse when compared with gray. By 4 months, they can discriminate among most colors, and by 6 months, their color perception nearly equals that of adults (Bornstein, 1978; Maurer & Maurer, 1988; Teller & Bornstein, 1987).

From the beginning, as noted earlier, infants are selective in what they look at. They prefer novel and moderately complex patterns and human faces.

The newborn's senses are finely tuned. For example, an infant can recognize his mother's face as soon as 2 weeks after birth.

Some preferences change over the first year, however. Newborns look primarily at the edges of a face. By 2 months, they look at internal features such as the eyes. By 4 months, they prefer a regularly arranged face over a distorted one. By 5 months, they look at the mouth of a person who is talking, and by 7 months they respond to whole facial expressions.

Are such changes due partly to ways in which the infant's neural system matures? It has been found, for example (Bornstein, 1978), that 4-month-old infants prefer pure colors to other shades and look longer at perpendicular lines than at slanted lines. He suggests that infants prefer such stimuli because they trigger more "neural firings" in the brain. In other words, infants actively seek out things that excite neural activity.

Other marked improvements in vision occur during the first 6 months. Older infants are better able to control their eye movements; they can track moving objects more consistently and for longer periods (Aslin, 1987). They also spend more time scanning and surveying their environment. During the first month, only 5–10% of their time is spent scanning, in contrast to 35% at $2\frac{1}{2}$ months (White, 1971). By 3 or 4 months, infants can also use motion as well as shape and spatial positioning to help define the objects in their world (Mandler, 1990; Spelke, 1988).

DEPTH AND DISTANCE PERCEPTION   A key aspect of visual perception is seeing that some things are closer and others are farther away. Even with one eye closed (monocular vision), we can determine the approximate distance of objects. Objects that are close to us appear larger, and they block our view of more distant objects. If we close one eye and hold our head still, the view resembles a two-dimensional photograph. But if we move our head, the world comes to life with its three-dimensional aspect. If we use both eyes (binocular vision), we don't have to move our head. The left-eye view and the right-eye view differ slightly. The brain integrates the two images, giving us information about distance and depth.

A question that has long interested researchers is exactly when infants develop depth perception. Are their brains preprogrammed to integrate the images from the two eyes to gain information about distance or relative size? Can they use the information produced by moving their head to see the world in three dimensions?

Although lack of convergence of the eyes probably limits neonatal depth perception, it appears that the infant's brain can integrate binocular images in rudimentary form. Because the newborn's eyes are not well coordinated and the infant has not yet learned how to interpret all of the information transmitted by the eyes, early depth perception is probably not very sophisticated. It takes about 4 months for binocular vision to emerge (Aslin & Smith, 1988).

However, even infants as young as 6 weeks use spatial cues to react defensively. They dodge, blink, or show other forms of avoidance when an object appears to be coming directly at them (Dodwell et al., 1987). By 2 months, infants react defensively to an object on a collision course. In addition, they prefer three-dimensional figures to two-dimensional ones. At 4 months, infants can swipe with reasonable accuracy at a toy that is dangled in front of them. By 5 months, they also have a well-controlled, visually guided reach, as noted earlier. However, 5-month-olds with a patch over one eye are less accurate in reaching for objects. Similarly, when given a choice between two objects, one slightly closer than the other, they don't always pick the closer object (Granrud et al., 1984).

A classic approach to assessing infants' depth perception uses the "visual cliff" created by Eleanor Gibson and colleagues (Gibson & Walk, 1960) to simulate depth. On one side of the horizontal surface, a heavy piece of glass covers a solid surface. On the other side, the glass is well above the floor, simulating a cliff. Infants 6 months or older refuse to crawl across the cliff. Younger infants who are not yet able to crawl show interest, but not distress, when placed on the cliff (Campos et al., 1970). These findings indicate that younger infants are also able to discriminate among spatial cues for depth.

Further studies focused on the factors that determine whether babies will cross the deep side. If the mother is encouraging, the baby can be coaxed to cross the deep side if the depth is relatively shallow (Kermoian & Campos, 1988). However, the same baby will refuse to cross if the mother signals that the deep side is dangerous by speaking anxiously or otherwise expressing fear.

In sum, it appears that an understanding of visual cues for depth perception develops within the first 4 to 6 months (Yonas & Owsley, 1987). The meaning of distance or depth is learned more gradually, however, as the child begins to move about in its environment. Sensory-perceptual maturation and the psychosocial environment interact to guide development.

AUDITION

It is obvious that newborn infants can hear. They're startled by loud sounds. They're soothed by low-pitched sounds such as lullabies, and they fuss when they hear high-pitched squeaks and whistles. But how refined is neonatal hearing?

The anatomical structures for hearing are well developed in the newborn (Morse & Cowan, 1982). For the first few weeks, however, there is excess fluid and tissue in the middle ear, and hearing is therefore believed to be muffled—similar to the way you hear if you have a head cold. Moreover, the brain structures for transmitting and interpreting auditory information are not fully developed at birth. Brain structures pertaining to hearing will continue to develop until the child is about 2 years old (Aslin, 1987; Morse & Cowan, 1982; Shatz, 1992).

Despite such limitations, however, newborns can respond to a wide range of sounds. Even in the first month of life, they are especially sensitive to speech sounds (Eimas, 1975). They also show a preference for human voices. For example, they prefer to listen to a song sung by a woman rather than to the same song played on a musical instrument (Glen et al., 1981). Infants can localize the sources of sounds. Even in their first few days of life, they will turn their head toward a sound or a voice. Curiously, however, it has been found that babies temporarily lose this ability during the second month and regain it during the third month (Muir & Field, 1979).

EARLY DEVELOPMENT OF AUDITORY PERCEPTION   Acuity of hearing improves considerably over the first few months. Although it takes several weeks for the fluid in the middle ear to dissipate, neonates show changes in heart rate and breathing in response to moderate tone levels such as those that are typical of a telephone conversation. Over the next 8 months, they respond to progressively softer sounds (Hoversten & Moncur, 1969). Infants can also be soothed, alerted, or distressed by sounds. Low-frequency or rhythmic sounds generally soothe infants. Loud, sudden, or high-frequency tones cause them distress. Such behaviors imply that infants have fairly well-developed auditory perception within the first 6 months of life.

Infants are especially attentive to human voices. By 4 months, they will smile more in response to their mother's voice than to another female voice. By 6 months, they show distress on hearing their mother's voice if they cannot see

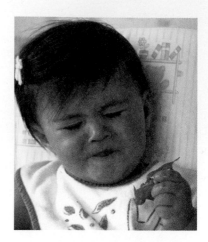

Even neonates have distinct taste preferences.

her, and the mother's mere talking to them from another room—perhaps while preparing food or a bottle—is no longer an effective soother.

A significant aspect of infants' hearing during the first year is their ability to differentiate between speech and nonspeech sounds. As early as 1 month, infants can also detect subtle differences between speech sounds, such as "lip" and "lap" (Eimas, 1975). Early on, they can discriminate among some consonants and vowels. In fact, during the first year, infants can sometimes detect differences in speech sounds that adults cannot detect (Maurer & Maurer, 1988).

TASTE, SMELL, AND TOUCH

The senses of taste and smell are fully operational at birth. Newborns discriminate among sweet, salty, sour, and bitter tastes, as evidenced by facial expressions (Rosenstein & Oster, 1988). They react negatively to strong odors and are selectively attracted to positive odors, such as those of a lactating mother (Makin & Porter, 1989). As early as 6 days of age, infants can distinguish the smell of their mother from that of another woman, and they prefer the familiar scent (MacFarlane, 1978; Makin & Porter, 1989).

The sense of touch is well developed even in preterm newborns. Regular stroking of tiny preterm infants in their incubators helps regulate their breathing and other bodily processes. The rooting reflex is one of the more dependable reflexes in premature infants. Simply holding newborns' arms or legs is often enough to soothe them. Swaddling has a similar effect (Brazelton, 1969).

SENSORY INTEGRATION

Researchers generally agree about the extent to which the individual senses are present at birth, but there has been much disagreement as to whether neonatal senses are fully *integrated,* or coordinated. For example, with regard to audition and vision, does a young infant know that a particular sound comes from a particular object?

Research indicates that either the senses are integrated at birth or integration occurs early and rapidly. In one study, infants were allowed to suck on either of two different pacifiers, one covered with bumps and the other smooth. When the pacifier was removed and the infants were simply shown each pacifier, they looked longer at the one that they had just felt in their mouth (Meltzoff & Borton, 1979). In another experiment, 4-month-olds were shown two novel films with a sound track that matched only one film. The infants preferred to look at the film that matched the sound (Kuhl & Meltzoff, 1988), indicating visual-auditory integration.

Sensory and especially perceptual integration must also be learned, of course. Infants must learn which sounds go with which sights, what soft fur feels and looks like, what the noisy puppy looks like, and so on. Nevertheless, it appears that infants have a built-in tendency to seek out such cognitive links. Integration then advances rapidly over the first year. In one study (Rose et al., 1981), it was found that even though 6-month-olds could sometimes visually identify an object that they had touched or were touching, older infants were much better at it. Research on the visual cliff makes a similar point. Although young infants recognize depth in the visual cliff, they do not necessarily recognize it as unsafe; they are more interested than afraid. Older infants with a higher level of integration are warier of the deep side. Behavior and emotions become integrated over time as a result of the interaction of experience and maturation.

Even when coaxed by their mothers, infants will not crawl over the edge of the visual cliff.

1. Summarize neonatal visual capabilities and their implications for parent-child interactions.
2. Summarize neonatal auditory capabilities and their implications for parent-child interactions.
3. How do researchers apply the novelty and preference paradigms in setting up experiments on infant perceptual development?
4. Why do researchers believe that the senses are integrated either at birth or soon afterward?

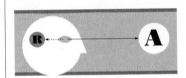

REVIEW & APPLY

COGNITIVE DEVELOPMENT

Cognition is a set of interrelated processes through which we gain and use knowledge about our world. It includes thinking, learning, perceiving, remembering, and understanding. *Cognitive development* refers to the growth and refinement of intellectual processes. In this section we'll explore various approaches to studying and describing cognitive development during the first 2 years of life.

THE ACTIVE MIND
Many theorists believe that infants take an active role in their cognitive development. That's the basic position of Jean Piaget. Piaget saw humans as active, alert, creative beings who possess mental structures, called *schemes* or *schemas*, that process and organize information. Over time, schemes develop into more complex cognitive structures, as discussed in Chapter 1. This development occurs in a series of stages that may begin at somewhat different ages but always follow the same sequence.

Infants have a limited number of behavioral schemes in their repertoire. Looking, mouthing, grasping, and banging are ways they interact with their environment.

THE SENSORIMOTOR PERIOD

Piaget called the first period of development the **sensorimotor period.** Infants enter the world prepared to respond to their environment with extensive sensory-perceptual and motor capabilities. According to Piaget, basic sensorimotor behavior patterns—which begin as reflexes—enable infants to form schemes through the process of assimilation and accommodation. Ready-made behavioral schemes such as looking, visually following, sucking, grasping, and crying are the building blocks for cognitive development. Over the next 24 months, they are transformed into early concepts of objects, people, and self. Thus, sensorimotor behavior is where intelligence begins.

ADAPTATION   Infant schemes are developed and modified by the process that Piaget (1962) called **adaptation,** which refers to the general tendency to adjust to and mentally incorporate elements of our environment. As an example, he described how his 7-month-old daughter, Lucienne, played with a pack of cigarettes. Unlike a 2-year-old, who might (regrettably) take out a cigarette and pretend to smoke it, Lucienne treated the pack of cigarettes as if it were any other toy or object that she was accustomed to handling. Looking, mouthing, grasping, and banging were her only toy-manipulating schemes. In other words, she *assimilated* the pack of cigarettes into her existing schemes (see Chapter 1).

With each new object, children make minor changes in their action patterns. Grasping and mouthing *accommodate* new objects. Gradually these action patterns become modified, and the infant's basic sensorimotor schemes develop into more complex cognitive capacities. Beginning with *circular reactions*, which are simple, repetitive behaviors that are primarily reflexive in nature, much of young infants' learning takes place quite by accident. An action occurs, and infants see, hear, or feel it. For example, babies may notice their hands in front of their face. By moving their hands, they discover that they can change what they see. They can prolong the event, repeat it, stop it, or start it again. Infants' early circular reactions involve the discovery of their own bodies. Later circular reactions involve how they use their bodies or themselves to change the environment, as in making a toy move.

SENSORIMOTOR STAGES   Piaget viewed the sensorimotor period as six fairly discrete stages, which are briefly outlined in Table 4–4. A detailed

sensorimotor period   Piaget's first period of cognitive development (from birth to about 2 years). Infants use action schemes—looking, grasping, and so on—to learn about their world.

adaptation   In Piaget's theory, the process by which infant schemes are elaborated, modified, and developed.

TABLE 4–4   A SKETCH OF PIAGET'S SIX STAGES OF SENSORIMOTOR DEVELOPMENT

STAGE	AGE	KEY FEATURES
One	0–1 month	Exercising reflexes: sucking, grasping, looking, listening
Two	1–4 months	Adaptations of basic sensory and motor patterns (e.g., sucking different objects)
Three	4–8 months	Developing strategies for making interesting sights last
Four	8–12 months	Actions becoming more purposeful; brief search for hidden objects
Five	12–18 months	Active exploration through trial and error (the "little scientist")
Six	18–24 months	Thinking before doing, using mental combinations

discussion of each stage is beyond the scope of this book, but we will consider some of the processes and cognitive achievements of development that occur as Piaget's stages unfold.

PLAY WITH OBJECTS Often-subtle accomplishments in object play are important to children's cognitive development. By 4 or 5 months, infants generally reach out, grasp, and hold objects. Such seemingly simple skills—together with advancing perceptual skills—equip infants for progressively more varied play with objects. Infants remember repeated events, match their actions appropriately with various objects, and develop their understanding of the social world through pretending and imitating. Play, in other words, lays the groundwork for further complex thought and language.

Object play goes through identifiable stages, starting with simple explorations at about 5 months (Garvey, 1977). By 9 months, most infants explore objects; they wave them around, turn them over, and test them by hitting them against other objects. But they are not yet aware of their use or function. By 12 months, infants examine objects closely before putting them in their mouth. By 15 to 18 months, they try to use objects appropriately. For example, they may pretend to drink from a cup or brush their hair with a toy brush. By 21 months, they use many objects appropriately. They try to feed a doll with a spoon, put a doll in the driver's seat of a toy truck, or use keys to unlock an imaginary door. Play becomes more realistic by 24 months. Toddlers take dolls out for walks and line up trucks and trailers in the right order. By 3 years, preschool children may see dolls as imaginary people. They may have a doll go outdoors, chop wood, bring it back inside, and put it in an imaginary fireplace (Bornstein & O'Reilly, 1993; Fein, 1981).

IMITATION It can easily be seen that the object play of 2-year-olds is rich with imitations of the world as they see it. Imitation, however, also has simple beginnings in early infancy.

Within the first 2 months, infants do some sporadic imitation in the context of play with caregivers. As noted earlier, a neonate may imitate facial expressions. But early imitations of facial expressions disappear at 2–3 months, not to reappear until several months later (Meltzoff & Moore, 1989).

At 3 to 4 months, babies and mothers often begin to play a game of "talking" to each other in which the infant appears to be trying to match the sounds of the mother's voice. Typically, however, the mother begins the game by imitating the infant, and it can be hard to tell who is imitating whom (Uzgiris, 1984). By 6 or 7 months, infants can imitate gestures and actions fairly accurately. The first hand gestures to be imitated are those for which infants already have action schemes such as reaching and grasping. By 9 months, infants can imitate novel gestures such as banging two objects together. During the second year, infants begin to imitate entire series of actions or gestures. At first children imitate only actions that they choose themselves. Later they imitate brushing their teeth or using a fork or spoon. Some toddlers even toilet train themselves by imitating an older child or a caregiver.

Does imitation require a mental representation of the action? Is it thinking? Piaget believed that even simple imitation is a complex mix of behavioral schemes. Thus, he predicted that infants would not be capable of imitating novel actions until they were at least 9 months old. And he believed that *deferred imitation*—imitating something that happened hours or even days before—requires cognitive skills that are not present in the first 18 months.

However, infants seem to be able to imitate novel action somewhat earlier than Piaget predicted. For example, children of deaf parents begin to learn and

By 6 or 7 months, infants are greatly improved in their ability to imitate gestures and actions.

use sign language as early as 6 or 7 months (Mandler, 1988). Researchers have also demonstrated that infants are capable of deferred imitation well before 18 months. One study (Meltzoff, 1988a, 1988b) used novel toys, such as a box with a hidden button that would sound a beep and a toy bear that would dance when jiggled with a string. Infants were shown these actions but were not given the opportunity to perform them right away. The researchers found that 11-month-olds could imitate the actions up to 24 hours later and that 14-month-olds could imitate them as much as a week later.

Object Permanence   According to Piaget, **object permanence** is a major accomplishment of the sensorimotor period. Object permanence is the awareness that objects exist in time and space, whether or not they are present and in view. According to Piaget, the development of object permanence is not complete before about 18 months, although infants form an idea of their mother's or father's permanence as early as 8 months. With regard to objects in general, "out of sight, out of mind" seems to be literally true throughout much of infancy. If an infant doesn't see something, it doesn't exist. Thus, a covered toy holds no interest even if the infant continues to hold on to it under the cover.

The development of object permanence involves a series of cognitive accomplishments. First, as early as 2 months, infants are able to recognize familiar objects. For example, they become excited at the sight of a bottle or their caregivers. Second, at about 2 months, infants may watch a moving object disappear behind one side of a screen and then shift their eyes to the other side to see whether the object reappears. Their visual tracking is excellent and well timed, and they are surprised if something does not reappear. But they do not seem to mind when a completely different object appears from behind the screen. In fact, infants up to 5 months old will accept a wide variety of changes in disappearing objects with no distress (Bower, 1971).

Infants more than 5 months old are more discriminating trackers. They are disturbed if a different object appears or if the same object reappears but moves faster or more slowly than before. Even these older infants, however, can be fooled. Imagine two screens side by side with a gap in the middle. An object disappears behind one screen, say from the left; the object does not appear in the gap, but it does reappear from behind the second screen, to the right. Not until infants are 9 months old will they be surprised at what happens (Moore et al., 1978).

Searching for hidden objects also proceeds through a predictable sequence. Infants less than 5 months old typically do not search or hunt; they seem to forget about an object once it is hidden. Beginning between 5 and 8 months, however, infants will engage in and greatly enjoy hiding-and-finding games with objects. They also like being hidden under a blanket or covering their eyes with their hands and having the world reappear when they take their hands away. The searching abilities of infants up to 12 months old still have limitations, however. If a toy disappears through a trapdoor and another reappears when the door is reopened, they are surprised, but they accept the new toy. Older infants, between 12 and 18 months, are puzzled; they search for the first toy.

Some irregularities persist in 12-month-olds' searching behavior. If a toy is hidden in one place and they expect to find it there, 12-month-olds will continue looking for it there even when they have seen it hidden in another place. Piaget (1952) suggested that at this age, infants have two memories—one of seeing the object hidden and another of finding it. Not everyone agrees with Piaget's interpretation of such hiding experiments, however (Mandler, 1990).

object permanence   According to Piaget, the beginning realization in infants at about 8 months that objects continue to exist when they are out of sight.

In Bower's multiple mothers experiment, infants younger than 20 weeks are not disturbed by seeing more than one mother. But older infants become upset at the sight of such images.

As noted earlier, infants grasp the idea of person permanence somewhat before that of object permanence. T. G. R. Bower (1971) arranged mirrors so that infants would see multiple images of their mother. He found that most infants less than 5 months old were not disturbed at seeing more than one mother; instead, they were amused and delighted. Infants older than 5 months or so, however, expected to see only one mother and were highly disturbed at seeing more than one.

MEMORY The sensorimotor abilities discussed so far generally require some form of memory. Earlier it was noted that 4-month-old infants prefer to look at novel objects, showing that they have already established memory for the familiar (Cohen & Gelber, 1975). An infant who imitates must remember the sounds and actions of another person, at least briefly. Infants who search for a toy where they have seen it hidden are remembering the location of that toy.

Very young infants appear to have powerful visual memory (Cohen & Gelber, 1975; McCall et al., 1977). Habituation studies have shown that infants as young as 2 months store visual patterns (Cohen & Gelber, 1975). Fagan (1977) found that 5-month-olds recognize patterns 48 hours later and photographs of faces 2 weeks later. A few studies indicate that infants have even longer-term memory, at least for dramatic events. For example, children who participated in an unusual experiment at a very young age remembered it when they were reintroduced to the same setting several months later (Rovee-Collier, 1987). Indeed, in one study, children recalled aspects of an experiment 2 years later (Myers et al., 1987). Further research has demonstrated various factors that determine the extent to which early memories are retained (Hayne & Rovee-Collier, 1995), notably whether movement and motion are involved when the infants are first exposed to objects later to be recalled. Music associated with an object can also enhance later recall (Fagen et al., 1997).

SYMBOLIC REPRESENTATION During infancy, some of the earliest forms of mental representation are actions. Infants smack their lips before food or a bottle reaches their mouth. They may continue to make eating motions after feeding time is over. They may drop a rattle, yet continue to shake the hand that held it. They may wave bye-bye before they are able to say the words. Such

Children generally start pretending between 6 and 12 months—particularly if they have the help of an older sibling.

actions are the simplest forerunners of **symbolic representation**—the ability to visualize or otherwise think about something that isn't physically present.

Pretending is evidence of an underlying process of symbolic representation (Mandler, 1983). Between 6 and 12 months, children begin pretending, that is, using actions to represent objects, events, or ideas. Pretending behavior also develops in a predictable sequence (Fein, 1981; Rubin et al., 1983). The first stage occurs by about 11 or 12 months; most children of this age pretend to eat, drink, or sleep—all familiar actions. In the next few months, the range and amount of pretend activity increases dramatically. At first, infants do not need objects to pretend, as when a child pretends to sleep curled up on a rug. But as children grow older, toys and other objects are used too. By 15 to 18 months, children feed their brothers and sisters, dolls, and adults with real cups and toy cups, spoons, and forks. By 20 to 26 months, they may pretend that an object is something other than what it is; a broom may become a horse, a paper sack a hat, a wood floor a pool of water. Such pretending represents a further step in cognitive development. By noting the rough similarities between a horse and a broom, children combine a distant concept with a familiar one and thus establish a symbolic relationship between the two.

Language, of course, is the ultimate system of symbolic representation. We will explore infants' language development in the next section of this chapter. Before we do, however, it is important to examine how Piaget's theories of cognitive development are viewed today.

A CRITIQUE OF PIAGET'S THEORY

Piaget's theory of infant cognitive development has fueled decades of research and debate. His careful, naturalistic observations of infants have challenged others to look more closely. His emphasis on the interaction between maturation and experience and on the infant's active, adaptive, constructive role in his or her own learning brought a new respect to infant research. For Piaget, the toddler is a "little scientist" who tests and discovers the nature of physical objects and the social world.

But Piaget's findings were not always accurate, as we have seen with regard to imitation and object permanence. Object permanence in particular doesn't occur precisely in the fashion that Piaget describes. Critics suggest that infants may have more sophisticated knowledge of objects that is based on their perceptual development but that their motor development may lag, in which case they cannot show through actual behavior that they have acquired the idea of object permanence (Baillargeon, 1987; Gratch & Schatz, 1987; Mandler, 1990).

Among Piaget's critics are proponents of information-processing theory. Like Piaget, they are cognitive psychologists because they study thought and the mind. Unlike Piaget, however, they are skeptical of a theory based on qualitatively different stages. They tend to believe that human development, particularly cognitive development, is a continuous, incremental process.

Piaget has also been criticized for paying too much attention to motor development and too little attention to perception. From an early age, infants recognize and remember the regular aspects of their world. Not only do infants learn by doing, but they also learn by seeing as they select, sort, and organize the sensory information available to them. Let's take a closer look at these perceptual abilities.

PERCEPTUAL ORGANIZATION AND CATEGORIES

When we look at objects, we automatically consider the possibilities they offer. A cup of coffee or a glass of juice is something to drink. An empty windowsill

symbolic representation The use of a word, picture, gesture, or other sign to represent past and present events, experiences, and concepts.

in a crowded lecture hall may provide a place to sit. Eleanor Gibson, whose research on depth perception was discussed earlier, believed that such thinking occurs even in infancy. **Affordances,** the potential uses of objects, depend on the individual's needs at the time, as well as on her or his past experience with and cognitive awareness of the object. An orange, for example, may look different to a thirsty adult, an artist, and a teething baby. Possible affordances of an orange are smelling, tasting, touching, viewing, throwing, and squeezing. Gibson contends that almost from the beginning of life, infants examine what they see and hear for possible uses. The affordances are limited at first but become increasingly refined. Eyeglasses, hair, and ears are graspable; eyes are not. Similarly, babies may test these objects for their suckability, squeezability, and noise-making ability. Babies often squeeze furry objects but suck plastic objects. Such behaviors are considered to be early attempts at categorization (Gibson & Walker, 1984).

PERCEPTUAL CATEGORIES Research on infant perception indicates that infants may be neurologically wired to perceive some categories in the same way that older children and adults do. Researchers (Cook & Birch, 1984) showed infants as young as 3 months of age a series of squares followed by a very similar parallelogram (see Figure 4–4). When the infants saw the parallelogram, they looked at it much longer than at the squares, as if it violated their expectations. Did the infants have a perceptual category of "squareness"? To investigate, the researchers gave the objects one-quarter of a turn and showed the same series. Then the objects all looked like diamonds. The final object appeared to be a somewhat more narrow diamond. Now the infants did not stare at the last object longer but behaved as older children do.

As noted earlier, by 3 months, infants can discriminate among the basic colors and many shades and hues. They also seem to have perceptual schemes for more complex categories. They can discriminate between male and female faces and voices almost as well as adults can. They can tell the difference when they look at two versus three objects. This ability doesn't mean that infants have conceptual knowledge about men and women or that they understand the concept of number, but it does indicate that they notice things in perceptual displays (Mandler, 1992). At 7 or 8 months, for example, infants have at least a global concept of animals versus vehicles, and at 9 months, they can differentiate between birds and airplanes. Thus, it appears that perceptual analysis is working even in very young infants. They are sorting, organizing, and noticing differences and similarities early on.

Is this the beginning of true concepts? Both doing and seeing probably contribute to the development of most concepts. One-year-olds know about containers like cups. They know that containers have to be right side up to hold things. Most infants have played with and watched many containers; they have put things into containers and taken things out of them. For Piaget, it is

Initially, affordances are limited, but then they become more refined, with babies testing objects for their "suck-ability," "squeeze-ability," and noisemaking ability.

affordances The different opportunities for interaction offered by a perception; for example, halls are for moving through.

FIGURE 4–4

When shown this series of geometric objects, infants as young as 3 months old find the last one in the top row strange, but not the last one in the second row.

Source: Cook and Birch (1984).

Lev Semenovich Vygotsky, proponent of the importance of social context in cognitive development.

zone of proximal development Vygotsky's concept that children develop through participation in activities slightly beyond their competence, with the help of adults or older children.

this active exploration—doing and seeing what happens—that matters. Yet a physically handicapped infant who cannot manipulate objects learns such concepts too. Could it be that perceptual analysis alone is enough?

COGNITIVE DEVELOPMENT IN SOCIAL CONTEXT

According to Piaget, the child is an "active scientist" who interacts with the physical environment and develops increasingly complex thought strategies. This active, constructing child often seems to be working alone at solving problems and forming concepts. Increasingly, however, some social scientists emphasize that the child is also a social being who plays and talks with others and learns from these interactions (Bruner & Haste, 1987). In a psychologist's lab, children may work alone to solve the problems given to them by researchers. Yet in real life, children experience events in the company of adults and older peers, who translate and make sense of these events for them. Thus, children's cognitive development is often an "apprenticeship" in which they are guided in their understanding and skills by more knowledgeable companions (Rogoff, 1990).

VYGOTSKY The origins of a different branch of cognitive psychology can be found in the work of a noted Russian scholar, Lev Vygotsky (1896–1934). Vygotsky was interested not only in the development of the mind in a social context but also in the historical development of the community's knowledge and understanding. His central question was, How do we collectively make sense of our world? Vygotsky tried to incorporate aspects of sociology, anthropology, and history into his understanding of individual development. He concluded that we make sense of our world only by learning the *shared meanings* of others around us.

Together, people construct shared meanings of objects and events, which are passed from generation to generation through observation, as well as through language. Simple activities like cooking or more complex ones like playing sports in the particular style of our culture are shared. Shared meaning also applies to much more complex things, such as the systematic learning of history, mathematics, literature, and social customs. We develop understanding and expertise primarily through apprenticeship with more knowledgeable learners. We join with others and are guided in our participation, thus enabling us to understand more and more about our world and to develop an increasing number of skills.

Vygotsky defined two levels of cognitive development. The first is the child's actual developmental level, as determined by independent problem solving. The second is the child's level of potential development, as determined by the kind of problem solving that the child can do under adult guidance or in collaboration with a more capable peer (Vygotsky, 1935/1978).

Vygotsky called the distance between these two points the **zone of proximal development** (Rogoff & Wertsch, 1984). He illustrated this concept by studying two children, each of whom had a tested mental age of 7 years. One child, with the help of leading questions and demonstrations, could easily solve problems 2 years above his actual level of development. However, the other child, even with guidance and demonstration, could solve problems only 6 months ahead. Vygotsky emphasized that we need to know both the actual and the potential levels of development in children to understand fully their cognitive development and to design appropriate instruction for them.

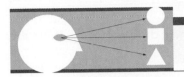

EYE ON DIVERSITY

DYSFUNCTIONAL FAMILIES AND INTERVENTION

Children must be raised in a responsive social environment if they are to develop well. That necessity becomes especially clear when we contrast children raised in dysfunctional families with those raised in well-functioning ones.

The general effect of the home environment on development has been demonstrated in a number of studies. A longitudinal study compared children with sex chromosomal anomalies in well-functioning and dysfunctional families. The dysfunctional families were characterized by ineffective parenting and were subject to stresses such as poverty, drug and alcohol abuse, or the death of a family member. In general, both groups of children showed some motor and cognitive problems compared with their normal siblings. However, the nature and extent of these problems were more pronounced if the child came from a dysfunctional family (Bender et al., 1987).

Another study followed 670 children who were born on the Hawaiian island of Kauai in 1955 (Werner, 1989a, 1989b). Among the children with birth defects, those from dysfunctional families—especially poor families—showed the most negative effects. For example, the IQs of children with severe birth defects who were living in dysfunctional and poor families were 19 to 37 points lower than those children with mild or moderate deficiencies. By contrast, the scores of children with severe birth defects who were born into stable, higher-income families were only 5 to 7 points lower than those of peers who had been born with mild or moderate deficiencies.

Early intervention for children living in dysfunctional families can be highly effective. In the past three decades various programs have offered supportive services to parents and infants in high-risk groups. Because funding is limited, however, many of the programs serve fewer than half of the children who need them. Thus, it is possible to compare the progress of infants and their families within the programs with the progress of others who are not enrolled. By and large, these programs demonstrate a real difference. They show that an optimal environment is crucial for high-risk children to flourish and thrive (Horowitz, 1982; Korner, 1987).

One of the first major home-based, parent-oriented intervention programs for infants was developed by Ira Gordon in the late 1960s (Gordon, 1969). Working with poor families in rural Florida, Gordon set the goal of enhancing the intellectual and personality development of the infants and the self-esteem of the parents. He trained women from the community in child development, and they made weekly visits to the families. The women learned about activities that would be appropriate at each stage of development for the infants whom they visited, and they were taught interviewing skills to use in working with the mothers. Infants who participated in the weekly program on a regular basis for 2 or 3 years demonstrated significantly more advanced development than matched infants who did not. In follow-up studies, fewer children who participated for at least 2 years were later placed in special classes in public schools.

For Vygotsky and his adherents, cognitive development is therefore embedded in life's social and cultural context. The child's best performance demonstrates that what she or he knows comes from collaboration with more competent peers or with adults (Berke, 1994). Barbara Rogoff (1990) describes this process as an "apprenticeship in thinking," in which children and other inexperienced learners are given guided participation in culturally valued activities—everything from acquiring self-help skills to conducting themselves appropriately in social situations. The caregivers and companions in these activities structure the child's participation while providing support and challenge. They build bridges from the child's present understanding to new understanding and skills, thereby gradually increasing the child's participation and responsibility.

In sum, to understand the child's cognitive development, we must examine the processes that contribute to the social construction of knowledge as well as its physical construction. We must also consider characteristics of families and the way they interact with cognitive development, and sometimes intervene (see "Eye on Diversity," above).

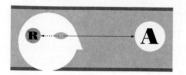

REVIEW & APPLY

1. Describe Piaget's theory of cognitive development during infancy. What are some major criticisms of this theory?
2. What is object permanence, and what is its significance for infant development?
3. What is symbolic representation, and what is its significance for infant development?
4. What are perceptual affordances, and what role do they play in cognition?
5. In what key ways does Vygotsky's approach to cognitive development differ from Piaget's?

LANGUAGE DEVELOPMENT

Even newborn infants communicate. It doesn't take long for them to discover how to let their parents know that they are hungry, wet, or bored. By about 1 year of age, most children say their first word; by 18 months, they put two or more words together; and by two years, they have mastered more than 100 words and can have conversations. Their vocabulary may be severely limited and their grammar flawed, but their implicit grasp of language and its structure is remarkable.

Language is based on the use of symbols for communicating information. The acquisition of language is a complex yet natural process. Perhaps better than any other single accomplishment, it illustrates the range and potential of the human organism, and it sets us apart from other animals (see "A Matter for Debate," page 155).

ELEMENTS OF LANGUAGE

Language has three major dimensions (Bloom & Lahey, 1978). **Content** refers to the meaning of a written or spoken message. **Form** involves the symbols used to represent that content—sounds and words—along with how words are combined to produce sentences and paragraphs. **Use** refers to social exchange between two or more people: the speaker and the person spoken to. The details of the social exchange depend on the situation, the relationship between the speaker and the listener, and the intentions and attitudes of the participants.

The social use of language is complex and is learned simultaneously with content and form. Children learn to be polite and deferential to their elders, to simplify their language when speaking to babies, to take turns in a conversation, and to understand indirect as well as direct speech. They learn to determine the speaker's intention as well as to understand the actual words. For example, a sentence such as "What's that?" can have different meanings depending on the situation. It can serve as a simple request for information, but it can also be an expression of fear.

In the discussions that follow, it will be helpful to have a frame of reference for talking about language. The study chart on page 156 summarizes the "language" of linguistics with regard to phonemes, morphemes, semantics, syntax, and grammar.

THE BEGINNINGS OF LANGUAGE

Language development involves learning to speak or produce oral language, learning the meaning of words, learning rules of syntax and grammar, and—eventually—learning to read and write. Language development takes two

content The meaning of any written or spoken message.

form The particular symbol used to represent content.

use The way in which a speaker employs language to give it one meaning as opposed to another.

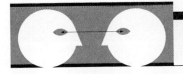

A MATTER FOR DEBATE

IS LANGUAGE EXCLUSIVELY HUMAN?

Are humans the only animals that are capable of using language to express simple and complex thoughts? During the past three decades, a number of chimpanzees and apes have been able to learn at least the rudiments of human communication. Chimps have learned to associate names with objects, put two words together, and use words in novel contexts. But they have been unable to master the complex use of syntax that is an essential part of language.

Because chimps have only limited control of their vocal tracts, speech is impossible for them. Researchers made their first breakthrough in teaching human language to chimps when they moved from vocal speech to other forms, such as sign language. After quickly learning the signs for 200 or more nouns, including the names of people and things around them, as well as verbs and significant adjectives like "big" and "sweet," the chimps extended the use of many of these signs to refer to new objects and events. For example, Washoe, the first chimpanzee to learn sign language, initially learned the sign for "hurt" in connection with scratches and bruises. Later, when she saw a person's navel for the first time, she signed "hurt." (Klima & Bellugi, 1973).

With a few months of training, chimps start to combine signs to express specific thoughts. For example, when Washoe heard the sound of a barking dog, she combined the signs for "listen" and "dog." When she wanted someone to continue tickling her, she signed "more" and "tickle." When she saw a duck, she signed "water bird."

To test the logical and grammatical abilities of chimps, the trainers of a chimp named Sarah took a different approach. Sarah learned to associate magnetized pieces of plastic of various shapes and colors with the objects, people, and actions around her, and to express her thoughts on a metal board. She learned to use plastic symbols that had no resemblance to the objects they represented, and she learned the rudi-ments of grammar. When tested, Sarah correctly understood such complex sentences as "Sarah banana pail" and "cracker dish insert"; she put the banana in the pail and the cracker in the dish 8 out of 10 times.

Chimps can learn to use symbols to represent objects and events and to communicate their insights. But there is considerable debate as to what this ability indicates about their cognitive processes. Chomsky (1975) notes that there is a vast difference between the language learning of humans and the rudimentary responses of chimps. Chimps, he says, never learn the subtleties of word order, nor do they use language in a creative, spontaneous way. It has also been argued that although apes can be trained to produce behaviors that have some of the properties of human linguistic behavior, they do not have the inner motivation to produce language that a child does. Therefore, the communication of the chimp differs profoundly from that of the child (Sugarman, 1983).

What do you think?

---

forms. **Receptive language** refers to understanding spoken or written words and sentences. **Productive language** refers to producing language through speaking or writing.

Among the most common first words in an American-English-speaking infant's receptive vocabulary are "mommy," "daddy," "peekaboo," "bye," "bottle," "no," and the child's name. Infants as young as 8 months usually understand such words. The most common first words in children's productive vocabularies are "daddy," "mommy," "bye," "hi," and "uh-oh." Children can generally produce single words like these by the time they're 14 months old (Fenson et al., 1994). Productive and receptive language evolve simultaneously, although receptive language leads productive language. For example, a parent may ask her 14-month-old, "Will you go into the kitchen and bring back the cookies?" The child may be incapable of producing such a sentence but will return with the cookies. Throughout the lifespan, receptive vocabulary tends to be larger than productive vocabulary, that is, we can understand more words than we can use.

BEFORE THE FIRST WORDS Language production begins with undifferentiated cries at birth. Infants soon develop a range of different cries and, by about 6 weeks, cooing sounds. At birth, infants have a large area in the left hemisphere

receptive language The repertoire of words and commands that a child understands, even though he or she may not be able to use them.

productive language The spoken or written communication of preschool children.

STUDY CHART ▸ LINGUISTIC TERMINOLOGY

Phonemes: The basic units of sound in a language. English, for example, has about 45 phonemes. These include the sounds indicated by the letters of the alphabet plus the variations in those sounds for vowels and some consonants. Distinct combinations, such as *th* in words like "the" or "that" and *ng* in "talking" or "thinking," are also phonemes.

Morphemes: The basic units of meaning in a language. A word can be a single morpheme, or it can include additional morphemes such as *s* for plural, *'s* for possessive, and *ed* for past tense.

Semantics: The way in which meaning is assigned to morphemes or morpheme combinations. Semantics includes connotation and context, i.e., how word meanings change according to the situation.

Syntax: The way in which words are combined into meaningful statements such as sentences.

Grammar: A comprehensive term that includes all of the above.

of the brain (the hemisphere that controls language) that allows them to listen to and respond to language (Brooks & Obrzut, 1981). By the second or third month, infants are sensitive to speech and can distinguish between similar sounds such as "b" and "p" or "d" and "t" (Eimas, 1974). In the first year of life, long before the first words are spoken, infants learn a great deal about language. Major milestones in the development of language are presented in Table 4–5.

Three interesting aspects of language learning during early infancy are babbling, receptive vocabulary, and social communication.

BABBLING From their earliest moments, infants make a variety of sounds. Often they start with vowel sounds and front-of-the-mouth consonants: "Ahh, bahh, bahh, bahh." By 6 months, they have a much more varied and complex repertoire. They string together a wide range of sounds, draw them out, cut them off, and vary their pitch and rhythm. Increasingly they seem to control

TABLE 4–5 MILESTONES IN LANGUAGE DEVELOPMENT*

AVERAGE AGE	LANGUAGE BEHAVIOR DEMONSTRATED BY THE CHILD
12 weeks	Smiles when talked to; makes cooing sounds
16 weeks	Turns the head in response to the human voice
20 weeks	Makes vowel and consonant sounds while cooing
6 months	Cooing changes to babbling, which contains all the sounds of human speech
8 months	Certain syllables repeated (e.g., "ma-ma")
12 months	Understands some words; may say a few
18 months	Can produce up to 50 words
24 months	Has vocabulary of more than 50 words; uses some 2-word phrases
30 months	Vocabulary increases to several hundred words; uses phrases of 3 to 5 words
36 months	Vocabulary of about 1000 words
48 months	Most basic aspects of language are well established

*These are strictly averages; individual children may differ.

Source: From Robert A. Baron, *Psychology, Fourth Edition.* Copyright © 1998 by Allyn & Bacon. Reprinted by permission.

their vocalizations. They purposefully repeat sounds, elongate them, and pause in a kind of self-imitating precursor to speech called *iteration*.

The earliest vocalizations involve only a few different phonemes. Sound production increases rapidly, however, and by the second month, infants are forming a large number of phonemes as well as clicks, gurgles, grunts, and other sounds. Many of these sounds do not appear in the language of the infant's caregivers. This "random" phoneme production continues to increase until about 6 months; then the range of phonemes that infants use begins to narrow, eventually including only those of their native language.

Sometime after 6 months, parents may hear something suspiciously like "ma-ma" or "da-da" and interpret it as their precocious infant's first word. Usually, however, these are chance repetitions of sounds that have no real meaning. Babbling takes on inflections and patterns like those of the parents' language and may sound so much like coherent speech that the parents strain to listen, thinking that it is. This **expressive jargon,** a highly developed form of babbling, is the same for infants in all language groups and cultures (Roug et al., 1989).

How important is babbling? How does it prepare a baby for speaking? A baby's babbling is an irresistible form of verbal communication, and caregivers throughout the world delight in imitating and encouraging it. In the course of babbling, it appears that babies are learning how to produce the sounds they will later use in speaking. Thus, the sounds or phonemes that babies produce are influenced by what they hear before they use words. Although babbling is a means for babies to communicate and interact with other people, it is also a problem-solving activity. Babies babble as a way of figuring out how to make the specific sounds needed to say words. This practice may be the reason that babies do not stop babbling when they start producing words. In fact, new words seem to influence babbling, and babbling, in turn, affects the preferred sounds that babies use in selecting new words (Elbers & Ton, 1985).

Babies are language *universalists* who can distinguish among all the possible sounds in human language, whereas adults are language *specialists* who perceive and reproduce only the sounds of their native tongue. In one study, 6-month-old infants were taught to look over their shoulder when they heard a difference in pairs of sounds and to ignore sounds that seemed alike. The

expressive jargon The babbling produced when an infant uses inflections and patterns that mimic adult speech.

By eight months babies understand first words such as "mommy" and "daddy."

babies were able to distinguish variations in unfamiliar languages but ignored the familiar similarities of their own language, indicating that language perception is clearly shaped by experience—and at an earlier age than was once thought. The study also indicated that "conversations" between parents and infants are instrumental in producing spoken language (Kuhl et al., 1992).

Comparisons of the babbling of hearing babies and deaf babies also demonstrate the importance of what the baby hears, even at the babbling stage. Although the babbling of hearing babies and deaf babies is comparable at first, over time only the babbling of the hearing infants moves closer to the sounds used in their language (Oller & Eilers, 1988). Moreover, the babbling of deaf babies appears to lessen significantly after about 6 months.

Babbling therefore plays a key role in normal babies' learning to use the specific sounds needed to speak the language of their caregivers. For example, a comparison of the babbling of 10-month-olds in Paris, London, Hong Kong, and Algiers found that differences in how the infants pronounced vowel sounds paralleled the pronunciations of vowels in their native languages (de Boysson-Bardies et al., 1989).

RECEPTIVE VOCABULARY   As noted earlier, very young children understand words before they can say them. Infants as young as 1 year can follow directions from adults and show by their behavior that they know the meaning of words like "bye-bye." However, it is very difficult to study infant comprehension. It is hard to identify and describe concepts that very young children associate with specific words. Even when the evidence seems clear—for example, when a 1-year-old follows the instruction "Put the spoon in the cup"—the child's understanding may not be as complete as we might think. It is, after all, unlikely that the infant will instead try to put the cup in the spoon, even if that is what the infant mistakenly comprehended. Also, children may receive clues, such as gestures, that help them perform tasks correctly when they don't fully comprehend spoken instructions.

SOCIAL COMMUNICATION   Throughout the first year, infants learn nonverbal aspects of communication as part of their "mutual dialogue" with the caregiver (see Chapter 5). They learn to signal, take turns, gesture, and pay attention to facial expressions. Infants learn a lot about communication while playing simple games like peekaboo (Ross & Lollis, 1987). Indeed, some parents are skilled at structuring social games that teach their infants aspects of conversation in an enjoyable way. The parents provide a structure for the game that helps the child learn the rules of give-and-take and turn-taking (Bruner, 1983). Along the way, they provide a support system for early language acquisition. As mothers and their infants focus together on objects of play ("Look, a kitten"), infants learn the names of objects and activities (de Villiers & de Villiers, 1992). But social communication with the infant goes beyond such games. By 1 year of age, most infants are alert to the people around them, including strangers, and they respond appropriately to the emotional expressions of adults (Klinnert et al., 1986).

WORDS AND SENTENCES

Most children utter their first words around the end of the first year. Their vocabulary grows slowly at first, then much more rapidly. However, there is wide individual variation in the rate at which language learning progresses. Toddlers who seem to progress rather slowly are not necessarily developmentally delayed; they may be preoccupied with other tasks, such as learning to walk. Some children start late but catch up quickly; others seem to be stuck at particular stages for long periods. Regardless of the pace of language learning, however, the language development follows a regular and predictable *sequence* in every language (Slobin, 1972).

EARLY WORDS AND MEANINGS Around the world, infants' first utterances are single words—most often nouns and usually names of people and things in their immediate environment. At first, children do not have the ability to use words in combination. Instead, they engage in **holophrastic speech**—one-word utterances that apparently convey more complex ideas. Thus, in different contexts and with different intonations and gestures, "mama" may mean "I want my mama" or "Mama, tie my shoe" or "There she is, my mama."

What words form an infant's early vocabulary? The choice of words depends upon the vocabulary being used around them, but first words do fall into predictable categories. Names—that is, nouns that refer to specific things such as "dada," "bottie," and "car"—comprise much of a child's early vocabulary (Nelson, 1974). However, children in the holophrastic stage also use words that indicate function or relationship, such as "there," "no," "gone," and "up," sometimes before they use nouns (Bloom et al., 1985).

The individual words and the categories of words that a child uses most may also depend on the child's personal speech style. Katherine Nelson (1981), one of the first researchers to study children's language-learning styles, identified children with a "referential" style, who tended to use nouns, and "expressive" children, who were more inclined to use active verbs and pronouns. By 18 months, when children have vocabularies of about 50 words, the two styles were distinct. The referential children's vocabularies were dominated by naming words—mostly nouns indicating persons or objects. The expressive children, on the other hand, had learned the naming words but used a higher percentage of words pertaining to social interactions (e.g., "go away," "I want," "give me"). The later language development of expressive and referential children also differed. Expressive children typically had smaller vocabularies than did referential children. In addition, expressive children were more likely to create and use "dummy words"—words with no apparent meaning—to substitute for words they didn't know. Other researchers have noted even more stylistic variation in children's language usage at the one-word stage (Pine et al., 1997), partly as a function of their mother's speech characteristics.

CATEGORIZING OBJECTS A child's first words are often **overextensions.** Although first words refer to a specific person, object, or situation, the child overgeneralizes them to refer to all similar objects. Suppose a child has a dog named "Pookie." The child may use "Pookie" as the name for all other dogs or even for all other four-legged animals. Only after learning new words, such as "doggie," does the child redefine the erroneous categories (Schlesinger, 1982). Children tend to overextend, underextend, or overlap the categories that they use to determine what words refer to because they often do not share adults' knowledge of appropriate functions and characteristics of objects. Instead, they may emphasize characteristics that adults ignore (Mervis, 1987). Some examples are given in Table 4–6.

As children learn additional contrasting names for objects, such as "kitty," "cat," "lion," and "tiger," they reassign words to more specific categories (Clark, 1987; Merriman, 1987). In other words, although a lion and a tiger are different, they are both cats. Over time, the child's linguistic categories take on the structure of the linguistic culture in which the child is being raised; children adopt their language's approaches to grouping and sorting objects and concepts. The process of categorizing appears to follow the same pattern as intellectual or cognitive development in general (Chapman & Mervis, 1989). Children's words and their meanings are closely linked to the concepts that the children are forming.

holophrastic speech In the early stages of language acquisition, the young child's use of single words to convey complete thoughts or sentences.

overextensions The young child's tendency to overgeneralize specific words as when a child uses "chihuahua" as the term for all dogs.

TABLE 4–6 EXAMPLES OF OVEREXTENSIONS OF FIRST WORDS

CHILD'S WORD	FIRST REFERENT	POSSIBLE COMMON EXTENSIONS	PROPERTY
Bird	Sparrows	Cows, dogs, cats, any moving animal	Movement
Mooi	Moon	Cakes, round marks on a window, round shapes in books, postmarks	Shape
Fly	Fly	Specks of dirt, dust, all small insects, crumbs	Size
Wau-wau	Dogs	All animals, toy dog, soft slippers, someone in a furry coat	Texture

Source: Adapted from deVilliers and de Villiers (1979).

Which comes first, the word or the concept? Researchers differ in their interpretations of the evidence. Some, including Piaget, argue that the concept usually comes first. The child forms a concept and then attaches a name to it, whether real or invented. Twins sometimes create their own private language, and deaf children create signs or gestures even when they are not taught sign language (Clark, 1983). This finding implies that concepts come first. Other researchers emphasize that words help shape concepts. When a young child calls the family pet "dog," the child is simply naming that object. When the child extends and refines categories, the concept "dog" follows (Schlesinger, 1982). Thus, it is difficult to determine whether concepts precede words or vice versa. The two processes probably occur simultaneously and complement each other.

TELEGRAPHIC SPEECH AND EARLY GRAMMAR Around the middle of the second year, children begin to put words together. The first attempts typically are two words that represent two ideas: "Daddy see," "Sock off," "More juice." Implicit rules of syntax soon appear, and children use two-word sentences in consistent ways. They may say "See dog" or "See truck" as they point at things. But they don't say "Truck see."

What sort of linguistic rules do children use at this stage? When children start putting words together, their sentences are sharply limited. At first they're restricted to two elements, then three, and so on. At each stage, the number of words or thoughts in a sentence is limited; children retain informative words and omit less significant ones. The result is what Brown (1965) calls **telegraphic speech.** The informative words, which Brown calls *contentives*, are nouns, verbs, and adjectives. The less important words are called *functors* or simply *function words*; they include articles, prepositions, and auxiliary verbs.

The concept of **pivot grammar** (Braine, 1963) describes the two-word phase. *Pivot words* are usually action words ("go") or possessives ("my"). They are few in number and frequently occur in combination with *open words*, which are usually nouns. "See," for example, is a pivot word that can be combined with any number of open words to form two-word sentences: "See milk," "See Daddy," or "Daddy see." Pivot words almost never occur alone or with other pivots (McNeill, 1972). Open words may, however, be paired or used singly. Thus, children follow rules in their two-word utterances; the word combinations are not random.

With the help of gestures, tone, and context, children can communicate numerous meanings with a small vocabulary and limited syntax. Dan Slobin (1972) studied the variety of meanings conveyed by two-word sentences spo-

telegraphic speech The utterances of 1½- and 2-year-olds that omit the less significant words and include the words that carry the most meaning.

pivot grammar A two-word, sentence-forming system used by 1½- and 2-year-olds, and involves action words, prepositions, or possessives (pivot words) in combination with x-words, which are usually nouns.

ken by 2-year-olds. Although the children were from different linguistic cultures (English, German, Russian, Turkish, and Samoan), they used speech in the same ways. Among the concepts that they were able to communicate by two-word utterances were the following:

Identification: See doggie.
Location: Book there.
Nonexistence: Allgone thing.
Negation: Not wolf.
Possession: My candy.
Attribution: Big car.
Agent-action: Mama walk.
Action-location: Sit chair.
Action-direct object: Hit you.
Action-indirect object: Give papa.
Action-instrument: Cut knife.
Question: Where ball?

In sum, the language development that occurs during infancy sets the stage for the expanding vocabulary, understanding of complex grammar, use of language as a social act, and ability to engage in conversation that occur during the preschool years. But what causes all that to happen?

PROCESSES OF LANGUAGE LEARNING

Over the years, a great deal of research and theorizing has been devoted to understanding how we progress from crying to babbling to speaking an adult language. Although there has been considerable controversy as to precisely how language development works, it is possible to highlight four components: imitation, conditioning, innate language structures, and cognitive development.

IMITATION Imitation plays a large role in many aspects of human learning, and language learning is no exception. Children's first words are obviously learned by hearing and imitating. In fact, most early vocabulary must be learned in this way; children cannot make themselves understood with words they invent. But the development of syntax is not as easily explained. Although some phrases result from imitation, a form such as "amn't I" is clearly original. So is a phrase like "me go"; it is unlikely that the child has heard anyone speak this way. Even when adults use baby talk or attempt to correct children's errors, the children tend to adhere to their own consistent speech patterns.

CONDITIONING As we saw in Chapter 3, conditioning through reinforcement and punishment is a powerful learning device, and this observation holds true for certain aspects of language acquisition. Certainly, children are influenced by the way people react to their speech. Smiles, hugs, and increased attention will encourage learning of words. Also, when particular words produce favorable results, children are likely to repeat them. If an infant calls "Mommy" and she comes, or says "Cookie" and is given one, the infant will use these words again—they have been reinforced. Punishment plays a role too. Uttering certain socially unacceptable words can produce consequences that will cause the child to refrain from using these words again—at least in the presence of adults.

But like imitation, reinforcement by itself does not explain the acquisition of syntax. Much of children's speech is original and therefore has never been reinforced. Even if some forms are encouraged and others discouraged, it would not be possible to reinforce all correct forms and extinguish all incorrect ones. Also, especially when children first begin to talk, adults tend to reinforce any

Imitation plays an important part in language learning, particularly in the early stages of development.

speech at all, however unintelligible or incorrect. They are more likely to respond to content than to form. For example, if a child says, "I eated my peas," the parents will probably praise the child—unless, of course, the statement isn't true. In general, research indicates that parents rarely reinforce their young children for correct syntax.

INNATE LANGUAGE STRUCTURES The famous linguist Noam Chomsky (1959) drew attention to the limitations of imitation and conditioning theory, proposing instead that we are born with cognitive structures for acquiring language. This **language acquisition device** or **LAD** (sometimes referred to as a "black box" because it is not an actual organic structure) enables children to process linguistic information and "extract" rules with which they create language. That is, when children hear people talk, they automatically acquire rules and produce their own language accordingly. The process follows a predictable sequence; children can assimilate certain kinds of rules and information before they can assimilate other kinds. According to Chomsky, children are preprogrammed to learn language, and they do it actively if not entirely consciously. Thus, at first they develop simple rules in accord with pivot grammar, and then over the first several years of life, their syntax gradually becomes more complex and closer to that of an adult as they add function words and make other adjustments.

One piece of evidence for the existence of an LAD is deaf children's ability to develop spontaneous systems of language-like gestures (Goldin-Meadow & Mylander, 1984). Another is the observation that deaf children babble just like hearing children during the first 6 months or so. Yet another is the observation that there are certain language universals that are found in all linguistic cultures; these include the orderly sequence of development of babbling, first words, and telegraphic speech.

Chomsky's approach has been criticized, however. For one thing, as yet there is no anatomical evidence of an LAD, beyond the observation that the brain hemispheres specialize in language functions (see Chapter 6). For another, Chomsky's reasoning is circular (Brown, 1973; Maratsos, 1983): Why do children learn language? Because of the LAD. How do we know there's an LAD? Because children learn language. Still another criticism involves Chomsky's proposal that a common grammar underlies all languages; scientists have been unable to agree on what that grammar is (Moerk, 1989). Despite such criticisms, the theory has been useful and has stimulated considerable study of children's language development.

COGNITIVE DEVELOPMENT The fourth major approach to language acquisition emphasizes the link between language learning and a child's developing cognitive abilities. This approach stems from the observation that basic grammatical structures are not present in children's earliest speech but develop progressively over time. Learning them depends on prior cognitive development (Bloom, 1970). Thus, a particular speech pattern will not emerge before the child has grasped the concept behind it. Between the ages of 1 and $4\frac{1}{2}$, children are actively constructing their own grammar, gradually approaching the full grammar of the adults around them. At any given time, however, children are capable of expressing only concepts that they have mastered.

There are many parallels between cognitive development and language development. At about the time that a child is gaining an understanding of object permanence and is interested in games that involve hiding and finding objects, the child's beginning language reflects these cognitive processes with words like "see," "all gone," "more?" and "bye-bye." Comings and goings and hidings and findings become the focus of language and vocabulary. Later, as

language acquisition device or LAD Chomsky's term for an innate set of mental structures that aid humans in language learning.

children become concerned with possessions, they learn aspects of syntax that reflect the possessive case: "Daddy sock," "baby bed," and eventually "mine" and "Mommy's cup." At about the end of their second year, children typically learn a burst of new words, especially object names. This learning appears to be tied to their emerging ability to categorize objects and events in their world (de Villiers & de Villiers, 1992). Thus, the development of language and the development of cognition often go hand in hand.

1. Define the key elements of language, and give examples of each.
2. Differentiate between receptive and productive language.
3. Describe the sequence of language development in infancy.
4. What is babbling, and how important is it to the infant's language development?
5. Discuss the implications of holophrastic and then telegraphic speech.

REVIEW & APPLY

SUMMARY

Neonates

■ There are six newborn behavioral states: waking activity, crying, alert inactivity, drowsiness, regular sleep, and irregular sleep.

■ Infants enter the world with survival reflexes (those necessary for adaptation and survival) and primitive reflexes (which may have been important at some point in our evolutionary history).

■ Infants are capable of habituation, a form of learning that involves becoming accustomed to stimuli and then no longer responding to them.

■ During the first few days of life, a baby may be given a neurological examination and a behavioral assessment.

Physical and Motor Development

■ Arnold Gesell believed that behaviors such as crawling and walking emerge as a function of maturation, given a normal environment. (See the study chart on page 132 for a summary of infant competencies.)

■ Later research showed that children raised in different social, cultural, or historical contexts may develop quite differently.

■ In the first four months, most infants nearly double in weight. Around age 4 months, the body starts to grow and lengthen more rapidly than the head. Most reflexes normally disappear.

■ By about 5 months, most infants can accurately reach out and grasp an object and bring it to them; this ability is known as visually guided reach. Fine motor skills continue to be refined, and gross motor skills show refinement as well—most 8-month-olds can sit without support, and many can stand while holding on to a support.

■ Half of infants 12 months old are standing alone and taking their first steps. They have developed a pincer grasp, with thumb opposing forefinger, and can play simple games such as rolling a ball back and forth.

■ At 18 months, children weigh up to four times their birth weight. Almost all are walking alone. They may be able to stack two to four blocks and feed themselves.

■ Two-year-olds have a number of motor skills, including jumping, throwing, climbing steps, manipulating objects, and pouring water. They can dress and undress with assistance.

■ Malnutrition in infancy—either insufficient total quantity of food or inadequate quantities of certain kinds of food—can have serious long-term effects. Food supplement programs can reverse some of those effects.

■ Under most conditions, breast milk is better for a baby's health. However, bottle-feeding causes no problems for the majority of infants in developed countries.

Sensory and Perceptual Development

■ Researchers use the novelty paradigm to determine how small a difference in a stimulus young infants can detect. In the preference method, infants are given a choice between stimuli to look at or listen to.

The surprise paradigm involves assessing infants' surprise reactions by measuring changes in their breathing and heart rate.

■ Newborns have some control over eye movements and can visually track an object. They are selective about what they look at, preferring moderately complex patterns such as those of the human face. They are able to imitate facial expressions.

■ In the first few months, infants' visual abilities improve rapidly. Focusing ability, visual acuity, and color discrimination improve. Older infants are better able to control their eye movements and spend more time scanning their environment.

■ It takes about 4 months for binocular vision to develop, but young infants can use spatial cues to react defensively.

■ Studies using the "visual cliff" have shown that infants are able to discriminate among spatial cues for depth.

■ Newborns can respond to a wide range of sounds. They are especially sensitive to speech sounds.

■ Acuity of hearing improves considerably over the first 6 months. By 4 months, infants can distinguish their mother's voice from that of another female.

■ The senses of taste and smell are fully operational at birth.

■ Either the senses are integrated (coordinated) at birth, or integration occurs early and rapidly.

Cognitive Development

■ Cognitive development refers to the growth and refinement of intellectual processes. According to Piaget, this occurs in a series of stages beginning with the sensorimotor period.

■ Infant schemes are developed and modified by the process of adaptation. Children make minor changes in their action patterns to accommodate new objects.

■ Play with objects is important to children's cognitive development. Object play goes through identifiable stages, starting with simple explorations and developing through close examination, attempts to use objects appropriately, and more realistic play.

■ Imitation begins as early as 2 months. By 6 or 7 months, infants can imitate gestures and actions fairly accurately.

■ Object permanence is the awareness that objects exist in time and space whether or not they are in view. Infants develop this awareness gradually between 8 months and 18 months. Tracking of objects and searching for hidden objects proceed through a predictable sequence. Infants grasp the idea of per-

son permanence somewhat before that of object permanence.

■ Very young infants appear to have powerful visual memory.

■ Evidence of symbolic representation can be seen in pretending, which begins between 6 and 12 months.

■ Piaget's theory has been criticized because his findings were not always accurate. Some theorists are skeptical also of a theory based on qualitatively different stages.

■ Young infants examine what they see and hear for possible uses, or affordances.

■ Infants may be able to perceive some categories in the same way that older children and adults do.

■ Children's cognitive development occurs in a social context; children are guided in their understanding and skills by more knowledgeable companions. This aspect of development was emphasized by Vygotsky, who believed that we make sense of our world only by learning the shared meanings of others around us.

Language Development

■ Language is based on the use of symbols for communicating information. It has three major dimensions: content (meaning), form (symbols), and use (social exchange between two or more people). (See the study chart on page 156.)

■ Receptive language refers to understanding spoken or written words and sentences. Productive language refers to producing language through speaking or writing.

■ Babies can distinguish among all the possible sounds in human language. Through babbling they learn to use the specific sounds needed to speak the language of their caregivers.

■ Most children utter their first words around the end of the first year. Their first utterances are single words, usually names of people and things in their immediate environment.

■ Holophrastic speech consists of one-word utterances that apparently convey more complex ideas.

■ A child's first words are often overextensions, in which a word is overgeneralized to refer to all similar objects.

■ Around the middle of the second year, children begin to put words together. They engage in telegraphic speech, which retains informative words and omits less significant ones.

■ The main processes of language learning are imitation, conditioning, innate language structures, and cognitive development. The idea of innate language structures, proposed by Chomsky, is controversial.

KEY TERMS

survival reflexes	preference method	use
primitive reflexes	surprise paradigm	receptive language
habituation	sensorimotor period	productive language
habituation method	adaptation	expressive jargon
fine motor skills	object permanence	holophrastic speech
gross motor skills	symbolic representation	overextensions
pincer grasp	affordances	telegraphic speech
sensation	zone of proximal development	pivot grammar
perception	content	language acquisition device
novelty paradigm	form	or LAD

USING WHAT YOU'VE LEARNED

What can we learn about infants' mental development from observing their play with objects? Take a simple object, such as a set of keys on a ring, and hand it to babies of different ages. What do 4-month-old babies do with the keys? How about babies aged 8 months, 12 months, 18 months, and 2 years? What perceptual affordances seem to be operating?

Remember that at first, infants may be limited to grasping and sucking. Then there may be some shaking to create noise, or perhaps some careful visual exploration while moving the keys from hand to hand. If a child hunts for a door or a small hole in which to insert a key, how old is the child likely to be? If a child sits on a toy truck, turns the keys in the air, and says "brumm, brumm," how old? Considering the close links among perception, motor development, and cognitive development, what can you say about the cognitive development of the infants and toddlers whom you observe?

SUGGESTED READINGS

BARON, N. S. (1993). *Growing up with language: How children learn to talk.* Reading, MA: Addison-Wesley. This linguistics professor describes how humans create speech and language. Very readable approach.

BRAZELTON, T. B. (1994). *Infants and mothers: Differences in development* (rev. ed.). New York: Delta/Seymour Lawrence. Three infant-mother pairs with different personalities and temperamental styles are described just after childbirth and at selected periods during the children's first 2 years. Written in a highly readable fashion.

EISENBERG, A., MURKOFF, H. E., & HATHAWAY, S. E. (1996). *What to expect the first year* (rev. ed.). New York: Workman Publishing. A comprehensive, month-by-month guide that explains everything parents need to know about their first year with a new baby.

ELKIND, D. (1993). *Images of the young child.* Washington, DC: National Association for the Education of Young Children. A delightful collection of essays from this wise, popular, and provocative psychologist.

FIELD, T. (1990) *Infancy.* Cambridge, MA: Harvard University Press. A title in the popular and highly readable *Developing Child* series. This book surveys the latest infant research and highlights the infant's surprising abilities. It also makes applications to practical concerns, including day care, maternal drug use, and infants at risk.

LEACH, P. (1997). *Your baby, your child: From birth to age five.* New York: Knopf. One of the better parent guides about children, their health, and their experiences from before birth through the preschool period. It reflects the realities of today's changing lifestyles and new approaches to parenting.

SIEGLER, R. (1991). Children's thinking (2nd ed.). Englewood Cliffs, NJ: Prentice-Hall. An excellent text that integrates the latest research with central themes from several theoretical perspectives. It presents a coherent picture of cognitive development from infancy to adolescence.

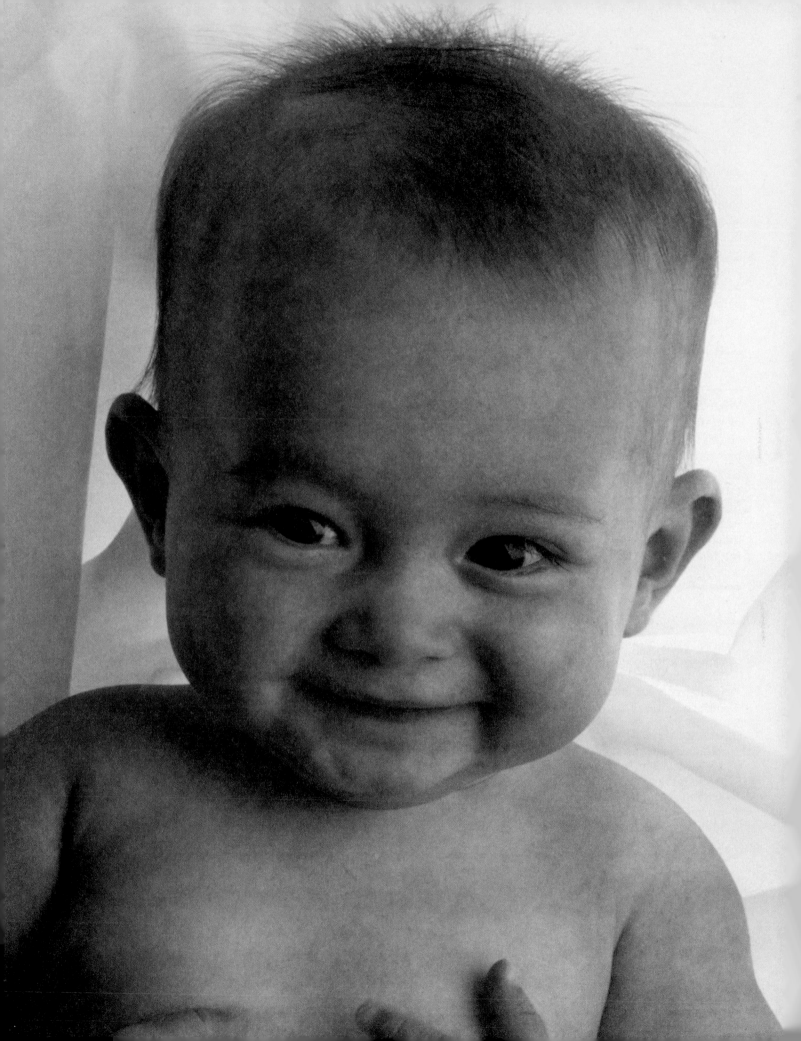

Infants and Toddlers: Personality Development and Socialization

CHAPTER

5

CHAPTER OUTLINE

CHAPTER OBJECTIVES

By the time you have finished this chapter, you should be able to do the following:

1. List milestones in the emotional development of the infant.
2. Discuss the process of attachment between the infant and the primary caregiver.
3. Characterize the infant's growing repertoire of emotional responses.
4. List key factors that affect the quality of the relationship between the infant and the primary caregiver.
5. Examine attachment problems faced by families with infants with special needs.
6. Describe attachment between the infant and the father, siblings, and grandparents.
7. Compare the effects of specific child-rearing practices on personality development in the second year of life.
8. Discuss the implications of parental employment for child care and the psychosocial development of the infant.

Human infants are born into an environment that is rich with expectations, norms, values, and traditions. All of these and more will help shape their **personality**—their characteristic beliefs, attitudes, and ways of interacting with others. From a somewhat different perspective, over the first 2 years, infants are **socialized:** They begin to learn and assimilate their society's standards for behavior, meaning their society's laws, norms, and values, both written and unwritten. They will later learn to cope with their society's contradictions and hypocrisies as well. At the same time, as they grow older, they help shape their own personality: They actively accept or reject norms and rules, as opposed to being passive recipients of socialization.

Newborns are unaware of their relationship to those around them. At birth, an infant apparently has no understanding of self versus others, male versus female, child versus adult. A newborn also has no expectations about the behavior of others; things simply happen, or they don't. In other words, at first the infant lives in the present, and whatever is out of sight is "out of mind," as we saw in Chapter 4 with regard to development of object permanence.

Dramatic changes take place during the first 2 years of life. Newborns become aware of their environment and the way they can interact with it, aware of the responsiveness or unresponsiveness of the world around them, and aware that they can do some things for themselves or get help when necessary. As they become toddlers, they become more aware of family relationships and of what is "good" and "bad." They become conscious of being a girl or a boy and begin to learn how gender imposes certain styles of behavior on the person.

Babies are not born devoid of **temperament,** however. They come into the world with certain behavioral styles, which, taken together, constitute temperament. Some neonates are more sensitive to light or sudden loud sounds than others. Some react more quickly and dramatically to discomfort. Some are

personality Characteristic beliefs, attitudes, and ways of interacting with others.

socialization The process by which we learn our society's standards, laws, norms, and values.

temperament Inborn behavioral styles.

fussy, some placid, some active and vigorous. In turn, most infants fall in one of three categories (Thomas & Chess, 1977): *easy* (often in a good mood and predictable), *difficult* (often irritable and unpredictable), and *slow to warm up* (moody and resistant to attention). As we'll see, early infant temperament can have a profound effect on the quality of early parent-child interactions.

More generally, in this chapter we look at how the infant's personality develops within relationships with caregivers and others. We focus on the first relationships—those that establish patterns for the development of future relationships and for the acquisition of basic attitudes, expectations, and behavior. Specifically, we examine the social and emotional development of the infant during the first and second years; the process of attachment between the infant and the primary caregiver—usually the mother; factors that affect the quality of early relationships; the infant's emotional ties with the father, siblings, and grandparents; and the potential effects of parental employment on psychosocial development.

SOCIAL AND EMOTIONAL DEVELOPMENT IN INFANCY

In the course of a lifetime, most individuals are involved in a number of significant interpersonal relationships. The first—and undoubtedly the most influential—occurs between the infant and the mother or other primary caregiver. The relationship normally becomes firmly established by 8 or 9 months. Since the mid-1960s, psychologists have used the term **attachment** in referring to this first relationship—a relationship that is characterized by interdependence, intense mutual feelings, and strong emotional ties.

FIRST RELATIONSHIPS

Children go through phases of emotional and social growth that result in the establishment of their first relationship. Although the emotional states of newborns are limited, consisting mainly of distress and relaxed interest, a range of self-oriented emotions quickly emerges—sadness, anger, disgust, and pleasure. These are nurtured and given meaning in the context of relationships. Later, primarily in the second year, socially oriented emotions such as pride, shame, embarrassment, guilt, and empathy emerge as the toddler gains greater understanding of self and others. Stanley and Nancy Greenspan (1985) describe six stages in the emotional development of the infant and preschool child within the first relationships. These are summarized in Table 5–1. Note that, as with other developmental sequences, the timing varies from one child to another but the order of the stages is presumed to be the same—each builds on the one before.

THE ATTACHMENT PROCESS

Since attachment is so crucial to the infant's overall psychosocial development, it is important to examine the mechanisms through which it occurs. Mary Ainsworth (1983) defines attachment behaviors as those that primarily promote nearness to a *specific* person. Such behaviors include signaling (crying, smiling, vocalizing), orienting (looking), movements relating to another person (following, approaching), and active attempts at physical contact (clambering up, embracing, clinging). Attachment is mutual and reciprocal—it works both ways and involves sharing experiences in a cooperative manner

attachment The bond that develops between a child and another individual. The infant's first bond is usually characterized by strong interdependence, intense mutual feelings, and vital emotional ties.

TABLE 5–1 MILESTONES IN EARLY EMOTIONAL DEVELOPMENT

1. *Self-regulation and interest in the world—birth to 3 months*. In the early weeks, infants seek to feel regulated and calm, but at the same time, they try to use all their senses and to experience the world around them. Infants seek a balance between over- and under-stimulation. Gradually they become increasingly socially responsive as they use signaling and orienting behavior—crying, vocalizing, visual following—to establish contact. At this stage, infants do not discriminate between primary caregivers and other people; they react to everyone in much the same way.

2. *Falling in love—2 to 7 months*. By 2 months, self-regulated infants become more alert to the world around them. They recognize familiar figures and increasingly direct their attention toward significant caregivers rather than strangers. Infants now find the human world pleasurable and exciting—and they show it. They smile eagerly and respond with their whole body.

3. *Developing intentional communication—3 to 10 months*. This milestone overlaps considerably with the last, but now infants begin to engage in dialogues with others. Mother and baby initiate their own playful sequences of communication, including looking at each other, playing short games, and taking rests. Fathers and babies and siblings and babies do as well.

4. *Emergence of an organized sense of self—9 to 18 months*. One-year-old infants can do more things for themselves and take a more active role in the emotional partnership with their mothers and fathers. They can signal their needs more effectively and precisely than before. They begin using words to communicate. By now a number of emotions—including anger, sadness, and happiness—have emerged. At the end of this period, the infant has a sense of self.

5. *Creating emotional ideas—18 to 36 months*. Toddlers are now able to symbolize, pretend, and form mental images of people and things. They can learn about the social world through make-believe and pretend play. Now that they have a sense of self, they can feel the ambivalent needs of autonomy and dependency. During this period, toddlers' emotional repertoire expands to include such social emotions as empathy and embarrassment and gradually shame, pride, and guilt. This expansion coincides with their new sense of self and their growing knowledge of social rules.

6. *Emotional thinking: the basis for fantasy, reality, and self-esteem—30 to 48 months*. By this time the give-and-take of close relationships with significant people has settled into a kind of partnership. Young children can discern what the caregiver expects of them and can try to modify their behavior to meet those expectations and thus achieve their own goals.

(Kochanska, 1997). Thus, child-to-caregiver attachment is intertwined with caregiver-to-child attachment.

Ainsworth describes these behaviors as criteria of attachment because if they do not occur, attachment can be difficult to establish. Consider, for example, how hard it would be for a mother to develop a sense of emotional closeness to an infant who constantly stiff-arms her instead of embracing her. Or what if an infant does not smile or vocalize much in response to the caregiver? Ainsworth and colleagues (1979) have found that when a baby dislikes being touched or has a disability such as blindness, mutual attachment is at risk.

Thus, infant and caregiver alike must behave in ways that foster attachment. Normally the infant's behaviors invite nurturing responses from the caregiver, who not only feeds the infant and cares for the infant's physical needs but also communicates with the infant by talking, smiling, and touching.

The baby's behavior prompts the caregiver to act in certain ways, and the caregiver's actions prompt the baby as well.

Is attachment a conditioned response, or are innate needs involved? For a long time, developmental psychologists with a conditioning orientation thought that infant-to-caregiver attachment occurred through the fulfillment of the infant's primary drives, such as hunger and thirst. Essentially through classical conditioning, the infant learns to associate the caregiver's nearness with the reduction of primary drives (Sears, 1963). Similarly, psychoanalytic theorists argued that a child's first emotional bonds occur through the gratification of the child's needs: When those needs are met, the infant forms a positive inner image of the mother. But experimental research with animals indicates that drive satisfaction is only part of how infants form their first attachments, as discussed in "A Matter for Debate" on page 172.

British psychologist and ethologist John Bowlby (1973) argued that human babies are born with preprogrammed behaviors that function to keep their parents close by and responsive. In his view, such behaviors have evolved in humans and other animals partly because they increase the infant's chances of being protected from danger, and therefore surviving, eventually reaching sexual maturity and passing the relevant genes along to the next generation.

Bowlby proposed that preprogrammed behaviors affect both the infant and the caregiver. Attachment is initiated by those behaviors and is then maintained by pleasurable events, such as physical closeness and warmth between mother and child, reduction of hunger and other drives, and comfort. His theory thus combines heredity and environment in explaining the development and maintenance of attachment. According to Bowlby, the infant's attachment to the primary caregiver becomes internalized as a working model—or scheme—by the end of the first year. The infant uses the model to predict and interpret the mother's behavior and respond to it. Once the model has been formed, the infant tends to hold on to it even when the caregiver's behavior changes. Thus, for example, a mother who provides little early nurturance because of prolonged illness may later be rebuffed by the infant when she recovers, since the infant's working model includes prior feelings of rejection. It is then harder for the mother to be responsive because of the infant's behavior (Bretherton, 1992).

In sum, Bowlby and Ainsworth (1973; Ainsworth et al., 1978) were convinced that the nature of the parent-child interaction that emerges from the development of attachment in the first 2 years of life forms the basis for all future relationships. This observation closely parallels Erikson's theory of early psychosocial development, discussed in Chapter 1.

EMOTIONAL COMMUNICATION AND ATTACHMENT

The attachment behaviors of both mother and infant evolve gradually and constitute a *dynamic* system in which the behaviors of the infant reciprocally influence those of the mother and vice versa (Fogel et al., 1997). For example, a sociable and easy baby who seeks close contact and derives pleasure from it can encourage even the most tentative new mother. In contrast, an often-fussy, difficult baby interrupts a caretaker's efforts at soothing or verbal give-and-take (Belsky et al., 1984; Lewis & Feiring, 1989).

To learn more about the two-way affective (emotional) communication system that defines the infant's interaction with the primary caregiver during the first 6 months of life, Ed Tronick (1989) devised a laboratory experiment that focused on the mutual expectations of parents and infants. In what was called the "still face" experiment, parents were first asked to sit and play with their

A MATTER FOR DEBATE

GEESE, MONKEYS, AND HUMANS

Half a century ago Konrad Lorenz (1903–1989), an Austrian zoologist and ethologist, observed that goslings begin to follow their mother very soon after hatching. They develop a bond that is important in helping the mother protect and train her offspring. Interestingly, Lorenz also found that during their first hours after hatching, orphaned greylag goslings developed a pattern of following *him*, as if he were their mother. The pattern was relatively permanent—and sometimes annoyingly persistent. Some of Lorenz's greylag geese preferred to spend the night in his bedroom rather than on the banks of the Danube!

The critical period for *imprinting*—forming the bond between goslings and their mother—occurs soon after hatching, when the gosling is strong enough to move around but before it develops a strong fear of large, moving objects. If imprinting is delayed, the gosling will either fear the parent or simply give up and become limp, tired, and listless.

Researchers disagree about the parallels between imprinting in birds and attachment behavior in humans. There is no clear evidence that a critical period exists for human bonding. Parents and infants may be particularly receptive to bonding in the first few days after birth, but this is hardly a critical period. On the other hand, it is clearly necessary for human infants to establish some kind of relationship with one or more major caregivers within the first 8 months or so if normal development is to occur. Because monkeys have much closer biological ties to humans, studies of their social development—and deprivation—are more directly relevant to understanding human development than are studies of goslings. An important series of ob-

Orphaned goslings nurtured by Konrad Lorenz during the critical imprinting period follow him as if he were their real mother.

In Harlow's studies of attachment, young monkeys showed a distinct preference for the cloth-covered surrogate mother over the wire mother regardless of which one supplied food.

servations on social deprivation in monkeys began somewhat by accident when Harry Harlow (1959) was studying learning and conceptual development in monkeys. To control the learning environment, Harlow decided to rear each young monkey without its mother, thus ruling out her influence as a teacher and model. Unexpectedly, Harlow found that separation from the mother had a disastrous effect on the young monkeys. Some died. Others were frightened, irritable, and reluctant to eat or play. Obviously, the monkeys needed something more than regular feeding to thrive and develop.

Harlow and colleagues next conducted experiments with artificial *surrogate* mothers (Harlow & Harlow, 1962). For each infant monkey, there was a wire surrogate with a bottle from which the monkey was fed, as well as a terrycloth-covered surrogate from which it was not fed. In spite of the feeding provided by the wire surro-

gate, the young monkeys showed a distinct preference for the terrycloth form: They spent more time clinging and vocalizing to it, and they ran to it when they were frightened. As a result, Harlow proposed that *contact-comfort* is an important factor in early attachment.

Monkeys who were reared with surrogates still didn't develop normally, however. As adults they avoided or attacked other monkeys and did not engage in normal sexual activity. Subsequent research indicates, however, that peer contact among infant monkeys can compensate for the deprivation (Coster, 1972). Infant monkeys who are raised with surrogate mothers and are given an opportunity to play with other infant monkeys develop reasonably normal social behavior. Thus, mutually responsive social interaction is crucial for normal development in monkeys, and it seems plausible to generalize this conclusion to humans.

3-month-old infants in their usual manner. Play patterns differed markedly among parent-infant pairs, but in each case, at some points the infants would turn away or close their eyes before returning to the fun.

After 3 minutes the experimenter asked the parents to stop communicating with their infants. The parents were instructed to continue looking at their infants but to put on a blank, still face. The infants responded with surprise and tried to engage their parents with smiles, coos, and general activity, but the parents maintained the blank expression. Within a few minutes, the infants' behavior began to deteriorate. They looked away, sucked their thumbs, and looked pained. Some began to whimper and cry, while others had involuntary responses such as drooling or hiccuping. Thus, although the parents were still present and attending, they were suddenly and unexpectedly unavailable emotionally, and the infants had difficulty coping with the change. This experiment provided a clear demonstration of the strength and importance of emotional communication between caregivers and infants as young as 3 months of age. According to Tronick (1989), emotional communication is a major determinant of children's emotional development. When the bidirectional, reciprocal communication system fails—as it does, for example, when the primary caregiver is chronically depressed or ill—the infant cannot achieve his or her interactive goals.

At about 7 months, infants become wary of strangers. This stranger-anxiety is a landmark in the infant's social development.

STRANGER ANXIETY, SEPARATION ANXIETY, AND ATTACHMENT

A key landmark in the development of the attachment relationship is the appearance of **stranger anxiety and separation anxiety.** Pediatricians and psychologists often make little distinction between the two, referring to both as "7-months anxiety" because they often appear suddenly at about that age. Babies who have been smiling, welcoming, friendly, and accepting toward strangers suddenly become shy and wary of them. At the same time, some babies become extremely upset by being left alone in a strange place, even for a moment. Although many babies do not experience intense stranger and separation anxiety, for those who do, such reactions often continue throughout the rest of the first year and much of the second year.

THE DISCREPANCY HYPOTHESIS   Most psychologists see stranger and separation anxiety as a sign of the infant's intellectual development. As cognitive processes mature, infants develop schemes for what is familiar, and they notice anything that is new and strange. They distinguish caregivers from strangers and become keenly aware when the primary caregiver is absent. Thus, according to the **discrepancy hypothesis,** they experience anxiety when they become capable of detecting departures from the known or the expected (Ainsworth et al., 1978). The anxiety is based on the infant's new awareness that the caregiver's presence coincides with safety. Things seem secure when familiar caregivers are present but uncertain when they are not.

Some psychologists believe that by 9 months, the anxiety reaction is further complicated by learning. Wanda Bronson (1978) found that 9-month-old babies sometimes cry when they first notice a stranger, even before the stranger comes close. This crying implies that they may have had negative experiences with strangers and so anticipate another disturbing encounter. But the learning process may be more subtle than that. Perhaps the mother signals her baby by her facial expression or tone of voice. In one study, one group of mothers of 8- to 9-month-old babies were trained to knit their eyebrows, widen their eyes, pull down their lips, and otherwise demonstrate worry while greeting a

stranger anxiety and separation anxiety   An infant's fear of strangers or of being separated from the caregiver. Both occur in the second half of the first year and indicate, in part, a new cognitive ability to respond to differences in the environment.

discrepancy hypothesis   A cognitive theory stating that at around 7 months, infants acquire schemes for familiar objects. When a new image or object is presented that differs from the old one, the child experiences uncertainty and anxiety.

stranger with a troubled "Hello." A second group was trained to show pleasure with a smile and a cheery "Hello." As predicted, the infants accurately picked up their mothers' signals: Infants whose mothers displayed pleasure smiled more and cried less when the stranger picked them up than did infants whose mothers displayed worry (Boccia & Campos, 1989). Emotional signaling by the mother is called **social referencing;** we will investigate this process further later in the chapter. Through such signaling, parents can assist their infants and toddlers in adjusting to strangers and strange situations by monitoring their own emotional reactions and giving children time to *acclimate* (Feiring et al., 1984).

Stranger anxiety is also a milestone in social development (Bretherton & Waters, 1985). Once children learn to identify the caregiver as a source of comfort and security, they feel free to explore new objects while in the caregiver's reassuring presence. Children who fail to explore, preferring to hover near their mother, miss out on new learning. On the other hand, infants who are too readily comforted by strangers or who show wariness when returned to their mother may also be maladjusted (Sroufe & Fleeson, 1986). The latter children may suffer pervasive and unresolved anxiety about their caregivers that can interfere with emotional development. For more on what happens to children when circumstances prevent or disrupt attachment, see "Eye on Diversity" on page 175.

Stranger anxiety and separation anxiety can also be used to assess the *quality* of infant-to-caregiver attachment, as we'll see in the next section.

REVIEW & APPLY

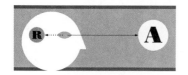

1. What is attachment, and what is its significance for the relationship between the infant and the primary caregiver?
2. Discuss Bowlby's ethological view of attachment.
3. What do stranger anxiety and separation anxiety tell us about infants' emotional development?

PATTERNS OF EARLY RELATIONSHIPS

Infants all over the world normally show similar responses to their social environments; they gradually establish attachment relationships with their primary caregivers. Although the sequence of development of these first relationships is fairly consistent across cultures, the details vary dramatically, depending on the personality of the parents, their child-rearing practices, and the temperament and personality of the child.

How do we assess the quality of the relationship between the infant and the primary caregiver? As we'll see, researchers in Western cultures have focused on security of attachment, responsiveness of the mother and its effects on the infant, mutual relationships with key caregivers, and multiple versus exclusive attachments.

For perspective, however, it is worthwhile to take a cross-cultural view of attachment. In the United States and much of Western Europe, child development experts have assumed that a single primary relationship—usually with the mother—is ideal for healthy infant development. The relationship is

social referencing Subtle emotional signals, usually from the parent, that influence the infant's behavior.

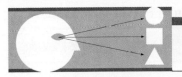

EYE ON DIVERSITY

REACTIONS TO SEPARATION AND LOSS

If attachment is essential to normal development and if attachment relationships progress through predictable stages, what happens to a child who does not have such a relationship or whose progress toward attachment is interrupted? What happens to a child who is reared in an orphanage by numerous caregivers? What happens to an infant who spends a prolonged period in a hospital? And what about the child who has begun to establish an attachment relationship and is suddenly separated from the caregiver?

Social deprivation has a devastating effect on children's emotional development. Infants who are cared for by numerous different caregivers who meet only their basic physical needs don't develop an attachment relationship. The mutual responses between child and caregiver do not occur consistently; the social interaction that permits expression of emotion is missing (Bowlby, 1973, 1980, 1988). Typically, the result is apathy, withdrawal, and depressed functioning, which lead to distorted personality development.

When securely attached infants are separated from their parents through prolonged hospitalization or loss, a series of dramatic reactions tend to occur. Bowlby (1973) divides these reactions into three stages: *protest, despair,* and *detachment.* At first infants protest and do not accept the separation; they cry and scream and refuse to respond to anyone who tries to comfort them. Then they enter a stage of despair, in which they withdraw and become very quiet and appear to lose all hope. Eventually they begin to accept attention from others and appear to recover, although they react with detachment if the primary caregiver returns. Have they actually recovered? Bowlby (1960, page 143) summed up the situation as follows:

A child living in an institution or hospital who has reached this state will no longer be upset when nurses change or leave. He will cease to show feelings when his parents come and go on visiting day; and it may cause them pain when they realize that, although he has an avid interest in the presents they bring, he has little interest in them as social people. He will appear cheerful and adapted to his unusual situation and apparently easy and unafraid of anyone. But this sociability is superficial: he appears no longer to care for anyone.

As this description shows, it is easy to underestimate the complexity of young children's emotional reactions and behavior.

---

mutually responsive and is characterized by game playing and interactive dialogues. But that's not the norm in many other cultures. In some cultures, for example, infants have close physical contact with caregivers—including being carried in a back sling and sleeping with a parent or another adult—but do not have frequent face-to-face interactions. In other cultures, a primary adult-infant relationship is supplemented by many relationships. Grandmothers, aunts, fathers, siblings, and neighbors take turns caring for the infant. To the extent that these relationships are reasonably consistent, healthy attachment emerges. Thus, although the quality of relationships is important, many cultural and subcultural variations can foster healthy attachment.

QUALITY OF ATTACHMENT

Mary Ainsworth's *strange situation test* (1973) is used to assess the quality of infant attachment to the primary caregiver. Ainsworth's test is a kind of minidrama with a simple cast of characters: the mother, her 1-year-old baby, and a stranger. The setting is an unfamiliar playroom that contains toys. Table 5–2 summarizes the eight scenes involved in the test and what is observed during each scene.

Using the strange situation test, Ainsworth found three basic types of attachment. Between 60% and 70% of middle-class babies are **securely attached.** They can separate themselves fairly easily from their mother and go exploring in the room, even when the stranger is present. Although they may become upset when their mother leaves, they greet her warmly and become calm

secure attachment   A strong emotional bond between child and caregiver that develops as a result of responsive caregiving.

TABLE 5–2   AINSWORTH'S STRANGE SITUATION PARADIGM*

EPISODE	EVENTS	VARIABLES OBSERVED
1	Experimenter introduces parents and baby to playroom and then leaves.	
2	Parent is seated while baby plays with toys.	Parent as a secure base
3	Stranger enters, seats self, and talks to parent.	Reaction to an unfamiliar adult
4	Parent leaves; stranger responds to baby and offers comfort if upset.	Separation anxiety
5	Parent returns, greets baby, and offers comfort if needed; stranger leaves.	Reaction to reunion
6	Parent leaves room; baby is alone.	Separation anxiety
7	Stranger enters and offers comfort.	Ability to be soothed by stranger
8	Parent returns, greets baby, and offers comfort if needed; tries to reinterest baby in toys.	Reaction to reunion

*While each episode lasts for about 3 minutes, the separation episodes may be cut short if the baby becomes too distressed.
Source: Ainsworth et al., (1978).

quickly when she returns. Correlational research by Ainsworth indicates that securely attached infants had warm, affectionate, and responsive interactions with their mothers in the 12 months prior to the tests. Follow-up studies indicate that securely attached children are more curious, sociable, independent, and competent than their peers at ages 2, 3, 4, and 5 (Matas et al., 1978; Sroufe et al., 1983; Waters et al., 1979). The studies also conform to Erikson's predictions, as discussed in Chapter 1, regarding the effects of an early sense of trust on later development.

Ainsworth found that the remaining infants—about a third—were **insecurely attached.** Insecure attachment takes two forms. In one, the child becomes angry when the mother leaves and avoids her when she returns. In the other, the child responds to the mother ambivalently, simultaneously seeking and rejecting affection. Both types are often associated with unresponsive, indifferent, or perhaps resentful caregiving during the first year of life.

Longitudinal research contrasting the two basic types of attachment (Sroufe, 1977; Arend et al., 1979; Bretherton & Waters, 1985) has found dramatic differences in personality and social development as early as 18 months of age. Securely attached infants are more enthusiastic, persistent, and cooperative than infants in the two insecure categories. By age 2, they are also more effective in coping with peers. They spontaneously invent more imaginative and symbolic play. Later, in elementary school, children who have experienced secure attachment during infancy persist in their work longer, are more eager to learn new skills, and exhibit more highly developed social skills in interacting with adults and peers—which is highly consistent with Erikson's stages of autonomy versus shame and doubt, and initiative versus guilt.

insecure attachment   The result of inconsistent or unresponsive caregiving.

Numerous other studies have yielded similar findings (see Belsky & Rovine, 1990a). Although the evidence is correlational—which means that we can't say absolutely that responsive caregiving *causes* secure attachment and its later benefits—it does strongly point in that direction. Securely attached toddlers and preschoolers do even simple things—like exploring playrooms—better than children who are insecurely attached. They maneuver around the furniture, find their way to interesting toys, and position themselves comfortably for play with greater ease than insecurely attached children (Cassidy, 1986). Also, securely attached 3-year-olds tend to be better liked by their peers (Jacobson & Wille, 1986).

Thus, we can conclude that a warm, supportive relationship between caregiver and infant leads to higher levels of cognitive competence and greater social skills (Olson et al., 1984). It promotes active exploration and early mastery of object play and the social environment. From the beginning, the quality of the relationship between caregiver and infant provides the foundation for many aspects of child development.

Children who spend long hours strapped to their mothers' backs form strong attachments.

WHAT CONSTITUTES RESPONSIVE CAREGIVING? Numerous studies have shown that the mother's sensitivity to her baby's signals and her overall responsiveness have important implications for the social and personality development of the child (De Wolff & van Ijzendoorn, 1997). In early studies of children in Uganda, for example, Ainsworth (1967) found that the children with the strongest attachment behavior had a highly responsive relationship with their mothers. In the United States, she reported that securely attached 1-year-olds had mothers who were more responsive to their cries, more affectionate, more tender, more competent in providing close bodily contact, and more likely than mothers of insecure 1-year-olds to synchronize their rate of feeding and their play behavior with the baby's own pace (Ainsworth et al., 1978). Since then, researchers have consistently found that infants who were securely attached at age 1 had mothers who were more responsive to their physical needs, distress signals, and attempts to communicate with facial expressions or vocalizations (Bornstein, 1989).

Does this finding mean that a mother must respond to every little thing her infant does? Of course not. Even highly responsive mothers don't respond 100% of the time. Marc Bornstein and Catherine Tamis-LeMonda (1989) found that mothers' responsiveness varies according to the situation. When infants are in distress, for example, the typical responsive mother responds quickly about 75% of the time. In contrast, mothers respond differently to bids for attention, vocalization, and smiling. Some mothers respond to these cues as little as 5% of the time, whereas others respond about half the time. Moreover, different mothers respond in different ways—some with physical play, others with vocal imitation, and still others with touching, playing, patting, and feeding.

Other researchers (Clarke-Stewart & Hevey, 1981) have studied the interactions of mothers with their securely or insecurely attached children. Mothers who are more verbally responsive and attentive to their children tend to have children who are more autonomous and communicative. Interactions between the securely attached infant and mother are gentler and warmer, and these interactions elicit more compliant and cooperative behavior from the infant (see also Londerville & Main, 1981).

MUTUAL DIALOGUES AND ATTACHMENT Many researchers have studied the two-way affective communication system between mother and infant, which was discussed earlier in the context of the still-face experiment. Heinz

A mother and her young son illustrate mutuality while reading a book.

Early mutuality and signaling lay the foundation for long-term patterns of interaction.

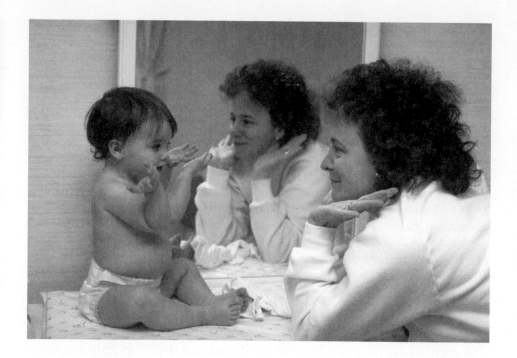

Schaffer (1977) investigated the way in which **mutuality, or interactive synchrony,** develops between infant and caregiver. He observed that most infant behavior follows an alternating on-off pattern. For example, while visually exploring new objects, babies stare at them and then look away. Some caregivers respond to these patterns more skillfully than others. Films of some mothers face-to-face with their 3-month-old infants reveal a pattern of mutual approach and withdrawal; they take turns looking and turning, touching and responding, vocalizing and answering. Synchrony between infant and caregiver during the first few months is a good predictor of secure attachment at age 1, as well as more sophisticated patterns of mutual communication at that age (Isabella et al., 1989).

Caregivers do not merely respond to the child's behavior. They also change the pace and nature of the dialogue with a variety of techniques: introducing a new object, imitating and elaborating on the infant's sounds or actions, making it easier for the child to reach something of interest. By monitoring the baby's responses, caregivers gradually learn when the child is most receptive to new cues. It takes months for this mutual process to develop fully.

Some techniques seem to be especially effective in developing synchrony (Field, 1977; Paulby, 1977). Tiffany Field compared infant reactions to three different maternal behaviors: the mother's spontaneous behavior, her deliberate attempts to catch and hold the child's attention, and her imitations of the child. The infants responded most to the imitations, perhaps because of the slowed-down, exaggerated nature of imitative action. The closer the similarity between maternal and infant behavior, the less discrepancy babies have to deal with; thus, the more attentive they will be. Further, each mother carefully observed her infant's "gaze-away" point. Field suggested that respecting the child's need for pauses in the action is one of the earliest rules of "conversation" that a responsive caregiver must learn.

Some parents overstimulate their infants despite signals of resistance from the babies such as turning away, hiding their faces, or closing their eyes. Some parents continue the stimulation until the child actually cries. Other parents

mutuality, or interactive synchrony The pattern of interchange between caregiver and infant in which each responds to and influences the other's movements and rhythms.

understimulate their infants. They often ignore their babies' smiles and babbling or other bids for attention. An infant whose cues for attention are ignored may cry or soon give up trying. Still other parents have mixed patterns of sensitivity. Sometimes they overstimulate, sometimes they understimulate. They regularly misidentify the infant's cues. This pattern is particularly common in abusive mothers (Kropp & Haynes, 1987), depressed mothers (Field, 1986; Teti et al., 1995), some adolescent mothers (Lamb, 1987), and mothers whose temperament is very different from that of their child (Weber et al., 1986). Relatively short maternal leave in combination with factors such as maternal depression is also associated with inappropriate maternal sensitivity (Clark et al., 1997).

The behavior of a sensitive and responsive mother changes as the infant grows older (Crockenberg & McCluskey, 1986). Indeed, some developmental psychologists use the term **scaffolding** to describe the mother's or father's role in progressively structuring the parent-child interaction (Ratner & Bruner, 1978; Vandell & Wilson, 1987). That is, parents provide the framework within which they interact with their infant. With a younger child, they uses games like imitation or peekaboo. As the child grows older, the games become more sophisticated. The child learns increasingly complex rules of social interaction—rules of pacing and give-and-take, rules of observing and imitating, the way to maintain the game, and so on.

Early mutuality and signaling lay the foundation for long-standing patterns of interaction. This practice is illustrated in studies of maternal responses to crying. Mothers who respond promptly and consistently to their infant's crying in the first few months are more likely to have infants who cry *less* by the end of the first year. A quick response gives babies confidence in the effectiveness of their communications and encourages them to develop other ways of signaling their mother (Bell & Ainsworth, 1972). On the other hand, if responses to crying are inconsistent, infants may fail to develop confidence and later may cry more, be more insistent, or be less responsive themselves.

During the second year, mutuality blossoms into a variety of behaviors. For example, some securely attached toddlers spontaneously exhibit sharing behavior, both with parents and with other children—showing a toy, placing it in someone's lap, or using it to invite another child to play. In general, whether or not children are born "selfish," the quality of early parent-child interactions has a profound influence on behaviors such as sharing and helping.

MULTIPLE ATTACHMENTS VERSUS EXCLUSIVITY Infants who have a relatively exclusive relationship with one parent tend to exhibit more intense stranger and separation anxiety. They also show these anxieties at an earlier age than infants whose relationship with the parent is not exclusive (Ainsworth, 1967). A child who is constantly with the parent and sleeps in the same room exhibits dramatic and intense separation reactions. By contrast, a child who has more than one caregiver from birth tends to accept strangers or separation with far less anxiety (Maccoby & Feldman, 1972).

Is attachment impaired if caregiving is done by too many different people? Every year over 5.5 million children receive care from many different people in nurseries and day-care centers. If the *quantity* of attachments is a factor, children who spend less time with their parents might suffer.

Research indicates, however, that day care and multiple caregivers may have no adverse effects on attachment (but see "A Matter for Debate" on page 172). These children form multiple attachments (Clarke-Stewart & Fein, 1983; Welles-Nystrom, 1988) that can vary in quality just as child-parent attachment can.

scaffolding The progressive structuring by the parents of the parent-child interaction.

When toddlers first attend a day-care program, they often experience separation distress, especially if they're between 15 and 18 months old. Some toddlers adjust more readily than others. Toddlers who have had an exclusive relationship with one person experience the most trouble. Those who have already had too many separations and too many caregivers also display separation distress. Adjustment is easiest for toddlers who have had some experience with other caregivers and have had a moderate degree of separation experience (Jacobson & Wille, 1984).

Besides becoming attached to their mothers, children form attachments with fathers, siblings, and other family members, as we'll see later in the chapter. And they form attachments with peers. The power of peers as attachment figures was revealed in Anna Freud's famous study (Freud & Dann, 1951) of six German-Jewish orphans who were separated from their parents at an early age during World War II. They were placed in a country home at Bulldog Banks, England, that had been transformed into a nursery for war children. They had previously been in large institutions, so that this was their first experience in a small, intimate setting. At first the children were hostile toward their adult caregivers or ignored them, showing much more concern for one another. For example, when a caregiver accidentally knocked over one of the smaller children, two other children threw bricks at her and called her abusive names. The orphans also depended on each other when frightened, a reaction that clearly illustrates the strength of their attachment to each other.

EFFECTS OF NEGLECT AND ABUSE Neglect is a factor in **failure-to-thrive syndrome,** in which infants are small and emaciated, appear sick, and are unable to digest food properly. Failure-to-thrive can occur as a result of malnutrition, but in many cases it appears to be due to lack of affection and attention—including poor-quality (or nonexistent) attachment. Often there is disruption in the home and the social environment; sometimes well-intentioned but busy, dual-earner parents inadvertently "neglect" their child. The infants are often listless and withdrawn, perhaps immobile. They avoid eye contact by staring with a wide-eyed gaze, turning away, or covering their face or eyes. By definition, infants with failure-to-thrive syndrome weigh in the lower 3% of the normal weight range for their age group and show no evidence of disease or abnormality that would explain their failure to grow. Such infants may exhibit developmental retardation, which can be reversed with appropriate feeding and attention (Barbero, 1983; Drotar, 1985).

Child abuse also interferes with attachment. When abuse begins in infancy, it betrays the nurturant relationship on which the infant depends and may have devastating effects throughout life. Studies have shown that toddlers who have suffered physical maltreatment and insecure attachment experience distortions and delays in the development of their sense of self and in their language and cognitive development. When infants are securely attached during the first year, abuse during the second year is less damaging (Beeghly & Cicchetti, 1994) though equally regrettable. Other studies point to a potentially malignant combination of negligent or inconsistent mothering and a biologically or temperamentally vulnerable infant. In combination, the result is an infant who shows insecure attachment and experiences frequent distress and episodes of angry behavior—along with later maladjustment (Cassidy & Berlin, 1994). Abuse is sometimes related to an intrusive, interfering style of caregiving that ignores the baby's wishes and disrupts the baby's activities. One study found that when a mother's style of interaction with her 6-month-old infant is highly intrusive and persistent, the child may later demonstrate

failure-to-thrive syndrome A condition in which infants are small for age and often sick, as a result of malnutrition or unresponsive caregiving.

poor academic, social, emotional, and behavioral skills (Egeland, Pianta, & O'Brien, 1993).

In some cases, mothers of failure-to-thrive and abused or neglected infants are themselves mentally or physically ill, depressed, or inclined toward alcohol or other drug abuse. Such parents often experienced similar deprivation as infants. Some studies show that as many as 85% of abusive or neglectful parents had negative early childhood experiences themselves; that is, they too were abused or neglected. Certainly, not all people who were abused as children grow up to abuse their children, but too often the cycle is repeated (Helfer, 1982). Issues in child abuse are considered in more detail in Chapter 9.

ATTACHMENT AND INFANTS WITH SPECIAL NEEDS

Blind infants cannot search their caregivers' faces or smile back at them. Deaf babies may appear to be disobedient. Infants with other severe handicaps cannot respond to signals the way normal babies do. Obvious handicaps that are evident from birth, such as Down syndrome and cerebral palsy, create serious adjustment problems for all concerned. Formerly, researchers ignored how infants affect caregivers and concentrated instead on the impact of caregivers' behavior on infants. In the past two decades, however, researchers have devoted more attention to the child's role in the relationship.

INFANTS WHO CAN'T SEE   Visual communication between caregiver and child is normally a key factor in the establishment of attachment. Caregivers depend heavily on subtle responses from their infants—looking back, smiling, and visually following—to maintain and support their own behavior. They may feel that a blind infant is unresponsive. It is essential that a parent and an unseeing child establish a mutually intelligible communication system that compensates for the child's disability.

In early life, one of the normal infant's best-developed resources for learning is the visual-perceptual system. Babies look at and visually follow everything new, and have distinct visual preferences. They especially like to look at human faces. Blind infants, however, cannot observe the subtle changes in caregivers' facial expressions or follow their movements. Thus, they fail to receive the kinds of information that sighted babies use in formulating their own responses.

Caregivers of sighted infants rely on visual signals of discrimination, recognition, and preference. Blind infants who are otherwise competent do not develop signals for "I want that" or "Pick me up" until near the end of the first year. Thus, the first few months of life are extremely difficult for both caregiver and infant. The child's seeming lack of responsiveness can be emotionally devastating for the caregiver. The danger is that communication and mutuality will break down and that the caregiver will tend to avoid the child (Fraiberg, 1974). Blind babies do not develop a selective, responsive smile as early as sighted children do; they do not smile as often or as ecstatically. They have very few facial expressions. Yet they rapidly develop a large, expressive vocabulary of hand signals. Eventually they are able to direct these signals to unseen people and objects. Training parents and caregivers of blind infants to talk all the time to their children and to watch for and interpret hand signals greatly enhances parent-child interaction, attachment formation, and subsequent socialization (Fraiberg, 1974).

INFANTS WHO CAN'T HEAR   The developmental difficulties of deaf-but-sighted infants follow a different pattern. In the first few months of life, their well-developed visual sense generally makes up for the problems imposed by deafness. After the first 6 months, however, communication between parent and infant can begin to break down. The child's responses are not complete enough to meet parents' expectations. To make matters worse, the discovery that the child is deaf often doesn't occur until the second year, by which time the child has already missed a great deal of communication via language. One of the first indications of hearing impairment in 1-year-olds is seeming disobedience, as well as startled reactions when people approach (the child simply doesn't hear them coming). In 2-year-olds, there may be temper tantrums and frequent disobedience owing to failure to hear what the parents want. This behavior may be accompanied by an overall failure to develop normal expectations about the world.

The diagnosis of deafness may come as a shock to parents who have been talking to the child all along. Like parents of blind children, parents of deaf children need special training and counseling. Without careful attention during infancy, deafness can result in poor communication during the preschool years and later can lead to severe social, intellectual, and psychological deficits (Meadow, 1975).

INFANTS WITH SEVERE HANDICAPS   When an infant is born with a severe handicap such as cerebral palsy, there is a high risk of parental rejection, withdrawal, and depression. A severely handicapped infant strains marital ties and may trigger a variety of disturbances in other children in the family. Child-care workers can help with a family's early adjustment problems, and they should be consulted from birth. Early success or failure in coping with initial traumas can greatly affect parents' ability to make wise decisions about child care and education (Turnbull & Turnbull, 1990).

REVIEW & APPLY

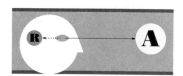

1. Describe the strange situation test and the way it is used to measure the infant's attachment to the primary caregiver.
2. How does a responsive environment affect the development of attachment behavior?
3. Just what is responsive caregiving?
4. How do special needs influence the attachment between infant and caregiver?

FATHERS, SIBLINGS, AND THE FAMILY SYSTEM

Most children develop within a social context that encourages early attachments to the father, as well as to any siblings, grandparents, and other family members who are regularly present. In other words, the infant's emotional development often doesn't depend on the strengths and weaknesses of a single attachment.

FATHERS
Much has been learned from research on fathers and fathering in the American family system. Fathers are spending more time with their infants than they did in the past (Pleck, 1985; Ricks, 1985). They provide routine child care and can bathe, diaper, feed, and rock as skillfully as mothers. They can be as responsive to the infant's cues as mothers (Parke, 1981), and infants can become as

Fathers today are taking a more active role in caring for infants.

attached to their fathers as they are to their mothers. In turn, fathers who spend more time taking care of young children form stronger attachments to them, and the children benefit (Ricks, 1985). Despite these shared capabilities, however, most fathers still don't take primary responsibility for infant care. As a result, the father's relationship with the infant is often different from the mother's.

FATHERING STYLES The father's role in child rearing continues to evolve as more and more mothers work outside the home. However, some traditional differences in how fathers and mothers interact with their infants persist. For example, whereas mothers are likely to hold infants for care-taking purposes, fathers are more likely to hold infants during play (Parke, 1981). Fathers are also more physical and spontaneous. Play between fathers and infants occurs in cycles, with peaks of excitement and attention followed by periods of minimal activity. In contrast, mothers engage their infants in subtle, shifting, gradual play, or initiate conventional games such as pat-a-cake. Fathers tend toward unusual, vigorous, and unpredictable games, which infants find highly exciting (Lamb & Lamb, 1976). This practice changes, though, when the father is the primary or sole caregiver: Of necessity, he acts more like a traditional mother (Field, 1978). Surprisingly, recent research also suggests that older fathers are more likely to behave like traditional mothers when playing with their children, whereas younger fathers are more likely to conform to the traditional "father" role (Neville & Parke, 1997).

As infants grow older and require less direct care, father-infant interaction is likely to increase. Fathers may engage in more rough-and-tumble play and interact more frequently with the young child in public places such as zoos or parks (Lewis, 1987).

Fathers who frequently interact with their infants, are responsive to their signals, and become significant figures in their children's world are likely to develop into forceful agents of socialization. As the child grows older, the father becomes an important and positive role model. In contrast, fathers who are inaccessible to their infants may have difficulty establishing strong emotional ties later on. It is even possible that they will have a negative influence as the child grows older (Ricks, 1985). Fathers who are most influential in their young children's lives not only spend time with them but also are sensitive to their wants, cries, and needs (Esterbrook & Goldberg, 1984; Parke, 1981). Indeed, today fathers are broadening their parenting role, even during infancy (Lamb et al., 1987; Parke, 1981).

FATHERS AND THE FAMILY SYSTEM There are both social and psychological reasons why fathers usually are not equal partners in infant care. In one study, mothers and fathers were recruited from a childbirth class in which the fathers were active participants and were expected to share in the care of the infant. It did not work out that way, however (Grossman et al., 1988). Soon after childbirth, both the mothers and the fathers rated the fathers as less competent in most infant-care skills. As a result, the fathers tended to be relegated to the role of helper. Indeed, no father in the study ever mentioned the reverse situation, in which the mother helped the father. The more competent adult— the mother—generally took primary responsibility for infant care and became more adept at meeting the baby's needs and interpreting his or her signals. In general, fathers' backseat role may be related to feelings of incompetence in caring for the child (Entwisle & Doering, 1988).

Most couples work through their differing responses to infant care by selecting complementary roles for the father and the mother. Those who aren't successful, however, tend to become impatient with each other, and the father takes on the role of reluctant and occasional helper who plays with the child but does little else.

Whether as partner or as helper, the father's influence on the infant (and the family) is considerable. Numerous studies indicate that the father's emotional support of the mother during pregnancy and early infancy is important in the establishment of positive relationships. The absence of the father during infancy places considerable stress on the family system (Lewis, 1987). Although in our culture the father often remains a secondary caregiver, he plays an important part in a complex system of interactions.

The addition of an infant, especially a first-born child, affects the marriage itself. Studies have shown that the birth of the first child can place profound stress on the marital relationship. A newborn makes heavy demands on the time and energy of both parents. Complementary roles need to be established, child-care arrangements made, and decisions reached about the mother's return to work (Baruch & Barnett, 1986a). The stress on the marriage may be greater if the infant is demanding, frequently sick, or handicapped. Fortunately, it is possible for stress to bring the couple closer together (Turnbull & Turnbull, 1990). Yet if the marriage was vulnerable at the start, stress may create increased dissatisfaction and turmoil. In other words, contrary to some folk wisdom, having a baby is often not the solution to a marriage that is on the rocks—it is just as likely to make things worse.

SIBLINGS

Siblings form significant and long-lasting attachments to each other beginning in infancy, although younger siblings are often more attached to older siblings than the reverse (Lewis, 1987). Infants often form very strong attachments to an older sibling and are upset when they are separated from him or her even overnight (Dunn & Kendrick, 1979).

Often, older siblings are important social models. Children learn how to share, cooperate, help, and empathize by watching their older brothers or

Older siblings may be rivals, but they are also important social models.

sisters. They learn appropriate gender roles and family customs and values. In some cultures the older sibling is the principal caretaker of the younger child (Whiting & Whiting, 1975). In many families the positive aspects of sibling roles—helping, protecting, and providing an ally—last throughout life.

It is therefore somewhat surprising that the negative aspects of sibling relationships have received more research attention than the positive aspects (Lewis, 1987). Two negative aspects of sibling relationships are *sibling rivalry* and the *dethroning of the older sibling*. With the birth of a new infant, parents pay less attention to and have less time and energy for the firstborn child. The way they handle these changes influences the degree of strife, competition, and rivalry that develops between siblings (Dunn & Kendrick, 1980; Lewis, 1987; Lewis et al., 1984). For example, if parents attempt to enlist the older sibling in the care of the newborn, an alliance is often created both between the siblings and between the older sibling and the parents. The mother and father and the older child may refer to the newborn as "our baby." In general, if parents set aside special time for the first child after the birth of a second child, it is more likely that the firstborn child will feel special rather than disregarded.

GRANDPARENTS

In many cultures, including our own, grandparents see their adult children and grandchildren on at least a weekly basis. In families where both parents work, grandparents frequently are the primary caregivers; they also often serve as babysitters. Grandparents can be particularly important to the stability of single-parent households, in which one out of every five U.S. children now live, and to the 60 percent of all families with children under age 3 whose mothers are in the labor force (U.S. Census Bureau, 1997). Grandparents' roles are usually different from parents' roles, however, and different attachment relationships are formed. Grandparents frequently offer more approval, support, empathy, and sympathy, and they use less discipline. The relationship tends to be more playful and relaxed (Lewis, 1987). Grandparents also have more time

In families where both parents work, grandparents are frequently the primary caregivers for much of the time.

to tell the child stories about "way-back-when," which can help create a sense of family identity and tradition.

REVIEW & APPLY

1. Describe the traditional differences between father-child interactions and mother-child interactions.
2. What are the negative and positive effects of sibling relationships?
3. What differences are there between the ways in which parents and grandparents interact with infants?

PERSONALITY DEVELOPMENT IN THE SECOND YEAR

The ways in which we convey our culture to our children, beginning in infancy, are far from subtle. Almost from birth we try to instill attitudes and values about bodily functions—the acceptability of erotic self-stimulation, the degree and kinds of physical contact that are acceptable—as well as the goodness or badness of their behaviors and their basic nature as human beings. Culturally based attitudes and values are communicated through specific child-rearing practices and have a wide-ranging effect on personality development.

It is in the context of broad, cross-cultural child-rearing patterns that we can see how differing practices affect psychosocial development. Four important aspects of infant development are the development of trust and nurturance; the way that children receive culturally laden signals through social referencing; the way that parents respond to children's attempts at autonomy; and the effects of child-rearing practices on the infant's self-awareness and sense of self.

TRUST, NURTURANCE, AND A SECURE BASE

To Erikson, the development of trust marks the first stage of psychosocial development and occurs during the first year of life. It is during this stage that infants learn whether they can depend on the people around them and whether their social environment is consistent and predictable. If we examine child-rearing practices in other cultures, we see dramatic differences in approaches to the development of trust.

A sense of trust is conveyed to the infant through the mother's (or other primary caregiver's) nurturing behavior, that is, her responsiveness to the infant's needs. Through their reactions to feeding, weaning, and comfort-seeking behaviors, mothers and other caregivers convey their values and attitudes. From these reactions children learn whether they are considered good or bad, whether they should feel anxious or guilty, and when to feel comfortable and secure. In all, they learn a great deal more than merely whether they should suck their thumbs or carry a security blanket.

FEEDING AND COMFORTING   Researchers who study the development of trust focus on how feeding fits into the total pattern of nurturant care. Feeding, whether by breast or bottle, allows for a special closeness between mother and child as it expresses the mother's sensitivity and responsiveness.

The total pattern nurturance helps build trust and security or the lack of it.

In some cultures, the transition period between the infant's birth and separation from the mother lasts 3 years or more. Feeding is an integral part of the prolonged relationship (Mead & Newton, 1967). Children may sleep close to their mothers, be carried around during most of the first year, and be breast-fed until the age of 3 (Richman et al., 1988). In other cultures—especially in the United States—some infants are weaned almost immediately and placed in a separate bedroom.

In Italy, nurturance of the infant is a social affair. Mothers and infants are rarely alone. Mothers do most of the feeding, dressing, and cleaning of their infants in an indulgent and caring fashion, but family members, friends, and neighbors also contribute. In one study, people other than the mother tended to the baby—through hugging, talking, teaching, and even teasing—70% of the time, even when the mother was present. The American observer was especially surprised at the amount of teasing that occurred, even when the infant became upset and cried. Pacifiers were held just out of reach; adults said, "Here comes Daddy!" only to laugh and declare "He isn't here anymore!" Infants were jiggled and pinched to wake them up when adults wanted to play with them. Yet the infants learned to cope remarkably well and developed trust in the adults (New, 1988).

Much research has been devoted to thumb sucking and other self-comforting behaviors, but remarkably few conclusions have been reached about these behaviors. For the most part, sucking seems to be a natural need. Yet parents respond to it in a wide variety of ways (Goldberg, 1972; Richman et al., 1988). In Europe in the early twentieth century, for example, thumb sucking was considered a dirty habit that was harmful to a child's general personality development. Elaborate devices, vile-tasting applications, and sleeves were used to prevent it.

That era is clearly over. Today some children are given a pacifier on the assumption that they can give it up more easily than thumb sucking. Most children who use either thumbs or pacifiers give them up as regular comfort devices by the end of the preschool years. For those who remain avid thumb suckers or comfort seekers, it is assumed that they have other needs that are not being met. For example, some children may continue sucking their thumbs simply because it is one of the few ways they get attention when parents try to dissuade them from doing it.

SOCIAL REFERENCING AND CULTURAL MEANING

An important area of parental influence is social referencing. When infants are not sure whether a situation is safe or unsafe, good or bad, they often look to the parent for emotional signals. For example, in Chapter 4 we saw the effectiveness of social referencing in encouraging or discouraging an infant to cross the visual cliff, and earlier in this chapter we saw how social referencing can affect children's behavior toward a stranger. Infants look for emotional signals in many circumstances, including how far to wander away from the mother and whether or not to explore a strange toy. Infants reference fathers as well as mothers. Although they look more at mothers than at fathers when both are present, the father's signals seem to be equally effective in regulating behavior (Hirshberg & Svejda, 1990).

What are the consequences of one parent's encouraging the child to explore an unusual toy while the other frowns and appears worried? In a study of 1-year-olds (Hirshberg, 1990), parents were coached to give either consistent or conflicting emotional signals. The infants adapted much more easily to consistent emotional signals—either both parents happy or both parents fearful—

than to conflicting ones. In fact, when they were given conflicting facial responses—say, "happy" from the mother and "afraid" from the father—the infants expressed their confusion with a wide range of anxious behaviors. Some sucked their thumbs or rocked in an agitated way; others avoided the situation altogether; still others wandered aimlessly or seemed disoriented. Thus, even 1-year-olds are remarkably sensitive to emotional signals from their parents.

Through social referencing and selective attention, parents teach infants as young as 1 year the values of their culture. Communication of cultural meaning has been demonstrated in a series of studies of the !Kung San, a hunter-gatherer culture in Botswana. For the !Kung San, sharing is highly valued. When cultural anthropologists looked at mothers and their 10- to 12-month-old infants, they were surprised to find that, in contrast to many American parents, the !Kung San parents seemed to pay no attention to the infant's exploration of objects. They did not smile or talk about the objects, nor did they punish their children as they picked up twigs, grass, parts of food, nut shells, bones, and the like. Instead, they said the equivalent of "He's teaching himself." However, the adults paid close attention to the sharing of objects, with commands like "Give it to me" or "Here, take this" (Bakeman & Adamson, 1990).

Parents also convey cultural meaning by including toddlers in social interactions, even though the toddlers are often peripheral to the ongoing social life of the family and community. Barbara Rogoff and colleagues (1993) visited four communities—a Mayan Indian town in Guatemala, a middle-class urban community in the United States, a tribal village in India, and a middle-class urban neighborhood in Turkey—to study how adults help toddlers learn appropriate social behavior. Sometimes toddlers were given direct instruction and help, but often they learned through their own keen observation, imitation, and participation in adult activities. Thus, through guided participation, adults bridge the gap created by the child's limited knowledge of events, and they structure small tasks that are within the group's activity. For example, at dinnertime toddlers may eat with the family (finger foods instead of adult foods), imitate the conversation and gestures of adults and older siblings, enjoy good feelings and laughter, and be encouraged to take small adultlike actions like lifting a cup for a toast.

AUTONOMY, DISCIPLINE, AND PROSOCIAL BEHAVIOR

When infants are a year old their parents have already taught them some guidelines for acceptable behavior, especially with regard to dependency and their need for physical closeness. But in the second year, caregivers must cope with a whole new set of issues. Toward the end of the second year, toddlers experience increased emotional conflict between their greater need for autonomy and their obvious dependence and limited skills.

The changes that occur in children at this age were observed at length by Margaret Mahler and her colleagues (1975). They noted an extraordinary ambivalence in 18-month-old children. The toddlers were torn between a desire to stay close to their mother and a desire to be independent. Their new sense of separateness seemed to frighten them. They tried to deny it by acting as if their mothers were extensions of themselves. For example, a child might pull the mother's hand in an effort to have her pick up an object the child wanted. In addition, the toddlers experienced a wider range of emotions and were developing new ways of dealing with them, such as suppressing crying. The way parents deal with the conflict between autonomy and dependence is expressed in their approach to discipline.

DISCIPLINE What limits should a parent or caregiver set on a child's behavior? Some parents, afraid that any kind of control over their children's behavior will interfere with creative exploration and independence, passively stand by while their 2-year-olds do whatever they please. Discipline, when it comes, is often harsh, reflecting the adults' sense of frustration. Other parents, determined not to "spoil" their children and convinced that 2-year-olds should act like responsible little adults, set so many limits on behavior that their children literally cannot do anything right. Although it is easy to see the errors in these extremes, it is not easy to provide guidelines that work for every situation. For example, adults who encourage exploration and manipulation sooner or later may have to cope with a child who wants to stick a fork into an electrical outlet. Obviously, guidelines must be tempered with common sense and must consider children's needs for safety, independence, and creative expression.

Parental feedback helps children see how their actions affect others. Children need feedback if they are to become sensitive to the needs of others. Feedback might consist of praise for good behavior, such as "What a good helper you are." Or it might take the form of mild scolding, such as "Don't do that, it hurts your brother." The key to feedback is that it should focus on the *behavior*—not the child—as the object of criticism. Children who have a strong attachment relationship and whose needs are met through loving interaction with an adult are neither spoiled by attention nor frightened or threatened by reasonable limits. They are stronger and more confident because they have a secure base from which to venture forth into independent activities. The secure-base phenomenon is robust indeed and has been demonstrated across many cultures in addition to the United States, including China, Germany, Japan, and Israel (Posada et al., 1995). The researchers also found, however, that mothers in different cultures differ with regard to what they perceive as the "ideal" child in this respect, such as what constitutes appropriate proximity to the mother and how much physical contact is preferable.

TOILET TRAINING Although much early theory and research, inspired by Freudian theory, focused on the methods and presumed long-range effects of toilet training, recent studies view it as part of a cluster of child-rearing issues. Toilet training is only one aspect of behavior that is affected by adult attitudes toward children's explorations, the way children handle their own bodies, and children's need for autonomy. By itself, it is not a major issue in social and personality development.

Those who are severe and harsh in toilet training are usually just as strict about other behaviors that require self-mastery and independence, such as feeding, dressing, and general exploration. Some adults demand that a child have early and total bowel and bladder control; they regard "accidents" as intolerable. Such parents are also likely to be severe when their child breaks a plate, plays in the dirt, and explores new places and objects. This strict discipline can have pronounced effects on personality development, creating a child who is inhibited and fearful of anything new.

DEVELOPMENT OF PROSOCIAL BEHAVIOR Many studies have focused on the development of **prosocial behaviors** such as empathy, cooperation, sharing, and general concern about the well-being of others. Between 18 and 24 months toddlers begin to cooperate, share, help, and respond empathically to emotional distress in others. The development of empathy in particular may be related to the toddler's developing sense of self, as Carolyn Zahn-Waxler and her colleagues (1992, page 126) explain:

Going to the potty with a book. Does she plan to be there for a while?

prosocial behavior Helping, sharing, or cooperative actions that are intended to benefit others.

As children begin to differentiate self and other during the second year of life and hence to develop understanding of others as separate beings, their emotional involvement in another's distress begins to be transformed from personal self-distress to sympathetic concern for the victim.

These researchers also believe that the roots of empathy in toddlers are linked to secure attachments and to the way that the child is treated when hurt or in need of help.

Concern for others does not emerge smoothly. Often toddlers are confused when they see others in distress. They don't know how to react and may even laugh. In one series of studies (Radke-Yarrow et al., 1983), mothers were asked to make believe that they had just hurt themselves. At 21 months, toddlers were confused and anxious about the mother's distress. However, 3 months later some of the toddlers had learned soothing, comforting behaviors by observing the behavior of their mothers, who regularly responded with empathy when the child was in distress.

In studies of cooperation in simple tasks, almost no 12-month-old infants cooperate with each other. At 18 months, cooperation is infrequent and appears accidental. At 24 months, with a little coaching, nearly all toddlers can cooperate (Brownell & Carriger, 1990).

DEVELOPMENT OF THE SELF

Many theories of adult and child development emphasize the individual's **self-concept**—his or her perception of personal identity. Self-concept is viewed as an integrator, a filter, and a mediator for much of human behavior. That is, people tend to behave in ways that are consistent with their self-image and self-concept.

At first, infants cannot differentiate between themselves and the world around them. Gradually, however, they begin to realize that they are separate and unique beings. Much of infancy is devoted to making this distinction. From 3 to 8 months, infants actively learn about their bodies. First, they discover their hands, their feet, and some of the things they can do with them. Later, they use their hands to explore and manipulate objects and to see what happens. At 7 or 8 months, they become wary of strangers. They also become capable of delaying their actions for a short time. Infants now become more deliberate in testing and exploring their own responses and events they cause to happen. Also, by observing and imitating the behavior of people around them, infants begin to learn how they should behave.

Between 12 and 18 months, infants are hard at work learning social expectations and the results of their testing or exploring the social world. By the end of this period, they clearly recognize themselves in pictures and in the mirror (see Table 5–3 for an overview of stages in self-recognition), and they are ready for more detailed socialization (Lewis & Feinman, 1991). Finally, from 18 to 30 months, children learn a great deal about themselves. They learn about their gender, their physical features and characteristics, their goodness and badness, the things they can and cannot do. With the growing sense of self come more emotional reactions to others, sometimes in the form of temper tantrums. As toddlers become more aware of their own feelings, they react more personally to frustration and hurt, and they may respond with intense emotion (Dunn & Munn, 1985).

Michael Lewis (1995) studied the development of "self-conscious" emotions such as pride, shame, guilt, and embarrassment, which begin to appear after the infant's first birthday. Such emotions depend on a fairly well-developed

self-concept   Your perception of your personal identity.

TABLE 5–3   WHO IS THAT BABY IN THE MIRROR?

At 9 months, an infant studies "that baby" in the mirror. At about 18 months, infants make the amazing discovery of an independent self.

During the first 2 years, infants make giant leaps in self-knowledge. From experiments involving infants of various ages looking at themselves in the mirror, it appears that self-knowledge develops in the following stages:

Before 8 months: Infants appear to be attracted to the image of an infant in the mirror, but it is unclear whether they recognize it as their own image. Sometimes infants 6–8 months old will recognize that their own movements correspond with the movements they observe in the mirror.

Between 8 and 16 months: Infants can tell the difference between their own image and the images of others who are clearly different from themselves, such as an older child. During this period infants begin to associate specific features with their sense of self. Nevertheless, an infant will sometimes crawl around the mirror to try to find the "other" baby. If a researcher puts a dot of red rouge on the infant's nose, the infant notices it but points to the nose in the mirror and not to his or her own nose.

At about 18 months: Toddlers no longer need environmental clues to make the connection between the baby in the mirror and themselves. That is, they recognize that the image they see is their own image. Now, if the researcher puts a dot of red rouge on the toddler's nose, there is a classic reaction. The infant points to her own nose, turns her head away from the mirror, drops her eyes, smiles, and looks embarrassed.

By age 2: Self-knowledge expands to include awareness of activities as well as appearance. A 2-year-old who preens in front of a mirror is engaging in a self-admiring activity (Cicchetti, D., & Beeghly, 1990).

Source: Lewis and Brooks-Gunn (1979).

understanding of social rules along with a sense of self. That is, the infant must be able to determine how personal behavior compares with the standards set by the culture, along with whether she or he is succeeding or failing at meeting those standards.

Awareness of sex roles begins to develop at around 21 months (Goldberg & Lewis, 1969). Girls and boys begin to exhibit gender-specific behaviors. Boys are likely to disengage themselves from their mothers, whereas girls seek greater closeness to them and have more ambivalent feelings about being separate. This behavior seems to be linked to awareness of gender differences.

By the end of the second year, children's language is filled with references to themselves. Children know their names and use them, often describing their needs and feelings in the third person: "Terri wants water." The words "me" and "mine" take on new significance, and the concept of ownership is clearly and strongly acted out. Even in families that emphasize sharing and minimize ownership, toddlers can be extremely possessive. It may be that they develop the concept of ownership in rounding out their understanding of self.

STUDY CHART ▸ SELECTED FACTORS IN PERSONALITY DEVELOPMENT
OVER THE FIRST TWO YEARS OF LIFE

Temperament:	At birth, children display behavioral styles that can influence how their parents react to and care for them, in turn reciprocally influencing the children's personality development. Some infants are *easy*, some are *difficult*, and some are *slow to warm up*.
Attachment:	Responsive caregiving fosters *securely attached* infants who later are highly curious, sociable, independent, and competent during the preschool years. Unresponsive or indifferent caregiving fosters *insecurely attached* infants who later are less enthusiastic, persistent, and cooperative compared with securely attached infants.
Neglect and abuse:	Infants and toddlers who suffer neglect and physical abuse experience distortions and delays in developing a sense of self and self-control, as well as social skills. As adolescents and adults, they are more inclined toward mental disorders and alcohol or other drug abuse and may become child abusers themselves.
Siblings:	In addition to parents, older siblings are often attachment objects for infants and toddlers, and they can serve as important role models. On the positive side, young children learn to share, cooperate, and emphathize by observing their older siblings. On the negative side, sibling rivalry may disrupt the family, and older siblings may model undesirable behaviors for young children.
Social referencing:	Personality development and behavior are strongly influenced by emotional and other signals that parents provide for their children in social situations. Cultural values and meanings are also conveyed through social referencing.
Parental discipline:	Especially during toddlerhood, how parents balance the child's attempts at autonomy with necessary discipline and limits is important. Either extreme—placing too few or too many limits—can interfere with healthy personality development.
Self-concept:	Personality revolves around a sense of self or personal identity. Children and adults tend to behave in ways that are consistent with their self-concept, which is based in part on gender, physical abilities, and physical appearance. In turn, even young children reflect on matters such as whether they are good or bad, how others view them, and whether they are acceptable, competent human beings, in forming their self-concept.

Logically, sharing and cooperation come more easily once toddlers are confident about what is theirs.

In sum, self-awareness is a function of self-exploration, cognitive maturation, and reflections about self. Toddlers can frequently be heard talking to and admonishing themselves ("No, Lee, don't touch") or rewarding themselves ("Me good girl!"). They incorporate cultural and social expectations into their reflections as well as into their behavior, and they begin to judge themselves and others in light of these expectations. If they enjoy consistent, loving interaction with the caregiver in an environment that they are free to explore and can begin to control, they learn to make valid predictions about the world around them. Gradually they develop a perception of self—hopefully as acceptable, competent individuals.

REVIEW & APPLY

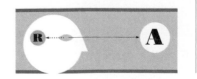

1. Describe how child-rearing practices with regard to social and personality development vary in different cultures, and explain how different practices might influence personality development.
2. Explain the process of social referencing.
3. Summarize stages and issues in the development of self.

PARENTAL EMPLOYMENT

In exploring the implications of parental employment, we often refer to the employment of mothers. The reason is simple: Traditionally the mother has had the primary responsibility for caregiving. However, an increasing number of fathers are taking on this responsibility. They may do so for a variety of reasons, including a divorce that grants them custody of the children, the illness or death of the mother, a situation in which the mother can earn more money to support the family, and the recognition that the father can be an effective, nurturing parent.

THE SOCIAL ECOLOGY OF CHILD CARE

The *social ecology* of child care refers to the environment in which child care takes place, including government policy and support, community approval or disapproval, and cost. Not unexpectedly, the social ecology of child care differs from one country to another. In Sweden, for example, 85% of mothers with children under school age work part-time or full-time outside the home. As a result, there is an enormous need for child care, which is met by a publicly funded child-care system (Andersson, 1989; Hwang & Broberg, 1992). Child care is provided for every family that requests it. There are day-care centers as well as family-based day-care providers, called *day mothers.* Both the day-care centers and the day mothers are licensed and regulated. There is also a system of open preschools where mothers or day mothers may take children to play with other children and receive advice and support.

In comparison, parents in the United States receive little public support. They are financially responsible for providing whatever supplemental child care they need and are assisted in this responsibility only if their income is low. Because about 60% of American mothers of infants and toddlers work outside the home, many families face the difficult task of finding suitable child care at an affordable price. (Figure 5–1 shows the percentages of working mothers with children under age 6 in selected years.)

About 3 out of 4 preschool children in the United States receive care from someone other than their parents. About 25% percent are enrolled in nursery school or center-based programs, and the remainder are cared for by relatives or other caregivers (see Figure 5–2). It is clear that American parents are willing to use both formal and informal child-care arrangements.

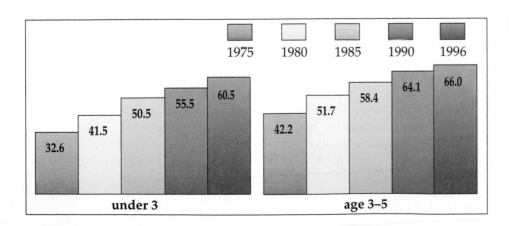

FIGURE 5–1   LABOR FORCE PARTICIPATION RATES FOR WIVES WITH HUSBAND PRESENT BY AGE OF YOUNGEST CHILD FROM 1975–1996

Source: U.S. Census Bureau, 1997.

FIGURE 5–2 CHILD-CARE
ARRANGEMENTS FOR
CHILDREN UNDER
5 YEARS OLD

*Source: Data from U.S. Census Bureau,
(1995).*

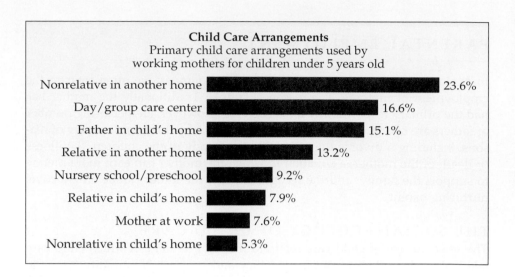

Child Care Arrangements
Primary child care arrangements used by
working mothers for children under 5 years old

Arrangement	Percentage
Nonrelative in another home	23.6%
Day/group care center	16.6%
Father in child's home	15.1%
Relative in another home	13.2%
Nursery school/preschool	9.2%
Relative in child's home	7.9%
Mother at work	7.6%
Nonrelative in child's home	5.3%

INFANT DAY CARE

Swedish employers must provide 9 months of parental leave (Welles-Nystrom, 1988). In the United States, under the current Family and Medical Leave Act, employers must provide only 12 weeks, beginning at childbirth. Mothers (or fathers who take on the primary caregiving role) who return to work after only 12 weeks must arrange for the safe and reliable supervision of their children. Some hire a relative or friend or used an unlicensed "sitter" from their neighborhood. Others seek licensed, high-quality day-care centers, which can be expensive and often have waiting lists. Still others seek local "family" day-care homes, which may or may not employ adequately trained personnel.

Both family day-care homes and well-run day-care centers are capable of fostering normal development in infants and toddlers. Several studies have shown that children ranging in age from 3 to 30 months developed at least as well in a group-care situation as children from similar backgrounds who were reared at home (Clarke-Stewart, 1982; Kagan, 1978; Keister, 1970; National Institute of Child Heath and Human Development, 1997). In contrast, however, in Sweden children who begin day care before age 1 are generally rated more favorably and perform better in elementary school than children who are reared at home by parents. They are more competent in cognitive tests of reasoning and vocabulary, and they are rated by teachers as better in school subjects like reading and arithmetic and as more socially competent than their home-reared peers (Andersson, 1989). Some researchers in the United States find similar but smaller positive effects on cognitive or social development for children in early group care (Clarke-Stewart & Fein, 1983); however, first-year nonparental care remains controversial (see "A Matter for Debate," page 195).

The day-care services available to many American families are not ideal, however. Staff members are often poorly trained and poorly paid, and staff turnover rates are high. Such facilities rarely admit researchers, but one study (Vandell & Corasaniti, 1990) was able to assess third-graders in an area characterized by poor-quality day care. The children who had been in day care displayed highly significant and pervasive negative effects compared with children reared at home: Extensive day care was associated with lower ratings on peer relations, work habits, and emotional health, and lower scores on standardized tests. The day-care children also earned lower grades in school. Some had serious behavior problems, including extreme aggressiveness. It is not

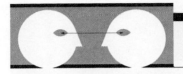

A MATTER FOR DEBATE

EARLY INFANT DAY CARE

In the mid-1980s, Jay Belsky published a startling warning to parents and infant-care professionals. After reviewing studies that compared children who had begun day care in their first year with children who started later, he cautiously concluded that entry into day care during the first year is a "risk factor" for the development of insecure attachments in infancy and increased aggressiveness, noncompliance, and withdrawal in preschool and later (Belsky, 1986).

The report drew immediate and intense reactions from many researchers, day-care workers, and parents. If it were true that infants are at risk when both parents work and place their infants in early alternative care, there were serious implications for all concerned. Clearly, the lifestyle of dual-income parents was being challenged. Some day-care workers felt personally insulted, although a few suggested that the possibility of harm due to less than ideal day-care arrangements deserved closer scrutiny (Fitzcharles, 1987; Miringoff, 1987). Other experts warned of a hasty conclusion drawn from diverse studies conducted under a variety of circumstances (Chess, 1987).

Before the 1980s, Belsky noted, virtually all research was done in high-quality, research-oriented centers that were often affiliated with universities. As a result, there was little evidence to suggest that nonparental care was a problem. In fact, infants in high-quality centers tended to show better social, cognitive, and emotional development than home-reared infants. But recently researchers have studied infants in a wide range of nonparental care arrangements of varying quality. In addition, a more representative cross section of families was studied, including single-parent families, families at risk for abuse or neglect, and dual-parent families at all socioeconomic levels.

When Belsky looked closely at such studies as well as at his own, he found disturbing commonalities. Among children who had nonparental care starting in the first year and for more than 20 hours per week, more were insecurely attached to their mothers—even when the nonparental caregiver was a neighbor or relative at home with her own child. The proportion of infants who were insecurely attached was nearly double (Belsky, 1986; Belsky & Rovine, 1988, 1990b).

Other researchers have reached different conclusions from the same studies. The quality of alternative care, for example, appears to be more important than the number of hours spent in the alternative care setting. Infants who receive low-quality care or who experience changes in their primary caregiver are particularly vulnerable. Also, when families that are under stress place their infants in a low-quality care arrangement, the risk to the child's well-being is greater (Phillips et al., 1987).

Finally, a recent large-scale study by the National Institute of Child Health and Human Development (NICHD) (1997) concluded that age of entry into day care and amount of day care *by themselves* were not good predictors of quality of attachment. The NICHD researchers did find, however, that low maternal responsiveness and sensitivity in combination with poor quality day care or extensive day care were associated with insecure attachment. Relatedly, in an extensive review of the literature on nonparental child care, Michael Lamb (1996) concluded that the quality of the care as well as the age and temperament of individual children are important factors to consider.

Thus, the picture is a complex one—more so than Belsky's research implied—that will undoubtedly continue to be a matter for debate.

possible to determine conclusively whether the infant care interrupted the mother-infant attachment and caused these problem behaviors.

Other research indicates that how infants fare in day care is influenced by their gender, the family's economic status, and the quality of care that the infant receives. Poor children seem to do better when cared for by their mothers or grandmothers, whereas in more affluent families, girls do better with babysitters and boys do better with their mothers (Baydar & Brooks-Gunn, 1991). Other studies suggest that the timing of the mother's return to work is crucial. When a mother resumes working before her child's first birthday, the child later tends to do less well on cognitive and behavioral measures than children whose mothers waited until after that age. Other studies have found that children whose mothers return to work almost immediately, exhibit less negative effects than children whose mothers return to work during the second quarter of the first year (Baydar & Brooks-Gunn, 1991; Field, 1991). Obviously, further research is needed to unscramble the effects of early day care.

The day care services available to many families are not ideal, like this overcrowded infant center.

TWO CHILD-CARE ADAPTATION MODELS   What is it that causes trouble for some infants who receive nonparental care after the first year? Researchers suggest two models of adaptation (Jaeger & Weinraub, 1990). According to the *maternal separation model*, the infant experiences daily, repeated separations from the mother as either maternal absence or maternal rejection. The infant begins to doubt the mother's availability or responsiveness. It is the absence of the mother that leads to insecurity.

In the *quality of mothering model*, it is not maternal employment or separation per se that determines the infant's reactions. Instead, the key factor is how maternal employment affects maternal behavior. The employed mother can't be as sensitive and responsive a caregiver as she might be if she had more time and practice, and the result is insecurity in the infant. Current research based on the quality-of-mothering model focuses on the competing demands of the mother's work and family, the quality of the child care (and whether she has to worry about it), the characteristics of the infant, and whether the mother thinks her infant is sturdy and capable of coping with the situation. Researchers are also examining the general quality of the mother's life and the satisfaction she experiences in her various roles, as well as any role conflict, marital strain, and fatigue she may experience. If the mother feels strong separation anxiety when she leaves her child each day, the child tends not to do well (McBride, 1990; Stifter, Coulehan, & Fish, 1993).

REVIEW & APPLY

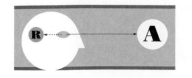

1. Discuss why early infant day care is controversial.
2. Contrast day care in Sweden with that in the United States.
3. Contrast Jaeger and Weinraub's two child-care adaptation models.

SUMMARY

Social and Emotional Development in Infancy

- Researchers have identified six stages in the emotional development of the infant and preschool child.
- Attachment behaviors are those that primarily promote nearness to a specific person. Both infant and caregiver must behave in ways that foster attachment.
- According to Bowlby, human babies are born with preprogrammed behaviors that function to keep their parents close by and responsive.
- The attachment behaviors of both mother and infant evolve gradually and reciprocally.
- Stranger anxiety and separation anxiety appear at about 7 months. At that time, babies suddenly become shy and wary of strangers and upset by being left alone.
- According to the discrepancy hypothesis, infants experience anxiety when they become capable of detecting departures from the known or the expected.
- Infants are also affected by social referencing, or emotional signaling by the mother.

Patterns of Early Relationships

- In Western cultures attachment usually develops between the infant and a single primary caregiver, usually the mother. In other cultures the primary relationship may be supplemented by other relationships.
- The Ainsworth strange situation test is used to assess the quality of infant attachment to the primary caregiver.
- Securely attached infants can separate themselves fairly easily from their mother and go exploring in the room, even when a stranger is present.
- Insecure attachment takes two forms. In one, the child becomes angry when the mother leaves, and then avoids the mother when she returns. In the other, the child responds to the mother ambivalently, simultaneously seeking and rejecting affection.
- Mothers who are more verbally responsive and attentive to their children tend to have children who are more autonomous and communicative.
- By monitoring the baby's responses, caregivers gradually learn when the child is most receptive to new cues. The closer the similarity between maternal and infant behavior, the more attentive babies will be.

- The term *scaffolding* is used to describe the mother's or father's role in progressively structuring the parent-child interaction.
- Early mutuality and signaling lay the foundation for long-standing patterns of interaction.
- Research indicates that day care and multiple caregivers may have no adverse effects on attachment. Adjustment to day care is easiest for toddlers who have had some experience with other caregivers and have had a moderate degree of separation experience.
- Infants with failure-to-thrive syndrome are small and emaciated, appear sick, and are unable to digest food properly. The syndrome can occur as a result of malnutrition but often appears to be due to lack of affection and attention.
- Child abuse beginning in infancy results in insecure attachment and delays in the child's development of a sense of self and in language and cognitive development.
- When an infant cannot see, there is a danger that communication and mutuality will break down and that the caregiver will avoid the child. Caregivers can be trained to watch for and interpret infants' hand signals.
- When an infant cannot hear, communication may break down when the infant's responses do not meet parents' expetations. Parents of deaf children need special training and counseling.

Fathers, Siblings, and the Family System

- Fathers can be as responsive to infants as mothers, and infants can become as attached to their fathers as they are to their mothers.
- Fathers are more likely to hold infants during play and tend to be more physical and spontaneous.
- Fathers who become significant figures in their children's world become important positive role models.
- Most couples develop complementary infant care roles for the father and the mother.
- The birth of the first child can place profound stress on the marital relationship.
- Siblings form significnt and long-lasting attachments to each other beginning in infancy.
- Two negative aspects of sibling relationships are sibling rivalry and the dethroning of the older sibling.
- Grandparents frequently offer more approval, support, empathy, and sympathy, and use less discipline, than parents.

Personality Development in the Second Year

- According to Erikson, the development of trust marks the first stage of psychosocial development and occurs during the first year of life.
- A sense of trust is conveyed to the infant through the caregiver's nurturant behavior—that is, his or her responsiveness to the infant's needs.
- When infants are not sure whether a situation is safe, they often look to the parent for emotional signals. This behavior is known as emotional referencing.
- Through social referencing and selective attention, parents teach infants the values of their culture.
- Toward the end of the second year, toddlers experience increased emotional conflict between their greater need for autonomy and their obvious dependence and limited skills.
- Parental discipline must be tempered with common sense and must consider children's needs for safety, independence, and creative expression.
- Prosocial behaviors such as cooperation begin to develop between 18 and 24 months.
- At first, infants cannot differentiate between themselves and the world around them, but they gradually realize that they are separate and unique beings.

- Self-awareness is a function of self-exploration, cognitive maturation, and reflections about self.

Parental Employment

- The social ecology of child care refers to the environment within which child care takes place, including government policy and support, community approval or disapproval, and cost.
- Parents in the United States receive little public support, and statistics show that they are willing to use both formal and informal child-care arrangements.
- Both family day-care homes and well-run day-care centers are capable of fostering normal development in infants and toddlers.
- How infants fare in day care is influenced by their gender, the family's economic status, and the quality of care that the infant receives.
- According to the maternal separation model, the infant experiences daily, repeated separations from the mother as either maternal absence or maternal rejection. In the quality of mothering model, the infant is insecure because the employed mother cannot be as sensitive and responsive as she might otherwise be.

KEY TERMS

personality	discrepancy hypothesis	scaffolding
socialization	social referencing	failure-to-thrive syndrome
temperament	secure attachment	prosocial behavior
attachment	insecure attachment	self-concept
stranger anxiety	mutuality	
separation anxiety	interactive synchrony	

USING WHAT YOU'VE LEARNED

This exercise involves observing the emotional communication between parent and infant. You will need the cooperation of two infants and their parents. Ask family members or friends with infants for help.

Part I: Your first observation requires a 2- to 7-month-old infant and the infant's parent. Your goal is to reproduce the still-face experiment described in this chapter. As you observe the pair at play, ask yourself these questions: Who initiates the interactions? How does the infant signal that a pause is needed? How does the parent adjust to the infant's temperament and style?

Now ask the parent to put on a blank expression and not respond to the infant for a few minutes. What happens to the infant's behavior? If you observe any behavioral changes, what do you think they mean? What does the parent think they mean?

Part II: Observe an older infant or toddler at play with the parent, and then consider the following questions: Do you notice any social referencing and guided participation between parent and child? What forms do they take?

How does the parent structure the social situation?

How does the child react to subtle communications such as glances, smiles, and frowns? How does the child react to more intense communications like orders or commands?

Finally, how do your observations compare with the research findings reported in this chapter?

SUGGESTED READINGS

BOWLBY, J. (1988). *A secure base: Parent-child attachment and healthy human development.* New York: Basic Books. Bowlby's latest integration of his influential theory presented in a very readable style.

BRAZELTON, T. B. (1994). *Touchpoints: Your child's emotional and behavioral development.* Reading, MA: Addison-Wesley. The well-known pediatrician discusses 30 infant and early childhood problems, accompanied by the potential turning points in a young child's life.

BROTT, A. A. (1998). *The new father: A dad's guide to the toddler years.* New York: Abbeville Press. This handbook explores fatherhood during the second and third years. It incorporates the author's and other father's personal experiences, plus some of the top research in the area.

LIEBERMAN, A. (1995). *The emotional life of the toddler.* New York: Free Press. A splendid, easily under-standable book, based on observations of toddlers and their families, showing how each child discovers his or her own way of mastering the environment.

SPOCK, B., & ROTHENBERG, M. B. (1997). *Dr. Spock's baby and child care.* New York: Simon & Schuster Pocket Books. Benjamin Spock and a coauthor thoroughly revised Spock's classic guide to reflect the changing medical practices and cultural shifts of the 1980s in an earlier revision, less so those of the 1990s in this one. It remains a classic well worth reading nontheless.

ZIGLER, E. F., & LANG, M. E. (1991). *Child-care choices: Balancing the needs of children, families, and society.* New York: Free Press. A thorough overview of children's needs and a comprehensive look at current available child-care options in light of today's economic and social realities.

Preschool Children: Physical, Cognitive, and Language Development

CHAPTER

6

CHAPTER OBJECTIVES

By the time you have finished this chapter, you should be able to do the following:

1. Discuss the physical development of preschool children in terms of body size and proportion, skeletal maturation, and overall growth.
2. List the major aspects of brain development during the preschool years and their impact on motor skills.
3. Explain the major changes in gross and fine motor skills during early childhood.
4. Characterize preoperational thought according to Piaget, and then discuss limitations of Piaget's theory.
5. Analyze how the social perspective and information processing theories help explain cognitive development during the preschool years.
6. Describe how language develops in preschool children.
7. Explain the influence of caregivers on children's language development.
8. Describe the cultural and social values that children assimilate in the context of language development.
9. Discuss how subdialects and bilingualism raise important issues in language development.
10. Explain the major types of children's play and how they influence development.

As relative newcomers to our world, 2- to 6-year-olds often demonstrate their thinking in ways that are both amusing and thought provoking. Consider the following excerpt from *Winnie-the-Pooh*, which captures the preschool child's cognitive and social egocentrism—that is, the child's tendency to see and interpret things primarily from his or her own point of view:

> One day when he was out walking, he came to an open place in the middle of the forest, and in the middle of this place was a large oak-tree, and, from the top of the tree, there came a loud buzzing-noise.
>
> Winnie-the-Pooh sat down at the foot of the tree, put his head between his paws and began to think.
>
> First of all he said to himself: "That buzzing-noise means something. You don't get a buzzing-noise like that, just buzzing and buzzing, without its meaning something. If there's a buzzing-noise, somebody's making a buzzing noise, and the only reason for making a buzzing-noise that *I* know of is because you're a bee."
>
> Then he thought another long time, and said: "And the only reason for being a bee that I know of is making honey."
>
> And then he got up, and said: "And the only reason for making honey is so as *I* can eat it." So he began to climb the tree.
>
> He climbed and he climbed and he climbed, and as he climbed he sang a little song to himself. It went like this:
>
> "Isn't it funny
> How a bear likes honey?

Buzz! Buzz! Buzz!
I wonder why he does?"

A. A. Milne (1926/1961), pages 5–7

Winnie-the-Pooh: The essence of a preschool child.

Such attitudes reveal a great deal about children. Preschool children's errors indicate that there's an enormous distance to be covered between the ages of 2 and 6 in developing the thought processes necessary for formal schooling. Young children gradually develop into concept-forming, linguistically competent realists (Fraiberg, 1959). They discover what they can and cannot control. They generalize from experience. Their reasoning changes from forming simple concepts to using the beginnings of logic.

They also acquire the language necessary to express their needs, thoughts, and feelings. Preschoolers' language develops rapidly in interaction with cognitive and social development. Younger preschool children manage with two- or three-word sentences based on their limited and at times idiosyncratic grammar; 6-year-olds speak in complete sentences with essentially correct grammatical structure. As preschoolers learn syntax and vocabulary, they also absorb culturally appropriate social values such as politeness, obedience, and gender roles. Thus, language is a bridge between infancy and childhood: Children come to understand and communicate their wants, needs, and observations, and others respond to them accordingly.

Accompanying cognitive and linguistic development are rapid and dramatic changes in children's appearance and physical competence. Chubby toddlers with large heads and short limbs become slimmer 6-year-olds with smoother coordination and increased strength. Children refine their ability to skip and run, and develop the fine motor skills they need to write the alphabet, button a sweater, or place puzzle pieces in the right places.

The developmental strides that preschool children make in thinking, language, and motor skills are interrelated. As children become physically stronger and more capable, they are motivated to use their developing skills to explore and learn. Exploration leads to further skill development. Thus, the ways in which children behave and think form an integrated system (Thelen, 1989).

PHYSICAL AND MOTOR DEVELOPMENT

Between the ages of 2 and 6, a child's body loses the look of infancy as it changes in size, body proportions, and shape. At the same time, rapid brain development leads to more sophisticated and complex learning abilities and refinement of gross and fine motor skills.

BODY SIZE AND PROPORTIONS

A visit to a pediatrician's office often includes an evaluation of the child's height and weight. Although children vary considerably, extreme deviations from the average for a given age can indicate developmental problems. Developmental psychologists not only share the pediatrician's interest in the physiological aspects of growth but also focus on the relationship between growth and the acquisition of new skills.

It cannot be overemphasized that generalized statements about growth may or may not apply to individual children. Each child's physical growth is the result of genetics, nutrition, and the opportunity to play and exercise. The relationship between nutrition and growth is demonstrated by the physical differences between children in developed and developing nations. For example, because a significant number of children in Bangladesh are malnourished, the average 6-year-old in Bangladesh is only as tall as the average 4-year-old in Sweden (Eveleth & Tanner, 1976; United Nations, 1991). As we saw in Chapter 3, prolonged deprivation of essential nutrients can have pronounced effects on children's physical and motor development.

Sustained periods of malnutrition during early childhood limit children's cognitive development both directly and indirectly (Brown & Pollitt, 1996). As the authors point out, the situation is much more complex than a simple malnutrion, then brain damage, then delayed cognitive development scenario. Malnutrition does directly produce brain damage that is sometimes reversible, sometimes not. At the same time, however, it sets off a dynamic and reciprocal process in which, for example, the child becomes lethargic and only minimally explores and learns from the environment—thus interfering with cognitive development. Malnutrition also produces delayed physical growth and development of motor skills that feed into lowered parental expectations and, in turn, delayed cognitive development.

BODY PROPORTIONS Throughout childhood, body proportions change dramatically, as shown in Figure 6–1. For example, at birth, the head comprises one-quarter of overall body length. By age 16, the head has doubled in size, but now it accounts for only one-eighth of body length. Elongation of the lower body and legs accelerates as children begin to lose the "baby fat" associated with infancy and toddlerhood. From age 2 to age 6, the rate of growth slows compared with the first two years of life. Healthy preschool children may grow in spurts but gain an average of $4\frac{1}{2}$ pounds (2 kilograms) per year and grow almost 3 inches (7.6 centimeters) taller each year. As with other aspects of physical development, however, it's important to remember that children vary widely in growth rates and gains during the preschool period, and parents should not attempt to "accelerate" growth through overfeeding or overexercising their children.

In young children the center of gravity is higher than in adults; children carry a greater proportion of their weight in their upper body. Being top-heavy makes it more difficult to control the body. Preschool children lose their

FIGURE 6–1 CHANGING BODY PROPORTIONS IN GIRLS AND BOYS FROM BIRTH TO MATURITY

Source: Nichols, B. (1990). Moving and learning: The elementary school physical education experience. *St. Louis, MO: Times Mirror/Mosby College Publishing.*

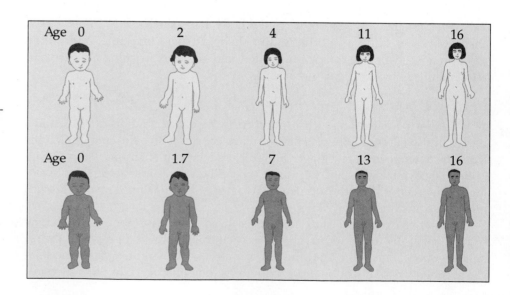

balance more easily and have difficulty coming to a quick stop without tipping forward. It is also hard for them to catch a large ball without falling backward (Nichols, 1990). The center of gravity gradually descends to the pelvic area as body proportions continue to change.

SKELETAL MATURATION   As the skeletal system matures, bones develop and harden through *ossification*, in which soft tissue or cartilage is transformed into bone. *Skeletal age* is determined by bone maturation and can be measured by X-rays of the wrist bones. Skeletal age may vary by as much as 2 years in either direction with respect to chronological age. For example, the skeletal age of a 6-year-old may range from 4 to 8 years (Nichols, 1990).

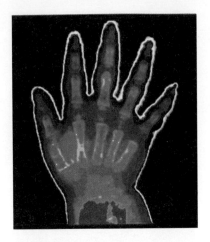

X-ray of a 2-year-old's hand and wrist.

BRAIN DEVELOPMENT

Rapid changes in body size and proportion are obvious signs of growth, but unseen changes are also taking place in the brain. By age 5, a child's brain is nearly the size of an adult's. Brain development makes possible increasingly complex learning, problem solving, and language use; in turn, sensory-perceptual and motor activity create and strengthen neural connections. The myriad neural connections that are formed throughout the lifespan are the physical basis of learning, memory, and knowledge in general.

Neurons—the specialized cells that make up the nervous system—began forming during the embryonic period, and by birth nearly all of the perhaps 200 billion neurons that make up the adult human brain are present. **Glial cells**, which insulate the neurons and improve the efficiency of transmission of neural impulses, continue to grow rapidly throughout the second year. Rapid growth in the size of neurons, the number of glial cells, and the complexity of neural interconnections produce a *brain growth spurt* during infancy and toddlerhood, which continues (although at a slower rate) into the early preschool period. In many respects, the brain growth spurt is a "window of opportunity" for brain development as a result of experience. The brain growth spurt is also a period of considerable plasticity, during which children can more readily recover from brain injury than at later ages; also, plasticity does continue to an extent into adulthood (Nelson & Bloom, 1997).

Maturation of the brain and central nervous system includes **myelination**—the formation of sheathing cells that "insulate" the neurons and make transmission of neural impulses much more efficient (Cratty, 1986). Myelination of neurons for motor reflexes and vision begins in early infancy. It is followed by myelination of neurons for the complex motor activities and then those controlling eye-hand coordination, attention span, memory, and self-control. Myelination of the central nervous system closely parallels the development of cognitive and motor abilities during the preschool years.

Two aspects of brain development during early childhood are of particular interest to psychologists: *lateralization* and *hand preference*.

LATERALIZATION   The surface of the brain, or *cortex* (Latin for "bark"), is divided into two cerebral hemispheres—the left and the right. In processing information and controlling behavior, the hemispheres specialize to some extent; this process is called **lateralization**. In the 1960s, Roger Sperry and colleagues verified the presence of lateralization by studying the effects of surgery designed to reduce major epileptic seizures. They found that severing the neural tissue that connects the two hemispheres (the *corpus callosum*) could reduce seizures while leaving intact most abilities needed for daily functioning, although it did create a person with two largely independent hemispheres that

neurons   The cells that make up the nervous system. They form prenatally and continue to grow and branch throughout life.

glial cells   Cells that insulate the neurons and improve efficiency of transmission of nerve impulses.

myelination   The formation of the myelin sheath covering the fast-acting central nervous system pathways. This sheath increases the speed of transmission and the precision of the nervous system.

lateralization   The process whereby specific skills and competencies become localized in particular hemispheres of the brain.

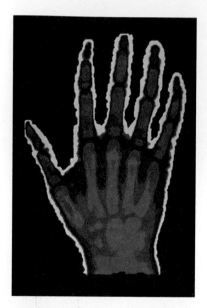

X-ray of a 6-year-old's hand and wrist. Note the greater degree of ossification in the older child's bones.

couldn't communicate with each other (Sperry, 1970). Nowadays, seizure-related surgery is much more specific and refined.

The left hemisphere controls motor behavior for the right side of the body, and the right hemisphere controls the left side (Cratty, 1986; Hellige, 1993). In some aspects of functioning, however, one hemisphere may be more active. Figure 6–2 illustrates some of these functions for a right-handed person; in left-handed people, some functions may be reversed. Bear in mind, however, that in normal people the *entire* brain is involved in most functioning (Hellige, 1993). Lateralized (or otherwise specialized) functions simply indicate the degree of activity; the brain always functions as a whole.

Taking into account how children's skills develop, it is not surprising that the hemispheres develop at different rates (Thatcher et al., 1987). For example, language develops very rapidly from age 3 to age 6, and the left hemisphere shows accelerated growth during that period. In contrast, the right hemisphere matures more slowly during early childhood; its growth accelerates during middle childhood. Lateral specialization continues throughout childhood and into adolescence.

HANDEDNESS Researchers have long been intrigued by right- or left-hand preference, which is a function of lateralization. The majority of people are right-handed and therefore display strong left-hemisphere dominance. Even when a strong preference exists, however, young children can learn to use their nonfavored hand—a flexibility that decreases with age. Research on hemisphere dominance indicates that for the majority of right-handed people, language is highly localized in areas of the left hemisphere. For the remaining 10% of the population who are left-handed, language is often shared by the two sides of the brain, suggesting that the brains of left-handed people may be

FIGURE 6–2
THE FUNCTIONS OF THE RIGHT AND LEFT CEREBRAL HEMISPHERES

Source: Shea, C. H., Shebilske, W. L., and Worchel, S. (1993). Motor learning and control. Englewood Cliffs, NJ: Prentice-Hall, p. 38.

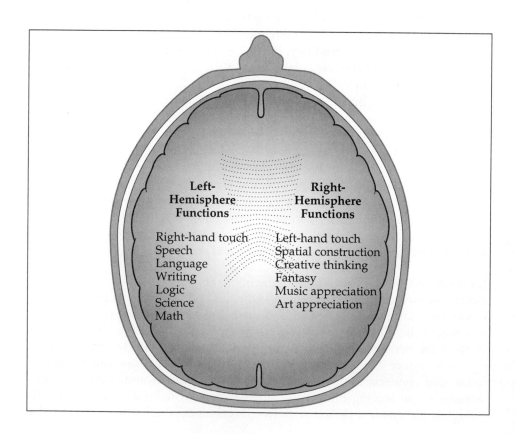

less lateralized in general (Hiscock & Kinsbourne, 1987). Additional evidence is provided by the observation that left-handed people are more likely to be *ambidextrous*—capable of using either hand with good coordination and fine motor skills.

In most children, handedness is established by early to middle childhood (Gesell & Ames, 1947). In addition to brain maturation, hand preference may reflect pressures by parents and teachers toward use of the "socially preferable" right hand (Coren and Porac, 1980). The prevailing opinion, however, is that hand preference should be allowed to develop naturally, without coercion.

The majority of 3- to 5-year-olds also shows a well-established foot preference that is further refined during middle childhood. Researchers suggest that since "footedness" is less socially influenced than handedness—parents may force a left-handed child to be right-handed—failure to develop foot preference may actually be a more sensitive indicator of developmental delays associated with establishing preference (Bradshaw, 1989; Gabbard et al., 1991).

DEVELOPING MOTOR SKILLS

Children's motor skills improve markedly during the preschool years (Clark & Phillips, 1985). The most dramatic changes are in gross motor skills such as running, hopping, and throwing. In contrast, fine motor skills such as writing and handling eating utensils develop more slowly.

However, distinguishing perceptual-motor development from overall cognitive development is difficult. Almost everything a child does during the early years of life involves interaction between the two, along with social and emotional development. For example, when a preschooler walks on a log, the child not only learns how to balance but also experiences the cognitive concept "narrow" and the emotional concept "confidence." Although much of what preschool children do appears to be sheer sensory exploration, children's actions are usually purposeful and directed toward goals (von Hofsten, 1989).

Some developmental sequences involve what's called **functional subordination.** Actions that are initially performed for their own sake later become integrated into more complex, purposeful skills. A child's early markings with crayon and paper, for example, are an end in themselves. Later, putting marks on paper becomes functionally subordinate to more complex skills such as writing and creating designs.

The roots of complex behavior and thought are not always as obvious. We'll return to that issue after we survey gross and fine motor development during the preschool period. Table 6–1 summarizes the major motor developmental achievements of the preschool years. Again, note that the age designations are strictly averages; individual children can vary considerably from these norms.

GROSS MOTOR SKILLS   Compared with infants, 2-year-olds are amazingly competent, but they still have a long way to go. They can walk and run, but they're still relatively short and round. They walk with a wide stance and a swaying gait. Toddlers also tend to use both arms (or legs) when only one is necessary (Woodcock, 1941). When handed a cookie, for example, a 2-year-old is likely to extend both hands.

By age 3, children's legs stay closer together during walking and running, and the children no longer need to pay attention to what their legs and feet are doing (Cratty, 1970). Thus, their gross motor behavior is showing signs of **automaticity**—the ability to perform motor behaviors without consciously thinking about them (Shiffrin & Schneider, 1977). Three-year-olds run, turn, and

functional subordination   The integration of a number of separate simple actions or schemes into a more complex pattern of behavior.

automaticity   Performing well-practiced motor behaviors without having to think about them consciously.

TABLE 6–1 MOTOR DEVELOPMENT OF PRESCHOOL CHILDREN

2-YEAR-OLDS	3-YEAR-OLDS	4-YEAR-OLDS	5-YEAR-OLDS
Walk with wide stance and body sway.	Keep legs closer together when walking and running.	Can vary rhythm of running.	Can walk a balance beam.
Can climb, push, pull, run, hang by both hands.	Can run and move more smoothly.	Skip awkwardly; jump.	Skip smoothly; stand on one foot.
Have little endurance.	Reach for objects with one hand.	Have greater strength, endurance, and coordination.	Can manage buttons and zippers; may tie shoelaces.
Reach for objects with two hands.	Smear and daub paint; stack blocks.	Draw shapes and simple figures; make paintings; use blocks for buildings.	Use utensils and tools correctly.

The gait of 2-year-olds is characterized by a wide stance and a body sway. They love to walk and run but have little endurance. In contrast, the legs of 3-year-olds stay closer together when they run.

stop more smoothly than 2-year-olds do, although their ankles and wrists are not as flexible as they will be by age 4 or 5 (Woodcock, 1941). They are also more likely to extend only the preferred hand to receive an object such as a cookie.

By age 4, children can vary the rhythm of their running. Many 4-year-olds can also skip (though awkwardly) and execute a running jump or a standing broad jump; 5-year-olds can skip smoothly, walk along a balance beam confidently, stand on one foot for several seconds, and imitate dance steps (Gesell, 1940). Many 5-year-olds can throw a ball overhead and catch a large ball thrown to them (Cratty, 1970), although such skills continue to be refined over the next several years (Robertson, 1984).

Whereas 3-year-olds may push a doll carriage or a large truck for the fun of pushing it, 4-year-olds functionally subordinate their pushing to fantasy play or games, although they may continue to perform some motor activity for its own sake.

Children's overall activity level peaks between the ages of 2 and 3, gradually declining in the remaining preschool years. The decline is earlier for girls than for boys, which is why boys may have more trouble sitting still in kindergarten than girls (Eaton & Yu, 1989).

FINE MOTOR SKILLS Fine motor skills require the coordinated and dexterous use of hand, fingers, and thumb. Abilities involving the hands and fingers result from a series of overlapping processes beginning before birth. (Recall, for example, how the infant's grasp reflex evolves into a voluntary grasp and then a pincer grasp.) Near the end of the third year, new manual abilities emerge as the child begins to integrate and coordinate manual schemes with other motor, perceptual, or verbal behaviors. Fine motor skills also begin to display automaticity. For example, 4-year-olds can carry on a dinner conversation while successfully manipulating a fork (Cratty, 1986). Despite their increasing competence, however, preschoolers still have trouble with precise fine motor movements. This difficulty is linked to the immaturity of the child's central nervous system (myelination is still in progress) as well as to the child's limited patience and relatively short attention span.

As children gain fine motor skills, they become increasingly competent at taking care of themselves and carrying out their daily activities. From 2 to 3 years of age, for example, children can put on and remove simple items of clothing. They can handle large zippers and use a spoon effectively.

A 3- to 4-year-old child can fasten and unfasten large buttons and independently "serve" food—though sometimes making a mess while doing so. By the time children are 4 to 5 years old, they can dress and undress themselves without assistance and can use eating utensils well. Five- to 6-year-olds can tie a simple knot, and 6-year-olds can usually tie their own shoelaces—although many still find it difficult and may ask for help instead.

A preschool girl concentrates on tying her shoelaces.

LEARNING AND MOTOR SKILLS The first motor skills that preschool children begin to learn are usually everyday actions such as tying shoes, cutting with scissors, skipping, and jumping, although they won't master them until the end of the preschool period. Such skills increase the young child's ability to move around, perform self-care, and behave creatively. Some young children also learn more highly skilled activities, such as gymnastics, playing the piano, or even horseback riding.

Researchers have identified important conditions for motor learning. These include readiness, practice, attention, competence, motivation, and feedback.

Readiness is generally required for learning any new skill—cognitive or motor. A certain level of maturation and certain basic skills must be present before the child can profit from training. Although it can be difficult to know just when a child is "ready," American and Russian studies indicate that if children are introduced to new motor learning at the optimal point of readiness, they learn quickly and with little training or effort (Lisina & Neverovich, 1971). The children want to learn, enjoy the practice, and are excited about their performance. Children frequently give clues to the time when they have reached optimal readiness for a given skill: Watch for them to begin imitating the behavior on their own.

Practice is also essential to motor development. Children cannot master climbing stairs without actually climbing stairs. They can't learn to throw a ball unless they practice throwing. When children live in limited, restricted environments, their motor-skills development lags. Children who lack objects to play with, places to explore, tools to use, or people to imitate will have trouble developing motor skills. On the other hand, given a rich, active environment, children tend to pace their own learning appropriately. They imitate behaviors, often repeating them endlessly. They do things like repeatedly pouring water from one container to another to explore the concepts of "full" and "empty," "fast" and "slow." Such self-designed and self-paced schedules of learning are often more efficient than lessons programmed by adults (Karlson, 1972).

For a young child to learn a highly skilled activity like playing the piano, certain conditions have to be in place, including readiness, motivation, and attention.

Motor learning is also enhanced by *attention*, which requires an alert and engaged state of mind. How can children's attending be improved? Young children can't simply be told what to do and how to do it. Instead, 2- and 3-year-old children learn new motor skills most efficiently by being led through activities. Exercises and games can be used to teach them to move their arms and legs in special ways. Such techniques show that children between the ages of 3 and 5 focus their attention most effectively through active imitation. Only when children have reached age 6 or 7 can they can attend closely to verbal instructions and follow them reasonably well, at least while participating in familiar tasks and activities (Zaporozlets & Elkonin, 1971).

Competence motivation (White, 1959) is reflected in the observation that children often attempt things just to see whether they can do them, to perfect their skills, to test their muscles and abilities, and to enjoy how it all feels. Children run, jump, climb, and skip for the sheer pleasure and challenge of it. In other words, child often engage in **intrinsically motivated behavior,** behavior that is

intrinsically motivated behavior Behavior performed for its own sake, with no particular goal.

performed for its own sake, with no identifiable goal except perhaps competence and mastery. In contrast, **extrinsically motivated behavior** is performed to gain reinforcement.

Finally, the *feedback* children receive for their efforts helps them acquire and refine motor skills. Parents and peers tell them how well they're doing and encourage them to do more. Feedback can also come from the behavior itself. For example, when climbing a play ladder, children may derive pleasure from the tension in their muscles and from the experience of being up high and seeing things that are not visible from the ground. Parents and teachers can be particularly helpful by highlighting such internal feedback. Specific statements like "Now you have a strong grip on the bar" are more helpful than general praise such as "What a good job you're doing climbing that ladder."

REVIEW & APPLY

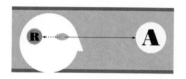

1. Describe the major physical changes in the preschool child's body as they relate to the child's growing sense of competence.
2. How does brain lateralization interact with physical and motor development?
3. Summarize key milestones in the development of preschool children's gross and fine motor skills, and describe the conditions necessary for the development of these skills.

COGNITIVE DEVELOPMENT

When we look at all the developmental changes that occur in the preschool child, it is often difficult to disentangle the contributions of increasing physical competence from those of cognitive development. Children often use their bodies as the testing ground for their developing intellectual skills.

Decades after Piaget's initial research, his theories still provide an important base for understanding cognitive development, although other theories challenge some of Piaget's conclusions about young children's cognitive abilities and the way they develop. We'll begin with Piaget's observations about the preschool period and then consider other perspectives.

AN OVERVIEW OF PREOPERATIONAL THINKING

Recall from Chapter 1 that Piaget described cognitive development in terms of discrete stages through which children progress on their way to understanding the world. According to Piaget, children actively construct a personal understanding. They build their own reality through experimentation; they are like little scientists working diligently to figure out how the world works. They explore their surroundings and comprehend new information on the basis of their current level and ways of understanding. When they encounter something familiar, they assimilate it. When they encounter something new, they accommodate their thinking to incorporate it.

During the *preoperational stage*, preschool children continue to expand their understanding of the world by using their growing language and problem-solving skills. According to Piaget, however, preschool children have not yet achieved the mental abilities necessary to understand logical operations and to interpret reality more fully. Such operations include cause and effect, percep-

extrinsically motivated behavior Behavior performed to obtain rewards or avoid aversive events.

tions of reality, time and space, and most concepts of number. These abilities will be acquired during the next stage—the *concrete operational stage*. The cognitive skills and understanding acquired during the preoperational stage lay the groundwork.

In Piaget's view, children enter the preoperational stage with only rudimentary language and thought abilities, and they leave it asking sophisticated questions such as "Where did Grandma go when she died?"

What is preoperational thinking like? Let's consider the question in conjunction with the dramatic cognitive advances that preschoolers make during this stage.

PREOPERATIONAL SUBSTAGES AND THOUGHT   The preoperational period lasts from age 2 to about age 7 and is divided into two parts—*the preconceptual period* (age 2 to about age 4) and the *intuitive or transitional period* (age 5 to age 7).

The preconceptual period is highlighted by increasing use and complexity of symbols and symbolic (pretend) play. Previously the child's thinking was limited to the immediate physical environment. Now symbols enable the child to think about things that are not immediately present. The child's thinking is more flexible (Siegler, 1991). Words now have the power to communicate, even in the absence of the things they name.

Preoperational children, however, still have difficulty with major categories of reality. They don't distinguish between mental, physical, and social reality. For example, their thinking displays *animism*: They may think that anything that moves is alive—the sun, the moon, clouds, an automobile or a train. They also display *reification*: Objects and people in their thoughts and dreams are real to them; they represent things as real as those actually present in the child's environment. Such approaches to thinking stem partly from another characteristic of preschool (and younger) children's thinking: **egocentrism.** This term refers to the child's tendency to see and understand things in terms of her or his personal point of view—very much like Winnie-the-Pooh at the beginning of the chapter. Preschool children are unable to separate the realm of personal existence from everything else (Siegler, 1991).

The intuitive, or transitional, period begins around age 5. The transitional child now begins to separate mental from physical reality and to understand causation apart from social norms. For example, before this stage, children may think that everything was created by their parents or some other adult. Now they begin to grasp the significance of other forces. Intuitive children understand multiple points of view and relational concepts, though in an inconsistent and incomplete way. Compared with older children, they are unable to perform many basic mental operations. Although rational thinking increases during this period, preschool children are also willing to use magical thinking to explain things. While 4- to 6-year-olds basically understand that an adult cannot be transformed into a child and that people can't pass through solid objects, the majority will change their opinion if an adult relates a fairy tale as if it were true (Subbotsky, 1994).

SYMBOLIC REPRESENTATION   The most dramatic cognitive difference between infants and 2-year-olds is in their use of *symbolic representation*. As defined in Chapter 4, this term refers to the use of actions, images, or words to represent objects and events. The difference can be seen most clearly in language development and symbolic play (Flavell et al., 1993). Two-year-olds can imitate past events, roles, and actions. A preschooler might use gestures to act out an extensive sequence of events such as a car ride. Given props, preschool-

egocentrism   A self-centered view of the world, perceiving everything in relation to yourself.

Preschoolers develop the ability to use symbols to represent actions, events, and objects—one of the milestones in cognitive development. This young businesswoman is reading her newspaper during her commute to work.

ers may act out a family dinner or imitate a mean baby-sitter or enact a story from a favorite book.

The ability to employ numbers to represent quantity is another use of symbolic representation. Still another is the acquisition of skills in drawing and artistic representation, which begins during the preoperational stage.

How does symbolic representation develop? Donald Marzoff and Judy De-Loache (1994) performed a series of experiments on preschool children's understanding of spatial representations. They found that early experiences with symbolic relations contribute to the child's readiness to recognize that one object may stand for another. One study (DeLoache, 1987) found that children's understanding of some symbolic relationships occurs fairly suddenly. For example, although $2\frac{1}{2}$-year-olds do not understand the relationship between a scale model of a room and the actual room that it represents, 3-year-olds easily see the connection. The younger child's failure may involve inability to understand that a scale model is *both* an object and a symbol of something else.

Although symbolic representation starts at the end of the sensorimotor period, it continues to be refined; a child is much better at symbolization at age 4 than at age 2. In one experiment (Elder & Pederson, 1978), researchers found that the younger children—$2\frac{1}{2}$-year-olds—needed props similar to real objects for their pretend games. In contrast, $3\frac{1}{2}$-year-olds could represent objects with quite different props or could act out a situation without props. They could pretend that a hairbrush was a pitcher or even pretend to use a pitcher with no props at all, whereas $2\frac{1}{2}$-year-olds could not.

Thought processes become more complex with the use of symbols (Piaget, 1950, 1951). Children show that they perceive similarities between two objects by giving the objects the same name. They become aware of the past and form expectations for the future. They distinguish between themselves and the person they are addressing. Symbolic representation may help children in other ways as well (Fein, 1981): It may help them become more sensitive to the feelings and viewpoints of others. That sensitivity, in turn, helps the child make the transition to less egocentric and more *sociocentric* thinking. Such socially oriented thought, however, requires many more years to mature.

LIMITATIONS ON PREOPERATIONAL THINKING

In spite of the development of symbolic representation, preoperational children have a long way to go before they are logical thinkers. Their thought processes are limited in many ways, as evidenced by observations of their behavior and especially by experiments designed to test the limits of their thinking. The limitations on children's thinking include concreteness, irreversibility, egocentrism, centration, and difficulties with concepts of time, space, and sequence.

CONCRETENESS The thinking of preschool children is *concrete*. Preoperational children can't deal well with abstractions. They are concerned with the here-and-now and with physical things that they can easily represent mentally.

IRREVERSIBILITY Young children's thinking is *irreversible*. That is, children see events as occurring in only one direction. Preoperational children cannot imagine how things might return to their original state or how relationships can exist in two directions. Consider the following example: A 3-year-old girl is asked, "Do you have a sister?" She says, "Yes." "What's her name?" "Jessica." "Does Jessica have a sister?" "No." Here, the relationship is solely one way; the younger girl knows that she has a sister but does not yet recognize that she is Jessica's sister.

EGOCENTRISM As noted earlier, preoperational children's thought is egocentric and centered on their own perspective, so that it's hard for them to take another person's point of view. Preoperational children concentrate on their own perceptions and assume that everyone else's outlook is the same as theirs. Piaget (1954) used the "mountains problem" illustrated in Figure 6–3 to study children's egocentrism. The child sits at one side of a table that has a plaster model of a mountain range on it. The child is shown pictures taken from the four possible views of the model—the child's and the three other seats at the table. When asked to select a picture that corresponds to their own view, most preschool children can easily do so. However, when asked to select the picture representing the view of a doll placed in one of the other seats, most children cannot.

CENTRATION Preoperational children's thought also tends to focus on only one aspect or dimension of an object or a situation to the exclusion of others. This limitation—called *centration*—can be seen in *class inclusion* problems. For example, when preoperational children are shown a collection of wooden beads, some red and some yellow, and asked whether there are more red beads or more wooden beads, they apparently cannot simultaneously consider what the color of the beads is and what the beads are made of.

TIME, SPACE, AND SEQUENCE A 3-year-old may be able to say, "Grandpa will come visit next week." Even 2-year-olds use words that seem to indicate a knowledge of time and space, such as "later," "tomorrow," "last night," "next time," and "far away." But a child of 2 or 3 apparently has very little appreciation of what the words really mean. "Noon" may mean lunchtime, but if lunchtime is delayed an hour, it is still noon to the child. Upon waking from a nap, a child may not even know whether it is the same day. Conceptualizing days, weeks, and months is difficult for preoperational children, as is acquiring the more general concept that time exists along a continuum of past, present, and future.

Stated differently, young children have little idea of cause-and-effect sequences. In fact, their early use of the words "cause" and "because" may have nothing to do with the adult understanding of the terms. The same possibility is true of the word "why"—the 4-year-old's favorite question. A child may ask, "Why do we drink out of bottles *and* cans?" The parent replies, "Because some things are better in bottles, some in cans." The child asks, "But juice comes in bottles and cans too! Why?" The parent answers, "Well, sometimes it's cheaper that way." The child asks, "Why?" And perhaps the parent says, "Go wash up

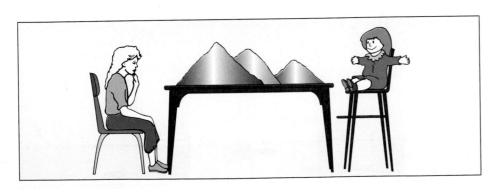

FIGURE 6–3 A VIEW OF THE "MOUNTAINS" PROBLEM

Even though this preschooler is pointing to a number on the clock, the concepts of minutes and hours are very difficult for her to understand.

for dinner, we'll talk about it later!" Meanwhile, the child may have been concerned with the appearance of the containers all along—not the real "why."

The understanding of spatial relations also develops during the preschool period. The meanings of words such as "in," "out," "near," "far," "over," "under," "up," and "down" are learned directly through the child's experiences with his or her own body (Weikart et al., 1971). The authors suggest that the usual progression is for children to learn a concept first with their bodies (crawling under a table) and then with objects (pushing a toy truck under a table). Later they learn to identify the concept in pictures ("See the boat go under the bridge!").

CONSERVATION

Piaget's **conservation** problems are used to illustrate some of the limitations of preoperational thinking. The term *conservation* refers to understanding that changing the shape or appearance of objects and materials doesn't change their amount. Consider the following examples.

CONSERVATION OF VOLUME　Piaget observed that preoperational children do not conserve *volume*, as indicated by his classic liquid/beakers problem (see Figure 6–4). The child is first presented with two identical beakers containing the same amount of liquid. When asked, "Are they the same?" the child readily says, "Yes." Then, as the child watches, the contents of one of the original beakers is poured into a tall, slender beaker. Now the child is asked, "Are they the same, or are they different?" Preoperational children tend to say that they're different, perhaps adding that the taller beaker contains more liquid. Centration apparently gets in the way, in that the child attends to only one dimension, such as height, and doesn't realize that a compensating change occurs in the beaker's width. For the child, it's a *perceptual* problem, not a logical one—the child simply focuses on the here-and-now, and in effect, the state of the liquids before the pouring is a different problem from the state of the liquids afterward. In other words, from the child's point of view, the pouring is irrelevant.

Irreversibility is a factor too: It doesn't occur to the child that the liquid in the taller beaker could be poured back into the original one and therefore must be the same—again, the child's thinking lacks the necessary logical approach.

CONSERVATION OF MASS　Figure 6–5 shows possible tests for conservation of *mass*, which illustrate preoperational thinking very similar to that revealed by the liquid/beakers problem. Here a child is presented with two identical balls of clay. As the child watches, one ball is transformed into various shapes while the other ball remains untouched. Consider the case in which the ball is

conservation　The understanding that changing the shape or appearance of objects doesn't change their amount or volume.

FIGURE 6–4　THE CLASSIC "LIQUID/BEAKERS" PROBLEM

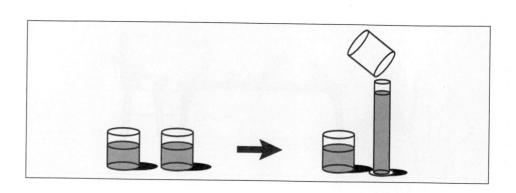

STUDY CHART ▸ CHARACTERISTICS OF PREOPERATIONAL THINKING

Preconceptual Period	animism	Belief that anything that moves is alive	Sun, moon, cars, trains, etc., are seen as living creatures.
	reification	Belief that objects and people in thoughts and dreams are real	A monster in a dream actually lurks under the child's bed.
	egocentrism	Tendency to see and understand things from the child's point of view	The sky is blue because that's the child's favorite color.
Intuitive Period	symbolic representation	Use of actions, images, or words to represent objects and events	Blocks represent houses and towers.
	sociocentric thinking	Ability to take other people's points of view	The child understands that another child may not want to play house today.
Limitations	concreteness	Inability to deal with abstractions	That's not a mountain; it's a pile of sand.
	irreversibility	Inability to see events as occurring in more than one direction	I have a sister, but she doesn't have any sisters or brothers.
	centration	Inability to focus on more than one aspect of a problem at a time	The child cannot consider color and material at the same time.

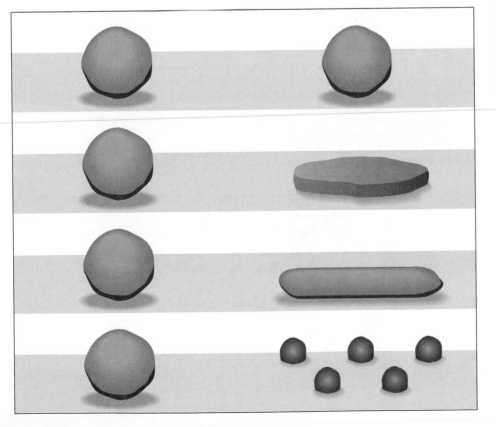

FIGURE 6–5

In this conservation experiment, a child is shown two identical balls of clay. One ball remains the same, while the other is transformed into various shapes.

rolled into a longish sausage shape. Because of centration, the child might say either that the sausage contains more clay or that it contains less, depending on whether the child attends to length or height. And as before, the child, caught up in the here-and-now, fails to realize that the process is reversible.

CONSERVATION OF NUMBER The development of numerical abilities is an especially intriguing area—both because of the amount of formal education we invest in teaching children to use numbers and because of the many practical applications of numbers in everyday life. A number-conservation task is shown in Figure 6–6. The researcher first places six candies in each of two rows, one above the other and spaced in the same way. After the child agrees that the two rows contain the same number of candies, the experimenter removes one of the candies from one row and spreads out the remaining candies. To conserve number, the child must recognize that the longer row actually contains one fewer candy despite its "wider" appearance. Children younger than age 5 or 6 are often fooled and judge that the longer row contains more candies.

LIMITATIONS OF PIAGET'S THEORY

Do Piaget's experiments place preoperational children at a disadvantage and thus underestimate their cognitive abilities? In some respects, research indicates that they do. For example, although preschool children do tend to be egocentric and preoccupied with their own perspective on things, in some situations they can take another person's point of view. When Piagetian problems are presented in such a way that they make "human sense," they become clear even to young preschool children (Donaldson, 1978). For example, in one study, preoperational children who couldn't solve the mountains problem were instead asked whether a naughty boy could hide so that he would not be

FIGURE 6–6 PIAGET'S EXPERIMENT ON THE CONSERVATION OF NUMBERS

When shown the arrangement of candies in the top two rows and asked whether one line has more or both lines are the same, the 4- or 5-year-old will generally answer that both lines contain the same number of candies. Using the same candies, those in the lower row were pushed closer together, and one candy was removed from the upper row, but the line was spread out so that it was longer. The child has watched this operation and has been told that he or she may eat the candies in the line that contains more. Even preoperational children, who can count, will insist that the longer line has more, although they have gone through the exercise of counting the candies in each line.

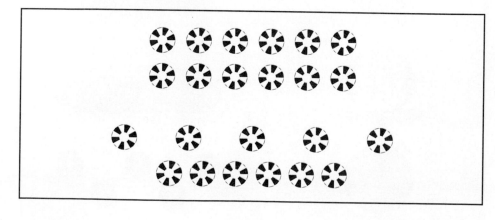

seen by a police officer. Although none of the children in the study had ever actually hidden from the police, they had all played hide-and-seek and had no difficulty taking the naughty boy's point of view. Even 3-year-olds were successful at this (Hughes & Donaldson, 1979). Numerous studies also show that preschool children at least occasionally attend to more than one dimension at a time and think in terms of transformations instead of concrete beginning and end states—thus in effect displaying elements of conservation. These simply aren't their *dominant* modes of thinking (Siegler & Ellis, 1996).

Rochel Gelman and colleagues (1986) have demonstrated that preschool children are also more competent in using numbers than Piaget believed. For example, they identified two major types of numerical skills displayed by young children: *number-abstraction abilities* and *numerical-reasoning principles*. Number-abstraction abilities refer to cognitive processes that children use in counting; even a 3-year-old might count the number of cookies on a table and accurately arrive at "four." Numerical reasoning principles are cognitive processes by which children determine the correct way to operate on or transform an array (Flavell et al., 1993). For example, a child might know that the only way a number of objects can be increased is by adding an object. Not until children gain more advanced reasoning abilities, however, can they add, subtract, multiply, and divide (Becker, 1993).

BEYOND PIAGET: SOCIAL PERSPECTIVES

As discussed in Chapter 4, some developmental psychologists look at cognitive development from a very different perspective. Rather than seeing children as active scientists, they emphasize the children's social nature and dispute Piaget's view of the child as a solitary explorer attempting to make sense of the world on her or his own. Active exploration is not excluded, but the child more often acquires cognitive abilities through interactions with more experienced people—parents, teachers, and older children. In the course of these interactions, parents and others also pass on society's rules and expectations (Bruner & Haste, 1987).

According to the social perspective, the ways in which adults demonstrate how to solve problems help children learn to think. As noted in Chapters 4 and 5, all cultures initiate children into myriad activities through guided participation. When young children help to set or to clear the table or join in singing "Happy Birthday," specific aspects of culture are transmitted from the more experienced members (adults) to the less experienced members (children). Katherine Nelson argues that knowledge of events is the key to understanding the child's mind (1986). Whereas Piaget focused on what young children *don't* know, Nelson is interested in what they *do* know and what they learn from daily experiences. She views the child's knowledge of and participation in routine daily activities as material both for the child's mental life and for the development of cognitive abilities. Thus, the child's understanding of the world is embedded in cultural knowledge.

Vygotsky's zone of proximal development (see Chapter 4) includes the view that children develop through participation in activities that are slightly beyond their competence, given the assistance of others who are more skilled and knowledgeable (Vygotsky, 1934/1978). Social play is important as a means of moving children toward more advanced levels of social and cognitive skills (Nicolopoulou, 1993). Play also provides an excellent opportunity to study the way children learn in widely diverse cultures (Rogoff, 1993). We'll return to the relationship between play and learning later in the chapter.

These children have learned birthday rituals through guided participation.

THE ROLE OF MEMORY IN COGNITIVE DEVELOPMENT

Memory is a key aspect of cognitive development. Perceiving selectively, reasoning, classifying, and generally progressing toward more complex concepts all occur along with the maturation and development of memory processes. In this section we begin with an overview of the information-processing model of memory. Then we look at evidence for developmental changes (and limitations) in memory during the preschool period.

MEMORY PROCESSES When visual sensory information enters an adult human "computer," the *sensory register* retains that information very briefly—often much less than a second—before it is either replaced by new information or passed along for further processing. Auditory sensory memory lasts longer—up to 3 seconds or so.

Information that we attend to passes to *short-term memory (STM)*, also known as *working memory*, for processing. STM or working memory is essentially "consciousness"—what you're thinking about at a given moment, what's in your mind right now. In the absence of rehearsal (e.g., repeating a new phone number long enough to dial it), information remains in working memory for 15 to 20 seconds. If you make an effort to remember the information, it passes to *long-term memory (LTM)*. Most researchers regard long-term memory as permanent and based on structural changes in the brain. Thus, barring brain damage, long-term memories are potentially accessible throughout life and constitute the cumulative store of knowledge that we regularly access both in recognizing the familiar and in learning about the new (Atkinson & Shriffrin, 1971; Hagen et al., 1975).

Memory can consist of images, actions, or words. Thus, researchers often refer to visual, motor, and verbal (semantic) memory. Visual memory is the first to develop. Yet if we are asked to remember our very early years, we typically can't remember much before age 3. This inability presumably has something to do with encoding, but researchers aren't sure exactly what processes are involved. Verbally encoded recollections that can be described appear after age 4 to 6. One reason for this timing is that the development of language may enable preoperational children to encode new information better.

RECOGNITION AND RECALL   Studies of preschool children's memory skills have focused on two basic memory abilities. **Recognition** refers to the ability to identify objects or situations as having previously been seen or experienced. For example, children may recognize a picture or a person they have seen before even though they may not be able to tell us much about the memory. **Recall** refers to the ability to retrieve long-term memories with little in the way of cues or prompts; recall is much harder both for children and for adults. For example, a child might be asked to tell a story from memory. Or you might be asked to relate everything you've learned so far in this chapter. Both tasks would be quite difficult.

Researchers have found that preschool children perform quite well on recognition tasks but that their recall performance is poor, although both forms of remembering improve between the ages of 2 and 5 (Myers & Perlmutter, 1978). In a recognition task in which many objects were shown only once to children between the ages of 2 and 5, even the youngest children could correctly point to 81% of the objects as having been seen before; the older children recognized 92% of the objects. However, when children between the ages of 2 and 4 were asked to recall objects by naming them, 3-year-olds could name only 22% of the items, and 4-year-olds only 40%. Preschool children are clearly better at recognition than recall but may perform better on the latter if their caregivers routinely ask questions that require recall (Ratner, 1984).

REHEARSAL AND ORGANIZATION   It is generally assumed that young children's difficulties with recall are due to limited strategies for encoding and retrieval (Flavell, 1977; Myers & Perlmutter, 1978), in conjunction with limited attention span and working memory. Preschool children don't spontaneously organize or mentally rehearse (repeat to themselves) information the way older children and adults do. If you ask an adult to memorize a list such as "cat, chair, airplane, dog, desk, car," the adult automatically classifies the items as "animals," "furniture," and "vehicles," and then rehearses the items within each category; young children do not. Children age 6 and older also improve in their ability to recall information when they are trained in memory strategies, but it is difficult to teach preschoolers to organize and rehearse information.

Preschoolers do use some memory strategies. In one study, 18- to 24-month-old toddlers watched an experimenter hide a Big Bird replica under a pillow and were told to remember where Big Bird had been hidden because they would later be asked where he was. The experimenter then distracted the children with other toys for several minutes. During the delay period, the children frequently interrupted their play to talk about Big Bird, point at the hiding place, stand near it, or even attempt to retrieve Big Bird, clearly indicating that they were trying to remember his location (DeLoache et al., 1985). In another study, the researchers determined that preschoolers group spatial information—but not conceptual information—into categories while trying to remember the information (DeLoache & Todd, 1988). For example, when very young children were asked to remember the location of a hidden object, they frequently used rehearsal-like verbalizations such as referring to the hidden toy, the fact that it was hidden, the hiding place, and their having discovered it. The researchers in both studies concluded that such behaviors may be

recognition   The ability to correctly identify items previously experienced when they appear again.

recall   The ability to retreive information and events that are not present, with or without cues.

precursors to more mature strategies for keeping material in short-term memory (Flavell et al., 1993).

Some researchers have focused on teaching preschool children memory strategies such as sorting, naming, or categorizing. Preschoolers learned more advanced memory techniques and retained them for several days, but then they ceased using them, possibly because they forgot them or simply became bored with the activity. In addition, learning advanced memory strategies appeared to have little effect on children's recall (Lange & Pierce, 1992). Similar results have been found in studies of mothers who use memory strategies to teach young children skills such as wrapping gifts or naming characters in stories. Preschool children employ simpler and fewer techniques than their mothers (Harris & Hamidullah, 1993) and often don't apply them spontaneously.

Overall, such studies demonstrate that with carefully planned learning experiences and instructional techniques, young children may learn cognitive skills beyond their current repertoire of abilities. But the learning doesn't endure—either because children cannot fit the skills comfortably into their current set of abilities or because they are too busy learning about the world in other, more comfortable ways. It is interesting to note that when studies compared a group of children who were asked to "remember" toys with another group who were asked to "play with" the toys, the children involved in active play demonstrated better memory. The finding suggests that the active play contributes to children's mental organization (Newman, 1990). Indeed, a growing body of research is focusing on the role of the physical and social contexts in children's ability to remember. Two-year-olds who engage in and talk about an activity in a naturalistic setting such as the home demonstrate increased memory competence. However, when formal strategies such as rehearsal are simply taught and replace informal contextual interactions, children's memory performance actually declines (Fivush & Hudson, 1990).

EVENT SCRIPTS AND SEQUENTIAL UNDERSTANDING It is becoming increasingly clear that children can remember information that is ordered *temporally*, that is, in a time sequence. They can structure a series of occurrences into an ordered, meaningful whole. In one study, children were asked to describe how they had made objects from clay 2 weeks earlier (Smith et al., 1987). When the children were given the opportunity to make the same objects again, they could describe how they had worked step by step. Apparently preschool children can organize and remember sequences of actions even after a single experience with them.

Young children are aware that an occasion such as a birthday party is composed of an orderly progression of events: a beginning, the time when the guests arrive with presents; a series of events in the middle, including playing games, singing "Happy Birthday," blowing out the candles, and eating cake and ice cream; and an end, when the guests leave. Children can also remember the elements of repeated events, such as dinnertime, grocery shopping, or a day at nursery school. It is as if they develop *scripts* for routine events (Friedman, 1990; Mandler, 1983; Nelson et al., 1983). When mothers talk to their young children about objects and events that are not immediately present, such as describing errands to be done after lunch, they help their children develop scripts and thereby remember events in a series (Lucariello & Nelson, 1987). Younger children remember events only in the order in which they actually occur, however. Only when young children become extremely familiar with an event can they reverse the order of steps (Bauer & Thal, 1990). Scripts are therefore a *mnemonic*—a memory aid—used to remember sequences of events. They "may be the young child's most powerful mental tool for understanding the world" (Flavell et al., 1993).

REVIEW & APPLY

1. Explain how Piaget characterized preoperational children's thought and why the limits of their thought largely define preschool children's cognitive abilities.
2. Discuss ways in which Piaget apparently underestimated the cognitive abilities of preschool children.
3. How does the social-perspective theory of cognitive development differ from Piaget's theories?
4. How does memory play a central role in cognitive development?

LANGUAGE DEVELOPMENT

Throughout the preschool years, children rapidly expand their vocabularies, their use of grammatical forms, and their understanding of language as a social activity. In this section we'll look at the preschool child's expanding grasp of grammar, words, and concepts; the influence of parents' speech; and the characteristics of children's conversations, including the social context of language. We also discuss two important current topics: ethnic subdialects and bilingualism.

AN EXPANDING GRAMMAR

One of the more influential works on language acquisition was written by Roger Brown (1973). Brown and his colleagues recorded the speech patterns of three young children named Adam, Eve, and Sarah. Using **mean length of utterance (MLU)** as the primary measure of the children's language acquisition, Brown identified five distinct, increasingly complex stages in language development. Although the three children progressed at different rates, the order was similar for each, as it is for most children. Certain skills and rules are mastered before others, and certain errors are peculiar to specific stages.

STAGE 1   The first stage is characterized by two-word utterances, in the form of telegraphic speech and pivot and open words, as discussed in Chapter 4. However, Brown went beyond structure to focus on the meanings children attempt to convey with word order and position—concepts such as that objects exist, that they disappear and recur, and that people possess them.

STAGE 2   This stage of language acquisition is characterized by utterances that are slightly longer than two words. Early preschool children begin to generalize the rules of *inflection* to words that they already know. For example, they can form the regular past tense of many verbs, such as "play/played," and the regular plurals of many nouns. Are they simply imitating the speech of others, or are they using linguistic rules? The latter seems to be the case (Berko, 1958). Preschool and first-grade children reveal a surprising grasp of rules for conjugating verbs and forming plurals and possessives. Indirect evidence for this ability is their tendency to **overregularize** inflections. Whereas they previously used the irregular verbs they were hearing in everyday speech, they now temporarily overapply inflection rules to *all* verbs. They use

mean length of utterance (MLU)   The average length of the sentences that a child produces.

overregularize   To generalize complex language principles, typically by preschool children who are rapidly expanding their vocabularies.

This 3-year-old is able to demonstrate the sentence "The rabbit chases the dog" but not "The dog is chased by the rabbit." Mastery of the passive concept is still to come.

past-tense constructions such as "goed" instead of "went," "breaked" instead of "broke," "seed" instead of "saw." Their tendency to overregularize is quite resistant to correction by parents and teachers. Only later do they return to irregular forms that depend on rote learning (Marcus et al., 1992).

STAGE 3 Now children learn to modify simple sentences. They create negative and imperative forms, ask yes-no questions, and depart in other ways from the simple statements of earlier stages. The negative form is an excellent example of how complex language learning can be. Earlier, children negated by putting the negative word at the beginning of an utterance, as in "no pocket," "no more," and "no dirty." By the third stage, however, they use auxiliary verbs and embed negatives in sentences. They easily use sentences such as "Paul didn't laugh" and "Jeannie won't let go" (Klima & Bellugi, 1966).

However, preschool children still do not comprehend the passive voice. For example, if 3-year-olds are given stuffed animals and asked to act out "The cat chases the dog" and "The dog chases the cat," they have no trouble doing so (Bellugi et al., 1970). But when told "The boy washes the girl" and "The girl is washed by the boy," children often do not recognize that the intent is the same.

STAGES 4 AND 5 In the fourth and fifth stages, children learn to deal with increasingly sophisticated language elements. They begin to use subordinate clauses and fragments within compound and complex sentences. By the age of $4\frac{1}{2}$, children have a good grasp of correct syntax, but they continue to refine it in the next few years (Chomsky, 1969).

MORE WORDS AND CONCEPTS

Throughout the preschool period, children learn words rapidly—often at a rate of two or three a day. Some words have meaning only in context—for example, "this" and "that." Some words express relationships between objects: "softer," "lower," "shorter." Frequently children understand one concept, such as "more," much earlier than they know the word or the concept that contrasts with it, such as "less." Thus, a 3-year-old may easily be able to tell you which dish has more candy but not which dish has less. Often, too, preschool children want to say things but don't know the right word, so they invent a word. They use nouns in place of verbs, as in "Mommy, pencil it" for "Mommy, write it." At least through age 3, children also have difficulty with pronouns. For example, a child might say "us need to take a nap." Even when corrected, such errors persist until age 4 or 5, sometimes longer.

THE INFLUENCE OF PARENTS' LANGUAGE USE

Every culture transmits language to its children. Many methods of talking and relating to infants facilitate language development. Researchers studying American children have found that caregivers ask questions to check children's understanding, expand children's utterances, and make ritualized use of play speech. Adults often speak for their children; that is, they express the child's wants, wishes, and actions in correct language. The child's language develops most from everyday communication with adults who seek to communicate—that is, to understand and to be understood (Schacter & Strage, 1982).

However, it is not entirely clear how parents' language use and children's language development interact (Chesnick et al., 1983). Individual differences in children's language development are inherited to some extent and are also influenced by the child's environment. For example, twins often display delayed language development, a tendency that might suggest a genetic basis. Yet it may be that they receive significantly less verbal input than nontwins because mothers of twins must divide their attention between two children. In addition, twins sometimes communicate with each other using a "primitive" language all their own (Tomasello et al., 1986).

When parents speak with their children, they communicate far more than words, sentences, and syntax. They demonstrate how thoughts are expressed and how ideas are exchanged. They teach the child about categories and symbols, about how to translate the complexities of the world into ideas and words. Conceptual tools provide a "scaffold" for the child to use in understanding the world and expressing his or her place in it (Bruner & Haste, 1987).

Studies have also shown that reading picture books to children can facilitate language learning. This result is especially true when parents ask open-ended questions that encourage the child to expand the story and when they respond appropriately to the child's attempts to answer the questions and to minimize simple reading (Whitehurst et al., 1988).

LANGUAGE AND GENDER   Language is also one of the ways in which children learn who they are and how they should relate to other people. Gender is a case in point. Assumptions about gender are often culturally embedded in parents' thinking and cause them to talk differently to male and female children (Lloyd, 1987). However, language development may also be influenced by factors inherent in the sex-typed toys children play with. In one study (O'Brien & Nagle, 1987), researchers analyzed the language used by mothers and fathers while playing with their toddlers with toys such as vehicles or dolls. Playing with dolls elicited more verbal interaction, whereas play with vehicles involved little talking—whether the parents were playing with either daughters or sons. Thus, children who play with dolls may have more opportunities to learn and practice language than would children who play with other toys. Then, because boys and girls play with sex-stereotyped toys starting at age 2, girls may experience more sophisticated early language environments—causing them to develop verbal skills somewhat ahead of boys.

CHILDREN'S CONVERSATIONS

Young children do more than say words and simple sentences. They have conversations with adults and other children, and even with themselves (see "In Theory, In Fact," page 224). Their conversations typically follow certain patterns.

MONITORING THE MESSAGE   First, children realize that it's necessary to get the other person's attention. A child who is just learning the art of conversation may yank on another child's clothing. As time passes, the child may instead say something like "Know what?" Children also discover that conversation means taking turns. They learn that conversations have a beginning, a middle, and an end. Eventually they learn to talk about the same subject and to monitor whether the other person is listening and understanding, and to make sounds or nod to indicate their own understanding (Garvey, 1984).

If you listen to younger children's conversations, however, the first thing you'll notice is they don't run smoothly. Very young children's conversations are often **collective monologues**—two children may know that they need to take turns speaking, but they may be talking about entirely different, unrelated subjects. Later, when talking about the same subject, children often stop abruptly to see whether the other person is listening. They pause and repeat and correct themselves, all of which is a normal part of developing effective

collective monologues Children's conversations that include taking turns talking, but not necessarily about the same topic.

IN THEORY, IN FACT

WHEN CHILDREN TALK TO THEMSELVES, IS IT A SIGN OF IMMATURITY?

Josh is alone in his room playing a game in which he tries to fit pieces into a puzzle. If we were observing him, we might overhear him say to himself, "This piece doesn't fit. Where's a round one? No, it doesn't. It's too big. This one is small. . . ." Children between the ages of 4 and 8 have been observed talking to themselves about 20% of the time in schools that permit it (Berk, 1985). Why do children talk to themselves? Is it a good thing or a bad one?

Psychologists call talking aloud to oneself *private speech*. All people, young and old, talk to themselves. But young children engage in private speech aloud and in public settings. Young children even sing to themselves about what they are doing—songs that are generated spontaneously. They also talk aloud to themselves far more often than adults do. Jean Piaget made early observations of private speech by preschool children and suggested that it simply indicated immaturity; social speech was more mature because it required consideration of the listener's perspective. He called children's self-talk *egocentric speech* (Piaget, 1926). However, other theorists and researchers have raised questions about

Often young children talk out loud while they work or play. Sometimes the talk is pretend dialogue, but more often it fulfills other funcitons.

Piaget's explanation. They have found that the amount of private speech varies a great deal, depending on the situation, and that even the youngest children use far more social speech than private speech. Perhaps private speech serves a distinct and separate purpose.

Vygotsky (1934/1987) observed that private speech often mirrors adult social speech and helps develop inner

thought and self-direction. More recently, researchers have identified three stages in the development of children's private speech. In its earliest stage, private speech occurs *after* an action—"I made a big picture." In the second stage, self-talk *accompanies* actions—"It's getting darker and darker with lots of paint." In the third stage, it *precedes* an action—"I want to make a scary picture with dark paint." Private speech, then, corresponds to the developing thought processes in a child's mind. In the third stage, when speech comes before behavior, the child is planning a course of action. The changes in private speech thus illustrate the development of thought processes in guiding behavior and accompanying linguistic development (Berk, 1992; Winsler et al., 1997).

Some studies have failed to show a connection between private speech and the development of cognitive abilities, but these were done in school settings where children were discouraged from talking while doing things. Other research shows that when children are given tasks and encouraged to speak, they often talk to themselves (Frauenglass & Diaz, 1985). Researchers have also found that children in comfortable school environments tend to use more private speech if adults are not present.

---

communication (Garvey, 1984; Reich, 1986). Even school-age children sometimes have considerable difficulty communicating what they want to say to a listener, and first- and second-grade children have difficulty comprehending each other fully (Beal, 1987).

Finally, children must learn to adjust their conversations so as to reduce social friction, conflict, and embarrassment. Adjustment means using courtesy markers like "please" and "thank you"; paying attention; and selecting suitable topics and the proper forms of address and phrasing. It also means being aware of the social status of the other person.

pragmatics The social and practical aspects of language use.

THE SOCIAL CONTEXT OF LANGUAGE   At the same time that children learn the meaning and syntax of language, they also learn **pragmatics,** the social aspects of language. They learn that language expresses social status, roles, and values. They learn that the specific words, syntax, tone of voice, and mode of address used depend on the relationship between speaker and listener. They learn to talk in one way to younger children, in another way to their peers, and in still another way to older children and adults. They are aided with reminders like "Don't talk to your grandmother like that" (Garvey, 1984). In general, children are quick to learn nuances of speech and to conform to social status. They are also quick to perceive degrees of status and the appropriate speech behavior in a wide variety of social settings.

Cross-cultural research has shown that pragmatics of speech differ throughout the world in accordance with the cultural values that parents communicate to their children (Shatz, 1991). For example, researchers studying differences between German and American child-rearing practices noted that German parents tend to speak to their children in more authoritative, dominating ways than do American parents. American parents focus more on satisfying their children's desires and intentions. The societal values that underlie these tendencies are communicated, in part, through the use of *modal* verbs. Verbs such as "must," "may," "might," "can," "could," and "should" express cultural concepts such as necessity, possibility, obligation, and permission. Thus, German mothers focus more on necessity ("You will have to tell me what you want") and obligation ("You must pick up your toys"). In contrast, American mothers emphasize intention ("I'm going to take you to the movies") and possibility ("That might happen"). Young children then adopt such tendencies in their own speech (Shatz, 1991).

In another cross-cultural study, Judy Dunn and Jane Brown (1991) examined how the child-rearing language used by parents in Pennsylvania differs from that used in Cambridge, England, with regard to societal values. When the researchers focused on how "prescriptive" messages were sent, they found that American mothers tend to define acceptable or unacceptable behavior in terms of their children's specific actions (Mother to child: "Don't do that in here!"). In contrast, English mothers tend to discuss their children's behavior in terms of societal norms (Child to mother: "I want to kick you!" Mother to child: "You mustn't kick people"). In addition, English mothers are much more likely than American mothers to use evaluative words ("bad," "good"). Such language differences clearly reflect cultural values: Whereas parents in the United States focus more on personal actions, parents in Great Britain focus more on complying with norms.

SUBDIALECTS

Often children are presented with more than one form of language usage because of subcultural differences within a society. This experience is especially true in the United States, where numerous racial/ethnic groups, as well as distinct social and economic classes, coexist. Subcultural differences can produce **subdialects**—variations of a language that can usually be understood by most speakers, though at times with difficulty. In contrast, true *dialect* differences occur when speakers of a language group usually cannot understand each other, as is the case with American Standard English versus some British English dialects in terms of pronunciation, inflection, and vocabulary.

The status of Black English, as spoken by many African-Americans and with its own regional variations, has been debated for decades. Before linguists studied it systematically, Black English was considered to be simply poor English. Experts now agree that it is one of many subdialects of American

These girls are playing pretend. One of them is having a conversation with the help of the telephone. Through play, children can practice their conversational skills; for example, they learn to take turns speaking.

subdialects   Subcultural language differences; speakers of different subdialects usually can understand each other.

Standard English. That is, it is different, as opposed to deficient or substandard (Williams, 1970).

Black English has its own rules and is frequently employed in richly expressive ways (Labov, 1970). Linguists have found that the so-called errors made by speakers of Black English are better viewed as alternative grammatical forms. For example, the word "be" in Black English, as used in the sentence "I be sick," expresses an ongoing rather than a transitory condition. The situation expressed concisely by "I be sick" might be rephrased in American Standard English as "I have been sick and still am feeling sick." Similar considerations apply to Hispanic English and its variations, to certain forms of Asian English and Native American English, and to the many regional variations of "White" English—all of which can be viewed as subdialects of American Standard English.

What position should schools take regarding subdialects? When, for example, Hispanic English is the primary language spoken in the child's home environment and by the child, its use at school can be an important mode of self-expression. But most children who speak Hispanic English or one of the many other American subdialects will ultimately have to use American Standard English in addition to the language they learned at home. Ideally, speakers of English subdialects become competent in the mainstream language while retaining their own distinct linguistic identity.

BILINGUALISM

Language is not only a means of communication. It is also a symbol of social or group identity. Thus, language conveys attitudes and values, and it contributes to socialization. The child who grows up hearing two languages and becomes bilingual goes through both a linguistic and a socializing process (Grosjean, 1982).

The status of bilingualism in different nations is strongly affected by issues of social class and political power. In Europe, for example, bilingualism is associated with being a cultured "citizen of the world." In the United States, bilingualism is more often associated with first- or second-generation immigrant status, which is not always viewed positively by the majority. Although cultural pluralism has become more widely accepted, the millions of American children growing up in bilingual environments still experience pressures to conform.

Learning two languages by the age of 5 is a complex task involving two systems of rules, two sets of vocabulary, and different pronunciation. Many children who are bilingual in their earliest years nonetheless show little confusion between the two languages by the age of 3, although they sometimes use words in the two languages interchangeably. Thus, some psycholinguists theorize that the young child uses a single, "hybrid" language system and only later is able to distinguish between two languages. Other evidence, however, indicates that bilingual children use two separate language systems even as infants (Genesee, 1989).

Does learning two languages during the preschool years hinder a child's language learning or interfere with cognitive development? Early studies in the United States and Great Britain concluded that learning two languages at too young an age is detrimental to cognitive development. In that research, bilingual children scored lower on standardized English tests than did monolingual English-speaking children. Most of those studies, however, did not take into account the socioeconomic level of either the children or their parents. In other words, the scores of the bilingual children may have been lower

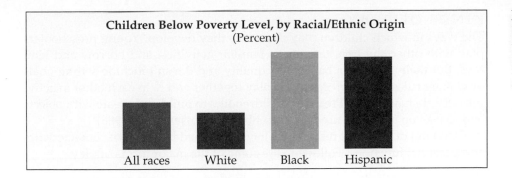

FIGURE 6–7 CHILDREN BELOW POVERTY LEVEL, BY RACIAL/ETHNIC ORIGIN (PERCENTAGE)

Source: U.S. Census Bureau, 1997.

for other reasons, such as poverty, poor schooling, or lack of familiarity with their new culture. Figure 6–7 gives percentages of children below poverty level by racial/ethnic origin.

Most researchers now believe that linguistically, culturally, and probably cognitively, it is an advantage to grow up bilingual (e.g., Diaz, 1985; Goncz, 1988). On each count, children are exposed to different ways of thinking about and doing things that may later make them more flexible and therefore more adaptive to our changing world.

1. List and describe Brown's five stages of language acquisition.
2. What is pragmatics, and how is it communicated through language? What do cross-cultural studies tell us about pragmatics in different cultures?
3. What are subdialects, and how do they affect children's language development?

REVIEW & APPLY

PLAY AND LEARNING

Every aspect of preschool children's development is enhanced through play. Play is children's unique way of experiencing the world and practicing and improving their skills, and it is found in all cultures.

Play satisfies many needs in a child's life: the need to be stimulated and diverted, to express natural exuberance, to experience change for its own sake, to satisfy curiosity, to explore, and to experiment under risk-free conditions. Play has been called the "work of childhood" because of its central role in the young child's development. It promotes the growth of sensory-perceptual capabilities and physical skills while providing endless opportunities to exercise and expand intellectual skills. Play is different from any other kind of activity. By its very nature, it is not directed toward goals; it is intrinsically rewarding. As Catherine Garvey (1990) has pointed out, play is behavior that is engaged in simply for pleasure, has no purpose other than itself, is chosen by the player(s), requires players to be actively engaged, and is related to other areas of life—that is, it promotes social development and enhances creativity. In other words, in a very real sense, play is developmental business.

Sensory play.

KINDS OF PLAY

The ways in which children play change as they develop. Young preschoolers play with other children, talk about familiar activities, and borrow and lend toys. But their play has a haphazard quality and doesn't include setting goals or making rules. Older preschoolers play together and help each other in activities that do have goals. Preschool children like to build and create with objects and to take on roles and use props (Isenberg & Quisenberry, 1988).

Each kind of play that researchers have identified has its own characteristics and potential functions. Following are some of the major forms of play.

SENSORY PLEASURE   The aim of this kind of play is sensory experience in and of itself. Young children may endlessly splash water, bang pots, and pluck flower petals simply to experience new sounds, tastes, odors, and textures. Sensory play teaches children essential facts about their bodies and the qualities of things in their environment.

PLAY WITH MOTION   Running, jumping, twirling, and skipping are just some of the countless forms of play with motion that are enjoyed for their own sake. Play involving the continuously changing sensation of movement is one of the earliest forms of play—infants rock back and forth or blow bubbles with their food. Infants frequently engage in movement routines that not only are exciting and stimulating but also give them practice in body coordination. Play with motion is often initiated by an adult or older child and thus gives infants some of their earliest social experiences. Children typically do not initiate or share this kind of activity with other children until about age 3 (Garvey, 1990).

ROUGH-AND-TUMBLE PLAY   Parents and teachers may try to discourage the rough-and-tumble, mock-fighting play that young children are fond of. They may try to reduce aggression and real fighting among children. But rough-and-tumble is *play* fighting, not real fighting. Recent research suggests that it provides real benefits, within limits. Not only does it offer a chance to

Play with motion.

exercise and release energy, but it also helps children learn to handle their feelings, control their impulses, and avoid behaviors that are inappropriate in groups. Moreover, it helps children learn to distinguish between pretend and real (Pellegrini, 1987). Rough-and-tumble play is observed in cultures throughout the world (Boulton & Smith, 1989). Regardless of the culture, however, boys are more likely to engage in this kind of play than girls are, with one study showing that boys in the United States spend about three times as much time in rough-and-tumble play as girls do (DiPietro, 1981).

Rough-and-tumble play.

PLAY WITH LANGUAGE   Young children love to play with language. They experiment with its rhythm and cadences. They mix up words to create new meanings. They play with language to poke fun at the world and to verify their grasp of reality. They use it as a buffer against expressions of anger. The primary function of language—meaningful communication—tends to be lost in language play. Children concentrate on the language itself, playfully manipulating its sounds, patterns, and meanings for their own amusement.

Judith Schwartz (1981) provided some examples of language play. Sometimes children play with sound and rhythm, regularly repeating letters and words in a steady beat: *La la la / Lol li pop / La la la / Lol li pop.* They also make patterns with words as if practicing a grammatical drill: *Hit it. / Sit it. / Slit it. / Mitt it.* Or, *There is the light. / Where is the light? / Here is the light.* Why do children play with language? Partly because it's simply funny. Other people laugh when a young child says something like "I'm gonna telly 'cause you put jelly in my belly and made me smelly."

Playing with language also gives young children practice in mastering the grammar and words they're learning. By ages 3 and 4, children are using some basic linguistic rules and structures of meaning. They ask questions such as "Couldn't table legs be fitted with shoes?" and "Since there is running water, is there sitting water?" (Chukovsky, 1963; Garvey, 1977). Children also use language to control their experiences. Older children use language to structure their play. They create sometimes elaborate rituals that must be followed: Always do this first, then this, before that—and do it all in highly specific ways. By following the rituals carefully, they control the experience (Schwartz, 1981).

DRAMATIC PLAY AND MODELING   An important kind of play involves taking on roles or imitating models: playing house; mimicking a parent going to work; pretending to be a nurse, an astronaut, or a truck driver. Such play, called *sociodramatic play,* involves not only imitation of whole patterns of behavior but also considerable fantasy and novel ways of interaction. Children learn various social relationships, rules, and other aspects of their culture through dramatic play. Dramatic play also interacts with the beginnings of literacy (Davidson, 1996).

Language play.

GAMES, RITUALS, AND COMPETITIVE PLAY   As children grow older, their play develops rules and specific goals. Children make decisions about taking turns, set up guidelines about what is and what is not permitted, and enjoy situations in which someone wins and someone loses. Although the intricate rules of baseball and chess are beyond most preschoolers, they can cope with the rituals and rules of simpler games like tag and hide-and-go-seek. Such games help them develop cognitive skills like learning rules, understanding cause and effect, realizing the consequences of various actions, and learning about winning and losing (Flavell et al., 1993; Herron & Sutton-Smith, 1971; Kamii & DeVries, 1980).

Dramatic play and modeling.

Constructive play or play with games and rituals.

PLAY AND COGNITIVE DEVELOPMENT

Play promotes cognitive development in many ways. Preoperational children use play to learn about their physical surroundings. Although, as Piaget noted, the youngest preschoolers are often egocentric, they use dramatic play to master symbolic representation and to increase their social knowledge.

EXPLORING PHYSICAL OBJECTS When preschool children play with physical objects—sand, stones, and water, for example—they learn the properties and physical laws that govern these objects. When playing in a sandbox, a child learns that different objects leave different marks in the sand. When bouncing a ball on the floor, a child learns that throwing the ball harder will make it bounce higher. By engaging in constructive play, children acquire bits of information that they use to build their knowledge. Greater knowledge, in turn, gives them increasingly higher levels of understanding and competence (Forman & Hill, 1980). Gradually, they learn to compare and classify events and objects, and they develop a better understanding of concepts such as size, shape, and texture. In addition, through active play, children develop skills that make them feel physically confident and self-assured (Athey, 1984).

PLAY AND EGOCENTRISM The egocentrism that Piaget ascribed to preoperational children is particularly evident in their play with others. Two-year-olds will watch other children and seem interested in them, but they will not usually approach them. If they do approach, the interaction typically centers on playing with the same toy or object—not with the other child per se (Hughes, 1991). Children 2 years old and younger may seem to be playing together but are almost always playing out separate fantasies.

Dramatic play reflects greater social maturity. The play of 3-year-olds shows a better understanding of others' views, which allows them to be better at role-playing games. In role playing, success depends on cooperation among the players; if children don't act out their parts, the game doesn't work. By age 4, some children can reliably identify play situations that are likely to produce happiness, sadness, fear, and anger (Borke, 1971, 1973).

In one study (Shatz & Gelman, 1973), researchers asked 4-year-olds to describe to 2-year-olds how a specific toy worked. Even 4-year-olds understood the need to address younger children in simpler terms. The researchers found that 4-year-olds spoke slowly, used short sentences, employed many attention-getting words such as "look" and "here," and frequently repeated the child's name. Four-year-olds did not speak to older children or adults in that way.

As with all behaviors, however, social maturity is relative. At the age of 3 or even 4, children can still be very stubborn and negative. But by age 3, children are likely to be more willing to conform to others' expectations. Other people are more important to 3-year-olds than they were a year earlier, and the children therefore seek out more social interaction. By now they are more interested in the effects of their behaviors on the world around them, and they gain considerable satisfaction from showing things that they make to others (Hughes, 1991).

DRAMATIC PLAY AND SOCIAL KNOWLEDGE Older preoperational children test their social knowledge in dramatic play. Through imitation, pretending, and role taking, dramatic play promotes the growth of symbolic representation. It also enables children to project themselves into other personalities, experiment with different roles, and experience a broader range of thought and feeling (see "A Matter for Debate," facing page). Role playing thus leads to

A MATTER FOR DEBATE

PRETEND AND REAL

Adults might be tempted to dismiss young children's pretend play as unimportant, perhaps even unhealthy. Quite the reverse is true, according to research findings.

When children are involved in pretend play, they often display two levels of meaning—the level of the reality-based meaning and the level of the pretend meaning. Children maintain two frames of meaning: a real frame and a play frame (Bateson, 1955). For example, when in the real frame, children playing cops and robbers know that they are actually children; yet they are deep in the pretend frame, too. When there are disagreements, children often "break frame" to resolve their disputes before returning to the pretend frame.

Pretend play becomes increasingly sophisticated during the preschool years (Rubin et al., 1983). Children make greater and greater leaps from the real to the pretend meaning of an object or action, and they extend the duration and complexity of their pretend roles and activities. The ability to tell the difference between fantasy and reality continues to develop, however; 4- to 6-year-olds sometimes actually believe that what they imagine is real (Harris et al., 1991).

Preschoolers are capable of various types of pretense (Lillard, 1991). They can pretend about the identity or characteristics of themselves, another person, an object, an event or action, or a situation. As children become older, they rely less on concrete props. Another developmental change is growing flexibility in using self versus another as either the actor or the recipient of action. At first, in solitary play, the child is both the agent and the recipient; the child pretends to go to sleep and covers up. Later, the child uses an object as the active agent—a doll lies down and goes to sleep as though it were doing this itself.

There seems to be a relationship between pretend play and distinctions between appearance and reality. Children who have had lots of practice with pretend play at ages 3 and 4 are better able to understand that objects can look like something else (Flavell et al., 1986; Flavell et al., 1987). Children who are experienced at pretend play are also better at taking someone else's perspective or understanding someone else's feelings. Researchers suggest that seemingly innocent make-believe play provides key experiences for children's development of structured (organized) knowledge (Flavell, 1985; Garvey, 1977).

better understanding of others as well as to a clearer definition of self (Fein, 1984).

Role playing allows children to experiment with behaviors and to experience the reactions and consequences of those behaviors. For example, children who play hospital with dolls, friends, or alone will play many different roles: patient, doctor, nurse, visitor. In acting out these roles, they may be motivated by real fears and anxieties about illness and dependence on others. Whatever the dramatic situation, role playing allows children to express intense feelings (such as anger or fears), helps them resolve conflicts (such as between them and parents or siblings), and helps them resolve those feelings and conflicts in ways they can understand.

THE ROLE OF PEERS   Given the opportunity, preschool children often spend more time interacting directly with each other than with adults. Children play with siblings and other children at home, in the neighborhood, and at school. In many cultures the significance of children's interactions with other children is even greater than it is in the American middle-class culture (Rogoff, 1990). In some societies younger children are cared for largely by 5- to 10-year-old children (Watson-Gegeo & Gegeo, 1989). Children may carry a younger sibling or cousin around on their backs or hips, thus enabling the younger children to experience the sights and sounds of the community (Rogoff, 1990).

Informal neighborhood groups often include children of various ages. Mixed-age peer groups can offer older children the opportunity to practice teaching and child care with younger children, while younger children can imitate and practice role relations with older children (Whiting & Edwards, 1988). The play activities of mixed-group children may encourage the development of new ways of thinking and problem solving.

REVIEW & APPLY

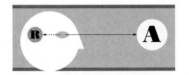

1. Describe the major forms of children's play.
2. How do children use play to explore their physical and social world?
3. Why is dramatic play so important to the development of cognitive skills in the preoperational child?

SUMMARY

Physical and Motor Development

- Throughout childhood, body proportions change dramatically. At birth, the head comprises one-quarter of overall body length, but by age 16, it accounts for only one-eighth of body length.
- As the skeletal system matures, bones develop and harden through ossification. Skeletal age may vary with respect to chronological age.
- By age 5, a child's brain is nearly the size of an adult's.
- Neurons begin forming during the embryonic period and are almost all present at birth.
- Myelination is the formation of insulating cells that cover the neurons. It is essential for the development of motor skills and coordination.
- The left and right hemispheres of the brain generally control functions of the opposite side of the body; this process is known as lateralization. Lateralization also includes specialization and dominance in certain areas of the hemispheres.
- For the majority of right-handed people, language is highly localized in areas of the left hemisphere. For left-handed people, language is often shared by the two sides of the brain.
- In a process termed *functional subordination*, actions that are initially performed for their own sake later become integrated into more complex, purposeful skills.
- Gross motor skills develop steadily during the preschool years. By age 3, gross motor behavior shows signs of automaticity—the ability to perform motor behaviors without consciously thinking about them.
- Fine motor skills—those involving coordinated and dexterous use of hand, fingers, and thumb—also begin to display automaticity near the end of the third year.
- Readiness is generally required for learning any new skill. Readiness refers to a certain level of maturation and the presence of certain basic skills.
- Motor learning is enhanced by practice, attention, competence motivation, and feedback.

Cognitive Development

- During the preoperational stage, preschool children expand their understanding of the world by using their growing language and problem-solving skills.
- The preoperational stage is divided into the preconceptual period (age 2–4) and the intuitive or transitional period (age 5–7).
- The thinking of peroperational children is characterized by animism (belief that anything that moves is alive) and reification (belief that objects and people in thoughts and dreams are real). These characteristics stem from egocentrism, the child's tendency to see and understand things in terms of her or his personal point of view.
- Rational thinking increases during the intuitive period, but children are also willing to use magical thinking to explain things.
- Symbolic representation—the use of actions, images, or words to represent objects and events—be-

gins at the end of the sensorimotor stage and is refined during the preoperational stage.

■ Thought processes become more complex with the use of symbols. Children's thinking becomes less egocentric and more sociocentric.

■ The thinking of preschool children is concrete; preoperational children do not understand abstractions. It is also irreversible; children see events as occurring in only one direction. It is characterized by egocentrism and centration (the tendency to focus on only one aspect or dimension of an object or situation). Young children also have little idea of cause-and-effect sequences. (See the study chart on page 215.)

■ Limitations of preoperational thinking are illustrated by Piaget's conservation problems. Preoperational children do not understand conservation of volume, mass, or number.

■ Further research has revealed some limitations of Piaget's theory. Preoperational children have been found to be less egocentric and to have more numerical skills than Piaget believed.

■ According to the social perspective, the ways in which adults demonstrate how to solve problems help children learn to think. All cultures initiate children into complex, meaningful activities through guided participation.

■ Memory is a key aspect of cognitive development. Memory processes begin when visual sensory information enters the brain's sensory register. Information that is attended to enters short-term or working memory. If an effort is made to remember the information, it passes to long-term memory. Memory can consist of images, actions, or words.

■ Recognition refers to the ability to identify objects or situations as having previously been seen or experienced. Recall refers to the ability to retrieve long-term memories with few cues or prompts.

■ Recall can be improved by organizing and rehearsing information. Preschool children are able to use such strategies but do not often do so unless they are taught—and even then the learning does not endure.

■ Children can remember information that is ordered temporally, or in a time sequence.

Language Development

■ Children's grammar expands in several stages: two-word utterances; slightly longer utterances, often including overregularizing of inflections; modifica-

tion of simple sentences, including creating negative and imperative forms; and utterances including increasingly sophisticated language elements.

■ Throughout the preschool period, children learn words rapidly. Although many methods of talking and relating to children facilitate language development, it is not entirely clear how parents' language use and children's language development interact.

■ Parents talk differently to male and female children, thereby contributing to gender differences.

■ Young children's conversations are often collective monologues in which children take turns speaking but may be talking about unrelated subjects.

■ In learning pragmatics, or the social aspects of language, children learn that language expresses social status, roles, and values.

■ Some children speak subdialects, such as Black English, in addition to American Standard English. Use of subdialects in school can be an important mode of self-expression, as long as students also become competent in the mainstream language.

■ Many children grow up in bilingual environments. Most researchers believe that bilingualism does not hamper development and can be an advantage in cultural and cognitive terms.

Play and Learning

■ Children play in a variety of ways. Play aimed at sensory play is engaged in for the sake of sensory experiences. Play with motion includes activities such as running, jumping, and skipping. Rough-and-tumble play offers a chance to exercise and release energy and helps children learn to handle their feelings, control their impulses, and avoid inappropriate behaviors. Play with language gives children practice in mastering the grammar and words they're learning. Other kinds of play include dramatic play and modeling, and games, rituals, and competitive play.

■ Play promotes cognitive development in that it gives children opportunities to explore physical objects and to develop a better understanding of concepts such as size, shape, and texture.

■ Children's play becomes less egocentric with age.

■ Older preoperational children test their social knowledge in dramatic play.

■ The play activities of mixed-group children may encourage the development of new ways of thinking and problem solving.

KEY TERMS

neurons	intrinsically motivated behavior	mean length of utterance (MLU)
glial cells	extrinsically motivated behavior	overregularize
myelination	egocentrism	collective monologues
lateralization	conservation	pragmatics
functional subordination	recognition	subdialects
automaticity	recall	

USING WHAT YOU'VE LEARNED

Experts on early childhood believe that pretend play is valuable for preschoolers. Through pretend play, children practice language, test their knowledge, and rehearse social roles. Conduct an inconspicuous 5-minute observation of two or more preschool children involved in pretend play to consider what they might be learning. Divide a sheet of paper into two columns. In one column, record the behaviors and language of two children at play, describing it in as much detail as possible. Try to be like a video camera, capturing the sequencing and style of play as well as the children's actions and words, using telegraphic comments as necessary. For example, you might write "José puffed chest, shouted, 'Dummy!'"

In the other column, try to interpret each behavior that you observed. Try to assess the children's thoughts, feelings, and intentions. For example, you might decide this: "José, playing father, appeared angry at his 'son's' mistakes. Might he be imitating his father or fearing the results of his own mistakes?"

Also consider whether your interpretations might be mistaken, and why. (You may wish to review the discussion of research methods in Chapter 1.)

SUGGESTED READINGS

BERK, L., & WINSLER, A. (1995). *Scaffolding children's learning: Vygotsky and early childhood education.* Washington, DC: National Association for the Education of Young Children. The authors describe effective ways to structure preschoolers' play and learning activities consistent with a vygotskian perspective.

BRUBE, M. (1998) *Life as we know it: A father, a family and an exceptional child.* New York: Vintage. A personal account of raising a son with Down Syndrome, written by a father for whom the experience raises serious questions about the nature of social justice, natural rights, and our obligations to one another.

GARVEY, C. (1990). *Play.* Cambridge, MA: Harvard University Press. A concise description of the developmental forms of children's play.

JONES, E., & NIMMO, J. (1994). *Emergent curriculum.* Washington, DC: National Association for the Education of Young Children. Some excellent ideas for designing education for young children. Each year, this organization publishes four or five paperback books on timely topics aimed at preschool, kindergarten, or primary school educators.

PALEY, V. G. (1990). *The boy who would be helicopter: The uses of storytelling in the classroom.* Cambridge, MA: Harvard University Press. An engaging account of one boy's odyssey from social isolation to integration woven into an insightful essay on excellent early childhood education.

PAUL, J. L., & SIMEONSSON, R. J. (Eds.) (1993). *Children with special needs: Family, culture and society* (2nd ed.). New York: Harcourt Brace Jovanovich. A collection of insightful articles on the meaning and experience of a child with disabilities in different family and cultural contexts.

SHEA, C. H., SHEBILSKE, W. L., & WORCHEL, S. (1993). *Motor learning and control.* Englewood Cliffs, NJ: Prentice Hall. An excellent overview of the princi-ples involved in motor control and training, with case examples.

SINGER, D. G., & REVENSON, T. A. (1996). *How a child thinks: A Piaget primer* (revised ed.). New York: Plume. A very readable book replete with examples of Pooh and preoperational thinking.

Preschool Children: Personality Development and Socialization

CHAPTER

7

CHAPTER OBJECTIVES

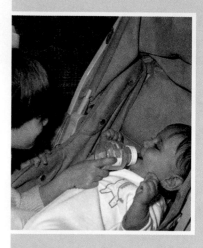

By the time you have finished this chapter, you should be able to do the following:

1. Explain the strong feelings and conflicts that preschool children face.
2. List potential sources of fear and anxiety, and describe ways in which children cope with them.
3. Discuss factors that influence aggressive and prosocial behavior.
4. Analyze the development of the self-concept during the preschool period.
5. Describe how children internalize social concepts and gender schemes in forming their self-concept.
6. Explain the impact of parenting styles and parental warmth and control on psychosocial development during early childhood.
7. List and analyze some of the ways in which siblings influence each other's social development.
8. Discuss how disciplinary techniques have changed over the years, and describe current child-rearing goals.

The preschool period is a time when the pace of children's learning about their social world accelerates. Ideally, children learn what constitutes good and bad behavior; how to handle their feelings, wants, and needs in socially appropriate ways; and what their family, community, and society at large expect of them. They begin to acquire the norms, rules, and mores of their culture. At the same time, they develop a keen and perhaps lasting concept of self.

Normally, children's self-control and social competence improve dramatically from age 2 to age 6. Although 2-year-olds have all the basic emotions of 6-year-olds (and adults), they express them differently. During the "terrible twos," children can truly be difficult (often unintentionally), but they are often wonderfully charming and affectionate as well. Immediate gratification is the rule, however; deviations from it can produce dramatic emotional outbursts. If a mother promises her 2-year-old an ice-cream cone, the 2-year-old wants it *now*, not after the mother has a chat with a friend whom she happens to meet in front of the ice-cream parlor. Expressions of dependency are also direct and physical. In unfamiliar settings, 2-year-olds stay close to their mother or father, perhaps clinging. If they venture away, they often return to the parent, using him or her as a "secure base." If they are forcibly separated from the parent, they may throw themselves on the floor and howl in protest. Anger in particular is expressed in physical ways. Instead of expressing themselves verbally, 2-year-olds may kick or bite.

In contrast, 6-year-olds are much more verbal and thoughtful; they are less quick to anger, and they control themselves better. They cope with anger and frustration in far more diverse ways. For example, 6-year-olds can vent anger by kicking a door or a teddy bear rather than a brother or a sister or a parent's shin. Some can even hold in their anger and not express it outwardly at all. Some can assume an assertive posture to defend their rights or can use fantasy to see themselves through unpleasant situations. Six-year-olds are also much less likely to kick and howl. Instead, they talk out their anger or fear, or express it indirectly—for example, by being uncooperative and grumpy.

In sum, by age 6, most children's abilities to cope are quite refined, and they have their own personal style based on their developing self-image.

THREE PERSPECTIVES REVISITED

Socialization during the preschool years is complex; it is no wonder that experts disagree about the major influences and critical interactions that take place, as well as about how to study them. Three major theoretical perspectives govern much contemporary research on socialization during the preschool years. As we'll see, each has its merits and its shortcomings.

Psychodynamic perspectives emphasize the child's feelings, drives, and developmental conflicts. Freud emphasized that preschool children must learn to cope with powerful innate emotions in socially acceptable ways. Erikson emphasized the growth of autonomy and the need to balance it with dependence on parents during this period.

In contrast, *social-learning perspectives* emphasize links between cognition, behavior, and the environment. The child's behavior is shaped by external rewards and punishments, as well as by role models. Rewards can also be internal, in that children may behave in ways that augment self-esteem and pride and a sense of accomplishment.

Finally, *cognitive-developmental perspectives* emphasize children's thoughts and concepts as organizers of their social behavior. Preschool children develop increasingly complex concepts; they learn what it means to be a girl or a boy, a sister or a brother. Children also learn to fit their behavior into accepted gender schemes: They judge what behaviors are appropriate for boys and for girls.

Each perspective has led to important theories and conclusions about socialization and personality development, as discussed next.

Preschoolers have intense feelings that they must learn to handle during these early years. Learning that losing a race is not the end of the world may take away some of this child's sadness.

PSYCHODYNAMIC PERSPECTIVES

Children must learn to manage a wide range of feelings or emotions. Some of these are good—such as joy, affection, and pride. Others—such as anger, fear, anxiety, jealousy, frustration, and pain—obviously are not. Whether the feelings are good or bad, however, preschool children must acquire some means of moderating their feelings and expressing them in socially acceptable ways.

Children must also find ways of resolving developmental conflicts. They must learn to deal with their dependence on others and find ways to relate to the authority figures in their lives. They must deal with their need for **autonomy**—the strong drive to do things for themselves, to master their physical and social environments, to be competent and successful. How children master these tasks has been explored extensively by psychodynamic theorists, especially Erikson. As Erikson suggests, children who are unable to resolve these early psychosocial conflicts may have difficulty with adjustment later in life (Erikson, 1963).

The sense of personal and cultural identity that children form between the ages of 2 and 6 is accompanied by many strong feelings. Finding acceptable ways of coping with feelings of fear and anxiety, distress and anger, affection

autonomy   The strong drive to do things for yourself, to master physical and social environments, and to be competent and successful.

and joy, and sensuality and sexual curiosity is no easy task, and children often experience conflict while doing so.

FEAR AND ANXIETY

One of the most important forces that children must learn to deal with is the stress caused by fear and anxiety. The two emotions are not synonymous. **Fear** is a response to a specific stimulus or situation: A child may fear the dark or lightning and thunder, or have a phobia of big dogs or high places. In contrast, **anxiety** is a more generalized emotional state. Whereas some children may become anxious in specific situations, those who are characterized as "anxious" experience regular and continuing feelings of apprehension and unease, often without knowing why. A move to a new neighborhood or a sudden change in parental expectations, such as the beginning of toilet training, may induce anxiety that seems to come from nowhere. Many psychologists believe that anxiety inevitably accompanies the socialization process as the child attempts to avoid the pain of parental displeasure and discipline (Wenar, 1990).

CAUSES OF FEAR AND ANXIETY   Fear and anxiety can have many causes. Young children may be afraid that their parents will leave them or stop loving them. Parents usually act in a loving and accepting fashion, but sometimes they withdraw their love, attention, and protection as a means of punishment. Withdrawal of love threatens children and makes them feel anxious. Anticipation of other types of punishment, especially physical punishment, is another source of anxiety for young children. Two-year-olds sometimes have no realistic idea of how far their parents will go in punishing them. When an exasperated parent shouts, "I'm going to break every bone in your body!" the young child may not fully appreciate that the threat is an empty one.

Fear and anxiety may be increased or even created by the child's imagination. For example, children often imagine that the birth of a new baby will cause their parents to reject them. Sometimes anxiety results from children's awareness of their own unacceptable feelings—anger at a parent or other caregiver, jealousy of a sibling or a friend, or a recurrent desire to be held like a baby.

The sources of some fears are easily identified—fear of the doctor who gives inoculations, dread inspired by the smell of a hospital or the sound of a dentist's drill. Other fears are harder to understand. Many preschoolers develop a fear of the dark that is related more to fantasies and dreams than to real events in the child's life. Sometimes the fantasies stem directly from developmental conflicts with which the child is currently struggling; for example, fearsome imaginary tigers or ghosts may arise from the child's struggle with dependency and autonomy.

A classic study of children's fears (Jersild & Holmes, 1935) found that younger children were most likely to be afraid of specific objects or situations, such as strangers, unfamiliar things, the dark, loud noises, or falling. In contrast, children aged 5 or 6 were more likely to fear imaginary or abstract things—monsters, robbers, death, being alone, or being ridiculed. Fifty years later, researchers found most of the same fears in preschool children, except that fear of the dark, of being alone, and of unfamiliar things now appear at earlier ages (Draper & James, 1985).

In today's world there are many sources of fear, anxiety, and stress. Some are a normal part of growing up, such as being yelled at for accidentally breaking something or being teased by an older sibling. Others are more serious: internal stresses like illness and pain and the chronic long-term stresses created

fear   A state of arousal, tension, or apprehension caused by a specific, identifiable circumstance.

anxiety   A feeling of uneasiness, apprehension, or fear that has a vague or unknown source.

by unfavorable social environments—poverty, parental conflict or drug use, dangerous neighborhoods (Greene & Brooks, 1985). Some children must cope with major disasters or terrors, such as earthquakes, floods, and wars. Severe or long-term stressful situations can drain the psychological resources of even the most resilient child (Honig, 1986; Rutter, 1983).

Although we naturally try to avoid and minimize fear and anxiety, it's important to bear in mind that these are normal feelings that are necessary to development. In mild forms, they can be a spur to new learning. Many kinds of fear are necessary for our very survival in a world full of potentially dangerous things such as hot stoves, electrical appliances, fast-moving cars and trucks, and stray animals.

COPING WITH FEAR AND ANXIETY   How can we help children cope with fear and anxiety? Using force or ridicule is likely to have negative results, and ignoring children's fears will not always make them go away. Instead, at least when their fears are mild, children can be gently and sympathetically encouraged to confront and overcome them. Parents can help by demonstrating that there is little to fear. For example, to help a child who is afraid of night-time "robbers," parents can have the child watch while they check the locks on all the doors and otherwise verify the home's security. With fears that have acquired phobia status, however, children (and adults as well) may need professional treatment in the form of **systematic desensitization.** In this procedure, after learning certain relaxation techniques, the person works through a "hierarchy" that begins with minimally fearsome versions of the object or situation and eventually progresses to the real thing. For example, a child who is afraid of dogs might practice staying relaxed while looking at a simple drawing of a dog, then at a more detailed drawing, then at a photograph, and eventually at a real dog.

systematic desensitization   In behavior therapy, a technique that gradually reduces an individual's anxiety about a specific object or situation.

Often the best way to help children cope with anxiety is to reduce unnecessary stress in their lives. When children show unusually high levels of tension or have frequent temper tantrums, it's helpful to simplify their lives by stick-

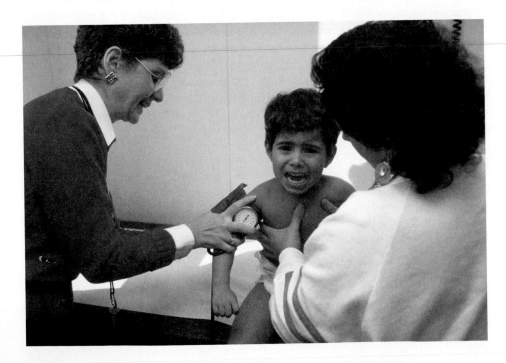

No child really enjoys going to the doctor. Often a trip to the doctor's office is linked in a child's mind with a painful injection.

ing to daily routines, specifying clearly what is expected of them, and helping them anticipate special events such as visits by friends and relatives. Other helpful strategies include reducing their exposure to parental fighting or violent television programs and protecting them from being teased or tormented by neighborhood bullies or gangs.

Not all life stresses can be avoided or minimized, of course. Children must learn to cope with the birth of a sibling, moving to a new home, or entering day care, as well as, sometimes, with divorce, the death of a parent, or natural catastrophes. Under such circumstances parents and teachers are encouraged to do the following (Honig, 1986):

1. Learn to recognize and interpret stress reactions in their children.
2. Provide a warm, secure base to help children regain confidence.
3. Allow opportunities for children to discuss their feelings—a shared trauma is easier to handle.
4. Temporarily allow immature or regressive behavior, such as thumb sucking, cuddling a blanket, fussing, or sitting on laps.
5. Help children give meaning to the event or circumstance by providing explanations that are appropriate to their age level.

Bear in mind that children also develop their own means of coping with fears and anxiety. For example, quite normal 2- to 4-year-olds often display highly repetitive, ritualized behaviors that in adults would be deemed "obsessive-compulsive" (Evans et al., 1997). A child who is afraid of the dark, for example, might develop a highly specific ritual for saying good night to parents in a certain order and with an exact number of kisses or hugs, thus reducing anxiety about going to bed.

DEFENSE MECHANISMS   In response to more generalized feelings of anxiety—especially those that arise in the intense emotional climate of the family and involve issues of morality or sex roles—children learn strategies called **defense mechanisms.** In psychoanalytic theory, a defense mechanism is a way of reducing or at least disguising anxiety. We often employ defense mechanisms in coping with anxiety and frustration. For example, we occasionally use *rationalization* when we don't get something we want. If you don't get that promotion you were hoping for, you might rationalize away your disappointment by telling yourself that you wouldn't have liked the increased responsibility anyway. If a child isn't invited to a party, the child might rationalize that he or she wouldn't have had a good time at the party anyway. Common defense mechanisms—many of which were clarified or identified by Freud's daughter Anna (1966)—are listed in Table 7–1. By age 5 or 6, most children have learned to use basic defense mechanisms.

HISTORICAL AND CULTURAL INFLUENCES   As a result of differences in cultural and family backgrounds, children experience fear and anxiety about different things. A hundred years ago, children were afraid of wolves and bears. Fifty years ago, they worried more about goblins and "bogeymen." Nowadays their nightmares are populated with extraterrestrials and killer robots. There are also striking cultural differences in the way children express their fears, indeed whether they express their fears at all. In contemporary Western culture, showing fear is generally frowned upon. Children (especially boys) are supposed to be brave; most parents worry about a child who is unusually fearful. In contrast, traditional Navajo parents believe that it is healthy and normal for a child to be afraid; they consider a fearless child foolhardy. In one study, Navajo parents reported an average of 22 fears in their children,

defense mechanisms   The cognitive "tricks" that individuals use to reduce tensions that lead to anxiety.

TABLE 7–1 COMMON DEFENSE MECHANISMS USED BY CHILDREN

Identification: The process of incorporating the values, attitudes, and beliefs of others. Children adopt the attitudes of powerful figures, such as parents, in order to become more like these figures—more lovable, powerful, and accepted—to help reduce the anxiety they often feel about their own relative helplessness.

Denial: Refusal to admit that a situation exists or that an event happened. Children may react to an upsetting situation such as the death of a pet by pretending that the pet is still living in the house and sleeping with them at night.

Displacement: Substituting something or someone else for the real source of anger or fear. For example, Tyler may be angry with his baby sister, but he can't hit her—perhaps he can't even admit to himself that he wants to hit her. Instead, then, he torments the family dog or cat.

Projection: Attributing undesirable thoughts or actions to someone else and in the process distorting reality. "She did it, not me" is a projective statement. "She wants to hurt me" may seem more acceptable than "I want to hurt her." Projection thus sets the stage for a distorted form of "self-defense": "If she wants to hurt me, I'd better do it to her first."

Rationalization: Persuading yourself that you don't want what you can't have. Even relatively young children are capable of talking themselves out of things. A child who doesn't get invited to a party might decide, "Oh, well. I wouldn't have had a good time anyway." Rationalization is a common defense mechanism that continues to develop and refine well into adulthood.

Reaction formation: Behaving in ways opposite to your inclinations. When children have thoughts or desires that make them anxious, they may react by behaving in a contradictory way. For example, they might like to cling to their parents, but instead they push them away and behave with exaggerated independence and assertiveness.

Regression: Returning to an earlier or more infantile form of behavior as a way of coping with a stressful situation. Perhaps when frustrated, an eight-year-old suddenly reverts to sucking her thumb and carrying around her "blankie"—behaviors that were given up years before.

Repression: An extreme form of denial in which the person *unconsciously* erases a frightening event or circumstance from awareness. There is no need to rely on fantasy because the child literally does not remember that the event ever occurred.

Withdrawal: Simply removing yourself from an unpleasant situation. This is a very common defense mechanism in young children. It is the most direct defense possible. If a situation seems too difficult, the child withdraws from it either physically or mentally.

including fears of supernatural beings. In contrast, a group of Anglo-American parents from rural Montana reported an average of only 4 fears in their children (Tikalsky & Wallace, 1988).

OTHER EMOTIONS

Western societies also expect children to inhibit the display of other emotions, both negative and positive, such as anger and distress, affection and joy, sensuality and sexual curiosity. Most parents expect their children to learn what Claire Kopp (1989) calls *emotion regulation*, meaning dealing with emotions in socially acceptable ways.

Kopp calls children's growing ability to control their behavior *self-regulation*: Children adopt and internalize a composite of specific standards for behavior,

Different cultures often elicit fears about different things as well as sanctioning different ways of expressing them. This Korean child tries to hide her tearful anxiety rather than "let it all hang out."

such as safety concerns and respect for the property of others. *Compliance*, a component of self-regulation, refers to obeying the requests of caregivers. During toddlerhood, parents' requests, such as "stay indoors" or "pick up your toys," may be met with crying. During the third year, crying occurs infrequently, but "resistive behavior" such as refusal to obey requests increases and peaks. By age 4, resistance declines. Kopp argues that resistance does not decline simply because language skills and communication between child and parents are improving; instead, a 4-year-old's cognitive skills have improved to a point where the child can convey personal needs in more socially acceptable and less emotional ways.

Emotion regulation is a normal part of children's psychosocial development, especially during the first 7 years of life. Children who fail to learn the bounds of acceptable behavior may develop mild to severe emotional problems, such as disruptive behaviors and personality disorders (Cole et al., 1994).

DISTRESS AND ANGER   Children learn very early that open displays of negative feelings are unacceptable in public places—including nursery schools and day-care centers (Dencik, 1989). As children grow older, their parents' expectations for emotional regulation increase: It's okay for babies to cry when they're hungry, but it is not okay for 6-year-olds to do so. Children who do not learn such lessons at home are at risk of being socially rejected outside the home. In particular, preschoolers who cry a lot are likely to be unpopular with their peers (Kopp, 1989).

Learning to manage anger is even more important. In one longitudinal study, children who were still having temper tantrums at the age of 10 were tracked into adulthood (Caspi et al., 1987). The researchers found that the children tended to be unsuccessful as adults as a result of their continuing outbursts of anger. They had difficulty holding jobs, and their marriages often ended in divorce.

Learning to manage negative emotions is not the same as not having them—negative emotions are an inevitable part of life. Children can come to accept their angry feelings as a normal part of themselves while at the same time learning to control or redirect their reactions to such feelings. They may use anger as a motivating force, as a way of overcoming obstacles, or as a means of standing up for themselves or others.

AFFECTION AND JOY   In our culture, children must also learn to restrain their positive emotions. Spontaneous feelings such as joy, affection, excitement, and playfulness are dealt with quite differently by 2-year-olds and 6-year-olds. Just as 2-year-olds are direct in expressing distress, they are also likely to openly display positive feelings—they freely jump up and down or clap their hands when excited. As preschool socialization continues, children learn to subdue such open expressiveness. Spontaneous joy and affection become embarrassing because they are considered babyish, so most children learn to limit their spontaneity to acceptable occasions such as parties and games.

SENSUALITY AND SEXUAL CURIOSITY   Two-year-olds are very sensual creatures. They like the feel of messy, gooey things. They are conscious of the softness or stiffness of clothes against their skin; they are fascinated by sounds, lights, tastes, and smells. Consistent with psychoanalytic theory, such sensuality is primarily oral during infancy, but the preschooler has a new awareness of and fascination with the anal and then the genital regions. Masturbation and sex play are quite common during the preschool period, although most

Young children are very open about showing positive feelings like joy. But by the age of 6 they have learned to somewhat mask even these feelings.

children in our culture quickly learn not to display such behaviors when adults are present. As children discover that self-stimulation is pleasurable, most develop active curiosity about their bodies and ask many sex-related questions.

The ways in which the culture and the family react to the child's developing sensuality and sexual curiosity can have a powerful effect, just as the reactions of others affect the way children handle hostility and joy. Until recently, parents in our society were advised to prevent their children from engaging in sexual exploration (Wolfenstein, 1951), and many parents still do. Whether openly or in private, however, sensual exploration is a natural and vital part of experience, beginning in early childhood and continuing into adolescence and adulthood.

DEVELOPMENTAL CONFLICTS

Trying to express their feelings in socially acceptable ways is not the only task young children face during the preschool years. Developmental conflicts also arise as children adjust to their own changing needs. Preschool children are pulled in one direction by their need for autonomy and in another direction by their continuing dependence on their parents. They must also deal with issues of mastery and competence.

AUTONOMY AND CONNECTEDNESS   Preschoolers constantly struggle with themselves and others. Out of the close sense of "connectedness" that 2-year-olds have with their caregivers emerges a new sense of autonomy—the conviction that they can do *it* (whatever *it* is) themselves. Ambivalence between the opposing forces of autonomy and connectedness is characteristic of the early preschool period.

Although dependence and independence are commonly considered opposite types of behavior, things aren't necessarily that simple for young children. Independence follows a complex trajectory during the preschool period. Whereas infants are usually fairly cooperative, everything changes at about

All children need to feel a sense of mastery over their environment. This feeling of mastery may lead to chaos at times, but it is still a key aspect of development.

age 2. Many children now become quite uncooperative, the hallmark of the "terrible twos." Temper tantrums become common. When 2-year-olds are asked to do something, they show their independence by saying "No!" As they get older, however, children tend to become compliant and cooperative again. Three-year-olds are more likely to do what their parents tell them and less likely to break rules when their parents aren't looking, perhaps as a result of their developing sense of morality (Emde & Buchsbaum, 1990; Howes & Olenick, 1986).

One study (Craig & Garney, 1972) traced developmental trends in expressions of dependency by observing how children at ages 2, 2½, and 3 maintained contact with their mothers in an unfamiliar situation. The 2-year-olds spent most of their time physically close to their mothers, staying in the same part of the room and looking up often to make sure that their mother was still there. The older children (2½- and 3-year-olds) neither stayed as close to their mother nor checked as often to see whether she had left the room. The older the child, the more the child maintained verbal rather than physical contact. All three age groups made a point of drawing attention to their activities, but the older children were more inclined to demonstrate them from afar.

MASTERY AND COMPETENCE   Preschoolers are discovering their own bodies and learning to control them. If they are successful in doing things for themselves, they become self-confident. If their efforts at autonomy are frustrated by criticism or punishment, they think that they have failed and feel ashamed and doubtful about themselves (Erikson, 1963; Murphy, 1962; White, 1959).

In Erikson's third stage, *initiative versus guilt*, the primary developmental conflict from age 3 to age 6 directly involves mastery and competence. Initiative refers to the purposefulness of young children as they ambitiously explore their surroundings. They eagerly learn new skills, interact with peers, and seek the guidance of parents in their social interactions. Guilt is inevitable too, as when children go against their parents' wishes in exploring their world.

The key is to achieve a balance between initiative and guilt. As Erikson pointed out, excessive guilt can dampen the child's initiative, especially if parents harshly suppress or criticize their children's natural curiosity. Children's self-confidence and initiative-taking breaks down, resulting in timidity and fearfulness that remain a part of personality for life.

The conflict between initiative and guilt is an extension of the toddler's struggle with autonomy. Toddlers gain control and competence starting with their own bodies—feeding, dressing, toileting, handling objects, and getting around. Ideally, preschoolers learn how things work, what social situations and relationships mean, and how to influence people in constructive and appropriate ways. Concepts of right and wrong, good and bad, become important; labels such as "sissy," "baby," or "brat" can have devastating effects. The job of the parent or teacher is to guide and discipline the child without creating too much anxiety or guilt. In the often confusing and complex social world of the preschool child, initiative can lead either to success and feelings of competence or to failure and feelings of frustration.

LEARNING COMPETENCE   What happens when children's attempts at mastery or autonomy meet with constant failure or frustration? What happens when children have little or no opportunity to try things on their own, or when their environment is so chaotic that they can't see the consequences of their acts? All children need to master their environment and to feel competent and successful. If they do not, they may give up trying to learn and then become passive in their interactions with the world. Many studies have shown that such children fail to develop an active, exploratory, self-confident approach to learning; they lack *learning competence* (White & Watts, 1973). Moreover, when children are made to feel anxious about their need for autonomy, they generally learn to deny, minimize, or disguise their needs.

Some children are restricted in their drive toward autonomy. Children who are physically handicapped or chronically ill may have little opportunity to test their skills in mastering the environment (Rutter, 1979). Children who grow up in dangerous or crowded surroundings and have to be restrained for their own safety, or who are supervised by excessively vigilant caregivers, may also develop exaggerated passivity or anxiety (Zuravin, 1985).

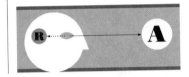

REVIEW & APPLY

1. What are the primary causes of fear and anxiety in preschool children? List some ways in which children cope with fear and anxiety.
2. Describe the role of regulation of emotion in the psychosocial development of the preschool child.
3. Discuss the major developmental conflicts during the preschool years.

SOCIAL-LEARNING PERSPECTIVES

Preschool children must also learn to control their aggressive tendencies and must engage in positive behaviors such as helping and sharing. Although Freud considered aggression to be an inherent drive, the social-learning perspective is quite different. In this view, whether we are born with aggressive tendencies or not, actual aggressive behavior varies considerably from one person to the next as a result of reinforcement, punishment, and imitation of models. Behaviors such as helping and sharing are similarly affected by learning, even though we may also have inherent tendencies in this respect. Thus, the focus of research on both negative and positive behaviors is directed at studying how children are influenced by interactions with parents, siblings, peers, and others.

The preschool child's social repertoire is also strongly affected by play and other peer interactions. Although theorists disagree about the origins and purposes of play, it is clear that play enhances social skills by giving children practice in getting along with others.

AGGRESSION

In the language of social psychology, **hostile aggression** is behavior that is intended to harm another or to establish dominance over another. A child hits another child as an act of revenge, a child pushes another child down as a sort of preschool terrorism. **Instrumental aggression** involves harm caused as a byproduct of some goal-directed behavior. A child pushes another child down while trying to grab a toy; the resulting harm is unintentional. Both forms of aggression differ from *assertiveness*, which does not involve harm and instead takes forms such as standing up for your rights, perhaps in self-defense.

Aggression may be physical or verbal. It may be directed at people or "displaced" onto animals or objects. In preschool children, aggression is a common

hostile aggression   Aggression that is intended to harm another person.

instrumental aggression   Aggression that is not intended to harm, but is instead incidental to gaining something from another person.

response to anger and hostility. Typically, physical aggression increases during the early preschool period and then declines as verbal aggression begins to replace it (Achenbach et al., 1991; Parke & Slahy, 1983). The decline in aggression is also associated with children's growing ability to resolve conflicts in nonaggressive ways—through negotiation, for example—and with their improving experience in *how* to play (Shantz, 1987). In addition, by the age of 6 or 7, children are less egocentric and better able to understand another child's point of view. This understanding helps in two ways: Children are less likely to misinterpret another child's behavior as aggression that might invite retaliation, and they are better able to empathize with how another child feels when harmed.

FRUSTRATION AND AGGRESSION   Learning theorists once argued that *frustration*—a typically angry state produced when goals are blocked or thwarted—leads to aggression. Can frustration cause aggression? Of course, whenever someone does something that makes you angry and you retaliate verbally or even physically, frustration leads to aggression. However, the *frustration-aggression hypothesis* (Dollard et al., 1939) has been shown to be incorrect. This hypothesis stated that *all* aggression is derived from frustration, and that sooner or later all frustration results in some form of aggression, either direct or disguised. The aggression might be directed toward the source of the frustration, or it might be displaced onto another person or object—for example, a parent scolds a child and takes away a toy, and a little while later the child kicks the family pet.

The frustration-aggression hypothesis was challenged by a classic study of the behavior of preschool children in a frustrating situation (Barker et al., 1943). The children were given access to attractive toys, which were then removed and placed behind a wire screen; the toys thus remained visible but beyond reach. How did the children react? A few did display aggressive behaviors. Others, however, simply tried to leave the room, or waited patiently, or turned their attention to something else. Some engaged in behaviors such as thumb sucking.

The other half of the frustration-aggression hypothesis—the idea that all aggression is derived from frustration—has been similarly discredited (Dollard & Miller, 1950). Aggression can occur as a result of imitation, as we saw in Bandura's classic experiment on observational learning in Chapter 1. Simply rewarding children for aggressive behavior causes it to increase (Parke & Slahy, 1983). Thus, frustration *can* lead to aggression, and vice versa, but aggression can occur for many other reasons as well.

PUNISHMENT AND AGGRESSION   Punishment can also ceate a tendency to behave aggressively—especially if the punishment is harsh and frequent. If children are punished for aggressive acts, they will avoid these behaviors—in the presence of the person who has punished them. Ironically, however, they may become more aggressive in general. For example, their aggression at home may decrease, but they may become more aggressive at school. They may express aggression in different ways, such as tattling or name-calling. Adults who use physical punishment to curb a child's aggression also provide a model of aggressive behavior. One study (Strassberg et al., 1994) found that preschool children who received spankings at home were more aggressive than children who did not. Moreover, the more often the children were spanked, the more aggressive they were. In other words, a young child who is spanked may learn that if someone is smaller than you, it's okay to use force.

The mother's pointing finger tells the story about the child's behavior.

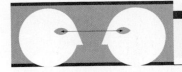

A MATTER FOR DEBATE

THE EFFECTS OF TELEVISION

Television is not merely an electronic toy or a casual means of entertainment. It is a pervasive influence that has a major impact on family relationships and especially on children. In 1950, only 1 family in 20 had a TV set. Ten years later, about 90% of American homes had TV sets. Today virtually every family in the United States, Western Europe, and Japan has at least one TV set; many families have several, one for each member of the household.

In developed nations, children spend more time watching TV than doing anything else except sleeping (Fabes, Wilson, & Christopher, 1989; Huston et al., 1989). The average child watches about $7\frac{1}{2}$ hours of television programming per day (Bennett, 1993). For better or worse, therefore, television programming is a major socializing force in our society.

Many researchers have concluded that exposing children to large doses of casual violence on the TV screen teaches them to think of aggression as a commonplace and acceptable way of dealing with frustration and anger.

Others have taken the opposite view, arguing that viewing violent acts on television may serve as a substitute for overt aggression, thus providing *catharsis*—an acceptable outlet for aggressive impulses that decreases aggressiveness (Feshback & Singer, 1971). Research evidence does not support the latter view, however. A large number of studies have shown that exposure to televised violence produces a small but significant increase in the aggressiveness of viewers (Heath, 1989; Huston et al., 1989).

For some children, habitual viewing of aggressive programs may be combined with an environment in which many role models—parents, siblings, or friends—are also aggressive or antisocial. This combination seems to increase aggressive behavior, especially in children with behavioral or emotional problems (Heath, 1989; Huesmann et al., 1984).

Many other aspects of televised program content affect children. Often certain kinds of people are presented in a stereotyped fashion: Members of minority groups may be depicted in unfavorable ways; women may be shown in passive, subordinate roles; and older people may be made to appear senile or burdensome. Children can therefore develop unrealistic social beliefs and concepts by watching television. Even their overall view of the world may be affected. One study found that heavy television-viewing causes people to see the world as a mean and threatening place—probably because there are more frightening incidents on television than occur in most people's everyday experience (Rubinstein, 1983).

Despite numerous studies that have identified negative effects of television viewing, television can also have a positive influence on children's thoughts and actions. Television can teach children many forms of prosocial behavior. Carefully designed children's programs interweave themes such as cooperation, sharing, affection, friendship, persistence at tasks, control of aggression, and coping with frustration. Children who watch such programs, even for relatively short periods, become more cooperative, sympathetic, and nurturant (Stein & Friedrich, 1975).

MODELING AND AGGRESSION As noted earlier, observing aggressive models can strongly influence antisocial behavior. Imitation of models is more likely to occur when the observers sense a similarity between themselves and the model or when the model is perceived as powerful or competent (Eisenberg, 1988). Thus, boys are more likely to imitate other boys or men than to imitate girls or women. Children are also more likely to imitate other children who have dominant personalities—that is, who are socially powerful (Abramovitch & Grusec, 1978). Well-liked children dominate their peers through the force of their personalities, not through physical aggression. In contrast, preschool children dislike physically aggressive playmates (Ladd et al., 1988). Not all models come from the child's immediate environment, of course; many varieties of potentially powerful models appear on television, as discussed in "A Matter for Debate" above.

Just how many television sets are there? Figure 7–1 gives a global view. Social learning also takes place via a wide array of other media, including radio, music, and other sources as illustrated in Figure 7–2.

FIGURE 7–1   THE AVAILABILITY OF RADIOS AND TELEVISION SETS
IN THE NATIONS OF THE WORLD

Source: U.S. Census Bureau, 1997.

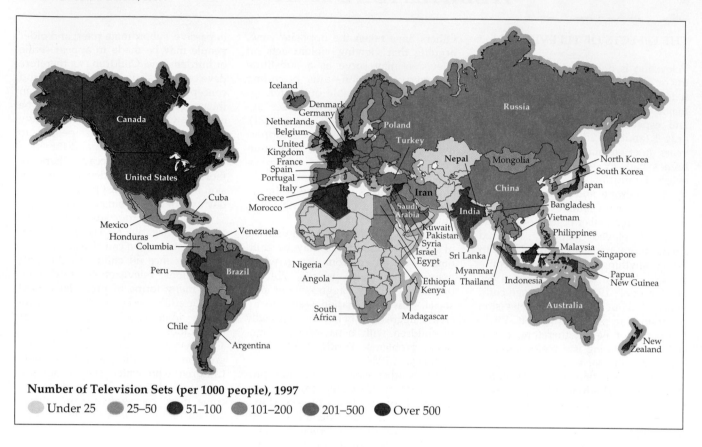

Number of Television Sets (per 1000 people), 1997

⬤ Under 25   ⬤ 25–50   ⬤ 51–100   ⬤ 101–200   ⬤ 201–500   ⬤ Over 500

PROSOCIAL BEHAVIOR

Prosocial behavior is defined as actions that are intended to benefit others, with no anticipation of external rewards (Eisenberg, 1988). Such actions, which include comforting, sympathizing, assisting, sharing, cooperating, rescuing, protecting, and defending (Zahn-Waxler & Smith, 1992), mostly fit the definition of *altruism*—unselfish concern for the welfare of others. Prosocial behavior also frequently involves some cost, sacrifice, or risk to the individual. Prosocial behavior is not just a set of social skills, however. When fully developed, it is accompanied by feelings of friendship, caring, and warmth—including empathy with regard to the feelings of others (Zahn-Waxler & Smith, 1992).

Prosocial behavior begins to develop during the preschool years and may be displayed by children as early as age 2. Parents exert a powerful influence on the development of prosocial behaviors, as do siblings. Preschool children who have secure relationships with their caregivers are more likely to attempt to comfort younger siblings than children with fragile relationships (Teti & Ablard, 1989). There are limits to young children's ability to share and cooperate, however; prosocial behavior continues to develop into adolescence and beyond.

Whether behavior is considered socially appropriate depends on the situation and on the standards of the family and the culture. Aggression is not always bad, altruism not always appropriate. Unaggressive soldiers would be useless in combat; altruistic football players would never win a game. More-

prosocial behavior   Helping, sharing, or cooperative actions that are intended to benefit others.

FIGURE 7–2   MEDIA USAGE, UNITED STATES (HOURS PER PERSON PER YEAR)*

Source: U.S. Census Bureau, 1997.
*1998, projected.

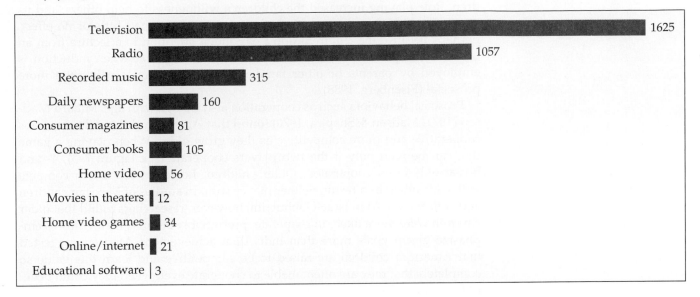

over, overly altruistic people may be intrusive, moralistic, and conforming (Bryan, 1975).

MODELING AND PROSOCIAL BEHAVIOR   Many studies have demonstrated the influence of modeling on prosocial behavior. In a typical experiment, a group of children observe a person performing a prosocial act, such as putting toys or money into a box designated for "needy children." After watching the generous model, each child is given an opportunity to donate something. Researchers usually find that children who witness another person's generosity become more generous themselves (Eisenberg, 1988). Prosocial models are also more effective when the model is perceived as nurturant or has a special relationship with the child, but note again that models often appear in movies and on TV.

CONDITIONING, LEARNING, AND PROSOCIAL BEHAVIOR   Because reward and punishment affect aggression, it is natural to assume that they also affect helping and sharing behaviors. However, it has been difficult to prove that this assumption is true. One problem is that researchers are understandably reluctant to conduct experiments in which prosocial behavior is punished. Another is that experiments in which prosocial behavior is rewarded are often inconclusive because the results may be due to modeling: When experimenters give a reward, they are also modeling the act of giving (Rushton, 1976). Even so, one study found that 4-year-old children who were given many chores to do at home were more likely to be helpful outside the home. It is interesting to note that the most helpful children in this study were black males. The experimenters hypothesized that because more of the black children came from fatherless homes, their mothers had turned to their sons for help and emotional support. Thus, these children had learned helping and comforting behaviors very early in life (Richman et al., 1988).

Two other approaches to enhancing prosocial behavior are *role playing* and *induction*. In the former, children are encouraged to act out roles as a way of helping them see things from another person's point of view. In the latter, children are given reasons for behaving in positive ways; for example, they may be told what consequences their actions will have for others. In one experiment (Staub, 1971) both procedures were employed with kindergarten children. Role playing increased the children's willingness to help others, and its effects lasted as long as a week. In contrast, induction had little or no effect, perhaps because the children didn't pay much attention to a lecture from an unfamiliar experimenter. Other research has shown that when induction is employed by parents or other familiar people, children can become more prosocial (Eisenberg, 1988).

Prosocial behaviors such as cooperation also change with age. Millard Madsen (1971; Madsen & Shapira, 1970) found that American children become less cooperative and more competitive as they grow older. When playing a game that can be won only if the two players cooperate (see Figure 7–3), 4- and 5-year-olds often cooperated. Older children, however, tended to compete with each other; as a result, neither player won. In studies of Mexican children and children raised in Israeli kibbutzim, however, researchers found that older children were more likely to cooperate, presumably because their cultures emphasize group goals more than individual achievement. Madsen suggested that American children are raised to be competitive and learn this value so completely that they are often unable to cooperate even when they could benefit from doing so.

PEERS, PLAY, AND DEVELOPMENT OF SOCIAL SKILLS

Children influence one another in many ways. They provide emotional support in a variety of situations. They serve as models, reinforce behavior, and encourage complex, imaginative play. They also encourage—or discourage—both prosocial and aggressive behaviors.

Children help one another learn a variety of physical, cognitive, and social skills (Asher et al., 1982; Hartup, 1983). For example, young boys playing aggressively may first imitate characters seen on television and then imitate each other. They continue to respond and react to each other in a way that supports and escalates the play, a form of *social reciprocity* (Hall & Cairns, 1984).

PLAY AND SOCIAL SKILLS An early study of peer relations (Parten, 1932–33) identified five developmental levels of social interaction in young children: (1) *solitary play*; (2) *onlooker play*, in which a child simply observes other children; (3) *parallel play*, in which children play alongside each other but do not directly interact; (4) *associative play*, in which children share materials

FIGURE 7–3

In Madsen's game, two children sit at opposite ends of a game board that features a cup at each end, a gutter down each side, and a marble holder with a marble inside. To play the game, the children move the marble holder by pulling on strings; if the holder is moved over a cup, the child earns the marble as it drops into the cup. The children must cooperate to earn marbles; if they both pull on the strings at the same time, the marble holder comes apart, and the marble rolls into the gutter.

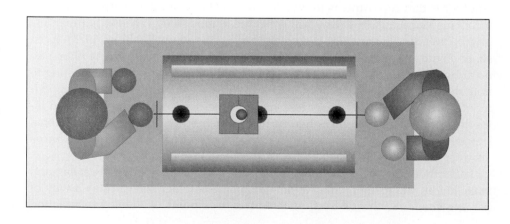

American children become more competitive in their play as they grow older.

and interact but do not coordinate their activities within a single theme; and (5) *cooperative play*, in which children engage in a single activity together—such as building a house with blocks or playing hide-and-seek. Two-year-olds mostly engage in onlooker and parallel play, whereas 4- and 5-year-olds show increasing periods of associative and cooperative play. Children at ages 5, 6, and 7 can interact for relatively long periods while sharing materials, establishing rules, resolving conflicts, helping one another, and exchanging roles.

Beginning around age 4, preschool children often engage in *social pretend play*, which involves imagination and the sharing of fantasies in accordance with agreed-upon rules. According to Vygotsky (as discussed in Chapter 4), it is partly through social pretend play that children learn cooperation and other social skills along with the ability to think about and regulate their own behavior. Pretend play offers many opportunities for discussion, reflective thought, and joint problem solving. Together, the preschoolers negotiate mutually acceptable activities and construct the play framework. For example, if two 5-year-olds pretend that they are astronauts, both children share their limited knowledge and develop play sequences in a cooperative fashion (Berk, 1994; Goncu, 1993; Kane & Furth, 1993). There are also pronounced cultural variations in styles and meanings of social play, as discussed in "Eye on Diversity," page 254.

POPULARITY AND DEVELOPMENT OF SOCIAL SKILLS   When we observe children in nursery schools, day-care centers, or kindergartens, it is apparent that some children are popular with their peers, whereas others are not. Popularity can be remarkably stable over the years: Children who are rejected by their peers in kindergarten are likely to be rejected in elementary school as well. They are also more likely to have adjustment problems in adolescence and adulthood (Parker & Asher, 1987). It is therefore important to understand what social skills are involved in popularity and to identify unpopular children early to teach them the skills they lack.

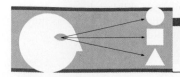

EYE ON DIVERSITY

CULTURAL VARIATIONS IN THE MEANING OF PLAY

Play has long been recognized as important to cognitive development. Play is also a primary vehicle for practicing the values, behaviors, and roles of society. Through play, for example, children act out themes, stories, or episodes that express their understanding of their culture (Nicolopoulou, 1993).

Children in all cultures develop and learn in social contexts that include older peers and adults who pass on their cultural heritage. When children pretend, the roles that they imitate "channel" their behavior. For example, a child who is playing "father" or "mother" parallels the parent's behavior as the child understands it. When a little girl plays mother, she attends to and makes explicit her understanding of the rules embedded in the role of mother (Nicolopoulou, 1993; Oppen-

heim et al., 1997). Because the role of mother—and other major social roles and values—differs from one culture to another, we would expect to find that the specifics of play also vary across cultures (e.g., see Farver & Shin, 1997). This appears to be the case even though play itself is found in all cultures.

Even in cultures in which there is little time for play, children frequently create play situations by integrating chores and fun. Kenyan Kipsigis children, for example, play tag while tending herds, or they climb trees while watching younger siblings (Harkness & Super, 1983). Work songs are common among Amish children as they collectively wash potatoes or shuck peas. Children in countries that are at war play games of war. Children have even been found to playact funerals (Timnick, 1989).

There are vast differences in the amount and type of play observed both

across and within cultures. In some societies, children's games are simple; in others, they are complex and elaborate. In some societies, competitive games are virtually nonexistent, and cooperative games are the rule. For example, the day nurseries of the former Soviet Union, emphasized collective play— "not only group games, but special complex toys are designed which require the cooperation of two or three children to make them work" (Bronfenbrenner, 1972). In cultures in which daily survival depends on motor skills, games of physical skill are generally the only forms of competition. For example, in hunting-and-gathering societies where machetes are used to cut through dense undergrowth, playful competition in speed of machete use is the norm. In other societies, foot races, competitive tracking, and spear-throwing contests are the main types of play (Huges, 1991).

Popular children are more cooperative and generally display more prosocial and other-oriented behaviors during play with their peers; these behaviors are summarized in Table 7–2 (Asher, 1983; Asher et al., 1982). Such behaviors are also good predictors of social status in the first grade (Putallaz, 1983).

In contrast, unpopular, rejected children may be either more aggressive or more withdrawn. They may also simply be "out of sync" with their peers' activities and social interactions (Rubin, 1983). Which comes first: Do rejected children engage in negative behaviors because they are rejected, or are they rejected because of their negative behaviors? Why do some children lack the social skills that make others popular? Abuse or neglect during the preschool years can be a factor. Research indicates that young children who are physically maltreated by their caregivers are more likely to be rejected by their peers. Unable to form effective peer relationships, abused children are often more disliked, less popular, and more socially withdrawn than children who aren't abused, and the extent to which they are rejected by peers increases with age (Dodge et al., 1994). Less dramatic but nonetheless potentially important contributors to unpopularity include being "sheltered" and allowed little interaction with peers, being singled out as "different" by peers, or simply getting off to a bad start when first entering a group-care setting. Remember too, as discussed earlier, that highly aggressive children are unlikely to be popular.

Given that peer relations are a significant socializing influence in the lives of children and that the success of these relations depends on the development of social skills, it is important to help children during the preschool period, when

TABLE 7–2 CHARACTERISTICS OF POPULAR CHILDREN IN KINDERGARTEN

Initiate activity by moving into the group slowly, making relevant comments and sharing information

Sensitive to the needs and activities of others

Don't force themselves on other children

Content to play alongside other children

Possess strategies for maintaining friendships

Show helpful behavior

Are good at maintaining communication

Are good at sharing information

Are responsive to other children's suggestions

Possess strategies for conflict resolution

When faced with conflict, are less likely to use aggressive or physical solutions

Source: Asher (1983), Asher et al., (1982).

rejection first occurs (Asher, 1990). Adults can help in at least two ways. First, they can teach social skills directly, through modeling and induction. Second, they can offer and encourage opportunities for successful social experiences with peers. Especially in group-care settings, adults can draw unpopular children into group activities and help them learn how to get along with others. Children need opportunities to play with other children, as well as appropriate space and play materials. Dolls, clothes for dress-up activities, toy cars and trucks, blocks, and puppets promote cooperative play and offer opportunities for interaction. With preschoolers, adult caregivers must be available to help initiate activities, negotiate conflicts, and provide social information (Asher et al., 1982).

THE ROLE OF IMAGINARY COMPANIONS Many preschool children create **imaginary companions** and playmates who become a regular part of their daily routines. An imaginary companion is an invisible character that may seem quite real to the child (Taylor et al., 1993). Children give these characters names, mention them in their conversations, and play with them. Imaginary companions help children deal with fears, provide companionship during periods of loneliness, and provide reassurance.

Research indicates that as many as 65% of preschoolers have imaginary companions. Normally, creating imaginary friends is associated with positive personality characteristics. For example, compared with children who don't have imaginary companions, those who do have such companions have been found to be more sociable and less shy, have more real friends, be more creative, and participate more in family activities (Mauro, 1991). Imaginary companions also seem to help children learn social skills and practice conversations. Children who have imaginary companions will play happily with peers and will be cooperative and friendly with both peers and adults (Singer & Singer, 1990).

Finally, there may be cognitive as well as emotional benefits to having an imaginary companion. It is possible that children who are adept at imagination and fantasy are better at mastering symbolic representation and the real world. Pretending may facilitate children's understanding that their mental images are distinct from external objects.

imaginary companions Companions children "make up" and pretend are real.

HOW GENDER INTERACTS WITH SOCIAL LEARNING

Sex is genetically determined and biological; *gender* is culturally based and therefore acquired, as discussed in Chapter 5. Some theorists suggest that sex dramatically determines differences in intellect, personality, adult adjustment, and style biologically. In everyday language, think how often you hear statements like "Women are . . ." and "Men are . . .," which clearly indicate underlying beliefs in built-in, immutable differences between the sexes.

The alternate view is that men and women differ primarily because of the way they are treated by their parents, teachers, friends, and culture from early childhood on—in other words, they differ because of differences in their environment. But when we argue about whether heredity or environment is more important in determining gender-specific behaviors, we are actually missing the point. Genetics and culture may each set limits on **gender roles**—what is appropriate for a male or a female to be and do—but they interact like two strands of a rope. In addition, children play an active role in developing their own sense of gender, as we'll see later in the chapter.

Early in the preschool period, children begin to acquire social behaviors, skills, and roles that their culture deems appropriate for their gender. For perspective, let's look first at some differences between the sexes that might set the stage for this process.

MALE-FEMALE DIFFERENCES ACROSS THE LIFESPAN Studies have shown that male babies, on average, are born slightly longer and heavier than female babies. Newborn girls have slightly more mature skeletons and are a bit more responsive to touch. As toddlers, again on average, boys are more aggressive, and girls have a slight edge in verbal abilities. In the United States, by age 8 or 10, boys begin to outperform girls in mathematics. By age 12, the average girl is well into adolescence, whereas physically the average boy is still a preadolescent.

By midadolescence, girls' superiority in verbal skills increases, as does boys' edge in mathematics and spatial reasoning. By age 18, the average female has roughly 50% less upper-body muscular strength than the average male. In adulthood, the average male body carries more muscle and bone, and the average female body carries more fat. By middle age, males are much more likely to die from arteriosclerosis, heart attacks, liver disease, homicide, suicide, or drug addiction. By age 65, there are only 68 men alive for every 100 women; at age 85, women outnumber men almost two to one; and at the age of 100, there are five times as many women as men (McLoughlin et al., 1988).

Equally important are areas in which males and females do *not* differ. One review of the research (Ruble, 1988) discovered many areas in which gender differences were not found. For example, there appeared to be no consistent differences in sociability, self-esteem, motivation to achieve, or even rote learning and certain analytical skills.

Finally, actual differences between males and females are small, and there is considerable overlap between the sexes—there are, for example, many women who are more aggressive than many men. It's also important to note that many studies conducted in the mid-1980s found less significant gender differences than those reported in earlier studies (Halpern, 1986; Ruble, 1988). These findings suggest that cultural changes—specifically, changed views of gender-appropriate behavior—have influenced the social roles open to women and men.

GENDER AND SOCIALIZATION Gender has at least two interrelated components: gender-related behaviors and gender concepts. Social-learning theorists focus on how gender-specific behaviors are learned and combined to create gender roles.

gender roles Roles we adopt with regard to being male or female.

In most cultures, children display gender-specific behaviors by age 5; many children learn some of those behaviors by age 2½ (Weinraub et al., 1984). In nursery schools, for example, girls are often observed playing with dolls, helping with snacks, and showing interest in art and music, while boys build bridges, engage in rough-and-tumble play, and play with cars and trucks (Pitcher & Schultz, 1983).

Young children often exaggerate gender-specific behaviors and rigidly conform to **gender-role stereotypes**—fixed ideas about masculine and feminine behavior. Such stereotypes imply a belief that "masculine" and "feminine" are two distinct and mutually exclusive categories. This belief appears in nearly every culture, although cultures vary considerably in the specific attributes they ascribe to females and males. In the United States, for example, traditional parents expect their male children to be "real boys"—reserved, forceful, self-confident, tough, realistic, and assertive—and their female children to be "real girls"—gentle, dependent, high-strung, talkative, frivolous, and impractical (Bem, 1975; Williams et al., 1975). In traditional families, children are pressured to conform to these gender stereotypes, regardless of their natural dispositions.

How are gender attributes learned? As with aggressive behavior and prosocial behavior, rewards, punishment, and modeling that are appropriate for the child's gender begin early. In one study (Smith & Lloyd, 1978), mothers were observed interacting with 6-month-old infants who were not their own. Sometimes baby girls were presented to the mothers as boys, sometimes boys were presented as girls; sometimes the babies were presented in accordance with their actual sex. Invariably the mothers encouraged babies whom they thought were boys to walk, crawl, and engage in physical play. Girls were handled more gently and encouraged to talk.

As children grow older, parents often react more favorably when they engage in behavior that is appropriate to their sex. Fathers may be especially important in the development of the child's gender role (Honig, 1980; Parke, 1981). Even more than mothers, fathers teach specific gender roles by reinforcing femininity in daughters and masculinity in sons.

gender-role stereotypes Rigid, fixed ideas of what is appropriate masculine or feminine behavior.

---

1. How do social-learning theorists explain aggression and prosocial behavior during the preschool years?
2. Describe the five developmental levels of social interaction in young children.
3. How is popularity linked to the development of social skills?
4. Briefly discuss the role of imaginary companions in the development of social skills.
5. Discuss how parents convey gender roles to their children.

REVIEW & APPLY

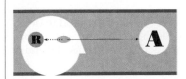

COGNITIVE-DEVELOPMENTAL PERSPECTIVES: UNDERSTANDING SELF AND OTHERS

So far we have focused mostly on specific types of behavior—how children learn to share or to be aggressive or to handle feelings. But children also act in a more comprehensive way. They put together various specific behaviors to create overall patterns of behavior that are appropriate for their gender, family, and culture. As children grow older, they become less dependent on the rules, expectations, rewards, and punishments of others, and more capable of making judgments and regulating their behavior on their own. Cognitive-developmental theorists believe that the integration of patterns of social behavior coincides with the development of a concept of self, which includes gender schemes and social concepts that help mediate the child's behavior.

SELF-CONCEPT

Even a 2-year-old has some understanding of self. As we saw in Chapter 5, by 21 months a child can recognize herself in the mirror; if she sees a red mark on her nose, she may show embarrassment. The language of 2-year-olds is full of assertions of possession, which imply "me" versus "you." In one study of 2-year-olds playing in pairs, most of the children began their play with numerous self-assertions. They defined their boundaries and their possessions—"my shoe, my doll, my car." Assertiveness can be viewed as a cognitive achievement, not mere selfishness: The children are increasing their understanding of self and others as separate beings (Levine, 1983). A review of studies of children's self-concepts and social play concluded that the children who are most social also have more fully developed self-concepts (Harter, 1983). Thus, self-understanding is closely linked to the child's understanding of the social world.

During the preschool years, children develop certain generalized attitudes about themselves—a sense of well-being, for example, or a feeling that they are "slow" or "bratty." Many of these ideas begin to emerge very early and at a nonverbal level. Children may develop strong anxieties about some of their feelings and ideas while being quite comfortable with others. They also begin to develop a set of ideals, and they begin measuring themselves against who they think they ought to be. Often children's self-evaluation is a direct reflection of what other people think of them. Imagine a lovable 2-year-old with a talent for getting into mischief, whose older siblings call him "Bad Buster" whenever he gets into trouble. By the age of 7, the child might be making a conscious effort to maintain his reputation for being bad. Early attitudes thus can eventually become basic elements of a person's self-concept.

Preschool children are fascinated with themselves; many of their activities and thoughts center on learning about themselves. They compare themselves with other children in terms of height, hair color, family background, and likes or dislikes. They compare themselves with their parents and imitate their parents' behavior. As part of their drive to find out about themselves, preschool children ask a variety of questions about where they came from, why their feet grow, whether they are good or bad, and on and on.

Awareness of how you appear to others is a key step in the development of self-knowledge and self-concept. Young preschoolers tend to define themselves in terms of physical characteristics ("I have brown hair") or possessions ("I have a bike"). Older preschoolers are more likely to describe themselves in terms of their activities: "I walk to school," "I play baseball" (Damon & Hart, 1982). They also define themselves through their interpersonal relationships and experiences. According to Peggy Miller and colleagues (1992), preschoolers commonly describe themselves through stories about their families. Children's tendency to portray themselves through social connections increases during the preschool years. In turn, personal storytelling by parents can be an important means of conveying moral and social standards to children (Miller et al., 1997).

As children learn who and what they are and begin to evaluate themselves as active forces in the world, they put together a cognitive theory, or *personal*

Older preschoolers tend to describe themselves according to their activities such as "I stand on my head."

script, about themselves that helps to regulate their behavior. In other words, human beings apparently need to feel that they are consistent and do not act randomly: Even as children, we try to bring our behavior in line with our beliefs and attitudes.

SOCIAL CONCEPTS AND RULES

Preschool children busily sort things out, classify behaviors as good or bad, and attempt to find meaning in the *social* world—just as they do with regard to the physical world. Central to the development of social concepts and rules is a process called **internalization:** Ideally, children learn to incorporate the values and moral standards of their society into their self-concept. Some values are related to appropriate gender-role behavior, some to moral standards, and some simply to customary ways of doing things.

How do children internalize values and rules? At first they may simply imitate verbal patterns: A 2-year-old says "No, no, no!" as she marks on the wall with crayons. She continues doing what she wants to do, but at the same time she shows the beginnings of self-restraint by telling herself that she shouldn't be doing it. In a few months, she should have developed enough self-control to arrest such impulses. Cognitive theorists point out that children's attempts to regulate their own behavior are influenced not only by their developing self-concept but also by their developing social concepts. Such concepts reflect increased understanding about others as well as about self. For example, a preschool child may be learning what it means to be a big brother or sister or to be a friend. The child is also learning about concepts such as fairness, honesty, and respect for others. Many such concepts are far too abstract for young children, but they struggle to understand them anyway.

Young children learning about social concepts often ask, "Why did he or she do that?" The answers often involve attributions about personality and character. For example, the question "Why did Kevin give me his cookie?" may be answered with "Because Kevin is a nice boy." As children grow older, they become progressively more likely to see other people—as well as themselves—as having stable character attributes (Miller & Aloise, 1989). Caregivers can encourage children to be helpful or altruistic by teaching them that they are kind to others because they want to be—because they are "nice" people (Eisenberg et al., 1984; Grusec & Arnason, 1982; Perry & Bussey, 1984).

Children's Friendships Social concepts and rules surrounding children's friendships have been studied extensively. Children do not acquire a clear understanding of friendship until middle childhood; notions of mutual trust and reciprocity are too complex for the preschool child. However, preschool children do behave differently with friends than with strangers, and some 4- and 5-year-olds can maintain close, caring relationships over an extended period. They may not be able to verbalize what friendship is, but they follow some of its implied rules (Gottman, 1983). In one study, for example, preschoolers who watched puppet scenarios involving either a friend or an acquaintance in trouble reacted differently depending on which character was involved. They responded with more empathy to the friend and showed greater willingness to help the friend (Costin & Jones, 1992).

Children's Disputes When children argue with peers, siblings, and parents, they often demonstrate a surprisingly sophisticated level of social understanding and an ability to reason from social rules and concepts. Children as young as 3 years of age can justify their behavior in terms of social rules ("Now it's my turn!") or the consequences of an action ("Stop, you'll break it if you do that!") (Dunn & Munn, 1987). A close look at children's verbal disputes

internalization Making social rules and standards of behavior part of yourself and adopting them as your own set of values.

Children's developing understanding of gender-appropriate behavior and gender schemes often involves modeling and dramatic play.

gender schemes Cognitive standards (including stereotypes) as to what behavior and attitudes are appropriate for males and females.

gender identity The knowledge that you are male or female and the ability to make that judgment about other people.

gender constancy The older child's understanding that gender is stable and stays the same despite changes in superficial appearance.

in the preschool years demonstrates systematic development in their understanding of social rules, their understanding of another person's perspective, and their ability to reason from social rules or from the consequences of their actions (Shantz, 1987).

GENDER SCHEMES

Most experts agree that the development of **gender schemes**—gender-based cultural standards or stereotypes—depends in part on the child's level of cognitive development and in part on aspects of the culture that the child attends to (Levy & Carter, 1989). That is, children progressively become more capable of understanding what it means to be a girl or a boy, and as they do, they elaborate their knowledge of what is culturally "appropriate" for females and males.

Gender schemes, in turn, give rise to **gender identity,** our sense of who we are as males or females. Gender identity develops in a particular sequence over the first 7 or 8 years of life. Very young children learn to label themselves as "boy" or "girl." However, young children don't fully understand that they will be male or female throughout life or that gender doesn't change with changes of clothing or hairstyle. It is not unusual for a preschooler to ask a a parent whether he or she was a boy or a girl as a baby. By age 6 or 7, however, most children no longer make such mistakes (Stangor & Ruble, 1987).

Children develop gender schemes directly, from what they are taught and from the models they see around them, and indirectly, from stories, movies, and television. Studies of stereotypical models in television programs indicate that over the years, the gender roles conveyed by these models have been quite traditional (Signorelli, 1989). Even studies of children's elementary school reading books, conducted in 1972 and again in 1989, indicate a preponderance of gender-stereotyped roles (Purcell & Sewart, 1990). It is therefore not surprising that children's concepts about gender are often stereotypical.

As we saw earlier, children learn some aspects of gender roles by imitating significant others and by being reinforced for gender-appropriate behavior. But children are active participants in this process and are selective about what they imitate and internalize. Research suggests that children's developing understanding of gender-related schemes helps determine what attitudes and behaviors they learn. Moreover, gender-related schemes and a sense of gender identity develop in predictable ways over the preschool period. By age $2\frac{1}{2}$ most children can readily label people as boys or girls or as men or women, and they can accurately answer the question "Are you a girl or a boy?" (Thompson, 1975). But even though they can easily discriminate between males and females, they may be confused about what this distinction means. Many 3-year-olds believe, for instance, that if a boy puts on a dress, he becomes a girl. They may not realize that only boys can become fathers and only girls can become mothers. By age 5 to 7, children understand that their gender is stable and permanent. Thus, children acquire **gender constancy**—the understanding that boys invariably become men, girls become women, and gender is consistent over time and situations (Kohlberg, 1966; Shaffer, 1988)(see Table 7–3).

During early childhood, children also acquire a sense of the meaning underlying gender stereotypes. In research settings, 4-year-olds offer fierce toy bears to boys and fluffy toy kittens to girls; this finding suggests that the cultural associations of objects and qualities with one gender or the other do not depend solely on observing or being taught *specific* associations—such as that dolls are for girls and trucks are for boys. Instead, children readily generalize what *classes* of toys are appropriate for each gender. As one group of researchers concluded,

"Children, even at these early ages, may have begun to connect certain qualities with males and other qualities with females" (Fagot et al., 1992).

Many cognitive-developmental psychologists believe that children are intrinsically motivated to acquire values, interests, and behaviors consistent with their own gender—a process called *self-socialization*. Children develop rigid concepts of "what boys do" and "what girls do." For example, boys play with cars and don't cry; girls play with dolls and like to dress up. Typically, a child will be more interested in the details of behaviors that are gender-appropriate and less so in gender-inappropriate behaviors (Martin & Halverson, 1981).

Are young children better at attending to and remembering things that are consistent with their gender schemes? Research indicates that they are. In memory tests, for example, boys tend to remember more "boy items," and girls remember more "girl items." Children make memory errors when a story violates their gender stereotypes. For example, they may remember that a boy was chopping wood when in fact a girl was. Such results indicate that children's developing gender concepts have a powerful influence on their attention and learning (Martin & Halverson, 1981). When concepts of gender stability and consistency are developing, children tend to have stereotyped concepts of gender-appropriate behavior that organize and structure their behavior and feelings. If stereotypes are violated, children may feel embarrassed, anxious, or uncomfortable—although they may also be amused, depending on the situation.

ANDROGYNY

In our culture, parents and teachers have traditionally been urged to help children establish clear, gender-specific behavior by the time they enter elementary school. It was believed that failure to do so could lead to psychological maladjustment—possibly to homosexuality, which was viewed negatively. Recent research suggests, however, that exaggerated gender-specific behavior severely limits the emotional and intellectual development of both men and women (Bem, 1985).

Sandra Bem and colleagues argue that "feminine" and "masculine" are not opposite ends of a single dimension. They are two separate dimensions; that is, it is possible for a person to be high or low on either or both. Stated differently, desirable masculine and feminine traits can easily exist in the same

TABLE 7–3   THE DEVELOPMENT OF GENDER SCHEMES ACROSS EARLY CHILDHOOD

LEVEL OF SCHEMES	APPROXIMATE AGE	CHARACTERISTICS OF BEHAVIOR
Gender identity	2 to 5 years	By $2\frac{1}{2}$ children can label people as boys or girls; are confused about the meaning of being a boy or girl; believe gender is changed by surface appearance—for example, changing clothes changes gender.
Gender constancy	5 to 7 years	Children can understand that gender is stable and permanent; boys grow up to become daddies or men, girls grow up to become mommies or women; gender is consistent over time and situations.

person regardless of gender. Both men and women are capable of being ambitious, self-reliant, and assertive (traditional masculine roles), as well as affectionate, gentle, sensitive, and nurturant (traditional feminine roles). Such a blend of traits in either a woman or a man is called **androgynous personality.** Depending on the situation, androgynous men can be independent and assertive, yet able to cuddle an infant or offer a sensitive ear to another person's troubles. Likewise, androgynous women can be assertive and self-reliant, yet expressive and nurturant when warranted.

Androgynous personality is formed by specific child-rearing practices and parental attitudes that encourage desirable cross-gender behaviors. Traditionally, parents have accepted more cross-gender behavior in girls than in boys (Martin, 1990). Lifelong androgynous gender identities that combine aspects of both traditional masculinity and femininity are most likely to develop when such behavior is modeled and accepted. It helps for the same-sex parent to provide a model of the cross-sex behavior and for the opposite-sex parent to reward the pattern (Ruble, 1988). Dad can vacuum the rug, clean bathrooms, and mend clothing, just as Mom can mow the lawn, repair appliances, and take out the trash.

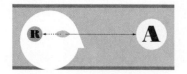

REVIEW & APPLY

1. List some ways in which children's self-concept develops during the preschool years.
2. Describe how children internalize social concepts and rules and use them in forming friendships and handling disputes.
3. What is gender identity, and how is it acquired?
4. What is androgynous personality?

FAMILY DYNAMICS

Many family dynamics—parenting styles, number and spacing of children, interactions among siblings, discipline techniques—affect development during the preschool years. Development is also influenced by the structure and circumstances of the family, such as whether there are two parents or only one, whether family members are employed, whether grandparents or other relatives live in the household, and whether the family lives in a comfortable house in the suburbs or a crowded apartment in the city.

PARENTING STYLES

Just as each individual is unique, each family is unique. Parents use their own versions of child-rearing techniques, depending on the situation, the child, the child's behavior at the moment, and the culture. Ideally, parents place reasonable limits on the child's autonomy and instill values and self-control while being careful not to undermine the child's curiosity, initiative, and growing sense of competence. Crucial dimensions in parenting are control and warmth.

Parental control refers to how restrictive the parents are. Restrictive parents limit their children's freedom; they actively enforce compliance with rules and see that children fulfill their responsibilities. In contrast, nonrestrictive parents are minimally controlling, make fewer demands, and place fewer restraints on their children's behavior and expression of emotions. *Parental warmth* refers to

androgynous personality People who are high both on desirable masculine and feminine characteristics.

the amount of affection and approval that the parents display. Warm, nurturing parents smile at their children frequently and give praise and encouragement. They limit criticism, punishment, and signs of disapproval. In contrast, hostile parents criticize, punish, and ignore their children, rarely expressing affection or approval. Parental control and warmth directly affect children's aggressiveness and prosocial behavior, their self-concepts, their internalization of moral values, and their development of social competence (Becker, 1964; Maccoby, 1984).

FOUR PARENTING STYLES Diana Baumrind (1975, 1980) used these dimensions in classifying parenting styles. She identified three distinct patterns of parenting: *authoritative*, *authoritarian*, and *permissive*. To complete the picture, we also include *indifferent* parenting (Maccoby & Martin, 1983). Bear in mind that these are general tendencies, not absolutes; parenting style varies somewhat from one situation to the next.

Authoritative parents combine a moderately high degree of control with warmth, acceptance, and encouragement of autonomy. Although they set limits on behavior, the limits are reasonable, and the parents provide explanations appropriate to the child's level of comprehension. Their actions do not seem arbitrary or unfair; as a result, their children more willingly accept restrictions. Authoritative parents also listen to their children's objections and are flexible when it is appropriate. For example, if a young girl wants to visit at a friend's house beyond the hour when she is normally expected to be home, authoritative parents might ask her why she wants to do so, what the circumstances will be (such as whether the friend's parents will be there), and whether it will interfere with responsibilities such as homework or chores. If there are no problems, the parents might allow the small deviation from the rule.

Authoritarian parents are highly controlling and tend to show little warmth toward their children. They adhere rigidly to rules. In the situation just de-

authoritative parents Those parents who use firm control with children but encourage communication and negotiation in rule setting within the family.

authoritarian parents Those parents who adhere to rigid rule structures and dictate rules to the children; in this situation, children do not contribute to the family's decision-making process.

Authoritative parents encourage the developing autonomy of their children while at the same time setting reasonable limits.

Study Chart · Parenting Styles Combining Warmth and Control

Authoritative	Moderately high control	Accept and encourage the growing autonomy of their children.
	High warmth	Have open communication with children; flexible rules; children found to be the best adjusted—most self-reliant, self-controlled, and socially competent; better school performance and higher self-esteem.
Authoritarian	High control	Issue commands and expect them to be obeyed.
	Low warmth	Have little communication with children; inflexible rules; allow children to gain little independence from them; children found to be withdrawn, fearful, moody, unassertive, and irritable; girls tend to remain passive and dependent during adolescence; boys may become rebellious and aggressive.
Permissive	Low control	Have few or no restraints on child; unconditional love by parents.
	High warmth	There is communication from child to parent; much freedom and little guidance for children; no setting of limits by parents; children tend to be aggressive and rebellious; also tend to be socially inept, self-indulgent, and impulsive; in some cases, children may be active, outgoing, and creative.
Indifferent	Low control	Set no limits for children; lack affection for children.
	Low warmth	Focus on stress in their own lives; no energy left for their children; if indifferent parents also show hostility (as neglectful parents do), children tend to show high expression of destructive impulses and delinquent behavior.

permissive parents Those parents who exercise little control over their children but are high in warmth; in this situation, children may have trouble inhibiting their impulses or deferring gratification.

indifferent parents Those parents who are not interested in their role as parents or in their children; they exercise little control over and demonstrate little warmth toward their children.

scribed, their response to their daughter's request would probably be refusal accompanied by statements like "A rule is a rule" or "Because I said so!" If the child argues or resists, the parents might become angry and impose punishment—often physical. Authoritarian parents issue commands and expect them to be obeyed; they avoid lengthy verbal exchanges with their children. They behave as if their rules are set in concrete and can't be changed, a response that can make the child's attempts at autonomy highly frustrating.

Permissive parents show a great deal of warmth and exercise little control, placing few or no restraints on their children's behavior. The issue of staying out later than usual would probably not even arise because there would be few curfews in the first place, along with no fixed times for going to bed and no rule that the child must always keep her parents informed of her whereabouts. Rather than asking her parents if she can stay out later than usual, the young girl might simply tell her parents what she plans to do or perhaps just let them find out about it afterward. When permissive parents are annoyed or impatient with their children, they often suppress these feelings. According to Baumrind (1975), many permissive parents are so intent on showing their children "unconditional love" that they fail to perform other important parental functions—in particular, setting necessary limits on their children's behavior.

Indifferent parents neither set limits nor display much affection or approval—perhaps because they don't care or because their own lives are so stressful that they don't have enough energy left over to provide guidance and support for their children.

EFFECTS OF DIFFERENT PARENTING STYLES   As indicated by Baumrind (1972, 1975) and other researchers, authoritarian parents tend to produce withdrawn, fearful children who are dependent, moody, unassertive, and irritable. As adolescents, these children—especially boys—may overreact to the restrictive, punishing environment in which they were reared and become rebellious and aggressive. Girls are more likely to remain passive and dependent (Kagan & Moss, 1962).

Although permissiveness in parenting is the opposite of restrictiveness, it does not necessarily produce the opposite results: Children of permissive parents may also be rebellious and aggressive. In addition, they tend to be self-indulgent, impulsive, and socially inept, although some may instead be active, outgoing, and creative (Baumrind, 1975; Watson, 1957).

Children of authoritative parents have been found to fare well in most respects. They are most likely to be self-reliant, self-controlled, and socially competent. In the long run, these children develop higher self-esteem and do better in school than children reared with the other parenting styles (Buri et al., 1988; Dornbusch et al., 1987).

The worst outcome is found in children of indifferent parents. When permissiveness is accompanied by hostility and lack of warmth, the child feels free to give rein to even the most destructive impulses. Studies of young delinquents show that in many cases, their home environments have exactly this combination of permissiveness and hostility (Bandura & Walters, 1959; McCord et al., 1959).

Still, the effects of parenting styles can vary considerably across cultures and subcultures, and we can't say that any one style is universally "best" (Darling & Steinberg, 1993). Moreover, the methods by which authoritative parents convey standards for behavior can vary considerably across cultures. Some research also indicates that certain elements of the authoritarian style have advantages. Traditional Chinese parents, for example, are often described as authoritarian and highly controlling, yet the "training" approach they take to child rearing fosters high academic achievement (Chao, 1994).

"TRADITIONAL PARENTS"   In two-parent families, each parent may have a different parenting style. For example, in what has been called the *traditional style*, parents conform to traditional male and female stereotypes. The father may be quite authoritarian, the mother more nurturant and permissive (Baumrind, 1989). Here the impact of either parenting style is balanced by that of the other parent.

NEGOTIATION OF SHARED GOALS   Eleanor Maccoby (1979, 1980) looked at styles of parenting from a perspective similar to Baumrind's, but she expanded the dimensions of the model to include the effects of children's behavior on their parents. Parents, of course, are in a better position than children to control the home environment. But the reciprocal interaction between parents and children affects the climate of family life. In some families, the parents are highly controlling. At the other extreme, the children are in control.

Ideally, neither parents nor children dominate the family all the time. Maccoby (1980) focused on the ways in which parents and children interact. As children grow older, parents need to negotiate with them in making decisions and defining rules. Rather than simply establishing rules and requiring compliance, it is better to help the child develop his or her own ways of thinking problems through and learning the give-and-take of getting along with others—in a warm, supportive atmosphere. Thus, the family relationship evolves; children exert more self-control and self-responsibility as they grow older.

Through long-term dialogue and interaction, parents and children come to agree on what Maccoby calls *shared goals*. The result is a harmonious atmosphere in which decisions are reached without much struggle for control. Families that achieve such a balance have a fairly high degree of intimacy, and their interactions are stable and mutually rewarding. Families that are unable to achieve shared goals must negotiate everything—from what to have for supper to where to go on vacation. This too can be an effective family style, despite the need for constant discussion.

If either the parents or the children dominate the situation, negotiation is difficult, and the family atmosphere becomes unstable. Parents who continue to be highly controlling tend to produce preadolescent children who concentrate on avoiding control. They stay away from home as much as possible. On the other hand, when the children are in control, the parents may avoid the family situation as much as possible. Either extreme weakens the socialization process during middle childhood and adolescence, making it more difficult for children to effect a smooth transition from dependence on the family to independence and close peer friendships.

SIBLING DYNAMICS

Siblings are the first and closest peers who affect children's personality development. Sibling relationships provide experiences that are different from parent-child interactions (Bossard & Boll, 1960). The down-to-earth openness of brothers and sisters gives them a chance to experience the ups and downs of human relationships on the most basic level. Siblings can be devotedly loyal to each other, despise each other, or form an ambivalent love-hate relationship that may continue for life. Preschoolers may engage in sibling rivalry that leads to arguments and hitting, but brothers and sisters are actually more likely to give each other affection and friendship and have enormous influence on what the other does. Even when children are far apart in age, they are directly affected by the experience of living with others who are both equal (as children in the same family) and unequal (differing in age, size, sex, competence, intelligence, attractiveness, and so on). Indeed, siblings are important in helping each other identify social concepts and social roles by prompting and inhibiting certain patterns of behavior (Dunn, 1983, 1985).

Judy Dunn (1993) describes five major dimensions of sibling relationships: rivalry, attachment, security, connectedness (including self-disclosure and humor), and shared fantasy. With regard to attachment security, for example, some toddlers and preschoolers are so attached to their siblings that they miss them terribly when they are absent, are delighted when they appear, and join forces with them to explore the world in novel and imaginative ways. Sibling attachment may be as strong as child-to-parent attachment. Or, in contrast, siblings may have little to do with each other and lead separate emotional lives.

How does birth order, or **sibling status,** affect each child's personality? Although psychologists have devoted much speculation to the effects on personality of being the oldest, youngest, or middle sibling, current research findings do not support earlier views on this question. In fact, no consistent personality differences appear to result solely from birth order. This outcome doesn't mean, of course, that all children in a family will be similar in personality. Siblings raised in the same family are likely to have very different personalities— often as different as those of unrelated children (Plomin & Daniels, 1987).

One reason for personality differences is that children *need* to establish distinct identities for themselves (Dreikurs & Soltz, 1964). Thus, if an older sibling is serious and studious, a younger one may be boisterous. A girl who has four

Families provide a powerful context for learning attitudes, beliefs, and appropriate behavior—sometimes down to the last detail of posture and dress.

sibling status Birth order.

sisters and no brothers may carve out her own niche in the family by taking on a masculine role. Another reason has to do with the nature of shared versus nonshared experiences (see Chapter 3). Although siblings in the same family share many experiences, including living in the same home with the same set of parents, they also have many nonshared experiences and relationships. As Robert Plomin (1990) explains, DNA, not shared experiences, runs in families. Environmental effects are specific to each child rather than common to the entire family.

Some nonshared experiences are linked to birth order. For example, a firstborn son may receive more favorable treatment than his brothers and sisters. Other nonshared experiences, such as illness, changes in family finances, and peer and school relationships, have nothing to do with birth order (Bower, 1991a).

Although birth order seems to have few clear, consistent, and predictable effects on personality, many studies have found that the oldest child does have some advantages. On average, firstborns have higher IQs and achieve more in school and in their careers. "Only" children are also high achievers, although their IQs tend to be slightly lower, on the average, than that of the oldest child in a family of two or three children (Zajonc & Markus, 1975). One possible explanation for this tendency is that only children lack the opportunity to serve as teachers for their younger siblings, an experience that can enhance intellectual development (Zajonc & Hall, 1986).

Average differences in IQ based on birth order tend to be small, however, and—as with gender differences—they tell us nothing about individual children. Larger and more consistent differences appear when researchers look at family size. The more children there are in a family, the lower their IQs tend to be, and the less likely they are to graduate from high school. This remains the case even when other factors are taken into account (Blake, 1989). Family structure (whether there are two parents or one) and income can also have strong effects on IQ and achievement—effects that are noticeably greater than those of birth order or number of siblings (Ernst & Angst, 1983).

Older siblings are powerful models; children who have older same-sex siblings tend to show stronger gender-typed behavior than those with older siblings of the opposite sex. The spacing between siblings also affects sibling status. Siblings who are closer in age have more intense relationships (Sutton-Smith & Rosenberg, 1970).

The effects of birth order vary across cultures, however. Robert LeVine (1990) notes that the concept of birth order has vastly different implications for a family in a "high-fertility" agrarian society like Kenya than it does for a family in the United States. In many agrarian societies, several families share communal living quarters, with the result that children of several mothers are raised together. Whereas the firstborn child in a U.S. family usually is the only child in the home and has his or her own room and possessions, as well as liberal access to parents for conversation and games, firstborn children in agrarian cultures live with older children from other families, who function much like older siblings, caring for and socializing the young. As a result, says LeVine, "the early social experience of only or firstborn children in agrarian societies is rarely as differentiated from that of later-borns as it is in middle-class America" (LeVine, 1990).

DISCIPLINE AND SELF-REGULATION
Disciplinary techniques vary widely in different historical periods. There have been periods when harsh physical punishment was in vogue, and there have been periods of relative permissiveness. Methods of disciplining children—

IN THEORY, IN FACT

TEACHING CHILDREN SELF-REGULATION

In raising healthy and achieving children, isn't it enough for parents to be warm, loving, and in control? Evidently not, according to research by John Gottman and colleagues Lynn Katz and Carole Hooven (Gottman et al., 1996). The researchers found that the way parents deal with both their own and their children's emotions may strongly affect not only the children's psychological and physical health but also their academic achievement. Regardless of their IQs, children whose parents had taught them how to cope emotionally had longer attention spans, scored higher on reading and math achievement tests, exhibited fewer behavior problems, and had

slower heart rates; in addition, urine samples from these children contained smaller amounts of stress hormones.

Four types of parents were identified: those who helped their children think about their emotions and express them constructively, those who ignored their children's feelings of anger or sadness, those who disapproved of their children's having such feelings, and those who believed that the parental role consisted of simply accepting all their children's emotions. Children of parents in the first category scored highest both intellectually and physically.

The researchers believe that their findings can help parents teach children better ways of coping with their emotions. As Gottman explains, "So much of the popular parenting litera-

ture is oriented toward getting obedience, control, and consistent discipline. But so little really talks about how to make an emotional connection with the child." One father, for example, held his daughter in his arms or tried to distract her by putting her in front of the TV. Although the father was concerned, he was not actively helping his daughter understand and control her feelings of sadness. A more effective approach would be to ask the child what is making her sad and what she can do about it to make her feel better. Thus, if a girl is angry at her brother, a parent can talk with her about what happened to make her angry and say, "You can't hit your brother, but you can tell me when you're angry."

setting rules and limits and enforcing them—are subject to changes in fashion just as other aspects of culture are. The child-rearing literature of the 1950s and early 1960s, for example, warned against strong, overbearing disciplinary methods. Parents worried about stifling their children's emotions and turning them into anxious and repressed adults. Then the trend changed: The literature of the 1970s and 1980s emphasized that children need external social control, firmness, and consistency to feel safe and secure.

The 1990s continued the trend toward firm parental control. Of course, children's need for affection and approval also continues to be recognized (Perry & Bussey, 1984). Based on accumulated research findings, parents are advised to follow these guidelines:

1. Foster an atmosphere of warmth, caring, and mutual support among family members. Affection tends to be reciprocated, and children who are generally happy show more self-control, maturity, and prosocial behavior.

2. Concentrate more on promoting desirable behaviors than on eliminating undesirable ones. Deliberately suggest, model, and reward children's helping and caring behaviors.

3. Set realistic expectations and demands, firmly enforce demands, and above all, *be consistent*.

4. Avoid unnecessary use of power, including use of force and threats to control children's behavior. The assertion of power fosters similar behavior in children and may cause anger, bitterness, and resistance.

5. Help children gain a sense of control over themselves and their environment.

6. Use verbal reasoning (induction) to help children understand social rules.

To this list we might add this: Tell children personal stories and fables that exemplify social and moral values (Miller et al., 1997).

In sum, children need to know the consequences of their behavior, including how other people will feel. Children also need opportunities to discuss or explain their actions to their parents. Such interchanges help them develop a sense of responsibility for their behavior. In the long run, self-regulated behavior is determined by children's understanding of the situation in addition to parental warmth and control (see also "In Theory, In Fact," on facing page).

REVIEW & APPLY

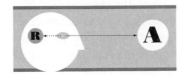

1. Describe four different parenting styles and how they tend to affect children's personality development.
2. What is meant by "negotiating shared goals"?
3. Why are sibling relationships important during preschool?
4. List six child-rearing guidelines that combine parental control with affection and approval.

SUMMARY

Three Perspectives Revisited

- Psychodynamic perspectives emphasize the child's feelings, drives, and developmental conflicts.
- Social-learning perspectives emphasize links between cognition, behavior, and the environment.
- Cognitive-developmental perspectives emphasize children's thoughts and concepts as organizers of their social behavior.

Psychodynamic Perspectives

- One of the most important forces that children must learn to deal with is the stress caused by fear and anxiety. These emotions, which can have many causes, may be increased or even created by the child's imagination.
- Parents can help children cope with fears by encouraging them to confront and overcome them and demonstrating that there is little to fear.
- Often the best way to help children cope with anxiety is to reduce unnecessary stress in their lives. It is also helpful to provide a warm, secure base to help children regain confidence and to allow opportunities for children to discuss their feelings.
- Children often respond to generalized feelings of anxiety through a variety of defense mechanisms.
- Emotion regulation refers to dealing with emotions in socially acceptable ways. Children's growing ability to control their behavior is termed *self-regulation.*
- Children learn very early that open displays of negative emotions are unacceptable in public places.

Learning to manage negative emotions is not the same as not having them at all.

- Children's expressions of positive feelings become less open and spontaneous as they grow older.
- Most children develop active curiosity about their bodies and ask many sex-related questions. The ways in which others react to the child's developing sensuality and sexual curiosity can have a powerful effect.
- Several developmental conflicts arise during the preschool years. One of these is the conflict between autonomy and connectedness. The development of independence follows a complex trajectory during the preschool period.
- Another conflict is between initiative and guilt. Excessive guilt can dampen the child's initiative.
- All children need to master their environment and to feel competent and successful. If they do not, they may fail to develop *learning competence,* an active, exploratory, self-confident approach to learning.

Social-Learning Perspectives

- Aggression may be physical or verbal. Typically, physical aggression increases during the early preschool period and then declines as verbal aggression begins to replace it.
- Frustration may give rise to aggressive behavior, either toward the source of the frustration or toward another person or object, but it does not necessarily have that effect.

- Punishment can create a tendency to behave aggressively, especially if the punishment is harsh and frequent.
- Observing aggressive models can strongly influence antisocial behavior, especially when the observers sense a similarity between themselves and the model or when the model is perceived as powerful or competent.
- Prosocial behavior, or actions that are intended to benefit others, begins to develop during the preschool years. Many studies have demonstrated the influence of modeling on prosocial behavior.
- Prosocial behavior can be enhanced through role playing (encouraging children to act out roles so as to see things from another person's point of view) and induction (giving children reasons for behaving in positive ways).
- Peers and play influence the development of children's social skills. Preschool children often engage in social pretend play, which helps them learn cooperation and the ability to regulate their own behavior.
- Popular children are more cooperative and generally display more prosocial behaviors during play with their peers. Rejected children may be either more aggressive or more withdrawn.
- Many preschool children create imaginary companions who seem real to them. Research has found that this practice has beneficial effects for the child.
- There are a number of biological differences between males and females across the lifespan. However, the areas in which males and females do not differ are equally important.
- In most cultures, children display gender-specific behaviors by age 5. Often they exaggerate those behaviors and rigidly conform to gender-role stereotypes.
- Gender attributes are learned through rewards, punishment, and modeling that are appropriate for the child's gender.

*Cognitive-Developmental Perspectives:
Understanding Self and Others*

- By age 2, children have some understanding of self. During the preschool years, they develop certain generalized attitudes about themselves and are often fascinated with themselves.
- Central to the development of social concepts and rules is the process of internalization, in which children incorporate the values and moral standards of their society into their self-concept.
- Children begin to internalize values and rules by imitating verbal patterns. They are also influenced by their developing social concepts.

- Children do not acquire a clear understanding of friendship until middle childhood.
- The development of gender schemes depends in part on the child's level of cognitive development and in part on aspects of the culture that the child attends to. Gender schemes, in turn, give rise to gender identity.
- Children develop gender schemes directly, from what they are taught and from the models they see around them, and indirectly, from stories, movies, and television.
- During early childhood, children acquire a sense of the meaning underlying gender stereotypes. Much of this process occurs through self-socialization.
- A blend of "feminine" and "masculine" traits in either a woman or a man is called androgynous personality. It is formed by specific child-rearing practices and parental attitudes.

Family Dynamics

- Parenting styles depend on parental control (how restrictive the parents are) and the amount of parental warmth (the amount of affection and approval the parents display).
- Diana Baumrind has identified three parenting styles: authoritative, authoritarian, and permissive. In addition, some parents are indifferent to their children. (See the study chart on page 264.)
- Authoritative parents combine a high degree of control with warmth, acceptance, and encouragement of autonomy.
- Authoritarian parents are highly controlling and tend to show little warmth toward their children.
- Permissive parents show a great deal of warmth and place few or no restraints on their children's behavior.
- Children of authoritative parents are most likely to be self-reliant, self-controlled, and socially competent. They develop higher self-esteem and do better in school than children reared with the other parenting styles.
- The reciprocal interaction between parents and children affects the climate of family life. Ideally, neither parents nor children dominate the family all the time. Through long-term dialogue and interaction, parents and children come to agree on shared goals.
- Siblings have an important effect on children's personality development. Major dimensions of sibling relationships are rivalry, attachment, security, connectedness, and shared fantasy.

■ There is no consistent evidence that sibling status (i.e., birth order) affects personality. Family size has been shown to affect intelligence, however.

■ Disciplinary techniques vary widely in different historical periods. Currently most experts agree that children need external social control, firmness, and consistency to feel safe and secure.

KEY TERMS

autonomy

fear

anxiety

systematic desensitization

defense mechanisms

hostile aggression

instrumental aggression

prosocial behavior

imaginary companions

gender roles

gender-role stereotypes

internalization

gender schemes

gender identity

gender constancy

androgynous personality

authoritative parents

authoritarian parents

permissive parents

indifferent parents

sibling status

USING WHAT YOU'VE LEARNED

Television is an ever-present influence in the lives of many preschoolers, but just what do children learn from television? How are they influenced? What do they understand about the events unfolding on the screen?

Try observing a young child during three different types of programs. What is the child watching? When does the child lose interest? What aspects or events seem to capture the child's attention? Does the child comment on or ask questions about what he or she has seen? After the child has watched a program, ask her or him a few questions about what happened. See what the child understands about the action. Is the child able to follow the story line?

It isn't easy to interview a preschooler. You may need to ask simple questions about each character—their actions, feelings, intentions, and the consequences of their actions. For example, "What did Bart do?" "Why did he do that?" "And then what happened?" "How did his sister feel about that?"

SUGGESTED READINGS

DAMON, W. (1991). *The moral child: Nurturing children's natural moral growth.* New York: Free Press. Approaches to moral education, both at home and in the community, are clearly and concisely linked to the normal course of moral development from infancy through adolescence.

DUNN, J. (1995). *From one child to two: What to expect, how to cope, and how to enjoy your growing family.* New York: Fawcett. A down-to-earth text that provides a wealth of detail on such key concerns as differences between children, providing the firstborn with private space one-on-one time with the parents, sources of ambivalence in sibling relationships, and ways to handle feelings of displacement.

EISENBERG, N. (1992). *The caring child (The developing child series).* Cambridge, MA: Harvard University Press. Dr. Eisenberg steps out of her role as scholar to discuss what we know about raising responsible, caring children.

LEWIS, M. (1991). *Shame: The exposed self.* New York: Free Press. This "history of shame" as a human response during infancy and early childhood looks at the many ways in which shame is induced and expressed, reacted to, and handled.

PALEY, V. G. (1993). *You say you can't play.* Cambridge, MA: Harvard University Press. A fascinating look at the moral dimensions of the classroom. The author interweaves her conversations with children and her private reflections into a story about what happened when she instituted a radical new order in her classroom.

SINGER, D. G., & SINGER, J. L. (1990). *The house of make believe: Children's play and the developing imagination.* Cambridge, MA: Harvard University Press. A comprehensive review of children's evolving fantasy play and its function in child development.

Middle Childhood and Elementary School Children: Physical and Cognitive Development

CHAPTER

8

CHAPTER OBJECTIVES

By the time you have finished this chapter, you should be able to do the following:

1. Discuss the physical development of the school-age child, including changes in gross motor and fine motor skills.
2. Identify major health and safety concerns for school-age children.
3. Describe the cognitive ability of the young child in terms of the transition between preoperational and concrete operational thought.
4. Explain how Piaget's concepts of thinking in middle childhood can be used in the classroom.
5. Discuss cognitive development during middle childhood as described by information-processing theorists.
6. Describe the expansion of language development into literacy.
7. Explain learning and thinking in terms of increased demands and expectations, and discuss ways in which schools and parents can encourage competent learning and critical thinking.
8. Discuss the controversy regarding definitions of intelligence and the uses and abuses of intelligence testing.
9. Define mental retardation and describe levels of mental retardation.
10. Describe learning disorders and the various views of their causes and treatments.

Middle childhood—the age range from 6 to 12—is an exciting time for learning and refining skills from reading and writing and arithmetic to playing basketball, dancing, skateboarding, or rollerblading. Children focus on testing themselves, on meeting their own challenges as well as those imposed by their world. The child who is successful will become capable and self-assured; the child who is unsuccessful may develop feelings of inferiority or a weak sense of self. Erikson called middle childhood the period of *industry*, a word that captures the spirit of the age range—it is derived from the Latin word meaning "to build."

In this chapter we look at ways in which children build both physical and cognitive competencies. We also look at schooling and developmental problems encountered in middle childhood, including the ways that academic development and intellectual development are measured and current approaches to understanding learning disorders and mental retardation.

It's important to remember that physical, cognitive, and psychosocial factors interact to produce individual development. In part because neurological functioning improves (through myelination of the reticular formation), children can focus their attention for longer periods. Because their cognitive skills improve, children can anticipate the moves of others and can plan strategies. These and other changes influence their choices of activities as well as their successes or failures.

PHYSICAL AND MOTOR DEVELOPMENT

During the elementary school years, children refine their motor abilities and become more independent. Given appropriate opportunities or training, children can learn to ride a bicycle, jump rope, swim, dance, write, or play a musical instrument. Group sports like football, baseball, basketball, and soccer become important as children's coordination and physical abilities improve. In this section we survey changes in physical characteristics and motor skills in middle childhood, along with important health-related issues such as obesity, physical fitness, and accidents and injuries. Then we look at physical environments at school and at home that promote healthy activity and exercise.

PHYSICAL GROWTH AND CHANGE

Growth is slower and steadier during middle childhood than during the first 2 years of life. The average 6-year-old weighs 45 pounds (20.4 kilos) and is 3½ feet (just over a meter) tall. Gradual, regular growth continues until about age 9 for girls and age 11 for boys; at that point, the "adolescent growth spurt" begins (see Chapter 10). The changes in body size and proportion that are typical of middle childhood are illustrated in Figure 8–1. Note, however, that there is wide variability in the timing of growth; not all children mature at the same rate. Activity level, exercise, nutrition, genetic factors, and gender interact. For example, girls tend to be slightly shorter and lighter than boys until age 9, after which their growth accelerates because their growth spurt begins earlier. Moreover, some girls and boys are structurally smaller than others. Such differences may affect the child's body image and self-concept and thus cause yet another way in which physical, social, and cognitive development interact.

Their enhanced motor skills and coordination open the door for school-age children to participate in sports such as tennis.

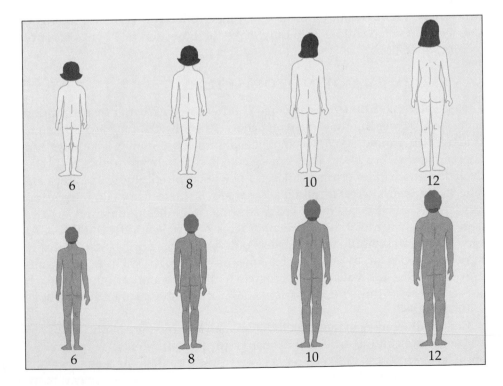

FIGURE 8–1

During middle childhood, there are tremendous variations in growth patterns, but these changes in body size and proportion are typical of this period.

INTERNAL CHANGES

SKELETAL MATURATION Bones grow longer as the body lengthens and broadens; sometimes these changes cause growing pains. Episodes of stiffness and aching caused by skeletal growth are particularly common at night. Rapidly growing children experience such pains as early as age 4; other children don't experience them until adolescence. In either case, children may need reassurance that they're experiencing a normal response to growth (Nichols, 1990; Sheiman & Slomin, 1988). Parents should also be aware that since the skeleton and ligaments of the school-age child are not mature, overly stringent physical training may cause injuries. It is common, for example, for Little League pitchers to injure their shoulders and elbows. Wrist, ankle, and knee injuries are also associated with rigorous sports.

Beginning at age 6 or 7, children also lose their primary or "baby" teeth. When the first permanent teeth emerge, they appear too big for the child's mouth until facial growth catches up. Two noticeable landmarks of middle childhood are the toothless smile of a 6-year-old and the "beaver-toothed" grin of an 8-year-old.

FAT AND MUSCLE TISSUE After about 6 months of age, fat deposits gradually decrease until age 6 to 8; this decrease is more marked in boys. In both sexes, muscles increase in length, breadth, and width (Nichols, 1990). The strength of girls and boys is similar throughout middle childhood.

BRAIN DEVELOPMENT Between 6 and 8 years, the forebrain undergoes a temporary growth spurt, and by age 8 the brain is 90% of its adult size. Brain development during this period produces more efficient functioning—especially in the frontal lobes of the cortex, which is intimately involved in thought and consciousness. The surface area of the frontal lobes increases slightly because of continuing branching of neurons. In addition, lateralization of the brain's hemispheres becomes more pronounced during the school years (Thatcher et al., 1987). The corpus callosum becomes more mature both in structure and in function. Whether or not there is a direct relationship, this is also the time when children typically make the transition to Piaget's stage of concrete operations.

DEVELOPMENT OF MOTOR SKILLS

GROSS MOTOR SKILLS School-age children become better at performing controlled, purposeful movements (Nichols, 1990). By the time a child enters kindergarten around age 5, locomotive skills such as running, jumping, and hopping are well in place. They are executed with an even rhythm and relatively few mechanical errors. Children's newly acquired physical abilities are reflected in their interest in sports and daredevil stunts. They climb trees and use logs as balance beams to cross streams or gullies. Numerous studies demonstrate how motor development progresses during middle childhood. At age 7, a boy can typically throw a ball about 34 feet. By age 10, he can probably throw it twice as far; by age 12, three times as far (Keogh, 1965). Accuracy improves as well. Girls make similar progress in throwing and catching, although at each age their throwing distance is, on average, shorter than that of boys (Williams, 1983).

Gender differences in motor skills before puberty are more a function of opportunity and cultural expectations than of physical differences (Cratty, 1986; Nichols, 1990). These differences are closely linked to the time a child spends practicing a skill. Girls who participate in Little League develop longer, more

By middle childhood children are developing the fine motor skills required to draw, write, paint, cut, and shape materials like clay and papier-mâché.

accurate throws than girls who sit on the sidelines. Boys and girls who play soccer and other sports develop skills at a similar pace.

FINE MOTOR SKILLS   Fine motor skills also develop rapidly during middle childhood, growing out of skills taught in nursery schools and day-care centers. Preschool teachers help build writing readiness as they offer children opportunities to draw, paint, cut, and mold with clay. Thus, children discover how to draw circles, then squares, and then triangles. Each increasingly complex shape requires greater hand-eye coordination, which leads to the ability to write. Most of the fine motor skills required for writing develop between the ages of 6 and 7, although some quite normal children cannot draw a diamond or master many letter shapes until age 8.

Ideally, children develop mastery over their bodies and gain feelings of competence and self-worth that are essential to good mental health. Controlling their bodies also helps them win the acceptance of peers. Awkward, poorly coordinated children are often left out of group activities and may continue to feel rejected long after their awkwardness disappears.

HEALTH, ILLNESS, AND ACCIDENTS

Middle childhood can be one of the healthiest periods in life. Although minor illnesses such as ear infections, colds, and upset stomachs are prevalent in the preschool period, most 6- to 12-year-olds experience few such illnesses. That healthiness is partly a result of greater immunity due to previous exposure, and partly because most school-age children have somewhat better nutrition, health, and safety habits (O'Connor-Francoeur, 1983; Starfield, 1992). Minor illnesses do occur, however. **Myopia** (nearsightedness) is often diagnosed during middle childhood. For example, by the sixth grade, 25% of white middle-class children have been fitted with glasses or contact lenses. Table 8–1 lists the annual incidence of selected common childhood diseases in the U.S.

myopia   Nearsightedness.

STUDY CHART ▸ PHYSICAL DEVELOPMENT DURING MIDDLE CHILDHOOD

5- TO 6-YEAR OLDS

- Steady increases in height and weight
- Steady growth in strength for both boys and girls
- Growing awareness of the placement and actions of large body parts
- Increased use of all body parts
- Improvement in gross motor skills
- Performance of motor skills singly

7- TO 8-YEAR-OLDS

- Steady increase in height and weight
- Steady increase in strength for both boys and girls
- Increased use of all body parts
- Refinement of gross motor skills
- Improvement in fine motor skills
- Increasing variability in motor skill performance but still performed singly

9- TO 10-YEAR-OLDS

- Beginning of growth spurt for girls
- Increase in strength for girls accompanied by loss of flexibility
- Awareness and development of all body parts and systems
- Ability to combine motor skills more fluidly
- Balance improvement

11-YEAR-OLDS

- Girls generally taller and heavier than boys
- Beginning of growth spurt for boys
- Accurate judgment in intercepting moving objects
- Continued combination of more fluid motor skills
- Continued improvement of fine motor skills
- Continued increasing variability in motor skill performance

One author (Parmelee, 1986) suggests that minor illnesses such as colds play a positive role in children's psychological development. Although common illnesses disrupt school, family social roles, and work schedules, children and their families generally recover quickly. In the process, children learn how to cope with stress. They also develop a realistic understanding of the role of "being sick" and therefore learn to empathize with others who get sick.

OBESITY   **Obesity** is a common problem for school-age children in developed nations. An individual who weighs at least 20% more than her or his ideal weight is considered obese. About one-quarter of American school-age children are significantly overweight (Gortmaker, Dietz, Sobol, & Wehler, 1987), and nearly 70% of obese 10- to 13-year-olds will continue to be overweight as adults (Epstein & Wing, 1987). Obesity predisposes them to heart disease, high blood pressure, diabetes, and other medical problems.

Genetic factors apparently play an important role in obesity. A child with one obese parent has a 40% chance of becoming obese, and the proportion

obesity   Weighing at least 20% more in body weight than would be predicted by your height.

TABLE 8–1   ANNUAL INCIDENCE OF SELECTED DISEASES, UNITED STATES

DISEASE	NUMBER OF CASES
Mumps	906
Whooping cough	5,137
Polio	2
Measles	281
German measles	128
Chicken pox	120,624
Pneumonia (under age 5)	1,100,000
Pneumonia (ages 5–17)	550,000
Influenza (under age 5)	7,600,000
Influenza (ages 5–17)	22,900,000
Acute ear infections (under age 5)	12,800,000
Acute ear infections (ages 5–17)	6,700,000
Common cold (under age 5)	14,000,000
Common cold (ages 5–17)	14,500,000

Source: U.S. Census Bureau, 1997.

leaps to 80% if both parents are obese. Further evidence for genetic factors is that adopted children more closely resemble their biological parents than their adoptive parents with regard to body weight (Rosenthal, 1990; Stunkard, 1988).

Genetics are not the whole story, however, and should not be used as an "excuse" for being overweight. Environmental factors are important also, as can be seen in the fact that childhood obesity is more common now than it was 20 years ago. One environmental factor is television viewing, which has increased steadily. Children who spend a lot of time sitting in front of TV sets don't get the exercise they need to develop physical skills or burn excess calories. At the same time, if they spend their viewing hours munching the snacks and drinking the sweetened beverages that they see advertised on TV, then they lose their appetite for more nutritious, less fattening foods (Dietz, 1987). Home computers have a similar impact in that many children spend inordinate amounts of time playing computer games, exchanging e-mail, visiting chat rooms, and "surfing the Net."

Even seriously overweight children should not be placed on drastic weight-loss programs. They need a balanced, nutritious diet to support their energy level and growth. Parents should instead try to encourage overweight children to develop better eating habits that they can maintain. In particular, children should increase their intake of healthful foods like fruits and vegetables and should decrease their intake of foods that are high in fats, such as pizza. Equally important is physical activity to develop muscles and burn calories. Successful weight-loss programs may involve treating the parents as well as the children (Epstein et al., 1990), since obese parents may be less concerned about obesity in their children and may also model bad eating and exercise habits.

Physical education classes may encourage children to develop a lifelong interest in their own fitness by engaging them in physical activities such as aerobics.

Because their improved mobility exposes school-age children to greater accident risk, they often need guidance on ways to protect themselves from injury.

Overweight children face far fewer medical risks than overweight adults, but their obesity can still have serious social and psychological consequences. Peers may reject or stereotype them and call them names. The result can be a negative self-image that may make overweight children even more reluctant to play with peers and engage in physical activities and sports that might help them lose weight.

PHYSICAL FITNESS   Health is often measured in terms of the absence of illness. A better measure is *physical fitness*—optimal functioning of the heart, lungs, muscles, and blood vessels. Physical fitness does not require that children become star athletes. It simply requires that they engage in regular exercise that involves four aspects of conditioning: flexibility, muscle endurance, muscle strength, and cardiovascular efficiency. Some activities help more than others. Basketball, soccer, tennis, bicycling, and swimming exercise the whole body continuously, in contrast to football and baseball, in which players are often idle (Nichols, 1990).

A national survey of 8000 10- to 18-year-olds found that in the 1990s, children tend to be less physically active and fit than were children 30 years earlier. The survey also found that more than half of the children did not engage in physical activity and that many did not participate in fitness activities at school. Given the number of hours school-age children spend watching television and playing video games, it is not surprising that many live sedentary lives. In addition, "latchkey" children, who must care for themselves after school, may not be allowed to play outside for safety reasons—a situation that reduces their activity level still further.

ACCIDENTS AND INJURIES   As children grow in size, strength, and coordination, they engage in increasingly dangerous activities such as cycling, skateboarding, and rollerblading. Many participate in team sports like baseball and football, which employ potentially harmful projectiles and crippling body contact (Maddux et al., 1986). From infancy on, children's need to exercise their newfound skills often conflicts with their need for protection against the dangers associated with many physical activities. In addition, children's risk of harming themselves typically exceeds their ability to foresee the consequences of their actions (Achenbach, 1982). Parental warnings against riding a bicycle or skateboard on a busy street may be ignored or forgotten in the excitement of play.

Accidents—especially motor vehicle accidents—cause more deaths in children than six other major causes of death combined: cancer, homicide, congenital anomalies, suicide, heart disease, and AIDS (see Figure 8–2 for selected comparisons). About half of all childhood deaths result from injuries and accidents. Accidents are also the leading cause of physical disability in childhood.

PHYSICAL EDUCATION IN SCHOOLS   Although we generally think of school in terms of cognitive or social development, schools also promote physical and motor development. Elementary schools include physical education partly because physical activity in childhood often sets a pattern for lifelong activity. *Physical education* is defined as a program of carefully planned and conducted motor activities that prepare students for skillful, fit, and knowledgeable performance (Nichols, 1990). It can be carried out in different school settings: classroom, gymnasium, multipurpose room, playground, or playing field.

Because of the poor average level of physical fitness in the U.S. population, current national health objectives call for increasing children's participation in

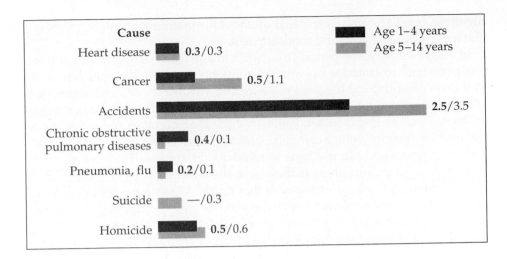

Cause	Age 1–4 years ■ Age 5–14 years ▦
Heart disease	0.3/0.3
Cancer	0.5/1.1
Accidents	2.5/3.5
Chronic obstructive pulmonary diseases	0.4/0.1
Pneumonia, flu	0.2/0.1
Suicide	—/0.3
Homicide	0.5/0.6

FIGURE 8–2 MAJOR CAUSES OF DEATH IN CHILDHOOD, UNITED STATES (IN THOUSANDS OF DEATHS PER YEAR)

Source: U.S. Census Bureau, 1997.

daily physical education classes and regular physical activity (U.S. Department of Health and Human Services, 1992). Such programs may assist in increasing children's overall physical activity and eventual interest in fitness as adults. A national health objective therefore calls for programs that engage students in active physical exercise—preferably lifelong activities such as jogging and swimming—for at least 50% of the time devoted to physical education. (U.S. Department of Health and Human Services, 1992).

1. Trace the development of bones, fat, muscle tissue, and the brain during middle childhood.
2. What factors contribute to childhood obesity?
3. What are the objectives of school-based physical education programs, and why are these programs so important to physical fitness?

REVIEW & APPLY

COGNITIVE DEVELOPMENT

Here we return to the two major approaches to studying cognition, this time with respect to middle childhood: cognitive-developmental theory and information-processing theory. Language and literacy are considered as well.

PIAGET AND CONCRETE OPERATIONAL THINKING

The thinking of a 12-year-old child is very different from that of a 5-year-old. This difference is partly due to the larger body of knowledge and information that a 12-year-old has accumulated, but it is also due to the different ways in which children think and process information. In Piaget's terms, elementary schoolchildren develop *concrete operational thought*.

COGNITIVE ABILITIES A large part of cognitive development occurs in schoolrooms, beginning at age 5 to 7 in most cultures. At those ages, many cognitive, language, and perceptual-motor skills mature and interact in ways that make learning easier and more efficient.

In Piaget's theory, the period from age 5 to age 7 marks the transition from preoperational to concrete operational thought: Thought becomes less intuitive and egocentric and becomes more logical. Toward the end of the preoperational stage, the rigid, static, irreversible qualities of children's thought begin to "thaw out," as Piaget put it. Children's thinking becomes reversible, flexible, and considerably more complex. Children now notice more than one aspect of an object and can use logic to reconcile differences. They can evaluate cause-and-effect relationships if they have the concrete object or situation in front of them and can see changes as they occur. When a piece of clay looks like a sausage, they no longer find it inconsistent that the clay was once a ball or that it can be molded into a new shape, such as a cube. The emerging ability mentally to go beyond the immediate situation or state lays the foundation for systematic reasoning in the concrete operational stage and, later, in the formal operational stage. Table 8–2 contrasts the basics of preoperational and concrete operational thought.

An important difference between preoperational and concrete operational thought can be illustrated by school-age children's use of logical inference (Flavell, 1985). Recall Piaget's liquid/beakers conservation problem (Chapter 6). Preoperational children consistently judge that a tall, narrow glass holds more liquid than a short, wide one, even though both quantities of liquid have been shown to be identical at the start. In contrast, concrete operational children recognize that both containers must hold the same amount of liquid. They begin to think differently about states and transformations and can remember how the liquid appeared before it was poured into the tall, thin container. They can think about how its shape changed as it was poured from one

TABLE 8–2 A COMPARISON OF PREOPERATIONAL AND CONCRETE OPERATIONAL THOUGHT

STAGE	AGE	THE CHILD'S THINKING IS:
Preoperational	2 to 5–7 years	Rigid and static
		Irreversible
		Focused on the here and now
		Centered on one dimension
		Egocentric
		Focused on perceptual evidence
		Intuitive
Concrete operational	5–7 to 12 years	Flexible
		Reversible
		Not limited to the here and now
		Multidimensional
		Less egocentric
		Marked by the use of logical inferences
		Marked by the search for cause-and-effect relationships

glass into the other, and they can imagine the liquid's being poured back. In short, their thinking is reversible.

In addition, concrete operational children know that differences between similar objects can be measured. In Piaget's (1970) matchstick problem, illustrated in Figure 8–3, children are shown a zigzag row of six matchsticks and a straight row of five matchsticks placed end to end. When asked which row has more matchsticks, preoperational children center only on the distance between the end points of the rows and therefore pick the "longer" row with five matchsticks. Concrete operational children, however, can take into account what lies between the end points of the rows and therefore correctly choose the one with six matchsticks.

Unlike preoperational children, concrete operational children can also theorize about the world around them. They think about and anticipate what will happen; they make guesses about things and then test their hunches. They may estimate, for example, how many more breaths of air they can blow into a balloon before it pops, and they will keep blowing until they reach the mark. Their ability to theorize is limited to objects and social relationships that they can see or concretely imagine, however. They don't develop theories about abstract concepts, thoughts, or relationships until they reach the stage of formal operations, which occurs around age 11 or 12.

The transition from preoperational to concrete operational thought does not happen overnight. It requires years of experience in manipulating and learning about objects and materials in the environment. According to Piaget, children learn concrete operational thought largely on their own. As they actively explore their physical environment, asking themselves questions and finding the answers, they acquire more complex, sophisticated forms of thinking.

PIAGET AND EDUCATION As we saw in Chapter 4, infants benefit from stimulation that is slightly ahead of their developmental level. Some researchers believe that appropriate training can also accelerate the cognitive development of preoperational children, hastening their entry into concrete operational thinking. Training is most effective when children have reached a state of readiness, an optimal period that occurs just before they make the transition to the next stage (Bruner et al., 1966).

Many of the basic concepts presented by Piaget have been applied to education, especially in the areas of science and math. One such application includes the use of concrete objects for teaching 5- to 7-year-olds. By combining, comparing, and contrasting objects (e.g., blocks and rods of different shapes and

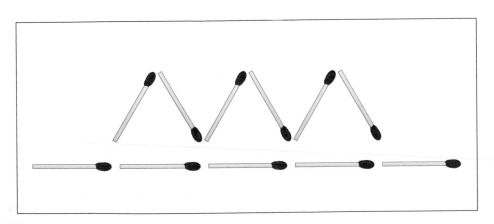

FIGURE 8–3 PIAGET'S MATCHSTICK PROBLEM

Concrete operational children realize that the six matchsticks in the zigzag top row will make a longer line than the five matchsticks in the straight bottom row. Younger children will say that the bottom row is the longest because they tend to center only on the end points of the two lines and not on what lies between them.

sizes; seeds that grow in sand, water, or soil), children discover similarities, differences, and relationships.

An example of this technique is arranging objects in simple patterns (see Figure 8–4). In introducing first- or second-graders to the number concept of 16, a teacher might present several different spatial arrays of 16 cubes—grouped into two towers of 8, one row of 16, four rows of 4, and so on. The teacher might then give verbal cues to help the children conserve, pointing out that the number of cubes remains the same even though the length and width of the rows change.

There are many other applications of Piaget's concepts. For example, addition and subtraction involve an understanding of reversibility (5 + 8 = 13; 13 – 5 = 8). Again, children can learn most readily by manipulating real objects. Parents and teachers who understand the basic principles of Piaget's theory of cognitive development can develop effective educational lessons and organize them into a logical sequence. Piagetian concepts have also been applied to social studies, music, and art.

Piaget's theory therefore extends to learning as a component of cognitive development. Children are active learners who construct their own theories about how the world operates, and they are self-motivated to change their theories when pieces of information do not fit (Bruner, 1973). Educational psychologists warn against structuring education in ways that encourage children to seek praise from teachers rather than solving problems for their own sake. They emphasize that children's interest in learning depends on the intrinsic rewards they find in the encounter with the subject matter itself. Children gain confidence from mastering problems and discovering principles, and they learn by *doing*—just as adults do (Gronlund, 1995).

Educators also point out that, all too often, teachers fall into the trap of telling instead of showing. Some teachers remove the real-life, concrete context of many subjects. They present rules for children to memorize by rote without motivating the children to understand the rules. Children are then left with an arid body of facts without the ability to apply facts and principles beyond the immediate situation. Children need to learn by actively exploring ideas and relationships and solving problems in realistic contexts.

FIGURE 8–4

Some possible spatial arrays of 16 cubes. By arranging the cubes in different ways, a teacher can help young schoolchildren understand the number concept of 16.

4 x 4 array

2 x 8 array

16 cubes in an open design

Two "towers" of 8

1 x 16 array

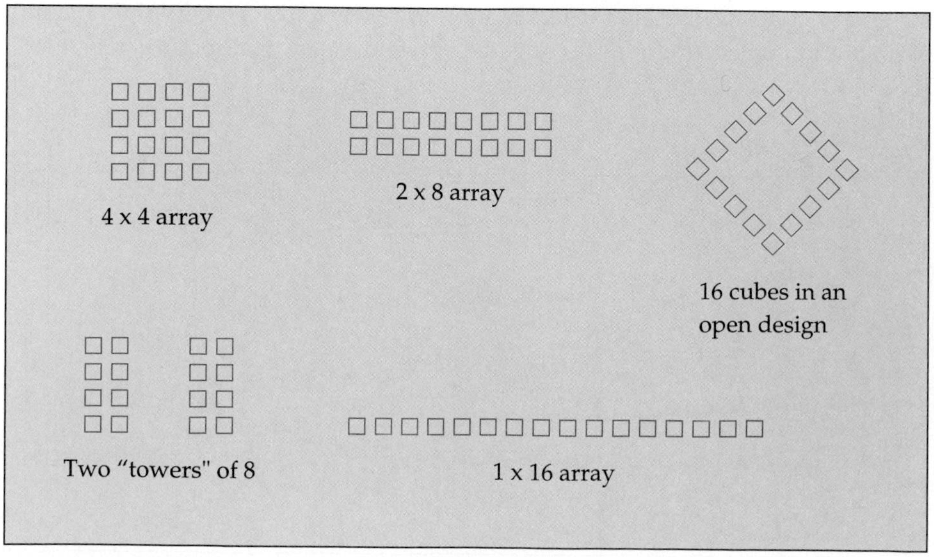

Piaget was a remarkable observer of young children's cognitive development. But there are some aspects of cognitive development that he didn't assess, and these are also important for school learning. Many of these come under the heading of the information-processing perspective.

INFORMATION PROCESSING

Recall that information-processing theorists see the human mind as analogous to a computer. Thus, the focus shifts to cognitive functions such as attention and problem solving, along with two crucial functions that show considerable development during middle childhood: memory and metacognition.

MEMORY   A number of significant developments occur in the memory abilities of concrete operational children. Recall from Chapter 6 that preoperational children do well at recognition tasks but poorly at recall tasks; they have trouble using memory strategies like rehearsal. However, their ability to recall lists of items improves significantly between the ages of 5 and 7. Most children begin making conscious efforts to memorize information. They look at material to be remembered and repeat it over and over. Later they organize material into categories, and eventually they may create stories or visual images to help them remember particular items. The increasingly deliberate use of memory strategies makes the older child's recall more effective and efficient (Flavell, 1985).

To put it another way, elementary schoolchildren learn **control processes**—strategies and techniques that enhance memory. Following are examples of such processes, with indications of the ages at which they develop.

1. *Rehearsal:* At first, children rehearse simply by saying items to themselves over and over, one at a time. At about age 9, however, they begin to group or "chunk" items together (Ornstein et al., 1975; Ornstein et al., 1977). This process improves their ability both to hold information in short-term memory and to transfer it to long-term memory.

control processes   Higher cognitive processes that enhance memory.

When spelling a word, children usually need to retrieve the proper letters from their memory.

2. *Organization:* Another major development in the use of memory strategies is the ability to organize. Whereas younger school-age children tend to relate words by simple association (such as the arrangement of words in a list), older children organize groups of words by common features and meaning; for example, apples, pears, and grapes are "fruit." Children who group words into categories can remember more items than those who do not. However, children seldom use organizational strategies on their own before age 9 (Bjorklund, 1988).

3. *Semantic elaboration:* It is clear that elementary-school children can often remember what they infer from statements in addition to what is actually said to them. In a series of studies by Scott Paris and colleagues, children were given sentences like "Her friend swept the floor." They were then asked whether the friend had a broom. Eleven-year-olds were able to infer the presence of a broom; 7-year-olds were not (Paris et al., 1977). Semantic elaboration involves the use of logical inferences to reconstruct an event, as opposed to simply recalling a "perfect," unedited copy (Flavell et al., 1993).

4. *Mental imagery:* Younger children can be taught to remember unusual material by constructing images or "pictures" in their minds. Older children are more likely to construct such images on their own, and their images tend to be more vivid (Siegler, 1986).

5. *Retrieval:* Often when younger children try to spell a word, they search their memory for the proper letters. They may know the letter that the word begins with, but they need to sound out possibilities for the rest of the word. Older children become much better at retrieval strategies (Flavell et al., 1993).

6. *Scripts:* Memory for routine events may be organized in the form of "scripts." This method has the advantage that an event that occurs over and over again need not be stored separately in memory each time. The event can be remembered in the form of a standard sequence of events, along with fill-in "slots" for aspects that vary. For example, the script for a school morning might specify the events that typically occur on such a morning: get up, get dressed, eat breakfast, go to school. The slots would be filled with variable items, such as which clothes are worn, what's for breakfast, and what form of transportation is used to get to school (Nelson & Gruendel, 1986). By age 4 or 5, children apparently use specific scripts for familiar routines, but during middle childhood they become capable of "merging" specific scripts into broader categories (Case, 1996).

METACOGNITION **Metacognition** refers to the sophisticated intellectual processes that enable children to monitor their own thinking, memory, knowledge, goals, and actions; in other words, metacognition is "thinking about thinking." During middle childhood, children develop metacognitive abilities that they use in planning, making decisions, and solving problems.

In his description of metacognition, Flavell (1985) cites the following example: Preschool and elementary-school children were asked to study a group of items until they were certain that they could remember them perfectly. When the children said that they were ready, they usually were: When tested, they remembered each item without error. In contrast, preschool children often said that they were ready when in fact they were not. Despite the good intentions of the preschoolers, they did not have sufficient cognitive abilities to complete the task *and* to know when they had completed it; they could not monitor their own intellectual processes. The ability to monitor thinking and memory begins at about age 6 and emerges more fully between the ages of 7 and 10. Even

metacognition The process of monitoring your own thinking, memory, knowledge, goals, and actions.

then, however, metacognition is better when the material to be learned is typical or familiar (Hasselhorn, 1992).

Like other aspects of cognitive ability, metacognitive skills continue to develop into adolescence. Just as a 9-year-old has greater metacognitive ability than a 4-year-old, a 15-year-old's self-monitoring skills far surpass those of a 9-year-old.

LANGUAGE AND LITERACY

Oral and written language skills become much more refined during middle childhood. As their vocabulary continues to expand, children master increasingly complex grammatical structures and more sophisticated language usage. For example, they begin to use and understand the passive voice, although their syntax may still be shaky. They are also able to infer that sentences like "John was watched as he walked along the beach" include participants who are not explicitly named.

LITERACY   Although oral language development is often dramatic, it frequently takes a back seat to the development of literacy—skills in reading and writing. Preschoolers focus on learning to produce and understand spoken language; school-age children learn to read and write. Reading includes learning phonetics and the way to decode the alphabet, and writing includes refining the fine motor skills needed to form letters. But there's much more. Reading requires the ability to elicit *meaning* from print, and writing requires the ability to convey meaning in print. Both reading and writing are forms of symbolic communication that also involve attention, perception, and memory.

Through symbolic communication, children learn to relate the external world to their inner thoughts and feelings. "Members of a culture share common ways of infusing various forms (such as sounds, actions, marks on paper, and monuments in the park) with meaning," comments Anne Haas Dyson (1993), a researcher in the field of literacy development. "These symbols— these connections between forms and meanings—connect us to others and, at the same time, organize our own feelings, experiences, and thoughts."

Reading and writing are natural outgrowths of the child's growing language skills. The recognition that oral and written language learning are interconnected has led to the *whole-language* approach to literacy (Fields & Spanglier, 1995). Rather than looking for a distinct point at which children develop reading and writing readiness, whole-language theorists focus on the concept of "emergent" literacy: The skills associated with oral and written language acquisition begin to develop in infancy and gradually improve over a period of years (Teale & Sulzby, 1986). Thus, the stories that an infant can only listen to, the "writing" that a toddler does with a crayon, and the preschooler's "reading" from memory are all precursors to reading and writing. Parents and teachers can encourage the development of literacy by providing a rich home and school environment (see Table 8–3 for details).

The development of reading and writing skills during middle childhood is a complex, multidimensional process that also emerges out of a social-cultural context. Children learn to read and write in the context of relevant social situations. They acquire the basics of literacy while interacting with their parents, siblings, teachers, and peers. The interactions differ, as do the contributions each interaction makes to the child's growing literacy. Parents, for example, may make their greatest contributions by having conversations with their children rather than focusing exclusively on print-related activities (Snow, 1993). Similarly, children respond differently when they are actively engaged with

Some children like to read more than others.

TABLE 8–3 CONDITIONS THAT PROMOTE LITERACY

1. A print-rich environment
   - adults who read for their own purposes
   - adults who write for their own purposes
   - frequent story-time experiences
   - dictation experiences
   - high-quality literature
   - contextualized print
   - functional print
   - answers to questions about print
2. A rich oral language environment
   - adult language models
   - adults who listen to children
   - free exploration of oral language
   - peer conversation
   - dramatic play roles
   - experiences for vocabulary enrichment
   - vocabulary information as requested
3. Firsthand experiences of interest
   - play
   - daily living
   - field trips
   - nature exploration
4. Symbolic representation experiences
   - dramatic play
   - drawing and painting
   - music and dance
5. Pressure-free experimentation with writing
   - drawing
   - scribbling
   - nonphonetic writing
   - invented spelling
6. Pressure-free exploration of reading
   - reading from memory
   - reading with context clues
   - matching print to oral language

Source: From *Let's begin reading right: Developmentally appropriate beginning literacy,* Third Edition, by M. V. Fields and K. L. Spangler, p. 104. Copyright © 1995 by Prentice-Hall. Reprinted by permission.

their peers in learning to read than when they are working with a teacher (Daiute et al., 1993). Whereas teachers help children learn the knowledge and skills they need to become expert readers and writers, peer interactions give children the opportunity to discuss ideas and problems spontaneously. When children work with each other on a collaborative basis, they also tend to talk more than when they work with a teacher.

Taken together, children's social interactions lay the groundwork for literacy in a much more important way than merely mastering units of written language. Just as communication or problem solving occurs in social context, children learn to read and write in a social environment (Vygotsky, 1934/1987). When problems of literacy occur, educators take into consideration the family, peer, and teacher relationships that make up the child's social world (Daiute, 1993).

---

1. How does children's thinking change as they make the transition from pre-operational to concrete operational thought?
2. Why is the growing ability to use logical inferences so important in this stage of cognitive development?
3. Describe the major developments in memory and metacognition that occur during middle childhood.
4. How do metacognitive skills increase children's intellectual competence?
5. Describe how the concept of emergent literacy fits into the whole-language approach to literacy.

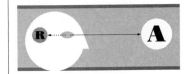

REVIEW & APPLY

INTELLIGENCE AND ACHIEVEMENT

In the 1940s and 1950s, achievement, personality, and career aptitude tests were widely administered to U.S. schoolchildren. As a result, school files were filled with test scores that often varied in accuracy and significance. In the 1960s, many parents and educators became alarmed at what they considered the abuse of school-based tests. Although intelligence, diagnostic, and achievement tests are still widely used, educators are now more aware of the dangers of misinterpreting (or overinterpreting) test results and labeling children incorrectly. Indeed, whether the label is accurate or not, the very fact of being labeled as "retarded" or "dyslexic" (terms defined later in the chapter) can haunt the child for life and create a "self-fulfilling prophecy" that prevents the child from obtaining a quality education (Tobias, 1989; Howard, 1995).

When used appropriately, however, tests are vital educational tools. They identify what children can and cannot do, allowing teachers to prescribe steps in learning that are tailored to the individual child. Preferably, a child is not simply labeled as "superior" or a "slow learner" but instead is assessed with regard to specific behaviors and skills.

In addition to classroom observation and "diagnostic" lessons, children are given **criterion-referenced tests** that measure the extent to which they have mastered specific skills and objectives (Glaser, 1963). Because criterion-referenced tests focus on the specific achievements of an individual, they differ radically from the more familiar **norm-referenced tests,** which compare children's scores to those of other children of the same age. Most IQ and general achievement tests are norm-referenced, meaning that they are first given to a large sample of people and *standardized* with regard to procedures and scoring criteria. Thus, whereas a criterion-referenced math test describes a child's accuracy and speed in specific math skills, a norm-referenced test assesses whether a child is performing at a level that is higher or lower than average compared with the standardization group. A norm-referenced test might iden-

criterion-referenced tests
Tests that evaluate an individual's performance in relation to mastery of specified skills or objectives.

norm-referenced tests Tests that compare an indiviual's performance with the performances of others in the same age group.

tify a child as being in the bottom 10% of the class in math skills, yet may reveal little about what the child actually knows, why the child answers specific items incorrectly, or what skills the child needs to acquire.

INTELLIGENCE TESTING

Perhaps no issue in developmental psychology has been more controversial than intelligence and intelligence testing. The academic debate has often gone public because of the broad impact that intelligence test scores can have on educational and social opportunities and because intelligence tests are administered widely and taken seriously in the United States. When young children are labeled on the basis of intelligence test scores, the results can be far-reaching. Children's scores may affect the extent and quality of their education, determine the jobs they can obtain as adults, and have a lasting impact on their self-image. Why do we hold intelligence in such high regard? What are we trying to measure in the first place? In this section we look at attempts to measure intelligence and then consider how to define it.

THE STANFORD-BINET TEST   The first comprehensive intelligence test was designed in the early twentieth century by Alfred Binet, a psychologist who was commissioned by the French government to devise an objective method for identifying children who would not benefit from school. In 1916, an American version of Binet's test was created by Lewis Terman and colleagues at Stanford University and referred to as the Stanford-Binet Test. This individually administered test gained wide acceptance during the 1940s and 1950s and—with modern revision—is still widely used.

Binet's initial concept of intelligence focused on complex intellectual processes such as judgment, reasoning, memory, and comprehension. Through extensive trial and error, he developed test items involving problem solving, word definitions, and general knowledge that appeared to differentiate children according to *mental age* (MA). For example, if more than half of all 5-year-olds but fewer than half of all 4-year-olds could define the word *ball*, that would be an item on the test for 5-year-olds (Binet & Simon, 1905, 1916).

THE INTELLIGENCE QUOTIENT   According to Binet's approach, a 4-year-old who could answer questions at the level of a 5-year-old would have a mental age of 5, and this analysis was as far as Binet went in developing his early tests. (Remember, his purpose was to test schoolchildren and determine which ones were not progressing well.) Later, however, other test researchers developed a formula for expressing the child's intellectual level that made it possible to compare children of different *chronological ages* (CA). This measure, the **intelligence quotient (IQ)**, was obtained as follows:

$$IQ = MA\ /\ CA \times 100$$

Thus, an average 4-year-old should score an MA of 4 on the test; then her or his IQ would be 100 ($4/4 \times 100 = 100$). An above-average 4-year-old with an MA score of 5 would obtain an IQ of 125 ($5/4 \times 100 = 125$); a below-average child with an MA of 3 would have an IQ of 75.

THE WECHSLER TESTS   There were problems with the "ratio" approach, however. Although the formula worked reasonably well with children and adolescents whose cognitive abilities were continuing to improve in predictable ways, it was difficult to assess adult intelligence by this means. What kinds of test items would uniformly and fairly assess the mental age of a 30-year-old compared with that of a 40-year-old? Because of this drawback, IQ is now

intelligence quotient (IQ) An individual's mental age divided by chronological age, multiplied by 100 to eliminate the decimal point.

assessed by what's called **deviation IQ**. This measure was developed primarily by David Weschler and applied to IQ tests that he and his colleagues developed for early childhood, childhood and adolescence, and adulthood. An individual who takes the test obtains a score that is compared statistically with the scores of other people in the same age range. In other words, today's IQ tests (including the modern Stanford-Binet) are norm-referenced, as noted earlier.

Figure 8–5 illustrates the distribution of deviation-based IQ scores in the general population; it is based on the Wechsler IQ tests, which are widely used. Note the familiar "bell-shaped" curve: IQ is assumed to be normally distributed around an average of 100, with about two-thirds of the general population scoring between 85 and 115, and almost 96% of the population scoring between 70 and 130. That result leaves roughly 2% scoring below 70, which is one criterion for mental retardation, and roughly 2% scoring above 130, which is typically the cutoff point for "giftedness."

IQ test scores are by no means the whole story, however. Even though modern versions of the Stanford-Binet and Weschler tests provide "subscores" on performance in specific areas such as language and math abilities, the consensus is that they do not measure all of what we commonly think of as intelligence. Their purpose is primarily to measure abilities associated with academic performance—which is appropriate, since that's what they were designed for. A related point is that the tests measure an individual's intellectual abilities only at the time when they are administered; in other words, they measure *current* intellectual functioning. A popular misconception is that they assess intellectual *potential*, which is definitely not the case. Thus, as noted earlier, labeling children as "bright" or "dull" on the basis of IQ scores can be misleading and even detrimental to the child—IQ scores can change substantially over time as a function of schooling and other cognitive experiences; nevertheless, an early label may persist.

THE NATURE OF INTELLIGENCE

The development of sophisticated models for testing and measuring intelligence naturally stimulated inquiry into what intelligence actually is. Here are some of the highlights of the continuing debate.

deviation IQ The approach that assigns an IQ score by comparing an individual's raw score with the scores of other subjects of the same age range.

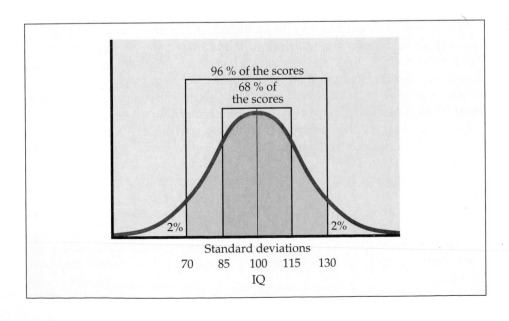

FIGURE 8–5 DISTRIBUTION OF IQ IN THE GENERAL POPULATION

INNATE VERSUS LEARNED?   The nature-nurture controversy still produces fireworks in academic journals and the popular press. Arthur Jensen (1969), for example, generated a great deal of controversy when he stated that 80% of what is measured on IQ tests is inherited and that only 20% is determined by a child's environment, and further that intelligence is racially determined, with the intellectual gene pool of blacks inferior to that of whites. In research conducted in the 1960s African-Americans did on average score 10–15 points lower on IQ tests than did whites. But the difference has progressively decreased in recent years, and researchers now argue that "adjustments for economic and social differences in the lives of black and white children all but eliminate differences in the IQ scores between these two groups" (Brooks-Gunn et al., 1996).

Jensen's research has been thoroughly discredited and need not be discussed further here, except to note that the criticism he invoked helped produce a backlash with regard to the possible genetic contribution to intelligence. Some psychologists even took the view that there is no evidence for any genetic effect on IQ (Kamin, 1974).

The current view is more balanced: Genetic and environmental factors are about equally important in determining how well a child will do on an IQ test (Weinberg, 1989; Plomin & DeFries, 1998). But the pendulum may once again be tipping toward the side of those who think that intelligence is largely innate: A recent paper on identical twins who were reared apart claims that IQ is 70% inherited (Bouchard et al., 1990). For further discussion of environmental factors that influence intellectual development and achievement, see "Eye on Diversity," on facing page.

GENERAL AND SPECIFIC ABILITIES   Although some intelligence tests define intelligence as a single, unitary attribute, most tests define it as a composite of abilities. The Wechsler Intelligence Scale for Children, for example, has separate subtests for information, comprehension, mathematics, vocabulary, digit span, picture arrangement, and others. This test yields a Verbal IQ score, a Performance (nonverbal) IQ score, and a Full-Scale score that combines the two. The current version of the Stanford-Binet test takes a similar approach in breaking down general intelligence into separate components.

One proponent of the view that intelligence comprises independent abilities is Howard Gardner (1983). On the basis of studies of neurology, psychology, and human evolutionary history, he identified at least seven distinct categories of intelligence, divided into two groups. In the first group are linguistic, musical, logical-mathematical, and spatial intelligence. The second group includes kinesthetic, interpersonal, and intrapersonal intelligence. Thus, although a particular child may be below average in the academic intelligence measured by most IQ tests, he or she may be high in other types of intelligence, such as the ability to understand the feelings and motivations of others. Of course, it's also important to consider whether the child actually *uses* his or her different types of intelligence (Hatch, 1997).

Robert Sternberg (1985) incorporates another perspective in his "triarchic" (three-part) concept of intelligence. According to Sternberg, *contextual intelligence* involves adaptation to the environment and the characteristic that we might call "common sense"; *experiential intelligence* involves the ability to cope with new tasks or situations as well as with old ones; and *componential intelligence* corresponds roughly to the abilities measured by commonly employed IQ tests.

In schools today, skills that are not easily measured, like the ability to appreciate art, tend to be ignored.

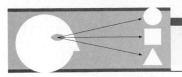

EYE ON DIVERSITY

SOUTHEAST ASIAN REFUGEES AND ACADEMIC ACHIEVEMENT

The scholastic success of Asian children in science and math in particular is widely recognized. Schools in Japan and Taiwan, for example, have longer school years and more rigorous work requirements than do American schools. But is that all there is to it?

An answer to this question may be found by studying Southeast Asian "boat people" who migrated to the United States in the late 1970s and early 1980s. At first glance, it might seem that the children of these refugee families would be doomed to failure in American schools. Devastating economic and political circumstances forced their families to flee their countries. The children often went for months, even years, without formal schooling while living in relocation camps. Many suffered hunger and physical trauma. In addition, they had little knowledge of English.

Nevertheless, in a study of 200 Southeast Asian families who had been in the United States an average of $3\frac{1}{2}$ years, researchers found that the chil-

dren had surprisingly high grade-point averages and math test scores. Despite their many disadvantages, the majority of the children adapted to their urban schools and quickly began to achieve at or above their grade level (Kaplan et al., 1992).

What factors were responsible for these children's academic success? Parental encouragement and dedication to learning were especially significant. Parents helped their children overcome poor English skills, initial poverty, and the often disruptive environment of urban schools. They had a strong tradition of collective family responsibility. Parents and children alike expressed their obligations, not only to each member of the family but also to the family's overall success. The children's academic achievement was highly valued because it was linked to the future success of the entire family.

Nowhere was the family's commitment to academic excellence more obvious than in attitudes toward homework. During the evenings, homework was the dominant family activity. Despite their poor English skills, parents set standards and goals for the evening's activity and did many of the chil-

dren's chores so that they could study. Older siblings helped younger ones. This sibling involvement indicates how a large family can encourage academic success in its members, in contrast to the lower educational achievement typically encountered in large, poor American families.

In about half of the families, the parents read aloud to their children regularly. Children whose parents read to them got higher grades, whether the reading was in English or in their native language. Reading aloud fosters shared knowledge, strengthens emotional ties, and maintains an environment in which learning and discussion are valued. The more successful refugee families also displayed egalitarianism in gender roles. Husbands helped with the dishes and laundry. Both boys and girls were expected to help with chores. And it was expected that both boys and girls would go to college.

Finally, the families believed that their efforts would enable them to achieve change or desired goals—not just immediately but also in the future. They did not depend on luck or fate for their success.

LIMITATIONS OF TESTING

Schools use many kinds of tests to assess students' skills and competencies. Their tendency to concentrate on measurable abilities reflects the popularity of behavioral objectives, meaning the specific kinds of knowledge and skills that a student is expected to display after a specified amount of instruction. In a very real sense, the tests provide a way of testing schools as well as students. At various points during each academic year, schools are expected to provide objective data on what their students are learning. As valuable as this approach can be in keeping schools up to par, however, emphasizing a school's success can mean that children spend much of the school day focusing on the particular competencies that are measured by the tests. As a result, less tangible competencies, ways of thinking, and personality traits may be overlooked. Tests do not tell the whole story about ability, and some personal qualities and skills are difficult or impossible to measure.

There is also the question of possible cultural bias in the tests themselves. To demonstrate the absurdity of culturally linked intelligence tests, Stephen Jay

Gould (1981) gave a class of Harvard students a nonverbal test of intelligence designed for World War I army recruits. (A sample of the test is shown in Figure 8–6.) He found that many of his students could not identify a horn as the missing part of a Victrola record player (item 18), despite the test makers' claim that the subjects' "innate" intelligence would guide them to the correct answer.

Minority groups object to having their skills and abilities measured by tests that assume wide exposure to the dominant culture; they feel that the tests are unfair to people from different cultural backgrounds. Support for this view is provided by a study of black and interracial children who had been adopted by white middle-class parents. The IQ scores and school achievements of these children were well above average—and well above those of children with similar backgrounds but different cultural experiences (Weinberg, 1989). Research also suggests that minority children may be victims of a self-fulfilling

Figure 8–6

This is part 6 of the Army Beta mental test given to recruits during World War I. (Answers:
1. mouth; **2.** eye; **3.** nose; **4.** spoon in right hand; **5.** chimney; **6.** left ear; **7.** filament; **8.** stamp; **9.** strings; **10.** rivet; **11.** trigger; **12.** tail; **13.** leg; **14.** shadow; **15.** bowling ball in man's right hand; **16.** net; **17.** left hand; **18.** horn of Victrola; **19.** arm and powder puff in mirror image; **20.** diamond.)

prophecy. They acquire low expectations about their academic performance on tests designed primarily for white students, and the low expectations further lower their self-confidence and, hence, their test scores. To be fair, in recent years designers of tests such as the Stanford-Binet and the Weschler tests have gone to great lengths to eliminate as much cultural bias as possible, but the tests are still oriented toward the mainstream culture.

It is not always necessary to use tests to assess children's progress. Teachers, parents, and caregivers can learn a lot by informally observing what children do and say. By merely listening as a child reads a book, a skilled teacher can determine much about the child's progress toward reading mastery. We will return to problems associated with standardized testing later in the chapter in the context of developmental disorders.

1. What is the difference between criterion-referenced and norm-referenced tests?
2. How do ratio-IQ tests differ from deviation-IQ tests?
3. Briefly discuss the controversy over the nature of intelligence.

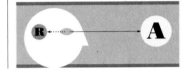

REVIEW & APPLY

LEARNING AND THINKING IN SCHOOL

Schools play a critical role in healthy development. At school, children test their intellectual, physical, social, and emotional competencies to find out whether they can meet the standards set for them by their parents, their teachers, and society in general. They also gain confidence in their ability to master their world and develop good relationships with peers.

At school, children encounter demands and expectations that differ markedly from those they have faced at home. Children vary greatly in their capacity to adapt to these demands, in their ability to use critical thinking, in their overall success in school, and in the role their parents play in helping them learn. Around the world, children also vary widely with regard to opportunities to attend school and the extent to which they reach at least the fifth grade (see Figure 8–7).

NEW DEMANDS AND EXPECTATIONS

Children entering school are separated from their parents, some for the first time, and they must learn to trust unfamiliar adults. At the same time, greater independence is expected of them. No longer can a little boy yell to his mother, "Put on my boots!" The teacher expects him to do it himself. Even in small classes, children must now compete for adult attention and assistance.

Regardless of the school, there is always a gap between what is expected at home and what is expected in the classroom. The greater the gap, the more difficult the child's adjustment will be. Children who have just begun to internalize the rules of family life are suddenly expected to adapt to a new set of standards. Their success will depend on their family background, the school environment, and their own individuality. How well a child has coped with dependency, autonomy, authority, aggression, and conscience will influence

Figure 8–7 Primary School Enrollment around the World

Source: The Progress of Nations, 1995, UNICEF.

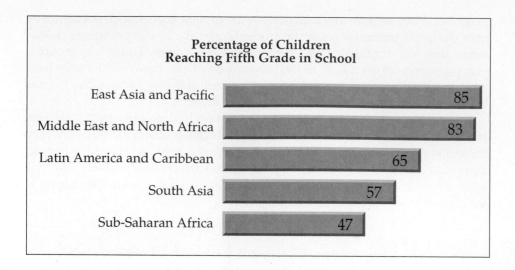

Percentage of Children Reaching Fifth Grade in School

East Asia and Pacific	85
Middle East and North Africa	83
Latin America and Caribbean	65
South Asia	57
Sub-Saharan Africa	47

his or her adjustment to school. Although teachers recognize that the inner resources of a child who has just started school may be shaky, they nonetheless insist that the child adapt—and quickly.

From the first day of school, children are expected to learn the complex social rules that govern the social life of the classroom. Relations with classmates involve finding the right balance between cooperation and competition. Similarly, relations with teachers involve achieving a compromise between autonomy and obedience.

Some schools have elaborate codes of behavior: Children must listen when the teacher speaks, line up to go outside for recess, obtain permission to go to the bathroom, and raise a hand before speaking. Initially, a great deal of class time may be spent enforcing such rules. Public school classrooms have been studied with respect to how much time teachers spend on the following activities: (1) teaching facts or concepts; (2) giving directions for a particular lesson; (3) stating general rules of behavior; (4) correcting, disciplining, and praising children; and (5) miscellaneous activities (Sieber & Gordon, 1981). The results are startling: In a half-hour lesson, it is not unusual for a teacher to spend only 10–15% of the time on academic work (categories 1 and 2). Research indicates that children learn more in classes in which time on task is maximized—that is, in which the teacher spends at least half the time on actual teaching and less on such concerns as maintaining order (Brophy, 1986). Time and energy invested in socializing children to the specific demands of the classroom is only indirectly connected to intellectual or social growth.

DEVELOPING COMPETENT LEARNERS AND CRITICAL THINKERS

In a rapidly changing world, there is much to learn and little time in which to learn it. With knowledge becoming obsolete literally overnight, people need to become lifelong learners who are able to integrate and organize barrages of changing information. Thus, many educators are no longer focusing on disconnected facts and principles but instead are helping children become self-directed, competent learners and critical thinkers.

Educational psychologists recommend a range of teaching strategies to develop student thinking. Children need to develop six kinds of thought (Costa, 1985). We might call these the six Rs:

1. *Remembering:* Recalling a fact, an idea, or a concept.
2. *Repeating:* Following a model or procedure.
3. *Reasoning:* Relating a specific instance to a general principle or concept.
4. *Reorganizing:* Extending knowledge to new contexts and devising original solutions to problems.
5. *Relating:* Connecting newly acquired knowledge with past or personal experience.
6. *Reflecting:* Exploring the thought itself and the way it occurred.

Teaching students to develop critical thinking is more difficult than simply imparting facts and principles (Costa, 1985). To develop reasoning, for example, teachers must challenge students with interesting problems and materials. The goal is to increase curiosity, foster questioning, develop related concepts, encourage evaluation of alternatives, and help students construct and test hypotheses.

During the past decade, U.S. schools have placed greater emphasis on teaching learning and thinking skills; tailoring instruction to the child's individual learning style and developmental level; and fostering independent, self-regulated, self-paced learning. One way of achieving such goals is to assign students small-group projects and activities. When small-group instruction is done effectively, children experience cooperative rather than competitive learning. Cooperative learning techniques have been found to increase overall performance (Johnson et al., 1992). It has also been found to raise the self-esteem of female students significantly more than when individual-centered teaching strategies are employed (Petersen et al., 1992). However, despite the success of these strategies, students in U.S. classrooms still don't perform as well in math and science as Asian students do (see "A Matter for Debate," page 298.

SUCCESS IN SCHOOL

Success in school is influenced by many factors. Children who are in poor health, do not get enough to eat, are preoccupied with problems at home, or have low self-esteem don't fare as well. Self-perceived competence may also

In order to do well in school, children need to eat well.

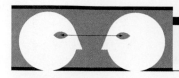

A MATTER FOR DEBATE

THE MATH GAP

We have known for some time that college students coming from Japan and Taiwan to study in the United States outperform their American counterparts in math and science. Why? Are these students a select group—the gifted, the elite, the highly motivated?

No. The overall superiority of Asian students in mathematics and science was confirmed by studies conducted in the late 1960s and early 1970s (Comber & Keeves, 1973; Husen, 1976). The average achievements of Asian junior high and high school students were consistently higher than those of American students. Later studies showed similar accomplishments in math as early as kindergarten (Stevenson et al., 1986). By the first grade, the difference increased; and by the fifth grade, it was so large that when 60 fifth-grade classes in Japan, Taiwan, and the United States were compared, the average math score of the highest-scoring American classroom was below that of all the Japanese classrooms and all but one of the Taiwanese classrooms.

Even after two decades of greater emphasis on math in U.S. classrooms, the math gap between U.S. elementary schoolchildren and their counterparts in China and Japan was as great in 1990 as it was in 1980 (Stevenson et al., 1993). Why? Although the American and Asian school systems have some things in common, such as the age at which kindergarten begins, universal education at least through junior high school, and a cultural emphasis on ed-ucational achievement, there are also significant differences. Test scores on nationwide examinations determine entry into high school in Japan, Taiwan, and many European countries, but not in the United States. Career paths, too, are more closely linked to educational achievement in the two Asian countries. As a result, even the youngest children in Japan and Taiwan are under enormous pressure to succeed in school—far less than for young children in the United States.

There are also striking differences in classroom instruction. American children spend far less time in school, and while in school, they spend less time on tasks. One study (Stigler et al., 1987), found that fifth-graders in the United States spend an average of only 19.6 hours per week on academic activities, whereas Taiwanese and Japanese children spend, respectively, 40.4 and 32.6 hours per week on academic activities. American children also spend less of their academic time on math: U.S. fifth-grade classrooms average 3.4 hours per week on math compared with 11.4 hours in Taiwan and 7.6 hours in Japan.

That finding alone might be enough to explain the differences in performance, but there's more. Classroom organization, teacher behavior, and child behavior differ as well. Classes in the United States are smaller, and the children tend to work alone or in small groups. In contrast, Asian children spend most of their math classes working, watching, and listening as a class. Although the U.S. approach gives teachers an opportunity to individualize assignments, encourage individual problem solving, and tutor individuals and small groups, the approach has built-in inefficiencies. Much of the time, the children's work is not closely supervised or guided. In addition, teachers in Taiwanese and Japanese classes are better prepared, more intensely involved in their subject matter, and more lively in their presentations. Student attention and involvement are higher, too.

Should U.S. schools shift their emphasis away from individualized instruction and small, cooperative learning groups? The researchers suggest simpler changes, such as increasing the percentage of elementary school time spent on math and cutting back on irrelevant activities. Further, they recommend more direct teacher-student communication and better math preparation for teachers. In assessing differences between the U.S. and Asian educational systems that may contribute to the math gap, Harold Stevenson (1992) points to the greater amount of time that Asian teachers devote to nonclassroom activities that may indirectly improve their effectiveness. For example, teachers in Japan and Taiwan are responsible for classes only 60% of the time that they spend in school. They spend their remaining work time in planning lessons, consulting each other about curriculum and effective teaching methods, and providing feedback to students.

Sources: Adapted from Stigler et al., 1987; Stevenson et al., 1973; and Husen, 1976.

affect school performance. In one study, 20% of school-age children underestimated their actual abilities, set lower expectations for themselves, and were surprised when they made high grades (Phillips, 1984).

According to David McClelland (1955), the reason that some children achieve more than others may stem from the values of the culture in which they are reared. After comparing several cultures during different periods of history, McClelland concluded that **achievement motivation**—persistence to-

achievement motivation
A learned motive to excel and succeed.

ward success and excellence—is an acquired, culturally based drive. In any given society at any time, some groups value achievement more highly than others (DeCharms & Moeller, 1962). Different cultures or subcultures may also value different kinds of achievement; one group may stress educational goals; another may place more value on social success. Children whose parents stress values that are different from those of the school may bring less motivation to academic tasks.

GENDER DIFFERENCES AND SCHOOL SUCCESS   Success in school is also influenced by gender differences. A pioneering review of the literature on gender differences (Maccoby & Jacklin, 1974) found—on average—that girls tend to outperform boys in verbal skills and that boys tend to do better in quantitative and spatial tasks. There are many possible reasons for this finding. For example, although there may be small sex differences in relevant brain development (Kimura, 1992), different social expectations for boys and girls profoundly influence their behavior. As Carol Gilligan (1987) points out, girls in middle childhood who are self-confident and have a strong sense of identity sometimes confront major obstacles to their intellectual development during the preadolescent and adolescent years. As their bodies mature, they must reconcile their notions of what it means to be a woman with what they observe around them. Attractiveness and fitting in may become more important than academic achievement. To put it another way, girls may find themselves "dumbing down" in order to be desirable in a traditionally male-dominated society.

Increasingly, success in school is also aided by computer-assisted instruction, as discussed in "In Theory, In Fact," page 300.

In addition, the broader society has traditionally defined mathematics and science as male-oriented and literature and language as female-oriented. Many adults—even teachers—may therefore assume that boys will do better in math and thus put more effort into teaching math to boys than to girls.

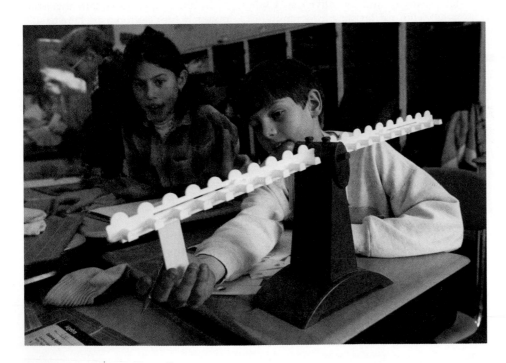

Girls who do well in mathematics during middle childhood may put less effort into this subject when they become adolescents because of societal stereotypes that mathematical thinking is typically more "masculine" than "feminine."

IN THEORY, IN FACT

COMPUTER-ASSISTED INSTRUCTION IN THE SCHOOLS

Today's learning environments continue to be in transition as more and more grade-school students—and younger students as well—have access to computer workstations with multimedia capability and Internet access. Do children actually benefit from computer-assisted instruction (CAI) in the classroom? In what ways? Do teachers generally view CAI favorably?

Nowadays, it is rare to find research that isn't positive with regard to CAI's effects on children. As educators continue to develop ways in which CAI can be used to enhance learning and thinking, computers become "personal tutors" that make many different kinds of learning more efficient and effective. Although the benefits of CAI depend upon many variables such as the type of instructional setting, the teacher's approach to computer use, and of course the quality of the computer programs deployed (Brown, 1996), an increasing body of research indicates favorable outcomes. Some examples follow.

Computer programs permit ongoing interaction between student and machine. Acting as a surrogate teacher,

computers provide *programmed instruction* that structures learning in sequential steps, adjusts the "size" of the steps to individual abilities, and provides ongoing feedback about performance. At the same time, contrary to what you might expect, computer use actually tends to foster individual interaction with peers and teachers (Schofield, 1997a) rather than interfere with it—students and teacher alike interact in goal-oriented ways as the students acquire basic computer skills and apply them to learning. Of particular interest is that computers can also be used to teach skills such as how to keep from getting in trouble and how to solve personal problems or problems with others (Elias, 1997). Yet another approach uses "paired" keyboards where students work together in exploring the Internet, having been assigned according to Vygotsky's zone of proximal development (Peters, 1996); as they explore, those less familiar with computers learn from those who are more familiar. The range of applications seems limitless and goes well beyond the teaching of basic academic skills such as reading, writing, and arithmetic.

Computers can also be used to foster creativity and inventiveness. Children who are learning programming

skills, for example, become responsible for what the computer does. Using LOGO, a longstanding, child-oriented programming language, children can increase their thinking and reasoning abilities as well as become computer literate (Narrol, 1996).

Multimedia CD-ROMs have opened many avenues for the teaching of concepts that were once abstract and theoretical (Stoddart & Niederhauser, 1993). Multimedia software allows children to view text, hear stereo sound, and watch video clips as they learn. A single CD may contain an entire encyclopedia that, for example, not only presents text and a picture of a dinosaur but also shows how it moves. Similarly, literature, history, and art come to life on personal computers with the click of a mouse.

What do teachers think of CAI? Again, it depends on the setting and the subject, but research generally indicates that educators are spending substantial amounts of money and personal time on obtaining computer equipment and using it for activities such as exploring the Internet (Schofield, 1997b), as well as for more traditional forms of CAI.

In all, it appears certain that computers in the classroom are here to stay.

Research indicates that although gender differences still emerge on standardized tests, they are declining in some respects (Feingold, 1988). For example, in studying the results of the Preliminary Scholastic Aptitude Test (PSAT) between 1960 and 1983, researchers found significant gender differences. On average, girls scored higher than boys in grammar, spelling, and perceptual speed; boys scored higher in spatial visualization, high school mathematics, and mechanical aptitude. No differences were found in verbal reasoning, arithmetic, and figural reasoning. However, the gender gap remains constant at higher levels of performance in high school mathematics. Negative experiences in the classroom and at home, combined with outmoded yet still widely accepted stereotypes of males and females, do much more to produce gender differences than actual brain physiology.

PARENTAL INFLUENCES ON SCHOOL SUCCESS Parents can play a large role in creating a supportive environment and encouraging the development

Children who perform well in school tend to have parents who strongly value education and encourage their child's self-esteem.

of specific skills that help children succeed. On the negative side, children from homes characterized by severe marital distress, parental criminality or psychiatric disorder, or overcrowding, along with intermittent placement in foster care, are at special risk for school failure (Sameroff et al., 1993).

If we look at the parents of children who succeed in school, we find behaviors that almost any parent can practice, regardless of economic circumstances. Reviews of the research point to three important parental factors associated with children's success at school (Hess & Holloway, 1984):

1. Parents of successful children have realistic beliefs about their children's current abilities but also have high expectations for the future. These parents help their children develop self-confidence by encouraging them to perform age-appropriate tasks both at school and at home.
2. Parent-child relationships are warm and affectionate, and parents have discipline and control strategies that are authoritative rather than authoritarian (see Chapter 7). Parents place limits on their children's behavior, but the children feel safe and accepted.
3. Finally, and perhaps most important, parents talk to their children. They read to them, listen to them, and have regular conversations with them. They support and enrich their children's exploration and inquiry, acting as role models in the process.

In general, children tend to succeed academically when their parents provide support and guidance. This supportive atmosphere is common among Southeast Asian families. The parents, who value learning and hard work, believe that children can succeed at any task through determination and effort (Kaplan et al., 1992). Similarly, the parents of African-American children who excel academically tend to stress the importance of education and to encourage the development of self-esteem and belief in personal efficacy—the ability to get things done. At the same time, they acknowledge that their children may encounter racial bias and try to prepare them to cope with it (Patterson et al., 1990).

Although poverty and minority status may be major factors lowering children's intellectual performance, it is not only poor, minority children who have school problems. Middle- and upper-income families may also have underachieving children. Children of parents who emphasize fun, excitement, or material possessions tend to perform more poorly in school than children of parents who value educational achievement (Kaplan et al., 1992).

REVIEW & APPLY

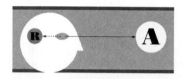

1. What major demands and expectations do schools place on school-age children?
2. List the six cognitive "Rs" that children need to develop in order to become self-directed, competent learners and critical thinkers.
3. Explain three basic strategies that parents can use in helping their children succeed in school.

DEVELOPMENTAL DISORDERS

MENTAL RETARDATION

In Chapters 2 and 3, we discussed four possible causes of **mental retardation:** genetic defects, prenatal exposure to diseases and drugs, anoxia at birth, and extreme malnutrition before birth or during infancy. We have also seen that the family or other caregiving environment can have either a facilitating or a debilitating effect on a child's intellectual development. In this section we'll look briefly at mental retardation, noting that it often goes undetected until age 5 or 6, when the child enters formal schooling.

The *Diagnostic and Statistical Manual* (DSM-IV) of the American Psychiatric Association (1994), based on guidelines originally developed by the American Association on Mental Deficiency, lists three criteria that a child must meet to be diagnosed as mentally retarded:

1. Significantly subaverage intellectual functioning (an IQ of *about* 70 or below)
2. Significantly impaired adaptive behaviors in areas such as self-care, self-direction, and general functioning at home and in the community
3. Onset before age 18

There are four levels of mental retardation: *mild* (IQ of about 55 to 70), *moderate* (40 to 55), *severe* (25 to 40), and *profound* (below 25). What are children (and adults) with mental retardation like at each level? It's important to remember that they are individuals just like intellectually typical people. Nevertheless, their level of impairment does produce certain common characteristics.

Children with mild mental retardation generally attend public schools, although they often have special help and may be placed in special education classes or resource rooms for part of the day. They can learn to read, and in time many can achieve at least an elementary school education and corre-

mental retardation Significantly subaverage intellectual functioning and self-help skills, with onset prior to age 18.

sponding social skills. Most can also hold a job, although they may require continuing support and assistance.

Children with moderate mental retardation were once inappropriately labeled as merely "trainable," but they too can benefit to some extent from academic and vocational education. They often can care for themselves with supervision, learn to get around in their neighborhood, and support themselves at jobs that don't exceed their mental and social capabilities.

Children who are severely or profoundly retarded don't fare as well. They often require close supervision and generally are not able to perform more than the simplest of tasks. Although they are capable of limited self-care, they generally don't profit from training or education beyond a preschool level and are unlikely to be able to support themselves. Such individuals can still adapt to structured home and community settings, however, and are not merely "custodial" or "vegetative" as they were once labeled. Known neurological defects and a variety of physical disabilities often accompany their mental retardation—hence the term *organic* mental retardation. The contrasting term, *cultural-familial* retardation, is applied to people in the mild-to-moderate range, and their retardation is thought to arise more from social and environmental factors than from neurological problems.

What about children with mental retardation and the public school system? Since landmark federal legislation in 1975, all American children are entitled to a publicly funded education. (Prior to that time, each year, nearly a million children and youth with mental retardation or other disabilities were receiving no education at all.) In Public Law 94-142, the Education for All Handicapped Children Act, a set of principles and guidelines were laid out to provide each child with special needs an appropriate and individually tailored educational plan. The act requires that children be educated in the "least restrictive" environment possible, which often means in normal public school classrooms rather than "special education" classes. Studies over the past 20 years have shown that some children with moderate to even severe handicaps have been able to progress to higher academic levels than previously imagined. Gains in social skills and self-concept have at times been remarkable, and they extend into adulthood (Turnbull & Turnbull, 1997).

LEARNING DISORDERS

Learning disorders, also termed *learning disabilities*, involve difficulty in acquiring specific academic skills but not others. The child may have average or above-average general intellectual ability, yet be markedly substandard in one particular area, such as reading. Such a child's overall academic achievement often suffers—a child who can't read adequately, for example, is at a major disadvantage in all areas of schooling and will eventually encounter vocational difficulties as well. Perhaps understandably, the school dropout rate for older children with unremediated learning disorders is much higher than the rate for the general student population.

Children with learning disorders often have no more in common than the label itself. In school systems today, children with normal intelligence and no sensory or motor defects are considered to have a learning disorder when they require special attention in the classroom—that is, when they have trouble learning to read, write, spell, or do arithmetic. For reasons that remain unclear, up to 80% of children with learning disorders are boys.

The DSM-IV recognizes three main categories of learning disorders: *reading disorder* (dyslexia); *disorder of written expression* (dysgraphia), which can involve anything from spelling and handwriting to syntax; and *mathematics disorder*

learning disorders Extreme difficulty in learning school subjects such as reading, writing, or math, despite normal intelligence and absence of sensory or motor defects.

(dyscalculia), which can involve anything having to do with recognizing mathematical symbols and performing mathematical operations. Each category typically also involves poor perceptual skills.

Day after day, children with learning disorders are unable to do things that their classmates seem to accomplish effortlessly. With each failure they become increasingly insecure about their ability to perform, and their self-esteem suffers. Classmates tend not to interact with a child who doesn't succeed. Children with learning disorders often have difficulty with social as well as academic skills (Kavale & Forness, 1996). They may become increasingly isolated from peers and even from family members, who find life with a child who has a learning disorder to be highly stressful (Dyson, 1996). Some children with these disorders become shy and withdrawn; others become boastful; still others are prone to impulsive or angry outbursts. It can be difficult indeed to find ways to help a child with a learning disorder develop confidence and experience success in other areas.

The study of learning disorders is a challenging puzzle with a confusing array of expert opinions about their causes, symptoms, and treatments. If there is a consensus, it is that learning disorders are associated with one or more basic mental processes. For example, a child with a learning disorder may experience difficulty with attention, memory, auditory or visual perception, or cognitive control processes. Many of the classic controversies about child development are also evident in the questions raised about learning disorders. Is the child abnormal, deficient, or disabled, or is the child just different in temperament and style? Is the problem organic, or is it a result of the home or school environment? Should the child be "treated" medically, "managed" through behavioral programs, or "educated" creatively? One thing is clear, however: The earlier that intervention begins, the better the child's chances of later success (see Slavin, 1996).

READING DISORDER   Reading disorder, or dyslexia, is one of the most common types of learning disorders. Because children with dyslexia often confuse letters such as *b* and *d*, or read *star* as *rats*, it was long believed that these children simply "see things backward." Very few of them actually have anything wrong with their visual system, however. In other contexts, children with dyslexia may have no perceptual problems. They have no trouble finding their way around, so they aren't deficient in spatial relationships. They may be exceptionally good at putting together puzzles. Why, then, do they make errors like confusing *b* and *d*? One observation is that these are very common errors for beginning readers. Most children make reversal errors when they first learn to read, but most get through this stage quickly. Dyslexic children somehow remain stuck in the early stages of reading (Richardson, 1992; Vogel, 1989).

Children with dyslexia also have problems outside of school. Many have pervasive language problems. They may be delayed in learning to speak, or their speech may be at a lower developmental level than that of their agemates. Their difficulty in naming letters and written words is matched by their difficulty in naming objects or colors; it takes them longer than usual to recall an ordinary word like *key* or *blue*. They also have trouble hearing the two separate syllables in a two-syllable word or recognizing that the spoken word *sat* starts with an *s* sound and ends with a *t* sound (Shaywitz et al., 1991; Wagner & Torgerson, 1987).

Although the hypothesized "brain dysfunction" that underlies dyslexia has not yet been identified, it is clear that heredity plays a role in the disorder.

Many children with reading disorders have a parent or a sibling with the same problem (Scarborough, 1989). It is also interesting to note that dyslexia tends to run in families that exhibit left-handedness. However, left-handedness itself is only weakly associated with dyslexia; most children with reading disorders are right-handed (Hiscock & Kinsbourne, 1987).

Treatment of dyslexia generally involves intensive remedial work in reading and language, including carefully sequenced tutorial instruction. One approach (Stanton, 1981) emphasizes the need to improve the child's confidence. Although no single educational plan seems to work with all children, most programs help children learn. Graduates of one especially successful program—a British residential school for children with dyslexia—usually can attend college. In contrast, children who attend the least successful programs generally become high school dropouts (Bruck, 1987). Children who manage to overcome their dyslexia may emerge with renewed self-confidence and have successful adult lives. Thomas Edison, Nelson Rockefeller, and Hans Christian Andersen were all dyslexic as children.

ATTENTION-DEFICIT/HYPERACTIVITY DISORDER

Attention-deficit/hyperactivity disorder (ADHD) involves inattentiveness, difficulty sustaining attention or concentrating long enough to follow through on tasks, distractibility, and forgetfulness—each to an extreme. Perhaps contrary to what the term *ADHD* implies, attention deficit is not always associated with hyperactivity, which involves inability to sit still or remain quiet, as well as impulsiveness and impatience, again to extremes. Nor is hyperactivity always associated with attention deficit. However, most children with the disorder display at least some of each aspect of the disorder; hence the combined name.

Researchers have suggested many possible causes of ADHD, including malnutrition, lead poisoning, organic brain damage, heredity, intrauterine abnormalities, prenatal exposure to drugs like crack cocaine, and anoxia during fetal development or childbirth. Many children with symptoms of ADHD (and also learning disorders) experienced some form of birth irregularity, including prematurity (Buchoff, 1990). In addition, studies of identical and fraternal twins suggest that ADHD has a strong genetic link (Gillis, 1992).

Just as there are different possible causes of ADHD, there are also differences in recommended treatments. Many children who display symptoms of ADHD respond to an amphetamine, Ritalin. They calm down in response to a drug that ordinarily speeds up behavior and CNS activity. This result has given rise to the hypothesis that ADHD children are either understimulated or unable to focus on tasks because all stimulation comes in at equal levels. Perhaps their high activity level is an attempt to provide more environmental stimulation. In that case, Ritalin lowers children's threshold of sensitivity to events around them. An alternate hypothesis is that by speeding up neural processing, Ritalin enables ADHD children to control their overall cognitive functioning better, thereby improving their attention and behavioral control.

Although not all ADHD children benefit from taking Ritalin, the benefits can outweigh the risk of possible side effects for those who do respond when the treatment program is monitored carefully. Research has consistently shown improvements in these children's schoolwork and family and peer relationships (Campbell & Spencer, 1988).

An alternate form of treatment for children with ADHD is educational management, which takes place both at home and at school. This method restructures the child's environment by simplifying it, reducing distractions, making

For children with attention-deficit disorder and hyperactivity, there is no single treatment or approach that "solves" the problem.

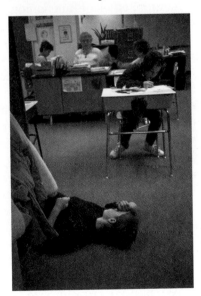

Attention-deficit/hyperactivity disorder (ADHD) An inability to keep focused on something long enough to learn it, often accompanied by poor impulse control.

expectations more explicit, and generally reducing confusion. The specific educational plan depends on the theoretical position of the therapist or educator. One position (Cruickshank, 1977) advocates an instructional program involving various training tasks that require specific skills. Another (Ross, 1977) focuses more on the development of selective attention. Yet another focuses on finding acceptable and constructive outlets for the boundless energy often associated with ADHD (Armstrong, 1996).

REVIEW & APPLY

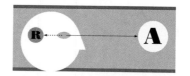

1. List the criteria for a diagnosis of mental retardation.
2. Describe learning problems faced by children with reading disorder.
3. What are the symptoms and treatment approaches for ADHD?
4. What is the connection between developmental disorders and low self-esteem?

SUMMARY

Physical and Motor Development

■ Growth is slower and steadier during middle childhood than during the first 2 years of life. There is wide variability in the timing of growth.

■ Bones grow longer as the body lengthens and broadens, and fat deposits gradually decrease.

■ By age 8, the brain is 90% of its adult size, resulting in more efficient functioning.

■ School-age children become better at performing controlled, purposeful movements.

■ Gender differences in motor skills are more a function of opportunity and cultural expectations than of physical differences.

■ Fine motor skills develop rapidly during middle childhood. (See the study chart on page 278.)

■ Middle childhood is usually a very healthy period, but minor illnesses may occur.

■ Obesity is a common problem for school-age children in developed nations. Obesity can have serious social and psychological consequences.

■ Physical fitness refers to optimal functioning of the heart, lungs, muscles, and blood vessels. Children today are less physically active and fit than were children 30 years earlier.

■ As children grow in size, strength, and coordination, they engage in increasingly dangerous activities. As a result, the greatest number of deaths of children are caused by accidents.

■ Because of the poor average level of physical fitness in the U.S. population, current national health objectives call for increasing children's participation in daily physical education classes.

Cognitive Development

■ A large part of cognitive development occurs in school. Many cognitive, language, and perceptual-motor skills mature and interact in ways that make learning easier and more efficient.

■ In Piaget's theory, the period from age 5 to age 7 marks the transition from preoperational to concrete operational thought.

■ Unlike preoperational children, concrete operational children can theorize about the world around them.

■ Many of the basic concepts presented by Piaget have been applied to education, such as the use of concrete objects for teaching.

■ Children's ability to recall lists of items improves significantly between the ages of 5 and 7. This is the age when they usually learn control processes-strategies and techniques that enhance memory. These processes include rehearsal, organization, semantic elaboration, and mental imagery.

■ Metacognition refers to the intellectual processes that enable children to monitor their own thinking. It develops during middle childhood.

■ School-age children learn to read and write, both of which are forms of symbolic communication that enable children to mediate the relationship between the external world and their inner thoughts and feelings.

- Children acquire the basics of literacy while interacting with their parents, siblings, teachers, and peers.

Intelligence and Achievement

- When used appropriately, intelligence, diagnostic, and achievement tests are vital educational tools.
- Criterion-referenced tests measure the extent to which a child has mastered specific skills and objectives; norm-referenced tests compare children's scores with those of other children of the same age.
- The first comprehensive intelligence test was designed by Alfred Binet as a method for identifying children who weren't doing well in school. An American version of this test was developed by Lewis Terman and colleagues at Stanford University and referred to as the Stanford-Binet test.
- The intelligence quotient or IQ is a measure of a child's mental age in relation to his or her chronological age.
- Intelligence tests now measure deviation IQ, meaning that they are norm-referenced.
- Most experts agree that genetic and environmental factors are about equally important in determining how well a child will do on an IQ test.
- Most intelligence tests define intelligence as a composite of abilities. Howard Gardner believes that there are at least seven distinct categories of intelligence.
- Robert Sternberg's triarchic concept of intelligence includes contextual, experiential, and componential intelligence.
- Testing has some limitations, including the fact that much of the school day may be spent focusing on the particular competencies that are measured by the tests.
- Minority groups object to having their skills and abilities measured by tests that assume wide exposure to the dominant culture. Although test designers have made a serious effort to eliminate cultural bias, the tests are still oriented toward the mainstream culture.

Learning and Thinking in School

- Children entering school must learn to deal with new demands and expectations. The greater the gap between what is expected at home and in the classroom, the more difficult the child's adjustment will be.
- Educational psychologists believe that children need to develop six kinds of thought; remembering, repeating, reasoning, reorganizing, relating, and reflecting.
- Cooperative learning techniques have been found to increase overall performance.
- According to David McClelland, achievement motivation is an acquired, culturally based drive. Some cultures value achievement more highly than others, and different cultures may value different kinds of achievement.
- Success in school is influenced by gender differences. As Carol Gilligan points out, girls sometimes confront major obstacles to their intellectual development during the preadolescent and adolescent years. Attractiveness and fitting in may become more important than academic achievement.
- Research indicates that although gender differences still emerge on standardized tests, they are declining.
- Parents can play a large role in creating a supportive environment and encouraging the development of specific skills that help children succeed.

Developmental Disorders

- Mental retardation may be caused by genetic defects, prenatal exposure to diseases and drugs, anoxia at birth, and extreme malnutrition before birth or during infancy.
- There are four levels of mental retardation: mild, moderate, severe, and profound.
- Children with mild or moderate mental retardation can benefit from academic and vocational schooling, but children with severe or profound mental retardation often require close supervision and cannot perform more than the simplest of tasks.
- Learning disorders, or learning disabilities, involve difficulty in acquiring specific academic skills but not other skills.
- There are three main categories of learning disorders; reading disorder (dyslexia), disorder of written expression (dysgraphia), and mathematics disorder (dyscalculia).
- Children with dyslexia seem to remain stuck in the early stages of reading, in which letters are often reversed. Many of these children also have pervasive language problems.
- Treatment of dyslexia generally involves intensive remedial work in reading and language, including carefully sequenced tutorial instruction.
- Attention-deficit/hyperactivity disorder involves inattentiveness, difficulty sustaining attention or concentrating, distractibility, and forgetfulness.

■ Many children who display symptoms of ADHD respond to treatment with Ritalin. An alternate form of treatment is educational management, which involves simplifying the child's environment, reducing distractions, making expectations more explicit, and generally reducing confusion.

KEY TERMS

myopia
obesity
control processes
metacognition
criterion-referenced tests

norm-referenced tests
intelligence quotient (IQ)
deviation IQ
achievement motivation
mental retardation

learning disorders
attention-deficit/hyperactivity disorder (ADHD)

USING WHAT YOU'VE LEARNED

Try to observe (unobtrusively) elementary-school-age children engaging in a freely chosen leisure activity. Watch them in a video arcade, on a playground, or at home, while they are playing, watching television, or using a computer. Record their activities for perhaps 5 or 10 minutes, as you did with preschoolers in Chapter 6. What skills and knowledge do these children display that prepare them for that particular activity?

What are they learning from the activity? How does this activity contrast with school learning with respect to the organization, motivation, and pace of learning? What kinds of feedback seem to be necessary to sustain this activity?

Finally, if you know the children, ask them questions about what they're doing and why. See whether their answers are consistent with your observations.

SUGGESTED READINGS

CAHILL-FOWLER, M. (1990). *Maybe you know my kids.* New York: Carroll Publishing Group. A personal account of the disruptive impact that a child's ADHD has on his family, his classmates, and his own learning activities. Offers helpful suggestions and resources to parents and teachers.

DELPIT, L. (1995). *Other people's children: Cultural conflict in the classroom.* New York: New Press. Drawing upon her extensive teaching experience in classrooms from Alaska to New Guinea, the author argues that all children must be given access to opportunities in mainstream society.

FARNHAM-DIGGORY, S. (1990). *Schooling.* Cambridge, MA: Harvard University Press. An excellent review and discussion of several key aspects of schooling today's children. Another selection in the popular *Developing Child* series.

FIELDS, M. V., & SPANGLER, K. L. (1995). *Let's begin reading right: Developmentally appropriate beginning literacy* (3rd ed.). Englewood Cliffs, NJ: Merrill. A balanced whole-language approach to early reading and writing.

GARDNER, H. (1983). *Frames of mind.* New York: Basic Books. A challenging, readable, well-developed presentation of a new way of thinking about intelligence.

GARDNER, H. (1992). *To open minds: Chinese clues to the dilemma of contemporary education.* New York: Basic Books. A thoughtful discussion of two radically different approaches to education in their respective social contexts.

KREMENTZ, J. (1992). *How it feels to live with a physical disability.* New York: Simon and Schuster. Fifteen children and adolescents tell, in their own words, what living with a disability means to them. Beautiful photographs strengthen the book's presentation of the normal lives that these children live. Even though this book was intended for a late childhood audience, it is appropriate for readers of all ages.

KOHL, H. (1995). *Should we burn Babar?: Essays on children's literature and the power of stories.* New York: New Press. A controversial book that provides new perspectives on well-known children's stories, highlighting instances of racism and sexism that detract from the tale being told.

LANDAU, S., & MCANINCH, C. (1993). Young children with attention deficits. *Young Children, 48(5)*, 49–58. A highly readable and descriptive article on ADHD signs and treatment.

SADKER, M., & SADKER, D. (1995). *Failing at fairness: How our schools cheat girls.* New York: Touchstone. A well-researched and provocative disclosure of inequality in American schools. It chronicles how girls start school testing higher in every academic subject but finish high school feeling less confident and scoring an average of 50 points lower than boys on the Scholastic Aptitude Test.

Middle Childhood and Elementary School Children: Personality Development and Socialization

CHAPTER OUTLINE

CHAPTER OBJECTIVES

By the time you have finished this chapter, you should be able to do the following:

1. Describe children's developing self-concept during the elementary school years.
2. Discuss the development of social cognition and moral reasoning during middle childhood.
3. List the ways in which the American family is changing and the ways in which parents can help children cope with the stresses that accompany these changes.
4. Discuss the effects of divorce on children and the factors that influence how children react to and are affected by divorce.
5. Explain factors that can lead to child abuse, and list various types of psychological abuse.
6. Summarize the characteristics of childhood friendships and peer groups.
7. Explain how children develop racial awareness and how their attitudes toward members of other groups change as they grow older.

If Shakespeare was right and all the world's a stage, then the stage on which children perform broadens dramatically during middle childhood. The emotional and social attachments of infants, toddlers, and preschoolers centered primarily on the family; now school-age children move into a broader world made up of peers, teachers, and other people in the wider community. The expansion of the child's world is gradual, yet it is punctuated with milestones like beginning first grade, joining clubs, and venturing beyond the immediate neighborhood.

As their social world expands, so does children's perspective on the conflicts and stresses in their own families. Children who experience abuse, divorce, or life in a single-parent household must find ways of coping. These in turn produce patterns of social and emotional behavior that help determine personality. Children's growing alliances with peers also influence how they come to see themselves and their place in the world.

In all, broadened experiences teach children about the complexities of family relationships and friendships and the conduct that society expects of them. These experiences also prepare children to make moral judgments.

PERSONALITY DEVELOPMENT IN AN EXPANDING SOCIAL WORLD

How does a child's personality develop and change during middle childhood? Again, the answer depends on your theoretical perspective. In this section we'll begin with how psychodynamic, cognitive-developmental, and social-learning theories generally apply to middle childhood. We'll then focus on how the child's developing sense of self interacts with personality development.

THREE PERSPECTIVES ON MIDDLE CHILDHOOD

Freud described middle childhood as a period of *latency*. In his view, the period from age 6 to 12 was a time during which family jealousies and turmoil (along with sexual impulses) became submerged. If so, children could turn their emotional energies toward peer relationships, creative efforts, and learning the culturally prescribed tasks in the school or the community. As noted in Chapter 1, however, Freud had much less to say about the latency period (and the adolescent *genital* period beyond that) than he did about the first 6 or 7 years of life. It was therefore up to Erikson to expand on Freud's ideas and to develop a more comprehensive theory. Unlike Freud, however, Erikson emphasized *psychosocial* factors in personality development.

Erikson proposed that the central focus of middle childhood is the conflict of **industry versus inferiority**. In middle childhood, with the impetus of formal schooling, much of the child's time and energy is directed toward acquiring new knowledge and skills. Children are better at channeling their energies into learning, problem solving, and achievement. When children succeed in school, they incorporate a sense of industry into their self-image—they come to realize that hard work produces results, and they continue to progress toward mastering their environment. In contrast, children who do not progress toward academic mastery begin to feel inferior compared with their peers. This sense of inferiority may be part of their personality throughout life. Lack of success in schoolwork, however, can be compensated for by success in other activities that are valued, such as sports, music, or art.

The second theoretical perspective—the cognitive-developmental approach—has been increasingly applied to personality and social development. Piaget and Lawrence Kohlberg, for example, have written extensively about the development of children's concepts about self and *morality*—ideas about fairness and justice, right and wrong, good and bad. Other researchers have focused more broadly on the importance of children's self-concepts as determinants of their behavior.

Finally, social-learning theory has made major contributions to the understanding of how specific behaviors are learned via the family and the peer group. During middle childhood, peers increasingly serve as models and reinforce or punish behaviors.

All three theoretical perspectives merge to help us understand how children become socialized into their culture during middle childhood. The ways in which children interact with peers, adults, and family members change: The impatient 4-year-old becomes the cooperative 8-year-old, who in turn may become the rebellious 13-year-old. Although neither of the three perspectives alone explains all social development during middle childhood, taken together they provide a more complete picture.

SELF-CONCEPT

Self-concept in particular helps us understand development during middle childhood, in that self-concept interweaves personality and social behavior. Children form increasingly stable pictures of themselves, and their self-concept also becomes more realistic. They understand their skills and limitations more accurately, and they use their understanding of themselves to organize their behavior.

As children grow older, they form more complex pictures of their own physical, intellectual, and personality characteristics as well as those of other people. They attribute increasingly specific *traits*—stable personality characteristics—to themselves and others. They make efforts to behave consistently, and they expect consistency in the behavior of others.

industry versus inferiority
Erikson's psychosocial conflict during middle childhood, in which children either work industriously and are rewarded for their efforts in school or fail and develop a sense of inferiority.

Children compare themselves with their age-mates (Marsh et al., 1991) and conclude, "I'm better than Susan at sports, but I'm not as good in math as Jose," or "I may not be as pretty as Courtney, but I'm better at making friends." Children's emerging self-concept, in turn, provides a "filter" through which they evaluate their own behavior and that of others (Harter, 1982). Early self-concepts are not always accurate, however. For example, first-grade boys tend to have more positive perceptions of their competence in areas like sports than do older children (Eccles, 1993). During the elementary school years, children also learn gender stereotypes, refine their gender-typed personal preferences, and develop greater flexibility (Serbin et al., 1993).

SELF-ESTEEM   Whereas self-concept involves who you are and what you can do, **self-esteem** adds an evaluative component; it refers to whether you see yourself in a favorable or an unfavorable light. High self-esteem means that you basically like yourself and often feel competent in your social and other skills; low self-esteem means that you often dislike yourself and feel incompetent. Like self-concept, self-esteem has roots in the preschool period and is influenced both by the child's experiences with success and failure and by his or her interactions with parents (Chapter 7). During the school years, self-esteem is significantly correlated with academic achievement. Children who do well in school have higher self-esteem than those who do poorly (Alpert-Gillis & Connell, 1989).

The correlation between self-esteem and academic achievement is far from perfect, however: Many children who don't do well in school nonetheless manage to develop a healthy respect for themselves. If they come from a culture or subculture in which school is not regarded as important, their self-esteem may not be related to their academic achievement. Depending on how their parents treat them and what their friends think of them, children who don't do well in some activity, such as sports, can often find other areas in which to excel. A child's self-esteem can also be strongly affected by being viewed positively by family, peers, and the immediate community. That's how many African-American children manage to develop a healthy self-esteem despite their frequent encounters with racial prejudice in the larger society (Spencer, 1988).

Development of self-esteem is a circular process. Children tend to do well if they are confident in their own abilities; their success then bolsters and increases their self-esteem. In the same way, a "vicious circle" may set in when children perform poorly because of low self-esteem; because of their poor performance, their self-esteem tends to decrease still further. In all, personal successes or failures can lead children to see themselves as leaders or losers, champions or chumps. Fortunately, however, many children who start off with social or academic deficits eventually find something they can do well and thus turn the process around.

Many teachers use praise to build self-esteem in their students. Used in moderation and given only for legitimate accomplishments, praise can be quite helpful. However, too much praise without appropriate links to achievement can prevent children from developing an accurate sense of their weaknesses as well as their strengths. They may begin to think, "I am great no matter what I do." This attitude can create confusion and problems in peer and school relations (Damon & Hart, 1992), as well as lead to frustration when achievements do not match expectations.

In recent years, researchers have warned that when children are told that the most important thing in the world is how highly they regard themselves,

Effective praise goes a long way in building self-esteem.

self-esteem   Seeing yourself as an individual with positive characteristics—as someone who will do well in the things that you think are important.

they hear an implicit message that they are the center of the universe, which can hinder their progress beyond egocentrism. Further, critics contend that overpraised children don't acquire a real sense of right and wrong. For example, they may deny misdeeds even when caught red-handed because they're convinced of their own rightness (Damon, 1991).

REVIEW & APPLY

1. Briefly contrast the three theoretical perspectives on personality development in middle childhood.
2. Discuss how self-concept develops during middle childhood.
3. Discuss the interaction between self-esteem and achievement.

SOCIAL KNOWLEDGE AND REASONING

Elementary-school children must come to terms with the subtleties of friendship and authority, expanding or conflicting gender roles, and a host of social rules and regulations. One way they do this is through what we might call "direct socialization" by parents and teachers: rewards for desirable behavior, punishments for undesirable behavior. Another way is through observation and imitation of models. In general, conditioning and observational learning play a large role in helping children understand right and wrong. Children also learn about the social world through psychodynamic processes. They develop anxious feelings in certain situations, and then they learn defense mechanisms to reduce anxiety (see Chapter 7).

Central to socialization during middle childhood is **social cognition:** thought, knowledge, and understanding pertaining to the world of self in social interactions with others. The social-cognitive approach shifts the emphasis to what the child thinks, partly as a result of reward, punishment, observation, and psychodynamics, but also partly as a result of what the child actively figures out for himself or herself. First we'll focus on how social cognition develops during middle childhood; then we'll consider links to the development of moral reasoning.

THE DEVELOPMENT OF SOCIAL COGNITION

During middle childhood and into adolescence, social cognition becomes an increasingly important determinant of behavior. Children begin to look at their social world and gradually come to understand the principles and rules that govern it (Ross, 1981). Social-cognitive theorists believe that all knowledge, whether scientific, social, or personal, exists as an organized system or structure, not as unrelated bits and pieces. Children's understanding of the world does not develop in a piecemeal fashion; rather, children try to make sense of their experience as an organized whole.

As we saw in Chapter 6, preschool children's understanding of the world is limited by egocentrism. During middle childhood, children gradually develop a less self-centered focus that takes into account what other people are thinking and feeling. A primary component of social cognition is **social inference—** guesses and assumptions about what another person is feeling, thinking, or

social cognition Thought, knowledge, and understanding that involve the social world.

social inference Guesses and assumptions about what another person is feeling, thinking, or intending.

intending (Flavell, 1985; Flavell et al., 1993). A young child, for example, hears Mom laughing and so assumes that she is happy. An adult might hear something forced about the mother's laughter and thus infer that she is covering up feelings of unhappiness. Although young children cannot make sophisticated inferences, by age 6, they can usually infer when another person's thoughts differ from their own. Around age 8, they understand that people can think about each other's thoughts. By age 10, they can infer what another person is thinking while at the same time inferring that their own thoughts are the subject of another person's thoughts. A child might think, "Johnny is angry with me, and he knows that I know he's angry." Accuracy in social inference develops gradually through late adolescence (Shantz, 1983).

A second component of social cognition is the child's understanding of **social responsibility.** Children gradually accumulate information and understanding about obligations of friendship (such as fairness and loyalty), respect for authority, and concepts of legality and justice. A third component is the understanding of **social regulations** such as customs and conventions. Many customs are first learned by rote or imitation and then applied rigidly. Later, children become more flexible and thoughtful about conforming to the customs of their culture.

PIAGET ON MORAL REASONING AND JUDGMENT

As they grow up, most children somehow learn how to tell good from bad and to distinguish between kindness and cruelty, generosity and selfishness. Mature moral judgment involves more than rote learning of social rules and conventions. It involves making decisions about right and wrong.

There is considerable debate as to how children develop morality. Social-learning theorists believe that conditioning and observational learning are primarily responsible. Psychodynamic theorists believe that morality develops as a defense against anxiety and shame. Cognitive theorists believe that, like intellectual development, morality develops in progressive, age-related stages. The latter view is presented here.

Piaget defined morality as an individual's respect for the rules of social order and sense of justice—justice being a concern for give-and-take and equality among individuals (see Hoffman, 1970). According to Piaget (1965), children's moral sense arises from the interaction between their developing thought structures and their gradually widening social experience. The moral sense develops in two stages. At the stage of **moral realism** (early middle childhood), children think that all rules must be obeyed as if they were written in stone. To them rules are real, indestructible things, not abstract principles. Games, for example, must be played strictly according to the rules. A child at this stage also judges the morality of an act in terms of its consequences and is unable to judge intentions. For example, a young child will think that a child who accidentally breaks 12 dishes while setting a table is much more guilty than a child who intentionally breaks 1 dish simply out of anger.

Toward the end of middle childhood, children reach the stage of **moral relativism.** Now they realize that rules are created and agreed upon cooperatively by individuals and that they can be changed as the need arises. This understanding leads to the realization that there is no absolute right or wrong and that morality depends not on consequences but on intentions.

KOHLBERG'S SIX-STAGE THEORY

Lawrence Kohlberg (1981, 1984) expanded Piaget's two-stage theory of moral development into a six-stage theory. In developing his theory, he presented subjects (children, adolescents, and adults) with morally problematic stories

social responsibility Obligations to family, friends, and society at large.

social regulations The rules and conventions governing social interactions.

moral realism Piaget's term for the first stage of moral development, in which children believe in rules as real, indestructible things.

moral relativism Piaget's term for the second stage of moral development, in which children realize that rules are agreements that may be changed, if necessary.

and then asked them questions about the stories in order to discover the kinds of reasoning they used. The leading character in each story was faced with a moral dilemma, and the subject being interviewed was asked to resolve the dilemma. Here is a classic example:

In Europe, a woman was near death from a special kind of cancer. There was one drug that the doctors thought might save her. It was a form of radium that a druggist in the same town had recently discovered. The drug was expensive to make, but the druggist was charging 10 times what the drug cost him to make. He paid $200 for the radium and charged $2,000 for a small dose of the drug. The sick woman's husband, Heinz, went to everyone he knew to borrow the money, but he could only get together $1,000, which is half of what it cost. He told the druggist that his wife was dying and asked him to sell it cheaper or let him pay later. But the druggist said, "No, I discovered the drug, and I am going to make money from it." So Heinz got desperate and broke into the man's store to steal the drug for his wife (Kohlberg, 1969, page 379).

Should Heinz have stolen the drug? What do you think? Why? Was the druggist right to have charged so much more than it cost to make the drug? Why?

Subjects' answers to such questions provided evidence that moral reasoning develops in an orderly fashion and in distinct stages. Kohlberg defined three broad levels of moral reasoning: *preconventional. conventional*, and *postconventional*. Each of these is subdivided into two stages, as presented in the study chart on page 318. Note two interrelated trends that characterize progress through the six stages: (1) At first, reasoning is based on external consequences, whereas later it is based on internalized moral principles; and (2) at first, reasoning is highly concrete, whereas later it is quite abstract.

Support for Kohlberg's theory was provided by studies showing that young boys, at least in Western societies, generally go through the stages in the predicted order. In a 20-year longitudinal study of 48 boys, Kohlberg and his associates found remarkable support for the theory (Colby et al., 1983).

Many objections have been raised to Kohlberg's theory and research, however. Researchers have pointed out that it can be very difficult to follow Kohlberg's procedures exactly and to agree on how a child's response to the test should be scored (Rubin & Trotten, 1977). Others have attacked the theory on grounds of **moral absolutism:** It disregards significant cultural differences that determine what is or is not considered moral in a given culture (Baumrind, 1978; Wainryb, 1995; Carlo et al., 1996). Kohlberg (1978) himself acknowledged that it is necessary to take into account the social and moral norms of the group to which a person belongs. In particular, he concluded that his sixth stage of moral development may not apply to all people in all cultures.

There are other other weaknesses in Kohlberg's theory (Power & Reimer, 1978). Kohlberg's research assesses moral attitudes, not moral behavior, and there can be a great difference between thinking about moral questions and behaving morally. Here's a quick example: In most cultures, stealing is wrong, and the trait of honesty is highly prized. You, of course, are an honest person. So suppose you see someone on the sidewalk unknowingly drop a quarter. You'll pick it and give it back. Suppose it's a ten-dollar bill. You'll do the same, right? Suppose it's a stack of hundred-dollar bills, and the person looks a bit shady and has already turned the corner, and there's no one else around. Ask yourself honestly what you would do. Also ask yourself what a poor but honest person in a deteriorating urban neighborhood would do.

Developing a sense of right and wrong involves understanding social rules and gaining experiences in social relationships.

moral absolutism   Any theory of morality that disregards cultural differences in moral beliefs.

STUDY CHART ‣ KOHLBERG'S STAGES OF MORAL DEVELOPMENT

STAGE		ILLUSTRATIVE REASONING	
LEVEL I. PRECONVENTIONAL (BASED ON PUNISHMENTS AND REWARDS)	**Stage 1**	Punishment and obedience orientation	Obey rules in order to avoid punishment.
	Stage 2	Naive instrumental hedonism	Obey to obtain rewards, to have favors returned.
LEVEL II. CONVENTIONAL (BASED ON SOCIAL CONFORMITY)	**Stage 3**	"Good-boy" morality of maintaining good relations, approval of others	Conform to avoid disapproval or dislike of others.
	Stage 4	Authority-maintaining morality	Conform to avoid censure by legitimate authorities, with resulting guilt.
LEVEL III. POSTCONVENTIONAL (BASED ON MORAL PRINCIPLES)	**Stage 5**	Morality of contract, of individual rights, and of democratically accepted law	Abide by laws of the land for community welfare
	Stage 6	Morality of individual principles of conscience	Abide by universal ethical principles.

Source: Kohlberg, L., *Stages of moral development*. Unpublished doctoral dissertation, University of Chicago, 1958. Used by permission. Also adapted from Kohlberg, L., *The philosophy of moral development*. New York: Harper & Row, 1981.

Moral decisions are not made in a vacuum; instead, they are usually made in "crisis situations." No matter how high our moral principles may be, when the time comes to act on them, our behavior may not reflect our thoughts or beliefs.

GILLIGAN'S ALTERNATIVE VIEW

Carol Gilligan (1982) proposed that because Kohlberg based his theory entirely on interviews with male subjects, he failed to consider the possibility that moral development might proceed differently in females than in males. In other words, she accused Kohlberg of sex bias, noting that females' responses to Kohlberg's moral dilemmas generally place them at lower levels in his model of moral development. According to Gilligan, this difference arises because males and females use different criteria in making moral judgments. In traditional American culture, girls and boys are taught from early childhood to value different qualities. Boys are trained to strive for independence and to value abstract thinking. In contrast, girls are taught to be nurturing and caring and to value relationships with others. Gilligan believes that there are two distinct types of moral reasoning. One is based primarily on the concept of justice, the other primarily on human relationships and caring. The justice perspective is characteristic of masculine thinking, whereas caring for others is more common in feminine thought. Traditional men often focus on rights, whereas traditional women see moral issues in terms of concern for the needs of others. However, Gilligan notes that gender differences in moral reasoning (like other gender differences) are not absolute. Some women make moral judgments from a justice perspective, and some men make moral judgments from a caring perspective.

Gilligan's subjects were mostly adolescents and young adults. Other researchers have looked at younger children and failed to find sex differences in moral judgments made by children younger than age 10. However, some 10- or 11-year-old boys give rather aggressive responses to test questions—the sorts of responses that are rarely given by girls. For example, in one study, children listened to a story about a porcupine who, needing a home for the winter, moved in with a family of moles. The moles soon found that they were constantly being pricked by the porcupine's sharp needles. What should they do? Only boys responded with suggestions like "Shoot the porcupine" or "Pluck out his quills." Girls tended to look for solutions that would harm neither the moles nor the porcupine—in other words, caring solutions (Garrod et al., 1989).

EISENBERG'S VIEW

Nancy Eisenberg (1989a, 1989b) feels that Kohlberg's mistake was not in placing too much emphasis on abstract justice; rather, it was in making the stages too rigid and absolute. Her argument is that children's moral development is not predictable and narrowly determined. Many factors go into children's moral judgments, ranging from the social customs of the culture in which they are reared to how they feel at a particular moment. Children (and adults) are capable of making moral judgments at a higher level one moment and at a lower level the next. They may even make judgments at a higher level for some issues (e.g., whether they would help someone who was injured) than for others (e.g., whether they would invite someone they didn't like to their home).

With regard to gender differences, Eisenberg also finds that girls between the ages of 10 and 12 give more caring and empathetic responses than boys at these ages. However, she believes that this finding stems from the fact that girls mature more rapidly than boys. By late adolescence, boys catch up. Eisenberg and her colleagues have found few gender differences in the responses of older adolescents (Eisenberg, 1989a; Eisenberg et al., 1987).

1. Describe the development of social cognition during middle childhood.
2. Discuss Kohlberg's cognitive theory of moral development.
3. List Gilligan's and Eisenberg's criticisms of Kohlberg's theory.

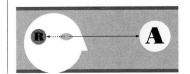

REVIEW & APPLY

CONTINUING FAMILY INFLUENCES

In spite of the time that children spend in school, the family normally continues to be the most important socializing influence. At the same time, their expanding cognitive abilities enable children to learn ever more sophisticated social concepts and rules, whether the rules are taught explicitly or simply implied by the behavior of others.

Social learning occurs in the context of relationships that are sometimes close and secure, sometimes anxiety provoking, and sometimes full of conflict.

Parents teach the value of warmth and affection by their own behavior.

In this section we will examine the family as the context of personality development and socialization. We will look closely at the changing forces in family life that affect children, including stress, divorce, the permanent absence of a parent, and child abuse.

PARENT-CHILD INTERACTIONS AND RELATIONSHIPS

In the elementary-school years, the overall nature of parent-child interactions changes. Children express less direct anger toward their parents and are less likely to whine, yell, or hit than when they were younger. Parents are less concerned with promoting autonomy and establishing daily routines and are more concerned with children's work habits and achievement (Lamb et al., 1992). School-age children need more subtle monitoring of their behavior than previously, but parental monitoring is still very important. Monitoring means knowing where your children are and what they're doing, and also that what they are doing is appropriate—both socially and with regard to schoolwork and other responsibilities. Researchers find that well-monitored boys, for example, receive higher grades than those who are less well monitored (Crosler, 1990).

OPTIMAL PARENTING   What is *optimal* parenting? Opinions on this subject have differed over the years. Contemporary research emphasizes that a major goal of parenting is to increase children's **self-regulated behavior**—basically, their ability to control and direct their behavior and meet requirements that parents and others impose upon them. As we saw in Chapter 7, authoritative approaches to discipline are more successful than other approaches in helping children develop self-regulation. When a parent relies on verbal reasoning and suggestions, the child tends to negotiate rather than react with defiance (Lamb et al., 1992).

Reasoning is related both to prosocial behavior and to compliance with social rules. Parents who remind their children of the effects of their actions on others tend to have children who are more popular and whose moral standards are more fully internalized. In contrast, when parents simply assert their power over the child (as in authoritarian parenting), their children tend not to develop internalized standards and controls. Studies consistently find that children who comply with adults' demands when the adults are present, but not when the adults are absent, are more likely to have parents who used power-assertive techniques.

Parents are more successful in developing self-regulated behavior if they gradually increase the child's involvement in family decisions. In a series of studies on parental dialogue and discipline, Eleanor Maccoby (1992) concluded that children adjust best when their parents foster what she calls **coregulation.** The parents gradually build cooperation and share responsibility in anticipation of the teenage years, by which time they expect their children to make most decisions for themselves. In preparation, they engage in frequent discussions and negotiations with their children. The parents see themselves as building a framework for responsible decision making.

The concept of scaffolding (Chapter 5) is especially useful in understanding optimal parenting. Children learn about the social world in complex social contexts in which they are accompanied by parents or other, more competent partners (Rogoff, 1990). Imagine a family attending a large wedding. Socially competent parents help their children anticipate what will happen. They may discuss the meaning of the event and specific rituals, cueing their children as

self-regulated behavior   Personal behavior regulated by the child.

coregulation   Development of a sense of shared responsibility between parents and children.

to how adults expect them to behave. Only small parts of the broad set of shared meanings of "marriage" and "wedding" are conveyed at one time, ideally at a level just beyond the child's current understanding.

It has been argued that socialization should not be viewed as a process in which control shifts from parents to child as the child becomes more autonomous and self-regulating. Instead, it is a process of mutual or shared coregulation that will last throughout the participants' lives—or until the relationship ends. Maccoby (1992) suggests that enduring parental influence stems from the strength and health of the parent-child relationship, which is particularly important during middle childhood.

THE CHANGING NATURE OF THE FAMILY

Until recently, research on parenting was based primarily on the so-called traditional American family: mother, father, and two or three children. Things have changed. Having children isn't going out of style—over 3 million babies were born in the United States in 1995. What has changed is getting married in the first place, as well as the likelihood of staying married. Either way, single parenthood has become commonplace. About 30% of all births are to unmarried mothers; in African-American families, the proportion is about 70% (U.S. Census Bureau, 1997). In 1997, 8 million American children were being raised in single-parent families (U.S. Census Bureau, 1997). Table 9–1 gives percentages of family (child-present) households by race/ethnicity and type, 1980–1995.

The American family has also undergone rapid change with regard to mothers' working. Once children enter school, the majority of American mothers enter the paid workforce. In 1948, only 26% of the mothers of school-age children (ages 6 to 17) worked outside the home; in 1975, the figure was 51%; and in 1996, it was over 76% (U.S. Census Bureau, 1997). Since the early 1950s,

TABLE 9–1   FAMILY (CHILD-PRESENT) HOUSEHOLDS BY RACE/ETHNICITY AND TYPE, 1980–1995

RACE/ETHNICITY AND TYPE OF FAMILY HOUSEHOLDS	PERCENT DISTRIBUTION			
	1980	1985	1990	1995
White				
Married couple	86	84	83	82
Male householder	3	3	4	4
Female householder	12	13	13	14
Black				
Married couple	56	51	50	47
Male householder	4	5	6	7
Female householder	40	44	44	46
Hispanic				
Married couple	75	72	70	68
Male householder	5	5	7	8
Female householder	20	23	23	24

Source: U.S. Census Bureau, 1997.

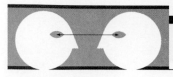

A MATTER FOR DEBATE

LATCHKEY KIDS

"Latchkey" children are often at home alone out of economic necessity. Their parents have to work outside the home and either cannot afford or cannot locate appropriate after-school care. This problem has grown dramatically along with the increase in the number of mothers who work outside the home. With about three-quarters of mothers of school-age children now in the workforce, it is no surprise that 4 out of 10 children in this age group are left unsupervised on a frequent or at least an occasional basis. The problem is especially severe among children of single mothers, who are often forced to work at two or three jobs to make ends meet.

There are conflicting opinions about the effects of leaving elementary-school children at home alone. In one study, sociologist Hyman Rodman found no differences in self-esteem or behavior between latchkey and nonlatchkey

children. But Thomas Long, a child psychologist, disagrees. According to Long, latchkey children fall into two groups: those who view themselves as capable and independent, and those who feel abandoned and rejected and hence are emotionally vulnerable. In general, Long believes that children younger than age 10 should not be left alone for extended periods.

In deciding whether a child is ready to be left alone, parents should assess the child's ability to take care of herself or himself and to keep out of harm's way. For example, can the child lock and unlock the door, dial the phone, tell time, recognize dangerous situations and take appropriate action, and follow simple instructions? Can the parent trust the child to stay away from the stove, sharp knives, and open windows in high-rise apartments? Parents should also assess whether the child is emotionally prepared to be alone. Does past behavior indicate that the child is confident in new situations

or easily frightened? Can the child handle boredom? Can the child settle squabbles with brothers or sisters who may also be home?

An established routine—especially if it involves contact with the parent—helps children adjust to being alone. Some parents call their children at a specified time every day, preferably as soon as the child returns from school. It also helps if parents return home at approximately the same time every day. In addition, they can give children the information and resources that they need to handle the unexpected—a list of emergency phone numbers, an escape plan in case of fire, a first-aid kit, money. Loving notes and warm, reassuring phone calls also help. So do nourishing snacks and meals.

Primary source: James Willwerth, "Hello, I'm Home Alone . . ." *Time*, March 1, 1993, pages 46–47.

---

mothers of elementary-school children have been more likely to work than married women without children—partly because of the greater financial needs of families with children, partly because of the larger number of single-parent women (Scarr et al., 1989). One important consideration is that more and more "latchkey children" are coming home from school to an empty home, as discussed in "A Matter for Debate," above.

Another consideration in changing families is the stress experienced both by parents and by children. This is so significant that we discuss it in detail in the following section.

FAMILIES AND STRESS   Many life situations are inherently stressful for children and their families. They include poverty, divorce, moving to a new town, suffering a serious illness or injury, or growing up in a dangerous neighborhood. (See "Eye on Diversity," on facing page). What determines a child's ability to cope constructively with these stresses? One factor is the sheer number of stressful situations in a child's life; a child (or adult) who can deal successfully with one stressful event may be overwhelmed if forced to deal with several at the same time (Hetherington, 1984). A second factor is the child's perception or understanding of the event. For example, the first day of school is a major event in a child's life. A child who knows what to expect and can use this milestone as a sign of increasing maturity will experience less stress in making the transition.

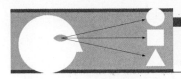

EYE ON DIVERSITY

GROWING UP IN DANGER

It was morning, and a 19-year-old gang member who had been gunned down in the Watts neighborhood of Los Angeles lay on the sidewalk in a pool of blood as hundreds of children walked by, lunch boxes and school bags in hand, on their way to the 102nd Street Elementary School. A few months later, children playing in the schoolyard dropped to the ground as five shots nearby claimed another victim. On yet another occasion, an outdoor assembly was disrupted by gunshots and wailing sirens as students watched a neighborhood man scuffle with police officers (Timnick, 1989).

Such experiences are no longer rare for children living in inner cities, some suburbs, and even rural areas. Children often fall asleep to the sound of gunfire. Children as young as age 6 are recruited as drug runners. Some babies' first words and gestures are the names and signs of their parents' gangs (Timnick, 1989). Researchers have found that children growing up in

inner-city "war zones" are often anxious and depressed. Children who experienced violence themselves or who witness the brutal murder of a parent, sibling, or friend are especially prone to severe psychological distress.

Posttraumatic stress disorder was first used to describe the psychological problems exhibited by some war veterans. These veterans had vivid nightmares, flashbacks about combat, and difficulty in sleeping, concentrating, and controlling their impulses. They were either withdrawn, aggressive, or both. Research indicates that children living in inner-city war zones have similar behavioral patterns. Many engage in aggressive play, have nightmares, and are troubled by sudden memories that intrude during school or other activities.

Chronic, ongoing violence produces a state of sustained stress. Young children who live with constant violence are fearful, depressed, and anxious (Garbarino et al., 1991). Many have trouble concentrating in school and suffer other school-related problems.

They may fear being abandoned and may become overly aggressive and cocky in order to disguise their fears. Many develop blunted emotions—they're afraid to develop affection for people who may be killed or who may abandon them. In turn, parents are likely to underestimate the extent of their children's psychological distress, either because the children don't talk about their fears or because the parents cannot acknowledge their children's emotional pain, which they feel helpless to remedy (Elkind, 1981).

The American Psychological Association's Committee on Violence and Youth recommends a community approach to the problem of children living in violent surroundings. Programs involving health care, recreation, and vocational training should be built around children's developmental needs. In addition, role models from the community and peer support groups should be available to help children find alternatives to activities involving violence and drug use.

Research clearly indicates that close-knit, adaptable families with open communication patterns and good problem-solving skills are better able to weather stressful events (Brenner, 1984). Social support systems such as neighbors, relatives, friendship networks, or self-help groups are also valuable.

From a different perspective, temperament and early personality characteristics influence children's ability to cope with stressful environments. Over a 30-year period, Emmy Werner (1989b, 1995) studied a group of what she terms **resilient children.** The children had been born on one of the Hawaiian islands and raised in family environments that were marred by poverty, parental conflict or divorce, alcoholism, and mental illness. Yet they developed into self-confident, successful, and emotionally stable adults. Since most children reared under such conditions do not fare nearly as well, Werner was interested in learning how these children managed to thrive in spite of their unfavorable environment. She found that they had been temperamentally "easy" and lovable babies who had developed secure attachment to a parent or grandparent in the first year of life. Later, if that parent or grandparent was no longer available, these children had the ability to find someone else—another adult or even a sibling or friend—who could provide the emotional support they needed. Other researchers have found that positive self-esteem and good self-

resilient children Children who overcome difficult environments to lead socially competent lives.

organization are strongly related to resilience in children—especially those who are maltreated (Chicchetti & Rogosch, 1997).

COPING WITH SINGLE-PARENTING   About 13% of American families with two parents have incomes below the poverty line, but nearly half of all families headed by single women live in poverty (U.S. Census Bureau, 1997). If a mother did not graduate from high school, the likelihood that the family income will be below the poverty level is almost 90% (Children's Defense Fund, 1992).

Some single mothers do an excellent job, and many have support from family and friends. But children who grow up in poverty in a home headed only by a mother are at risk in many ways (McLoyd & Wilson, 1990). Not having a father lowers a family's social status as well as its economic status. Housing is likely to be crowded; frequent moves are common. Meals may be skimpy and nutritionally poor. Medical care may be lacking. Also, the women who head these homes are often psychologically stressed by their struggle for survival. Many suffer from depression or anxiety, which interferes with their ability to be supportive and attentive parents.

Children who grow up in these homes may be handicapped in a number of ways that affect both their psychological health and their intellectual development. As a result, they are less likely than other American children to improve their socioeconomic status when they become adults. They are also more likely to become single parents themselves. Thus, the problems are passed on to the next generation (McLanahan & Booth, 1989).

Researchers have tried to identify factors that can break the cycle of depression and hopelessness that is characteristic of many low-income, single-parent families. They have found, for example, that when mothers in single-parent families work at jobs that they like, their children have greater self-esteem and a greater sense of family organization and togetherness compared with children whose mothers do not work or who work at jobs that they intensely dislike. Working single mothers have an especially strong impact on their daughters, who place greater emphasis on independence and achievement than mothers who do not work (Alessandri, 1992).

Researchers are also examining specific factors in single-parenting that negatively affect children's relationship with their mothers and their feelings about themselves. When Vonnie McLoyd (1994) and colleagues studied how maternal unemployment and work interruption affected a sample of 241 single African-American mothers and their children, they found an indirect negative effect on children's well-being. That is, economic hardship took a toll on the mother's psychological functioning, in turn affecting her ability to be an effective parent and, thus, the mother-child relationship. The mothers in the study showed symptoms of depression when they were unemployed; when depressed, they tended to punish their children more frequently. In turn, children who were punished frequently showed greater signs of cognitive distress and depression.

What, if anything, can break this cycle of economic hardship, maternal depression, and psychological consequences for children in single-parent families? McLoyd and her colleagues found that when mothers perceived that tangible help was available in the form of goods and services—when they knew, for example, that someone outside their family would help them run errands if they were sick—they had fewer depressive symptoms, felt better about their role as mothers, and punished their children less.

Social support helps, but not always. In a recent study (Chase-Lansdale et al., 1994), the researchers examined the disciplinary styles, problem-solving strategies, and emotionality of African-American grandmothers, mothers, and children who shared the same residence. In this built-in support system, a complex interplay of helpful, though sometimes conflicting, parenting was exhibited by both the mothers and the grandmothers. The effects of coresidence on parenting were most likely to be positive when teenage mothers were involved. Older mothers were more likely to provide positive parenting when they did not live in a three-generation household. In addition, part-time grandmothers provided better parenting and social support than grandmothers who lived in the same family unit.

Despite the stresses that single-parent families face, many do succeed. Table 9–2 provides some guidelines for making a single-parent family work.

CHILDREN OF DIVORCE

Since about half of all marriages end in divorce, each year over a million children experience the breakup of their families (Table 9–3 gives specific percentages, 1970–1990). Primarily because of divorce, only 40% of the children born nowadays will reach the age of 18 in an intact, two-parent home (Otto, 1988). Here we look mainly at the effects of divorce on children; we'll return to the effects on the parents in Chapter 15.

PSYCHOLOGICAL CONSEQUENCES OF DIVORCE   Family breakup affects children in a number of ways. Both parents strongly influence their children's development; a divorce means that both parents will no longer be equally available to their children. Moreover, usually the family has already been in a state of tension and stress for a long time. The children may have heard the word *divorce* spoken (or shouted) in their homes for months or even years, often accompanied by anger, fights, and crying. Even very young children know when their parents' relationship is disturbed. Children wonder what will happen to them if their parents divorce.

When one parent finally leaves, children may fear that the other parent will also abandon them. They may feel sad, confused, angry, or anxious. They may become depressed or disruptive at home or at school. Many children—especially younger ones—feel that they are to blame for the divorce: Were it not for

TABLE 9–2   SEVEN GUIDELINES FOR SINGLE PARENTING

1. Accept responsibilities and challenges. Maintain a positive attitude and the feeling that solutions are possible.

2. Give the parental role high priority. Successful single parents are willing to sacrifice time, money, and energy to meet their children's needs.

3. Use consistent, nonpunitive discipline.

4. Emphasize open communication. Encourage trust and the open expression of feelings.

5. Foster individuality within a supportive family unit.

6. Recognize the need for self-nurturance. Parents must understand the need to take care of themselves in order to be able to help their children.

7. Emphasize rituals and traditions, including bedtime routines, holiday celebrations, and special family activities.

Source: Adapted from Olson and Haynes, 1993.

Children in close-knit adaptable families generally tend to be best-equipped to cope with stressful situations.

TABLE 9–3 ESTIMATED NUMBER OF CHILDREN INVOLVED IN DIVORCE, UNITED STATES, 1970–1990

YEAR	NUMBER
1970	870,000
1975	1,123,000
1980	1,174,000
1985	1,091,000
1990	1,075,000

Source: U.S. Census Bureau, 1997.

something that they did wrong, maybe their parents would still be together. Children may even try to bring their parents back together, perhaps by being very good; they may also fantasize about a reconciliation (Hetherington, 1992; Hetherington et al., 1989; Wallerstein et al., 1988). Some parents complicate things even further by not being sure about their divorce at first, perhaps making failed attempts to get back together and falsely raising their children's hopes.

Relationships with both parents change during and after a divorce. Children may become defiant and argumentative; as adolescents, they may disengage themselves emotionally. Often children are forced to serve as sounding boards for their parents, listening to each parent criticize the other at length. They may be at the center of a custody battle and may be asked to choose sides. The parents may compete for their children's affection and try to bribe them with gifts or privileges. Parents often are under considerable stress right after the divorce and may be incapable of providing warmth or control; they may be less affectionate, inconsistent in applying discipline, uncommunicative, or unsupportive. Also, children may become upset when their parents start new relationships. For example, a boy who is living with his mother may take over the role of "man of the house" and feel threatened when a "rival" appears on the scene (Hetherington et al., 1989).

Among the most important factors that determine how children react to divorce are these:

1. *The amount of hostility accompanying the divorce.* If there is a great deal of hostility and bitterness, it is much harder for children to adjust. Parental conflict lowers children's sense of well-being. When parents fight, children develop fear and anger. They are especially vulnerable when they are forced to choose between their parents (Amato, 1993). Ongoing squabbles or legal battles over custody, division of property, child support, visitation, or child care arrangements make the situation much more difficult for both children and parents (Rutter & Garmezy, 1983).

2. *The amount of actual change in the child's life.* If children continue to live in the same home, attend the same school, and have the same friends after a divorce, their adjustment problems are likely to be less severe. In contrast, if their daily life is disrupted in major ways—moving back and forth from one parent's household to the other's, losing friends, entering a new school—their self-confidence and sense of order are likely to be shaken. The more

changes a child is forced to make, especially in the period immediately following the divorce, the more difficult the adjustment (Hetherington & Camara, 1984).

3. *The nature of the parent-child relationship.* Long-term involvement and emotional support from *both* parents help considerably. Some researchers have observed that the nature of ongoing parent-child interactions is much more important than whether both parents are present in the home (Rutter & Garmezy, 1983). In fact, sometimes children of divorce are better off than they would have been had their parents stayed together and continued to argue and fight.

CONSEQUENCES IN DAILY LIFE Immediately after a divorce, children—especially those between the ages of 5 and 7—often appear confused. They exhibit behavioral difficulties at home and at school. Their daily lives and their understanding of their social world are severely disrupted. The long-established patterns of their family life have broken down. Whereas in the past the world was predictable—Daddy came home from work every evening, the entire family sat down to dinner, and bedtime was at 8:00 P.M.—unpredictability is now the rule. Consequently, children often test the rules to see whether the world still works the way it did before. They may have to be told by their mother, "I know it's upsetting that Daddy's not coming home any more. But that doesn't mean you don't have to go to bed at 8:00. You still have to get up early in the morning and go to school. And you still need your rest." Teachers can help by gently reminding the child of the school's rules and expectations and by being emotionally supportive. Children who are seriously hurt by divorce are more likely to repeat a grade or be expelled from school and be treated for emotional and behavioral problems than children of intact families.

RECONSTITUTED FAMILIES When the custodial parent remarries and therefore forms a **reconstituted family,** as a majority do nowadays, some children welcome the arrival of the stepparent. For others, though, a parent's remarriage represents yet another difficult adjustment. Children may be distressed because there is no longer any chance of reuniting their parents. They may resent the stepparent's attempts to win their affection or to discipline them. They may feel divided loyalties to their original parents and may feel guilty about "abandoning" the noncustodial parent by giving affection to the stepparent. Children may also be unhappy about having to "share" their parent with his or her new partner, and they may worry about being "left out" of the new family. Many children have the additional problem of having to learn to live with stepsiblings (Hetherington et al., 1989).

In most cases, the major disruptions associated with divorce and reconstituted families subside in about 2 years. By that time, most children and parents have adjusted and are moving ahead with their lives, although remnants of divorce may reappear in adolescence and again in young adulthood. Divorce-related problems that persist may seriously interfere with a child's emotional, social, and academic progress.

CHILD ABUSE

As noted at various points in this book, one of the most serious and disturbing examples of family breakdown is child abuse. Regardless of the child's age, an abusing parent destroys the expectations of love, trust, and dependence that are so essential to healthy personality and social development. Severe developmental problems frequently result. In this section we'll look at child abuse and its dynamics in more detail.

reconstituted family Also known as stepfamily; families when parents have remarried to produce a new family.

Child abuse refers to physical or psychological injuries that are *intentionally* inflicted by an adult (Burgess & Conger, 1978). It is distinguished from child neglect in that the latter is usually unintentional. *Neglect* is failure of a caregiver to respond to or care for children. Though not as serious as abuse, it can nonetheless cause children to suffer or die, as discussed in Chapter 5. The deliberate nature of child abuse, however, is more horrifying—whether it takes blatant physical forms such as violent punishment or sexual abuse, or subtler psychological forms such as ridicule and direct attacks on the child's self-concept and self-esteem.

It can be difficult to draw the line between child abuse and acceptable punishment, partly because the distinction varies according to community and cultural standards. Historically, many cultures have condoned, even encouraged, physical mistreatment that is now generally considered shocking and brutal. Harsh physical punishment was at one time viewed as necessary in disciplining and educating children. Some cultures imbued certain forms of physical cruelty, such as foot binding, skull shaping, or ritual scarring, with deep symbolic meaning and reverence. Since children were viewed as property, parents had the legal right to treat them any way they saw fit. Infanticide and abandonment of unwanted babies were time-honored methods used by desperate parents trying to cope with hunger, illegitimacy, or birth defects (Radbill, 1974).

Today, deliberately causing serious injury or death to a child is a serious crime—a felony with consequences ranging from removal of the child from the parents to imprisonment or capital punishment. But, sadly, child abuse is still not uncommon.

PHYSICAL ABUSE   In the United States, official reports of child abuse and neglect total about 1 million a year; three children die every day as a result of physical abuse or neglect. These figures may be appalling, but they are not unique to the United States; similar rates are found in Canada, Australia, Great Britain, and Germany (Emery, 1989).

Physical abuse most often occurs at the hands of the child's parents, both mothers and fathers. When someone other than a parent is responsible, however, male abusers outnumber females by four to one. The proportion of male *sexual* abusers is even higher—nearly 95%. Sexual abuse of little girls usually is not committed by the child's own father. Stepfathers are five times more likely to abuse female children than are biological fathers (Sedlack, 1989; Wolfe et al., 1988). Sexual abuse is more often inflicted on girls, physical abuse more often on boys. Younger children sustain more serious injuries than older ones; about half of cases involving serious injury or death involve children under the age of 3 (Rosenthal, 1988).

PSYCHOLOGICAL ABUSE   Physical abuse is always accompanied by psychological components that may be even more damaging than the abuse itself (Emery, 1989). Psychological abuse takes six distinct forms (Hart et al., 1987); these are summarized in Table 9–4. Psychological abuse is so common that virtually no one grows up without experiencing some form of it. Fortunately, however, in most cases the abuse is not intense or frequent enough to do permanent damage (Hart et al., 1987).

EFFECTS OF CHILD ABUSE   Sexual and other physical abuse have long-term effects on the child's emotional well-being. Children's self-esteem can be irreparably damaged, and they may find it difficult to trust anyone because of the fear of exploitation and pain. Thus, abused children tend to isolate

child abuse Intentional psychological or physical injuries inflicted on a child.

TABLE 9–4   SIX FORMS OF PSYCHOLOGICAL CHILD ABUSE

1. *Rejection:* Actively refusing the requests or needs of a child in a way that implies strong dislike.

2. *Denial of emotional responsiveness:* Passive withholding of affection that involves behaviors such as coldness or failing to respond to attempts to communicate.

3. *Degradation:* Humiliating children in public or calling them names like "dummy." Children's self-esteem is lowered by frequent assaults on their dignity or intelligence.

4. *Terrorization:* Being forced to witness the abuse of a loved one or being threatened with personal abuse. A child who suffers regular beatings or is told "I'll break every bone in your body" is being terrorized. A more subtle form of terrorism occurs when a parent abandons a misbehaving child on the street.

5. *Isolation:* Refusing to allow a child to play with friends or to take part in family activities. Some forms of isolation, such as locking a child in a closet, may also be terrorization

6. *Exploitation:* Taking advantage of a child's innocence or weakness. The most obvious example of exploitation is sexual abuse.

themselves and may display highly aggressive behaviors when approached (Hart & Brassard, 1989; Haskett & Kistner, 1991; Mueller & Silverman, 1989). In addition, abused children tend to have more school-related problems than children raised in nonabusive homes (Hanson, 1989; Vondra, 1990). Adolescents and adults who were abused as children are at greater risk of psychological problems, including depression, alcoholism, and drug abuse (Schaefer et al., 1988). Their incidence of suicide attempts is also higher than average.

Abused children also have trouble controlling their emotions and behavior and tend to be less socially competent than children who are not abused (Shields et al., 1994). When researchers conducted a longitudinal study of a sample of physically abused 5-year-olds, they found that the children were less popular and more socially withdrawn than their nonabused peers and that such peer-related problems increased during each of the 5 years of the study (Dodge et al., 1994).

Researchers also speculate that a history of family conflict involving verbal and physical abuse may have a cumulative impact on children's reaction to anger, even when the anger does not directly involve them (Cummings et al., 1994). Abused children are caught in damaged relationships and aren't socialized in positive, supportive ways. They may learn defiance, manipulation, and other problem behaviors as ways of escaping abuse; they learn to exploit, degrade, or terrorize. They also come to *expect* interpersonal relationships to be painful—with pervasive, long-term consequences.

EXPLANATIONS OF CHILD ABUSE

Extensive research on child abuse has centered on three theoretical explanations: psychiatric, sociological, and situational (Parke & Collmer, 1975). Let's look briefly at each of these.

PSYCHIATRIC EXPLANATIONS   The psychiatric model focuses on the personality and family background of the parents. The basic view is that abusive parents are sick and in need of psychiatric treatment, although researchers have not found a particular cluster of personality or other traits associated with child abuse. Child abusers come from all walks of life.

One consistent finding, however, is that many child abusers were themselves abused as children (Ney, 1988). Although it remains unclear how child abuse is passed from one generation to the next, a plausible explanation is that adults who were abused as children pattern their abusive parenting behavior after role models—their parents—in the same way that acceptable behaviors are learned during childhood. For example, their parents may have taught them that needs like dependency or autonomy are unacceptable—that crying or asking for help is useless or inappropriate. To underscore that theory, consider the behavior of a child who became distressed when his father quit beating him. The child asked the social worker, "How come Daddy doesn't love me anymore?" Thus, children absorb such lessons at an early age, and when they become parents, they apply what they learned to their own children.

SOCIOLOGICAL EXPLANATIONS   An aspect of American culture that may be related to child abuse is violence. The United States ranks higher in murders and other violent crimes than all other industrialized nations. Violent television programming suggests that violence is an acceptable way to resolve conflicts. Also significant is that when physical spouse abuse occurs, physical child abuse is also likely. Child abuse is also linked to the widespread acceptance of physical punishment as a form of discipline; 93% of all U.S. parents spank their children, although the majority do it sparingly and within acceptable limits. In comparison, more peaceful societies that tend to use love-oriented disciplinary techniques have less overall violence and child abuse (Parke & Collmer, 1975).

Poverty also plays a role in child abuse. Although physical abuse of children is found at all socioeconomic levels, it is almost seven times more likely to be reported in homes whose annual income is below $15,000 (Sedlack, 1989). This statistic may result partly from the fact that abuse in middle-class homes is less likely to come to the attention of authorities. It is also true, however, that general family stresses such as those associated with poverty increase the risk of child abuse.

Unemployment is another risk factor. In periods of high unemployment, male violence against wives and children increases. Fathers or mothers who are suddenly and unexpectedly out of work may begin to abuse their children. Aside from the financial problems, unemployment lowers the parent's social status and self-esteem. An unemployed father may try to compensate by wielding authority at home through physical domination.

Social isolation is another common characteristic of families in which child abuse occurs. These parents are often isolated from relatives, friends, and other support systems. They have difficulty sustaining friendships and rarely belong to social organizations. Thus, they may have no one to ask for help when they need it, and they may take out their frustrations on their children.

SITUATIONAL EXPLANATIONS   Like the sociological model, the situational model looks at environmental factors. Here, however, the emphasis is on interactions among family members and the recognition that children are active participants in the process (Parke & Collmer, 1975). When we examine the child's role in abusive families, we find that parents usually single out one child for mistreatment. Infants and very young children are the most frequent targets. Those with physical or mental abnormalities or difficult temperaments are at especially high risk. Infants who cry constantly can drive parents to the breaking point. Or there may simply be a mismatch between the parent's expectations and the child's characteristics. For example, a mother who wants to touch and

STUDY CHART ▸ APPROACHES TO UNDERSTANDING CHILD ABUSE

EXPLANATION	CAUSE	PERSPECTIVE
Psychiatric	Parents	Focuses on the personalities of the parents as being sick and in need of extensive psychotherapy; most child abusers were themselves abused as children; presence of poor parenting models leads to family cycles of violence.
Sociological	Society	Views American families as living in a culture of violence reflected in television programming; physical punishment is widely used and can get out of control when the family is under stress; socioeconomic conditions such as unemployment and poverty increase stress and therefore encourage abuse.
Situational	Immediate circumstances and patterns or interaction	Seeks environmental causes for the abuse, such as dysfunctional family interaction patterns; often the abused child has some trait that is considered undesirable by the parents and thus becomes the focus of abuse.

comfort her child may have a child that doesn't like to be touched. Another possibility is that the parent has unrealistic views of what kinds of behavior are appropriate in a child (Parke & Collmer, 1975; Vasta, 1982). For example, a father may become angry when his 3-year-old son fails to clean his room.

Although each approach sheds light on possible causes of child abuse, none tells us how to stop it. Programs for preventing child abuse focus on giving parents social support and teaching them better methods of discipline. Although these programs usually reduce the level of abuse, approximately one in four participants continues to abuse his or her children (Ferleger et al., 1988). Criminal prosecution of offenders and removal of the child from the home are sometimes the only alternatives.

1. What is meant by parental monitoring, and why is it important to the child's development?
2. What is self-regulation, and how do children develop it?
3. List some of the stresses associated with single parenting.
4. Discuss three important factors that determine how children react to divorce.
5. Contrast physical and psychological child abuse.
6. Discuss the main points in the three approaches to explaining why caregivers abuse their children.

REVIEW & APPLY

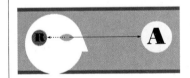

PEER RELATIONSHIPS AND SOCIAL COMPETENCE

Peer relationships become increasingly important in middle childhood and exert a major influence on social and personality development. In this section we begin with a look at individual friendships, the way they form, and the

Friendship and fun go hand-in-hand.

way they benefit children. Then we'll consider peer relationships on a larger scale, with emphasis on peer pressure.

CONCEPTS OF FRIENDSHIP

The ability to infer the thoughts, expectations, feelings, and intentions of others plays a central role in understanding what it means to be a friend. Children who can view things from another person's perspective are better able to develop strong, intimate relationships with others.

Robert Selman (1976, 1981) studied the friendships of children aged 7 to 12. His approach was similar to that used in Kohlberg's studies of moral development: Tell children stories involving a "relationship" dilemma, and then ask them questions to assess their concepts of other people, their self-awareness and ability to reflect, their concepts of personality, and their ideas about friendship. Here's an example of the stories Selman used:

> Kathy and Debbie have been best friends since they were 5. A new girl, Jeannette, moves into their neighborhood, but Debbie dislikes her because she considers Jeannette a showoff. Later, Jeannette invites Kathy to go to the circus on its one day in town. Kathy's problem is that she has promised to play with Debbie that same day. What will Kathy do?

Such stories raise questions about the nature of relationships, old friendships versus new ones, and loyalty and trust. They require children to think and talk about how friendships are formed and maintained, and about what is important in a friendship. On the basis of the children's responses, Selman (1981) described four stages of friendship; these are summarized in Table 9–5. At the first stage (age 6 and younger), a friend is just a playmate—someone who lives nearby, goes to the same school, or has desirable toys. There is no understanding of the other person's perspective, so Kathy simply goes to the circus. At the second stage (7 to 9), awareness of another person's feelings begins to appear. A child at this stage might say that Kathy could go to the circus

TABLE 9–5 SELMAN'S STAGES OF FRIENDSHIP DEVELOPMENT

STAGE	AGE	CHARACTERISTICS
1	6 and under	Friendship is based on physical or geographic factors; children are self-centered, with no understanding of the perspectives of others.
2	7–9	Friendship begins to be based on reciprocity and awareness of others' feelings; it begins to be based on social actions and evaluation by each other.
3	9–12	Friendship is based on genuine give-and-take; friends are seen as people who help each other; mutual evaluation of each other's actions occurs; the concept of trust appears.
4	11–12 and older	Friendship is seen as a stable, continuing relationship based on trust; children can observe the relationship from the perspective of a third party.

Source: Adapted from Selman (1981).

with Jeannette and remain friends with Debbie only if Debbie did not object. At the third stage (9 to 12), friends are seen as people who help each other, and the concept of trust appears. The child realizes that the friendship between Kathy and Debbie is different from the friendship between Kathy and Jeannette because the older friendship is based on long-standing trust. At the fourth stage, which was rare among the 11- and 12-year-olds studied, children are fully capable of looking at a relationship from another's perspective. A child at this level might say, "Kathy and Debbie should be able to understand each other and work it out."

Selman argues that the key to developmental changes in children's friendships is the ability to take another person's perspective. Not all researchers agree, however. For example, there is evidence that younger children implicitly know more about the rules and expectations of being a friend than they can explain to an interviewer (Rizzo & Corsaro, 1988). Also, real friendships are more complicated and changing than Selman's model implies. They may involve mutuality, trust, and reciprocity at one time, competitiveness and conflict at another (Hartup, 1996). Conflict in particular may be intrinsic to friendship. Such complexities are not easily handled by a model that looks only at the cognitive aspects of children's friendships and ignores the emotional aspects (Berndt, 1983).

FUNCTIONS OF FRIENDSHIP

Children and adults alike benefit from having close, confiding relationships. Friendships help children to learn social concepts and social skills and to develop self-esteem. Friendship provides structure for activity; reinforces and solidifies group norms, attitudes, and values; and serves as a backdrop for individual and group competition (Hartup, 1970a, 1996). Children with stable, "satisfying" friendships have better attitudes toward school and achieve more (Ladd et al., 1996).

Friendship patterns shift during childhood (Piaget, 1965). The egocentric pattern of Selman's first stage changes during middle childhood, when

Friendship pairs allow children to share feelings and fears and to reinforce activities, values, and norms.

children begin to form closer relationships and have "best" friends. In later childhood and adolescence, *group friendships* become common. The groups are generally large, with several boys or girls regularly participating together in various activities.

Children who are friends may complement each other. One may be dominant, the other submissive. One friend may use the other as a model, whereas the other may enjoy "teaching." Friendship can also be a vehicle of self-expression. Children sometimes choose friends whose personalities are quite different from their own. An outgoing or impulsive child may choose a more reserved or restrained child as a close friend. As a pair, the children may demonstrate more personality traits than either child could alone (Hartup, 1970a, 1970b). Of course, friends are rarely complete opposites. Friendship pairs that last usually have many shared values, attitudes, and expectations. Indeed, the relationship may be egalitarian, with neither friend playing a clear or consistent role.

With a friend, children can share their feelings, their fears, every detail of their lives. Having a best friend to confide in teaches a child how to relate to others openly without being self-conscious. Having friends also allows for sharing secrets, although the kinds of secrets children understand and share (or don't share) change during middle childhood. Younger children are less likely to "keep" secrets from adults (Watson & Valtin, 1997). Otherwise, close friendships are more common among girls; boys tend to reveal less of themselves to their friends (Maccoby, 1990; Rubin, 1980).

Some childhood friendships last throughout life; more often, however, friendships change. Best friends may move away or transfer to another school, and when this kind of event happens, children may feel a real sense of loss—until they make new friends. Sometimes friends become interested in other people who meet their needs in new and different ways. Sometimes friends just grow apart or develop new interests. As children mature and change, they may form new friendships (Rubin, 1980).

Finally, although research indicates that virtually all children have at least one *unilateral* friendship, many children lack *reciprocal* friendships characterized by give-and-take (George & Hartmann, 1996). Some children are consistently unsuccessful at forming meaningful friendships. Children who are rejected by their peers are at risk for maladjustment later in life, but not all children who are rejected by peers are "friendless." Even a single close friend helps a child cope with the negative effects of being disliked and isolated from peers (Rubin & Coplan, 1992). Research has also shown that many children who are consistently rejected by their peers still believe they have friends, although the friendships are weak and unsatisfying (Parker & Asher, 1993).

PEER GROUPS

A **peer group** is more than just a group of kids. It is relatively stable and stays together, and its members interact with one another regularly and share values. Group norms govern interactions and influence each member. Finally, there are status differences within the group—some members are leaders, and others are followers.

peer group A group of two or more people of similar status who interact with each other and who share norms and goals.

DEVELOPMENTAL TRENDS Peer groups are important throughout middle childhood, but a general shift occurs in both their organization and their significance during the years from 6 to 12.

In early middle childhood, peer groups are relatively informal. They are usually created by the children themselves, they have very few operating rules, and turnover in their membership is rapid. It is true that many of the group's activities, such as playing games or riding bikes, may be carried out according to precise rules. But the structure of the group itself is quite flexible.

The group takes on greater significance for its members when they reach the ages of 10 to 12. Conformity to group norms becomes extremely important, and peer pressure becomes much more effective. Groups also develop a more formal structure. They may have special membership requirements, club meetings, and initiation rites. At this time, also, separation of the sexes becomes especially noticeable. Peer groups are now almost invariably composed of one sex, and groups of different sexes maintain different interests, activities, and styles of interaction (Maccoby, 1990). Strict attitudes about rules, conformity, and sex segregation usually do not diminish until mid-adolescence.

GROUP FORMATION   Children are constantly thrown together in schools, camps, and neighborhoods. Groups form quickly. Role differentiation develops within groups, and shared values and interests emerge. Mutual influences and expectations grow, and a feeling of tradition takes shape. This process is almost universal across cultures.

Classic research on how fifth-grade boys in summer camp form peer groups indicated that groups formed quickly and developed shared values and norms; the boys even named their groups. Of most importance, when groups competed against each other, feelings of exclusiveness and hostility quickly developed. When the groups were later required to cooperate, hostility was greatly reduced (Sherif & Sherif, 1953; Sherif et al., 1961). Such findings are typical of how groups form and compete in classrooms, athletic competitions, and neighborhood or ethnic rivalries.

Peer groups form wherever children with common values, interests, or goals are thrown together.

STATUS WITHIN THE PEER GROUP If we watch schoolchildren during free time, such as at lunch or recess, we can observe the development of roles within groups. One girl is surrounded by children who are eager to get her attention. Another stands on the fringes, ignored. Three boys run by, shouting. A muscular child grabs a smaller child's toy, and the child cries. Scenes like this occur throughout the world, wherever there are children.

Each peer group has some members who are popular and some who are not. In addition to the factors discussed in Chapter 8, peer acceptance is often related to an individual's overall adjustment—enthusiasm and active participation, ability to cooperate, and responsiveness to social overtures. "Getting in sync" tends to be reinforced because of its effects on self-esteem and social self-confidence. The adjustment of well-liked children is bolstered by their popularity; inept children become even more ill at ease when ignored or rejected by the group (Glidewell et al., 1966).

Academic performance and athletic ability also influence popularity. In general, popular children are brighter than average and do well in school. Slow learners are often made fun of or ignored. Athletic ability is particularly important in settings like camps or playgrounds, where the peer group is involved in sports.

Peer acceptance can be influenced by teacher feedback. In one study (White & Kistner, 1992), a group of first- and second-graders viewed a videotape of a problem child (an actor) who was rejected by his peers. The positive comments that the teacher made about the child when the video was over encouraged students to change their negative perceptions. Thus, by accepting problem children—but not their problem *behavior*—teachers can influence peer group status.

Popularity is affected by both extreme aggressiveness and extreme timidity. No one likes a bully, so the overly aggressive child is shunned. The child may then become even more aggressive out of frustration or in an attempt to win by force what she or he cannot win by persuasion. Similarly, a timid, anxious child is at risk of becoming a chronic victim, picked on not just by bullies but even by nonagressive children (Dodge et al., 1990; Newcomb et al., 1993; Perry et al., 1990). Timid children also show little prosocial behavior and suffer most from peer rejection. They tend to be lonelier and to worry more about their peer relationships than aggressive children who are rejected by peers (Parkhurst & Asher, 1992).

Status within the group affects the way children feel about themselves. In one study (Crick & Ladd, 1993) researchers assessed the feelings of loneliness, social anxiety, and social avoidance reported by a group of third- and fifth-graders. It was found that how children feel about themselves and whether they blame themselves or others for what happens to them depend on their experiences with peers. Rejected children reported a higher degree of loneliness and had a greater tendency to blame unsatisfactory relationships on others than did children who were accepted peer-group members. Unpopular children often have traits that make them different from their classmates—obesity, skin of the "wrong" color, or even an unusual name (as discussed in "In Theory, In Fact," on facing page). These traits can reduce children's conformity to group standards.

PEER GROUP CONFORMITY How insistent is the pressure to conform to group standards? Conforming to the peer group can be a normal, healthy, and often desirable behavior. As part of their daily behavior, children conform to

Conformity with a peer is normal and often desirable behavior.

IN THEORY, IN FACT

NICKNAMES

Remember the good old days in grade school, when you were called everything but the name your parents gave you? You may have been lucky enough to have borne the nickname "Chief" or "Coach" or "Ace," or unfortunate enough to be called "Dumbo" or "Four-Eyes" or even "Sewage." Such labels may seem amusing to adults, but they can be painful for children. Nicknames teach children about social status, friendship, and morality.

To understand better the significance of nicknames, Rom Harré and colleagues (1980) surveyed thousands of youngsters and adults in the United States, Great Britain, Spain, Mexico, Japan, and the Arab nations. They found that children between the ages of 5 and 15 often create separate, secret worlds for themselves and that nicknames may perform important social functions in these worlds. One of the main reasons that children bestow nicknames on each other is to separate "us" from "them." Children who have no nicknames are considered too insignificant to bother with. They tend to be unpopular and isolated from the rest of the group. As Harré and his colleagues (1980) point out, "To be nicknamed is to be seen as having an attribute that entitles one to social attention, even if that attention is unpleasant. Thus, it may be better to be called 'Sewage' than merely John." In other words, having even a bad nickname is better than having no nickname at all.

The "Fatties" and "Lame-brains" of the group are used as examples by group leaders to show what people are *not* supposed to be like. They are walking advertisements of violated group standards. Through nicknames, children proclaim what is acceptable to society and what is not. Any behavior, style, or physical characteristic that does not meet society's standards can become the source of a nickname. Thus, when children call others "Stinky," "Pimples," or "Eagle Nose," they indicate that they have internalized adult norms for cleanliness and appearance.

Unfortunately, nicknaming can be very painful. However, children are often willing victims of the process: "It is not necessarily the fattest, stupidest, and dirtiest who acquire the names 'Hippo' or 'Tapeworm-Woman,' but those who willingly bear the humiliation of being symbols of childhood greed, improvidence, and aversion to washing" (Harré, 1980).

Children use nicknames differently in various cultures. Nicknames like "The Lame One" or "The Three-Legged One," which poke fun at physical deformities, are much more common in the Arab nations than in England or Japan. Japanese children are more likely to use animal and insect analogies. In any culture, though, it seems that nicknames help children build the social reality that they take with them into adulthood. What's in a name? In the case of nicknames, there's a lot more than you might expect.

peer group standards as well as to adult expectations. But children sometimes conform excessively to group norms—even when these standards are not helpful to the individual child, to the group as a whole, or to the society at large.

Several characteristics are common among highly conforming children. They have feelings of inferiority and low "ego strength" (Hartup, 1970a; Rubin & Coplan, 1992). They tend to be more dependent or anxious than other children and are exceptionally sensitive to social cues for behavior. They also tend to *self-monitor* what they do and say very closely. They are especially concerned with how they appear to others and constantly compare themselves with their peers.

Of course, peer pressure can be positive as well as negative. Studies have shown, for example, that peer group influence can encourage academic motivation. When peer group formation was studied in classes of fourth- and fifth-graders, researchers found that peer groups tend to be composed of students with similar motivations regarding school (Kindermann, 1993). Thus, because peer group members identify with each other, the peer group can foster learning and academic success. Children are actually more likely to conform to peer pressure when it is positive than when it involves misbehavior such as stealing, drinking, or using illegal drugs. When peer pressure involves antisocial

Each peer group has members who are popular and members who are not.

acts, boys are more likely than girls to yield to it (Brown et al., 1986). Children who are unsupervised after school also tend to conform to antisocial peer pressure more than those who are monitored by adults (Steinberg, 1986).

Conformity is especially meaningful to children during late middle childhood, when they begin moving beyond the security of family life. Preadolescents typically have a strong need to belong, to feel accepted, and to be part of a group. These needs coexist with an equally strong need for autonomy or mastery. Children try to exert some control over their social and physical environments, to understand the rules and limits, and to find a place within these limits. Thus, they become very involved in making rules and learning rituals.

Unfortunately, peer groups sometimes breed conformity that manifests itself in prejudice toward people who are different. The final section of this chapter examines how prejudice develops during middle childhood, with emphasis on the development of racial prejudice.

IN-GROUPS, OUT-GROUPS, AND PREJUDICE

Prejudice means having negative attitudes toward people because of their membership in a group that is defined on the basis of race, religion, ethnicity, or some other noticeable attribute. Prejudice implies the existence of an *in-group*—people who believe that they possess desirable characteristics—and of an out-group—people who are different and undesirable. **Discrimination** means acting on the basis of prejudice—for example, by not hiring members of a particular racial or ethnic group.

Racial awareness begins to develop during the preschool years. Just as a child learns that she is a girl or that he is a boy, an African-American child learns that he or she has darker skin and other differences in physical features compared with whites. Just as a little girl learns that her body is different from that of a boy before she understands what it means to be female in our society, a black child learns that she is different from white children before she understands what it means to be an African-American in our society. Thus, she learns first that she is different from white children in appearance; and second, she learns that these differences may make her unwelcome or may be held against her. The same situation holds for a white child in a predominantly black setting. What the child does not understand is *why* race or ethnicity results in social discrimination. Answering that question can be a lifelong task (Spencer, 1988).

Understanding what group differences signify and what it means to be a member of a group requires social cognition, which in turn depends on cognitive development. Thus, a child whose thought is still egocentric and who can focus on only one dimension at a time assumes that people who are similar in one dimension (such as skin color) must be similar in other dimensions as well. As children grow older, they become more skilled at seeing people as multidimensional. In an experiment with English-speaking and French-speaking Canadian children (Doyle et al., 1988), the researchers found that older children had more flexible attitudes about members of the other language-speaking group. Children capable of concrete operational thought were less likely to attribute negative characteristics to members of the other group than were children still in the preoperational period. Other researchers have found, however, that the level of cognitive development is not directly related to children's understanding of their own racial or ethnic identity (Ocampo et al., 1997).

A greater ability to see people as multidimensional is offset by the strong tendency of older school-age children to conform to group standards and

prejudice A negative attitude formed without adequate reason and usually directed toward people because of their membership in a certain group.

discrimination Treating others in a prejudiced manner.

reject those who are different from them in any way. A study done in a California town in which the schools were about 50% African-American and 50% white found that older children were actually less likely than younger ones to have a friend of a different race. Interracial friendships declined steadily from the fourth through the seventh grade. The researchers concluded that as children grow older, similarity becomes an increasingly powerful basis for friendship.

There may also be pressure from other members of a peer group to avoid forming friendships with members of a different group (Hallinan & Teixeira, 1987). It works both ways with regard to blacks and whites. African-American children who become friendly with white children may be pressured to give up such friendships because they are being "disloyal" to their race (Schofield, 1981). Recently, studies have also found that black children who succeed at school may be perceived as being disloyal. They may be taunted by their peers and excluded from group activities (Reuter News Service, 1993).

Racial awareness is an important issue during middle childhood. Children absorb the cultural attitudes of those around them. In return for adhering to the standards of their society, children must receive some assurance that they belong to a larger, more powerful group. But African-American parents have had to adapt to a majority culture that does not reward them as it does whites. They are expected to teach their children the values of a society that holds them in low esteem. The children naturally sense this conflict, which affects their attitudes toward society.

Peer pressures aggravate this situation. Minority peer groups often have norms that differ widely from those of white, middle-class peer groups. An African-American child growing up in an innercity environment belongs to a different culture from that of most middle-class whites or blacks. The degree of acceptance that African-American children find in the larger society often depends on their ability to conform to its norms. When minority children get together with other members of their racial or ethnic group, their adjustment is easier during middle childhood. Group membership tends to improve their self-esteem and to increase both in-group solidarity and out-group hostility. But minority children eventually face the problem of integrating their own self-concept with society's image of them, which can cause conflict, anxiety, or anger at any age.

1. Discuss the importance of friendship during middle childhood.
2. Discuss developmental trends in peer groups and some characteristics of peer group formation.
3. Discuss some of the problems children face as a result of prejudice and discrimination. Why is racial awareness a particularly significant issue in middle childhood?

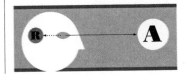

REVIEW & APPLY

SUMMARY

Personality Development in an Expanding Social World

■ Freud described middle childhood as a period of latency in which children could turn their emotional energies toward peer relationships, creative efforts, and learning.

■ Erikson proposed that the central focus of middle childhood is the conflict of industry versus inferiority.

- Piaget and Kohlberg focused on the development of children's concepts about self and morality.
- Social-learning theory has made major contributions to the understanding of how specific behaviors are learned via the family and the peer group.
- During middle childhood, children form increasingly stable pictures of themselves, and their self-concept also becomes more realistic.
- As children grow older, they form more complex pictures of their own physical, intellectual, and personality characteristics as well as those of other people.
- Self-esteem refers to whether you see yourself in a favorable or an unfavorable light. During the school years, it is significantly correlated with academic achievement.

Social Knowledge and Reasoning

- Central to socialization during middle childhood is social cognition: thought, knowledge, and understanding pertaining to the world of self in social interactions with others.
- A primary component of social cognition is social inference—guesses and assumptions about what another person is feeling, thinking, or intending.
- Other components of social cognition are an understanding of social responsibility and an understanding of social regulations such as customs and conventions.
- According to Piaget, children's moral sense develops in two stages. At the stage of moral realism (early middle childhood), children think that all rules must be obeyed. At the stage of moral relativism, they realize that rules can be changed as the need arises.
- Kohlberg defined three broad levels of moral reasoning; preconventional, conventional, and postconventional, each of which is subdivided into two stages. (See the Study Chart on page 318.)
- Critics have attacked Kohlberg's theory on grounds of moral absolutism, arguing that it disregards significant cultural differences. The theory has also been criticized because it assesses moral attitudes, not behavior.
- Gilligan believes that there are two distinct types of moral reasoning, one based primarily on the concept of justice, the other primarily on human relationships and caring. The justice perspective is characteristic of masculine thinking, whereas caring for others is more common in feminine thought.

- Eisenberg believes that many factors go into children's moral judgments, such as the social customs of the culture in which they are reared and the way they feel at a particular moment.

Continuing Family Influences

- In the elementary-school years, parents are less concerned with promoting autonomy and establishing daily routines and more concerned with children's work habits and achievement.
- A major goal of parenting is to increase children's self-regulated behavior.
- According to Maccoby, children adjust best when their parents foster coregulation; that is, they gradually build cooperation and share responsibility in anticipation of the teenage years.
- In recent decades, single parenthood has become commonplace. In addition, over three-quarters of mothers of school-age children work outside the home. These trends have increased the general level of stress experienced both by parents and by children.
- Close-knit, adaptable families with open communication patterns and good problem-solving skills are better able to weather stressful events.
- Resilient children manage to thrive in spite of unfavorable environments. Most such children develop a secure attachment to a parent or grandparent in the first year of life; if that person later is no longer available, the child is able to find someone else who can provide emotional support.
- Children who grow up in a poor single-parent home are at risk in many ways, including low social and economic status, crowded housing, frequent moves, skimpy and nonnutritious meals, and lack of medical care. These problems affect both their psychological health and their intellectual development.
- Social support can sometimes help single-parent families break out of the cycle of economic hardship, maternal depression, and psychological consequences for children.
- Children whose parents divorce feel sad, confused, angry, or anxious. They may become depressed or disruptive at home or at school. Many feel that they are to blame for the divorce.
- Relationships with parents change during and after a divorce. Children may become defiant and argumentative; as adolescents, they may disengage themselves emotionally.
- Among the most important factors that determine how children react to divorce are the amount of hos-

tility accompanying the divorce, the amount of actual change in the child's life, and the nature of the parent-child relationship.

■ Immediately after a divorce, children's daily lives and their understanding of their social world are severly disrupted.

■ For many children of divorce, a parent's remarriage represents yet another difficult adjustment.

■ Child abuse refers to physical or psychological injuries that are intentionally inflicted by an adult.

■ Physical abuse most often occurs at the hands of the child's parents. Sexual abuse of little girls is usually not committed by the child's father. Whereas sexual abuse is more often inflicted on girls, physical abuse is more often suffered by boys; younger children sustain more serious injuries than older ones.

■ Abuse can have long-term effects on the child's emotional well-being, self-esteem, and ability to trust others. Abused children have trouble controlling their emotions and behavior, and they tend to be less socially competent than children who are not abused.

■ There are three theoretical explanations of child abuse. The psychiatric model focuses on the personality and family background of the parents. Sociological explanations emphasize the role of a culture of violence and the prevalence of poverty, unemployment, and social isolation in families in which abuse occurs. Situational explanations look at interactions among family members, including the child's role in incurring abuse.

Peer Relationships and Social Competence

■ Selman described four stages of friendship. At the first stage, a friend is just a playmate; at the second stage, awareness of another person's feelings begins to appear; at the third stage, friends are seen as people who help and trust each other; at the fourth stage, children are capable of looking at a relationship from another's perspective.

■ Friendships help children learn social concepts and skills, and develop self-esteem; provide structure for activity; solidify group norms, attitudes, and values; and serve as a backdrop for individual and group competition.

■ Friendship patterns shift during childhood, with "best friends" appearing during middle childhood and group friendships becoming more common in later childhood. Although some childhood friendships last throughout life, most of them change for various reasons, such as moves or transfers, development of new interests, or simply growing apart.

■ A peer group is relatively stable and stays together, and its members interact regularly and share values.

■ In early middle childhood, peer groups are relatively informal. In later childhod, conformity to group norms becomes extremely important, and peer pressure becomes much more effective.

■ Each peer group has some members who are popular and some who are not. Peer acceptance is often related to an individual's overall adjustment—enthusiasm and active participation, ability to cooperate, and responsiveness to social overtures.

■ Popularity is affected by both extreme aggressiveness and extreme timidity.

■ Status within the group affects the way children feel about themselves. Rejected children report a higher degree of loneliness and have a greater tendency to blame unsatisfactory relationships on others.

■ Children sometimes conform excessively to group norms. They tend to have feelings of inferiority and low ego strength, and to be more dependent or anxious than other children.

■ Conformity is especially meaningful to children during late middle childhood. Preadolescents typically have a strong need to belong, to feel accepted, and to be part of a group.

■ Prejudice means having negative attitudes toward people because of their membership in a particular group. Discrimination means actually acting on the basis of prejudice.

■ Racial awareness, like gender awareness, begins to develop during the preschool years. However, understanding what group differences signify and what it means to be a member of a group requires social cognition, which in turn depends on cognitive development.

■ Racial awareness is an important issue during middle childhood. African-American parents are expected to teach their children the values of a society that holds them in low esteem, which produces conflict that affects the children's attitudes toward society.

■ Membership in a peer group tends to improve minority children's self-esteem and ease their adjustment during middle childhood.

KEY TERMS

industry versus inferiority
self-esteem
social cognition
social inference
social responsibility
social regulations

moral realism
moral relativism
moral absolutism
self-regulated behavior
coregulation
resilient children

reconstituted family
child abuse
peer group
prejudice
discrimination

USING WHAT YOU'VE LEARNED

For better or worse, the peer group becomes an important influence in children's lives during the elementary-school years. Sometimes peer group experiences are structured by adults, as in organized team sports, clubs, scouting, and group lessons like band practice or gymnastics. Other peer experiences take place away from adult supervision.

Think back to your own experiences with peers in elementary school. What were some of the most positive skills, values, and "lessons" you learned from friends and the peer group? Were there identifiable cir-

cumstances that fostered these benefits? Did adults hinder or help shape these benefits, or were adults simply irrelevant?

What negative experiences were associated with peer influences? What circumstances shaped those experiences? How might they have been avoided or prevented? Did any of your classmates have exceptionally negative interactions with their peers? Perhaps they were ridiculed or led into misbehavior. How might some of these experiences have been prevented?

SUGGESTED READINGS

BILLINGS, G. L. (1994). *The dreamkeepers: Successful teachers of African American children.* San Francisco: Jossey-Bass. A beautifully written, inspiring book about the lives and experiences of eight successful teachers who keep hope and discovery alive for their students.

DUNN, J. (1985). *Sisters and brothers.* Cambridge, MA: Harvard University Press. In a challenging review of the literature, Dunn examines the intensity of the sibling relationship as it develops throughout childhood and into adulthood.

GARBARINO, J., DUBROW, N., KOSTELNY, K., & PARDO, C. (1992). *Children in danger: Coping with the consequences of community violence.* San Francisco: Jossey-Bass, 1992. Several child development specialists examine the effects of growing up in the "war zones" of some of our inner cities like Washington, D.C., Chicago, and Los Angeles and suggest what can be done to help.

KAGEN, S., & WEISSBOURD, B. (Eds.) (1994). *Putting families first: America's family support movement and the challenge of change.* San Francisco: Jossey-Bass. A scholarly yet rich collection of articles on the evolution of family support practices and creative ideas for the future.

KOZOL, J. (1988). *Rachel and her children: Homeless families in America.* New York: Crown. A highly readable documentary of life on the edge of society.

MILLER, A. (1997). *Breaking down the wall of silence: The liberating experience of facing painful truth.* New York: Plume. The author explores the roots and results of child abuse, with a close look at why society often suppresses the truth and how the cycle can be broken.

SELIGMAN, M. E. P., RELVICH, K., JAYCOX, L., & GILLHAM, J. (1995). *The optimistic child.* Boston: Houghton Mifflin. Based on the remarkable Penn Depression Prevention Project, psychologist Martin Seligman and colleagues offer helpful guidelines for parents with regard to rearing mentally healthy, resilient children.

WALLERSTEIN, J. S., & KELLY, J. B. (1996). *Surviving the breakup: How children and parents cope with divorce.* New York: Basic Books. This intriguing book is based on a study of child and parent coping during the first 5 years after divorce. In particular, it shows how the child is affected as much by what happens afterward as by conditions in the family before the divorce.

Adolescence: Physical and Cognitive Development

CHAPTER OBJECTIVES

By the time you have finished this chapter, you should be able to do the following:

1. Discuss cultural factors that influence adolescent development.
2. Describe physical maturation during pubescence for males and females and the difficulty that many adolescents have in adjusting to their changing body image.
3. Analyze the attitudes, behaviors, and relationships that influence the adolescent's emerging sexuality and gender identity.
4. Identify the problems associated with teenage parenthood.
5. Describe the cognitive changes that occur during adolescence and explain how these changes affect the scope and content of adolescent thought.

In our culture, adolescence often extends over a period of a decade or more. Both the beginning and the end of adolescence are often ambiguous. Children frequently begin to act like adolescents before they start to change physically. And how can we define when an adolescent truly becomes an adult? Perhaps the best indicator of adulthood is emotional maturity rather than more obvious criteria such as completing an education, earning a living, marrying, or becoming a parent (Baldwin, 1986); however, emotional maturity is difficult to define.

Despite mixed opinions about its boundaries, there's complete agreement that the prolonged transitional period from childhood to adulthood is a modern phenomenon found mainly in developed nations. As discussed in Chapter 1, adolescence historically was a much shorter stage. This is still true in some less developed societies, where young people go through a symbolic ceremony, name change, or physical challenge at puberty. Such transition rituals are called **rites of passage.** An apprenticeship of a year or two may follow, and by age 16 or 17, the young person achieves full, unqualified adulthood. Such a relatively rapid transformation is possible because the skills necessary for adult life in less complex societies can be mastered without a lengthy education. Still, the need for some period of transition is recognized everywhere; no society demands that a child become an adult overnight, and no society fails to recognize the attainment of adulthood.

ADOLESCENCE TODAY

To understand adolescents and what adolescence is, it helps to be aware of the special cultural niche—the social environment—in which today's adolescents live. One factor is age segregation: In our society, adolescents interact mostly with other adolescents and much less with younger children or adults. This arrangement is largely the choice of the adolescents, perhaps because they don't want to be considered children by virtue of associating with them, or perhaps because they want to figure out things for themselves without the

rites of passage Symbolic events or rituals to mark life transitions, such as one from childhood to adult status.

constraints often imposed by adults. However, age-graded schools are a factor as well in industrialized nations (Elder, 1980; Elder & Casp, 1990).

Age segregation can have negative effects. Being separated from younger children deprives adolescents of opportunities to guide and tutor those who are less knowledgeable than themselves, the only exceptions being the limited periods they may spend caring for younger siblings or working as baby-sitters or camp counselors. Separation from the adult world means that adolescents miss opportunities to serve apprenticeships—to learn jobs by working alongside older, experienced people. Adolescents are separated for many hours every day from the major activities, customs, and responsibilities of society, except for the limited time they may spend helping their parents with chores or working at after-school jobs.

Prolonged economic dependence is another characteristic of adolescence. In a society like ours, adolescents often depend on financial support from their parents while they acquire the extended education necessary for jobs requiring technologically sophisticated skills. For those who don't obtain sufficient education, the low-level jobs available to them are usually neither interesting nor financially rewarding. Either way, adolescents often become frustrated and restless with their place in the world. Thus, some theorists view adolescence as a time of restricted rights and opportunities and rigidly prescribed roles (Farber, 1970). Others, like Erikson (see Chapter 11), take a more positive view, seeing adolescence as a time when individuals are allowed to explore and experiment with various roles before taking on the responsibilities of the adult world.

Adolescents are also affected by the events of the time in which they live. Every era has its wars, religious movements, and economic ups and downs. Adolescents are especially vulnerable to such crises. The state of the world affects adolescents much more than it does younger children. Adolescents and young adults fight in wars, participate in riots, and sustain movements for social reform. Adolescents and young adults support radical political and religious movements with their idealism. They lose their jobs during economic downturns and are hired during economic booms. Today's adolescents are affected not only by local and regional crises but also by crises in distant parts of the world.

Finally, the mass media have specific effects on adolescents. As we have seen repeatedly, theories of human development emphasize the importance of an emotionally supportive and responsive environment. Individuals of any age learn best when they can act on their environment, perceive the consequences of their actions, and have some power to cause change. But there is no way to alter events portrayed by television and other mass media. It seems that adolescents, with their rapidly developing physical and cognitive capacities, are particularly vulnerable to the passive role of mass-media consumer. They accept tragedy and brutality in a matter-of-fact way; perhaps they develop a thirst for excessive stimulation. Perhaps they model their behavior on the trite or bizarre events that they see portrayed. Perhaps they become absorbed with the often angry, socially deviant worlds portrayed by "heavy metal" and "rap" music in particular. The list of potentially harmful influences is endless.

According to Keniston, adolescents use introspection as a way of redefining and changing themselves in order to escape what they feel to be society's too constricting views of them.

---

1. What is meant by the term "adolescent cultural niche"?
2. Discuss how age segregation, prolonged economic dependence, global crises, and the mass media help determine the environment of adolescents?

REVIEW & APPLY

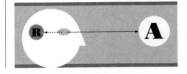

PHYSICAL DEVELOPMENT AND ADJUSTMENT

Physiologically, adolescence ranks with the fetal period and the first 2 years of life as times of extremely rapid biological change. Adolescents, however, have the pains and pleasures of observing the process; they watch themselves with alternating feelings of fascination, delight, and horror as their bodies change. Surprised, embarrassed, and uncertain, they constantly compare themselves with others and revise their self-image. Both sexes anxiously monitor their development—or lack of it—basing their judgments on both knowledge and misinformation. They compare themselves with the prevailing ideals for their sex; in fact, trying to reconcile differences between the real and the ideal is a major problem for adolescents. How parents react to their child's physical changes can also have a profound impact on the adolescent's adjustment.

PHYSICAL GROWTH AND CHANGE

The biological hallmarks of adolescence are a marked increase in the rate of growth, rapid development of the reproductive organs, and the appearance of secondary sex characteristics such as body hair, increases in body fat and muscle, and enlargement and maturation of sexual organs. Some changes are the same for boys and girls—increased size, improved strength and stamina—but most changes are sex-specific.

HORMONE CHANGES　　The physical changes that occur upon entry into adolescence are controlled by **hormones,** biochemical substances that are secreted into the bloodstream in minute amounts by internal organs called *endocrine glands*. Hormones that eventually trigger adolescent growth and change are present in trace amounts from the fetal period on, but their production greatly increases at about age $10\frac{1}{2}$ for girls and age 12–13 for boys. Then comes the **adolescent growth spurt,** a period of rapid growth in physical size and strength accompanied by changes in body proportions (Malina & Bouchard,

hormones　Biochemical secretions of the endocrine gland that is carried by the blood or other body fluids to a particular organ or tissue and acts as a stimulant or an accelerator.

adolescent growth spurt　The sudden increase in rate of growth that accompanies entrance into puberty.

The onset of puberty requires considerable adaption whether to a suddenly crackly voice, longer legs, or unfamiliar passions or feelings.

1990). Especially for girls, the growth spurt is a sign of entry into adolescence; the more noticeable changes associated with **puberty** (sexual maturity) follow the growth spurt by about a year (see Figure 10–1).

The growth spurt is typically accompanied by clumsiness and awkwardness as children learn to control their "new" bodies. Some of the clumsiness also stems from the fact that the growth spurt is not always symmetrical; one leg may temporarily be longer than the other, one hand larger than the other. As you might imagine, the growth spurt is also accompanied by a ravenous appetite as the body seeks the nutrients necessary for such rapid growth. Another change is an increase in the size and activity of *sebaceous* (oil-producing) glands in the skin, which can cause the teenager's face to break out in acne. A new kind of sweat gland also develops in the skin, resulting in a stronger body odor.

Subtle changes preceding the growth spurt may include an increase in body fat; some preadolescents become noticeably pudgy. In both males and females, fat is deposited in the breast area; this deposit is permanent in females but temporary in males. As the growth spurt kicks in, boys generally lose most of the extra fat, whereas girls tend to keep it.

Both sexes display wide variability in the timing of the hormone changes associated with entry into adolescence. As discussed later in this section, there are "early maturers" and "late maturers," and the timing of maturation can have pronounced effects on adjustment. "Male" and "female" hormones are present in members of both sexes, but males begin to produce more of the hormones called *androgens*, of which the most important is *testosterone*, and females begin to produce more of the hormones *estrogen* and *progesterone* (Tanner, 1978).

Each hormone influences a specific set of targets or *receptors*. For example, the secretion of testosterone causes the penis to grow, the shoulders to broaden, and hair to grow in the genital area and on the face. Similarly,

puberty   The attainment of sexual maturity in males and females.

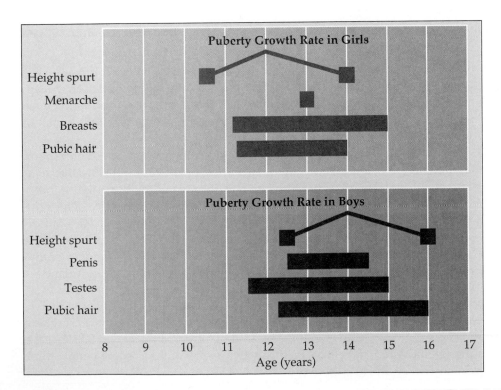

FIGURE 10–1   GROWTH RATES AND SEXUAL DEVELOPMENT DURING PUBERTY

The peak in the line labeled "height spurt" represents the point of most rapid growth. The bars below represent the average beginning and end of the events of puberty.

IN THEORY, IN FACT

ARE ADOLESCENTS VICTIMS OF RAGING HORMONES?

In most Western cultures, adolescence is marked by major changes in behavior and appearance. Historically, many of these changes have been described as negative and attributed to biological factors—especially hormones. Adolescents have been portrayed as victims of their own "raging hormones." But is this a realistic portrayal?

From a physiological perspective, hormones act on the brain in two ways. First, sex hormones can influence personality and behavior through their early influence on brain development. Such effects are permanent and therefore are not affected by changes in hormone levels during puberty. Second, hormones may activate specific behaviors through their effects on the nervous system. These effects tend to be immediate or only slightly delayed. Physical and sexual maturation result from interactions among the hormonal levels, health factors, and genetic makeup of the developing person.

Researchers have found only a very limited *direct* relationship between hormone levels during adolescence and the following behaviors (Buchanan et al., 1992):

> Moodiness
> Depression
> Restlessness and lack
>   of concentration
> Irritability
> Impulsiveness
> Anxiety
> Aggression and behavior problems

It should also be recognized that not all adolescents exhibit dramatic changes in these behaviors, even though they all experience increases in hormone levels. Therefore, it is likely that other factors are involved. Among these are changing roles, social or cultural expectations, specific situations in the home or school, and even the influence of the media.

If there are problems in the family during early and middle childhood, for example, they may become worse during adolescence. Adolescents in dysfunctional families may have problems with inappropriate sexual behavior, running away, aggression, and drug use. In contrast, if parent-child relationships are good before adolescence, they generally remain good throughout adolescence, and the parents continue to have a positive influence on their children (Buchanan et al., 1992).

This is not to say that hormones have no effect on behavior. But their effect is often determined by psychological or social factors. For example, in one study, testosterone level was found to be a strong predictor of sexual activity among 12- to 16-year-old girls (Udry, 1988). But its effect was reduced or eliminated by having a father in the home or by the girl's participation in sports. Fathers who are present tend to raise girls' self-esteem in ways that lessen their need to be sexually active. In conjunction with the mother's guidance and role modeling, fathers are also more likely to create situations that stress relationships rather than sexual behavior alone. In other words, environmental factors override hormonal effects on behavior. Researchers therefore conclude that the notion that raging hormones are a direct cause of adolescent behaviors is a myth.

---

estrogen causes the uterus and breasts to grow and the hips to broaden. Receptor cells are sensitive to minute quantities of the appropriate hormones, even though the hormones are present only in amounts comparable to a pinch of sugar dissolved in a swimming pool (Tanner, 1978).

The endocrine glands secrete a delicate and complex balance of hormones. Maintaining the balance is the job of two areas of the brain: the *hypothalamus* and the *pituitary gland*. The hypothalamus is the part of the brain that initiates growth and eventual reproductive capability during adolescence. The pituitary, located on the underside of the brain, produces several varieties of hormones, including *growth hormone*, which controls the overall growth of the body, as well as some secondary *trophic* hormones. Trophic hormones stimulate and regulate the functioning of other glands, including the sex glands—the testes in the male and the ovaries in the female. In males, the sex glands secrete androgens and produce sperm; in females, the sex glands secrete estrogens and regulate ovulation. Hormones secreted by the pituitary gland and the sex glands have emotional as well as physical effects on adolescents, although the emotional effects aren't always as profound as some people think (see "In Theory, In Fact," above.)

PUBERTY

As noted earlier, puberty refers to the attainment of sexual maturity and the ability to have children. For females, the approach of puberty is marked by the first menstrual period, or **menarche,** although contrary to popular belief, the first ovulation may occur a year or more later (Tanner, 1978). For boys, puberty is marked by the first emission of semen containing viable sperm cells.

In earlier times, puberty occurred later than it does now. In the 1880s, for example, the average age at puberty was $15\frac{1}{2}$ for girls (Frisch, 1988), and the social transition from youth to adulthood followed closely behind. In the United States and other industrialized nations today, there is usually an interval of several years between the attainment of biological maturity and the social transition to adulthood.

SEXUAL MATURATION IN MALES   In males the first indication of puberty is accelerating growth of the testes and scrotum. The penis undergoes a similar acceleration in growth about 1 year later. In the meantime, pubic hair begins to appear but does not mature completely until after genital development is complete. During this period there are also increases in the size of the heart and lungs. Because of the presence of testosterone, boys develop more red blood cells than girls. The extensive production of red blood cells may be one factor in the superior strength and athletic ability of adolescent boys. The first emission of semen may take place as early as age 11 or as late as age 16. A boy's first ejaculation usually occurs during the growth spurt and may be a result of masturbation or come in a "wet dream." These first emissions generally do not contain fertile sperm (Money, 1980).

Characteristically, descriptions of adolescent boys include their awkwardly cracking voices. The actual voice change takes place relatively late in the sequence of pubertal changes, however, and in many boys it occurs too gradually to constitute a developmental milestone (Tanner, 1978).

SEXUAL MATURATION IN FEMALES   In girls the "breast buds" are usually the first signal that changes leading to puberty are under way. The uterus and vagina also begin to develop, accompanied by enlargement of the labia and clitoris.

Menarche, which is the most dramatic and symbolic sign of a girl's changing status, actually occurs late in the sequence, after the peak of the growth spurt. It may occur as early as age $9\frac{1}{2}$ or as late as age $16\frac{1}{2}$; the average age at menarche for American girls is about $12\frac{1}{2}$. In other parts of the world, menarche occurs considerably later: The average Czechoslovakian girl has her first period at age 14; among the Kikuyu of Kenya, the average age is 16; and for the Bindi of New Guinea, it is 18 (Powers et al., 1989). Menarche typically occurs when a girl is nearing her adult height and has stored some body fat. For a girl of average height, menarche typically occurs when she weighs about 100 pounds (Frisch, 1988).

The first few menstrual cycles vary greatly from one girl to another; they also tend to vary from one month to another. In many cases the early cycles are irregular and *anovulatory*—that is, an ovum is not produced (Tanner, 1978). But it is unwise for a young teenage girl to assume that she is infertile. (We will return to the subject of teenage pregnancy later in the chapter.)

Menstruation is accompanied by menstrual "cramping" in nearly half of all teenage girls (Wildholm, 1985). Premenstrual tension is common and is often accompanied by irritability, depression, crying, bloating, and breast tenderness.

One reason girls often feel more mature than boys their own age is that the female growth spurt during puberty occurs about 2 years before the male growth spurt.

menarche   The time of the first menstrual period.

STUDY CHART ‣ TYPICAL PHYSICAL CHANGES IN ADOLESCENCE

CHANGES IN GIRLS

- Breast development
- Growth of pubic hair
- Growth of underarm hair
- Body growth
- Menarche
- Increased output of oil and sweat-producing glands

CHANGES IN BOYS

- Growth of testes and scrotal sac
- Growth of pubic hair
- Growth of facial and underarm hair
- Body growth
- Growth of penis
- Change in voice
- First ejaculation of semen
- Increased output of oil- and sweat-producing glands

BODY IMAGE AND ADJUSTMENT

As mentioned earlier, adolescents continually appraise their changing bodies. Are they the right shape and size? Are they coordinated or clumsy? How do they compare with the ideals portrayed by their culture?

Adolescents belong to what sociologists call a *marginal* group—a group between cultures or on the fringe of a dominant culture—that typically exhibits an intensified need to conform. Adolescents can be extremely intolerant of deviation, whether in body type (being too fat or too thin) or timing (maturing late or early). The mass media contribute to this intolerance by presenting stereotypical images of attractive, exuberant youths who glide through adolescence without pimples, braces, awkwardness, or weight problems. Because many adolescents are extremely sensitive about their appearance, discrepancies between their less-than-perfect self-image and the glowing ideals that they see in the media often foster considerable anxiety and self-doubt.

CONCERN WITH BODY IMAGE During middle childhood, children become keenly aware of different body types and ideals and gain a fairly clear idea of their own body type, proportions, and skills. In adolescence, body type receives even closer scrutiny. Some young people subject themselves to intense dieting, whereas others engage in rigorous regimens of physical fitness and strength training. For boys, the primary concern is with physical strength (Lerner, Orlos, & Knapp, 1976). Height and muscles are most important. Girls, in contrast, worry about being too fat or too tall. They focus on weight largely because of their concern with social acceptance. Thus, many normal, even lean, adolescent girls consider themselves overweight. When carried to an extreme, such concerns can lead to eating disorders, particularly *anorexia nervosa* and *bulimia nervosa*, which are discussed in "A Matter for Debate," on facing page.

Height, weight, and complexion are the major sources of concern for 10th graders of both sexes. About two-thirds wish for one or more physical changes in themselves (Peterson & Taylor, 1980). Such self-consciousness diminishes in late adolescence. One longitudinal study found that satisfaction with one's own body image is lowest for girls at age 13 and for boys at age 15; then it rises steadily. At every age from 11 to 18, however, it is lower for girls than for boys (Rauste-von Wright, 1989). For adolescent girls, having a positive body image

A MATTER FOR DEBATE

ANOREXIA NERVOSA AND BULIMIA NERVOSA

Victims of the disorder known as anorexia nervosa can literally starve themselves to death. Obsessed by thoughts of food and an unattainable image of "perfect" thinness, they refuse to eat and may also engage in behaviors such as purging and abusing laxatives. Even though they may feel that they are becoming increasingly attractive, they actually become emaciated and physically ill. In the United States today, there are more than 100,000 anorexics (ten times as many as there were two decades ago); 10,000 to 15,000 will die because of medical problems associated with the disorder.

Almost all anorexics are women under age 25. Although the disorder has no single identifiable cause, many anorexics are apparently victims of our culture's obsession with thinness and its emphasis on feminine attractiveness (Nagel & Jones, 1992). Constantly getting the message that thin is beautiful and fat is repugnant, they fear that the curves and added weight that come with adolescence will make them unattractive and undesirable. Family pressures to remain thin or be attractive

may make matters worse. A father who makes a habit of teasing his daughter about putting on a few extra pounds may increase her negative self-concept and contribute to the disorder.

To date there is no cure for anorexia nervosa and no generally accepted method of treatment. Some therapists take a behaviorist approach, rewarding their patients with praise and approval when they eat. Others attempt to analyze childhood problems that they believe may cause the disease. Still others focus on the patient's feelings and attitudes about food and eating. However, regardless of the theoretical orientation of the therapist, hospitalization with intravenous feeding may be required to reverse the life-threatening weight loss that anorexics often experience. The goal of all therapy with anorexics is to help them learn to separate their feelings about food from their feelings about themselves and to develop a sense of self-worth and autonomy.

Bulimia nervosa has some things in common with anorexia nervosa, but it is classified as a separate disorder in the DSM-IV. A major difference is that bulimics typically don't lose weight and actually are often slightly overweight. Although they are terribly anxious

about weighing too much, bulimics, like anorexics, have a periodic uncontrollable urge to eat, especially sweets and salty snacks. Bulimics on a "binge" consume huge quantities of carbohydrates in a very short time, usually an hour or two. They then feel despondent and out of control. To compensate, they purge or take laxatives.

Like anorexics, most bulimics are female. Bulimia usually afflicts people in late adolescence (in contrast, many anorexics are in early or mid-adolescence). Some researchers estimate that about 20% of college-age women have engaged in bulimic eating patterns (Muuss, 1986).

Although bulimia does not have fatal consequences, it is highly self-destructive and requires treatment. Bulimics develop gastrointestinal disorders, ulceration of the throat and mouth caused by frequent passage of stomach acids, and sometimes hernias caused by purging. Fortunately, bulimics tend to be more responsive to treatment than anorexics. Antidepressant drugs are often helpful in treating this disorder—even among patients who show no signs of depression—suggesting that a biochemical abnormality may be involved (Walsh, 1988).

---

is positively correlated with whether their mothers have a positive body image (Usmiani & Daniluk, 1997).

There are some interesting differences in the changes that adolescent girls and boys would like to make in their bodies. Girls want specific changes: "I would make my ears lie back," or "I would make my forehead lower." Boys are less precise. A boy might say this: "I'd make myself look handsome and not fat. I'd change my whole physical appearance so that I'd be handsome and with a good build." Both sexes worry about their skin, however: Almost half of all adolescents voice concerns about pimples and blackheads.

EARLY AND LATE MATURERS The effects of timing of maturation have engrossed researchers almost as much as adolescence itself. Although many teenagers have a fairly positive attitude toward their own rate of maturation (Pelletz, 1995), ill-timed maturation can be a problem. This situation is especially true for late-maturing boys. Because girls mature, on the average, 2 years earlier than boys, the late-maturing boy is last of all to begin the growth spurt

With regard to body image, boys tend to be concerned more with exercises to increase physical strength, girls more with exercises that help control weight.

and reach puberty. Thus, because he is smaller and less muscular than his age-mates, he is at a disadvantage in most sports and in many social situations. Other children and adults tend to treat a late maturer as though he were a younger child, and the late maturer has lower social status among his peers and is perceived as less competent by adults (Brackbill & Nevill, 1981).

Sometimes this perception becomes a self-fulfilling prophecy, and the boy reacts with childish dependence and immature behavior. In other cases, the boy may overcompensate and become highly aggressive. In contrast, early-maturing boys tend to gain social and athletic advantages among their peers and enjoy a positive self-fulfilling prophecy. From middle childhood on, early-maturing boys are likely to be the leaders of their peer groups (Weisfeld & Billings, 1988).

Early maturation is a mixed blessing for girls. Late maturation can be advantageous in that the girl matures at about the same time as most of her male peers. She is therefore in a better position to share their interests and privileges. She is more popular with her peers than early-maturing girls. On the other hand, early-maturing girls are taller and more developed than all their peers, both male and female. One effect is that they have fewer opportunities to discuss their physical and emotional changes with friends. Another is that they are significantly more likely to experience psychological distress over their changes (Ge, Conger, & Elder, 1996). But there are compensations. Early-maturing girls frequently feel more attractive, are more popular with older boys, and are more likely to date than their late-maturing age-mates (Blyth et al., 1981).

GIRLS' REACTIONS TO MENARCHE   Menarche is a unique event, a milestone on the path to physical maturity. It occurs without warning and is heralded by a bloody vaginal discharge. In some parts of the world, it has major religious, cultural, or economic significance, and it may trigger elaborate rites and ceremonies. Although there is no such drama in the United States, menarche still holds considerable significance for American girls and their parents (Greif & Ulman, 1982).

Studies of adolescent girls confirm that menarche is a memorable event. Only those girls who were not informed about it in advance by their parents or who experienced it very early describe it as traumatic. Some girls who receive information about menarche from men react negatively to the experience. But most girls are well informed by their mothers or female relatives about what to expect, and they report a positive reaction to menarche—a feeling that they are coming of age (Ruble & Brooks-Gunn, 1982).

1. List the major changes that take place in males and females during adolescence.
2. Give examples of how cultural ideals affect body image and adjustment during adolescence.
3. Discuss advantages and disadvantages of early and late maturation.

REVIEW & APPLY

SEXUAL ATTITUDES AND BEHAVIOR

During middle and late childhood, children associate mostly in same-sex peer groups, but in a sexually neutral way. At puberty, however, the biological changes experienced by adolescents are accompanied by interest in members of the opposite sex and a need to integrate sexuality with other aspects of the personality. During adolescence, therefore, young people begin forming relationships in which sex plays a central role.

Adolescents' evolving gender identity includes changing attitudes, behaviors, and relationships. In some unfortunate cases, how adolescents feel about their bodies is influenced by incidents of sexual abuse. In other cases, adolescents sense that they are different from their peers because of homosexual feelings or experiences.

THE SEXUAL "REVOLUTION"
Historical changes in social attitudes are clearly visible in the way people respond to sexuality. In large part, adolescents view themselves in terms of the cultural norms of the time and place in which they live. Their sexual behavior varies accordingly.

Before the mid-1960s, most young people felt that premarital sex was immoral, although peer pressure often impelled older adolescent boys to gain sexual experience before marriage. Girls, in contrast, were under pressure to remain virginal until marriage. By the late 1960s and early 1970s, sexual attitudes had changed considerably, partly because of the development and widespread distribution of birth control pills, partly because of the "free love" movement that accompanied protests against the Vietnam War and against "the establishment" in general. In a study of adolescent sexual attitudes during that era (Sorensen, 1973), the majority of adolescents did not think of premarital sex as inherently right or wrong but instead judged it on the basis of the relationship between the participants. A majority rejected the traditional double standard

The biological changes that occur during adolescence lead to the development of a sexual identity.

that gave sexual freedom to boys but not to girls. Almost 70% agreed that two people should not have to marry in order to have sex or live together. A surprising 50% approved of homosexuality between consenting individuals, although 80% stated that they had never engaged in homosexual acts and would never want to. In all, their attitudes were quite different from those of their parents.

By the late 1970s, the sexual "revolution" was in full swing. In 1979, Catherine Chilman reviewed the findings of numerous studies and reported an increasing trend toward sexual liberalization, reflected both by an increase in sexual activity among adolescents and by a change in societal attitudes. Society had become more accepting of a wide range of sexual activities, including masturbation, homosexuality, and unmarried couples living together (Dreyer, 1982). In another study (Hass, 1979), 83% of the boys and 64% of the girls interviewed approved of premarital intercourse; 56% of the boys and 44% of the girls reported having actually had intercourse.

Note that there was little difference between the responses of boys and girls. This finding is consistent with the continuing decline in the double standard. The sexual revolution affected girls' behavior much more than it did that of boys: Even in the 1940s, 1950s, and 1960s, between one-third and two-thirds of teenage boys had already lost their virginity—a statistic comparable to that reported in the 1970s. In contrast, the proportion of 16-year-old girls who had lost their virginity rose from 7% in the 1940s to 33% in 1971 and 44% in 1982 (Brooks-Gunn & Furstenberg, 1989).

The sexual revolution was accompanied by a variety of problems. Large numbers of adolescents were having sexual intercourse without using birth control. As a result, the rate of pregnancy among teenage girls tripled between 1940 and 1975. Another problem was the spread of sexually transmitted diseases (STDs)—first syphilis, gonorrhea, and genital herpes, and later HIV/AIDS. Although AIDS is still rare among adolescents (because it often takes years for symptoms to appear and is undetected in many of them), teenagers have a high rate of other STDs (Ehrhardt, 1992). In the United States, for example, one in seven teenagers has an STD (Quadrel et al., 1993). In addition, although few teenagers suffer from full-blown AIDS, an increasing number are HIV positive. Experts believe that many of the approximately 30,000 young adults age 20 to 29 diagnosed with AIDS in 1996 probably were infected with the virus while they were adolescents (U.S. Census Bureau, 1997; Millstein, 1990).

The sexual revolution began to decline in the 1980s. Young people became more cautious about sexual activity, and monogamy—or at least "serial" monogamy—became fashionable again. During the 1980s, when adolescents were asked what they thought of the sexual attitudes of the 1960s and 1970s, a sizable proportion viewed them as irresponsible. College students were also more likely to consider sexual promiscuity immoral (Leo, 1984; Robinson & Jedlicka, 1982).

The late 1980s saw a continuation of the trend toward more conservative attitudes about sexual matters (Murstein et al., 1989). Although young people still considered sex an essential part of romance, they were generally not in favor of casual sex (Abler & Sedlacek, 1989). Attitudes toward homosexuality also turned negative again (Williams & Jacoby, 1989). The increase in *homophobia* (fear or dislike of homosexuals) seems to be related to fear of sexually transmitted diseases, especially AIDS—even though AIDS is now spread primarily through heterosexual contact.

Part of The Annual Gay Pride Parade down New York City's Fifth Avenue.

HOMOSEXUALITY

Many young people have one or more homosexual experiences, often in early adolescence (Dreyer, 1982). Such isolated experiences do not determine future sexual orientation, however. In nearly all societies and ethnic groups, approximately 5% of adults are actively homosexual, and about that many are bisexual. Many famous personages have been homosexual, including Aristotle, Alexander the Great, Leonardo da Vinci, Michelangelo, Rock Hudson, Oscar Wilde, Tennessee Williams, Greg Luganis, Gertrude Stein, Willa Cather, and Martina Navratilova (Rubin, 1994).

Although theorists disagree about the causes of homosexuality, most believe that sexual preference is not something people choose. Is homosexuality primarily biological in origin? In a recent review of the literature from a developmental perspective, Charlotte Patterson (1995) cites evidence for both environmental and biological causes. On the environment side, historical and cultural influences may be involved. Add to Patterson's view the possibility that homosexuality can result from sexual abuse, which yields an extreme aversion to contact with the opposite sex—thus the person may turn toward same-sex relationships for lack of an alternative.   As Patterson points out, however, the recent focus of research has been on biological factors. Some children, for example, realize that they're "different" very early and engage in cross-gender behavior that turns out to be a good predictor of homosexuality later in life. More to the point, as cited in a review by Robert Finn (1996), some studies have shown relatively high correspondence between identical twins with regard to homosexuality: Among pairs of male twins, in 52% of the cases, if one twin is gay, the other is also; for pairs of female twins, the figure is 48%. Finn also cites research on possible genetic material on the X chromosome that may be related to homosexuality. Many questions remain to be answered, however, and not all researchers agree that such markers exist.

Regardless of the origins of homosexuality, gender identity can be intensely stressful for a gay or lesbian adolescent. Homosexuals represent a small minority, and peer pressure to conform is extremely strong during adolescence. Often they receive little or no support from parents or peers and have few acceptable role models. As a result, homosexual teenagers may feel unbearably alone with their feelings and may choose to stay "in the closet." Those who do "come out" often experience verbal and even physical abuse (Hershberger & D'Augelli, 1995). Their self-esteem plummets, and depression is common. It is therefore not surprising that perhaps 30% of teenagers who attempt suicide are homosexual.

Since the early 1980s, the spread of AIDS has made it even more difficult for gay teenagers to come to grips with their homosexuality and find acceptance in their community. Data from the Centers for Disease Control show that almost one-third of male adolescents infected with the AIDS virus contracted the disease through homosexual activity (Millstein, 1990). Thus, adolescents who are grappling with their sexual identity realize that their decision may have life-threatening implications. They also realize that AIDS has made them an even greater target for "gay bashing."

MASTURBATION

In adolescence, girls spend more time fantasizing about romance as an outlet for their sexual impulses; boys are more likely to masturbate. But masturbation and fantasizing are common in both sexes. According to one study, about one-half of adolescent girls and three-quarters of boys masturbate (Hass, 1979). Social-class differences play a part too, or at least they did in the past. Enjoyment of fantasies during masturbation was reportedly more common in middle-class males, whereas guilt over the "unmanliness" of masturbation was of greater concern to working-class males. These differences are gradually disappearing, however (Dreyer, 1982), as are male-female differences in attitudes toward masturbation.

GENDER DIFFERENCES IN SEXUAL EXPRESSION

Class differences in sexual behavior have traditionally been less significant among females, partly because of the limited roles that were available to women in the past. Girls were discouraged from overt sexuality; instead, they received early training in enhancing their desirability in subtle ways, evaluating potential mates, and "holding out" until marriage. Dating and courtship then provided the setting in which members of each sex learned from each other about desires and expectations. In our society, femininity formerly connoted passivity, nurturance, and ability to fit in. Girls had to remain flexible enough to conform to the value systems of potential spouses. But now girls are encouraged to acquire skills that they can employ to support themselves regardless of their future marital plans, and expression of sexuality by members of both sexes is encouraged by the media.

The expression of sexuality for both sexes always depends on the society's prevailing norms; it changes as these norms change. Some societies reserve sexuality exclusively for procreation. Others view restrictions on sex as silly or even as a crime against nature.

FACTORS INFLUENCING EARLY SEXUAL RELATIONSHIPS

Although societal attitudes toward sexual behavior have become more conservative, teenagers continue to be highly active sexually. The age at which they first have sex still varies by gender; it also varies by racial and subcultural group. In 1990 the Centers for Disease Control reported the results of a

Despite the more conservative attitudes of society toward sex, adolescents are still very active sexually.

national survey of high school students. The median age of first intercourse was 16.1 years for boys and 16.9 years for girls (Ehrhardt, 1992). Among whites, over 60% of boys and just under 60% of girls have had intercourse by age 18. Sexual activity begins at an earlier age for black men and women, also for Hispanic men—but later for Hispanic women (Michael et al., 1994) (see Figure 10–2).

Boys start having sex earlier and tend to have different attitudes toward it than girls do. For boys, sexual initiation is more likely to be with a casual partner than with a "steady," and they receive more social approval for losing their virginity than do girls. Boys are also more likely to seek another sexual experience soon afterward, more likely to talk about their activity, and less likely to feel guilty about it than girls are (Zelnick & Kantner, 1977).

Several factors influence adolescent sexual behavior, including education, psychological makeup, family relationships, and biological maturation (Chilman, 1979). Let's consider these factors in more detail.

EDUCATION   Education is related to sexual behavior partly because those who attain higher levels of education more frequently come from the middle and upper middle classes, which tend to have more conservative views about sex. This tendency is especially true for adolescents who emphasize careers, intellectual pursuits, and educational goals. Another factor is the relationship between sexual behavior and academic success in high school: Good students are less likely to initiate sexual activity at an early age (Miller & Sneesby, 1988). Perhaps adolescents who are failing academically turn to sexual activity (and drugs, which lower inhibitions about sex) as a way of gratifying their needs. In the past, this tendency may have been more true for girls than for boys because girls had fewer opportunities for achievement in nonacademic areas such as sports. With the current emphasis on opportunities for women in all aspects of society, including sports, this situation may be changing.

Education is also the way most teenagers learn about sex nowadays; in the past they generally learned about it from their parents or peers. What children

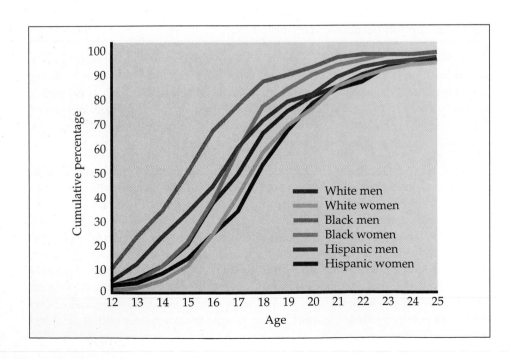

FIGURE 10–2   AGE AND FIRST SEXUAL INTERCOURSE

Source: Data from Michael et al., 1994.
Sex in America (Boston: Little, Brown).

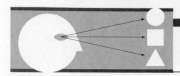

EYE ON DIVERSITY

TEACHING SEX IN JAPAN AND SCANDINAVIA

How is sex taught to children and teenagers in conservative societies like Japan and in liberal societies like Scandinavia? The differences are striking.

In Japan, classroom sex education begins at age 10 or 11. The approach is limited and strictly scientific: Children learn about the male and female reproductive systems, including menstruation and ejaculation. If the curriculum is so limited, from whom do Japanese children and teenagers learn about sex? Evidently not from their parents, who tend to avoid the subject. Says one mother of two daughters, "We never discuss sex at home. I feel we should, but . . . I do remember giving my children a book on where babies come from." Because of traditional parents' embarrassment about sex, Japanese teenagers learn the important details mostly from their friends and what they read. One consequence is that

only 4% of Japanese girls and 6% of Japanese boys have lost their virginity by the age of 15. (In contrast, about 25% of American girls and 33% of American boys are no longer virgins by age 15.)

There are other explanations for the relative chastity of Japanese youth. Hisayo Arai of the Japanese Association for Sex Education explains that it is "partly because [teenagers are] so busy with their college entrance examinations. Also, people are always keeping a watch on each other." The strictness applies especially to girls, who are supposed to wait until marriage to have sex. Finally, the school they attend influences teenagers' sexuality. In some Japanese schools, even dating is prohibited.

In contrast, the Scandinavian countries are far more sexually permissive. Says Stefan Laack of the Swedish Association for Sex Information, "There is not much talk about sex between teenagers, yet it is widely accepted that

they sleep with their boyfriends or girlfriends."

One expression of this cultural freedom is that Scandinavian children and teenagers learn about sex not in special classes but throughout the curriculum. For example, Danish students discuss sexuality in any class in which it is relevant. In Sweden, starting at the age of 7, children learn about the physical aspects of sex in biology class and about gender roles in history class. Every 15-year-old student in Finland receives a sex packet containing a condom, a cartoon love story, and an informational pamphlet.

Has this liberal view of sex caused Scandinavian teenagers to be more sexually promiscuous than their Japanese or American peers? Apparently not. In Sweden, teenagers still typically lose their virginity at about age 17, just as they did before such education existed.

Source: Toufexis, A. (1993).

learn about sex in school depends to a large extent on their culture, as discussed in "Eye on Diversity," above.

PSYCHOLOGICAL FACTORS To some extent the psychological factors associated with early sexual experience are different for males and females. Sexually experienced male adolescents tend to have relatively high self-esteem, whereas sexually experienced females tend to have low self-esteem. However, for both sexes, early sexual activity is associated with other problem behaviors, such as drug use and delinquency (Donovan et al., 1988).

FAMILY RELATIONSHIPS A number of studies have found that parent-child interactions influence adolescent sexual behavior. Both overly restrictive parenting and overly permissive parenting are associated with earlier sexual activity in adolescents; moderate restrictiveness tends to work best with this age group (Miller et al., 1986). Another significant factor is communication between parents and offspring: Adolescents who are sexually active are more likely to report poor communication with their parents. In contrast, "quality" parent-child communication has been found to be correlated with adolescent sexual abstinence (Miller et al., 1998). Good parent-child relationships, however, will not necessarily prevent young people from experimenting with sex (Chilman, 1979).

Recent research suggests that the changing structure of the American family also influences adolescent sexual behavior. The higher divorce rate and the larger number of single-parent families are social realities that affect teenage sexual activity. In general, male and female teenagers from two-parent families have less and later sexual experience than those from single-parent families (Young et al., 1991).

BIOLOGICAL FACTORS According to Chilman, the biological factors that influence early sexual behavior constitute an important area of research that has frequently been overlooked. For example, adolescents may become sexually active earlier today than in the past because of the decline in the average age at which puberty occurs. This is consistent with the observation that individuals who mature early are likely to engage in sexual activity at a younger age than those who mature late (Miller et al., 1998). There's a major exception, however: Although boys reach sexual maturity about 2 years later than girls, they lose their virginity about a year earlier (Brooks-Gunn & Furstenberg, 1989).

SEXUAL ABUSE OF ADOLESCENTS

Unfortunately, for a significant number of children and adolescents at all socioeconomic levels, their first sexual experiences occur without their consent; they are sexually abused or exploited. Reported cases probably represent only a small fraction of the actual number of such incidents. In one study, a large random sample of women was interviewed about their sexual experiences in childhood and adolescence (Russell, 1983). The researchers found that 32% had been sexually abused at least once before age 18, and 20% had been victimized before age 14. Fewer than 5% of these women had reported the incidents to the police, although nowadays reporting is much more likely.

The impact of sexual abuse on children depends on a variety of factors, including the nature of the abusive act, the age and vulnerability of the victim, whether the offender is a stranger or a family member, whether there was a single incident or an ongoing pattern of abuse, and the reactions of adults in whom the child confides (Kempe & Kempe, 1984). The impact on the individual's identity and self-esteem often lasts throughout life.

The most common form of sexual abuse occurs between a young adolescent girl and an adult male relative or family friend (Finkelhor, 1984). A stepfather or the mother's boyfriend is more likely to be the culprit than the girl's natural father (Wolfe et al., 1988). The abuse often continues and becomes a secret between the abuser and the victim. Sometimes the victim's mother is unaware that the abuse is taking place. At other times, the mother steadfastly refuses to believe her child's claims, or if she does believe them, does nothing to protect the child against further abuse.

Sexually abused adolescent girls often feel guilty and ashamed, yet powerless to avoid the abuse. They may feel isolated and alienated from their peers and distrustful of adults in general. Some have academic problems, others have physical complaints, and still others become sexually promiscuous. Some girls turn their anger inward, becoming depressed or contemplating suicide (Brassard & McNeill, 1987). Some inappropriately blame themselves for having "enticed" the abuser.

In general, these girls' attitudes about intimate relationships become distorted. As adults, they have difficulty establishing normal sexual relationships; they may even have difficulty establishing normal relationships with their own children. Many have distorted views of sexuality and are actually more likely than nonabused women to marry abusive men. When abuse begins in their own family—say, between their husband and daughter—they may deny the problem or feel powerless to do anything about it (Kempe & Kempe, 1984).

Sexual abuse also involves young boys, mainly in homosexual encounters. The abusers usually are not family members, and the abuse generally takes place outside the home. Molestation is especially traumatic for boys; they feel ashamed that they were forced to engage in homosexual acts and were powerless to defend themselves against their attacker (Bolton, 1989).

TEENAGE PARENTS

Although the overall proportion of babies born to U.S. adolescents has declined since the 1960s, the proportion born to adolescents outside of marriage has increased. Every day several thousand teenage girls in the United States become pregnant. The number of babies born to unmarried American teenagers quadrupled between 1940 and 1985 (National Center for Health Statistics, 1987). More than 1 million adolescent girls become pregnant each year; over 65% of them are not married. About 50% of the pregnancies end in miscarriage or abortion; the other 50% result in delivery (Sonenstein, 1987; Brooks-Gunn & Furstenberg, 1989; Alan Guttmacher Institute, 1994). Table 10–1 contrasts the intention and outcome of pregnancy for all women of reproductive age with the intention and outcome for 15- to 19-year-olds. Older teenagers in particular are significantly more likely to experience unintended pregnancies, miscarriages, and abortions.

WHY TEENAGERS BECOME PREGNANT   There is a great deal of sexual activity among American teenagers. Teenagers in most Western European countries are equally active, but the pregnancy rates in those countries are much lower (Hechtman, 1989; Coley & Chase-Lansdale, 1998). Why so many American girls become pregnant is a major cause of concern. One basic factor seems to be that although American adolescents are not more sexually active than those of other nations, they are less likely to use contraception. Another likely factor is that there is less social stigma attached to illegitimate births than there

It is generally difficult for teenage mothers to care for the needs of an infant as well as their own developmental needs.

TABLE 10–1   ESTIMATED PREGNANCY RATES FOR WOMEN OF REPRODUCTIVE AGE BY PREGNANCY INTENTION AND OUTCOME (PER 1000 WOMEN)

PREGNANCY INTENTION AND OUTCOME	WOMEN AGED 15–44	WOMEN AGED 15–19
Total	109.2	126.8
Births	66.3	64.0
Abortions	26.9	45.5
Miscarriages	16.0	17.3
Intended	47.8	24.7
Births	39.9	20.5
Miscarriages	8.0	4.1
Unintended	61.3	102.1
Births	26.5	43.4
Abortions	26.9	45.5
Miscarriages	8.0	13.2

Source: *Statistical Handbook on the American Family* (1992).

was in the past. Instead of expelling pregnant teenagers from high school, many school systems have special programs to help young mothers complete their education. In some subcultural groups, an unmarried mother may receive support both from her family and from the father of her child (Chilman, 1979). Finally, some teenage girls wish to have and keep children because of their own need to be loved. These young mothers have usually been deprived of affection and expect their children to supply what they have missed (Fosburgh, 1977).

About 3 out of 10 sexually active adolescents do not use contraceptives (Fielding & Williams, 1991). The most common reasons are ignorance about the facts of reproduction, unwillingness to accept responsibility for sexual activity, or a generally passive attitude toward life (Dreyer, 1982)—coupled with a belief that "it can't happen to me." The double standard continues to play a role too: Both sexes tend to view the male as the sexual initiator and the female as the one who is responsible for setting limits on sexual activity. At the same time, adolescents tend to believe that it is more proper for a female to be "swept off her feet by passion" than to prepare for sex by taking contraceptive precautions (Goodchilds & Zellman, 1984; Morrison, 1985). An important point is that studies have shown that sexually active teenagers who attend sex education classes are more likely to use contraceptives than those who do not attend such classes (Fielding & Williams, 1991).

EFFECTS OF EARLY PARENTHOOD   What is the impact of early parenthood on a teenage girl's later development? Teenage mothers usually drop out of school and therefore work at lower-paying jobs, experience greater job dissatisfaction, and are likely to become dependent on government support (Coley & Chase-Lansdale, 1998). Adolescent mothers also must deal with their own personal and social development while trying to adapt to the needs of an infant or a small child (Rogel & Peterson, 1984).

Many teenage fathers have an especially hard time because of the pressures they feel to drop out of school to support their new family. Often in such situations only low-paying jobs are available.

The effects of parenthood on the lives of teenage boys may also be negative and long-lasting. Because of the pressures that they feel to support their new family, many teenage fathers also tend to leave school and take low-skilled, low-paying jobs. As the years pass, they are more likely to have marital problems (Card & Wise, 1978).

Often adolescents who become pregnant encounter strong disapproval at home. Yet if they do not marry, they may have no choice but to continue living at home in a dependent situation during and after their pregnancy. Thus, some teenagers are motivated to get married in order to set up their own households (Reiss, 1971). But marriage is not necessarily the best solution to an adolescent mother's problems. Some researchers believe that even though early motherhood obstructs adult growth, in many cases it is preferable to early motherhood combined with early marriage. Adolescent marriage is more likely to lead to dropping out of high school than is adolescent pregnancy. Similarly, those who marry young are more likely to divorce than those who bear a child and marry later (Furstenberg, 1976).

Children of teenage parents are at a disadvantage compared with children of older parents. They may suffer from their parents' lack of experience in handling adult responsibilities and caring for others. Because young parents are often stressed and frustrated, they are more likely to neglect or abuse their children. Children of teenage parents more often exhibit slow development and cognitive growth (Brooks-Gunn & Furstenberg, 1986). If poverty, marital discord, and poor education exist simultaneously in the family, and if they persist over time, the child's chances of developing cognitive and emotional problems increase (McLoyd, 1998).

Some teenage parents, however, do an excellent job of nurturing their young while continuing to grow toward adulthood themselves—given assistance. Helping young parents and their offspring thrive and become productive remains an overriding social concern and challenge, as discussed in "Eye on Diversity," on facing page.

REVIEW & APPLY

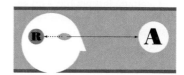

1. Discuss how attitudes toward male and female sexuality have changed in recent decades.
2. What are some of the major factors that influence adolescent sexual behavior?
3. What special problems do homosexuals face during adolescence?
4. Discuss immediate and long-range problems experienced by sexually abused adolescents.
5. What special problems do teenage parents face?

COGNITIVE CHANGES IN ADOLESCENCE

During adolescence there is normally an expansion in the capacity and style of thought that broadens the young person's awareness, imagination, judgment, and insight. These enhanced abilities lead to a rapid accumulation of knowledge that opens up a range of issues and problems that can both enrich and complicate adolescents' lives.

Cognitive development during adolescence is defined by increased abstract thinking and use of metacognition. Both exert a dramatic influence on the

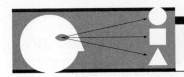

EYE ON DIVERSITY

HELPING TEENAGE MOTHERS IN THE CONTEXT OF POVERTY

What characteristics are crucial if teenage mothers are to escape from poverty? According to Judith Musick (1994), young mothers who free themselves and their children from poverty achieve a strong sense of self-worth, self-efficacy, and personal responsibility. "In a context where many forces act to divert young women and hold them back," says Musick, "only those with steady will and self-determination keep moving forward against the tide" (page 7).

Teenage mothers face enormous obstacles. Many have grown up in a disorganized family and are continually reexposed to its negative influence, making it more difficult for them to change their lives. Musick explains: "Chronic disorganization takes on a life of its own within a family; an enduring mode of transmitting cycles of inadequacy from generation to generation, unnoticed and unbroken" (1994, page 1).

Teenage mothers with a strong sense of self-worth define a special role for themselves as protectors of their children. A young mother living in a Chicago housing project defines her parenting role as follows:

No way would I send my children through these buildings at five years old.... So many kids get snatched off.... Not only will somebody snatch them, the older kids, they take their money. They beat them up. All kinds of things.... Maybe I'm over protective.... Mine wouldn't be doing it. (Musick, 1994, page 6)

At the same time that a mother is protecting her children from harm, she must also nurture their cognitive and psychosocial development and instill in them a sense of self-worth. Unfortunately, says Musick, many adolescent mothers are unable to dedicate themselves to fostering their children's well-being. This inability is especially true when adolescent mothers are involved in destructive, violent relationships with a series of men on whom they are financially dependent. Thus, even when a young mother wants to improve the quality of her life, her relationships may stand in the way.

The more effective programs for teenage mothers work on many levels. They include education or work training as well as guidance in improving parenting skills and family relationships. The programs offer counseling to help the teenage mother with problem solving, as well as direct help with matters such as housing, meal preparation, child care, and other aspects of daily life. Some programs focus on the teenager's need to develop and mature as a person. The program may provide role models, mentoring, and guidance, or simply a view of a wider world beyond the home and community.

Do intervention programs help? According to Musick, the results so far have been modest, mainly because these programs must compete against the powerful negative forces that shape the lives of these young women. However, one thing is fairly certain: Intervention programs can help only those who discover a sense of self-worth and are willing to make an effort on their own to climb out of poverty.

---

scope and content of the adolescent's thoughts and on his or her ability to make moral judgments.

ABSTRACT THINKING

Piaget characterized the abstract thinking of the adolescent as the hallmark of the final stage of cognitive development. Theorists are still arguing about whether the onset of abstract thinking is dramatic and sudden or part of a gradual, continuous process. In this section we take a closer look at this developmental stage.

FORMAL OPERATIONAL THOUGHT   In Piaget's developmental theory, the final stage is *formal operational thinking*. This new form of intellectual processing is abstract, speculative, and independent of the immediate environment and circumstances. It involves thinking about possibilities as well as comparing reality with things that might or might not be. Whereas younger children are more comfortable with concrete, observable events, adolescents show a growing inclination to treat everything as a mere variation on what *could* be (Keating, 1980). Formal operational thought requires the ability to formulate, test, and evaluate hypotheses. It involves manipulation not only of known, verifiable events but also of things that are contrary to fact ("Let's just suppose, for the sake of discussion, that. . . .").

Adolescents also show increasing ability to plan and think ahead. In one study (Greene, 1990), the researcher asked tenth graders, twelfth graders, college sophomores, and college seniors to describe what they thought might happen to them in the future and to say how old they thought they would be when these events occurred. The older subjects could look further into the future than the younger ones, and the narratives of the older subjects were more specific. Formal operational thought thus can be characterized as a *second-order* process. Whereas the first order of thinking is discovering and examining relationships between objects, the second order involves thinking about one's thoughts, looking for links between relationships, and maneuvering between reality and possibility (Inhelder & Piaget, 1958). Three notable characteristics of adolescent thought are the following:

1. The capacity to combine relevant variables in finding a solution to a problem.
2. The ability to offer conjecture about what effect one variable will have on another.
3. The ability to combine and separate variables in a hypothetical-deductive fashion ("If X is present, then Y will occur") (Gallagher, 1973).

It is generally agreed that not all individuals become capable of formal operational thought. Moreover, adolescents and adults who attain this level don't always use it consistently. For example, people who find themselves facing unfamiliar problems in unfamiliar situations are likely to fall back on more concrete reasoning. A certain level of intelligence seems to be necessary for formal operational thought. Cultural and socioeconomic factors, particularly educational level, also play a role (Neimark, 1975). The observation that not all individuals achieve formal operational thought has led some psychologists to suggest that it should be considered an extension of concrete operations rather than a stage in its own right. Piaget (1972) even admitted that this may be the case. Nevertheless, he emphasized that elements of this type of thought are essential for the study of advanced science and mathematics.

A Continuous Process or a Dramatic Shift?   Piaget's notion of dramatic, qualitative shifts in cognitive ability is not shared by all developmental theorists. Some theorists contend that the transition is much more gradual, with shifts back and forth between formal operational thought and earlier cognitive modes (as discussed in Chapter 1 with regard to stages in general). For example, Daniel Keating (1976, 1988) argued that the lines drawn between the thinking of children, adolescents, and adults are artificial; cognitive development is a continuous process, and even young children may have latent formal operational abilities. Some children are able to handle abstract thought. Perhaps better language skills and more experience with the world, instead of new cognitive capability per se, are responsible for the appearance of these abilities in adolescents.

INFORMATION PROCESSING AND ADOLESCENT COGNITIVE DEVELOPMENT

In contrast, information-processing theorists emphasize the adolescent's improvement in metacognition (as defined in Chapter 8). Because of their improved skills in thinking about thinking, forming strategies, and planning, teenagers learn to examine and consciously alter their thought processes.

Cognitive development during adolescence thus includes the following:

1. More efficient use of separate information-processing components such as memory, retention, and transfer of information.
2. More complex strategies for different types of problem solving.
3. More effective ways of acquiring information and storing it symbolically.
4. Higher-order executive functions, including planning, decision making, and flexibility in choosing strategies from a broader base of scripts (Sternberg, 1988).

From the perspective of intelligence, Robert Sternberg (1984, 1985) specified three measurable information-processing components, each with a different function:

1. *Meta components*—the higher-order control processes for planning and decision making. Examples are the ability to select a particular memory strategy and to monitor how well it is working (metamemory).
2. *Performance components*—the processes used to carry out problem solving. These include selection and retrieval of relevant information from stored, long-term memory.
3. *Knowledge acquisition (storage) components*—the processes used in learning new information.

Essentially, "the metacomponents serve as a strategy construction mechanism, orchestrating the other two types of components into goal-oriented procedures" (Siegler, 1991). All of these processes are thought to increase gradually throughout childhood and adolescence. Sternberg's theory is illustrated in Figure 10–3.

In sum, cognitive development, and therefore the growth of intelligence, involve both the accumulation of knowledge and the improvement of information processing. The two are interrelated. Problem solving is more efficient and effective when there is a larger store of relevant information. Individuals with more efficient storage and retrieval strategies develop a more complete knowledge base. Adolescents are more efficient and effective in solving problems and making inferences than school-age children, but they also have a broader range of scripts or schemes to employ in doing so. Remember that preschool

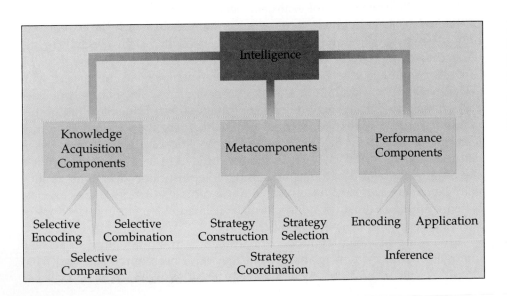

FIGURE 10–3   A DIAGRAM OF STERNBERG'S THEORY OF INTELLIGENCE (AS ADAPTED BY SIEGLER, 1991)

Source: R. S. Siegler (1991). Children's thinking (2nd ed.). Upper Saddle River, NJ: Prentice Hall.

children develop simple scripts for everyday activities. In contrast, adolescents develop more complicated scripts for special circumstances (a ball game) or special procedures (the election of a president). When adolescents attempt to solve a problem or to understand a social event, they can make inferences about the meaning of such things by relating them to their more elaborate social scripts.

CHANGES IN THE SCOPE AND CONTENT OF THOUGHT

Adolescents also use their developing cognitive skills in intellectual and moral pursuits that focus on themselves, their families, and the world. Because of new and improved cognitive skills, adolescents develop a much broader scope and richer complexity in the content of their thoughts. Since the adolescent can now deal with contrary-to-fact situations, reading or viewing science fiction and fantasy is a popular hobby. Experimentation with the occult, cults, or altered states of consciousness caused by anything from meditation to drug-induced conditions is often intriguing to adolescents. Abstract thinking influences not only those pursuits and the study of science and math but also the way that adolescents examine the social world.

EXAMINING WORLD AND FAMILY   The ability to understand contrary-to-fact situations affects the parent-child relationship. Adolescents contrast their ideal parent with the real parent they see on a daily basis. Often they are critical of all social institutions, including family and especially their parents.

Family bickering therefore tends to escalate during early adolescence. Many researchers believe, however, that the battles that rage over such daily activities as chores, dress, schoolwork, and family meals serve a useful purpose. They allow the adolescent to test her or his independence over relatively minor issues and in the safety of the home. Indeed, *negotiation* has become a popular word in the psychology of adolescence. Instead of talking about rebellion and the painful separation of teenagers from their families, many researchers prefer to describe adolescence as a time in which parents and teenagers negotiate new relationships with one another. The teenager must gain more independence; the parents must learn to see their child as more of an equal, with the right to differing opinions. For most adolescents the interplay between these competing needs is conducted within a caring, close relationship with their parents. In a recent study, for example, teenagers who had the strongest sense of themselves as individuals were raised in families in which the parents not only offered guidance and comfort but also permitted their children to develop their own points of view (Flaste, 1988).

During middle and late adolescence, there may be increasing concern with social, political, and moral issues. Adolescents begin to develop holistic concepts of society and its institutions, along with ethical principles that go beyond those they have experienced in specific interpersonal relationships. Adolescents construct their own beliefs about the political system within a social, cultural, and historical context (Haste & Torney-Purta, 1992). Their understanding of the world becomes increasingly sophisticated over time as they gain experience and can conceptualize more complex theories and scenarios. When conflicts occur, their concepts of civil liberties—including freedom of speech and religion—change (Helwig, 1995).

Adolescents also employ rational analysis of issues in an effort to achieve internal consistency; they evaluate what they have been in the past and what they hope to become in the future. Some of their swings and extremes of behavior occur when they start taking stock of themselves intellectually. They restructure their behavior, thoughts, and attitudes, either toward a new, more individualized self-image or toward greater conformity with group norms.

The improved cognitive abilities that develop during adolescence also help young people make vocational decisions. They analyze both real and hypothetical options in relation to their talents and abilities. Often, however, it is not until late adolescence that vocational choices become based on realistic self-appraisal and attainable career options (Ginsburg, 1972).

Adolescence is a time of self-absorption and self-reflection. Sometimes adolescents feel terribly alone and may believe that no one else has ever thought or felt the way they do.

SELF-INSIGHT AND EGOCENTRISM   As noted earlier, an important aspect of formal operational thought is the ability to analyze one's own thought processes. Adolescents typically do this a great deal, and in addition to gaining insight into themselves, they indirectly gain insight into others. Taking others' thoughts into account, combined with the adolescent's preoccupation with his or her own "metamorphosis," leads to a peculiar kind of egocentrism. Adolescents assume that other people are as fascinated with them as they are with themselves. They may fail to distinguish between their own concerns and those of others. As a result, adolescents tend to jump to conclusions about the reactions of those around them and to assume that others will be as approving or as critical of them as they are of themselves. In particular, research indicates that adolescents are far more concerned than younger children about having their inadequacies revealed to others (Elkind & Bowen, 1979).

The adolescent's idea that she or he is constantly being watched and judged has been dubbed the **imaginary audience** (Elkind, 1967). As a product of the adolescent's self-involved imagination, the imaginary audience shares the adolescent's involvement with personal thoughts and feelings. Adolescents use the imaginary audience to "try on" various attitudes and behaviors. The imaginary audience is also a source of self-consciousness—a feeling of being constantly and painfully on display. Because adolescents are unsure of their identities, they overreact to other people's views in trying to figure out who they are (Elkind, 1967).

At the same time, adolescents are absorbed in their own feelings. They sometimes believe that their emotions are unique and that no one has ever known or will ever know the same degree of agony or ecstasy. As part of this variation of egocentrism, some adolescents develop a **personal fable**—the feeling that they are so special that they should be exempt from the ordinary laws of nature, that nothing bad can happen to them, and that they will live forever. This feeling of invulnerability and immortality may be the basis for the risk-taking behavior that is so common during adolescence (Buis & Thompson, 1989).

Related to the personal fable is the *foundling fantasy* (Elkind, 1974). Adolescents become convinced that their parents have a large number of failings. Then they have trouble imagining how two such ordinary and limited individuals could have possibly produced such a sensitive and unique "me." Since this is obviously not possible, the adolescent must have been a foundling. Fortunately, however, egocentrism typically starts receding by the age of 15 or 16 as adolescents realize that most people are not paying all that much attention to them and that they are indeed subject to the laws of nature just like everyone else.

In sum, adolescence can be an intellectually intoxicating experience. New powers of thought are turned inward to a close examination of the self and, at

imaginary audience Adolescents' assumption that others are focusing a great deal of critical attention on them.

personal fable Adolescents' feeling that they are special and invulnerable—exempt from the laws of nature that control the destinies of ordinary mortals.

the same time, outward to a world that has suddenly grown much more complex.

CONTINUING MORAL DEVELOPMENT As they progress toward adulthood, adolescents are forced to confront aspects of morality that they haven't encountered before. Now that they are capable of having sex, for example, they have to decide what sex means to them and whether or not to have intercourse before marriage. They have to evaluate the behaviors and attitudes of peers who might be involved with drugs or gangs. They have to decide whether doing well in school is important, how they feel about fitting into a society that measures success largely in terms of money and power, and what role, if any, religion will play in their life. As a result, adolescents start considering the broader issues that will define their adult years.

Some of their decisions—including those about sex—have complex, even life-threatening consequences. Rosemary Jadack and her colleagues (1995) investigated the moral reasoning of 18-year-olds and 20-year-olds about sexual behavior that could lead to STDs, including AIDS. The researchers found that only subjects in their early 20s carefully considered the moral dilemmas associated with STDs. Apparently, even the ability to make moral judgments about life-threatening behaviors takes time to develop.

The thinking of adolescents changes within the context of their developing sense of morality. By the time they reach their teens, a majority of children in U.S. society have moved beyond the first level of Kohlberg's moral development (the preconventional level; see Chapter 9) and have arrived at the conventional level (which is based on social conformity). They are motivated to avoid punishment, oriented toward obedience, and ready to abide by conventional moral stereotypes. They may remain at this "law-and-order" level throughout their lives, especially if they have no reason to move beyond it—in many day-to-day situations, this level of thinking works in the sense that it avoids trouble with society. They may never reach the final stages of moral development, in which morality is seen as based on a social contract and derived from personal ethical principles.

Can more advanced moral thinking be learned? Kohlberg and others have set up experimental moral education classes for children and adolescents from a variety of social backgrounds. The results, even with juvenile delinquents, suggest that higher levels of moral judgment can indeed be taught. The classes center on discussions of hypothetical moral dilemmas. The adolescent is presented with a problem and asked to give a solution. If the answer is argued at stage 4, the discussion leader suggests a stage 5 rationale to see whether the teenager thinks it is a good alternative. The students almost always find that slightly more advanced reasoning is more appealing, and through repeated discussions they sooner or later begin to form judgments at higher stages (Kohlberg, 1966).

Educators in particular are concerned with how morality develops during childhood and adolescence. They feel that if they could understand it better, they could do something about such problems as delinquency and drug abuse and could help create a better social order. According to Kohlberg's framework, presenting a child with increasingly complex moral issues creates *disequilibrium* in his or her mind, forcing the child to think and to try to resolve contradictions. Considering moral paradoxes and conflicts requires the child to use higher levels of moral reasoning. However, it is not entirely clear that superior moral judgments lead to superior moral behavior; to date, very little research has been done on the relationship between the two.

1. What is formal operational thought? How did Piaget view the cognitive changes that occur during adolescence?
2. How do information-processing theorists describe cognitive development during adolescence?
3. Describe the impact of cognitive development on changes in the scope and content of adolescent thought.

REVIEW & APPLY

SUMMARY

Adolescence Today

■ Several factors combine to make adolescence a unique cultural niche in modern societies. Those factors are age segregation, prolonged economic dependence, major events of the era in which adolescents live, and the influence of the mass media.

Physical Development and Adjustment

■ The biological hallmarks of adolescence are a marked increase in the rate of growth, the rapid development of the reproductive organs, and the appearance of secondary sex characteristics.

■ The physical changes that occur upon entry into adolescence are controlled by hormones, substances secreted into the bloodstream by endocrine glands.

■ The adolescent growth spurt is a period of rapid growth in physical size and strength accompanied by changes in body proportions.

■ Puberty, the attainment of sexual maturity, usually follows the growth spurt by about a year.

■ During adolescence, males begin to produce more of the hormones called androgens, of which the most important is testosterone, and females begin to produce more estrogen and progesterone. The balance among these hormones is maintained by the hypothalamus and the pituitary gland. The pituitary also produces growth hormone and trophic hormones, which stimulate and regulate the functioning of other glands.

■ For girls, puberty is marked by the first menstrual period, or menarche. For males, it is marked by the first emission of semen containing viable sperm cells.

■ In males, the first indication of puberty is accelerating growth of the testes and scrotum, followed by similar growth of the penis a year later. There are also increases in the size of the heart and lungs.

■ In females, "breast buds" are usually the first sign of puberty. The uterus and vagina also begin to develop. Menarche occurs later, after the peak of the growth spurt. The first few menstrual cycles are often irregular and do not produce an ovum.

■ Many adolescents are extremely sensitive about their appearance. When their self-image does not match the ideal that they see in the media, they may subject themselves to intense dieting or rigorous regimens of physical fitness. Concern with body image can lead to eating disorders such as anorexia nervosa or bulimia.

■ Early or late maturation can create problems for adolescents. Late-maturing boys are smaller and less muscular than their age-mates, so that they are placed at a disadvantage. For girls, late maturation can be an advantage because the girl matures at about the same time as most of her male peers.

■ Menarche is a memorable event for most girls. For those who are ill informed beforehand, it can be traumatic. But most girls are well prepared and report a positive reaction.

Sexual Attitudes and Behavior

■ The sexual "revolution" of the 1960s and 1970s was reflected in increased sexual activity among adolescents and in a reduction in the "double standard" that had allowed greater sexual freedom for males than for females.

■ Problems associated with increased sexual activity include high rates of teenage pregnancy and the spread of sexually transmitted diseases, including AIDS.

■ In the late 1980s, attitudes toward sexual matters became more conservative.

■ For gay or lesbian adolescents, gender identity can be intensely stressful because they lack support from parents or peers. This situation has been made much worse by the spread of AIDS.

■ The age at which teenagers first engage in sex varies by gender and by racial and subcultural group.

Boys start having sex earlier and tend to have different attitudes toward it than girls do.

■ Education is related to sexual behavior. Students who are doing well in high school are less likely to initiate sexual activity at an early age.

■ Parent-child interactions influence adolescent sexual behavior. Adolescents who are sexually active are more likely to report poor communication with their parents.

■ For a significant number of children and adolescents, the first sexual experience takes the form of abuse. The most common form of sexual abuse occurs between a young adolescent girl and an adult male relative or a family friend.

■ Abuse can have negative effects that last throughout life. The girl may feel guilty and ashamed, feel isolated from peers and distrustful of adults, and have academic problems or become sexually promiscuous. In general, their attitudes about intimate relationships become distorted.

■ Each year more than 1 million adolescent girls become pregnant, and half of these pregnancies result in delivery. Among the reasons for these high rates are failure to use contraception and the reduced social stigma attached to illegitimacy.

■ Teenage mothers usually drop out of school and work at low-paying jobs or become dependent on government support. If they do not marry, they may be forced to continue living at home in a dependent situation.

Cognitive Changes in Adolescence

■ Most adolescents become capable of formal operational thinking, which is abstract, speculative, and independent of the immediate environment and circumstances.

■ Adolescents also show increasing ability to plan and think ahead.

■ Not all individuals become capable of formal operational thought, and those who do attain this level do not always use it consistently.

■ Information-processing theorists emphasize adolescents' improved metacognition, which enables them to examine and consciously alter their thought processes.

■ Sternberg identifies three information-processing components: meta components (higher-order control processes), performance components (those used to carry out problem solving), and knowledge acquisition components (those used in learning new information). With these abilities, adolescents are more efficient and effective in solving problems and making inferences than school-age children.

■ Adolescents use their developing skills in intellectual and moral pursuits that focus on themselves, their families, and the world. This practice may affect the parent-child relationship. Many researchers describe adolescence as a time in which parents and teenagers negotiate new relationships with one another.

■ Adolescents may also become more concerned with social, political, and moral issues. Their understanding of the world becomes increasingly sophisticated, and they employ rational analysis of issues.

■ Adolescents develop a form of egocentrism in which they fail to distinguish between their own concerns and those of others. The adolescent's feeling of constantly being watched and judged is referred to as the *imaginary audience*. Some adolescents develop a *personal fable*—the feeling that they are so special that they should be exempt from the ordinary laws of nature.

■ As they progress toward adulthood, adolescents must consider aspects of morality that they haven't encountered before. Their decisions take on greater importance, and their sense of morality develops further. Some reach the final stages in Kohlberg's model of moral development, in which morality is derived from personal ethical principles.

KEY TERMS

rites of passage	puberty	imaginary audience
hormones	menarche	personal fable
adolescent growth spurt		

USING WHAT YOU'VE LEARNED

Gradually, between the ages of 10 and 20, most adolescents develop the ability to think in more abstract terms than they could when they were younger. By age 10, children know something about fair play through interactions with their parents, teachers, and peers. They also know something about friendship through interactions with peers. By age 20, young adults have a much more complete, and typically more abstract, understanding of justice and friendship. They are no longer bound by specific instances and events but instead can apply general principles and consider hypothetical situations.

To verify this transition for yourself, interview two teenagers who are at least 4 years apart in age. Select a couple of abstract issues and encourage your respondents to tell you what they believe to be important considerations and why. For example,

- What makes a good friend?
- Can a black person obtain justice in American courts?
- Are women treated equitably in our society?
- Is censorship ever justified?
- What would you do to create a perfect world?

Consider any differences that you observe in your respondents' answers, and relate them to the material in this chapter. What do the answers tell you about each respondent's level of abstract thinking and moral development?

SUGGESTED READINGS

COLES, R., & STOKES, G. (1985). *Sex and the American teenager.* New York: Harper & Row. Presentation and discussion of a detailed, interview-based survey of American teenage sexual attitudes and behavior.

COLMAN, W. (1988). *Understanding and preventing AIDS.* Chicago: Children's Press. A detailed, well-illustrated overview for teenagers and their parents, including a clear presentation of the immune system and realistic profiles of young AIDS patients.

ERIKSON, E. (1968). *Identity: Youth and crisis.* New York: Norton. A full discussion of adolescent identity formation, with many examples taken from case studies.

FELDMAN, S. S., & ELLIOTT, G. R. (1990). *At the threshold: The developing adolescent.* Cambridge, MA: Harvard University Press. Results of the extensive Carnegie Foundation study of adolescent development in a social context, presented for professionals and nonprofessionals alike.

KEMPE, R. S., & KEMPE, C. H. (1984). *The common secret: Sexual abuse of children and adolescents.* New York: W. H. Freeman. A hard-hitting, statistics-packed presentation of the range, extent, and impact of sexual abuse in America.

PIPHER, M. B. (1995). *Reviving Ophelia: Saving the selves of adolescent girls.* New York: Ballantine. A highly recommended and sympathetic book based on case histories of young women's struggles to stay within our traditional narrow definition of "female." Includes concrete suggestions on building and maintaining a strong sense of self.

ROSENBERG, E. (1983). *Growing up feeling good.* New York: Beaufort Books. One of the best self-help guides for early adolescents, it is also valuable for the parents of adolescents and for teachers.

RUBIN, N. J. (1994). *Ask me if I care: Voices from an American high school.* Berkeley, CA: Ten Speed Press. A popular, respected high school teacher presents the candid concerns of her students about the issues facing today's teenagers.

SHENGOLD, L. (1989). *Soul murder: The effects of childhood abuse and deprivation.* New Haven, CT: Yale University Press. This psychiatrist explores the adult results of the psychological trauma of childhood abuse. The lives of Dickens, Kipling, Chekhov, and Orwell are examined, along with those of contemporary, less well known victims of abuse.

UNKS, G. (Ed.) (1995). *The gay teen.* New York: Routledge. This popular collection of articles, originally published in a special issue of the *High School Journal,* covers many aspects of gay and straight gender identity in today's high schools.

Adolescence: Personality Development and Socialization

CHAPTER

11

CHAPTER OBJECTIVES

By the time you have finished this chapter, you should be able to do the following:

1. Discuss the major developmental conflicts that adolescents must resolve in making a successful transition to adulthood.
2. Explain the concept of identity status.
3. Describe how intergenerational communication, including parenting styles and family dynamics, continues to influence behavior during adolescence.
4. Identify key characteristics of successful family functioning during the adolescent's move toward increasing independence.
5. Explain the importance of peers in an adolescent's life and the way that relationships change over the adolescent years.
6. Describe factors and processes that help shape moral development and the selection of values during adolescence.
7. Discuss patterns of adolescent risk-taking, including drug use and delinquency.
8. Explain the relationship between stress and depression in adolescents.

dolescents frequently display a curious combination of maturity and childishness during their transition to adulthood. The mixture is awkward and sometimes comical, but it serves an important developmental function. How adolescents cope with the stresses created by changing bodies and new roles depends on their personality development in earlier years. To meet new challenges, they draw upon the skills, resources, and strengths they began to develop much earlier.

In the preceding chapter, we observed that the transitional period between childhood and adulthood varies considerably from one culture to another. In some societies, adult skills are mastered quickly and easily; new adult members are urgently needed and promptly recruited immediately following puberty. In contrast, in developed nations, successful transition to adult status often requires lengthy education and occupational training. In modern societies, adolescence often stretches from puberty to the late teenage years. Adolescents thus live in an extended period of limbo: Despite their physical and intellectual maturity, many are excluded from meaningful work.

On the one hand, prolonged adolescence gives the young person repeated opportunities to experiment with different adult styles without making irrevocable commitments. On the other hand, a decade of adolescence generates certain pressures and conflicts, such as the need to appear independent and sophisticated while still being financially dependent on one's parents.

Some adolescents experience a great deal of pressure from their parents, who transfer to them their own compulsions to succeed and attain higher social status (Elkind, 1997). Adolescents must cope with these pressures as well as with those that come from within themselves. They must also accomplish significant developmental tasks and weave the results into a coherent, functioning identity.

In this chapter we look at how teenagers cope with the dilemmas of adolescence and the resulting triumphs and setbacks. We examine how young people adopt values and form loyalties and become more mature. Involved are parents and peers—including crowds, cliques, and intimate friends—and choices as wide and varied as society itself. Also involved are stresses and maladaptive coping patterns that sometimes lead to risk-taking behaviors, drug abuse, delinquency, and even depression and suicide.

DEVELOPMENTAL TASKS OF ADOLESCENCE

Each period in life presents developmental challenges and difficulties that require new skills and responses. Most theorists agree that adolescents must confront two major tasks:

1. Achieving autonomy and independence from their parents
2. Forming an identity, which means creating an integrated self that harmoniously combines different elements of the personality.

Adolescence has traditionally been viewed as a period of "storm and stress," a dramatic upheaval of emotions and behavior. The term derives from a German literary movement of the late eighteenth and early nineteenth centuries (Sturm und Drang). It was adopted by Anna Freud as a label for the emotional state that she believed to be characteristic of adolescence. She went so far as to say, "To be normal during the adolescent period is by itself abnormal" (1958). She and other Freudians argued that the onset of biological maturation and increased sexual drive produces pronounced conflicts between adolescents and their parents, their peers, and themselves.

Are adolescents habitually troubled? Some are, but we now know that most are not. The majority are well adjusted and have no major conflicts with their parents, peers, or selves. Only an estimated 10% to 20% experience psychological disturbances, a percentage comparable to that of adults in the general population (Powers et al., 1989).

INDEPENDENCE AND INTERDEPENDENCE

In the prevailing view, adolescents use conflict and rebelliousness as a means of achieving autonomy and independence from their parents. Especially since the mid-1960s, the media have focused on the "generation gap" (see "Eye on Diversity," page 378) and turbulent conflicts between parents and their children. Stories with this theme are dramatic and interesting, but there is limited research evidence to support them. Most research in this area indicates that the degree of conflict between adolescents and their families has been exaggerated.

Although the emotional distance between teenagers and their parents tends to increase in early adolescence (Steinberg, 1988), this tendency does not necessarily lead to rebellion or to rejection of parental values. In a study of 6000 adolescents in ten diverse nations—Australia, Bangladesh, Hungary, Israel, Italy, Japan, Taiwan, Turkey, the United States, and the former West Germany—Daniel Offer and his colleagues (1988) administered a questionnaire that focused on how teenagers perceived their family relations. They found that the vast majority of teenagers in each nation got along well with their parents and had positive attitudes toward their families. Only small percentages of respondents endorsed the following negative statements:

Contrary to popular belief, adolescence is not inevitably marked by rebellion against parents.

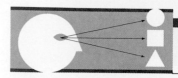

EYE ON DIVERSITY

GENERATION X VERSUS THE BABY BOOMERS

It seems that adolescents inevitably lock horns with the previous generation, who believe that they "know better." This tendency has never been clearer than it is today. On one side is what has come to be known as Generation X—the 80 million adolescents and young adults born between 1961 and 1981. On the other side are the Baby Boomers—the 70 million people born between 1943 and 1960.

Neil Howe and William Strauss (1992) have carried out a provocative analysis of the striking differences between Generation X and the Baby Boomers. Many Baby Boomers started life as indulged children. They were raised in the permissive environment encouraged by Dr. Benjamin Spock in his classic book *Baby and Child Care*—a volume that has sold nearly as many copies as the Bible. By the time they reached adolescence, they were disenchanted by what they saw around them. They wanted to build a better world and were willing to create a social revolution to achieve it. Their anger at "the establishment" was expressed through major, often violent demonstrations protesting U.S. involvement in the Vietnam War. Although the protesters accounted for only about 15% of all young people, they set the tone for the entire generation.

As the generation aged, its tendency toward self-involvement took the form

of moral wisdom—a sense of knowing exactly what was right—that was aimed largely at the next generation. In other words, Baby Boomers enjoyed telling other people what to do. But the next generation didn't necessarily see things their way. Generation X came of age without many of the advantages Baby Boomers took for granted. Many young people in this generation could not find decent jobs; many were forced by economic necessity to continue living with their parents; and many felt that the Baby Boomers' lack of self-discipline had created an uncertain and even dangerous future for the following generation.

Moreover, as the first generation to bear the brunt of the rapid increase in the rate of divorce, many Xers grew up in single-parent families. What's worse, their parents valued material goods over children-rearing concerns. Howe and Strauss explain: "From the 1960s until the early 1980s America's preadolescents grasped what nurture they could through the most virulently antichild period in modern American history. Ugly new phrases (like 'latchkey child') joined the sad new lexicon of youth. America's priorities lay elsewhere" (pages 77–78). When Xers joined the workforce, they found that their inflation-adjusted income was far below that of Baby Boomers and that the poverty rate of people under 30 was rising. As a result, Generation X felt increasing anger and resentment at the Baby Boomers.

The Baby Boomers, in turn, labeled the Xers as a "lost generation." According to Howe and Strauss,

This generation—more accurately, this generation's reputation—has become a Boomer metaphor for America's loss of purpose, disappointment with institutions, despair over the culture, and fear for the future. Many Boomers are by now of the settled opinion that [Xers] are—front to back—a disappointing bunch. This attitude is rooted partly in observation, partly in blurry nostalgia, partly in self-serving sermonizing, but the very fact that it is becoming a consensus is a major problem for today's young people. No one can blame them if they feel like a demographic black hole whose only elder-anointed mission is somehow to pass through the next three quarters of a century without causing too much damage to the nation during their time. (page 79)

What Boomers and Xers are left with is a serious generation gap. As one generation ages and the next enters adulthood, the conflict is bound to get worse.

Source: Neil Howe and William Strauss, "The New Generation Gap." *The Atlantic Monthly*, December 1992, pages 67–89.

My parents are ashamed of me. (7%)
I have been carrying a grudge against my parents for years. (9%)
Very often I feel that my mother is no good. (9%)
Very often I feel that my father is no good. (13%)
My parents will be disappointed in me in the future. (11%)

The adolescents' responses differed somewhat from one nation to another, underlining the importance of cultural context in adolescent development. Israeli youth, for example, reported the most positive family relations—probably because of the emphasis placed on family relations by traditional Jewish culture. In general, Offer's findings clearly contradict the Freudian view of inevitable conflict stemming from biological drives and changes.

Definitions of autonomy that stress freedom from parental influence need to be reconsidered. Independence must take into account the continuing influence of parents during and after adolescence. John Hill (1987) has suggested an interesting approach to adolescent independence-seeking. He believes that autonomy should be defined as *self-regulation*. Independence involves making your own judgments and regulating your own behavior, as in the expression "Think for yourself." Many adolescents learn to do precisely that. They reevaluate the rules, values, and boundaries that they experienced as children at home and at school. Sometimes they encounter considerable resistance from their parents, which may lead to conflict. More often, however, their parents work through the process with them, minimizing areas of conflict and helping them develop independent thought and self-regulated behavior (Hill, 1987).

Becoming an adult is, of course, a gradual transformation. It requires being simultaneously independent and interdependent. **Interdependence** can be defined as reciprocal dependence. Social relationships are interdependent—as, for example, in the workplace. Bosses depend on their workers to produce, while workers depend on their bosses to manage the enterprise. Interdependence thus involves long-term commitments and interpersonal attachments (Gilligan, 1987).

IDENTITY FORMATION

Before adolescence we view ourselves in terms of an assortment of roles—friend, enemy, student, ballplayer, guitar player—and in terms of membership in cliques, clubs, or gangs. In adolescence our improved cognitive powers (see Chapter 10) allow us to analyze our roles, identify inconsistencies and conflicts in them, and restructure them in forging an identity. Sometimes we abandon earlier roles; sometimes we establish new relationships with parents, siblings, and peers. Erikson (1968) sees the task of **identity formation** as the major hurdle that adolescents must cross in making a successful transition to adulthood. Ideally, adolescents enter adulthood with a stable and consistent sense of who they are and how they fit into society.

INFLUENCES ON IDENTITY   Adolescents derive many of their ideas about roles and values from reference groups. *Reference groups* may consist of individuals with whom adolescents interact often and have close relationships, or they may be broader social groups with whom they share attitudes and ideals: religious, ethnic, generational, or interest groups, even chat groups on the Internet. Reference groups, whether broad or narrow, confirm or reject values and sometimes impose new ones.

Adolescents must come to terms with a variety of reference groups. Group memberships that were almost automatic in childhood—in the family, the neighborhood gang, or the church youth group, for example—are no longer as comfortable or fulfilling as they were earlier. Often the adolescent feels conflicting loyalties to family, peer groups, and other reference groups.

Sometimes adolescents are drawn to the values and attitudes of a special person rather than to those of a group. This *significant other* may be a close friend, an admired teacher, an older sibling, a movie or sports or music star, or anyone whose ideas and behaviors the adolescent admires. Although the influence of significant others may be felt at any stage of life, it often has its greatest impact during adolescence.

Much can be learned about a teenager's sense of identity by a tour of his or her room.

interdependence   Reciprocal dependence.

identity formation   Gaining a sense of who you are and how you fit into society.

In sum, adolescents are surrounded by a bewildering variety of roles offered by a multitude of reference groups and people. These roles must be integrated into a personal identity, and conflicting ones must be reconciled or discarded. This process is even more difficult when there is conflict between roles (for instance, between being a member of a fun-loving peer group and being a good student) or between significant others (for example, between an older sibling and a romantic partner).

ERIKSON'S CONCEPT OF IDENTITY   Erikson spent much of his professional life as a clinical psychologist working with adolescents and young adults. His writings on the process of establishing an "inner sense of identity" have had an enormous impact on developmental psychology. According to Erikson, identity formation is an often lengthy and complex process of *self-definition*. Identity formation provides continuity between the individual's past, present, and future. It forms a framework for organizing and integrating behaviors in diverse areas of life. It reconciles the person's own inclinations and talents with earlier roles that were supplied by parents, peers, or society. By helping the individual know where he or she stands in comparison with others, identity formation also provides a basis for social comparisons. Finally, a sense of identity helps give direction, purpose, and meaning to life (Erikson, 1959, 1963, 1968; Waterman, 1985).

MODES OF IDENTITY FORMATION   James Marcia (1980) refined Erikson's theory and defined four different states, or modes, of identity formation. The four modes, or "identity statuses," are *foreclosure, diffusion, moratorium,* and *identity achievement;* these are summarized in the study chart on facing page. At issue is whether the individual has gone through a decision-making period called an **identity crisis** and whether the individual has made a commitment to a specific set of choices, such as a system of values or a plan for a future occupation.

Adolescents who are in **foreclosure status** have made commitments without going through much decision-making. They have chosen an occupation, a religious outlook, an ideological viewpoint, and other aspects of their identity, but the choices were made early and determined more by their parents or teachers than by themselves. Their transition to adulthood occurs smoothly and with little conflict, but also with little experimentation.

Young people who lack a sense of direction and seem to have little motivation to find one are in **diffusion status.** They have not experienced a crisis, nor have they selected an occupational role or a moral code. They are simply avoiding the issue. For some, life revolves around immediate gratification; others experiment, seemingly at random, with various kinds of attitudes and behaviors (Coté & Levine, 1988).

Adolescents or young adults in **moratorium status** are in the midst of an ongoing identity crisis or decision-making period. The decisions may concern occupational choices, religious or ethical values, or political philosophies. Young people in this status are preoccupied with "finding themselves."

Finally, **identity achievement** is the status attained by people who have passed through an identity crisis and made their commitments. As a result, they pursue work of their own choosing and attempt to live by their own individually formulated moral code. Identity achievement is usually viewed as the most desirable and the most mature status (Marcia, 1980).

EFFECTS OF IDENTITY STATUS   Research indicates that identity status profoundly influences an adolescent's social expectations, self-image, and reac-

identity crisis   A period of making decisions about important issues, such as "Who am I, and where am I going?"

foreclosure status   The identity status of those who have made commitments without going through an identity crisis.

diffusion status   The identity status of those who have neither gone through an identity crisis nor made commitments.

moratorium status   The identity status of those who are currently in the midst of an identity crisis.

identity achievement   The identity status of those who have gone through an identity crisis and have made commitments.

STUDY CHART ▸ MARCIA'S MODES OF IDENTITY FORMATION

MODE	DESCRIPTION	EFFECTS ON THE ADOLESCENT
Foreclosure	Commitments are made without doing much decision-making.	Has minimal anxiety; more authoritarian values, and strong, positive ties to significant others.
Diffusion	Commitments are not yet made; has little sense of direction; avoids the issue.	May drop out, or turn to alcohol or other drug use as a way of evading responsibility.
Moratorium	Undergoes ongoing identity crisis or decision-making period.	Has anxiety due to unresolved decisions; struggles with conflicting values and choices.
Identity achievement	Commitments are made after passing through an identity crisis.	Has balanced feelings toward parents and family; has less difficulty achieving independence.

tions to stress. Moreover, cross-cultural research in the United States, Denmark, Israel, and other societies suggests that Marcia's four statuses are part of a relatively universal developmental process, at least in cultures characterized by an extended period of adolescence. Let's consider next how the four identity statuses interact with some of the problems of adolescence.

Anxiety is a dominant emotion for young people in moratorium status because of their unresolved decisions. These young people often struggle with conflicting values and choices, and they are constantly faced with unpredictability and contradictions. They are often tied to their parents in an ambivalent relationship: They struggle for freedom yet fear or resent parental disapproval. Many college students are in moratorium status.

In contrast, adolescents in foreclosure status experience a minimum of anxiety. They have more authoritarian values than adolescents in the other statuses, and they have strong, positive ties to significant others. Young men in foreclosure status tend to have lower self-esteem than those in moratorium status and are more easily persuaded by others (Marcia, 1980).

Diffusion status is seen most frequently in teenagers who have experienced rejection or neglect from detached or uncaring parents. They may become dropouts, perhaps turning to alcohol or other drug use as a way of evading responsibility. Diana Baumrind (1991) has shown that drug and alcohol abuse are most common in children of "indifferent" parents (see Chapter 7).

Adolescents who have attained identity achievement have the most balanced feelings toward their parents and family. Their quest for independence is less emotionally charged than that of youths in moratorium, and that quest is not tainted with the isolation and sense of abandonment that troubles individuals in the diffusion status (Marcia, 1980).

The proportion of people in identity achievement status naturally increases with age. In high school, there are far more individuals in diffusion and foreclosure statuses than in moratorium and identity achievement statuses. Identity status may also vary according to what aspect of identity is under consideration: A high school student may be in foreclosure status regarding sex-role preference, moratorium status regarding vocational choice or religious beliefs, and diffusion status regarding political philosophy.

SEX DIFFERENCES Marcia and other researchers have noted a marked difference between males and females in the behavior and attitudes associated with the various identity statuses. For example, males in identity achievement and moratorium statuses seem to have a great deal of self-esteem. Females in these statuses appear to have more unresolved conflicts, especially regarding family and career choices.

Later studies partially confirm the earlier findings but present a more complex picture. Sally Archer (1985), for example, found that for family and career choices, girls in the later high school years are most likely to be in foreclosure status, whereas boys are most likely to be in diffusion status. Further, girls in foreclosure and moratorium statuses express a great deal of uncertainty about reconciling conflicts stemming from their family and career preferences. Although both boys and girls say that they plan to marry, have children, and pursue careers, girls are more likely to express concern about possible conflicts between family and career. When asked how much concern they had, 75% of males and 16% of females said none, 25% of males and 42% of females said some, and 0% of males and 42% of females said they felt a lot of concern about potential conflicts between family and career.

In the other major areas of interest—religious and political beliefs—results are mixed. For religion, research indicates no significant gender differences. But with respect to political beliefs, there seems to be a significant difference in identity status between older male and female adolescents. Males have more often been found to be in identity achievement status, whereas females are more often in foreclosure status (Waterman, 1985).

REVIEW & APPLY

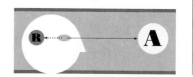

1. What are the major developmental challenges of adolescence?
2. Describe the processes of achieving independence and interdependence as they relate to adolescent development.
3. Describe Erikson's concept of identity formation.
4. Discuss Marcia's four identity statuses.

FAMILY DYNAMICS

Throughout the process of identity formation, adolescents are forced to assess their own values and behaviors in relation to those of their family. In turn, the most important tasks of parenthood often seem paradoxical. On the one hand, successful parents provide their children with a sense of security and roots in an environment in which the children feel loved and accepted. On the other hand, successful parents encourage their children to become self-directing adults who can function independently in society.

How parents interact with their adolescents affects the adolescents' moves toward adulthood in dramatic ways. Family systems are dynamic: Behavioral changes in one family member influence every other member of the family. Since adolescence is a time of significant and often dramatic change, the family as a social system also changes, as does the nature of intergenerational communication.

INTERGENERATIONAL COMMUNICATION

The adolescent's emerging need for autonomy and self-definition normally leads to at least some conflict within the family and an increased need to talk with parents about certain issues. Adolescents remain very much influenced by their families, although their ties to the family may become strained. Studies over the past 25 years have consistently shown that there is much less conflict between adolescents and their families than was previously believed. Surveys report serious conflicts in only 15% to 25% of families. Most conflicts revolve around such ordinary issues as family chores, curfew hours, dating, grades, personal appearance, and eating habits. Conflicts between parents and adolescents about basic economic, religious, social, and political values are much less common (Hill, 1987). The relatively few adolescents who form truly independent opinions about ideological matters generally do so late in high school or in college (Waterman, 1985).

Generally, early adolescence is more conflict-laden than later adolescence. When teenagers and their parents are older, both are better able to come to grips with potentially difficult autonomy and separation issues. It is important for parents and adolescents alike to realize that if they can maintain communication and share views during adolescence, the difficult issues can be negotiated successfully.

Mothers and fathers influence their teenagers in different ways. Although there is little difference between how adolescent males and females describe their family relations (Hauser et al., 1987; Youniss & Ketterlinus, 1987), there is considerable difference between the behavior and roles of mothers and those of fathers (Steinberg, 1987a). Traditionally, fathers tend to encourage intellectual development and are frequently involved in discussing and solving family problems. As a result, both boys and girls generally discuss their ideas and concerns with their fathers (Hauser et al., 1987). Adolescents' involvement with their mothers is far more complex. Mothers and adolescents are more likely to interact in areas such as household responsibilities, homework, discipline both in and out of the home, and leisure activities (Montemayor & Brownlee, 1987). Although these interactions may cause greater strain and conflict between mothers and their children, they also tend to create greater closeness (Youniss & Ketterlinus, 1987).

In general, the great involvement of mothers in their adolescent children's daily life activities such as homework tends to make this relationship more complex than the adolescents' relationships with their fathers.

PARENTING STYLES   In Chapter 7, we discussed the influences of different parenting styles (Baumrind, 1975, 1980) on children's psychological make-up. These influences continue into adolescence. The authoritative parenting style is most likely to result in normal or healthy adolescent behavior (Baumrind, 1991; Hill, 1987), characterized by responsible, independent actions and good self-acceptance and self-control. In contrast, adolescents who have experienced authoritarian parenting may be dependent and anxious in the presence of authority figures, or they may become defiant and resentful. The negative impact of authoritarian parenting also holds up for racial/ethnic groups, as does the positive impact of authoritative parenting (Lamborn et al., 1996).

The warmth and the confident control provided by authoritative parents is reassuring to most adolescents. The parent provides the experimenting adolescent with a safety net. The consequences of failure are not irreparable because the parents help pick up the pieces. Authoritative parenting also takes into account the adolescent's increased cognitive ability. For the first time, both parents and children can communicate, using the same or similar levels of reasoning and logic (Baumrind, 1987).

FAMILY ALLIANCES   Family alliances also play a powerful role in communication. Like parenting styles, they begin to shape behavior long before adolescence. An older brother who dominated his younger brother during childhood will probably have the same influence in adolescence; a daughter who was "Daddy's girl" at age 6 will probably remain close to her father when she is 16.

Although alliances between various family members are natural and healthy, it is important that parents maintain a united front and a distinct boundary between themselves and their children. Parents also need to work together to nurture and discipline their children; a close bond between a child and one parent that excludes the other parent can be disruptive. The excluded parent loses stature as a socializing agent and an authority figure. Problems also arise from other kinds of imbalance, such as the absence of one parent due to divorce or separation. When an adolescent is testing new roles and struggling to achieve a new identity, parental authority may be severely tested in a single-parent home.

THE CHANGING AMERICAN FAMILY

The effects of families in transition, discussed in earlier chapters, also continue into adolescence. Figure 11–1 shows the living arrangements of children under 18. Also note that adolescents are often latchkey children, as discussed on page 322.

It is interesting to observe how changes in the American family have affected adolescents' responsibility for household chores. One study yielded some surprising findings (Benin & Edwards, 1990). Teenagers in dual-income families tend to help less around the house than those in families in which the mother is a homemaker. Moreover, the demands made on adolescents are divided along gender lines. Whereas sons in dual-income households spend only one-third as much time on chores as sons in traditional families, daughters in dual-income families spend one-fourth *more* time on chores than daughters in traditional families. In contrast, full-time homemakers expect their teenage sons and daughters to do an equal amount of work around the house.

FIGURE 11–1   LIVING ARRANGEMENTS OF CHILDREN UNDER AGE 18

Sources: U.S. Census Bureau, (1990). A. Cherlin & J. McCarthy. (February 1985). Remarried couple households: Journal of Marriage and the Family, *47, 23–30.*

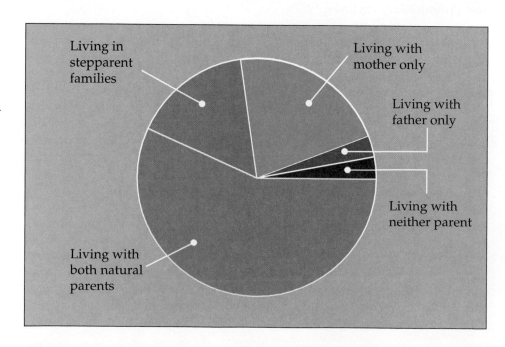

Living in stepparent families

Living with mother only

Living with father only

Living with neither parent

Living with both natural parents

Why? The researchers suggest that working mothers may trust their daughters more than their sons to complete their assigned chores while unsupervised, and therefore give them a larger workload. Homemakers may succeed in getting their sons to do an equal amount of work by monitoring them closely.

How do adolescents respond to the stresses and pressures associated with the changing American family? Some take on added responsibilities. Others externalize their negative feelings and conflicts by becoming involved in anti-social, noncompliant behavior. Still others disengage themselves from the family by focusing on activities involving peers.

LEAVING HOME

For all concerned, making adjustments as adolescents become increasingly in-dependent and prepare to leave home is not an easy task. Parents and children must renegotiate roles. Adolescents need different support than younger chil-dren because they explore their independence more actively. Separateness and self-assertion are not harmful characteristics; they are crucial to development. Some families encourage these characteristics; others oppose them.

Researchers have identified three dimensions of family functioning that are relevant here: *cohesion, adaptability,* and *quality of communication* (Barnes & Olsen, 1985). During the separation process, it helps if families have moderate but not extreme levels of cohesion and adaptability. It's best if families are somewhat flexible and adaptable, but not so loosely structured as to be chaotic. Also, families should be cohesive but not "smothering." Families adapt best if they can negotiate changes rationally, taking each member's wants and needs into consideration. Family cohesiveness can be maintained when parents and the departing adolescent can deal with one another as indi-viduals and establish reciprocal relationships (Grotevant & Cooper, 1985). Open communication helps preserve family cohesiveness because it enables family members to talk things out and minimize friction.

Some studies suggest that fathers play a key role in helping adolescents find the right balance between separateness and connectedness, a balance that ex-tends to the time when they are ready to leave home. Fathers who emphasize separateness give their adolescents the "space" they need to form their own identity and begin to take responsibility for their own actions. The fact that adolescents generally have fewer conflicts with their fathers than with their mothers suggests that fathers tend to interfere less and have greater respect for their adolescent's independence. Thus, instead of expending energy opposing their fathers, many adolescents are free to pursue their own interests (Shulman & Klein, 1993).

Helping adolescents form their own identity and separate themselves from their parents may be more difficult in single-parent households. In such cases, the involvement of another adult, such as a grandparent, an aunt, an uncle, or a teacher, makes the transition easier for both the parent and the adolescent (Dornbusch et al., 1985).

---

1. What role does conflict play in communication between adolescents and their parents? Why are most conflicts likely to occur during early adoles-cence?
2. How do parenting styles affect intergenerational communication?
3. Describe the dimensions of family functioning that help the adolescent be-come an independent adult.

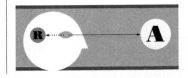

REVIEW & APPLY

PEERS AND FRIENDS

As individuals become more independent of their families, they depend increasingly on friendships to provide emotional support and serve as testing grounds for new values (Douvan & Adelson, 1966; Douvan & Gold, 1966). Close friends in particular help in identity formation. To accept her or his identity, the adolescent must feel accepted and liked by others.

During adolescence the importance of peer groups increases enormously. Teenagers seek support from others in coping with the physical, emotional, and social changes of adolescence. Understandably, they are most likely to seek support from peers, who are going through the same experiences. In a study of how much time adolescents spend with peers versus parents (Csikszentmihalyi & Larson, 1984), high school students were given electronic pagers and were beeped at different times during the day and evening. On each of these occasions, they were to call the researchers and report what they were doing. As expected, the students spent significantly more of their free time with friends and classmates than with their families (including parents and siblings)—about 50% versus about 20%. They spent the rest of their free time alone.

Peer networks are essential to the development of social skills. The reciprocal equality that characterizes teenage relationships also helps develop positive responses to the various crises that young people face (Epstein, 1983; Hawkins & Berndt, 1985). Teenagers learn from their friends and age-mates the kinds of behavior that will be socially rewarded and the roles that suit them best. *Social competence* is a major element in a teenager's ability to make new friends and maintain old ones (Fischer et al., 1986).

Social competence is based in part on the adolescent's ability to make *social comparisons*. Social comparisons enable the adolescent to form a personal identity and to evaluate characteristics of others. On the basis of these evaluations, adolescents choose close and intimate friends and sort through the cliques and crowds that are part of their environment. Adolescents are also faced with analyzing the often conflicting values of peers, parents, and others. Here we look at these processes in some detail.

SOCIAL COMPARISON

Social comparison is the process we all use to evaluate our abilities, behaviors, personality characteristics, appearance, reactions, and general sense of self in comparison with those of others, and it takes on tremendous importance during adolescence. Social comparison takes different forms during the adolescent years (Seltzer, 1989). During early adolescence, teenagers spend their time and energy defining themselves in a diverse "peer arena" made up of many different kinds of young people; they use this arena to explore and define who they are and who they want to become. They focus on their appearance and on personality characteristics that make them popular, such as a sense of humor and friendliness. This process involves a wide circle of acquaintances but few close friends; many of their relationships lack intimacy. Teenagers need time by themselves during this stage to sort out the different messages they receive, to consolidate their identity, and to develop a secure sense of self.

Social comparison changes during later adolescence. Teenagers now seek friends with whom they share similar characteristics as they substitute the quality provided by a few close friendships for a larger quantity of relatively loose friendships. Intimacy in same-sex friendships increases (Seltzer, 1989; Shulman et al., 1997).

social comparison The process by which we evaluate ourselves as compared to others.

Peers serve as audience, critic, and emotional support for their friends' ideas, innovations, and behavior.

Between ages 12 and 17, adolescents are increasingly likely to agree with statements like "I feel free to talk with my friend about almost anything" and "I know how my friend feels about things without his or her telling me." Most adolescents report that they have one or two "best friends" as well as several "good friends." These friendships tend to be stable and usually last for at least a year. It is not surprising that the stability of relationships also increases as adolescence progresses. Teenagers tend to choose friends on the basis of shared interests and activities, with equality, commitment, and especially loyalty playing major roles. Disloyalty is one of the main reasons teenagers cite for ending a friendship (Hartup, 1993).

As friendships become more intimate, teenagers tend to turn to close friends instead of to their parents for advice. As Table 11–1 shows, adolescents are likely to ask their peers for advice on many matters. However, they continue to seek advice from their parents on such matters as education, finances, and career plans (Sebald, 1989).

DATING

At the same time that the intimacy of same-sex friendships is increasing, friendships with members of the opposite sex are being formed. Close relationships with opposite-sex friends are reported at an earlier age by girls than by boys (Sharabany, Gershoni, & Hoffman, 1981); this tendency is probably due in part to the fact that puberty occurs earlier in girls than in boys.

During early adolescence, most interactions with the opposite sex take place in group settings. Many 14- or 15-year-olds prefer group contact to the closer relationship of dating. "Just hanging out" (sitting around and chatting in a pizzeria, standing on a street corner, milling around a shopping mall) is a popular pastime throughout adolescence, and it becomes increasingly "coeducational" as adolescence progresses. This type of interaction is often the first step in learning how to relate to the opposite sex. Early adolescence is a stage of testing, imagining, and discovering what it's like to function in mixed groups and pairs. It gives adolescents a trial period to collect ideas and experiences

Intimacy takes many forms during adolescence.

TABLE 11–1   PERCENTAGES OF TEENAGERS SEEKING ADVICE FROM PEERS

ISSUES	GIRLS	BOYS
What to spend money on	2	19
Whom to date	47	41
Which clubs to join	60	54
Where to get advice on personal problems	53	27
How to dress	53	43
Which courses to take at school	16	8
Which hobbies to take up	36	46
How to choose the future occupation	2	0
Which social events to attend	60	66
Whether to go to college	0	0
What books to read	40	38
What magazines to buy	51	46
How often to date	24	35
Whether to participate in drinking parties	40	46
How to choose a future spouse	9	8
Whether to go steady	29	30
How intimate to be on a date	24	35
Where to get information about sex	44	30

Source: Adapted from H. Sebald (Winter 1989). Adolescents' Peer Orientation: Changes in the Support System During the Past Three Decades." *Adolescence*, pp. 940–941.

from which to form basic attitudes about gender roles and sexual behavior without feeling pressured to become too deeply involved (Douvan & Adelson, 1966).

Bruce Roscoe and colleagues (1987) note seven important functions that dating serves; these are summarized in Table 11–2. The researchers also noted certain developmental trends. Younger adolescents tend to think in terms of immediate gratification; they consider recreation and status to be the most important reasons for dating. Young adolescents look for dates who are physically attractive, dress well, and are liked by others. Older adolescents are less superficial in their attitudes toward dating; they are more concerned about personality characteristics and the person's plans for the future. Older adolescents consider companionship and mate selection important reasons for dating. In addition, an interesting gender difference emerges for both younger and older adolescents: Females consider intimacy more important than sex, whereas males consider sex far more important than intimacy.

In general, adolescents tend to select friends and dating partners who are similar to themselves in terms of social class, interests, moral values, and academic ambitions (Berndt, 1982). They become increasingly aware of peer groups and are very concerned about whether their group is "with it" or "out of it." Adolescents know which kind of group they belong to and consider its effect on their status and reputation. Teenagers who belong to high-status groups tend to have high self-esteem (Brown & Lohr, 1987). Also teenagers who have

TABLE 11–2   FUNCTIONS OF DATING

Recreation: An opportunity to have fun with a person of the opposite sex.

Socialization: An opportunity for persons of opposite sexes to get to know each other and to learn how to interact appropriately.

Status: An opportunity to increase status by being seen with someone who is considered desirable.

Companionship: An opportunity to have a friend of the opposite sex with whom to interact and to share experiences.

Intimacy: An opportunity to establish a close, meaningful relationship with a person of the opposite sex.

Sex: An opportunity to engage in sexual experimentation or to obtain sexual satisfaction.

Mate selection: An opportunity to associate with members of the opposite sex for the purpose of selecting a husband or wife.

a strong sense of ethnic-group identity (especially African-Americans and Hispanic-Americans) tend to have higher self-esteem than those who do not (Martinez & Dukes, 1997).

CLIQUES, CROWDS, AND LONERS

There are two basic types of peer groups, distinguished by size. The larger type, with perhaps fifteen to thirty members, is called a *crowd*; the smaller type, which might have as few as three members or as many as nine, is called a *clique*, and is more cohesive. Peer crowds typically have cliques within them. Clique members share similar backgrounds, characteristics, interests, or reputations; examples include "jocks," "populars," "brains," and "druggies" (Brown & Lohr, 1987; Dunphy, 1963, 1980). During early adolescence, cliques

As adolescence proceeds, cliques expand to include both males and females.

tend to be all-male or all-female; later, teenagers become involved in opposite-sex cliques as well. This change coincides with the beginning of dating. Small same-sex cliques merge or relate to other same-sex groups, expand to include opposite-sex groups, and finally reemerge as groups that include both males and females (Dunphy, 1980; Atwater, 1992).

Although about 80% of adolescents belong to identifiable groups, 20% don't and are therefore "loners." Most of us think of being alone as a sad state of affairs that no one would willingly choose, but that isn't necessarily the case. For example, creative work such as painting, composing music, or writing requires solitude. Creative people want to be alone much of the time. Solitude may have many other positive attributes as well. Some people experience a sense of renewal or healing when alone. Also, many seek solitude for the same reasons as the artist or the writer does—they can think best while alone and can work through their problems (Marcoen et al., 1987). In each case the aloneness is *voluntary*—an opportunity for creativity, relief from pressures, or psychological renewal.

Sometimes, however, adolescents wind up as loners because they feel that they're different and strange and so can't really "belong." That result can happen for many reasons, but a striking one is having grown up in a markedly different neighborhood, city, or region of the country. An extreme example—having lived overseas in childhood and then having returned to the United States—is discussed in "Eye on Diversity," on facing page. Also on the negative side, *involuntary* aloneness imposed by others through arguments and rejection can bring on severe feelings of isolation and depression (Marcoen et al., 1987).

NEGOTIATING THE BORDERS: PEERS AND PARENTS

As we've seen, the backdrop for adolescents' relationships with their peers is their relationship with their family. Adolescents respond to their peers in the context of the cultural practices they grew up with at home, including their parents' socioeconomic status, occupation, and ethnic and religious background. Inevitably, there will be some difference between the worldviews of family members and those of peers. All teenagers must "negotiate the border" between differing worldviews in defining their own identities.

For some adolescents, that task is especially difficult. For example, Hindu adolescents whose parents have immigrated to the United States from India face a double set of standards, many of which are in direct conflict. They must decide how to dress and wear their hair—in the traditional way, perhaps demanded by their parents, or in a way that conforms to that of their new American peers. When one researcher investigated how Hindu adolescents handle this conflict (Miller, 1995), she found that such conflicts are more serious for girls than for boys. Girls must choose between strict Hindu standards, which require extreme modesty in attire and long, braided hair, and the more liberal clothing and hairstyles that are popular in the United States. Miller reported that time and again, the influence of the peer group was stronger than that of parents. Even at events held at religious temples, some adolescent girls wore shorts while their parents wore the traditional sari or kurta/pajama wear. Similarly, Hindu adolescent girls in the United States frequently wear their hair short and unbound.

Conflicts also occur when Hindu values about dating and premarital sex clash with the more liberal values of the U.S. adolescent culture. As Indian psychoanalyst Sudhir Kakar (1986) explains,

In sexual terms, the West is perceived as a gigantic brothel, whereas the "good" Indian woman is idealized nostalgically in all her purity, modesty,

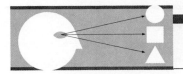

EYE ON DIVERSITY

REPATRIATED ADOLESCENTS

Roughly a quarter of a million American children and adolescents currently live overseas with their families, go to "American-sponsored" or "international" schools, and are part of a small American community living in the midst of a local culture that may be quite different from their own. What is it like when they are repatriated—that is, when they and their families eventually return to the United States?

This experience, often termed *reentry*, has been compared with coming back to the earth from outer space. It is often stressful and psychologically difficult for adolescents—especially if they have spent extended portions of their childhood away from the United States. They feel different and may even look different; they find it hard to answer questions like "Where are you from?" They experience "reverse culture shock" when they encounter aspects of American culture that are unfamiliar to them. It can take months, even years, to learn how to fit in and feel comfortable in American society.

For adolescents who have had this experience, identity formation may be particularly difficult. They may have to retrace the steps toward identity achievement outlined by Erikson and Marcia. And they are frequently treated as outsiders by peers. It is difficult for them to gain acceptance in already-established crowds or cliques, especially since their outlooks and values may be very different from those of their peers. Thus, at least for a time, they often become loners. Some will never feel that they are truly "Americans."

On the positive side, repatriated Americans often have a much more re- alistic view of the United States and the way that its actions and policies affect other nations and peoples. Moreover, they often feel like "global citizens," avoiding the ethnocentric view of many Americans that the United States is the center of the universe. The skills they developed while living overseas— such as language ability and the ability to bridge cultural gaps—stand them in good stead as they pursue careers in such fields as intercultural counseling and international relations. In the long run, then—after their difficult period of adjustment—they may actually become better citizens than many Americans who have not had an opportunity to view their nation from the outside.

Source: C. D. Smith. (1994). *The Absentee American: Repatriates' Perspectives on America.*

---

and chastity. For Indians living in the West, this idealization and the splitting that underlies it are more emotionally charged and more intense than would be the case in India itself. The inevitable Westernization of wives and daughters is, therefore, the cause of deep emotional stress in men, and of explosive conflicts in the family. (page 39)

The difficult act of negotiating the borders between parental and peer values and practices is, of course, common to all adolescents, not just new immigrants. Some urban adolescents, for example, must negotiate between a peer culture that glorifies drugs and crime, and parental values that stress working within the system and obeying the rules. For adolescents who are still in the process of defining themselves, there is a tendency to draw the borders too narrowly or to adhere slavishly to a narrow set of peer prescriptions for behavior, dress, and all the other things that matter so much to adolescents.

---

1. Describe the stages that adolescents pass through in developing intimate relationships.
2. What is the difference between a crowd and a clique, and why is it important for adolescents to be alone at times?
3. Why is it sometimes difficult for adolescents to negotiate the border between the worldviews of their parents and those of their peers?

REVIEW & APPLY

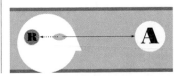

WHEN ADOLESCENCE GOES AWRY

Experimenting with different attitudes and behaviors, defining and redefining oneself, and gradually moving away from parental control are hallmarks of adolescence that serve an important and healthy purpose—they help transform a child into an adult. These same tendencies, however, can yield extremely unhealthy behaviors during adolescence—such as risk-taking in general and drug use in particular. In this section we look at these and other aspects of the "downside" of adolescence, along with some of their causes.

RISK-TAKING

Many adolescents engage in unprotected sex, sometimes with multiple partners and with outcomes ranging from unwanted pregnancy to life-threatening diseases as noted in the preceding chapter. Many also use and abuse drugs. Teenagers are notorious for reckless driving and a variety of other dangerous activities. Violence, often gang-related, continues at an alarming rate. In fact, people from 10 to 19 years of age represent the only segment of the U.S. population in which mortality rates have not declined rapidly in recent years (U.S. Department of Health and Human Services, 1991).

Naturally, some teenagers are more prone to engage in high-risk activities than others, often engaging in more such activities as they get older (Jessor et al., 1992). For other teenagers, the increase in energy and intellectual curiosity that accompanies adolescence is harnessed in different ways, perhaps in sports, or put to constructive rather than potentially destructive uses. For example, many teenagers become involved in social activism, engaging in environmental cleanups, helping to build houses for poor families, or working with sick children. It is important to keep in mind that only a minority of adolescents engage in high-risk behaviors for destructive purposes.

Adolescents engage in high-risk behaviors for a variety of reasons. They may get into trouble because they don't understand the risks they're taking. They may have too little information; the warnings that adolescents receive from adults may be ineffective, or they may choose to ignore them. Many researchers believe that adolescents who take risks underestimate the likelihood of bad outcomes; in other words, they see themselves as invulnerable. They focus mainly on the anticipated benefits of high-risk behaviors, such as higher status with peers. This explanation is consistent with David Elkind's (1967) concept of the *personal fable*, discussed in Chapter 10, in which adolescents believe that they won't get hurt, sick, or pregnant as a result of their behavior.

The results of over two decades of research on adolescent risk-taking point to multiple causes for these behaviors (see Figure 11–2). Factors producing high-risk behaviors are divided into five domains: biology/genetics, the social environment, the perceived environment, personality, and actual behavior. These domains interact to cause adolescents to engage in high-risk behaviors or lifestyles. Note that both hereditary and social-environmental factors contribute. For example, a child with a family history of alcohol or other drug use might be predisposed to such behavior, experience environmental poverty and deviant role models, and be more like to engage in drug-related behavior than a child who doesn't experience each domain.

FIGURE 11–2   A CONCEPTUAL FRAMEWORK FOR ADOLESCENT RISK BEHAVIOR

Source: "Risk Behavior in Adolescence: A Psychosocial Framework for Understanding and Action," (page 27) by Richard Jessor, 1992, in Adolescents at Risk: Medical and Social Perspectives, *edited by D. E. Rogers and E. Ginzberg. Reprinted by permission of Richard Jessor.*

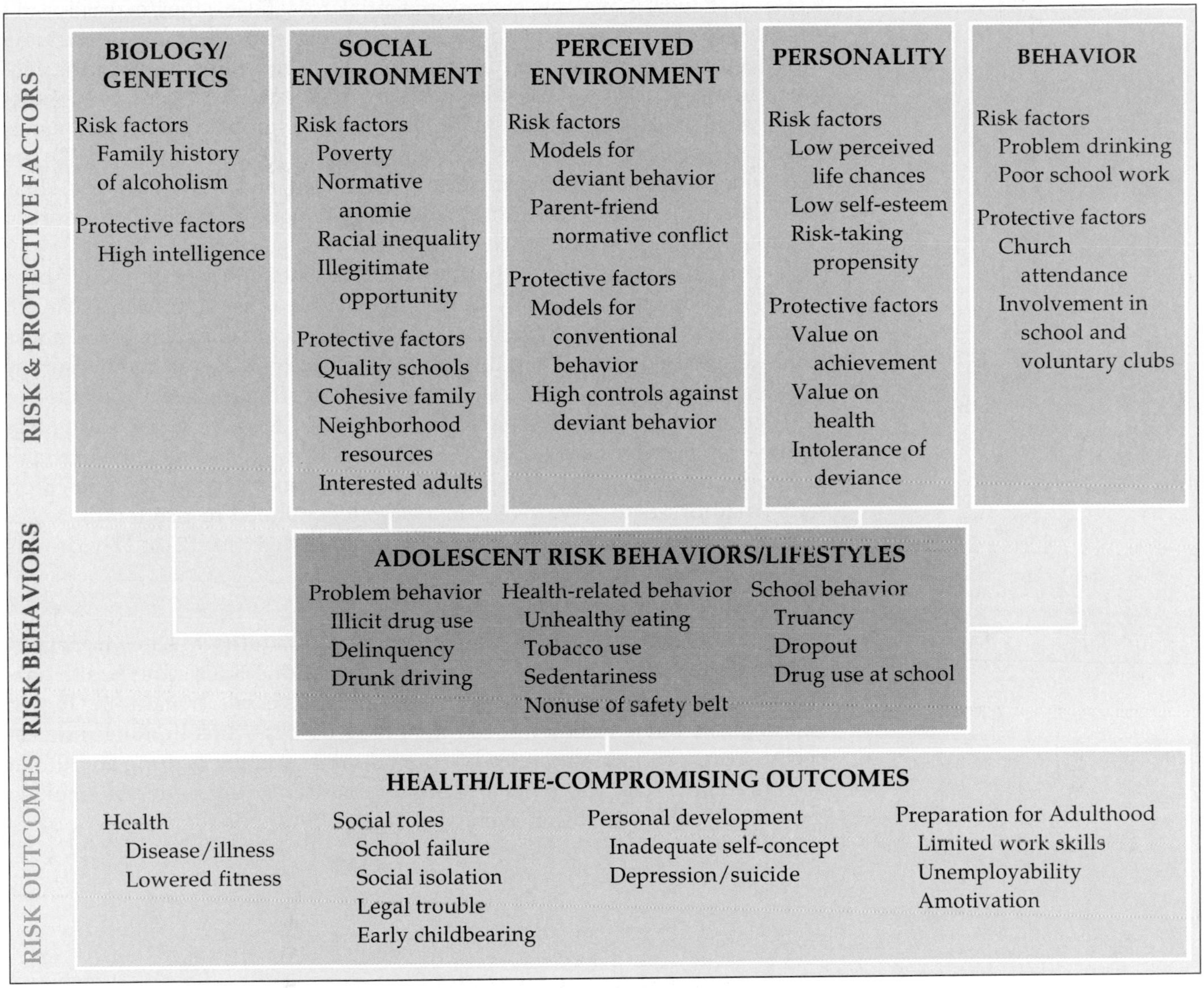

How can parents prevent adolescents from engaging in dangerous activities? Many families become involved in their children's schools, contact public officials and teachers when their child is having trouble, and take action to prevent drug use and other destructive behaviors at home. Some families move their child to a safer environment, such as a private school, to avoid negative neighborhood or peer group influences (Jessor, 1993). In general, when adolescents develop self-esteem, a sense of competence, and a sense of belonging to a stable family and social order, they are less likely to engage in high-risk behaviors (Jessor, 1993; Quadrel et al., 1993). However, there is no truly safe environment, and no child is completely invulnerable to the destructive forces that are ubiquitous in our society. In the remainder of this section, we will take a closer look at some of these forces, beginning with perhaps the most destructive of all: drugs.

DRUG USE AND ABUSE

A pervasive high-risk behavior during adolescence and young adulthood is the use and abuse of alcohol and other drugs. Of all the legal and illegal drugs that are widely available in this country, nicotine (cigarettes) and alcohol (beer, wine, or liquor) have the highest potential for abuse—they're easily and cheaply obtained, and many adults serve as models for their use. Aside from the effects of these drugs, and in spite of public-service messages to the contrary, many adolescents consider smoking and drinking "safe" habits that make them look more adult. Marijuana, cocaine, amphetamine stimulants, heroin, and *hallucinogenic drugs* such as lysergic acid diethylamide (LSD) are also widely available in inner cities and suburbs and outlying areas alike. Given limited funds, some adolescents (and younger children) also resort to "huffing" volatile inhalants such as glues and even gasoline.

As described in Chapter 1, the National Household Survey on Drug Abuse (NHSDA), conducted annually by the Substance Abuse and Mental Health Services Administration (SAMSHA), assesses the extent of drug use and abuse in age ranges beginning at age 12. Although most experts agree that the survey underestimates actual drug use, it nonetheless provides a clear picture of trends over the years, as illustrated in Figure 11–3. Aside from the alarmingly high percentages for persons aged 12 to 17 and 18 to 25, also note the rise in illicit drug use in these age groups in the 1990s—which apparently tapered off somewhat for 12- to 17-year-olds in 1996 but continued to rise for 18- to 25-year olds. Table 11–3 breaks down drug use percentages for 12- to 17-year-olds by type of drug.

TOBACCO Cigarettes are an alluring symbol of maturity to some teenagers, despite overwhelming evidence that cigarette smoking is a serious health hazard. Smoking increases heart rate, constricts blood vessels, irritates the throat, and deposits foreign matter in sensitive lung tissues—thus limiting lung capacity. Years of smoking can lead to premature heart attacks, lung and throat cancer, emphysema, and other respiratory diseases. Even moderate smoking shortens a person's life by an average of 7 years (Eddy, 1991).

FIGURE 11–3 PAST MONTH* ILLICIT DRUG USE, BY AGE, 1979–1996

**"Past Month" drug use means at least once in the month preceding the interview.*

Source: Substance Abuse and Mental Health Services Administration (1997). National Household Survey on Drug Abuse.

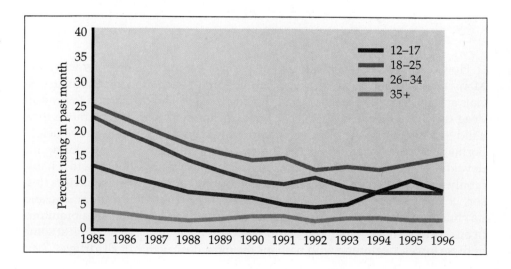

TABLE 11–3   PERCENTAGES OF ADOLESCENTS AGED 12 TO 17 REPORTING PAST MONTH ALCOHOL AND OTHER DRUG USE

	1985	1988	1990	1991	1992	1993	1994	1995	1996
Any alcohol	41	33	33	27	21	24	22	21	19
"Heavy" alcohol	8	6	6	7	6	7	6	6	5
Cigarettes	39	35	33	33	32	30	29	29	29
Marijuana	10	6	5	5	5	5	5	5	5
Cocaine	3	2	1	1	1	1	1	1	1
Any illicit drug	13	8	7	6	5	6	8	11	9

Source: Substance Abuse and Mental Health Services Administration (1997), *National Household Survey on Drug Abuse.*

Tobacco smoking by adolescents showed a sharp decline in the 1970s and early 1980s, but since then, it has remained relatively stable (about 29% of adolescents smoked at least occasionally in 1996). In the past, boys began smoking earlier than girls and smoked more. Since 1977, however, more adolescent girls than boys have reported daily smoking. More than half of both boys and girls who smoke begin by the ninth grade, sometimes as a result of peer pressure. In the years just after high school, many light smokers begin smoking more heavily. One in four young adults is a daily smoker, and one in five smokes half a pack of cigarettes or more per day (National Institute on Drug Abuse, 1987). As adults, many continue to smoke because nicotine is a highly addictive drug.

Many cigarette ads now target teenagers. Adolescent girls smoke more frequently than boys.

FIGURE 11–4 USE OF ILLICIT DRUGS AND ALCOHOL BY 12- TO 17-YEAR-OLD SMOKERS AND NONSMOKERS, 1996

Source: Substance Abuse and Mental Health Services Administration (1997), National Household Survey on Drug Abuse.

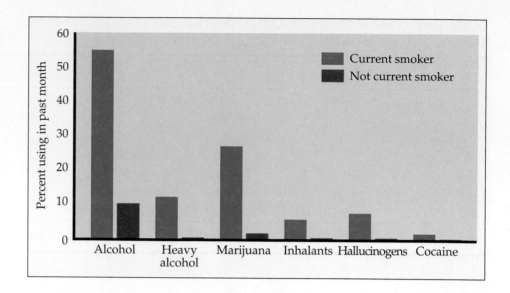

It is interesting that smoking is highly correlated with adolescent use of other drugs, as illustrated in Figure 11–4. For example, of the adolescents classified as "current" smokers, about 55% also use alcohol at least occasionally, compared with only 10% of nonsmokers.

ALCOHOL   Alcohol is a central nervous system (CNS) depressant with effects similar to those of sleeping pills or tranquilizers. When alcohol is consumed in small amounts, the psychological effects include reduced inhibition and self-restraint, a heightened feeling of well-being, and an accelerated sense of time. Many drinkers use alcohol to ease tension and facilitate social interaction—which it does, but only up to a point. Larger doses distort vision, impair motor coordination, and slur speech; still larger doses lead to loss of consciousness or even death. These effects depend not only on the amount of alcohol consumed but also on individual levels of tolerance for the substance. Long-term habitual use of alcohol increases tolerance but eventually causes damage to the liver and brain. Gender is a factor, too: Women typically don't metabolize alcohol out of their system as rapidly as men, so that smaller amounts can make them relatively more inebriated.

Like cigarettes, a powerful factor in teenage alcohol use is the notion that alcohol consumption is a symbol of adulthood and social maturity. In 1996, there were about 9 million current drinkers in the 12 to 20 age range (SAMSHA, 1997). By early adolescence more than half of American teenagers have used alcohol; the proportion grows to 92% by the end of high school (Newcomb & Bentler, 1989). Although only one in twenty high school seniors reports drinking every day, heavy drinking on weekends has become quite common among adolescents. Fully 35% of high school seniors report having had five or more drinks in a row at least once in the past 2 weeks, and 32% report that most or all of their friends get drunk at least once a week. Young adults who can drink legally tend to consume more alcohol because they may drink on a more regular basis at bars and social gatherings. These patterns of alcohol consumption have remained relatively stable in recent years, with only a slight decline since the early 1980s.

Alcohol consumption by young people varies according to age, ethnic and religious background, locality, and gender. For example, the pattern of occasional heavy drinking is highest for those in the four years immediately after high school (above 40%); for males (50% versus 26% for females); for noncollege youth; and for those who live in cities rather than in rural areas (National Institute on Drug Abuse, 1987).

The typical alcohol-abusing adolescent is a male with low grades and a family history of alcohol abuse. He is likely to have friends who also drink, and he may also use other drugs. Many alcohol abusers have serious psychological problems such as depression, a poor sense of identity, lack of goals, or a tendency constantly to seek new sensations and experiences. In addition, poor self-efficacy and low personal competence are predictors of adolescent alcohol use (Scheier & Botvin, 1998).

MARIJUANA   After alcohol and nicotine, marijuana is the most widely used drug in the United States. This drug, which is illegal (except for medicinal purposes in some states), produces at least mild physical and psychological symptoms in those who use it regularly (Witters & Venturelli, 1988). A report by the National Academy of Sciences states that marijuana has undesirable short-term effects but that little is known about its long-term effects. The short-term effects include impaired coordination and perception, along with a rise in heart rate and blood pressure (Reinhold, 1982). Possible long-term effects are the same as those of smoking cigarettes, especially since marijuana is typically smoked without filtering; marijuana "joints" or "bowls" are smoked all the way because of the cost of the drug, with harsh effects on the respiratory system.

Use of marijuana by adolescents and young adults rose sharply during the 1970s, then declined, but began to rise again in the 1990s—at least 7% of 12- to 17-year-olds reported at least occasional use in 1996 (SAMSHA, 1997). Interestingly, marijuana also became a much more "egalitarian" drug in the 1990s, as shown in Figure 11–5. Whereas white adolescents were significantly more likely to use marijuana in the 1980s, white, Hispanic, and black adolescents now use marijuana at virtually the same rate.

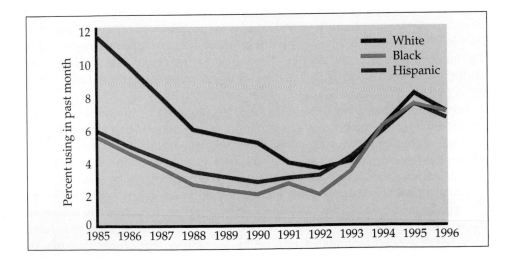

FIGURE 11–5   PAST MONTH* MARIJUANA USE AMONG YOUTH AGED 12 TO 17, 1985–1996

*"Past Month" drug use means at least once in the month preceding the interview.

Source: Substance Abuse and Mental Health Services Administration (1997), National Household Survey on Drug Abuse.

COCAINE Cocaine is an extract of the coca plant and is medically classified as a CNS stimulant, although it is legally classified as a narcotic. It is highly addictive in any form—powder, which is sniffed or injected in solution, or "crack," which is usually smoked. Crack is the most addictive form. Crack smokers experience the greatest initial "rush" of exhilaration; they also feel the most intense craving as the dose wears off. The full range of physical and psychological risks of cocaine use has not been studied fully, but the known risks include death from stroke, heart attack, or respiratory failure (Kaku, 1991; Witters & Venturelli, 1988). Using cocaine in conjunction with other drugs, such as alcohol and heroin, is popular and obviously increases the risks.

Because cocaine is very expensive, its use has never been common among adolescents; it is more likely to be used by young adults who can afford it, although it is also associated with prostitution at all ages. In fact, crack cocaine use is heavily implicated in the transmission of HIV/AIDS because some users engage in prostitution to support their habit; unprotected sex with multiple partners is routine in "crack houses."

As indicated in Table 11–3, cocaine use by younger adolescents has always been minimal and has remained stable at about 1% during the 1990s. Moreover, adolescents' attitudes toward cocaine use have undergone a striking change: 97% disapprove of regular use of the drug (Newcomb & Bentler, 1989).

HEROIN Heroin is a central nervous system depressant that alleviates pain, produces strong feelings of euphoria, and therefore is highly addictive. It is usually injected for maximum effect, although it can also be sniffed or smoked. As with cocaine, heroin use is relatively low among adolescents; however, heroin use has increased during the 1990s (University of Michigan, 1997). Among adolescents between the ages of 12 and 17, heroin use nearly doubled from 1994 to 1996 (SAMSHA, 1997).

OTHER DRUGS According to the University of Michigan's Monitoring the Future study (1997), an annual survey of junior high and high school students, hallucinogen use (including LSD) increased steadily in the 1990s and leveled off in 1997. Adolescent use of "designer" drugs such as ecstasy ("X") and other amphetamine derivatives has also been on the rise. Adolescent use of volatile inhalants increased in the early 1990s but has recently declined.

DELINQUENCY

Risk-taking sometimes takes the form of delinquent behavior, which often—but not necessarily—goes hand in hand with drug use. Delinquent acts range in seriousness from shoplifting and vandalism to robbery, rape, and murder. People under age 16 or 18 who commit criminal acts are called *delinquents;* the age cutoff varies by state and by the nature of the crime. Although people under age 18 make up only 38% of the U.S. population, they commit more than 50% of all serious crimes (Garbarino et al., 1984).

At some point in their lives, most children engage in some form of delinquent behavior. Shoplifting is very common, as are minor acts of vandalism—damage or desecration of property. Whether individuals are labeled as delinquent depends mainly on the frequency with which they commit misdemeanors or felonies and, of course, on whether they're arrested.

Statistically, delinquency rates are highest in poor urban areas, although this trend may be due in part to the tendency of police to make more arrests in those areas. Delinquency is also more likely among ethnic groups that have only recently been assimilated into urban life, either from other cultures or from rural areas—especially if they form gangs. Young males from single-parent homes headed by a mother are more likely to engage in delinquent behavior, regardless of the family's socioeconomic level. It is not merely the absence of a male role model that is responsible; an adolescent boy with a stepfather is as likely to get into trouble as one who lives with his mother alone (Steinberg, 1987b).

Sociologists and psychologists explain delinquent behavior in different ways. Sociological statistics and theories link delinquency to factors in the youth's social environment, but they do not address psychological factors. Psychological theories maintain that environmental factors alone do not explain why adolescents commit crimes. Individuals are not delinquent because they are poor or live in a city. They may be delinquent because they are unable or unwilling to adjust to society or to develop adequate self-control or outlets for anger or frustration. Some adolescents also become delinquent mainly because they are members of delinquent peer groups (Vitaro et al., 1997).

The distinction between sociological and psychological causes of delinquency is artificial, however (Gibbons, 1976). As we have seen, sociological factors often lead to psychological consequences, and vice versa. Sociological influences such as crowding, mobility, and rapid change are linked to psychological problems. Like the other patterns we have studied in this chapter, delinquency is a form of adjustment to the social and psychological realities of adolescence—an extreme adjustment that society disapproves of. Delinquency may satisfy the need for self-esteem; it provides acceptance and status within deviant peer groups (such as gangs) and a sense of autonomy. Some delinquents engage in high-risk behaviors just for thrills.

In addition to individual factors, the mass media may be implicated in the development of violent or delinquent behaviors among vulnerable teenagers. Movies, for example, may affect troubled adolescents through social learning. Identification with a violent movie and its characters may lead to imitation of the characters' behaviors with regard to assault and battery, stealing, using and selling drugs, and even "copy-cat" acts of violence.

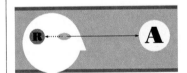

REVIEW & APPLY

1. Discuss reasons for risk-taking behaviors during adolescence, including alcohol and abuse of other drugs.
2. Describe recent trends in alcohol and drug use by adolescents and young adults.
3. How do sociologists and psychologists explain delinquent behavior?

STRESS, DEPRESSION, AND ADOLESCENT COPING

Many articles and discussions about adolescents are filled with dramatic rhetoric. One article may claim that all adolescents are depressed or rebellious or potential runaways; another may state, "Wait until your child turns 12; then the storm and stress will begin." Two problems arise from such overstatements of the psychological traumas of adolescence. First, all adolescents are labeled as experiencing psychological distress, which is not the case. Second, adolescents who need help are not taken seriously because their behavior and feelings are considered part of a normal developmental phase (Connelly et al., 1993). Clearly, it is important to distinguish between normal adolescents and those who are experiencing real psychological distress. In this section, therefore, we'll take a close look at adolescent depression and other stress-related disorders, the factors that help protect adolescents from these disorders or make them vulnerable to them, and common coping responses.

DEPRESSION

In general, studies of psychiatric disorders during adolescence have found a fairly low incidence of moderate to severe depression, but in those who are affected, the symptoms may be life-threatening (Peterson, et al., 1993). In a recent study, for example, although the results show an increase in depression over the teenage years, the percentage experiencing depression is consistently low, peaking at age 16 and again at age 19 (see Table 11–4).

Symptoms vary by gender. Troubled boys are likely to engage in antisocial behaviors like delinquency and drug abuse. Troubled girls are more likely to direct their symptoms inward and become depressed (Ostrov et al., 1989). Overall, depression is about twice as common in female adolescents (and adults) as in males. Although the reasons for these gender differences aren't clear, psychologists believe that they may be related to the substantial drop in self-esteem that sometimes occurs in girls when they enter junior high school (Bower, 1991b; Orenstein, 1994). As we have seen, girls are pressured by peers and the media to become more attractive and to value relationships above achievements (Connelly et al., 1993). In general, the combination of less effective coping styles and greater challenges may increase the likelihood of depression for girls as they move through adolescence.

Researchers have also found ethnic and other group differences in the incidence of depression in adolescence. For example, European- and Asian-

TABLE 11–4   PERCENTAGE OF STUDENTS EXPERIENCING NONE TO MILD AND MODERATE TO SEVERE DEPRESSION, BY AGE AND GENDER (N = 2698)

SEVERITY	AGE							
	13	14	15	16	17	18	19	Total
Males								
None to mild	96%	97%	93%	88%	93%	94%	89%	93%
Moderate to severe	4%	3%	7%	12%	7%	6%	11%	7%
Female								
None to mild	93%	90%	89%	84%	87%	87%	82%	88%
Moderate to severe	7%	10%	11%	16%	13%	13%	18%	12%

Source: Connelly et al. (1993).

A MATTER FOR DEBATE

WHAT CAUSES ADOLESCENT SUICIDE?

In recent years, public concern over the increasing rate of adolescent suicide has led to increased suicide prevention efforts at the local, state, and federal levels. The concern is justified. In 1992, 4693 adolescents and youth between the ages 15 and 24, and 314 children under age 15, committed suicide (National Center for Health Statistics, 1995). Suicide is the third leading cause of death among adolescents, behind accidents and homicide, and the statistics probably underestimate the actual number of suicides. Suicide tends to be underreported because of religious taboos against it and concern for the feelings of other family members (Garland & Zigler, 1993). Surveys of high school students have found that from 54% to 62.6% of students have either engaged in suicidal behavior or thought about suicide (Meehan et al., 1992).

Risk Factors

Studies of adolescents who have attempted suicide, together with "psychological autopsies" of successful suicides, have revealed certain risk factors. Although many adolescents who experience these risk factors do not contemplate or attempt suicide, these factors can provide early warnings that suicide is a possibility. Generally accepted risk factors for adolescent suicide include the following (see Norton, 1994, for a review of risk factors and warning signs):

1. A previous suicide attempt (the best single predictor)
2. Depression, including strong feelings of helplessness and hopelessness (perhaps the next best predictor)
3. Other psychiatric problems, such as conduct disorder or antisocial personality
4. Abuse of alcohol and other drugs
5. Stressful life events, such as serious family turmoil, divorce, or separation
6. Access to and use of firearms

In general, adolescents who attempt suicide are not responding to one particular upsetting event. Instead, suicides generally occur within the context of long-standing personal or family problems, although the attempt itself may be done on impulse (Curran, 1987).

David Elkind (1997) attributes the dramatic increase in adolescent suicides to increased pressure on young children to achieve and be responsible at earlier ages. Others have blamed the mass media: There is a significant increase in adolescent suicidal behavior following television or newspaper coverage of suicides. Fictional stories about suicide have also been found to be associated with an increase in suicidal behavior (Garland & Zigler, 1993). "Copycat suicides" are particularly likely in adolescence, when individuals are most vulnerable to the belief that the future is beyond their control or is unlikely to meet their dreams.

Prevention Efforts

Crisis intervention services and telephone hotlines have been established throughout the nation to help prevent suicide. There are over 1000 suicide hotlines available to adolescents. A relatively new approach, preventive education, is usually directed at secondary school students, their parents, and educators. These programs typically include a review of the statistics on suicide, the warning signs for suicide, a list of community resources and the way to contact them, and the listening skills needed to convince a suicidal friend or family member to seek help (Garland & Zigler, 1993).

The American Psychological Association has developed a suicide prevention program (Garland & Zigler, 1993) that includes the following recommendations:

1. Professional education for educators, health workers, and mental health workers.
2. Restricting access to firearms by passing strict gun control laws.
3. Suicide education for media personnel to ensure correct information and appropriate reporting.
4. Identification and treatment of at-risk youth.

Given the severity of the problem, a comprehensive program such as this may offer the best means of preventing adolescent suicide. Prevention, of course, must be followed by treatment. Through psychotherapy, adolescents with suicidal tendencies gain insight into their problems and develop coping strategies. Therapy also helps troubled teenagers to feel better about themselves and to develop increased self-efficacy. Treatment may also include antidepressive medications such as Elavil, Tofranil, and Prozac (Shuchman & Wilkes, 1990).

Contact with a close friend is a positive way for teenagers to relieve moderate stress.

Americans are more likely to show symptoms of depression when under stress than are African-Americans or Hispanic-Americans. Native American teenagers have elevated rates of depression. Homosexual adolescents also show higher rates of depression and are two to three times more likely to commit suicide than heterosexual adolescents (Connelly et al., 1993), presumably because of the social pressures they encounter. Factors in adolescent suicide are discussed in more detail in "A Matter for Debate," page 401.

DEPRESSION AND OTHER DISORDERS

In a recent review of the research literature on depression, Dante Cicchetti and Sheree Toth (1998) note that understanding childhood and adolescent depression requires the understanding of the interrelationships among biological, psychological, and social-systems components. Several such interrelationships are discussed here.

Depression in adolescence often occurs at the same time as other disorders in response to internal and external stresses. Thus, depression and anxiety disorders often occur together, and so do depression and conduct disorders. Boys are more likely to be disruptive when depressed, whereas depressed girls are more likely to develop eating disorders such as anorexia or bulimia (Connelly et al., 1993), discussed in the preceding chapter. A high proportion of adolescents of either sex who attempt suicide are depressed, both before and after the attempt. Depression, thoughts of suicide, and substance abuse are also interrelated (Kandel et al., 1991).

On the other hand, poor body image may lead to eating disorders and then to depression. An elevated risk of depression has been found to be associated with illness, and this too can work in either direction—chronic illness is depressing, and depression can increase vulnerability to illness. Depression may also cause other problems because of its impact on interpersonal functioning, and vice versa. Poor social functioning may worsen the parent-child relationship during adolescence and may also affect friendships and romantic relationships. For example, pregnancy is three times more likely among depressed teenage girls than among those who are not depressed (Horowitz et al., 1991).

PROTECTIVE FACTORS AND COPING BEHAVIORS

The biological changes of puberty, as well as the social changes related to the move from elementary school to middle and high school, all demand extensive psychological adjustment. Here we'll look at risk factors, protective factors, and coping behaviors.

RISK FACTORS　Factors that place adolescents at risk for depression and stress reactions include the following:

1. Negative body image, which is believed to lead to depression and eating disorders
2. Increased capacity to reflect about oneself and the future, which can lead to depression as adolescents dwell on negative possibilities
3. Family dysfunction or parental mental health problems, which can lead to stress reactions and depression as well as conduct disorders
4. Marital discord or divorce and economic hardship in the family, which lead to depression and stress
5. Low popularity with peers, which is related to depression in adolescence and is among the strongest predictors of adult depression

6. Low achievement in school, which leads to depression and disruptive behavior in boys but does not appear to affect girls

Many girls emerge from early adolescence with a poor self-image, relatively low expectations of life, and much less confidence in themselves and their abilities than is true of boys (American Association of University Women, 1991; Orenstein, 1994; Zimmerman et al., 1997). At age 9, a majority of girls feel positive about themselves, but by the time they reach high school, less than a third feel that way. Although boys lose some self-esteem during the middle school years, their loss isn't nearly as great as that of girls.

There are significant racial and ethnic differences in this loss of self-esteem: It appears to be largely a white phenomenon. Surveys indicate that African-American girls seem to derive self-esteem from their families and communities rather than from their experiences in school. African-American girls may be surrounded by strong women whom they admire. In addition, African-American parents often teach their children that there is nothing wrong with them, only with the way the world treats them. White girls, on the other hand, may overreact to social cues in schools where boys are favored, as noted in earlier chapters. By the age of 15 or 16, many white girls are filled with self-doubt. When they have problems with academic subjects such as math, they are more likely to blame themselves, whereas boys are more likely to blame the course (Daley, 1991). As Carol Gilligan has put it,

> This [research] makes it impossible to say that what happens to girls is simply a matter of hormones . . . . If that was it, then the loss of self-esteem would happen to all girls and at roughly the same time. This work raises all kinds of issues about cultural contributions and it raises questions about the role of the schools, both in the drop of self-esteem and in the potential for intervention. (Quoted by Daley, 1991)

PROTECTIVE FACTORS   There are three sets of counterbalancing factors that help adolescents cope with the transitions of this period. First, good relationships with parents and peers serve as buffers against stress. The importance of protective, supportive relationships cannot be overstated. Second, a particular area of competence or expertise, such as in sports, music, a craft, or an academic subject, can give the teenager a basis for realistic self-confidence. Finally, a role that includes responsibility for others (perhaps team members or younger siblings) can help an adolescent set priorities and respond to challenges or crises with greater resilience.

COPING RESPONSES   Adolescents use a variety of coping responses to deal with the stress of their daily lives. Positive coping strategies, such as careful planning and organization, setting priorities, or finding a close friend or confidante, can help relieve moderate stress. When an adolescent is under heavy stress, the use of more negative defensive strategies increases. In general, research has found that substance use, diversions, and rebelliousness are major ways in which adolescents cope with stress. Students at all levels report drinking alcohol, smoking cigarettes, and using drugs to reduce feelings of stress. The diversions they report include shopping, taking a hot bath or shower, going out with friends, sleeping, watching television, and eating. These activities do not deal with problems directly, but at least they divert attention from them. In all, few adolescents who are under extreme stress feel that they can deal with the stress directly—they often lack the personal resources (Mates & Allison, 1992).

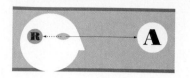

REVIEW & APPLY

1. What are the factors that place adolescents at increased risk for depression?
2. Why do teenage girls tend to suffer more from depression than teenage boys?
3. What are some of the protective factors that help adolescents cope with the stresses in their lives?

SUMMARY

Developmental Tasks of Adolescence

■ Adolescence has traditionally been viewed as a period of "storm and stress." However, most adolescents are well adjusted and have no major conflicts with their parents, peers, or selves.

■ Although the emotional distance between teenagers and their parents tends to increase, this increase does not necessarily lead to rebellion or to rejection of parental values.

■ An important goal of adolescence is independence, particularly self-regulation. Becoming an adult also requires interdependence in various kinds of social relationships.

■ According to Erikson, identity formation is the major hurdle that must be overcome in making a successful transition to adulthood.

■ Adolescents derive many of their ideas about roles and values from reference groups of various kinds, or in some cases from a special person, known as a significant other.

■ Identity formation is an often lengthy and complex process of self-definition.

■ Marcia has identified four identity statuses: foreclosure, diffusion, moratorium, and identity achievement. The status of an individual depends on whether he or she has gone through a decision-making period called an identity crisis. (See the study chart on page 381.)

■ Adolescents in foreclosure status have made commitments without going through much decision making. Those in diffusion status have not experienced a crisis or selected a role or moral code. Those in moratorium status are in the midst of an ongoing identity crisis or decision-making period. Identity achievement is the status attained by those who have passed through an identity crisis and made their commitments.

■ Anxiety is a dominant emotion for people in moratorium status because of their unresolved decisions;

in contrast, those in foreclosure status experience little anxiety. Those in diffusion status are prone to drug and alcohol abuse. Those who have attained identity achievement have the most balanced feelings toward their parents and family.

■ Girls in the later high school years are most likely to be in foreclosure status, whereas boys are most likely to be in diffusion status. Girls are more likely to express concern about possible conflicts between family and career.

Family Dynamics

■ Adolescents continue to be influenced by their families, although their ties to the family may become strained. Most conflicts revolve around issues such as chores, dating, grades, and personal appearance.

■ Generally, early adolescence is more conflict-laden than later adolescence.

■ The influences of different parenting styles continue into adolescence. The warmth and the confident control provided by authoritative parents are reassuring to most adolescents.

■ Changes in the family have affected adolescents' responsibility for household chores. Daughters now have more responsibilities than sons.

■ When teenagers are preparing to leave home, three dimensions of family function become important. They are cohesion, adaptability, and quality of communication.

■ Some studies suggest that fathers play a key role in helping adolescents find the right balance between separateness and connectedness.

Peers and Friends

■ During adolescence, the importance of peer groups increases enormously. Peer networks are essential to the development of social skills.

■ Social competence is based in part on the adolescent's ability to make social comparisons. This process is used to evaluate one's abilities, behaviors, appearance, and other characteristics in comparison with others.

■ During later adolescence, teenagers seek friends with whom they share similar characteristics. Intimacy in same-sex friendships increases.

■ As friendships become more intimate, teenagers tend to turn to close friends instead of to their parents for advice.

■ During early adolescence, most interactions with the opposite sex take place in group settings; recreation and status are the most important reasons for dating at this stage.

■ Older adolescents consider companionship and mate selection important reasons for dating. Females consider intimacy more important than sex, whereas males consider sex far more important than intimacy.

■ There are two basic types of peer groups: crowds, which have fifteen to thirty members, and cliques, which have three to nine members. Clique members share similar backgrounds, characteristics, interests, or reputations.

■ About 20% of adolescents do not belong to identifiable groups and are therefore "loners." Solitude can have some positive qualities, but involuntary aloneness imposed by others can bring on severe feelings of isolation and depression.

■ In defining their own identities, all teenagers must negotiate the border between differing worldviews of family members and peers.

Emerging Choices, Patterns, and Lifestyles

■ Many adolescents engage in risk-taking behaviors such as unprotected sex and drug use. Others harness their increased energy and intellectual curiosity in different says, such as sports.

■ Adolescents engage in high-risk behaviors for a variety of reasons. They may not understand the risks they are taking or underestimate the likelihood of bad outcomes. They focus mainly on the anticipated benefits, such as higher status with peers.

■ Adolescents with self-esteem, a sense of competence, and a sense of belonging to a stable family and social order are less likely to engage in high-risk behaviors.

■ A pervasive high-risk behavior during adolescence and young adulthood is use and abuse of alcohol and other drugs. National data show high rates of drug use among young people, and the rates for some drugs have apparently risen in the 1990s.

■ One in four young adults smokes, and smoking is highly correlated with use of other drugs.

■ As with cigarettes, a powerful factor in teenage alcohol use is the notion that alcohol consumption is a symbol of adulthood and social maturity.

■ Alcohol use by young people varies according to age, ethnic and religious background, locality, and gender. The typical alcohol-abusing adolescent is a male with low grades and a family history of alcohol abuse.

■ After alcohol and nicotine, marijuana is the most widely used drug in the United States. After declining during the 1980s, marijuana use by adolescents and young adults began to rise again in the 1990s.

■ Because cocaine is very expensive, its use has never been common among adolescents. Heroin use is also relatively low among adolescents; however, heroin use has increased during the 1990s.

■ People under age 16 or 18 who commit criminal acts are called delinquents. At some point, most children engage in some form of delinquent behavior such as shoplifting. Young males from single-parent homes headed by a mother are more likely to engage in delinquent behavior, regardless of the family's socioeconomic level.

Stress, Depression, and Adolescent Coping

■ Studies of psychiatric disorders during adolescence have found a fairly low incidence of moderate to severe depression, but in those who are affected, the symptoms may be life-threatening.

■ Troubled boys are likely to engage in antisocial behaviors, whereas troubled girls are more likely to direct their symptoms inward and become depressed.

■ Depression in adolescence often occurs at the same time as other disorders, such as anxiety disorders. Boys are more likely to be disruptive when depressed, whereas girls are more likely to develop eating disorders.

■ Risk factors for depression include negative body image, increased capacity to reflect about oneself and the future, family dysfunction, and low popularity with peers.

■ Many girls emerge from early adolescence with a poor self-image, relatively low expectations of life, and much less confidence in themselves and their abilities than is true of boys.

■ Factors that help adolescents cope with the transitions of this period include a good relationship with parents and peers, a particular area of competence or expertise, and a role that includes responsibility for others.

KEY TERMS

interdependence
identity formation
identity crisis

foreclosure status
diffusion status
moratorium status

identity achievement
social comparison

USING WHAT YOU'VE LEARNED

As we've seen in this chapter, adolescents often must negotiate the borders of home and school, family and peers, and the broader social arena. Sometimes these groups' values, practices, and expectations conflict. Basic decisions—what to wear, what kinds of music to listen to, how to spend time after school—may be sources of conflict. Major attitudes and values may be at issue, including those related to achievement in school, use of alcohol and other drugs, and sex.

Interview two adolescents about the cultural borders in their lives. (If an interview can't be arranged, consider using your own and a friend's adolescence as points of reference.) Try to make the adolescents feel comfortable enough to tell you in detail about the conflicting contexts of their lives. Here are examples of the kinds of questions you might ask:

■ What are some of the major things your parents and peers agree on?
■ What are some of the major conflicts?
■ What makes you most uncomfortable with the expectations of family, peers, and friends?

Their answers to these and similar questions should give you a sense of the adolescent "balancing act."

SUGGESTED READINGS

CARY, L. (1991). *Black ice.* New York: Knopf. Lorene Cary presents a compelling autobiographical account of her journey at age 15 from the black ghetto of Philadelphia, through the pioneering experience of integration, and into the privileged world of an exclusive prep school.

EDER, D., EVANS, C. C., & PARKER, S. (1995). *School talk: Gender and adolescent culture.* Brunswick, NJ: Rutgers University Press. Sociologists enter the harsh world of the middle school cafeteria and try to learn the cultural prescriptions of tough guys and wimps, of friendships and segregation of unpopular kids. An amazingly readable paperback despite its strong research base.

ELKIND, D. (1997). *All grown up and no place to go: Teenagers in crisis.* Reading, MA: Addison Wesley. Drawing from research and clinical practice, David Elkind looks at the pressures placed on adolescents now as compared with earlier decades. He warns of the dangers to mental health from overstimulation and exaggerated expectations in childhood.

GILLIGAN, C. (1983). *In a different voice: Psychological theory and women's development.* Cambridge, MA: Harvard University Press. A thoughtful and compelling discussion of the different roots of moral thought in women compared with men. The author contrasts theories and draws from her own research, particularly with adolescent girls.

HAUSER, S. (1991). *Adolescents and their families: Paths of ego development.* New York: Free Press. Scholarly, readable, and filled with case studies. Hauser presents four main "paths" through adolescence and the ways parents subtly guide their teenagers.

ORENSTEIN, P. (1995). *Schoolgirls: Young women, self-esteem, and the confidence gap.* New York: Anchor. A thorough and highly readable follow-up of the 1990 American Association of University Women survey on adolescent women and loss of self-esteem.

RUBIN, N. (1994). *Ask me if I care: Voices from an American high school*. Berkeley, CA: Ten Speed Press, 1994. Teenagers talk and write about sex, drugs, violence, racial identity, stress, and self-image as they make decisions and find their way through daily life.

SMITH, C. D. (1996). *Strangers at home: Essays on the effects of living overseas and coming "home" to a strange land*. Bayside, NY: Aletheia. An intriguing collection of personal reflections by Americans who spent their childhood or adolescence abroad.

Young Adults: Physical and Cognitive Development

CHAPTER OBJECTIVES

By the time you have finished this chapter, you should be able to do the following:

1. Explain why the absence of age-related markers makes it difficult to discuss developmental processes that take place during young adulthood.
2. Analyze how age clocks and coping capacity help researchers assess adult development.
3. Discuss the important aspects of physical development in early adulthood, including strength and stamina, fitness and health, fertility, and sexuality.
4. Discuss evidence for continuing cognitive growth and development during adulthood.
5. Give the pros and cons of assessing adult development in stages.
6. Describe the various ways in which theorists have sought to explain cognitive development in adulthood.
7. Identify some of the central developmental tasks of early adulthood.
8. Discuss how "seasons" might apply differently to male and female development in adulthood.
9. Summarize cognitive "transformations" that might apply to adult development.

Development continues throughout life. Although some theorists argue that there are recognizable developmental stages in adulthood, the developmental processes that occur during the adult years differ from those that occur during childhood and adolescence. Changes in adult thought, personality, and behavior are much less a result of chronological age or specific biological changes than of personal, social, and cultural forces or events. The social milestones and cultural demands of the young adult may support, expand, or disrupt behavior patterns laid down in the adolescent years. Decisions must be made and problems solved on a daily basis. A hallmark of maturity is the increasing ability to respond to change and adapt to new conditions. Positive resolution of contradictions and difficulties is the basis for mature adult activity (Datan & Ginsberg, 1975). Not all adults progress the same way or structure their lives the same way. Pathways can diverge considerably during adulthood, and adults therefore have less in common than children.

As we'll see, however, there are some commonalities in the developmental processes of adulthood. Although there are no adult physical markers comparable to pubescence, and no clear-cut cognitive stages, we do have culturally defined *social* milestones to go by, such as roles and relationships that are part of the cycles of family and career. Social and emotional development is blended with the gradual physical changes that take place during the adult years, as well as with the individual's growing body of knowledge, skills, and experience—all of which may be influenced by sudden, traumatic events that can occur on both a personal and a cultural/societal level.

The timing of social milestones such as marriage, parenting, and career choice varies widely from one individual to another. The ways in which different people react to these events, as well as the nature of the roles they must play, vary according to the demands and restrictions of the culture. Some social events—and the transitions that surround them—are *normative*; others are *idiosyncratic*. Normative events and transitions occur at relatively specific times and are shared with most people in a particular age cohort. Such events aren't usually associated with extreme, acute stress. There is time for planning, and social support and cultural meaning are often available to provide guidance. Examples of such events include looking for a first job and moving out of the parental home.

In contrast, idiosyncratic events and transitions can happen at any time. Examples include losing a job, having a spouse die suddenly, contracting a major illness, or—on a happier note—winning the lottery. Because these events often are not anticipated or emotionally shared with others, they create considerable stress and a need for major reorganization of the person's life both personally and socially.

In this chapter, in addition to exploring physical and cognitive development in young adulthood, we lay the groundwork for the chapters that follow. We examine fundamental concepts and theories of adult development, looking at how theorists define adulthood in terms of *age clocks*. Next we turn more specifically to young adulthood, first in terms of physical development and then in terms of cognitive functioning from the perspectives of both continuity and change. We examine whether there are identifiable stages of adult cognitive development, along with characteristics of adult cognition—which interacts with social and personality development. Finally, we look at some of the developmental tasks of early adulthood.

Personality factors—such as resilience and optimism—positively affect an individual's ability to cope with catastrophic life events such as an earthquake.

PERSPECTIVES ON ADULT DEVELOPMENT

As discussed in Chapter 1, we conventionally divide the adult years into young adulthood (the 20s and 30s), middle adulthood (the 40s and 50s), and later adulthood (age 60 or 65 and up). We have also noted that what age means to a given individual can vary considerably. How can we classify and study adult development if so much of it is based on individual behavior and judgment? In the absence of markers other than arbitrary age ranges, we turn to the concepts of age clocks and social norms.

AGE CLOCKS AND SOCIAL NORMS

Since it is difficult, if not impossible, to pinpoint stages of adult development solely on the basis of age, researchers have devised the concept of the **age clock** (Neugarten, 1968a). Age clocks are a form of internal timing; they let us know whether we are progressing through life too slowly or too quickly. For example, a 35-year-old who is still in college might be considered to be lagging behind his or her peers, whereas a 35-year-old who is thinking about retirement might be considered to be far ahead of them. Age clocks let us know when certain events in our life should occur. If these events happen earlier or later than expected, we may experience distress and less peer support than when we accomplish things according to schedule.

In other words, we have built-in expectations, constraints, and pressures for various periods of life that we apply to ourselves and others. Although these boundaries sometimes have a biological or psychological basis—a woman normally can't conceive after menopause, or an older man might not welcome the

age clock A form of internal timing used as a measure of adult development; a way of knowing that we are progressing too slowly or too quickly in terms of key social events that occur during adulthood.

Although age clocks let us know when events generally should occur, they are more flexible than previously. Many people, like this woman, are returning to school in their 30s or even later.

rigors of rearing an infant—the boundaries are more often socially based. For example, if we observe a couple proudly introducing their newborn child, we will probably have quite different reactions depending on whether the couple are in their twenties or their forties. We will interpret the motivations of the couple differently, and we may also behave differently toward them. To complicate matters further, the behaviors expected of an individual and the reactions of others can vary considerably according to historical and cultural contexts, as discussed in "Eye on Diversity," on the facing page.

In examining cultural changes in the United States over recent decades, Bernice and Dail Neugarten (1987) suggest that there has been a "blurring of traditional life periods," with the result that age clocks are more flexible now than they were in earlier decades. "Nontraditional" students return to school at age 35, 45, or even older; many couples postpone having their first child until they are in their mid to late thirties; marriage, divorce, and remarriage occur throughout the lifespan, not just during early adulthood. Whereas in 1950, 80% of men and 90% of women believed that the best age for a man to marry was between 20 and 25, by 1970 only 42% felt this way. Researchers continue to suggest that we have become an "age-irrelevant" society in which members of a given adult age cohort may be involved in vastly different activities and life events.

THREE COMPONENTS OF AGE It is important to keep in mind that an adult's **chronological age** (number of years of life) has relatively little meaning by itself. **Biological age** is a preferable way of looking at things, in interaction with **social age** and **psychological age** (Birren & Cunningham, 1985). Biological age, which is the person's position with regard to her or his expected lifespan, varies tremendously from one individual to another. A 40-year-old with emphysema and a severe heart condition who is likely to die in the near future differs greatly in biological age from a healthy 40-year-old who can expect to live another 35 years or more. In turn, social age refers to how an individual's current status compares with cultural norms. A 40-year-old married person with three children is developmentally different from a 40-year-old single person who engages in casual dating and doesn't plan to have children. Finally, psychological age refers to how well a person can adapt to social and other environmental demands. It includes such things as intelligence, learning ability, and motor skills, as well as subjective dimensions like feelings, attitudes, and motives.

What is maturity? Although biological, social, and psychological age combine to determine maturity, certain psychological characteristics are the primary ingredients. Although they vary somewhat according to the culture, they include physical and social independence and autonomy; independent decision making; and some degree of stability, wisdom, reliability, integrity, and compassion. Different investigators put different characteristics into the blend, and different cultures make different demands, with the result that there is no universal definition of maturity.

CONTEXTUAL PARADIGMS OR APPROACHES

A *paradigm* is a hypothetical model or framework, or, more simply, a systematic way of looking at things. **Contextual paradigms** for human development seek to describe and organize the effects of different kinds of forces on development. The term *context* is used here in the way it has been used at other points in this text: We speak of the environmental context, the social context, the psychological context, and the historical context, each of which influences development in interaction with the others.

chronological age The number of years of life.

biological age The person's position with regard to his or her expected lifespan.

social age An individual's current status as compared with cultural norms.

psychological age An individual's current ability to cope with and adapt to social and environmental demands.

contextual paradigms The view that numerous environmental, social, psychological, and historical factors interact to determine development.

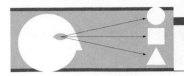

EYE ON DIVERSITY

HISTORY, CULTURE, AND THE LIFE COURSE

The study of adult development is in many ways a study of the life course—the ways in which an individual's personal biography intertwines with the historical period in which she or he lives and with the person's place in the social system. Research reveals that social, cultural, and historical factors affect crucial transitions in an adult's life in dramatic ways and that these factors help define personal expectations (Hagestad, 1990; Stoller & Gibson, 1994).

It is important, therefore, to examine how historical factors define the demographic conditions of a period and influence the normal expectations and life scripts of people living in that period. It is clear that a poor black woman born in a slum in 1950 will have a very different life course than a white woman born at the same time into a socially well-connected family in an affluent section of the city. It is also clear that a black women born in 1870 had a very different life course than a black woman born 100 years later will have had.

Perhaps the most important historical change affecting the life course is the increasing length of the lifespan. Whereas in 1900, only about 14% of

U.S. women reached age 80 or older, by 1980, more than half of them expected to reach that age (Watkins et al., 1987). In Germany in 1600, nearly half of all children never reached adulthood, with the result that for centuries "it took two infants to make one adult" (Imhof, 1986). These changes affect how families experience a child's death. Whereas losing a child was once a normal and expected event, it is now an abnormal part of the social script. In 1800, by the time an average woman reached age 35, she had lost one-third of her children. In 1990, less than 1% of 35-year-old women had lost a child. As a result, the death of a child is now a shattering personal loss instead of an event that touches almost every woman's life at one time or another.

Historical periods also affect the "time budgets" of adulthood, with the result that today's adults spend their lives in very different ways than the adults of earlier periods. When Ellen Gee (1986, 1987, 1988) studied the demographic conditions prevailing in 1830, she found that after a woman married, 90% of her life was spent raising children. In contrast, in 1950, the percentage had dropped to 40%. Another interesting observation was that in 1860, only 16% of 50-year-olds had living parents, whereas by 1960, the figure had risen to 60%.

The death of a parent is a more age-graded transition today than ever before; that is, it occurs during predictable times in the lifespan. The death of parents now occurs significantly later in a child's life and is likely to be encountered during a relatively narrow band of time (Winsborough, 1980). As a result, it is common to hear the Baby Boomers referred to as the "sandwich" generation because they are responsible both for raising children and for caring for aging, often infirm, parents.

When the effects of factors such as gender, race, socioeconomic status, personality, and intelligence are considered in addition to historical periods, each individual's life course is unique. Nevertheless, researchers remain fascinated with discernible patterns shared by members of the same adult cohorts. They wonder how these patterns will evolve over the next 100 years as medicine and technology prolong life and reduce disease and suffering, as gender roles continue to change, and as African-Americans, Hispanics, and other minority groups become an ever-larger part of the "gorgeous mosaic" of the U.S. population.

Context is a large part of what make us unique as individuals: No two individuals experience exactly the same combination of contexts. Contextual paradigms attempt to pull the various contexts together into an orderly package and thereby provide insights into both commonalities and idiosyncrasies in development. They focus on developmental forces as a whole, whether those forces are within or external to the individual, meaning biological/maturational or experiential/historical (Dixon, 1992). The contrasting (and outdated) approach is to view development from only one perspective at a time, excluding all the rest.

Needless to say, contextual approaches are complex. They also apply throughout the lifespan, beginning in early childhood. At no point, however, do contextual considerations become more important than in adult development, when, as noted earlier, pathways of life begin to diverge markedly compared with those of childhood and adolescence.

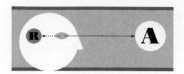

REVIEW & APPLY

1. What are age clocks, and in what ways are they less rigid now than in earlier decades?
2. Explain how the three components of age apply to the concept of adult maturity.
3. What are contextual paradigms, and how do they apply in understanding human development?

PHYSICAL DEVELOPMENT IN YOUNG ADULTHOOD

In part, our responses to life events are determined by our physical capacity—our health, fitness, strength, and stamina. Almost every aspect of physical development reaches its peak in early adulthood. Most young adults are stronger, healthier, and more fertile than they have ever been or will ever be. As a rule, they are also more sexually active and responsive and have a clear sense of sexual identity.

STRENGTH AND STAMINA

In young adulthood—the twenties and thirties—most people enjoy peak vitality, strength, and endurance compared with people in other age ranges. This is a normative, age-graded expectation, as discussed in Chapter 3. Most cultures capitalize on these prime years by putting professional apprentices through grueling regimens of internships, bar exams, and dissertation defenses; sending the young to do battle; idolizing young athletes and fashion models; and expecting women to have children.

For the most part, organ functioning, reaction time, strength, motor skills, and sensorimotor coordination are at their maximum between the ages of 25 and 30; after that, they gradually decline. However, the decline that occurs during the thirties and forties is less than most people imagine. As Figure 12–1 illustrates, the major functional dropoff of most of the body's biological systems occurs after about age 40. Thus, although the decline from peak performance that occurs after the mid-twenties may be important to star athletes, it barely affects the rest of us. Not all systems are at their peak between 25 and 30, however. Visual accommodation, for example, declines gradually but steadily beginning in middle childhood, and visual acuity begins a very slow decline from about age 20 that accelerates markedly after about age 40 (Meisami, 1994).

Declines in physical skills and capabilities are most noticeable in emergency situations and at other times when physical demands are extreme (Troll, 1985). For example, when a woman is in her late thirties a pregnancy draws more heavily on her reserve physical stamina than if she were in her twenties. In addition, it may take longer for the older woman to return to normal after the child is born. Similarly, it is easier for a 25-year-old man to work at more than one job to get his family through a financial crisis than it is for a 40-year-old.

FITNESS AND HEALTH

By and large, young adulthood is a healthy period. This condition is especially true for people who follow a sensible diet, get regular exercise, avoid tobacco and other drugs, and use alcohol in moderation, if at all. Compared with older adults, young adults also are least likely to be overweight.

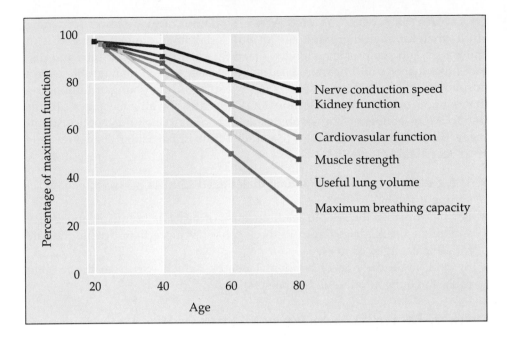

FIGURE 12–1

Average declines in biological systems. These declines can be improved dramatically by health and fitness practices, including regular exercise.

Source: Adapted from J. Fries and L. Crapo, Vitality and Aging. *San Francisco: W. H. Freemand and Company, 1981.*

The health and exercise habits formed during young adulthood often persist throughout the adult years. Many of these patterns have beneficial effects, which we will examine in greater depth in Chapter 14. Although attitudes and behaviors related to health and fitness can change at any point, people often tend to resist such change, making it especially important to establish good health habits in young adulthood.

PHYSICAL FITNESS   Many athletes reach their peak skills and conditioning during young adulthood. Between ages 23 and 27, the *striated* (voluntary) muscles, including the biceps and triceps, achieve their maximum physical strength (Hershey, 1974). Peak leg strength comes between the ages of 20 and 30, peak hand strength at about age 20 (Buskirk, 1985). Of course, the age at which athletes reach their peak *performance* varies according to the sport (Fries & Crapo, 1981). Swimmers generally peak during adolescence, runners and tennis players in their early twenties (Schulz & Salthouse, in press). In contrast (and with some notable exceptions), golfers tend to perform best in their late twenties and on into their thirties. Major league baseball players generally peak around age 27 to 30, although the players with the greatest ability may peak several years after that (Schulz et al., 1994).

In recent decades, improvements in exercise and diet have added so much to adult fitness that older adults are now capable of higher performance levels than adults in their prime 100 years ago. When Anders Ericsson (1990) compared the winning times of younger runners in the 1896 Olympics with the best performances of "master" athletes aged 50 to 69 in 1979, he found that the older athletes were usually faster than the younger gold medal winners. For example, in 1896, the winning time for a marathon was 2 hours and 59 minutes; in 1979, the winning time for master athletes running the same distance ranged from 2 hours and 25 minutes for those in the 50 to 54 age group, to 2 hours and 53 minutes for those aged 65 to 69. In general, better nutrition and better training throughout the adult years more than compensate for advanced age.

A pregnancy in the late 30s will probably draw on the woman's reserve capacity of physical stamina more than would a pregnancy in the 20s.

Today, HIV infection, resulting in AIDS, is the leading cause of death among males between 25 and 44.

DEATH RATES AMONG YOUNG ADULTS Death rates are lower for young adults than for any other adult age group. Today few younger women die in childbirth. Tuberculosis is no longer a leading killer of young adults, and diseases like diabetes and heart and kidney disease are often manageable over a normal lifespan. Yet the rate of *preventable* deaths during young adulthood remains high. Despite overall declines in death rates for all age ranges, deaths due to AIDS, accidents, and stabbings and shootings (including police shootings) still pose significant threats to young adults in particular. Here are some specifics (see also Table 12–1):

■ The leading cause of death among males aged 25 to 44 is HIV infection, resulting in AIDS.
■ For black males, the second leading cause of death is homicide and police shootings. Black males die from these causes at more than double the rate for all males aged 25 to 44.
■ By and large, the rate of accidental deaths (which was once the leading cause in young adulthood) has been falling.

DISEASE, DISABILITY, AND PHYSICAL LIMITATIONS While death rates for young adults are lower than those for other age groups, many of the diseases that will cause trouble later in life begin during young adulthood (Scanlon, 1979). Young adults may feel no symptoms, but lung, heart, and kidney diseases, as well as arthritis, joint and bone problems, atherosclerosis, and cirrhosis of the liver, may be in their initial stages. Diseases and disorders that do yield symptoms during young adulthood include multiple sclerosis and rheumatoid arthritis, stress-linked diseases such as hypertension, ulcers, and

TABLE 12–1 LEADING CAUSES OF DEATH FOR U.S. MALES AND FEMALES, 25 TO 44 YEARS, 1994 (RATES PER 100,000 POPULATION IN SPECIFIED GROUP)

CAUSE	NUMBER	RATE
Males		
HIV infection	25,773	62.4
Accidents	20,729	50.2
Heart disease	11,903	28.8
Suicide	10,265	24.8
Malignant neoplasms (cancer)	10,091	24.4
Homicide and legal intervention	8,987	21.7
Females		
Malignant neoplasms (cancer)	11,808	28.3
Accidents	6,283	15.1
Heart disease	4,860	11.7
HIV infection	4,703	11.3
Suicide	2,464	5.9
Homicide and legal intervention	2,432	5.8

Source: U.S. Census Bureau, 1997.

depression, and some genetically based diseases such as diabetes or sickle-cell anemia.

Sometimes sociocultural factors lead to disease or even death. In times of war, young adults are killed or permanently injured. In urban areas with high crime rates, youths are often victims of homicide or drug abuse. Most recently, the AIDS epidemic has hit young adults at disproportionate rates, sometimes stemming from HIV infection during adolescence (Chapter 10). Individual psychological development and adjustment is especially difficult when a young adult's physical condition counteracts normal biological changes. In general, any physical handicap or disease is likely to affect both biological age and social age expectations (see "Eye on Diversity," page 418).

FERTILITY

During the young adult years, a woman's supply of ova remains relatively stable. Females are born with their lifetime supply of about 400,000 ova, which are released monthly, beginning soon after menarche and ending at menopause. This process is relatively stable between the ages of 25 and 38. After age 38, however, there is a rapid decline in the number and regularity of ova released. This decline does not mean that older women can't become pregnant. On the contrary: Increasing numbers of women are choosing to have children in their late thirties and early forties, when they are more secure emotionally and financially, and perhaps well established in a career. Genetic screening procedures such as amniocentesis and chorionic villus sampling (Chapter 3) help make late pregnancies less risky.

Men produce sperm continually from puberty on. Most men remain fertile throughout their later adult years (Troll, 1985), although seminal emissions contain progressively fewer viable sperm. Only during adolescence and the early adult years are both men and women are at their peak levels of fertility.

SEX AND SEXUALITY

Researchers at the University of Chicago recently conducted a random survey on the sexual habits of nearly 3500 Americans aged 18 to 59 (Laumann et al., 1994; Michael et al., 1994). Bearing in mind the usual problems associated with surveys on sensitive matters such as sex, such as underreporting of socially "undesirable" behaviors (see Chapter 1), their findings included the following:

■ There are three basic patterns of sexual relations: One-third of Americans have sex at least twice a week, one-third several times a month, and one-third a few times a year or not at all.

■ The vast majority of Americans are monogamous. More than eight out of ten have just one sexual partner a year (or no partner at all). Over the course of a lifetime, a typical woman has just two partners, whereas a man has six.

■ The group who have the most sex and are most likely to have orgasms during sex are married couples. Whereas only one out of four single people has sex twice a week, nearly two out of five married people do.

■ Contrary to popular stereotypes, there are only very minor variations across racial/ethnic groups with regard to frequency of sex.

Earlier researchers noted important changes in American marital sexual behavior in the past few decades. The median duration of intercourse has increased markedly, suggesting that married partners are experiencing greater enjoyment, relaxation, and mutuality during intercourse (Hunt, 1974). It appears that attitudes and priorities have changed. More couples seek to maximize the pleasure of the entire act rather than reaching release quickly.

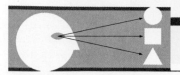

EYE ON DIVERSITY

COPING WITH PHYSICAL DISABILITY IN YOUNG ADULTHOOD

Normally, young adults are in their physical prime. They enjoy peak strength, stamina, and energy. They are generally in good health and have few illnesses. If they are physically fit, they enjoy the self-esteem and sense of efficacy and competence that go along with their physical prowess. But what about young adults who are physically disabled? How do they adjust psychologically while their age mates are performing at optimal levels?

Adjusting to a physical disability is difficult at any age. However, late adolescence and young adulthood can be a particularly difficult period (Wright, 1983). At this stage in life, individuals normally are developing intimate relationships and making major decisions such as choosing an occupation. Physically disabled people may become overwhelmed by their limitations during this future-oriented period.

There are at least three factors that influence how people adapt to physical disabilities (Wright, 1983). First, it is important to understand the disability and its limitations. Any handicap is defined by the interaction between the individual's abilities and the environ-

mental task—if you can't speak Japanese, you will be handicapped in a Japanese classroom. The second aspect of adaptation to a physical disability involves coping with the attitudes and values of others and their social expectations. Physically disabled people are often stereotyped and must deal with strong prejudices. They may be pitied or demeaned, or looked upon as passive and incompetent. There is often a sweeping set of generalizations that may be applied to any physically disabled individual regardless of the particular disability.

Finally, coping with a physical disability involves coping with an array of hopes, fears, dreams, frustrations, lost opportunities, and guilt and anger. When a person becomes disabled suddenly, perhaps because of an accident, there may initially be a crisis period accompanied by grief and mourning as well as shock and disbelief. There will be periods of anger and frustration as the disabled person attempts to cope with everyday tasks that are easy and routine for others. There is likely to be further anger and frustration at unnecessary social handicaps or obstacles.

In the process, some individuals adopt a definition of themselves as "physically challenged" rather than disabled (Wright, 1983). The attitude is

particularly common among disabled athletes. Simply by changing the definition and the terminology, it is sometimes easier to see the specific physical obstacle as a challenge to be overcome, perhaps with the help of others, rather than as a label or category that defines the person. Unfortunately, however, the term "challenged" has become somewhat of a cliché and is often used in a derogatory way in jokes.

Young adults with physical disabilities have been in the forefront of efforts to change social attitudes and laws that affect all those disabled people. In 1990, as a result of their actions and those of other interested individuals and groups, the Americans with Disabilities Act (ADA) was passed. This law makes it illegal to discriminate against individuals with disabilities in employment, public accommodations, transportation, and telecommunications. Among other things, this law requires companies to make "reasonable accommodations" for the needs of disabled employees so that they can do work for which they are trained; if it is not possible to do so, those employees must be trained for comparably skilled work. Of most importance, people cannot be fired because of a disability alone; the ADA demands a policy of inclusion rather than exclusion.

Flexibility has also increased; intercourse now may include previously "forbidden" acts such as initiation of sex by the woman, masturbation, and oral sex (Hunt, 1974; McCary, 1978).

Trends in adult sexual behavior have shifted considerably over the decades. In 1937 and again in 1959, only 22% of the U.S. population condoned premarital sex for both men, and women. In the 1974 survey (Hunt, 1974), 75% of the men approved of premarital sex for men, and over 50% found it acceptable for women. Some behaviors have not increased significantly, however; these include mate swapping, group sex, and extramarital sex. The double standard persisted into the 1970s, with 50% of college men approving of premarital sex for women but 75% still preferring a virgin bride (McCary, 1978).

Although sexuality is certainly more open and accepted now than it was before the 1960s, it appears that college students engaged in less sexual intercourse during the 1980s than during the 1960s and 1970s. For example, one study reported that in 1978, 51% of sophomore women were engaging in sex at least once a month, but in 1983, the figure had fallen to 37% (Gerrard, 1987). The continuing shift toward more conservative sexual behavior among college women is almost certainly attributable in part to increased fear of sexually transmitted diseases. It may also reflect the growing self-assurance of young women, who feel less compelled to have sex merely to "please" their boyfriends. Women are more likely to follow their own belief systems rather than those imposed upon them by others (Gerrard, 1987).

SEXUAL RESPONSIVENESS The dominant pattern of sexual intimacy between men and women in the 1990s appears to be one of increased communication and mutual satisfaction. Yet a frequent finding of studies of sexual attitudes and behavior has been a marked difference in the patterns of male and female satisfaction. In the 1970s (Hite, 1976; Hunt, 1974; McCary, 1978) research indicated that for some couples, men routinely achieved physical gratification, but women did not. Women complained that men are in too much of a hurry, are rough and perfunctory, and fail to appreciate the erotic and romantic importance of gentle, slow arousal. Men complained that women are frigid and unresponsive. It appeared that sexual intimacy is not always as mutually satisfying as the popular media present it.

The University of Chicago study suggests otherwise (Michael et al., 1994; Laumann et al., 1994). As Figure 12–2 indicates, large percentages of married or cohabiting men and women reported being extremely physically and emotionally satisfied by sex with their primary partner. Notably, since less than 30% of the women reported always having an orgasm (consistent with earlier research), the authors concluded that "Despite the fascination with orgasms, despite the popular notion that frequent orgasms are essential to a happy sex life, there was not a strong relationship between having orgasms and having a satisfying sexual life" (Michael et al., 1994). In addition, as you might expect, the highest frequencies of sexual activity regardless of marital status were reported by people in their twenties and thirties. We will return to how sexuality changes with age in Chapter 14.

In the 1990s, the key components of sexual intimacy between men and women are greater communication and mutual satisfaction.

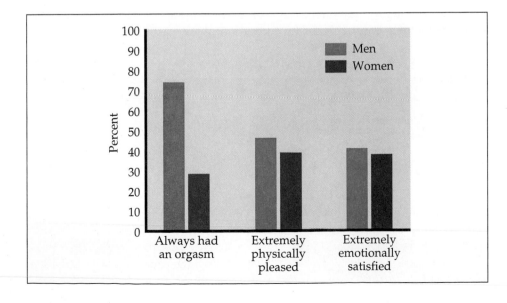

FIGURE 12–2 THREE MEASURES OF SEXUAL SATISFACTION WITH PRIMARY PARTNER

Source: From Sex in America *by Robert T. Michael et al. Copyright © 1994 by CSG Enterprises, Inc., Edward O. Laumann, Robert T. Michael, and Gina Kolata. By permission of Little, Brown and Company.*

For both young homosexuals and heterosexuals, there is now caution and concern about multiple sexual partners.

HOMOSEXUALITY Homosexuality—sexual or erotic attraction to people of your own sex—often becomes apparent in adolescence or even earlier, as discussed in Chapter 10. Here we'll look more closely at what homosexuality is and how it affects adult lifestyles, with emphasis on two important points: Homosexuality is not a disorder, and it does not predict more serious adjustment problems than those occurring in the general population—except to the extent that homophobic individuals make life difficult for homosexuals.

The word *homosexual* applies to same-sex-oriented men and women, as does the word *gay*. However, homosexual men more often refer to themselves as gay, whereas homosexual women more often call themselves lesbians. Although homosexuals sometimes are attracted exclusively to individuals of the same sex, most people have both homosexual and heterosexual leanings in varying degrees (whether they display them or not). Thus, homosexuality and heterosexuality are perhaps better conceptualized as opposite ends of a continuum rather than as a dichotomy. Somewhere in between are *bisexuals*, who are attracted to and may engage in sexual activity with members of both sexes, although they may prefer one sex over the other.

The incidence of homosexuality is difficult to assess; many homosexuals are reluctant to acknowledge their sexual preference. In 1948, the Kinsey Report estimated that one in every ten American men was homosexual and that one-third of American men and one-eighth of American women had had homosexual experiences to the point of orgasm at least once in their lives (see McCary, 1978). In contrast, the 1994 University of Chicago survey discussed earlier found that only 2.8% of men and 1.4% of women considered themselves homosexual or bisexual (Dunlap, 1994; Laumann et al., 1994). According to the researchers, the incidence of homosexuality varies widely by location (urban versus rural) and educational level (see Figure 12–3). Whereas 10.2% of men in the nation's twelve largest cities reported having had homosexual relations during the past year, only 1% of men in rural areas reported similar encounters. Similarly, whereas 3.5% of male college graduates reported a recent homosexual experience, only 1.4% of high school graduates reported similar relations. These figures may, however, reflect the greater tolerance toward homosexuals found in large cities and the greater psychological and financial security that accompanies a college degree. Without this security, many homosexuals are unwilling to declare their sexual identity or even report it on a survey.

A classic study of gay men in the San Francisco area before the appearance of AIDS yielded a great deal of information about gay lifestyles. This study

FIGURE 12–3 DIFFERENCES IN THE HOMOSEXUAL POPULATION

Men and women who reported that they had sexual partners of the same sex in the last year.

Source: "The Social Organization of Sexuality by Laumann et al." University of Chicago Press, 1994. Reprinted with permission. Reported in The New York Times, *October 18, 1994.*

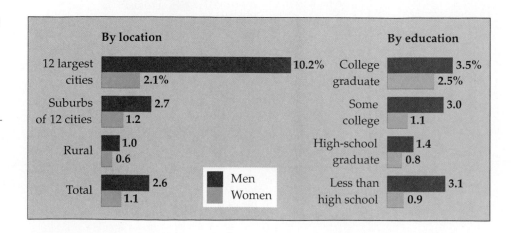

By location

	Men	Women
12 largest cities	10.2%	2.1%
Suburbs of 12 cities	2.7	1.2
Rural	1.0	0.6
Total	2.6	1.1

By education

	Men	Women
College graduate	3.5%	2.5%
Some college	3.0	1.1
High-school graduate	1.4	0.8
Less than high school	3.1	0.9

(Bell & Weinberg, 1978) used good sampling and interviewing techniques. Their major conclusion was that there is as much diversity of attitudes and behavior among gays as there is among "straights." Most of the respondents, however, concealed their homosexuality from friends and acquaintances. The study also found that gay men tended to be more sexually promiscuous than gay women, whereas gay women tended to form strong emotional ties and have fewer partners.

Many gays and lesbians live together in sustained relationships. Almost 40% of gay men and over 60% of lesbian women have monogamous same-sex relationships (Bell and Weinberg, 1978). More than half of gay men belong to "open couples," in which monogamy isn't required. But most lesbians are in "closed couples," in which monogamy is expected. This finding underscores an important difference between homosexual and heterosexual couples. Gay men are much more likely than heterosexual men to have at least one affair outside of their marriage or steady relationship. One study reported that during the first two years of the relationship, 66% of gay men but only 15% of heterosexual men were unfaithful (Blumstein & Schwartz, 1983). By contrast, lesbian women are about as monogamous as heterosexual women. Only about 15% of lesbians and 13% of heterosexual wives had sexual relations with someone other than their partner during the first two years of the relationship (Blumstein & Schwartz, 1983).

SEXUALLY TRANSMITTED DISEASES AND SOCIAL CHANGE As noted earlier, AIDS is the leading cause of death for men aged 25 to 44. However, the response to the AIDS epidemic has not always been constructive. At first, many heterosexuals ignored the threat of AIDS because it appeared to affect only homosexual men (because of the increased likelihood of torn tissues and blood contact during anal sex) and intravenous (IV) drug users (through sharing of syringes). The gay community, too, responded with resistance and denial. Early warnings about the spread of HIV through unsafe sex were labeled as homophobic messages intended to violate the rights of gay men.

By 1984, however, people were beginning to take the epidemic seriously. It had spread across the United States and to most European nations, having already decimated the young adult heterosexual populations of many African countries. It affected not only homosexual men and IV drug users but also hemophiliacs (through tainted blood transfusions), sexual partners of bisexuals or IV drug users, and newborn babies of mothers who had the disease. What's more, it was estimated that perhaps 10% of the gay community in San Francisco and twice that many in New York were infected with the virus. These facts—together with the long latency period between HIV infection and development of AIDS symptoms, which makes HIV harder to detect—led to more serious action. Medical research on AIDS took on greater urgency, and the gay community began to educate its members and to promote safer sexual practices.

Social change does not happen smoothly, however. Many HIV-positive people continued to infect others; they also avoided HIV testing. In the late 1980s, the heterosexual community was still far behind the gay community in responding to the epidemic, even though by then AIDS was being transmitted primarily through heterosexual activity. Sporadic incidents of panic and discrimination against individuals who had AIDS, who might have AIDS, or who might contract AIDS because of their lifestyle received more attention from the press than the educational information needed to reduce the spread of the disease.

Table 12–2   Major Sexually Transmitted Diseases Other Than AIDS

Chlamydia trachomatis: The leading cause of urinary tract infections in men; also responsible for about half of reported cases of testicular infection. In women, chlamydia can cause inflammation of the cervix and fallopian tubes. Although the infection is easily treated with antibiotics, failure to treat it may result in permanent damage, including infertility. Approximately 3 to 4 million cases of chlamydia are reported every year.

Nongonococcal urethritis: A sexually transmitted urinary tract inflammation that affects about 2.5 million Americans a year. It is caused by several different organisms.

Gonorrhea: This disease can cause sterility and other chronic problems if left untreated or if treated only at an advanced stage. Approximately 1 million people are infected with gonorrhea each year.

Syphilis: This disease can cause severe health problems, including sterility and even death if left untreated. Pregnant women with untreated syphilis can infect their developing fetus.

Herpes: A group of viruses that includes herpes simplex virus, types I and II, and affects about 500,000 Americans a year. Although there is no cure for herpes, there are treatments that can limit the severity of outbreaks. Currently about 20 million Americans suffer from herpes.

Source: DeVilliers and deVilliers (1979).

During the second half of the 1980s and in the 1990s, sexual behavior of both heterosexuals and homosexuals continued to change. Today most young people report exercising greater caution in their sexual activities. In the University of Chicago study, 76% of those who reported having five or more sex partners in the past year claimed either to be decreasing their sexual activity, being tested for HIV regularly, or always using condoms (Laumann et al., 1994). Prostitution without condoms is also declining. Some observers have even suggested that the sexual revolution is over and that American society has entered a period of new restraint comparable to the 1950s.

OTHER SEXUALLY TRANSMITTED DISEASES In addition to AIDS, over twenty different organisms cause STDs that affect millions of sexually active adolescents and adults each year (Stevens-Long & Commons, 1992). The effects include urinary tract infections, gonorrhea, syphilis, and herpes, as described in Table 12–2.

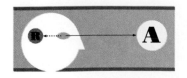

REVIEW & APPLY

1. Describe the typical levels of strength and stamina of healthy individuals during young adulthood.
2. What are the leading preventable causes of death that affect young adults?
3. Discuss the heterosexuality-homosexuality continuum.
4. How have sexual patterns in American society changed as a result of the increased prevalence of sexually transmitted diseases?

COGNITIVE CONTINUITY AND CHANGE

At the same time that the body is reaching its physical peak, so is cognitive functioning. However, although stages of cognitive development are relatively clear in childhood and adolescence, they are not easily defined in adulthood. Theorists disagree over whether the concept of stages even applies in adulthood. Thus, in the absence of a universally accepted theory, exploring cognitive development in adulthood involves assessing different theoretical perspectives that address specific aspects of the evolution of adult intellectual functioning.

COGNITIVE GROWTH OR DECLINE?

An obvious consequence of learning, memory, problem solving, and other cognitive processes we use as we grow older is that we accumulate a broader knowledge base; we know more about ourselves and the physical and social world around us. But changes occur in what we call intelligence or cognitive capacity, or in intellectual competence. Is there continued cognitive *development* after adolescence?

During young adulthood, frequently used cognitive skills are maintained better than those more rarely used.

The evidence is not clear, especially with regard to timing. Early theorists and researchers argued that intellectual capacities peak during the late teens or early twenties, but it is now clear that this conclusion was based on misinterpretation of the limited research findings available at the time. In a study conducted during World War I, for example, all draftees took a group intelligence test called the Army alpha. The younger recruits—those between the ages of 15 and 25—did better on average than the older ones. Several other studies conducted in the 1930s and 1940s produced somewhat similar results. Older people scored consistently lower than younger people. What was wrong with this research? The problem began with the Army alpha itself, which was a "quick" paper-and-pencil test designed to assess large numbers of recruits as efficiently as possible, not necessarily as accurately as possible; also, it emphasized verbal skills over basic reasoning skills. In all, since the research used a cross-sectional design, the tests were measuring age-cohort differences instead of developmental differences (see Chapter 1). Stated differently, older adults had different historical contexts (especially lower educational levels) that caused them on average to score lower on the tests—quite apart from how intelligent they might actually have been.

In the late 1940s, when researchers began using better IQ tests and longitudinal designs, quite a different picture emerged. Individuals usually showed some increase in intelligence test performance through their twenties and thirties, leveling off at around age 45 (Whitbourne, 1986). Longitudinal studies also suggest that continuing education tends to increase IQ test scores in adulthood (Schaie, 1983), which makes sense when we remember that IQ tests primarily assess academic skills and knowledge.

What specific cognitive abilities increase in young adulthood? Some skills peak in the late teens and early twenties; they include speed-related performance, rote memory, and the manipulation of matrices and other patterns. This trend may have a biological basis, or it may occur because many young people are full-time students who practice, develop, and rely on these skills on a daily basis. Note, too, that specific disciplines are associated with specific reasoning skills. Psychology majors, for example, tend to develop probabilistic reasoning because of their frequent use of statistical procedures; in contrast, humanities majors tend to develop skills in written analysis and exposition. In any case, people in their thirties, forties, fifties, and beyond perform better with training in specific cognitive skills such as approaches to reasoning and processing information (Willis, 1990).

Similarly, skills that are exercised frequently are maintained better than those that aren't. Architects, for example, retain their visual-spatial skills at above-average levels for longer periods (Salthouse et al., 1990; Salthouse & Mitchell, 1990). Other cognitive abilities, especially judgment and reasoning, normally continue to develop throughout the lifespan. However, it still isn't clear which cognitive abilities change and in what ways. We'll return to these issues in Chapters 14 and 16.

"STAGES" OF THOUGHT IN THE COLLEGE YEARS

Are there stages of cognitive development after adolescence and the achievement of formal operational thought? Are there qualitative differences between the way an adult understands the world and the way an adolescent understands it? In 1970, William Perry conducted a classic study of change in the thought processes of 140 Harvard and Radcliffe students during their four years in college that sheds some light on these questions. At the end of each year, the students were asked questions about how they made sense of their college experiences—how they interpreted those experiences, what those experiences meant to them. Of particular interest was how the students came to grips with the many conflicting points of view and frames of reference that they encountered in their studies.

The results provided evidence for stages of cognitive development. At first the students interpreted the world and their educational experiences in authoritarian, dualistic terms. They were seeking absolute truth and knowledge. The world could be divided into good and bad, right and wrong. The faculty's role was to teach them, and they would learn through hard work.

Inevitably, however, the students were confronted with differences of opinion, uncertainty, and confusion. Perhaps professors presented subject matter in ways that encouraged students to figure out things for themselves. Or perhaps the professors themselves didn't have all the answers. Gradually, in the face of contradictory points of view, the students began to accept and even respect diversity of opinion. They began to adopt the perspective that people have a right to hold different opinions, and they began to understand that things can be seen in different ways, depending on context. This *relativistic* perspective, however, eventually gave way to a stage in which the students made personal commitments and affirmations to particular values and points of view, although they did so in a testing, exploratory manner at first.

In sum, the students moved from a basic dualism (e.g., truth versus falsehood) to tolerance for many competing points of view (conceptual relativism) to self-chosen ideas and convictions. Perry viewed this aspect of intellectual development as characteristic of young adults.

BEYOND FORMAL OPERATIONS Other theorists have elaborated on the types of thinking that are characteristic of young adulthood. Klaus Riegel (1975, 1984) emphasized understanding of contradictions as an important achievement of adult cognitive development and proposed a fifth stage of cognitive development, which he called **dialectical thinking.** The individual considers and contemplates, then attempts to integrate opposing or conflicting thoughts and observations. One particularly important aspect of dialectical thinking is the integration of the ideal and the real. According to Riegel, this

dialectical thinking Thought that seeks to integrate opposing or conflicting ideas and observations.

ability is the strength of the adult mind. Riegel also points out, with respect to contextual paradigms, that the process is ongoing and dynamic—never static.

Both Perry's and Riegel's studies were based primarily on young adults in college. The changes they observed may have been specifically related to college experiences rather than to the more general experiences of young adulthood. Another theorist, Gisela Labouvie-Vief (1984), emphasizes "commitment and responsibility" as the hallmark of adult cognitive maturity. In her view, the course of cognitive development should involve both the evolution of logic, as described by Piaget, and the evolution of self-regulation from childhood well into adulthood. She recognizes that logic may reach its final stage in adolescence with the development of formal operational thought. Like Perry and Riegel, however, she argues that individuals need exposure to complex social issues, different points of view, and the practicalities of life in the real world if they are to escape from dualistic thinking. She describes a somewhat longer process of evolution in which adults become truly autonomous and can handle the contradictions and ambiguities of their life experiences. Adult cognitive maturity is marked by the development of independent decision-making skills (Labouvie-Vief, 1987).

FLEXIBILITY IN INTELLIGENCE

Not all researchers believe that there is a fifth stage of cognitive development. Some focus on how adults use whatever intelligence they have acquired to meet life's demands and how cognitive functioning evolves in the face of new experiences that force us to change our "systems of meaning." Let's take a closer look at each of these approaches.

SCHAIE'S STAGES OF ADULT THINKING Warner Schaie (1986) believes that the distinctive feature of adult thinking is the flexible way in which adults use the cognitive abilities that they already possess. He suggests that during childhood and adolescence, we acquire increasingly complex structures for understanding the world. The powerful tools of formal operational thinking are

In the acquisition period, young adults use their intellectual abilities to choose a lifestyle and pursue a career.

the key achievement of this period, which he calls the *acquisition* period. In young adulthood, we use our intellectual abilities to pursue a career and to choose a lifestyle; Schaie calls this the *achieving* period. We apply our intellectual, problem-solving, and decision-making abilities toward accomplishing goals and a life plan—aspects of cognition that do not show up on IQ tests.

Individuals who successfully do this planning acquire a certain degree of independence and move on to another phase in the application of cognitive skills, a period involving *social responsibility*. In middle age, according to Schaie, we use our cognitive abilities to solve problems for others in the family, in the community, and on the job. For some people these responsibilities may be quite complex, involving the understanding of organizations and different levels of knowledge. Such individuals exercise their cognitive abilities in *executive* functions in addition to assuming social responsibilities. Finally, in the later years, the nature of problem solving shifts again. The central task is one of *reintegrating* the elements experienced earlier in life—making sense of your life as a whole and exploring questions of purpose. For Schaie, then, the focus of cognitive development in adulthood is not expanded capacity or a change in cognitive structures. Instead, it is the flexible use of intelligence at different stages of the lifespan (see Figure 12–4).

SYSTEMS OF MEANING   Several theorists view adulthood as a time of continued change and growth. A leader in this field is Robert Kegan (1982), who has drawn upon various developmental theories to present an integrated perspective on the evolving, cognitive self. Much of Kegan's theorizing was influenced by the work of Jane Loevinger (1976), who attempted to describe how individuals form a consistent idea of themselves and whether such self-concepts might develop in a sequence of predictable stages. Loevinger combined psychoanalytic theory and aspects of Kohlberg's theory of moral development with a variety of research findings to create a new model of personality development. She also developed a series of tests to determine whether or not the model fits actual experience.

Like Loevinger, Kegan emphasizes the importance of meaning. The developing individual is continually differentiating the self from the world and at the same time integrating the self into the broader world. Kegan is also one of the few theorists who has looked at both masculine and feminine tendencies in development. Kegan's stages of development are summarized in Table 12–3.

FIGURE 12–4   SCHAIE'S STAGES OF ADULT COGNITIVE DEVELOPMENT

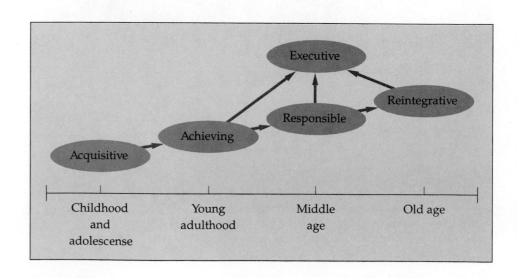

TABLE 12–3   KEGAN'S STAGES OF PERSONALITY DEVELOPMENT

STAGE	ILLUSTRATIVE BEHAVIOR
0. Incorporative (Infancy)	No separation of self and other.
1. Impulsive (2–7 years)	Impulsive behavior, self-centered (similar to Loevinger's Impulsive stage).
2. Imperial (7–12 years)	Strives for independence, works toward achievement and skill building.
3. Interpersonal (13–19 years)	Restructuring of relationships; some marked sex differences.
4. Institutions (early adulthood)	Reintegration of the interconnectedness of the evolving self.
5. Interindividual (adulthood)	

Source: Adapted from R. Kegan (1982). *The Evolving Self: Problem and Process in Human Development,* (Cambridge, MA: Harvard University Press.

In particular, Kegan emphasizes that we continue to develop **systems of meaning** well into adulthood. Such systems can take many forms: religious, political, cultural, personal. We actively construct systems of beliefs and values through experience, and in turn they shape our experiences, organize our thoughts and feelings, and underlie our behavior.

Kegan's theory is too complex to present adequately here, but the basics are as follows. He builds on the tradition of Piaget and theories of cognitive development, defining several levels or stages of "meaning making" that yield systems of meaning. As we progress through adulthood, each individual's systems of meaning become more idiosyncratic, yet have some things in common with the meaning systems of others at the same developmental level. At each stage, the old becomes part of the new, just as children's concrete understanding of the world becomes raw data for their formal operational thought. For theorists like Kegan, most people continue to structure and restructure their systematic understanding of themselves and the world well into their thirties and even beyond—a rather optimistic view of adult development.

1. Summarize the findings of Perry's study of young-adult intellectual development.
2. Explain why Riegel considers dialectical thinking the "fifth stage of cognitive development."
3. Why do some theorists point to flexible thinking as a hallmark of adult cognition?

REVIEW & APPLY

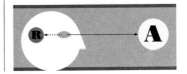

SEASONS AND TASKS OF ADULT DEVELOPMENT

Various researchers have examined the interweaving of adult intellectual competence, personal needs, and social expectations in attempting to define stages or periods of adult development. The data underlying their theories often

systems of meaning   Belief systems that shape our experiences, organize our thoughts and feelings, and determine our behavior.

come from extensive interview studies of particular age cohorts. Specific developmental periods emerge, based on "crises" or conflicts that we all supposedly experience. Thus, the theories often provide insightful descriptions of the issues and concerns of adulthood, but how broadly and universally they apply to adult development remains open to question. "Milestones" in particular should be viewed as tentative.

Also note that the theories or frameworks presented here go well beyond young adulthood; as we will see in later chapters.

HAVIGHURST'S DEVELOPMENTAL TASKS

Robert Havighurst (1953) described development over the lifespan in a very pragmatic way. He saw adulthood as a series of periods in which certain developmental tasks must be accomplished; these tasks are summarized in Table 12–4. In a sense, the tasks provide the broad context in which development takes place. They are demands that shape our use of intelligence. In young

TABLE 12–4 HAVIGHURST'S DEVELOPMENTAL TASKS

TASKS OF EARLY ADULTHOOD

1. Selecting a mate
2. Learning to live with a marriage partner
3. Starting a family
4. Rearing children
5. Managing a home
6. Getting started in an occupation
7. Taking on civic responsibility
8. Finding a congenial social group

TASKS OF MIDDLE AGE

1. Achieving adult civic and social responsibility
2. Establishing and maintaining an economic standard of living
3. Developing adult leisure-time activities
4. Assisting teenage children to become responsible and happy adults
5. Relating oneself to one's spouse as a person
6. Accepting and adjusting to the physiological changes of middle age
7. Adjusting to aging parents

TASKS OF LATER MATURITY

1. Adjusting to decreasing physical strength and health
2. Adjusting to retirement and reduced income
3. Adjusting to death of spouse
4. Establishing an explicit affiliation with one's age group
5. Meeting social and civic obligations
6. Establishing satisfactory physical living arrangements

Source: *Human Development and Education,* by Robert J. Havighurst. Copyright © 1953 by Longman, Inc. Reprinted by permission of Longman, Inc., New York.

adulthood, the tasks mostly involve starting a family and establishing a career. In middle age, they center on maintaining what was established earlier and adjusting to physical changes as well as to changes in the family. In the later years, still other adjustments must be made, as we'll return to in Chapter 17.

Do these concepts still apply to adult development during the 1990s? Yes, but not for all people. For many, the developmental tasks of middle age include settling into a single lifestyle or starting a family and raising young children, learning to live with a new mate after a divorce, and beginning a new occupation or facing early retirement as a result of corporate "downsizing." Although most people's lives still conform to the timing of Havighurst's developmental tasks, there are more exceptions now than ever before. Again we see how the particular path an individual takes depends in large part on his or her cultural environment.

ERIKSON'S DEVELOPMENTAL TASKS

Many theorists look to Erikson's theory of psychosocial stages in defining the central developmental tasks of adulthood. Recall from Chapter 1 that Erikson's theory includes eight psychosocial stages (crises) and that each stage builds on the one before. Adult development depends on resolution of the problems of earlier periods—issues of trust and autonomy, initiative and industry. In adolescence, the central issues to be resolved were identity achievement versus identity confusion. These can persist into young adulthood and give a sense of continuity to adult experiences (Erikson, 1959). Individuals define and redefine themselves, their priorities, and their place in the world.

The crisis of *intimacy versus isolation* is the other issue that is most characteristic of young adulthood. Intimacy involves establishing a mutually satisfying, close relationship with another person. It represents the union of two identities without the loss of each individual's unique qualities. By contrast, isolation involves inability or failure to achieve mutuality, sometimes because the individual's identity is too weak to risk a close union with another person (Erikson, 1963).

Erikson's theory is basically a stage theory, but he applies it in a much more flexible fashion (Erikson & Erikson, 1981). Like Havighurst's theory, it can be considered normative. Issues of identity and intimacy are present throughout life. Major events such as a death in the family may create simultaneous identity and intimacy crises as a person struggles with the loss and tries to redefine herself or himself in the absence of an intimate partner. Moving to a new town, starting a new job, and going back to college are major changes that require psychosocial adjustment. Erikson's theory therefore provides guidelines for issues that may have to be resolved again and again throughout life. After a major move to a new area of the country, for example, it may be necessary to "back up" all the way to reestablishing trust, developing autonomy, and rediscovering competence and industry before you can truly feel like an adult again.

Hence, for many contemporary thinkers, both identity and intimacy processes are central to an understanding of adult development (Whitbourne, 1986b). It is interesting, however, that intimacy and identity achievement may be specific to Western culture. Asian graduate students who come to the United States may find independent identity and more intimacy in their marriage to be very unfamiliar concepts.

LEVINSON'S SEASONS OF A MAN'S LIFE

Daniel Levinson (1978, 1986) conducted an intensive study of adult development; the participants were forty men aged 35 to 45, drawn from different racial, ethnic, and professional groups. Over a period of several months,

Young adults who are successful tend to be practical, organized individuals with an integrated personality.

interviews were conducted in which the men introspected about their feelings, attitudes, and life experiences. Along with the men's reconstructed biographies, Levinson and colleagues also studied the biographies of great figures such as Dante and Gandhi for clues to patterns of adult growth. Objective tests and scales were not used, however. In all, Levinson's approach was not unlike that of Freud (Chapter 1), and his theory should be viewed accordingly.

The researchers identified three major eras in the adult male life cycle, each extending for roughly 15 to 20 years (see Figure 12–5). During each era, the person constructs what Levinson calls a **life structure.** This is the pattern underlying a person's life. It serves both as a boundary between the inner person and the outside world and as a means by which the person deals with the outside world. The life structure is composed mainly of the person's social and environmental relationships, including what the individual gains from and must contribute to each relationship. The relationships may be with individuals, groups, systems, or even objects. For most men, relationships at work and within the family are central. At specific ages, people begin to question their existing life structure. They then construct a new structure that is consistent with their current needs, which dominates until the person "outgrows" it and starts the process again.

life structure The overall pattern that underlies a person's life.

Although Levinson was interested primarily in the midlife decade from age 35 to age 45, he found that maturation and adjustment at this stage are largely

FIGURE 12–5 LEVINSON'S SEASONS OF A MAN'S LIFE

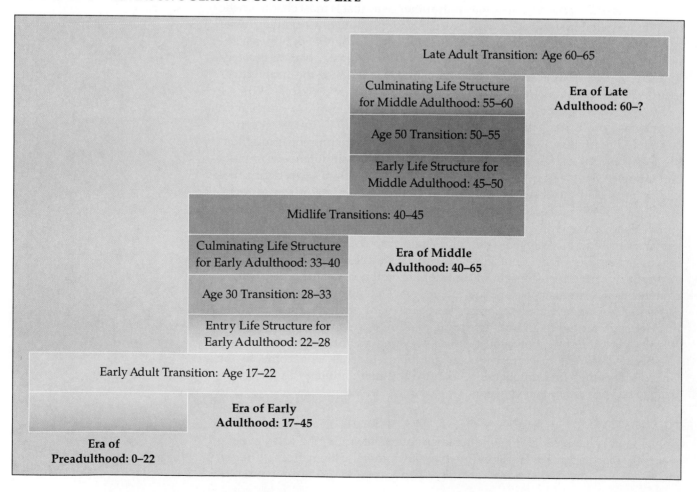

dependent on the individual's growth in a *novice* phase that extends from age 17 to age 33 (not labeled in the figure). This is the time when young American men resolve adolescent conflicts, create a place for themselves in adult society, and commit themselves to stable, predictable patterns of behavior and life. Within the novice phase, Levinson saw three distinct periods: early adult transition (about ages 17 to 22); entering the adult world (ages 22 to 28); and the age-30 transition (ages 28 to 33). Developmental "crises" then occur when people have difficulty making the transitions.

To achieve complete entry into adulthood, according to Levinson, the young man must master four developmental tasks: (1) defining a "dream" of what adult accomplishment will consist of, (2) finding a mentor, (3) developing a career, and (4) establishing intimacy. Let's take a closer look at each of these tasks.

DEFINING A DREAM   At the beginning of the novice phase, a man's dream of adult accomplishment is not necessarily linked to reality. It may consist of a specific goal such as winning a Pulitzer Prize, or a grandiose role such as becoming a movie producer, business tycoon, or famous writer or athlete. Some men have more modest aspirations, such as being a master craftsman, village philosopher, or loving family man. The most important aspect of the dream is its ability to inspire a man in his present endeavors. Ideally, the young man begins to structure his adult life in realistic, optimistic ways that will help him realize this dream. Hopeless fantasies and utterly unattainable goals are not conducive to growth.

Besides being unrealistic, the dream may not be realized because of lack of opportunity, parental pressures in other directions, individual traits such as passivity and laziness, or special skills that the person lacks and can't acquire. Consequently, a young man may enter and master an occupation that is beneath his dream, one that holds no magic for him. According to Levinson, such decisions bring about continual career conflicts and are responsible for lack of excitement and limited investment in work. Levinson believes that those who struggle to achieve at least some semblance of their dream are more likely to achieve a sense of fulfillment. Also note that the dream itself undergoes change. A young man who enters the early adult transition hoping to become a basketball star may later find satisfaction as a coach, thus incorporating some but not all elements of his dream.

FINDING A MENTOR   In pursuing their dream, young people can be aided enormously by mentors. A mentor can instill self-confidence by sharing and approving of the dream as well as imparting skills and wisdom. As a sponsor, the mentor may influence advancement of the apprentice's career. The major function of the mentor, however, is to provide a transition from the parent-child relationship to the world of adult peers. The mentor must be sufficiently parental and authoritative, yet sufficiently sympathetic to overcome the generation gap and establish a peer bond. Gradually the apprentice may acquire a sense of autonomy and competence; he may eventually overtake the mentor. Frequently the mentor and young man drift apart at this point.

DEVELOPING A CAREER   Besides forming the dream and acquiring a mentor, the youth faces a complex process of career formation that goes well beyond the mere selection of an occupation. Levinson views this developmental task as spanning the entire novice phase as the young man attempts to define himself vocationally. (This topic is discussed more fully in Chapter 13.)

Signs of successful career development.

ESTABLISHING INTIMACY   Similarly, the formation of intimate relationships does not begin and end with the "marker" events of marriage and the birth of the first child. Both before and after these events, the young man is learning about himself and the way he relates to women. He must ascertain what he likes about women and what they like about him; he must define his inner strengths and vulnerabilities in sexual intimacy. Although some self-discovery along these lines takes place in adolescence, young men often are still puzzled about these matters. Not until their early thirties do they develop the capacity for a serious romantic partnership.

A primary relationship with a *special woman* (Levinson's term) fills a need similar to that of the mentor-apprentice bond. The special woman may facilitate realization of the young man's dream by sanctifying it and by believing that the young man has what it takes. She aids his entry into the adult world by encouraging adult hopes and tolerating dependent behavior or other shortcomings. According to Levinson, a man's need for the special woman decreases later, during the midlife transition, at the period when most men achieve a high degree of autonomy and competence.

SEASONS OF A WOMAN'S LIFE

As you might imagine, Levinson's study stimulated numerous criticisms, of which the most persistent was that he had not included women. That criticism was addressed in subsequent research (Levinson, 1990; Levinson, 1996). Levinson studied a group of 45 women, 15 of whom were homemakers, 15 businesswomen, and 15 academicians. In part, the findings supported his theory that entry into adulthood involves defining a dream, finding a mentor, choosing an occupation, and establishing a relationship with a special person; and his model for women is very similar to the one for men in Figure 12–5. There was also a critical transition around age 30, a time of stress as career objectives and lifestyles were reexamined. The women's experiences, however, appeared to be quite different from those of men. Moreover, although Levinson claimed that both men's and women's transitions are closely linked to age, other researchers have found that for women, the stage of the family life cycle seems to be a better indicator of transitions than age alone (Harris et al., 1986). Women's transitions (and crises) may be linked less to age than to events like the birth or the departure of children.

DIFFERING DREAMS   Perhaps the most striking difference between the sexes was in their dream definitions. Indeed, the difference was so significant that Levinson labels it *gender splitting*. Whereas men tend to have a unified vision of their future focused on their career, many women tend to have "split" dreams. Both the academicians and businesswomen in Levinson's study wanted to combine career and marriage, albeit in different ways. The academic women were less ambitious and more willing to forgo their careers as long as they could engage in intellectually stimulating activities in the community after their children were born. The businesswomen wanted to maintain their careers, but to do so on a reduced level after they had children. Only the homemakers had unified dreams comparable to those of men: They wanted to be full-time wives and mothers, much as their own mothers had been.

Similarly, most women in other studies using Levinson's methods had dreams that incorporated both career and marriage, and the majority of these women gave greater weight to marriage. Only a minority focused exclusively on career achievement in their dreams; even fewer restricted their visions of the future to the traditional roles of wife and mother. However, even women who had dreams of both career and marriage moderated their dreams in the context of their husbands' goals, thereby fulfilling traditional expectations within a more contemporary lifestyle (Roberts & Newton, 1987).

Many women express dissatisfaction with one or another aspect of their split dream (Droege, 1982). It seems to some that careers and marriage are incompatible. The women in Levinson's study also found it extremely difficult to integrate career and family. None of the businesswomen, for example, viewed her solution as more than "adequate." Although colleagues and family members often judge career women to be successful, the women themselves often feel that they have sacrificed one aspect of their dream in order to fulfill the other (Roberts & Newton, 1987).

DIFFERING RELATIONSHIPS WITH MENTORS   Another area in which men and women apparently have very different experiences is in the mentoring relationship. Women have been found to enter into such relationships less frequently than men. Part of the problem is that there are fewer women in positions to guide, counsel, or sponsor young women seeking professional careers. When men act as mentors to women, the relationship between them may be disrupted by sexual attractions (Roberts & Newton, 1987). Sometimes husbands or lovers serve as mentors, but in these cases the mentoring function is often complicated by conflicting demands. When women assert their independence and either pursue their career fully or claim equality in the relationship, their mate sometimes withdraws his support.

Women may also have trouble finding a *special man* to support their dream (Droege, 1982). Although a husband or lover sometimes serves as the special man, particularly in the early adult phase of separation from parental dominance, a traditional male mate rarely sustains the female's dream if it starts to threaten his preeminence in the relationship. In other words, a male mate doesn't necessarily perform all the functions of the special man in facilitating the woman's personal and career growth.

DIFFERING CAREER TRAJECTORIES   Not only do women have greater difficulty than men in finding a special person, but also they tend to settle on a career much later than men. In an earlier study (Levinson et al., 1978), it was observed that most men "complete [their] occupational novitiate and assume a fully adult status in the work world" by the end of their age-30 transition—they are no longer novices. By contrast, women often do not achieve this status

Unlike young males, who generally focus on their jobs, many young females want to combine career and marriage.

until well into middle age (Droege, 1982; Furst, 1983; Stewart, 1977). Ruth Droege found that even women who had settled on a career path in their twenties had, for the most part, not completed their "occupational novitiate" until age 40 or later. Droege also noted that women in middle adulthood were still preoccupied with trying to succeed in the workplace and were not yet ready to reevaluate their occupational goals or achievements. Another study (Adams, 1983) found that a group of female lawyers followed the male career pattern until the age-30 transition, but at that point, most of them began to shift their focus from achieving success in their career to gaining satisfaction from their personal relationships.

DIFFERING REEVALUATION   The age-30 transition is stressful for both men and women. However, men and women react differently to the reevaluative process that takes place at that point. Men may make changes in their careers or lifestyles, but they do not change their focus on job and career. In contrast, women generally reverse the priorities that they established during young adulthood (Adams, 1983; Droege, 1982; Levinson, 1990; Stewart, 1977). Women who are oriented toward marriage and child rearing tend to shift toward occupational goals, whereas those who are career-centered generally move toward marriage and child rearing. Their more complex dream makes it much more difficult for them to achieve their goals.

WOMEN'S DREAMS AND SOCIAL CHANGE   Perhaps one reason a woman's dream is more complex is that it has been more strongly affected by social changes in the twentieth century. In one study (Helson & Picano, 1990), it was noted that in the late 1950s and 1960s, the "best-adjusted" women had a clear dream: to be a full-time homemaker. That dream became outdated as social changes brought women into the workforce at all levels. By middle age, the traditional women were no longer the best adjusted in the study. Instead, they were more dependent or overcontrolled than the less traditional women. Apparently, being in congruence with societal roles is important to individual well-being. The roles open to young adult women today usually combine career and family. Young men, on the other hand, still are expected to pursue a career and not make a full commitment to homemaking (Kalleberg & Rosenfeld, 1990).

GOULD'S TRANSFORMATIONS

Researchers on the course of development during adulthood often face the difficult task of deciding how to organize extensive biographical data. The results depend in part on the focus and interests of the investigator. In his original study, Levinson obtained 15 hours of biographical interviews from 40 men. He chose to look at various aspects of the process of establishing a career and a lifestyle.

Roger Gould (1978) had a more cognitive focus. He was interested in the individual's assumptions, ideas, myths, and worldviews during different periods of adulthood. Gould's studies of adults included both men and women. He and his colleagues examined the life histories of a large group of men and women aged 16 to 60. On the basis of these profiles, they developed descriptions of the way people look at the the world around them that are characteristic of different adult stages. For Gould, growth is a process of casting off childish illusions and false assumptions in favor of self-reliance and self-acceptance. Like Kegan, he believes that an individual's system of meaning-making shapes his or her behavior and life decisions.

According to Gould, from age 16 to age 22, the major false assumption to be challenged is "I'll always belong to my parents and believe in their world." To penetrate and discard this illusion, young adults must start building an adult identity that their parents cannot control or dominate. Young people's sense of self, however, is still fragile at this point, and self-doubt makes them highly sensitive to criticism. Young adults also begin to see their parents as imperfect and fallible people rather than the all-powerful, controlling forces they once were.

Between the ages of 22 and 28, young adults often make another false assumption that reflects their continuing doubts about self-sufficiency: "Doing things my parents' way, with willpower and perseverance, will bring results. But if I become too frustrated, confused, or tired, or am simply unable to cope, they will step in and show me the right way." To combat this notion, the young adult must accept full responsibility for his or her own life, surrendering the expectation of continuous parental assistance. This acceptance involves far more than removing yourself from a mother's or father's domination; it requires the active, positive construction of an adult life. Conquering the world on your own also diverts energy from constant introspection and self-centeredness. Gould finds that the predominant thinking mode during this period progresses from flashes of insight to perseverance, discipline, controlled experimentation, and goal orientation.

From age 28 to age 34, a significant shift toward adult attitudes occurs. The major false assumption during this period is this: "Life is simple and controllable. There are no significant coexisting contradictory forces within me." This impression differs from those of previous stages in two important respects: It indicates a sense of competence and an acknowledgment of limitations. Enough adult understanding has been achieved to admit inner turmoil without calling strength or integrity into doubt. Talents, strengths, and desires that were suppressed during the twenties because they didn't fit into the unfolding blueprint of adulthood may resurface. Gould cites the example of an ambitious young partner in a prestigious law firm who begins to consider public service, and the example of a suave, carefree bachelor who suddenly realizes that his many relationships with women are not satisfying because of some inadequacy of his own. (This development closely resembles Levinson's prediction about the dream: Those who ignore and suppress it in young adulthood will be haunted by this unresolved conflict later in life).

Even those who have fulfilled youthful ambitions still experience some doubt, confusion, and depression during this period. They may begin to question the very values that helped them gain independence from their parents. Growth involves breaking out of the rigid expectations of the twenties and embracing a more reasonable attitude: "What I get is directly related to how much effort I'm willing to make." Individuals cease to believe in magic and begin to put their faith in disciplined, well-directed work. At the same time, they begin to cultivate the interests, values, and qualities that will endure and develop throughout adult life.

The years between 35 and 45 bring full involvement in the adult world. Parents no longer have control over people at this age, and their children have not yet effectively challenged them. They are, as Gould says, "in the thicket of life." At the same time, they experience time pressure and fear that they won't accomplish all of their goals. The physical changes of middle age frighten and dismay them; reduced career mobility makes them feel penned in. The drive for stability and security, which was paramount when they were in their

STUDY CHART ▸ SELECTED THEORISTS' VIEWS OF THE MAJOR TASKS OF EARLY ADULTHOOD

THEORIST	VIEW
Perry	Progressing from dualistic thinking to relativistic thinking
Riegel	Achieving dialectical thinking
Labouvie-Vief	Developing autonomy and independent decision-making
Schaie	Flexibly applying intellectual abilities toward accomplishing personal and career goals—the *achieving* period.
Kegan	Structuring and restructuring personal systems of meaning
Havighurst	Starting a family and establishing a career
Erikson	Continuing to develop a sense of identity; resolving intimacy versus isolation
Levinson	Developing an early life structure and making the age-30 and other transitions, which include defining a dream, finding a mentor, developing a career, and establishing intimacy with a special partner
Gould	Casting off erroneous assumptions about dependency and accepting responsibility for one's life; developing competence and acknowledging personal limitations

thirties, is replaced by a need for immediate action and results. There can be no more procrastination. The deaths of their parents and their awareness of their own mortality bring them face to face with the frequent unfairness and pain of life. In acknowledging the ugly side of human existence, they let go of their childish need for safety. They also become free at last to examine and discard the sense of their own worthlessness and wickedness left over from childhood. This freedom, Gould believes, represents a full, autonomous adult consciousness.

In closing, it is important to remember that theories that emphasize periods or stages are valuable in understanding adult development but should not be interpreted too rigidly, for several reasons. First, the notion of stages tends to obscure the stable aspects of personality during adulthood. Second, these theories pay little attention to the unpredictability of life events (Neugarten, 1979). Third, thus far, most subjects in studies of adult development have been men, and much of the research has concentrated on the same age cohorts—individuals born in the first half of the twentieth century.

REVIEW & APPLY

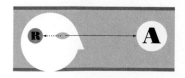

1. Summarize Havighurst's developmental tasks of adulthood.
2. Describe the central developmental tasks of young adulthood according to Erikson.
3. According to Levinson and studies inspired by his theories, what are the four developmental tasks that a young adult must master to enter adulthood? In what ways do men and women experience these tasks differently?
4. Describe Gould's cognitive view of transformations during adult development.

SUMMARY

Perspectives on Adult Development

■ Age clocks are a form of internal timing; they let us know whether we are progressing through life too slowly or too quickly.

■ Age clocks are socially based and are more flexible today than they were in earlier decades.

■ Chronological age refers to the number of years lived; biological age is a person's position with regard to his or her expected lifespan; and psychological age refers to how well a person can adapt to social and other environmental demands.

■ Contextual paradigms seek to describe and organize the effects of different kinds of forces on development. No two individuals experience exactly the same combination of contexts.

Physical Development in Young Adulthood

■ In young adulthood, most people enjoy peak vitality, strength, and endurance.

■ Organ functioning, reaction time, strength, motor skills, and sensorimotor coordination are at their maximum between the ages of 25 and 30; after that, they gradually decline.

■ Declines in physical skills and capabilities are most noticeable in emergency situations and at other times when physical demands are extreme.

■ The health and exercise habits formed during young adulthood often persist throughout the adult years.

■ In recent decades, improvements in exercise and diet have added greatly to adult fitness.

■ Death rates are lower for young adults than for any other adult age group, but the rate of preventable deaths during young adulthood remains high.

■ Many diseases that will cause trouble later in life begin during young adulthood.

■ Sometimes sociocultural factors lead to disease or even death.

■ The process of ovulation is relatively stable between the ages of 25 and 38, but then it declines. Men produce sperm from puberty on, although seminal emissions contain progressively fewer viable sperm.

■ Researchers have found that the median duration of intercourse has increased markedly, as has flexibility in attitudes toward intercourse.

■ Although sexuality is more open and accepted now than it was before the 1960s, there is a trend back toward more conservative behavior, partly because of fear of sexually transmitted diseases.

■ The dominant pattern of sexual intimacy between men and women in the 1990s appears to be one of increased communication and mutual satisfaction.

■ Homosexuality often becomes apparent in adolescence or earlier. Its incidence is difficult to assess and varies widely by location.

■ Many gays and lesbians live together in sustained relationships. Gay men are more likely to belong to "open couples," in which monogamy isn't required.

■ Because of the spread of AIDS, sexual behavior of both heterosexuals and homosexuals has changed. Today most young couples report exercising greater caution in their sexual activities.

Cognitive Continuity and Change

■ The evidence regarding cognitive capacity after adolescence is not clear, but it appears that intelligence increases until around age 45 and then levels off.

■ Continuing education tends to increase IQ test scores in adulthood. People over 30 perform better with training in specific cognitive skills, and skills that are exercised frequently are maintained better than those that aren't.

■ A study of college students found that they begin by interpreting the world and their educational experiences in authoritarian, dualistic terms, but gradually begin to accept and even respect diversity of opinion. This relativistic perspective, in turn, eventually gives way to a stage in which students make personal commitments and affirmations to particular values and points of view.

■ According to Riegel, there is a fifth stage of cognitive development, dialectical thinking, in which the individual considers opposing thoughts and observations and then integrates them.

■ Labouvie-Vief emphasizes commitment and responsibility as the hallmark of adult cognitive maturity.

■ Schaie believes that the distinctive feature of adult thinking is the flexible way in which adults use the cognitive abilities they already possess. He has divided adult thinking into four stages: the acquisition period, the achieving period, the period of social responsibility, and a period in which the central task is reintegrating elements experienced earlier in life.

■ According to Kegan, the individual is continually differentiating the self from the world and at the same time is integrating the self into the broader world. He emphasizes that we continue to develop systems of meaning well into adulthood.

Seasons and Tasks of Adult Development

■ Havighurst sees adulthood as a series of periods in which certain developmental tasks must be accomplished. In young adulthood, the tasks mainly involve starting a family and establishing a career. In middle age, they center on maintaining what was established earlier and adjusting to physical and family changes. In later years, new adjustments must be made.

■ According to Erikson, the central task of adulthood is to resolve the crisis of intimacy versus isolation. Intimacy involves establishing a mutually satisfying, close relationship with another person.

■ Levinson believes that the adult male life cycle consists of three major eras, each extending for roughly 15–20 years. During each era, the person constructs a life structure, the pattern underlying his life.

■ To achieve complete entry into adulthood, according to Levinson, the young man must master four developmental tasks: (1) defining a "dream," (2) finding a mentor, (3) developing a career, and (4) establishing intimacy.

■ Subsequent studies included women and found both similarities and differences. The most striking difference involves the nature of the "dream." Levinson refers to this as gender splitting: Whereas men tend to have a unified vision of their future focused on their career, women tend to have "split" dreams involving various combinations of career and marriage.

■ Men and women also differ in their relationships with mentors. When a woman has a male mentor, the relationship between them may be disrupted by sexual attractions.

■ Women tend to settle on a career much later than men and often do not achieve fully adult status in the work world until after age 30.

■ According to Gould, growth is a process of casting off childish illusions and false assumptions in favor of self-reliance and self-acceptance. Full, autonomous adult consciousness is achieved when a person becomes able to face the unfairness and pain of life and free to examine and discard the sense of worthlessness and wickedness left over from childhood.

KEY TERMS

age clock	social age	dialectical thinking
chronological age	psychological age	systems of meaning
biological age	contextual paradigms	life structure

USING WHAT YOU'VE LEARNED

Is there cognitive development after adolescence? Are we wiser, and do we have better judgment, at age 35 than at age 20? Clients tend to prefer to hire a lawyer who is over 35 rather than one in his or her twenties. Why might this be so?

To explore factors that contribute to adult cognitive development, find two adults who are equally well educated for their job but differ in age by 15 or more years. With each of them, discuss some of the more puzzling or controversial aspects of their job. How do they describe the key issues? What frameworks do they use for finding solutions or making decisions? How do their responses differ? Is one more complex or more efficient than the other?

Then see whether you can relate the differences that you observe to the material presented in this chapter.

SUGGESTED READINGS

BELENSKY, M. F. (1986). *Women's ways of knowing: The development of self, voice and mind.* New York: Basic Books. A landmark book, based on in-depth interviews, that chronicles women's adult development of self-confidence and thought.

GILOVICH, T. (1991). *How we know what isn't so: The fallibility of human reason in everyday life.* New York: Free Press. Despite the cognitive abilities of well-educated adults, how and why do they sometimes become convinced of false beliefs?

HIDE, J. S. (1989). *Understanding human sexuality* (4th ed.). New York: McGraw-Hill. A comprehensive text on the many aspects of human sexuality—heterosexual and homosexual attitudes and behavior together with the biological base.

LEVINSON, D. J. (1978). *The seasons of a man's life.* New York: Knopf. A report on the common patterns of development from a ten-year study of adult males, with particular attention to the novice phase, the settling-down period, and the midlife transition.

LEVINSON, D. J. (1996). *The seasons of a woman's life.* New York: Ballantine. In this report of a longitudinal study of women comparable to his earlier study of men, Levinson explores similarities and differences between the genders with regard to seasons, and he attempts to formulate an overall human life cycle.

LEWIS, M. (1997). *Altering fates: Why the past does not predict the future.* New York: Guilford Press. Michael Lewis, noted developmental researcher, challenges some popular models for predicting adulthood personality from childhood events. Adult adaptability, and circumstances plus the personal meanings of those earlier events, strongly shape adult psychological development, he contends.

MICHAEL, R. T., GAGNON, J. H., LAUMANN, E. O., and KOLATA, G. (1994). *Sex in America: A definitive survey.* Boston: Little, Brown. Movies, magazines, and advertisements give one impression. This comprehensive survey of adult sexual practices, preferences, and lifestyles gives another!

ROSE, M. (1989). *Lives on the boundary: The struggles and achievements of America's underprepared.* New York: Free Press. Real-life stories of young adults breaking out of the poorly educated underclass.

Young Adults: Personality Development and Socialization

Early in the history of the study of adult development, Freud defined success in adulthood as the ability to love and to work. Erikson emphasized achieving intimacy, and later generativity, which includes productive work of any kind. Other theorists talk about affiliation and achievement; still others about acceptance and competence. Clearly, a successful journey through adulthood is intimately tied to a person's involvement with a career and, for most people, with a romantic partner and a family.

In this chapter, we focus on the importance of love and work in development during early adulthood. With regard to love, crucial social contexts are the family and evolving personal lifestyles. We will look at the various ways in which adults establish intimate relationships and will use these relationships to structure and restructure their sense of identity. With regard to work, we'll focus on how adults apply their energy and skills and pursue their ambitions. Work shapes our lifestyles, friendships, prestige, and socioeconomic status, as well as our attitudes and values. Ideally, work challenges us and helps us grow. It requires us to solve problems. It can be a means for finding pleasure, satisfaction, and fulfillment. On the downside, it can cause frustration, boredom, worry, humiliation, and a sense of hopelessness. It can create stress and damage health. Either way, however, work is a central context for and contributor to adult development.

CONTINUITY AND CHANGE IN PERSONALITY DEVELOPMENT AND SOCIALIZATION

Socialization continues into young adulthood and beyond; we become socialized to new roles within the contexts of work, independent living, sustained intimacy with another person, marriage, and family. Many people assume new roles in their community as well by joining clubs, civic groups, and religious institutions.

Is it the same for personality? Do we continue to develop and change during early adulthood and beyond? Many theorists think so, as discussed in the preceding chapter. The role changes of young adulthood constitute transitions and turning points in our lives (Clausen, 1995), and we are changed by them. We see things differently; we behave differently; we adjust our beliefs, attitudes, and values in accordance with the roles and contexts we experience. That indeed is personality development—although the changes are subtler and less systematic than those of childhood and adolescence, and there is much continuity as well. *Stable* personality, however, typically is not achieved until the latter part of young adulthood or in early middle adulthood. Even then, personality is not cast in concrete: Abrupt changes in family, social, or vocational contexts can influence personality at any point in the lifespan.

SELF, FAMILY, AND WORK

Adult development can be described in the context of three separate but interacting systems that focus on various aspects of the self. These involve the development of the personal self, the self as family member (adult child, member of a couple, and parent), and the self as worker (Okum, 1984) (see Figure 13–1).

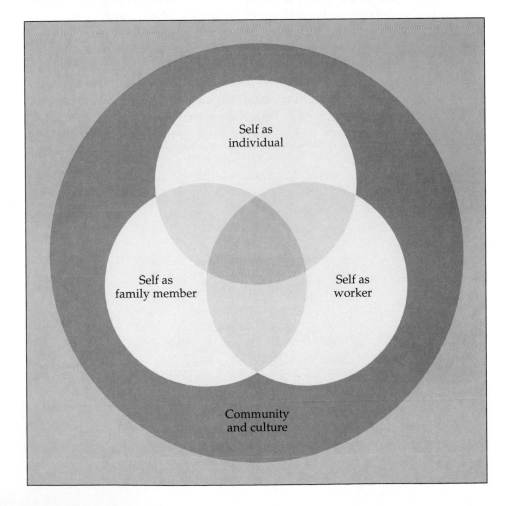

FIGURE 13–1

The three systems of adult development involve dynamic interactions among the self as an individual, a family member, and a worker. These interactions take place in the broad context of community and culture.

Source: Adapted from B. Okum. (1984). Working with Adults: Individual Family and Career Development. Monterey, CA: Brooks/Cole.

Interactions abound. For example, research has shown that the more positive a father's work experience, the higher his self-esteem and the more likely he is to have an accepting, warm, and positive parenting style (Grimm-Thomas & Perry-Jenkins, 1994).

These systems change as a result of events and circumstances and as a result of interactions with the broader community and culture. As discussed in Chapter 3, Urie Bronfenbrenner's (1979, 1989) ecological systems model presents development as a dynamic, multidirectional process involving the individual's immediate surroundings, the social environment, and the values, laws, and customs of the culture in which the individual lives. These interactions and the personal changes that emerge from them occur throughout the lifespan.

THE PERSONAL SELF: SELF-ACTUALIZATION AND SELF-REGARD

There are many conceptualizations of self, as we have seen in previous chapters with regard to childhood and adolescence. A classic formulation of what is important to the adult self is that of Abraham Maslow (1908–1970). Maslow's theory has distinct developmental overtones. Instead of stages, however, it emphasizes *needs* that each individual must meet in striving to reach his or her unique potential and sense of self. The goal is **self-actualization,** which means full development and utilization of talents and abilities (Maslow, 1954, 1979). Self-actualization is at the top of Maslow's classic "hierarchy of needs," which is often illustrated as a pyramid as in Figure 13–2. **Humanistic psychologists** like Maslow maintain that we actively make choices about our own lives. We are influenced by our experiences with others, but we also determine the directions we take and strive to achieve our own goals (May, 1983).

This need for self-actualization can be expressed or pursued only after lower needs such as those for food and shelter and safety have been met. People living in conditions of deprivation or terror are not likely to be concerned with achieving their full potential. People also need to love and to feel loved and to "belong" in contexts such as family and community. Beyond that, we

self-actualization Realizing one's full unique potential.

humanistic psychology The view that humans actively make choices and seek to fulfill positive personal and social goals.

FIGURE 13–2 MASLOW'S HIERARCHY OF NEEDS

Although higher needs are no less important than lower needs, individuals must satisfy lower needs, such as those for survival and safety, before meeting higher needs such as belongingness and esteem. Later in life, adults must work out their needs for self-actualization in order to develop their fullest potential.

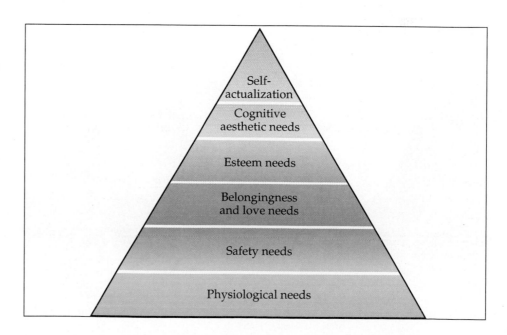

Self-actualization

Cognitive aesthetic needs

Esteem needs

Belongingness and love needs

Safety needs

Physiological needs

need self-esteem; we need positive responses from others, which can range from simple confirmation of our personality, skills, and accomplishments by family and friends to acclamation and fame in society at large. We also seek to satisfy higher cognitive and aesthetic needs.

For evidence of self-actualization and of its composition, Maslow looked primarily at case studies of important personages and others who seemed to be well along the road to realizing their potential. What are self-actualizers like? They tend to be realistic, have a good sense of humor, be creative, be productive, and have a positive self-concept. But they aren't necessarily perfect. They can be cranky, absentminded, and single-minded in pursuit of their unique potential. Also, they aren't necessarily happy all the time, although they do have *peak experiences* in which they feel extremely good about themselves and their place in the world.

A person can only begin the journey toward self-actualization in young adulthood; it is a lifelong quest that can never be fully satisfied. It is better viewed as a "search for truth and understanding, the attempt to secure equality and justice, and the creation and love of beauty" (Shaffer, 1978).

Carl Rogers (1902–1987), another humanistic psychologist, approached these issues from the viewpoint of a psychotherapist. He was attempting to discover the causes of his patients' anxieties, low self-esteem and sense of self-worth, and interpersonal difficulties. For him, the core of human nature consists of healthy and constructive impulses (1980). At birth, we are prepared to be "good" both as individuals and as members of society, but as we develop, society often "corrupts" us. Various significant others, beginning with our parents, impose **conditions of worth** on us: Do this, don't do that, or you will be a worthless human being. An individual who internalizes such conditions develops low self-esteem, a sense of failure, and recurrent anxiety and despair. The internalized conditions become standards of perfection that can never be attained. Misbehave once, and you're a rotten child. Fall just the least bit short as a spouse or a worker, and you're a worthless human being.

Rogers proposed that we should view ourselves and others with **unconditional positive regard,** by which he meant warmly accepting another person as a worthwhile human being, without reservations or conditions. As a parent, love your child unconditionally, regardless of his or her behavior. When the child misbehaves, punish if necessary, but never attack the child's sense of being loved and having worth as a person. Similar admonitions apply to interactions with family members, friends, and coworkers.

SELF AS FAMILY MEMBER

Individuals view their family as an extremely important context for adult development. In one national survey, women and men of all ages said that their family roles were very important in defining who they are (Beroff et al., 1981). In a more recent and detailed study of adult identity, fully 90% of the men and women who were interviewed indicated that their family roles and responsibilities were the most important components in defining who they were (Whitbourne, 1986a). They talked about their roles as parents, spouses, siblings, and children; about family tasks and responsibilities; about closeness, communication, companionship, and personal fulfillment. Broadly speaking, they talked about the people whom they had become within these family relationships and experiences. Very few men and women defined themselves primarily in terms of their career rather than their family.

Young adults, whether married or not, are often in transition, moving from the family they grew up in to the family they will create. Lois Hoffman (1984)

Young, unmarried adults may be viewed as moving from their family of origin to their family of procreation.

conditions of worth   Conditions others impose upon us if we are to be worthwhile as human beings—conditions that are often impossible to fulfill.

unconditional positive regard Rogers's proposition that we should warmly accept another person as a worthwhile human being, without reservations or conditions.

identifies four aspects of this process. The first is *emotional independence*, in which the young adult becomes less dependent on the parents for social and psychological support. The second form is *attitudinal independence*. The young adult develops attitudes, values, and belief systems that may differ from those of the parents. *Functional independence*, the third form, refers to the young adult's ability to support himself or herself financially and to take care of day-to-day problems. Finally, *conflictual independence*—which can occur at any point along the way—involves separating from parents without feelings of guilt or betrayal.

Studies of college students (Lapsley et al., 1989) indicate substantial progress in each form of independence over the college years. Substantial functional dependence often remains, however, even in the senior year. Many students still rely on their parents financially. Finally, young adults who fail to complete the separation process, especially with regard to conflictual independence, are more likely to develop psychological adjustment problems (Friedlander & Siegel, 1990; Lapsley et al., 1989).

SELF AS WORKER

Children are often asked, "What do you want to be when you grow up?" Many of our thoughts and fantasies are occupied by this question, which we may continue asking ourselves well beyond childhood. In adulthood, how we answer the question contributes greatly to our identity—who we are and who we are not. Erikson's stage of *generativity versus stagnation* (Chapter 15) is intimately related to work as well, in that many people achieve a sense of being productive, worthwhile members of society in part through their trade or profession.

Whatever our occupation, we carry with us the attitudes, beliefs, and experiences of our jobs. We are members of a corporation, a profession, a trade or craft, perhaps a union. Work often defines our status, income, and prestige. It defines our daily schedule, social contacts, and opportunities for personal development.

Because low-ceiling jobs often offer less intrinsic satisfaction, work friendships may be an especially important source of extrinsic satisfaction.

What does work give people in return for the time and energy they devote to it? Industrial/organizational psychologists note that for some people, work is merely a means of survival. It provides them with money to feed, clothe, and shelter themselves and their families, and they "live their lives" away from their jobs. For other people, work provides a chance to be creative or productive; offers welcome challenge and stimulates growth; and provides an opportunity to gain self-esteem or respect. For still others, work is an addiction—"workaholics" are driven to perform and define their lives in terms of their work.

When researchers ask adults what is important to them about their work, there are two typical kinds of answers. On the one hand, people talk about the characteristics of their job together with the particular abilities they possess to do the work. These are **intrinsic factors of work.** People who focus on intrinsic factors might describe their work in terms of its challenge or interest and might talk about their work competence and achievements. On the other hand, some people focus on **extrinsic factors of work.** These include salary and status, the comfort or convenience of the work environment and hours of work, the adequacy of supervision and other employer practices, the attitudes and support of coworkers, and the opportunities for advancement (Whitbourne, 1986a).

What workers say about their jobs depends in part on the job. Many, many jobs in our society offer little challenge and opportunity for personal growth, and the people who perform them can talk only about extrinsic factors and financial survival. The fortunate workers whose jobs do provide for intrinsic factors and who do talk about them tend, on average, to report more job satisfaction and higher motivation and personal involvement in their jobs. These workers also are more likely to define their identity largely in terms of their work or career. They are aware of and do not wish to lose the personal satisfaction they derive from work. In a study of middle-class workers between the ages of 46 and 71 (Pfeiffer & Davis, 1971), 90% of the men and 82% of the women questioned said that they would continue to work even if they did not have to. They indicated that they derived more satisfaction from work than from leisure activities. Even people approaching retirement age preferred to continue working, at least part-time.

Figure 13-3 presents a model of the way in which intrinsic work motivation is tied to identity as a competent worker. When a worker is intrinsically motivated, there is more job involvement, better job performance, and stronger identity as a competent worker. This condition in turn increases intrinsic work motivation. But the cycle can go in a negative direction as well. For example, feeling incompetent or overwhelmed decreases intrinsic motivation, job involvement, and job performance (Maehr & Breskamp, 1986; Whitbourne, 1986b).

Friendships can be important extrinsic factors in the workplace. Friendships formed on the job may be especially important to people in "low-ceiling" jobs (Kanter, 1977), for which the pay may be adequate but there is no ladder of success to climb; instead, there is a "ceiling" beyond which the worker can't advance. Socializing with fellow employees may add meaning to such a job. Women in particular may find social relationships at work important (Repetti et al., 1989). These relationships provide emotional support and may be one reason why women who work outside the home typically have better mental and physical health than those who do not. (This point is discussed more fully later in the chapter.)

Other extrinsic factors are related to health. When high job demands are combined with unclear supervision, stress and the risk of heart attacks in-

intrinsic factors of work Satisfactions workers obtain from doing the work in and of itself.

extrinsic factors of work Satisfaction in the form of pay, status, and other rewards for work.

FIGURE 13–3

The interaction between intrinsic work motivation and worker identity.

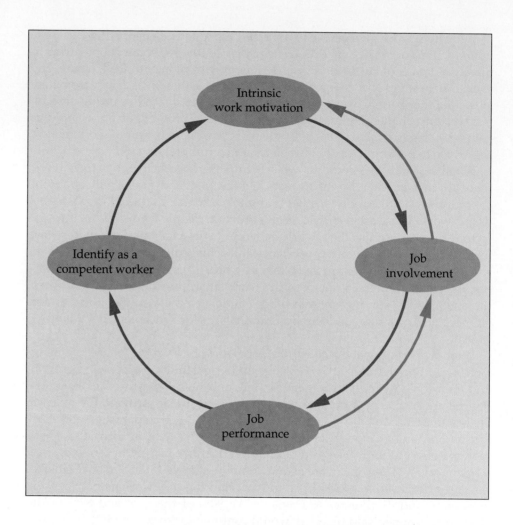

crease (Repetti et al., 1989). Thus, extrinsic factors are important not only to job satisfaction but also to overall physical and mental health.

Finally, attitudes and values toward work shifted during the 1980s. The majority of workers no longer defined themselves exclusively or even primarily with respect to work. Far more workers sought a balance among family, work, and personal interests and pastimes (Derr, 1986; Whitbourne, 1986b). Nevertheless, the majority of respondents reported high levels of personal satisfaction in their work. In this study, intrinsic rewards outweighed extrinsic rewards.

FORMING INTIMATE RELATIONSHIPS

Whether they are single, married, widowed, divorced, or cohabiting, most adults actively seek or maintain intimate relationships—as romantic partners and as close friends. Intimacy, the essential part of an enduring, satisfying emotional bond, is the basis for both friendship and love.

ADULT FRIENDSHIPS

As noted by Beverly Fehr (1996), friendships are a core aspect of adult life. Although as Fehr puts it, "There are as many definitions of friendship as there are social scientists studying the topic," there are some things that friendships have in common. Close friends are people whom we trust and rely on in times of difficulty, who are always ready to help, and whom we enjoy spending time with. Like romantic relationships, friendships are usually characterized by positive emotional attachment, need fulfillment, and interdependence (Brehm, 1992). We'll return to adult friendships in Chapter 15; for now, note that friendship also includes elements that are closely akin to those of love.

STERNBERG'S TRIANGULAR THEORY OF LOVE

Robert Sternberg's triangular theory of love (1986) demonstrates the complexities of achieving love relationships. Sternberg suggests that love has three components, as illustrated in Figure 13–4. First, there is **intimacy,** the feeling of closeness that occurs in love relationships. Intimacy is the sense of being connected or bonded to the loved one. We want to do things to make life better for people we love. We genuinely like them and are happiest when they are around. We count on them to be there when we need them, and we try to provide the same support in return. People who are in love share activities, possessions, thoughts, and feelings. Indeed, sharing may be one of the most crucial factors in turning a dating relationship into a loving marriage or marriagelike relationship.

Passion is the second component of love. This refers to physical attraction, arousal, and sexual behavior in a relationship. Sexual needs are important but are not the only motivational needs involved. For example, needs for self-esteem, affiliation, and nurturance may also play a role. Sometimes intimacy leads to passion; at other times, passion precedes intimacy. In still other cases, there is passion without intimacy or intimacy without passion (as in a sibling relationship).

The final component of Sternberg's love triangle is **decision/commitment.** This component has both short- and long-term aspects. The short-term aspect is the decision or realization of being in love. The long-term aspect is a commitment to maintain that love. Again, the relationship between decision/commitment and the other components of love can vary. To demonstrate

intimacy The feeling of closeness that occurs in love relationships.

passion The second component of love that refers to physical attraction, arousal, and sexual behavior in a relationship.

decision/commitment The realization of being in love and making a commitment to maintain it.

According to Sternberg, intimacy is a key characteristic of a love relationship.

FIGURE 13–4 STERNBERG'S
TRIANGULAR THEORY
OF LOVE

Source: Adapted from Feldman (1998).

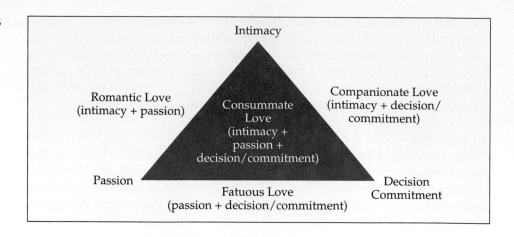

the possible combinations, Sternberg (1986) developed the taxonomy of love relationships shown in Table 13–1. Clearly, most of us hope for a marriage relationship marked by consummate love. But more than one couple has mistaken infatuation for love, and in many marriages, passion ebbs, and the relationship becomes essentially nonromantic.

Intimacy can be destroyed by denial of feelings, particularly anger. Fear of rejection also blocks intimacy, especially when it leads to a false identity designed to cater to another person rather than to fulfill important personal needs. Traditional courtship and dating patterns may even discourage intimacy if they involve only ritual exchanges and facades. Some behaviors are even more harmful to intimacy: Casual sex, brutal candor, and contrived aloofness are not fertile ground for intimacy (McCary, 1978).

TABLE 13–1 TAXONOMY OF KINDS OF LOVE BASED ON STERNBERG'S
TRIANGULAR THEORY

Kind of Love	COMPONENT		
	Intimacy	Passion	Decision/Commitment
Liking	+	–	–
Infatuated love	–	+	–
Empty love	–	–	–
Romantic love	+	+	–
Companionate love	+	–	+
Fatuous love	–	+	+
Consummate love	+	+	+

Note: + = component present; – = component absent. These kinds of love represent limiting cases based on the triangular theory. Most loving relationships fit between categories because the various components of love are expressed along continua, not discretely.

Source: Sternberg (1986).

COUPLE FORMATION AND DEVELOPMENT

Couple formation and development are a major part of adult development. Individuals achieve part of their personal identity as a member of a relatively stable couple. It is therefore important to understand how people choose their mates and why some decide to marry and others to cohabit.

When Arland Thornton (1989) analyzed how attitudes and values about family life changed from the late 1950s to the mid-1980s, he found a dramatic and pervasive weakening of the norms requiring couples to marry, remain married, have children, engage in intimate relations only within the marriage, and maintain separate roles for males and females. As we'll see, the power of socially shared beliefs that individuals "ought to" or "should" follow certain patterns in marriage and family formation has diminished. Still, whereas there is greater acceptance of different family patterns, most people still choose a traditional family lifestyle—one that includes marriage and parenthood.

MARITAL CHOICE How do people choose their marital partners? Do they make this all-important choice on the basis of similarity, choosing partners who are "like" them? Or do more complex emotional and environmental factors steer them toward a certain kind of person? Over the years, a number of theorists have tried to answer these questions. If nothing else, their conclusions show that marital choice is a far more complex issue than it might appear to be at first glance.

Freud was one of the early theorists who speculated about why people marry. A cornerstone of his psychoanalytic theory was the love attraction that children feel toward the opposite-sex parent (Chapter 1), which they later "transfer" to a socially acceptable object—their potential mate. (Hence, perhaps, the old song that goes, "I want a girl just like the girl that married dear old Dad.") As with many other aspects of Freud's theory, however, conclusive research evidence is lacking.

The *complementary needs theory* (Winch, 1958) is based on the age-old principle that opposites attract. Thus, a domineering man may be attracted to a deferential woman, or a quiet man to a dynamic and outspoken woman, and vice versa. The *instrumental theory of mate selection* developed by Richard Centers (1975) also focuses on gratification of needs, but it states that some needs (such as sex and affiliation) are more important than others and that some needs are more appropriate for men and others for women. According to Centers, people are attracted to others with similar or complementary needs.

The *stimulus-value-role theory* developed by Bernard Murstein (1982) states that mate selection is motivated by each partner's attempt to get the best possible deal. Each person examines the assets and liabilities of the other partner to determine whether the relationship is worthwhile. This examination takes place during three stages of courtship. During the *stimulus* stage, when a man and woman meet or see each other for the first time, they make initial judgments about each other's appearance, personality, and intelligence. If the mutual first impressions are favorable, the couple progresses to the second stage of courtship, *value-comparison*. During this stage, their conversations reveal whether their interests, attitudes, beliefs, and needs are compatible. During the final *role* stage, the couple determines whether they can function in compatible roles in a marriage or similarly long-term relationship.

According to one study of seriously involved college-age couples over a period of six months (Adams, 1979), initial attraction is based on fairly superficial qualities such as physical appeal, gregariousness, poise, and shared interests. The relationship is reinforced by the reactions of others (including being labeled as a couple) and by feeling comfortable in each other's presence. The

Marriage takes different forms in different cultures, but it is a major milestone in adult development in virtually all cultures.

couple then enters a stage of commitment and intimacy, which leads to deeper attraction and involvement. Each person examines the other's viewpoints and value systems in making a commitment. At this point, the couple often feels prepared to make decisions about marriage.

Finally, there's the *family system perspective* (McGoldrick, 1980), which emphasizes that couple formation involves the development of a new structure as well as a process of getting to know each other. Negotiating boundaries is crucial to couple formation. Gradually, a couple redefines their relationships with others—their family and friends—as well as with each other. Many informal shifts in relationships occur. In addition, more formal events, such as the marriage ritual, establish specific boundaries for the couple.

MARRIAGE We are a nation of subcultures with many different patterns of adult lifestyles. Yet monogamous marriage is by far the most popular and most frequently chosen lifestyle. In the United States, over 90% of men and women will marry at some point in their lives. Many cultures approve of sexual intimacy only within the confines of marriage. Preparation for marriage may involve elaborate rituals of dating, courtship, and engagement. The bond is symbolized by a wedding rite; subsequently, the new roles of husband and wife in relation to each other and to the rest of society are defined. The community sanctions the union, which is expected to provide emotional sustenance, sexual gratification, and financial security for young couples and their families. Cultures (and individuals) vary considerably, however, in the extent to which sexual fidelity is expected.

In traditional Arab cultures, for example, the transition to married life is carefully orchestrated by older relatives. As soon as girls reach puberty, maintaining chastity through constant family vigilance takes on an urgent, life-or-death quality. All contact with men—including the fiancé—is forbidden once he has been selected. Young men are also excluded from the courtship process. Older relatives of the young man screen eligible young girls and their families. Male elders conduct bride-price negotiations. To conserve family assets and protect family honor, "cousin marriages" with the daughter of the father's brother are strongly favored. In this manner, a family can be sure that the young bride will be chaperoned and guarded in an acceptable manner (Goode, 1970).

Although American marriages generally are free of such prenuptial investigation and negotiation, there are strong constraints for relationships that violate social, economic, religious, or ethnic/racial boundaries. Community groups and social institutions, as well as parents, often frown on "mixed" marriages of any kind. Mixed marriages are becoming more socially acceptable, however. For example, studies indicate that one out of five Americans has dated someone of a different race (Porterfield, 1973) and that, as of 1996, there were 1,260,000 interracial couples in the United States (U.S. Census Bureau, 1997).

Although all couples must deal with the issues of fidelity, commitment, and permanence, for cohabiting couples these issues may be especially significant.

ALTERNATIVES TO FORMAL MARRIAGE Depending on the couple, cohabiting or "living together" may or may not be similar to marriage. It lacks the social approval and legalized responsibilities of traditional marriage but offers greater freedom for the partners to design their roles as they see fit. It is characterized by an overt acknowledgment that the couple is not married. Accurate statistics are hard to come by because of the reluctance of some couples to proclaim their relationship, and also because of the often transient nature of cohabitation. The U.S. Census Bureau nonetheless documents a large increase in the number of couples openly acknowledging cohabitation, especially young adults. For the population as a whole, cohabitation increased almost eightfold from 1970 to 1996, from 523,000 to 3,958,000 couples (U.S. Census Bureau, 1997). Among

people under age 25, a fifteenfold increase was reported—from 55,000 couples in 1970 to 816,000 in 1996. Most cohabiting couples (64%) have no children, but that percentage still leaves more than a million such households that do include children. Most cohabitors are young adults; 59% are between ages 25 and 44 (U.S. Census Bureau, 1997). As cohabitation without marriage becomes increasingly acceptable, marriage may become less important as a means of formally sanctioning sex (Thornton, 1989).

It has been estimated that about one-third of all cohabiting couples eventually marry. Although the great majority of such couples plan to marry, they feel less urgency than those who have never cohabited. Cohabiting couples who eventually marry do not necessarily communicate better or find greater satisfaction in marriage than couples who do not live together before marriage (Demaris & Leslie, 1984). Because cohabiting couples who do not marry typically break up, it is rare to find a long-established cohabiting couple. Philip Blumstein and Pepper Schwartz (1983) could not locate enough heterosexual cohabitors who had been together for more than ten years to permit data analysis, although they did find enough gay and lesbian couples who had been together this long. The latter finding is undoubtedly related to laws against homosexual marriage, which have only recently begun to be reconsidered—often in the face of vocal protests by heterosexuals.

Living together in an informal arrangement entails many of the same relationship-building tasks that newlyweds face. Conflicts must be resolved through a complex process of "negotiation and collective bargaining" (Almo, 1978). Constant and effective communication is essential. As in marriage, good communication is a constant struggle. In fact, it may be even more important and more difficult within the vague boundaries of cohabitation.

Finally, a couple that lives together must deal with issues of commitment, fidelity, and permanence. Both men and women in cohabiting relationships are more likely than married people to have affairs outside the relationship (Blumstein & Schwartz, 1983). This likelihood may contribute to the greater tension reported by cohabiting couples compared with married, gay, or lesbian couples (Kurdek & Schmitt, 1986). According to one study (Almo, 1978), couples find it difficult to deal explicitly with such concerns even though the partners have strong feelings about each other. Most couples make a definite, if unspoken, commitment to each other before moving in together. That commitment is based on a mutual desire for some kind of permanence that will allow them to plan for the future but retain flexibility. They may or may not require sexual exclusivity and fidelity. Some couples view outside relationships as taboo. Others explicitly agree that each partner may pursue other relationships, although this arrangement is usually desired by one partner and acquiesced to by the other.

An alternative to marriage or cohabitation is remaining single, as discussed in "In Theory, In Fact," page 454.

---

1. Describe the three components of Sternberg's triangular theory of love and the seven types of love relationships that emerge from the theory.
2. How do the following theories explain mate selection: psychoanalytic theory, the complementary needs theory, the instrumental theory of mate selection, and the stimulus-value-role theory?
3. How does "living together" differ from being married?

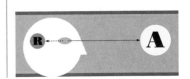

REVIEW & APPLY

IN THEORY, IN FACT

SINGLES

In many historical periods, remaining single was often an unfortunate result of disaster or war. It was also considered a sign of abnormality or immaturity, and to an extent it still is. Some married people hold stereotyped images of singles, such as "swingers" and "losers." Swingers supposedly live wild, exciting lives with few restraints. The stereotyped loser is a physically unattractive person with no compensating personality or intellectual characteristics, who would like to get married but can't find anyone who's willing. Is there any truth to the stereotypes?

Sometimes there is. There are individuals who fit the descriptions, at least for a while; but people change. A real understanding of single-hood, however, requires placing it in a historical perspective. Periodically, large groups of people have remained single. During the late 1930s, for example, when the country was recovering from the Great Depression, fewer people married, and those who did marry did so at later ages. This trend continued during World War II, when millions of temporarily single women joined the labor force while their boyfriends or husbands were overseas fighting and dying. After the war, the picture changed dramatically. By the mid-1950s, only 4% of marriage-age adults remained single, and the age at first marriage was the youngest on record. Remaining single became popular once again in the 1970s and 1980s: The marriage rate among single people under 45 years of age fell to equal the post-Depression low. In 1996, 26.8% of the population over 18 years of age was single, 2.7% widowed, and 8.4% divorced (U.S. Census Bureau, 1997).

The choice of a single lifestyle may also be deliberate—a balance between freedom and constraint, self-sufficiency and interdependence. Some commentators worry about the trend toward fewer marriages and more divorces. Are we as a society too fascinated with freedom and autonomy at the expense of interpersonal obligations (Weiss, 1987)? More than one observer has expressed fears about the effects of our individualistic lifestyles and our emphasis on free choice at the expense of transgenerational ties and interdependent roles (Hunt & Hunt, 1987).

Many singles choose the single life as a way of enjoying intimate relationships while avoiding the possible constraints and problems of marriage. They do not want to feel trapped by a mate who stands in the way of their own personal development. Nor do they want to feel bored, unhappy, angry, sexually frustrated, or lonely with a person from whom they have grown apart. Watching the marriages of their friends fall apart, they feel that the single life is a far better choice.

PARENTHOOD AND ADULT DEVELOPMENT

Parenthood imposes new roles and responsibilities on both the mother and the father. It also confers a new social status on them (Hill & Aldous, 1969). The actual birth brings an onslaught of physical and emotional strains—disruption of sleep and other routines, financial drain, increased tension, and conflicts of various kinds. The mother is tired, the father feels neglected, and both partners feel that their freedom has been curtailed. The closeness and companionship of husband and wife can be diluted by the introduction of a new family member, and the focus of either or both partners may shift to the baby (Komarovsky, 1964).

The challenges and demands of parenthood are a major developmental phase for the parents as individuals and for the couple as a system (Osofsky & Osofsky, 1984). Important factors are the transition to parenthood and learning to cope with childrearing.

THE FAMILY LIFE CYCLE

Families go through a predictable family life cycle marked by specific events (Birchler, 1992). The first milestone occurs when the individual leaves his or her family of origin. Separation may come at the time of marriage, or earlier if the individual opts for independence and lives alone or with others. The second milestone is usually marriage, with all the attendant adjustments of establishing a relationship with a new individual and a new family network—the spouse's. The third milestone is the birth of the first child and the beginning of parenthood, which is referred to as the establishment of a family or simply as the transition to parenthood. There are other milestones, such as the first child's enrollment in school, the birth of the last child, the departure of the last child from the family, and the death of a spouse.

During the past 50 to 100 years, family life cycles have changed in timing as well as in nature. Not only are more people living longer, but their ages at various points in the family cycle and the length of time between milestones have changed. For example, the time between the last child's leaving and the parent's retirement or death has increased and continues to do so.

THE TRANSITION TO PARENTHOOD

The transition to parenthood is one of the major periods in the family life cycle. Often there is considerable family and cultural pressure to have a child—a change that is irrevocable. In contrast to those of marriage by itself, the roles and responsibilities of parenting endure despite changing life circumstances (Rossi, 1979). Parenthood calls for numerous adaptations and adjustments. Newlywed couples often enjoy a relatively high standard of living when both spouses are working and there is no child to provide for. They buy cars, furniture, and clothes. They eat out often and enjoy numerous recreational activities. This lifestyle all comes to an abrupt end with the arrival of the first child (Aldous, 1978).

Effects of the transition to parenthood on specific domains of personal and family life include the following (Cowan & Cowan, 1992):

- *Changes in identity and inner life*: Each parent's sense of self changes, along with assumptions about how family life works.
- *Shifts in roles and relationships within the marriage*: The division of labor between the parents changes at a time when both are stressed by sleep disruptions and by not being able to be alone together as much as they would like.
- *Shifts in generational roles and relationships*: The transition affects grandparents as well as parents.
- *Changing roles and relationships outside the family*: Outside changes affect the mother most, as she is likely to put her career on hold, at least temporarily.
- *New parenting roles and relationships*: The couple must navigate the new responsibilities associated with raising a child.

During the wife's pregnancy, both spouses can offer emotional support to each other.

Although they share many concerns, fathers and mothers also display different reactions to the arrival of the first child. Women characteristically adjust their lifestyles to give priority to parenting and family roles. Men, on the other hand, more often intensify their work efforts to become better or more stable providers. When the child arrives, there are new stresses and challenges, and the role changes are rapid (Rossi, 1979). Both parents experience new feelings of pride and excitement coupled with a greater sense of responsibility that can be overwhelming. Some men are envious of their partner's ability to reproduce and of the close emotional bond established between mother and infant. Couples need to find time for each other and for other interests. Sexual problems, less communication and sharing of interests, and increased conflict occur in many marriages after the birth of a child (Osofsky & Osofsky, 1984).

The arrival of the first child usually constitutes a transition rather than a crisis, however (Entwisle, 1985). Most couples say that they experienced only slight difficulty in adjusting (Hobbs & Cole, 1976). For example, most mothers

Parents with high self-esteem adjust better to parenthood than parents with low self-esteem.

do not experience postpartum depression (Chapter 2). Instead they experience two to three days of much milder "baby blues." Perhaps 10% to 20% of new mothers do not even experience that (O'Hara et al., 1990). In addition, a recent study (Belsky & Rovine, 1990) reported that 20% to 35% of couples actually experience increased marital satisfaction.

A variety of factors influence how well the new parents adjust to their roles. Social support, especially from the husband, is crucial to a new mother (Cutrona & Troutman, 1986). Marital happiness during pregnancy is another important factor in the adjustment of both husband and wife (Wallace & Gotlib, 1990). In fact, the father's adjustment is strongly affected by the mother's evaluation of her marriage and pregnancy (Wallace & Gotlib, 1990).

Parental self-esteem can be an issue too, in that parents with higher self-esteem are more likely to adjust well (Belsky & Rovine, 1990b). The baby's characteristics are also important. For example, parents of "difficult" babies (see Chapter 5) often report a decline in marital satisfaction (Belsky & Rovine, 1990b; Crockenberg, 1986). Finally, as discussed in "Eye on Diversity," on facing page, the age at which parents have a child can markedly affect their adaptation to parenthood.

COPING WITH CHILDREN'S DEVELOPMENTAL STAGES

The demands on parents vary at each period in the family life cycle. A young infant requires almost total and constant nurturance, which some parents provide more easily than others. Some parents are overwhelmed by the infant's intense dependency. Some can't bear to hear an infant cry. The baby's wails may trigger feelings of helplessness, even anger, in the father or mother.

Each critical period for the child produces or reactivates a critical period for the parents (Benedek, 1970). According to one theory (Galinsky, 1980), there are six separate stages of parenthood. In the *image-making stage*, from conception to birth, couples create images of the kind of parents they will be and will

Parents may be better at dealing with children at one stage of development than at another.

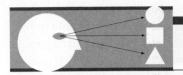

EYE ON DIVERSITY

DELAYING PARENTHOOD

In the Plymouth colony, the average number of children per family was nine. In 1850, the average American family produced six children, and it was unlikely for both parents to survive much beyond age 50. Nowadays, the average family includes only two or three children, the average lifespan continues well into the seventies, and the timing of parenthood is therefore much more flexible. For example, a woman may stop working temporarily to devote her time to raising children—perhaps 9 years if she has three children—and still spend 35 to 40 years in the workforce (Daniels & Weingarten, 1982). What are the effects on adult development and the family life cycle when parenting is delayed by 5, 10, or 15 years? What are the pros and cons?

Leila Josephs (1982) followed several older first-time mothers during their first two years with their first children. Most of the women had developed stability and security in their lives. They had already worked through some of the issues of adult development and had acquired financial resources. Their professions had taught them how to be organized, competent, and motivated, and they typically used this training to educate themselves thoroughly and to prepare for childbirth and child rearing.

But no amount of education could prepare these mothers for the disorganization that a new baby brought to their lives. As professional women accustomed to having control over their lives, they were often upset by their lack of control over the new baby and their own need for flexibility and patience. They often found it difficult simply to relax with the baby. Accustomed to having time to pursue personal and professional interests, they were often too tired to do so, or too busy caring for their babies. Their adult need for intellectual stimulation was not fulfilled by their relationship with their baby. In general, their expectations differed from the realities they faced as new mothers.

A broader study of both mothers and fathers in their thirties, forties, and fifties (Daniels & Weingarten, 1982) compared the effects of having first children at ages 20, 30, and 40. The researchers found numerous differences. One age was not necessarily better than another for coping with the tasks of parenting, but nearly all parents agreed that the many demands of parenting were an important challenge in their own development. Some fathers reported that they were not involved in parenting at first but became "hooked" when their children reached a certain stage of development or because of a particular event. For some, this change occurred when they could share special interests with their child; others felt closer to their children when they reached adolescence. A child's illness was a dramatic event that awakened some men to the realities of fatherhood.

Late parenting may require numerous initial adjustments in lifestyle and attitudes, yet most parents who start their families later than average report appreciating the full range of parenting experiences more than they thought they would have appreciated it at a younger age. In addition, many feel that when they were younger, they were too absorbed in their own needs and goals or in their marital relationship to appreciate fully the parenting role (Daniels & Weingarten, 1982).

---

measure their anticipated performance against their own standards of perfection. In the *nurturing stage*, from birth to about 2 years (specifically, until the child starts saying "No!"), parents become attached to their baby and try to balance the baby's needs with the emotional commitment and time that they devote to spouse, job, friends, and parents. During the *authority stage*, the time roughly between the child's second and fifth birthdays, parents begin to question the kind of parents they have been and will be. Growth comes when parents realize that they, along with their child, sometimes fall short of their images of perfection.

During the *interpretive stage*—the middle childhood years—parents reexamine and test many of their long-held theories. When their children become teenagers, parents pass through the *interdependence stage*, in which they must redefine the authority relationship they have with their nearly grown children. They may find themselves competing with or comparing themselves with their children. Finally, during the *departure stage* when grown children leave home, parents not only have to "let go" but must also face the difficult and sometimes unpleasant task of taking stock of their experiences as parents.

During each stage, parents must be able to resolve their own conflicts at a new and more advanced level of integration; otherwise, they may be unable to cope with their feelings. Unresolved tensions may interfere with the marriage relationship or with the ability to function well as parents.

Parents who are unable to deal effectively with children at one stage may be quite good at dealing with them at another stage. For example, parents who have a lot of difficulty with an infant may cope quite effectively with a preschool child or an adolescent. The reverse may also be true; the parent who is quite at ease with a helpless baby may have problems with an increasingly independent teenager.

At each phase in the family life cycle, parents not only have to cope with the new challenges and demands of their changing and developing children but also must renegotiate their own relationship (Carter & McGoldrick, 1980). Couples must establish ways of making decisions and resolving conflicts that will maintain the integrity and respect of each partner. Systems in which one person is always dominant and the other is always passive tend to dissolve over time. The new pressures created by adolescent rebellion and the quest for independence, for example, require that the couple adapt the family system to make room for the nearly autonomous child. The family system that is too rigid or too unstructured doesn't cope well with the child's emerging needs.

COPING WITH SINGLE PARENTHOOD

The pressures of parenthood are particularly acute for single parents, the overwhelming majority of whom are working mothers. Single-parent families are becoming increasingly common in the United States. In the mid-1970s, one of every seven children spent part of childhood without a father in the home. Since then, single-parent families have increased at a rate ten times faster than traditional two-parent families. The trend is greatest among young women. In 1995, almost one-third of all families were maintained by single mothers (U.S. Census Bureau, 1997).

For perspective, in 1994, 1,191,000 marriages ended in divorce. In the same year, the divorce rate per 1000 was 4.6, 11% lower than it was in 1979 and 1981, which were peak years for divorce (Clarke, 1995; National Center for Health Statistics, 1995). For every three marriages that succeed, two are expected to fail (Clarke, 1995). Failures are concentrated in the first 7 years of marriage, with divorcing couples having a median marriage duration of 7.2 years. Although divorce can happen at any age, they are more likely in young adulthood. In 1995, for example, the divorce rate for men was 32.8 per 1000 married men in the 15 to 19 age group and 50.2 per 1000 for men in the 20 to 24 age group (see Figure 13–5). For couples involved in a first marriage, only one in eight can expect a divorce after age 40 (Uhlerberg et al., 1990).

SINGLE-MOTHER FAMILIES What's responsible for the exploding number of single-parent families headed by women? There are a number of factors (Ross & Sawhill, 1975). In the 1960s and 1970s, the main cause was the rising divorce rate, accompanied by the tradition of awarding custody of the children to the mother. The divorce rate peaked in 1979 and again in 1981, but since then, it has dropped back to the 1974 level (National Center for Health Statistics, 1995). The next greatest increase was in never-married mothers. In 1994, 32.6% of all births were to unmarried women; for African-American women, the figure was 70.4% (U.S. Census Bureau, 1997). Third, there was a substantial increase in the number of mothers who were separated from their spouses but not divorced.

FIGURE 13–5   AGE-SPECIFIC DIVORCE RATES FOR MEN AND WOMEN

Divorce rates peak for men and women in early adulthood and then decline steadily throughout middle and old age.

Source: National Center for Health Statistics. Monthly Vital Statistics Report *(March 22, 1995).*

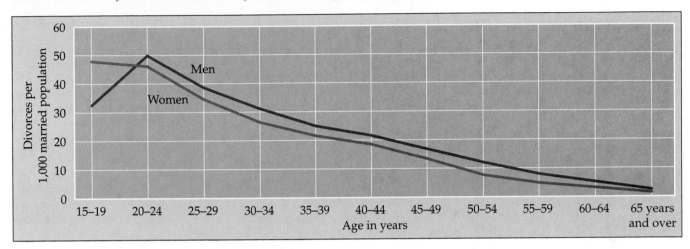

Researchers point to improved social and economic conditions for women as an important factor in these changes (Ross & Sawhill, 1975). They conclude that better job opportunities and improved status have enabled mothers and children to survive without their husbands and fathers, at least in the short run. Indeed, for many single mothers, the status is only temporary because a large percentage eventually remarry.

Single parenthood can be an exhausting struggle, even in middle- and working-class families. Single parents experience frequent and destructive levels of stress (McAdoo, 1995). Single mothers consistently earn less than single fathers. For women without education, making ends meet is extremely difficult. For those who formerly depended on public assistance, welfare reform has brought new demands and pressures, as discussed in "A Matter for Debate," page 460.

Single-mother homes are more numerous and more often poor among African-Americans. Fully 58% of all African-American families with children under 18 years are headed by single women (U.S. Census Bureau, 1997). Although less than 3% of all poor families remain poor indefinitely, 62% of them are African-American (Klein & Rones, 1989). The majority of black children will spend at least half of their childhood in poverty (Ellwood & Cranc, 1990). In 1994, the median family income for white single-mother households was only about 65% of that for white married couples. For black or Hispanic single mothers, the income was less than half that of white married couples (U.S. Census Bureau, 1997). All this information indicates the special hardships faced by African-American and Hispanic-American single parents.

On the other hand, poor African-Americans and Hispanic-Americans are more likely to live in intergenerational households (Harrison et al., 1990; Jackson et al., 1990). These extended families most often include one of the single mother's parents in addition to other family or nonfamily members. Thus, additional financial, psychological, and social resources are available to the single mother, and so she may feel less isolated and overwhelmed. There will also be less general housework to do if other members of the household contribute,

Single parents, whatever their socioeconomic status, may find the continual responsibility overwhelming.

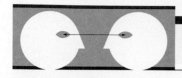

A MATTER FOR DEBATE

THE IMPACT OF WELFARE REFORM ON SINGLE PARENTING

The Personal Responsibility and Work Opportunity Reconciliation Act (PRWORA) was enacted by Congress and signed into law in August 1996. This was the first major welfare reform effort in the 60 years since passage of the Aid to Families with Dependent Children (AFDC) program. The intent of the PRWORA was to change public assistance into a system that helps welfare mothers become independent, self-sufficient workers instead of encouraging them to be dependent, passive-aid recipients who tended to pass their dependency along to the next generation. Exactly how to accomplish this was to be determined by the states, within guidelines that (1) set a relatively tight schedule for implementation of state programs, (2) established immediate and lifetime limits on a mother's receipt of welfare payments, and (3) most important, required the mother to work to receive payments and other assistance. The intent, in other words, was to reverse the welfare/poverty cycle.

How well the welfare reform act is faring is unclear at this point; the results are just starting to come in. Suffice it to say—largely on the basis of anecdotal evidence—that it appears to be working better in some states than in

others, and better for some mothers than for others. For example, for mothers who are semiskilled and have some work history, the transition to employment isn't as difficult as it is for those who are capable of only unskilled labor and have little or no work history. At the outset, most states have focused on the easier cases; the difficult ones are yet to come.

It is possible, however, to discuss some of the problems that welfare has created for single mothers, who constitute over 90% of welfare recipients. Of crucial importance is the question of who takes care of the children while the mothers are at work. For mothers who live in extended families, as discussed on page 459, satisfactory childcare arrangements can often be made within the home. For two-parent welfare families, alternating shifts are a possibility. But for single mothers who are on their own, the transition is proving difficult. Day-care facilities are limited, and most have long waiting lists as a result of the PRWORA—up to several months in many communities. In turn, federal funds to assist with child care are limited—and day care can be very expensive. An additional problem for unskilled single mothers in particular is that whatever jobs they can find often involve working at times when day-care centers aren't open. Entry-level positions in factories, ware-

houses, and service industries (such as building cleaning and maintenance and food preparation and service in fast-food outlets) often require night and weekend work; but day-care centers cater to nine-to-five employees who are at home on weekends.

Finally, for mothers who do solve child-care problems and find full-time employment, the job is typically paid the minimum wage, which is still well below the poverty line for a family of three (Children's Defense Fund, 1998). The simple fact is that many single mothers cannot support their children adequately even when they work, and the disparity between what people earn and what they can buy with it is increasing (Children's Defense Fund, 1998). What will happen to single mothers, working or not, when their Temporary Cash Assistance (TCA) runs out? Will their children have to be placed in foster care? Will the states start making exceptions—which they can do under extenuating circumstances—at such a rate that the outcome will resemble the former welfare system? Or will increasing numbers of single mothers and their children become destitute and homeless as suggested by Bassuk et al. (1996)?

It all remains to be seen. The only certainty is that welfare as we knew it is history; what is much less clear is exactly what we have replaced it with.

---

but there is a downside: Living with her parents makes it significantly less likely that the mother will receive public assistance (Folk, 1996).

SINGLE-FATHER FAMILIES   Although it is still true that only a small proportion of fathers gain custody of their children after divorce, the number is growing and is currently about 10%. Another 16% participate in joint custody settlements (National Center for Health Statistics, 1995).

Single fathers experience many of the same problems and tensions as single mothers. However, they are usually better off financially (Hetherington & Camara, 1984). One profile of single fathers revealed that many had taken on extensive parenting roles before the divorce (Pichitino, 1983). Most single fathers maintain high levels of emotional involvement with their children, are heavily invested in and committed to their care, and worry about failing them or not spending enough time with them. However, their parenting experience does not always prepare them for the demands that they face when they must maintain a job and a family simultaneously. Many single fathers have the same feelings of loneliness and depression that single mothers have. Single fathers also find, as do single mothers, that it is difficult to maintain an active circle of friends and other sources of emotional support (Pichitino, 1983).

1. List and define the major milestones in the family life cycle.
2. How does the transition to parenthood affect the personal and family life of the parents?
3. Discuss the child-rearing challenges faced by single parents.

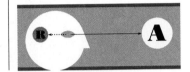

REVIEW & APPLY

THE OCCUPATIONAL CYCLE

An adult's working life follows what is called the **occupational cycle**. The cycle begins in adolescence with thoughts and experiences that lead to a choice of occupation; it continues with pursuit of the chosen career; and it ends with retirement from the workforce. The cycle isn't usually that simple, however, and it doesn't always run smoothly. An adult must make important choices throughout his or her working life, choices that can include changing careers more than once. In any career there are moments of doubt and crisis, and special events such as receiving a promotion or being fired can affect the course of an individual's career.

To a great extent, people's work influences their attitudes and lifestyle. Their work may determine whether they will lead mobile or relatively settled lives, the kind of community they will live in, and the kind of home and standard of living they will have. Work may also contribute to their friendships, opinions, prejudices, and political affiliations.

In this section we'll examine the stages that individuals go through in their vocational lives, some factors that affect occupational choice and preparation, and the process of entering the workforce and consolidating and maintaining, or perhaps changing, a career.

STAGES OF VOCATIONAL LIFE

According to Robert Havighurst (1964), the occupational cycle starts in middle childhood. He divides the cycle into a series of stages based on how people are involved with work at various times in their lives, with emphasis on the acquisition of attitudes and work skills. Those stages are as follows:

1. *Identification with a worker* (ages 5 to 10): Children identify with working fathers and mothers, and thus the idea of working enters their self-concept.
2. *Acquiring basic habits of industry* (ages 10 to 15): Students learn to organize their time and efforts so as to accomplish tasks like schoolwork or chores. They also learn to give work priority over play when necessary.

Single parenting is no easier for fathers than for mothers.

occupational cycle   A variable sequence of periods or stages in a worker's life, from occupational exploration and choice, through education and training, novice status, promotions and more experienced periods.

3. *Acquiring an identity as a worker* (ages 15 to 25): People choose their occupation and begin to prepare for it. They acquire work experience that helps them choose their career and get started in it.

4. *Becoming a productive person* (ages 25 to 40): Adults perfect the skills required for their chosen occupation and move ahead in their career.

5. *Maintaining a productive society* (ages 40 to 70): Workers are now at the high point of their career. They begin to pay attention to and give time to civic and social responsibilities related to and beyond their jobs.

6. *Contemplating a productive and responsible life* (age 70 on): Workers are now retired. They look back on their careers and contributions, hopefully with satisfaction (see also Erikson's stage of *integrity versus despair* in Chapter 17).

Although Havighurst's model is useful, it doesn't always apply in today's rapidly changing, highly technological society. Not everyone goes through a single, forward-moving set of stages and a single occupational cycle (Okun, 1984). Young people often change jobs frequently before they make a major occupational commitment; many adults make one or more major midcareer shifts. These shifts may be the result of factors beyond the person's control, such as when a company downsizes and lays off the worker or when the worker's job simply becomes obsolete. Alternatively, the shifts may result from personal career reevaluation, as when a person hits a "ceiling" and can progress no further in his or her present occupation, or perhaps simply "burns out" and feels compelled to find something else to do.

OCCUPATIONAL CHOICE AND PREPARATION

Why does one person become an accountant, another a police officer, another a doctor, another a plumber or an electrician? A multitude of factors influence the choice of an occupation, including socioeconomic status, ethnic background, intelligence, skills, gender, and parents' occupations. Here, we'll look specifically at gender and race, parental attitudes, self-concept, personality traits, and practical considerations.

SEX AND RACE As Table 13–2 indicates, African-Americans and women are overrepresented in lower-status, lower-paying jobs and are underrepresented in more highly paid professions (see also Walsh, 1997). Researchers explain these discrepancies in two ways. One explanation is that individuals make early choices that ultimately determine what occupations they can or cannot pursue. For example, blacks are less likely to finish high school than whites, and those who drop out cannot compete for the jobs that require a high school or college education. Women limit their choices when they question their competence in the sciences (Ware & Steckler, 1983) and avoid careers in technology-based fields such as engineering. Some women choose careers that will give them the flexibility to raise a family. They may choose part-time work; move in and out of the job market during their child-rearing years; and look for jobs involving limited stress and time pressure—which also have limited career and financial potential (Council of Economic Advisers, 1987; Kalleberg & Rosenfeld, 1990). Role modeling by parents may also influence career choice. Once they are established, such job-limiting patterns can be self-perpetuating.

A second explanation for these occupational patterns is discrimination. African-Americans and women may be subtly (or not so subtly) channeled into some jobs rather than others, in spite of federal equal opportunity requirements. The better positions still tend to be given to men more frequently than to women—even when women have equal skills (Bielby & Baron, 1986).

TABLE 13–2 REPRESENTATION OF FEMALES, BLACKS, AND HISPANICS IN VARIOUS OCCUPATIONS

Occupation	PERCENTAGE OF TOTAL		
	Females	Black	Hispanic
Total percent employed*	46.2	10.7	9.2
Architects	16.7	2.7	4.3
Engineers	8.5	4.2	3.8
Registered nurses	93.3	8.6	2.6
Teachers, college and university	43.5	6.5	4.1
Teachers, prekindergarten and kindergarten	98.1	13.6	5.8
Teachers, elementary school	83.3	9.9	4.8
Social workers	68.5	22.6	7.7
Secretaries	98.6	9.3	6.2
Duplicating, mail, and other office machine operators	63.6	13.2	13.1
Mail clerks	49.3	29.8	11.1
Data entry keyers	84.5	17.0	10.8
Teachers' aides	92.1	15.9	14.4
Private household cleaners and servants	93.6	18.5	32.4
Correctional institution officers	21.7	22.1	8.4
Dental assistants	99.1	6.2	11.2
Nursing aides, orderlies, and attendants	88.4	33.2	8.1
Maids and housemen	81.8	29.6	21.1
Janitors and cleaners	34.9	21.1	19.7
Automobile mechanics	1.2	7.6	13.9
Pressing machine operators	76.3	22.7	38.4
Farmworkers	18.8	3.4	37.3

*Civilian noninstitutionalized population 16 years old and over, 1996.
Source: U.S. Census Bureau, 1997.

Promotions also may not be equally available. Such discrimination is illegal, but as affirmative action and employment "quotas" have come under increasing pressure, it has become easier for employers to hire or promote in discriminatory ways for "legitimate" reasons—such as exaggerated performance reviews. Thus, the education and skills that predict high salaries for white men do not result in equally high salaries for African-Americans and women (Ferber et al., 1986; Klein & Rones, 1989).

HOW PARENTAL ATTITUDES AND CHILD REARING CONTRIBUTE The relationship between parents and their children can give rise to attitudes, needs, and interests that later affect the children's occupational choices (Roe, 1957). For example, a child who is the center of the family's attention may become preoccupied with belongingness and esteem needs and thus in later years be overly concerned with the opinions and attitudes of others.

Career choice is often a defining feature in self-concept.

Consequently, he or she will be attracted to occupations that involve frequent contact with people and that hold out the possibility for gaining their esteem. Such individuals tend to choose careers in which they can serve others or to gravitate toward culturally oriented work—perhaps in the arts or entertainment.

Children who are neglected or avoided by their parents often suffer from a lack of love and do not develop the same kind of dependence. In later years, they will not seek out people to gratify their needs and may be attracted to solitary activities. They tend to pursue careers in science, technology, or other professions that do not require frequent interactions with other people.

Families influence their children's career choices in other ways, too: They model certain lifestyles, values, and beliefs. The degree of individuality and autonomy allowed within the family system can also affect career choices (Bratcher, 1982). For example, girls with working mothers tend to have higher achievement motivation and career aspirations than girls whose mothers do not work outside the home (Hoffman, 1989).

Self-Concept Theory versus Trait Theory The essence of self-concept theory as it applies to occupational choices is that people seek careers that fit their self-concept (Super, 1963). By establishing themselves in occupations that fit their notions of self, individuals progress toward self-actualization. That is, they act in ways that they believe are best for their own satisfaction and individual growth. A man who sees himself as quiet, scholarly, intelligent, and eloquent, for example, may become a college professor. A woman who sees herself as socially concerned, energetic, and a charismatic leader might become a politician.

Like self-concept theory, trait theory addresses the link between personality and occupational choice. Trait theory, however, investigates objectively measured personality traits, as opposed to the individual's perception of self. The idea is that there is a close fit between the kinds of occupations people choose and their personality traits. In the opposite direction, jobs can be defined by the kinds of personality traits that they seem to require. If an individual exhibits the traits demanded by a particular job, then the job and the person are potentially a good match. In one approach (Holland, 1973), six individual personality traits are assessed and matched with occupations. The traits are (1) realistic, (2) investigative, (3) social, (4) conventional, (5) enterprising, and (6) artistic. Thus, a person who is high in traits 2 and 5 might become a research scientist; a person who is high in traits 3 and 4 might become, say, a hospital worker.

The trait theory has stimulated considerable research. As you might expect, however, the matching of individuals and occupations by personality traits doesn't always work and is perhaps best viewed as providing very general indications of the direction people might take in their working lives.

Formal and Informal Preparation Before entering the workforce, people acquire certain skills, values, and attitudes, both formally and informally. Formal occupational preparation includes structured learning in high school, vocational training programs, and college, as well as on-the-job training (OJT). Informal occupational preparation takes subtler forms: It involves adopting the attitudes, norms, and role expectations that are appropriate to a particular job. Long before we begin formal preparation, we are acquiring informal norms and values from our parents and teachers, members of the trades and professions, even television and movie portrayals. We learn by observing others and from our day-to-day experiences. Informal socialization is so pervasive that it often determines the formal steps we take to prepare for a career (Moore, 1969).

For many people, college is considered a mandatory step in preparing for a career, although educational attainment (especially college) and other job-related training varies considerably across nations (see Table 13–3). In many areas of college work, particularly in the liberal arts, little or no training is specifically aimed at developing marketable skills. Liberal arts curricula try to develop basic communication skills, expose students to a variety of ideas and perspectives, and develop analytical skills. Although they are essential to intellectual maturity, these skills are not directly related to specific job titles—except perhaps for future teachers of these skills. In contrast, programs such as engineering, health sciences, business, and education provide substantive knowledge and practical skills. They usually attract motivated, determined students who have already defined their goals.

A survey of hundreds of thousands of college students in the early 1970s (Astin, 1977) found that, for most students, the emotional and attitudinal changes that occur during the college years are far more significant than preparation for a career. Beliefs and self-concepts are revised. Young adults learn to rate and assess themselves in increasingly complex and realistic ways, and they become more specific in analyzing various assets like originality, artistic ability, mechanical skill, effective writing skill, and personal communication. They tend to develop higher opinions of their intellectual abilities, leadership skills, and popularity. These changes often are more lasting than the specific career training that the student receives in college and may help a student make better occupational choices.

SOME PRACTICAL ISSUES   The preceding sections explain in part how occupational choices are made. But practical issues often are equally or even more important than these factors. In times of recession and high unemployment, for example, people may not have much choice and may be forced to focus on simply finding some kind of job that will make ends meet. Under such conditions, it is not uncommon to hear about individuals who want to be architects or musicians but instead wind up as civil servants or hospital workers, depending on what jobs are available. In extreme cases, people with college degrees may be sacking groceries and mowing lawns. The need to support a spouse or children may also cause people to look for a job in a different field than they would choose if they did not have these constraints. An aspiring painter, for example, may get by with advertising or public relations work (or even house painting), with little time left for artistic pursuits.

Finally, many people let family pressures determine their choice of a career. Some children are "groomed" to take over family businesses or to follow in a parent's footsteps, even though they might have preferred to pursue a different career. Alternatively, people without definite plans or with varied interests and abilities may take any job that is available and may frequently change jobs.

GAINING A PLACE IN THE WORKFORCE

Having made at least tentative occupational choices and acquired appropriate training or education, young adults are ready to enter the workforce. This entry involves an adjustment period that can be eased somewhat by the assistance of a mentor. It also involves a growing sense of loyalty and commitment. To set the stage, however, let's first consider how attitudes about work have changed in recent decades.

TABLE 13–3 EDUCATIONAL ATTAINMENT AND OTHER JOB-RELATED TRAINING ACROSS NATIONS

EDUCATIONAL ATTAINMENT, BY COUNTRY: 1994
(PERCENT DISTRIBUTION, PERSONS 25 TO 84 YEARS OLD)

Country	Total	Early childhood, primary, and lower secondary education only	Upper secondary education only	Nonuniversity tertiary education only	University education only
Australia	100	50	27	10	13
Austria	100	32	60	2	6
Belgium	100	51	27	12	10
Canada	100	26	28	29	17
Denmark	100	40	40	6	14
Finland	100	36	44	9	11
France	100	33	50	8	9
Germany	100	16	62	10	13
Greece	100	55	27	6	12
Ireland	100	55	27	10	9
Italy	100	67	26	—	8
Netherlands	100	40	38	—	21
New Zealand	100	43	34	14	9
Norway	100	19	53	11	16
Portugal	100	81	8	3	7
Spain	100	74	11	4	11
Sweden	100	28	46	14	12
Switzerland	100	18	61	13	8
Turkey	100	60	13	—	7
United Kingdom	100	26	54	9	12
United States	100	15	53	8	24

PARTICIPATION IN JOB-RELATED CONTINUING EDUCATION AND TRAINING, BY COUNTRY

Country	Year	Total	Male	Female
United States	1995	34	31	36
Australia	1993	38	37	40
Belgium	1994	3	3	2
Canada	1993	28	27	30
Denmark	1994	15	13	18
Finland	1993	41	38	44
France	1994	40	38	43
Germany	1994	33	35	31
Greece	1994	1	1	1
Ireland	1994	4	3	6
Italy	1994	1	1	2
Spain	1994	3	2	4
Sweden	1995	44	40	47
Switzerland	1993	38	42	34
United Kingdom	1994	13	12	14

Source: U.S. Census Bureau, 1997.

CHANGING ATTITUDES ABOUT WORK Before the 1970s, a coherent value system dominated the attitudes of most American workers (Yankelovich, 1978). The old value system had several distinct components. It was considered desirable for women to stay home if their husbands could afford it, and many husbands were strongly opposed to the idea of their wives' working outside the home. In turn, men often tolerated unsatisfying jobs for the sake of economic security. The main motivations for workers were money, status, and achieving the "American dream": Work hard, own your home, and retire comfortably. If you did your job well, society—including your company—would provide for you.

This value system has eroded considerably in recent decades. The civil rights movement, the Vietnam War, the counterculture, the women's movement, Watergate, and other social phenomena challenged the old order. Many young adults entering the workforce view work in very different ways, primarily as a means to an end. Another factor is the corporate downsizing that began in the late 1980s, which left millions of workers uncertain about their future. In industries as unrelated as banking and steel, workers no longer believe that companies have any loyalty to their employees, and workers realize that they may suddenly be unemployed through no fault of their own. They also realize that they are responsible for advancing their own career and cannot depend on the corporation for anything—such as a long-term career path and retirement benefits, or short-term benefits like health insurance.

Forced by circumstances to reassess what work means to them, many young adults attempt to find work that they can do at home. This new pattern is largely the result of modern technology. Architects, writers, and computer programmers, among others, are working at home, thanks to computers, e-mail, fax machines, cellular phones, and conference calls. *Someone* has actually to go to the factory or office, however. What they find there, especially if they're young adults entering the workforce, can be quite different from what they might expect.

EXPECTATION MEETS REALITY When young adults start working, they may experience what could be termed *reality shock*. During adolescence and preparation for a career, people often have high expectations about what their work will be like and what they will accomplish. When the training ends and the job begins, novices quickly learn that some of their expectations were unrealistic. Their training may be inadequate for the actual work; many employers view novices as people who have yet to be trained. The work may be dull and mechanical, supervisors unfair, and peers difficult to work with. The goals of the job may be lost in a maze of bureaucratic politics, or subject to the whims of superiors. The shock of reality may result in a period of frustration and anger as the young worker adjusts to the new situation.

In a longitudinal study of young, lower-level managers at AT&T, the results supported some of Levinson's concepts (discussed in Chapter 12) about molding the dream into a realistic pathway. A total of 422 young men, half of whom were college educated and half of whom had been promoted to management positions in crafts and trades, were followed for much of their careers. At the outset, the young men had very high expectations regarding their potential for success; but over the first seven years, their expectations became much more realistic. Fewer expected promotions; many realized that promotions might well mean transferring to a new location, disrupting their families, or working harder and having more responsibility and less time for family life. These young managers were not necessarily dissatisfied with their jobs, however.

A formal system of mentor relationships might help more young women obtain managerial, executive, and administrative positions.

Most found considerable satisfaction in the challenge of doing their jobs well and meeting personal standards of achievement. The extrinsic rewards of salary and status appeared to become somewhat less important over time (Bray & Howard, 1983).

THE ROLE OF MENTORS   Gradually, the entry phase gives way to growing competence and autonomy. Remember that Levinson emphasized the role of mentors, who help younger workers acquire appropriate values and norms. In the context of work, apprentices acquire skills and self-confidence with the help of mentors. They soon establish themselves and may begin to outperform their mentors and break away from them. Later, they acquire authority over others and serve as mentors themselves.

Several authors have noted the positive role of good mentors in the development of young workers (Kanter, 1977). Mentors perform teaching and training roles. They sponsor the young worker's advancement. They serve as models for social as well as work-related behavior. Generally, they ease the transition to independent work status. In executive and academic careers, male workers frequently report having a mentor. However, because only 12% of men and 7% of women are in executive, administrative, or managerial roles, the number of available upper-level mentors available is very limited. Most women executives report that no steady female mentor was available to them (Busch, 1985). Some women find male mentors, or their husbands serve as mentors, but that kind of relationship can become complicated, as we saw in Chapter 12. If the woman's career threatens to reduce the amount of time devoted to her husband and family, the husband often becomes less supportive of the wife's career development (Roberts & Newton, 1987). In an effort to help more women achieve executive, administrative, and managerial roles, some have suggested that one of the most successful strategies would be to promote a formal, company-based system of mentor relationships (Swoboda & Millar, 1986).

GROWTH OF LOYALTY AND COMMITMENT   Levinson also emphasized that maintaining a sense of excitement and commitment to work throughout adulthood is essential to mature job satisfaction. Commitment to a trade or career varies greatly, depending both on individual traits and on broader social and economic factors. People with low-paying, unpleasant work will naturally have difficulty maintaining commitment to the job. There is also little motivation for good performance when there is little chance of upward mobility (Moore, 1969).

A young adult's commitment to a job or profession becomes stronger as a result of growing loyalty and adjustment to particular occupational expectations and norms. Loyalty develops as young adults begin to identify personally with their occupation. Loyalty to an employer will grow to the extent that employees want continued employment and rewards from the employer—and believe that the employer will reciprocate.

As a result of many years of involvement in an occupation, people identify themselves with an entire occupational group or industry. They learn to behave according to the particular rules and expectations of their occupational group. Beginners are given the least desirable job assignments—those with the most tedium or drudgery. At the same time, however, the beginners have an opportunity to observe what their superiors do and to gain information and skills that will help them advance. Beginners are also introduced to the jargon and shop talk that will help them become part of the occupational in-group. As they develop experience on the job, they learn to use time-tested techniques for solving problems and getting work done. They also begin to realize that they must defer to authority and live up to certain standards of work performance (Moore, 1969).

CONSOLIDATION, MAINTENANCE, AND CHANGE   For those who conform to the classic occupational cycle, the midcareer period is a time of consolidation—settling down and coming to grips with the realities of one's occupational situation. For the men studied by Levinson (1978), the late thirties was a time of establishing a niche in society, forgetting about attractive alternative careers, and striving for advancement. This effort involved striving to be as good as possible at their chosen profession. It also involved attempting to create some stability at work and in life in general. For some, it involved increasing responsibility and prestige, drawing away from the mentor, and becoming autonomous.

Climbing the ladder of success generally is not as easy as anticipated. The higher you climb, the less room there is for advancement. Hence, by their early forties, many workers are disillusioned and somewhat cynical. The original dream is gone; they face lower levels of accomplishment. The study of AT&T managers discussed earlier found such a pattern at mid-career. Although some managers had reached upper-management levels, many were still at low- or middle-management levels and had downgraded their goals and aspirations. Indeed, many reported that further advancement in their careers was not crucial to their life satisfaction and that other areas of their lives—such as family and personal pursuits—had become more important (Bray & Howard, 1983). The high-level managers in the AT&T study, however, rated work as crucial to their sense of self and overall life satisfaction.

In sum, the classic occupational cycle is no longer the dominant pattern, even for white-collar managers and executives. Only a minority of workers now stay with the same company throughout their careers. Many people change jobs within a field, looking for better pay, more responsibility, promotion, or better working conditions. So-called "headhunters" earn fees by enticing talented and accomplished workers—especially managers and those with skills that are in high demand, such as computer programming—to move to another company. In addition, an increasing number of people are making career shifts and changing fields to pursue different interests. Some workers don't experience much occupational stability at all, and they may encounter frequent or protracted periods of unemployment and career crisis—often accompanied by financial, social, and adjustment problems.

Review & Apply

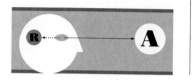

1. List and describe the stages of vocational life identified by Havighurst.
2. Summarize how the following factors affect occupational choice: sex and race, parental attitudes, self-concept, and possession of specific traits.
3. Why is a period of adjustment necessary when a young adult enters the workforce, and how can a mentor help ease that adjustment?

WORK AND GENDER

For women, occupational career patterns are even more complex (LaSalle & Spokane, 1987). Indeed, in the coming century, the most common occupational pattern for women in midlife will probably be one of change rather than consolidation and maintenance.

The vocational life stages proposed by Havighurst describe career progressions that are more typical for men than for women. Specifically, Havighurst's fourth stage says nothing about the vocational choices that many women are likely to make if they are raising children during their young adult years. Whereas some women follow the same path as men in their working lives, the majority try to combine work and family roles by taking a more flexible approach to their careers. Some stop working during their child-rearing years; others work part-time; and still others find a way to continue earning money by working at home.

In this section, we look at work from the perspective of gender, paying special attention to how women combine work and family roles. We'll examine how women's work patterns differ from what was once considered the norm for all workers but actually applied only to men. We'll also consider what work really means to women—despite stereotypes to the contrary. Finally, we'll look at what it means to be a member of a dual-earner couple. Let's begin with some dramatic statistics on women's growing presence in the workforce.

A CHANGING STATISTICAL PICTURE

One of the most notable developments in the employment world is the great increase in the percentage of women in the workforce in recent decades. In 1960, approximately 38% of all women age 16 and older were in the labor force; by 1996, the figure had risen to 59.3%, and it is projected to increase to 61% or more by 2005 (U.S. Census Bureau, 1997). The increase has been most dramatic for white women. It has been less so for black women, who have always worked in greater numbers out of greater economic necessity. In all, less than 11% of married women are full-time homemakers.

As more women have entered the workforce, they have made some advances. In 1970, for example, only 8% of all doctors were women, but by 1986, the figure had nearly doubled. Even more dramatically, in 1970, only 5% of all lawyers and judges were women. By 1986, the figure for all women was 18%, rising to 29% for women under 35 years of age (Council of Economic Advisers, 1987). Virtually all professions have seen similarly significant increases.

Nevertheless, by far the largest number of women are still limited to lower-paying "women's jobs" such as nursing, primary and secondary school teaching, and secretarial/clerical work (Matthews & Rodin, 1989) (again see Table 13–2). One out of every two women is employed in low-paying, low-advancement jobs. Moreover, women still make less money than men—about 75 cents for every dollar men earn. Among full-time permanent employees, the median salary for white women is only about 74% of that for white men, and for black women the figure drops to about 67% (U.S. Census Bureau, 1997).

CHANGES IN WORK PATTERNS

Paid employment for women is not a new phenomenon, of course. Women have always worked outside the home, especially during periods of economic hardship. Many worked in factories and offices during the two World Wars when large numbers of male workers were overseas fighting. Before the rise of industrialism in the early 1800s, men and women often combined their efforts in family businesses and farms (as some still do). Not until the late nineteenth century did men come to be regarded as the "natural" providers for their families (Bernard, 1981). They worked at jobs outside the home while their wives cared for the children and the home. In the 1970s, however, the picture changed again as more and more women entered the workforce and established careers.

Women who work outside the home do not necessarily follow the same career patterns that men do. Although there are no formal theories dealing with women's career development, it is clear that women follow a greater *variety* of patterns. An increasing number of women follow the traditional male pattern of pursuing a career without interruption. Others plan to stop work and have children when their careers are well established. Women who wish to devote themselves exclusively to raising a family in early adulthood sometimes establish careers outside the home after the last child has entered first grade, or perhaps even later, when the child enters college. The average woman can devote 10 years to full-time child care while her children are young and still have 35 years left to enter the workforce, establish a career, or pursue other interests (Daniels & Weingarten, 1982). Most women still interrupt work at least temporarily to take care of children, however, whereas men rarely do so (Kalleberg & Rosenfeld, 1990; Shaw, 1983). These interruptions may contribute to the wage gap between men and women (Hewlett, 1984).

THE MANY MEANINGS OF WORK

Like men, women participate in the world of work for many reasons. The primary reason is economic necessity. Single mothers are often the sole source of income for their families. Even many married couples could not make ends meet without income from both spouses. Female factory and mill workers, for example, contribute almost as much money to the family as their husbands (Thompson & Walker, 1989). This situation is especially true in African-

For women who are not career oriented, self-esteem seems related more to family life than to full-time employment.

American and Hispanic-American households, where husbands tend to have lower wages and higher rates of unemployment compared with European-Americans. Like men, however, many women find satisfaction and fulfillment in employment outside the home. They find their work interesting and challenging; they consider it an opportunity for self-direction or increased responsibility; they like the benefits of salary, greater future security, and the possibility of advancement (Whitbourne, 1986a).

There are some differences, however. In some studies, women more often report that the opportunity to interact with people—as clients, coworkers, supervisors—is a particularly important reason for working outside the home. For some women, interpersonal relations at work are particularly important in helping define their own self-concept (Forrest & Mikolaitis, 1986).

Whatever the reasons, working women tend to be both physically and psychologically healthier than nonworking women (Baruch & Barnett, 1986; Kessler & McRae, 1982; McBride, 1990; Repetti, Mathews, and Waldron, 1989; Rodin & Ickovics, 1990). They suffer fewer heart attacks and ulcers and have higher self-esteem. Unmarried women reap the most benefits, but married women gain as well, especially if their husbands are supportive of their career. Either way, women who enjoy their work benefit more. This enjoyment may be one reason that professional women actually gain more physical and psychological benefits than do clerical workers, despite the greater responsibilities and stresses of their jobs. Given the potential role strains, family problems, and stress, it is surprising that there is virtually no evidence indicating detrimental effects of employment, regardless of the types of work.

There is a more dramatic contrast between career-oriented and noncareer-oriented women. Some women find homemaking meaningful and fulfilling; others consider it sheer drudgery. In one survey (Pietromonaco et al., 1987), the reports on self-esteem, life satisfaction, and self-perception differed dramatically between career-oriented and noncareer-oriented women. Those who described themselves as career oriented and were employed full-time were much happier. Those who were temporarily unemployed or were working at part-time jobs or jobs that underutilized their skills were much less happy and had lower self-esteem and poorer self-concepts. The results were quite different for women who described themselves as noncareer-oriented. Their self-esteem and life satisfaction were not related to whether they were employed full-time or part-time. They agreed with such statements as "I cannot imagine having a fully satisfying life without having children" or "I would not take a job that would interfere with the things I like to do with my family."

MYTHS AND STEREOTYPES THAT AFFECT WOMEN IN THE WORKPLACE

Although there are real differences in the ways in which men and women approach work, there are also certain myths and stereotypes that deny women's real motivations and can delay or block their career advancement. One such myth is that women in managerial, professional, or technical positions are less willing to take risks or make the sacrifices associated with career advancement. Another is that women do not want, need, or expect the same salaries as men, even when they accept a promotion. In reality, it has repeatedly been found that many women are quite similar to men in their attitudes about risk-taking, salaries, and advancement (Rynes & Rosen, 1983). Nor do women have less motivation to achieve or less specific career plans than men. Although women in traditionally "female" fields such as education, social work, and nursing are sometimes less ambitious and expect to make accommodations to fulfill marriage and family responsibilities, women in traditionally "male" professions such as business, law, and medicine have career plans that are very similar to those of men pursuing the same careers.

DYNAMICS OF DUAL-EARNER COUPLES

The dramatic increase in the number of women in the work force has led to an increasingly common phenomenon known as the **dual-earner couple** or *dual-earner marriage.* A dual-earner couple is defined as one in which the husband works full-time and the wife works 20 or more hours per week (Pleck & Staines, 1982; Rapoport & Rapoport, 1980). Today millions of women fully share the provider role with their husbands.

There are obvious advantages to dual-earner marriages. A higher total income makes possible a higher standard of living. There is more money for daily necessities, emergencies, a better place to live, a better education for the children. For college-educated dual-earner couples in particular, perhaps the most important benefit is the wife's equal chance to gain self-fulfillment through a job or career.

There are stresses and role conflicts too, of course. These stem in part from the need to juggle the roles of the wife as a worker, the husband as a worker, and both partners as family members. At times, one role may require more time and energy than the others. During early adulthood, for example, the needs of young children and the struggle to establish a career often collide, forcing the couple to set priorities and resolve conflicts.

Husbands in dual-earner families often report more marital dissatisfaction than other husbands (Burke & Weir, 1976; Kessler & McRae, 1982; Staines et al., 1986). In one study, over a third of dual-earner couples reported experiencing severe role conflicts in their attempts to meet both work and family responsibilities (Pleck & Staines, 1982). The conflicts stemmed from job demands, work hours, family and work scheduling conflicts, and family crises. Although both men and women in dual-earner couples experience these conflicts, women report higher levels of conflict between work and family roles. The role conflict experienced by professional women is particularly acute when they work long hours and are under time pressures (Guelzow et al., 1991). For both partners, dissatisfaction and stress can be eased somewhat by a flexible work schedule that allows them to take care of family needs (Guelzow et al., 1991).

Domestic tasks—especially child care—are shared more equally in some dual-earner families than in others. However, women who work still tend to have the primary responsibility for housework and child care (Barnett & Baruch, 1987; Berardo et al., 1987; Bergmann, 1986; Kalleberg & Rosenfeld, 1990; Maret & Finlay, 1984; Rapoport & Rapoport, 1980). This arrangement is true when the children are infants as well as when they are in school, and it remains true in spite of the recently enacted federal law requiring that companies offer their employees, both male and female, a minimum 12 weeks of **family leave.** It is true whether the woman is working full-time or part-time. Indeed, some people have suggested that working mothers really have two full-time jobs—that when they come home from work, they begin a "second shift" (Hochschild, 1989). Many are up at six o'clock in the morning, in the workplace by nine, and back home at six or seven in the evening. During the evenings and weekends, they face a

dual-earner couple A married or unmarried couple sharing a household, in which both husband and wife contribute to family income, as members of the paid labor force.

family leave Leave required by law to deal with family affairs and problems, especially those involving taking care of children.

mountain of household chores—everything from child care to cooking to laundry to cleaning.

It would seem logical and fair to assume that dual-earner couples should share household chores equally, but that is rarely the case. Study after study has shown that even when both spouses are employed full-time, women continue to do the lion's share of the housework (Berk, 1985; Pleck, 1985). Research consistently indicates that husbands of employed women do not spend significantly more time doing housework than husbands of women who are not employed outside the home (Ferber, 1982). Other studies have shown that the amount of work men do around the house decreases as their income increases (Antill & Cottin, 1988; Smith & Reid, 1986).

Men who have positive attitudes about sharing the provider role are more likely to share household chores than men who resent their wife's income-earning role (Hood, 1986; Perry-Jenkins & Crouter, 1990). "Who does what and how much" around the house apparently is only part of the story, however (Perry-Jenkins & Polk, 1994). Where overall marital satisfaction is concerned, how fair each spouse *perceives* the distribution of labor to be, can be as important as the actual amount of housework each spouse does (Blair & Johnson, 1992; Thompson, 1991; Wilkie et al., 1992).

There are other strains in dual-career marriages. Although social attitudes now favor women in the workforce, there is still some disapproval of mothers who work full-time when they have very young children. Some working women experience negative reactions from friends, neighbors, and colleagues. Some experience considerable role conflicts themselves. Their ambivalence is accentuated when they have difficulty finding adequate, affordable day care for their children. Women may feel particularly uneasy about leaving an infant in someone else's care, yet they may be subject to financial pressures that require them to do so as soon as possible. Federal law does not require that workers be paid while on family leave. Larger companies tend to provide pay during family leave, but many smaller ones do not.

The ambivalence that many women feel about their dual roles may be a result of gender socialization. Traditionally women have been expected to be less active than men, to focus on marriage, and not to develop a work or career orientation (Hansen, 1974). Alternatively, working women's ambivalence toward their roles may be attributable to the day-to-day pressures created by attempting to satisfy two competing sets of demands. In that case, role conflict is a result of the circumstances of dual-earner couples and not a psychological "problem."

Women who pursue professional or managerial careers face additional strains. There are strains in the marriage when decisions must be made about whose career takes precedence—especially during promotions or transfers. Since men generally have greater earning power, favoring the husband's career may maximize the family's income and standard of living but may place obstacles in the path of the woman's career development (Favia & Genovese, 1983).

Again, despite all the strains, women can gain substantial benefits from working. The job satisfactions described earlier often spill over into the families of working women, especially if the women have high-status jobs. This enables the family to adjust better to the woman's limited flexibility and time as well as to the increased stresses dual-earner families experience (Piotrkowski & Crits-Christoph, 1981). Job satisfactions may also be why most studies have found that dual-career marriages are no less happy than other marriages. In fact, several studies have found higher levels of marital satisfaction among employed wives than among nonemployed wives in both working-class and professional families (Burke & Weir, 1976; Walker & Wallston, 1985). Why might working women benefit despite the strains? One possibility is social support. Women can turn to their colleagues at work for friendship, advice, and emotional bolstering. Work may also provide an alternative source of self-esteem and even a sense of control when things are going poorly at home (Rodin & Ickovics, 1990). Thus, work may serve as a buffer against stresses experienced at home.

1. Discuss changes in the participation of women in the workplace in recent decades.
2. How do men and women differ in the meaning they attach to work?
3. How do common myths and stereotypes affect women's career opportunities?
4. Describe some of the strains in the lives of dual-earner couples.

REVIEW & APPLY

SUMMARY

Continuity and Change in Personality Development and Socialization

■ The role changes of young adulthood constitute transitions and turning points in our lives, and we are changed by them, but the changes are subtler and less systematic than those of childhood and adolescence.

■ Adult development occurs in the context of three separate but interacting systems. These involve the development of the personal self, the self as family member, and the self as worker.

■ According to humanistic psychologists such as Maslow, every individual strives toward self-actualization or full development and utilization of talents and abilities.

■ The need for self-actualization can be pursued only after lower needs, such as those for food and shelter, have been met.

■ According to Rogers, society "corrupts" the individual by imposing conditions of worth, which become internalized as standards of perfection. He proposed that we should view ourselves and others with unconditional positive regard—that is, as a worthwhile human being, without reservations or conditions.

■ The family is an extremely important context for adult development; most people define themselves primarily in terms of their family.

■ Young adults are often in a period of transition toward greater independence—emotional, attitudinal, functional, and conflictual.

■ Erikson's stage of generativity versus stagnation is intimately related to work, in that many people achieve a sense of being productive, worthwhile members of society in part through their trade or profession.

■ Some people focus on intrinsic factors of work, such as its challenge or interest; others focus on extrinsic factors such as salary and status.

■ Friendships can be important extrinsic factors in the workplace.

Forming Intimate Relationships

■ Friendships are a core aspect of adult life. Like romantic relationships, they are usually characterized by positive emotional attachment, need fulfillment, and interdependence.

■ According to Sternberg's triangular theory of love, love has three components: intimacy, or the feeling of closeness; passion, or physical attraction, arousal, and sexual behavior; and decision/commitment, the realization of being in love and a commitment to maintain that love.

■ Individuals achieve part of their personal identity as a member of a relatively stable couple.

■ The instrumental theory of mate selection states that some needs (such as sex and affiliation) are more important than others, and people are attracted to others with similar or complementary needs.

■ In the stimulus-value-role theory, courtship has three stages: the stimulus stage, when a man and woman make initial judgments about each other; the value-comparison stage, in which they discover whether they are compatible; and the role stage, in which they determine whether they can function in a long-term relationship.

■ The family system perspective emphasizes that couple formation involves the negotiation of boundaries and redefining of relationships with family and friends as well as with each other.

■ Monogamous marriage is by far the most popular and most frequently chosen lifestyle. It is symbolized by a wedding rite and sanctioned by the community. Cultures vary in the extent to which sexual fidelity is expected.

■ Cohabiting may be similar to marriage, but it lacks the social approval and legalized responsibilities of traditional marriage. About one-third of cohabiting couples eventually marry.

■ A couple that lives together must deal with issues of commitment, fidelity, and permanence.

Parenthood and Adult Development

■ The family life cycle begins when the individual leaves his or her family of origin and continues with marriage, the birth of the first child, the birth of the last child, the departure of the last child from the family, and the death of a spouse.

■ The transition to parenthood calls for numerous adaptations and adjustments, including changes in identity and inner life, shifts in roles and relationships within the marriage, shifts in generational roles and relationships, changing roles and relationships outside the family, and new parenting roles and relationships.

■ Mothers characteristically adjust their lifestyles to give priority to parenting. Men more often intensify their work efforts to become better providers.

■ A variety of factors influence how well new parents adjust. These factors include social support, marital happiness during pregnancy, parental self-esteem, and the baby's characteristics.

■ Six stages of parenthood have been identified: the image-making stage (conception to birth), the nurturing stage (birth to age 2), the authority stage (ages 2 to 5), the interpretive stage (middle childhood), and interdependence stage (adolescence), and the departure stage.

■ At each stage in the family life cycle, parents not only have to cope with the new challenges and demands of their children but must also renegotiate their own relationship.

■ The pressures of parenthood are particularly acute for single parents. Single mothers consistently earn less than single fathers, especially if they lack education.

■ Single-mother homes are more numerous and more likely to be poor among African-Americans. However, they are more often extended families, making additional financial, psychological and social resources available to the single mother.

■ Single fathers experience many of the same problems and tensions as single mothers. However, single fathers are usually better off financially. Most of them maintain high levels of emotional involvement with their children.

The Occupational Cycle

■ The occupational cycle begins with thoughts and experiences that lead to a choice of occupation, continues with pursuit of the chosen career, and ends with retirement. However, the cycle usually isn't that simple, and it doesn't always run smoothly.

■ According to Havighurst, the occupational cycle consists of a series of stages: identification with a worker (ages 5 to 10), acquiring basic habits of industry (ages 10 to 15), acquiring an identity as a worker (ages 15 to 25), becoming a productive person (ages 25 to 40), maintaining a productive society (ages 40 to 70), and contemplating a productive and responsible life (age 70 on).

■ Factors that influence occupational choice include socioeconomic status, ethnic background, intelligence, skills, gender, and parents' occupations.

■ African-Americans and women are overrepresented in lower-status, lower-paying jobs and underrepresented in more highly paid professions. This discrepancy may be due to choices such as dropping out of school or choosing part-time work, or it may be a result of discrimination.

■ The relationship between parents and their children can give rise to attitudes, needs, and interests that later affect the children's occupational choices.

- According to self-concept theory, people seek careers that fit their self-concept. Trait theory is similar, but it investigates objectively measured personality traits, as opposed to the individual's perception of self.
- Formal occupational preparation includes structured learning in high school, vocational training programs, and college, as well as on-the-job training. Informal preparation involves adopting the attitudes, norms, and role expectations that are appropriate to a particular job.
- Practical issues also affect occupational choice. Among these are economic conditions and family pressures.
- In recent decades, workers have come to realize that they are responsible for advancing their own career and cannot depend on the corporation for a long-term career path or even short-term benefits such as health insurance.
- When young adults start working, they often find that their expectations are not matched by reality. This discovery may result in a period of frustration and anger as the young worker adjusts to the new situation.
- Mentors can play a positive role in the development of young workers through teaching, training, sponsoring the young worker's advancement, and serving as models for social as well as work-related behavior.
- Maintaining a sense of excitement and commitment to work throughout adulthood is essential to mature job satisfaction.
- The midcareer period is a time of consolidation—settling down and coming to grips with the realities of one's occupational situation.

Work and Gender

- Although women have entered the workforce in large numbers and have made significant advances, by far the largest number of women are still limited to lower-paying jobs such as nursing, teaching, and secretarial/clerical work. Moreover, women, especially black women, still make less money than men.
- Women who work outside the home follow a greater variety of career patterns than men do. Whereas some follow the traditional male pattern of pursuing a career without interruption, others plan to stop work and have children, or to establish careers outside the home when their children are in school.
- Many women work out of simple economic necessity, but many others find satisfaction and fulfillment in employment outside the home. For some women, the opportunity to interact with people is a particularly important reason for working.
- Working women tend to be both physically and psychologically healthier than nonworking women.
- Women often suffer from the effects of myths and stereotypes. One myth is that women and men differ in their attitudes about risk taking, salaries, and advancement; studies have repeatedly found that this myth is untrue. Nor is it true that women have less motivation to achieve or less specific career plans than men.
- Dual-earner couples have a higher total income, which makes possible a higher standard of living. However, there are stresses and role conflicts stemming from the need to juggle roles and set priorities.
- Studies have found that even when both spouses are employed full-time, women continue to do most of the housework, which amounts to a "second shift" for the working women.
- Some working women experience considerable role conflicts because of factors such as the difficulty of finding adequate child care, the effects of gender socialization, and the pressures created by attempting to satisfy two competing sets of demands.
- Women can gain substantial benefits from working, and these often spill over into their families. In addition, work may serve as a buffer against stresses experienced at home.

KEY TERMS

self-actualization
humanistic psychologists
conditions of worth
unconditional positive regard

intrinsic factors of work
extrinsic factors of work
intimacy
passion

decision/commitment
occupational cycle
dual-earner couple
family leave

USING WHAT YOU'VE LEARNED

In young adulthood, the combined tasks of establishing independence and a personal identity, beginning a family, and developing a career can be a difficult juggling act. Some young adults manage to handle the three sets of roles in an orderly fashion, but for many, the roles and responsibilities of family, work, and self are in some degree of conflict for extended periods.

Make a list of four or five young adults whom you know well. Try to include at least one who is single and one who has not yet established a work-role identity. How would you describe and compare their sta-

tus with respect to each of the three areas of psychosocial development—personal self, self in family roles, and self as worker? Are any of them experiencing role strains or conflicts? If you were to give them advice, what might you suggest to help them relieve the situation or to set priorities? Are your suggestions realistic and practical in both the short and the long term?

Sometimes it's helpful to redefine the problem. If you examine the problem from another perspective, the priorities may shift.

SUGGESTED READINGS

ANDERSON, J. (1990). *The single mother's book.* Atlanta: Peachtree Publishers. A well-organized guide to managing life—children, work, home, finances, and everything else—as a single mother.

APTER, T. (1995). *Working women don't have wives: Professional success in the 1990s.* New York: St. Martin's Press. An insightful collection of interviews with women regarding conflicts between work and family life.

COSBY, F. (1991). *Juggling: The unexpected advantages of balancing career and home for women, their families and society.* New York: Free Press. Drawing on extensive research, Faye Crosby dispels myths about working and motherhood, and she highlights the benefits of complex roles for both parents and children.

COWAN, C. P., & COWAN, P. A. (1992). *When partners become parents: The big life change for couples.* New York: Basic Books. The results of interviews with a sample of couples, presented in a readable, insightful style.

GILL, B. (1998). *Changed by a child: Companion notes for parents of a child with a disability.* New York: Doubleday. Parenting is often tough, but parenting a child with a disability can be a life-changing, disruptive experience. Barbara Gill writes about the experience with wisdom and compassion.

MILLMAN, M. (1991). *Warm hearts, cold cash: The intimate dynamics of families and money.* New York: Free Press. A sociologist presents the uncomfortable truth about the ways we use money within the intimate, sometimes stormy, relationships of the family.

REGISTER, C. (1991). *"Are those kids yours?" American families with children adopted from other countries.* New York: Free Press. A thought-provoking examination of international adoption, from the viewpoints of adoptive parents and adopted children ages 6 to 30, highlighting both its normality and its special challenges.

ROGERS, C. R. (1961). *On becoming a person.* Cambridge, MA: Riverside Press. In very readable style, Carl

Rogers presents a perceptive and hopeful model for personal growth throughout the lifespan.

ROSENBERG, E. B. (1992). *The adoptive life cycle.* Lexington, MA: Lexington Books. A most unusual and authoritative source on the complex experience of adoptive parenting.

RUBIN, L. B. (1995). *Families on the fault line: America's working class speaks about the family, the economy, race,* *and ethnicity.* New York: Harperperennial Library. Noted sociologist Lillian Rubin interviews 162 families, mostly white, but including substantial numbers of blacks, Latinos, and Asians, to present this portrait of the experiences, attitudes, and circumstances of today's working class families.

Middle-Aged Adults: Physical and Cognitive Development

CHAPTER

14

By the time you have finished this chapter, you should be able to do the following:

1. Explain the developmental issues that characterize middle age.
2. Describe the physical changes that take place in middle age and factors that contribute to these changes.
3. Discuss sexuality in the middle years.
4. Identify the factors that influence the onset of disease during middle age, including poor health habits, poverty, and stress.
5. Explain the cognitive changes that occur in middle age and the research problems associated with assessing these changes.

We have looked at childhood, adolescence, and young adulthood. We have seen the developmental steps through which a child becomes an adult, an individual with a relatively stable outlook and personality. We have noted the social milestones that mark the adolescent's entry into the world of the adult—moving away from home, getting married, becoming a parent, establishing a career. What's next?

Middle adulthood (arbitrarily considered to begin at age 40), along with older adulthood, may constitute 50% or more of a person's lifespan. Does it pose new challenges, or is it merely a time in which to live out the decisions made earlier in life, possibly making a few corrections and adjustments here and there? How much continuity is there during these years? Is Guy Smith the same person at age 50 that he was at age 30? If not, what makes him change, how much, and in what ways? Does he embrace new experiences and accumulate wisdom, or do his perspective and opinions narrow? What role does his inevitable biological decline play in his psychological functioning?

As in young adulthood, the theme of the middle years is continuity and change—there is some of each. We'll begin with an overview that includes exposing popular myths about middle-aged people, such as the midlife "crisis." Then we'll look at changes in sensorimotor skills and other biological factors, as well as both biological and psychological aspects of sexuality. Health and disease are considered next. Finally, we'll take a detailed look at what happens to intelligence and cognitive skills during middle age, with emphasis on which skills decline and which ones do not.

DEVELOPMENT IN MIDDLE AGE

When do people start thinking of themselves as middle-aged? What cues tell them that they are no longer young, and how do they react to this realization? There are many signals of middle age. By popular convention, middle age covers roughly the years from age 40 to age 60 or 65. On a person's fortieth birthday, it is common practice to proclaim the milestone loudly, tell jokes about being "over the hill," send disparaging greeting cards, and maybe put up a sign and "flamingo" the person's lawn. In our culture, turning 40 is often heralded as the beginning of the end.

Developmental theories differ considerably on the question of when middle age begins and when it ends. Much depends on the life experiences that the person is going through: Does a 43-year-old woman with a newborn baby think of herself as middle-aged? Does a 41-year-old man in a job-training program consider himself in the middle years of his career—and life—or does he view himself as making a new start? Health is a factor too: How much do 40-year-olds who are physically fit and full of vim and vigor have in common with 40-year-olds who have "let themselves go" through alcohol or drug use and lack of exercise?

Moreover, the period defined as middle age may begin earlier or later, and may be longer or shorter for different people because there are so many different cues associated with aging (Neugarten, 1980). Some cues have to do with social and family status. Middle age is an in-between period, a bridge between two generations. People in midlife are aware of being separate not only from youngsters and young adults but also from older people, especially retirees. Some people feel that they are middle-aged when their children begin to leave home. Other cues may be physical and biological. A woman may suddenly realize that her son is taller than she is; a man may find that a certain skill, such as drawing or playing the piano, is hampered by the beginnings of arthritis.

There are also psychological cues, most of which involve issues of continuity and change. People realize that they have made certain basic decisions about their career or family that are now fairly set and remain to be played out or fulfilled. The future is never certain, but it no longer holds as many different possibilities as it once did. Cues also come from people's careers; their advancement at work may have stopped. They may have reached a position of seniority, or they may realize that they have reached a plateau well below their original goal.

PRIME TIME OR THE BEGINNING OF THE END?

How do people feel about being middle-aged? Theorists and middle-aged people themselves do not agree on whether this is a time of new fulfillment, stability, and potential leadership, or a period of dissatisfaction, inner turmoil, and depression. Economic conditions, social class, and the times in which people live affect how they view middle age. Many realize that they are no longer young, yet they feel satisfied and believe that they are now in the "prime of life" (Hunt & Hunt, 1975; Neugarten, 1968b). Middle-aged people often feel "safe," settled, and secure (Helson, 1997). For many, physical abilities may be slightly diminished, but experience and self-knowledge allow them to manage their own lives to a greater extent than at any other age. They can make decisions with ease, expertise, and self-confidence that were previously beyond their grasp. This ability explains why the 40- to 60-year-old age group has been called the *command generation* and why most of the decision makers in government, corporations, and society at large are middle-aged.

Of course, many middle-aged people do not make weighty decisions and run corporations or government agencies. Many do not feel that they even control their own lives, let alone those of others. Some people lose their vitality after age 40. Else Frenkel-Brunswik (1963), for example, does not see middle-aged people as the command generation. Instead, she sees the period as one of declining activity whose onset, around the age of 48, is usually marked by both psychological and biological crises. Levinson (1978, 1996) and his colleagues

Upon entry into middle age, many people may slightly reduce their physical activity.

also found that "the midlife transition is a time of moderate to severe crisis" for both men and women.

Most people experience a sense of ambivalence during middle age (Chiriboga, 1981; Sherman, 1987). It may be the prime of life with respect to family, career, or creative talents, but most people are also keenly aware of their own mortality and have recurrent thoughts about how their time is running out—also that the years seem to pass more quickly. Some people in midlife become preoccupied with questions of creativity and ongoing contributions to the next generation, with fears of stagnation or lost opportunities, and with concerns about maintaining intimate relationships with family and friends. With each major event—birth, death, job change, divorce—adults reexamine the meaning of their lives (Sherman, 1987). This practice applies to events that happen to them as well as events that happen to others around them. For some, the theme of middle age becomes "Whatever we do must be done now" (Gould, 1978). How people interpret this sense of urgency, together with the particular events they experience, determines whether middle age is a period of gradual transition and reassessment or a period of crisis.

MIDLIFE CRISIS AND RELATED MYTHS

Although some researchers believe that adults perceive middle age as "a period in which some hopes are blighted, some opportunities are seen as forever lost" (Clausen, 1986), a substantial and persuasive body of research indicates the opposite. Studies have shown that most adults experience the middle years simply as years of gradual transitions—both positive and negative—associated with growing older. Whereas the crisis model links the normative developmental changes of the period to predictable crises, the **transition model** rejects the idea that midlife crisis is the norm (Hunter & Sundel, 1989; Helson, 1997).

According to the transition model, development is marked by a series of expected major life events that can be anticipated and planned for. Although the transitions associated with these events can be difficult both psychologically and socially, most people adapt successfully because they know that these life

transition model The view that changes in midlife are gradual.

changes are coming. For example, knowing that he will probably retire sometime in his sixties, a 40-year-old small-business owner makes regular deposits into a tax-deferred individual retirement account (IRA). By the time he's 50, he may have found the ideal home to retire in, and he regularly discusses his retirement plans with his wife and children. Thus, individuals who expect to confront change during their middle years are not likely to wait for these changes to hit them over the head before acting. Through anticipation, they can plan for these life events and avoid midlife crises (Clausen, 1986; Troll, 1985).

The **crisis model** also has certain methodological weaknesses that limit its appeal. Many of the studies that support it were based on clinical populations rather than on normal samples, which reflect the overall adult population more accurately. Moreover, the classic studies of Levinson (1978), Gould (1978), and Vaillant (1977) focused exclusively on middle-class white males. For example, Levinson and his colleagues (1978) found that at about the age of 40, a man may begin to question, or at least put into perspective, the "driven" life he has been leading. If he has been successful in reaching his goals, he may suddenly ask, "Was it worth the struggle?" If he has not achieved what he wanted in life, he may become keenly aware that he does not have many more chances to change things. Thus, he questions his entire life structure, including both work and family relationships (Levinson, 1986). Women—and their unique midlife concerns—were excluded from this and other classic studies of the middle years. Indeed, some researchers question whether such male themes as "anguish over mortality and over the inadequacy of one's achievements" even apply to women (Baruch & Brooks-Gunn, 1984). They also question whether the negative impact of major life events such as menopause and the "empty nest" have been exaggerated.

Middle age, then, is a time when people begin to take stock of their lives. Some may feel effective, competent, and at the peak of their powers (Chiriboga, 1981). Others may find it painful to examine their lives. Although age-graded influences such as graying hair, an expanding midsection, or menopause may combine with nonnormative events such as divorce or unemployment to precipitate a crisis, if any of these influences is anticipated or regarded as a normal event, it is less likely to lead to a crisis (Neugarten, 1980).

Still, it is difficult for many adolescents and young adults to think of middle age as anything but a giant black hole in which they will spend at least 20 years of their lives. By middle age, they argue, growth and development are over. So are youthful dreams and passions about career and relationships, as well as the plans and strategies to make them happen. Whereas youth is about hope, middle age is about being stuck in a quagmire. Wrong, says Ronald Kessler, a sociologist and fellow at the MacArthur Foundation Research Network on Successful Midlife Development:

> The data show that middle age is the very best time in life. When looking at the total U.S. population, the best year is 50. You don't have to deal with the aches and pains of old age or the anxieties of youth: Is anyone going to love me? Will I ever get my career off the ground? Rates of general distress are low—the incidences of depression and anxiety fall at about 35 and don't climb again until the late sixties. You're healthy. You're productive. You have enough money to do some of the things you like to do. You've come to terms with your relationships, and the chance of divorce is very low. Midlife is the "it" you've been working toward. You can turn your attention toward being rather than becoming. (Quoted in Gallagher, 1993)

crisis model The view that changes in midlife are abrupt and often stressful.

Kessler also believes that midlife crisis is the exception rather than the rule. The overwhelming majority of people shift gently into midlife as they trade their youthful goals of fame, wealth, accomplishment, and beauty for more realistic expectations. A 42-year-old tennis player, accomplished enough to be ranked among the top 100 players in her state as an adolescent, has accepted that she will never make it to Wimbledon and has instead become a high school physical education teacher or a tennis pro. A politician with youthful aspirations to run for the U.S. Senate settles for being the mayor of a small town. Such "redirection" involves measuring ourselves against people with similar goals and accomplishments. When facing trouble, mature people are likely to compare themselves with people who are worse off. Thus, a middle-aged couple whose house was just flooded and their belongings destroyed may compare themselves with neighbors who experienced the same fate but who are also unemployed.

Those who are most likely to experience a midlife crisis tend to avoid introspection and instead use denial to avoid thinking about their changing bodies and lives. As a result, a 45-year-old who thinks he is still a great athlete may be emotionally devastated when his 15-year-old son beats him at basketball. "Such individuals have to work hard to maintain their illusions," said Kessler. "They spend a lot of energy on the cognitive effort of self-delusion, until reality finally intervenes" (Gallagher, 1993). Kessler also believes that midlife crises are more common among the affluent than among the poor and working class. Apparently, it is easier to delude yourself about the realities of middle age when money in the bank shields you from the burdens and struggles of life.

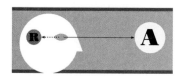

REVIEW & APPLY

1. Discuss some of the feelings people have about being middle-aged. What kinds of factors determine how people respond?
2. Describe the differences between the crisis model and the transition model of middle age.
3. Is there such a thing as a midlife crisis? Why or why not?

PHYSICAL CONTINUITY AND CHANGE

The most obvious changes associated with the middle years are physical ones. It is generally during middle age that people receive the first clear reminders that their bodies are aging.

"Age is like love; it cannot be hid," wrote a seventeenth-century dramatist. For many middle-aged people, there is a "moment of truth" when the mirror reveals new wrinkles, midriff bulge, a receding hairline, or gray hair at the temples that no longer seems distinguished—just depressing. These warning signals are more disturbing to some than to others, depending on their attitudes toward aging and eventually dying. Are these signs of maturity or of decline?

Some obvious biological events, such as menopause for women, increased difficulty in achieving erection for men, and decreasing visual acuity for both sexes, are events that require a change in self-image or activities and must be incorporated into a satisfactory lifestyle (Newman, 1982; Timiras, 1994). Most physical abilities peak during adolescence or early adulthood and level off in middle age; then the first signs of physical decline begin to appear. As we examine these changes, however, bear in mind that people age and develop at different rates. Many factors influence aging. By taking these into account, people can often ease the process and alleviate many of its unpleasant effects.

CHANGES IN CAPABILITIES

Some physical decline or slowing down is likely to occur during middle age (Birren et al., 1980). This decline involves sensory and motor skills as well as the body's internal functioning.

SENSATION Visual capabilities are fairly stable from adolescence through the forties or early fifties; then visual acuity declines (Kline & Schieber, 1985; Pollack & Atkeson, 1978). A partial exception is nearsightedness: People often see distant objects better in middle age than they could as young adults. Hearing typically becomes less acute after age 20 and declines gradually, especially with regard to high-frequency sounds. This hearing loss is more common in men than in women, a fact that may be attributable to environmental factors such as traditionally "male" jobs, such as construction work, that include sustained exposure to loud or high-frequency noises. In any case, it is rarely severe enough to affect normal conversation in middle age (Olsho et al., 1985). Taste, smell, and sensitivity to pain decline at different points in middle age, although these changes are more gradual and less noticeable than visual or auditory changes. Sensitivity to temperature changes remains high in middle age (Newman, 1982).

MOTOR SKILLS AND REACTION TIME Reaction time and sensorimotor skills are likely to slow down. Reaction time drops off slowly throughout adulthood and more quickly during old age. Motor skills may decline, but actual performance remains constant, probably as a result of continuing practice and experience (Newman, 1982). For example, someone who chops firewood or plays tennis every day will experience little decline in performance during middle age. Learning new skills, however, gradually becomes more and more difficult as middle age progresses.

INTERNAL CHANGES Internal changes begin to occur as well. The nervous system begins to slow down, particularly after age 50 (Newman, 1982). The skeleton stiffens and shrinks a bit over the course of adulthood; gravity gradually takes its toll, and the person becomes shorter in stature. Skin and muscles begin to lose elasticity, and wrinkles develop. There is a tendency to accumulate more subcutaneous fat, especially in areas like the midriff. The heart pumps an average of 8% less blood to the body for each decade after the beginning of adulthood, and by middle age, the opening of the coronary arteries is nearly one-third less than it is in the twenties. Lung capacity decreases as well. Because endurance depends on the amount of oxygen supplied to body tissues, people generally can't perform as much sustained hard labor in middle age as they can in young adulthood (Brody, 1979).

MENOPAUSE AND THE CLIMACTERIC

For women, the most dramatic internal change is **menopause**—cessation of ovulation and menstruation—which is an event with varied physical and psychological implications. Menopause is part of the **climacteric**, which refers to the overall complex of physical and emotional effects that accompany

Visual acuity often declines in middle adulthood.

menopause The permanent end of menstruation; it occurs in middle age and may be accompanied by physical symptoms and intense emotional reactions, more so in some women than in others.

climacteric The broad complex of physical and emotional symptoms that accompany reproductive changes in middle age. The climacteric affects both men and women.

hormonal changes in middle age. Because of its broad implications for women's lives, we will devote this section to both the immediate and the long-term physical and emotional changes associated with menopause. Although there is no comparable "male menopause," despite its occasional coverage in the popular media, many professionals believe that men also undergo biological changes in middle age that are accompanied by emotional readjustments and changes in sexual behavior. We will consider these changes as well.

PHYSICAL CHANGES AND SYMPTOMS   On average, menopause begins between age 48 and 51, although for some women, it may occur somewhat earlier or considerably later. Ovulation and the menstrual cycle become erratic at first, then stop altogether. At the same time, less estrogen is produced, and the reproductive system "shuts down." Slowly the uterus shrinks; there is a gradual reduction in breast size as glandular tissue atrophies and is replaced with fat tissue. Menopause is accompanied by physical symptoms such as hot flashes and night sweats, and, less frequently, headaches, dizziness, palpitations, and pain in the joints. However, research indicates that of these symptoms, hot flashes and night sweats are the only ones that are directly caused by menopause—specifically, by the decrease in estrogen levels (Asso, 1983). Up to 75% of all women report hot flashes during menopause (Asso, 1983; Greenwood, 1984). Night sweats may be extensive enough to cause insomnia. The other symptoms, such as the headaches and pains that some women experience, tend to occur mainly in women who have a history of the problem or are experiencing a particularly intense menopause (Asso, 1983). In all, probably only about 15% of all menopausal women require medical treatment for their symptoms (Shepard & Shepard, 1982).

IMMEDIATE EMOTIONAL EFFECTS   For some women, the physical changes are accompanied by emotional changes such as feelings of depression and a sense of being somehow less feminine because their reproductive function is gone. In particular, women who have not had children and had not completely made up their minds about childbearing may experience a sense of regret or loss, or depression. Most women, however, do not encounter such difficulties during menopause (Asso, 1983). Indeed, some researchers report a *decrease* in emotional difficulties during and after menopause compared with the years immediately preceding it.

In general, considerable research indicates that most women do not respond negatively to menopause in either the short run or the long term (Goodman, 1980; Neugarten, 1967; Neugarten et al., 1968). Half of the menopausal and postmenopausal women in one survey reported that the change was "easy" or at least "moderately easy" (Goodman, 1980). Many women feel freer and more in control of their own lives, with a sense of elation because they no longer need to be concerned with menstrual periods or the possibility of pregnancy. At the same time, their active mothering role is usually ending, and they will have more time for themselves. Even women who are not particularly pleased about menopause tend not to be worried or distressed—they simply take it in stride. During this period of their lives, women are more likely to be worried about becoming widows than about passing through menopause (Neugarten, 1967).

The cultural context of menopause can also affect the woman's feelings about herself, her behavior, and her actual physical symptoms. In the words of Margaret Lock (1993), menopause and other universal aging experiences are "the products . . . of an ongoing dialectic between biology and culture in which both are contingent." In some castes in India, for example, menopause

Many menopausal and postmenopausal women feel happy, now that their active mothering is drawing to an end, to have more time for themselves.

traditionally brings with it a new positive status for the woman. She is no longer required to remain isolated from much of society, associating only with her husband and immediate family. She may enjoy the company of both men and women in a greater variety of social circumstances. In one study of a group of Indian women, none reported the range of symptoms often associated with menopause—such as excessive moodiness, depression, or headaches (Flint, 1982). Some researchers have suggested that the excessive focus on youth and attractiveness in Western cultures may contribute to the symptoms that some women in these cultures experience during menopause.

LONG-TERM EFFECTS The estrogen loss that accompanies menopause has two, possibly three, long-term effects. The two clear-cut effects are changes in bone mass and in the genitals. The more controversial one is increased risk of coronary disease.

The mineral mass of bones peaks between the ages of 25 and 40 and then remains steady for several years. Both men and women experience a loss in bone mass as they age, but the loss is about twice as great in women and occurs more rapidly (Asso, 1983). As a result, bone fractures are six to ten times more common in women than in men after age 50 (Nathanson & Lorenz, 1982). Women's loss of bone mass accelerates greatly after menopause, apparently owing to estrogen deprivation. **Osteoporosis**, the medical term for loss of bone mass and increased bone fragility (regardless of the cause), affects 25 million Americans—most of whom are women. Nearly half of all postmenopausal women over the age of 50 will experience a bone fracture related to osteoporosis (McBean et al., 1994).

The second well-established long-term physical change involves the genitals. Vaginal atrophy occurs as a result of decreased estrogen. The tissues of the vagina, as well as the labia and other surrounding tissues, shrink and become thinner and drier. The vagina becomes shorter and narrower, and less lubrication occurs during intercourse. These and other changes may cause pain or bleeding during intercourse (Asso, 1983; Shepard & Shepard, 1982).

Such changes do not mean that intercourse is no longer possible, however. The changes are gradual, so a menopausal or immediately postmenopausal woman can easily continue intercourse. Lubricating cream or jelly can be used. Hormone replacement therapy (HRT) will alleviate and even reverse many of these symptoms (Asso, 1983; Shepard & Shepard, 1982), although it is not a panacea—as discussed in "In Theory, In Fact" on page 490.

The more controversial long-term effect concerns the relationship between menopause and cardiovascular disease and heart attacks. Women have a much lower rate of cardiovascular disease than men until menopause; then the rate for women rises nearly as high as the male rate. However, it remains unclear whether this rise is due to menopausal changes per se; it could have to do with other aspects of the aging process.

CHANGES IN MEN For men there is no single, relatively abrupt event comparable to menopause (Masters et al., 1982). We do know, however, that men undergo changes in sexual interest and activity, generally in their late forties. As with women, the amount of change varies widely and depends on the individual's personality and lifestyle as well as on cultural factors. Some changes in men are a result of biological factors, especially decreased production of androgens such as testosterone. Unlike estrogen, however, which decreases dramatically during menopause, androgens decline very gradually over a longer period. Even so, men occasionally experience symptoms such as impotence, frequent urination, and ulcers (Ruebsaat & Hull, 1975). Some experience loss

osteoporosis Loss of bone mass and increased bone fragility in middle age and beyond.

IN THEORY, IN FACT

HORMONE REPLACEMENT THERAPY AND OTHER TREATMENTS

Hormone replacement therapy, in the form of either estrogen or progesterone supplements or a combination of the two, is used to treat the short- and long-term effects of menopause (Dan & Bernhard, 1989). Hormone therapy helps alleviate symptoms such as hot flashes, and appears to be of some value in slowing or even stopping the progress of bone loss, although it will not reverse damage already done (Shepard & Shepard, 1982). During the first five years after menopause, bone loss is linked almost entirely to withdrawal of estrogen, and only estrogen replacement therapy slows this loss (McBean et al., 1994).

Hormone replacement therapy is also associated with reduced incidence of coronary heart disease, as well as fewer deaths associated with cardiovascular disease (Stampfer et al., 1991). In a longitudinal study of over 121,000 nurses, medical researchers found that replacement hormone users have a signficantly lower risk of death due to heart disease, at least in the early years; the benefits decline with long-term use (Grodstein et al., 1997). In sum, ". . . the benefits of estrogen use appear to far outweigh the risks" (*New England Journal of Medicine*, 1997), again in the short run. It is not clear, however, whether estrogen replacement therapy helps

women cope with the emotional symptoms that often accompany menopause.

On the downside, hormone replacement therapy in the form of estrogen alone may be associated with an increased overall risk of cancer, especially uterine cancer (Lee et al., 1986; Davidson, 1996). Studies also suggest a specific link between long-term use and increased risk of breast cancer (Grodstein et al., 1997; see also *Scientific American*, 1997), although the evidence remains inconclusive (Petrovitch et al., 1997). It is believed that using a combination of estrogen and progesterone minimizes these risks and may increase the estrogen's ability to prevent osteoporosis (Gambrell, 1987); progesterone also minimizes the uterine bleeding associated with intermittent use of estrogen alone (*Journal of the American Medical Association*, 1996). In all cases, however, the particular combination of hormone-replacing agents must be carefully tailored to the individual. In addition, feminists argue that defining menopause as a de facto "disease" requiring long-term treatment "medicalizes" a normal developmental process and turns an otherwise healthy population of women into patients (Gonyea, 1998).

There are partial alternatives to HRT. Evidence is mounting that increased calcium intake may also reduce the bone loss associated with osteoporosis. Adequate calcium during

childhood and early adulthood helps build the bone mass needed throughout life. Studies have shown that older postmenopausal women who consume 800 milligrams of calcium a day have less bone loss than similar women who consume less than 400 milligrams of calcium a day. However, calcium's positive effects are not seen in the five years immediately following menopause (Dawson-Hughes et al., 1990). Other drugs to prevent or minimize postmenopausal osteoporosis are currently being developed (Rizzoli & Bonjour, 1997; Mestel, 1997).

Finally, regular weight-bearing exercise throughout life helps increase bone density and may reduce the risk of osteoporosis. Postmenopausal women who exercise increase their strength, stability, flexibility, and balance, and thus are less likely to fall and suffer bone fractures (McBean et al., 1994). Among the exercises believed to increase bone mass are running, tennis, weight training, and low-impact aerobics. To be effective, these exercises must be performed at least three times a week for 30 to 45 minutes. However, the bone mass gained through exercise may be lost when exercise is discontinued. According to research physiologist Barbara Drinkwater, "We are sometimes told that exercise will put bone in our bank. I think it's more like putting bone in our savings and loan associations" (Skolnick, 1990).

of self-confidence; others become irritable, fatigued, and depressed. Some of these symptoms may be related to changes in hormone levels, but many are probably due to psychological stresses such as job pressures, boredom with a sexual partner, family responsibilities, or fear of ill health.

SEXUALITY IN THE MIDDLE YEARS

As we have seen, the physiological and psychological changes associated with middle age markedly affect sexual functioning in both men and women. How people respond to midlife changes has a major influence on their sexual satisfaction.

Although sexual capabilities decline during middle adulthood, sexual and romantic interests continue both for men and women.

Frequency of sexual activity—as well as the number of different sexual partners a person is likely to have—generally slows down in middle age (Michael et al., 1994; Laumann et al., 1994). Nevertheless, many healthy individuals can—and do—enjoy satisfying sex lives until age 70 and beyond, and frequency of sexual behavior knows no racial or ethnic bounds. Physiological changes account for some of the slowdown, but sexual activity may also drop off in the middle years because of ill health. Health problems that inhibit sexual activity include physical conditions such as hypertension, diabetes, and coronary artery disease, and emotional problems such as depression. In addition, medications used to treat these illnesses may have adverse effects on sexual activity. For example, the biochemicals used in the treatment of coronary artery disease may cause impotence as a side effect. Similarly, tranquilizers tend to reduce sexual desire.

Lack of opportunity is also a factor. The time pressures associated with the middle years may interfere with sexual interest. The pressures of career and family leave many couples with little time or energy for sex. For many people, interpersonal and family problems further interfere with sexual interactions (Weg, 1989).

For many adults, sexuality is redefined during the middle years to place more emphasis on sensuality, which includes a range of physical expressions that may or may not lead to a sexual act. Hugging, hand holding, and touching and stroking are as much expressions of mature sexuality as they are of caring and affection (Weg, 1989). For women, physiological changes associated with menopause do not eliminate the ability to function sexually. However, more time may be needed to achieve orgasm. A similar slowdown occurs in men, who may take longer to achieve an erection and reach orgasm. Thus, since both men and women require more time during sex, the result is often a more sharing kind of lovemaking—in contrast to lovemaking in former years, which may have been directed more urgently toward orgasm (Weg, 1989). One compensation is that middle-aged men often can maintain erection for a longer time (Masters et al., 1982).

On the downside, there is often an increase in sexual anxiety and dissatisfaction among middle-aged men (Featherstone & Hepworth, 1985). In addition to job stresses and boredom with a long-term sexual partner, poor physical conditioning may affect men's sexual activity. Men who are anxious about sex and have even a single episode of impotence or partial erection may start believing that age has diminished their sexual ability. To protect themselves from additional "failures," they avoid sex—or perhaps turn to an affair, often with a younger woman.

One pattern consistently emerges, however. Middle-aged people who engage in sex infrequently often mistakenly believe that others around them are enjoying active, fulfilling sex lives; many men also believe that there is a male "seven-year-itch" that others around them are pursuing even though they're not (Michael et al., 1994). Such misconceptions can compound their own dissatisfaction. Indeed, as Robert Michael and colleagues point out, media give the impression that everyone is doing it all the time, both within their marriage and extramaritally as well. Not so. The results of their broad-scale survey "support an extraordinarily conventional view of love, sex, and marriage," with monogamy predominant and many people having sex relatively infrequently.

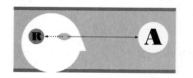

REVIEW & APPLY

1. What are some of the major changes that take place in sensory and motor functioning during the middle adult years?
2. Describe the short-term and long-term physical and emotional changes associated with menopause.
3. What are some of the ways in which sexuality changes during the middle years?

HEALTH AND DISEASE

Associated with the normal physical changes that occur during the middle years are changes in health, some of which are linked to the diseases associated with middle age. As the body ages, it becomes increasingly vulnerable to disease. Middle-aged people often become more aware of their own mortality as they or their friends become ill. In this section, we will look at the major diseases that affect people in their middle years; the cumulative effects of good or poor health habits; the relationships among race, poverty, and health; and the link between stress and disease. First, however, let's take a look at some statistics on the good news.

THE GOOD NEWS ABOUT AGING AND HEALTH
The large-scale Baltimore Longitudinal Study of Aging (as summarized by Nancy Shute, 1997) reported the following positive findings:

■ Many losses of function associated with aging can be stopped or slowed.
■ Even past age 70, only 20 to 30% of people have symptoms of heart disease.
■ Only about 10% of people over age 65 ever develop Alzheimer's disease, and much of the cognitive decline that old people do experience (discussed later in the chapter) is attributable to treatable diseases.

- It's actually healthy to gain a pound or so a year from age 40 on—middle-agers should avoid obesity, of course, but being concerned about losing 5 or 10 pounds is trivial.
- Finally, an aside: People don't get crankier as they age. Cranky older folks were just as cranky when they were young.

MAJOR DISEASES OF MIDDLE AGE

The single highest cause of death for U.S. adults in middle age is accidents. However, during the same period, people increasingly begin to die as a result of disease (National Center for Health Statistics, 1995). Certain diseases become major problems, and some of them affect one sex more than the other (see Table 14–1). Throughout much of the lifespan, the death rate of men at any particular age is about twice that of women of the same age, partly because men are more likely to work in dangerous occupations. Psychological factors contribute, too: Men are likely to be less concerned about their health than women because they have been taught that it is masculine to ignore pain, and they may be less likely to visit a doctor when ill or for a checkup. It is also possible that men have a higher genetic predisposition to certain diseases than women do.

Major diseases that affect people in the United States during their middle years are discussed in the following sections.

CARDIOVASCULAR DISEASES   These diseases, which include heart disease, arteriosclerosis, and hypertension, among others, are the leading fatal diseases. Heart disease accounts for 35% of all deaths and 28% of deaths for people between the ages of 45 and 64 (National Center for Health Statistics, 1995). Throughout middle age, cardiovascular disease is a greater threat to men than to women. Before menopause, women are less prone to heart attacks than men, partly because their bodies are producing estrogen. After menopause, heart disease becomes an increasing problem for women too, but even then, fewer women in each age bracket die of heart attacks.

TABLE 14–1   LEADING CAUSES OF DEATH FOR MALES AND FEMALES BETWEEN THE AGES OF 45 AND 64*

CAUSE	MALE	FEMALE
Heart disease	314.1	122.7
Cancer	306.7	245.0
Accidents	42.6	15.8
Cerebrovascular disease	33.7	26.5
Chronic liver diseases	31.3	12.2
Chronic lung diseases	29.0	22.5
HIV	28.7	less than 3.0
Suicide	23.1	6.9
Diabetes	23.0	9.8
Pneumonia	13.6	7.7

*Rank ordered by the rates for males.
Note: Figures represent annual numbers of deaths per 100,000 population.
Source: National Center for Health Statistics (1995).

CANCER   Cancer is the second highest cause of death overall but has recently become the leading cause of death for people between the ages of 45 and 64 (National Center for Health Statistics, 1995). The overall death rate from cancer continues to rise. Cancer, too, claims more men than women, but the difference is not as dramatic as it is for heart disease. Middle-aged men are more likely to die of lung cancer, although the rate for women is increasing (National Center for Health Statistics, 1995).

DIABETES   This is another disease that occurs in increasing rates and severity in middle age; it may also complicate other physical problems, with fatal consequences. One-half of the 3 million diabetics in the United States are between 45 and 64 years old (Ebersole, 1979), and the disease claims nearly the same number of women as men (National Center for Health Statistics, 1995).

RESPIRATORY DISEASES   These diseases are also a problem in middle age. Men are far more likely than women to have bronchitis, asthma, and emphysema (National Center for Health Statistics, 1990).

HIV-RELATED DISEASES   These are the seventh leading cause of death for middle-aged men, but the rate is lower for women.

Some diseases of middle age are less serious but nonetheless cause considerable discomfort and interfere with daily living. Arthritis, for example, troubles many middle-aged people of both sexes.

CUMULATIVE EFFECTS OF HEALTH HABITS

Fortunately, most middle-aged people will not suffer serious, life-threatening forms of any of the diseases just discussed. The life expectancy for individuals who make it to age 45 in the United States is about 79 years (National Center for Health Statistics, 1995). Over 80% of people who reach age 45 survive and remain in reasonably good health at least until age 65. Various researchers have noted that although the average lifespan has not increased much beyond 85 years for any subset of the population, a sizable proportion maintain relatively good health in middle age.

GOOD HEALTH HABITS   In part, longevity is attributable to good health habits. With a balanced and nutritious diet, a reasonable amount of exercise, and regular health care, many people will experience an active and extended adulthood (Fries & Crapo, 1981; Siegler & Costa, 1985). Indeed, many health experts believe that by following a program of regular exercise, lessened stress, and good diet, people can slow the aging process and continue to function with youthful vitality and a sense of well-being through middle age and beyond (Fries & Crapo, 1981). Numerous studies have shown that exercise before and during middle age can increase physical capacities and endurance (Weg, 1983). Certain kinds of exercise—especially aerobic exercises—are designed to increase heart and lung capacity, thus supplying the body with more oxygen and, in turn, more energy. Even short-term, mild exercise training programs for formerly sedentary older adults produce impressive gains in strength and heart and lung functioning (Sidney, 1981). Regular exercise can also slow the deterioration of muscle tissue, reduce body fat, help prevent deterioration of the joints, and combat some kinds of arthritis (Brody, 1979).

POOR HEALTH HABITS   The cumulative effects of poor health habits during early adulthood take their toll in middle age. Most chronic disorders begin to develop long before they are diagnosed. Chief among these are conditions related to cigarette smoking. Smoking contributes to cancer (of the lung, mouth,

Middle-aged people who exercise tend to maintain their youthful vitality and sense of well-being.

STUDY CHART ▸ PHYSICAL CHANGES OF MIDDLE AGE

TYPE OF CHANGE	CHARACTERISTICS
Sensation	Decline in visual acuity, except for distant objects. Hearing loss, especially for high-frequency sounds.
	Decline in taste, smell, and sensitivity to pain.
Reaction time	Slow decline in reaction time.
Internal changes	Slowing of the nervous system.
	Stiffening and shrinking of the skeleton.
	Loss of elasticity in skin and muscles; development of wrinkles.
	Accumulation of subcutaneous fat.
	Decrease in heart and lung capacity.
Sex-related changes	
Menopause in women	Cessation of ovulation and menstruation.
	Reduced production of estrogen.
	Shrinking of uterus and reduction of breast size.
	Hot flashes; night sweats.
	Loss of bone mass (osteoporosis).
	Vaginal atrophy.
Changes in men	Gradual decline in production of androgens.
	Increased difficulty in achieving erection.
Health	Increased susceptibility to certain diseases, including cardiovascular diseases, cancer, diabetes, respiratory diseases, and HIV-related diseases.

pharynx, larynx, esophagus, colon, stomach, pancreas, uterine cervix, kidney, ureter, and bladder), respiratory and cardiovascular diseases, arteriosclerosis, hypertension, and other diseases. Of the more than 2 million deaths in the United States in 1990, 20% (400,000) were caused by smoking-related illnesses. Among people between the ages of 35 and 64, smoking is responsible for more than 25% of all deaths. This finding should be no surprise, since in addition to nicotine, there are forty-two other substances in cigarette smoke that can cause cancer (Bartecchi et al., 1995).

Despite 40 years of media campaigns about the dangers of smoking, about one out of four American adults continues to smoke. Although the percentage has dropped significantly since the 1960s, when 41% of adults smoked, health officials are concerned that the percentage of smokers remained constant between 1990 and 1993 despite continuing efforts to alert the public to smoking-related health risks. The continuing popularity of smoking can be traced in part to the effectiveness of tobacco manufacturers' marketing programs, including the increasing prevalence of discount brands that have made cigarettes more affordable. In 1987, these brands accounted for only 10% of the market; six years later, their market share had risen to 36%. Demographic groups that are disproportionately affected by the lure of cigarette smoking include black males, Native Americans, and Alaskan natives, as well as people

The long-term effects of alcohol abuse becomes apparent in middle age.

with the least education and those below the poverty level (Bartecchi et al., 1995).

Regular smoking is just one habit that can lead to chronic disorders. Heavy use of any drug, including alcohol, has long-term consequences. As the liver and kidneys age, they become less efficient at clearing unusual amounts of drugs from the body. Cumulative damage to these two organs begins to become apparent in middle age (Rowe, 1982). In 1990, alcohol consumption was linked to approximately 100,000 preventable deaths in the United States; illicit use of other drugs was linked to 20,000 deaths (Bartecchi et al., 1995).

The long-term effects of smoking, alcohol abuse, and habitual use of other drugs are often compounded by other long-term habits, such as poor nutrition and lack of regular exercise. Table 14–2 summarizes some of the lifestyle habits and other factors that contribute to chronic disorders (Weg, 1983).

STRESS AND HEALTH

A person's subjective reaction to an event or situation determines his or her level of stress.

Increasing evidence shows that the way people live has a marked effect on their health. Stress in particular plays a role in many of the diseases of middle age. In the case of heart disease, for example, there is a complex interrelationship among lifestyle, personality, genetic factors, and stress. Because men experience heart disease more often than women, most studies of stress and coronary disease have focused on men.

An important question is what kinds of stress are dangerous. Is just being middle-aged stressful enough? What about the need to redefine goals, adjust to changing family roles, relinquish power to younger competitors, or cope with the first signs of biological aging? Table 14–3 lists potentially stressful events that people encounter throughout life. To determine the stress values in the table, each situation was rated by individuals of all ages for the amount of stress it produced. The death of a spouse, for example, was judged to be the highest stress producer and was assigned a value of 100. At the other extreme, a change in eating habits was rated as only mildly disruptive and assigned a value of only 15. Because middle age is a time when people do lose spouses

TABLE 14–2   DISEASE CONDITIONS AND LIFESTYLES

DISORDERS/DISEASES	LIFESTYLE FACTORS
Diseases of the heart and circulatory system	High-fat, refined-carbohydrate, high-salt diet; overweight; sedentary lifestyle; cigarette smoking; heavy drinking, alcoholism; unresolved, continual stress; personality type
Strokes	Sedentary lifestyle; low-fiber, high-fat, or high-salt diet; heavy drinking, alcoholism (which contribute to atherosclerosis, arteriosclerosis, and hypertension, risk factors for cerebrovascular accidents)
Osteoporosis and dental and gum diseases	Malnutrition—inadequate calcium, protein, vitamin K, fluoride, magnesium, and vitamin D; lack of exercise; immobility; for women, low estrogen
Lung diseases such as emphysema	Cigarette smoking; air pollution; stress; sedentary habits
Obesity	Low caloric output (sedentary lifestyle), high caloric intake; high stress levels; heavy drinking, alcoholism; low self-esteem
Cancer	Possible correlation with personality type; stress; exposure to environmental carcinogens over a long period of time; nutritional deficiencies and excesses; radiation; sex steroid hormones; food additives; cigarette smoking; occupational carcinogens (for example, asbestos); viruses; reduced immunity
Dementia and other forms of memory loss	Malnutrition; long illness and bed rest; drug abuse; anemia; other organ system disease; bereavement; social isolation
Sexual dysfunction	Ignorance (the older individual and society at large); societal stereotypic attitudes; early socialization; inappropriate or no partner; drug effects (for example, antihypertensive drugs); long periods of abstinence; serious disease

Source: From *Aging: Scientific Perspectives and Social Issues*, by D. W. Woodruff and J. E. Birren. Copyright © 1983, 1975 Brooks/Cole Publishing Company, Pacific Grove, CA 93950, a division of International Thomson Publishing Inc. By permission of the publisher.

through death, divorce, and separation, and do suffer changes such as early retirement and illness, it's easy to see that the middle years have the potential for extremely high stress levels.

Stress is not caused solely by life events, however. How an individual perceives and interprets an event plays an important role as well. Researchers have repeatedly pointed out that the same event may cause considerable distress for one person but be viewed as a positive "challenge" by another (Chiriboga & Cutler, 1980; Lazarus, 1981). Occasional exposure to stressful events may be an important stimulus to continuing personality development. Another factor is that if an event is anticipated or expected, it may be less stressful than if it occurs suddenly and without warning. Yet another is that the effects of stressful events are *additive*: If several stressful events occur at the same time, the impact is much worse than if only one or two events occur. To put it another way, the impact of a particular stressful event depends on what other

TABLE 14–3 STRESS SCALE FOR LIFE EVENTS

EVENT	VALUE	EVENT	VALUE
Death of spouse	100	Pregnancy	40
Son or daughter leaving home	29	Change in recreational habits	19
Divorce	73	Sex difficulties	39
Trouble with in-laws	29	Change in church activities	19
Marital separation	65	Addition to family	39
Outstanding personal achievement	28	Change in social activities	18
Jail term	63	Business readjustment	39
Spouse begins or stops work	26	Mortgage or loan under $10,000 [as of 1967]	17
Death of close family member	63	Change in financial status	38
Starting or finishing school	26	Change in sleeping habits	16
Personal injury or illness	53	Death of close friend	37
Change in living conditions	25	Change in number of family gatherings	15
Marriage	50	Change to different line of work	36
Revision of personal habits	24	Change in eating habits	15
Being fired from work	47	Change in number of marital arguments	35
Trouble with boss	23	Vacations	13
Marital reconciliation	45	Mortgage or loan over $10,000 [as of 1967]	31
Change in work hours, conditions	20	Christmas season	12
Retirement	45	Foreclosure of mortgage or loan	30
Change in residence	20	Minor violation of the law	11
Change in family member's health	44	Change in work responsibilities	29
Change in schools	20		

Source: The Social Readjustment Rating Scale, by T. H. Holmes and R. H. Rahe, *Journal of Psychosomatic Research,* 1967, 11(2), 213–218. Copyright 1967, Pergamon Press, Ltd. Reprinted with permission.

conditions are present at the time (such as concerns about money, legal problems, or family life), how seriously the event affects daily routines, and to what extent the event is a personal hazard. Richard Lazarus (1981) suggests that an accumulation of little hassles sometimes is more stressful in the long run than major life changes (see In Theory, In Fact, on facing page).

RACE, POVERTY, AND HEALTH

Minority groups and the poor bear the heaviest burden of disease and death. This burden is present throughout life, but it is especially evident during the middle and older years. In large part, poor health in these populations is linked to a higher incidence of unhealthy behaviors, including smoking, drinking, and drug abuse, as well as obesity. The consequences are devastating. For example, in the 45- to 64-year-old group, the death rate for blacks is nearly twice the rate for whites (Kovar, 1992; National Center for Health Statistics, 1995), although higher murder rates in some lower-income black neighborhoods are also a factor.

In addition to homicides, statistics show that black people are more likely to die from heart disease, hypertension, cancer, diabetes, accidents, and AIDS than are whites. Similarly, Hispanic-Americans have higher death rates from

IN THEORY, IN FACT

LITTLE HASSLES AND STRESS

Have you ever felt like exploding when life's little hassles get to be too much, such as when your friendly neighborhood dry cleaner burned a hole in your new suit or when you spent an hour watching the taillights of the car in front of you instead of the first act of a hit play that you had waited months to see? Minor blowups, frustration, and anger have long been thought to be consequences of petty annoyances like these. But according to Richard Lazarus (1981) and his colleagues at the University of California at Berkeley, the effects of little hassles may be far more serious.

To test this premise and determine whether pleasant, satisfying, and uplifting experiences counterbalance the negative effects of daily hassles, the researchers studied 100 men and women between the ages of 48 and 52 for one year. At the beginning of the study, each person filled out a 24-item life events scale, similar to the one presented in Table 14–3. On a monthly basis, they also completed a 117-item "hassle" checklist and a 135-item "uplift" checklist. To learn how the hassles and uplifts affected the participants' health, questionnaires measuring physical and mental health were completed at the beginning and end of the year, along with other measures of health changes.

The results of this study raise serious doubts about the belief that major

life events are the main sources of stress. According to Lazarus, everyday hassles predict a person's physical and mental health far better than major life events. Study participants who were overburdened with hassles had more mental and physical health problems than those whose lives were relatively calm. In contrast, people who experienced major life events such as divorce or the death of a close relative showed no serious health problems during the period of the study. Participants whose mental and physical health were affected by major life events had experienced these events during the two-and-a-half years before the study began. Thus, although there is a link between major life events and long-term health, little hassles seem to determine well-being in the short term.

That's not to say that major life events and hassles are unrelated. Divorce, the death of a spouse, or even marriage can have a ripple effect that creates a seemingly inexhaustible supply of little hassles. A man who divorces after 30 years of marriage may find, for example, that he has difficulty coping with cooking his own meals, cleaning his own house, and having no readily available sex partner. Of course, not everyone responds to daily frustrations in the same way. Personality and coping style affect the way we respond. In addition, Lazarus found that frequency, duration, and intensity of stress interact to determine whether we feel overwhelmed. Misplace a wal-

let or a purse or get a splinter in your foot; then you'll be less prepared to cope with a notice from the bank that a check bounced.

Do the small uplifts of life help? Do news of a raise or the good feelings we get from our families offset the pressures that everyday hassles cause? Unfortunately, the study found that daily uplifts do little to compensate.

Lazarus's Top 10 Hassles and Uplifts

Hassles
1. Concern about weight
2. Health of a family member
3. Rising prices of common goods
4. Home maintenance
5. Too many things to do
6. Misplacing or losing things
7. Yard work or outside home maintenance
8. Property, investment, or taxes
9. Crime
10. Physical appearance

Uplifts
1. Relating well with your spouse or lover
2. Relating well with friends
3. Completing a task
4. Feeling healthy
5. Getting enough sleep
6. Eating out
7. Meeting responsibilities
8. Visiting, phoning, or writing someone
9. Spending time with family
10. Having a home pleasing to you

infectious and parasitic diseases, diabetes, hypertension, and AIDS than European-Americans (National Center for Health Statistics, 1990, 1995).

A number of social factors are responsible for these differences. Although medical and lifestyle interventions can reduce the effects of many diseases, African-Americans and Hispanic-Americans tend to underutilize the health care system until they are in a state of emergency (and therefore won't be turned away from hospital emergency rooms). Higher levels of poverty, along with lack of health insurance, discourage some members of these groups from taking advantage of health screenings, physical examinations, and other early detection methods (Harlan et al., 1991; Kravitz et al., 1990; Solis et al., 1990).

Hispanic-Americans in particular are less likely to have private health insurance than either whites or African-Americans, and twice as many Hispanic-Americans as whites use hospital emergency rooms as their primary source of health care. Hispanic-Americans' access to preventive health care is also made more difficult by cultural and language barriers. Studies have shown that English-speaking Hispanic-Americans are more likely to have a regular source of medical care than Hispanic-Americans who speak only Spanish (Council on Scientific Affairs, 1991).

Poor health habits that lead to increased risk factors are inextricably linked to a sense of hopelessness and to life in difficult social conditions (Williams, 1992). Cigarettes, alcohol, drugs, and overeating help people cope with daily stresses, which is one reason why the incidence of such bad habits is higher in minority groups. One researcher looking at smoking noted that for African-Americans, cigarettes "make it possible to get up and face the world, to calm down when tension becomes too great to bear" (Mausner, 1973). According to an American Cancer Society study, one-third of African-Americans smoke to relieve stress (U.S. Department of Health and Human Services, 1985). Thus, there is a trade-off: Although these health habits may have negative long-term consequences, they provide the poor and disadvantaged with immediate physiological and psychological compensations that enable them to cope with the stresses of their daily lives (Williams, 1992).

REVIEW & APPLY

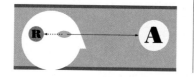

1. Identify the major diseases that affect middle-aged adults, and discuss the relationship between poor health habits and the onset of these problems.
2. Discuss how stress affects health in middle age.
3. Why do minority groups and the poor bear the heaviest burden of health problems?

COGNITIVE CONTINUITY AND CHANGE

Longitudinal studies have repeatedly indicated that aging is accompanied by decline in cognitive functioning, but we now know that the decline is much more gradual than researchers assumed as recently as 20 years ago. Serious cognitive decline occurs later than was previously thought, and then only in certain areas of intellectual functioning. Some aspects of intelligence actually increase during middle age and beyond, especially for college-educated adults who remain active (Schaie, 1983, 1995). Contrary to the stereotype that intellectual development peaks in adolescence or young adulthood, the development of some cognitive abilities continues throughout the middle years, especially in areas related to work and daily living (Willis, 1989).

FLUID VERSUS CRYSTALLIZED INTELLIGENCE

One way of looking at cognitive changes in middle and older adulthood was proposed by John Horn (1982), who distinguished between **fluid intelligence** and **crystallized intelligence.** Both types contribute to IQ test scores, but they can be analyzed separately. Fluid intelligence consists of abilities that we apply to new learning, including memorizing, reasoning inductively, and per-

fluid intelligence A broad area of intelligence that encompasses the abilities used in new learning, including memorization, inductive reasoning, and the rapid perception of spatial relationships. This form of intelligence is believed to reach its peak in late adolescence.

crystallized intelligence A broad area of intelligence that includes making judgments, analyzing problems, and drawing conclusions from experienced-based information and knowledge. This form of intelligence, which is drawn from education and the broader culture, increases across the lifespan.

ceiving new relationships between objects and events. The term *fluid intelligence* is a metaphor suggesting that these basic processes "flow into" various other intellectual activities, including recognizing, learning, analyzing, and solving problems (Horn, 1982; Neugarten, 1976). Fluid intelligence has been thought to increase until late adolescence or early adulthood and then decline gradually throughout the remainder of the lifespan, paralleling changes in the efficiency and integrity of the nervous system (Horn, 1982).

In contrast, crystallized intelligence is the knowledge that comes with education and life experiences in general; it is the body of knowledge and information that a person accumulates over the years. As with fluid intelligence, it is used in finding new relationships, making judgments, and analyzing problems, but it differs in that previously learned strategies are employed to a greater extent. People acquire this form of intelligence through formal education as well as daily contact with their culture. Unlike fluid intelligence, crystallized intelligence tends to increase over the lifespan in people who are free from brain damage, as long as they remain alert and capable of taking in and recording information (Neugarten, 1976). When people are tested for skills involving this kind of intelligence, they often score higher in their fifties than they do in their twenties. This finding helps explain why scholars and scientists, whose work is based on a great deal of accumulated knowledge and experience, are usually more productive in their forties, fifties, and even sixties and seventies than they were in their twenties (Dennis, 1966; Simonton, 1990). Thus, in a sense, increasing crystallized intelligence compensates for declining fluid intelligence.

RESEARCH PROBLEMS What evidence is there for the decline in fluid intelligence and the increase in crystallized intelligence? This isn't an easy research problem, and, as with all research problems, the results depend on how we study it. In Chapters 1 and 13 we talked about some of the differences between longitudinal and cross-sectional studies. Remember that longitudinal studies involve repeated measures of the same individuals over time, whereas cross-sectional studies involve measures of different individuals of different ages. In studying intelligence in adulthood, Horn and his colleagues (1980) used a cross-sectional approach with several different types of tests. As shown in Figure 14–1, measures of vocabulary, general information, and an element called

According to Lazarus, home maintenance is one of life's top hassles.

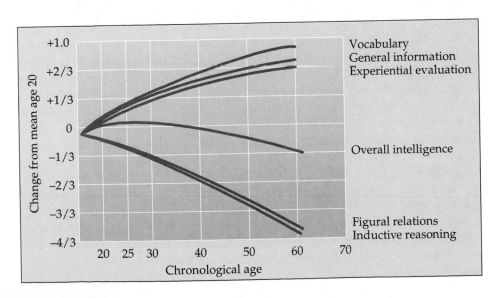

FIGURE 14–1

Comparison of changes in fluid and crystallized intelligence during adulthood.

According to Lazarus, a pleasing home environment is one of life's top emotional uplifts.

experiential evaluation were much higher for individuals in their forties and fifties than for individuals in their twenties and thirties. On the other hand, measures of figural relations and inductive reasoning were much lower for people in their fifties and sixties than for younger people (Horn & Donaldson, 1980).

Recall, however, that in a cross-sectional study, the individuals at each age level are from a different cohort. They were born in different eras and have had different life experiences. Younger cohorts are better educated, have better health, and have had better nutrition over a longer period. Older cohorts have been educated in a very different fashion than the younger cohorts. They may have had an education that emphasized certain types of intellectual abilities over others; for example, in the early twentieth century, educators placed much more emphasis on rote memorization of facts than on understanding what was being memorized.

So what happens when we use a longitudinal approach? The results vary somewhat from one study to the next, but in well-educated populations, many of the tested abilities generally continue to rise. According to a broad-based study conducted by Warner Schaie (1983, 1995), it appears that several different kinds of intellectual abilities, both fluid and crystallized, either increase or are maintained throughout much of adulthood, declining only after age 60. Recall, however, that there are problems with extended longitudinal studies as well. It is difficult to get subjects to come back and be tested again and again—some refuse to participate further; some become ill; some die. Comparisons of people who continue participating with those who drop out indicate that the dropouts score lower, on average, at the earlier testings. Therefore, the increase in certain scores may be due to the loss of a disproportionate number of low scorers.

What if we look at individual changes rather than at averages? By and large, we find that between 45% and 60% of people maintain a stable level of overall intellectual performance—both fluid and crystallized—well into their seventies. Some people (10 to 15%) often show increases in performance until their mid-seventies. A slightly larger group (roughly 30%) declines, at least by the time they reach their sixties.

Individuals thus vary considerably in intellectual growth and decline. Some show declines in word fluency and numerical reasoning, but not in other cognitive areas. A few remain stable or actually show increases on tests that involve verbal and numerical skills. Notably, inductive reasoning does not seem to decline any more dramatically than other abilities (Schaie, 1983). In all, losses during middle age are very limited. Indeed, there are often increases in full-scale intelligence test scores until the late thirties or early forties, followed by a period of relative stability until the middle fifties or early sixties. On average, it now appears that only word fluency and numerical reasoning show any statistically significant declines before age 60 (Schaie, 1990).

IMPLICATIONS FOR INTELLECTUAL FUNCTIONING Thus, it appears that many adults maintain a high level of functioning across a broad spectrum of intellectual abilities throughout middle age. There are also wide individual differences. Some of the abilities that are classified as fluid intelligence do decline somewhat more rapidly in some individuals, but such declines are not an inevitable consequence of aging. In one study, the decline was clearly found to be related to the complexity of individuals' lives. People who had more opportunity for environmental stimulation, greater satisfaction with life, less noise in their environment, an intact family, a lot of social interaction, and ongoing cultural influences showed longer maintenance of and even increases in intellectual abilities (Schaie, 1983).

There is one factor that does seem to decline in middle adulthood, however. Skills that require speed become increasingly difficult as people grow older—various psychomotor processes gradually begin to slow down because of physical/neurological decline. Middle-aged adults compensate for declines in speed with increases in efficiency and general knowledge (Salthouse, 1990). Intellectual activities that are well practiced and used regularly in daily problem solving or in work settings are maintained at high levels of efficiency (Botwinick, 1977).

People adapt their intellectual development to meet environmental demands. To succeed at a particular job or within a certain social network, a person may emphasize the development of some skills while neglecting others (Lerner, 1990). This tendency may be one reason why many middle-aged and older people perform more poorly than young adults on tests of abstract reasoning (Labouvie-Vief, 1985). They tend to place problems in context and make them concrete, thinking in terms of practical meaning and downplaying abstract reasoning—to the detriment of their test scores.

It is clear that one of the central influences on cognition in middle adulthood is the wealth of past life experience. Thus, if you think about it, it's a bit odd to conduct learning and memory studies comparing college students and older people on tests that use exclusively novel tasks and new, perhaps meaningless, information, as most studies do. They do so, however, to avoid confounding accumulated knowledge with "basic" abilities to think and reason. College students are in a period of life in which coping with new information is an important adaptive skill. People in middle adulthood function best when they can use the wealth of background and experience that they have accumulated (Labouvie-Vief, 1985). Thus, rather than measuring the cognitive capacities of middle-aged adults according to strategies appropriate to young adults, perhaps we should measure adult cognition in terms of experience and expertise (Salthouse, 1987).

Apparently, many middle-aged adults continue to function on a high intellectual level.

Experience is one factor that enables middle-aged adults to continue being productive.

EXPERIENCE AND EXPERTISE

As we've just seen, some aspects of cognitive functioning do gradually decline starting in middle age; how is it that so many of us—especially those in leadership positions—remain competent at work? How do aging experts differ from youthful novices? Given that the person remains intellectually active, age brings *more* knowledge—both **declarative** (factual) and **procedural** (action or "how-to" information)—through deliberate practice and refinement of skills.

Expertise, then, compensates for cognitive decline in middle age. Extensive research supports this view. Expert knowledge is better organized; there are more interconnections between units of information, such as schemas. Expert skills display more in the way of *automaticity* (Chapter 6), thus freeing up conscious brain power at the same time that certain abilities in memory and concentration may be declining. Experts quickly and easily recognize patterns and link these to appropriate procedures and responses (Glaser, 1987). This process applies across the board, to experts as diverse as physicists, computer programmers, musicians, bridge players, cooks, and gardeners.

Although experts remember relevant and crucial information better, however, they do not differ from novices in recalling material that is unorganized, unstructured, or unrelated to a particular problem. A study of chess players illustrates this point. Subjects were classified as older versus younger and as expert versus intermediate in ability, and there were two tasks. The subjects were first shown chess boards with a game in progress and asked to remember the position of every piece. The younger chess players did better on this task than the older ones, but skill level was not a factor. Then the subjects were asked to make an appropriate move. The experts (both old and young) were much better at this task, since they did not need to remember where all the pieces were to make a good move. Experts' memory was selective and organized, and focused on connections between the patterns of the pieces and the appropriate moves (Charness, 1981; Salthouse, 1987).

Experience, then, doesn't guarantee the maintenance of a particular skill—the older chess players could not remember the position of every piece. Older

declarative knowledge
Factual knowledge; knowing "what."

procedural knowledge Action knowledge; knowing "how to."

typists are slower under controlled conditions; older architects suffer losses in visual-spatial skills (Salthouse et al., 1990). But experience compensates. The more experienced architect knows almost automatically which building materials will work best. The older typist may read longer spans of words, thereby maintaining speedy typing. These compensations allow adults in their middle and later years to remain productive at work (Salthouse, 1990). The opportunities provided by the environment to develop and practice these compensations clearly influence functioning. These findings show that development often involves a trade-off: As one skill declines, another improves (Baltes, 1987).

In sum, elements of expertise include continuing development of competence; knowledge and skills that are specific to a particular area or field; knowledge that is highly procedural or goal-oriented; rapid recognition that minimizes the need for an extensive memory search; and generalized thinking and problem-solving skills (Glaser, 1987). Again, extended experience tends to increase not only the amount of information but also its organization. Individuals continually restructure their knowledge system to make it more cohesive, correct, and accessible. This process may be true for common knowledge, such as how to use the Yellow Pages, or for occupational knowledge, such as how to perform a technical procedure more efficiently. Cognitive tests rarely measure experiential influences on the knowledge and problem solving of older adults (Salthouse, 1987).

COGNITIVE SKILLS IN CONTEXT

For most middle-aged adults, the context for continued development of cognitive skills is the workplace. Adults' cognitive abilities are closely linked to the demands of their job. Those who are continually challenged by complexity in their work achieve higher scores on tests of intellectual flexibility than those who perform routine work (Kohn, 1980; Kohn & Schooler, 1983, 1990). That is, adults with a high degree of *occupational self-direction*—regular use of thought, initiative, and independent judgment—also have a high degree of intellectual flexibility (Schooler, 1987).

Increasingly, workers need flexibility in today's workplace. Technological change demands that most of us learn new skills, either to keep our jobs or to find new ones (see Eye on Diversity, page 506). Middle-aged adults who have the cognitive ability and skill to learn new tasks and the flexibility to take on more challenging assignments are better able to meet the demands of a changing workplace (Willis, 1989). This capacity is especially true in fields such as medicine, engineering, and computer technology, in which knowledge quickly becomes obsolete as new requirements and changes in the disciplines occur. With regard to computers in particular, keeping up with hardware, operating systems, and new programs is almost a full-time job in itself. In fact, as much as half of a computer scientist's knowledge may be obsolete within only two to three years (Cross, 1981; Dubin, 1972).

The concept of obsolescence is particularly important in middle age because formal schooling typically ends years earlier, yet the length of time most adults are involved in active work has increased dramatically in the last century. In today's rapidly changing workplace, obsolescence is almost inevitable if workers don't adapt to new technology and methods. Whereas in 1900, the average adult spent 21 years in the labor force, by 1980, that figure had jumped to 37 years. In addition, the work years are now marked by multiple job changes requiring the latest knowledge and skills. As a result, "the relevant knowledge one needs in one's career cannot be fully obtained in the years of formal schooling. The individual must continue to update throughout the adult

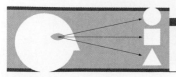

EYE ON DIVERSITY

BACK TO SCHOOL AT MIDDLE AGE

Visualize a "typical" college student. What do you see? A young adult? Someone who has gone straight from high school to college? Someone who is still supported by his or her parents during an "extended adolescence"? Someone who is a full-time student? The answer is not necessarily any of these choices. Although today's college campuses are filled with 18- to 22-year-olds, they are also filled with older, nontraditional students who return to school. More than 2.8 million people over age 35 are attending college—in 2-year programs, 4-year programs, and graduate school. From 1980 to 1995, the number of students over age 35 increased by 46% (U.S. Census Bureau, 1997).

This dramatic trend coincides with the recognition that humans are lifelong learners with cognitive abilities that adapt to life's demands. Despite societal stereotypes that the time for education is over after adolescence and young adulthood, middle-aged adults often need to gain the information and skills required to meet the changing demands of their jobs (Willis, 1989). This need is as true for bankers as it is for computer scientists, both of whom work in fields that have changed radically in recent years.

Although some middle-aged students are there to gain self-enrichment or to complete the education they abandoned earlier, many are there because they have to be. Some are unemployed—victims of corporate downsizing. Others, both men and women, are moving into the job market after spending many years at home as full-time parents. A financial planner who stopped working for five years to raise her daughter may need to be recertified before a firm will hire her. Even adults who worked part-time during their child-rearing years may have to return to school to acquire the knowledge and skills they need to qualify for a full-time job. This situation is especially true in fields with a high degree of professional obsolescence. Whatever the reason for their return, however, studies show that the majority of middle-aged students are conscientious about their work. They attend classes regularly and get better grades, on average, than other segments of the college student population (Saslow, 1981).

Returning to school requires many adjustments, and usually the support of other family members. It also involves a personal assessment of one's skills and abilities. The student role is generally very different from other roles that middle-aged adults have assumed; considerable adaptation may be necessary to become a student who is subordinate to younger faculty members. Mature adults also find themselves among a large number of students who are considerably younger than they are, and the age difference may be disconcerting. Self-doubt is also common when the older student returns to the school environment and must perform unfamiliar tasks in a prescribed fashion.

In the past, colleges and universities sometimes made it difficult for older students to succeed (Women's Reentry Project, 1981). Some middle-aged adults had trouble arranging time for other responsibilities because of rigid, full-time class schedules. Appropriate counseling was not always available, and the older part-time student often found that transferring credits, obtaining financial aid, and even gaining admission were geared exclusively to the needs of 18- to 22-year-old full-time students.

Nowadays the situation has changed at most colleges. With the realization that nontraditional students are here to stay and that they are increasingly important in maintaining enrollments, many colleges and universities have made substantial adjustments to meet their needs. Some schools have evening programs for nontraditional students; others attempt to incorporate them into the mainstream by offering a full program of day, evening, and weekend courses that are available to all students, both traditional and nontraditional.

---

years" (Willis, 1987). Fortunately, continued cognitive development is possible in middle age in area of ability that are "exercised" regularly on the job, especially in careers that involve complex decision making and independent judgment—both of which can foster cognitive development (Willis, 1989).

FUNCTIONAL CHANGES IN COGNITION

Another way to look at adult cognitive development is to consider *functional* changes. Schaie (1977–1978) has suggested that it is the function, not the nature, of intelligence that changes over time. Recall from Chapter 12 that the young adult is in the *achieving* stage. Intelligence is used primarily to solve real-life problems with long-term implications, such as selecting a job or a spouse. In middle age, we enter the *responsibility* stage. Now responsibilities to spouse, children, coworkers, and the community play a major role in decision making. For some middle-aged people, this stage takes a somewhat different form and is called the *executive* stage, which applies to people managers, government officials, and corporate executives, whose decisions affect many people's lives.

In old age, the uses of intellect shift again. In the *reintegrative* stage, people get back in touch with their own interests, values, and attitudes. They may balk at performing tasks such as IQ tests, which have little relevance for daily living. They can think abstractly, but they don't typically engage in solving such problems just for the sake of doing them, as young adults might.

Thus, intellectual changes, especially during the middle years, mainly consist of a person's orientation and emphasis in how intelligence is applied; they definitely do not constitute intellectual decline.

1. Describe the differences between fluid and crystallized intelligence.
2. What is the relationship between adult cognitive functioning, and technological change and professional obsolescence?
3. What role does experience play in cognitive development and functioning during middle age?

REVIEW & APPLY

SUMMARY

Development in Middle Age

- Developmental theorists differ considerably on the question of when middle age begins and when it ends. Much depends on the life experiences that the person is going through.
- Several different sets of cues are associated with aging. These include social and family status, physical and biological changes, and psychological cues.
- Economic conditions, social class, and the times in which people live affect how they view middle age.
- Most people experience a sense of ambivalence during middle age. It may be the prime of life, but most people have recurrent thoughts about how their time is running out.
- Although some researchers believe that most adults experience a midlife crisis, the transition model views development as marked by a series of expected major life events that can be anticipated and planned for.
- Middle age is a time when people begin to take stock of their lives. Some may feel effective and competent; others find it painful to examine their lives.
- Those who are most likely to experience a midlife crisis tend to avoid introspection and use denial to

avoid thinking about their changing bodies and lives.

Physical Continuity and Change

- The most obvious changes associated with the middle years are physical ones.
- Visual capabilities are fairly stable until the forties or early fifties and then decline. Hearing becomes less acute after age 20 and declines gradually. Taste, smell, and sensitivity to pain decline more gradually and less noticeably.
- Reaction time and sensorimotor skills are likely to slow down, but performance remains constant as a result of continuing practice and experience.
- Internal changes include a slowing down of the nervous system, stiffening and shrinking of the skeleton, and loss of elasticity in the skin and muscles.
- For women, the most dramatic internal change is menopause—cessation of ovulation and menstruation. This is part of the climacteric, the overall complex of physical and emotional effects that accompany hormonal changes in middle age.
- Menopause is accompanied by physical symptoms such as hot flashes and night sweats. Some women

also experience emotional changes such as feelings of depression. Research indicates that most women do not respond negatively to menopause.

■ The estrogen loss that accompanies menopause produces loss of bone mass (osteoporosis) and thinning and drying of vaginal tissue. There may also be increased risk of coronary disease.

■ For men, there is no single, relatively abrupt event comparable to menopause, but men do undergo changes in sexual interest and activity, depending on the individual's personality and lifestyle.

■ Frequency of sexual activity generally slows down in middle age. Nevertheless, many healthy individuals enjoy satisfying sex lives throughout this period. For many adults, sexuality is redefined to place more emphasis on a range of physical expressions such as hugging, hand holding, and stroking.

Health and Disease

■ Many losses of function associated with aging can be stopped or slowed, and much of the cognitive decline experienced by older people is attributable to treatable diseases.

■ Major diseases of middle age include cardiovascular diseases, cancer, diabetes, respiratory diseases, and HIV-related diseases. (See the Study Chart on page 495.)

■ In part, longevity is attributable to good health habits: a balanced and nutritious diet, a reasonable amount of exercise, and regular health care.

■ Poor health habits during early adulthood take their toll in middle age. Those habits include smoking, alcohol abuse, and habitual use of other drugs.

■ Stress plays a role in many of the diseases of middle age. Major life events such as the death of a spouse produce stress, but their impact depends on how the individual perceives and interprets them. Moreover, an accumulation of little hassles sometimes is more stressful in the long run than major life events.

■ Poor health in minority populations is linked to a higher incidence of unhealthy behaviors. In addition, minorities tend to underutilize the health care system until they are in a state of emergency.

Cognitive Continuity and Change

■ John Horn distinguishes between fluid and crystallized intelligence. Fluid intelligence consists of abilities that we apply to new learning, whereas crystallized intelligence is the knowledge that comes with education and life experiences.

■ Unlike fluid intelligence, crystallized intelligence tends to increase over the lifespan as long as the person remains alert and capable of taking in and recording information.

■ Most people maintain a stable level of overall intellectual performance well into their seventies, but individuals vary considerably in intellectual growth and decline.

■ Declines in fluid intelligence appear to be related to the complexity of individuals' lives. Environmental stimulation, satisfaction with life, an intact family, and similar factors help maintain intellectual abilities.

■ Skills that require speed become increasingly difficult as people grow older.

■ Expertise compensates for cognitive decline in middle age. Experts quickly and easily recognize patterns and link these to appropriate procedures and responses.

■ Elements of expertise include continuing development of competence; knowledge and skills that are specific to a particular area or field; knowledge that is highly procedural or goal-oriented; rapid recognition; and generalized thinking and problem-solving skills.

■ For most middle-aged adults, the context for continued development of cognitive skills is the workplace. Adults with a high degree of occupational self-direction also have a high degree of intellectual flexibility, which is increasingly necessary in the modern workplace.

■ According to Schaie, there are several functional changes in adult cognitive development. In the achieving stage, intelligence is used primarily to solve real-life problems; in the responsibility or executive stage, responsibilities to others play a major role in decision making; in the regenerative stage, people get back in touch with their own interests, values, and attitudes.

KEY TERMS

transition model	climacteric	crystallized intelligence
crisis model	osteoporosis	declarative knowledge
menopause	fluid intelligence	procedural knowledge

USING WHAT YOU'VE LEARNED

It is sometimes difficult to separate myth from reality. Nowadays, as people live longer and are in better health, we find that some of our impressions of middle age—those perpetuated in the media and popular literature—are too narrow, exaggerated, or simply mistaken.

Make a list of adjectives about middle age that come quickly to mind. Do your first impressions fit the concepts of midlife crisis, "the beginning of the end," and the stereotypes and myths associated with middle age? Are the characteristics on your list consistent with the research results presented in this chapter? Do they accurately fit neighbors and family members who are in middle adulthood?

SUGGESTED READINGS

CUTLER, W. B., & GARCIA, C. R. (1992). *Menopause: A guide for women and those who love them* (revised ed.). New York: Norton. An informative guide to women's health, with particular attention to symptoms of menopause and the health choices that women make.

GALLAGHER, W. (1993). Midlife myths. *The Atlantic* (May), 51–55, 58–65, 68–69. A refreshing, well-researched article about the facts and fiction of middle age.

GARDNER, H. (1993). *Creating minds: An anatomy of creativity seen through the lives of Freud, Einstein, Picasso, Stravinsky, Eliot, Graham and Gandhi.* New York: Basic Books. This scientist, humanist, and scholar, who has spent a lifetime looking at the emergence of human thought, takes a new look at creative genius. This engaging analysis and biography provides a fresh look at expertise and generativity.

GENOVESE, R. G. (1997). *Americans at midlife: Caught between generations.* New York: Bergin and Garvey. In a scholarly but readable presentation, Rosalie Genovese explores the middle years within the framework of trends in the larger society. Trends include longer life expectancy, an aging population, changes in marriage, divorce, and family composition and the growth of the two-income family.

HUNTER, S., & SUNDEL, M. (1989). *Midlife myths: Issues, findings, and practice implications.* Newbury Park, CA: Sage. An excellent collection of scholarly reviews of several aspects of middle age.

McCRAE, R. P., & COSTA, P. T. (1990). *Personality in adulthood.* New York: Guilford Press. This updated presentation of these authors contains theory and research that emphasizes continuity of personality characteristics.

NOTELOVITZ, M., & TONNESSEN, D. (1993). *Menopause and midlife health.* New York: St. Martin's Press. A leading medical authority presents this comprehensive guide to women's health in midlife. Nutrition, exercise, stress, and alcohol and drug issues, as well as the many facets of menopause, hormone replacement therapy, cancer risk, and many more topics, are fully explored.

OPPENHEIM, M. (1994). *The man's health book.* Englewood Cliffs, NJ: Prentice Hall. A helpful comprehensive guide for men of all ages.

SHEEHY, G. (1998). *The Silent Passage.* New York: Pocket Books. This pocketbook edition of Gail Sheehy's bestseller is candid, inspiring, and witty and covers everything from early menopause to Chinese remedies.

Middle-Aged Adults: Personality Development and Socialization

CHAPTER

15

CHAPTER OBJECTIVES

By the time you have finished this chapter, you should be able to do the following:

1. Identify the major developmental tasks that occur in middle age.
2. Describe some of the major problems that middle-aged people face as the parents of young adult children.
3. Describe some of the major problems that middle-aged people face as the children of aging parents.
4. Discuss the problems and issues of divorce and remarriage in middle adulthood.
5. Discuss the problems and issues of reconstituted families.
6. Explain some of the major occupational changes that take place during middle age, including career reassessment, burnout, and job loss.

The title of a book by Robert Kegan is *In Over Our Heads* (1995). He uses this phrase to describe the complexity of adult roles and responsibilities in the modern world. As the comments on the book jacket put it, "If contemporary culture were a school, with all the tasks and expectations meted out by modern life as its curriculum, would anyone graduate?" This view is especially apt during middle age, which is a time when adults try to make sense of the continually changing demands of parenting, shifting roles in intimate relationships, and the changing world of work, as well as issues in the world at large, such as racism, sexism, and emerging technologies—altogether a bewildering array of concerns.

Although it can be argued that there is little firm ground on which to stand during middle adulthood as life events race by and trigger a continual stream of social and cognitive changes, it can also be argued that the middle adult years are a period of continuity in personality and outlook. Even when we experience an onslaught of external changes and major life events, internal change can be gradual.

It is in the context of continuity and change during the middle years that reflection and reassessment occur. Between the ages of 40 and 65, we mentally rewrite our autobiographies as we go. We review our life scripts as we experience major events and transitions (the death of a parent, a friend's serious illness, a new job, the birth of a midlife baby, the "launching" of the youngest child into high school or college). We take stock, contemplate our own mortality (especially when a relative or friend dies or becomes critically ill), and sort out our values in a continuing attempt to decide what really matters in life. As we reflect, we think less about how long we have lived and more about how much time we have left.

These reflections and reassessments take place within the context of three interconnecting worlds: self, family, and work (see Chapter 13). Each adult expresses his or her development uniquely in each of these areas. For example, those who choose to have a child at 40, to enter and leave the workforce many times during a career, or to divorce and remarry will have vastly different lifestyles and experiences than those who have children early, have a steady career, and maintain a lifelong commitment to one spouse.

This chapter examines the complexity of psychosocial development during middle age, focusing on interpersonal relationships and work. Change—and the need to adjust to it—are constant during this period, as is a reordering of our notion of the way things ought to be. For example, it is during middle age that many families must adjust to the aftermath of divorce, the demands of stepfamilies, and unemployment. We begin by looking at personality continuity and change during the middle years.

PERSONALITY CONTINUITY AND CHANGE

In discussing the events of adulthood, most theories refer to role shifts, marker events, milestones, critical issues, and developmental tasks. The specific expression of these elements of continuity and change is tied to the family life cycle and to a model of development based on the timing of events. Certain developmental tasks define middle age, although the tasks of early and late adulthood may be mingled with those of middle age. These tasks also differ for men and women.

THE TASKS OF MIDDLE AGE

Numerous recent studies have provided evidence that the course of midlife is extremely diverse and varied (Lachman & James, 1997) and at times tumultuous. In other words, middle-aged adults "grow" too, often as a result of physical and social stressors (Fiske & Chiriboga, 1990).

Carl Jung (1933/1960) was one of the first theorists to emphasize the second half of life: He believed that older people mainly need to find meaning in their lives. Since then, various models of adult development have been proposed that emphasize how much more complex the middle and later years can be. Most middle-aged people have adolescent or young adult children and aging parents (Troll, 1989). However, an increasing number of people, including those in their forties with very young children, experience many normative life events at a later age than most others in their generation. Having young children in middle age is particularly common among career women who decide late in life to become mothers, and among divorced men who marry younger women who want children of their own. These middle-aged adults tend to share activities and establish friendships with others who are at the same stage of the family life cycle, even though they are older chronologically.

GENERATIVITY VERSUS SELF-ABSORPTION   According to Erik Erikson (1981), the basic issue facing people at this time of life is *generativity versus self-absorption*. With regard to generativity, Erikson suggests that people act within three domains: a *procreative* one, by giving and responding to the needs of the next generation; a *productive* one, by integrating work with family life and caring for the next generation; and a *creative* one, by contributing to society on a larger scale. In addition, generativity is traditionally expressed in women through prosocial activities, work, and immersion in parenting and caring for other loved ones (Peterson & Klohnen, 1995). More recent research provides further evidence that women's generativity is often expressed across multiple roles, including both family and work roles (MacDermid et al., 1997).

The alternative for both men and women is self-absorption and a sense of stagnation and boredom. Some people fail to find value in helping the next

Increasingly, middle-aged adults are becoming the parents of young children, thereby experiencing normative life events at an older age than most of their peers.

generation and have recurrent feelings of living an unsatisfying life. They also lack much in the way of accomplishments or devalue whatever accomplishments they have (Monte, 1987).

Havighurst's model as it applies to middle age (Chapter 12) is distinctly similar to Erikson's. Both models emphasize the importance of establishing increasingly complex relationships with others and of adjusting to the many changes that middle age brings. According to Erikson, however, the most important responsibilities of this period are derived from the simple fact of being literally "in the middle" of life, sandwiched between an older generation and a younger one. We'll return to the implications of this later in the chapter.

PECK'S EXTENSION OF ERIKSON'S THEORY   As summarized in Chapter 1, Erikson described a lifelong process of development consisting of eight stages. We have dealt with the first six earlier and will cover the seventh stage here. But the later years present other important issues as well. Robert Peck (1968) has been especially concerned with expanding Erikson's picture of the second half of the lifespan.

Peck's main criticism of Erikson is that the eight stages place too much emphasis on childhood, adolescence, and young adulthood. The six developmental issues of those periods—trust versus mistrust, autonomy versus shame and doubt, initiative versus guilt, industry versus inferiority, ego identity versus ego diffusion, and intimacy versus isolation—all pose important crises that each individual must resolve in the early years. Peck suggests that far too many new issues and tasks arise in the middle and older years to be summed up in two stages: generativity versus self-absorption and later *integrity versus despair* (when older people look back and evaluate their lives; see Chapter 17).

During these later years, all of the earlier issues and their resolutions reappear from time to time—especially during times of stress or change. A sudden physical impairment such as a heart attack may revive struggles with autonomy and dependence in a 45-year-old. The death of a spouse may renew strong intimacy needs in the survivor. In fact, each major life adjustment may

By middle age, some people may rearrange their priorities, for example, an individual may decide to switch careers—to be an artist rather than an accountant, a teacher rather than an advertising executive.

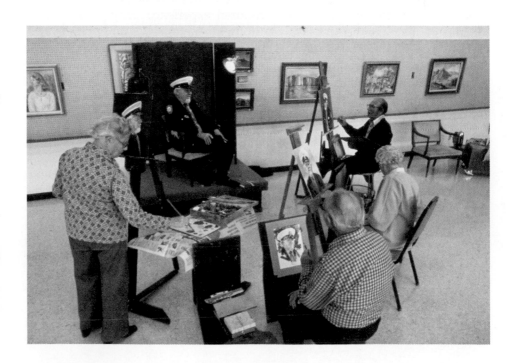

necessitate reevaluations and revisions of earlier solutions. Erikson believed that when we are uprooted by such major life circumstances as the death of a spouse, we *must* revisit issues of basic trust, autonomy, initiative, identity, and intimacy before we can pursue adult generativity.

In accounting for the special challenges of adult life, Peck proposes seven issues or conflicts of adult development; these are summarized in Table 15–1. The first four issues are particularly important in middle age; the latter three become important in old age, although the individual is already beginning to deal with them during middle age.

Like Erikson's stages, none of Peck's issues are strictly confined to middle age or old age. The decisions made early in life act as building blocks for all the solutions of the adult years, and middle-aged people are already starting to resolve the issues of old age. In fact, research suggests that the period from age 50 to age 60 is often a critical time for making adjustments that will determine the way people live out the rest of their lives (Peck & Berkowitz, 1964).

TABLE 15–1   PECK'S ISSUES (CONFLICTS) OF ADULT DEVELOPMENT

MIDDLE AGE

Valuing wisdom versus valuing physical powers: As physical stamina and health begin to wane, people must shift much of their energy from physical activities to mental ones.

Socializing versus sexualizing in human relationships: This, too, is an adjustment imposed by social constraints as well as by biological changes. Physical changes may force people to redefine their relationships with members of both sexes—to stress companionship rather than sexual intimacy or competitiveness.

Cathectic (emotional) flexibility versus cathectic impoverishment: Emotional flexibility underlies the various adjustments that people must make in middle age as families split up, friends move away, and old interests cease being the central focus of life.

Mental flexibility versus mental rigidity: Individuals must fight the inclination to become too set in their ways or too distrustful of new ideas. Mental rigidity is the tendency to become dominated by past experiences and former judgments—to decide, for example, that "I've disapproved of Republicans (or Democrats or Independents) all my life, so I don't see why I should change my mind now."

OLD AGE

Ego differentiation versus work-role preoccupation: If people define themselves exclusively in terms of job or family, such events as retirement, a change in occupation, a divorce, or a child's leaving home will create a gulf in which they are likely to flounder. Ego differentiation means defining yourself as a person in ways that go beyond what work you do or what family roles you fulfill.

Body transcendence versus body preoccupation: This centers on the individual's ability to avoid becoming preoccupied with the increasing aches, pains, and physical annoyances that accompany the aging process.

Ego transcendence versus ego preoccupation: This is particularly important in old age. It requires that people not become mired in thoughts of death (the "night of the ego," as Peck calls it). People who age successfully transcend the prospect of their own mortality by becoming involved in the younger generation—the legacy that will outlive them.

PERSONAL REACTIONS TO MIDDLE AGE

In middle age, both men and women reassess their goals and reflect on whether their original goals have been met. They made choices and established themselves in careers in young adulthood, but by middle age they often take a second look at their choices. Most people then realize that they have made career choices that they must live with for better or worse. Some who are dissatisfied with their work or are unemployed or have not advanced as far as they had hoped become bitter and discouraged. Others simply rearrange their priorities. For example, some people at midlife may decide to direct more attention to family and other interpersonal or even moral commitments and less to occupational development (Fiske, 1980).

MEN'S REACTIONS TO MIDDLE AGE   In one study of attitudes toward family, work, and physical self (Farrell & Rosenberg, 1981), researchers interviewed 300 middle-aged men. They found that men react to middle age in individual ways but with some similarities. Most of the men felt committed to both work and family. Most had developed a routine way of life that helped them cope as problems arose. Many had to face the same problems: caring for aging and dependent parents, dealing with adolescent children, coming to terms with personal limitations, and recognizing increasing physical vulnerability.

Although men's psychological well-being has traditionally been linked to their job role, it is now clear that family relations at midlife are extremely important as well. In the words of the researchers, "Our contact with families demonstrated the ways in which a man's experience at midlife is very much dependent on the culture and structure of his family. The changing relationships to wife and children act as precipitants for development in men. . . . This interlocking of individual and family developmental processes is a critical element in men's experience at midlife" (Farrell & Rosenberg, 1981). Indeed, midlife has been characterized as the "prime" of fathers, as their influence over their young adult children tends to increase (Nydegger & Mitteness, 1996). Other research supports the importance of family to men during midlife. In one study, the quality of men's marital and parental roles significantly predicted their level of psychological distress and affected how much distress they experienced on the job (Barnett et al., 1992).

From the foregoing research, it appears that there are four general paths in middle age for men. The first path is that of the *transcendent-generative man*. He does not experience a midlife crisis and has found adequate solutions to most problems of life, so midlife can be a time of fulfillment and accomplishment. The second path is that of the *pseudo-developed man*. This man copes with problems by maintaining the facade that everything is under control even when it isn't; underneath, he feels lost, confused, or bored. A *man in midlife crisis*—the third path—is confused and feels that his whole world is disintegrating. He is unable to meet demands and solve problems. For some men, this may be a temporary phase; for others, it may be the beginning of a continuous decline. The final path is that of the *punitive-disenchanted man*, who has been unhappy or alienated for much of his life and also displays signs of a midlife crisis and inability to cope with problems.

It should be noted that our society has traditionally forced men to conform to one standard of success and masculinity and that most men still try to conform to this standard. A number of the problems men experience at midlife come from having to cope with the idea that they have not lived up to this standard or that they have had to put aside many of their other interests and

According to Farrell and Rosenberg, most middle-aged men feel that they have not lived up to our society's standard of success and masculinity.

desires in trying to reach the standard. Only a few men manage to avoid at least some feelings of failure, self-estrangement, or loss of self-esteem in middle age.

WOMEN'S REACTIONS TO MIDDLE AGE Women, too, often experience difficult transitions and reassessments. Although there are wide individual differences, again there are some common patterns. Traditionally, women define themselves more in terms of the family cycle than by their place in the career cycle. One study of midwestern women (Reinke et al., 1985) found that the women tended to report major life transitions at three points in the family cycle. Fully 80% reported major role changes associated with the birth of their children and their early child-rearing years in young adulthood. Two other major transitions occurred in midlife. About 40% reported a major transition when their children left home, although very few described the transition as particularly traumatic. The final major transition (33% of the women) was menopause.

In our society, women are usually judged by their looks, and in order to be considered attractive, they must appear youthful. It is not surprising, then, that researchers report a high incidence of depression in middle-aged women.

From a different perspective and on the basis of more recent research, Terri Apter (1995) identified four "types of midlife women" in a sample of 80 women between the ages of 39 and 55. *Traditional women* (18 of the 80 studied), having previously defined themselves in terms of family roles, had relatively little difficulty shifting into the role of mature woman responsible for her own future. Their main issues were concerns about past compromises and unused potential. *Innovative women* (24), who had pursued careers, were beginning to view the climb to the top as too demanding and were reassessing "the work they had done on themselves" in their pursuits and the effects that it had. *Expansive women* (18) made marked changes in their goals in midlife in an attempt to expand their horizons. They were going back to school, some to qualify for new kinds of work, or they were turning hobbies into vocations. Finally, there were *protesters* (13), who had been thrust into a premature adulthood during late adolescence and were attempting to postpone midlife as long as possible. Apter notes, however, that only a small minority of the women had much trouble with the transition to midlife.

The timing-of-events model of development applies especially to women during middle age. That is, the timing of key events in the family life cycle and careers defines women's status, lifestyle, and options at middle age—their major activities, their pleasures and stresses, their friends and colleagues. A woman who postpones marriage and childbearing until she is 40 usually does so to pursue a career. Once her child is born, she may enter and leave the workforce many times during her child-rearing years. Her decision to combine family with a full-blown career may reduce her chance of poverty in old age (Baruch & Brooks-Gunn, 1984). The timing of events also defines the specific nature of role conflicts and role strains (see Chapter 13). Common *role conflicts* for middle-aged women involve finding time for both family and career. For example, how does a busy executive cook dinner every night while at the same time meeting business deadlines that may require overtime work? *Role strain* is associated with an overload of demands within the same role, such as when a mother trying to give each of her three teenage children the attention they need and feels incapable of fully satisfying any of them (Lopata & Barnewolt, 1984).

Women react more strongly than men to the physical changes of aging. In our society, women who appear youthful are often judged as more attractive than older women. Some women perceive wrinkles, graying hair, and other signs of aging as indications that they are no longer sexually desirable. As we saw in Chapter 14, some women also react negatively to menopause and regret losing the capacity to bear children. It is not surprising, then, that researchers report a high incidence of depression in middle-aged women compared with women in other age groups (Boyd & Weissman, 1981).

African-American women share many of the reactions of white women to middle age, as the following description indicates:

> We are never-married, married, separated and/or divorced, and widowed.... Some of us may be more preoccupied about our weight, age spots, and dry skin than we were about color in our adolescence. At middle age, many of us are more concerned about the thinning of our hair than about its texture. Others are taking the physical signs of middle age in stride, and fret little, if any, about the natural youthfulness of some of our sisters. We are represented in the statistics of the depressed and well-adjusted. Some of us are involved in midcareer changes; others are adjusting to early retirement. We are represented among blue- and white-collar workers, as well as among the self-employed in both stable and unstable businesses (Spurlock, 1984, page 246).

Despite the similarities between African-American and white women, the combined effects of race and gender create meaningful differences for African-American women in middle age. Memories of past discrimination engender anger in some, psychological denial in others. In addition, socioeconomic factors funnel many middle-aged black women into low-paying, dead-end jobs and often into poverty. Many suffer health problems associated with limited access to health care (Spurlock, 1984).

REVIEW & APPLY

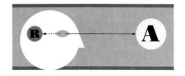

1. According to Erikson, what are the tasks that people must accomplish in middle age to feel satisfied with their lives?
2. Describe how Peck has expanded Erikson's stages of human development. Do the developmental conflicts that characterize earlier stages of development reappear in midlife? Explain.
3. What are the differences and similarities between men's and women's reactions to midlife?

FAMILY AND FRIENDS: INTERPERSONAL CONTEXTS

For both men and women, interpersonal relationships are crucial during the middle adult years. It can be argued that the key element that defines middle age is relationships with family members and friends. We begin by looking at the complex and changing relationships between middle-aged people and their young adult children, including the task of launching children into their own independent lives and the (typically easier) task of adjusting to a home without children. We then turn to the relationship between middle-aged people and their aging parents, and to their new role of grandparent. We will also examine the importance of relationships with friends.

THE GENERATION THAT RUNS THINGS

Middle-aged people act as a bridge between the younger generation (which usually means their children) and the older generation (their aging parents). As they adjust to their changing roles in these relationships, they often gain a new perspective on their own lives. They are now the generation that must run things. This new responsibility entails taking stock. They may regret goals not achieved and may have to acknowledge that some goals will never be reached. More than any other group, the middle-aged must live in the present. The young can look ahead, and the elderly often look back; people in their middle years, with shifting responsibilities to two generations as well as to themselves, must live in the here and now. As they do so, they serve as family **"kinkeepers"**: They are the ones who maintain family rituals, celebrate achievements, keep family histories alive, reach out to family members who are far away, and gather the family together for holiday celebrations.

RELATIONSHIPS WITH ADULT CHILDREN

Relationships with adult children include launching the children into their own independent lives and adjusting to life without them. They also involve learning to relate to adult children in a reciprocal way.

LAUNCHING ADOLESCENTS AND YOUNG ADULTS   Redefinition of the parent-child relationship begins with the *launching of adolescents* into the adult world. Some families are good at letting go. Adolescents on the verge of assuming responsible adult roles are best supported by parents who maintain a dialogue with them but increasingly trust and respect their judgments, decisions, and progress toward maturity. Parents must learn to let go, up to a point, and accept who their children really are.

There is no doubt that the launching of adolescents is an important transition for the parents (Harris et al., 1986). Although many women report unhappiness during this transition, the source of their dissatisfaction is more commonly related to work or marriage than to the children's departure (Harris et al., 1986). Men may also feel torn as the children leave home, especially if they feel that they somehow missed seeing their kids grow up (Rubin, 1980).

Parents repeatedly say that although they are glad that they had children, the increase in freedom, privacy, and discretionary income once the children are gone makes this a pleasant time of life (Alpert & Richardson, 1980; Cooper & Guttman, 1987; Nock, 1982; Rubin, 1980). Women especially benefit from being freed from daily parenting responsibilities and report greater assertiveness and freedom to explore their own interests.

Because of the high divorce rate in the United States, many Americans are raising children alone, at least temporarily. Others have chosen to be single parents without marrying in the first place. Single parents may find themselves in sharp conflict or shifting relationships with their adolescent children (Alpert & Richardson, 1980). Some studies suggest that this situation may be particularly true when the children are preadolescents. During this period, there may be almost daily conflicts over rights and responsibilities (Smetana, 1988). When children marry, parents are suddenly confronted with a new family member in the form of a son- or daughter-in-law. This abrupt demand for intimacy with someone who may be a total stranger is another common adjustment that must be made during this period (Neugarten, 1976).

Finally, it should be noted that not all children who are launched into the world manage to stay there the first time or two out. Because of aborted mar-

At this point in their lives, many middle-aged parents must begin to let go of their teenage children so that they may start the process of entering the adult world.

kinkeepers   The role assumed by middle-aged people that includes maintaining family rituals, celebrating achievements and holidays, keeping family histories alive, and reaching out to family members who live far away.

riage, job loss, and the difficulty of earning enough to live independently in today's world, many adult children "bounce" and return home to recuperate before giving the outside world another try. A few even return home with the intent to stay. How does a returning adult child affect parents? In general, negatively. Aside from issues as simple as having to share space and resources with another adult, a young adult's return to dependency tends to violate parents' expectations about their children's development and thereby to lower parental satisfaction and to put strain on the parent-child relationship (Aquilino, 1996). Moreover, the return often happens as the parents are trying to deal with their own midlife issues, complicating matters further.

THE "EMPTY NEST SYNDROME" After successfully launching their last child, parents turn to roles and interests beyond the sometimes all-encompassing role of parenthood. This process is becoming more important as people live longer. Whereas at the beginning of the nineteenth century, only 41% of adults could expect to live to age 65 or older, in 1990, over 75% of U.S. adults could expect to live that long. Given this dramatic increase in life expectancy, parents who remain married can anticipate spending a lengthy period together after the launching of the last child. This stage of the family life cycle, sometimes referred to as the **empty nest**, can be difficult if the partners have grown apart over the years, developed different interests, and become unaccustomed to spending much time together.

Many middle-aged couples, however, have a history of mutual parenting that includes shared traditions, values, and experiences. Even couples who no longer enjoy the high level of companionship that is characteristic of early marriage may have a strong emotional support system and be materially and functionally interdependent. They have a home and its furnishings and have grown accustomed to their daily routines. Marital satisfaction in this later period is not necessarily based on the same patterns of interaction or solutions to joint problems as it was in earlier phases of the family cycle (Troll, 1985).

MUTUALLY RECIPROCAL RELATIONSHIPS By middle age the relationship between parents and their children is more reciprocal than it has ever been before. The relationship evolves into one in which two adults interact on a more equal basis than was possible when the young adult was a child. The shift to a reciprocal relationship rarely takes place suddenly or smoothly; it usually occurs in a series of jolts over a period of years. In turn, the nature of the parenting relationship can make this shift easier or harder. If the parenting relationship was authoritarian, the roles and obligations tend to be formal, rigid, and resistant to change. Middle-aged parents and their young adult children will have to struggle for years to create a reciprocal relationship, if indeed they ever do.

Adult children often feel the need to distance themselves, at least for a while, from their parents—and from perceived parental judgment—before they can see their parents in a realistic way. When this distancing happens, middle-aged parents may feel cut off or unappreciated. It is often during times of family crisis—the death or illness of a family member, financial hardship, divorce, or unemployment—that adult children and their parents find ways to renegotiate their relationship so that they can interact with each other in new, more reciprocal ways. In some families this process can take many years, whereas in others, mutual respect emerges as adolescence wanes.

empty nest The period in the family life cycle that occurs after the last child has left home.

RELATIONSHIPS WITH AGING PARENTS

In 1900, one in four children experienced the death of a parent before they were 15 years old. In the 1980s, fewer than one in twenty children did. Conversely, in 1980, 40% of people in their late fifties had at least one surviving parent (Brody, 1985). Estimates indicate that of the women born in the 1930s, fully one-quarter will have living mothers when they turn 60 (Gatz et al., 1990), and these numbers are continuing to rise. As a result, middle-aged adults will need to adjust to the changing needs and roles of an aged parent (Brody, 1985). When parents are in good health and can live independently, the relationship is often characterized by reciprocity; the parent and adult child help each other in concrete ways. The relationship changes when parents become ill or too frail to live on their own.

How adult children behave toward their parents depends to a large extent on their life experiences and, more specifically, on their stage in the family life cycle. A 42-year-old woman with grown children who is at the peak of her professional life and lives 1000 miles away from her parents must take a different approach to them than would a woman of similar age who is a full-time homemaker and lives near her parents. The backdrop for adult-parent relationships is the repertoire of beliefs and practices that has defined their unique relationship over the years. With time come diverse strategies and understandings between parent and child that ultimately lead to different patterns of interaction and coping. Moreover, the degree to which children are called on to help their parents varies from one individual to another and from one family to another (Stueve & O'Donnell, 1984).

As you read about the evolving relationships between middle-aged adults and their aging parents, keep in mind that gender differences often affect these relationships. "Daughters of aging parents are different from sons of aging parents; the difference even depends on whether the aging parent is a father or a mother" (Troll, 1989). Traditionally, the primary parent-child relationship at this stage of life generally involves the daughter as caregiver. Ethnic and social class may also influence intergenerational relationships.

RECIPROCAL EXCHANGE OF ASSISTANCE Most middle-aged people have an ongoing relationship with their aging parents that includes regular contact, shared memories, and reciprocal exchange of assistance. Numerous surveys have revealed lasting social, emotional, and material exchanges between adult children and their parents (Stueve & O'Donnell, 1984). Many older parents provide financial assistance to their middle-aged children and to their grandchildren (Giordano & Beckman, 1985; Hill et al., 1970), at least in middle- and upper-middle-class families. In African-American families, the older generation often does not have the financial resources to contribute (Jackson et al., 1990). On the other hand, they are more likely to provide social support and perhaps caregiving services to their children—especially to those who are coping with single parenthood.

In all, contrary to widespread public opinion, it appears that most middle-aged people remain quite concerned about and close to both their parents and their children (see "In Theory, In Fact," page 522). Table 15–2 summarizes various myths with regard to intergenerational estrangement during midlife.

ROLE REVERSALS With age, role reversals gradually take place for middle-aged people and their parents. The middle-aged become the generation in charge—working, raising children, and generally functioning as the "doers" in society. Their parents, if they are still living, may be in poor health, retired, and in need of financial aid. Over a period of years, power gradually and naturally

IN THEORY, IN FACT

DO MIDDLE-AGED PEOPLE BECOME ESTRANGED FROM THEIR PARENTS AND CHILDREN?

Middle-aged people are often described as being "caught in the middle" between the conflicting needs of their young adult children (and their children's children) and their aging parents. When middle-aged people find themselves in this situation, they supposedly choose to focus on their own needs and have little contact with either the younger or the older generation.

Despite the prevalence of this belief, research on intergenerational relationships has shown that it is more fiction than fact. In the words of Lillian Troll (1989), "The myth that parents and their adult children are essentially estranged from each other in today's Western society is so widespread and persistent that it is difficult to convince the general public that it is untrue." Intergenerational myths can make it harder for middle-aged people to perceive positive feelings about family members as normal, so it is important to examine where the truth lies.

Despite the widespread belief that estrangement and isolation are the norm and contact is held to a minimum, surveys show that middle-aged children are likely to live relatively close to their parents and to see or speak with them on a regular basis. However, this finding does not mean that the generations are likely to share a home. Because independence is valued by each generation, fewer than 10% of aging parents share a home with their middle-aged children, and many do so only when economic hardship or physical disability gives them little choice.

Most middle-aged parents also have regular contact with their grown children, and this contact is likely to in-

Usually, middle-aged women assume most of the responsibilities for the care of aging parents.

crease when problems arise for either the children or the parents. However, while family members tend to come together to support one another during times of crisis, they are likely to return to their normal interaction patterns after the crisis is over (Belsky & Rovine, 1984; Morgan, 1984).

When the generations come together, they try to help each other in concrete ways. When help is needed—and given—it is in the context of a mutual, reciprocal relationship whose balance changes over time. During an individual's early adult years, most of the help given during times of illness flows from parent to child. During middle age, the flow often shifts toward the older generation as adults are forced to take care of their aging parents. The responsibility—and burden—of caring for both young and old usually falls on the "woman in the middle"

(Brody, 1985), who may have to juggle the needs of her aging parents, her young adult children, her marriage, and the health of her husband, as well as her own career and personal needs. Most women manage to meet these responsibilities but have little time left for themselves.

Relationships between the middle generation and their children and parents are often characterized by attempts to influence behavior (Hagestad, 1985). In most cases, such attempts are directed at children rather than parents, and regardless of the target, the advice is usually intended to be practical. Attempts to change poor health habits are common to all generations as the middle-aged, their parents, and their children try to persuade each other to stop smoking, eat sensibly, see their doctor regularly, and take their medications.

TABLE 15–2   Some Midlife Intergenerational Myths

1. Midlife men and women live as far apart from their children and their parents as they can.
2. Midlife men and women rarely visit or receive visits from their adult children or their parents.
3. Midlife men and women rarely phone (or get phone calls) or write (or receive letters) from their adult children or their parents.
4. Midlife men and women abandon their parents when they get old and sick.
5. Midlife parents and their adult children are more likely to stay in touch and feel close if they share values and personality.
6. Grandparents feel they know how to raise their grandchildren better than their children are doing and are eager to interfere.
7. Extensive extended family contact is deleterious to mental health.

Source: Myths of Midlife: Intergenerational Relationships. In S. Hunter and M. Surdel (eds.), *Midlife Myths: Issues, Funding, and Practice Implications.* Newbury Park, CA: Sage Publications, Inc., page 211.

shifts to their middle-aged child. Unless both generations realize that this role reversal is an inevitable part of the life cycle, it can cause resentments on both sides and can lead to conflicts (Gould, 1978; Neugarten, 1976).

Some adult children do not look after their aging or ill parents; instead they abandon them to nursing homes and other impersonal social services. However, they are by far the minority. Today people are living longer after the onset of chronic diseases or disabilities, and few people reach the end of life without experiencing a period in which they are dependent on their children. The responsibility of long-term care for parents has become more the norm than the exception. One study (Marks, 1996) found that one in five adults aged 35 to 64 had cared for a relative or a friend in the last year. Several studies conducted in the 1970s demonstrated that 80 to 90% of medically related and personal care, household tasks, and transportation and shopping for aging parents was managed by family members, not the social system (Brody, 1985).

Family members react to emergencies, but they also respond to the need for long-term assistance of the chronically disabled (Matthews & Rosner, 1988). In the Long-Term-Care Survey of caregivers of very frail elderly persons, 75% of the daughter caregivers provided daily assistance. Only 10% of the caregivers used formal services (Stone et al., 1987). Families also provide social support, affection, and a sense of having someone to rely on. It is also true, however, that family resources can become exhausted or the parent can become so debilitated that family members must turn over primary responsibility to someone else, such as a nursing home. Nevertheless, conservative estimates indicate that well over 5 million people in the United States are involved in parent care at any given time (Brody, 1985).

Daughters are much more likely than sons to provide care for aging parents (Brody et al., 1987; Gatz et al., 1990; Spitze & Logan, 1990). The same applies to daughters-in-law (Globerman, 1996), but there are fewer differences between working and nonworking women (Brody & Schoonover, 1986). Working daughters provide comparable amounts of help with tasks such as shopping, transportation, and emotional support. A survey has shown that nonemployed daughters are more likely to help with cooking and personal care. Substantial numbers of working daughters also change their work schedules to accommodate their parents' needs (Brody et al., 1987). Surveys indicate that 20 to 30% of caregiver daughters had rearranged their schedules to provide care. In fact, caring for ill relatives is the second most common reason given by middle-aged women for leaving the workforce (the first is problems with their own health).

Siblings may work together to care for their ailing parents (Goetting, 1982). The distribution of labor between the siblings is not always equal, however, with daughters again more likely than sons to provide care. In fact, parents expect more assistance from daughters than from sons (Brody et al., 1984). If there are two daughters and only one of them works outside the home, the unemployed one will provide more of the daily care and assistance in last-minute emergencies (Matthews et al., 1989). Nevertheless, the working daughter is expected to make significant contributions, typically providing aid in the evenings and on weekends.

How a daughter responds to the needs of her aging parents depends to a large extent on her life circumstances, including her age (is she in her thirties, forties, or fifties?), her position in the family life cycle (does she have grown children, or is she raising preschoolers?), and her involvement in the workforce (does she have a full-time job, or is she a full-time homemaker?) (Stueve & O'Donnell, 1984). Daughters may experience physical strain as a result of their caregiving efforts. However, when daughters have dependent children of their own, they experience less strain and a greater sense of well-being than those without dependent children (Stull et al., 1994).

In sum, responsibility for parent care is both rewarding and stressful. For some, it creates tension between dependence and independence. It may reactivate old dependency conflicts or other relationship problems between parent and child or between siblings. Old loyalties and alliances or rivalries sometimes reappear. The need to care for parents also foreshadows the future of the caregivers, who will be dependent on their children when they become old. It may be a preview and model for relinquishing autonomy, control, and responsibility. These internal conflicts—together with the very real demands on time and freedom, competing responsibilities, and interference with lifestyle, and social and recreational activities—can create a stressful environment. It is remarkable that 80 to 90% of middle-aged adults persist in the tasks and responsibilities of parental care. Indeed, some women practically make a career of serving as a caregiver to one aging relative after another. Despite the extent of their caregiving, however, fully three-fifths of caregiving women in one study reported that they felt guilty about not doing enough, and three-quarters of them agreed that nowadays children do not take care of their elderly parents to the extent that they did in the past (Brody, 1985).

INTRODUCTION TO GRANDPARENTING

Many people in middle age find themselves in the new role of grandparent. Grandparenting is highly satisfying for many people; they can help raise a new generation without having the daily responsibilities of a parent and without being involved in the intense relationships and conflicts that may develop between parent and child (Robertson, 1977).

The majority of Americans become grandparents in middle age; minorities and women tend to become grandparents somewhat earlier than whites and men (Szinovacz, 1998). If their adult children divorce or encounter other problems, some grandparents become full-time surrogate parents to their grandchildren; others care for their grandchildren part-time even though they themselves may still be working full-time (Szinovacz, 1998). Thus, in many ways, our concept of a grandparent has evolved from that of an old person in a rocking chair to that of an active, involved family member (Troll, 1989).

Although grandparenting is a highly individualized activity, there are some distinct roles that grandparents can play, depending on their relationships with their grandchildren (Troll, 1980). If a single mother or both parents work, grandparents can take care of children during the day. Some grandparents become "fun people" to their grandchildren, taking them on trips, out shopping, or to other interesting places. In certain ethnic groups, a grandfather maintains his status and position as formal head of the family.

One author suggests that there are four important, yet often largely symbolic, roles that grandparents fulfill (Bengston, 1985).

1. *Being there:* Sometimes grandparents describe their most important role as simply being there. They are a calming presence in the face of family disruption or an external catastrophe. They provide an anchor of stability to both grandchildren and parents. Sometimes they even act as a deterrent to family disruption.
2. *Family national guard:* Some grandparents report that their most important function is to be available in times of emergency. During these times they often need to go well beyond the role of simply being there and actively manage the grandchildren.
3. *Arbitrator:* Some grandparents see their role as one of imparting and negotiating family values, maintaining family continuity, and helping out in times of conflict. Although there are often differences in values between generations, some grandparents see themselves as better able to handle the conflicts between their adult children and their grandchildren because of their relative distance and greater experience.
4. *Maintaining the family's biography:* Grandparents can provide a sense of continuity for the family, teaching grandchildren about the heritage and traditions of their family.

Each of these roles may be either real or symbolic. Sometimes family values are maintained more because adult children and grandchildren worry about how a grandparent might react than through actual intervention by the grandparent (Bengtson, 1985). For example, a grandchild may choose not to marry outside her or his racial, ethnic, or religious group because of the way the grandparents might respond.

FRIENDSHIPS: A LIFELONG PERSPECTIVE

Although many important life stages are defined by family relationships, many people in midlife rely more on friends than on family. Although the majority of people marry and raise children, a significant and growing number remain single or raise children by themselves. For them, friendships are often a central part of life. Such important life tasks as establishing intimacy, for example, must be accomplished through friendships rather than through marriage and family. For older people whose children are grown or who are widowed, friendship often fills many vital emotional needs.

In a twelve-year study by Marjorie Fiske and colleagues (1990), people at four different stages of life were interviewed about their attitudes toward friendship and the kinds of friendships they had. The study involved high school students, newlyweds, people in early middle age, and people in late

By late middle age, friends become appreciated for what makes them unique.

middle age. Most middle-aged people reported that they had several friends with whom they had been close for at least six years, whereas adolescents and newlyweds tended to have more short-term friendships. When asked what qualities were important in real friendships and what qualities characterized an ideal friend, people at all four life stages had similar views. Reciprocity was considered very important, with a strong emphasis on helping and sharing. People saw their friends as similar to themselves in many ways and stressed the importance of shared experiences and being able to communicate well. Sex differences were more significant than age differences. Women responded in more detail than men and seemed to be more deeply involved in their friendships. Women considered reciprocity most important in their close friendships, whereas men tended to choose their friends on the basis of similarity. It should be noted, however, that many of today's middle-aged people are Baby Boomers who grew up in a time of relaxed norms regarding friends and acquaintances; thus, as Rebecca Adams and Rosemary Blieszner (1998) suggest, middle-age friendships today are now much more heterogeneous with regard to ethnicity, race, and gender.

In general, the most complex friendships occurred among the late-middle-aged group. In early middle age, people were more involved with their families and jobs. They had less time to devote to friends. But by late middle age, highly complex and multidimensional relationships were the rule. People at this stage were likely to appreciate the unique characteristics of their friends. This appreciation may be a result of certain personality shifts during middle age. Jung described the period from age 40 to age 60 as a time of inner awareness, when people turn away from the activities of the conscious mind and confront the unconscious. It is possible that as people become aware of the subtleties of their own natures, they also begin to appreciate complexity in others more than they did earlier in life (Fiske & Chiraboga, 1990).

1. Why do we characterize the relationship between middle-aged parents and their young adult children as "evolving"?
2. What is the most prevalent attitude that middle-aged people have toward their aging parents?
3. List some of the major difficulties that middle-aged people face in dealing with their aging parents.
4. How are friendships during midlife both different from and similar to friendships during other periods of the lifespan?

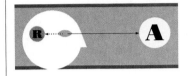

REVIEW & APPLY

THE CHANGING FAMILY

Increasingly, as we have seen in earlier chapters, family relationships must be viewed in the context of a changing family unit characterized by divorce, re-marriage, and reconstituted families. Here we'll look at the impact of the changing family on middle-aged adults.

No one—not even the most radical social critic—would claim that the traditional nuclear family is dead or even dying. But few families still fit the traditional mold in which the father works and the mother stays home to care for the children. Just as individuals are tailoring their lifestyles to suit their own needs and priorities, the idea of the family is adapting to changes in the social and personal needs and priorities of its members. As shown in Figure 15–1, marital (and therefore family) status in the U.S. population has changed markedly in recent decades: There are fewer married couples, and there are more single and divorced people.

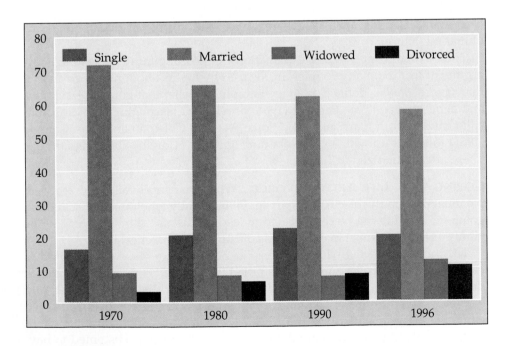

FIGURE 15–1
THE CHANGING MARITAL STATUS OF THE U.S. POPULATION, AGE 18 AND OVER, 1970–1996 (IN PERCENT)

Source: U.S. Census Bureau, 1997.

DIVORCE AND REMARRIAGE

As discussed in Chapter 13, for every three marriages that succeed, two fail. Although divorce is much more likely during young adulthood, it still occurs at significant rates in middle adulthood and beyond (see Figure 13–5, page 459). What are some of the reasons that people divorce, and what happens when so many of them remarry?

WHY COUPLES DIVORCE   Marriages rarely fall apart suddenly. More often a breakup is the culmination of a long process of emotional distancing. The final months of the marriage are usually remembered as unhappy by both partners. But the eventual decision to divorce is usually made by one partner. The wife usually raises the issue first. Wives often are dissatisfied with a marriage earlier than husbands, although that dissatisfaction does not always cause them to decide to divorce (Kelly, 1982).

In middle adulthood, couples get divorced for many of the same reasons that younger couples do. They want more from their marriage than they are currently getting, and divorce appears preferable to continuing an unhappy relationship. In addition, if the marriage is shaky, the empty nest stage of the family life cycle may create a personal or marital crisis. Couples observe that it's no longer necessary to stay together for the sake of the children; they may wonder whether they want to spend the rest of their lives together. In addition, divorce is often associated with misconceptions about marriage. Churches, lawyers, marriage counselors, the media, family, and friends all pay homage to myths about what marriage is supposed to be. These myths often include unrealistic expectations that set the stage for failure.

MYTHS ABOUT MARRIAGE, DIVORCE, AND REMARRIAGE   In 1994, about 2.36 million Americans got married, and 1.19 million got divorced. In other words, almost half as many individuals divorced each other as married. Actually, some scholars are encouraged by these figures because both marriage and divorce rates are down slightly from their respective highs in 1981, and the ratio of divorce to marriage has also declined somewhat from its earlier high (Clarke, 1995). Over 40% of contemporary marriages involve the remarriage of one or both individuals, and almost half of all remarriages end in divorce (Coleman & Ganong, 1985). What are the reasons for this persistently high rate of marital failure?

There are, of course, many explanations. One of the most interesting is the argument that too many couples are swayed by myths about marriage and remarriage. A *myth* is defined as an oversimplified belief that guides perceptions and expectations. Jessie Bernard (1981) provided a fascinating comparison of eight myths about marriage and divorce. Marilyn Coleman and John Ganong (1985) followed up with a corresponding analysis of myths about remarriage. These are summarized in Table 15–3.

COPING WITH LIFE AFTER DIVORCE   When marriages fail, divorced people must pick up the pieces and start again. Especially when there are children, going on with life can be complicated indeed, as discussed in Chapter 13. The family as a system must make serious adjustments in practical living.

To find out exactly what happens to people after they divorce, Mavis Hetherington and colleagues (1978) studied 96 divorced couples with children during a two-year period. They found that many of the divorced men and women suffered from a wide range of problems that they had not encountered while they were married. The practical problems of organizing and maintaining a household plagued many divorced men, who were accustomed to hav-

TABLE 15–3   MYTHS OF MARRIAGE, DIVORCE, AND REMARRIAGE

MARRIAGE

Everything will work out well if we love each other.

Always consider the other person first.

Emphasize the positive; keep criticisms to oneself.

If things go wrong, focus on the future.

See oneself as part of a couple first and then as an individual.

What's mine is yours.

Marriage makes people happier than they were before marriage.

What is best for the children will be best for us.

DIVORCE

Because we no longer love each other, nothing can work out anymore.

Always consider oneself first.

Emphasize the negative and criticize everything.

If things go wrong, focus on the past.

See oneself as an individual first and then as part of a couple.

What's yours is mine.

Divorce makes people unhappy.

What is best for us must be devastating for the children.

REMARRIAGE

This time we'll make it work by doing everything right.

Always consider everyone first.

Emphasize the positive and overlook the negative.

If things go wrong, think of what went wrong in the past and make sure it does not happen again.

Depending on one's personality, one might duplicate the marriage or divorce myth and see oneself either as part of a couple first or as an individual first.

What's mine is mine and what's yours is yours.

Marriage makes people significantly happier than they were before marriage.

What is best for us must be harmful to the children.

ing their wives perform these tasks. Financial hardship was also reported by both men and women. With two households to support instead of one, some men found that their incomes were spread too thin to make ends meet. Many men took a second job or worked overtime to make extra money. Women who had been homemakers before their divorce usually suffered financial strain—especially if their husbands failed to make court-ordered alimony or child support payments. Strapped by these new economic burdens, many women were forced to spend less time with their children and had little or no time for themselves (Goetting, 1981).

Divorce can be particularly difficult in middle age because the partners have grown accustomed to their way of life. The new financial and social circumstances that result from divorce may be wrenching to people in middle age, especially if they are forced to concentrate on developmental tasks (going back to school, finding a new job, dating) that are considered more appropriate for people in early adulthood.

Disruption of the marital relationship, whether through divorce or death, is a stressful event. There is often grief and mourning over the loss of an intimate relationship, even when it was an unhappy one—people usually have second thoughts about whether they should have divorced. There is disruption of normal routines and patterns. There is the new independence and autonomy, whether welcome or unwelcome, as well as sheer loneliness at times. There are, however, marked differences between divorce and widowhood, as we'll see in Chapter 17.

Most people who are experiencing divorce perceive it as a kind of failure. For the partner who did not make the decision to divorce, there is often a feeling of rejection. Feelings of humiliation and powerlessness are not uncommon. Even if the marriage was unsatisfactory, the final decision comes as a shock. For the partner who makes the decision, the stress is often higher during the agonizing months or years before the separation. The spouse who initiates the divorce may feel sadness, guilt, and anger, but there is at least a compensating sense of control. He or she has also rehearsed and mentally prepared for the separation (Kelly, 1982), which may come as a complete surprise to the other partner.

STARTING A NEW LIFE Establishing a new lifestyle after divorce is easier for some people than for others. For some, the freedom from constraint, obligation, and emotional turmoil is a welcome relief. Women especially are likely to feel that they have a "new chance" after a divorce (Caldwell et al., 1984; Kelly, 1982). For others, the idea of living alone is frightening. After a long period of marriage, older women often experience considerable difficulty relinquishing their previous role. In the past, women often had more difficulty than men maintaining friendships with their married peers and in managing financial and legal matters such as obtaining credit cards or securing a bank loan or mortgage. That situation has changed, but many divorced women still lack enough income to obtain credit. Individuals who married young have never been on their own and have little experience in coping with the independence that now confronts them. These newly single people often underestimate the problems of adjusting to being alone. Finally, regardless of the duration of the marriage, recently divorced men and women have higher rates of alcoholism, physical illness, and depression, sometimes as a direct result of the life changes resulting from separation.

Most divorced individuals experience considerable improvement in well-being within two or three years of the final separation (Spanier & Furstenberg, 1982). Divorced women are likely to have greater self-esteem (Wallerstein & Blakeslee, 1989). Divorced people with the strongest sense of well-being are likely to remarry within three or four years. In fact, divorced men have the highest rate of remarriage among all single groups. Overall, divorced men are three times as likely as divorced women to remarry. After age forty, most divorced men remarry, compared with only a third of divorced women (Spanier & Furstenberg, 1982). Many middle-aged men marry younger women and start a second family. Divorced people who develop new intimate relationships are more likely to experience a positive adjustment after divorce, partly because their new relationships diminish their attachments to their ex-spouse (Tschann et al., 1989).

People who become single in middle age may find it very difficult to begin to date again, especially since this activity is associated with being young.

A sizable minority of divorced people remain bitter and isolated even 10 years after the divorce. Some men virtually lose contact with their children and, despite adequate resources, refuse to help cover costs such as college expenses (Wallerstein & Blakelee, 1989). Some divorced women use their children as "weapons" against their ex-husbands, in an effort to produce guilt and shame.

Since divorce is so common, some researchers are studying why couples stay together instead of why they divorce (Lauer & Lauer, 1985). Although middle-aged men and women cite different reasons for remaining married, both list "My spouse is my best friend" as their primary reason. It is interesting that the top seven reasons listed by men and women who have been married for 15 years or more are the same:

- My spouse is my best friend.
- I like my spouse as a person.
- Marriage is a long-term commitment.
- Marriage is sacred.
- We agree on aims and goals.
- My spouse has grown more interesting.
- I want the relationship to succeed.

Although most happily married couples in the study were satisfied with their sex lives, it was not a primary factor in their happiness or marital satisfaction. Men listed satisfaction with sex as the twelfth most important reason for staying together; women listed it as number fourteen.

Middle-aged people who remain married or remarry report higher levels of general happiness and satisfaction than those who are single. Marriage helps older people deal with stressful life events such as retirement, loss of income, illness, and disability. These positive effects stem from the sense of intimacy, interdependence, and belonging that marriage brings (Gilford, 1986).

RECONSTITUTED FAMILIES

When divorced or widowed people with children remarry, they form **reconstituted or blended families**, also known as stepfamilies. These families present many more role adjustment problems for both stepparents and stepchildren than primary families do. With little preparation to handle their new roles and little support from the society around them, stepparents often find that achieving a satisfactory family relationship is harder than they ever imagined. Done properly, however, remarriage can reduce stress—particularly for the parent who has custody of the child (Furstenberg, 1987). A partner who is willing to share financial responsibilities, household tasks, child-rearing decisions, and so on can offer welcome relief to a divorced parent. Men who remarry, however, may have to deal with additional pressures if they are expected to provide financial support to two households.

In any event, second marriages are different from first marriages. They operate within a more complex family organization—stepchildren, ex-spouses, and former in-laws, for example—that can cause considerable conflict. Yet second marriages are often characterized by more open communication, greater acceptance of conflict, and more trust that any disagreements that arise can be resolved satisfactorily (Furstenberg, 1987).

RECONSTITUTED FAMILIES IN PERSPECTIVE There is a tendency to think that the current high divorce rate and the resulting high remarriage rate have created an entirely new phenomenon. After all, nearly 40% of marriages are re-

reconstituted or blended families Families in which mothers or fathers with children have remarried.

Most stepparents and children ultimately make a positive adjustment to each other.

marriages for at least one of the partners. But reconstituted families are not a new phenomenon. In fact, the current remarriage rate closely parallels remarriage rates in Europe and the United States in the seventeenth and eighteenth centuries. There is, however, a major difference. Today, most stepfamilies are created as a result of a marriage-divorce-remarriage sequence. In the past, most stepfamilies were a result of a marriage-death-remarriage sequence (Ihinger-Tallman & Pasley, 1987).

The difference between these two types of stepfamilies is, of course, the presence of a living former spouse. Contact with that former spouse often continues and may include shared custody, financial support, and visitation. In some families it is difficult to maintain distance, resolve conflicts, and avoid feelings of rejection by one spouse or the other. For the children, remarriage often creates a situation characterized by ambivalence, conflict, uncertainty, and divided loyalties. It is therefore not surprising that previously widowed stepparents often report more positive relationships with each other and with their children following remarriage than do previously divorced stepparents (Ihinger-Tallman & Pasley, 1987).

LEARNING TO LIVE IN A RECONSTITUTED FAMILY The expectation that stepfamilies can simply pick up where the primary family left off is unrealistic and inevitably leads to frustration and disappointment. Both stepparents and stepchildren need time to adjust to one another—to learn about and test each other's personalities. To do this, the best advice is that stepparents try to establish a position in the children's lives that is different from the one held by the missing biological parent. If the stepparents try to compete with the child's real parent, they're more likely to fail.

When asked what the greatest difficulties are in a stepparent-stepchild relationship, most stepparents mention disciplining the children, adjusting to the habits and personalities of the children, and gaining the children's acceptance (Schlesinger, 1975; cited in Kompara, 1980). Stepmothers often have more problems than stepfathers in adjusting to their new roles. Partly because of the stereotype of the "wicked stepmother" and partly because stepmothers spend more time with children than stepfathers do, stepmothers must overcome tremendous odds if they are to succeed.

There is also the popular stereotype of the stepchild. Stepchildren are seen as neglected, perhaps abused, and definitely not loved as much as the "real" child. Surveys of the general public and even of professionals who help stepfamilies find that these stereotypes are fairly widespread (Coleman & Ganong, 1987). Fairy tales like those of Cinderella and Hansel and Gretel reinforce the stereotypes. In reality, such stereotypes are inaccurate. When such a situation does exist (and it often does not), the stepparent is always to blame. The children themselves may stand in the way. If they haven't accepted the divorce or loss of their biological parent, are used as pawns in a bitter, angry divorce, or hold an idealized view of the missing parent, children may reject the stepparent's love and make family harmony impossible.

Taking time to develop mutual trust, affection, a feeling of closeness, and respect for the child's point of view often helps in forming a workable relationship. Girls are likely to have greater difficulty forming a good relationship with a stepfather than boys are (Hetherington, 1989). This is probably the case because the girl typically had a close relationship with her mother before the divorce and sees the stepfather as an intruder. Boys, on the other hand, often have tumultuous, conflictual relationships with their stepmothers.

Even though stepparents rarely duplicate the idealized biological parent's place in the child's life, they can often provide a loving, nurturant, and secure environment—one that is often more satisfactory than the one that the child experienced before the divorce. Indeed, most stepparents and stepchildren eventually make positive adjustments (Clingempeel & Segal, 1986; Visher & Visher, 1983). This adjustment is more likely to occur if the stepfamily creates a new social unit that extends the characteristics of the children's biological family to include new relationship and communication styles, methods of discipline, and problem-solving strategies (Paernow, 1984; Pasley & Ihinger-Tallman, 1989; Whiteside, 1989).

---

1. What are some of the difficulties that divorce poses for individuals and for the family system as a whole?
2. What are some of the adjustment problems that parents and children must face in reconstituted families?
3. What factors make divorce, remarriage, and the formation of a stepfamily especially difficult during middle age?

REVIEW & APPLY

OCCUPATIONAL CONTINUITY AND CHANGE

Middle age is also a time when long-term career goals may be met, midcourse corrections may be needed, or disappointments become obvious. It is also a time when job-related stress can reach its peak.

Until recently it was thought that a person's working life consisted of—or should consist of—entering a particular occupation or career as a young adult and remaining in that occupation until retirement. Obviously, this "preferred" career course required a thoughtful choice of occupation and careful preparation at the outset. Once a person had begun a job, she or he was expected to lay the foundation for a lifetime career and climb the ladder of success as quickly as possible.

This scenario has changed considerably, partly because of the realization that adult development may produce many shifts in attitudes, career needs, and goals. Moreover, in today's technologically advanced and economically unstable world, jobs change so quickly or are eliminated in such numbers that the one-career pattern no longer applies to most people. As Phyllis Moen puts it, "The ground is shifting beneath them as the nature of work, family, careers, and retirement is being reconfigured." Downsizing and outsourcing are taking their toll on the American worker (see "A Matter for Debate," on facing page). People frequently change employers or change positions within a company.

Although most people do not make truly dramatic changes once their careers have been established, it is now considered unusual for individuals to begin and end their working lives in the same job or career. This perception is especially true for women who interrupt their careers to spend a decade or more raising a family. At middle age they are ready to channel their energies into another form of generativity. It is in the workplace that these women gain a new sense of accomplishment and form meaningful, sustaining relationships. With this likelihood in mind, we will examine the process of career reassessment that often takes place during middle adulthood, as well as responses to job change and stress.

MIDCAREER REASSESSMENT

As we have seen, when we look at the work histories of individuals in the past several decades, it seems that the occupational life cycles described by Havighurst (see Chapter 13) overlook a period of serious career reassessment or reexamination that often occurs at midlife, a time when workers report lower well-being than either younger or older workers (Warr, 1992). Reassessment occurs for a number of reasons. Two prominent ones are that workers find that they are not being promoted as rapidly as they had expected and that a job may turn out to be less desirable than anticipated.

Middle-aged people who experience major midlife transitions are more likely to make dramatic changes in their occupation. Levinson (1978) found that adults in their forties may experience a shift in their values and goals that leads them to consider changing the course of their career. Levinson explains the occurrence of this change in terms of the reappearance of the dream—the inspiration, ideals, and goals of youth (see Chapter 13). Research suggests that adults cope with this reassessment period best if they realistically and systematically assess their own abilities and the pluses and minuses of their current occupational position (Okun, 1984; Schein, 1978).

Eugene Thomas (1979) suggests that certain societal conditions permit people who experience such dramatic alterations in their values and attitudes to act on them. People now live longer and can work longer, so when their responsibilities to their children end, they are free to make changes that may even reduce their income or transform their way of living. When both spouses work, one spouse may continue to earn income while the other makes a career change. Thomas cites the greater tolerance for deviations from traditional social norms (including the wife's supporting the husband), which makes it easier for people to act upon their newfound beliefs and ideals.

Still, only a minority of people make dramatic career shifts during midlife (Levinson, 1983). One reason for their making such shifts is that they feel that their abilities are underutilized at their current job, perhaps because of changes

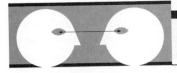

A MATTER FOR DEBATE

DOWNSIZING AND OUTSOURCING

Corporate restructuring can take many forms as upper management attempts to minimize costs and maximize profits (often earning huge year-end bonuses for themselves in the process). *Downsizing* is one approach: Jobs are eliminated, workers are laid off permanently, and the remaining workers are expected to do more, to work harder, and to put in longer hours. *Outsourcing* is another approach: Work that was previously performed in-house is farmed out to other companies, which often hire some of the same people who were doing the work before but reduce their benefits (especially retirement plans) and eliminate their job security. As with downsized workers, outsourced workers are also expected to work harder and increase their productivity, expectations that greatly increase job stress (Gowing et al., 1997).

For those who are laid off as a result of corporate restructuring, joblessness is far more than an economic misfortune. It can be a psychological catastrophe for the unemployed and their families. It can cause illness, divide families, and create feelings of worthlessness and lack of self-esteem. For

many, unemployment represents more than just loss of income. Unemployed workers commonly report an increased incidence of headaches, stomach problems, and insomnia. They also smoke, drink, and worry a lot more than they did when they were working (Liem, 1981). Men who were socialized to be the family breadwinner are especially hard hit by unemployment. They suffer more depression and anxiety and have a higher incidence of psychotic behavior than men who are employed (Liem, 1981). Beyond that, illness, suicide, alcoholism, divorce, and even crime occur at epidemic rates among the unemployed. Left without a job, many workers feel that they have nothing to look forward to. They miss their coworkers and the routine of going to work. For many, the sense of hopelessness grows worse every time they are rejected for a new job. When this process happens often enough, the worker may totally withdraw from the labor force. The rejection that unemployed workers feel may be exacerbated if friends and neighbors avoid them.

What about workers who survive restructuring? Constantly unsure of their future ("I might be the next to go") and with greater demands placed

on them, they are subject to many potential sources of stress (Burke & Nelson, 1997). They experience role confusion, work overload, more office politics and conflicts, increased conflict between their job and their personal/family life, and in general a tense climate at work—with accompanying symptoms such as dizziness, stomach problems, and high blood pressure. Their job satisfaction wanes, and they may become angry, cynical, and depressed; their company loyalty is likely to evaporate.

What will be the long-run effects of the increasing trend toward downsizing and outsourcing? For now, that remains a matter for debate. At present, unemployment is low, corporate profits and the stock markets are up, and the economy is generally viewed as healthy—with much of that health attributed to corporate restructuring. It's worth noting, however, that a similar condition existed around the beginning of the twentieth century, when those workers had few federally mandated rights and were exploited in every way imaginable. We might well wonder whether downsizing and outsourcing are modern business technology's way of turning back the clock.

---

in the job or because there are fewer challenges once a person has developed a high level of expertise. Another reason is **job burnout**—a feeling of being unable to endure the job anymore, accompanied by a strong sense of dread each morning when one must go to work. Burnout is not restricted to middle age, of course (Stagner, 1985). Indeed, the entire process of reappraising one's life structure, including work, is not restricted to middle age (Levinson, 1986). In all, older workers are less likely than young adults to change jobs (Rhodes, 1983).

JOB CHANGE AND STRESS

For many people, career changes are not welcome and may not go smoothly. Occupational instability can be harmful. Workers who move through predictable, on-schedule events in the course of their lives generally experience less stress than those who must cope with unpredictable, off-schedule ones. Careers in which progress and promotions do not occur as expected, forced ca-

job burnout The emotional exhaustion that often affects middle-aged people in the helping professions.

For the middle-aged, job loss may be far more difficult to cope with than for young adults, as more of the older person's identity tends to be invested in the job.

reer shifts or sudden unemployment may cause high levels of stress, anxiety, and disequilibrium. Other off-time events encountered by middle-aged workers may include the need to return to school to prepare for new careers or to take long periods away from work to upgrade their skills and continue progressing in their present careers.

JOB LOSS People who get fired, are laid off indefinitely, or experience forced retirement often face emotional problems that may outweigh the problem of loss of income (again see "A Matter for Debate," page 535). Many people's self-concept is destroyed and their self-esteem is shattered. Individuals often react to career loss in ways that are similar to the grief response triggered by the death of a loved one (Jones, 1979). The pattern of grieving that may follow sudden, involuntary job loss begins with initial shock and disbelief, followed by anger and protest. Some people even go through a bargaining stage similar to that experienced by terminally ill patients, in which they plead (with employers, spouses, or God) for more time, a second chance, and so on. This stage may be followed by depression, loneliness, or physical ailments. Jobless workers may feel panic, guilt about the loss, or resentment, and they may be unable to participate in their normal activities, even though these are unrelated to work. Occasionally they even "go postal"—an unfortunate term that refers to highly publicized postal workers who have sought murderous revenge on those whom they perceived as responsible for their job loss, along with anyone else who happened to be around at the time.

Once the grief and anger reactions have passed, the person can begin to accommodate the loss, develop hope, and redirect his or her energies toward finding another job or career. However, job loss may be more difficult to resolve for middle-aged people than for young adults. First, it is likely that the middle-aged individual has more of his or her identity invested in the job. Second, older people are likely to face age discrimination both in hiring and in training programs—in spite of federal laws barring such discrimination. Third, whatever job the worker can find is likely to have a lower salary and status than the previous one (Kelvin & Jarrett, 1985; Sinfeld, 1985). People who have worked their way up the job hierarchy in a company to a position that is beyond their educational qualifications are particularly vulnerable to reduced salary and loss of status because their skills are often specific to that particular company (DuBrin, 1978).

In general, those who cope best with job loss try to take it in stride and not turn their anger inward by blaming themselves or considering themselves professional and personal failures. Additional factors that determine how well people cope with job loss are summarized in Table 15–4.

JOB BURNOUT Burnout, as noted earlier, is a psychological state of emotional exhaustion, often accompanied by extreme cynicism, that is especially prevalent among individuals in the helping professions (Maslach & Jackson, 1979). Social workers, police officers, nurses, therapists, teachers, and others who must work in close personal contact with those whom they serve—often in strained, tension-filled situations—are especially at risk. In a different sense, burnout also applies to the effect on people who have worked hard and spent all their energies toward reaching a virtually impossible goal—and failed (Freudenberger & Richelson, 1980). Workers in low-status, subordinate positions who cannot respond to maltreatment that they sometimes experience on the job may also suffer burnout (Holt, 1982).

By and large, people in the helping professions who suffer job burnout are idealistic, highly motivated, extremely competent workers who finally realize

TABLE 15–4 FACTORS IN COPING WITH JOB LOSS

Physical health: One of the first ways of coping with losing a job is to find another one, and it is easier for individuals to present themselves effectively during job interviews if they are in good health. Being in good physical condition also adds to the ability to handle the stress, unforeseen challenges, and fatigue associated with losing a job.

Physical and financial resources: Losing a job places greater stress on individuals who have no financial resources than on those who can pay their bills while they are looking for work. Those without financial resources may be forced to sell their house and scale down their lifestyle—all of which adds to the stress created by the job loss.

Specific skills: People with marketable job skills will probably have less difficulty finding a job than those with inadequate or outmoded training.

Social support: An individual who is surrounded by a loving, supportive family can often cope better with job loss than someone who is alone or has troubled family relations.

Cognitive understanding of events: The ability to understand the reasons behind a job loss (was it corporate downsizing, poor performance, or a personality clash?) helps the individual handle the dislocation and gather the energy to search for a new job. This ability comes partly from education and past experience.

Anticipation and preparation: An aerospace engineer who understood the implications of the dismantling of the Soviet Union and the end of the cold war could anticipate the possibility of job loss and could train for employment in related fields well in advance of being laid off. People who can't or don't anticipate job loss are left with fewer options.

Personality factors: Personality traits such as flexibility, openness to experience, and resilience prepare the individual to handle the pressures associated with finding a new job.

Life history: Individuals who have lost jobs before and have lived through periods of unemployment may react differently to a job loss than those who have never had these experiences.

---

that they cannot make the difference they once thought they could. Here, the general cause of burnout is lack of rewards in a work situation in which great effort has been expended and high hopes originally predominated (Chance, 1981).

People who experience burnout often start out with high ideals and the best of intentions. In the course of their work, they realize that they are having little effect on the people they are trying to aid or that the problems they are trying to solve are so overwhelming and the tasks so difficult that they can never succeed. The problems that some have chosen to tackle—poverty, educational failure, disease and disease prevention, family violence, drug abuse—are difficult or impossible to solve. Also, the people whom they try to help may resent their efforts. To make matters even worse, they may also be forced to spend hours filling out forms to comply with institutional, state, and federal regulations, a thankless task that takes considerable time and energy away from helping people.

Early warning signs of burnout include increasingly frequent anger, frustration, and despair. Work becomes a burden that the individual can no longer handle. Burned-out workers may even turn on the people they are supposed to help or may withdraw from emotional involvement into cold detachment.

Physical exhaustion, psychosomatic illnesses, low morale, mediocre performance, and absenteeism commonly accompany burnout (Maslach & Jackson, 1979).

There is little anyone can do to eliminate the causes of burnout without completely transforming society and the situations in which people work. Workers can, however, avoid or at least minimize burnout by learning to be realistic in their approach to their work and their goals, promoting changes in their job requirements or work flow, attempting to keep the rest of their life separate from their work (i.e., not taking their work troubles home with them), and developing interests outside of their jobs. That's actually good advice for all workers, not just potential burnout victims.

JOB STRESS IN CONTEXT   Job stress is not simply a function of what goes on in the workplace. Both men and women have a large number of work and family roles that sometimes compete with one another. A subtle form of discrimination is sometimes practiced in the workplace when only women are thought to have such competing roles; sometimes it is feared that women will bring their family problems to work and therefore that they are less qualified than men to hold responsible jobs. Thus, they may quit or find themselves under too much stress to deal effectively with the demands of work. Some authors suggest that if we include the multiplicity of work and family roles in our models of work stress, we rediscover men's roles as fathers and husbands. With this type of model, men as well as women could feel free to acknowledge and deal with family-based as well as work-based sources of stress, and organizations could make adjustments to adapt to the conflicting demands of work and family (Baruch et al., 1987).

REVIEW & APPLY

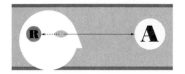

1. How does the occupational pattern that is characteristic of midlife today differ from the "classic" occupational cycle?
2. Why is middle age often a period of career reassessment?
3. List some problems and coping mechanisms that are associated with job loss.
4. Describe the causes and symptoms of job burnout.

SUMMARY

Personality Continuity and Change

- Numerous recent studies have provided evidence that the course of midlife is extremely diverse and varied.
- The middle and later years can be very complex because most middle-aged people have both adolescent or young adult children and aging parents.
- According to Erikson, the basic issue facing people at this time of life is generativity versus self-absorption. Generativity occurs within three domains: procreative, productive, and creative. The alternative is self-absorption and a sense of stagnation and boredom.

- Peck believes that the issues and tasks of middle and old age are more numerous than suggested by Erikson. He proposes seven issues or conflicts of adult development (see Table 15–1).
- Men in middle age feel committed to both work and family, have developed routines that help them cope as problems arise, and have to face the problems of caring for aging parents, dealing with adolescent children, coming to terms with personal limitations, and recognizing increasing physical vulnerability.
- There are four general paths in middle age for men. For transcendent-generative men, midlife is a time

of fulfillment and accomplishment; pseudo-developed men maintain a facade but feel lost, confused, or bored; men in midlife crisis feel unable to meet demands and solve problems; and punitive-disenchanted men are unhappy or alienated .

■ Traditionally, women define themselves more in terms of the family cycle than by their place in the career cycle. Apter has identified four "types of midlife women." Traditional women have relatively little difficulty shifting into the role of mature woman; innovative women reassess their roles; expansive women make marked changes in their goals in midlife in an attempt to expand their horizons; and protesters attempt to postpone midlife as long as possible.

■ Common role conflicts for middle-aged women involve finding time for both family and career. Role strain is associated with an overload of demands within the same role.

Family and Friends: Interpersonal Contacts

■ Middle-aged people act as a bridge between the younger and older generations. They often serve as family kinkeepers, maintaining family rituals, celebrating achievements, keeping alive family histories, and so on.

■ Relationships with adult children include launching the children into their own independent lives. This is an important transition for the parents. They may be unhappy during the transition itself but may enjoy the increase in freedom, privacy, and discretionary income once the children are gone.

■ Many Americans are raising children alone and may find themselves in sharp conflict or shifting relationships with their adolescent children.

■ After successfully launching their last child, parents turn to roles and interests other than parenthood. This stage of the family life cycle is sometimes referred to as the empty nest.

■ By middle age, the relationship between parents and their children is more reciprocal than it has ever been before.

■ How adult children behave toward their parents depends to a large extent on their life experiences and their stage in the family life cycle. Most middle-aged people have an ongoing relationship with their aging parents that includes regular contact, shared memories, and reciprocal exchange of assistance.

■ With age, role reversals gradually take place for middle-aged people and their parents. The middle-aged become the generation in charge.

■ Most middle-aged people take responsibility for the long-term care of their parents. They provide social support, affection, and a sense of having someone to rely on. Daughters are much more likely than sons to provide care for aging parents.

■ The majority of Americans become grandparents in middle age. Although grandparenting is highly individualized, there are four important roles that grandparents fulfill: providing stability, being available in times of emergency, acting as arbitrator, and maintaining the family's biography.

■ Friendships are often a central part of life for middle-aged people. For older people whose children are grown or who are widowed, friendship often fills many vital emotional needs.

The Changing Family

■ Divorce usually occurs as the culmination of a long process of emotional distancing. Many couples observe that it's no longer necessary to stay together for the sake of the children. Divorce is also associated with unrealistic expectations about marriage.

■ Divorced people suffer from a wide range of problems, including financial hardship and the practical problems of maintaining a household. Divorce can be particularly difficult in middle age because the partners have grown accustomed to their way of life.

■ Establishing a new lifestyle after divorce is easier for some people than for others. Some welcome a chance to start over, while for others the idea of living alone is frightening.

■ Most divorced individuals experience considerable improvement in well-being within two or three years of the final separation. However, a sizable minority remain bitter and isolated even ten years after the divorce.

■ The main reasons that couples stay together is that they like each other and consider each other their best friend.

■ Middle-aged people who remain married or remarry report higher levels of general happiness and satisfaction than those who are single.

■ Remarriage often creates a reconstituted or blended family. These families present many role adjustment problems for both stepparents and stepchildren. Also, second marriages operate within a more complex family organization that can cause considerable conflict.

■ The greatest difficulties in a stepparent-stepchild relationship are disciplining the children, adjusting to the habits and personalities of the children, and gaining the children's acceptance. Taking time to develop mutual trust, affection, and respect often helps in forming a workable relationship.

Occupational Continuity and Change

- Adult development may produce many shifts in attitudes, career needs, and goals. Also, jobs change so quickly or are eliminated in such numbers that the one-career pattern no longer applies to most people.
- A period of serious career reassessment or reexamination often occurs at midlife because workers find that they are not being promoted as rapidly as they had expected or that a job is less desirable than anticipated.
- Middle-aged people who experience major midlife transitions are more likely to make dramatic changes in their occupation, but only a minority of people make such dramatic career shifts.
- Career changes can cause high levels of stress, anxiety, and disequilibrium.

- People who get fired, are laid off indefinitely, or experience forced retirement often face emotional problems. They may react in ways that are similar to the grief response triggered by the death of a loved one.
- Job loss may be more difficult to resolve for middle-aged people than for young adults. Those who cope best with job loss try to take it in stride and not turn their anger inward by blaming themselves or considering themselves failures.
- Job burnout is a psychological state of emotional exhaustion, often accompanied by extreme cynicism, that is especially prevalent among individuals in the helping professions.

KEY TERMS

kinkeepers

empty nest

reconstituted or blended families

job burnout

USING WHAT YOU'VE LEARNED

What are the major issues and concerns for people in middle adulthood? Discuss this question with a friend or relative who is between the ages of 40 and 60. How do various aspects of family and work life affect her or his concerns? Encourage your respondent to compare his or her current concerns and interests with those of 10 years ago. How has this person's life changed in the last decade?

Has your respondent experienced some of the events and thoughts discussed in this chapter? Are they normative and predictable events and reactions, or is your respondent experiencing events that are off-time? Can he or she identify an area marked by continuity and an area marked by change? Does the greatest source of stress involve interpersonal relationships, or is it related to the person's career?

SUGGESTED READINGS

ANDERSON, J. (1990). *The single mother's book*. Atlanta: Peachtree Publishers. A well-organized guide to managing life—children, work, home, finances, and everything else—as a single mother.

APTER, T. E. (1995). Secret paths: Women in the new midlife. New York: W. W. Norton and Company. Social Psychologist, Terri Apter completes another one of her extensive interview studies and presents it in a popular form.

CARNOY, M., & CARNOY, D. (1995). *Fathers of a certain age: The joys and problems of middle-aged fatherhood*. Boston: Faber and Faber. Prompted by his own mid-

dle-aged second marriage and fatherhood, this father (Martin), collaborating with his adult son (David), explores the complexities of today's mixed families and shifting roles, using extensive interview data.

GEIST, W. (1997). *The big five-oh: Facing, fearing, and fighting fifty*. New York: William Morrow. Television commentator and humorist Bill Geist reacts to the seemingly unexpected phenomenon of growing older.

GOWING, M. K., KRAFT, J. D., & QUICK, J. C. (Eds.) (1998). *The new organizational reality: Downsizing, re-*

structuring, and revitalization. Washington, DC: American Psychological Association. A multidisciplinary collection of readings on recent business trends that cover both the corporation's and the worker's point of view.

KEGAN, R. (1995). *In over our heads: The mental demands of modern life.* Cambridge, MA: Harvard University Press. Robert Kegan, developmental scholar, describes the complex "mental demands" of public and private life that challenge today's adults and their personal struggles to make sense of it all.

LOPATA, H. Z. (Ed.) (1987). *Widows.* Durham, NC: Duke University Press. A collection of articles about widows in diverse cultures and the social support systems available.

MCCRAE, R. P., & COSTA, P. T. (1990). *Personality in adulthood.* New York: Guilford Press. An updated presentation by these authors, containing theory and research that emphasize continuity of personality characteristics.

RAWLINS, W. K. (1992). *Friendship matters.* Hawthorne, NY: Aldine de Gruyter. A review of studies demonstrating that friends are important as a buffer against stress and as a source of positive feedback.

ROUNDTREE, C. (1994). *On women turning 50: Celebrating midlife discoveries.* San Francisco: Harper. A delightful set of interviews, photographs, and profiles of contemporary women at midlife—from Charlayne Hunter-Gault to Gloria Steinam.

SCHREIBER, L. A. (1990). *Midstream: The story of a mother's death and a daughter's renewal.* New York: Penguin. A personal chronicle of this 40-year-old journalist's experiences with her mother's illness and death. It is a warm, caring memoir full of humor, hope, anger, and renewal.

SHEEHY, G. (1995). *New passages: Mapping your life across time.* New York: Random House. From her interviews, this journalist suggests that today's Baby Boomers reject the notion of middle age and instead begin a second adulthood at 45—one with deeper meaning and more playfulness.

Older Adults: Physical and Cognitive Development

CHAPTER OUTLINE

CHAPTER OBJECTIVES

By the time you have finished this chapter, you should be able to do the following:

1. Describe the myths and realities of aging.
2. Describe the physical changes that are characteristic of the aging process and the factors that contribute to these changes.
3. Compare and contrast the various theories and explanations of the aging process.
4. Explain the cognitive changes that occur with age, differentiating those that are intrinsic to the aging process from the secondary causes of cognitive decline.

Some years ago, Don and his 77-year-old father were huffing and puffing up a hilly trail in a national park; they were passed by two much younger men who were briskly taking the hill in stride. As the young men went by, one of them glanced back and then said to the other, "Man, I sure don't want to get old." Don's father quickly responded, with a twinkle in his eye, "Neither do I!" As this example shows, age is relative; how old you are depends in part on how old you *think* you are.

Later adulthood is an important period in its own right. It begins in the early sixties, and for some people it may span as many as 40 years. In some societies, people in their late adult years are recognized and awarded high status as elders. In contrast, Western society seems to have only recently rediscovered this large and growing segment of the population, often called "senior citizens."

In this chapter we'll look at the physical and intellectual development that occurs in later adulthood, along with the individual's reactions to developmental changes. Although it may seem odd to use the term *development* in the chapter title, the term actually refers to both growth and decline as a result of the influences of heredity and environment.

AGING TODAY

What is it like to grow old? For many people, the prospects are so grim that they never want to find out. In fact, some young people seem to view old age as a state of marginal existence. They fear the losses of energy, control, flexibility, sexuality, physical mobility, memory, and even intelligence that they think go hand in hand with aging. In this section we will examine some of the stereotypes of older adults and their impact. We will also take a decade-by-decade look at some of the characteristics of older adults.

AGEISM AND STEREOTYPES

Older people are often stereotyped. Polls of the general population, including older adults, have documented both negative and positive images of older people (see Table 16–1). Such stereotypes make it difficult to see older people accurately, to understand them as the varied individuals they really are. Stereotypes may even lead to attitudes and policies that discourage older adults from active participation in work and leisure activities. Studies also indicate that there are gender differences in people's perceptions of aging. For example, in a survey of popular movies over the last several decades, Doris Bazzini and colleagues (1997) found that older women are more often portrayed as unattractive, unfriendly, and unintelligent than are older men.

THE ERROR OF GENERALIZING FROM THE FEW TO THE MANY   Objectively, the situation of some older citizens seems unfulfilling. On average, today's older adults have a lower educational level than the younger popula-

One misperception of older people based on a negative stereotype is that they are less productive and efficient workers than younger people are.

TABLE 16–1   COMMON MISPERCEPTIONS ABOUT THE ELDERLY BASED ON STEREOTYPES

EXAMPLES OF MISPERCEPTIONS BASED ON NEGATIVE STEREOTYPES

Most older people are poor.

Most older people are unable to keep up with inflation.

Most older people are ill-housed.

Most older people are frail and in poor health.

The aged are impotent as a political force and require advocacy.

Most older people are inadequate employees; they are less productive, efficient, motivated, innovative, and creative than younger workers. Most older workers are accident-prone.

Older people are mentally slower and more forgetful; they are less able to learn new things.

Older people tend to be intellectually rigid and dogmatic. Most old persons are set in their ways and unable or unwilling to change.

A majority of older people are socially isolated and lonely. Most are disengaging or disengaged from society.

Most older people are confined to long-term-care institutions.

EXAMPLES OF MISPERCEPTIONS BASED ON POSITIVE STEREOTYPES

The aged are relatively well off; they are not poor but in good economic shape. Their benefits are generously provided by working members of society.

The aged are a potential political force that votes and participates in unity and in great numbers.

Older people make friends very easily. They are kind and amiable.

Most older people are mature, experienced, wise, and interesting.

Most older people are good listeners and are especially patient with children.

A majority of older people are very kind and generous to their children and grandchildren.

Source: S. Lubomudrov (1987). Congressional Perceptions of the Elderly: The Use of Stereotypes in the Legislative Process. *Journal of Gerontology, 27,* 77–81. Copyright © The Gerontological Society of America.

tion. Some nursing homes have become notorious for taking advantage of older people, giving them just enough care for survival and little reason to live and thrive. Aside from stories about nursing home abuses, newspapers are also filled with gruesome stories about elderly women being mugged and robbed and even raped by groups of vicious teenagers, and about desperate older people shoplifting hamburger meat or living on canned dog food. Until aggressive advocacy groups like the Gray Panthers began to voice the needs of older people and the American Association of Retired Persons (AARP) began organizing resources to help older adults, most people assumed that older people were not even able to speak for themselves. There has also been such a lack of interest in older people that almost no research was conducted on them until the past three decades. Bernice Neugarten (1970) uses the word **ageism** to describe this attitude of indifference and neglect. No wonder old age has often seemed to be a horrible fate.

Do the stereotypes of the past still exist now that people over age 65 account for almost 13% of the population and public awareness of them has greatly increased? At California State University, 160 students were asked a series of questions about what old people are like (Babladelis, 1987). The students estimated that 30% of the U.S. population was old and in need of services. They thought that the word *old* should apply to people over age 60. Also, they reported that although they had family members and neighbors who were old, they were "reluctant to spend time with old people." The students reported having a concerned, dutiful attitude toward old people, but feeling that they had a lot of undesirable characteristics—such as being senile, self-centered, boring, and too talkative. They viewed old people as generally physically disabled. Even though many of these students had grandparents in their sixties who were quite vigorous, their attitudes about the old had not changed dramatically from similar attitudes prevailing in the late 1970s (Babladelis, 1987).

In general, people of all ages tend to assign more negative stereotypes to older people and more positive ones to younger people (Hummert et al., 1995). Negative attitudes and stereotypes about older people are not necessarily the rule, however. Several studies have found that attitudes toward older people are often ambivalent, if not contradictory. Older people are often seen as both wise and senile, both kind and grouchy, and both concerned for others and inactive and unsociable (Crockett & Hummert, 1987). Thus, the stereotypes just presented are a mosaic of fact and fantasy. Some problems are only loosely associated with aging; failing health and loneliness do not have to be part of aging any more than acne and social awkwardness have to be part of adolescence. The population over age 65 has its marathoners and executives as well as its shut-ins and bench-sitters. Negative stereotypes not only instill fear of aging in the young but also have a powerful grip on older people. Polls have shown that most older adults have a much higher opinion of their own economic and social condition than does the general public. At the same time, however, they often believe that they are among the lucky few who have escaped the misery of aging in the United States.

A SOCIOLOGICAL/CULTURAL PERSPECTIVE People have not always dreaded old age. In the Bible, elders were considered to possess great wisdom. In American Indian tribes, older people have traditionally been venerated as wise elders, transmitters of culture, and a storehouse of historical lore. In China, Japan, and other Far Eastern countries, older people are venerated and respected in a tradition known as **filial piety**. In Japan, for example, more than three out of four older adults live with their children, and respect is demon-

ageism A widely prevalent social attitude that overvalues youth and discriminates against the elderly.

filial piety The veneration given the elderly in Eastern cultures. This respect is manifested in cultural traditions as well as everyday encounters.

strated through a variety of everyday activities. At home, meals are prepared with everyone's tastes in mind, and in public, people bow with respect when they pass an older person. However, although respect for older people remains strong in Japan, it is more pronounced among middle-aged and rural people than young adults and urban residents (Palmore & Maeda, 1985).

In colonial America, the biblical tradition of veneration for elders was a powerful cultural influence. Old age was viewed as an outward manifestation of divine grace and favor, the reward for an extraordinarily upright life. Benjamin Franklin played a major role in drafting the Constitution not only because he was a shrewd parliamentarian but also because he was over 80 years old at the time and was viewed as "crowned" with the glory of his years. From a pragmatic point of view, reverence for age was powerful because so few people managed to achieve it. The demographic contrast between then and now is startling; in the colonial period, the median age of the population was 16, and only 2% reached the age of 65. Some accounts of early colonists describe adults in their thirties as wrinkled, balding, or gray (Fischer, 1978).

Today, the median age of the U.S. population is 34.6 and climbing. Approximately one in eight Americans is 65 or older. As a result of the aging of the Baby Boomers and the trend toward lower birth rates and declining death rates, the percentage of the population over age 65 will rise dramatically in the next three decades. According to U.S. Census Bureau projections, by the year 2030, one out of every five Americans will be 65 or older (see Table 16–2). Modern medicine helps many people survive serious illnesses and injuries, and some people continue to live despite severe impairments. However, many other older people are vigorous, involved, and independent. Clearly, we are witnessing the emergence of an unprecedented group of healthy, educated, retired or partly retired older people, at least in the developed nations. Figure 16–1 shows population pyramids for men and women in selected nations (shaded areas represent percentages in the paid labor force). Note in particular the much larger number of people in the 65 and older age range in developed nations like the United States.

In many societies, including China, Japan, and other Asian nations, older people tend to be venerated and respected.

FOUR DECADES OF LATER LIFE

Nowadays, an average 60-year-old can expect to live another 21 years; those who are now 75 years old can look forward to an average of 11 more years (National Center for Health Statistics, 1995). Thus, old age has become a signif-

TABLE 16–2   AGING OF THE POPULATION: PERCENTAGE OF THE POPULATION 65 YEARS OF AGE AND OVER

ACTUAL		PROJECTED	
Year	Total	Year	Total
1950	8.1%	2000	12.8%
1960	9.2	2010	13.4
1970	9.8	2020	16.3
1980	11.3	2030	20.1
1990	12.5		

Source: U.S. Census Bureau, 1997.

FIGURE 16–1 POPULATION PYRAMID FOR SELECTED NATIONS

Source: U.S. Census Bureau.

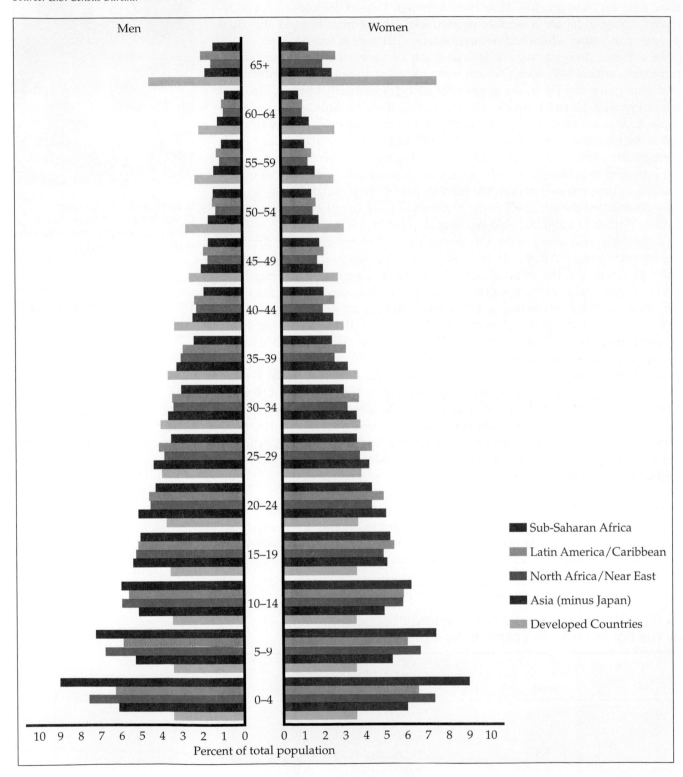

icant part of the lifespan. However, individuals in later adulthood are not a homogeneous group. A currently employed or newly retired and relatively hardy 65-year-old may be caring for an 85- or 90-year-old parent who may be quite frail. These people are members of two separate generations; they are clearly different cohorts with respect to historical events. In addition, many older people behave more like younger people. Medical advances as well as cultural factors influence the way older people live. Today, many active 70-year-olds are doing things that people in their fifties did just 30 years ago (Neugarten & Neugarten, 1987).

Irene Burnside and colleagues (1979) have analyzed older adulthood in terms of four decades of later life. Here we take a brief look at the major features of each decade.

"YOUNG-OLD": 60 TO 69   This decade marks a major transition. In our sixties, most of us must begin to adapt to a new role structure (Havighurst, 1972). Income is often reduced by retirement or reduced hours of work—whether voluntarily or otherwise—and some friends and colleagues die. Society frequently reduces its expectations of people in their sixties, demanding less energy, independence, and creativity. Burnside laments this social response, believing that it demoralizes older adults, especially those who remain healthy and vigorous. Many people in their sixties accept these expectations and respond by slowing the pace of their life, thereby creating a self-fulfilling prophecy.

Physical strength does wane somewhat, and reduced strength may pose problems for industrial workers who are still on the job. Yet many people in their sixties have plenty of energy and seek out new and different activities. Many recently retired people are healthy, hardy, and well educated. They may use their new leisure time for self-enhancement or for community or political activities. Some enjoy regular athletic and sexual activity. Some retirees are determined to remain givers, producers, and mentors. They become volunteer executives in small businesses, visitors to hospitals, or foster grandparents.

Many recently retired people become involved in community or political activities during their new leisure time.

There is tremendous variation in this age group with regard to retirement. Whereas most people retire at around age 65, others retire at age 55 and still others at age 75. Retirement decisions in any decade depend on such issues as health, energy level, and type of work. (As noted in an earlier chapter, those who perform hard physical labor are likely to be forced to retire much earlier than those who do white-collar work.) The decision to retire also depends on interpersonal factors such as the health of a spouse and the relocation of friends, as well as "environmental" issues such as family finances (Quinn & Burkhauser, 1990). Whereas one 68-year-old with little savings may be forced to continue working to pay the bills, another may be able to retire in comfort on a pension and invested savings supplemented by Social Security benefits.

"MIDDLE-AGED-OLD": 70 TO 79   A bigger shift occurs in our seventies than in the previous two decades. According to Burnside, the major developmental task of people in their seventies is to maintain the personality integration they achieved by their sixties. Many people in their seventies (*septuagenarians*) suffer loss and illness. More friends and family members die. Along with a contracting social world, many must cope with reduced participation in formal organizations. They often exhibit restlessness and irritability. Their own health problems tend to become more troublesome during this decade. There is often a decline in sexual activity for both men and women, in many cases because of the loss of a sexual partner. Despite these losses, many septuagenarians are able to avoid the more serious effects of the disabilities that often accompany advanced age. Often those who have suffered heart attacks, strokes, or cancer survive—most without serious disability—because of improved medical care and healthier lifestyles (see Figure 16–2). (Note that this figure is limited to patterns of disability for women because they far outnumber men in the later decades.)

"OLD-OLD": 80 TO 89   Although age is certainly one of the markers of the transition from young-old to old-old, it is not the only one. Old age in a person's eighties has been poignantly described as a "gradual process which be-

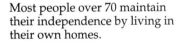

Most people over 70 maintain their independence by living in their own homes.

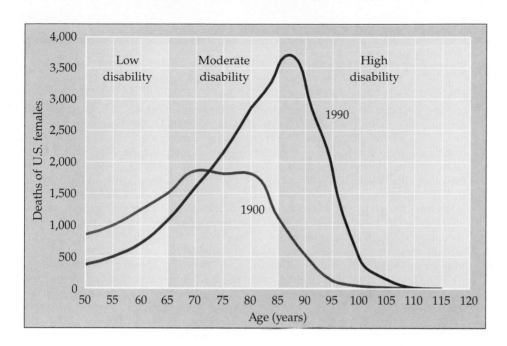

FIGURE 16–2

Patterns of disability and death are changing. Because of healthier lifestyles and improved medical care, people are living longer than ever before with heart disease, stroke, and cancer. As a result of extended life, people 85 years and older may live with a high level of disability.

Source: From "The Aging of the Human Species" by S. Jay Olshansky, Bruce A. Carnes, and Christine K. Cassel. Copyright © 1993 by Scientific American, Inc. All rights reserved.

gins the very first day one begins to live in his memories" (Burnside et al., 1979).

Most people in their eighties (*octogenarians*) experience increased difficulty in adapting to and interacting with their surroundings. Many need a streamlined, barrier-free environment that offers both privacy and stimulation. They need help in maintaining social and cultural contacts.

Most, but not all, 85-year-olds are frail. But frailty does not necessarily imply disability or total dependence. Although 25% of people currently in this age group were hospitalized for some time in the previous year, only 10% are seriously disabled. Most people over age 85 live in their own homes, including 30% who live alone. Only 25% reside in nursing homes or other institutions (Longino, 1987, 1988). Nevertheless, caring for the frail elderly is increasingly a matter of international concern, as discussed in "Eye on Diversity," page 552. We will consider social policy and the frail elderly in more detail in Chapter 17.

People over 85 make up the fastest-growing segment of the population. Whereas in 1980 there were 2.3 million people in this age group, it is estimated that there will be approximately 5 million by 2000. By 2040, when the Baby Boomers are over age 80, this group is expected to swell to between 8 million and 13 million people (Longino, 1988; U.S. Census Bureau, 1995).

"VERY OLD-OLD": 90 AND OVER   There are fewer data on people over age 90 (*nonagerians*) than on 60-, 70-, or 80-year-olds. It is difficult to obtain accurate information about the health and social circumstances of people in this age group.

Although health problems become more severe, nonagenarians can successfully alter their activities so as to make the most of what they have. One practicing psychiatrist in her nineties advises creating new fields of activity by removing the competitive element of earlier years. She emphasizes the advantages of old age, such as freedom from work pressures and responsibilities (Burnside et al., 1979). The changes that shape life in our nineties occur gradually and over a long period. If previous crises have been resolved in

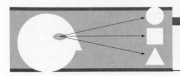

EYE ON DIVERSITY

CARING FOR THE FRAIL ELDERLY

How best to care for the frailest and oldest members of society is a concern shared by older adults, family members, and policy makers throughout the world. As the focus of public policy, care of the elderly has undergone dramatic changes in thinking and implementation over the past decade in such countries as Great Britain, Sweden, Denmark, the Netherlands, and Australia. The purpose of these policy changes has been to reduce costs to taxpayers and to improve the effectiveness and efficiency of elder care.

Pressure from the users of elder-care services—older people themselves—is especially potent in countries with organized senior citizen groups. In Sweden, for example, 30% of all older adults belong to pensioners' associations that make their members' voices heard at both the national and local levels. Even in countries with few organized groups, government officials have gotten the message that they must listen to what older people and their families want and must adapt existing programs to fit their needs. In general, after listening to constituents' voices, policy makers have embraced three goals that are changing the nature of elder care.

The first goal is to do as much as possible to keep older adults integrated into society while at the same time trying to improve the quality of their life and the care they receive. Doing this involves improving care in nursing homes and other residential facilities. It also involves trying to make existing residential facilities less restrictive and, when possible, moving older people out of these facilities into home and day-care situations. Bleddyn Davies (1993), who has analyzed the elder-care policies of various nations, comments on this trend:

> The official authors of policy documents the world over seem to be working hard to express the same sentiments, sometimes using almost the same words. The English version is typical: One of the three main aims of the comprehensive new policy is "to enable persons as far as possible to live in their own homes or in a homelike environment in the local community." (Cm. 849, 1989; Davies 1993)

The goal of caring for older people in their own homes entails a second goal: to recognize the burdens and stresses experienced by caregivers and devise programs to help avoid caregiver burnout. Policy statements from Great Britain give high priority to pro-viding practical support to caregivers. In Sweden, legislation requires that local governments listen to what caregivers say and provide support for their efforts. Since 1989, part of this support has been given in the form of up to 30 days' paid leave, reimbursed through sick-leave insurance policies. Both Great Britain and Australia have elevated the issue of rest for long-time caregivers to a national concern.

Naturally, these ambitious goals result in higher costs for taxpayers. Limiting these costs and improving the effectiveness and efficiency of elder care programs is the third policy goal. In the Netherlands, for example, a committee on health care financing was charged with the task of providing "strategies for volume and cost containment against the background of an aging population" (Dekker et al., 1987). Similarly, the Australian Aged Care Reform Strategy is committed to efficient and equitable use of public funds.

In most countries, meeting the evolving needs of frail older adults and their caregivers requires major changes in societal assumptions, behaviors, and practices. Meeting these needs also requires overcoming public resistance to allocating scarce resources to elder care at the expense of other social programs.

---

satisfactory ways, this decade can be joyful, serene, and fulfilling. It is also noteworthy that people who survive to their nineties are often healthier, more agile, and more active than people 20 years younger (Perls, 1995); the reason is that they have survived the diseases and other afflictions that cause some people to die in their seventies and eighties.

To reiterate, "the aged" are not a single cohesive group but, rather, a collection of subgroups, ranging from the active 65-year-old to the frail nonagenarian. Each group has its unique problems and abilities. To an extent, many share age-related difficulties of reduced income, failing health, and loss of loved ones. But *having* a problem is not the same as *being* a problem. The all-too-popular view of people over age 65 as needy, unproductive, and unhappy is an inaccurate one indeed.

STUDY CHART ▸ FOUR DECADES OF LATER LIFE

"Young-old" (60 to 69): For many people in their sixties, physical strength begins to wane, yet many others remain strong, healthy, and hardy. Depending upon their trade or profession, some people retire in their sixties and others do not.

"Middle-aged-old" (70 to 79): Health problems increase, and there is often a marked decline in sexual activity. A major life task is maintaining personality integration in the face of waning sensory capabilities and increased likelihood of disabilities.

"Old-old" (80 to 89): Most people now experience increased difficulty in daily functioning, and most begin to become frail and in need of some form of care. People over 85 are currently the fastest-growing segment of the population.

"Very-old-old" (90 and over): Health and psychological problems become severe for many people ninety and older, although many are instead healthier and more active than younger old people. This possibility occurs for those who have survived the diseases and afflictions that cause some people to die or to become debilitated in their seventies and eighties.

1. What are some of the positive and negative views of aging held by our society? Distinguish between stereotypes and realities.
2. How do attitudes toward older people differ in other cultures?
3. How does lumping older adults into a single all-encompassing category misrepresent them?

REVIEW & APPLY

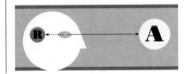

PHYSICAL ASPECTS OF AGING

The physical aspects of aging determine many of the changes and limitations that occur in later adulthood. Physical aging is universal. It comes sooner for some people and later for others, but it is inevitable. All bodily systems age, even under optimal genetic and environmental circumstances, although they do not age at the same rate. Yet, for most bodily systems, the processes of aging begin in early and middle adulthood. Many of the effects of aging are not noticed until later adulthood because aging is gradual and most physical systems have considerable reserve capacity. Most individuals do not experience interruptions in daily living or major health problems until well into their seventies. With regard to life expectancy, Figure 16–3 shows that both black men and white men tend to have shorter lifespans than women, and that white women have the longest life expectancy of all.

The sensory and systemic slowdowns that we will examine here commonly accompany age, but not all old people show these signs of aging. Studies have found that people who remain physically fit and active can perform as well as younger people who are not physically fit (Birren et al., 1980). In addition, we cannot say that the predictable biological course of nature is the only explanation for physical aging. Many people who become partially or completely deaf in old age do so because of experiences earlier in life—such as a firecracker's going off close to their ear or frequent attendance at loud music concerts. Similarly, for most sensory deficiencies and defects of the internal organs,

Figure 16–3 Life Expectancy by Sex and Race: 1970–1992

Source: National Center for Health Statistics, 1995.

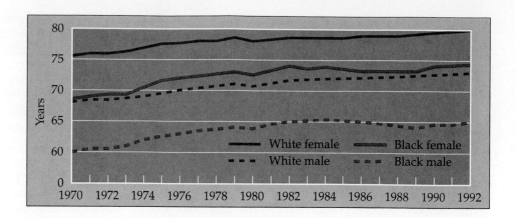

individual experiences begin the process of decline. Lifelong smokers may develop breathing problems in later years. An older woman with back trouble may have suffered strain as a young mother when she lifted her children. A 65-year-old man with heart trouble may have had early warning signs with a brief illness at age 40. Thus, not all of the changes that come with age are part of a normal aging process. The kind of life that individuals have led and the illnesses and accidents that they have experienced all contribute. These factors are sometimes called **pathological aging factors** (Elias, 1987). Some experts believe that the cumulative effects of disease and accidents are so much a part of life that it is impossible to separate them from the normal aspects of aging (Kohn, 1985).

We begin this section by looking at some of the more common physical changes that are the result of aging. Then we discuss some diseases and personal habits that contribute to physical decline.

THE CHANGING BODY

The body changes in a number of ways during later adulthood. Specifically, changes occur in appearance, the senses, muscles, bones, mobility, and internal organs. Daily cycles change as well, though not always as a result of aging per se—as discussed in "In Theory, In Fact," on facing page.

APPEARANCE A look in the mirror provides regular evidence of the aging process. The gray hair, the aging skin, a shift in posture, and deepening wrinkles are telltale signs. The skin becomes drier, thinner, and less elastic. In earlier years, wrinkles were formed by the use of particular muscles; "laugh lines" are an example. In old age, wrinkles are caused partly by loss of fat tissue under the skin and partly by the decrease in the skin's elasticity. The skin may take on the crisscrossed look of soft, crumpled paper or fine parchment (Rossman, 1977). There may be an increase in warts on the trunk, face, and scalp. Small blood vessels often break, producing tiny black-and-blue marks. Age spots may appear; these brown areas of pigmentation are popularly called "liver spots" even though they have nothing to do with the liver's functioning.

Some changes in appearance are a result of the normal aging that we all experience, although they can be modified by genetic factors. Identical twins, for example, show very similar patterns of aging. For many people, however, skin changes are closely related to exposure to wind, climate, abrasions, and especially ultraviolet rays from the sun. The sun diminishes the skin's ability to renew itself; a "healthy tan" leads to thin, wrinkled skin for some people and skin cancer for others. Some of these signs of aging skin can be controlled by

pathological aging factors
Cumulative effects of diseases and accidents that may accelerate aging.

SLEEP PATTERNS OF OLDER ADULTS

Is insomnia as normal in old age as white hair and wrinkles? Changes in sleep patterns are, but insomnia is not. Although about half of people over the age of 65 who live at home and about two-thirds of those in nursing homes and other long-term care facilities suffer from sleep problems, these problems are not an inevitable part of aging (Becker & Jamieson, 1992). They may be linked to a primary sleep disorder, an illness, or even medication. Depending on the problem, older insomniacs can often be helped.

Sleep problems must first be viewed in the context of the normal changes in sleep that occur as we age. According to researchers, the following sleep patterns are typical in individuals between the ages of 60 and 80 (Bachman, 1992; Becker & Jamieson, 1992):

- Older people average between 6 and $6\frac{1}{2}$ hours of sleep a night, although many remain in bed for up to 8 hours.
- Although many older people sleep more than younger adults, the amount of nightly sleep that older people get varies from fewer than 5 hours to more than 9 hours. Many older people have trouble going to sleep and may toss and turn for up to 30 minutes before falling asleep.
- After older people fall asleep, they experience significantly more early awakenings than younger people. It is considered normal for older people to spend up to 20% of their time in bed awake and to compensate by spending more time in bed.
- A change in the distribution of sleep stages results in an increase in stage 1 sleep (light sleep) and a decrease in stages 3 and 4 sleep (deep sleep). Thus, even when sleep occurs, generally it is not deep, satisfying sleep.

Adjustment sleep disorders occur in about one-third of older people, many of whom have a prior history of sound sleep. In these cases, insomnia is related to recent stresses in the older person's life, such as a recent hospitalization, retirement, or the death of a spouse or close friend. The individual

Changes in sleep patterns in older people are normal, but sleep disturbances are not.

reacts to these problems by being unable to fall asleep or to remain asleep for extended periods. Deprived of sleep, they may be irritable, anxious, or lethargic during the day and worried about their sleeplessness at night, thus making falling asleep even harder. Adjustment sleep disorder generally disappears over time as the older person learns to deal with the stress that causes it.

Poor sleep hygiene—sleep-related habits and behaviors that are incompatible with sleep—is another cause of insomnia. For example, individuals who drink caffeinated beverages before bedtime, who work until bedtime, or who watch the clock may experience heightened arousal, which is incompatible with sleep. Going to bed at irregular hours may also worsen the problem. Many older adults who experience these problems become preoccupied by their inability to sleep. They attempt to nap during the day or drink coffee to stay awake—both of which make the insomnia worse. Problems related to inadequate sleep hygiene can often be remedied by behavior modification. For example, individuals are encouraged to go to sleep at regular hours and to avoid caffeine.

Psychophysiologic insomnia is sometimes linked to adjustment sleep disorders and poor sleep hygiene. Individuals suffering from psychophysiologic insomnia associate bedtime and the bedroom with mental and physical

arousal and high levels of frustration. Philip Becker and Andrew Jamieson, psychiatrists who specialize in sleep disorders, explain:

> These sleep disturbances continue as a result of conditioned, learned arousal, even after normal coping and sleep habits are reestablished. Following her retirement, one of our older patients began lying in bed to plan her investments. Twelve months later, she successfully invested her money but could not fall asleep until after 1:00 A.M. To her surprise, however, she was able to fall asleep quickly in a motel room. Without realizing it, she had associated her bed and bedtime with thinking and problem solving rather than with rapid sleep onset (Becker & Jamieson, 1992, pages 48–49).

Behavioral therapies that stress positive sleep hygiene are often used to treat psychophysiologic insomnia.

Insomnia in older people is sometimes linked to a variety of psychiatric disorders, including major depression and anxiety. In these cases, appropriate medication may help alleviate the symptoms. Insomnia is also linked to symptoms of medical illness. The pain of arthritis, for example, may interrupt sleep. In addition, medications designed to treat medical disorders may have the unfortunate side effect of disturbing sleep.

Finally, sleep disturbances are also related to sleep apnea and periodic limb movements. *Sleep apnea* is an interruption in breathing that lasts at least ten seconds and occurs at least five times per hour. Individuals suffering from this disorder may be plagued by loud snoring, restless sleep, daytime sleepiness, and depression. *Periodic limb movements* are repeated jerks of the legs that arouse the sleeper. Individuals suffering from these disorders often benefit from medical treatment.

In sum, although severe sleep problems are not an inevitable part of growing old, they occur frequently in older people and should be viewed as problems that can often be treated successfully.

Older people generally suffer some sensory impairment, although the pattern and degree of loss vary widely.

eating well, staying healthy, and protecting your skin against lengthy exposure to the sun—either by avoiding exposure or using high-level sunblocking lotions.

THE SENSES The senses—hearing, vision, taste, and smell—generally become less efficient as we age. Many older people find that it takes longer to perceive and process an event through the sensory systems (Hoyer & Plude, 1980). However, although each kind of sensory decline described here is common among older individuals, not all older people are affected. Again, there is wide variation in the overall aging process.

Hearing deficits are quite common. In fact, hearing impairments hamper daily living for as many as a third of all older people (Fozard, 1990). These impairments are usually mild to moderate and often involve detecting voices in the midst of background noise (Olsho et al., 1985). In addition, there is greater hearing loss in the higher-frequency tones—those that occur in speech sounds such as *s*, *sh*, *ch*, and *f*. Sometimes, hearing aids are helpful in dealing with these problems, but often they are frustrating as well. Most hearing aids amplify all sound frequencies, including background noise, and therefore do not provide much help in picking out the details of what someone is saying. With or without hearing aids, older individuals with hearing loss may appear inattentive or embarrassed when in fact they simply can't understand what is being said. Others withdraw or become suspicious of what they cannot hear.

Several kinds of visual impairments are common in aging individuals. The ability to focus on objects declines as the lenses of the eyes become less flexible and able to accommodate. Depth perception may also be affected by loss of flexibility in the lens. Another problem associated with aging is that the lens may become cloudy and may eventually develop a **cataract**—an almost complete blockage of light and visual sensation. Yet another problem is **glaucoma**, an increase of pressure within the eyeball that can result in damage and gradual loss of vision. Fortunately, most cataracts can be removed through outpatient laser surgery, and glaucoma can often be treated with medication. Subtler problems like loss of flexibility in the lens are less easily remedied (Kline & Schieber, 1985).

Older individuals often lose some *visual acuity*—the ability to distinguish fine detail. It is not uncommon for older people to have difficulty perceiving visual details—whether it's reading names or numbers on mailboxes, distinguishing a staircase from a confusing carpet pattern, or simply reading a newspaper (Perlmutter, 1978). This difficulty may be due partly to the inflexibility of the lens and partly to the loss of visual "receptor" cells in the rear of the eye. Visual acuity can be increased with corrective lenses, including bifocals and trifocals (Kline & Schieber, 1985). Surgical procedures to improve visual acuity are still regarded as experimental, however.

From a perceptual viewpoint, many older people also have trouble ignoring irrelevant stimuli. For example, detecting a particular road sign in a crowded display of signs becomes more difficult with age. *Redundancy*, in the form of repeated, standard signs that convey the same instructions, helps older adults understand visual signals (Allen et al., 1992). Still, sooner or later there usually comes a point when older adults should avoid driving because of limited visual acuity (and reaction time), which is not an easy transition in areas where people lack alternative means of transportation.

In contrast, the sense of taste shows considerable stability even into relatively old age. The ability to taste sugar is particularly consistent (Bartoshuk & Weiffenbach, 1990). However, there appears to be some decline in the ability to

cataract Clouding of the lens of the eye that obstructs vision.

glaucoma Increased, potentially damaging pressure within the eyeball.

detect and distinguish among bitter tastes (Spitzer, 1988). People with complications such as **hypertension** (high blood pressure) have more trouble distinguishing among different tastes. Medications associated with aging may also be a factor, although Mary Spitzer (1988) has hypothesized that higher sensory thresholds may be involved as well. With regard to salt in particular, older people need more salt if they are to taste it at all. However, increased consumption of salt may contribute to increased hypertension.

Aging people also have difficulty distinguishing tastes within blended foods. This difficulty appears to be attributable more to a decline in the sense of smell than to a decrease in taste sensitivity (Bartoshuk & Weiffenbach, 1990). The sense of smell often shows a marked decline compared with that of taste.

MUSCLES, BONES, AND MOBILITY   Muscle weight—and, hence, strength and endurance—decreases with age. The structure and composition of muscle cells change; body weight may be lower than it was in early and middle adulthood owing to loss of muscle tissue, unless increased fat tissue compensates for the loss.

Muscle function is affected by the changing structure and composition of the skeleton. Older adults are usually an inch or more shorter than they were in early adulthood as a result of compression of cartilage in the spine (a long-term effect attributable to the effects of gravity), as well as changes in posture and loss of bone calcium (Whitbourne, 1985). The bones become weaker, hollower, and more brittle. Because they are more porous, they are more likely to fracture and take longer to mend (see Chapter 14). Older women are particularly susceptible to this condition (Belsky, 1984). To make things worse, the tendency to fall increases because of changes in the *vestibular system* that regulates balance (Ochs et al., 1985). The sensitivity of vestibular sensory receptors, which detect bodily movement and changes in position, declines markedly in old age.

In general, muscle reaction and functioning slows down, and it takes longer for a muscle to achieve a state of relaxation and readiness after being exerted (Gutmann, 1977). Muscles also function less efficiently if the cardiovascular system doesn't deliver enough nutrients or if it does not remove toxic waste products well, problems that can result both from aging and from poor health habits earlier in life. The blood vessels become less elastic; some become clogged. Consequently, there is less blood flow to the muscles. Decreased lung functioning may reduce the supply of oxygen to the muscles as well as to the brain. Fine motor coordination and speed of reaction time therefore decrease as well (Botwinick, 1984; Shock, 1952b).

Studies have shown that high-intensity exercise training—within age-appropriate limits—helps counteract muscle weakness and related physical frailty in very old people. For example, in a study of 37 men with an average age of 87 years, regular exercise increased muscle strength by more than 113% (Fiatarone et al., 1994). Similarly, a 3-year study conducted by the National Institute on Aging and the National Center for Nursing Research showed how strength and balance exercises can benefit frail people in their eighties and nineties. Those who engaged in muscle-building exercises were able to double and even triple their strength and, for the first time in years, perform many strength-related tasks without assistance (Krucoff, 1994).

INTERNAL ORGANS   The heart is a highly specialized muscle that suffers from some of the same problems as other muscles during aging. The heart also depends on the efficiency of the cardiovascular system, which can develop a

hypertension   Abnormally high blood pressure, sometimes accompanied by headaches and dizziness.

variety of problems associated with aging. The result is decreased blood flow to and from the heart and increased recovery time after each heart contraction (Timiras, 1978).

In old age, the lungs often have less capacity for oxygen intake. Of course, much lung trouble may be attributable not to the normal aging process but to prolonged damage caused by smoking and air pollution.

The reserve capacity of the heart, lungs, and other organs also decreases with age. During early adulthood, these organs are able to function at between four and ten times their normal level when under stress. Reserve capacity drops slowly but steadily in middle age and beyond. Older people may not notice the diminished capacity in day-to-day living, but they may realize it when, for example, they attempt to shovel snow after the first storm of the season. Diminished reserve capacity may be especially severe in extreme heat or cold. Many older people adapt more slowly to cold environments than they did when they were younger, and they may chill more easily, with a resulting low body temperature that is a serious health risk. Thus, older people often complain of being cold, and they are, even at temperatures that younger people find normal or on the warm side. Older people often have similar difficulty coping with heat, particularly if they exert themselves, as in mowing the lawn on a hot summer day. Nevertheless, older adults can often perform many of the tasks that they did when they were younger as long as they do them more slowly, take frequent breaks, and consume extra liquids such as water and nutrient-replenishing products like "Gator Ade."

The immune system also changes during later adulthood; production of antibodies peaks during adolescence and then starts to decline. The result is that by old age, people have less protection against microorganisms and disease (La Rue & Jarvik, 1982). That lessened protection is, for example, why annual flu shots are often routinely recommended for older people (and not-so-old people as well). Influenza can be lethal to older people, not only by itself but also because it makes the individual vulnerable to secondary bacterial infections such as pneumonia.

HEALTH, DISEASE, AND NUTRITION

Most older people, however, report having good to excellent health most of the time. They may be forced to adapt to the slow development of arthritis or to the side effects of medication to control high blood pressure and other disorders, but they usually can adapt easily. Health-related changes that occur during later adulthood fall into three general categories: They may be chronic; they may be related to changing nutritional needs; or they may involve misuse of prescribed medications.

CHRONIC HEALTH PROBLEMS   When health problems occur, they may become chronic—that is, lasting and recurrent. One major difference between childhood and late adulthood is in the incidence of acute versus chronic diseases. In childhood, acute diseases—which last a brief time and often climax with a fever and a rash—are very common. Older adults, however, often suffer from chronic conditions—illnesses that occur repeatedly and never go away. The most common chronic conditions are arthritis, heart problems, and high blood pressure, as well as the visual and hearing impairments discussed previously (Belsky, 1984). Accidental falls also produce chronic effects. In all, chronic diseases and impairments touch the lives of a substantial number of older adults, with 85% of people over age 65 reporting at least one chronic condition and 50% reporting two or more (Belsky, 1984).

To a great extent, this increase in health problems reflects the body's decreased ability to cope with stress, including the stress of disease. A disease that a young person can handle easily—for example, a respiratory infection—may linger on in an older person and cause permanent damage. Ironically, as the ability to cope with stress declines in old age, the number of stressful events in the person's life tends to increase (Timiras, 1978). Aside from health problems, stress comes about as a result of life-cycle crises such as retirement and widowhood.

Socioeconomic factors, race, and sex all play a part in the occurrence of illness in old age. In fact, in people over age 25, the number of days of restricted activity due to sickness is more highly correlated with socioeconomic background than with age (Kimmel, 1974). Similar data exist for the leading causes of death among older people. The majority of deaths in people over age 65 are attributable to three categories: cardiovascular disease, cancer, and stroke. The rates are higher for men than for women in all age categories. The rate of cardiovascular disease for whites is twice as high as the rate for Asians (National Center for Health Statistics, 1990).

Although it is not uncommon for older Americans to be overweight and undernourished, it is important to note that many others are well nourished.

NUTRITION   Some of the poor health of old age may be due to poor diet or improper nutrition. Because of the reduced physical activity of old age and the slowdown in body metabolism, older adults do not require as much food as younger adults. In fact, by the time they reach age 65, individuals require at least 20% fewer calories than younger adults. But they still need nearly as many basic nutrients. As a result, it is not unusual for older Americans to be both overweight and undernourished. Some older people are anemic and malnourished because they are too poor, uninformed, or depressed to buy and consume sufficient quantities of nutritious food. The most common deficiencies are in iron, calcium, and vitamins A and C (National Dairy Council, 1977).

Much of the problem lies in overconsumption of fats. As the body ages, it becomes less able to use the various kinds of fat that are present in many foods. Fat that is not used is stored in special *lipid* cells and within the walls of the arteries. There it may harden and form plates that reduce the flow of blood. This condition, called **atherosclerosis,** or hardening of the arteries, is responsible for many of the heart conditions that are prevalent in old age. Atherosclerosis is so common in older people in the United States and Western Europe that it is almost considered a normal part of aging. The condition is rare, however, in some non-Western countries with radically different diets (Belsky, 1984).

Thus, with age, bodily changes require changes in diet. As noted earlier and in Chapter 14, the bones of older adults become fragile and porous. Over the years, bones lose more calcium than they can absorb from food. To counteract this loss, middle-aged and older people are advised to supplement their diets with calcium. Also, the muscle tone of the intestines decreases with age, often causing constipation and a temptation to rely on laxatives—which can be extremely habit-forming. Nutritionists recommend that older people suffering from constipation add high-fiber foods such as bran to their diets and drink plenty of water to maintain proper bowel function (National Dairy Council, 1977).

atherosclerosis   Hardening of the arteries, which is a common condition of aging caused by the body's increasing inability to use excess fats in the diet. These fats are stored along the walls of arteries and restrict the flow of blood when they harden.

MISUSE OF PRESCRIBED MEDICATION   Serious intentional drug abuse is not a major problem among older adults. In fact, the most popular "recreational drug" used by this age group is alcohol, and by and large, older Americans are more moderate drinkers than members of younger age groups (Snyder & Way, 1979). Nevertheless, some researchers are convinced that as much as one-third of older adults are hospitalized because of overuse, misuse, or abuse of drugs (Poe & Holloway, 1980). Why? For many older people, the problem may relate to changes in body chemistry that result in reduced need for a particular prescription drug, a condition that may go undetected for months or even years. In addition, older people often take combinations of medications for different conditions, and those who are experiencing cognitive decline may simply become confused as to when to take and how much to take of each medication. They may also fail to mention all of their medications to nurses or physicians. In turn, some physicians may prescribe inappropriately: A recent study (Spore et al., 1997) found that among elderly people in residential facilities, some 20 to 25% had at least one inappropriate prescription.

Interactions between medications can have toxic effects. In fact, there have been cases of octogenarians who enter the hospital with numerous symptoms and a depressed level of functioning, suggesting that they are close to death. Yet when certain medications are given in reduced dosages or completely withheld, some of these patients return to a level of functioning that they have not enjoyed for years (Poe & Holloway, 1980).

Drug effects may produce symptoms that mimic **dementia**. The various forms of dementia (including dementia associated with Alzheimer's disease, as discussed later in this chapter) have in common cognitive deficits such as impaired memory and learning ability, deterioration of language and motor functions, progressive inability to recognize familiar people and objects, and frequent confusion (DSM-IV, 1994). Personality changes often accompany dementia. Tranquilizers such as Valium or Librium and cardiac medication such as digitalis can produce dementialike disorientation and confusion (Rudd & Balaschke, 1982; Salzman, 1982). Another factor contributing to involuntary abuse of drugs is that older people have greater difficulty clearing drugs through declining organ systems such as the liver and kidneys, with the effect that larger amounts of drugs remain in their system longer.

REVIEW & APPLY

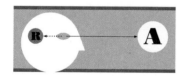

1. Describe the physical changes that occur during the aging process. Do all individuals experience these changes? Explain.
2. Describe chronic health problems in later adulthood.
3. How do improper nutrition and misuse of prescribed medication contribute to health problems in older adults?

CAUSES OF AGING

Aside from the effects of stress, disease, poor nutrition, and so on as contributors to aging, what about normal aging processes? What is the physiology of aging? What happens to cells and organs, and can that process be slowed or stopped by advances in medical science or environmental controls? Many plausible theories have been proposed, but none is conclusive. Some are too complex for a full treatment here, so we'll limit our discussion to the central issues. We begin by examining hereditary and environmental factors associated with aging; then we look at theories of aging.

dementia The confusion, forgetfulness, and personality changes that may be associated with old age and are linked to a variety of primary and secondary causes.

HEREDITARY AND ENVIRONMENTAL FACTORS

Many kinds of aging are observed in nature: Many plants flower, go to seed, die, and regenerate annually according to a preprogrammed genetic code; trees grow until they can no longer raise nutrients and fluid to their highest points—a lifespan of many years, predictable according to the species. In lower mammals, aging and death usually occur at about the same time as loss of fertility; as soon as the younger generation is successfully launched into the world, the parent generation dies. Humans and other primates (as well as elephants) are among the few exceptions to this rule. The human life cycle extends well beyond reproductive capacity, which ends roughly at age 50 for women and later for men (Kimmel, 1974).

It is clear from studies across species that each plant's or animal's characteristic lifespan has a hereditary component. In humans, the genetic influence is particularly striking in studies of identical twins. Identical twins grow bald, accumulate wrinkles, and shrink at the same rate, despite long separations that may expose them to markedly different environmental influences. Identical twins who die of natural causes often die at the same time. Fraternal twins, on the other hand, may age at different rates and have thoroughly dissimilar lifespans (Kallman & Sander, 1949). For the hereditary components in the aging process to be completely expressed, however, all other factors such as stress, accidents, and diseases would have to be held constant. Because this task is impossible, we must consider other processes, both inside and outside the body, that determine how much of the genetic potential will be fulfilled— along with whether we can extend that potential.

In addition to those factors discussed previously, there are a number of reversible and permanent external factors that lengthen or shorten life expectancy (Jones, 1959). For example, rural life adds about 5 years to the lifespan compared with city life, as does being married compared with being single. Obesity has a consistently negative effect, taking 3.6 years off the lives of people who are 25% overweight and about 15 years off the lives of those who are 67% overweight.

THEORIES OF AGING

How does aging actually happen? Does the "genetic clock" simply run down, or is the process more one of wear and tear? **Senescence**, or normal aging, refers to the universal biological processes of aging; it does not include the effects of disease.

The majority of theories of aging can be grouped into two categories—the stochastic theories and the preprogrammed or "clock" theories.

STOCHASTIC THEORIES According to **stochastic theories of aging**, the body ages as a result of random assaults from both the internal and external environments (Schneider, 1992). These theories, which are sometimes called *wear-and-tear* theories, compare the human body to a machine that simply wears out as a result of constant use and accumulated cellular insults and injuries. In one such theory, for example, it is thought that as cells age, they are less efficient in disposing of wastes. Extra substances, particularly a fatty substance called *lipofusein*, accumulate, especially in blood and muscle cells. Eventually these substances take up space and slow down normal cell processes. Most gerontologists, however, think that the accumulation of chemicals such as lipofusein is a result rather than a cause of aging.

senescence The normal aging process, not connected with the occurrence of disease in the individual.

stochastic theories of aging Theories suggesting that the body ages as a result of random assaults from both internal and external environments.

A more popular stochastic theory involves the action of pieces of molecules called *free radicals*. In the course of normal use of oxygen for virtually every cellular process, small, highly charged, unpaired electrons are left over. These free radicals react with other chemical compounds in the cell and may interrupt normal cell functioning. Normally, the cell has repair mechanisms that reduce the damage done by free radicals. But after a major injury such as a heart attack or exposure to radiation, substantial free radical damage occurs. Researchers are exploring the effects of some dietary substances, such as vitamins C and E, that seem to reduce the effects of free radicals. But excessive amounts of vitamin E, for example, can have negative side effects as well. As yet, there is also no conclusive evidence that increased levels of vitamins C or E can increase life expectancy (Walford, 1983).

There are still other stochastic theories. Damage might be done to DNA in the genes, for example. It is known that the ultraviolet light in sunshine can damage the DNA in skin cells. Usually, when the genes in a cell are damaged, the cell either repairs itself or dies and is replaced by other cells. In older people, such repairs are less efficient, and damage tends to remain. Perhaps aging is nothing more than a decline in self-repair capacity.

Wear and tear affects tissues and systems as well. Sometimes connective tissue, or the cross-links between cells, is affected. The tissue loses some of its flexibility and become rigid. In aging, the immune system also becomes less efficient. Sometimes the immune cells attack their own body's healthy cells, as in *rheumatoid arthritis* or certain kidney ailments. Still, the processes described by stochastic theories, though fairly common, might be a result of some deeper aging process rather than the cause of aging itself.

In sum, although stochastic theories are appealing, they do not fully explain aging. They do not, for example, explain why the functions of the body's internal "repair shop" decline. In addition, they do not explain why exercise—a potential form of wear and tear—can have beneficial rather than negative effects.

BIOLOGICAL CLOCK THEORIES The second general type of theory of aging focuses on genetic programming. Preprogrammed theories of aging suggest that the programmed actions of specific inherited genes determine aging. It is believed that approximately 200 human genes determine the average lifespan of a human being (Schneider, 1992). The notion of biological clocks is associated with that of programmed aging. The idea is that there are built-in timers, or clocks, that are set to go off according to a schedule. These clocks may be located in each cell or in the brain. At the cellular level, it has been found that particular kinds of cells seem to be preprogrammed to divide (and therefore replace damaged or worn out cells) only a certain number of times. For example, some human embryo cells divide only about 50 times. Even if you freeze these cells after 30 divisions, when you thaw them, they will divide only another 20 times. The maximum number of reproductions varies in different types of cells and in different species. Individuals may also vary in the potential number of cellular reproductions for different kinds of cells.

Another biological clock theory suggests that there is some sort of pacemaker, or timer, housed in the hypothalamus and the pituitary gland. In this view, the pituitary gland releases a hormone shortly after puberty that begins the process of decline throughout the rest of the lifespan at a programmed rate.

Biological clocks in humans appear to control the female menstrual cycle, which begins at around age 12 and ends somewhere around age 50. A biological clock also appears to control the human immune system, which gains strength until age 20 and then gradually weakens. Some theorists suggest that this decline in immune function is linked to many age-related conditions, including susceptibility to cancer and infections like influenza and pneumonia, as well as to alteration in the walls of the blood vessels and arteriosclerosis (Schneider, 1992).

In sum, no single theory can explain aging. A combination of theories works better, and future discoveries will undoubtedly contribute further to our understanding of the normal aging process. Researchers are also keenly interested in studying ways to slow the process so that we can all live longer. Some of this research is disease-related. The study of the relationship between childhood cancer or juvenile arthritis and premature aging is an example. Other research is aimed at helping people live a healthy, disease-free life until close to the end of their natural lifespan. However, despite recent advances, the likelihood of dramatically extending the normal lifespan seems a long way off.

1. How do heredity and environment interact in the aging process?
2. Describe and compare the stochastic and preprogrammed theories of aging.

REVIEW & APPLY

COGNITIVE CHANGES IN ADVANCED AGE

Having examined various processes and theories of aging, we next take a close look at changes that occur in cognition as a result of aging.

Many people assume that older people's intellect automatically decays. For example, if a young or middle-aged man prepares to leaves a party and doesn't remember where he left his coat, people think nothing of it. If the same forgetfulness is observed in an old man, however, people shrug their shoulders and say, "His memory is going" or "He's losing his mind." Here we'll consider facts and fictions about cognitive changes associated with advanced age and the ways that older adults cope with those changes.

COGNITION IN THE LATER YEARS

As noted in Chapter 14, with regard to fluid and crystallized intelligence, there is some controversy over the extent of decline in intellectual functioning as a result of normal aging. However, it is agreed that most mental skills remain relatively intact. Extensive research has demonstrated that age-related decline in memory is not as general or as severe as was previously thought (Perlmutter et al., 1987). Many of the memory problems that some older people suffer are not the inevitable consequences of age but are due to other factors, such as depression, inactivity, or side effects of prescription drugs. When cognitive decline does occur—and there is a well-documented decline in the *speed* of cognitive processing—there are compensations. The effect is that any loss normally has very little effect on daily living (Perlmutter et al., 1987; Salthouse, 1985, 1990). Let's look at selected cognitive changes as they relate to speed of performance, memory, and the development of wisdom.

SPEED OF COGNITION Old age brings a decline in the speed of both mental and physical performance (Birren et al., 1980). Many studies have shown that intellectual functions that depend heavily on speed of performance decline in older people (Salthouse, 1985, 1990). Older people have slower reaction times, slower perceptual processing, and slower cognitive processes in general. Although some of this slowness is clearly attributable to aging, some may be due to the fact that older people value accuracy more than younger people do. When tested, older people make fewer guesses and try to answer each item correctly. Also, they may be less familiar with some of the tasks used in testing situations. For example, older people are often compared with college students in tests of recall of nonsense syllables. Students regularly practice learning new vocabularies for examinations, but older people usually have not engaged in such practice for a long time. On many such tasks, older people are sometimes slower because they haven't practiced the relevant cognitive skills recently, and therefore such comparisons are unrealistic and lead to inaccurate conclusions (Labouvie-Vief, 1985). Thus, although the decline in cognitive processing associated with aging is real, much of it appears to be exaggerated.

Studies of performance on standard memory tasks typically reveal a difference in speed between the performances of 30- and 70-year-olds. In relatively simple cognitive tasks, such as those that ask subjects to compare the size of different objects, older people take approximately 50% longer to complete the task than younger people. As cognitive problems become more complex—requiring, for example, simultaneous comparisons of size and location—older adults require about twice as much time as younger adults to complete the task (Baltes, 1993).

There are, however, certain compensations that older people use to make up for their loss of speed. In one study, older typists did just as well as younger typists despite seemingly slower visual processing and reaction time and reduced dexterity. Why? When the researcher limited the number of words that the typists could read ahead, the older typists slowed down considerably, and the younger ones were much less affected. It appears that older typists had learned to look farther ahead and thereby to type quickly (Salthouse, 1985). With fairly limited training, older people are often able to compensate for loss of speed on such tasks and in many cases to recover much of their former speed (Willis, 1985).

MEMORY Perhaps no single aspect of aging has been studied more thoroughly than memory. Recall the information-processing model of memory discussed in Chapter 6. Information is first fleetingly retained in sensory memory in the form of visual or auditory images, then transferred to short-term memory for organization and encoding, and finally transferred to long-term memory for retention. In studies of adult memory, we also find evidence of even more permanent, or *tertiary*, memory, which holds extremely remote information. Each of these presumed levels of memory has been studied in some detail (Poon, 1985).

Sensory storage is very brief visual or auditory memory that holds sensory input for fractions of a second while the information is being processed. It appears that older individuals are able to pick up and hold slightly less sensory information than young adults. On average, they have a slightly shorter perceptual span, particularly when two things are happening at once. It is not clear why this difference is so. Is there a decline in the visual or auditory system? Is there less selective attention or pattern recognition? Or is there perhaps less motivation to succeed in these very precise tasks? In any case, it is unlikely

Most mental skills remain relatively intact in older people.

that the modest sensory memory loss observed in later adulthood has much effect on daily living. The older person can often compensate by looking at or listening to things longer (Poon, 1985), although doing that isn't always possible: Highway signs that whiz by can create difficulty for older drivers.

Short-term memory, which is limited-capacity storage that holds things that are "in mind" at the moment, also changes little with age. Most studies find no significant difference between older and younger adults in short-term memory capacity per se.

When it comes to *long-term memory*, however, most studies show clear age differences. In studies of learning and recall, older people often remember fewer items on a list or fewer details in a design. But are these differences due to the storage capacity of the older person or to the processes of learning or remembering (that is, the *transfer* of information from short-term to long-term memory)? In some memory studies, it appears that older individuals are less efficient in organizing, rehearsing, and encoding material to be learned—all of which are short-term memory functions. Yet, with careful instruction and a little practice, older people improve markedly (Willis, 1985). Even people near age 80 show some benefits from training in how to organize and rehearse information for permanent retention (Poon, 1985; Willis & Nesselroade, 1990).

The effectiveness of such training is not unlimited, however. Even after memory training, individuals in their seventies may not reach the same levels as young adults (Campbell & Charness, 1990). In some studies comparing older and younger people, the training actually increased the gap in performance because young adults made even greater gains than older adults (Kleigl et al., 1990). This result may imply that older adults may have less reserve capacity (Baltes, 1987) than young adults, at least in some skills. In other words, older adults have less room for improvement and less plasticity in their thinking.

Paul Baltes (1993) demonstrated the limitation of reserve capacity in older adults in a study in which young adult and older adult subjects with similar educational backgrounds were asked to remember long lists of words, such as thirty nouns, in correct order. Realizing that under normal conditions, most people can remember a string of only about five to seven words presented at a rate of about two words per second, the researchers trained the subjects to use a mnemonic device—that is, a memory strategy—known as the *method of loci*. In this strategy, subjects associate items to be remembered with objects in a setting that is very familiar to them, such as a room or the neighborhood they live in. They then form bizarre or humorous mental images as an aid to recall. When asked to recall the items, they easily remember the familiar objects and then the associated items on the list.

The researchers found that healthy older adults could apply the method of loci fairly well. However, there were clear age-related performance differences. These involved both speed and accuracy of performance. For example, even after 38 training sessions, most older adults failed to reach the level of performance achieved by young adults after only a few training sessions. In fact, the researchers found no subjects over age 70 who performed above the average for the young adults.

There are other age differences in performance of long-term memory tasks. Older subjects tend to do better on recognition tasks than on recall of such things as vocabulary lists (Craik & McDowd, 1987). They tend to be somewhat selective in what they retain. Also, they may balk at memorizing useless word lists but do very well in the comprehension of paragraphs (Meyer, 1987). One study found that older people remembered interesting metaphors such as "the

Older adults seem to have more wisdom than younger adults.

wisdom An expert knowledge system focusing on the pragmatics of life that involves excellent judgment and advice on critical life issues, including the meaning of life and the human condition; wisdom represents the capstone of human intelligence.

seasons are the costumes of nature" better than college students did. They did not try to reproduce the sentence exactly; rather, they understood and remembered its meaning (Labouvie-Vief & Schell, 1982). In other words, older people tend to remember what appears to them to be useful and important. This finding reminds us, then, that development and behavior occur in context, and that even as we age, environmental demands and opportunities shape our skills and abilities (Lerner, 1990).

Tertiary memory, or memory for extremely remote events, appears to remain fairly intact in older adults. Indeed, in some studies, older adults are better at recalling details of historical events than younger adults. This tendency is especially true of historical events that the older adults experienced but that the young adults learned about secondhand. It is also consistent with the ease with which older adults can often vividly describe memorable events of their childhood.

In sum, very few significant age differences are found in each of the memory stages except long-term memory, and the differences found in this stage depend on several factors. Older individuals may do poorly if the memory task requires unusual organizational and rehearsal techniques that are not well practiced. Most will improve, however, if they are taught organization and memory strategies. Memory in older people is also selective. More interesting and meaningful material is remembered more easily. In all, the notion of major memory decline associated with aging is best categorized as a myth.

WISDOM Although the mechanics of memory are somewhat stronger in young adults than in older adults, the reverse is often true with regard to **wisdom**—expert knowledge that focuses on the pragmatics of life and involves judgment and advice on crucial life issues. "To understand wisdom fully and correctly probably requires more wisdom than any of us have," wrote Robert Sternberg (1990). Nevertheless, Paul Baltes has proposed that the expert knowledge associated with wisdom can be classified into five categories: factual knowledge, procedural knowledge, lifespan contextualism, value relativism, and uncertainty (see Figure 16–4). At the very least, wisdom is a cognitive quality founded on crystallized, culture-based intelligence (see Chapter 14) that is related to experience and personality. Remember that crystallized

FIGURE 16–4 A MODEL OF WISDOM

Source: Baltes (1993).

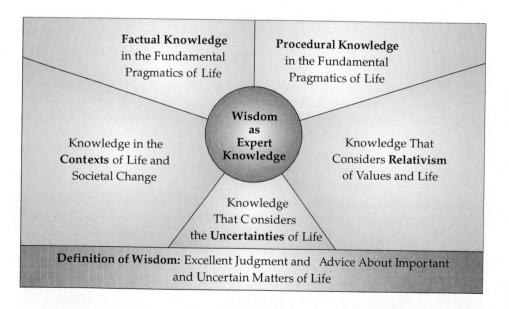

intelligence stems from the knowledge and information that an individual gathers about the world and human relationships throughout life.

According to Baltes (1993), wisdom has five general characteristics. First, it appears to focus on important and difficult matters that are often associated with the meaning of life and the human condition. Second, the level of knowledge, judgment, and advice reflected in wisdom is superior. Third, the knowledge associated with wisdom has extraordinary scope, depth, and balance, and is applicable to specific situations. Fourth, wisdom combines mind and virtue (character) and is employed for personal well-being as well as for the benefit of humankind. Fifth, though difficult to achieve, wisdom is easily recognized by most people.

To measure the body of knowledge associated with wisdom, Baltes (1993) asked research participants to consider dilemmas like this one: A 15-year-old girl wants to get married right away. What should she do? Baltes asked participants to "think aloud" about this problem. Their thoughts were taped, transcribed, and evaluated on the basis of the degree to which they approached the five criteria of wisdom-related knowledge: factual knowledge, procedural knowledge, lifespan contextualism, value relativism, and recognition and management of uncertainty. Subjects' answers were rated to evaluate how much and what kind of wisdom-related knowledge they had. The various criteria and the evaluation are summarized in Table 16–3.

According to Baltes, there are two reasons why growing old might increase the quantity and quality of an individual's wisdom-related knowledge and make a high score more likely than a low one. First, it takes years of experience in diverse life circumstances to understand fully and work with wisdom-enhancing factors. This experience comes with age. Second, as adults age, they develop personal attributes that are conducive to the development of wisdom. These attributes involve personality and cognitive growth. However, the development of wisdom is not irreversible. The losses in cognitive processing experienced by very old people may limit their wisdom or their ability to apply it.

COGNITIVE DECLINE

Despite the retention of memory skills and the development of wisdom in many older adults, some individuals experience a marked decline in cognitive functioning. This decline may be temporary, progressive, or intermittent. It is relatively minor and fleeting in some cases but can be severe and progressive in others.

Cognitive decline may have primary or secondary causes. Among the primary causes of decline are Alzheimer's disease and strokes. However, it should be remembered that most cognitive decline is not intrinsic to the aging process itself; rather, it is attributable to other factors such as failing health, poor formal education, poverty, or low motivation. These secondary causes of decline deserve consideration as well, although they can be difficult to distinguish from primary causes. Let's begin our consideration of cognitive decline with its ultimate manifestation, dementia.

DEMENTIA   As noted earlier, dementia refers to the chronic confusion, forgetfulness, and accompanying personality changes that are sometimes associated with old age. It can have many causes, one of which is Alzheimer's disease. Many people fear dementia in the mistaken belief that it is an inevitable curse of old age. To them, growing old means losing emotional and intellectual control and becoming a helpless, useless person who becomes a "burden" on his or her family.

TABLE 16–3 USE OF THE WISDOM-RELATED CRITERIA TO EVALUATE DISCOURSE ABOUT LIFE MATTERS

Example: A 15-year-old girl wants to get married right away. What should one/she consider and do?

Factual knowledge:

___Who, when, where?

___Examples of possible different situations

___Multiple options (forms of love and marriage)

Procedural knowledge:

___Strategies of information search, decision making, and advice giving

___Timing of advice, monitoring of emotional reactions

___Cost/benefit analysis: scenarios

___Means-ends analysis

Lifespan contextualism:

___Age-graded (e.g., issues of adolescence), culturally graded (e.g., change in norms), idiosyncratic (e.g., terminal illness) contexts across time and life domains

Value relativism:

___Separating personal values from those of others

___Religious preferences

___Current/future values

___Cultural-historical relativism

Uncertainty:

___No perfect solution

___Optimization of gain/loss ratio

___Future not fully predictable

___Backup solutions

ILLUSTRATION OF TWO EXTREME RESPONSES (ABBREVIATED)

Low score

A 15-year-old girl wants to get married? No, no way; marryng at age 15 would be utterly wrong. One has to tell the girl that marriage is not possible. (After further probing) It would be irresponsible to support such an idea. No, this is just a crazy idea.

High score

Well, on the surface, this seems like an easy problem. On average, marriage for 15-year-old girls is not a good thing. I guess many girls might think about it when they fall in love for the first time. And, then, there are situations where the average case does not fit. Perhaps in this instance, special life circumstances are involved, such that the girl has a terminal illness. Or this girl may not be from this country. Perhaps she lives in another culture and historical period. Before I offer a final evaluation, I would need more information.

According to gerontologists, the actual incidence and nature of dementia have been exaggerated and distorted. Far from being inevitable, dementia affects only 3 to 4% of people over 65 (Brocklehurst, 1977, cited in Wershow, 1981). Unfortunately, however, a recent community-based survey indicates that the rate increases dramatically in old-old age. The Boston-based survey indicated that nearly 20% of the 75- to 84-year-olds tested appeared to suffer from dementia in the form of Alzheimer's disease. The rate among community dwellers 85 years old and older approached 50% (Evans et al., 1989).

People who suffer from dementia have a limited ability to grasp abstractions; they may lack ideas, repeat the same statements over and over again, think more slowly than normal people, and be unable to pay attention to those around them. They also lose their train of thought in the middle of a sentence. Memory for recent events may be impaired. A person suffering from dementia may clearly recall a childhood event but be unable to remember something that happened an hour ago. Because of these symptoms of mental deterioration, the person may be unable to cope with such routine tasks as keeping clean and groomed. Operating within the confines of a shrinking mental world, she or he can no longer think, behave, or relate to people normally (Kastenbaum, 1979).

Unfortunately, the label *senile* is all too often attached to older people who show even the slightest signs of confusion, mental lapses, or disoriented behavior, even though these problems may be attributable to a number of other causes. A clear diagnosis is difficult, given the wide range of secondary causes. Improper nutrition, as well as chronic insufficient sleep related to illness, anxiety, depression, grief, or fear, can distort thinking in young as well as old people. Heart or kidney problems that cause changes in normal body rhythms or metabolism, or the accumulation of toxic body wastes may also affect the ability to think clearly. Confusion, agitation, and drowsiness can also be induced by drugs used to treat other illnesses. In each of these cases, when the physical or emotional illness is treated effectively, the senility-like symptoms disappear (Kastenbaum, 1979).

Of those diagnosed as having dementia, approximately 50% have Alzheimer's disease. Another 30% or so have had a series of ministrokes that damaged brain tissue. The remainder suffer from a wide variety of diseases or disorders, including brain trauma as a result of accidents.

PRIMARY CAUSES OF DECLINE   As noted earlier, the leading primary cause of dementia and other forms of cognitive decline is Alzheimer's disease. Alzheimer's disease is also the fourth leading cause of death among older people (Schneck et al., 1982).

Alzheimer's disease involves a progressive deterioration of brain cells, beginning in the outer cerebral cortex. Autopsies have revealed a characteristic pattern of damaged areas that look like little bits of braided yarn. While the patient is alive, the diagnosis of Alzheimer's disease is based on patterns of regressive memory loss and disorientation.

The causes of Alzheimer's disease are not yet known, although the high incidence of the disease in some families leads researchers to suspect a genetic cause (Miller, 1993). Other suspected causes, such as high levels of aluminum in the brain, have not been substantiated by research findings (Doll, 1993; Mason, 1993).

Whatever its causes, the effects of Alzheimer's disease are devastating both to the patient and to his or her family. Generally, the first symptoms are forgetfulness and minor disruptions in speech. In the beginning, only little things are

Dealing with a loved one suffering from Alzheimer's disease is usually emotionally wrenching to family members.

Alzheimer's disease   A disease that causes dementia due to a progressive deterioration of brain cells, especially those in the cerebral cortex.

forgotten; as the disease progresses, places, names, and routines may not be recalled; and finally, even events that may have just occurred are forgotten. The forgetful phase is followed by a sense of confusion. It is much more difficult to plan and perform even simple routines; for example, it is hard to get something to eat because you can't find the refrigerator. This loss of contact with the routine and familiar aspects of life causes serious disorientation, confusion, and anxiety. At this point it becomes clear that the person cannot be left alone because of the potential for injury. Finally, full dementia sets in. The patient is unable to complete the simplest tasks, such as dressing or even eating. Familiar people are not recognized; even a devoted spouse who has cared for the patient through years of decline may be perceived as a complete stranger.

Alzheimer's disease typically has a substantial impact on the patient's family. Within a few years, an independent, cognizant adult becomes childlike and requires 24-hour care and supervision. In the early stages, adaptations are relatively easy. The environment can be simplified and objects—even furniture—can be labeled. The person can still be alone, at least for short periods, and things like a sandwich prepared earlier by a family member may prevent an accident in the kitchen at mealtime. Later, when 24-hour care becomes necessary, major adaptations must be made. Aside from practical matters, family members often must deal with grief and despair and perhaps with anger and frustration. Feelings of resentment, guilt, embarrassment, and isolation are likely. Although such feelings are understandable, family members must continue to consider the feelings of the patient. In addition, the support of other families with similar experiences is particularly helpful (Cohen & Eisdorfer, 1986; Zarit et al., 1985). Often the difficult decision to place the person in a nursing home must be made. Sometimes this decision is easier in the final stages if the person seems not to know where she or he is, even at home with familiar family members. Sometimes, too, the simpler, more predictable environment of the institution makes life easier for an Alzheimer's patient (but see "In Theory, In Fact" in Chapter 17, page 598, which discusses elder abuse).

Strokes, including ministrokes, are another primary cause of dementia. This form of cognitive decline is sometimes called multi-infarct dementia (MID). An *infarct* is an obstruction of a blood vessel that prevents a sufficient supply of blood from reaching a particular area of the brain. This insufficiency causes destruction of brain tissue and is commonly referred to as a stroke or ministroke. If these events are very small and temporary, they are referred to as *transient ischemic attacks* (TIAs). Often the person is not even aware that the event has occurred. As the name implies, MID is caused by a series of events that damage brain tissue.

Often the underlying cause of ministrokes and the resulting destruction of brain tissue is atherosclerosis—the buildup of fatty plates on the lining of the arteries. People who have atherosclerosis or existing heart problems, hypertension, or diabetes are at particular risk for strokes. Those at risk are advised to pay attention to measures to improve their circulation, such as moderate exercise, and to control their hypertension and diabetes through diet and medication.

Secondary Causes of Decline Psychological expectations, mental health, and other factors can profoundly influence cognitive functioning in older adults.

At any age, our beliefs or judgments about our own abilities have an effect on how well we perform. Some older adults fully believe that they are going to

stroke Blockage of blood to the brain, which can cause brain damage.

Even moderate drinking over time causes impairment of primary and secondary memory.

lose their memory and become less able to do things than they were in the past. They expect to be helpless and dependent on others and to lose control of their lives. Older people often imagine that their fate will rest in the hands of luck, chance, or powerful others. In a self-fulfilling prophecy, individuals who have these expectations become less competent and less in control. They have less self-esteem and show less persistence and effort. On the other hand, if they can be convinced that they can take more control of their lives and that cognitive loss is not inevitable, they often improve markedly (Perlmutter et al., 1987).

An individual's mental health directly affects his or her performance on cognitive tasks. Depression is a common psychological reaction in old age, partly because of the loss of loved ones and friends; many old people have several such experiences. Depression causes reduced concentration and attention and, hence, lowers the overall level of cognitive functioning.

There are a number of other secondary factors that cause cognitive decline (Perlmutter et al., 1987). Some of the more important ones include the following:

■ Physical fitness affects mental tasks as well as physical tasks. On a wide range of tests of cognitive functions, individuals who are more physically fit perform at a higher level.
■ Nutritional deficits such as anemia, vitamin deficiencies, or choline deficiency result in poor performance on intellectual tasks. Choline, which is found in meat, fish, and egg yolks, is used by the brain to manufacture acetylcholine, a chemical that is essential for efficient neural processing (Wurtman, 1979).
■ Use of alcohol over an extended period—even in moderate amounts—results in reduced short- and long-term memory. More extensive drinking tends to interfere with daily functioning, also with adequate nutrition. Both

Social isolation or depression may impair mental functioning among the old.

directly and indirectly, alcohol use impairs mental functions even when the person is not under the influence.

■ Prescription and over-the-counter drugs, ranging from sleeping pills to pain relievers and drugs for hypertension, have side effects that reduce alertness and attention. Drugs are not always easily cleared from the kidneys or liver. As an individual grows older, smaller doses of a drug may be just as potent as large ones. Sometimes a reduction in the amount of a drug used can dramatically improve mental functioning.

■ Disuse of mental functioning. After periods of prolonged illness, social isolation, or depression, some individuals do not return to their former level of mental functioning. The old adage "Use it or lose it" holds true in such cases (Perlmutter et al., 1987).

COMPENSATING FOR AN AGING MIND

Research conducted by Baltes (1993) focused on the mechanisms that older adults use to coordinate the gains and losses of an aging mind. These mechanisms are especially important as biological and health-related losses shift the balance of cognitive functioning. The model that Baltes developed is based on "selective optimization with compensation." He uses the following example to describe how this adaptive process works:

When the concert pianist Rubinstein was asked, in a television interview, how he managed to remain such a successful pianist in his old age, he mentioned three strategies: (1) In old age he performed fewer pieces, (2) he now practiced each piece more frequently, and (3) he introduced more ritardandos in his playing before fast segments, so that the playing speed sounded faster than it was in reality. These are examples of selection (fewer pieces), optimization (more practice), and compensation (increased use of contrast in speed). My contention is that this is the kind of life knowledge that is another facet of the pragmatics of the aging mind. (Baltes, 1993, page 590)

Baltes contends that as older adults recognize their objective and subjective cognitive losses, as well as the changing balance between gains and losses, they reorganize and adjust their sense of self in response. This readjustment, Baltes believes, may explain why most older adults do not experience a major reduction in their sense of either subjective well-being or personal control. Other research supports this view. For example, factors such as higher education (Leibovici et al., 1996) and sustained overall activity level (Christensen et al., 1996) help the individual compensate for, and to some extent minimize, some aspects of cognitive decline in very old age.

REVIEW & APPLY

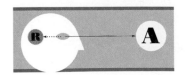

1. Discuss in detail the cognitive changes that take place in later adulthood, including those that affect speed of performance and memory.
2. Identify the five general properties of wisdom.
3. Is cognitive decline intrinsic to the aging process? Describe the primary and secondary factors that contribute to cognitive decline, including those linked to Alzheimer's disease.
4. Discuss how older individuals compensate for losses in cognitive functioning.

SUMMARY

Aging Today

- Stereotypes about the elderly make it difficult to understand them as the varied individuals they really are.

- The term *ageism* is used to describe an attitude of indifference and neglect toward the elderly.

- People of all ages tend to assign more negative stereotypes to older people and more positive ones to younger people.

- In some cultures and historical eras, older people have been respected as wise elders, transmitters of culture, and a storehouse of historical lore.

- The median age of the U.S. population is increasing and will result in ever-larger proportions of older people in the population in coming decades.

- Burnside and colleagues have analyzed older adulthood in terms of four decades of later life: "young-old" (60 to 69), "middle-aged-old" (70 to 79), "old-old" (80 to 89), and "very old-old" (90 and over). Each of these decades has characteristic features, which are summarized in the study chart on page 553.

Physical Aspects of Aging

- Many of the effects of aging are not noticed until later adulthood because aging is gradual and most physical systems have considerable reserve capacity.

- Not all old people show the signs of aging to the same degree. Much depends on whether they remain physically fit and active.

- The kind of life that individuals have led and the illnesses and accidents they have experienced contribute to aging; these are sometimes called pathological aging factors.

- Signs of aging include gray hair, less elastic skin, a shift in posture, and deepening wrinkles.

- The senses generally become less efficient with age; many older people find that it takes longer to perceive and process an event through the sensory systems.

- Hearing deficits are quite common but are usually mild to moderate. There is greater hearing loss in the higher-frequency tones.

- Several kinds of visual impairments are common in aging individuals. They include cataracts (a clouding of the lens that blocks light), glaucoma (a buildup of pressure within the eyeball), decreased ability to focus on objects, and decreased visual acuity (ability to distinguish fine detail).

- The sense of taste shows considerable stability into old age.

- Muscle weight—and strength and endurance—decreases with age. The bones become weaker, hollower, and more brittle, and therefore they are more likely to fracture and take longer to mend.

- High-intensity exercise training helps counteract muscle weakness and related physical frailty in very old people.

- The cardiovascular system becomes less efficient with age, and the capacity of the lungs decreases. The reserve capacity of the heart, lungs, and other organs is reduced.

- The immune system changes during later adulthood, making older people more vulnerable to disease.

- Older people are more likely to have chronic health problems than acute illnesses. These largely reflect the body's decreased ability to cope with stress; socioeconomic factors, race, and sex also play a part.

- Some of the poor health of old age may be due to poor diet or improper nutrition. Overconsumption of fats results in atherosclerosis, or hardening of the arteries, which is responsible for many of the heart conditions that are prevalent in old age.

- Overuse, misuse, or abuse of drugs can sometimes cause health problems in older people.

Causes of Aging

- Any organism's characteristic lifespan has a genetic component, but other factors, such as stress, accidents, and diseases, also play a role.

- For humans, rural life and marriage tend to extend life, whereas obesity and exposure to radiation tend to shorten it.

- Senescence, or normal aging, refers to the universal biological processes of aging.

- According to stochastic theories, the body ages as a result of random assaults from both the internal and external environments; these are sometimes called wear-and-tear theories.

- Programmed or biological clock theories suggest that the programmed actions of specific inherited genes determine aging. Evidence of biological clocks can be seen in the immune system and in the female menstrual cycle.

Cognitive Changes in Advanced Age

- Many people assume that older people's intellect automatically decays. However, most mental skills remain relatively intact, although there is a decline in the speed of cognitive processing. With training, older people can make up for this loss of speed.

- Sensory storage and short-term memory change little with age, but long-term memory declines. With careful instruction and a little practice, older people can improve their memory capability.

- Tertiary memory, or memory for extremely remote events, appears to remain fairly intact in older adults.

- Wisdom refers to expert knowledge that focuses on the pragmatics of life and involves judgment and advice on crucial life issues.

- Growing old often increases the quantity and quality of an individual's wisdom-related knowledge.

- Among the primary causes of cognitive decline in older adults are Alzheimer's disease and strokes. Secondary causes include such factors as poverty or failing health.

- Dementia refers to the chronic confusion, forgetfulness, and accompanying personality changes that are sometimes associated with old age.

- Confusion, mental lapses, or disoriented behavior in older people may be attributable to a number of causes, including physical or emotional illnesses that can be treated.

- Approximately 50% of people diagnosed as having dementia are suffering from Alzheimer's disease, which involves a progressive deterioration of brain cells. The eventual result is serious disorientation, making it impossible to leave the person alone. Caring for a patient with the disease places major strains on family members.

- Strokes or ministrokes are another primary cause of dementia. They are often caused by atherosclerosis—the buildup of fatty plates on the lining of the arteries.

- Psychological expectations, mental health, and other factors can profoundly influence cognitive functioning in older adults. Those who expect to be helpless and dependent often become so. Depression is also common in old age, partly because of the loss of loved ones and friends.

- Other factors that can cause cognitive decline include lack of physical fitness, nutritional deficits, use of alcohol over an extended period, side effects of drugs, and disuse of mental functioning.

- As older adults recognize their objective and subjective cognitive losses, they reorganize and adjust their sense of self in response.

KEY TERMS

ageism	hypertension	stochastic theories of aging
filial piety	atherosclerosis	wisdom
pathological aging factors	dementia	Alzheimer's disease
cataract	senescence	strokes
glaucoma		

USING WHAT YOU'VE LEARNED

What makes people wise? Make a list of five to ten of the wisest people you know. Your list might include national and world leaders in many fields or people in your neighborhood, campus, or town. Try to include both men and women and at least one individual whom you know personally. Now look at Baltes's five criteria for wisdom. Do the people on your list fit those criteria? Would you like to add some other characteristics of wisdom? Researchers who study wisdom often note the wise person's ability to integrate different kinds of knowledge or even to integrate feelings, thoughts, and actions. Is this true of the people on your list? What factors, life experiences, education, or training contributed to the development of wisdom in these individuals?

SUGGESTED READINGS

COHEN, D., & EISDORFER, K. (1986). *The loss of self: A family resource for the care of Alzheimer's disease and related disorders.* New York: Norton. A helpful resource for understanding Alzheimer's disease and coping with the stress and turmoil of long-term care.

FOWLER, M., & McCUTCHEON, P. (Eds.) (1991). *Songs of experience: An anthology of literature on growing old.* New York: Ballantine. Poems, diary entries, stories, musings, and inspiring words of wisdom from men and women in their final years, including E. B. White, Helen Hayes, Robert Coles, Eleanor Roosevelt, and many others.

PALMORE, E. B. (1988). *The facts of aging quiz: A handbook of uses and results.* New York: Springer. A glimpse of attitude research on aging, including results that show stereotypes of aging among both young and old.

WHITBOURNE, S. K. (1985). *The aging body: Physiological changes and psychological consequences.* New York: Springer-Verlag. An excellent review of physical aging, with extensive discussion of individual adaptations, adjustments, and reactions.

ZARIT, S., ORR, N. K., & ZARIT, J. N. (1985). *The hidden victims of Alzheimer's disease: Families under stress.* New York: New York University Press. Another helpful and insightful resource for families.

CHAPTER
17

Older Adults: Personality Development and Socialization

CHAPTER OUTLINE

- **Personality and Aging**
    Developmental Tasks in Later Life
    Continuity and Change in Later Life
    Successful Aging

- **Retirement: A Major Change in Status**
    Physical, Economic, and Social Conditions
    Deciding to Retire

- **Family and Personal Relationships**
    When Parenting Is Over
    Caring for an Ill Spouse
    Widows and Widowers
    Siblings and Friends

- **Social Policy and the Elderly**
    The Demographics of Aging in America
    The Frail Elderly in America
    Lifestyle Options for Older Americans

CHAPTER OBJECTIVES

By the time you have finished this chapter, you should be able to do the following:

1. Discuss personality changes and developmental tasks in older adulthood.
2. Describe the physical, economic, and social conditions that influence how well older adults adjust to retirement.
3. Summarize factors that contribute to the decision to retire.
4. Describe patterns of family and personal relationships that define many of the stresses and satisfactions of older adulthood.
5. Discuss the relationship between the needs of the elderly and the social policies and attitudes that apply to older people in the United States.

A major change in role and social position is called a **status passage**. Changes in status occur throughout the lifespan. The adolescent becomes a young adult; the young adult enters middle adulthood; in each case, the individual takes on enlarged roles and responsibilities, typically with gains in status and power. The status passage into older adulthood, however, is quite different. The transition to retirement, to becoming a widow or widower, or to failing health may result in loss of power, responsibility, and autonomy (Rosow, 1974).

On the positive side, retiring can yield new freedom to pursue personal interests, and becoming a great-grandparent can provide the opportunity to spend more time with loved ones. Thus, the way a person interprets status passages and the changes that accompany them is often at least as important as the events themselves. The effect of many life events of later adulthood depends in large part on the meaning attached to them. You may view retirement as signaling the end of your usefulness or productiveness in the workforce, perhaps the end of a major part of your identity—whether as a truck driver, a dentist, a dancer, or a corporate executive. You may view retirement quite differently if you have spent the last 30 to 40 years hating your job and everything about it. In this case, retirement may mean release from tedium, drudgery, and subservience to authority. (Indeed, one factor that predicts successful adjustment to retirement is "dislike of your job.") Similarly, becoming a widower or widow may bring a sudden release from the toil of caring for a chronically ill spouse, along with new freedoms. It may also mean no longer having to live with someone you have disliked for many years but have been unwilling to divorce. On the other hand, it can bring considerable and enduring grief over the loss.

Illness and physical disabilities are among the most difficult circumstances that we may have to cope with in later adulthood. Even here, however, there is wide variation in styles of coping. As one older man commented, "I don't get around the way I used to, but I've never enjoyed my garden like I have these last few years, and that last grandchild is a sheer joy."

When Gail Sheehy interviewed adults in their sixties and seventies, she found that many older people continue to see life as full of potential rather than limitations. They anticipate a life "in which they can concentrate on

status passage A change in the role and position that occurs when an individual enters adolescence, becomes a parent, retires, or becomes a widow or widower.

becoming better, stronger, deeper, wiser, funnier, freer, sexier, and more attentive to living the privileged moments" (Sheehy, 1995). In their sixties, many older adults experience a wonderful combination of good health and freedom from work and worry. In their seventies and beyond, these same adults fine-tune their priorities and focus on what they can do rather than on what they cannot do any longer.

In this chapter, we'll explore the status changes that mark later adulthood with regard to personality, adjustment to developmental tasks such as retirement, and family relationships with grandchildren and great-grandchildren. We'll also look at topics such as caring for an ill spouse, adjusting to being a widow or widower, and reaffirming relationships with siblings and friends. Finally, we'll consider in detail how older people are affected by social policy in such areas as health care and housing.

PERSONALITY AND AGING

It is easy to overgeneralize about personality, life satisfaction, and developmental tasks in later adulthood. Recall from the last chapter that there are many differences between the vigorous, healthy, recently retired young-old, the often frail old-old, and those in between. Each individual, regardless of age, also has a unique pattern of attitudes, values, and beliefs about old age and about himself or herself, along with a pattern of life experiences that reinforces that pattern. Yet, given all the differences, there are still some events and concerns that are common to most people in later life. How these are dealt with plays a major role in successful aging.

DEVELOPMENTAL TASKS IN LATER LIFE

At the outset, it is helpful to return to Erikson's theory to look for central developmental tasks. In his view, people who can face and cope with such tasks maintain better mental health.

MAINTAINING IDENTITY   One of the central tasks from adolescence on is maintaining a relatively consistent identity. As the term is used here, **identity** refers to the reasonably consistent set of concepts that a person has about his or her physical, psychological, and social attributes. For theorist Susan Whitbourne (1987), the process of maintaining a consistent identity is a lot like Piaget's ongoing process of adaptation (Chapter 1): It involves assimilating new events and changing circumstances into existing self-concepts, and accommodating major life events or threats that cannot be readily assimilated. In the face of a major chronic illness, for example, physical, psychological, and social aspects of self-concept are threatened and may require considerable accommodation.

Ideally, according to Whitbourne, individuals maintain a balance between assimilation and accommodation. Refusal to accommodate may mean that the individual is denying reality. Such a person may be defensive and rigid and may unjustifiably blame other people. On the other hand, accommodating too readily can make a person hysterical, impulsive, or hypersensitive. In all, maintaining a balance between consistency of identity and openness to new experiences is an important developmental task of older adulthood, just as it is in earlier periods of the lifespan.

For the very old, maintaining a sense of consistency in personal identity may be particularly important. In one study of over 600 individuals, mostly in

identity   Reasonably consistent set of concepts that a person has about his or her physical, psychological, and social attributes.

Older people seem to need to remember and reflect on the past in a search for the meaning of their lives.

their seventies and eighties, who experienced major changes in their health and living arrangements (Lieberman & Tobin, 1983), the researchers found that accommodating was an enormously difficult task, especially for those who were frail and highly dependent on others. Those who were most successful in adapting managed to do so by maintaining and "validating" their identities. In spite of the adversity, they were able to say, "I am who I have always been." How were they able to do this in the face of very real shifts in their lives and physical abilities? Generally they shifted from thinking about the present to thinking about the past. For example, one woman at first described herself by saying, "I am important to my family and friends; you should see how many birthday cards I got." Two years later, after some major changes in her life, she instead defined herself by saying, "I think I am important to my family; I have always done the best I could for my family, and they appreciate it." Her past became evidence that allowed her to maintain a concept of her present personal identity that was in accordance with the person she used to be (Tobin, 1988).

INTEGRITY VERSUS DESPAIR   The final stage in Erikson's theory is the psychosocial conflict of *integrity versus despair*. In his view, older people ponder whether their lives have fulfilled their earlier expectations. Those who can look back and feel satisfied that their lives have had meaning and that they have done the best that they could, develop a strong sense of personal integrity. Those who look back and see nothing but a long succession of wrong turns, missed opportunities, and failures develop a sense of despair. Ideally, resolution of this conflict involves a preponderance of integrity tinged with realistic despair (Erikson et al., 1986), which is an aid to wisdom (see Chapter 18). Wisdom enables older adults to maintain dignity and an integrated self in the face of physical deterioration and even impending death.

Part of the adjustment to old age includes the psychological need to reminisce and reflect on past events. Older people often spend time searching for themes and images that give their lives meaning and coherence. Sometimes they need to sort out and make sense of episodes and situations in their past (Kübler-Ross, 1969; Neugarten, 1976). Some people ruminate over what sort of legacy they will leave, what contributions they have made, and how the world will remember them—whether through works of art, social service, their accomplishments at work, the children they bore and raised, or the material wealth they will pass along to their children or to society. Many look to their children and grandchildren as a legacy in whom traces of their own personality and values will live on.

An 85-year-old woman eloquently expressed some of the musings, sighings, and expressions of minor regrets that are typical of this process:

If I had my life to live over, I'd dare to make more mistakes next time. I'd relax. I'd limber up. I'd be sillier than I've been this trip. I'd take fewer things seriously. I'd take more chances. I'd take more trips. I'd climb more mountains and swim more rivers. I'd eat more ice cream and less beans. I'd perhaps have more actual troubles, but I'd have fewer imaginary ones.

You see, I'm one of those people who live sensibly and sanely hour after hour, day after day. Oh, I've had my moments and if I had it to do over again, I'd have more of them. In fact, I'd try to have nothing else. Just moments, one after another, instead of living so many years ahead of each day. I've been one of those persons who never goes anywhere without a thermometer, a hot water bottle, a raincoat, and a parachute. If I had it to do again, I would travel lighter than I have.

If I had my life to live over, I would start barefoot earlier in the spring and stay that way later in the fall. I would go to more dances. I would ride more merry-go-rounds. I would pick more daisies. (Burnside, 1979a, page 425)

CONTINUITY AND CHANGE IN LATER LIFE

As we have seen in earlier chapters, most contemporary theorists tend to see development as a lifelong phenomenon; thus, adjustment to old age is an extension of earlier personality styles. Even in older adulthood, however, theorists differ on the issue of continuity and change.

"Stage" theorists believe that new life structures or organizations emerge in old age, built on the earlier stages. Levinson (1978, 1986, 1996), for example, believes that there is a period of transition (ages 60 to 65) that links the individual's previous life structure to that of late adulthood. Erikson sees ego integrity (or its counterpart, despair) as the outcome of a long process of development (Erikson et al., 1986). Peck (1968) views old age in terms of the resolution of the conflict between *ego transcendence* (achieving a state of mind that goes beyond one's prospects of dying) and *ego preoccupation* (with dying) (see Chapter 15).

Other theorists see even more continuity between previous adjustment and reactions to aging. Robert Atchley (1989) suggests that continuity provides people with an identity, a sense of who they are. People strive to be consistent in their behavior because it makes them feel more secure. Consistency enables people to say things like "I would never do that" or "That's just like me" with confidence. Similarly, there are external pressures for consistency. Other people expect us to we behave in a similar way in various kinds of situations, and they become uncomfortable if we are often unpredictable. Atchley is quick to emphasize, however, that continuity does not mean that there are no changes at all. Certainly, people's roles, abilities, and relationships all change. This change requires them to make certain alterations in their behaviors, their expectations, even their values. Atchley suggests that these changes are in line with a relatively constant "inner core" that we use to define ourselves. Let's look at that inner core in more detail.

PERSONALITY As adults, do we fit the following pronouncement by William James (1842–1910) that "In most of us, by the age of thirty, the character has set like plaster, and will never soften again. . . ." (cited in Costa & McCrae, 1994)?

Apparently we do. Several longitudinal studies have looked at the maintenance of basic personality traits or types over the decades in adulthood, and they have found the kind of continuity described by James. In one study, Paul Costa and Robert McCrae (1989) assessed three aspects of personality in a group of 2000 adult men. First, they looked at *neuroticism*—the amount of anxiety, depression, self-consciousness, vulnerability, impulsiveness, and hostility the men displayed. By and large, they found no real changes in the men's neuroticism over a ten-year period. Those who were highly neurotic tended to complain about their health; smoke heavily; have problems with drinking, sex, and finances; and feel generally dissatisfied with their lives. In particular, those who were high in neuroticism tended to be hypochondriacs, in accordance with one popular stereotype of older people. The evidence, however, showed that they had probably been hypochondriacs all their lives (Costa & McCrae, 1985).

Second, the researchers looked at *extraversion* versus *introversion*. Extraverted people are assertive and outgoing; they seek excitement and activity. Introverted people are more inclined to be shy and keep to themselves. The men in the study who were highly extraverted tended to stay that way. They were also happier and more satisfied with their lives than those who were highly introverted. There was a minor shift toward introversion, however, when circumstances required the men to become more dependent upon others. Other researchers have studied extraversion and introversion over longer periods and have found that many of their subjects become more introverted in old age.

The third dimension studied was *openness to experience*. The men who were open to new experiences had a wider range of interests. They tended to experience events intensely, whether the events were positive or negative. Men who were open to experience also showed more life satisfaction than those who were more defensive, cautious, and conforming. This aspect of personality also remained consistent from middle to later adulthood.

Many such studies show general consistency in personality. People have organized, coherent, integrated patterns or beliefs about themselves, and they tend to act in ways that are consistent with their self-image. When they are able—despite major life changes—to judge themselves as having acted in accordance with their self-concept, by and large they express more life satisfaction and self-esteem. Self-concept is, of course, vulnerable to life events and major changes in health, finances, social involvement, social class, sex, housing conditions, and marriage. Major changes in self-concept can, in turn, affect a person's sense of well-being (Thomae, 1980). Yet, aging per se seems to have no direct effect on self-concept.

Although few universal personality changes occur in later life, some researchers have studied whether any distinct pattern of personality change occurs as people grow older. One longitudinal study (Gutman, 1964) used the Thematic Apperception Test (TAT), in which subjects tell stories about ambiguous pictures and researchers infer attitudes and feelings from the stories. The question was whether any consistent changes would occur over the twenty-year period of the study. The researchers found that 40-year-old men tended to view their environment as being within their control, rewarding boldness and risk taking; they saw themselves as equal to the challenges presented by the outside world. In contrast, 60-year-old men saw the world as more complex and dangerous, no longer within their power to be changed according to their will. They instead saw themselves as accommodating and conforming to their environment.

COPING STYLES Whereas the research just discussed suggests that coping skills decline during old age, other research puts a different spin on the changes, indicating that people become more mature in their coping skills (Valliant, 1977). For example, they show increases in the use of wise detachment and humor in the face of stress. Still others have argued that there are age-related differences in coping but that they are determined by the different stressors faced by older versus younger adults (Folkman & Lazarus, 1980; McCrae, 1982). Stressors that present positive challenges (for example, a promotion at work) become less frequent with age. Although losses don't increase appreciably with age, it may be that the losses experienced by older adults are more centrally related to their identity and, hence, more threatening. Similarly, the nature of daily hassles—which also create stress—also varies with age (Folkman et al., 1987).

Some theorists, beginning with Jung (1933/1960), have suggested that men's and women's coping styles change in different ways. Men seem to move from an active to a passive style. After a lifetime of responsibility and decision making, they feel free to express more of the complexity of their personalities—including traits that are traditionally considered feminine (Gutmann, 1969, 1975). Very old men move beyond passivity to a style called *magical mastery*, in which they deal with reality through projection and distortion. As women age, they seem to become more aggressive, instrumental, and domineering—in accordance with masculine stereotypes. Perhaps both sexes respond to being liberated from the *parental imperative*, the social pressures for women to conform to nurturing roles and for men to be financially responsible and to suppress any traits that conflict with that role (Gutmann, 1969, 1975).

Cross-sectional research has also indicated that there are age-related changes in coping styles. Susan Folkman and her colleagues (1987) found that younger adults are more likely to use active, problem-focused coping styles, whereas older adults are more passive and focused on emotions. For example, an older woman might downplay the importance of the traffic accident she just had, or she might view it in a more positive light by saying "I really needed to get rid of that car anyway" or "At least no one was injured." A younger woman might instead handle the situation by confronting the other driver, getting his or her name and address, contacting the insurance company, and getting estimates to repair the damage. As in all cross-sectional research, the differences could also be attributable to cohort differences (see Chapter 1). Generally, however, longitudinal research has also tended to find continuity in coping styles as people age (e.g., McCrae, 1989).

In sum, adjustments in later life are often very similar to the adjustments that occur in earlier life. People develop an identity; they create themes that they carry with them through life. When they reach old age, their reactions to aging and to new situations will be highly individual and consistent with the identity and themes that they have created for themselves throughout their lives. Personality development in old age, then, consists of personal interpretation of events and reactions to events in keeping with the individual's past reactions (Ryff, 1985).

SUCCESSFUL AGING

Eventually, many older individuals must confront the problems of sensory decline or ill health, both in themselves and in friends and relatives. Many must confront the realities of lower status or productivity and reduced income. The longer they live, the more likely they are to experience the death of friends and family members, including their spouse. For some, the problems are overwhelming. They become preoccupied with their health, restricted circumstances, hardships, and increasing lack of autonomy.

What, then, is successful aging? First, note that the preceding description is not the predominant pattern in later adulthood. All too often, stereotypical thinking about aging paints a bleak picture that many older people themselves accept and conform to. In reality, the great majority of older people perceive themselves in quite different, more positive ways. One survey, for example, noted that although many older people agreed that "life is really tough for most people over 65," they and their friends were, for some reason, exceptions to the rule (Harris and Associates, 1978).

As noted by Paul and Margaret Baltes (1990), the Roman statesman Cicero (106–43 B.C.) produced perhaps the first essay on positive aspects of aging. He contended that in advanced age, it is finally possible for a person to enjoy life and contemplation without being distracted by "bodily pleasures." Life satisfaction and adjustment in older adulthood actually depend on a number of factors, but such satisfaction has little relationship to age itself (Larson, 1978). Health is the most important factor. After that, money, social class, marital

Most older people must cope with a sense of their own vulnerability.

status, adequacy of housing, amount of social interaction, and even transportation are important factors that influence whether or not older adults feel satisfied with their lives. Earlier life satisfaction also influences feelings of satisfaction in later adulthood. Although life satisfaction itself is comparable in young and old adults, the sources of satisfaction may change. Younger adults gain the most satisfaction from achievements and advances in work, self-development, and other areas; older adults may be satisfied simply to maintain their ability to function (Bearon, 1989). In addition, many older people look to religion and an extended social network for support and validation, as discussed in "Eye on Diversity" on facing page.

Life satisfaction in later adulthood is also determined by how older people define positive functioning. In a study of 171 middle-aged and older adults, Carol Ryff (1989) found that both cohorts defined psychological well-being in terms of an "other" orientation—being a caring, compassionate person and having good relationships with others. Older subjects also pointed to acceptance of change as an important quality of positive functioning.

When Ryff and colleagues (Heidrich & Ryff, 1993b) tried to determine why many older people maintain a positive outlook in spite of failing health and declining abilities, they found that **social comparison** plays a crucial role. Social comparison means evaluating yourself and your own situation relative to that of others. Older adults who compared their situations with those of other older people around them modified their perspectives accordingly. In particular, older women facing health problems frequently engaged in social comparison. The more positive the comparisons, the better the women's mental health—even in the face of severe physical problems. It is interesting that the women who were in poorest health showed the strongest effects of social comparison and achieved a degree of psychological adaptation comparable to that of healthy women—they came to perceive themselves as better off than they actually were. Another study (Heidrich & Ryff, 1993a) found that social comparison and social integration—maintenance of meaningful roles, normative guidelines, and reference groups—offset the negative effects of poor physical health and had a positive impact on maintaining well-being and minimizing psychological distress.

In sum, maintaining activities you're good at and actively compensating for any physical or mental decline you experience are important factors in successful aging (Schulz & Heckhausen, 1996; also see Chapter 16). Stated somewhat differently, successful aging involves avoiding disease and disability, maintaining physical and cognitive functioning, and especially staying engaged in social and productive activities (Rowe & Kahn, 1997). Old age, then, is very much what you yourself make of it.

social comparison Evaluating yourself and your situation relative to others.

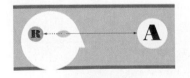

REVIEW & APPLY

1. Explain the process of identity maintenance in older adulthood, and give an example of how older people can maintain a consistent identity in the face of major shifts in their lives.
2. How is Erikson's psychosocial crisis of integrity versus despair expressed in later adulthood?
3. How do personality type and coping styles affect adjustment to aging? Does research indicate consistency or change in personality type from middle to later adulthood?
4. What factors are involved in successful aging?

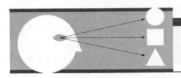

EYE ON DIVERSITY

AGING IN THE AFRICAN-AMERICAN COMMUNITY

There is a paradox between the plight of many older African-Americans and their remarkable ability to sustain themselves psychologically as they age. No one can dispute that African-American adults are more likely than whites to live in poverty, have less education, be single mothers, and experience substandard medical care. Yet survey after survey has shown that many older African-Americans have resources that enable them to cope with aging—often more effectively than their white counterparts.

Researchers have identified two key factors that are largely responsible for the staying power of many African-Americans: (1) prayer and affiliation with a church and (2) help from family and friends. "The adaptive value of these two strategies," says researcher Rose Gibson (1986), "may make blacks' entry into old age more transition than crisis."

Gibson based her conclusion on an analysis of the 1957 and 1976 versions of the *Americans View Their Mental Health* surveys, which asked respondents how they handled problems or worries. Several important findings emerged.

The surveys showed the importance of prayer in the lives of many African-Americans. In fact, African-Americans are much more likely than whites to turn to prayer as a source of help and comfort. This finding was true in both 1957 and 1976, when African-Americans used prayer more often than any other coping strategy. By 1976, however, there was a significant lessening in prayer among middle-aged African-Americans. Whereas in 1957, a clear majority of middle-aged African-Americans continued to turn to prayer as they grew older, in 1976, far fewer (27.3%) of their middle-aged counterparts prayed as a way of coping with problems.

African-Americans' reliance on prayer can be explained in part by the role of the church in the black community. Many African-Americans look to the church for a range of social services as well as religious activity. Research has shown that they are more likely than whites to rely on their church for practical assistance, especially when the community offers little help (Haber, 1984; Hirsch et al., 1972). As a result, older African-Americans perceive the church as providing practical support while family members provide emotional support (Walls, 1992). Older African-Americans who receive strong support from their church and their families are more likely to report a sense of well-being than those who receive moderate support.

The surveys also showed a pattern among African-Americans of seeking informal help from varied family members and friends. Whereas in both 1957 and 1976, whites were much more likely than blacks to turn to an internal network in times of worry, the helper they chose was likely to be a spouse or another family member. In contrast, African-Americans were more likely to turn to friends for help in 1957 and to combinations of family members in 1976. According to Gibson (1986), "The use of multiple family members for help with worries seems to increase as blacks move from middle to old age." This informal social support network plays a crucial role in the lives of low-income, older African-Americans, who rely on second- and third-generation adult kin for the physical and emotional help they need during their later years (Luckey, 1994).

Thus, although older African-Americans endure many more hardships over their lifetimes and have fewer economic resources to sustain them in old age, they find enormous comfort and sustenance in family and friends and in prayer. However, it is important to remember that this sense of psychological well-being is no substitute for adequate economic and social support. Despite the inner peace experienced by many older African-Americans, their lives continue to be marred by limited resources (Gibson, 1986).

RETIREMENT: A MAJOR CHANGE IN STATUS

One of the primary tasks of old age is adjusting to retirement. Historically, this adjustment affected men much more than women because of men's greater participation in the workforce. In the past 30 years, however, the gender difference has changed dramatically as increasing numbers of women have entered and remained in the workforce all the way to retirement. In the past, also, retirement was the culmination of a long and stable career. That, too, has changed (see Chapter 15). Nowadays, a great many workers do not stay in the same job and work for the same company throughout their working years; this circumstance often has a negative impact on their social and economic circumstances after retirement (Hayward et al., 1998). Indeed, one of the most important considerations in how people fare after retirement is whether they actually choose to retire (Reitzes et al., 1996), as opposed to being forced to retire because of their age, because of being squeezed out by a younger person, or as a result of corporate downsizing.

Either way, however, retirement is a significant status change of later adulthood. Work provides a structure for living, a daily schedule. It provides coworkers and other people with whom to interact regularly. Work also provides roles and functions, and thereby contributes to personal identity. Thus, retirement may require considerable adjustment.

Retirement does not involve just dealing with greatly increased free time. The individual must work out choices, negotiations, and coping patterns consistent with his or her personal set of meanings; in effect, each person constructs his or her own social reality for retirement. How easily the individual adopts the new role depends on a number of factors. If the shift to retirement is sudden and dramatic or if an individual's identity has been closely tied to an occupational role, the transition will probably be very difficult.

PHYSICAL, ECONOMIC, AND SOCIAL CONDITIONS

The pattern of and adjustment to retirement are the results of many factors: physical health, economic status, the attitudes of others, and the need for work-related fulfillment. As we'll also see, men and women often face different circumstances when they retire.

PHYSICAL HEALTH   An important consideration that influences the way a person reacts to retirement is health. A great number of older people leave the workforce—willingly or otherwise—because of ill health. One study of a large group of men who were about to retire (Levy, 1978) found that healthy men who wanted to retire fared the best. Those in ill health fared poorly, whether or not they wanted to retire. Their poor outcome may be because retirement frequently occurs more suddenly for people in ill health (Ekerdt et al., 1989).

Of those who retire, the healthy generally fare better than those retiring because of poor health.

They may therefore be less prepared financially and psychologically than those who have time to anticipate and plan for retirement. Moreover, their health expenses may create a financial burden, especially if they have a disability; disabled retirees rely much more on Social Security than other retirees do (Social Security Administration, 1986). Social Security benefits make up 67% of the income of unmarried disabled retirees but only 50% of unmarried nondisabled retirees' income.

Attitudes often change in the first few years of retirement (Levy, 1978). It was found that healthy men who are unwilling to retire quickly become dissatisfied; they withdraw socially and tend to be bitter and angry. They eventually tend to recover, however, and gradually take on attitudes similar to those of people who want to retire. In contrast, those who are ill when they retire show little improvement in attitude over time, even if they had looked forward to retirement.

ECONOMIC STATUS Economic status is another major factor that affects a retiree's adjustment to a new way of life. Contrary to what you might think, most older Americans have sufficient financial assets to live on. In terms of net worth, older adults tend to be wealthier than young adults (Radner, 1989). Still, some 10.5% of older adults live below the poverty line (U.S. Census Bureau, 1997). This is a lower rate than among young adults, but it masks the circumstances of certain subgroups of older people. Single people are much more likely to be poor than those who are married (Radner, 1989). Members of minority groups are more likely to be poor (Dressel, 1988; Jackson, 1985). For example, 27% of Hispanic-American older adults are below the poverty line (Ford Foundation, 1989). Women are more likely than men to be poor. Among single older white women, over 25% live in poverty. Those suffering the discrimination that often comes with being both female and a member of a minority group are the most likely to be poor. Over 60% of single black older women are impoverished (Ford Foundation, 1989). Moreover, older adults are less likely than young adults to escape poverty. This tendency is particularly true when the older person has been poor for more than three years. Whereas the majority of young adults living in poverty will improve their situation within a decade, only 5% of older adults will do so (Coe, 1988).

NEED FOR WORK-RELATED FULFILLMENT As discussed earlier, an individual's lifelong attitude toward work also affects his or her feelings about retirement. In some segments of our society, there is an almost religious devotion to work (Tilgher, 1962). Many men have invested so much time and energy in their jobs that their overall sense of self-worth and self-esteem depends on the work they do. For many, leisure activities are superficial and therefore lack meaning. In a very real sense, retirement for such men means stepping out of their previous life. Disengagement is especially hard for people who have never found satisfaction outside of their jobs in the form of hobbies, reading, continued education, or involvement in civic organizations. The problem tends to be worse for the less educated, the financially strained, and those with few social or political involvements, but professionals or business executives may also have difficulty finding something to do with their greatly increased leisure time. This is one reason why substantial numbers of people continue to work part-time after retiring (Quinn & Burkhauser, 1990).

GENDER DIFFERENCES IN RETIREMENT? Until the past decade, studies that include both men and women (and in some cases, women only) reported findings similar to those of earlier studies that included only men: Factors such as good health, economic security, and higher educational level predict a positive adjustment to retirement for women as well as men (Atchley, 1982; Block, 1981). Unfortunately, however, many women receive lower salaries and are often less financially secure than men after retirement—particularly if they are single or recently widowed or divorced. In addition, women's satisfaction after retirement can be markedly reduced if the retirement was forced upon them because of the need to care for an ailing spouse or parent.

Otherwise, it is popularly thought that women adjust to retirement more easily than men because many women have had interrupted work histories and therefore have experience with being unemployed. This view, however, is not entirely supported by research evidence. Indeed, in one study, women who had a continuous work history for an extended portion of their adult lives adapted more easily to retirement (Block, 1981). However, on average, the women with continuous work experience had greater financial security and were better prepared for retirement than those who had intermittent experience in the workforce.

DECIDING TO RETIRE

Retirement is not necessarily hazardous to your health, of course. In fact, fully a third of retirees report improvement in their mental and physical health in the period immediately after retirement. Another 50% report no change. Overall, many recent retirees experience an increase in life satisfaction (Ekerdt, 1987).

PREPARING FOR RETIREMENT As noted, adjusting to retirement is easier if you are prepared for it. In one view (Thompson, 1977), preparing for retirement consists of three elements:

1. *Decelerating*: As people grow older, they begin to let go or taper off their work responsibilities in order to avoid a sudden drop in activity at retirement.
2. *Retirement planning*: People plan specifically for the life they will lead after retirement.
3. *Retirement living*: People come to grips with concerns about stopping work and think about what it will be like to live as a retired person.

Some companies provide retirement counselors who can guide people through the process and help them determine the best time to retire. Several specific factors are considered (Johnson & Riker, 1981). How long has the potential retiree worked? Does the retiree have adequate savings and income, a place to live, and plans for further work or activities after retirement? Is he or she old enough to consider retirement? Some retirement counselors refer to the answers to these questions as an index of **retirement maturity**—how prepared a person is to retire. In general, people with a higher degree of retirement maturity have more positive attitudes toward retirement and an easier time adjusting to it.

RETIREMENT OPTIONS Of course, complete withdrawal from the workforce is not the only option for people in later adulthood. Some experts suggest that society may face a work shortage in the future (Forman, 1984), that we may be needlessly losing talented and productive workers, and that the increase in the number of full-time retirees may put severe strains on the pension plans of the future (Alsop, 1984; Wojahn, 1983). Therefore, creative solutions such as part-time, perhaps less physically demanding work options are needed for older people. Although formerly there was little or no financial

retirement maturity How prepared a person is to retire.

incentive for older workers to remain in the labor force, recent changes in Social Security regulations have made it less costly for older people to continue to work part-time (Quinn & Burkhauser, 1990).

Pilot programs to employ retired people have been remarkably successful. For example, retired businesspeople have been hired to train young and inexperienced workers. Another approach trains older people to work with handicapped children. Numerous other options are being explored (Donovan, 1984; Kieffer, 1984). When we look at how retirement has changed in the past 50 years and how it is likely to change in the years ahead, it becomes clear that retirement must be viewed in a historical context. Whereas in 1950, about half of all men over age 65 were still working, in 1995, only about 12% of this age group still had a job or were looking for work (Quinn & Burkhauser, 1990; Kaye et al., 1995). Increases in Social Security benefits, retirement funds, and pensions are partially responsible for many early-retirement decisions. Those who continue working after retirement are more likely to be employed part-time or self-employed than younger workers (Quinn & Burkhauser, 1990).

However, if current economic trends continue, fewer people may have the option of early retirement in the years to come. Experts predict that many of the 76 million Baby Boomers will be forced to continue working to age 70 and beyond because they cannot afford to retire. According to the federal Committee for Economic Development, a combination of factors is putting pressure on Baby Boomers to remain employed. These include the government's decision to raise the minimum age for Social Security retirement benefits, the uncertain future of the Social Security system, and Baby Boomers' notoriously poor rates of savings (Kaye et al., 1995).

Part-time work is one creative solution for older people who have not lost their productivity or talent.

1. Describe factors that influence how a person reacts to retirement.
2. How can a person best prepare for retirement? How can society be of assistance?

REVIEW & APPLY

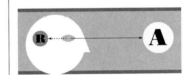

FAMILY AND PERSONAL RELATIONSHIPS

An age-related status change equal in importance to retirement involves changes in family and personal relationships, often including coping with illness and death and making a new life as a widow or widower.

As in any period of life, the social context of family and personal relationships helps define our roles and responsibilities and our life satisfactions. In today's world, this social context is shifting for older adults much as it is for younger adults. Divorce and remarriage are more common. Kinship relations with grandchildren and stepgrandchildren are more complicated. There is also a wider range of single lifestyles. Nevertheless, close interpersonal relationships continue to define many of the stresses and satisfactions of life in later adulthood. We will explore these relationships first by focusing on the "postparental" period and then by examining the role of many older people as caregiver to an ill or a dying spouse. The importance of support from siblings and friends will also be considered.

Older couples, without the responsibilities of work and children, often report increased satisfaction and harmony.

WHEN PARENTING IS OVER

Marital satisfaction often changes during the postparental period, as do relationships with children and grandchildren. For most older adults, the direct responsibilities of parenting are over (assuming that they had children). On average, older married couples report being more satisfied with their marriage after the children leave home. There may be some initial difficulty in adjusting to each other as a couple, but most couples who remain married report less stress and increased feelings of satisfaction and harmony (Lee, 1988; Olson & Lavee, 1989). Couples who report greater than average satisfaction are also likely to be those whose marriage is at the emotional center of their lives. Marriage now brings them more comfort, emotional support, and intimacy. Happy marriages that survive into later adulthood characteristically are more egalitarian and cooperative. There is reasonable equality with regard to love, status, and money (Reynolds et al., 1995). Traditional gender roles also become less important (Troll et al., 1979).

RELATIONSHIPS WITH CHILDREN AND GRANDCHILDREN Despite high mobility and social change, most older adults report having relatively frequent contact with their children and grandchildren—if not in person, at least by phone. Typically, they still feel responsible for helping their children as needed, although they are also anxious not to interfere (Blieszner & Mancini, 1987; Greenberg & Becker, 1988; Hagestad, 1987). Aside from advice—whether solicited or not—parents often provide their adult children with various forms of assistance, such as money and babysitting.

Grandparenthood (see Chapter 15) is often seen as one of the most satisfying roles of older age. Studies have shown that many grandparents develop strong, companionable relationships with their grandchildren. These bonds, which are based on regular contact, are the basis for close, loving relationships (Cherlin & Furstenberg, 1986).

Over 40% of older Americans have great-grandchildren (Doka & Mertz, 1988). In general, great-grandparents are also pleased with their role and attach emotional significance to it. The role can provide a sense of personal and family renewal, a new diversion in their lives, and a proud marker of longevity (Doka & Mertz, 1988). Thus, great-grandparents may be given a special status in the family.

Still, kinship patterns have undergone stress and change in the past few decades. The high rates of divorce and remarriage have made those patterns more complex. It is therefore not surprising that grandparents often report greater closeness to their grandchildren in situations in which their adult child is the custodial parent. Some grandparents feel that they have a particularly important role in helping to maintain stability and a sense of values during periods of family disruption (Johnson & Barer, 1987).

CARING FOR AN ILL SPOUSE

Although most older people do not need much help with daily living, those who do tend to rely heavily on their families (Gatz et al., 1990; Stone et al., 1987). If there is a surviving spouse, she or he is the most likely caregiver, with wives being more likely to play this role than husbands. Therefore, the caregiver is also likely to be old and have health problems. In one national survey, the average age of such caregivers was slightly over 57 years, with 25% in the 65- to 74-year-old range, and 10% over age 75 (Stone et al., 1987).

Caregiver wives often report more stress than caregiver husbands, although some studies find that the differences are small (Miller, 1990). There are probably many contributing factors; research suggests that gender-role changes that occur in old age may be involved (Pruchno & Resch, 1989). As men become more oriented to the family, they may actually be more interested in providing such care than women, who may feel that they have already spent most of their lives taking care of other people. It is also possible, however, that the differences in caregiver stress and strain are due to factors such as women's greater willingness to admit to having health or psychological problems (Miller, 1990).

Caring for someone with Alzheimer's disease entails unique strains. It is particularly stressful when the afflicted person's behavior becomes disruptive or socially embarrassing (Deimling & Bass, 1986). Moreover, these caregivers tend to have smaller support systems than people who are caring for physically but not mentally impaired older persons (Birkel & Jones, 1989). Even organized respite programs do not seem to be particularly helpful (Lawton et al., 1989). In spite of the stresses and strains, however, caregivers often report considerable gratification from providing care for a person who has meant so much to them (Motenko, 1989).

WIDOWS AND WIDOWERS

In later adulthood, it is all too common to suffer the loss of a close family member, friend, or spouse, a loss that is usually marked by grief and bereavement, followed by a long period of readjustment (as discussed in Chapter 18). At the same time, men and women who experience the death of their spouse also assume a new status in life—that of widower or widow. For many, this is a very difficult transition involving major changes in daily life patterns and the risk of social isolation. For others, it may provide a long-awaited opportunity to assume control of their lives, especially if they have been caring for an ill or a frail spouse.

There are more than five times more older-adult widows than widowers in the United States—some 9.2 million in all as of 1992 (see Figure 17–1). In addition, most older men are married, whereas most older women are not. By age 85, four out of every five women are widows (U.S. Census Bureau, 1993). These numbers are due in part to longevity. On average, older widows survive about 50% longer than older widowers after the spouse's death (Burnside, 1979).

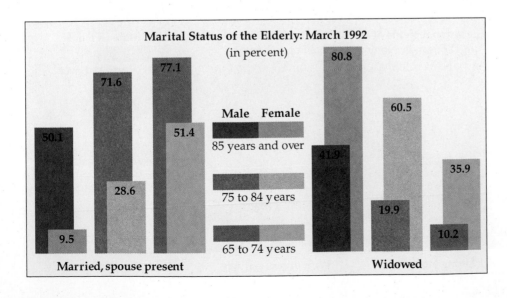

Marital Status of the Elderly: March 1992
(in percent)

Married, spouse present: 50.1, 9.5, 71.6, 28.6, 77.1, 51.4

Male / Female
85 years and over
75 to 84 years
65 to 74 years

Widowed: 80.8, 41.9, 60.5, 19.9, 35.9, 10.2

FIGURE 17–1

There are far more widows than widowers in the elderly U.S. population.

Source: U.S. Census Bureau, 1993.

LIVING ARRANGEMENTS The statistics just discussed spell loneliness for many older people, but a woman's experience of forced independence is often quite different from a man's. As with divorce, after the death of a spouse, women of all ages are less likely than men to remarry; on average, older-adult women are more than eight times less likely to remarry than older-adult men (Burnside, 1979). This trend occurs partly because our society traditionally favors the pairing of older men and younger women, which is also one of the reasons for the disproportionate number of widows in the first place: Older husbands die sooner. Obviously, it is also partly because fewer men are available, since women live longer. Of American women over age 65, nearly half are widowed, and more than 40% live alone; another 40% live with their husbands. Of American men over 65, only 15% are widowed, and less than 20% live alone; the large majority are still married and living with their wives. Among the oldest-old (people in their eighties), one study found that only 10% of the women were married and that about two-thirds lived alone; in contrast, 50% of the men were married, and less than half lived alone (Barer, 1994). In all, some 9.5 million older adults live alone, and eight out of ten are women (see Figure 17–2). The morbid preoccupation about becoming widows sometimes seen in middle-aged and older married women therefore has roots in reality.

There are many practical and psychological realities that widows and widowers must face if they live alone. They must run errands, maintain social contacts, and make financial decisions on their own. Some may welcome the opportunity; others may have difficulty because their spouses have always taken care of certain matters, such as finances.

SOCIAL SUPPORT Many potential support systems are available for widows and widowers, including family, friends, work associates (or former ones), and participants in leisure activities (Lopata, 1979). The majority of older Americans have at least one child living within 10 miles of them, and adult children who have moved away often return when their parents need help (Lin & Rogerson, 1995). Both mothers and fathers are likely to receive assistance from

FIGURE 17–2

Living arrangements for the elderly differ considerably for men and women.

Source: U.S. Census Bureau, 1993.

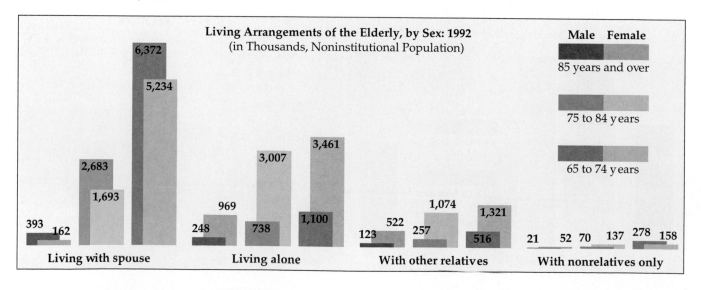

their children, especially if they have daughters (Spitze & Logan, 1989, 1990). A widowed father may see his children less often than a widowed mother, although the difference is typically small (Spitze & Logan, 1989). In the immediate aftermath of the spouse's death, there is increased contact, help, and perception of kinship obligations. Relationships between the surviving parent and his or her children may be disrupted. In time, however, mother-child relationships usually improve or remain close, with exchanges of help and finances. Father-child relationships are less predictable and may be affected negatively. In such cases, the wife has often been the family's kinkeeper (Aquilino, 1994).

Widows may have an easier time than widowers in maintaining a social life because wives traditionally maintain communication with family members and initiate social activities with friends (Lopata, 1975; Stevens, 1995). Widowers are therefore more likely to become isolated from the couple's previous social contacts. They are also generally less active in social organizations than widows. Finally, widowers are prone to certain sexual problems following bereavement. Attempts to end prolonged sexual inactivity, particularly when a wife dies after a long illness, may cause intense guilt and in turn may bring about a form of impotence known as *widower's impotency* (Comfort, 1976).

Widows who cope well generally have a wide support network, including close female friends.

In general, then, the ways in which men and women adapt to widowhood differ significantly. According to the results of two studies conducted in the Netherlands in which older men and women who had been widowed for three to five years and were living alone were interviewed, widowers generally have greater income, education, freedom from health problems, and access to more partnerlike relationships than do widows. However, they have more trouble coping emotionally than widows, who tend to have a broader support network that includes close female friends, children, and helpful neighbors (Stevens, 1995). The loneliest widows are those who have few or no children, were widowed suddenly and early, and have been widowed for less than six years (Lopata et al., 1982).

SIBLINGS AND FRIENDS

In later adulthood, many people report increased contact with and concern for siblings. Relationships that were quite distant in the busy, middle part of adult life are sometimes renewed and revitalized. Siblings share living quarters, provide comfort and support in times of crisis, and nurture each other in times of ill health. They are valuable companions for the kind of reminiscing that leads to ego integrity. They may also work together to organize and provide help to an ailing parent (Goetting, 1982). Siblings are also important to a widow's recovery from bereavement after the death of her husband, as well as to her subsequent well-being. Research has shown that the support a widow receives from her siblings depends on a variety of factors, including the sex, marital status, and proximity of her siblings as well as the proximity of her own children. Sometimes the most helpful relationships are those between a widow and her married sisters (O'Bryant, 1988).

Sibling relationships are not always smooth and congenial, of course. Nevertheless, at least a modicum of kinship responsibility among siblings is a common part of the social network of older adults. It is particularly important for single adults or for older individuals who need care and assistance but do not have grown children who can help.

As discussed in Chapter 15, friendships also provide considerable stability and life satisfaction for both married and unmarried individuals. Still, most studies that compare friendships and family relationships find clear distinctions. Most older adults think of kinship relationships as permanent. We can

call upon kin for long-term commitments; we cannot make quite the same demands on a friendship. The prevailing view is that friends will help in handling an immediate emergency such as a sudden illness, but long-term responsibilities should be handled by kin (Aizenberg & Treas, 1985). Friends can,
however, take on special importance for adults who lack siblings. Friendships
are also an important source of social support for older adults living in retirement communities (Potts, 1997).

REVIEW & APPLY

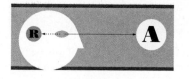

1. What are some characteristic patterns of relationships during the postparental period?
2. Discuss some of the major adjustments that must be made by a widow or
   widower.
3. Characterize sibling relationships during later adulthood.

SOCIAL POLICY AND THE ELDERLY

Although personality stability and change, retirement, and family and personal relationships are issues that older adults face as individuals, the needs of
older adults have social policy implications as well.

Social policy that affects older adults is influenced by the demographic composition of the population. These policies are most important to the frail elderly, who often must rely on others for their care. Often, social policy translates into lifestyle options for older Americans.

THE DEMOGRAPHICS OF AGING IN AMERICA

As Figure 17–3 shows, the demographics of the older adult population in the
United States have changed dramatically since 1900 and will continue to
change as we move toward 2050. Whereas in 1900 there were only 3.1 million
older people in the United States—about one in twenty-five Americans—in
1990, there were 31.1 million—about one in every eight people. By 2050, this
segment of the population is expected to grow to about 79 million people and
represent one in five Americans (U.S. Census Bureau, 1993). Many of these
older people are expected to remain healthy into their seventies and beyond.

The fastest-growing segment of the older adult population is age 85 and
older. Although the general population increased by 30% in the past 35 years,
the population age 85 and older increased by 232% during the same period.
Today the oldest-old represent 1.2% of the population, a figure that could increase to nearly 10% by 2050 (Angier, 1995). Although most people believe that
this demographic shift will place enormous financial strains on the health-care
system, and particularly on Medicare, current data indicate that the oldest-old
may actually be healthier than people in the young-old age group. Richard
Suzman of the National Institute on Aging explains: "There seems to be a selection process, and once you're over the hump, you start a less steep trajectory
of disablement" (cited in Angier, 1995). Moreover, the oldest-old usually die
quickly as a result of such illnesses as pneumonia, and they are less likely to
suffer prolonged hospitalizations than people in their sixties and seventies.

When researchers at the Health Care Financing Administration calculated
the impact of increased longevity on Medicare spending, they found that

FIGURE 17–3

Over the last one hundred and the next fifty years, the elderly population
of the United States grows from one in twenty-five to one in five.

Source: U.S. Census Bureau, 1993.

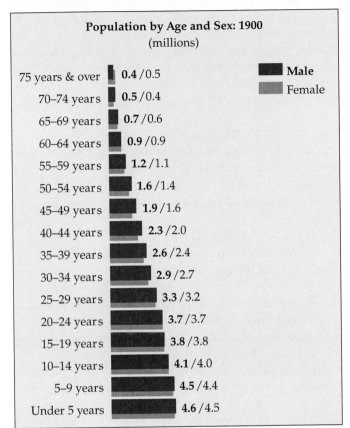

Population by Age and Sex: 1900
(millions)

75 years & over	0.4 /0.5	■ Male
70–74 years	0.5 /0.4	Female
65–69 years	0.7 /0.6	
60–64 years	0.9 /0.9	
55–59 years	1.2 /1.1	
50–54 years	1.6 /1.4	
45–49 years	1.9 /1.6	
40–44 years	2.3 /2.0	
35–39 years	2.6 /2.4	
30–34 years	2.9 /2.7	
25–29 years	3.3 /3.2	
20–24 years	3.7 /3.7	
15–19 years	3.8 /3.8	
10–14 years	4.1 /4.0	
5–9 years	4.5 /4.4	
Under 5 years	4.6 /4.5	

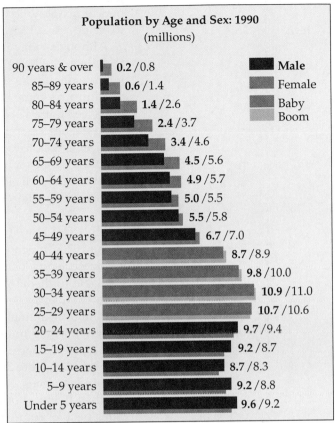

Population by Age and Sex: 1990
(millions)

90 years & over	0.2 /0.8	■ Male
85–89 years	0.6 /1.4	Female
80–84 years	1.4 /2.6	Baby
75–79 years	2.4 /3.7	Boom
70–74 years	3.4 /4.6	
65–69 years	4.5 /5.6	
60–64 years	4.9 /5.7	
55–59 years	5.0 /5.5	
50–54 years	5.5 /5.8	
45–49 years	6.7 /7.0	
40–44 years	8.7 /8.9	
35–39 years	9.8 /10.0	
30–34 years	10.9 /11.0	
25–29 years	10.7 /10.6	
20–24 years	9.7 /9.4	
15–19 years	9.2 /8.7	
10–14 years	8.7 /8.3	
5–9 years	9.2 /8.8	
Under 5 years	9.6 /9.2	

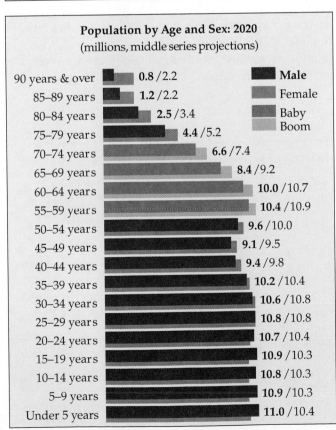

Population by Age and Sex: 2020
(millions, middle series projections)

90 years & over	0.8 /2.2	■ Male
85–89 years	1.2 /2.2	Female
80–84 years	2.5 /3.4	Baby
75–79 years	4.4 /5.2	Boom
70–74 years	6.6 /7.4	
65–69 years	8.4 /9.2	
60–64 years	10.0 /10.7	
55–59 years	10.4 /10.9	
50–54 years	9.6 /10.0	
45–49 years	9.1 /9.5	
40–44 years	9.4 /9.8	
35–39 years	10.2 /10.4	
30–34 years	10.6 /10.8	
25–29 years	10.8 /10.8	
20–24 years	10.7 /10.4	
15–19 years	10.9 /10.3	
10–14 years	10.8 /10.3	
5–9 years	10.9 /10.3	
Under 5 years	11.0 /10.4	

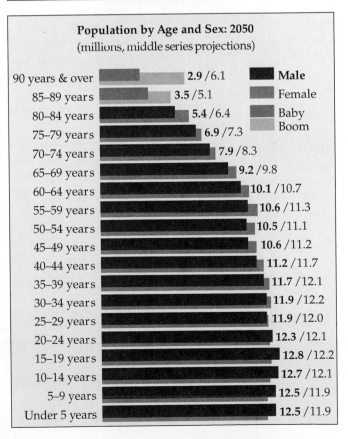

Population by Age and Sex: 2050
(millions, middle series projections)

90 years & over	2.9 /6.1	■ Male
85–89 years	3.5 /5.1	Female
80–84 years	5.4 /6.4	Baby
75–79 years	6.9 /7.3	Boom
70–74 years	7.9 /8.3	
65–69 years	9.2 /9.8	
60–64 years	10.1 /10.7	
55–59 years	10.6 /11.3	
50–54 years	10.5 /11.1	
45–49 years	10.6 /11.2	
40–44 years	11.2 /11.7	
35–39 years	11.7 /12.1	
30–34 years	11.9 /12.2	
25–29 years	11.9 /12.0	
20–24 years	12.3 /12.1	
15–19 years	12.8 /12.2	
10–14 years	12.7 /12.1	
5–9 years	12.5 /11.9	
Under 5 years	12.5 /11.9	

improved life expectancy had only a small financial impact on the system (Angier, 1995). Instead, it is the sheer size of the Baby Boom cohort—the vast numbers of people who will reach age 65 over the next 25 years—that is expected to drive up annual Medicare costs by about $98 billion (Angier, 1995).

Although today most older people are white, this group will become more racially and ethnically diverse in the years ahead. By 2050, the percentage of white older adults is expected to decline from its 1990 level of 87% to 67% as other groups come to represent a significantly larger share of the older population (see Figure 17–4).

As the older population grows, more attention is being given to the quality of services available to the aged. Only a small fraction of the total number of older people are frail and in need of extensive services. However, despite their small numbers, the frail elderly are often the most vulnerable members of society. Social services are needed to address the specific needs of these individuals.

THE FRAIL ELDERLY IN AMERICA

In the 1970s, much public attention focused on the poverty, ill health, and inadequate living conditions of older people and the limited social services available to them. Many services were improved. Although, as noted earlier, poverty still exists among older adults, most older individuals are guaranteed a minimum annual income and basic health-care services. Far more low-income housing units were allocated to older people, and some communities developed a range of social services for them (Kutza, 1981).

It has been more difficult to identify the next level of problems and to develop possible solutions. For example, living in near poverty isn't much less depressing than living in poverty. Public housing does not always meet the needs of older people. Some housing may not provide the opportunity to share living space with others; in other cases, it might not be safe to walk in the corridors of community projects. Also, transportation can become a major problem for those who must stop driving because of failing vision or slow reaction time.

There are at least 1.6 million noninstitutionalized older adults receiving help in daily living from one or more unpaid caregivers (Steon et al., 1987).

FIGURE 17–4

The U.S. elderly population will become more racially and ethnically diverse in the years ahead.

Source: U.S. Census Bureau, 1993.

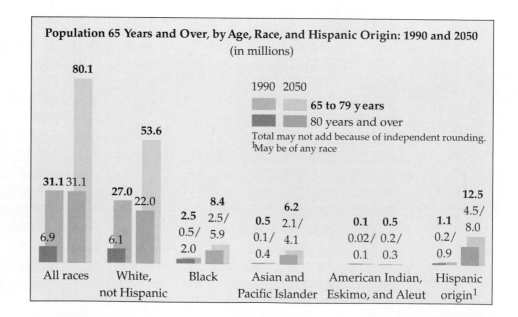

Hundreds of thousands more live in residential-care homes in the community (Mor et al., 1986). Only a small percentage of people over age 65 are in nursing homes (Shanas & Maddox, 1985). Those who end up in nursing homes are likely to be single, suffering from mental impairment, and over age 85 (Birkel & Jones, 1989; Mor et al., 1986; Shapiro & Tate, 1988). Although most receive adequate care, some frail elderly are subject to physical and mental abuse (see "In Theory, In Fact," page 598).

Social programs for the frail elderly are not fine-tuned to meet the needs of the individual. Critics have often warned that people sometimes opt for nursing home placement when other services might be more appropriate. We are anxious to avoid medical and economic catastrophes for older adults, but we have difficulty with the range of lesser services that might help the individual maintain a higher quality of life and prevent catastrophe (Brody, 1987). Other critics warn that we must remember that aging per se is not the problem— older individuals with physical and mental disabilities need to be treated for those disabilities. Similarly, some older individuals lack the social support of family or friends, or display unusual behavior patterns, or have trouble with self-care; they need help in those areas in particular, not necessarily complete nursing home care. They may need education, counseling, legal aid, social networking, or just more interesting things to do (Knight & Walker, 1985).

The institutional care received by older people varies widely in quality. Although there are many well-planned and caring institutions, in the past few years, many nursing homes have been exposed as boring, meaningless places where people often have little to do but wait for the end of their lives. Thus, people who are about to enter an institution often feel great anxiety and dread, and their children often feel guilty. People entering nursing homes may also exhibit many characteristics of people who are already institutionalized, such as apathy, passivity, bitterness, or depression (Tobin & Lieberman, 1976). They are facing a break with the continuity of their lives, losing their independence, becoming separated from many of their possessions and familiar routines. Once they do enter an institution, they may find that their identity is further submerged (they are now "Honey" or "Dearie" instead of Mr. or Mrs. or Ms. Somebody), and they may have to conform to unfamiliar and unpleasant daily routines (Kastenbaum, 1979).

For the elderly, living in near poverty may be just as depressing as living in poverty.

LIFESTYLE OPTIONS FOR OLDER AMERICANS

As we have seen, older Americans constitute a remarkably varied group; they are not a single, uniform mass of humanity. Catch-all phrases such as "the elderly" and "senior citizens" are inadequate to describe the multitude of individual qualities found in aging individuals. Moreover, the period of old age covers a long span of time. Consequently (as discussed in Chapter 16), there are sharp differences between the young-old, who are recently retired and are often healthy and vigorous, and the old-old, who are more likely to experience ill health, restricted mobility, and social isolation. Social policies designed to assist older people must take account of this diversity if they are to be effective (Kane & Kane, 1980).

Social policies center on caregiving and living facilities and other services that provide older adults with the assistance that they need to live with dignity. The push for recognition comes from older people themselves.

DAY CENTERS FOR OLDER ADULTS   Of individuals over age 65, one in four can expect to be disabled to such an extent that **institutionalization**— long-term, typically permanent, placement—will be necessary. Far more will

institutionalization Long-term, usually permanent placement in an institution.

IN THEORY, IN FACT

ELDER ABUSE

In the late 1970s, Americans discovered the existence and prevalence of elder abuse (Callahan, 1988). To their astonishment and dismay, they began hearing about old people who were neglected, belittled, and mistreated—in their homes, on the streets, and in institutions. Given the attention that "granny bashing" received on the evening news, most Americans came to believe that elder abuse was a widespread problem. Indeed, early estimates indicated that there were over 1 million cases of elder abuse annually (Callahan, 1988; Salend et al., 1984). Although we do not have reliable estimates on how common elder abuse is, testimony during hearings held by the House Select Committee on Aging in 1989 indicated that it may affect as many as one in twenty-five Americans over age 65 (Weith, 1994).

Elder abuse can take a variety of forms (Pillemer & Finkelhor, 1988; Salend et al., 1984). These include physical violence, neglect (such as withholding food or medicine), psychological abuse, or financial exploitation. There is debate over which form is most common. Some researchers report that physical violence, with a rate of 20 cases per 1000 individuals, is the most common form (Pillemer & Finkelhor, 1988). Social service agencies have found that neglect is the most common form, although these figures often include self-neglect as well as neglect by caregivers (Salend et al., 1984). It may be, however, that financial exploitation is actually the most common form. There is simply not enough information to know.

Who are the victims and victimizers? Older people who are in ill health are three to four times more likely than healthy ones to be abused (Pillemer & Finkelhor, 1988). Female victims are more likely to come to the attention of social service agencies, as are the very old (Callahan, 1988). Those who live with another person are actually more likely to be abused. Not surprisingly, then, the most common abuser is the victim's spouse (Pillemer & Finkelhor, 1988). Spouses with a long history of conflict and violence are particularly likely to engage in elder abuse. However, when we take into account that more older adults live with their spouses than with their children, the rate of abuse is actually slightly higher for the latter group (Pillemer & Finkel-hor, 1988). Caregivers who abuse alcohol or other drugs, or are mentally incompetent, are more likely to be abusive—as are those who are forced to provide care by other family members (Kosberg, 1988).

Jordan Kosberg (1988) has argued that societal attitudes are a major factor in elder abuse. He suggests that as long as the United States is an ageist, violent society, we will have elder abuse. Other societal values, such as discrimination against the disabled and women, also play a role. In addition, factors that increase the likelihood of family dysfunction—including poverty, unemployment, lack of community resources, and cyclic familial violence—will all need to be addressed before elder abuse is eliminated.

Finally, significant cultural differences make it difficult to generalize findings about elder abuse in the United States to other countries. Researchers in Great Britain and other countries are currently investigating how this problem affects their own older adult populations and the actions that can be taken to reduce the incidence of abuse (McCreadie & Tinker, 1993).

need limited health, social, and living assistance. Day centers are one option (Irwin, 1978). They provide an attractive alternative to nursing homes for those who need care on a limited basis. To families who are willing to care for their older relatives in the evenings and at night, day centers offer periods of relief and the opportunity to maintain a normal working schedule. Consider the case of a 77-year-old stroke victim. She lived with her daughter and son-in-law but spent her days in a Baltimore day center, where she received therapy, kept busy, and made new friends. Her morale and temperament improved dramatically after only a few weeks of attendance, so that her family's burden of care became much lighter. Note, however, that the cost of day centers often is not covered by health insurance policies, even though these centers are more cost-effective than nursing homes. Thus, they may be prohibitively expensive for many families (Gurewitsch, 1983).

OTHER OPTIONS For older people in good health, there are various other options. Retirement communities allow older people to live together and share interests and activities in safe surroundings. One drawback is that they isolate

There is great diversity among older people with many adopting active lifestyles.

older adults from the rest of the world, a situation that most older Americans do not like. Polls show that most older people want to spend their postretirement years in their own communities and preferably in their own homes (Lord, 1995).

Other ideas are being tried by organizations such as the Gray Panthers and the Quakers. One successful experiment is the Life Center operated by the Quakers in Philadelphia. Here, older people live in a large converted house with students and people in other age groups. Costs, housework, and meals are shared, and the resulting sense of community keeps older people in the mainstream of life. Home sharing has also worked for older adults in such varied locations as Boulder, Colorado, and Rochester, Vermont (Lord, 1995).

COMMUNITY SERVICES   An array of services is increasingly being made available to older people: various modes of transportation, including door-to-door service and escort services in dangerous neighborhoods; "meals on wheels" services; in-home care, including both homemakers and health professionals; friendly visitors; telephone reassurance; cultural services, such as bookmobiles and other library programs and free or reduced-price admission to museums and concerts; opportunities to serve as foster grandparents or in some other volunteer capacity, possibly even work for pay; and free legal assistance.

Many communities and religious groups have also established senior centers at which older people can participate in varied activities, attend classes and parties, and receive needed services (Kaplan, 1979). Other communities have experimented with community care programs in which people who would otherwise be institutionalized receive around-the-clock care in a private home (Oktay & Volland, 1981).

PROGRESS THROUGH SELF-HELP   Although society is finally beginning to pay more attention to the needs of older people, older people themselves are an important resource for meeting their own needs and those of others. Older people are often unaware of the services and benefits already available to them. Better use of the media could inform them of their rights and

Senior shuttles help older people get around more easily.

opportunities. Even more effective as a means of self-help are activist organizations like the Gray Panthers (actually a coalition of older people and young people) and the AARP, which bring older people together as a political and social force (Miller, 1981; Rowe, 1982). These groups rightly see older people as a largely untapped resource in our society.

Members of these and other groups are working for more rights for older people both in the workplace and in society as a whole. Their work has led to greater autonomy and better living conditions both for older people and for other members of society. One badly crippled older woman made a great impact in Philadelphia by publicly demonstrating that the urban transportation system could not accommodate the weak or the old. The most serious shortcoming found was that the steps for getting onto buses were too high. Efforts like this have led to the use of "kneeling buses" and special vans for the handicapped. Finally, organizations like the Gray Panthers and AARP are giving older people a better self-image—something long neglected in a world that equates youth with beauty, maturity with power, and age with obsolescence (Mackenzie, 1978).

With a little flexibility in social policy and creative solutions to health, mobility, and social needs, numerous other adaptive living styles may be developed. A larger population of older people does not necessarily mean a larger burden on the younger adult population. The financial and creative resources of this segment of the population may more than pay for itself.

REVIEW & APPLY

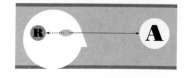

1. Describe the older adult population in the United States in terms of key demographic characteristics.
2. Describe some social programs for the frail elderly that take account of the diversity of individual needs.
3. How have the Gray Panthers and the AARP helped improve the lot of older people?

SUMMARY

Personality and Aging

- According to Erikson, a central developmental task from adolescence on is maintaining a relatively consistent identity—that is, a reasonably consistent set of concepts about one's physical, psychological, and social attributes.
- For the very old, maintaining a sense of consistency in personal identity may be particularly important as they experience major changes in their health and living arrangements.
- The final stage in Erikson's theory is the psychosocial conflict of integrity versus despair. Those who can look back and feel satisfied that their lives have had meaning develop a sense of personal integrity, whereas those who see nothing but wrong turns, missed opportunities, and failures develop a sense of despair.
- Part of the adjustment to old age includes the psychological need to reminisce and reflect on past events.
- Levinson believes that there is a period of transition that links the individual's previous life structure to that of late adulthood.
- Atchley believes that people strive to be consistent in their behavior because doing so makes them feel more secure as their roles, abilities, and relationships change.
- Research has shown that certain personality characteristics, such as neuroticism, extraversion versus introversion, and openness to experience remain consistent from middle to later adulthood.
- Some studies suggest that coping skills decline during old age, but others indicate that people become more mature in their coping styles. There is also evidence that men's and women's coping styles change in different ways.
- Some research indicates that there are age-related changes in coping styles. Younger adults are more likely to use active, problem-focused coping styles, whereas older adults are more passive and focused on emotions.
- Stereotypical thinking about aging paints a bleak picture that many older people themselves accept. In reality, the great majority of older people perceive themselves in positive ways.
- Life satisfaction and adjustment in older adulthood depend on several factors other than age. These include health, money, social class, marital status, adequacy of housing, and amount of social interaction.

- Social comparison, or evaluating yourself and your own situation relative to that of others, plays a crucial role in the outlook of older people.

Retirement: A Major Change in Status

- One of the most important considerations in how people fare after retirement is whether they actually choose to retire as opposed to experiencing mandatory retirement. Either way, retirement is the most significant status change of later adulthood.
- An important factor in reactions to retirement is health. Many people leave the workforce because of ill health. Others may be healthy yet forced to retire because of their age.
- Economic status is another important factor. Most older people have sufficient financial assets to live on. Single people, members of minority groups, and women are more likely to be poor.
- An individual's lifelong attitude toward work also affects his or her feelings about retirement. For those who have been devoted to work, retirement means stepping out of their previous life. It is especially difficult for people who have never found satisfaction outside of their jobs in the form of hobbies and other activities.
- On average, women with continuous work experience have greater financial security and are better prepared for retirement than those with intermittent experience in the workforce.
- Preparation for retirement consists of three elements: decelerating (tapering off work responsibilities), retirement planning, and retirement living. Some companies provide retirement counselors who can guide people through the process.
- Some experts suggest that we may be needlessly losing talented and productive workers and that creative solutions such as part-time, less demanding work options are needed for older people.

Family and Personal Relationships

- Close interpersonal relationships continue to define many of the stresses and satisfactions of life in later adulthood.
- On average, older married couples report being more satisfied with their marriage after the children leave home. Happy marriages that survive into later adulthood characteristically are more egalitarian and cooperative.

- Most older adults report having relatively frequent contact with their children and grandchildren. Typically, they still feel responsible for helping their children as needed.
- Grandparenthood is often seen as one of the most satisfying roles of older age. Great-grandparents are also pleased with their role.
- Older people who need help with daily living tend to rely heavily on their families. If there is a surviving spouse, he or she is the most likely caregiver. Caregiver wives often report more stress than caregiver husbands.
- Caring for someone with Alzheimer's disease entails unique strains, particularly when the afflicted person's behavior becomes disruptive or socially embarrassing.
- Becoming a widow or widower is a very difficult transition involving major changes in daily life patterns and the risk of social isolation.
- Since men are more likely than women to remarry after the death of a spouse, more older women than older men live alone. Living alone entails adjusting to many practical and psychological realities.
- Social support systems available for widows and widowers include family, friends, work associates, and participants in leisure activities.
- Widows may have an easier time than widowers in maintaining a social life; widowers are more likely to become isolated from the couple's previous social contacts.
- In later adulthood, many people report increased contact and concern for siblings. Siblings share living quarters, provide comfort and support in times of crisis, and nurture each other in times of ill health.
- Friendships also provide considerable stability and life satisfaction for both married and unmarried individuals.

Social Policy and the Elderly

- The fastest-growing segment of the older adult population is age 85 and older. Current data indicate that the oldest old may be healthier than people in the young-old age group.
- Although today most older people are white, this group will become more racially and ethnically diverse in the years ahead.
- As the older population grows, more attention is being given to the quality of services available to the aged.
- Many noninstitutionalized older adults receive help in daily living from one or more unpaid caregivers. Others live in residential-care homes in the community. Only a small percentage are in nursing homes.
- Social programs for the frail elderly are not fine-tuned to meet the needs of the individual. Some older adults have physical and mental disability, lack the support of family or friends or have trouble with self-care; they need help in those areas, not necessarily complete nursing-home care.
- Although about one in four individuals can expect to be disabled to such an extent that institutionalization will be necessary, far more will need limited health, social, and living assistance. These services can be provided by day centers, where older people are given care on a limited basis and return to their families in the evenings.
- For older people in good health, there are other options such as retirement communities. Most adults, however, want to spend their postretirement years in their own communities and preferably in their own homes.
- An array of services is increasingly being made available to older people. These include various modes of transportation, meals on wheels, in-home care, cultural services, and volunteer opportunities, among others.
- Activist organizations like the AARP bring older people together as a political and social force. They are working for more rights for older people both in the workplace and in society as a whole.

KEY TERMS

status passage
identity
social comparison

retirement maturity
institutionalization

USING WHAT YOU'VE LEARNED

What are the issues, concerns, and needs of individuals in their late sixties, as opposed to those in their late eighties? How well are individuals in each group managing in your community? Find two individuals (preferably not in nursing homes) who are both over 60 but differ in age by at least 20 years. Where do you find them? Are they on the golf course? In a senior center? In a service organization or church? Are they your neighbors or relatives? Are they still working, at least part-time? Try talking with them briefly, perhaps about community events, investment strategies, popular music, TV programs, computer programs, world news events, their siblings and grandchildren, or even recent changes in their lives. How are they dealing with the problems they are facing? Would the availability of simple services (transportation to the grocery store, yard work, etc.) help them?

SUGGESTED READINGS

ALLEN, K. R. (1989). *Single women/family ties: Life histories of older women.* Newbury Park, CA: Sage. Case studies of older women highlighting life change events are collected as part of the Syracuse Family Relative Project.

ELKIND, D. (1989). *Grandparenting: Understanding today's children.* Glenview, IL: Scott, Foresman. A popular author speaks to grandparents about generational similarities and differences.

LUSTRADER, W. (1991). *Counting on kindness: The dilemmas of dependency.* New York: Free Press. We often take our good health and independence for granted. This examination of the natural processes of illness, death, caregiving, and being "beholden" explores issues of power and dependency in disabled older people and those who care for them.

ROGERS, C. (1980). *A way of being.* Boston: Houghton Mifflin. This humanist provides a collection of his reflections on life, all written between the ages of 65 and 78. The essays express his continued openness to new experiences and a growing, changing philosophical perspective.

RUBENSTEIN, R. (1986). *Singular paths: Old men and living alone.* New York: Columbia University Press. A research-based presentation of the patterns of aged men living alone, with application to social services for life skills.

SHEEHY, GAIL. (1995). *New passages: Mapping your life across time.* New York: Random House. From her interviews, this journalist suggests a second adulthood beginning at around age 45—one with deeper meaning, fewer proscribed roles, and more playfulness.

Death and Dying

CHAPTER

18

CHAPTER OBJECTIVES

By the time you have finished this chapter, you should be able to do the following:

1. Discuss American and other cultural attitudes toward death and the terminally ill.
2. Explain stages of adjustment to death, and suggest ways of dealing with these stages.
3. Compare and contrast hospices and hospitals with regard to death and dying.
4. Discuss the controversy over the right-to-die issue.
5. Discuss the grieving process in detail.
6. Introspect about your own personal meaning of death on the basis of the factors discussed throughout the chapter.

Death is the ultimate milestone, the end of life as we know it. "Life is short. Shorter for some than for others," observed Gus, a leading character in the TV movie *Lonesome Dove*. To that observation—for most people—we might add the following as corollaries: (1) No matter how long you live, it will not be long enough, and (2) when the end arrives, it will seem to have arrived suddenly and abruptly.

Physiologically, death is an irrevocable cessation of life functions. Psychologically, of course, death has intense personal significance and meaning to the dying person as well as to family and friends. To die means to cease experiencing, to leave loved ones, to leave unfinished business, and to enter the unknown (Kalish, 1987). It is important, however, to bear in mind that death is a *natural* event—whether it occurs prematurely because of disease or accident, or at the end of a full and rich lifespan. All creatures die; death is as much a part of development as is living.

A person's death is also deeply embedded in the cultural context. There are collective meanings, many of which are expressed in literature, arts, music, religion, and philosophy of the culture. In most cultures, death is also elaborated with rituals and rites. According to your culture—in conjunction with your personal beliefs and interpretations—death may be an event to be feared, dreaded, abhorred, and postponed as long as possible. Alternately, many cultures and religions view death more as a transition than an end, a welcomed passage into another life and hopefully, a better world or plane of existence. For some individuals, it may be a welcomed relief from the extreme suffering that can accompany disease or old age. Or, for some—such as those who commit suicide—it may be a final, desperate escape from a life replete with pain and misery. Death indeed has many meanings.

If we knew more about the experience of dying and the process of grief and bereavement for those who remain, would we be better able to help people cope with the tragedies in their lives as well as with the triumphs? Historically, developmentalists mostly ignored the subject of death. Granted, it isn't easy to study, and perhaps they thought it inappropriate to scrutinize the attitudes and reactions of individuals who were dying; perhaps dying people were better left undisturbed. In recent decades, however, death has been studied thoroughly. In this chapter, we take a look at some of the things that have been discovered about death, and we consider some of the ways in which this knowledge might be applied. We examine thoughts and fears that surround death, the process of confronting your own death, the societal and individual search for a humane death, and the process of grief and bereavement in death's aftermath—with regard to "normal" death in old age and death at younger ages as well. In closing, we also consider what it means to complete the life cycle.

THOUGHTS AND FEARS OF DEATH

Birth and death are both natural events, the beginning and end of a life. However, their emotional impact and their personal meanings are of course vastly different. Birth is usually anticipated with excitement and optimism; death is usually avoided, even by those who believe in an afterlife. Sometimes people deny the reality of death.

DENIAL OF DEATH

Several authors have suggested that our Western technological, youth-oriented society has a curious habit of denying and avoiding death while, at the same time, being strangely preoccupied with it—especially in the media, although there, we are detached from it and don't usually think about its happening to us as well. Murders and fatal accidents, we tend to believe, happen only to *other* people.

We also tend to sidestep the subject of death when we're around someone who is dying. To illustrate that point, one author (Kalish, 1985) tells a tale of being invited to cocktails and dinner at the home of a friend. On entering the dining room, the man notices with astonishment that there is a brown horse sitting quietly on the dining room table. He turns to look at the reactions of the other guests and the host; all faces express shock and confusion. But no one wants to embarrass the host by mentioning what is so obviously discomforting. The dinner proceeds with long silences that are broken only by innocuous and inconsequential conversation. Is this, the author asks, analogous to what goes on when a person is dying and no one will speak with him or her about it or even permit the person to speak about it?

In earlier periods in history, death was a familiar event. It usually occurred at home with family members in attendance, who cared for the dying person up to the end. Even after death, the details of preparing the body for burial and performing the final rituals were family and community events. With regard to burial in particular, family members and friends even opened and closed the grave.

In the twentieth century, however, we turned death into something of a technological marvel. Most people now die in hospitals, with medical staff attending to their needs and family members only standing by. In many segments of our culture, professional morticians prepare the body for the final rituals and burial, and the body is presented for final viewing in a funeral home. In all, contact with the dying person before and after death is now often greatly restricted. Thus, some have suggested that we live in an era of "invisible death." Moreover, have we deceived ourselves into believing that death is just another problem to deal with, such as a disease for which we have not yet found a cure (Aris, 1981)?

Denial is a common mechanism for coping with stress—the person simply refuses to see or accept reality—and denial can interfere with coping. Actively coping with death means taking realistic precautions about the hazards of living without restricting ourselves unnecessarily. We must be able to accept the real limitations of life and our own vulnerability, even though violent, unrealistic images are popular. Some experts suggest that if our culture could deal more directly with death, we might present fewer distorted images of death to our children (Pattison, 1977). The average person, by age 21, has not seen one real death, but has seen over 13,000 on television (DeSpelder & Strickland, 1983). It is indeed a paradoxical picture of denial, ambiguity, and fascination.

Some researchers believe that our cultural taboo against death is weakening, however. There are available many books, articles, and death education classes that may change people's attitudes. Even members of the medical profession, who confront death and dying on a daily basis, need educational programs and seminars on how to cope with their feelings about it. In the mid-1960s, when Elisabeth Kübler-Ross began her study of the dying process (as discussed in the next section), she noted considerable resistance and denial by hospital staff members (Kübler-Ross, 1969). Her visits in the hospital wards disturbed her because of the behavior of the nurses and doctors. Once a diagnosis of terminal illness was made, both nurses and doctors paid less attention to the patient, seemingly avoiding all but the most necessary contact. They talked to the patient less, provided less in the way of routine care, and usually didn't tell the patient that she or he was terminal—even when the patient asked. Patients also were discouraged from discussing their feelings about dying.

Today, that treatment is changing. All nursing programs and many programs for doctors include seminars on death education, which stress maintaining contact with the patient and respecting the patient's "right to know." It is now recognized that medical professionals who understand the dying process are better able to set realistic goals for "good" outcomes in which the patient dies with dignity, has the chance to express final sentiments to family and friends, and faces death in a manner consistent with his or her lifestyle (Haber, 1987).

PREOCCUPATION WITH DEATH AND WHAT DEATH MEANS

Are older people more fearful or more preoccupied with death than younger people? Are those who are healthy and those who feel more in control of their lives less (or perhaps more) fearful of the prospect of death? Psychoanalytic theory asserts that anxiety or fearfulness at the prospect of your own death is normal, which may or may not be the case universally. Moreover, those who do experience significant anxiety differ in how they deal with it. Some people find meaning and purpose in life and incorporate death into that meaning. Religious fanatics who sacrifice themselves for their cause (such as in suicide bombings) are an extreme example of that "solution." In contrast, an existentialist or a devout atheist, perhaps whose primary purpose in life is life itself, may be terrified by the prospect of death—although this is certainly not always the case, noting that it is quite possible for people who do not believe in an afterlife to reconcile death as a natural, perhaps even peaceful, state. In the latter view, where there is nothingness, there can also be no stress or pain; nor can you worry about being dead.

For the wide range of individuals who fall somewhere in between, researchers find that personal and cultural meanings of death are often of prime

Older people, when confronted with the question what they would do if they had only 6 months to live, often focused on spending time with their families.

importance in determining whether individuals are fearful or preoccupied with thoughts of their own death. Studies have found that older adults actually tend to be less anxious about death than younger persons (Kastenbaum, 1986), that those with a strong sense of purpose in life fear death less (Durlak, 1979), and that although some older people think about death often, they feel surprisingly calm at the prospect of it. Religious beliefs are also a factor: Research has repeatedly shown that those who have strong religious convictions and a deep belief in an afterlife experience less depression and anxiety over dying (Alvarado et al., 1995). As the authors point out, however, it is the personal conviction itself that is the important thing; attempting to lower your anxiety about dying through increasing your religious participation and forcing yourself to believe "is not a guaranteed remedy."

When young people are asked how they would spend their six remaining months of life if that time was all they had, they describe activities such as traveling and trying to accomplish things that they have not yet done. Older people have different priorities. Sometimes they talk about contemplation or meditation and other inner-focused pursuits. Often they talk about spending time with their families and those closest to them (Kalish, 1987; Kalish & Reynolds, 1981). Indeed, in a comprehensive set of interviews with a large group of elderly volunteers, only 10% answered yes to the question "Are you afraid to die?" (Jeffers & Verwoerdt, 1977). Many participants did report, however, being afraid of a prolonged and painful death.

Although older people generally report low levels of anxiety about death, not all older people feel this way. There are substantial individual differences among older people with regard to their anxiety about death (Stillion, 1985). Is there a pattern that identifies who will be most or least anxious? The research is difficult to reconcile. In some studies, those who are psychologically well adjusted and who seem to have achieved Erikson's personality integrity are the least anxious. In other studies, older individuals who are both physically and mentally healthy and who feel in control of their own lives are the most anxious. Nor is anxiety about death a constant. Often, for example, individuals experience high death anxiety when they are diagnosed as having a potentially fatal disease, but they gradually reach a point of low anxiety several weeks or months later (Belsky, 1984). Death anxiety appears to be only one symptom in an ongoing process of establishing and accepting the meaning of death in the context of the meaning of life.

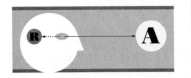

REVIEW & APPLY

1. How does American culture handle death today compared with a century ago?
2. Discuss how psychological denial is involved in coping with dying.
3. Are older people more fearful or more preoccupied with death than younger people? Explain.

CONFRONTING YOUR OWN DEATH

As people grow older or become ill, the realization comes that death is no longer a distant event, and its imminence increasingly crosses their minds. Young people have the luxury of pushing such thoughts into the background, but in illness or old age, thoughts of death are unavoidable. How do people react to this final stage of development? Many experience orderly stages of adjustment to dying, which ultimately includes acceptance of death. There are also alternate trajectories in dying.

DEATH AS THE FINAL STAGE OF DEVELOPMENT

Those who are not faced with the prospect of immediate death can spend more time adjusting to the idea. They often spend their last years looking back and reliving old pleasures and pains. According to one theorist (Butler, 1968, 1971), this life review is a very important step in the lifelong growth of the individual. At no other time is there as strong a force toward self-awareness as in old age. The process often leads to real personality growth; individuals resolve old conflicts, reestablish meaning in life, and even discover new things about themselves. Only in coping with the reality of approaching death can we ultimately make life's crucial decisions as to what is important and who we really are. Death lends the necessary perspective (Kübler-Ross, 1975). Paradoxically, then, dying can be "a process of re-commitment to life" (Imara, 1975).

As in earlier periods of life, the task of finding meaning and purpose involves active restructuring of philosophical, religious, and pragmatic thoughts and beliefs (Sherman, 1987). In 1974, when author Ernest Becker was hospitalized in the last stages of terminal cancer, he was interviewed about what he was experiencing. During his life he had written a great deal about facing up to death, so that he was aware of what he was experiencing on many levels. Becker had passed through several stages of adjusting to his own death, and by the time of the interview, he had apparently reached a final stage of transcendence. His own resolution was a religious one: "What makes death easier [is] to know that . . . beyond what is happening to us there is the fact of the tremendous creative energies of the cosmos that are using us for some purposes we don't know" (cited in Keen, 1974). Other individuals may use a quite different approach in coming to grips with their own death, and beliefs pertaining to death vary considerably across cultures and religions. In any case, however, Becker's testimony is a persuasive argument for allowing people to work out their own personal resolution and to face death with dignity and peace.

STAGES OF ADJUSTMENT

Elisabeth Kübler-Ross (1969) was one of the first to study the topics of death and dying in depth. She focused on the relatively short-term situation in which death becomes an immediate possibility—such as when a person is diagnosed as having terminal cancer or some other soon-to-be fatal illness. Through extensive interviews with such people, she identified five stages in the process of adjusting to the idea of death: denial, anger, bargaining, depression, and ultimately, acceptance.

- In the *denial* stage, the person rejects the possibility of death and searches for other, more promising opinions and diagnoses.
- Once the person realizes that she or he actually will die, there is anger, resentment, and envy—the *anger* stage. The person is frustrated that plans and dreams will not be fulfilled.
- The person in the *bargaining* stage looks for ways to buy time, making promises and negotiating with his or her God, doctors, nurses, or others for more time—also for relief from pain and suffering.
- When the bargaining fails or time runs out, helplessness and hopelessness take hold. The person in the *depression* stage mourns both for the losses that have already occurred and for the death and separation from family and friends to come.
- In the final stage of *acceptance*, the person accepts and awaits death calmly.

Although the stages that Kübler-Ross describes are common reactions to impending death and therefore are helpful in understanding how dying people feel, they are not universal. Not all people go through all the stages, and only a few go through them in the specified order. Many factors influence a person's reactions, including culture, personality, religion, personal philosophy, and the length and nature of the terminal disease. Some people remain angry or depressed until the end; others welcome death as a release from pain. People cope with death in individual ways and should not be forced into a set pattern of stages (Hudson, 1981). Instead, as Robert Kastenbaum (1979) advocates, people should be allowed to follow their own path to dying. If they want, they should talk about their feelings, concerns, and experiences; have their questions answered; set their lives in order; see relatives and friends; and forgive someone or ask forgiveness from someone for quarrels or petty misdeeds. These actions, Kastenbaum suggests, are more important to the individual than experiencing broad emotional states in a particular order. Figure 18–1 includes practical suggestions for caregivers attempting to provide support for dying loved ones.

ALTERNATIVE TRAJECTORIES

Often the course of the illness itself affects reactions to the dying process. If death is sudden, there is little time for life review and integration. An illness that causes considerable pain or limited mobility or that requires frequent and complex medical intervention may leave a person little time or energy to adjust to death. It would be a mistake for medical personnel or family members to assume casually that a person is in the "anger" stage when, in fact, the reaction is directly related to the person's current physical condition or medical treatment (Kastenbaum & Costa, 1977).

In no illness are reactions to the dying process more influenced by the nature of the illness than in AIDS, a disease that is often sexually transmitted and

FIGURE 18–1
YOUR CARING PRESENCE:
WAYS OF EFFECTIVELY
PROVIDING SUPPORT
TO OTHERS

Source: The Centre for Living with Dying.

1. Be honest about your own thoughts, concerns, and feelings.
2. When in doubt, ask questions:
   How is that for you?
   How do you feel right now?
   Can you tell me more about that?
   Am I intruding?
   What do you need?
   What are the ways you can take care of yourself?
3. When you are responding to a person facing a crisis situation, be sure to use statements such as:
   I feel _____
   I believe _____
   I would want _____
   Rather than:
   You should _____
   That's wrong.
   Everything will be okay.
   Which are statements that may not give the person the opportunity to express his/her own unique needs and feelings?
4. Stay in the present as much as possible: How do you feel RIGHT NOW? What do you need RIGHT NOW?
5. Listening is profoundly healing. You don't have to make it better. You don't have to have the answers. You don't have to take away the pain. It's his/her pain. He/she needs to experience it in his/her own time and in his/her own way.
6. People in crisis need to know they have decision-making power. It may be appropriate to point out alternatives.
7. Offer any practical assistance that you feel comfortable giving.
8. If the situation warrants it, feel free to refer the individual to the appropriate agency.

thus surrounded by strong emotions among those afflicted and those closest to them. Gay author Fenton Johnson (1994) focuses on the themes of memory and forgiveness that "lie at the heart of any community" and yet are challenged by this disease. He explains as follows:

> The wisest people I know, HIV-positive or negative, live not in denial [of death] but in acceptance—a state not of forgive and forget but of forgive and remember. The most difficult and necessary of the mourner's tasks are these contradictory imperatives: forgive and remember, accept and never shut up. (1994, page 15)

The prolonged dying process experienced by many AIDS patients makes acceptance and forgiveness difficult for those who must cope with the emotions that surround dying. This difficulty is heightened in some segments of the Hispanic- and African-American communities by the youth of many who succumb to AIDS. As Table 18–1 shows, HIV infection is the leading cause of death for Hispanics and African-Americans aged 25 to 44. In addition, grieving for multiple deaths while at the same time dealing with their own illnesses

TABLE 18–1   RANKING OF HIV AS A CAUSE OF DEATH

AGE	HISPANIC	AFRICAN-AMERICAN	WHITE/NON-HISPANIC
15–24	5	5	7
25–44	1	1	3
45–64	5	6	9

Source: K. D. Kochanek & B. L. Hudson (1995). *Advance Report of Final Mortality Statistics, 1992; 43*(6) Supplement. NCHS.

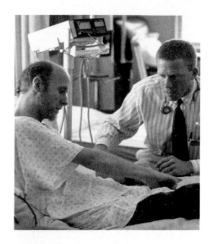

The often lengthy dying process of people with AIDS makes it especially difficult for both the ill and their personal community to cope with the emotions that surround dying.

eliminates the time and energy necessary to go through the traditional stages associated with accepting death (Horn, 1993).

Just as there are numerous and unique life trajectories in adult development, there is also a wide range of dying trajectories. The commonly accepted ideal trajectory is to be healthy to age 85 or more, put your affairs in order, and die suddenly and without pain by heart attack (Kalish, 1985), perhaps while asleep. Indeed, surveys show that far more people would prefer a sudden death—particularly the young (Kalish, 1985). When there is an illness with an expected trajectory, family members as well as the dying individual adjust and adapt to the presumed "time left to live." For many, there are tasks to be completed, arrangements to be made, things to be said—the unfinished business of living. Some people attempt to influence the expected trajectory by accepting treatment or rejecting it, by exerting their "will to live," or by resigning themselves to the inevitable. Many individuals need to maintain some control and dignity in this final trajectory, as they have done in life. All search for a humane way to die.

SUICIDE   Suicide is surprisingly common in middle-aged and older people. Although the most highly publicized suicides are those of young adults, adolescents, and even schoolchildren, by far the greatest number of suicides occurs among people over age 45; of this group, most occur among those age 65 and older (U.S. Census Bureau, 1990). Four times as many men as women commit suicide. The rate for men rises steadily with age, reaching a peak among those over age 80 (Manton et al., 1987; Miller, 1979; Riley & Waring, 1976). Both white and minority men show dramatic increases in suicide during old age (Manton et al., 1987). These statistics do not take into account the more passive forms of suicide, such as simply letting yourself die, which is called **submissive death** (Riley & Waring, 1976), or the indirect forms, such as through excessive drinking, smoking, or drug abuse, which is called **suicidal erosion** (Miller, 1979). Yet another indirect form of suicide is "going postal" and gunning down a group of innocent bystanders, which typically results in the perpetrator's being killed as well.

Suicide among the elderly is almost always a result of "vital losses," such as employment difficulties, retirement shock, and becoming a widow or widower. Both widows and widowers, therefore, fall into the high-risk group among potential suicides. The risk falls off sharply after the first year of bereavement but remains higher than average for several years (Miller, 1981). There is another important factor besides retirement and widow- or widowerhood. Old people who are chronically lonely or who have a history of

submissive death   Suicide in the form of simply letting yourself die.

suicidal erosion   An indirect form of suicide through excessive drinking, smoking, or other drug abuse.

emotional instability—especially those with deep-seated anxieties and feelings of inferiority—are highly prone to suicide.

One of the most effective treatments for widows and widowers to improve mental health and encourage ways of meeting social needs is self-help groups. Individuals who participate in such groups may find comfort in sharing their fears and feelings with others. The groups also provide a protective setting in which to form new relationships and try out new roles, so that people become less isolated and better able to help themselves. Systematic follow-up of participants in formal self-help groups has repeatedly demonstrated positive outcomes such as these for most participants (Gartner, 1984).

REVIEW & APPLY

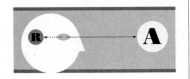

1. What are the stages of adjustment to death outlined by Kübler-Ross? Are these stages universal?
2. In what sense can death be considered a stage of growth?
3. What are alternative death trajectories, and how do they vary among individuals?
4. How does the nature of an illness affect the acceptance of death?
5. What age group is most prone to suicide, and why?

THE SEARCH FOR A HUMANE DEATH

As we have seen, a great deal of study has been conducted on the experience of dying, and our former ignorance and neglect of the subject are giving way. It may be a long time, however, before society's general attitude toward death catches up to the advanced thinking of some theorists. We are remarkably good at providing health care to dying patients, in the form of medication and life-support systems, but we are poor at dealing head-on with their worries and thoughts. The terminally ill are often treated as somehow less than human by those around them. They are isolated from their loved ones in a sterile environment; moreover, decisions are made for them without regard for their wishes. They are still often not told what their treatments are for, and if they become upset or rebellious, they are often sedated. Compared with the terrifyingly cold atmosphere of the hospital, an old-fashioned death at home, where the dying person is surrounded by familiar faces and objects, seems almost a luxury.

Doctors and other health-care professionals have at least become more honest with dying patients about their condition (Fixx, 1981). Along these lines, it is suggested that dying patients should be given some measure of autonomy (Birren & Birren, 1987). Having a say in how much pain medication or sedatives they receive, for example, can give them a sense that they still control some aspects of their lives. This sense is very important for patients who may otherwise feel that they are being swept along by forces beyond their control. In fact, some research indicates that almost any animal—whether a rat, a dog, or a cockroach—often simply relinquishes life if it feels that it has lost control of its life (Seligman, 1974). In one experiment in which rats were put in water to see how long they could swim, some lasted as long as 60 hours, whereas others sank below the surface and drowned almost instantly. What caused the different reactions? The rats that died quickly had been restrained for an extended period before being put in the water, acquired "learned helplessness," and simply gave up. Those that kept on struggling had not been restrained and therefore tried their best to survive. A similar thing happens when people are put in nursing homes or hospitals prematurely and feel that they can no longer control their own lives in any meaningful way. They respond by giving up the struggle. By contrast, individuals who have spent a lifetime controlling their environments may try to control the hospital or nursing staff. Although these patients may not be cooperative, easy-to-get-along-with patients, they do tend to live longer (Tobin, 1988).

We have already seen that only a relatively small proportion of the elderly report fearing death (Jeffers & Verwoerdt, 1970). Yet they often report other fears about the dying process. They do not want a long, painful terminal period, and they do not want to be dependent on others. Also, they fear the loss of their minds as well as their dignity. Some even talk about wanting a "good death," not an agonizing, degrading one. The quest for the good death has led to several proposed changes in the ways in which we provide services to the dying. These changes include hospices and the right to die.

In hospices, death is seen as a normal stage of life to be faced with dignity.

HOSPICES

The notion that dying people should maintain some control over their lives and, for that matter, over their deaths, has given rise to the recent widespread development of hospices for the dying. Hospices are designed to help terminally ill patients live out their days as fully and independently as possible by giving needed support both to the patients and to their families. The first hospice for the dying was started in England in 1967 as an inpatient program. The idea spread to the United States in 1974, with the launching of a hospice program in New Haven, Connecticut, and it caught on rapidly. Four years later, there were some 200 hospice programs in 39 states and the District of Columbia in various stages of planning and implementation (Abbott, 1978).

The hospice approach has now become widely adopted in this country, with a National Hospice Organization that sets standards and monitors programs (Birnbaum & Kidder, 1984). Some hospices are independent, but most are part of comprehensive health-care organizations. The comprehensive program usually includes an inpatient unit, home-care programs with a variety of home-based services, medical and psychological consultation, and ongoing medical and nursing services that relieve pain and help control symptoms (Haber, 1987). A law enacted in 1982 helped make hospice services more affordable and available to dying patients. Under Public Law 97-248, individuals covered by the Social Security system can receive home services for as much as two periods of three months each. These services include involvement of the regular physician, home nursing care, psychological counseling, nutrition evaluation, respite care, spiritual guidance, home support services, legal and financial advice, occupational, physical, and speech therapy, and bereavement care for the family. Not only is this kind of home service welcomed by the patient, but also, in many cases, it is more cost-effective than hospitalization (Haber, 1987).

Hospitals are devoted to life and life support; hospital personnel see death as the enemy. Sometimes the care they give to the dying reflects that attitude, as noted earlier. The hospice concept, however, views death not as a failure but as a normal and natural stage of life to be approached with dignity. Death is as natural as birth, and like birth, is sometimes hard work that requires assistance (Garrett, 1978). Hospices are designed to provide that assistance and comfort. Their first aim is to manage pain of all sorts: physical pain, mental pain, social pain, and spiritual pain (Garrett, 1978). Beyond that, they try as much as possible to "include the dying person as taking an active part in his own care and decision making" (Rosel, 1978), and to respect the dying person's rights with regard to choices—as far as possible—about death (Koff, 1980). In addition, they help the family understand the dying person's experience and needs, and they keep communication lines open so that the dying member feels less isolated. Hospice contact with the family continues up to and beyond death, extending throughout the period of bereavement.

THE RIGHT TO DIE

If, as many people believe, death is a natural, essentially positive experience, do we have the right to tamper with it? Do we rob people of a dignified death if we artificially maintain their life systems beyond the point where they can never recover? Is there a point at which a person is "meant" to die, where it would be better to let nature take its course? Do we prolong life because we fear death, even though the patients themselves may be ready to die? These questions have received a great deal of attention in recent years, and many people now demand a **right to die**.

The idea of letting nature take its course—or even lending a helping hand—is of course not entirely new. *Euthanasia*, or mercy killing, was practiced in ancient Greece and probably earlier. Reportedly, one of the more notable "victims" of euthanasia in this century was Sigmund Freud. In 1939, the 83-year-old Freud, who had been suffering from cancer of the jaw for 16 years, decided that he had had enough: "Now it is nothing but torture, and makes no sense anymore" (cited in Shapiro, 1978). He had previously made a pact with his physician to administer a lethal dose of morphine should Freud decide that he could no longer bear his intense pain and frustration. He then asked that the agreement be put into force, and the doctor honored his wish (Shapiro, 1978).

In Freud's case, nature was not simply allowed to take its course; positive steps were taken to bring about death. This process is generally called **active**

right to die The view that death is a right to be exercised at the individual's discretion.

active euthanasia Taking positive steps to bring about another person's death, as in cases of terminal illness. In the United States, active euthanasia is murder.

In contemporary American society, Dr. Jack Kevorkian has publicized the moral, ethical, and legal issues involved in active euthanasia.

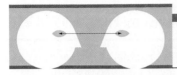

A MATTER FOR DEBATE

ASSISTED SUICIDE

According to John Horgan, staff writer for *Scientific American* (1997), among others, polls indicate that a majority of Americans now support the right of a patient to receive a lethal drug from their physician if they wish—as do a few health-related professional organizations. On the other hand, the American Medical Association (AMA), and the majority of such organizations, strongly oppose suicide assisted by a physician. What are some of the issues?

Proponents of assisted suicide argue that a significant number of people die in pain and agony after lengthy battles with diseases such as cancer and AIDS. In spite of major advances in the management of pain, modern narcotics often do not eliminate it. Moreover, current laws often prohibit doctors from prescribing excessive dosages of painkillers. Notably, narcotics tolerance increases with sustained use, requiring increasing and, therefore, excessive dosages—which also render the patient immobile and unconscious much of the time. Thus, for many terminally ill patients, quality of life declines rapidly. Advocates of assisted suicide question the point of it all. Why not instead allow the patient to choose a quick, easy, "good death," after saying good-bye to loved ones and putting

financial affairs and such in order? In addition, there is the point that "hastening death" behind the scenes, in less dramatic ways than openly assisted suicide, is not an uncommon practice with terminally ill patients and has been done for many years. In other words, the equivalent of assisted suicide is already a widespread practice, just as abortion was a widespread practice even before its legalization.

Opponents of assisted suicide argue that it constitutes a form of euthanasia, which makes them extremely wary of the precedent that would be set by legalization of assisted suicide. For example, would a next step be death for patients with nonterminal but nonetheless incurable and debilitating diseases such as major mental disorders? Who would make the decision in such cases, given that the mentally disordered patient is incapable of informed consent? Would family members have the right? In all, considering assisted suicide to be a "foot in the door" for euthanasia, where would we draw the line?

In the forefront of most discussions of assisted suicide is Jack Kevorkian, former M.D., who has now assisted numerous such patients (no one knows quite how many) and has thus far been acquitted of wrongdoing in each case for which he has been prosecuted. Kevorkian openly advocates euthana-

sia, not just for the dying but also for the disabled, the mentally ill, and infants with birth defects, among others (Betzold, 1997). Who would make the final decision in such cases? *Doctors* would decide, Kevorkian has said, a statement that many within the medical community and society at large also find alarming. In addition, critics contend that at least some of Kevorkian's patients have not been terminally ill, in keeping with his advocacy but at odds with the way his assisted suicides are usually portrayed in the press (see Guttman, 1996).

Thus, the debate continues. Legislative action, state referendums, and court challenges continue. Civil and criminal prosecutions of those who openly assist with suicide will no doubt continue as well. And while hospices increasingly offer services that offset much of the pain, misery, and isolation that often accompany dying (see pages 615–616), the fact remains, as Joe Loconte (1998) puts it, "Too many people in America are dying a bad death." To that we might add that far too many people in America are *afraid* of dying a bad death, which makes better death care—whatever its form—an issue that continues to deserve status as a national issue.

---

euthanasia, although many would consider the term euphemistic. In our society, such an act is considered murder, pure and simple—although it is sometimes treated with leniency (Shapiro, 1978). This situation is especially true in cases in which the final act of euthanasia is carried out by the dying person, so that it can legally be considered a suicide. Termed **assisted suicide,** this is what happens in the widely publicized cases of terminally ill patients' being provided with "death machines" that allow the patient to self-administer a lethal drug, as discussed in "A Matter for Debate: Assisted Suicide" above.

Passive euthanasia, on the other hand, involves withholding (or disconnecting) life-sustaining equipment so that death will come about naturally. Passive, voluntary euthanasia has become a conspicuous issue as well, because of continuing medical advances in the ability to sustain life—in some cases almost indefinitely. Indeed, a major issue is how to determine when to disconnect life support machines. Table 18–2 lists the Harvard Criteria for defining death. These have been widely used as a foundation for legal definitions of

assisted suicide Providing a terminally ill patient with the means to end his or her own life.

passive euthanasia Withholding or disconnecting life-sustaining equipment so that death can occur naturally.

TABLE 18–2 THE HARVARD CRITERIA FOR DETERMINATION OF A PERMANENTLY NONFUNCTIONING (OR DEAD) BRAIN

Unreceptive and unresponsive: No awareness is shown for external stimuli or inner need. The unresponsiveness is complete even under the application of stimuli that ordinarily would be extremely painful.

No movements and no breathing: There is a complete absence of spontaneous respiration and all other spontaneous muscular movement.

No reflexes: The usual reflexes that can be elicited in a neurophysiological examination are absent (for example, when a light is shined in the eye, the pupil does not constrict).

A flat electroencephalogram (EEG): Electrodes attached to the scalp elicit a printout of electrical activity from the living brain. These are popularly known as brain waves. The respirator brain does not provide the usual pattern of peaks and valleys. Instead, the moving automatic stylus records essentially a flat line. This is taken to demonstrate the lack of electrophysiological activity.

No circulation to or within the brain: Without the oxygen and nutrition provided to the brain by its blood supply, functioning will soon terminate. (Precisely how long the brain can retain its viability, the ability to survive, without circulation is a matter of much current investigation and varies somewhat with conditions.)

Source: R. Kastenbaum (1986). *Death, society, and human experience* (page 9). Columbus, OH: Merrill.

death. Although they seem straightforward and irrefutable, however, the criteria do not fully resolve all of the issues (Kastenbaum, 1986). For example, do functioning and blood flow have to be absent in all areas of the brain for the person to be considered dead, or is cessation of activity in the cerebral cortex sufficient? Such questions are most likely to be raised—and the criteria are most likely to be invoked—when there are differing opinions among family members or medical staff and a judge is asked to make the decision to terminate life support (Robbins, 1986).

One example of an effort to ensure some individual autonomy in the last stages of life is the living will, such as the one prepared by Concern for Dying, an Educational Council (see Figure 18–2). This document informs the signer's family, or others who may be concerned, of the signer's wish to avoid the use of "heroic measures" to maintain life in the event of irreversible illness. Although the living will is not legally binding, it does protect those who observe its terms from legal liability for doing so (Shapiro, 1978).

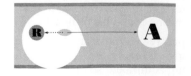

REVIEW & APPLY

1. What is the difference between a hospital and a hospice? Discuss the advantages of hospice care and its philosophy.
2. What are the controversial issues involved in euthanasia? How does our society deal with these issues?
3. Describe how a living will helps dying people ensure their own humane death.

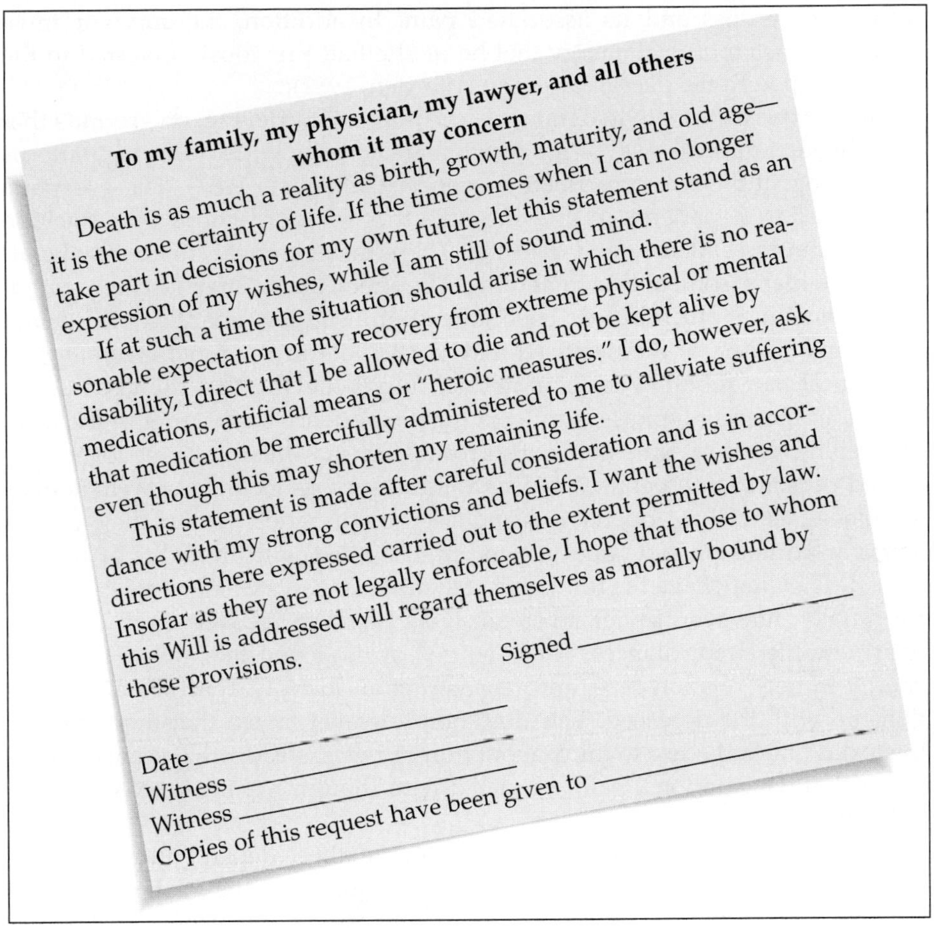

To my family, my physician, my lawyer, and all others whom it may concern

Death is as much a reality as birth, growth, maturity, and old age— it is the one certainty of life. If the time comes when I can no longer take part in decisions for my own future, let this statement stand as an expression of my wishes, while I am still of sound mind.

If at such a time the situation should arise in which there is no reasonable expectation of my recovery from extreme physical or mental disability, I direct that I be allowed to die and not be kept alive by medications, artificial means or "heroic measures." I do, however, ask that medication be mercifully administered to me to alleviate suffering even though this may shorten my remaining life.

This statement is made after careful consideration and is in accordance with my strong convictions and beliefs. I want the wishes and directions here expressed carried out to the extent permitted by law. Insofar as they are not legally enforceable, I hope that those to whom this Will is addressed will regard themselves as morally bound by these provisions.

Signed _____

Date _____
Witness _____
Witness _____
Copies of this request have been given to _____

FIGURE 18–2
THE LIVING WILL

This is a formal request prepared by Concern for Dying, an Educational Council. It informs the signer's family, or others who may be concerned, of the signer's wish to avoid the use of "heroic measures" to maintain life in the event of irreversible illness.

GRIEF AND BEREAVEMENT

What of those who are left behind? Often, surviving family members and close friends must make major adjustments to a loved one's death, beginning during the dying process. For them, life must go on.

Family members and close friends must make short- and long-term adjustments to the death of a loved one. Short-term adjustments include initial emotional reactions to the personal loss—the **grief work,** as it is often called—plus the practical matters of funeral arrangements, financial matters, and legal proceedings. Long-term adjustments, particularly for a widow or widower, include changes in life patterns, routines, roles, and activities that may be necessary to cope with the social void left by death, as discussed in the preceding chapter. Each of these adjustments may require more time and involvement than anticipated. The grieving process may also differ from culture to culture, and it often involves differing rituals and customs. As we'll also see, grieving may be especially difficult when a child dies.

GRIEVING

Is it actually necessary to grieve? Do sorrow and mental anguish serve some essential function? What is the purpose of grief work?

The prevailing view is that certain psychological tasks need to be accomplished following the loss of a loved one. The survivor needs to accept the

grief work Dealing with emotional reactions to the loss of a loved one.

reality of the loss and its associated pain. In addition, the survivor must rechannel the emotional energy that he or she had previously invested in the relationship with the deceased person (Worden, 1982).

Many experts hesitate to define specific phases of grieving, on grounds that it might encourage people to "force" what are actually widely varying patterns of grieving into some prescribed sequence (Gallagher, 1987). Those experts who do address patterns in grieving note that initial reactions often include shock, numbness, denial, and disbelief. There may be anger, there may be attempts to blame someone or something. The shock phase often lasts for several days, sometimes much longer. Especially after a sudden, unanticipated death, the people closest to the deceased may participate in the funeral ceremonies and burial in a robotlike fashion, not yet fully believing that the loss has occurred. In the second phase, survivors may experience active grief in the form of weeping or other expressions of sorrow. They may yearn or pine for the deceased person. Some people have symptoms such as feelings of weakness or emptiness, as well as appetite loss and sleep disturbances. Often, they lose interest in normal pursuits and become preoccupied with thoughts of the deceased. They may have the full range of symptoms associated with depression. Eventually, however, by far most survivors begin to recover. They adjust to their new life circumstances. They "let go" of the loved one, invest time and energy in new relationships, and reconstruct an identity apart from the relationship with the deceased. This does not, however, mean that they "forget" the loved one and cease to think about him or her; instead, what seems to happen is that the emotional pain associated with thoughts of the loved one gradually diminishes.

As noted, there are many patterns of grieving; these depend on personality, age, sex, and cultural traditions, also upon the quality of the relationship with the deceased. In addition, there are factors that can aid the recovery process. If the death is preceded by a long illness or loss of functioning, for example, the survivors can to an extent prepare themselves for the loss; they experience **anticipatory grief**. Perhaps feelings of loss, guilt, or missed opportunities are discussed with the dying person. Anticipatory grief, however, will not eliminate postdeath grieving. Indeed, it may not even reduce the intensity of postdeath grief (Rando, 1986). It can, however, make the effects of the death less overwhelming because of plans and adjustments made in advance, and coping with the grief may thus be improved. On the other hand, if an illness lasts for more than about 18 months, the emotional drain of caring for the person tends to outweigh any compensations via anticipatory grief. Moreover, when an illness is prolonged, the survivor may become convinced that the terminally ill person will not really die, that she or he has "beaten the odds." Thus, the death can be even more shocking than a sudden death (Rando, 1986).

Social support also plays a role in grieving. Theoretical models of stress and coping frequently note the value of a strong social-support system in successfully negotiating life crises. Yet, not all social support is equally helpful (Bankoff, 1986; Morgan, 1989). In one study, about 40% of the comments made by widows about postbereavement social relationships were negative (Morgan, 1989). Another point is that support from peers, especially those who have also experienced the loss of their spouse, seems to be more helpful than family support. Widowhood self-help support groups can also be of value (Morgan, 1989). Similarly, parents who have lost a child often find it comforting to interact with others whose children have died (Edelstein, 1984).

anticipatory grief Emotionally preparing yourself for the death of a loved one, as in cases of prolonged terminal illness.

There are circumstances in which grief may be particularly overwhelming. For example, older people who happen to experience the loss of several friends or family members in a relatively short span of time may experience *bereavement overload*. Similarly, bereavement overload affects gay and minority communities that are hard hit by AIDS. Depression then becomes a serious risk during bereavement, especially for men (Stroebe & Stroebe, 1987). So does alcohol and other drug abuse, again especially among men. Physical health may also be affected; the recently bereaved visit their physicians more frequently than other groups (Mor et al., 1986). It is also possible, however, that such visits represent routine care that was neglected while the bereaved served as a caregiver to the deceased. Many of these visits may also be linked to depression more than to physical illness per se (Mor et al., 1986).

BEREAVEMENT IN CROSS-CULTURAL PERSPECTIVE

Are there universal grief responses after the death of a loved one? Studies have shown that some responses long considered the norm (1) may not be shared by a majority of bereaved people, (2) may be culturally bound, and (3) may not even be healthy adaptations. When Margaret Stroebe and her colleagues (1992) explored the universality of grief responses, they found that responses are both historically and culturally determined. Although the modern Western view of grief requires that people engage in "proper grieving" by recovering from their grief as quickly as possible and returning to normal functioning, many non-Western cultures stress a continuing bond with the deceased. In Japan, mourners traditionally have a home altar dedicated to family ancestors, offer food at the altar, and talk to the ancestors, who they believe are accessible to them. In Egypt, mourners are encouraged to express their grief through emotional outpourings. For a detailed look at the traditional celebration of ancestors in Mexico, see "Eye on Diversity," page 622.

Similarly, whereas current Western thought about grief emphasizes a rational response as the means of returning to normal functioning, grief was viewed differently during the nineteenth-century Romantic period. Stroebe explains as follows:

> Because close relationships were matters of bonding in depth, the death of an intimate other constituted a critical point of life definition. To grieve was to signal the significance of the relationship, and the depth of one's own spirit. Dissolving bonds with the deceased would not only define the relationship as superficial, but would deny as well one's own sense of profundity and self-worth. It would make a sham of a spiritual commitment and undermine one's sense of living a meaningful life. In contrast with the breaking bonds orientation of modernism, in romanticism valor was found in sustaining these bonds, despite a "broken heart." (Stroebe et al., 1993).

Stroebe and her colleagues point out that despite the modern Western emphasis on "breaking bonds," many widows and widowers tend to maintain their ties just as the bereaved did during the Romantic age. Widows and widowers "sense" their spouse's presence perhaps for years after their spouse dies, and the deceased continues to have a strong psychological influence on the survivor's life.

Other theorists (Wortman & Silver, 1989) take issue with contemporary views of bereavement that focus on immediate, intense emotionality. They dispute the popular view of bereavement, which states that distress or depression

For widows, the greatest sense of support comes from peers, particularly those who are also widowed.

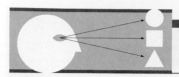

EYE ON DIVERSITY

TODOS SANTOS: THE DAY OF THE DEAD

The strength of cultural influences on bereavement and death is clearly seen in traditional Mexican culture. During the festival of *Todos Santos* (All Saints), Mexicans from every walk of life—the rich and the poor, the educated and the illiterate, the urban and the rural—stop their worldly business to remember and respect the dead. This commemoration contrasts sharply with bereavement practices in most of the United States, which instead seem to be motivated more by anxiety and discomfort than by celebration and remembrance.

Todos Santos stems from a belief that death is a natural element of the life cycle—an element to be celebrated with a community festival (Cohen, 1992). The celebration combines pre-Columbian customs and beliefs of the Indian cultures with those of Catholic Spain.

At the center of the celebration are community altars that welcome the an-

cestors' return. Each family has its own altarpiece, known as an *ofrenda*, to honor and remember deceased family members. Each *ofrenda* includes the favorite food and drink of the deceased, as well as articles of the deceased's clothing and personal belongings. Special offerings are made for the souls of deceased children, which Mexicans believe return first. These offerings are prepared in miniature and include ample sweets. After the souls of the dead have made their presence felt, the living take part in the celebration. Family members consume some of the food and drink; they share some with neighbors and friends; and they place a final offering on the graves of the deceased. What might these customs mean?

> This joyful sharing creates a form of communal reciprocity: it helps connect the community with their dead and, in turn, creates a symbolic presence of the deceased within the community. (Cohen, 1992, page 108)

Rather than being shielded from the realities of death, Mexican children are at the center of the Todos Santos festivities. The children help prepare the *ofrenda* and take part in graveside celebrations. They help decorate the graves with brightly colored flowers and light candles of remembrance. From this, children learn that death is a natural part of life and is not to be feared. Thus,

> In many [cultures], death is . . . not regarded as a termination but as an elevation to another level of existing. It is an event initially tinged with uncertain emotions, but ultimately one to be celebrated as the dead are reaccommodated as ancestors. (Carmichael & Sayer, 1991, page 7)

In Mexico, this reaccommodation has the status of a national tradition.

---

is inevitable; that failure to experience distress is pathological; that "working through" a loss is important; and that the bereaved should have an expectation of recovery. For example, they cite studies showing that despite the belief that those who are depressed after a loss adapt more successfully than those who experience no depression, people with the greatest degree of distress and depression are likely still to be the most distressed one or two years later. Similarly, they identify **chronic grief**, or failure ever to recover from a loss, as a pathological mourning process that is clearly identifiable in many grievers.

A lengthy longitudinal study of the bereavement response (Cleiren, 1993) focused on loss reaction, health, and social functioning of 309 family members who were the immediate relatives of people who had died from suicides, traffic accidents, and long-term illnesses. The study, which was known as the *Leiden Bereavement Study* after the Dutch town in which it was conducted, found wide variations in bereavement responses based on the meaning of the relationship before the death, the nature of the death, whether there was an opportunity to anticipate the death, and the practical support that the bereaved received from others after the death occurred.

Thus, grief reactions differ markedly from person to person and from culture to culture. There is no universal or "right" way to grieve, although societal expectations are a powerful influence that can make it appear that there is.

chronic grief A pathological mourning process in which the person never overcomes the grief.

RITUALS AND CUSTOMS

The customs and rituals of death in the United States have changed considerably throughout history. It used to be customary, for example, for a widow to wear black and refrain from most social activities for up to a year. This behavior symbolized her presumed and expected emotional distress. Other people were signaled to provide comfort and support, and the culture allowed for a long adaptation period (Aries, 1981). The opposite is true in much of contemporary Western culture. Normally, the survivor is expected to return to normal living in a few days.

Funerals and memorial services can impart a sense of order, decorum, and continuity. They can reaffirm the values and beliefs of the individuals and the community, and also can demonstrate the support of family and friends. The deceased person's life can be reviewed and celebrated in a public, shared forum. Sometimes, however, the public ceremonies clash with the values and experiences of the survivors, leaving them feeling further isolated. Sometimes, too, the rituals and institutions are too distant from the personal lives of the participants to be meaningful. Yet, it is hard for most of us to conceive of following up a loved one's death with no rituals whatsoever; rituals make the end "official."

WHEN A CHILD DIES

Many aspects of grief and bereavement are intensified when a child dies. If the death is sudden or unexpected, the reactions of parents and siblings are often prolonged and intense. There may also be confusion, guilt, and attempts to affix blame for the loss (Miles, 1984). The brothers and sisters of a dying child may be particularly confused and disoriented. Death is often seen as a punishment of some sort—to the child who died, to the parent, or to the surviving brothers or sisters—or perhaps the family simply resorts to platitudes such as "God moves in mysterious ways" to reconcile their loss. Often parents coping with their own grief may not be able to help the other children in the family or

Funerals can help survivors by providing, among other things, a sense of continuity.

even to think through answers to a child's questions on an appropriate developmental level. Many siblings do not disclose their secret fears, feelings of guilt, or misunderstandings, and yet many of the thoughts and feelings that arise during such a family crisis may last a lifetime (Coleman & Coleman, 1984).

When a child dies slowly of a terminal illness, there are other issues to deal with. What should the dying child be told? How can the child be helped to confront death? How do the parents deal with their likely feelings of failure, guilt, and helplessness? Often the medical caregivers as well become quite involved in the child's hopes for recovery. They, too, experience some of the parents' feelings of failure and anticipatory grief. There is the tendency for all involved to deny these painful feelings. In all, grief and recovery are particularly difficult when a child dies (Wass & Corr, 1984).

A crisis of values is not uncommon for survivors following the death of a child. Certainly the child did not deserve to die. Survivors struggle to reevaluate their most closely held beliefs and values—especially religious ones—at the same time that they are suffering from numerous symptoms of sorrow and depression (Kushner, 1981). Those who find some form of resolution to such issues often report sensing a deeper meaning in their own lives; those who do not find resolution may live out a lifetime of despair. In the case of unnecessary fatal accidents, they may also find meaning and resolution in joining advocacy groups such as Mothers Against Drunk Driving (MADD), which seek to prevent needless child deaths in the future.

REVIEW & APPLY

1. Describe the grieving process in general terms, noting what bereaved individuals are *likely* to experience.
2. How can rituals and customs for grieving sometimes be a source of further discomfort?
3. How do cultural and historical factors influence the grieving process?
4. What special issues are associated with the death of a child?

COMPLETING THE LIFE CYCLE

Ultimately, whether death involves a child, an elderly, frail adult, or anyone in between, it marks the completion of the individual's life cycle. We close this chapter (and this book) with some thoughts about what this completion means. Each individual life cycle is embedded in a cultural and historical context. Birth, first steps, first words, schooling, coming of age, finding a mate, working, building a family, finding wisdom, and facing your own mortality are common tasks, but they are played out in a rich tapestry of individual biology and cultural patterns—that is, heredity and environment in interaction. The social sciences have much to say about some common patterns and influences and the timing of same, but the immediate community has much to say about what it all means.

Some cultural practices make the links between death, birth, and the life cycle explicit. In traditional Chinese culture, for example, when a grandparent dies, a grandchild of the appropriate age may be urged to marry or to have a child. In Jewish culture, as in others, it is the custom to name a newborn child after a deceased member of the immediate family; renewal and continuity are thus celebrated in the new birth. Hence, what seem like polar opposites—birth and death—are linked as part of a continuous family thread.

Whatever the cultural backdrop, death and its prospects often give life new meaning for the individual and the community. As we try to make sense of a particular person's life and death, we reassess our own priorities and values. The death of a community leader or public figure may sharpen individual and community values. Yet, quite ordinary deaths often help just as much in defining the meaning of courage, loyalty, kindness, or virtue in lasting and personal ways.

Otherwise, as noted at the beginning of this chapter, death—regardless of its circumstances—is a part of nature. It is undeniable and clear-cut. It happens to all of us and every member of every other species as well. What lies beyond death for any particular one of us will always be debated and probably will never be known scientifically; but what lies beyond death for us as Homo sapiens is, in the end, new life for those who follow.

SUMMARY

Thoughts and Fears of Death

- Our technological, youth-oriented society has a tendency to deny death while at the same time being preoccupied with it.
- In earlier historical periods death was a familiar event that usually occurred at home. In the twentieth century, however, death became something of a technological marvel, and most people now die in hospitals.
- Actively coping with the reality of death means taking realistic precautions without restricting ourselves unnecessarily.
- In the past there was considerable resistance to discussing the dying process, but this is changing.
- Personal and cultural meanings of death often play a key role in determining whether individuals are fearful or preoccupied with thoughts of their own death.

Confronting Your Own Death

- People who are not faced with the prospect of immediate death can spend more time adjusting to the idea, especially by conducting a life review.
- The task of finding meaning and purpose in life involves active restructuring of philosophical, religious, and pragmatic thoughts and beliefs.
- Kübler-Ross identified five stages in the process of adjusting to the idea of death; denial, anger, bargaining, depression, and acceptance. Not all people go through all the stages, and few do so in the specified order.
- Reactions to the dying process are strongly influenced by the nature of the illness, especially in the

case of AIDS; many AIDS patients experience a prolonged dying process that makes acceptance and forgiveness difficult.
- Suicide is common in middle-aged and older people. There are also more passive forms of suicide, such as submissive death (letting oneself die) and suicidal erosion (killing oneself indirectly through excessive drinking, smoking, or drug abuse).
- Suicide among the elderly is almost always a result of vital losses such as the loss of a spouse. An effective means of improving the mental health of widows and widowers is self-help groups.

The Search for a Humane Death

- It has been suggested that dying patients should be informed of their condition and given some autonomy, for example, in determining how much pain medication they receive.
- People who feel that they can no longer control their own lives in any meaningful way may respond by simply giving up.
- Hospices are designed to help terminally ill patients live out their days as fully and independently as possible by giving needed support both to patients and to their families.
- The first goal of hospices is to manage pain of all sorts—physical, mental, social, and spiritual. They also try to respect the dying patient's wishes to the extent possible.
- Many people now demand a right to die, rather than to have bodily systems maintained artificially. Taking positive steps to bring about death is called

active euthanasia and includes assisted suicide. Passive euthanasia involves withholding or disconnecting life-sustaining equipment so that death will occur naturally.

■ An example of an effort to ensure individual autonomy in the last stages of life is a living will, a document that states the signer's wish to avoid the use of "heroic measures" to maintain life in the event of irreversible illness.

Grief and Bereavement

■ Family members and close friends must make short- and long-term adjustments to the death of a loved one. The short-term adjustments include initial emotional reactions, often called grief work, as well as practical matters. Long-term adjustments include changes in routines, roles, and activities.

■ It is generally agreed that certain psychological tasks need to be accomplished after the loss of a loved one. These include accepting the reality of the loss and rechanneling the emotional energy previously invested in the relationship with the deceased.

■ Initial reactions often include shock, numbness, denial, and disbelief, and sometimes anger and blame. This may be followed by active grieving, including weeping and yearning for the deceased. Eventually most survivors begin to adjust to their new circumstances.

■ If the death is preceded by a long illness or loss of functioning, the survivors may experience anticipatory grief. This does not eliminate postdeath grief, but it can make the effects of the death less overwhelming.

■ Social support, especially from peers, can be helpful in coping with grief.

■ People who experience several losses within a relatively short span of time may experience bereavement overload. This is common in gay and minority communities that lose many of their members to AIDS.

■ Grief responses are both historically and culturally determined.

■ Some theorists dispute the popular view of bereavement and note that people with the greatest degree of distress are likely to still be the most distressed one or two years later.

■ Chronic grief, or failure to ever recover from a loss, has been identified as a pathological mourning process.

■ Funerals and memorial services can impart a sense of order and continuity. They reaffirm the values and beliefs of the community as well as demonstrating support.

■ Many aspects of grief and bereavement are intensified when a child dies, especially if the death is sudden or unexpected.

Completing the Life Cycle

■ Each individual life cycle is embedded in a cultural and historical context. Biological and cultural patterns interact throughout the cycle.

■ Death and its prospects often give life new meaning for the individual and the community.

KEY TERMS

submissive death	active euthanasia	grief work
suicidal erosion	assisted suicide	anticipatory grief
right to die	passive euthanasia	chronic grief

USING WHAT YOU'VE LEARNED

Attitudes toward death and dying vary, depending on your age, your life stage, and your past experiences with death. Just as an 8-year-old has difficulty understanding the identity struggles of a 16-year-old, young, active adults may avoid serious thoughts about death until they are confronted with it. Even then, their reactions may be quite different from those of mourners in later adulthood.

Think about the recent death of someone you knew. How did the reactions of family members and friends vary, depending on the age and life experience of the mourner? Were the rituals more helpful to some than to others? Were the mourners able to find ways to reach across the generations to help one another?

SUGGESTED READINGS

Aris, P. (1990). *The hour of our death.* New York: Knopf, 1981. A historical survey of practices of handling the dying.

Beisser, A. (1990). *A graceful passage: Notes on the freedom to live or die.* New York: Doubleday. A candid and compassionate discussion of progressive terminal diseases and the issues concerning the right to die.

Cook, A. S., & Oltjenbruno, K. A. (1989). *Dying and grieving: Lifespan and family perspectives.* New York: Holt, Rinehart & Winston. A comprehensive text on death and dying and the related mourning process.

Fitzgerald, H. (1994). *The mourning handbook: A complete guide for the bereaved.* New York: Simon and Schuster. One of the more helpful guides that explores the practical and the traumatic with gentle, balanced advice and insight.

Kalish, R. (1985). *Death, grief, and caring relationships.* Monterey, CA: Brooks/Cole. A textbook on death and dying, with emphasis on the importance of allowing the dying patient, family, and friends to express their feelings and to cope with the concept of death.

Kübler-Ross, E. (1969). *On death and dying.* New York: Macmillan. On the basis of extensive interviews with dying patients, Kübler-Ross describes the most common reactions to approaching death.

Kushner, H. (1981). *When bad things happen to good people.* New York: Schocken. A sensitive, thoughtful discussion about coping with notions of justice and religious beliefs when facing situations such as death.

Mor, V. (1987). *Hospice care systems: Structure, process, costs and outcome.* New York: Springer. An overview and analysis of the range of hospice care systems now available.

Nuland, S. B. (1993). *How we die: Reflections on life's final chapter.* New York: Random House. An extraordinary, award-winning book that blends clear medical information with wise insights on the harsh realities of both life and death. This surgeon-author provides clear descriptions of the mechanisms of cancer, heart disease, stroke, AIDS, and Alzheimer's disease with clinical exactness yet poetic eloquence for a fresh and compassionate approach to this final life task.

Glossary

accommodation Piaget's term for the act of changing our thought processes when a new object or event does not fit existing schemas.

achievement motivation A learned motive to excel and succeed.

acquired immune deficiency syndrome (AIDS) A fatal disease caused by HIV. Anyone can be infected through sexual contact or through exposure to infected blood or needles.

active euthanasia Taking positive steps to bring about another person's death, as in cases of terminal illness. In the United States, active euthanasia is murder.

adaptation In Piaget's theory, the process by which infant schemes are elaborated, modified, and developed.

adolescent growth spurt The sudden increase in rate of growth that accompanies entrance into puberty.

affordances The different opportunities for interaction offered by a perception; for example, halls are for moving through.

afterbirth The third and last stage of childbirth, typically occurring within 20 minutes after delivery, during which the placenta and umbilical cord are expelled from the uterus.

age clock A form of internal timing used as a measure of adult development; a way of knowing that we are progressing too slowly or too quickly in terms of key social events that occur during adulthood.

age of viability The age (at about 24 weeks) at which the fetus has a 50-50 chance of surviving outside the womb.

ageism A widely prevalent social attitude that overvalues youth and discriminates against the elderly.

alleles A pair of genes, found on corresponding chromosomes, that affect the same trait.

Alzheimer's disease A disease that causes dementia due to a progressive deterioration of brain cells, especially those in the cerebral cortex.

amniocentesis A test for chromosomal abnormalities that is performed during the second trimester of pregnancy; it involves the withdrawal and analysis of amniotic fluid with a syringe.

amniotic fluid Fluid that cushions and protects the embryo or fetus.

amniotic sac A fluid-filled membrane that encloses the developing embryo or fetus.

androgynous personality People who are high both on desirable masculine and feminine characteristics.

anoxia Lack of oxygen that can cause brain damage.

anticipatory grief Emotionally preparing yourself for the death of a loved one, as in cases of prolonged terminal illness.

anxiety A feeling of uneasiness, apprehension, or fear that has a vague or unknown source.

Apgar Scale A standard scoring system that allows hospitals to evaluate an infant's condition quickly and objectively.

assimilation In Piaget's theory, the process of making new information part of existing schemas.

assisted suicide Providing a terminally ill patient with the means to end his or her own life.

atherosclerosis Hardening of the arteries, which is a common condition of aging caused by the body's increasing inability to use excess fats in the diet. These fats are stored along the walls of arteries and restrict the flow of blood when they harden.

attachment The emotional bond that develops between a child and another individual. The infant's first bond is usually characterized by strong interdependence, intense mutual feelings, and vital emotional ties.

attention-deficit/hyperactivity disorder (ADHD) An inability to keep focused on something long enough to learn it, often accompanied by poor impulse control.

authoritarian parents Those parents who adhere to rigid rule structures and dictates rules to the children; in this situation, children do not contribute to the family's decision-making process.

authoritative parents Those parents who use firm control with children but encourage communication and negotiation in rule setting within the family.

automaticity Performing well-practiced motor behaviors without having to think about them consciously.

autonomy The strong drive to do things for yourself, to master physical and social environments, and to be competent and successful.

autosomes All chromosomes except those that determine sex.

bacterial Microscopic creatures that cause infections but can't pass the placental barrier.

behavior modification A method that uses conditioning procedures such as reinforcement, reward, and shaping, to change behavior.

behavioral genetics The study of relationships between behavior and physical/genetic characteristics.

biological age The person's position with regard to his or her expected lifespan.

birthing centers Designed to accommodate the entire process, from labor through delivery and recovery.

blastula The hollow, fluid-filled sphere of cells that forms several days after conception.

breech presentation The baby's position in the uterus such that the buttocks will emerge first; assistance is usually needed in such cases to prevent injury to the infant, producing anoxia.

cataract Clouding of the lens of the eye that obstructs vision.

cephalocaudal trend The sequence of growth that occurs first in the head and progresses toward the feet.

Cesarean section Surgical procedure used to remove the baby and the placenta from the uterus by cutting through the abdominal wall.

child abuse Intentional psychological or physical injuries inflicted on a child.

chorionic villus sampling (CVS) In this procedure, cells are drawn from the membranes surrounding the fetus, either with a syringe or with a catheter. Because more cells are collected in this procedure than in amniocentesis, the test can be completed more quickly.

chromosome Chains of genes, visible under a microscope.

chronic grief A pathological mourning process in which the person never overcomes the grief.

chronological age The number of years of life.

classical conditioning A type of learning in which a neutral stimulus, such as a bell, comes to elicit a response, such as salivation, by repeated pairings with an unconditioned stimulus, such as food.

climacteric The broad complex of physical and emotional symptoms that accompany reproductive changes in middle age. The climacteric affects both men and women.

cloning Technique in which scientists can duplicate an animal from a single somatic cell.

cognitive-developmental theory An approach that focuses on the development of thinking, reasoning, and problem solving.

collective monologues Children's conversations that include taking turns talking, but not necessarily about the same topic.

conditions of worth Conditions others impose upon us if we are to be worthwhile as human beings—conditions that are often impossible to fulfill.

congenital Inborn or hereditary.

conservation The understanding that changing the shape or appearance of objects doesn't change their amount of volume.

content The meaning of any written or spoken message.

context The particular setting or situation in which development occurs; the "back drop" for development.

contextual paradigms The view that numerous environmental, social, psychological, and historical factors interact to determine development.

contingency A relationship between behavior and its consequences.

control processes Higher cognitive processes that enhance memory.

coregulation Development of a sense of shared responsibility between parents and children.

corrective gene therapy The repair or substitution of individual genes to correct defects.

correlation A mathematical statement of the relationship or correspondence between two variables.

crisis model The view that changes in midlife are abrupt and often stressful.

criterion-referenced tests Tests that evaluate an individual's performance in relation to mastery of specified skills or objectives.

critical period The only point in time when a particular environmental factor can have an effect.

cross-sectional designs A method of studying development in which a sample of individuals of one age are observed and compared with one or more samples of individuals of other ages.

crystallized intelligence A broad area of intelligence that includes making judgments, analyzing problems, and drawing conclusions from experienced-based information and knowledge. This form of intelligence, which is drawn from education and the broader culture, increases across the lifespan.

decision/commitment The realization of being in love and making a commitment to maintain it.

declarative knowledge Factual knowledge; knowing "what."

defense mechanisms The cognitive "tricks" that individuals use to reduce tensions that lead to anxiety.

dementia The confusion, forgetfulness, and personality changes that may be associated with old age and are linked to a variety of primary and secondary causes.

deoxyribonucleic acid (DNA) A large, complex molecule composed of carbon, hydrogen, oxygen, nitrogen, and phosphorus. It contains the genetic code that regulates the functioning and development of an organism.

dependent variable The variable in an experiment that changes as a result of manipulating the independent variable.

development The changes over time in the structure, thought, or behavior of a person as a result of both biological and environmental influences.

deviation IQ The approach that assigns an IQ score by comparing an individual's raw score with the scores of other subjects of the same age range.

dialectical thinking Thought that seeks to integrate opposing or conflicting ideas and observations.

diffusion status The identity status of those who have neither gone through an identity crisis nor made commitments.

discrepancy hypothesis A cognitive theory stating that at around 7 months, infants acquire schemes for familiar objects. When a new image or object is presented that differs from the old one, the child experiences uncertainty and anxiety.

discrimination Treating others in a prejudiced manner.

dizygotic (fraternal) twins Twins resulting from the fertilization of two separate ova by two separate sperm.

dominant In genetics, one gene of a gene pair that will cause a particular trait to be expressed.

dual-earner couple A married or unmarried couple sharing a household, in which both husband and wife contribute to family income, as members of the paid labor force.

ecological systems model A model of child development in which the growing child actively restructures aspects of the four environmental levels in which he or she lives while simultaneously being influenced by these environments and their interrelationships.

ecological validity   The extent to which research applies to what happens in the real world.

egocentrism   A self-centered view of the world, perceiving everything in relation to yourself.

ego   The conscious, reality-oriented component of personality.

embryonic period   The second prenatal period, which lasts from the end of the second week to the end of the second month after conception. All the major structures and organs of the individual are formed during this time.

embryo   From the Greek term "swell."

empty nest   The period in the family life cycle that occurs after the last child has left home.

episiotomy   An incision to enlarge the vaginal opening.

ethnocentrism   The tendency to assume that our own beliefs, perceptions, customs, and values are correct or normal, and that those of others are inferior or abnormal.

ethology   The study of patterns of animal behavior, especially behavior that is guided by instinct.

evolution   Process through which species change across generations, acquiring adaptive characteristics and losing characteristics that have become maladaptive or useless.

exosystem   The third level, which refers to social settings or organizations beyond the child's immediate experience that affect the child.

expressive jargon   The babbling produced when an infant uses inflections and patterns that mimic adult speech.

extrinsic factors of work   Satisfaction in the form of pay, status, and other rewards for work.

extrinsically motivated behavior   Behavior performed to obtain rewards or avoid adversive events.

failure-to-thrive syndrome   A condition in which infants are small for age and often sick, as a result of malnutrition or unresponsive caregiving.

fallopian tubes   Two passages that open out of the upper part of the uterus and carry the ova from the ovary to the uterus.

family leave   Leave required by law to deal with family affairs and problems, especially those involving taking care of children.

fear   A state of arousal, tension, or apprehension caused by a specific, identifiable circumstance.

fetal alcohol syndrome (FAS)   Congenital abnormalities, including small size, low birth weight, certain facial characteristics, and possible mental retardation, resulting from maternal alcohol consumption during pregnancy.

fetal alcohol effects (FAE)   Similar though milder abnormalities due to drinking during pregnancy.

fetal monitor   The external monitor records the intensity of uterine contractions and the baby's heartbeat by means of two belts placed around the mother's abdomen. The internal monitor consists of a plastic tube containing electrodes, which is inserted into the vagina and attached to the baby's head.

fetal period   The final period of prenatal development, lasting from the beginning of the second month after conception until birth. During this period, all organs mature and become functional.

fetus   French for "pregnant" or "fruitful."

filial piety   The veneration given the elderly in Eastern cultures. This respect is manifested in cultural traditions as well as everyday encounters.

fine motor skills   Competence in using the hands.

fluid intelligence   A broad area of intelligence that encompasses the abilities used in new learning, including memorization, inductive reasoning, and the rapid perception of spatial relationships. This form of intelligence is believed to reach its peak in late adolescence.

fontanelles   The soft, bony plates of the skull, connected only by cartilage.

foreclosure status   The identity status of those who have made commitments without going through an identity crisis.

form   The particular symbol used to represent content.

functional subordination   The integration of a number of separate simple actions or schemes into a more complex pattern of behavior.

gametes   reproductive cells (sperm and ova)

gender constancy   The older child's understanding that gender is stable and stays the same despite changes in superficial appearance.

gender identity   The knowledge that you are male or female and the ability to make that judgment about other people.

gender roles   Roles we adopt with regard to being male or female.

gender schemes   cognitive standards (including stereotypes) as to what behavior and attitudes are appropriate for males and females.

gender-role stereotypes   Rigid, fixed ideas of what is appropriate masculine or feminine behavior.

gene splicing   Transplantation of genetic material from one species into another, with the result being a hybrid with characteristics of both donors.

genes   The basic units of inheritance.

genetic counseling   Counseling that helps potential parents evaluate their risk factors for having a baby with genetic disorders.

genotype   The genetic makeup of a given individual or group.

germinal period   After conception, the period of very rapid cell division and initial cell differentiation, lasting for approximately two weeks.

glaucoma   Increased, potentially damaging pressure within the eyeball.

glial cells   Cells that insulate the neurons and improve efficiency of transmission of nerve impulses.

grief work   Dealing with emotional reactions to the loss of a loved one.

gross motor skills   Those skills that involve the larger muscles or the whole body and that show refinement as well.

gross-to-specific trend   The tendency to react to stimuli with generalized, whole-body movements at first, with these responses becoming more local and specific later.

habituation method   To study infant perceptual capabilities, researchers habituate infants to certain stimuli and then change the stimuli.

habituation The process of becoming accustomed to certain kinds of stimuli and no longer responding to them.

heterozygous Referring to the arrangement in which the two alleles for a simple dominant-recessive trait differ.

holistic approach People are "whole" creatures, not at all compartmentalized.

holophrastic speech In the early stages of language acquisition, the young child's use of single words to convey complete thoughts or sentences.

homozygous Referring to the arrangement in which the two alleles for a simple dominant-recessive trait are the same.

hormones Biochemical secretions of the endocrine gland that is carried by the blood or other body fluids to a particular organ or tissue and acts as a stimulant or an accelerator.

hostile aggression Aggression that is intended to harm another person.

humanistic psychology The view that humans actively make choices and seek to fulfill positive personal and social goals.

hypertension Abnormally high blood pressure, sometimes accompanied by headaches and dizziness.

identity achievement The identity status of those who have gone through an identity crisis and have made commitments.

identity crisis A period of making decisions about important issues, such as "Who am I, and where am I going?"

identity formation Gaining a sense of who you are and how you fit into society.

identity Reasonably consistent set of concepts that a person has about his or her physical, psychological, and social attributes.

id The primitive, hedonistic component of personality.

imaginary audience Adolescents' assumption that others are focusing a great deal of critical attention on them.

imaginary companions Companions children "make up" and pretend are real.

independent variable The variable in an experiment that is manipulated in order to observe its effects on the dependent variable.

indifferent parents Those parents who are not interested in their role as parents or in their children; they exercise little control over and demonstrate little warmth toward their children.

industry versus inferiority Erikson's psychosocial conflict during middle childhood, in which children either work industriously and are rewarded for their efforts in school or fail and develop a sense of inferiority.

information-processing theory A theory of human development that uses the computer as an analogy for the way the human mind receives, analyzes, and stores information.

initial labor The first stage is the period during which the cervical opening of the uterus begins to dilate to allow for passage of the baby.

insecure attachment The result of inconsistent or unresponsive caregiving.

instinct Behavior that occurs in all normal members of a species, under the same conditions, and in the same way.

institutionalization Long-term, usually permanent placement in an institution.

instrumental aggression Aggression that is not intended to harm, but is instead incidental to gaining something from another person.

intelligence quotient (IQ) An individual's mental age divided by chronological age, multiplied by 100 to eliminate the decimal point.

interdependence Reciprocal dependence.

internalization Making social rules and standards of behavior part of yourself and adopting them as your own set of values.

intimacy The feeling of closeness that occurs in love relationships.

intrinsic factors of work Satisfactions workers obtain from doing the work in and of itself.

intrinsically motivated behavior Behavior performed for its own sake, with no particular goal.

job burnout The emotional exhaustion that often affects middle-aged people in the helping professions.

karyotype A photograph of a cell's chromosomes arranged in pairs according to size.

kinkeepers The role assumed by middle-aged people that includes maintaining family rituals, celebrating achievements and holidays, keeping family histories alive, and reaching out to family members who live far away.

labor and delivery The second stage of childbirth, which begins with stronger and more regular contractions and ends with the actual birth of the baby. Once the cervix is fully dilated, contractions begin to push the baby through the birth canal.

laboratory observation The method in which researchers set up controlled situations designed to elicit the behavior of interest.

language acquisition device or LAD Chomsky's term for an innate set of mental structures that aid humans in language learning.

lateralization The process whereby specific skills and competencies become localized in particular hemispheres of the brain.

law of effect A principle of learning theory stating that a behavior's consequences determine the probability of its being repeated.

learning disorders Extreme difficulty in learning school subjects such as reading, writing, or math, despite normal intelligence and absence of sensory or motor defects.

learning theorists A term that usually refers to strict behaviorists who focused on learning.

learning The basic developmental process of change in the individual as a result of experience or practice.

life structure The overall pattern that underlies a person's life.

longitudinal design A study in which the same objects are observed continuously over a period of time.

macrosystem Unlike the other levels, this, the outermost level, does not refer to a specific setting. It consists of the values, laws, and customs of the society in which the individual lives.

mean length of utterance (MLU)   The average length of the sentences that a child produces.

meiosis   The process of cell division in reproductive cells that result in an infinite number of different chromosomal arrangements.

menarche   The time of the first menstrual period.

menopause   The permanent end of menstruation; it occurs in middle age and may be accompanied by physical symptoms and intense emotional reactions, more so in some women than in others.

mental retardation   Significantly subaverage intellectual functioning and self-help skills, with onset prior to age 18.

mesosystem   The second level, which is formed by the interrelationships among two or more microsystems.

metacognition   The process of monitoring your own thinking, memory, knowledge, goals, and actions.

microsystem   The first level, which refers to the activities, roles, and interactions of an individual and his or her immediate setting, such as the home, day-care center, or school.

mitosis   The process of ordinary cell division that results in two cells identical to the parent.

monozygotic (identical) twins   Twins resulting from the division of a single fertilized ovum.

moral absolutism   Any theory of morality that disregards cultural differences in moral beliefs.

moral realism   Piaget's term for the first stage of moral development, in which children believe in rules as real, indestructible things.

moral relativism   Piaget's term for the second stage of moral development, in which children realize that rules are agreements that may be changed, if necessary.

moratorium status   The identity status of those who are currently in the midst of an identity crisis.

mutuality, or interactive synchrony   The pattern of interchange between caregiver and infant in which each responds to and influences the other's movements and rhythms.

myelination   The formation of the myelin sheath covering the fast-acting central nervous system pathways. This sheath increases the speed of transmission and the precision of the nervous system.

myopia   Nearsightedness.

"natural" or prepared childbirth   This can take various forms but is based on procedures primarily developed by Fernand Lamaze, a French obstetrician.

natural selection   Darwin's theory of how evolution works.

naturalistic or field observation   The method in which researchers go into everyday settings and observe and record behavior while being as unobtrusive as possible.

neonates   Babies in the first month of life.

neurons   The cells that make up the nervous system. They form prenatally and continue to grow and branch throughout life.

nonnormative influences   Individual environmental factors that do not occur at any predictable time in a person's life.

norm-referenced tests   Tests that compare an individual's performance with the performances of others in the same age group.

normative age-graded influences   The biological and social changes that normally happen at predictable ages—a combination of species heredity and species environmental factors.

normative history-graded influences (also species environmental factors)   The historical events, such as wars, depressions, and epidemics, that affect large numbers of individuals at about the same time.

novelty paradigm   A research plan that uses infants' preferences for new stimuli over familiar ones to investigate their ability to detect small differences in sounds, patterns, or colors.

obesity   Weighing at least 20% more in body weight than would be predicted by your height.

object permanence   According to Piaget, the beginning realization in infants at about 8 months that objects continue to exist when they are out of sight.

occupational cycle   A variable sequence of periods or stages in a worker's life, from occupational exploration and choice, through education and training, novice status, promotions and more experienced periods.

operant conditioning   A type of conditioning that occurs when an organism is reinforced or punished for voluntarily emitting a response.

operational definitions   The actual procedures researchers use in conducting experiments.

osteoporosis   Loss of bone mass and increased bone fragility in middle age and beyond.

ova   Egg cells.

overextensions   The young child's tendency to overgeneralize specific words as when a child uses "chihuahua" as the term for all dogs.

overregularize   To generalize complex language principles, typically by preschool children who are rapidly expanding their vocabularies.

ovulation   The release of the ovum into one of the two Fallopian tubes; occurs approximately 14 days after menstruation.

partial reinforcement   A procedure in which only some responses are reinforced; produces much stronger habits than continuous reinforcement.

passion   The second component of love that refers to physical attraction, arousal, and sexual behavior in a relationship.

passive euthanasia   Withholding or disconnecting life-sustaining equipment so that death can occur naturally.

pathological aging factors   Cumulative effects of diseases and accidents that may accelerate aging.

peer group   A group of two or more people of similar status who interact with each other and who share norms and goals.

perception   The complex process by which the mind interprets and gives meaning to sensory information.

perinatology   A branch of medicine that deals with childbirth as a span of time including conception, the prenatal period, delivery, and the first few months of life.

periods   Stages.

permissive parents   Those parents who exercise little control over their children but are high in warmth; in this situation, children may have trouble inhibiting their impulses or deferring gratification.

personal fable   Adolescents' feeling that they are special and invulnerable—exempt from the laws of nature that control the destinies of ordinary mortals.

personality   Characteristic beliefs, attitudes, and ways of interacting with others.

phenotype   In genetics, those traits that are expressed in the individual.

phobias   Unreasonable fear of an object or situation.

pincer grasp   The method of holding objects, developed at around the age of 12 months, in which the thumb opposes the forefinger.

pivot grammar   A two-word, sentence-forming system used by $1\frac{1}{2}$- and 2-year-olds, and involves action words, prepositions, or possessives (pivot words) in combination with x-words, which are usually nouns.

placenta   A disk-shaped mass of tissue that forms along the wall of the uterus through which the embryo receives nutrients and discharges waste.

pragmatics   The social and practical aspects of language use.

preference method   Infants are given a choice between stimuli to look at or listen to. Researchers record which stimulus the infant attends to more. If an infant consistently spends more time attending to one of the two stimuli, the preference indicates that the infant can both perceive a difference and deliberately respond to it.

prejudice   A negative attitude formed without adequate reason and usually directed toward people because of their membership in a certain group.

preterm status   An infant born before a gestation period of 35 weeks.

primitive reflexes   These reflexes do not have apparent survival value but may have been important at some point in our evolutionary history.

procedural knowledge   Action knowledge; knowing "how to."

productive language   The spoken or written communication of preschool children.

prosocial behavior   Helping, sharing, or cooperative actions that are intended to benefit others.

proximodistal trend   The sequence of growth that occurs from the midline of the body outward.

psychoanalytic theory   A theory based on the theories of Freud, whose view of human nature was deterministic. He believed that personality is motivated by innate biological drives.

psychological age   An individual's current ability to cope with and adapt to social and environmental demands.

psychosexual stages   Freud's stages of personality developments used on erogenous zones.

psychosocial theory   In Erikson's theory, the phases of development during which the individual's capacity for experience dictates major adjustments to the social environment and the self.

puberty   The attainment of sexual maturity in males and females.

recall   The ability to retreive information and events that are not present, with or without cues.

receptive language   The repertoire of words and commands that a child understands, even though he or she may not be able to use them.

recessive   In genetics, one of a gene pair that determines a trait in an individual only if the other member of that pair is also recessive.

recognition   The ability to correctly identify items previously experienced when they appear again.

reconstituted family   Also known as stepfamily; families when parents have remarried to produce a new family.

reconstituted or blended families   Families in which mothers or fathers with children have remarried.

replication   Systematic repetitions of experiments to determine if findings are valid and generalizable.

resilient children   Children who overcome difficult environments to lead socially competent lives.

retirement maturity   How prepared a person is to retire.

ribonucleic acid (RNA)   A substance formed from, and similar to, DNA. It acts as a messenger in a cell and serves as a catalyst for the information of new tissue.

right to die   The view that death is a right to be exercised at the individual's discretion.

rites of passage   Symbolic events or rituals to mark life transitions, such as one from childhood to adult status.

scaffolding   The progressive structuring by the parents of the parent-child interaction.

schemes or schemas   Piaget's term for mental structures that process information, perceptions, and experiences; the schemes of individuals change as they grow.

secure attachment   A strong emotional bond between child and caregiver that develops as a result of responsive caregiving.

self-actualization   Realizing one's full unique potential.

self-concept   Your perception of your personal identity.

self-esteem   Seeing yourself as an individual with positive characteristics—as someone who will do well in the things that you think are important.

self-regulated behavior   Personal behavior regulated by the child.

senescence   The normal aging process, not connected with the occurrence of disease in the individual.

sensation   The simple registration of stimulus by a sense organ.

sensitive or optimal periods   The times during which certain types of learning and development occur best and most efficiently, but not exclusively.

sensorimotor period   Piaget's first period of cognitive development (from birth to about 2 years). Infants use action schemes—looking, grasping, and so on—to learn about their world.

sequential-cohort design A mix of the longitudinal and cross-sectional designs.

sex chromosomes The 23rd chromosome pair that determines sex.

shaping Systematically reinforcing successive approximates to a desired act.

sibling status Birth order.

significant others Anyone whose opinions an individual values highly.

small-for-date A full-term newborn who weighs less than $5\frac{1}{2}$ pounds.

social age An individual's current status as compared with cultural norms.

social cognition Thought, knowledge, and understanding that involve the social world.

social comparison Evaluating yourself and your situation relative to others.

social inference Guesses and assumptions about what another person is feeling, thinking, or intending.

social referencing Subtle emotional signals, usually from the parent, that influence the infant's behavior.

social regulations The rules and conventions governing social interactions.

social responsibility Obligations to family, friends, and society at large.

socialization The process by which we learn our society's standards, laws, norms, and values.

sociobiology A branch of ethology that maintains that social behavior is largely determined by an organism's biological inheritance.

spontaneous abortions Miscarriages; expulsion of the prenatal organism before it is viable.

stages Discrete periods often with abrupt transitions from one to the next.

status passage A change in the role and position that occurs when an individual enters adolescence, becomes a parent, retires, or becomes a widow or widower.

stochastic theories of aging Theories suggesting that the body ages as a result of random assaults from both internal and external environments.

stranger anxiety and separation anxiety An infant's fear of strangers or of being separated from the caregiver. Both occur in the second half of the first year and indicate, in part, a new cognitive ability to respond to differences in the environment.

strict behaviorism The view that only observable, measurable behavior can be studied scientifically.

stroke Blockage of blood to the brain, which can cause brain damage.

subdialects Subcultural language differences; speakers of different subdialects usually can understand each other.

submissive death Suicide in the form of simply letting yourself die.

suicidal erosion An indirect form of suicide through excessive drinking, smoking, or other drug abuse.

superego The conscience component, which includes the ego ideal.

surprise paradigm A research technique used to test infants' memory and expectations. Infants cannot report what they remember or expect, but if their expectations are violated they respond with surprise.

survival reflexes Reflexes necessary for adaptation and survival, especially during the first few weeks before the higher brain centers begin to take control.

symbolic representation The use of a word, picture, gesture, or other sign to represent past and present events, experiences, and concepts.

systematic desensitization In behavior therapy, a technique that gradually reduces an individual's anxiety about a specific object or situation.

systems of meaning Belief systems that shape our experiences, organize our thoughts and feelings, and determine our behavior.

telegraphic speech The utterances of $1\frac{1}{2}$- and 2-year-olds that omit the less significant words and include the words that carry the most meaning.

temperament Inborn behavioral styles.

teratogens Toxic agents of any kind that cause abnormalities or birth defects.

traditional childbirth Hospital labor and delivery.

transition model The view that changes in midlife are gradual.

trimesters The three equal time segments that comprise the gestation period.

ultrasound A technique that uses sound waves to produce a picture of the fetus in the uterus.

umbilical cord The "rope" of tissue connecting the placenta to the embryo; this rope contains two fetal arteries and one fetal vein.

unconditional positive regard Rogers's proposition that we should warmly accept another person as a worthwhile human being, without reservations or conditions.

use The way in which a speaker employs language to give it one meaning as opposed to another.

viruses Ultra microscopic organisms that reproduce only within living cells and can pass the placental barrier.

wisdom An expert knowledge system focusing on the pragmatics of life that involves excellent judgment and advice on critical life issues, including the meaning of life and the human condition; wisdom represents the capstone of human intelligence.

zone of proximal development Vygotsky's concept that children develop through participation in activities slightly beyond their competence, with the help of adults or older children.

zygote The first cell of a human being that occurs as a result of fertilization; a fertilized ovum.

▮▮▮▮▮ Bibliography

AAP TASK FORCE ON INFANT POSITIONING AND SIDS. (1992). Positioning and SIDS. *Pediatrics, 89(6),* 1120–1126.

ABBOTT, J. W. (1978). Hospice. *Aging, 5(3),* 38–40.

ABEL, E. L. (1995). An update on incidence of FAS: FAS is not an equal opportunity birth defect. *Neurotoxicology and Teratology, 17,* 437–443.

ABLER, R. M., & SEDLACEK, W. E. (1989). Freshman sexual attitudes and behaviors over a 15–year-period. *Journal of College Student Development, 30,* 201–209.

ABRAHAMS, B., FELDMAN, S. S., & NASH, S. C. (1978). Sex role self-concept and sex role attitudes: Enduring personality characteristics or adaptations to changing life situations? *Developmental Psychology, 14(4),* 393–400.

ABRAMOVITCH, R., & GRUSEC, J. E. (1978). Peer imitation in a natural setting. *Child Development, 49,* 60–65.

ACHENBACH ET AL. (1991). National survey of problems and competencies among four-to-sixteen-year olds. *Monographs of the Society for Research in Child Development, 56,* (Serial No. 225) 3.

ACHENBACH, T. M. (1982). *Developmental Psychopathology.* New York: Wiley.

ADAMS, B. B. (1979). Mate selection in the United States: A theoretical summarization. In W. Butt, R. Hill, I. Nye, & I. Reis (Eds.), *Contemporary theories about the family* (Vol. 1, pp. 259–267). New York: Free Press.

ADAMS, D. (1983). *The psychosocial development of professional black women's lives and the consequences of career for their personal happiness.* Unpublished doctoral dissertation. Wright Institute, Berkeley, CA.

ADAMS, R. G., & BLIESZNER, R. (1998). Baby boomer friendships. *Generations,* Spring, 70–75.

ADOLPH, K. E. (1997). Learning in the development of infant locomotion. *Monographs of the Society for Research in Child Development, 62* (3, Serial No. 251).

AINSWORTH, M. D. (1967). *Infancy in Uganda: Infant care and the growth of love.* Baltimore: Johns Hopkins University Press.

AINSWORTH, M. D. (1973). The development and infant–mother attachment. In B. M. Caldwell & H. N. Ricciuti (Eds.), *Review of child development research* (Vol. 3). Chicago: University of Chicago Press.

AINSWORTH, M. D. S. (1983). Patterns of infant–mother attachment as related to maternal care. In D. Magnusson & V. Allen (Eds.), *Human development: An interactional perspective.* New York: Academic Press.

AINSWORTH, M. D. S., & BOLBY, J. (April 1991). An ethological approach to personality development. *American Psychologist, 46(4),* 333–341.

AINSWORTH, M. D., BLEHAR, M., WATERS, E., & WALL, S. (1978). *Patterns of attachment.* Hillsdale, NJ: Erlbaum.

AINSWORTH, M. D. S., BLEHAR, M. C., WATERS, E., & WALL, S. (1979). *Patterns of attachment: A psychological study of the strange situation.* Hillsdale, NJ: Erlbaum.

AINSWORTH, M. D., BLEHAR, M. C., WATERS, E., & WALL, S. (1979). *Patterns of attachment.* New York: Halsted Press.

AIZENBERG, R., & TREAS, J. (1985). The family in late life: Psychosocial and demographic considerations. In J. Birren & K. Warner Schaie (Eds.), *Handbook of the psychology of aging* (2nd ed.). New York: Van Nostrand Reinhold.

ALAN GUTTMACHER INSTITUTE (1994). *Sex and America's teenagers.* New York: Alan Guttmacher Institute.

ALDOUS, J. (1978). *Family careers: Developmental change in families.* New York: Wiley.

ALESSANDRI, S. M. (1992). Effects of maternal work status in single-parent families on children's perception of self and family and school achievement. *Journal of Experimental Child Psychology, 54,* 417–433.

ALEXANDER, T. (November 1970). Psychologists are rediscovering the mind. *Fortune,* pp. 108–111ff.

ALLEN, M., DONOHUE, P., & DUSMAN, A. (1993). The limits of viability—Neonatal outcome of infants born at 22 to 25 weeks' gestation. *New England Journal of Medicine, 329(22),* 1597–1601.

ALLEN, P. A., ET AL. (1992). Impact of age, redundancy, and perceptual noise on visual search. *Journal of Gerontology: Psychological Sciences, 47(2),* 69–74.

ALLGAIER, A. (1978). Alternative birth centers offer family-centered care. *Hospitals, 52,* 97–112.

ALMO, H. S. (1978). Without benefit of clergy: Cohabitation as a noninstitutionalized marriage role. In K. Knafl & H. Grace (Eds.), *Families across the life cycle: Studies from nursing.* Boston: Little, Brown.

ALPERT, J. L., & RICHARDSON, M. (1980). Parenting. In L. W. Poon (Ed.), *Aging in the 1980s.* Washington, DC: American Psychological Association.

ALPERT-GILLIS, L. J., & CONNELL, J. P. (1989). Gender and sex-role influences on children's self-esteem. *Journal of Personality, 57,* 97–113.

ALSOP, R. (April 24, 1984). As early retirement grows in popularity, some have misgivings. *Wall Street Journal.*

AMATO, P. R. (February 1993). Children's adjustment to divorce: Theories, hypotheses, and empirical support. *Journal of Marriage and the Family, 55,* 23–38.

AMERICAN ACADEMY OF PEDIATRICS (1996). Policy statement: Drug-exposed infants. Washington, DC.

AMERICAN ASSOCIATION OF UNIVERSITY WOMEN. (1991) *Shortchanging girls, shortchanging America: Executive Summary.* Washington, DC: American Association of University Women Educational Foundation.

AMERICAN ASSOCIATION OF UNIVERSITY WOMEN. (1992) *How schools shortchange women: The AAUW Report.* Washington, DC: American Association of University Women Educational Foundation.

AMERICAN PSYCHIATRIC ASSOCIATION (1994). *Diagnostic andstatistical manual of mental disorders* (4th ed.). Washington, DC.

AMERICAN PSYCHOLOGICAL ASSOCIATION. (1973). *Ethical principles in the conduct of research with human participants.* Washington, DC: APA.

AMES, L. B. (December 1971). Don't push your preschooler. *Family Circle.*

ANCOLIE-ISRAEL, S., KRIPKE, D. F., MASON, W., & KAPLAN, O. J. (1985). Sleep apnea and periodic movements in an aging sample. *Journal of Gerontology, 40(4),* 419–425.

ANDERSON, D. R., & COLLINS, P. A. (1988). The impact on children's education: Television's influence on cognitive development. Washington, DC: U.S. Department of Education, Office of Educational Research and Improvement.

ANDERSON, D. R., LORCH, E. P., FIELD, D. E., & SANDERS, J. (1981). The effects of TV program comprehensibility on preschool children's visual attention to television. *Child Development, 52,* 151–157.

ANDERSON, E. S. (March 1979). *Register variation in young children's role-playing speech.* Paper presented at the Communicative Competence, Language Use, and Role-playing Symposium, Society for Research and Child Development.

ANDERSSON, B-E. (1989). Effects of public daycare: A longitudinal study. *Child Development, 60,* 857–866.

ANGIER, N. (June 11, 1995). If you're really ancient, you may be better off. *New York Times,* section 4, pp. 1, 5.

ANTHONY, E. J., & COHLER, B. J. (Eds.). (1987). *The invulnerable child.* New York: Guilford.

ANTIAL, J. K., & COTTIN, S. (1988). Factors affecting the division of labor in households. *Sex Roles, 18,* 531–553.

APA TASK FORCE ON WOMEN AND DEPRESSION. (Winter 1991). APA study finds no simple explanation for high rate of depression in women. *Quarterly Newsletter of the National Mental Health Association,* p. 5.

APGAR, V. (1953). Proposal for a new method of evaluating the newborn infant. *Anesthesia and Analgesia, 32,* 260–267.

APTER, T. E. (1995). *Secret paths: Women in the new midlife.* New York: Norton.

AQUILINO, W. S. (1990). The likelihood of parent–adult child coresidence: Effects of family structure and parental characteristics. *Journal of Marriage and the Family, 52,* 405–419.

AQUILINO, W. S. (November 1994). Late life parental divorce and widowhood: Impact on young adults' assessment of parent–child relations. *Journal of Marriage and the Family, 56,* 908–922.

AQUILINO, W. S. (1996). The returning child and parental experience at midlife. In C. D. Ryff & M. M. Seltzer (Eds.) *The parental experiment in midlife.* Chicago: University of Chicago Press.

ARCHER, S. L. (1985). Identity and the choice of social roles. *New Directions for Child Development, 30,* 79–100.

AREND, R. A., GORE, F. L., & SROUFE, L. A. (1979). Continuity of individual adaptation from infancy to kindergarten, *Child Development, 50,* 950–959.

ARIES, P. (1962). *Centuries of childhood.* (R. Baldick, Trans.). New York: Knopf.

ARIES, P. (1981). *The hour of our death.* New York: Knopf.

ARIES, P. (1989). Introduction. In R. Chartier (Ed.), *A history of a private life: Vol. 3. Passions of the Renaissance* (pp. 1–11). Cambridge, MA: Belknap Press of Harvard University Press.

ARMITAGE, S. E., BALDWIN, B. A., & VINCE, N. A. (1980). The fetal sound environment of sheep. *Science, 208,* 1173–1174.

ARMSTRONG, T. (1996). A holistic approach to attention deficit disorder. *Educational Leadership, 53,* 34–36.

ASHER, S. R. (1983). Social competence and peer status: Recent advances and future directions. *Child Development, 54,* 1427–1434.

ASHER, S. R. (1990). Recent advances in the study of peer rejection. In S. R. Asher & J. D. Coie (Eds.), *Peer rejection in childhood* (pp. 3–13). New York: Cambridge University Press.

ASHER, S. R., RENSHAW, P. D., & HYMEL, S. (1982). Peer relations and the development of social skills. In W. W. Hartup (Ed.), *The young child: Reviews of research* (Vol. 3). Washington, DC: National Association for the Education of Young Children.

ASLIN, R. (1987). Visual and auditory development in infancy. In J. Osofsky (Ed.), *Handbook of infant development* (2nd ed.). New York: Wiley.

ASLIN, R. N. (1987). Motor aspects of visual development in infancy. In P. Salapatek & L. Cohen (Eds.), *Handbook of infant perception: Vol. 1. From sensation to perception: Vol. 1.* New York: Academic Press.

ASLIN, R. N., PISONI, D. V., & JUSCZYK, P. W. (1983). Auditory development and speech perception in infancy. In P. H. Mussen (Ed.), *Handbook of child psychology* (Vol. 2). New York: Wiley.

ASLIN, R. N., & SMITH, L. B. (1988). Perceptual development. *Annual Review of Psychology, 39,* 435–473.

ASSO, D. (1983). *The real menstrual cycle.* Chichester, UK: Wiley.

ASTIN, A. W. (1977). *Four critical years.* San Francisco: Jossey-Bass.

ASTLEY, S. J., CLARREN, S. K., LITTLE, R. E., SAMPSON, P. D. & DALING, J. R. (1992).

Analysis of facial shape in children gestationally exposed to marijuana, alcohol and/or cocaine. *Pediatrics, 89,* 67–77.

ATCHLEY, R. (1989). A continuity theory of normal aging. *The Gerontologist, 29,* 183–190.

ATCHLEY, R. C. (1982). The process of retirement: Comparing women and men. In M. Szlnovacy (Ed.), *Women's retirement: Policy implications of recent research.* London: Sage.

ATHEY, I. J. (1984). Contributions of play to development. In T. D. Yawkey & A. D. Pellegrini (Eds.), *Child's play.* Hillsdale, NJ: Erlbaum.

ATKINSON, R. C., & SHIFFRIN, R. M. (1971). The control of short-term memory. *Scientific American, 225*(2), 82–90.

AUSUBEL, F., BECKWITH, J., & JANSSEN, K. (June 1974). The politics of genetic engineering: Who decides who's defective? *Psychology Today,* p. 30ff.

BABLADELIS, G. (1987). Young persons' attitudes toward aging. *Perceptual and Motor Skills, 65,* 553–554.

BABSON, S. G., & BENSON, R. C. (1966). *Primer on prematurity and high-risk pregnancy.* St. Louis: Mosby.

BACHMAN, D. L. (September 1992). Sleep disorders with aging: Evaluation and treatment. *Geriatrics, 47*(23), 41–52.

BAILLARGEON, R. (1987). Object permanence in three-and-a-half- and four-and-a-half-month-old infants. *Developmental Psychology, 23*(5), 655–674.

BAILLARGEON, R., & DEVOS, J. (1991). Object permanence in young infants: Further evidence. *Child Development, 62,* 1227–1246.

BAKEMAN, R., & ADAMSON, L. B. (1990). !Kung infancy: The social context of object exploration. *Child Development, 61,* 794–809.

BAKER, B. L., & BRIGHTMAN, A. J. (1989). *Steps to independence: A skills training guide for parents and teachers of children with special needs* (2nd ed.). Baltimore: Paul H. Brookes.

BALDWIN, B. A. (October 1986). Puberty and parents: Understanding your early adolescent. *PACE,* pp. 13, 15–19.

BALDWIN, J. M. (1906). *Mental development in the child and the race: Methods and processes* (3rd ed.). New York: Macmillan.

BALL, W., & TRONICK, E. (1971). Infant responses to impending collision: Optical and real. *Science, 171,* 818–820.

BALTES, P. B. (1979). Life-span developmental psychology: Some converging observations on history and theory. In P. B. Baltes & O. G. Brim, Jr. (Eds.), *Life-span development and behavior* (Vol. 2). New York: Academic Press.

BALTES, P. B. (1987). Theoretical propositions of life-span developmental psychology: On the dynamics of growth and decline. *Developmental Psychology, 23,* 611–626.

BALTES, P. B. (1993). The aging mind: Potential and limits. *Gerontologist, 33*(5), 580–594.

BALTES, P. B., & BALTES, M. M. (1990). Psychological perspectives on successful aging: The model of selective optimization with compensation. In P. B. Baltes & M. M. Baltes, (Eds.), *Successful aging: Perspectives from the behavioral sciences.* New York: Press Syndicate of the University of Cambridge.

BANDURA, A. (1964). The stormy decade: Fact or fiction. *Psychology in the Schools, 1,* 224–231.

BANDURA, A. (1965). Influence of models' reinforcement contingencies on the acquisition of imitative responses. *Journal of Personality and Social Psychology, 1,* 589–595.

BANDURA, A. (1969). *Principles of behavior modification.* New York: Holt, Rinehart and Winston.

BANDURA, A. (1977). *Social learning theory.* Englewood Cliffs, NJ: Prentice Hall.

BANDURA, A. (1982). The psychology of chance encounters and life paths. *American Psychologist, 37,* 747–755.

BANDURA, A. (1986). *Social foundations of thought and action.* Englewood Cliffs, NJ: Prentice Hall.

BANDURA, A., & WALTERS, R. H. (1959). *Adolescent aggression.* New York: Ronald Press.

BANDURA, A., & WALTERS, R. H. (1963). *Social learning and personality development.* New York: Holt, Rinehart & Winston.

BANDURA, A., ROSS, D., & ROSS, S. A. (1963). Imitation of film-mediated aggressive models. *Journal of Abnormal and Social Psychology, 66,* 3–11.

BANKOFF, E. (1986). Peer support for widows: Personal and structural characteristics related to its provision. In S. Hobfoll (Ed.), *Stress, social support, and women* (pp. 207–222). Washington, DC: Hemisphere.

BANKS, M., & DANNEMILLER, J. (1987). Infant visual psychophysics. In P. Salapatek & L. Cohen (Eds.), *Handbook of infant perception: Vol. 1. From sensation to perception.* New York: Academic Press.

BANKS, M. S., & SALAPATEK, P. (1983). Infant visual perception. In P. H. Mussen (Ed.), *Handbook of child psychology* (4th ed.). New York: Wiley.

BARBERO, G. (1983). Failure to thrive. In M. Klaus, T. Leger, & M. Trause (Eds.), *Maternal attachment and mothering disorders.* New Brunswick, NJ: Johnson & Johnson.

BARER, B. M. (1994). Men and women aging differently. *International Journal of Aging and Human Development, 38,* 29–40.

BARKER, R. G., DEMBO, T., & LEWIN, K. (1943). Frustration and regression. In R. G. Barker, J. S. Kounin, & H. F. Wright (Eds.), *Child behavior and development.* New York: McGraw-Hill.

BARNES, D. M. (1989). "Fragile X" syndrome and its puzzling genetics. *Research News,* pp. 171–172.

BARNES, H. L., & OLSEN, D. H. (1985). Parent-adolescent communication and the circumplex model. *Child Development, 56,* 438–447.

BARNETT, M., & PLEACK, M. (1992). Men's multiple roles and their relationship to men's psychological distress. *Journal of Marriage and the Family, 54,* 358–367.

BARNETT, R., & BARUCH, G. (1987). Social roles, gender, and psychological distress. In R. Barnett, L. Biener, & G. Baruch (Eds.), *Gender and stress* (pp. 122–143). New York: Free Press.

BARON, N. S. (1992). *Growing up with language: how children learn to talk.* Reading, Ma.: Addison-Wesley Publishing Co.

BARR, H. DARBY, B., STREISSGUTH, A., & SAMPSON, P. (1990). Prenatal exposure to alcohol, caffeine, tobacco, and aspirin: Effects on fine and gross motor performance in 4–year-old children. *Developmental Psychology, 26*(3), 339–348.

BARRETT, H. C. (March 1994). Technology-supported assessment portfolios. *The Computing Teacher,* 9–12.

BARTECCHI, C. E., MACKENZIE, T. D., & SCHRIER, R. W. (May 1995). The global tobacco epidemic. *Scientific American,* pp. 44–51.

BARTOSHUK, L., & WEIFFENBACH, J. (1990). Chemical senses and aging. In E. Schneider & J. Rowe (Eds.), *Handbook of the biology of aging* (pp. 429–444). San Diego: Academic Press.

BARUCH, G. K., & BARNETT, R. C. (1986a). *Consequences of fathers' participation in family work: Parent role strain and well-being* (Working Paper No. 159). Wellesley, MA: Wellesley College Center for Research on Women.

BARUCH, G., & BARNETT, R. (1986b). Role quality, multiple role involvement, and psychological well-being in midlife women. *Journal of Personality and Social Psychology, 51,* 578–585.

BARUCH, G. K., BIENER, L., & BARNETT, R. (February 1987). Women and gender in research on work and family stress. *American Psychologist,* pp. 130–135.

BARUCH, G., & BROOKS-GUNN, J. (1984). The study of women in mid-life. In G. Baruch & J. Brooks-Gunn (Eds.), *Women in midlife* (pp. 1–8). New York: Plenum.

BASIC BEHAVIORAL SCIENCE TASK FORCE (1996). Vulnerability and resilience. *American Psychologist, 51:1,* 22–28.

BASSUCK, E. L., BROWNE, A., & BUCKNER, J. C. (1996). Single mothers and welfare. *Scientific American, 275, October,* 60–67.

BATEMAN, D., NG, S., HANSEN, C., & HEAGARTY, M. (1993). The effects of interuterine cocaine exposure in newborns. *American Journal of Public Health, 83*(2), 190–194.

BATES, E., O'CONNELL, B., & SHORE, C. (1987). Language and communication in infancy. In J. D. Osofsy (Ed.), *Handbook of infant development* (2nd ed.). New York: Wiley.

BATES, J. E. (1987). Temperament in infancy. In J. D. Osofsky (Ed.), *Handbook of infant development* (2nd ed., pp. 1101–1149). New York: Wiley.

BATESON, G. (1955). *A theory of play and fantasy.* Psychiatric Research Reports, 2, 39–51.

BAUER, P. J., & THAL, D. J. (1990). Scripts or scraps: Reconsidering the development of sequential understanding. *Journal of Experimental Child Psychology, 50,* 287–304.

BAUMRIND, D. (1972). Socialization and instrumental competence in young children. In W. W. Hartup (Ed.), *The young child: Reviews of research* (Vol. 2). Washington, DC: National Association for the Education of Young Children.

BAUMRIND, D. (1975). *Early socialization and the discipline controversy.* Morristown, NJ: General Learning Press.

BAUMRIND, D. (1978). A dialectical materialist's perspective on knowing social reality. *New Directions for Child Development, 2.*

BAUMRIND, D. (1980). New directions in socialization research. *American Psychologist, 35,* 639–650.

BAUMRIND, D. (1987). A developmental perspective on adolescent risk-taking in contemporary America. *New Directions for Child Development, 37,* 93–125.

BAUMRIND, D. (1991). The influence of parenting style on adolescent competence and substance use. *Journal of Early Adolescence, 11*(1), 56–95.

BAYDAR, N. & BROOKS-GUNN, J. (1991). Effects of maternal employment and child-care arrangements on preschoolers' cognitive and behavioral outcomes: Evidence from the children of the National Longitudinal Survey of Youth. *Developmental Psychology, 27*(6), 932–945.

BAYLEY, N. (1965). Research in child development: A longitudinal perspective. *Merrill-Palmer Quarterly, 11,* 183–208.

BAYLEY, N. (1969). *Bayley scales of infant development.* New York: Psychological Corporation.

BAZZINI, D. G., MCINTOSH, W. D., SMITH, S. M., COOK, S., & HARRIS, C. (1997). The aging woman in popular film: Underrepresented, unattractive, unfriendly, and unintelligent. *Sex Roles, 36,* 531–543.

BEAL, C. R. (1987). Repairing the message: Children's monitoring and revision skills. *Child Development, 58,* 401–408.

BEARON, L. (1989). No great expectations: The underpinnings of life satisfaction for older women. *The Gerontologist, 29,* 772–776.

BECK, M. (August 15, 1988). Miscarriages. *Newsweek,* pp. 46–49.

BECKER, J. (1993). Young children's numerical use of number words: counting in many-to-one situations. *Developmental Psychology, 29*(3), 458–465.

BECKER, P. M., & JAMIESON, A. O. (March 1992). Common sleep disorders in the elderly: Diagnosis and treatment. *Geriatrics, 47*(3), 41–52.

BECKER, W. C. (1964). Consequences of different kinds of parental discipline. In M. L. Hoffman (Ed.), *Review of child developmental research* (Vol. 1). New York: Russell Sage Foundation.

BECKWITH, L., & COHEN, S. E. (1989). Maternal responsiveness with preterm infants and later competency. In M. H. Bornstein (Ed.), *New Directions for Child Development; Vol. 43. Maternal responsiveness: Characteristics and consequences.* San Francisco: Jossey-Bass.

BEEGLY, M., & CICCHETTI, D. (1994). Child maltreatment, attachment, and self system: Emergence of an internal state lexicon in toddlers at high social risk. *Development and Psychopathology, 6,* 5–30.

BEHRMAN, R.E. (1992). Introduction. *The future of children: U.S. health care for children. 2(2).* Los Angeles, CA: The David and Lucile Packard Foundation.

BEIT-HALLAHMI, B., & RABIN, A. (1977). The kibbutz as a social experiment and as a child-rearing laboratory. *American Psychologist, 32,* 532–541.

BELL, A. P., & WEINBERG, M. S. (1978). *Homosexualities: A study of diversity among men and women.* New York: Simon & Schuster.

BELL, B. D. (1978). Life satisfaction and occupational retirement: Beyond the impact years. *International Journal of Aging and Human Development, 9*(1), 31–49.

BELL, S. M., & AINSWORTH, M. D. (1972). Infant crying and maternal responsiveness. *Child Development, 43,* 1171–1190.

BELLER, E. K. (1955). Dependency and independence in young children. *Journal of Genetic Psychology, 87,* 25–35.

BELLER, F., & ZLATNIK, G. (1994). Medical aspects of the beginning of individual lives. In Fritz K. Beller and Robert F. Weir (Eds.), The beginning of human life (pp. 3–18). Dordrect, the Netherlands: Kluwer.

BELLUGI, U. (1970). Learning the language. *Psychology Today,* December, 32–38.

BELLUGI, U. (December 1970). Learning the language. *Psychology Today,* pp. 32–38.

BELMONT, I., & BELMONT, L. (1980). Is the slow learner in the classroom learning disabled? *Journal of Learning Disabilities, 13,* 32–33.

BELSKY, J. (1980). Child maltreatment: An ecological integration. *American Psychologist, 35,* 320–335.

BELSKY, J. (1984). *The psychology of aging: Theory and research and practice.* Monterey, CA: Brooks/Cole.

BELSKY, J. (1986). Infant day care: A cause for concern? *Zero to Three, 6,* 1–7.

BELSKY, J. (February 1987). Risks remain. *Zero to Three,* pp. 22–24.

BELSKY, J., & ROVINE, M. (1984). Social-network contact, family support, and the transition to parenthood. *Journal of Marriage and the Family, 46*(2), 455–462.

BELSKY, J., & ROVINE, M. (1988). Nonmaternal care in the first year of life and the security of infant–parent attachment. *Child Development, 59,* 157–167.

BELSKY, J., & ROVINE, M. (1990a). Q-sort security and first-year nonmaternal care. In *New Directions for Child Development: Vol. 49. Child care and maternal employment: A social ecology approach* (pp. 7–22).

BELSKY, J., & ROVINE, M. (1990b). Patterns of marital change across the transition to parenthood: Pregnancy to three years postpartum. *Journal of Marriage and the Family, 52,* 5–19.

BELSKY, J., ROVINE, M., & TAYLOR, D. (1984). The Pennsylvania infant and family development project III. The origins of individual differences in infant–mother attachment: Maternal and infant contributions. *Child Development, 58,* 718–728.

BEM, S. (1985). Androgyny and gender schema theory: A conceptual and empirical integration. In T. B. Sondegegger (Ed.), *Nebraska Symposium on Motivation, 1984: Psychology and gender.* Lincoln: University of Nebraska.

BEM, S. L. (September 1975). Androgyny vs. the tight little lives of fluffy women and chesty men. *Psychology Today,* pp. 59–62.

BENDER, B. G., LINDEN, M. G. & ROBINSON, A. (1987). Environment & developmental risk in children with sex chromosome abnormalities. *Journal of the Academy of Child and Adolescent Psychiatry, 26,* 499–503.

BENEDEK, T. (1970). Parenthood during the life cycle. In E. J. Anthony & T. Benedek

(Eds.), *Parenthood: Its psychology and psychopathology.* Boston: Little, Brown.

BENGSTON, V. L. (1985). Diversity and symbolism in grandparents' role. In V. L. Bengston & J. F. Robertson (Eds.), *Grandparenthood.* Beverly Hills, CA: Sage.

BENGSTON, V. L., & ROBERTSON, J. F. (Eds.). (1985). *Grandparenthood.* Beverly Hills, CA: Sage.

BENIN, M. H., & EDWARDS, D. A.(May 1990). Adolescents' chores: The differences between dual- and single-earner families. *Journal of Marriage and the Family*, 361–373.

BENNETT, D. A., & KNOPMAN, D. S. (August 1994). Alzheimer's disease: A comprehensive approach to patient management. *Geriatrics, 49*(8), 20–26.

BENNETT, N. (1976). *Teaching styles and pupil progress.* Cambridge, MA: Harvard University Press.

BENNETT, S. C., ROBINSON, N. M., & SELLS, C. J. (1983). Growth and development of infants weighing less than 800 grams at birth. *Pediatrics, 7*(3), 319–323.

BERARDO, D., SHEEHAN, C., & LESLIE, G. (1987). A residue of tradition: Jobs, careers, and spouses' time in housework. *Journal of Marriage and the Family, 49,* 381–390.

BEREITER, C., & ENGELMANN, S. (1966). *Teaching disadvantaged children in the preschool.* Englewood Cliffs, NJ: Prentice Hall.

BERGMANN, B. (1986). *The economic emergence of women.* New York: Basic Books.

BERK, L. E. (July 1985). Why children talk to themselves. *Young Children,* pp. 46–52.

BERK, L. E. (1986). Relationship of elementary school children's private speech to behavioral accompaniment to task, attention and task performance. *Developmental Psychology, 22*(5), 671–680.

BERK, L. E. (1992). Children's private speech: An overview of theory and the status of research. In R. M. Diaz & L. E. Berk (Eds.), *Private speech: From social interaction to self-regulation* (pp. 17–53). Hillsdale, NJ: Erlbaum.

BERK, L.E. (1994). Vygotsky's theory: The importance of make-believe play. *Young Children.* 30–39.

BERK, S. F. (1985). *The gender factory: The apportionment of work in American households.* New York: Plenum.

BERKE, L. E. (November 1994). Vygotsky's theory: The importance of make-believe play. *Young Children,* pp. 30–39.

BERKO, J. (1958). The child's learning of English morphology. *Word, 14,* 150–177.

BERNARD, J. (1981). The good-provider role: Its rise and fall. *American Psychologist, 36,* 1–12.

BERNDT, T. (1983). Social cognition, social behavior and children's friendships. In E. T. Higgins, D. Ruble, & W. Hartup, *Social cognition and social development: A socio-cultural perspective.* Cambridge, MA: Cambridge University Press.

BERNDT, T. J. (1982). The features and effects of friendship in early adolescence. *Child Development, 53,* 1447–1460.

BEROFF, J., DOUVAN, E., & JULKA, R. (1981). *The inner American: A self-portrait from 1957–1976.* New York: Basic Books.

BERTENTHAL, B. I., & CAMPOS, J. J. (1987). New directions in the study of early experience. *Child Development, 58,* 560–567.

BIELBY, W., & BARON, J. (1986). Sex segregation within occupations. *American Economic Review, 76,* 43–47.

BINET, A., & SIMON, T. (1905). Methodes nouvelles pour le diagnostic du niveau intellectual des anormaux. *L'Annee Psychologique, 11,* 191–244.

BINET, A., & SIMON, T. (1916). *The development of intelligence in children.* (E. S. Kite, Trans.). Baltimore: Williams & Wilkins.

BIRCH, H. G., & GUSSOW, J. D. (1970). *Disadvantaged children: Health, nutrition and school failure.* New York: Harcourt Brace Jovanovich.

BIRCHLER, G. R. (1992). Marriage. In V. B. Van Hasselt & M. Hersen (Eds.). *Handbook of social development: A lifespan perspective* (pp. 392–420). New York: Plenum.

BIRKEL, R., & JONES, C. (1989). A comparison of the caregiving networks of dependent elderly individuals who are lucid and those who are demented. *The Gerontologist, 29,* 114–119.

BIRNBAUM, H. G., & KIDDER, D. (1984). What does hospice cost? *American Journal of Public Health, 74*(7), 689–692.

BIRREN, J. E., & CUNNINGHAM, W. R. (1985). Research on the psychology in aging: Principles and experimentation. In J. E. Birren & K. W. Schaie (Eds.), *Handbook of the psychology of aging* (2nd ed.). New York: Van Nostrand Reinhold.

BIRREN, J. E., WOODS, A. M., & WILLIAMS, M. V. (1980). Behavioral slowing with age: Causes, organization, and consequences. In L. W. Poon (Ed.), *Aging in the 1980s.* Washington, DC: American Psychological Association.

BIRTH. (June 1988). Report for American College of Obstetricians and Gynecologists. *BIRTH, 15*(2), 113.

BJORKLUND, D. F. (1988). Acquiring a mnemonic: Age and category knowledge effects. *Journal of Experimental Child Psychology, 45,* 71–87.

BLAESE, R. M. (1997). Gene therapy for cancer. *Scientific American, 276 (6),* 111–115.

BLAIR, S. L., & JOHNSON, M. P. (1992). Wives' perceptions of fairness of the division of labor: The intersection of housework and ideology. *Journal of Marriage and the Family, 54,* 570–581.

BLAKE, J. (1989). Number of siblings and educational attainment. *Science, 245,* 32–36.

BLIESZNER, R., & MANCINI, J. (1987). Enduring ties: Older adults' parental role and responsibilities. *Family Relations, 36,* 176–180.

BLOCK, J. (1971). *Lives through time.* Berkeley, CA: Bancroft Books.

BLOCK, J. (1981). Some enduring and consequential structures of personality. In A. I. Rabin et al. (Eds.), *Further explorations in personality.* New York: Wiley.

BLOOM, B. S. (1964). *Stability and change in human characteristics.* New York: Wiley.

BLOOM, B. S., & KRATHWOHL, D. R. (1956). *Taxonomy of educational objectives: Handbook I: The cognitive domain.* New York: McKay.

BLOOM, L. (1970). *Language development: Form and function in emerging grammars.* Cambridge, MA: MIT Press.

BLOOM, L., & LAHEY, M. (1978). *Language development and language disorders.* New York: Wiley.

BLOOM, L., LIFTER, K., & BROUGHTON, J. (1985). The convergence of early cognition and language in the second year of life: Problems in conceptualization and measurement. In M. Barrett (Ed.), *Children's single-word speech.* New York: Wiley.

BLUMSTEIN, P., & SCHWARTZ, P. (1983). *American couples.* New York: Morrow.

BLYTH, D., BULCROFT, A. R., & SIMMONS, R. G. (1981). *The impact of puberty on adolescents: A longitudinal study.* Paper presented at the annual meeting of the American Psychological Association, Los Angeles.

BOCCIA, M., & CAMPOS, J. J. (1989). Maternal emotional signals, social referencing, and infants' reactions to strangers. In N. Eisenberg (Ed.), *New Directions for Child Development: Vol. 44. Empathy and related emotional responses.* (pp. 25–50).

BOHANNON, J. N., JR., & HIRSH-PASEK, K. (1984). Do children say as they're told? A new perspective on motherese. In L. Feagans, C. Garvey, & R. Golinkoff (Eds.), *The origins and growth of communication.* Norwood, NJ: Ablex.

BOLTON, F. G., MORRIS, L. A., AND MCEACHERON, A. E. (1989). *Males at risk: The other side of child sexual abuse.* Newbury Park, CA: Sage.

BOOTH-KEWLEY, S., & FRIEDMAN, H. (1987). Psychological predictors of heart disease: A quantitative review. *Psychological Bulletin, 101,* 343–362.

BORKE, H. (1971). Interpersonal perception of young children: Egocentrism or empathy? *Developmental Psychology, 5,* 263–269.

BORKE, H. (1973). The development of empathy in Chinese and American children between 3 and 6 years of age: A cross-cultural study. *Developmental Psychology, 9,* 102–108.

BORNSTEIN, M. H. (1978). Chromatic vision in infancy. In H. W. Reese & L. P. Lipsett (Eds.), *Advances in child development and behavior* (Vol. 12). New York: Academic Press.

BORNSTEIN, M. (Ed.). (1987). *Sensitive periods in development: Interdisciplinary perspectives.* Hillsdale, NJ: Erlbaum.

BORNSTEIN, M. H. (Ed.). (1989). *Maternal responsiveness: Characteristics and consequences.* San Francisco: Jossey-Bass.

BORNSTEIN, M. H., & BRUNER, J. (1986). *Interaction in human development.* Hillsdale, NJ: Erlbaum.

BORNSTEIN, M. H., & TAMIS-LEMONDA, C. S. (1989). Maternal responsiveness and cognitive development in children. In M. H. Bornstein (Ed.), *New Directions for Child Development: Vol. 43. Maternal responsiveness: Characteristics and consequences* (pp. 49–62).

BORNSTEIN, M. H., ET AL. (1992). Maternal responsiveness to infants in three societies: The United States, France, and Japan. *Child Development, 63,* 808–821.

BOSSARD, J. H. S., & BOLL, E. S. (1960). *The sociology of child development.* New York: Harper & Brothers.

BOSTON WOMEN'S HEALTH BOOK COLLECTIVE. (1976). *Our bodies, ourselves* (2nd ed.). New York: Simon & Schuster.

BOTWINICK, J. (1977). Intellectual abilities. In J. Birren & K. W. Schaie (Eds.), *Handbook of the psychology of aging.* New York: Van Nostrand Reinhold.

BOTWINICK, J. (1984). *Aging and behavior: A comprehensive integration of research findings* (3rd ed.). New York: Springer.

BOUCHARD, R. J., JR. (June 25, 1987). Environmental determinants of IQ similarity in identical twins reared apart. Paper presented at the 17th annual meeting of the Behavior Genetics Association, Minneapolis, MN.

BOUCHARD, T. J., JR., LYKKEN, D. T., MCGUE, M., SEGAL, N., & TELLEGEN, A. (1990). Sources of human psychological differences: The Minnesota study of twins reared apart. *Science, 250,* 223–228.

BOULTON, M., & SMITH, P. K. (1989). Issues in the study of children's rough-and-tumble play. In M. N. Block & A. D. Pelligrini (Eds.), *The ecological content of children's play.* Norwood, NJ: Ablex.

BOUVIER, L. (1980). America's baby boom generation: The fateful bulge. *Population Bulletin, 35,* 1–35.

BOWER, B. (1991). Emotional aid delivers labor-saving results. *Science News, 139,* 277.

BOWER, B. (1991a). Same family: Different lives. *Science News* (December 7), 375–478.

BOWER, B. (1991b). Teenage turning point: Does adolescence herald the twilight of girls' self-esteem? *Science News, 139*(12), 184–186.

BOWER, T. G. R. (October 1971). The object in the world of the infant. *Scientific American,* pp. 30–38.

BOWER, T. G. R. (1974). *Development in infancy.* San Francisco: Freeman.

BOWER, T. G. R. (1989). *The rational infant: Learning in infancy.* New York: Freeman. A closer look at infant cognitive studies from a most imaginative researcher.

BOWLBY, J. (1960). Separation anxiety. *International Journal of Psychoanalysis, 41,* 89–113.

BOWLBY, J. (1973). *Attachment and loss: Vol. 2. Separation.* New York: Basic Books.

BOWLBY, J. (1980). *Attachment and loss: Vol. 3. Loss, sadness and depression.* New York: Basic Books.

BOWLBY, J. (1982). *Attachment and loss: Vol. 1. Attachment* (2nd ed.). New York: Basic Books.

BOWLBY, J. (1988). *A secure base.* New York: Basic Books.

BOWLBY, J. (1990). *Charles Darwin: A new life.* New York: Norton.

BOYD, J. H., & WEISSMAN, M. M. (1981). The epidemiology of psychiatric disorders of middle age: Depression, alcoholism, and suicide. In J. G. Howels (Ed.), *Modern perspectives in the psychiatry of middle age.* New York: Brunner/Mazel.

BRACKBILL, Y. (1979). Obstetrical medication and infant behavior. In J. Osofsky (Ed.), *Handbook of infant development.* New York: Wiley.

BRACKBILL, Y., MCMANUS, K., & WOODWARD, L. (1985). *Medication in maternity: Infant exposure and maternal information.* International Academy for Research on Learning Disabilities. Monographs, Series Number 2. Ann Arbor: University of Michigan Press.

BRACKBILL, Y., & NEVILL, D. (1981). Parental expectations of achievement as affected by children's height. *Merrill-Palmer Quarterly, 27,* 429–441.

BRADLEY. R. H., ET AL. (1989). Home environment and cognitive development in the first 3 years of life: A collaborative study involving six sites and three ethnic groups in North America. *Developmental Psychology, 25*(2), 217–235.

BRADSHAW, J. (1989). *Hemispheric specialization and psychological function.* New York: Wiley.

BRADWAY, K. P., THOMPSON, C. W., & GRAVEN, S. B. (1958). Preschool IQs after 25 years. *Journal of Educational Psychology, 49,* 278–281.

BRAINE, M. D. S. (1963). The ontogeny of English phrase structure: The first phase. *Language, 39,* 1–13.

BRAND, H. J., & WELCH, K. (1989). Cognitive and social-emotional development of children in different preschool environments. *Psychological Reports, 65,* 480–482.

BRASSARD, M. R., & MCNEILL, L. E. (1987). Child sexual abuse. In M. Brassard, R. Germain, & S. Hart (Eds.), *Psychological maltreatment of children and youth.* New York: Pergamon.

BRATCHER, W. (October 1982). The influence of the family on career selection: A family systems perspective. *Personnel and Guidance Journal,* pp. 87–91.

BRAY, D. W., & HOWARD, A. (1983). The AT&T longitudinal studies of managers. In K. W. Schaie (Ed.), *Longitudinal studies of adult development.* New York: Guilford.

BRAZELTON, T. B. (1969). *Infants and mothers: Differences in development.* New York: Dell.

BRAZELTON, T. B. (1973). *Neonatal behavioral assessment scale.* London: Heinemann.

BRAZELTON, T. B., NUGENT, J. K., & LESTER, B. M. (1987). Neonatal behavioral assessment scale. In J. Osofsky (Ed.), *Handbook of infant development* (2nd ed., pp. 780–817). New York: Wiley.

BRAZELTON, T. B., YOGMAN, M., ALS, H., & TRONICK, E. (1979). The infant as a focus for family reciprocity. In M. Lewis & L. A. Rosenblum (Eds.), *The child and his family.* New York: Plenum.

BREHM, S. (1992). *Intimate relationships.* New York: McGraw-Hill.

BRENNER, A. (1984). *Helping children cope with stress.* Lexington, MA: D. C. Heath.

BRETHERTON, I. (1992). Attachment and bonding. In V. B. Van Hasselt & M. Hersen (Eds.), *Handbook of social development: A lifespan perspective* (pp. 133–155). New York: Plenum Press.

BRETHERTON, I., & WATERS, E. (Eds.). (1985). Growing points of attachment. *Monographs of the Society for Research in Child Development, 50*(1–2), Serial 209.

BRIESEMEISTER, L. A., & HAINES, B. A. (1988). The interactions of fathers and newborns.

In K. L. Michaelson (Ed.), *Childbirth in America: Anthropological perspectives.* South Hadley, MA: Bergin & Garvey.

BRIGGS, G. C., FREEMAN, R. K., & YAFFE, S. J. (1986). *Drugs in pregnancy and lactation* (2nd ed.). Baltimore: Williams & Wilkins.

BRODY, E. M. (1985). *Parent care as a normative family stress.* Donald P. Kent Memorial Lecture, presented at the 37th annual scientific meeting of the Gerontological Society of America, San Antonio, Texas.

BRODY, E., JOHNSEN, P., & FULCOMER, M. (1984). What should adult children do for elderly parents? Opinions and preferences of three generations of women. *Journal of Gerontology, 39,* 736–746.

BRODY, E., KLEBAN, M., JOHNSEN, P., HOFFMAN, C., & SCHOONOVER, C. (1987). Work status and parent care: A comparison of four groups of women. *The Gerontologist, 27,* 201–208.

BRODY, E., & SCHOONOVER, C. (1986). Patterns of parent-care when adult daughters work and when they do not. *The Gerontologist, 26,* 372–381.

BRODY, J. (June 6, 1979). Exercising to turn back the years. *New York Times,* pp. C18–19.

BRODY, S. J. (1987). Strategic planning: The catastrophic approach. *The Gerontologist, 27*(2), 131–138.

BROMAN, S. (1986). Obstetric medication: A review of the literature on outcomes in infancy and childhood. In Michael Lewis (Ed.), *Learning disabilities and prenatal risk.* Urbana: University of Illinois Press.

BRONFENBRENNER, U. (1970). *Two worlds of childhood: U.S. and U.S.S.R.* New York: Russell Sage Foundation.

BRONFENBRENNER, U. (1979). *The ecology of human development.* Cambridge, MA: Harvard University Press.

BRONFENBRENNER, U. (1989). Ecological systems theory. In R. Vasta (Ed.), *Annals of Child Development.* (Vol. 6, pp. 187–251). Greenwich, CT.: JAI Press.

BRONFENBRENNER, U., & CECI, S. J. (1993). Heredity, environment, and the question "How?"—A first approximation. In R. Plomin & G. E. McClearn (Eds.), *Nature, nurture and psychology* (pp. 313–339). Washington, DC: American Psychological Association.

BRONSON, G. (1978). Aversion reactions to strangers: A dual process interpretation. *Child Development, 49,* 495–499.

BRONSON, W. (1975). Developments in behavior with agemates during the second year of life. In M. Lewis & L. A. Rosenblum (Eds.), *Peer relations and friendship.* New York: Wiley.

BRONSON, W. C. (1981). Toddlers' behavior with agemates: Issues of interaction and cognition and affect. In L. P. Lipset (Ed.), *Monographs on Infancy* (Vol. 1). Norwood, NJ: Ablex.

BROOKS, R. L., & OBRZUT, J. E. (1981). Brain lateralization: Implications for infant stimulation and development. *Young Children, 26,* 9–16.

BROOKS-GUNN, J., & FURSTENBERG, F. F., JR. (1986). The children of adolescent mothers: Physical, academic, and psychological outcomes. *Developmental Review, 6,* 224–251.

BROOKS-GUNN, J., & FURSTENBERG, F. F., JR. (1989). Adolescent sexual behavior. *American Psychologist, 44,* 249–257.

BROOKS-GUNN, J., KLEBANOV, P. K., & DUNCAN, G. J. (1996). Ethnic differences in children's intelligence test scores: Role of economic deprivation, home environment, and maternal characteristics. *Child Development, 67,* 396–408.

BROPHY, J. (1986). Teacher influences on student achievement. *American Psychologist, 41,* 1069–1077.

BROUGHTON, J. (1977). Beyond formal operations: Theoretical thought in adolescence. *Teacher's College Record, 79,* 88–97.

BROUSSARD, E. R. (1989). The infant–family resource program: Facilitating optimal development. *Prevention in Human Services, 6*(2), 179–224.

BROWN, B. B., CLASEN, D. R., & EICHER, S. A. (1986). Perceptions of peer pressure, peer conformity dispositions, and self-reported behavior among adolescents. *Developmental Psychology, 22,* 521–530.

BROWN, B. B., & LOHR, M. J. (1987). Peer-group affiliation and adolescent self-esteem: An integration of ego-identity and symbolic-interaction theories. *Journal of Personality and Social Psychology, 52,* 47–55.

BROWN, D. L. (1996). Kids, computers, and constructivism. *Journal of Instructional Psychology, 23,* 189–195.

BROWN, J. L., & POLLITT, E. (1996). Malnutrition, poverty and intellectual development. *Scientific American, 276* (2), 38–43.

BROWN, R. (1965). *Social psychology.* New York: Free Press.

BROWN, R. (1973). *A first language: The early stages.* Cambridge, MA: Harvard University Press.

BROWNELL, C. A., & CARRIGER, M. S. (1990). Changes in cooperation and self-other differentiation during the second year. *Child Development, 61,* 1164–1174.

BRUCK, M. (1987). The adult outcomes of children with learning disabilities. *Annals of Dyslexia, 37,* 252–263.

BRUNER, J. S. (1960). *The process of education.* Cambridge, MA: Harvard University Press.

BRUNER, J. S. (1971). *The relevance of education.* New York: Norton.

BRUNER, J. S. (1973). *Beyond the information given: Studies in the psychology of knowing.* New York: Norton.

BRUNER, J. (1983). *Child's talk.* New York: Norton.

BRUNER, J., & HASTE, H. (Eds.). (1987). *Making sense: The child's construction of the world.* London & New York: Methuen.

BRUNER, J. S., & OLVER, R. R., & GREENFIELD, P. M. (1966). *Studies in cognitive growth.* New York: Wiley.

BRUSCHWEILER-STERN, N. (1997). Imagining the baby, imagining the mother: Clinical representations of perinatology. *Ab Initio: The Brazelton Institute Newsletter, 4,* 1–5.

BRYAN, J. H. (1975). Children's cooperation and helping behaviors. In E. M. Hetherington (Ed.), *Review of child development* (Vol. 5). Chicago: University of Chicago Press.

BUCHANAN, C. M., ECCLES, J. S., & BECKER, J. B. (1992). Are adolescents the victims of raging hormones: Evidence for activational effects of hormones on moods and behavior at adolescence. *Psychological Bulletin, 111*(1), 62–107.

BUCHOFF, R. (Winter 1990). Attention deficit disorder: help for the classroom teacher. *Childhood Education, 67*(2), 86–90.

BUIS, J. M., & THOMPSON, D. N. (1989). Imaginary audience and personal fable: A brief review. *Adolescence, 24,* 773–781.

BULTERYS, M. G., GREENLAND, S., & KRAUS, J. F. (1989). Cigarettes and pregnancy. *Pediatrics, 86*(4), 535–540.

BULTERYS, M. G., GREENLAND, S., & KRAUS, J. F. (October 1990). Chronic fetal hypoxia and sudden infant death syndrome: Interaction between maternal smoking and low hematocrit during pregnancy. *Pediatrics, 86*(4), 535–540.

BURGESS, R. L., & CONGER, R. D. (1978). Family interaction in abusive, neglectful, and normal families. *Child Development, 49,* 1163–1173.

BURI, J. R., LOUISELLE, P. A., MISUKANIS, T. M., & MUELLER, R. A. (1988). Effects of parental authoritarianism and authoritativeness on self-esteem. *Personality and Social Psychology Bulletin, 14,* 271–282.

BURKE, R. J., & NELSON, D. (1997). Mergers and acquisitions, downsizing, and privatization: A North American perspective. In M. K. Gowing, J. D. Kraft, & J. C. Quick (Eds.), *The new organizational reality: Downsizing, restructuring, and revitalization.* Washington, DC: American Psychological Association.

BURKE, R., & WEIR, T. (1976). Relationship of wives' employment status to husband, wife and pair satisfaction and performance. *Journal of Marriage and the Family,* 279–287.

BURNSIDE, I. M. (1979a). The later decades of life: Research and reflections. In I. M. Burnside, P. Ebersole, & H. E. Monea (Eds.), *Psychosocial caring throughout the life span.* New York: McGraw-Hill.

BURNSIDE, I. M. (1979b). Sensory and cognitive functioning in later life. In I. Burnside, P. Ebersole, & H. E. Monea (Eds.), *Psychosocial caring throughout the life span.* New York: McGraw-Hill.

BURNSIDE, I. M., EBERSOLE, P., & MONEA, H. E. (Eds.) (1979). *Psychosocial caring throughout the life span.* New York: McGraw-Hill.

BUSCH, J. W. (1985). Mentoring in graduate schools of education: Mentors' perceptions. *American Educational Research Journal, 22,* 257–265.

BUSHNELL, E., AND BOUDREAU, J. P. (1993). Motor development and the mind: The potential role of motor abilities as a determinant of aspects of perceptual development. *Child Development, 64,* 1005–1021.

BUSKIRK, E. R. (1985). Health maintenance and longevity: Exercise. In C. E. Finch & E. L. Schneider (Eds.), *Handbook of the biology of aging* (2nd ed.). New York: Van Nostrand Reinhold.

CALDWELL, R., BLOOM, B., & HODGES, W. (1984). Sex differences in separation and divorce: A longitudinal perspective. In A. Rickel, M. Gerrard, & I. Iscoe (Eds.), *Social and psychological problems of women* (pp. 103–119). Washington, DC: Hemisphere.

CALLAHAN, J. (1988). Elder abuse: Some questions for policymakers. *The Gerontologist, 28,* 453–458.

CAMPBELL, M., & SPENCER, E. K. (1988). Psychopharmacology in child and adolescent psychiatry: A review of the past five years. *Journal of the American Academy of Child and Adolescent Psychiatry, 27,* 269–279.

CAMPOS, J. J., LANGER, A., & KROWITZ, A. (1970). Cardiac responses on the visual cliff in prelocomotor human infants. *Science, 170,* 196–197.

CANTOR, J., & WILSON, B. J. (1988). Helping children cope with frightening media presentations. *Current Psychology: Research and Reviews, 7*(1), 58–75.

CAPELLI, C. A., NAKAGAWA, N., & MADDEN, C. M. (1990). How children understand sarcasm: The role of context and intonation. *Child Development, 61,* 1824–1841.

CAPLAN, N., CHOY, M. H., & WHITMORE, J. K. (February 1992). Indochinese refugee families and academic achievement. *Scientific American,* pp. 36–42.

CARD, J. J., & WISE, L. L. (1978). Teenage mothers and teenage fathers: The impact of early childbearing on the parents' personal and professional lives. *Family Planning Perspectives, 10,* 199–205.

CARLO, G., KOLLER, S. H., EISENBERG, N., DA SILVA, M. S., & FROHLICH, C. B. (1996). A cross-national study on the relations among prosocial moral reasoning, gender role orientations, and prosocial behaviors. *Developmental Psychology, 32,* 231–240.

CARLSON, C. I., COOPER, C. R., & SPRADLING, V. Y. (1991). Developmental implications of shared versus distant perspectives of the family in early adolescence. *New Directions in Child Development, 51,* 13–31.

CARMICHAEL, E., & SAYER, C. (1991). *The skeleton at the feast: The day of the dead in Mexico.* London: British Museum Press.

CARPENTER, G. (1974). Mother's face and the newborn. *New Scientist, 61,* 742–744.

CARSKADON, M. A., VAN DEN HOED, J., & DEMENT, W. C. (October 13, 1979). *Insomnia and sleep disturbances in the aged: Sleep and daytime sleepiness in the elderly.* Paper presented at a scientific meeting of the Boston Society for Gerontologic Psychiatry.

CARTER, B., & MCGOLDRICK, M. (1980). *The family life cycle.* New York: Gardner.

CARVER, C., & HUMPHRIES, C. (1982). Social psychology of the Type A coronary-prone behavior pattern. In G. Sanders & J. Suls (Eds.), *Social psychology of health and illness.* Hillsdale, NJ: Erlbaum.

CASE, R. (1996). Reconceptualizing the nature of children's conceptual structures and their development in middle childhood. *Monographs of the Society for Research in Child Development, 61,* 1–26.

CASPI, A. (1987). Personality in the life course. *Journal of Personality and Social Psychology, 53,* 1203–1213.

CASPI, A., & ELDER, G. H., JR. (1988). Childhood precursors of the life course: Early personality and life disorganization. In

E. M. Hetherington, R. N. Lerner, & M. Perlmutter (Eds.), *Child development* (pp. 259–276). Hillsdale, NJ: Erlbaum.

CASPI, A., ELDER, G. H., JR., & BEM, D. J. (1987). Moving against the world: Life-course patterns of explosive children. *Developmental Psychology, 23*, 308–313.

CASSIDY, J. (1986). The ability to negotiate the environment: An aspect of infant competence as related to quality of attachment. *Child Development, 57*, 331–337.

CASSIDY, J., & BERLIN, L. J. (1994). The insecure/ambivalent pattern of attachment: Theory and research. *Child Development, 65*, 971–991.

CAUDILL, W., & WEINSTEIN, H. (1969). Maternal care and infant behavior in Japan and America. *Psychiatry, 32*, 12–43.

CENTERS, R. (1975). *Sexual attraction and love: An instrumental theory.* Springfield, IL: Chas. C Thomas.

CHAN, M. (1987). Sudden Infant Death Syndrome and families at risk. *Pediatric Nursing, 13*(3), 166–168.

CHANCE, P. (January 1981). That drained-out, used-up feeling. *Psychology Today,* pp. 88–95.

CHAO, R. K. (1994). Beyond parental control and authoritarian parenting style: Understanding Chinese parenting through the cultural notion of training. *Child Development, 65*, 1111–1119.

CHAPMAN, K. L., & MERVIS, C. B. (1989). Patterns of object-name extension in production. *Journal of Child Language, 16*, 561–571.

CHARLESWORTH, W. (1988). Resources and resource acquisition during ontogeny. In K. B. MacDonald (Ed.), *Sociobiological perspectives on human development.* New York: Springer-Verlag.

CHARNESS, N. (1981). Search in chess: Age and skill differences. *Journal of Experimental Psychology: Human Perception and Performance, 7*, 467–476.

CHASE-LANSDALE, P. L., BROOKS-GUNN, J., & ZAMSKY, E. S. (1994). Young African-American multigenerational families in poverty: Quality of mothering and grandmothering. *Child Development, 65*, 373–393.

CHASNOFF, I. J. (1989). Cocaine, pregnancy and the neonate. *Women and Health, 5*(3), 33.

CHERLIN, A., & FURSTENBERG, F. F. (Summer 1986). Grandparents and family crisis. *Generations,* 26–28.

CHESNICK, M., MENYUK, P., LIEBERGOTT, J., FERRIER, L., & STRAND, K. (April 1983). *Who leads whom?* Paper presented at the meeting of the Society for Research in Child Development, Detroit.

CHESS, S. (1967). Temperament in the normal infant. In J. Hellmuth (Ed.), *The exceptional infant* (Vol. 1). Seattle: Special Child Publications.

CHESS, S. (February 1987). Comments: "Infant day care: A cause for concern." *Zero to Three,* pp. 24–25.

CHICCHETTI, D., & ROGOSCH, F. A. (1997). The role of self-organization in the promotion of resilience in maltreated children. *Development and Psychopathology, 9*, 797–815.

CHILDREN'S DEFENSE FUND. (1991). *The state of America's children, 1991.* Washington, DC: Children's Defense Fund.

CHILDREN'S DEFENSE FUND. (1992). *The State of America's Children 1992.* Washington, DC: Children's Defense Fund.

CHILDREN'S DEFENSE FUND (1994). *The state of America's children yearbook, 1994.* Washington, DC: The Fund.

CHILDREN'S DEFENSE FUND (1998). *The State of America's Children Yearbook 1998.* Washington, DC.

CHILMAN, C. (1979). *Adolescent sexuality in changing American society.* Washington, DC: Government Printing Office.

CHIRIBOGA, D. A. (1981). The developmental psychology of middle age. In J. Howells (Ed.), *Modern perspectives in the psychiatry of middle age.* New York: Brunner/Mazel.

CHIRIBOGA, D. A., & CUTLER, L. (1980). Stress and adaptation: Life span perspectives. In L. W. Poon, (Ed.), *Aging in the 1980s.* Washington, DC: American Psychological Association.

CHOMSKY, C. (1969). *The acquisition of syntax from 5 to 10.* Cambridge, MA: MIT Press.

CHOMSKY, N. (1959). Review of *Verbal Behavior* by B. F. Skinner, *Language, 35*, 26–58.

CHOMSKY, N. (1975). *Reflections on language.* New York: Pantheon.

CHOMSKY, N. (1975). *Reflections on language.* New York: Pantheon.

CHRISTENSEN, H., KORTEN, A., JORM, A. F., HENDERSON, A. S., SCOTT, R., & MACKINNON, A. J. (1996). Activity levels and cognitive functioning in an elderly community sample. *Age and Ageing, 25*, 72–80.

CHUKOVSKY, K. (1963). *From two to five.* (M. Morton Ed. & Trans.). Berkeley: University of California Press.

CICCHETTI, D., & BEEGHLY, M. (1990). Perspectives on the study of the self in transition. In D. Cicchetti & M. Beeghly (Eds.), *The self in transition: Infancy to childhood* (pp. 5–6). Chicago: University of Chicago Press.

CICCHETTI, D. & TOTH, S.L. (1998). The development of depression in children and adolescents. *American Psychologist, 53, 2,* 221–241.

CLARK, E. V. (1983). Meaning and concepts. In P. H. Mussen (Ed.), *Handbook of child psychology* (4th ed., Vol. 4). New York: Wiley.

CLARK, E. V. (1987). The principle of contrast: A constraint on acquisition. In B. Macwhinner (Ed.), *Mechanisms of language acquisition.* Hillsdale, NJ: Erlbaum.

CLARK, J. E., & PHILLIPS, S. J. (1985). A developmental sequence of the standing long jump. In J. E. Clark & J. H. Humphrey (Eds.), *Motor development: Current selected research.* Princeton, NJ: Princeton Book Company.

CLARK, K. (May 31, 1957). *Present threats to children and youth.* Draft Report, manuscript in the office of the National Committee on the Employment of Youth, New York City.

CLARK, R., HYDE, J. S., ESSEX, M. J., & KLEIN, M. H. (1997). *Child Development, 68,* 364–383.

CLARKE, S. C. (March 22, 1995). Advance report of final divorce statistics, 1989 and 1990. *Monthly vital statistics report, U. S. Department of Health and Human Services,* 43(9), 1–4. Washington, DC: Centers for Disease Control and Prevention.

CLARKE-STEWART, A. (1982). *Daycare.* Cambridge, MA: Harvard University Press.

CLARK-STEWART, A. (1988). Parent's effects on children's development: A decade of progress? *Journal of Applied Developmental Psychology, 9,* 41–84.

CLARKE-STEWART, K. A. (1978). And daddy makes three: The father's impact on mother and young child. *Child Development, 49,* 466–478.

CLARKE-STEWART, K. A., & FEIN, G. C. (1983). Early childhood programs. In M. Haith & J. Campos (Eds.), *Handbook of child psychology: Vol. 2. Infancy and developmental psychobiology* (4th ed.). New York: Wiley.

CLARKE-STEWART, K. A., & HEVEY, C. M. (1981). Longitudinal relations in repeated observations of mother–child interaction from 1 to 2½ years. *Developmental Psychology, 17,* 127–145.

CLAUSEN, J. A. (1995). Gender, contexts, and turning points in adults' lives. In Moen, P., Elder, G. H., & Luscher, K. (Eds.) *Examining lives in context: Perspectives on the ecology of human development.* Washington, DC: American Psychological Association.

CLAUSER, J. A. (1986). *The life course: A sociological perspective.* Englewood Cliffs, NJ: Prentice Hall.

CLEIREN, M. (1993). *Bereavement and adaptation: A comparative study of the aftermath of death.* Washington, DC: Hemisphere Publishing.

CLINGENPEEL, G., & SEGAL, S. (1986). Stepparent–stepchild relationships and the psychological adjustment of children in stepmother and stepfather families. *Child Development, 57,* 474–484.

COE, R. (1988). A longitudinal examination of poverty in the elderly years. *The Gerontologist, 28,* 540–544.

COHEN, D., & EISDORFER, K. (1986). *The loss of self: A family resource for the care of Alzheimer's disease and related disorders.* New York: Norton.

COHEN, J. S., & HOGAN, M. E. (1994). The new genetic medicines. *Scientific American 271*(6), 76–82.

COHEN, L. B., & GELBER, E. R. (1975). Infant visual memory. In L. B. Cohen & P. Salapatek (Eds.), *Infant perception: From sensation to cognition* (Vol. 1). New York: Academic Press.

COHEN, N. & FSTNER, L. (1983). *Silent knife: Caesarean prevention and vaginal birth after Caesarean.* South Hadley, MA: Bergin & Garvey.

COHEN, S. (Winter 1992). Life and death: A cross-cultural perspective. *Childhood Education,* 107–108.

COLBY, A., KOHLBERG, L., GIBBS, J., & LIEBERMAN, M. (1983). A longitudinal study of moral development. *Monographs of the Society for Research in Child Development, 48* (1–2 Serial No. 200).

COLE, M. A. (Winter 1979). Sex and marital status differences in death anxiety. *Omega, 9,* 139–147.

COLE, M., & BRUNER, J. S. (1971). Cultural differences and inferences about psychological processes. *American Psychologist, 26,* 867–876.

COLE, P. M., MICHEL, M. K., & TETI, L. O. (1994). The development of emotion regulation and dysregulation: A clinical perspective. In N. A. Fox (Ed.), *Monographs of the Society for Research in Child Development, 59*(2–3), Serial No. 240, 73–100.

COLEMAN, F. W., & COLEMAN, W. S. (1984). Helping siblings and other peers cope with dying. In H. Wass & C. A. Corr, *Childhood and death.* Washington, DC: Hemisphere.

COLEMAN, M., & GANONG, L. (1985). Remarriage myths; Implications for the helping professions. *Journal of Counseling and Development, 64,* 116–120.

COLEMAN, M., & GANONG, L. (1987). The cultural stereotyping of stepfamilies. In K. Pasley & M. Ihinger-Tallman (Eds.), *Remarriage and stepparenting: Current research and theory* (pp. 19–41). New York: Guilford.

COLES, R. (1968). Like it is in the alley. *Daedalus, 97,* 1315–1330.

COLES, R. (1980). *Children of crisis: Privileged ones.* Boston: Atlantic-Little, Brown.

COLEY, R. L., & CHASE-LANSDALE, P. L. (1998). Adolescent pregnancy and parenthood: Recent evidence and future directions. *American Psychologist, 53,* 152–166.

COLLINS, W. A., SOBOL, B. L., & WESTBY, S. (1981). Effects of adult commentary on children's comprehension and inferences about a televised aggressive portrayal. *Child Development, 52,* 158–163.

COLUMBIA UNIVERSITY COLLEGE OF PHYSICIANS AND SURGEONS (1985). *Complete home medical guide.* New York: Crown.

COMBER, L. C., & KEEVES, J. (1973). *Science achievement in nineteen countries.* New York: Wiley.

COMER, J. P., & POUSSAINT, A. F. (1975). *Black child care.* New York: Simon & Schuster.

COMFORT, A. (1976). *A good age.* New York: Crown.

COMMITTEE FOR ECONOMIC DEVELOPMENT. (1987). *Children in need.* Washington, DC: Committee for Economic Development, Research and Policy Committee.

CONNELLY, B., JOHNSTON, D., BROWN, I. D. R., MACKAY, S., & BLACKSTOCK, E. G. (1993). The prevalence of depression in a high school population. *Adolescence, 28*(109), 149–158.

CONNOR, E. M, SPERLING, R. S., GELBER, R., KISELEV, P., SCOTT, G., O'SULLIVAN, M. J., VANDYKE, R., BEY, M., SHEARER, W., JACOBSON, R. L., JIMENEZ, E., O'NEIL, E., BAZIN, B., DELFRAISSY, J., CULNANE, M., COOMBS, R., ELKINS, M., MOYE, J., STRATTON, P., & BALSEY, J. (1994). Reduction of maternal-infant transmission of human immunodeficienty virus type I with zidovudine treatment. *The New England Journal of Medicine, 331,* 1173–1180.

COOK, M., & BIRCH, R. (1984). Infant perception of the shapes of tilted plane forms. *Infant Behavior and Development, 7,* 389–402.

COOPER, K., & GUTTMAN, D. (1987). Gender identity and ego mastery style in middle-aged, pre- and post-empty nest women. *The Gerontologist, 27,* 347–352.

COPPLE, C. E., CLINE, M. G., & SMITH, A. N. (1987). *Path to the future: Long-term effects of Head Start in the Philadelphia school district.* Washington, DC: Office of Human Development Services.

COREN, S. & PORAC, C. (1980). Birth factors and laterality: The effect of birth order, parental age, and birth stress on four indices of lateral preference. *Behavioral Genetics, 10,* 123–138.

COSTA, A. (Ed.). (1985). *Developing minds: A resource book for teaching thinking.* Washington, DC: Association for Supervision and Curriculum Development.

COSTA, A., HANSON, R., SILVER, H., & STRONG, R. (1985). Building a repertoire of strategies. In A. Costa (Ed.), *Developing minds: A resource book for teaching thinking.* Washington, DC: Association for Supervision and Curriculum Development.

COSTA, P. T., & MCCRAE, R. R. (1980). Still stable after all these years: Personality as a key to some issues in adulthood and old age. In P. B. Baltes & O. G. Brim, *Lifespan development and behavior* (Vol. 3). New York: Academic Press.

COSTA, P. T., JR., & MCCRAE, R. R. (1982). An approach to the attribution of aging, period and cohort effects. *Psychological Bulletin, 92,* 238–250.

COSTA, P., & MCCRAE, R. (1985). Hypochondriasis, neuroticism, and aging: When are somatic complaints unfounded? *American Psychologist, 40,* 19–28.

COSTA, P. T., & MCCRAE, R. R. (1994). Set like plaster? Evidence for the stability of adult personality. In T. F. Heatherton, & J. L. Weinberger (Eds.), *Can personality change?* Washington, DC: American Psychological Association. PRIVATE

COSTER, G. (November 1972). *Scientific American,* p. 44.

COSTIN, S. E., & JONES, D.C. (1992). Friendship as a facilitator of emotional responsiveness and prosocial interventions among young children. *Developmental Psychology, 28*(5), 941–947.

CÔTÉ, J. E., & LEVINE, C. (1988). A critical examination of the ego identity status paradigm. *Developmental Review, 8,* 147–184.

COUNCIL OF ECONOMIC ADVISERS. (1987). *The economic report of the president.* Washington, DC.

COUNCIL OF ECONOMIC ADVISERS. (1990). *The economic report of the president.* Washington, DC.

COUNCIL ON SCIENTIFIC AFFAIRS (January 9, 1991). Hispanic health in the United States. *Journal of the American Medical Association, 365*(2), 248–252.

COWAN, C. P., & COWAN, P. A. (1992). When partners become parents: The big life change for couples. New York: Basic Books.

COWAN, P. A., & WALTERS, R. H. (1963). Studies of reinforcement of aggression: I. Effects of scheduling. *Child Development, 34,* 543–551.

COWGILL, D. O. (1972a). The role and status of the aged in Thailand. In D. O. Cowgill & L. D. Holmes (Eds.), *Aging and modernization.* New York: Appleton-Century-Crofts.

COWGILL, D. O. (1972b). Aging in American society. In D. O. Cowgill & L. D. Holmes (Eds.), *Aging and modernization.* New York: Appleton-Century-Crofts.

COX, H., & BHAK, A. (1979). Symbolic interaction and retirement adjustment: An empirical asset. *International Journal of Aging and Human Development, 9*(3), 279–286.

CRAIG, G. J., & GARNEY, P. (1972). *Attachment and separation behavior in the second and third years.* Unpublished manuscript. University of Massachusetts, Amherst.

CRAIK, F. I. M., & MCDOWD, J. M. (1987). Age differences in recall and recognition. *Journal of Experimental Psychology: Learning, Memory, and Cognition, 13*(3), 474–479.

CRATTY, B. (1986). *Perceptual and motor development in infants and children.* Englewood Cliffs, NJ: Prentice Hall.

CRATTY, B. J. (1970). *Perceptual and motor development in infants and children.* New York: Macmillan.

CRAWFORD, J. W. (1982). Mother–infant interaction in premature and full-term infants. *Child Development, 53,* 957–962.

CRICK, N. R., & LADD, G. W. (1993). Children's perceptions of their peer experiences: Attributions, loneliness, social anxiety, and social avoidance. *Developmental Psychology, 28*(2), 244–254.

CRIDER, C. (1981). Children's conceptions of body interior. In R. Bibace & M. E. Walsh (Eds.), *Children's conceptions of health, illness, and bodily functions.* San Francisco: Jossey-Bass.

CROCKENBERG, S. (1981). Infant irritability, mother responsiveness, and social support influences on the security of infant–mother attachment. *Child Development, 52,* 857–865.

CROCKENBERG, S., & MCCLUSKEY, K. (1986). Change in maternal behavior during the baby's first year of life. *Child Development, 57,* 746–753.

CROCKETT, W. H., & HUMMERT, M. L. (1987). Perceptions of aging and the elderly. In K. Warner Schaie & K. Eisdorfer (Eds.), *Annual review of gerontology and geriatrics* (Vol. 7, pp. 217–241). New York: Springer.

CROSS, K. P. (1981). *Adults as learners.* San Francisco: Jossey-Bass.

CRUICKSHANK, W. M. (1977). Myths and realities in learning disabilities. *Learning Disabilities, 10*(1), 57–64.

CSIKSZENTMIHALYI, M., & LARSON, R. (1984). *Being adolescent.* New York: Basic Books.

CUMMING, E., & HENRY, W. E. (1961). *Growing old: The process of disengagement.* New York: Basic Books.

CUMMINGS ET AL. (1994). Responses of physically abused boys to interadult anger involving their mothers. *Development and Psychopathology, 6,* 31–41.

CURRAN, D. K. (1987). Adolescent suicidal behavior. Washington, DC: Hemisphere Publishing.

CUTRONA, C., & TROUTMAN, B. (1986). Social support, infant temperament, and parenting self-efficacy: A mediational model of postpartum depression. *Child Development, 57,* 1507–1518.

CYTRYNBAUM, S., BLUM, L., PATRICK, R., STEIN, J., WADNER, D., & WILK, C. (1980). Midlife development: A personality and social systems perspective. In L. W. Poon (Ed.), *Aging in the 1980s.* Washington, DC: American Psychological Association.

DAHL, B. (1994). Windows on the world: Using literature to integrate curriculum. *The Computing Teacher, 27–30.*

DAIUTE, C. (1993). Synthesis. In C. Daiute (Ed.), *New directions in child development (61),* (pp. 121–124). San Francisco: Jossey-Bass.

DAIUTE, C., ET AL. (1993). Young authors' interactions with peers and a teacher: Toward a developmentally sensitive sociocultural literacy theory. In C. Daiute (Ed.), *New directions in child development (61)* (pp. 41–66). San Francisco: Jossey-Bass.

DALEY, S. (January 9, 1991) Girls self-esteem is lost on the way to adolescence, new study finds. *New York Times Magazine.*

DAMON, W. (1991). *The moral child: Nurturing children natural moral growth.* New York: Free Press.

DAMON, W., & HART, D. (1982). The development of self-understanding from infancy through adolescence. *Child Development, 53,* 841–864.

DAMON, W. & HART, D. (1992). Self understanding and it's role in social and moral development. In M. H. Bornstein & M. E. Lamb (Eds.), *Developmental Psychology: An advanced textbook.* Hillsdale, N.J.: Lawrence Erlbaum.

DAN, A. J., & BERNHARD, L. A. (1989). Menopause and other health issues for midlife women. In S. Hunter & M. Sundel, *Midlife myths: Issues, findings, and practice implications* (pp. 56–59). Newberry Park, CA: Sage.

DANIELS, P., & WEINGARTEN, K. (1982). *Sooner or later: The timing of parenthood in adult lives.* New York: Norton.

DANSEREAU, H. K. (1961). Work and the teenager. *Annals of the American Academy of Political and Social Sciences, 338,* 44–52.

DARGASSIES, S. S. (1986). *The neuromotor and psychoaffective development of the infant* (English language edition). Amsterdam, the Netherlands: Elsevier.

DARLING, N., & STEINBERG, L. (1993). Parenting style as context: An integrative model. *Psychological Bulletin, 113,* 487–496.

DARWIN, C. (1859). *On the origin of the species.* London: Murray.

DATAN, N., & GINSBERG, L. (Eds.). (1975). *Lifespan developmental psychology.* New York: Academic Press.

DAVIDSON, J. I. (1996). *Emergent literacy and dramatic play in early education.* New York: Delmar.

DAVIDSON, N. E. (1996). Current controversies: Is hormone replacement therapy a risk? *Scientific American, 275, September,* 101.

DAVIES, B. (Winter 1993). Caring for the frail elderly: An international perspective. *Generations,* Vol. 17, (4), 51–54.

DAWDAON-HUGHES, B., ET AL. (September 27, 1990). A controlled trial of the effect of calcium supplementation on bone density in postmenopausal women. *New England Journal of Medicine, 323(130),* 878–883.

DAWSON, D. A. (August 1991). Family structure and children's health and well-being: Data from the 1988 National Health Interview Survey on child health. *Journal of Marriage and the Family, 53,* 573–584.

DAY, D. E., PERKINS, E. P., & WEINTHALER, J. A. (1979). *Naturalistic evaluation for program improvement.* Unpublished monograph.

DEAN, P. G. (1986). Monitoring an apneic infant: Impact on the infant's mother. *Maternal-Child Nursing Journal, 15,* 65–76.

DE BOYSSON-BARDIES, B., HALLE, P., SAGART, L., & DURAND, C. (1989). A crosslinguistic investigation of vowel formants in babbling. *Journal of Child Language, 16,* 1–17.

DECHARMS, R., & MOELLER, G. H. (1962). Values expressed in American children's readers: 1800–1950. *Journal of Abnormal and Social Psychology, 64,* 136–142.

DEIMLING, G., & BASS, D. (1986). Symptoms of mental impairment among elderly adults and their effects on family caregivers. *Journal of Gerontology, 41,* 778–784.

DEKKER, R., ET AL. (1987). *Willingness to change.* The Hague: Ministry of Welfare, Health and Cultural Affairs.

DELOACHE, J. S., CASSIDY, D. J., & BROWN, A. L. (1985). Precursors of mnemonic strategies in very young children's memory. *Child Development, 56,* 125–137.

DELOACHE, J. S. (1987). Rapid change in the symbolic functioning of young children. *Science, 238,* 1556–1557.

DEMARIS, A., & LESLIE, G. (February 1984). Cohabitation with a future spouse: Its influence upon marital satisfaction and communication. *Journal of Marriage and the Family, 46,* 77–84.

DEMAUSE, L. (Ed.). (1974). *The history of childhood.* New York: Psychohistory Press.

DEMOTT, R. K., & SANDMIRE, H. F. (1990). *The Green Bay Caesarean section study: The physician factor as a determinant of Caesarean birth rates.* Presented at the fifty-seventh annual meeting of the Central Association of Obstetricians and Gynecologists, Scottsdale, AZ.

DENCIK, L. (1989). Growing up in the postmodern age: On the child's situation in the modern family, and on the position of the family in the modern welfare state. *Acta Sociologica, 32,* 155–180.

DENNEY, N. (1982). Aging and cognitive changes. In B. Wolman (Ed.), *Handbook of developmental psychology* (pp. 807–827). Englewood Cliffs, NJ: Prentice Hall.

DENNIS, W. (1960). Causes of retardation among institutional children: Iran. *Journal of Genetic Psychology, 96,* 47–59.

DENNIS, W. (1966a). Causes of retardation among institutional children: Iran. *Journal of Genetic Psychology, 96,* 47–59.

DENNIS, W. (1966b). Creative productivity between the ages of 20 and 80 years. *Journal of Gerontology, 21(1),* 1–8.

DENNIS, W. (1973). *Children of the creche.* New York: Appleton-Century-Crofts.

DENNIS, W., & NAJARIAN, P. (1957). Infant development under environmental handicap. *Psychological Monographs, 717* (Whole No. 436).

DERR, C. B. (1986). *Managing the new careerists.* San Francisco: Jossey-Bass.

DESPELDER, L., & STRICKLAND, A. (1983). *The last dance: Encountering death and dying.* Palo Alto, CA: Mayfield.

DE VILLIERS, P. A., & DE VILLIERS, J. G. (1979). *Early language.* Cambridge, MA: Harvard University Press.

DE VILLIERS, P. A., & DE VILLIERS, J. G. (1992). Language development. In M. H. Borstein & M. Lamb (Eds.), *Developmental psychology: An advanced textbook.* (3rd ed., pp. 344–345). Hillsdale, NJ: Erlbaum.

DEWEY, J. (1961). *Democracy and education.* New York: Macmillan.

DE WOLFF, M. S., & VAN IJZENDOORN, M. H. (1997). Sensitivity and attachment: A meta-analysis on parental antecedences of infant attachment. *Child Development, 68,* 571–591.

DIAZ, R. M. (1985). Bilingual cognitive development: Addressing three gaps in current research. *Child Development, 56,* 1376–1388.

DIAZ, R. M., & LOWE, J. R. (1987). The private speech of young children at risk: A test of three deficit hypotheses. *Early Childhood Research Quarterly, 2,* 181–184.

DICK-READ, G. (1953). *Childbirth without fear.* New York: Harper & Brothers.

DIETZ, W. H., JR. (1987). Childhood obesity. *Annals of the New York Academy of Sciences, 499,* 47–54.

DIPETRO, J. A. (1981). Rough and tumble play: A function of gender. *Developmental Psychology, 17,* 50–58.

DITZION, J. S., & WOLF, P. W. (1978). Beginning parenthood. In Boston Women's Book Collective (Ed.), *Ourselves and our children.* New York: Random House.

DIXON, R. A. (1992). Contextual approaches to adult intellectual development. In R. J. Sternberg & C. A. Berg (Eds.) *Intellectual development.* New York: Cambridge University Press.

DODGE, K. A., COIE, J. D., PETTIT, G. S., & PRICE, J. M. (1990). Peer status and aggression in boys' groups: Developmental and contextual analyses. *Child Development, 61,* 1289–1309.

DODGE, K. A., PETTIT, G. S., & BATES, J. E. (1994). Effects of physical maltreatment on the development of peer relations. *Development and Psychopathology, 6,* 43–55.

DODWELL, P., HUMPHREY, G. K., & MUIR, D. (1987). Shape and pattern perception. In P. Salapatek & L. Cohen (Eds.), *Handbook of infant perception.* New York: Academic Press.

DOKA, K., & MERTZ, M. (1988). The meaning and significance of great-grandparenthood. *The Gerontologist, 28,* 192–197.

DOLL, R. (March 1993). Alzheimer's disease and environmental aluminum. *Age and Aging, 22(2),* 138.

DOLLARD, J., DOOB, L. W., MILLER, N. E., MOWRER, O. H., & SEARS, R. R. (1939). *Frustration and aggression.* New Haven: Yale University Press.

DOLLARD, J., & MILLER, N. E. (1950). *Personality and psychotherapy: An analysis in terms of learning, thinking, and culture.* New York: McGraw-Hill.

DOMAN, G. (1963). *How to teach your baby to read.* New York: Random House.

DONALDSON, M. (1978). *Children's minds.* New York: Norton.

DONALDSON, M. (1979). The mismatch between school and children's minds. *Human Nature, 2,* 158–162.

DONOVAN, B. (1986). *The Caesarean birth experience.* Boston: Beacon Press.

DONOVAN, J. E., JESSOR, R., & COSTA, F. M. (1988). Syndrome of problem behavior in adolescence: A replication. *Journal of Consulting and Clinical Psychology, 56,* 762–765.

DONOVAN, J.E., JESSOR, R., & COSTA, F.M. (1988). Syndrome of problem behavior in adolescence: A replication. *Journal of Consulting and Clinical Psychology, 56,* 762–765.

DONOVAN, R. (February–March 1984). Planning for an aging work force. *Aging,* pp. 4–7.

DORNBUSCH, S. M., CARLSMITH, J. M., BUSHWALL, S. J., RITTER, P. L., LEIDERMAN, H., HASTORF, A. H., & GROSS, R. T. (1985). Single parents, extended households, and the control of adolescents. *Child Development, 56,* 326–341.

DORNBUSCH, S. M., RITTER, P. L., LEIDERMAN, P. H., ROBERTS, D. F., & FRALEIGH, M. J. (1987). The relation of parenting style to adolescent school performance. *Child Development, 58,* 1244–1257.

DOUVAN, E., & ADELSON, J. B. (1966). *The adolescent experience.* New York: Wiley.

DOUVAN, E., & GOLD, M. (1966). Modal patterns in American adolescence. In L. W. Hoffman & M. L. Hoffman (Eds.), *Review of child development research* (Vol. 2). New York: Russell Sage Foundation.

DOYLE, A. B., BEAUDET, J., & ABOUD, F. (1988). Developmental patterns in the flexibility of children's ethnic attitudes. *Journal of Cross-Cultural Research, 19*(1), 3–18.

DRAPER, T. W., & JAMES, R. S. (1985). Preschool fears: Longitudinal sequence and cohort changes. *Child Study Journal, 15*(2), 147–155.

DREIKURS, R., & SOLTZ, V. (1964). *Children: The challenge.* New York: Duell, Sloan & Pearce.

DRESSEL, P. (1988). Gender, race, and class: Beyond the feminization of poverty in later life. *The Gerontologist, 28,* 177–180.

DREYER, P. H. (1982). Sexuality during adolescence. In B. Wolman (Ed.), *Handbook of developmental psychology.* Englewood Cliffs, NJ: Prentice Hall.

DROEGE, R. (1982). *A psychosocial study of the formation of the middle adult life structure in women.* Unpublished doctoral dissertation. California School of Professional Psychology, Berkeley.

DROTAR, D. (Ed.). (1985). *New directions in failure to thrive: Implications for research and practice.* New York: Plenum.

DUBIN, S. (1972). Obsolescence or life-long education: A choice for the professional. *American Psychologist, 17,* 486–498.

DUBRIN, A. (1978). Psychological factors: Reentry and mid-career crises. In *Women in midlife-security and fulfillment* (pp. 180–185). Washington, DC: Government Printing Office.

DUCK, S. (1983). *Friends for life: The psychology of close relationships.* Brighton, UK: Harvester Press.

DUNLAP, D. W. (October 18, 1994). Gay survey raises a new question. *New York Times,* p. B8.

DUNN, J. (1983). Sibling relationships in early childhood. *Child Development, 54,* 787–811.

DUNN, J. (1985). *Sisters and brothers.* Cambridge, MA: Harvard University Press.

DUNN, J. (1986). Growing up in a family world: Issues in the study of social development of young children. In M. Richards & P. Light (Eds.), *Children of social worlds: Development in a social context.* Cambridge, MA: Harvard University Press.

DUNN, J. (1993). Young children's close relationships: Beyond attachment (pp. 48–51). Newberry Park, CA: Sage.

DUNN, J., & BROWN, J. (1991). Becoming American or English? Talking about the social world in England and the United States (pp. 155–171).

DUNN, J., & KENDRICK, C. (1979). Interaction between young siblings in the context of family relationships. In M. Lewis & L. Rosenblum (Eds.), *The child and its family: The genesis of behavior* (Vol. 2). New York: Plenum.

DUNN, J., & KENDRICK, C. (1980). The arrival of a sibling: Changes in interaction between mother and first-born child. *Journal of Child Psychology, 21,* 119–132.

DUNN, J., & KENDRICK, C. (1982). *Siblings: Love, envy and understanding.* Cambridge, MA: Harvard University Press.

DUNN, J., & MUNN, P. (1985). Becoming a family member: Family conflict and the development of social understanding in the second year. *Child Development, 56,* 480–492.

DUNN, J., & MUNN, P. (1987). Development of justification in disputes with mother and sibling. *Developmental Psychology, 23,* 791–798.

DUNPHY, D. C. (1963). The social structure of urban adolescent peer groups. *Sociometry, 26,* 230–246.

DUNPHY, D. C. (1980). Peer group socialization. In R. Muuss (Ed.). *Adolescent behavior and society* (3rd ed.). New York: Random House.

DURLAK, J. A. (1979). Comparison between experimental and didactic methods of death education. *Omega, 9,* 57–66.

DWYER, T., PONSONBY, A. B., NEWMAN, N. M. & GIBBONS, L. E. (1991). Prospective cohort study of prone sleeping position and sudden infant death syndrome. *The Lancet, 337,* 1244–1247.

DYSON, A. H. (1993). A sociocultural perspective on symbolic development in primary grade classrooms. In C. Daiute (Ed.), *New directions in child development, (61)* (pp. 25–40). San Francisco: Jossey-Bass.

DYSON, L. L. (1996). The experiences of families of children with learning disabilities: Parental stress, family functioning, and sibling self-concept. *Journal of Learning Disabilities, 29,* 280–286.

EAKINS, P. S. (Ed.), (1986). *The American way of birth.* Philadelphia: Temple University Press.

EATON, W. O., & YU, A. P. (1989). Are sex differences in child motor activity level a function of sex differences in maturational status? *Child Development, 60,* 1005–1011.

EBERSOLE, P. (1979). The vital vehicle: The body. In I. M. Burnside, P. Ebersole, & H. E. Monea (Eds.), *Psychosocial caring throughout the life span.* New York: McGraw-Hill.

ECCLES, J., ET AL. (1993). Age and gender differences in children's self- and task perceptions during elementary school. *Child Development, 64,* 830–847.

EDDY, D. M. (1991). The individual vs. society: Is there a conflict? *Journal of the American Medical Association, 265*(11), 1446–1450.

EDELSTEIN, L. (1984). *Maternal bereavement.* New York: Praeger.

EDWARDS, C. P., & GANDINI, L. (1989). Teachers' expectations about the timing of developmental skills: A cross-cultural study. *Young Children, 44*(4), 15–19.

EGELUND, B., PIANTA, R., & O'BRIEN, M. A. (1993). Maternal intrusiveness in infancy and child maladaptation in early school years. *Development and Psychopathology, 5,* 359–370.

EIBL-EIBESFELDT, I. (1989). *Human ethology.* New York: Aldine de Gruyter.

EICHORN, D. (1979). Physical development: Current foci of research. In J. D. Osofsky (Ed.), *Handbook of infant development* (pp. 253–282). New York: Wiley.

EIMAS, P. D. (1974). Linguistic processing of speech by young infants. In R. L. Schiefelbusch & L. L. Lloyd (Eds.), *Language perspectives: Acquisition, retardation, and intervention.* Baltimore: University Park Press.

EIMAS, P. D. (1975). Speech perception in early infancy. In Lin L. B. Cohen & P. Salapatek (Eds.), *Infant perception: From sensation to cognition* (Vol. 2), New York: Academic Press.

EIMAS, P. D., & QUINN, P. C. (1994). Studies on the formation of perceptually based basic-level categories in young infants. *Child Development, 65,* 903–917.

EISENBERG, N. (1988). The development of prosocial and aggressive behavior. In M. Bornstein & M. Lamb (Eds.), *Developmental psychology: An advanced textbook* (2nd ed.). Hillsdale, NJ: Erlbaum.

EISENBERG, N. (1989). Empathy and sympathy. In W. Damon (Ed.), *Child development today and tomorrow* (pp. 137–154). San Francisco: Jossey-Bass.

EISENBERG, N. (1989a). *The development of prosocial moral reasoning in childhood and mid-adolescence.* Paper presented at the April meeting of the Society for Research in Child Development, Kansas City.

EISENBERG, N. (1989b). The development of prosocial values. In N. Eisenberg, J. Reykowski, & E. Staub (Eds.), *Social and moral values: Individual and social perspectives.* Hillsdale, NJ: Erlbaum.

EISENBERG, N., PASTERNACK, J. F., CAMEROR, E., & TRYON, K. (1984). The relation of quantity and mode of prosocial behavior to moral cognitions and social style. *Child Development, 55,* 1479–1485.

EISENBERG, N., SHELL, R., PASTERNACK J., BELLER, R., LENNON, R., & MATHY, R. (1987). Prosocial development in middle childhood: A longitudinal study. *Developmental Psychology, 23*(5), 712–718.

EISENDORFER, D., & WILKIE, F. (1977). Stress, disease, aging and behavior. In J. E. Birren & K. W. Schaie (Eds.), *Handbook of the psychology of aging.* New York: Van Nostrand Reinhold.

EKERDT, D. (1987). Why the notion persists that retirement harms the health. *The Gerontologist, 27*(4), 454–457.

EKERDT, D., VINICK, B., & BOSSE, R. (1989). Orderly endings: Do men know when they will retire? *Journal of Gerontology, 44,* S28–35.

ELBEDOUR, S., BENSEL, R. T., & BASTIEN, D. T. (1993). Ecological integrated model of children of war: Individual and social psychology. *Child Abuse & Neglect, 17,* 805–819.

ELBERS, L., & TON, J. (1985). Play pen monologues: The interplay of words and babbles in the first words period. *Journal of Child Language, 12,* 551–565.

ELDER, G. H. (1980). Adolescence in historical perspective. In J. Adelson (Ed.), *Handbook of adolescent psychology.* New York: Wiley.

ELDER, G. II., & CASPI, I. (1990). Studying lives in a changing society. In Rubin, A. I., Zucher, R. A., Frank, S., & Emmons, R. (Eds.), *Study in persons and lives.* New York: Springer.

ELDER, J. L., & PEDERSON, D. R. (1978). Preschool children's use of objects in symbolic play. *Child Development, 49,* 500–504.

ELDER, L., CASPI, A., & BURTON, L. (1988). Adolescent transition in developmental perspective: Sociological and historical insights. In M. Gunnar & W. Collins (Eds.), *Minnesota Symposia on Child Development: Vol. 21. Development during the transition to adolescence* (pp. 151–179). Hillsdale, NJ: Erlbaum.

ELIAS, J. W., & MARSHALL, P. H. (Eds.). (1987). *Cardiovascular disease and behavior.* Washington, DC: Hemisphere.

ELIAS, M. J. (1997). Computer-facilitated counseling for at-risk students in a social problem solving "lab." *Elementary School Guidance and Counseling, 31,* 293–309.

ELKIND, D. (1967). Egocentrism in adolescence. *Child Development, 38,* 1025–1034.

ELKIND, D. (1974). *Children and adolescents: Interpretive essays on Jean Piaget.* New York: Oxford University Press.

ELKIND, D. (1981). *The hurried child.* Reading, MA: Addison-Wesley.

ELKIND, D. (1984). *All grown up and no place to go: Teenagers in crisis.* Reading, MA: Addison-Wesley.

ELKIND, D. (May 1986). Formal education and early childhood education: An essential difference. *Phi Delta Kappan,* pp. 631–636.

ELKIND, D. (1987). *Miseducation: Preschoolers at risk.* New York: Knopf.

ELKIND, D., & BOWEN, R. (1979). Imaginary audience behavior in children and adolescents. *Developmental Psychology, 15,* 38–44.

ELLWOOD, D., & CRANE, J. (1990). Family change among black Americans: What do we know? *Journal of Economic Perspectives, 4,* 65–84.

ELMER-DEWITT, P. (0ctober 17, 1994). Now for the truth about Americans and sex. *Time,* p. 62ff.

EMDE, R. N., & BUCHSBAUN, H. K. (1990). "Didn't you hear my Mommy?" Autonomy with connectedness in moral self-emergence. In D. Cicchetti & M. Beeghly (Eds.), The self in transition: Infancy to childhood (pp. 35–52). Chicago: University of Chicago Press.

EMERY, R. E. (1989). Family violence. *American Psychologist, 44,* 321–328.

ENTWISLE, D. (1985). Becoming a parent. In L. L'Abate (Ed.), *The handbook of family psychology and therapy.* (Vol. 1, pp. 560–578). Homewood IL: Dorsey.

ENTWISLE, D. R., & DOERING, S. (1988). The emergent father role. *Sex Roles, 18,* 119–141.

EPSTEIN, J. L. (1983). Selecting friends in contrasting secondary school environments. In J. L. Epstein & M. L. Karweit (Eds.), *Friends in school.* New York: Academic Press.

EPSTEIN, L. H., VALOSKI, A., WING, R. R., & MCCURLEY, J. (1990). Ten-year follow-up of behavioral, family-based treatment for obese children. *Journal of the American Medical Association, 264,* 2519–2523.

EPSTEIN, L. H., & WING, R. R. (1987). Behavioral treatment of childhood obesity. *Psychological Bulletin, 101,* 331–342.

ERICSSON, K. A. (1990). Peak performance in sports. In P. B. Baltes & M. M. Baltes (Eds.), *Successful Aging: Perspectives from the Behavioral Sciences.* New York: Cambridge University Press.

ERIKSON, E. H. (1959). The problem of ego identity. In E. H. Erikson (Ed.), *Identity and the life cycle: Selected papers. Psychological Issues Monograph,* No. 1.

ERIKSON, E. H. (1963). *Childhood and society* (2nd ed.). New York: Norton.

ERIKSON, E. H. (1968). *Identity, youth, and crisis.* New York: Norton.

ERIKSON, E. H. (1981). On generativity and identity. *Harvard Educational Review, 51,* 249–269.

ERIKSON, E. (1985). *Young man Luther.* New York: Norton.

ERIKSON, E. H., & ERIKSON, J. M. (1981). Generativity and identity. *Harvard Educational Review, 51,* 249–269.

ERIKSON, E. H., ERIKSON, J., & KIVNICK, H. (1986) *Vital involvement in old age.* New York: Norton.

ERNST, C., & ANGST, J. (1983). *Birth order: Its influence on personality.* New York: Springer-Verlag.

ESTERBROOK, M. A., & GOLDBERG, W. A. (1984). Toddler development in the family: Impact of father involvement and parenting characteristics. *Child Development, 55,* 740–752.

EVANS, D. W., LECKMAN, J. F., CARTER, A., REZNICK, J. S., HENSHAW, D., KING, R. A., & PAULS, D. (1997). Ritual, habit, and perfectionism: The prevalence and development of compulsive-like behavior in normal young children. *Child Development, 68,* 58–68.

EVANS, D., FUNKENSTEIN, H., ALBERT, M., SCHERR, P., COOK, N., CHOWN, M.,

HEBERT, L., HENNCKENS, C., & TAYLOR, D. (1989). Prevalence of Alzheimer's disease in a community population of older people. *Journal of the American Medical Association, 262,* 2551–2556.

EVANS, E. D. (1975). *Contemporary influences in early childhood education* (2nd ed.). New York: Holt, Rinehart & Winston.

EVELETH, P. B., & TANNER, J. M. (1976). *Worldwide variation in human growth.* New York: Cambridge University Press.

FABES, R. A., WILSON, P., & CHRISTOPHER, F. S. (1989). A time to reexamine the role of television in family life. *Family Relations, 38,* 337–341.

FADIMAN, A. (February 1982). The skeleton at the feast: A case study of anorexia nervosa. *Life,* pp. 63–78.

FAGAN, J. F., III. (1977). Infant recognition memory: Studies in forgetting. *Child Development, 48,* 66–78.

FAGEN, J., PRIGOT, J., CARROLL, M., PIOLI, L., STEIN, A., & FRANCO, A. (1997). Auditory context and memory retrieval in young infants. *Child Development, 68,* 1057–1066.

FAGOT, B. I., LEINBACH, M. A. & O'BOYLE, C. (1992). Gender labeling, gender stereotyping and parenting behaviors. *Developmental Psychology, 28,* 225–231.

FANTZ, R. L. (1958). Pattern vision in young infants. *Psychological Record, 8,* 43–47.

FANTZ, R. L. (May 1961). The origin of form perception. *Scientific American,* pp. 66–72.

FANTZ, R. L., ORDY, J. M., & UDELF, M. S. (1962). Maturation of pattern vision in infants during the first six months. *Journal of Comparative and Physiological Psychology, 55,* 907–917.

FARB, P. (1978). *Humankind.* Boston: Houghton Mifflin.

FARBER, J. (1970). *The student as nigger.* New York: Pocket Books.

FARBER, S. (January 1981). Telltale behavior of twins. *Psychology Today,* pp. 58–64.

FARRELL, M. P., & ROSENBERG, S. D. (1981). *Men at midlife.* Boston: Auburn House.

FARVER, J. A. M., & SHIN, Y. L. (1997). Social pretend play in Korean- and Anglo-American preschoolers. *Child Development, 68,* 544–556.

FAVIA, S., AND GENOVESE, R. (1983). Family, work and individual development in dual-career marriages. In H. Lopata & J. H. Pleck (Eds.), *Research in the interweave of social roles: Jobs and families* (Vol. 3). Greenwich, CT: JAI Press.

FEATHERMAN, D., HOGAN, D., & SORENSON, A. (1984). Entry into adulthood: Profiles of young men in the fifties. In *Life span development and behavior* (Vol. 6). New York: Academic Press.

FEATHERSTONE, H. (June 1985). Preschool: It does make a difference. *Harvard Education Letter,* pp. 16–21.

FEATHERSTONE, M., & HEPWORTH, M. (1985). The male menopause: Lifestyle and sexuality. *Maturitas, 7*(3), 235–246.

FEDOR-FREYBERGH, P., & VOGEL, M. L. V. (1988). *Prenatal and perinatal psychology and medicine.* Carnforth, Lanc: Parthenon.

FEHR, B. (1996). *Friendship processes.* Thousand Oaks, CA: Sage.

FEIN, G. G. (1981). Pretend play in childhood: An integrated review. *Child Development, 52,* 1095–1118.

FEIN, G. G. (1984). The self-building potential of pretend play, or "I gotta fish all by myself." In T. D. Yawkey & A. D. Pellegrini (Eds.), *Child's play.* Hillsdale, NJ: Erlbaum.

FEINGOLD, A. (1988). Cognitive gender differences are disappearing. *American Psychologist, 43(2),* 95–103.

FEIRING, C., LEWIS, M., & STARR, M. D. (1984). Indirect affects and infants' reactions to strangers. *Developmental Psychology, 20,* 485–491.

FEITELSEN, W., & ROSS, G. S. (1973). The neglected factor—play. *Human Development, 16,* 202–223.

FELDMAN, R. S. (1998). *Social psychology* (2nd ed.). Upper Saddle River, NJ: Prentice Hall.

FELGNER, T. (1997). Nonviral strategies for gene therapy. *Scientific American, 276 (6),* 102–106.

FENSON, L., ET AL. (1994). Variability in early communicative development. *Monographs of the Society for Research in Child Development, 59(5),* Serial No. 242, 92–93.

FERBER, M. (1982). Labor market participation of young married women: Causes and effects. *Journal of Marriage and the Family, 44,* 457–468.

FERBER, M., GREEN, C., & SPAITH, J. (1986). Work power and earnings of women and men. *American Economic Review, 76,* 53–56.

FERGUSON, C., & SNOW, C. (1977). *Talking to children: Language input and acquisition.* Cambridge, UK: Cambridge University Press.

FERLEGER, N., GLENWICK, D. S., GAINES, R. R. W., & GREEN, A. H. (1988). Identifying correlates of reabuse in maltreating parents. *Child Abuse and Neglect, 12,* 41–49.

FESHBACK, S., & SINGER, R. D. (1971). *Television and aggression: An experimental field study.* San Francisco: Jossey-Bass.

FIATARONE, M. A., ET AL. (June 23, 1994). Exercise training and nutritional supplementation for physical fraility in very elderly people. *New England Journal of Medicine, 330(25),* 1–6.

FIELD, T. (1977). Effects of early separation, interactive deficits, and experimental manipulations on infant–mother face-to-face interaction. *Child Development, 48,* 763–771.

FIELD, T. (1978). Interaction behaviors of primary vs. secondary caretaker fathers. *Developmental Psychology, 14(2),* 183–184.

FIELD, T. M. (1979). Interaction patterns of pre-term and term infants. In T. M. Field (Ed.), *Infants born at risk.* New York: Spectrum.

FIELD, T. (1986). Models for reactive and chronic depression in infancy. In E. Tronick & T. Fields (Eds.), *New Directions for Child Development, 34. Maternal depression and infant disturbance.*

FIELD, T. (1991). Quality infant day-care and grade school behavior and performance. *Child Development, 62,* 863–870.

FIELDING, J. E., & WILLIAMS, C. A. (1991). Adolescent pregnancy in the United States: A review and recommendations for clinicians and research needs. *American Journal of Preventive Medicine, 7(1),* 47–51.

FIELDS, M. V., & SPANGLIER, K. L. (1995). *Let's begin reading right: Developmentally appropriate beginning literacy* (3rd ed). Englewood Cliffs, NJ: Merrill.

FILIPOVIC, Z. (1994). *Zlata's Diary: A Child's Life in Sarajevo.* Quoted in *Newsweek,* February 28, 1994, pp. 25–27.

FILLMORE, C. J. (1968). The case for case. In E. Bach & R. T. Harms (Eds.), *Universals of linguistic theory.* New York: Holt, Rinehart & Winston.

FINCHER, J. (July/August 1982). Before their time. *Science 82 Magazine,* p. 94.

FINKELHOR, D. (1984). *Child sexual abuse: New theory and practice.* New York: Free Press.

FINN, R. (1996). Biological determination of sexuality heating up as a research field. *The Scientist, 10,* Jan. 8, 13–16.

FISCHER, D. H. (1978). *Growing old in America.* New York: Oxford University Press.

FISCHER, J. L., SOLLIE, D. L., & MORROW, K. B. (1986). Social networks in male and female adolescents. *Journal of Adolescent Research, 6(1),* 1–14.

FISKE, M. (1968). *Adult transitions: Theory and research from a longitudinal perspective.* Paper presented at the meeting of the Gerontological Society.

FISKE, M. (1980). Tasks and crises of the second half of life: The interrelationship of commitment, caring and adaptation. In J. E. Birren & R. B. Sloane (Eds.), *Handbook of mental health and aging.* Englewood Cliffs, NJ: Prentice Hall.

FISKE, M., & CHIRIBOGA, D. A. (1990). *Change and continuity in adult life.* San Francisco: Jossey-Bass.

FITZCHARLES, A. (February 1987). Model versus modal child care. *Zero to Three,* p. 26.

FIVUSH, R., & HUDSON, J. A. (1990). *Knowing and remembering in young children.* New York: Cambridge University Press.

FLASTE, R. (October 1988). The myth about teenagers. *New York Times Magazine,* pp. 19, 76, 82, 85.

FLAVELL, J. H. (1963). *The developmental psychology of Jean Piaget.* Princeton, NJ: Van Nostrand Reinhold.

FLAVELL, J. H. (1977). *Cognitive development.* Englewood Cliffs, NJ: Prentice Hall.

FLAVELL, J. H. (1985). *Cognitive development* (2nd ed.). Englewood Cliffs, NJ: Prentice Hall.

FLAVELL, J. H., FLAVELL, E. R., & GREEN, F. L. (1987). Young children's knowledge about the apparent-real and pretend-real distinctions. *Developmental Psychology, 23,* 816–822.

FLAVELL, J. H., GREEN, F., & FLAVELL, E. R. (1986). Development of knowledge about the appearance-reality distortion. *Monographs of the Society for Research in Child Development, 212.*

FLAVELL, J. H., MILLER, P. H. & MILLER, S. A. (1993). *Cognitive Development.* Englewood Cliffs, NJ: Prentice Hall.

FLINT, M. (1982). Male and female menopause: A cultural put-on. In A. Voda, M. Dennerstein, & S. O'Donnel (Eds.), *Changing perspectives in menopause* (pp. 363–375). Austin: University of Texas Press.

FOGEL, A., DICKSON, K. L., HSU, H., MESSINGER, D., NELSON-GOENS, G. C., & NWOKAH, E. (1997). Communication of smiling and laughter in mother-infant play: Research on emotion from a dynamic systems perspective. In Barrett, K. C. (Ed.), *The communication of emotion: Current research from diverse perspectives.* San Francisco: Jossey-Bass.

FOLK, K. F. (1996). Single mothers in various living arrangements: Differences in economic and time resources. *American Journal of Economics and Sociology, 55,* 277–291.

FOLKMAN, S., LAZARUS, R., PIMLEY, S., & NOVACEK, J. (1987). Age differences in stress and coping processes. *Psychology and Aging, 2,* 171–184.

FONTAINE, K. R., & JONES, L. C. (1997). *Journal of Clinical Psychology, 53,* 59–63.

FORD, D. H., & LERNER, R. M. (1992). *Developmental systems theory: An integrated approach.* Newbury Park, CA: Sage.

FORD FOUNDATION PROJECT ON SOCIAL WELFARE AND THE AMERICAN FUTURE. (1989). *The common good: Social welfare and the American future.* New York: Ford Foundation.

FORMAN, B. I. (June 1984). Reconsidering retirement: Understanding emerging trends. *The Futurist,* pp. 43–47.

FORMAN, G. (June 1985). The value of kinetic print in computer graphics for young children. In E. L. Klein (Ed.), *Children and Computers,* and issue of *New Directions for Child Development.* San Francisco: Jossey-Bass.

FORMAN, G. E. (April 1972). *The early growth of logic in children: Influences from the bilateral symmetry of human anatomy.* Paper presented at the conference of the Society for Research in Child Development, Philadelphia.

FORMAN, G. E., & FOSNOT, C. (1982). The use of Piaget's constructivism in early childhood education programs. In B. Spodek (Ed.), *Handbook on early childhood education.* Englewood Cliffs, NJ: Prentice Hall.

FORMAN, G. E., & HILL, F. (1980). *Constructive play: Applying Piaget in the preschool.* Monterey, CA: Brooks/Cole.

FORREST, L., & MIKOLAITIS, N. (December 1986). The relational component of identity: An expansion of career development theory. *The Career Development Quarterly,* pp. 76–85.

FOSBURGH, L. (August 7, 1977). The make-believe world of teenage pregnancy. *New York Times Magazine.*

FOUTS, R., with MILLS, S. T. (1997). *What chimpanzees have taught us about who we are.* New York: William Morrow.

FOZARD, J. L. (1990). Vision and hearing in aging. In J. E. Birren & K. W. Schaie (Eds.), *Handbook of the psychology of aging* (3rd ed., pp. 150–170). New York: Academic Press.

FRAIBERG, S. H. (1959). *The magic years.* New York: Scribner's.

FRAIBERG, S. H. (1974). Blind infants and their mothers: An examination of the sign system. In M. Lewis & L. Rosenblum (Eds.), *The effect of the infant on its caregiver.* New York: Wiley.

FRANK, S., & QUINLAN, D. M. (1976). Ego development and female delinquency: A cognitive-developmental approach. *Journal of Abnormal Psychology, 85,* 505–510.

FRANKENBURG, W. K., & DODDS, J. B. (1967). The Denver developmental screening test. *Journal of Pediatrics, 71,* 181–191.

FRAUENGLASS, M. H., & DIAZ, R. M. (1985). Self-regulatory functions of children's private speech: A critical analysis of recent challenges to Vygotsky's theory. *Developmental Psychology, 21,* 357–364.

FRAZIER, A., & LISONBEE, L. K. (1950). Adolescent concerns with physique. *School Review, 58,* 397–405.

FREDA, V. J., GORMAN, J. G., & POLLACK, W. (1966). Rh factor: Prevention of isoimmunization and clinical trial on mothers. *Science, 151,* 828–830.

FREEDMAN, D. G. (January 1979). Ethnic differences in babies. *Human Nature,* pp. 36–43.

FREEMAN, N. H. (1980). *Strategies of representation in young children.* London: Academic Press.

FRENKEL-BRUNSWIK, E. (1963). Adjustments and reorientation in the course of the life span. In R. G. Kuhlen & G. G. Thompson (Eds.), *Psychological studies of human development* (2nd ed.). New York: Appleton-Century-Crofts.

FREUD, A. (1958). Adolescence. In *Psychoanalytic study of the child* (Vol. 13). New York: International Universities Press.

FREUD, A. (1966). *The writings of Anna Freud, Vol. II, The ego and the mechanisms of defense.* New York: International Universities Press.

FREUD, A., & DANN, S. (1951). An experiment in group up-bringing. In R. S. Eisler, A. Freud, H. Hartmann & E. Kris (Eds.), *The Psychoanalytic study of the child* (Vol. 6). New York International Universities Press.

FREUDENBERGER, H., & RICHELSON, G. (1980). *Burnout: The high cost of high achievement.* New York: Anchor Press/Doubleday.

FRIED, P. A., & OXORN, H. (1980). *Smoking for two: Cigarettes and pregnancy.* New York: Free Press.

FRIEDLANDER, M., & SIEGEL, S. (1990). Separation-individuation difficulties and cognitive-behavior indicators of eating disorders among college women. *Journal of Counseling Psychology, 37,* 74–78.

FRIEDMANN, T. (1997). Overcoming the obstacles to gene therapy. *Scientific American, 276 (6),* 96–101.

FRIES, J. F., & CRAPO, L. M. (1981). *Vitality and aging.* San Francisco: Freeman.

FRISCH, R. E. (March 1988). Fatness and fertility. *Scientific American,* pp. 88–95.

FRISCHHOLZ, E. J. (1985). In R. P. Kluft (Ed.), *Childhood antecedents of multiple personality.* Washington, DC: American Psychiatric Press.

FROST, J. L., & SUNDERLINE, S. (Eds.). (1985). *When children play.* Proceedings of the International Conference on Play and Play Environments, Association for Childhood Education International, Weaton, MD.

FULLER, J., & SIMMEL, E. (1986). *Perspectives in behavioral genetics.* Hillsdale, NJ: Erlbaum.

FURST, K. (1983). *Origins and evolution of women's dreams in early adulthood.* Unpublished doctoral dissertation. California School of Professional Psychology, Berkeley.

FURSTENBERG, F. (1976). *Unplanned parenthood: The social consequences of teenage childbearing.* New York: Free Press.

FURSTENBERG, F. F., JR. (1987). The new extended family: The experience of parents and children after remarriage. In K. Pasley & M. Ihinger-Tallman (Eds.), *Remarriage and stepparenting: Current research and theory* (pp. 42–64). New York: Guilford.

FURTH, H. G. (1980). *The world of grown-ups: Children's conceptions of society.* New York: Elsevier.

GABBARD, C., DEAN, M., & HAENSLY, P. (1991). Foot preference behavior during early childhood. Journal of Applied *Developmental Psychology, 12,* 131–137.

GALINSKY, E. (1980). *Between generations: The six stages of parenthood.* New York: Times Books.

GALLAGHER, D. (1987). Bereavement. In G. L. Maddox ET AL. (Eds.), *The encyclopedia of aging.* New York: Springer.

GALLAGHER, J. M. (1973). Cognitive development and learning in the adolescent. In J. F. Adams (Ed.), *Understanding adolescence* (2nd ed.). Boston: Allyn & Bacon.

GALLAGHER, W. (May 1993). Midlife myths. *Atlantic,* pp. 51–55, 58–62, 65, 68–69.

GALLER, J. R. (1984). *Human nutrition: A comprehensive treatise:* (Vol. 5). *Nutrition and behavior.* New York: Plenum.

GANDINI, L., & EDWARDS, C. P. (1988). Early childhood integration of the visual arts. *Gifted International, 5(2),* 14–18.

GARBARINO, J., KOSTELNY, K., & DUBROW, N. (April 1991). What children can tell us about living in danger. *American Psychologist, 36(1),* 376–383.

GARBARINO, J., SEBES, J., & SCHELLENBACH, C. (1984). Families at risk for destructive parent–child relations in adolescence. *Child Development, 55,* 174–183.

GARBER, J. (December 1984). The developmental progression of depression in female children. In D. Chicchetti & K. Schneider-Rosen (Eds.), *New Directions for Child Development, 26.*

GARBER, K., & MARCHESE, S. (1986). *Genetic counseling for clinicians.* Chicago: Year Book Medical Publishers.

GARBER, K., & MARCHESE, S. (1986). *Genetic counseling for clinicians.* Chicago: Year Book Medical Publishers.

GARDNER, H. (1973). *The quest for mind: Piaget, Levi-Strauss, and the structuralist movement.* New York: Random House.

GARDNER, H. (1973a). *The arts and human development: A psychological study of the artistic process.* New York: Wiley-Interscience.

GARDNER, H. (1973b). *The quest for mind: Piaget, Levi-Strauss, and the structuralist movement.* New York: Random House.

GARDNER, H. (1983). *Frames of mind.* New York: Basic Books.

GARDNER, J. M., & KARMEL, B. Z. (1984). Arousal effects on visual preference in neonates. *Developmental Psychology, 20,* 374–377.

GARLAND, A. F. & ZIGLER, E. (1993). Adolescent suicide prevention: Current research and social policy implications. *American Psychologist, 48(2),* 169–182.

GARRETT, D. N. (1978). The needs of the seriously ill and their families: The haven concept. *Aging, 6(1),* 12–19.

GARROD, A., BEAL, C., & SHIN, P. (1989). *The development of moral orientation in elementary school children.* Paper presented at the April meeting of the Society for Research in Child Development, Kansas City.

GARTNER, A. (Winter 1984). Widower self-help groups: A preventive approach. *Social Policy,* pp. 37–38.

GARVEY, C. (1977). *Play.* Cambridge, MA: Harvard University Press.

GARVEY, C. (1984). *Children's talk.* Cambridge, MA: Harvard University Press.

GARVEY, C. (1990). *Play.* Cambridge, MA: Harvard University Press.

GATZ, M., BENGTSON, V., & BLUM, M. (1990). Caregiving families. In J. Birren & K. W. Schaie (Eds.) *Handbook of the psychology of aging* (3rd ed., pp. 405–426). San Diego: Academic Press.

GE, X., CONGER, R. D., & ELDER, G. H., JR. (1996). Coming of age too early: Pubertal influences on girls' vulnerability to psychological distress. *Child Development, 67,* 3386–3400.

GEE, E. M. (1986). The life course of Canadian women: A historical and demographic analysis. *Social Indicators Research, 18,* 263–283.

GEE, E. M. (1987). Historical change in the family life course of Canadian men and women. In V. Marshall (Ed.), *Aging in Canada* (2nd ed., pp. 265–287). Markham, ON: Fitzhenry & Whiteside.

GEE, E. M. (October 1988). The changing demography of intergenerational relations in Canada. Paper presented at the annual meeting of the Canadian Association of Gerontology, Halifax.

GELIS, J. (1989). The child: From anonymity to individuality. In R. Chartier (Ed.), *A history of a private life: Vol. 3. Passions of the Renaissance* (pp. 309–325). Cambridge, MA: Belknap Press of Harvard University Press.

GELMAN, R. & GALLISTEL, C. R. (1986). *The child's understanding of number.* Cambridge, MA: Harvard University Press.

GENESEE, F. (1989). Early bilingual development: One language or two? *Journal of Child Language, 16,* 161–179.

GEORGE, T. P., & HARTMANN, D. P. (1996). Friendship networks of unpopular, average, and popular children. *Child Development, 67,* 2301–2316.

GERRARD, M. (1987). Sex, sex guilt, and contraceptive use revisited: The 1980s. *Journal of Personality and Social Psychology, 52,* 975–980.

GESELL, A. (1940). *The first five years of life: The preschool years.* New York: Harper & Brothers.

GESELL, A. & AMES, L. B. (1947). The development of handedness. *Journal of Genetic Psychology, 70,* 155–175.

GIBBONS, D. C. (1976). *Delinquent behavior* (2nd ed.). Englewood Cliffs, NJ: Prentice Hall.

GIBSON, E. J., & SPELKE, E. S. (1983). The development of perception. In P. Mussen (Ed.), *The handbook of child psychology: Vol. 3. Cognitive development* (pp. 2–60). New York: Wiley.

GIBSON, E. J., & WALK, R. D. (April 1960). The "visual cliff." *Scientific American*, pp. 64–71.

GIBSON, E., & WALKER, A. S. (1984). Development of knowledge of visual–tactile affordances of substance. *Child Development, 55*, 453–456.

GIBSON, R. C. (Summer 1986). Older black Americans. *Generations*, 35–39.

GILFORD, R. (Summer 1986). Marriages in later life. *Generations*, pp. 16–20.

GILLIGAN, C. (1982). *In a different voice: Psychological theory and women's development.* Cambridge, MA: Harvard University Press.

GILLIGAN, C. (1987). Adolescent development reconsidered. *New Directions for Child Development, 37*, 63–92.

GILLIS, J. J., ET AL. (1992). Attention deficit disorder in reading-disabled twins: Evidence for a genetic etiology. *Journal of Abnormal Child Psychology, 20*(3), 303.

GINSBURG, E. (1972). Toward a theory of occupational choice: A restatement. *Vocational Guidance Quarterly, 20*, 169–176.

GIORDANO, J., & BECKMAN, K. (1985). The aged within a family context: Relationships, roles, and events. In L. L'Abate (Ed.) *The handbook of family psychology and therapy* (Vol. 1, pp. 284–320). Homewood, IL: Dorsey.

GLASER, R. (1963). Instructional technology and the measurement of learning outcomes: Some questions. *American Psychologist, 18*, 519–521.

GLASER, R. (1987). Thoughts on expertise. In C. Schooler & K. W. Schaie (Eds.). *Cognitive functioning and social structure over the life course* (pp. 81–91). Norwood, NJ: Ablex.

GLEITMAN, L., & WANNER, E. (1982). Language learning: State of the art. In E. Wanner & L. Gleitman (Eds.), *Language learning.* Cambridge, UK: Cambridge University Press.

GLICK, P. C. (1977). Updating the lifecycle of the family. *Journal of Marriage and the Family, 39*, 5–13.

GLICK, P., & LIN, S. (1986). More young adults are living with their parents: Who are they? *Journal of Marriage and the Family, 48*, 107–112.

GLIDEWELL, J. C., KANTOR, M. B., SMITH, L. M., & STRINGER, L. A. (1966). Socialization and social structure in the classroom. In L. W. Hoffman & M. L. Hoffman (Eds.), *Review of child development research* (Vol. 2). New York: Russell Sage Foundation.

GLOBERMAN, J. (1996). Daughters- and sons-in-law caring for relatives with Alzheimer's disease. *Family Relations, 45*, 37–45.

GOETTING, A. (1981). Divorce outcome research: Issues and perspectives. *Journal of Family Issues, 2*, 350–378.

GOETTING, A. (1982). The six stations of remarriage: Developmental tasks of remarriage after divorce. *Family Relations, 31*, 213–222.

GOLD, M. (1985). The baby makers. *Science, 6*(3), 26–38.

GOLDBERG, M., & HARVEY, J. (September 1983). A nation at risk: The report to the National Commission on Excellence in Education. *Phi Delta Kappan*, pp. 14–18.

GOLDBERG, S. (1972). Infant care and growth in urban Zambia. *Human Development, 15*, 77–89.

GOLDBERG, S. (1979). Premature birth: Consequences for the parent–infant relationship. *American Scientist, 67*, 214–220.

GOLDBERG, S. (1983). Parent–infant bonding: Another look. *Child Development, 54*, 1355–82.

GOLDBERG, S., & LEWIS, M. (1969). Play behavior in the year-old infant: Early sex differences. *Child Development, 40*, 21–31.

GOLDBERG, S., LOJKASEK, M., GARTNER, G., & CORTER, C. (1988). Maternal responsiveness and social development in preterm infants. In M. H. Bornstein (Ed.). *New Directions for Child Development: Vol. 43. Maternal responsiveness: Characteristics and consequences.* San Francisco: Jossey-Bass.

GOLDFIELD, E. C. (1989). Transition from rocking to crawling: Postural constraints on infant movement. *Developmental Psychology, 25*(6) 913–919.

GOLDIN-MEADOW, S., & MYLANDER, C. (1984). Gestural communication in deaf children: The effects and noneffects of parental input on early language development. *Monographs of the Society for Research in Child Development, 49* (3–4, Serial No. 207).

GOLDSMITH, H. H. (1983). Genetic influence on personality from infancy to adulthood. *Child Development, 54*, 331–355.

GONCU, A. (1993). Development of intersubjectivity in social pretend play. *Human Development, 36*, 185–198.

GONCZ, L. (1988). A research study on the relation between early bilingualism and cognitive development. *Psychologische Beitrage, 30*(1–2), 75–91.

GONYEA, J. G. (1998). Midlife and menopause: Uncharted territories for Baby Boomer women. *Generations, 21*, Spring, 87–89.

GOODCHILDS, J. D., & ZELLMAN, G. L. (1984). Sexual signalling and sexual aggression in adolescent relationships. In N. M. Malmuth & E. D. Donnerstein (Eds.), *Pornography and sexual aggression.* New York: Academic Press.

GOODE, W. J. (1970) *World revolution and family patterns.* New York: Free Press.

GOODLIN, R. C. (1979). History of fetal monitoring. *American Journal of Obstetrics and Gynecology, 133*, 323–347.

GOODMAN, M. (1980). Toward a biology of menopause. *Signs, 5*, 739–753.

GOODMAN, P. (1960). *Growing up absurd.* New York: Random House.

GOODNOW, J. (1977). *Children drawing.* Cambridge, MA: Harvard University Press.

GOODNOW, J. J., MILLER, P. J., & KESSEL, F. (Eds.) (1995). *Cultural practices as contexts for development.* New York: Jossey-Bass.

GOODWIN, F. (1991). From the alcohol, drug abuse, and mental health administration: Alcohol, caffeine and fetal cells. *Journal of the American Medical Association, 266*(8), 1056.

GOPNIK, A. (1988). Three types of early word: The emergence of social words, names and cognitive-relational words in the one-word stage and their relation to cognitive development. *First Language, 8*, 49–70.

GOPNIK, A., & MELTZOFF, A. N. (1987). The development of categorization in the second year and its relation to other cognitive and linguistic developments. *Child Development, 58*, 1523–1531.

GORDON, I. (1969). Early childhood stimulation through parent education. *Final Report to the Children's Bureau Social and Rehabilitation Services Department of HEW.* ED 038–166.

GORTMAKER, S. L., DIETZ, W. H., JR., SOBOL, A. M., & WEHLER, C. A. (1987). Increasing pediatric obesity in the United States. *American Journal of Diseases of Children, 141*, 535–540.

GOSLIN, D. A. (Ed.). (1969). *Handbook of socialization theory and research.* Chicago: Rand McNally.

GOTTMAN, J. M. (1983). How children become friends. *Monographs of the Society for Research in Child Development, 48*(3).

GOTTMAN, J. M., KATZ, L. F., & HOOVEN, C. (1996). Parental meta-emotion philosophy and the emotional life of families: Theoretical models and preliminary data. *Journal of Family Psychology, 10*, 243–268.

GOULD, R. L. (1978). *Transformations, growth and change in adult life.* New York: Simon & Schuster.

GOULD, S. J. (1981). *The mismeasure of man.* New York: Norton.

GOWING, M. K., KRAFT, J. D., & QUICK, J. C. (Eds.) (1997). Foreword to *The new organizational reality: Downsizing, restructuring, and revitalization.* Washington, DC: American Psychological Association.

GRANRUD, C. D., YONAS, A., & PETTERSON, L. (1984). A comparison of monocular and binocular depth perception in 5 and 7 month old infants. *Journal of Experimental Child Psychology, 38*, 19–32.

GRATCH, G., & SCHATZ, J. (1987). Cognitive development: The relevance of Piaget's infancy books. In J. Osofsy (Ed.), *Handbook of infant development* (2nd ed.). New York: Wiley.

GRAY, D. B., & YAFFE, S J. (1983). Prenatal drugs. In C. C. Brown (Ed.), *Prenatal Roundtable: Vol. 9. Childhood learning disabilities and prenatal risk.* (pp. 44–49). Rutherford, NJ: Johnson & Johnson.

GRAY, D. B., & YAFFE, S. J. (1986). Prenatal drugs and learning disabilities. In M. Lewis (Ed.), *Learning disabilities and prenatal risk.* Urbana: University of Illinois Press.

GRAY, S. (1976). *A report on the home-parent centered intervention programs: Home visiting with mothers of toddlers and their siblings.* DARCEE, Peabody College.

GREENBERG, J., & BECKER, M. (1988). Aging parents as family resources. *The Gerontologist, 28*, 786–791.

GREENBERG, M., & MORRIS, N. (July 1974). Engrossment: The newborn's impact upon the father. *American Journal of Orthopsychiatry, 44*(4), 520–531.

GREENE, A. L. (1990). Great expectations: Constructions of the life course during adolescence. *Journal of Youth and Adolescence, 19,* 289–303.

GREENE, A. L., & BROOKS, J. (April 1985). *Children's perceptions of stressful life events.* Paper presented at the Society for Research in Child Development, Toronto, Canada.

GREENFIELD, P. (1984). *Mind and media: The effects of television, video games and computers.* Cambridge, MA: Harvard University Press.

GREENOUGH, W. T., BLACK, J. E., & WALLACE, C. S. (1987). Experience and brain development. *Child Development, 58,* 539–559.

GREENSPAN, S., & GREENSPAN, N. (1985). *First feelings.* New York: Penguin.

GREENWOOD, S. (1984). *Menopause, naturally: Preparing for the second half of life.* San Francisco: Volcano Press.

GREIF, E. B., & ULMAN, K. J. (1982). The psychological impact of menarche on early adolescent females: A review of the literature. *Child Development, 53,* 1413–1430.

GRESS, L. D., & BAHR, R. T. (1984). *The aging person: A holistic perspective* (p. 145). St. Louis & Toronto: Mosby.

GRIMM-THOMAS, K., & PERRY-JENKINS, M. (April 1994). All in a day's work: Job experiences, self-esteem, and fathering in working-class families. *Family Relations, 43,* 174–181.

GROBESTEIN, C., FLOWER, M., & MENDELOFF, J. (1983). External human fertilization: An evaluation of policy. *Science, 22,* 127–133.

GRODSTEIN, F., STAMPFER, M. J., COLDITZ, G. A., WILLETT, W. C., MANSON, J. E., JOFFE, M., ROSNER, B., FUCHS, C., HANKINSON, S. E., HUNTER, D. J., HENNEKENS, C. H., & SPEIZER, F. E. (1997). Postmenopausal hormone therapy and mortality. *The New England Journal of Medicine, 336,* 1769–1775.

GRONLUND, G. (1995). Bringing the DAP message to kindergarten and primary teachers. *Young Children, 50 (5),* 4–13.

GROSJEAN, F. (1982). *Life with two languages: An introduction to bilingualism.* Cambridge, MA: Harvard University Press.

GROSS, T. F. (1985). *Cognitive development.* Monterey, CA: Brooks/Cole.

GROSSMAN, F. K., POLLACK, W. S., & GOLDING, E. (1988). Fathers and children: Predicting the quality and quantity of fathering. *Developmental Psychology, 24(1),* 82–91.

GROTEVANT, H. D., & COOPER, C. R. (1985). Patterns of interaction in family relationships and the development of identity exploration in adolescence. *Child Development, 56,* 415–428.

GRUSEC, J. E., & ARNASON, L. (1982). Consideration for others: Approaches to enhancing altruism. In S. Moore & C. Cooper (Eds.), *The young child: Reviews of research* (Vol. 3). Washington, DC: National Association for the Education of Young Children.

GUELZOW, M. G., BIRD, G. W., & KOBALL, E. H. (February 1991). An exploratory path analysis of the stress process for dual-career men and women. *Journal of Marriage and the Family, 53,* 151–164.

GUILFORD, J. P. (1959). Three faces of intellect. *American Psychologist, 14,* 469–479.

GUNNAR, M. R. (1989). Studies of the human infant's adrenocortical response to potentially stressful events. *New Directions for Child Development, 45.* San Francisco: Jossey-Bass.

GUREWITSCH, E. (July/August 1983). Geriatric day care: The options reconsidered. *Aging Magazine,* pp. 21–26.

GUTIERREZ DE PINEDA, V. (1948). Organizacion social en la Guajira. *Rev. Institute etnolog., 3.*

GUTMANN, D. L. (1964). An exploration of ego configurations in middle and later life. In B. L. Neugarten (Ed.), *Personality in middle and late life: Empirical studies.* New York: Atherton Press.

GUTMANN, D. L. (1969). The country of old men: Cross-cultural studies in the psychology of later life. *Occasional Papers in Gerontology, No. 5.* Ann Arbor: Institute of Gerontology, University of Michigan–Wayne State University.

GUTMANN, D. L. (1975). Parenthood: A key to the comparative study of the life cycle. In N. Datan & L. H. Ginsberg (Eds.), *Life-span developmental psychology: Normative life crises.* New York: Academic Press.

GUTMANN, D. (1987). *Reclaimed powers: Toward a new psychology of men and women in later life.* New York: Basic Books.

GUTMANN, E. (1977). In C. E. Finch & L. Hayflock (Eds.), *Handbook of the biology of aging.* New York: Van Nostrand Reinhold.

HABER, D. (1984). Church-based programs for black caregivers of noninstitutionalized elders. *Journal of Gerontological Social Work, 7,* 43–49.

HABER, P. (1987). Hospice. In G. L. Maddox et al. (Eds.), *The encyclopedia of aging.* New York: Springer.

HAGEN, J. W., LONGEWARD, R. H. J., & KAIL, R. V., JR. (1975). Cognitive perspectives on the development of memory. In H. W. Reese (Ed.), *Advances in child development and behavior* (Vol. 10). New York: Academic Press.

HAGESTAD, G. (1987). Able elderly in the family context: Changes, chances, and challenges. *The Gerontologist, 27,* 417–422.

HAGESTAD, G. O. (1985). Continuity and connectedness. In V. L. Bengston & J. Robertson (Eds.). *Grandparenthood* (pp. 31–48). Beverly Hills, CA: Sage.

HAGESTAD, G. O. (1990). Social perspectives on the life course. *Handbook of aging and the social sciences* (3rd ed., pp. 151–163). New York: Academic Press.

HALL, E. (April 1980). Interview of B. Neugarten, Acting one's age: New rules for old. *Psychology Today.*

HALL, W. M., & CAIRNS, R. B. (1984). Aggressive behavior in children: An outcome of modeling or social reciprocity? *Developmental Psychology, 20,* 739–745.

HALLIDAY, M. (1973). *Exploration in the functions of language.* London: Edward Arnold.

HALLINAN, M. T., & TEIXEIRA, R. A. (1987). Students' interracial friendships: Individual characteristics, structural effects, and racial differences. *American Journal of Education, 95,* 563–583.

HALPERN, D. F. (1986). *Sex differences in cognitive abilities.* Hillsdale, NJ: Erlbaum.

HALSEY, N. A., BOULOS, R., HOLT, E., RUFF, A. B., KISSINGER, P., QUINN, T. C., COBERLY, J. S., ADRIEN, M., & BOULOS, C. (October 1990). Transmission of HIV-1 infections from mothers to infants in Haiti. *Journal of the American Medical Association, 264(16).*

HANAWALT, B. A. (1995). *Growing up in medieval London: The experience of childhood in history.* New York: Oxford University Press.

HANDYSIDE, A. H., LESKO, J. G., TARIN, J. J., WINSTON, R. M. L. & HUGHES, M. R. (1992). Birth of a normal girl after in vitro fertilization and preimplantation diagnostic testing for cystic fibrosis. *New England Journal of Medicine, 327(13),* 905–909.

HANSEN, L. S. (1974). Counseling and career (self) development of women. *Focus on Guidance, 7,* 1–15.

HANSON, D., CONAWAY, L. P. & CHRISTOHER, J. S. (1989). Victims of child physical abuse. In Robert T. Ammerman and Micheal Hersen (Eds.), *Treatment of family violence.* New York: Wiley.

HARKNESS, S., & SUPER, C. M. (1983). *The cultural structuring of children's play in a rural African community.* Paper presented at the annual meeting of the Association for the Anthropological Study of Play, Baton Rouge, LA.

HARLAN, L. C., BERNSTEIN, A. B., & KESSLER, L. G. (1991). Cervical cancer screening: Who is not screened and why? *American Journal of Public Health, 81(7),* 885–890.

HARLOW, H. F. (June 1959). Love in infant monkeys. *Scientific American,* pp. 68–74.

HARLOW, H. F., & HARLOW, M. K. (November 1962). Social deprivation in monkeys. *Scientific American,* pp. 137–146.

HARRE, R. (January 1980). What's in a nickname? *Psychology Today,* pp. 78–84.

HARRIS, B. (1979). Whatever happened to Little Albert? *American Psychologist, 34(2),* 151–160.

HARRIS, K. R. (1990). Developing self-regulated learners: The role of private speech and self-instruction. *Educational Psychologist 25,* 35–49.

HARRIS, LOUIS, & ASSOCIATES. (1978). Myths and realities of life for older Americans. In R. Gross, B. Gross, & S. Seidman (Eds.), *The new old: Struggling for decent aging.* Garden City, NY: Anchor Press/Doubleday. (Originally published 1975)

HARRIS, P. L., BROWN, E., MARRIOTT, C., WHITTALL, S., & HARMER, S. (1991). Monsters, ghosts and witches: Testing the limits of the fantasy–reality distinction in young children. *British Journal of Developmental Psychology, 9,* 105–123.

HARRIS, R., ELLICOTT, A., & HOMMES, D. (1986). The timing of psychosocial transitions and changes in women's lives: An examination of women aged 45 to 60. *Journal of Personality and Social Psychology, 51,* 409–416.

HARRISON, A., WILSON, M., PINE, C., CHAN, S., & BURIEL, R. (1990). Family ecologies of ethnic minority children. *Child Development, 61,* 347–362.

HART, S. N. & BRASSARD, M. R. (1991). Psychological maltreatment: Progress achieved. *Development and Psychopathology, 3*, 61–70.

HART, S. N., GERMAIN, R. B., & BRASSARD, M. R. (1987). The challenge: To better understand and combat psychological maltreatment of children and youth. In M. R. Brassard, R. Germain, & S. N. Hart (Eds.), *Psychological maltreatment of children and youth* (pp. 3–24). New York: Pergamon.

HARTER, S. (1982). The perceived competence scale for children. *Child Development, 53*, 87–97.

HARTER, S. (1983). Developmental perspectives on the self system. In P. H. Mussen (Ed.), *Handbook of child psychology* (4th ed., Vol. 4). New York: Wiley.

HARTER, S. (1988). Developmental processes in the construction of the self. In T. D. Yawkey & J. E. Johnson (Eds.), *Integrative processes and socialization: Early to middle childhood*. Hillsdale, NJ: Erlbaum.

HARTUP, W. W. (1963). Dependence and independence. IN H. W. Stevenson, J. Kagan, & C. Spiker (Eds.), *Child psychology*. Chicago: National Society for the Study of Education.

HARTUP, W. W. (1970a). Peer interaction and social organization. In P. H. Mussen (ed.), *Carmichael's manual of child psychology* (3rd ed., Vol. 2). New York: Wiley.

HARTUP, W. W. (1970b). Peer relations. In T. D. Spencer & N. Kass (Eds.), *Perspectives in child psychology: Research and review*. New York: McGraw-Hill.

HARTUP, W. W. (1983). Peer relations. In P. H. Mussen (Ed.), *Handbook of child psychology* (4th ed., Vol. 4). New York: Wiley.

HARTUP, W. W. (1989). Social relationships and their developmental significance. *American Psychologist, 44*(2), 120–126.

HARTUP, W. W. (Summer 1993). Adolescents and their friends. *New Directions for Child Development, 60*, 3–19.

HARTUP, W. W. (1996). The company they keep: Friendships and their developmental significance. *Child Development, 67*, 1–13.

HASKETT, M. E. & KISTNER, J. A. (1991). Social interactions and peer perceptions of young physically abused children. *Child Development, 62*, 979–990.

HASS, A. (1979). *Teenage sexuality: A survey of teenage sexual behavior*. New York: Macmillan.

HASSETT, J. (September 1984). Computers in the classroom. *Psychology Today, 18*, 9.

HASTE, H., & TORNEY-PURTA, J. (Eds.) (Summer 1992). The development of political understanding: A new perspective (pp. 1–10). San Francisco: Jossey-Bass.

HATCH, T. (1997). Getting specific about multiple intelligences. *Educational Leadership, 54*, 26–29.

HAUSER, S. T. (1976). Loevinger's model and measure of ego development: A critical review. *Psychological Bulletin, 83*, 928–955.

HAUSER, S. T., BOOK, B. K., HOULIHAN, J., POWERS, S., WEISS-PERRY, B., FOLLANSBEE, D., JACOBSON, A. M., & NOAM, G. (1987). Sex differences within the family: Studies of adolescent and operent family interac-

tions. *Journal of Youth and Adolescence, 16*, 199–220.

HAVIGHURST, R. (1982). The world of work. In B. Wolman (Ed.), *The handbook of developmental psychology* (pp. 771–790). Englewood Cliffs, NJ: Prentice Hall.

HAVIGHURST, R. J. (1953). *Human development and education*. New York: Longman.

HAVIGHURST, R. J. (1964). Stages of vocational development. In H. Borow (Ed.), *Man in a world at work*. Boston: Houghton Mifflin.

HAVIGHURST, R. J. (1972). *Developmental tasks and education* (3rd ed.). New York: McKay.

HAVIGHURST, R. J., & DREYER, P. H. (1975). Youth and cultural pluralism. In R. J. Havighurst & P. H. Dreyer (Eds.), *Youth: The 74th yearbook of the NSSE*. Chicago: University of Chicago Press.

HAWKINS, J. A., & BERNDT, T. J. (1985). *Adjustment following the transition to junior high school*. Paper presented at the biennial meeting of the Society for Research in Child Development.

HAWKINS, J., SHEINGOLD, K., GEARHART, M., & BURGER, C. (1982). Microcomputers in schools: Impact on the social life of elementary classrooms. *Applied Developmental Psychology, 3*, 361–373.

HAYES, H. T. P. (June 12, 1977). The pursuit of reason. *New York Times Magazine*.

HAYNE, H., & ROVEE-COLLIER, C. (1995). The organization of reactivated memory in infancy. *Child Development, 66*, 893–906.

HAYWARD, M. D., FRIEDMAN, S., & CHEN, H. (1998). *Journal of Gerontology, 53B*, S91–S103.

HAZEN, N. L., & LOCKMAN, J. J. (1989). Skill in context. In J. J. Lockman & N. L. Hazen (Eds.) *Action in social context: Perspectives on early development* (pp. 1–22). New York: Plenum.

HEBB, D. O. (1966). *A textbook of psychology*. Philadelphia: Saunders.

HECHTMAN, L. (1989). Teenage mothers and their children: Risks and problems: A review. *Canadian Journal of Psychology, 34*, 569–575.

HECOX, K. (1975). Electrophysiological correlates of human auditory development. In L. B. Cohn & P. Salapatek (Eds.), *Infant perception: From sensation to cognition* (pp. 151–191). New York: Academia.

HEIDRICH, S. D., & RYFF, C. D. (1993a). Physical and mental health in later life: The self-system as mediator. *Psychology and Aging, 8*(3) 327–338.

HEIDRICH, S. D., & RYFF, C. D. (1993b). The role of social comparisons processes in the psychological adaptation of elderly adults. *Journal of Gerontology: Psychological Sciences, 48*(3), 127–136.

HELFER, R. (1982). The relationship between lack of bonding and child abuse and neglect. In *Round Table on Maternal Attachment and Nurturing Disorder* (Vol. 2). New Brunswick, NJ: Johnson & Johnson.

HELLIGE, J. B. (1993). Unity of thought and action. Varieties of interaction between the left and right cerebral hemispheres. *Current Directions in Psychological Science, 2*(1), 21–25.

HELSON, R. (1997). The self in middle age. In Lachman, M. E., & James, J. B. (Eds.), *Multiple paths of midlife development*. Chicago: University of Chicago Press.

HELSON, R., & PICANO, J. (1990). Is the traditional role bad for women? *Journal of Personality and Social Psychology, 59*, 311–320.

HELWIG, C. C. (1995). Adolescents' and young adults' conceptions of civil liberties: Freedom of speech and religion. *Child Development, 66*, 152–166.

HEPPER, P. (1989). Foetal learning: Implications for psychiatry? *British Journal of Psychiatry, 155*, 289–293.

HERKOWITZ, J. (1978). Sex-role expectations and motor behavior of the young child. In M. V. Ridenour (Ed.), *Motor development: Issues and applications*. Princeton, NJ: Princeton Book Co.

HERNANDEZ, D. J. (Spring 1994).Childrens changing access to resources: A historical perspective. *Social Policy Report: Society for Research in Child Development, 8*(1), 1–3.

HERRON, R. E., & SUTTON-SMITH, B. (1971). *Child's play*. New York: Wiley.

HERSHBERGER, S. L., & D'AUGELLI, A. R. (1995). The impact of victimization on the mental health and suicidality of lesbian, gay, and bisexual youths. *Developmental Psychology, 31*, 65–74.

HERSHEY, D. (1974). *Life-span and factors affecting it*. Springfield, IL: Charles C Thomas.

HESS, E. H. (1970). Ethology and developmental psychology. In P. H. Mussen (Ed.), *Carmichael's manual of child psychology* (3rd ed., Vol. 1). New York: Wiley.

HESS, E. H. (August 1972). "Imprinting" in a natural laboratory. *Scientific American*, pp. 24–31.

HESS, R. D. & HOLLOWAY, S. D. (1984). Family and school as educational institutions. In R. D. Parked (ed.), *Review of Child Development Reearch 7: The Family* (pp. 179–222). Chicago: University of Chicago Press.

HETHERINGTON, E. M. (1989). Coping with family transitions: Winners, losers, and survivors. *Child Development, 60*, 1–14.

HETHERINGTON, E. M. (1992). Coping with marital transitions: A family systems perspective. *Monographs of the Society for Research in Child Development, 57*(2–3), Serial No. 227, 1–14.

HETHERINGTON, E. M. (June 1984). Stress and coping in children and families. In A. Doyle, D. Gold, & D. Moskowitz (Eds.), *New Directions for Child Development, 24*.

HETHERINGTON, E. M., & BALTES, P. B. (1988). Child psychology and life-span development. In E. M. Hetherington, R. Lerner, & M. Perlmutter (Eds.) *Child development in life-span perspective* (pp. 1–20). Hillsdale, NJ: Erlbaum.

HETHERINGTON, E. M., & CAMARA, K. A. (1984). Families in transition: The process of dissolution and reconstitution. In R. D. Parke (Ed.), *Review of child development research* (Vol. 7). Chicago: University of Chicago Press.

HETHERINGTON, E. M., COX, M., & COX, R. (1982). Effects of divorce on parents and children. In M. L. Lamb (Ed.), *Nontradi-*

tional families: Parenting and child development. Hillsdale, NJ: Erlbaum.

HETHERINGTON, E. M., ET AL. (1978). The aftermath of divorce. In J. H. Stevens & M. Athews (Eds.), Mother–child, father–child relationships. Washington, DC: National Association for the Education of Young Children.

HETHERINGTON, E. M., STANLEY-HAGAN, M., & ANDERSON, E. R. (1989). Marital transitions: A child's perspective. American Psychologist, 44, 303–312.

HEWLETT, S. A. (1984). A lesser life: The myth of women's liberation in America. New York: Warner Books.

HILL, J. P. (1980). The family. In M. Johnson (Ed.), Toward adolescence: The middle school years. The seventy-ninth yearbook of the national society for the study of education. Chicago: University of Chicago Press.

HILL, J. P. (1980). Understanding early adolescence: A framework. Carrboro, NC: Center for Early Adolescence.

HILL, J. P. (1987). Research on adolescents and their families past and present. New Directions for Child Development, 37, 13–32.

HILL, R., & ALDOUS, J. (1969). Socialization for marriage and parenthood. In D. A. Goslin (Ed.), Handbook of socialization theory and research. Chicago: Rand McNally.

HILL, R., FOOTE, N., ALDOUS, J., CARLSON, R., & MACDONALD, R. (1970). Family development in three generations. Cambridge, MA: Schenkman.

HINDE, R. A. (1987). Individuals, relationships & culture: Links between ethology and the social sciences. Cambridge, UK, & New York: Cambridge University Press.

HIRSCH, B., KENT, D. P., & SILVERMAN. S. (1972). Homogeneity and heterogeneity among low-income Negro and white aged. In D. P. Kent, R. Kastenbaum, and S. Sherwood (Eds.), Research planning and action for the elderly: The power and potential of social science (pp. 400–500). New York: Behavioral Publishers.

HIRSHBERG, L. (1990). When infants look to their parents: II. Twelve-month-olds' response to conflicting parental emotional signals. Child Development, 61, 1187–1191.

HIRSHBERG, L. M., & SVEJDA, M. (1990). When infants look to their parents: I. Infants' social referencing of mothers compared to fathers. Child Development, 61, 1175–1186.

HIRSH-PASEK, K., NELSON, D. G., JUSCZYK, P. W., & WRIGHT, K. (April 1986). A moment of silence: How the prosaic cues in motherese might assist language learning. Paper presented at the International Conference on Infant Studies, Los Angeles.

HISCOCK, M., & KINSBOURNE, M. (1987). Specialization of the cerebral hemispheres: Implications for learning. Journal of Learning Disabilities, 20, 130–142.

HITE, S. (1976). The Hite report. New York: Macmillan.

HO, D. Y., & SAPOLSKY, R. M. Gene therapy for the nervous systems. Scientific American, 276 (6), 116–120.

HOBBS, D., & COLE, S. (1976). Transition to parenthood: A decade of replication. Journal of Marriage and the Family, 38, 723–731.

HOCHSCHILD, A. (1989). The second shift. New York: Avon Books.

HODGES, W., & COOPER, M. (1981). Head start and follow-through: Influences on intellectual development. Journal of Special Education, 15, 221–237.

HOFFMAN, J. (1984). Psychological separation of late adolescents from their parents. Journal of Counseling Psychology, 31, 170–178.

HOFFMAN, L. (1989). Effects of maternal unemployment in the two-parent family. American Psychologist, 44, 283–292.

HOFFMAN, M. L. (1970). Moral development. In P. H. Mussen (Ed.), Carmichael's manual of child psychology (3rd ed., Vol. 2). New York: Wiley.

HOFFMAN, M. L. (1977). Sex differences in empathy and related behaviors. Psychological Bulletin, 84(4), 712–722.

HOFFMAN, M. L. (1980). Moral development in adolescence. In J. Adelson (Ed.), Handbook of adolescent psychology. New York: Wiley.

HOFFMAN, M. L. (1981). Is altruism part of human nature? Journal of Personality and Social Psychology, 40, 121–137.

HOGAN, D. (1980). The transition to adulthood as a career contingency. American Sociological Review, 45, 261.

HOLDEN, C. (1980). Identical twins reared apart. Science, 207, 1323–1328.

HOLLAND, J. L. (1973). Making vocational choices: A theory of careers. Englewood Cliffs, NJ: Prentice Hall.

HOLT, J. (1964). How children fail. New York: Dell.

HOLT, R. R. (1982). Occupational stress. In L. Goldberger & S. Breznity (Eds.). Handbook of Stress (p. 4). New York: Free Press.

HONG, R., MATSUYAMA, E., & NUR, K. (1991). Cardiomyopathy associated with the smoking of crystal methamphetamine. Journal of the American Medical Association, 265(9), 1152–1154.

HONIG, A. S. (October 1980). The importance of fathering. Dimensions, pp. 33–38, 63.

HONIG, A. S. (May 1986). Stress and coping in young children. Young Children, pp. 50–63.

HONIG, A. (May 1989). Quality infant/toddler caregiving: Are there magic recipes? Young Children, pp. 4–10.

HOOD, J. C. (1986). The provider role: Its meaning and measurement. Journal of Marriage and the Family, 48, 349–359.

HOPKINS, B. (1991). Facilitating early motor development: An intercultural study of West Indian mothers and their infants living in Britain. In J. K. Nugent, B. M. Lester, and T. B. Brazelton (Eds.), The cultural context of infancy (Vol. 2, pp. 93–144). Norwood, NJ: Ablex.

HORGAN, J. (1993). Eugenics revisited. Scientific American, 268(6), 122–128, 130–131.

HORN, J. L. (1982). The theory of fluid and crystallized intelligence in relation to concepts of cognitive psychology and aging in adulthood. In F. I. M. Craik & S. Trehub (Eds.), Aging and cognitive processes. New York: Plenum.

HORN, J. L., & DONALDSON, G. (1980). Cognitive development in adulthood. In J. Kagan & O. G. Brim, Jr. (Eds.), Constancy and change in development. Cambridge, MA: Harvard University Press.

HORN, J. M. (1983). The Texas adoption project: Adopted children and their intellectual resemblance to biological and adoptive parents. Child Development, 54, 268–275.

HORN, M. (June 14, 1993). Grief re-examined: The AIDS epidemic is confounding the normal work of bereavement. U.S. News & World Report, pp. 81–84.

HOROWITZ, F. D. (1982). The first two years of life: Factors related to thriving. In S. Moore & C. Cooper (Eds.), The young child: Reviews of research (Vol. 3). Washington, DC: National Association for the Education of Young Children.

HOROWITZ, S. M., KLERMAN, L. V., SUNGKUO, H., AND JEKEL, J. F. (1991). Intergenerational transmission of school age parenthood. Family Planning Perspective, 23, 168–177.

HOVERSTEN, G. H., & MONCUR, J. P. (1969). Stimuli and intensity factors in testing infants. Journal of Speech and Hearing Research, 12, 687–702.

HOWARD, J. (1995). You can't get there from here: The need for a new logic in education reform. Daedalus, 124 (4), 85–93.

HOWARD, J., & HAMMOND, R. (September 9, 1985). Rumors of inferiority. The New Republic, pp. 17–21.

HOWE N. & STRAUSS, W. The new generation gap. The Atlantic Monthly. December 1992, pages 67–89.

HOWES, C., & OLENICK, M. (1986). Family and child care influences on toddler's compliance. Child Development, 57, 202–216.

HOYER, W. J., & PLUDE, D. J. (1980). Attentional and perceptual processes in the study of cognitive aging. In L. W. Poon (Ed.), Aging in the 1980s. Washington, DC: American Psychological Association.

HUDSON, H. (1981). As cited in H. J. Wershow, Controversial issues in gerontology. New York: Springer.

HUESMANN, L. R., LAGERSPETZ, K., & ERON, L. D. (1984). Intervening variables in the TV violence-aggression relation: Evidence from two countries. Developmental Psychology, 20, 746–775.

HUGES, F. P. (1991). Children, play and development. Boston: Allyn & Bacon.

HUGHES, M., & DONALDSON, M. (1979). The use of hiding games for studying the coordination of viewpoints. Educational Review, 31, 133–140.

HULL, C. L. (1943). Principles of behavior. New York: Appleton-Century.

HUMMERT, M. L., GARSTKA, T. A., SHANER, J. L., & STRAHM, S. (1995). Judgments about stereotypes of the elderly. Research on aging, 17, 168–189.

HUNT, B., & HUNT, M. (1975). Prime time. New York: Stein & Day.

HUNT, J. G., & HUNT, L. L. (1987). Here to play: From families to life-styles. Journal of Family Issues, 8, 440–443.

HUNT, J. M. (1961). Intelligence and experience. New York: Ronald Press.

HUNT, M. (1974). Sexual behavior in the 1970s. New York: Dell.

HUNTER, S., & SUNDEL, M. (1989). Midlife myths: Issues, findings, and practice implications. Newbury Park, CA: Sage.

HUSEN, T. (1967). *International study of achievement in mathematics: A comparison of twelve countries.* New York: Wiley.

HUSTON, A. (1983). Sex typing. In P. H. Mussen (Ed.), *Handbook of child psychology* (Vol. 4). New York: Wiley.

HUSTON, A. C., WATKINS, B. A., & KUNKEL, D. (1989). Public policy and children's television. *American Psychologist, 44,* 424–433.

HUTCHESON, R. H., JR. (1968). Iron deficiency anemia in Tennessee among rural poor children. *Public Health Reports, 83,* 939–943.

HWANG, C. P., & BROBERG, A. (1992). The historical and social context of child care in Sweden. In M. E. Lamb, & K. J. Sternberg (Eds.). *Child care in context.* Hillsdale, NJ: Erlbaum, 27–53.

HYDE, J. S. (1984). How large are gender differences in aggression? A developmental metaanalysis. *Developmental Psychology, 20,* 722–736.

HYDE, J. S. (1986). *Understanding human sexuality* (3rd ed.). New York: McGraw-Hill.

IHINGER-TALLMAN, M., & PASLEY, K. (1987). Divorce and remarriage in the American family: A historical review. In R. Pasley & M. Ihinger-Tallman (Eds.), *Remarriage and stepparenting: Current research and theory.* New York: Guilford.

IMARA, M. (1975). Dying as the last stage of growth. In E. Kübler-Ross (Ed.), *Death: The final stage of growth.* Englewood Cliffs, NJ: Prentice Hall.

IMHOF, A. E. (1986). Life course patterns of women and their husbands. In A. B. Sorensen, F. E. Weinert, & L. R. Sherrod (Eds.), *Human development and the life course: Multidisciplinary perspectives* (pp. 247–270). Hillsdale, NJ: Erlbaum.

INHELDER, B., & PIAGET, J. (1958). *The growth of logical thinking: From childhood to adolescence.* (A. Parsons & S. Milgram, Trans.). New York: Basic Books.

IRWIN, T. (1978). After 65: Resources for self-reliance. In R. Gross, B. Gross, & S. Seidman (Eds.), *The new old: Struggling for decent aging.* Garden City, NY: Anchor Press/Doubleday.

ISAACS, S. (1930). *Intellectual growth in young children.* London: Routledge & Kegan Paul.

ISABELLA, R. A., BELSKY, J., & VON EYE, A. (1989). Origins of infant–mother attachment: An examination of interactional synchrony during the infant's first year. *Developmental Psychology, 25*(1), 12–21.

ISENBERG, J., & QUISENBERRY, N. L. (February 1988). Play: A necessity for all children. *Childhood Education.*

JACACK, R. A., ET AL. (1995). Moral reasoning about sexually transmitted diseases. *Child Development, 66,* 167–177.

JACKSON, J. J. (1985). Race, national origin, ethnicity, and aging. In R. B. Binstock & E. Shanas (Eds.), *Handbook of aging and the social sciences.* New York: Van Nostrand Reinhold.

JACKSON, J., ANTONUCCI, T., & GIBSON, R. (1990). Cultural, racial, and ethnic minor-ity influences on aging. In J. Birren & K. W. Schaie (Eds.), *Handbook of the psychology of aging* (3rd ed., pp. 103–123). San Diego: Academic Press.

JACOBSON, A. L. (1978). Infant day care: Toward a more human environment. *Young Children, 33,* 14–23.

JACOBSON, J. L., & WILLE, D. E. (1984). Influence of attachment and separation experience on separation distress at 18 months. *Developmental Psychology, 70,* 477–484.

JACOBSON, J. & WILLE, D. (1986). The influence of attachment pattern on developmental changes in peer interaction from the toddler to the preschool period. *Child Development, 57,* 338–347.

JACOBSON, J. L., JACOBSON, S. W., SCHWARTZ, P. M., FEIN, G., & DOWLER, J. K. (1984). Prenatal exposure to an environmental toxin: A test of the multiple effects model. *Developmental Psychology, 20,* 523–532.

JAEGER, E., & WEINRAUB, M. (Fall 1990). Early nonmaternal care and infant attachment: In search of progress. In *New Directions for Child Development, 49,* 71–90.

JAMES, W. (1890). *Principles of psychology.* New York: Holt.

JEFFERS, F. C., & VERWOERDT, A. (1970). Factors associated with frequency of death thoughts in elderly community volunteers. In E. Palmore (Ed.), *Normal aging.* Durham, NC: Duke University Press.

JELLIFFE, D. B., JELLIFFE, E. F. P., GARCIA, L., & DE BARRIOS, G. (1961). The children of the San Blas Indians of Panama. *Journal of Pediatrics, 59,* 271–285.

JENSEN, A. R. (1969). How much can we boost IQ and scholastic achievement? *Harvard Educational Review, 39,* 1–123.

JENSH, R. (1986). Effects of prenatal irradiation on postnatal psychophysiologic development. In E. P. Riley & C. V. Vorhees (Eds.), *Handbook of behavioral periontology.* New York: Plenum.

JERSILD, A. T., & HOLMES, F. B. (1935). *Children's fears.* (Child Development Monograph No. 20). New York: Teachers College Press, Columbia University.

JESSNER, L., WEIGERT, E., & FOY, J. L. (1970). The development of parental attitudes during pregnancy. In E. J. Anthony & T. Benedek (Eds.), *Parenthood: Its psychology and psychopathology.* Boston: Little, Brown.

JESSOR, R. (1993). Successful adolescent among youth in high-risk settings. *American Psychologist, 48*(2), 117–126.

JOHNSON, C. L., & BARER, B. M. (June 1987). Marital instability and the changing kinship networks of grandparents. *The Gerontologist, 27*(3), 330–335.

JOHNSON, J. E., CHRISTIE, J. F., & YAWKEY, T. D. (1987). *Play and early childhood development.* Glenview, IL: Scott, Foresman.

JOHNSON, R. P., & RIKER, H. C. (1981). Retirement maturity: A valuable concept for preretirement counselors. *Personnel and Guidance Journal, 59,* 291–295.

JOHNSTON, L. D., O'MALLEY, P. M., & BACHMAN, G. J. (1987). *National trends in drug use and related factors among American high school students and young adults, 1975–1986.* Rockville, MD: U.S. Department of Health and Human Services, National Institute on Drug Abuse.

JONES, A. B. (1959). The relation of human health to age, place, and time. In J. E. Birren (Ed.), *Handbook of aging and the individual.* Chicago: University of Chicago Press.

JONES, A. P., & CRNIC, L. S. (1986). Maternal mediation of the effects of malnutrition. In E. P. Riley & C. V. Vorhees (Eds.), *Handbook of behavioral teratology.* New York: Plenum.

JONES, M. C. (1965). Psychological correlates of somatic development. *Child Development, 36,* 899–911.

JONES, M. C. (1979). Psychological correlates of somatic development. *Child Development, 36,* 899–911.

JORDANOVA, L. (1989). Children in history: Concepts of nature and society. In G. Scarr (Ed.), *Children, parents, and politics* (pp. 3–24). Cambridge, UK: Cambridge University Press.

JOSEPHS, L. (1982). *Professional women in the first two years of motherhood: A study of female-to-female support, nurturance, and autonomy.* Unpublished thesis, University of Massachusetts.

JOURNAL OF THE AMERICAN MEDICAL ASSOCIATION (1996). Boning up on estrogen: New options, new concerns (editorial). *Volume 276,* 1430–1432.

JUDD, L. J. (Winter 1991). Study finds mental disorders strike youth earlier than thought. *Quarterly Newsletter of the National Mental Health Association,* p. 4.

JUNG, C. G. (1931/1960). The stages of life. In H. Read, M. Fordham, & G. Adler (Eds.), *The collected works of C. G. Jung* (Vol. 8, pp. 387–402.) New York: Pantheon.

KADKAR, S. (1986). Male and female in India: Identity formation and its effects on cultural adaptation in tradition and transformation. In R. H. Brown & G. V. Coelho (Eds.). *Asian Indians in America.* Williamsburg, VA: College of William and Mary.

KAGAN, J. (1971). *Change and continuity in infancy.* New York: Wiley.

KAGAN, J. (1978). The baby's elastic mind. *Human Nature, I,* 66–73.

KAGAN, J., & MOSS, H. A. (1962). *Birth to maturity: A study in psychological development.* New York: Wiley.

KAGAN, J., & SNIDMAN, N. (1991). Temperamental factors in human development. *American Psychologist, 46*(8), 856–862.

KAGAN, J., ARCUS, D., & SNIDMAN, N. (1993). The idea of temperament: Where do we go from here? In R. Plomin & G. E. McClearn (Eds.), *Nature, nurture and psychology* (pp. 197–210). Washington, DC: American Psychological Association.

KAKU, D. A., ET AL. (1991). Emergence of recreational drug abuse as a major risk factor for stroke in young adults. *Journal of the American Medical Association, 265*(11), 1382.

KALES, J. D. (September 1979). Sleepwalking & night terrors related to febrile illness. *American Journal of Psychiatry, 136*(9), 1214–1215.

KALISH, R. A. (1985). *The final transition.* From the *Perspectives on Death & Dying* series. Farmingdale, NY: Baywood.

KALISH, R. (1987). Death. In G. L. Maddox et al. (Eds.), *The encyclopedia of aging.* New York: Springer.

KALISH, R. A., & REYNOLDS, D. K. (1981). *Death and ethnicity: A psychological study.* Farmingdale, NY: Baywood.

KALLEBERG, A., & ROSENFELD, R. (1990). Work in the family and in the labor market: A cross-national, reciprocal analysis. *Journal of Marriage and the Family, 52,* 331–346.

KALLMANN, F. J., & SANDER, G. (1949). Twin students on senescence. *American Journal of Psychiatry, 106,* 29–36.

KALNINS, I. V., & BRUNER, J. S. (1973). Infant sucking used to change the clarity of a visual display. In L. J. Stone, H. T. Smith, & L. B. Murphy (Eds.), *The competent infant: Research and commentary.* New York: Basic Books.

KAMII, C., & DEVRIES, R. (1980). *Group games in early education.* Washington, DC: National Association for the Education of Young Children.

KAMIN, L. (1974). *The science and politics of IQ.* Hillsdale, NJ: Erlbaum.

KAMMERMAN, S., KAHN, A., & KINGSTON, P. (1983). *Maternity policies and working women.* New York: Columbia University Press.

KANDEL, D. B., RAVEIS, V. H., & DAVIES, M. (1991). Suicidal ideation in adolescence: Depression, substance use & other risk factors. *Journal of Youth and Adolescence, 20,* 289–309.

KANE, R. L., & KANE, R. A. (1980). Alternatives to institutional care of the elderly: Beyond the dichotomy. *The Gerontologist, 20*(30), 197.

KANE, S. R., & FURTH, H. G. (1993). Children constructing social reality: A frame analysis of social pretend play. *Human Development, 36,* 199–214.

KANTER, R. (1977). *Men and women of the corporation.* New York: Basic Books.

KANTER, R. M. (March 1976). Why bosses turn bitchy. *Psychology Today,* pp. 56–59.

KANTROWITZ, B. (May 16, 1988). Preemies. *Newsweek,* pp. 62–67.

KAPLAN, L. J. (1984). *Adolescence: The farewell to childhood.* New York: Touchstone.

KAPLAN, M. (1979). *Leisure: Lifestyle and lifespan.* Philadelphia:

KAPLAN, N., CHOY, M. H., AND WHITMORE, J. K. (February 1992). Indochinese refugee families and academic achievement. *Scientific American,* 36–42.

KAREN, R. (February 1990). Becoming attached. *The Atlantic Monthly.*

KARLSON, A. L. (1972). *A naturalistic method for assessing cognitive acquisition of young children participating in preschool programs.* Unpublished doctoral dissertation, University of Chicago.

KASTENBAUM, R. (December 1971). Age: Getting there ahead of time. *Psychology Today,* pp. 52–54ff.

KASTENBAUM, R. (1979). *Growing old: Years of fulfillment.* New York: Harper & Row.

KASTENBAUM, R. (1986). *Death, society and human experience.* Columbus, OH: Merrill.

KASTENBAUM R., & COSTA, P. T. (1977). Psychological perspectives on death. In M. R. Rosenzweig & L. W. Porter (Eds.), *Annual review of psychology* (Vol. 28). Palo Alto, CA: Stanford University Press.

KATZ, L. G. (September 1990). Impressions of Reggio Emilia preschools. *Young Children, 45*(6), 4–10.

KAVALE, K. A., & FORNESS, S. R. (1996). Social skill deficits and learning disabilities. *Journal of Learning Disabilities, 29,* 226–237.

KEATING, D. (1976). Intellectual talent, research, and development: Proceedings. In D. Keating (Ed.), *Hyman Blumberg Symposium in Early Childhood Education.* Baltimore: Johns Hopkins University Press.

KEATING, D. P. (1980). Thinking processes in adolescence. In J. Adelson (Ed.), *Handbook of adolescent psychology.* New York: Wiley.

KEEN, S. (April 1974). The heroics of everyday life: A theorist of death confronts his own end. *Psychology Today,* pp. 71–75ff.

KEGAN, R. (1982). *The evolving self: Problem and process in human development.* Cambridge, MA: Harvard University Press.

KEGAN, R. (1995). *In over our heads: The mental demands of modern life.* Cambridge, MA: Harvard University Press.

KEISTER, M. E. (1970). *The good life for infants and toddlers.* New York: Harper & Row.

KEITH-SPIEGEL, R. (1976). Children's rights as participants in research. In G. P. Koocher (Ed.), *Children's rights in mental health professions.* New York: Wiley.

KELLOGG, R. (1970). *Analyzing children's art.* Palo Alto, CA: National Press.

KELLY, J. B. (1982). Divorce: The adult perspective. In B. Wolman (Ed.), *Handbook of developmental psychology.* Englewood Cliffs, N.J.: Prentice Hall.

KELLY, T. (1986). *Clinical genetics and genetic counseling* (3rd ed.). Chicago: Year Book Medical Publishers.

KELVIN, P., & JARRETT, J. (1985). *Unemployment: Its social psychological effects.* Cambridge, UK: Cambridge University Press.

KEMPE, R. S., & KEMPE, C. H. (1984). *The common secret: Sexual abuse of children and adolescents.* San Francisco: Freeman.

KENISTON, K. (Winter, 1968–69). Heads and seekers: Drugs on campus, counterculture, and American society. *American Scholar,* pp. 126–151.

KENISTON, K. (1975). Youth as a stage of life. In R. J. Havighurst & P. H. Dreyer (Eds.), *Youth: The 74th yearbook of the NSSE.* Chicago: University of Chicago Press.

KENISTON, K. (1977). *All our children: The American family under pressure.* Report of the Carnegie Council on Children. New York: Harcourt Brace Jovanovich.

KEOGH, J. F. (1965). *Motor performance of elementary school children.* Monograph of the Physical Education Department, University of California, Los Angeles.

KEPHART, W. M. (1966). The Oneida community. In W. M. Kephart (Ed.), *The family, society, and the individual* (2nd ed.). Boston: Houghton Mifflin.

KERMOIAN, R., & CAMPOS, J. J. (1988). Locomotor experience: A facilitation of spacial cognitive development. *Child Development, 59,* 908–17.

KESSLER, R., & MCRAE, J. (1982). The effect of wives' employment on the mental health of married men and women. *American Sociological Review, 47,* 216–227.

KETT, J. F. (1977). *Rites of passage: Adolescence in America, 1790 to the present.* New York: Basic Books.

KIEFFER, J. (February–March 1984). New roles for older workers. *Aging, 47,* 11–16.

KIESTER, E., JR. (October 1977). Healing babies before they're born. *Family Health,* pp. 26–30.

KIMMEL, D. C. (1974). *Adulthood and aging: An interdisciplinary view.* New York: Wiley.

KIMURA, D. (September 1992). Sex differences in the brain. *Scientific American.*

KINDERMANN, T. A. (1993). Natural peer groups as contexts for individual development: The case of children's motivation in school. *Developmental Psychology, 29*(6), 970–977.

KINSEY, A. C., POMEROY, W. B., & MARTIN, C. E. (1948). *Sexual behavior in the human male.* Philadelphia: Saunders.

KITZINGER, S. (1981). *The complete book of pregnancy and childbirth.* New York: Knopf.

KLAHR, D., LANGLEY, P., & NECHER, R. (Eds.). (1987). *Production system model of learning and development.* Cambridge, MA: MIT Press.

KLEIGL, R., SMITH, J., & BALTES, P. (1990). On the locus and process of magnification of age differences during mnemonic training. *Developmental Psychology, 26,* 894–904.

KLEIN, B., & RONES, P. (1989). A profile of the working poor. *Monthly Labor Review,* pp. 3–13.

KLEIN, N., HACK, N., GALLAGHER, J., & FANAROFF, A. A. (1985). Preschool performance of children with normal intelligence who were very low birth weight infants. *Pediatrics, 75,* 531–37.

KLIMA, E. S., & BELLUGI, U. (1966). Syntactic regularities. In J. Lyons & R. J. Wales (Eds.), *Psycholinguistics papers.* Edinburgh: University of Edinburgh Press.

KLIMA, E. S., & BELLUGI, U. (1973). As cited in P. de Villiers & J. de Villiers, *Early language.* Cambridge, MA: Harvard University Press, 1979.

KLINE, D. W., & SCHIEBER, F. (1985). Vision and aging. In J. E. Baron & K. W. Schaie (Eds.), *Handbook of the psychology of aging* (2nd ed.). New York: Van Nostrand Reinhold.

KLINNERT, M. D., EMDE, R. N., BUTTERFIELD, P., & CAMPOS, J. J. (1986). Social referencing: The infant's use of emotional signals from a friendly adult with mother present. *Developmental Psychology, 22,* 427–432.

KNIGHT, B., & WALKER, D. L. (1985). Toward a definition of alternatives to institutionalization for the frail elderly. *The Gerontologist, 25*(4), 358–363.

KNOBLOCH, H., MALONE, A., ELLISON, P. H., STEVENS, F., & ZDEB, M. (March 1982). Considerations in evaluating changes in outcome for infants weighing less than 1,501 grams. *Pediatrics, 69*(3), 285–295.

KNOBLOCH, H., PASAMANICK, B., HARPER, P. A., & RIDER, R. V. (1959). The effect of prematurity on health and growth. *American Journal of Public Health, 49,* 1164–1173.

KNOX, S. (1980). Ultra-sound diagnosis of foetal disorder. *Public Health, London, 94,* 362–367.

KOCH, H. L. (1956). Sissiness and tomboyishness in relation to sibling characteristics. *Journal of Genetic Psychology, 88,* 213–244.

KOCH, R., & KOCH, K. J. (1974). *Understanding the mentally retarded child: A new approach.* New York: Random House.

KOCHANSKA, G. (1997). Mutually responsive orientation between mothers and their young children: Implications for early socialization. *Child Development, 68,* 94–112.

KOFF, T. H. (1980). *Hospice: A caring community.* Englewood Cliffs, NJ: Prentice Hall.

KOHL, H. (1968). *36 children.* New York: Norton.

KOHLBERG, L. (1958). *Stages of moral development.* Unpublished dissertation. University of Chicago.

KOHLBERG, L. (1966). A cognitive developmental analysis of children's sex-role concepts and attitudes. In E. Maccoby (Ed.), *The development of sex differences.* Stanford: Stanford University Press.

KOHLBERG, L. (1966). Moral education in the schools: A developmental view. *School Review, 74,* 1–30.

KOHLBERG, L. (1969). Stage and sequence. The cognitive-developmental approach to socialization. In D. A. Goslin (Ed.), *Handbook of Socialization Theory & Research* (pp. 347–480). Chicago: Rand McNally.

KOHLBERG, L. (1978). Revisions in the theory and practice of moral development. *New Directions for Child Development, 2.*

KOHLBERG, L. (1981). *Essays on moral development: Vol. 1. The philosophy of moral development.* New York: Harper & Row.

KOHLBERG, L. (1984). *Essays on moral development: Vol. 2. The psychology of moral development.* New York: Harper & Row.

KOHN, M. L. (1980). Job complexity and adult personality. In N. J. Smelser & E. H. Erikson (Eds.), *Theories of work and love in adulthood.* Cambridge, MA: Harvard University Press.

KOHN, M. L., & SCHOOLER, C. (1978). The reciprocal effects of the substantive complexity of work and intellectual flexibility: A longitudinal assessment. *American Journal of Sociology, 84,* 24–52.

KOHN, M. L., & SCHOOLER, C. (1983). *Work and personality: Inquiry into the impact of social stratification.* Norwood, NJ: Ablex.

KOHN, R. R. (1985). Aging and age-related diseases: Normal processes. In H. A. Johnson (Ed.), *Relations between normal aging and disease* (pp. 1–43). New York: Raven.

KOMAROVSKY, M. (1964). *Blue-collar marriage.* New York: Random House.

KOMNER, M., & SHOSTAK, M. (February 1987). Timing and management of birth among the !Kung: Biocultural interaction and reproductive adaptation. *Cultural Anthropology, 2*(1), 11–28.

KOMPARA, D. R. (1980). Difficulties in the socialization process of stepparenting. *Family Relations, 29,* 69–73.

KOPP, C. B. (1989). Regulation of distress and negative emotions: A developmental view. *Developmental Psychology, 25,* 343–354.

KORNER, A. F. (1987). Preventive intervention with high-risk newborns: Theoretical, conceptual, and methodological perspectives.

In J. Osofsky (Ed.), *Handbook of infant development.* New York: Wiley.

KORTE, D., & SCAER, R. (1990). *A good birth, a safe birth.* New York: Bantam.

KOSBERG, L. (1988). Preventing elder abuse: Identification of high risk factors prior to placement decisions. *The Gerontologist, 28,* 43–50.

KOVAR, M. G. (Ed.) (August 1992). Morality among minority populations in the United States. *American Journal of Public Health, 82*(8), 1168–1170.

KOZOL, J. (1970). *Death at an early age.* New York: Bantam Books.

KRAVITZ, S. L., PELAEZ, M. B., & ROTHMAN, M. B. (1990). Delivering services to elders: Responsiveness to populations in need. In S. A. Bass, E. A. Kutza, & F. M. Torres-Gil (Eds.). *Diversity in Aging.* Glenview, IL: Scott, Foresman.

KREPPNER, K., & LERNER, N. (Eds.). (1989). *Family systems and life-span development.* Hillsdale, NJ: Erlbaum.

KREPPNER, K., PAULSEN, S., & SCHUETZ, Y. (1982). Infant and family development: From triads to tetrads. *Human Development, 25*(6), 373–391.

KROPP, J. P., & HAYNES, O. M. (1987). Abusive and nonabusive mothers' ability to identify general and specific emotion signals of infants. *Child Development, 58,* 187–190.

KRUCOFF, C. (March–April 1994). Use 'em or lose 'em. *Saturday Evening Post,* pp. 34–35.

KÜBLER-ROSS, E. (1969). *On death and dying.* New York: Macmillan.

KÜBLER-ROSS, E. (1975). *Death: The final stage of growth.* Englewood Cliffs, NJ: Prentice Hall.

KUHL, P. K., & MELTZOFF, A. N. (1988). Speech as an intermodel object of perception. In A. Yonas (Ed.), *The Minnesota Symposia on Child Psychology: Vol. 20. Perceptual development in infancy* (pp. 235–266). Hillsdale, NJ: Erlbaum.

KUHL, P. K., WILLIAMS, K. A., LACERDA, F., STEVEN, K. H., & LINDBLOM, B. (1992). Linguistic experience alters phonetic perception in infants by 6 months of age. *Science, 255,* 606–608.

KULIEV, A. M., MODELL, B., & JACKSON, L. (1992). Limb abnormalities and chorionic villus sampling. *The Lancet, 340,* 668.

KURDEK, L., & SCHMITT, J. (1986). Early development of relationship quality in heterosexual married, heterosexual cohabiting, gay, and lesbian couples. *Developmental Psychology, 48,* 305–309.

KUSHNER, H. S. (1981). *When bad things happen to good people.* New York: Schocken Books.

KUTZA, E. (1981). *The benefits of old age: Social welfare policy for the elderly.* Chicago: University of Chicago Press.

LABOUVIE-VIEF, G. (1984). Chapter in M. L. Commons, F. A. Richards, & C. Armon (Eds.), *Beyond formal operations: Late adolescence and adult cognitive development.* New York: Praeger.

LABOUVIE-VIEF, G. (1985). Intelligence and cognition. In J. Birren & K. Schaie (Eds.) *Handbook of the psychology of aging* (2nd ed., pp. 500–530) New York: Van Nostrand Reinhold.

LABOUVIE-VIEF, G. (1987). Article in *Psychology and Aging, 2.*

LABOUVIE-VIEF, G., & SCHELL, D. A. (1982). Learning and memory in later life. In B. Wolman (Ed.), *Handbook of developmental psychology.* Englewood Cliffs, NJ: Prentice Hall.

LABOV, W. (1970). The logic of nonstandard English. In F. Williams (Ed.), *Language and poverty.* Englewood Cliffs, NJ: Prentice Hall.

LABOV, W. (1972). *Language in the inner city: Studies in the black English vernacular.* Philadelphia: University of Pennsylvania Press.

LACHMAN, M. E., & JAMES, J. B. (Eds.) (1997). *Multiple paths of midlife development.* Chicago: University of Chicago Press.

LADD, G. W., KOCHENDERFER, B. J., & COLEMAN, C. C. (1996). Friendship quality as a predictor of young children's early school adjustment. *Child Development, 67,* 1103–1118.

LADD, G. W., PRICE, J. M., & HART, C. H. (1988). Predicting preschoolers' peer status from their playground behaviors. *Child Development, 59,* 986–992.

LAMAZE, F. (1958). *Painless childbirth: Psychoprophylactic method.* London: Burke.

LAMAZE, F. (1970). *Painless childbirth: The Lamaze method.* Chicago: Regnery.

LAMB, M. (1996). *The role of the father in child development.* New York: Wiley.

LAMB, M. E. (1979). Paternal influences and the father's role. *American Psychologist, 34,* 938–943.

LAMB, M. E. (1987). *The father's role: Cross-cultural perspectives.* New York: Wiley.

LAMB, M. E. (1996). Effects of nonparental child care on child development: An update. *Canadian Journal of Psychiatry, 41,* 330–342.

LAMB, M., & LAMB, J. (1976). The nature and importance of the father–infant relationship. *Family Coordinator, 4*(25), 379–386.

LAMB, M. E., KETTERLINUS, R. D., & FRACASSO, M. P. (1992). Parent-child relationships. In M. H. Bornstein, & M.E. Lamb (Eds.), *Developmental Psychology: An Advanced Textbook.* Hillsdale, NJ: Lawrence Erlbaum.

LAMBORN, S. D., DORNBUSCH, S. M., & STEINBERG, L. (1996). Ethnicity and community context as moderators of the relations between family decision making and adolescent adjustment. *Child Development, 67,* 283–301.

LANG, A. (1987). Nursing of families with an infant who requires home apnea monitoring. *Issues in Comprehensive Pediatric Nursing, 10,* 122–133.

LAPSLEY, D., RICE, K., & SHADID, G. (1989). Psychological separation and adjustment to college. *Journal of Counseling Psychology, 36,* 286–294.

LARSON, R. (1978). Thirty years of research on the subjective well-being of older Americans. *Journal of Gerontology, 33,* 109–125.

LA RUE, A., & JARVIK, L. F. (1982). Old age and behavioral changes. In B. Wolman (Ed.), *Handbook of developmental psychology.* Englewood Cliffs, NJ: Prentice Hall.

LA SALLE, A. D., & SPOKANE, A. R. (September 1987). Patterns of early labor force participation of American women. *Career Development Quarterly*, pp. 55–65.

LATHAM, M. C. (1977). Infant feeding in national and international perspective: An examination of the decline in human lactation, and the modern crisis in infant and young child feeding practices. *Annals of the New York Academy of Sciences, 300*, 197–209.

LAUERSEN, N. H. (1983). Childbirth with love. New York: Berkley Books.

LAUMANN, E. (1994). *The social organization of sexuality*. Chicago: University of Chicago Press.

LAUMANN, E. O., GAGNON, J. H., MICHAEL, R. T., & MICHAELS, S. (1994). *The social organization of sexuality: Sexual practices in the United States*. Chicago: The University of Chicago Press.

LAVER, J., & LAVER, R. (1985). Marriages made to last. *Psychology Today, 19*(6), 22–26.

LAWTON, M. P., BRODY, E., & SAPERSTEIN, A. (1989). A controlled study of respite service for care-givers of Alzheimer's patients. *The Gerontologist, 29*, 8–16.

LAZARUS, R. S. (July 1981). Little hassles can be hazardous to health. *Psychology Today*, pp. 58–62.

LEARMAN, L. A., ET AL. (1991). Pygmalion in the nursing home: The effects of care-giver expectations on patient outcomes. *Journal of the American Medical Association, 265*, 36.

LEBOYER, F. (1976). *Birth without violence*. New York: Knopf.

LEE, G. R. (1988). Marital satisfaction in later life: The effects of nonmarital roles. *Journal of Marriage and the Family, 50*, 775–783.

LEHANE, S. (1976). *Help your baby learn*. Englewood Cliffs, NJ: Prentice Hall.

LEHMAN, D., & NISBETT, R. (1990). A longitudinal study of the effects of undergraduate training on reasoning. *Developmental Psychology, 26*, 952–960.

LEO, J. (April 9, 1984). The revolution is over. *Time*, pp. 74–83.

LERNER, R. (1990). Plasticity, person-context relations and cognitive training in the aged years: A developmental contextual perspective. *Developmental Psychology, 26*, 911–915.

LERNER, R. M., ORLOS, J. B., & KNAPP, J. R. (1976). Physical attractiveness, physical effectiveness and self-concept in late adolescence. *Adolescence, 11*, 313–326.

LESTER, B. M., ALS, H., & BRAZELTON, T. B. (1982). Regional obstetric anesthesia and newborn behavior: A reanalysis toward synergistic effects. *Child Development, 53*, 687–692.

LESTER, B. M., & BRAZELTON, T. B. (1982). Cross-cultural assessment of neonatal behavior. In D. Wagner & H. Stevenson (Eds.), *Cultural perspectives on child development*. San Francisco: Freeman.

LESTER, B. M., & DREHER, M. (1989). Effects of marijuana use during pregnancy on newborn cry. *Child Development, 60*, 765–771.

LETTERI, C. A. (1985). Teaching students how to learn. *Theory into Practice*, pp. 112–122.

LEVENTHAL, E.A., LEVENTAL, H., SHACHAM, S. & EASTERLING, D.V. (1989). Active coping reduces reports of pain from childbirth.

Journal of Consulting and Clinical Psychology, 57(3), 365–371.

LEVINE, L. E. (1983). Mine: Self-definition in two-year-old boys. *Developmental Psychology, 19*, 544–549.

LEVINE, R. (1989). Cultural influences in child development: In William Damon (Ed.), *Child development today and tomorrow*. San Francisco: Jossey-Bass.

LEVINE, R. A. (1990). Enculturation: A biosocial perspective on the development of self. In D. Cicchetti & M. Beeghly (Eds.), *The self in transition: Infancy to childhood* (pp. 99–117). Chicago: University of Chicago Press.

LEVINSON, D. (1986). A conception of adult development. *American Psychologist, 41*, 3–13.

LEVINSON, D. (1990). *The seasons of a woman's life: Implications for women and men*. Presented at the 98th annual convention of the American Psychological Association, Boston.

LEVINSON, D. J. (1978). *The seasons of a man's life*. New York: Knopf.

LEVINSON, D. J. (1996). *The seasons of a woman's life*. New York: Ballantine.

LEVINSON, H. (1983). A second career: The possible dream. *Harvard Business Review*, pp. 122–129.

LEVY, B., WILKINSON, F., & MARINE, W. (1991). Reducing neonatal mortality rate with nurse-midwives. *American Journal of Obstetrics and Gynecology, 109*(1), 50–58.

LEVY, G. D., & CARTER, D. B. (1989). Gender schema, gender constancy and gender-role knowledge: The roles of cognitive factors in preschoolers' gender-role stereotype attributions. *Developmental Psychology, 25*(3), 444–449.

LEVY, S. M. (1978). Temporal experience in the aged: Body integrity and social milieu. *International Journal of Aging and Human Development, 9*(4), 319–343.

LEWIS, J. M., OWEN, M. T., & COX, M. J. (1988). The transition to parenthood: III, Incorporation of the child into the family. *Family Process, 237*, 411–421.

LEWIS, M. (1987). Social development in infancy and early childhood. In J. Osofsky (Ed.), *Handbook of infant development*. New York: Wiley.

LEWIS, M. Self-conscious emotions. (1995). *American Scientist, 83*, 68–78.

LEWIS, M., & BROOKS-GUNN, J. (1979). *Social cognition and the acquisition of self*. New York: Plenum Press.

LEWIS, M., & FEINMAN, S. (Eds.) (1991). *Social influences and socialization in infancy*. New York: Plenum.

LEWIS, M., & FEIRING, C. (1989). Infant, mother, and mother–infant interaction behavior and subsequent attachment. *Child Development, 60*, 831–837.

LEWIS, M., FEIRING, C., & KOTSONIS, M. (1984). The social network of the young child: A developmental perspective. In M. Lewis (Ed.), *Beyond the dyad: The genesis of behavior*. New York: Plenum.

LEWIS, M., & ROSENBLUM, L. (Eds.) (1974). *The effect of the infant on its caregiver*. New York: Wiley.

LIEBENBERG, B. (1967). Expectant fathers. *American Journal of Orthopsychiatry, 37*, 358–359.

LIEBERMAN, M. A., & TOBIN, S. S. (1983). *The experience of old age: Stress, coping and survival*. New York: Basic Books.

LIEBOVICI, D., RITCHIE, K., & LEDESERT, J. T. (1996). Does education level determine the course of cognitive decline? *Age and Ageing, 25*, 392–397.

LIEM, R. (December 1981). Unemployment and mental health implications for human service policy. *Policy Studies Journal, 10*, 350–364.

LIN, G., & ROGERSON, P. A. (1995). Elderly parents and the geographic availabiltiy of their adult children. *Research on Aging, 17*, 303–331.

LIPSITT, L. P., & KAYE, H. (1964). Conditioned sucking in the human newborn. *Psychonomic Science, 1*, 29–30.

LISINA, M. I., & NEVEROVICH, Y. Z. (1971). Development of movements and formation of motor habits. In A. Z. Zaporozlets & D. B. Elkonin (Eds.), *The psychology of preschool children*. Cambridge, MA: MIT Press.

LIVSON, F. (1976). Patterns of personality development in middle-aged women: A longitudinal study. *International Journal of Aging and Human Development, 1*, 107–115.

LIVSON, N., & PESKIN, H. (1980). Perspectives on adolescence from longitudinal research. In J. Adelson (Ed.), *Handbook of adolescent psychology*. New York: Wiley.

LLOYD, B. (1987). Social representations of gender. In J. Bruner & H. Haste (Eds.). *Making sense: The child's construction of the world*. London: Methuen.

LOCICERO, A. K. (1993). Explaining excessive rates of Cesareans and other childbirth interventions: Contributions from contemporary theories of gender and psychosocial development. *Social Science and Medicine, 37*, 1261–1269.

LOCK, M. (1993). *Encounters with aging*. Berkeley, CA: University of California Press.

LOCKMAN, J. J., AND THELAN, E. (1993). Developmental biodynamics: Brain, body, behavior connections. *Child Development, 64*, 953–959.

LOEVINGER, J. (1976). *Ego development: Conceptions and theories*. San Francisco: Jossey-Bass.

LOMBARDI, J. (September 1990). Head Start: The nation's pride, a nation's challenge. *Young Children*, pp. 22–29.

LONDERVILLE, S., & MAIN, M. (1981). Security of attachment, compliance, and maternal training methods in the second year of life. *Developmental Psychology, 17*, 289–299.

LONG, H. B., & ROSSING, B. E. (June 1978). Tuition waivers for older Americans. *Lifelong Learning: The Adult Years*, pp. 10–13.

LONGINO, C. F. (1987). *The oldest Americans: State profiles for data-based planning*. Coral Gables, FL: University of Miami Department of Sociology.

LOPATA, H., HEINEMANN, G. G., & BAUM, J. (1982). Loneliness: Antecedents and copying strategies in the lives of widows. In L. A. Peplau & D. Perlman (Eds.), *Loneliness: A sourcebook of current theory, research and therapy* (pp. 310–326). New York: Wiley.

LOPATA, H. Z. (1975). Widowhood: Societal factors in life-span disruptions and alterations. In N. Datan & L. H. Ginsberg (Eds.), *Life-span developmental psychology: Normative life crisis*. New York: Academic Press.

LOPATA, H. Z. (1979). *Women as widows: Support systems*. New York: Elsevier.

LOPATA, H. Z., & BARNEWOLT, D. (1984). The middle years: Changes and variations in social role commitments. In G Baruch & J. Brooks-Gunn (Eds.), *Women in midlife* (pp. 83–108). New York: Plenum.

LORD, L. J., SCHERSCHEL, P. M., THORNTON, J., MOORE, L. J., & QUICK, B. E. (October 5, 1987). Desperately seeking baby. *U.S. News & World Report*, pp. 58–64.

LORD, M. (June 12, 1995). Feathering a shared nest. *U.S. News & World Report*, pp. 86–88.

LORENZ, K. Z. (1952). *King Solomon's ring*. New York: Crowell.

LOURIE, I. S., CAMPIGLIA, P., JAMES, L. R., & DEWITT, J. (1979). Adolescent abuse and neglect: The role of runaway youth programs. *Children Today, 8*, 27–40.

LOVAAS, I. (1977). *The autistic child: Language development through behavior modification*. New York: Halsted Press.

LOVAAS, O. I. (1962). Effect of exposure to symbolic aggression on aggressive behavior. *Child Development, 32*, 37–44.

LOWENTHAL, M. F., THURNHER, M., CHIRIBOGA, D., & ASSOCIATES. (1977). *Four stages of life*. San Francisco: Jossey-Bass.

LOZOFF, B. (1989). Nutrition and behavior. *American Psychologist, 44(2)*, 231–236.

LUBIC, R. W., & ERNST, E. K. (1978). The childbearing center: An alternative to conventional care. *Nursing Outlook, 26*, 754–760.

LUCARIELLO, J., & NELSON, K. (1987). Remembering and planning talk between mothers and children. *Discourse Processes, 10*, 219–235.

LUCKEY, I. (1994). African American elders: The support network of generational kin. *Families in Society: Journal of Contemporary Human Services, 75(2)*, 33–36.

MACCOBY, E. E. (March 15, 1979). *Parent–child interaction*. Paper presented at the biennial meeting of the Society for Research in Child Development.

MACCOBY, E. E. (1980). *Social development: Psychological growth and the parent–child relationship*. New York: Harcourt Brace Jovanovich.

MACCOBY, E. E. (1984). Socialization and developmental change. *Child Development, 55*, 317–328.

MACCOBY, E. E. (1990). Gender and relationships: A developmental account. *American Psychologist, 45*, 513–520.

MACCOBY, E. E. (1992). The role of parents in the socialization of children: An historical overview. *Developmental Psychology, 28(6)*, 1006–1017.

MACCOBY, E. E., & FELDMAN, S. S. (1972). Mother-attachment and stranger-reactions in the third year of life. *Monographs of the Society for Research in Child Development, 37(1, Serial No. 146)*.

MACCOBY, E. E., & JACKLIN, C. N. (1974). *The psychology of sex differences*. Stanford: Stanford University Press.

MACCOBY, E. E., & JACKLIN, C. N. (1980). Sex differences in aggression: A rejoinder and reprise. *Child Development, 51*, 964–980.

MACCOBY, E. E., & MARTIN, J. A. (1983). Socialization in the context of the family: Parent–child interaction. In P. H. Mussen (Ed.), *Handbook of child psychology: Vol. 4. Socialization, personality, and social development*. New York: Wiley.

MACDERMID, S. M., HEILBRUN, G., & GILLESPIE, L. G. (1997). The generativity of employed mothers in multiple roles: 1979 and 1991. In M. E. Lachman, & J. B. James (Eds.), *Multiple paths of midlife development*. Chicago: University of Chicago Press.

MACFARLANE, A. (February 1978). What a baby knows. *Human Nature, 1*, 81–86.

MACGREGOR, S. N., KEITH, L. G., CHASNOFF, I. J., ROSNER, M. A., CHISUM, G. M., SHAW, P., & MINOGUE, J. P. (1987). Cocaine use during pregnancy: Adverse perinatal outcome. *American Journal of Obstetrics and Gynecology, 1(57)*, 66–90.

MACK, J., & HICKLER, H. (1981). *Vivienne: The life and suicide of an adolescent girl*. Boston: Little, Brown.

MACKENZIE, C. (1978). Gray panthers on the prowl. In R. Gross, B. Gross, & S. Seidman (Eds.), *The new old: Struggling for decent aging*. Garden City, NY: Anchor Press/Doubleday.

MACKEY, M. C. (1995). Women's evaluation of their childbirth performance. *Maternal-Child Nursing Journal, 23*, 57–72.

MADDEN, J. D., PAYNE, T. F., & MILLER, S. (1986). Maternal cocaine abuse and effect on the newborn. *Pediatrics, 77*, 209–211.

MADDUX, J. E., ROBERTS, M. C., SLEDDEN, E. A., & WRIGHT, L. (1986). Developmental issues in child health psychology. *American Psychologist, 41(1)*, 25–34.

MADSEN, M. C. (1971). Developmental and cross-cultural differences in the cooperative and competitive behavior of young children. *Journal of Cross-Cultural Psychology, 2*, 365–371.

MADSEN, M. C., & SHAPIRA, A. (1970). Cooperative and competitive behavior of urban Afro-American, Anglo-American, Mexican-American, and Mexican village children. *Developmental Psychology, 3*, 16–20.

MAEHR, M. L., & BRESKAMP, L. A. (1986). *The motivation factor: A theory of personal investment*. Lexington, MA: D. C. Heath.

MAHLER, M., PINE, F., & BERGMAN, A. (1975). *The psychological birth of the human infant: Symbiosis and individuation*. New York: Basic Books.

MAKIN, J. W., & PORTER, R. H. (1989). Attractiveness of lactating females' breast odors to neonates. *Child Development, 60*, 803–810.

MALINA, R., & BOUCHARD, C. (1990). *Growth, maturation, and physical activity*. Champaign, TL: Human Kinetics.

MANDELL, F., MCCLAIN, M., & REECE, R. (1987). Sudden and unexpected death. *American Journal of Diseases of Children, 141*, 748–750.

MANDLER, J. M. (1983). *Representation*. In J. H. Flavell & E. M. Markham (Eds.), *Handbook of child psychology: Cognitive development* (Vol. 3). New York: Wiley.

MANDLER, J. M. (1988). How to build a baby: On the development of an accurate representational system. *Cognitive Development, 3*, 113–136.

MANDLER, J. M. (May–June 1990). A new perspective on cognitive development in infancy. *American Scientist, 78*, 236–243.

MANDLER, J. M. (1992). Commentary. *Human Development, 35*, 246–253.

MANNING, B. H., & WHITE, C. S. (1990). Task-relevant private speech as a function of age and sociability. *Psychology in the Schools, 27*, 365–372.

MANTON, K., BLAZER, D., & WOODBURY, M. (1987). Suicide in middle age and later life: Sex and race specific life table and chart analyses. *Journal of Gerontology, 42*, 219–227.

MARATSOS, M. (1983). Some current issues in the study of the acquisition of grammar. In J. H. Flavell and E. M. Markham (Eds.), *Handbook of child psychology: Vol. 3 Cognitive Development*. New York: Wiley.

MARCIA, J. (1980). Identity in adolescence. In J. Adelson (Ed.), *Handbook of adolescent psychology*. New York: Wiley.

MARCOEN, A., GOOSSENS, L., & CAES, P. (1987). Loneliness in prethrough adolescence: Exploring the contributions of a multidimensional approach. *Journal of Youth and Adolescence, 16*.

MARCUS, G. F., PINKER, S., ULLMAN, M., HOLLANDER, M., ROSEN, T. J., & KU FEI, T. J. (1992). Overregularization in language acquisition. *Monographs of Society for Research in Child Development, 57(4)*, Serial No. 228, 1–164.

MARET, E., & FINLAY, B. (1984). The distribution of household labor among women in dual-earner families. *Journal of Marriage and the Family*, 357–364.

MARIESKIND, H. I. (1989). Caesarean section in the United States: Has it changed since 1979? In *An evaluation of Caesarean sections in the United States*. U.S. Department of Health, Education, & Welfare.

MARKS, N. F. (1996). Caregiving across the lifespan: National prevalence and predictors. *Family Relations, 45*, 27–36.

MARSH, H. W., CRAVEN, R. G., & DEBUS, R. (1991). Self-concepts of young children 5 to 8 years of age: Measurement and multidimensional structure. *Journal of Educational Psychology, 83(3)*, 377–392.

MARTIN, C. L. (1989). Children's use of gender-related information in making social judgments. *Developmental Psychology, 25(1)*, 80–88.

MARTIN, C. L. (1990). Attitudes and expectations about children with nontraditional and traditional gender roles. *Sex Roles, 22(3/4)*, 151.

MARTIN, C. L., & HALVERSON, C. F., JR. (1981). A schematic processing model of sex-typing and stereotyping in children. *Child Development, 52*, 1119–1134.

MARTINEZ, R. O., & DUKES, R. L. (1997). The effects of ethnic identity, ethnicity, and gender on adolescent well-being. *Journal of Youth and Adolescence, 26*, 503–511.

MARZOFF, D. P., & DELOACHE, J. S. (1994). Transfer in young children's understanding of spatial representations. *Child Development, 65,* 1–15.

MASLACH, C., & JACKSON, S. E. (May 1979). Burned-out cops and their families. *Psychology Today,* pp. 59–62.

MASLOW, A. H. (1954). *Motivation and personality.* New York: Harper & Brothers.

MASLOW, A. H. (1968). *Toward a psychology of being* (2nd ed.). Princeton, NJ: Van Nostrand Reinhold.

MASLOW, A. H. (1979). *The journals of A. H. Maslow.* (R. J. Lowry & B. G. Maslow, Eds.). Monterey, CA: Brooks/Cole.

MASON, R. P. (1993). Aluminum in Alzheimer's disease. *Journal of the American Medical Association, 270*(15), 1868.

MASTERS, W. H., JOHNSON, P. E., & KOLODNEY, R. C. (1982). *Human sexuality* (2nd ed.). Boston: Little, Brown.

MATAS, L., AREND, R. A., & SROUFE, L. A. (1978). Continuity of adaptation in the second year: The relationship between quality of attachment and later competence. *Child Development, 49,* 547–556.

MATES, D., & ALLISON, K. R. (1992). Sources of stress and coing responses of high school students. *Adolescence, 27(106),* 463–474.

MATTHEWS, K., & RODIN, J. (1989). Women's changing work roles: Impact on health, family and public policy. *American Psychologist, 44,* 1389–1393.

MATTHEWS, S. H., & ROSNER, T. T. (February 1988). Shared filial responsibility: The family as the primary care-giver. *Journal of Marriage and the Family, 50,* 185–195.

MATTHEWS, S., WERKNER, J., & DELANEY, P. (1989). Relative contributions of help by employed and nonemployed sisters to their elderly parents. *Journal of Gerontology, 44,* S36–44.

MAURER, D., & MAURER, C. (1988). *The world of the newborn.* New York: Basic Books.

MAURO, J. (1991). *The friend that only I can see: A longitudinal investigation of children's imaginary companions.* Unpublished doctoral dissertation. University of Oregon.

MAY, R. (1986). *Politics and innocence: A humanistic debate.* Dallas, TX: Saybrook, & New York: Norton.

MCADOO, H. P. (1995). Stress levels, family help patterns, and religiosity in middle- and working-class African American single mothers. *Journal of Black Psychology, 21,* 424–449.

MCBEAN, L. D., FORGAC, T., & FINN, S. C. (June 1994). Osteoporosis: Visions for care and prevention—A conference report. *Journal of the American Dietic Association, 94*(6), 668–671.

MCBRIDE, A. (1990). Mental health effects of women's multiple roles. *American Psychologist, 45,* 381–384.

MCBRIDE, S. L. (Fall 1990). Maternal moderators of child care: The role of maternal separation anxiety. *New Directions for Child Development, 49,* 53–70.

MCCALL, R. B., EICHORN, D. H., & HOGARTY, P. S. (1977). Transitions in early mental development. *Monographs of the Society for Research in Child Development, 42*(3, Serial No. 171), 1–75.

MCCARTNEY, K., HARRIS, M. J., & BERNIERI, F. (1990). Growing up and growing apart: A developmental meta-analysis of twin studies. *Psychological Bulletin, 107,* 226–237.

MCCARY, J. L. (1978). *Human sexuality* (3rd ed.). New York: Van Nostrand Reinhold.

MCCLELLAND, D. C. (1955). Some social consequences of achievement motivation. In M. R. Jones (Ed.), *Nebraska symposium on motivation* (Vol. 3). Lincoln: University of Nebraska Press.

MCCORD, W., MCCORD, J., & ZOLA, I. K. (1959). *Origins of crime.* New York: Columbia University Press.

MCCRAE, R. (1989). Age differences and changes in the use of coping mechanisms. *Journal of Gerontology, 44,* P161–169.

MCCRAE, R. R., & COSTA, P. T., JR. (1984). *Emerging lives, enduring dispositions: Personality in adulthood.* Boston: Little, Brown.

MCCREADIE, C., & TINKER, A. (1993). Review: Abuse of elderly people in the domestic setting: A UK perspective. *Age and Ageing, 22,* 65–69.

MCCUNE-NICOLICH, L. (1981). Toward symbolic functioning: Structure of early pretend games and potential parallels with language. *Child Development, 52,* 785–797.

MCGOLDRICK, M. (1980). The joining of families through marriage: The new couple. In E. A. Carter & M. McGoldrick (Eds.), *The family life cycle.* New York: Gardner Press.

MCGRAW, M. (1935). *Growth: A study of Johnny and Timmy.* New York: Appleton-Century.

MCKNEW, D. H., JR., CYTRYN, L., & YAHRAES, H. (1983). *Why isn't Johnny crying? Coping with depression in children.* New York: Norton.

MCKUSICK, V. A. (1994). *Mendelian inheritance in man: A catalog of human genes and geneitc disorders* (11th ed). Baltimore: Johns Hopkins University Press.

MCKUSICK, Y. (1986). *Mendelian inheritance in man* (7th ed.). Baltimore: Johns Hopkins University Press.

MCLANAHAN, S., & BOOTH, K. (1989). Mother-only families: Problems, prospects, and politics. *Journal of Marriage and the Family, 51,* 557–580.

MCLOUGHLIN, M., SHRYER, T. L., GOODE, E. E., & MCAULIFFE, K. (August 8, 1988). Men vs. women. *U.S. News World & Report.*

MCLOYD, V. C. (1998). Economic disadvantage and child development. *American Psychologist, 53,* 185–204.

MCLOYD, V. C., & WILSON, L. (1990). Maternal behavior, social support, and economic conditions as predictors of distress in children. *New Directions for Child Development, 46,* 49–69.

MCLOYD, V. C., ET AL. (1994). Unemployment and work interruption among African American single mothers: Effects on parenting and adolescent socioemotional functioning. *Child Development, 65,* 562–589.

MCNEILL, D. (1972). *The acquisition of language: The study of developmental psycholinguistics.* New York: Harper & Row.

MEAD, G. H. (1934). *Mind, self, and society: From the standpoint of a social behaviorist.* Chicago: University of Chicago Press.

MEAD, M. (January 1972). A new understanding of childhood. *Redbook,* p. 49ff.

MEAD, M., & NEWTON, N. (1967). Cultural patterning of perinatal behavior. In S. A. Richardson & A. F. Guttermacher (Eds.), *Childbearing: Its social and psychological aspects.* Baltimore: Williams & Wilkins.

MEADOW, K. P. (1975). The development of deaf children. In E. M. Hetherington (Ed.), *Review of child development research* (Vol. 5). Chicago: University of Chicago Press.

MEEHAN, P. J., LAMB, J. A., SALTZMAN, L. E. & O'CARROLL, P. W. (1992). Attempted suicide among young adults: Progress toward a meaningful estimate of prevalence. *American Journal of Psychiatry, 149,* 41–44.

MEISAMI, E. (1994). Aging of the sensory systems. In Timiras, P. S. (Ed.) *Physiological basis of aging and geriatrics* (2nd ed.). Ann Arbor, IN: CRC Press.

MELTZOFF, A. N. (1988a). Infant imitation and memory: Nine month olds in immediate and deferred tests. *Child Development, 59,* 217–225.

MELTZOFF, A. N. (1988b). Infant imitation after a 1–week delay: Long-term memory for novel acts and multiple stimuli. *Developmental Psychology, 24*(4), 470–476.

MELTZOFF, A. N., & BORTON, R. W. (1979). Intermodel matching by human neonates. *Nature, 282,* 403–404.

MELTZOFF, A. N., & MOORE, M. K. (1989). Imitation in newborn infants: Exploring the range of gestures imitated and the underlying mechanisms. National Institute of Child Health and Human Development (HD-22514).

MELTZOFF, A. N., & MOORE, M. K. (1989). Imitation in newborn infants: Exploring the range of gestures imitated and the underlying mechanisms. *Developmental Psychology, 25*(6), 954–962.

MERRIMAN, W. E. (1987). *Lexical contrast in toddlers: A re-analysis of the diary evidence.* Paper presented at the biennial meeting of the Society of Research in Child Development, Baltimore.

MERVIS, C. B. (1987). Child-basic object categories and early lexical development. In U. Neisser (Ed.), *Concepts and conceptual development: Ecological and intellectual factors in categorization.* London: Cambridge University Press.

MESTEL, R. (1997). A safer estrogen: Would you take it? *Health, 11, no. 8,* 73–75.

METCOFF, J., COSTILOE, J. P., CROSBY, W., BENTLE, L., SESHACHALAM, D., SANDSTEAD, H. H., BODWELL, C. E., WEAVER, F., & MCCLAIN, P. (1981). Maternal nutrition and fetal outcome. *American Journal of Clinical Nutrition, 34,* 708–721.

MEYER, B. J. F. (1987). Reading comprehension and aging. In K. W. Schaie (Ed.), *Annual review of gerontology and geriatrics* (Vol. 7) New York: Springer-Verlag.

MEYER, P. H. (1980). Between families: The unattached young adult. In E. A. Carter & M. McGoldrick (Eds.), *The family life cycle.* New York: Gardner Press.

MICHAEL, R. T., GAGNON, J. H., LAUMANN, E. O., & KOLATA, G. (1994). *Sex in America: A definitive survey.* Boston: Little, Brown.

MILES, M. S. (1984). Helping adults mourn the death of a child. In H. Wass & C. A. Corr

(Eds.), *Childhood and death*. Washington, DC: Hemisphere.

MILGRAM, S. (1963). Behavioral study of obedience. *Journal of Abnormal and Social Psychology, 67,* 371–378.

MILLER, B. (1990). Gender differences in spouse caregiver strain: Socialization and role explanations. *Journal of Marriage and the Family, 52,* 311–321.

MILLER, B. C., MCCOY, J. K., OLSON, T. D., & WALLACE, C. M. (1986). Parental discipline and control attempts in relation to adolescent sexual attitudes and behavior. *Journal of Marriage and the Family, 48,* 503–512.

MILLER, B. C., & SNEESBY, K. R. (1988). Educational correlates of adolescents' sexual attitudes and behavior. *Journal of Youth and Adolescence, 17,* 521–530.

MILLER, B. C., NORTON, M. C., FAN, X., & CHRISTOPHERSON, C. R. (1998). Pubertal development, parental communication, and sexual values in relation to adolescent sexual behavior. *Journal of Early Adolescence, 18,* 27–52.

MILLER, B. D. (Spring 1995). Percepts and practices: Researching identity formation among Indian Hindu adolescents in the United States. *New Directions for Child Development, 67,* 71–85.

MILLER, J., SCHOOLER, C., KOHN, M. L., & MILLER, R. (1979). Women and work: The psychological effects of occupational conditions. *American Journal of Sociology, 85,* 66–94.

MILLER, M. (1982). *Gray power: A survival manual for senior citizens.* Paradise, CA: Dust Books.

MILLER, P. (1989). *Theories of developmental psychology* (2nd ed.). New York: Freeman.

MILLER, P. H., & ALOISE, P. A. (1989). Young children's understanding of the psychological causes of behavior: A review. *Child Development, 60,* 257–285.

MILLER, P. J., MINTZ, J., HOOGSTRA, L., FUNG, H. J., & POTTS, R (1992). The narrated self: Young children's construction of self in relation to others in conversational stories of personal experience. *Merrill–Palmer Quarterly, 38*(1), 45–67.

MILLER, P., WILEY, A. R., FUNG, H., & LIANG, C.-H. (1997). Personal storytelling as a medium of socialization in Chinese and American families. *Child Development, 68,* 557–568.

MILLER, S. K. (1993). Alzheimer's gene "the most important ever found." *New Scientist, 139*(1887), 17.

MILLSTEIN, S. G. (Winter 1990). Risk factors for AIDS among adolescents. In W. Gardner, S. G. Millstein, & Brian L. Wilcox (Eds.), *New Directions for Child Development: Vol. 50. Adolescents in the AIDS epidemic.* San Francisco: Jossey-Bass.

MILLSTEIN, S. G. (Winter 1990). Risk factors for AIDS among adolescents. In W. Gardner, S. G. Millstein, & B. L. Wilcox (Eds.). *New Directions for Child Development, 50,* 3–4.

MILNE, A. A. (1926/1961). *Winnie-the-Pooh.* New York: Dutton.

MIRINGOFF, N. (February 1987). A timely and controversial article. *Zero to Three,* p. 26.

MOCK, N. B., BERTRAND, J. T., & MANGANI, N. (1986). Correlates and implications of

breastfeeding practices in Bas Zaire. *Journal of Biosocial Science, 18,* 231–245.

MOEN, P. (1998). Recasting careers: Changing reference groups, risks, and realities. *Generations,* Spring, 40–45.

MOERK, E. L. (1989). The LAD was a lady and the tasks were ill-defined. *Developmental Review, 9,* 21–57.

MONEY, J. (1980). *Love and love sickness: The science of sex, gender differences and pair-bonding.* Baltimore: Johns Hopkins University Press.

MONMANEY, T. (May 16, 1988). Preventing early births. *Newsweek.*

MONTAGU, M. F. (1950). Constitutional and prenatal factors in infant and child health. In M. J. Senn (Ed.), *Symposium on the healthy personality.* New York: Josiah Macy Jr. Foundation.

MONTE, C. F. (1987). *Beneath the mask: An introduction to theories of personality* (3rd ed.). New York: Holt, Rinehart and Winston.

MONTEMAYOR, R. (1983). Parents and adolescents in conflict: All families some of the time and some families all of the time. *Journal of Early Adolescence, 3,* 83–103.

MONTEMAYOR, R., & BROWNLEE, J. R. (1987). Fathers, mothers and adolescents: Gender-based differences in parental roles during adolescence. *Journal of Youth and Adolescence, 16,* 281–292.

MOORE, G. (June 1984). The superbaby myth. *Psychology Today,* pp. 6–7.

MOORE, K. (1988). *The developiong human: Clinically oriented embryology* (4th ed.). Philadelphia: Saunders.

MOORE, M. K., BORTON, R., & DARBY, B. L. (1978). Visual tracking in young infants: Evidence for object permanence? *Journal of Experimental Child Psychology, 25,* 183–198.

MOORE, W. E. (1969). Occupational socialization. In D. A. Goslin (Ed.), *Handbook of socialization theory and research.* Chicago: Rand McNally.

MOR, V., SHERWOOD, S., & GUTKIN, C. (1986). A national study of residential care for the aged. *The Gerontologist, 26,* 405–416.

MORGAN, D. (1989). Adjusting to widowhood: Do social networks really make it easier? *The Gerontologist, 29,* 101–107.

MORGAN, L. (1984). Changes in family interaction following widowhood. *Journal of Marriage and the Family, 46*(2), 323–331.

MORRISON, D. M. (1985). Adolescent contraceptive behavior: A review. *Psychological Bulletin, 98,* 538–568.

MOSES, B. (March 1983). The 59-cent dollar. *Vocational Guidance Quarterly.*

MOSHER, W. D., & PRATT, W. F. (1990). Fecundity and infertility in the United States, 1965–88. *Advanced Data from Vital and Health Statistics, 192.* Hyattsville, MD: National Center for Health Statistics.

MOTENKO, A. (1989). The frustrations, gratifications, and well-being of dementia caregivers. *The Gerontologist, 29,* 166–172.

MUELLER, E., & LUCAS, T. (1975). A developmental analysis of peer interaction among toddlers. In M. Lewis & L. A. Rosenblum (Eds.), *Peer relations and friendship.* New York: Wiley.

MUELLER, E. & SILVERMAN, N. (1989). Peer relations in maltreated children. In Dante Cicchettti and Vicki Carlson (Eds.), *Child maltreatment: Theory and research on the causes and consequences of child abuse and neglect.* Cambridge, England: Cambridge University Press.

MUIR, D., & FIELD, J. (1979). Newborn infants orient to sounds. *Child Development, 50,* 431–436.

MURPHY, J., & FLORIO, C. (1978). Older Americans: Facts and potential. In R. Gross, B. Gross, & S. Seidman (Eds.), *The new old: Struggling for decent aging.* Garden City, NY: Anchor Press/Doubleday.

MURPHY, L. B. (1962). *The widening world of childhood: Paths toward mastery.* New York: Basic Books.

MURPHY, P. A. (1993). Preterm birth prevention programs: A critique of current literature. *Journal of Nurse-Midwifery, 38*(6), 324–335.

MURRAY, A., DOLBY, R., NATION, R., & THOMAS, D. (1981). Effects of epidural anaesthesia on newborns and their mothers. *Child Development, 52,* 71–82.

MURSTEIN, B. I. (1980). Mate selection in the 1970s. *Journal of Marriage and the Family, 42,* 777–789.

MURSTEIN, B. I. (1982). Marital choice. In B. Wolman (Ed.), *Handbook of developmental psychology.* Englewood Cliffs, NJ: Prentice Hall.

MURSTEIN, B. I., CHALPIN, M. J., HEARD, K. V., & VYSE, S. A. (1989). Sexual behavior, drugs, and relationship patterns on a college campus over thirteen years. *Adolescence, 24,* 125–139.

MUSICK, J. S. (Fall 1994). Directions: Capturing the childbearing context. *SRCD Newsletter,* pp. 1, 6–7.

MUSSEN, P. H., CONGER J. J., & KAGAN, J. (1974). *Child development and personality.* New York: Harper & Row.

MUTRYN, C. S. (1993). Psychosocial impact of Cesarean section on the family: A literature review. *Social Science and Medicine, 37,* 1271–1281.

MUUSS, R. E. (Summer 1986). Adolescent eating disorder: Bulimia. *Adolescence,* pp. 257–267.

MYERS, N. A., CLIFTON, R. K., & CLARKSON, M. G. (1987). When they were very young: Almost-threes remember two years ago. *Infant Behavior and Development, 10,* 123–132.

MYERS, N. A., & PERLMUTTER, M. (1978). Memory in the years from two to five. In P. Ornstein (Ed.), *Memory development in children.* Hillsdale, NJ: Erlbaum.

MYERS, R. E., & MYERS, S. E. (1978). Use of sedative, analgesic, and anesthetic drugs during labor and delivery: Bane or boon? *American Journal of Obstetrics and Gynecology, 133,* 83.

NAEYE, R. L. (1979). Weight gain and the outcome of pregnancy. *American Journal of Obstetrics and Gynecology, 135,* 3.

NAEYE, R. L. (1980). Abruptio placentae and placenta previa: Frequency, perinatal mortality, and cigarette smoking. *Obstetrics and Gynecology, 55,* 701–704.

NAEYE, R. L. (1981). Influence of maternal cigarette smoking during pregnancy on fetal and childhood growth. *Obstetrics and Gynecology, 57,* 18–21.

NAGEL, K. L., & JONES, K. H. (1992). Sociological factors in the development of eating disorders. *Adolescence, 27,* 107–113.

NAROLL, H. G. (1996). Computers, thinking, and education. In M. G. Luther & E. Cole (eds.), *Dynamic assessment for instruction: From theory to application.* North York, ON, Canada: Captus Press.

NATIONAL ASSOCIATION FOR THE EDUCATION OF YOUNG CHILDREN. (1986). *NAEYC position statement on developmentally appropriate practice in early childhood programs: Birth through age eight.* Washington, DC: NAEYC.

NATIONAL CENTER FOR HEALTH STATISTICS. (1984). Trends in teenage childbearing, United States 1970–81. *Vital and Health Statistics* (Series 21, No. 41). U.S. Department of Health and Human Services.

NATIONAL CENTER FOR HEALTH STATISTICS. (June 3, 1987). Advance report of final marriage statistics, 1984. *Monthly Vital Statistics Report, 36*(2).

NATIONAL CENTER FOR HEALTH STATISTICS. (June 29, 1989). *Monthly Vital Statistics Report, 38*(3). Washington, DC: National Center for Health Statistics.

NATIONAL CENTER FOR HEALTH STATISTICS. (1990). *Health, United States, 1989.* Hyattsville, MD: Public Health Service.

NATIONAL CENTER FOR HEALTH STATISTICS. (August 1990). Advance report of final natality statistics, 1988. *Monthly Vital Statistics Report, 38*(4 Supplement). Hyattsville, MD: Public Health Service.

NATIONAL CENTER FOR HEALTH STATISTICS. (November 28, 1990). Advance report of final mortality statistics, 1988. *Monthly Vital Statistics Report, 39*(7). Hyattsville, MD: Public Health Service.

NATIONAL CENTER FOR HEALTH STATISTICS. (1991a). Births, marriages, divorces, and deaths for January 1991. *Monthly Vital Statistics Report, 40* (1). Hyattsville, MD: Public Health Service.

NATIONAL CENTER FOR HEALTH STATISTICS. (1991b). Advance report of final divorce statistics, 1988. *Monthly Vital Statistics Report, 39* (12, Supplement 2). Hyattsville, MD: Public Health Service.

NATIONAL CENTER FOR HEALTH STATISTICS. (1993a). *Health, United States, 1992.* Washington, D.C.: United States Government Printing 41(9).

NATIONAL CENTER FOR HEALTH STATISTICS. (1993b). Advance Report of Final Natality Statistics, 1990. *Monthly Vital Statistics Report, 41(9).*

NATIONAL CENTER FOR HEALTH STATISTICS. (1995). *Monthly vital statistics report* (March 22, 1995), 43, 6(S), 5.

NATIONAL DAIRY COUNCIL. (1977). Nutrition of the elderly. *Dairy Council Digest, 48,* 1.

NATIONAL INSTITUTE OF CHILD HEALTH AND HUMAN DEVELOPMENT (1997). The effects of infant child care on infant-mother attachment security: Results of the NICHD study of early child care. *Child Development, 68,* 860–879.

NATIONAL CENTER ON ADDICTION AND SUBSTANCE ABUSE AT COLUMBIA UNIVERSITY (1996). Substance abuse and the American Woman: Using the law. New York.

NATIONAL INSTITUTE ON DRUG ABUSE. (1984). *Student drug use in America: 1975–1983.* Washington, DC: Government Printing Office.

NATIONAL INSTITUTE ON DRUG ABUSE. (1987). *National trends in drug use and related factors among American high school students and young adults, 1975–1986.* U.S. Department of Health & Human Services.

NATIONAL INSTITUTE ON DRUG ABUSE. (1989). *National trends in drug use and related factors among American high school students and young adults, 1975–1988.* U.S. Department of Health & Human Services.

NEIMARK, E. D., (1975). Intellectual development during adolescence. In F. D. Horowitz (Ed.), *Review of child development* (Vol. 4). Chicago: University of Chicago Press.

NELSON, C. A., & BLOOM, F. E. (1997). Child development and neuroscience. *Child Development, 68,* 970–987.

NELSON, K. (1974). Concept, word and sentence: Interrelations in acquisition and development. *Psychological Review, 81,* 267–285.

NELSON, K. (1981). Individual differences in language development: Implications for development and language. *Developmental Psychology, 17,* 170–187.

NELSON, K. (1986). *Event knowledge: Structure and function in development.* Hillsdale, NJ: Erlbaum.

NELSON, K. (September 1987). What's in a name? Reply to Seidenberg and Petitto. *Journal of Experimental Psychology, 116*(3), 293–296.

NELSON, K., FIBUSH, R., HUDSON, J., & LUCARIELLO, J. (1983). *Scripts and the development of memory.* In M. T. C. Chi (Ed.), *Trends in memory development research.* Basil, Switzerland: Carger.

NELSON, K., & GRUENDEL, J. M. (1986). Generalized event representations: Basic building blocks of cognitive development. In A. Brown & M. Lamb (Eds.), *Advances in developmental psychology* (Vol. 1). Hillsdale, NJ: Erlbaum.

NEMETH, R. J., & BOWLING, J. M. (1985). Son preference and its effects on Korean lactation practices. *Journal of Biosocial Science, 17,* 451–459.

NEUGARTEN, B. (1968/1967). The awareness of middle age. In B. Neugarten (Ed.), *Middle age and aging.* Chicago: University of Chicago Press.

NEUGARTEN, B. L. (1968a). Adult personality: Toward a psychology of the life cycle. In B. L. Neugarten (Ed.), *Middle age and aging.* Chicago: University of Chicago Press.

NEUGARTEN, B. L. (1968b). The awareness of middle age. In B. L. Neugarten (Ed.), *Middle age and aging.* Chicago: University of Chicago Press.

NEUGARTEN, B. L. (1969). Continuities and discontinuities of psychological issues into adult life. *Human Development, 12,* 121–130.

NEUGARTEN, B. L. (1970). The old and the young in modern societies. *American Behavioral Scientist, 14,* 18–24.

NEUGARTEN, B. L. (December 1971). Grow old along with me! The best is yet to be. *Psychology Today,* pp. 45–48ff.

NEUGARTEN, B. L. (1976). *The psychology of aging: An overview.* Washington, DC: American Psychological Association.

NEUGARTEN, B. L. (1977). Personality and aging. In I. Birren & K. W. Schaie (Eds.), *Handbook of the psychology of aging.* New York: Van Nostrand Reinhold.

NEUGARTEN, B. L. (1978). The wise of the young-old. In R. Gross, B. Gross, & S. Seidman (Eds.), *The new old: Struggling for decent aging.* Garden City, NY: Anchor Books/Doubleday.

NEUGARTEN, B. L. (1979). Time, age and the life cycle. *American Journal of Psychiatry, 136,* 887–894.

NEUGARTEN, B. L. (February 1980). Must everything be a midlife crisis? *Prime Time,* pp. 263–264.

NEUGARTEN, B. L., & MOORE, J. W. (1968). The changing age status system. In B. L. Neugarten (Ed.), *Middle age and aging.* Chicago: University of Chicago Press.

NEUGARTEN, B. L., & NEUGARTEN D. A. (1987). The changing meanings of age. *Psychology Today, 21*(5), 29–33.

NEUGARTEN, B. L., WOOD, V., KRAINES, R., & LOOMIS, B. (1968). Women's attitudes toward the menopause. In B. L. Neugarten (Ed.), *Middle age and aging.* Chicago: University of Chicago Press.

NEVILLE, B., & PARKE, R. D. (1997). Waiting for paternity: Interpersonal and contextual implications of the time of fatherhood. *Sex Roles, 37,* 45–59.

NEWCOMB, A. F., BUKOWSKI, W. M., & PATTEE, L. (1992). The influence of teacher feedback on young children's peer preferences and perceptions. *Developmental Psychology, 28*(5), 933–940.

NEWCOMB, M. D., & BENTLER, P. M. (1989). Substance use and abuse among children and teenagers. *American Psychologist, 44,* 242–248.

NEW ENGLAND JOURNAL OF MEDICINE (1997). Postmenopausal hormone-replacement theory—time for a reappraisal? (editorial). *Volume 336,* 1821–1822.

NEWMAN, B. M. (1982). Mid-life development. In B. Wolman (Ed.), *Handbook of developmental psychology.* Englewood Cliffs, NJ: Prentice Hall.

NEWMAN, L. F., & BUKA, S. L. (1991). Clipped wings: The fullest look yet at how prenatal exposure to drugs, alcohol, and nicotine hobbles children's learning. *American Educator, 42,* 27–33.

NEWMAN, L. S. (1990). Intentional and unintentional memory in young children: Remembering vs. playing. *Journal of Experimental Child Psychology, 50,* 243–258.

NEWMAN, L., & BUKA, S. (Spring 1991). Clipped wings. *American Educator,* pp. 27–33, 42.

NEW, R. (1988). Parental goals and Italian infant care. In R. B. LeVine, P. Miller, & M. West (Eds.), *New Directions for Child Devel-*

opment: Vol. 40, Parental behavior in diverse societies (pp. 51–63). San Francisco: Jossey-Bass.

NEW, R. (1990). Excellent early education: A city in Italy has it. *Young Children, 45*(6), 11–12.

NEWSWEEK. (February 11, 1980). The children of divorce, pp. 58–63.

NEWSWEEK. (November 15, 1976). New science of birth, pp. 62–64.

NEW YORK TIMES. (August 1, 1989). Casual drug use is sharply down. P. A14.

NEW YORK TIMES. (March 4, 1991). Schools are not families. Editorial, p. A16.

NEY, P. G. (1988). Transgenerational child abuse. *Child Psychiatry and Human Development, 18,* 151–168.

NICHOLS, B. (1990). *Moving and Learning: The elementary school physical education experience.* St. Louis, MO: Times Mirror/Mosby College Publishing.

NICHOLS, P. L., & CHEN, T. C. (1981). *Minimal brain dysfunction: A prospective study.* Hillsdale, NJ: Erlbaum.

NICOLOPOULOU, A. (1993). Play, cognitive development, and the social world: Piage, Vygotsky, and Beyond. *Human Development, 36,* 1–23.

NILSSON, L. (1990). *A child is born.* New York: Delacorte.

NILSSON, L., & HAMBERGER, L. (1990). *A child is born* (rev. ed.). New York: Dell.

NOCK, S. (1982). The life-cycle approach to family analysis. In B. Wolman (Ed.), *Handbook of developmental psychology* (pp. 636–651). Englewood Cliffs, NJ: Prentice Hall.

NORTON, R. D. (1994). Adolescent suicide: Risk factors and countermeasures. *Journal of Health Education, November/December,* 358–361.

NOZYCE, M., HITTELMAN, J., MUENZ, L., DU-RAKO, S. J., FISCHER, M., & WILLOUGHBY, A. (1994). Effect of perinatally acquired human immunodeficiency virus infection on neurodevelopment during the first two years of life. *Pediatrics, 94,* 883–891.

NUGENT, J. K. (November 1994). Cross-cultural studies of child development: Implications for clinicians. *Zero to Three,* p. 6.

NUGENT, J. K., GREENE, S., & MAZOR, K. (October 1990). *The effects of maternal alcohol and nicotine use during pregnancy on birth outcome.* Paper presented at Bebe XXI Simposio Internacional, Lisbon, Portugal.

NUTRITION TODAY. (1982). Alcohol use during pregnancy: A report by the American Council on Science and Health. Reprint.

NYDEGGER, C. N., & MITENESS, L. S. (1996). Midlife: The prime of fathers. In Ryff, C. D., & Seltzer, M. M. (Eds.) *The parental experiment in midlife.* Chicago: University of Chicago Press.

OAKLEY, A., & RICHARDS, M. (1990). Women's experiences of Caesarean delivery. In J. Garcia, R. Kilpatrick, & M. Richards (Eds.), *The politics of maternity care.* Oxford: Clarendon Press.

OB/GYN NEWS. (June 15–30, 1984). In-vitro fertilization comes of age: Issues still unsettled, *19*(12), 3.

O'BRIEN, M., & NAGLE, K. J. (1987). Parents' speech to toddlers: The effect of play context. *Journal of Language Development, 14,* 269–279.

O'BRIEN, S. J., & DEAN, M. (1997). *Scientific American, 267 (9),* 44–51.

O'BRYANT, S. L. (February 1988). Sibling support and older widows' well-being. *Journal of Marriage and the Family, 50,* 173–183.

OCAMPO, K. A., KNIGHT, G. P., & BERNAL, M. E. (1977). The development of cognitive abilities and social identities in children: The case of ethnic identity. *International Journal of Behavioral Development, 21,* 479–500.

OCHS, A., NEWBERRY, J., LENHARDT, M., & HARKINS, S. (1985). Neural and vestibular aging associated with falls. In J. Birren & K. Schaie (Eds.), *The handbook of the psychology of aging* (2nd ed.). New York: Van Nostrand Reinhold.

OCHS, E. (1986). Introduction. In B. B. Schieffelin & E. Ochs (Eds.), *Language socialization across cultures.* Cambridge, UK: Cambridge University Press.

O'CONNOR-FRANCOEUR, P. (April 1983). *Children's concepts of health and their health behavior.* Paper presented at the meeting of the Society for Research in Child Development, Detroit.

O'HARA, M., ZEKOSKI, E., PHILIPPS, & WRIGHT, E. (1990). Controlled prospective study of postpartum mood disorders: Comparison of childbearing and nonchildbearing women. *Journal of Abnormal Psychology, 99,* 3–15.

O'HERON, C. A., & ORLOFSKY, J. L. (1990). Stereotypic and nonstereotypic sex role trait and behavior operations, gender identity and psychological adjustment. *Journal of Personality and Social Psychology, 58*(1), 134–143.

OFFER, D., OSTROV, E., HOWARD, K., & ATKINSON, R. (1988). *The teenage world: Adolescents' self-image in ten countries.* New York: Plenum Medical, 1988.

OHLSSON, A., SHENNAN, A. T., & ROSE, T. H. (1987). Review of causes of perinatal mortality in a regional perinatal center, 1980–84. *American Journal of Obstetrics and Gynecology, 1*(57), 443–445.

OKTAY, J. A., & VOLLAND, P. J. (1981). Community care program for the elderly. *Health and Social Work, 6,* 41–46.

OKUN, B. F. (1984). *Working with adults: Individual, family and career development.* Monterey, CA: Brooks/Cole.

O'LEARY, K. D., & SMITH, D. A. (1991). Marital interactions. *Annual Review of Psychology, 42,* 191–212.

OLLER, D. K., & EILERS, R. E. (1988). The role of audition in infant babbling. *Child Development, 59,* 441–449.

OLSHO, L. W., HARKINS, S. W., & LENHARDT, M. L. (1985). Aging and the auditory system. In J. E. Birren & K. W. Schaie (Eds.), *Handbook of the psychology of aging* (2nd ed. pp. 332–376). New York: Van Nostrand Reinhold.

OLSON, D. H., & LAVEE, Y. (1989). Family systems and family stress: A family life cycle perspective. In K. Kreppner & R. M. Lerner (Eds.), *Family systems and life-span development.* Hillsdale, NJ: Erlbaum.

OLSON, M. R. , & HAYNES, J. A. (1993). Successful single parents. *Families in Society: The Journal of Contemporary Human Services, 74*(5), 259–267.

OLSON, S. L., BATES, J. E., & BAYLES, K. (1984). Mother–infant interaction and the development of individual differences in children's cognitive competence. *Developmental Psychology, 20,* 166–179.

OLTON, R. M., & CRUTCHFIELD, R. S. (1969). Developing the skills of productive thinking. In P. H. Mussen, J. Langer, & M. Covington (Eds.), *Trends and issues in developmental psychology.* New York: Holt, Rinehart & Winston.

ONI, G. A. (October 1987). Breast-feeding pattern in an urban Nigerian community. *Journal of Biosocial Science, 19*(4), 453–462.

OPIE, I., & OPIE, P. (1959). *The lore and language of school children.* London: Oxford University Press.

OPPENHEIM, D., EMDE, R. N., & WARREN, S. (1997). Children's narrative representations of mothers: Their development and associations with child and mother adaptation. *Child Development, 68,* 127–138.

ORENSTEIN, P. (1994). *Schoolgirls: Young women, self-esteem, and the confidence gap.* NY: Anchor.

ORLOFSKY, J. L., & O'HERON, C. A. (1987). Stereotypic and nonstereotypic sex role trait and behavior orientation: Implications for personal adjustment. *Journal of Personality and Social Psychology, 52,* 1034–1042.

ORNSTEIN, P. A., NAUS, M. J., & LIBERTY, C. (1975). Rehearsal and organizational processes in children's memory. *Child Development, 46,* 818–830.

ORNSTEIN, P. A., NAUS, M. J., & STONE, B. P. (1977). Rehearsal training and developmental differences in memory. *Developmental Psychology, 13,* 15–24.

OSOFSKY, J. D., & OSOFSKY, H. J. (1984). Psychological and developmental perspectives on expectant and new parenthood. In R. D. Parke (Ed.), *The family: Review of child development research* (Vol. 7). Chicago: University of Chicago Press.

OSTROV, E., OFFER, D., & HOWARD, K. I. (1989). Gender differences in adolescent symptomatology: A normative study. *Journal of the American Academy of Child and Adolescent Psychiatry, 28,* 394–398.

OTTO, L. B. (1988). America's youth: A changing profile. *Family Relations, 37,* 385–391.

OUELLETTE, E. M., ET AL. (1977). Adverse effects on offspring of maternal alcohol abuse during pregnancy. *New England Journal of Medicine, 297,* 528–530.

PAERNOW, P. L. (1984). The stepfamily cycle: An experimental model of stepfamily development. *Family Relations, 33,* 355–363.

PALKOVITZ, R. (1985). Fathers' birth attendance, early contact and extended contact with their newborns: A critical review. *Child Development, 56,* 392–406.

PAPERT, S. (1980). *Mindstorms: Children, computers and powerful thinking.* New York: Basic Books.

PAPOUSEK, H. (1961). Conditioned head rotation reflexes in infants in the first three months of life. *Acta Paediatrica Scandinavica, 50,* 565–576.

PARIS, S. C., LINDAUER, B. K., & COX, G. I. (1977). The development of inferential comprehension. *Child Development, 48,* 1728–1733.

PARKE, R. D. (1972). Some effects of punishment on children's behavior. In W. W. Hartup (Ed.), *The young child: Reviews of research* (Vol. 2). Washington, DC: National Association for the Education of Young Children.

PARKE, R. D. (1979). Perceptions of father–infant interaction. In J. Osofsky (Ed.), *Handbook of infant development.* New York: Wiley.

PARKE, R. D. (1981). *Fathers.* Cambridge, MA: Harvard University Press.

PARKE, R. D., & COLLMER, C. (1975). Child abuse: An interdisciplinary analysis. In E. M. Hetherington (Ed.), *Review of child development research* (Vol. 5). Chicago: University of Chicago Press.

PARKE, R., & SLAHY, R. (1983). The development of aggression. In P. H. Mussen (Ed.), *Handbook of child psychology* (Vol. 4). New York: Wiley.

PARKE, R., & SLAHY, R. (1983). The development of aggression. In P. H. Mussen (Ed.), *Handbook of child psychology* (Vol. 4). New York: Wiley.

PARKE, R. D., & TINSLEY, B. J. (1987). Family interaction in infancy. In J. D. Osofsky (Ed.), *Handbook of infant development* (2nd ed., pp. 579–641). New York: Wiley.

PARKER, J. G., & ASHER, S. R. (1987). Peer relations and later personal adjustment: Are low-accepted children at risk? *Psychological Bulletin, 102,* 357–389.

PARKER, J. G., & ASHER, S. R. (1993). Friendship and friendship quality in middle childhood: Links with peer group acceptance and feelings of loneliness and social dissatisfaction. *Developmental Psychology, 29*(4), 611–621.

PARKER, W. A. (1980). Designing an environment for childbirth. In B. L. Blum (Ed.), *Psychological aspects of pregnancy, birthing, and bonding.* New York: Human Sciences Press.

PARKHURST, J. T., & ASHER, S. R. (1992). Peer rejection in middle school: Subgroup differences in behavior, loneliness, and interpersonal concerns. *Developmental Psychology, 28*(2), 244–254.

PARMELEE, A. H., JR. (1986). Children's illnesses: Their beneficial effects on behavioral development. *Child Development, 57,* 1–10.

PARTEN, M. B. (1932–33). Social participation among preschool children. *Journal of Abnormal and Social Psychology, 27,* 243–269.

PASLEY, B. K. & IHINGER-TALLMAN, M. (1989). Boundary ambiguity in remarriage: Does ambiguity differentiate degree of marital adjustment and integration? *Family Relations,* 38, 46.

PATTERSON, C. J. (1995). Sexual orientation and human development: An overview. *Developmental Psychology, 31,* 3–11.

PATTERSON, C. J., KUPERSMIDT, J. B. & VADEN, N. A. (1990). Income level, gender, ethnicity, and household composition as predic-

tors of children's school-based competence. *Child Development, 61,* 485–494.

PATTISON, E. M. (1977). *The experience of dying.* Englewood Cliffs, NJ: Prentice Hall.

PAULBY, S. T. (1977). Imitative interaction. In H. R. Schaffer (Ed.), *Studies of mother–infant interaction.* London: Academic Press.

PAVLOV, I. P. (1928). *Lectures on conditioned reflexes.* (W. H. Gantt, Trans.). New York: International Publishers.

PECK, R. C. (1968). Psychological developments in the second half of life. In B. L. Neugarten (Ed.), *Middle age and aging.* Chicago: University of Chicago Press.

PECK, R. F., & BERKOWITZ, H. (1964). Personality and adjustment in middle age. In B. L. Neugarten (Ed.), *Personality in middle and late life: Empirical studies.* New York: Atherton.

PEDERSON, F., ET AL. (1979). Infant development in father–absent families. *Journal of Genetic Psychology, 135,* 51–61.

PEDIATRICS. (1978). Effect of medication during labor and delivery on infant outcome, *62,* 402–403.

PEDIATRICS. (1979). The fetal monitoring debate, *63,* 942–948.

PELLEGRINI, A. D. (1987). Rough-and-tumble play: Developmental and educational significance. *Educational Psychologist, 22*(1), 23–43.

PELLETZ, L. (1995). *The effects of an interactive, interpersonal cirriculum upon the development of self in seventh-grade girls.* Ph.D. dissertation, University of Massachusetts, Amherst.

PERETTI, P. O., & WILSON, C. (1978). Contemplated suicide among voluntary and involuntary retirees. *Omega, 9*(2), 193–201.

PERKINS, S. A. (1977). Malnutrition and mental development. *Exceptional Children, 43*(4), 214–219.

PERLMUTTER, M. (1978). What is memory aging the aging of? *Developmental Psychology, 14,* 330–345.

PERLMUTTER, M., ADAMS, C., BARRY, J., KAPLAN, M., PERSON, D., & VERDONIK, F. (1987). Aging & memory. In K. W. Schaie & K. Eisdorfer (Eds.), *Annual review of gerontology and geriatrics* (Vol. 7). New York: Springer.

PERLS, T. T. (1995). The oldest old. *Scientific American, 272, (1),* 70–75.

PERRY, D. G., & BUSSEY, K. (1984). *Social development.* Englewood Cliffs, NJ: Prentice Hall.

PERRY, D. G., WILLIARD, J. C., & PERRY, L. C. (1990). Peers' perceptions of the consequences that victimized children provide aggressors. *Child Development, 61,* 1310–1325.

PERRY, W. G., JR. (1970). *Forms of intellectual and ethical development in the college years: A scheme.* New York: Holt, Rinehart & Winston.

PERRY-JENKINS, M., & CROUTER, A. C. (1990). Men's provider-role attitudes: Implications for household work and marital satisfaction. *Journal of Family Issues, 11*(2), 136–156.

PERRY-JENKINS, M., & FOLK, K. (February 1994). Class, couples, and conflict: Effects of the division of labor on assessments of marriage in dual-earner families. *Journal of Marriage and the Family, 56,* 165–180.

PETERS, J. M. (1996). Paired keyboards as a tool for Internet exploration of third grade students. *Journal of Educational Computing Research, 14,* 229–242.

PETERSON, A. C., & TAYLOR, B. (1980). The biological approach to adolescence: Biological change and psychological adaptation. In J. Adelson (Ed.), *Handbook of adolescent psychology.* New York: Wiley.

PETERSON, A. C., COMPAS, B. E., BROOKS-GUNN, J., STEMMLER, M., EY, S., AND GRANT, K. E. (1993). Depression in adolescence. *American Psychologist, 48*(2), 155–168.

PETERSON, B. E. , & KLOHNEN, E. C. (1995). Realization of generativity in two samples of women at midlife. *Psychology and Aging, 10*(1), 20–29.

PETROVICH, H., MASAKI, K., & RODRIGUEZ, B. (1997). Update on women's health: Pros and cons of postmenopausal hormone replacement therapy. *Generations, 20, no. 4,* 7–11.

PFEIFFER, D., & DAVIS, G. (1971). The use of leisure time in middle life. *The Gerontologist, 11,* 187–195.

PFEIFFER, J. (Ed.). (1964). *The cell.* New York: Time-Life Books.

PHILLIPS, D. (1984). The illusion of incompetence among academically competent children. *Child Development, 55,* 2000–2016.

PHILLIPS, D., MCCARTNEY, K., SCARR, S., & HOWES, C. (February 1987). Selective review of infant day care research: A cause for concern! *Zero to Three,* pp. 18–20.

PHILLIPS, J. L., JR. (1969). *The origins of intellect: Piaget's theory.* San Francisco: Freeman.

PHILLIPS, R. B., SHARMA, R., PREMACHANDRA, B. R., VAUGHN, A. J., & REYES-LEE, M. (1996). Intrauterine exposure to cocaine: Effect on neurobehavior of neonates. *Infant Behavior and Development, 19,* 71–81.

PIAGET, J. (1926). *The language and thought of the child.* London: Kegan, Paul, Trench & Trubner.

PIAGET, J. (1950). *The psychology of intelligence.* (M. Percy & D. E. Berlyne, Trans.). New York: Harcourt Brace.

PIAGET, J. (1951). *Play, dreams and imitation in childhood.* New York: Norton.

PIAGET, J. (1952). *The origins of intelligence in children.* (M. Cook, Trans.). New York: International Universities Press. (Originally published 1936)

PIAGET, J. (1954). *The construction of reality in the child.* (M. Cook, Trans.). New York: Basic Books.

PIAGET, J. (1962). *Plays, dreams, and imitation.* New York: Norton.

PIAGET, J. (1965). *The moral judgment of the child.* (M. Gabain, Trans.). New York: Free Press. (Originally published 1932)

PIAGET, J. (1970). Piaget's theory. In P. H. Mussen (Ed.), *Carmichael's manual of child psychology* (3rd ed., Vol. 1). New York: Wiley.

PIAGET, J. (1972). Intellectual evolution from adolescence to adulthood. *Human Development, 15,* 1–12.

PICHITINO, J. P. (January 1983). Profile of the single father: A thematic integration of the literature. *Personnel and Guidance Journal,* pp. 295–299.

PIETROMONACO, P., MANIS, J., & MARKUS, H. (1987). The relationship of employment to self-perception and well-being in women: A cognitive analysis. *Sex Roles,* 17(7–8), 467–476.

PILLEMER, K., & FINKELHOR, D. (1988). The prevalence of elder abuse: A random sample survey. *The Gerontologist, 28,* 51–57.

PINE, J. M., LIEVEN, E. V. M., & ROWLAND, C. F. (1997). Stylistic variation at the "single-word" stage: Relations between maternal speech characteristics and children's vocabulary composition and usage. *Child Development, 68,* 807–819.

PINES, M. (1979). Superkids. *Psychology Today,* 12(8), 53–63.

PINES, M. (September 1981). The civilizing of Genie. *Psychology Today,* pp. 28–34.

PINES, M. (1984). PT conversations: Resilient children. *Psychology Today,* 12(8), 53–63.

PIOTRKOWSKI, C. S., & CRITS-CHRISTOPH, P. (1981). Women's jobs and family adjustment. *Journal of Family Issues, 2,* 126–147.

PIPER, J. M., BAUM, C., & KENNEDY, D. L. (1987). Prescription drug use before and during pregnancy in a Medicaid population. *American Journal of Obstetrics and Gynecology,* 1(57), 148–156.

PITCHER, E. G., & SCHULTZ, L. H. (1983). *Boys and girls at play: The development of sex roles.* New York: Praeger.

PLECK, J. (1985). *Working wives/working husbands.* Beverly Hills, CA: Sage.

PLECK, J. H. (1985). *Working wives, working husbands.* Beverly Hills, CA: Sage.

PLECK, J. H., & STAINES, G. L. (1982). Work schedules and work family conflict in two-earner couples. In J. Aldous (Ed.), *Two paychecks: Life in dual-earner families.* Beverly Hills, CA: Sage.

PLOMIN, R. (1983). Developmental behavioral genetics. *Child Development, 54,* 25–29.

PLOMIN, R. (1990). *Nature and nurture: An introduction to human behavioral genetics.* Pacific Grove, CA: Brooks/Cole.

PLOMIN, R., & DANIELS, D. (1987). Why are children in the same family so different from one another? *Behavioral and Brain Sciences, 10,* 1–60.

PLOMIN, R., & DEFRIES, J. C. (1998). The genetics of cognitive abilities and disabilities. *Scientific American, 278 (5),* 62–69.

PLOWDEN, B. (1967). *Children and their primary schools: A report of the Central Advisory Council for Education in England* (Vol. 1). London: Her Majesty's Stationery Office.

PLUMB, J. H. (Winter 1971). The great change in children. *Horizon,* pp. 4–12.

POE, W., & HOLLOWAY, D. (1980). *Drugs and the aged.* New York: McGraw-Hill.

POEST, C. A., WILLIAMS, J. R., WITT, D. D., & ATWOOD, M. E. (1989). Physical activity patterns of preschool children. *Early Childhood Research Quarterly, 4,* 367–376.

POLLACK, R. H., & ATKESON, B. M. (1978). A lifespan approach to perceptual development. In P. B. Baltes (Ed.), *Lifespan development and behavior* (Vol. 1). New York: Academic Press.

POLLITT, E. (1994). Poverty and child development: Relevance of research in developing countries to the United States. *Child Development,* 65(2), 283–295.

POLLITT, E., GORMAN, K. S., ENGLE, P. L., MARTORELL, R., & RIVERA, J. (1993). Early supplementary feeding and cognition: Effects over two decades. *Monograph for the Society of Research in Child Development, 58* (Serial No. 235).

POLLOCK, L. A. (1983). *Forgotten children: Parent-child relations from 1500 to 1900.* Cambridge, UK: Cambridge University Press.

POLLOCK, L. A. (1987). *A lasting relationship: Parents and children over three centuries.* Hanover, NH: University Press of New England.

POMERLEAU, A., BOLDUC, D., MALCUIT, G., & COSSETTE, L. (1990). Pink or blue: Environmental gender stereotypes in the first two years of life. *Sex Roles,* 22(5/6), 359–367.

POOLE, W. (July/August 1987). The first 9 months of school. *Hippocrates,* pp. 66–73.

POON, L. (1985). Differences in human memory with aging: Nature, causes and clinical implications. In J. Birren & W. K. Schaie (Eds.), *Handbook of the psychology of aging* (2nd ed.). New York: Van Nostrand Reinhold.

POPE, H. G., IONESCU-PIOGGIA, M., AIZLEY, H. G., & VARMA, D. K. (1991). College student drug use: Twenty-year trends. *Harvard Mental Health Letter,* 7(9), 7.

PORTERFIELD, E. (January 1973). Mixed marriage. *Psychology Today,* pp. 71–78.

POSADA, G., GAO, Y., WU, F., POSADA, R., TASCON, M., SHOELMERICH, A., SAGI, A., KONDO-IKEMURA, K., HAALAND, W., & SYNNEVAAG, B. (1995). The secure-base phenomenon across cultures: Children's behavior, mothers' preferences, and experts' concepts. *Monographs of the Society for Research in Child Development, 60,* 27–48.

POTTS, M. K. (1997). Social support and depression among older adults living alone: The importance of friends with and outside of a retirement community. *Social Work, 42,* 348–361.

POWELL, A. G., FARRAR, E., & COHEN, D. K. (1985). *The shopping mall high school: Winners and losers in the education marketplace.* Boston: Houghton Mifflin.

POWER, C., & REIMER, J. (1978). Moral atmosphere: An educational bridge between moral judgment and action. *New Directions for Child Development, 2.*

POWERS, S. I., HAUSER, S. T., & KILNER, L. A. (1989). Adolescent mental health. *American Psychologist, 44,* 200–208.

PRATT, K. C. (1954). The neonate. In L. Carmichael (Ed.), *Manual of child psychology* (2nd ed.). New York: Wiley.

PRECHTL, H., & BEINTEMA, D. (1965). *The neurological examination of the full term newborn infant* (Clinics in Developmental Medicine Series No. 12). Philadelphia: Lippincott.

PRUCHNO, R., & RESCH, N. (1989). Husbands and wives as caregivers: Antecedents of depression and burden. *The Gerontologist, 29,* 159–165.

PRUETT, K. D. (1987). *The nurturing father: Journey toward the complete man.* New York: Warner Books.

PURCELL, P., & SEWART, L. (1990). Dick and Jane in 1989. *Sex Roles,* 22(3/4), 177–185.

PUTALLAZ, M. (1983). Predicting children's sociometric status from their behavior. *Child Development, 54,* 1417–1426.

QUADREL, M. J., FISCHOFF, B., & DAVIS, W. (1993). Adolescent (in) vulnerability. *American Psychologist,* 48(2), 102–116.

QUEENAN, J. T. (August 1975). The Rh-immunized pregnancy. *Consultant,* pp. 96–99.

QUINN, J. F., & BURKHAUSER, R. V. (1990). Work and retirement. In R. H. Binstock & L. K. George (Eds.), *Handbook of aging and the social sciences* (3rd ed., pp. 308–327). New York: Academic Press.

RADBILL, S. (1974). A history of child abuse and infanticide. In R. Helfer & C. Kempe (Eds.), *The battered child.* Chicago: University of Chicago Press.

RADKE, M. J., & TRAGER, H. G. (1950). Children's perceptions of the social role of Negroes and whites. *Journal of Psychology, 29,* 3–33.

RADKEY-YARROW, M., ZAHN-WAXLER, C., & CHAPMAN, M. (1983). Children's prosocial dispositions and behavior. In E. M. Hetherington (Ed.), *Handbook of child psychology: Vol. 4. Socialization, personality and social development.* New York: Wiley.

RAHBAR, F., MOMENI, J., FUMUFOD, A. K., & WESTNEY, L. (1985). Prenatal care and perinatal mortality in a black population. *Obstetrics and Gynecology, 65 (3),* 327–329.

RAMEY, C. T. (1981). Consequences of infant day care. In B. Weissbound & J. Musick (Eds.), *Infants: Their social environments.* Washington, DC: National Association for the Education of Young Children.

RAMEY, C. T., & RAMERY, S. L. (1998). Early intervention and early experience. *American Psychologist, 53,* 109–120.

RANDO, T. (1986). A comprehensive analysis of anticipatory grief: Perspectives, processes, promises, and problems. In T. Rando (Ed.), *Loss and anticipatory grief.* Lexington, MA: Lexington Books.

RAPOPORT, R., & RAPOPORT, R. M. (1980). Three generations of dual-career family research. In F. Pepitone-Rockwell (Ed.), *Dual-career couples.* Beverly Hills, CA: Sage.

RATNER, H. H. (1984). Memory demands and the development of young children's memory. *Child Development, 55,* 2173–2191.

RATNER, N. B., & PYE, C. (1984). Higher pitch in BT is not universal: Acoustic evidence from Quiche Mayan. *Journal of Child Language, 11,* 515–522.

RATNER, N., & BRUNER, J. S. (1978). Games, social exchange and the acquisition of language. *Journal of Child Development, 5,* 1–15.

RAUSTE-VON WRIGHT, M. (1989). Body image satisfaction in adolescent girls and boys: A longitudinal study. *Journal of Youth and Adolescence, 18,* 71–83.

REGESTEIN, Q. R. (October 13, 1979). *Insomnia and sleep disturbances in the aged: Sleep and insomnia in the elderly.* Paper presented at a scientific meeting of the Boston Society for Gerontologic Psychiatry.

REICH, P. A. (1986). *Language development.* Englewood Cliffs, NJ: Prentice Hall.

REID, M. (1990). Prenatal diagnosis and screening. In J. Garcia, R. Kilpatrick, & M. Richards (Eds.), *The politics of maternity care* (pp. 300–323). Oxford: Clarendon Press.

REID, M., RAMEY, S. L., & BURCHINAL, M. (1990). Dialogues with children about their families. In I. Bretherton & M. W. Watson (Eds.), *New Directions for Child Development, 48,* 5–28.

REINACH, L. (1901). *de Lelaos.* Paris: Charles.

REINHOLD, R. (June 27, 1981). Census finds unmarried couples have doubled from 1970 to 1978. *New York Times,* pp. A1, B5.

REINHOLD, R. (February 27, 1982). Study reaffirms general doubts over marijuana. *New York Times,* p. C7.

REINKE, B. J., ELLICOTT, A. M., HARRIS, R. L., & HANCOCK, E. (1985). Timing of psychosocial changes in women's lives. *Human Development, 28,* 259–280.

REISS, I. L. (1971). *The family system in America.* New York: Holt, Rinehart & Winston.

REITZES, D. C., MUTRAN, E. J., & FERNANDEZ, M. E. (1996). Does retirement hurt well-being? Factors influencing self-esteem and depression among retirees and workers. *The Gerontologist, 36,* 649–656.

REPETTI, R., MATTHEWS, K., & WALDRON, I. (1989). Employment and women's health: Effects of paid employment on women's mental and physical health. *American Psychologist, 44,* 1394–1401.

RESTAK, R. (1986). The infant mind. Garden City, NY: Doubleday.

REUHL, K. R., & CHANG, L. W. (1979). Effects of methylmercury on the development of the nervous system: A review. *Neurotoxicology, 1,* 21–55.

REYNOLDS, W., REMER, R., & JOHNSON, M. (1995). Marital satisfaction in later life: An examination of equity, equality, and reward theories. *International Journal of Aging and Human Development, 40(2),* 155–173.

RHEINGOLD, H. L., GEWIRTZ, J. L., & ROSS, H. W. (1959). Social conditioning of vocalizations in the infant. *Journal of Comparative and Physiological Psychology, 52,* 68–73.

RHODES, S. (1983). Age-related differences in work attitudes and behavior: A review and conceptual analysis. *Psychological Bulletin, 93,* 328–367.

RICE, M. L., & HAIGHT, P. L. (1986). "Motherese" of Mr. Rogers: A description of the dialogue of educational television programs. *Journal of Speech and Hearing Disorders, 51,* 282–287.

RICE, S. G. (1990). *Putting the play back in exercise.* Unpublished.

RICHARDSON, S. O. (1992). Historical perspectives on dyslexia. *Journal of Learning Disabilities, 25(1),* 40–47.

RICHMAN, A. L., LeVINE, R. A., NEW, R. A., HOWRIGAN, G. A., WELLES-NYSTROM, B., & LeVINE, S. E. (Summer 1988). Maternal behavior to infants in five cultures. In R. A. LeVine, P. M. Miller, & M. M. West (Eds.), *New Directions for Child Development: Vol. 40. Personal behavior in diverse societies* (pp. 81–98).

RICHMAN, C. L., BERRY, C., BITTLE, M., & HIMAN, K. (1988). Factors relating to help-

ing behavior in preschool-age children. *Journal of Applied Developmental Psychology, 9,* 151–165.

RICKS, S. S. (1985). Father–infant interactions: A review of empirical research. *Family Relations, 34,* 505–511.

RIEGEL, K. (1984). Chapter in M. L. Commons, F. A. Richards, & C. Armon (Eds.), *Beyond formal operations: Late adolescence and adult cognitive development.* New York: Praeger.

RIEGEL, K. F. (1975). Adult life crises: A dialectical interpretation of development. In N. Datan & L. H. Ginsberg (Eds.), *Life-span developmental psychology: Normative life crises.* New York: Academic Press.

RIGER, S., & GALLIGAN, P. (1980). Women in management. *American Psychologist, 35,* 902–910.

RILEY, M. W., & WARING, J. (1976). Age and aging. In R. Merton & R. Nisbet (Eds.), *Contemporary social problems* (4th ed.). New York: Harcourt Brace Jovanovich.

RILEY, M. W., & WARING, J. (1978). Most of the problems of aging are not biological, but social. In R. Gross, B. Gross, & S. Seidman (Eds.), *The new old: Struggling for decent aging.* Garden City, NY: Anchor Books/Doubleday.

RIZZO, T. A., & CORSARO, W. A. (1988). Toward a better understanding of Vygotsky's process of internalization: Its role in the development of the concept of friendship. *Developmental Review, 8,* 219–237.

RIZZOLI, R, & BONJOUR, J.-P. (1997). Hormones and bones. *The Lancet, 349, March.* SI20–23.

ROBBINS, D. (1986). Legal and ethical issues in terminal illness care for patients, families, care-givers, and institutions. In T. Rando (Ed.), *Loss and anticipatory grief* (pp. 215–228). Lexington, MA: Lexington Books.

ROBERTS, R., & NEWTON, P. M. (1987). Levinsonian studies of women's adult development. *Psychology and Aging, 2,* 154–163.

ROBERTSON, J. F. (1977). Grandmotherhood: A study of role conceptions. *Journal of Marriage and the Family, 39,* 165–174.

ROBERTSON, M. (1984). Changing motor patterns during childhood. In J. R. Thomas (Ed.), *Motor development during childhood and adolescence.* Minneapolis, MN: Burgess.

ROBINSON, I. E., & JEDLICKA, D. (1982). Change in sexual behavior of college students from 1965–1980: A research note. *Journal of Marriage and the Family, 44,* 237–240.

ROBINSON, R., COBERLY, S., & PAUL, C. (1985). Work and retirement. In R. Binstock & E. Shanas (Eds.), *Handbook of aging and the social sciences.* (2nd ed., pp. 503–527). New York: Van Nostrand Reinhold.

ROCHAT, P. (1989). Object manipulation and exploration in 2– to 5–month-old infants. *Developmental Psychology, 25(6),* 871–884.

RODIN, J., & ICKOVICS, J. (1990) Women's health: Review and research agenda as we approach the 21st century. *American Psychologist, 45,* 1018–1034.

ROE, A. (1957). Early determinants of vocational choice. *Journal of Counseling Psychology, 4,* 212–217.

ROGEL, M. J., & PETERSON, A. C. (1984). Some adolescent experiences of motherhood. In

R. Cohen, B. Cohler, & S. Weissman (Eds.), *Parenthood: A psychodynamic perspective.* New York: Guilford.

ROGERS, C. (1980). *A way of being.* Boston: Houghton Mifflin.

ROGERS, C. R. (1961). *On becoming a person.* New York: Houghton Mifflin.

ROGOFF, B. (1990). *Apprenticeship in thinking: Cognitive development in social context.* New York: Oxford University Press.

ROGOFF, B. (1993). Commentary. *Human Development, 36,* 24–26.

ROGOFF, B., & WERTSCH, J. (1984). Children's learning in the "zone of proximal development." *New Directions for Child Development, 23.* San Francisco: Jossey-Bass.

ROGOFF, B., ET AL. (1993). Guided participation in cultural activity by toddlers and caregivers. *Monographs of the Society for Research in Child Development, 58(8),* Serial No. 236, whole issue.

ROSCOE, B., DIANA, M. S., & BROOKS, R. H., II. (1987). Early, middle, and late adolescents' views on dating and factors influencing partner selection. *Adolescence, 12,* 59–68.

ROSE-KRASNOR, L. (1988). Social cognition. In T. D. Yawkey & J. E. Johnson (Eds.), *Integrative processes and socialization: Early to middle childhood* (pp. 79–95). Hillsdale, NJ: Erlbaum.

ROSEL, N. (1978). Toward a social theory of dying. *Omega, 9(1),* 49–55.

ROSENFELD, A. (March 23, 1974b). Starve the child, famish the future. *Saturday Review,* p. 59.

ROSENFELD, A. (September 7, 1974a). If Oedipus' parents had only known. *Saturday Review,* 49f.

ROSENMAN, R. H. (1974). The role of behavioral patterns and neurogenic factors in the pathogenesis of coronary heart disease. In R. S. Eliot (Ed.), *Stress and the heart.* New York: Futura.

ROSENMAN, R., & CHESNEY, M. (1982). Stress, Type A behavior, and coronary disease. In L. Goldberger & S. Breznitz (Eds.), *The handbook of stress: Theoretical and clinical applications* (pp. 547–565). New York: Macmillan.

ROSENSTEIN, D., & OSTER, H. (1988). Differential facial response to four basic tastes in newborns. *Child Development, 59,* 1555–1568.

ROSENTHAL, E. (January 4, 1990). New insights on why some children are fat offers clues on weight loss. *New York Times,* p. B8.

ROSENTHAL, J. A. (1988). Patterns of reported child abuse and neglect. *Child Abuse and Neglect, 12,* 263–271.

ROSENTHAL, R., & JACOBSON, L. (1968). *Pygmalion in the classroom: Teacher expectation and pupil's intellectual development.* New York: Harper & Row.

ROSENWASSER, S. M., LINGENFELTER, M., & HARRINGTON, A. F. (1989). Nontraditional gender role portrayals on television and children's gender role perceptions. *Journal of Applied Developmental Psychology, 10,* 97–105.

ROSE, S. A., GOTTFRIED, A. W., & BRIDGER, W. H. (1981). Cross-modal transfer in 6–month-old infants. *Developmental Psychology, 17,* 661–669.

ROSETT, H. L., ET AL. (1981). Strategies for prevention of fetal alcohol effects. *Obstetrics and Gynecology, 57,* 1–16.

ROSKINSKI, R. R. (1977). *The development of visual perception.* Santa Monica, CA: Goodyear.

ROSOW, I. (1974). *Socialization to old age.* Berkeley: University of California Press.

ROSS, A. O. (1977). *Learning disability, the unrealized potential.* New York: McGraw-Hill.

ROSS, H. S., & LOLLIS, S. P. (1987). Communication within infant social games. *Developmental Psychology, 23,* 241–248.

ROSS, H., & SAWHILL, I. (1975). *Time of transition: The growth of families headed by women.* Washington, DC: Urban Institute.

ROSS, L. (1981). The "intuitive scientist" formulation and its developmental implications. In J. H. Flavell & L. Ross (Eds.), *Social cognitive development.* Cambridge, UK: Cambridge University Press.

ROSSI, A. S. (Spring 1977). A biological perspective in parenting. *Daedalus.*

ROSSI, A. S. (1979). Transition to parenthood. In P. Rossi (Ed.), *Socialization and the life cycle.* New York: St. Martin's Press.

ROSSMAN, I. (1977). Anatomic and body-composition changes with aging. In C. E. Finch & L. Hayflick (Eds.), *Handbook of the biology of aging.* New York: Van Nostrand Reinhold.

ROUG, L., LANDBERG, I., & LUNDBERG, L. J. (February 1989). Phonetic development in early infancy: A study of four Swedish children during the first eighteen months of life. *Journal of Child Language, 16*(1), 19–40.

ROVEE-COLLIER, C. (1987). Learning and memory in infancy. In J. Osofsky (Ed.), *Handbook of infant development* (2nd ed.). New York: Wiley.

ROWE, J. W., & KAHN, R. L. (1997). Successful aging. *The Gerontologist, 37,* 433–440.

ROWE, P. (May/June 1982). Model project reduces alienation of aged from community. *Aging,* pp. 6–11.

ROWLAND, T. W., DONNELLY, J. H., LANDIS, J. N., LEMOINE, M. E., SIGELMAN, D. R., & TANELLA, C. J. (1987). Infant home apnea monitoring. *Clinical Pediatrics, 26*(8), 383–387.

RUBIN, K. H. (1983). Recent perspectives on social competence and peer status: Some introductory remarks. *Child Development, 54,* 1383–1385.

RUBIN, K. H. & COPLAN, R. J. (1992). Peer relationships in childhood. In M. H. Bornstein and M. E. Lamb, (Eds.), *Developmental Psychology: An advanced textbook.* Hillsdale, NJ: Lawrence Erlbaum.

RUBIN, K. H., FEIN, G. C., & VANDENBERG, B. (1983). In P. H. Mussen (Ed.), *Handbook of child psychology* (Vol. 4). New York: Wiley.

RUBIN, K. H., MALONI, T. L., & HORNUNG, M. (1976). Free play behaviors in middle- and lower-class preschoolers: Partner and Piaget revised. *Child Development, 47,* 414–419.

RUBIN, K., & TROTTEN, K. (1977). Kohlberg's moral judgment scale: Some methodological considerations. *Developmental Psychology, 13*(5), 535–536.

RUBIN, L. (1980). The empty nest: Beginning or end? In L. Bond & J. Rosen (Eds.), *Competence and coping during adulthood* (pp. 309–321). Hanover, NH: University Press of New England.

RUBIN, N. J. (1994). Ask me if I care: Voices from an American high school (p. 83). Berkeley, CA: Ten Speed Press.

RUBINSTEIN, C. (1994). *Helping teachers and schools to nip sex bias in the bud.* The New York Times, p. C4.

RUBINSTEIN, E. A. (1983). Television and behavior: Conclusion of the 1982 NIMH report and their policy implications. *American Psychologist, 38,* 820–825.

RUBIN, Z. (1980). *Children's friendships.* Cambridge, MA: Harvard University Press.

RUBLE, D. (1988). Sex-role development. In M. Bornstein & M. E. Lamb (Eds.), *Developmental psychology: An advanced textbook* (2nd ed., pp. 411–460). Hillsdale, NJ: Erlbaum.

RUBLE, D. N., & BROOKS-GUNN, J. (1982). The experience of menarche. *Child Development, 53,* 1557–1577.

RUDD, P., & BALASCHKE, T. (1982) Antihypertensive agents and the drug therapy of hypertension. In A. Gilman, L. Goodman, T. Rall, & F. Murad (Eds.), *Goodman and Gilman's the pharmacological basis of therapeutics* (7th ed., pp. 784–805.)

RUEBSAAT, H. J., & HULL, R. (1975). *The male climacteric.* New York: Hawthorn Books.

RUGH, R., & SHETTLES, L. B. (1971). *From conception to birth: The drama of life's beginnings.* New York: Harper & Row.

RUSHTON, T. P. (1976). Socialization and the altruistic behavior of children. *Psychological Bulletin, 83*(5), 898–913.

RUSSELL, D. (1983). The incidence and prevalence of intrafamilial and extrafamilial sexual abuse of female children. *Child Abuse and Neglect, 7,* 133–146.

RUTTER, M. (1979). Protective factors in children's responses to stress and disadvantage. In M. W. Kent & J. E. Rolf (Eds.), *Primary prevention of psychopathology: III. Social competence in children.* Hanover, NH: University Press of New England.

RUTTER, M. (1983). Stress, coping and development: Some issues and questions. In N. Garmezy & M. Rutter (Eds.), *Stress, coping and development in children.* New York: McGraw-Hill.

RUTTER, M. (1984). PT conversations: Resilient children. *Psychology Today, 18*(3), 60–62, 64–65.

RUTTER, M. L. (1997). Nature-nurture integration: The example of antisocial behavior. *American Psychologist, 52,* 390–398.

RUTTER, M., & GARMEZY, N. (1983). Developmental psychopathology. In P. H. Mussen (Ed.), *Handbook of child psychology* (Vol. 4). New York: Wiley.

RUTTER, M., DUNN, J., PLOMIN, R., SIMONOFF, E., PICKLES, A., MAUGHAN, B., ORMEL, J., MEYER, J., & EAVES, L. (1997). Integrating nature and nurture: Implications of person-environment correlations and interactions for developmental psychology. *Development and Psychopathology, 9,* 335–364.

RYAN, A. S., MARTINEZ, G. A., & MALEC, D. J. (Spring 1985). The effect of the WIC program on nutrient intakes of infants, 1984. *Medical Anthropology,* p. 153.

RYFF, C. D. (1985). The subjective experience of life-span transitions. In A. S. Rossi (Ed.), *Gender and the life course* (p. 97). New York: Aldine.

RYFF, C. D. (1989). In the eye of the beholder: Views of psychological well-being among middle-aged and older adults. *Psychology and Aging, 4*(2), 195–210.

RYNES, S., & ROSEN, B. (1983). A comparison of male and female reactions to career advancement opportunities. *Journal of Vocational Behavior, 22,* 105–116.

SADKER, M., & SADKER, D. (1994). *Failing at fairness: How America's schools cheat girls.* New York: Charles Scribner's Sons.

SAGI, A., ET AL. (1994). Sleeping out of home in a kibbutz communal arrangement: It makes a difference for infant–mother attachment. *Child Development, 65,* 992–1004.

SALEND, E., KANE, R., SATZ, M., & PYNOOS, J. (1984). Elder abuse reporting: Limitation of statutes. *The Gerontologist, 24,* 61–69.

SALT, P., GALLER, J. R., & RAMSEY, F. C. (1988).The influence of early malnutrition on subsequent behavioral development. VII. The effects of maternal depressive symptoms. *Developmental and Behavioral Pediatrics, 9,* 1–5.

SALTHOUSE, T. A. (1984). Effects of age and skill in typing. *Journal of Experimental Psychology: General, 113,* 345–371.

SALTHOUSE, T. (1985). Speed of behavior and its implications for cognition. In J. E. Birren & K. W. Schaie (Eds.), *Handbook of the psychology of aging* (2nd ed.). New York: Van Nostrand Reinhold.

SALTHOUSE, T. (1987). The role of experience in cognitive aging. In K. W. Schaie & K. Eisdorfer (Eds.), *Annual review of gerontology and geriatrics* (Vol. 7). New York: Springer.

SALTHOUSE, T. (1990). Cognitive competence and expertise in aging. In J. Birren & K. W. Schaie (Eds.), *Handbook of the psychology of aging* (3rd ed., pp. 311–319). San Diego: Academic Press.

SALTHOUSE, T., & MITCHELL, D. (1990). Effect of age and naturally occurring experience on spatial visualization performance. *Developmental Psychology, 26,* 845–854.

SALTHOUSE, T., BABCOCK, R., SKOVRONEK, E., MITCHELL, D., & PALMON, R. (1990). Age and experience effects in spatial visualization. *Developmental Psychology, 26,* 128–136.

SALZMAN, C. (1982) A primer on geriatric psychopharmacology. *American Journal of Psychiatry, 139,* 67–74.

SARASON, S. B., & DORIS, J. (1953). *Psychological problems in mental deficiency.* New York: Harper & Row.

SASLOW, R. (Fall 1981). A new student for the eighties: The mature woman. *Educational Horizons,* pp. 41–46.

SASSERATH, V. J. (Ed.). (1983). *Minimizing high-risk parenting.* Skillman, NJ: Johnson & Johnson.

SAUDINO, K. J., & PLOMIN, R. (1997). Cognitive and temperamental mediators of genetic contributions to the home environment during infancy. *Merrill-Palmer Quarterly, 43,* 1–23.

SAVAGE-RUMBAUGH, S., RUMBAUGH, D. M., & McDONALD, K. (September 1986). Spontaneous symbol acquisition and communicative use by pygmy chimpanzees. *Journal of Experimental Psychology, 115*(3), 211–235.

SCANLON, J. (1979). *Young adulthood.* New York: Academy for Educational Development.

SCARBOROUGH, H. S. (1989). Prediction of reading disability from familial and individual differences. *Journal of Educational Psychology, 81,* 101–108.

SCARR, S., & KIDD, K. K. (1983). Behavior genetics. In M. Haith & J. Campos (Eds.), *Manual of child psychology: Infancy and the biology of development* (Vol. 2). New York: Wiley.

SCARR, S., & McCARTNEY, K. (1983). How people make their own environments: A theory of genotype/environmental effects. *Child Development, 54,* 424–435.

SCARR, S., PHILLIPS, D., & McCARTNEY, K. (1989). Working mothers and their families. *American Psychologist, 44,* 1402–1409.

SCARR, S., & WEINBERG, R. A. (1983). The Minnesota adoption studies: Genetic differences and malleability. *Child Development, 54,* 260–267.

SCHACTER, F., & STRAGE, A. (1982). Adult's talk and children's language development. In S. Moore & C. Cooper (Eds.), *The young child: Reviews of research* (Vol. 3, pp. 79–96). Washington, DC: National Association for the Education of Young Children.

SCHAEFER, M. R., SOBIERAJ, K., & HOLLYFIELD, R. L. (1988). Prevalence of childhood physical abuse in adult male veteran alcoholics. *Child Abuse and Neglect, 12,* 141–149.

SCHAFFER, H. R. (1977). *Studies in mother–infant interaction.* London: Academic Press.

SCHAIE, K. W. (1977/1978). Toward a stage theory of adult cognitive development. *Journal of Aging and Human Development, 8,* 129–138.

SCHAIE, K. W. (1983a). The Seattle longitudinal study: A twenty-one year exploration of psychometric intelligence in adulthood. In K. W. Schaie (Ed.), *Longitudinal studies of adult psychological development.* New York: Guilford.

SCHAIE, K. W. (1983b). Twenty-one-year exploration of psychometric intelligence in adults. In K. W. Schaie (Ed.), *Longitudinal studies of adult psychological development.* New York: Guilford.

SCHAIE, K. W. (1986). Beyond calendar definitions of age, period and cohort: The general developmental model revisited. *Developmental Review, 6,* 252–277.

SCHAIE, K. W. (1990). Intellectual development in adulthood. In J. Birren & K. W. Schaie (Eds.), *Handbook of the psychology of aging* (3rd. ed., pp. 291–310). San Diego: Academic Press.

SCHAIE, K. W. (1995). *Intellectual development in adulthood: The Seattle longitudinal study.* New York: Cambridge University Press.

SCHAIE, K. W., & WILLIS, S. L. (1986). *Adult development and aging* (2nd ed.). Boston: Little, Brown.

SCHARDEIN, J. L. (1976). *Drugs as teratogens.* Cleveland, OH: Chemical Rubber Co. Press.

SCHEIER, L. M., & BOTVIN, G. J. (1998). Relations of social skills, personal competence, and adolescent alcohol use: A developmental exploratory study. *Journal of Early Adolescence, 18,* 77–114.

SCHEIN, E. H. (1978). *Career dynamics: Matching individual and organizational needs.* Reading, MA: Addison Wesley.

SCHIEFFELIN, B. B., & OCHS, E. (1983). A cultural perspective on the transition from prelinguistic to linguistic communication. In R. M. Golinkoff (Ed.), *The transition from prelinguistic to linguistic communication.* Hillsdale, NJ: Erlbaum.

SCHILDER, P., & WECHSLER, D. (1935). What do children know about the interior of the body? *International Journal of Psychoanalysis, 16,* 355–360.

SCHLESINGER, J. M. (1982). *Steps to language: Toward a theory of native language acquisition.* Hillsdale, NJ: Erlbaum.

SCHNECK, M. K., REISBERG, B., & FERRIS, S. H. (February 1982). An overview of current concepts of Alzheimer's disease. *American Journal of Psychiatry, 139*(2), 165–173.

SCHNEIDER, M. L., ROUGHTON, E. C., & LUBACH, G. R. (1997). Moderate alcohol consumption and psychological stress during pregnancy induce attention and neuromotor impairments in primate infants. *Child Development, 68,* 747–759.

SCHNEIDMAN, E. (1989). The Indian summer of life: A preliminary study of septuagenarians. *American Psychologist, 44,* 684–694.

SCHOCK, N. (1977). Biological theories of aging. In J. Birren & K. W. Schaie (Eds.), *Handbook of the psychology of aging.* New York: Van Nostrand Reinhold.

SCHOFIELD, J. W. (1981). Complementary and conflicting identities: Images and interaction in an interracial school. In S. R. Asher & J. M. Gottman (Eds.), *The development of children's friendships.* New York: Cambridge University Press.

SCHOFIELD, J. W. (1997a). Psychology: Computers and classroom social processes—a review of the literature. *Social Science Computer Review, 15,* 27–39.

SCHOFIELD, J. W. (1997b). The Internet in school: A case study of educator demand and its precursors. In S. Kiesler (Ed.), *Culture of the Internet.* Mahwah, NJ: Lawrence Erlbaum.

SCHOOLER, C. (1987). Psychological effects of complex environments during the life span: A review and theory. In C. Schooler & K. W. Schaie (Eds.). *Cognitive functioning and social structure over the life course* (pp. 24–49). Norwood, NJ: Ablex.

SCHOOLER, C. (1990). Pyschosocial factors and effective cognitive functioning in adulthood. In *Handbook of the psychology of aging* (3rd ed.). New York: Academic Press.

SCHULMAN, S., LAURSEN, B., KALMAN, Z., & KARPOVSKY, S. (1997). Adolescent intimacy revisited. *Journal of Youth and Adolescence, 26,* 597–603.

SCHULZ, R., & HECKHAUSEN, J. (1996). A lifespan model of successful aging. *American Psychologist, 51,* 702–714.

SCHULZ, R., & SALTHOUSE, T. (in press). *Adult development and aging: Myths and emerging realities.* Upper Saddle River, NJ: Prentice Hall.

SCHULZ, R., MUSA, D., STASZEWSKI, J., & SIEGLER, R. S. (1994). The relationship between age and major league baseball performance: Implications for development. *Psychology and Aging, 9,* 274–286.

SCHWARTZ, J. I. (1981). Children's experiments with language. *Young Children, 36,* 16–26.

SCIENTIFIC AMERICAN (1997). In focus: The start of something big? *276* (5), 15–16.

SCIENTIFIC AMERICAN (1997). Women's Health: Hold the hormones? *Volume 277,* September, 38–39.

SCOTT, J. P. (1990). Forward. In M. E. Hahn, J. K. Hewitt, N. D. Henderson, & R. H. Benno (Eds.), *Development behavior genetics: Neural, biometrical and evolutionary approaches.* New York: Oxford University Press.

SEARS, R. R. (1963). Dependency motivation. In M. R. Jones (Ed.), *The Nebraska symposium on motivation* (Vol. 11). Lincoln: University of Nebraska Press.

SEBALD, H. (Winter 1989). Adolescents' peer orientation: Changes in the support system during the past three decades. *Adolescence,* 940–941.

SEDLAK, A. J. (1989). *Supplementary analyses of data on the national incidence of child abuse and neglect.* Rockville, MD: Westat.

SEGAL, J., & YAHRAES, H. (November 1978). Bringing up mother. *Psychology Today,* pp. 80–85.

SELIGMAN, M. E. P. (May 1974). Submissive death: Giving up on life. *Psychology Today,* pp. 90–96.

SELMAN, R. L. (1976). The development of interpersonal reasoning. In A. Pick (Ed.), *Minnesota symposia on child psychology* (Vol. 1). Minneapolis: University of Minnesota Press.

SELMAN, R. L. (1981). The child as a friendship philosopher. In S. R. Asher & J. M. Gottman (Eds.), *The development of children's friendships.* Cambridge, UK: Cambridge University Press.

SELTZER, V. C. (1989). *The psychosocial worlds of the adolescent.* New York: Wiley.

SERBIN, L. A., POWLISHTA, K. K., & GULKO, J. (1993). The development of sex typing in middle childhood. *Monographs of the Society for Research in Child Development, 58*(2), Serial No. 232, 1–73.

SHAFFER, D. R. (1988). *Social and personality development* (2nd ed.). Pacific Grove, CA: Brooks/Cole.

SHAFFER, J. B. P. (1978). *Humanistic psychology.* Englewood Cliffs, NJ: Prentice Hall.

SHANAS, E., & MADDOX, G. (1985). Health, health resources, and the utilization of care. In R. Binstock & E. Shanas (Eds.). *Handbook of aging and the social sciences* (pp. 697–726). New York: Van Nostrand Reinhold.

SHANE, P. G. (1989). Changing patterns among homeless and runaway youth. *American Journal of Orthopsychiatry, 59*(2), 208–214.

SHANNON, D., & KELLY, D. (1982). SIDS and near-SIDS. *New England Journal of Medicine, 306,* 961–962.

SHANTZ, C. (1983). Social cognition. In P. H. Mussen (Ed.), *Handbook of child psychology* (Vol. 3). New York: Wiley.

SHANTZ, C. U. (1975). The development of social cognition. In E. M. Hetherington (Ed.), *Review of child development research* (Vol. 5). Chicago: University of Chicago Press.

SHANTZ, C. U. (1987). Conflicts between children. *Child Development, 51,* 283–305.

SHAPIRO, M. (1978). Legal rights of the terminally ill. *Aging, 5(3),* 23–27.

SHARABANY, R., GERSHONI, R., & HOFFMAN, J. E. (1981). Girlfriend, boyfriend: Age and sex differences in intimate friendship. *Developmental Psychology, 17,* 800–808.

SHATZ, C. (1992). The developing brain. *Scientific American (9),* 61–67.

SHATZ, M. (1991). *Using cross-cultural research to inform us about the role of language in development: Comparisons of Japanese, Korean, and English, and of German, American English, and British English* (pp. 139–153).

SHATZ, M., & GELMAN, R. (1973). The development of communication skills: Modifications in the speech of young children as a function of the listener. *Monographs of the Society for Research in Child Development, 38(152).*

SHAW, L. (1983). Problems of labor-market reentry. In L. B. Shaw (Ed.), *Unplanned careers: The working lives of middle-aged women.* Lexington, MA: Lexington Books.

SHAYWITZ, S. E., SHAYWITZ, B. A., FLETCHER, J. M., & ESCOBAR, M. D. (1991). Reading disability in children. *Journal of the American Medical Association, 265,* 725–726.

SHEA, C. H., SHEBILSKE, W. L. & WORCHEL, S. (1993). *Motor learning and control.* New Jersey: Prentice Hall.

SHEEHY, G. (1995a). *New passages: Mapping your life across time.* New York: Random House.

SHEEHY, G. (June 12, 1995b). New passages. *U.S. News & World Report,* p. 62.

SHEIMAN, D. L., & SLOMIN, M. (1988). *Resources for middle childhood.* New York, NY: Garland.

SHEPPARD, H. L., & HERRICK, N. Q. (1977). *Worker dissatisfaction in the '70s.* New York: Free Press.

SHERIF, M., & SHERIF, C. W. (1953). *Groups in harmony and tension.* New York: Harper & Brothers.

SHERIF, M., HARVEY, O. J., WHITE, B. J., HOOD, W. B., & SHERIF, C. W. (1961). *Intergroup conflict and cooperation: The robber's cave experiment.* Norman: University of Oklahoma Press.

SHERMAN, E. (1987). *Meaning in mid-life transitions.* Albany: State University of New York Press.

SHIELDS, A. M., CICCHETTI, D., & RYAN, R. M. (1994). The development of emotional and behavioral self-regulation and social competence among maltreated school-age children. *Development and Psychopathology, 6,* 57–75.

SHIFFRIN, R. M., & SCHNEIDER, W. (1977). Controlled and automatic human information processing: II. Perceptual learning, automatic attending, and a general theory. *Psychological Review, 84,* 127–190.

SHIRLEY, M. M. (1931). *The first two years: A study of twenty-five babies* (Institute of Child Welfare Monograph No. 7, Vol. 1). Minneapolis: University of Minnesota Press.

SHIRLEY, M. M. (1933). *The first two years: A study of twenty-five babies* (Institute of Child Welfare Monograph No. 7, Vol. 2). Minneapolis: University of Minnesota Press.

SHOCK, N. W. (1952a). Aging of homostatic mechanisms. In A. I. Lansing (Ed.), *Cowdry's problems of aging* (3rd ed.). Baltimore: Williams & Wilkins.

SHOCK, N. W. (1952b). Aging and psychological adjustment. *Review of Educational Research, 22,* 439–458.

SHORE, R. (1997). *Rethinking the brain: New insights in early development.* New York: Families and Work Institute.

SHUKIN, A., & NEUGARTEN, B. L. (1964). Personality and social interaction. In B. L. Neugarten (Ed.), *Personality in middle and late life: Empirical studies.* New York: Atherton.

SHULMAN, S., & KLEIN, M. M. (Winter 1993). Distinctive role of the father in adolescent separation–individuation. In S. Shulman & W. A. Collins (Eds.). *New Directions for Child Development, 62,* 41–58.

SHUTE, N. (1997). A study for the ages. *U.S. News and World Report, June 9,* 67–70, 72, 76–78, 80.

SIDNEY, K. H. (1981). Cardiovascular benefits of physical activity in the exercising aged. In E. L. Smith & R. C. Serfass (Eds.), *Exercise and aging: The scientific basis.* Hillside, NJ: Enslow.

SIEBER, R. T., & GORDON, A. J. (1981). Socialization implications of school discipline or how first graders are taught to listen. In *Children and their organizations: Investigations in American culture.* Boston: G. K. Hall.

SIEGLER, I. C., & COSTA, P. T., JR. (1985). Health behavior relationships. In J. E. Birren & K. W. Schaie (Eds.), *Handbook of the psychology of aging* (2nd ed.). New York: Van Nostrand Reinhold.

SIEGLER, R. S. (1986). *Children's thinking.* Englewood Cliffs, NJ: Prentice Hall.

SIEGLER, R. S. (1991). *Children's Thinking.* Englewood Cliffs, NJ: Prentice Hall.

SIEGLER, R. S., & ELLIS, S. (1996). Piaget on Childhood. *Psychological Science, 7,* 211–215.

SIGEL, I. (1987). Does hothousing rob children of their childhood? *Early Childhood Research Quarterly, 2,* 211–225.

SIGNORELLA, M. L. (1987). Gender schemata: Individual differences and context effects. *New Directions for Child Development, 38,* 23–38.

SIGNORIELLI, N. (1989). Television and conceptions about sex roles: Maintaining conventionality and the status quo. *Sex Roles, 21(5/6),* 341–350.

SILVER, C. B., & SILVER, R. C. (1989). The myths of coping with loss. *Journal of Consulting and Clinical Psychology, 57(3),* 349–357.

SILVER, L. B. (October 1990). Learning disabilities. *Harvard Mental Health Letter,* pp. 7, 3–5.

SIMMONS, R. G., BURGESON, R., CARLTON-FORD, S., & BLYTH, D. A. (1987). The impact of cumulative change in early adolescence. *Child Development, 58,* 1220–1234.

SIMONTON, D. (1988). Age and outstanding achievement: What do we know after a century of research? *Psychological Bulletin, 104,* 251–267.

SIMONTON, D. (1990). Creativity and wisdom in aging. In J. Birren & K. W. Schaie (Eds.), *Handbook of the psychology of aging* (3rd ed., pp. 320–329). San Diego: Academic Press.

SIMOPOULOS, A. P. (1983). Nutrition. In C. C. Brown (Ed.), *Prenatal Roundtable: Vol. 9. Childhood learning disabilities and prenatal risk* (pp. 44–49). Rutherford, NJ: Johnson & Johnson.

SIMPSON, W. J. (1957). A preliminary report on cigarette smoking and the incidence of prematurity. *American Journal of Obstetrics and Gynecology, 73,* 808–815.

SINFELD, A. (1985). Being out of work. In C. Littler (Ed.), *The experience of work* (pp. 190–208). New York: St. Martin's Press.

SINGER, D. G., & REVENSON, T. A. (1996). *How a child thinks: A Piaget primer* (rev. ed.). New York: Plume.

SINGER, D. G. & SINGER, J. L. (1990). *The house of make believe: Children's play and developing imagination.* Cambridge, MA: Harvard University Press.

SIQUELAND, E. R., & DeLUCIA, C. A. (1969). Visual reinforcement of nonnutritive sucking in human infants. *Science, 165,* 1144–1146.

SKINNER, B. F. (1953). *Science and human behavior.* New York: The Free Press.

SKINNER, B. F. (1968). *The technology of teaching.* New York: Appleton-Century-Crofts.

SKINNER, B. F. (1971). *Beyond freedom and dignity.* New York: Knopf.

SKOLNICK, A. (April 4, 1990). It's important, but don't bank on exercise alone to prevent osteoporosis, experts say. *Journal of the American Medical Association, 263(13),* 1751–1752.

SLADE, P., MACPHERSON, S. A., HUME, A., & MARESH, M. (1993). Expectations, experiences and satisfaction with labour. *British Journal of Clinical Psychology, 32,* 469–483.

SLAVIN, R. E. (1996). Neverstreaming: Preventing learning disabilities. *Educational Leadership, 53,* 4–7.

SLOBIN, D. (Ed.). (1982). *The cross-cultural study of language acquisition.* Hillsdale, NJ: Erlbaum.

SLOBIN, D. I. (July 1972). They learn the same way all around the world. *Psychology Today,* pp. 71–74ff.

SMETANA, J. (1988). Concepts of self and social convention: Adolescents' and parents' reasoning about hypothetical and actual family conflicts. In M. Gunnar & W. Collins (Eds.), *Minnesota Symposia on Child Development: Vol. 21. Development during the transition to adolescence* (pp. 79–122). Hillsdale, NJ: Erlbaum.

SMILANSKY, S. (1968). *The effects of sociodramatic play on disadvantaged children: Preschool children.* New York: Wiley.

SMITH, A. D., & REID, W. J. (1986). Role expectations and attitudes in dual-earner families. *Social Casework, 67,* 394–402.

SMITH, B. S., RATNER, H. H., & HOBART, C. J. (1987). The role of cuing and organization in children's memory for events. *Journal of Experimental Child Psychology, 44*, 1–24.

SMITH, C. D. (1994). *The absentee American: Repatriates' perspective on America.* Bayside, NY: Aletheia.

SMITH, C. D. (1996). *Strangers at home: Essays on the effects of living overseas and coming "home" to a strange land.* Bayside, NY: Aletheia.

SMITH, C., & LLOYD, B. (1978). Maternal behavior and perceived sex of infant: Revisited. *Child Development, 49*, 1263–1265.

SMITH, P. K., & DODSWORTH, C. (1978). Social class differences in the fantasy play of preschool children. *Journal of Genetic Psychology, 133*, 183–190.

SMITH, W. (1987). *Obstetrics, gynecology, & infant mortality.* New York: Facts on File Publications.

SNOW, C. (1989). Understanding social interaction and language acquisition: Sentences are not enough. In M. Bornstein & J. Bruner *Interaction in human development* (pp. 83–104). Hillsdale, NJ: Erlbaum.

SNOW, C. E. (1993). Families as social contexts for literacy development. In C. Daiute (Ed.), *New directions in child development, (61)* (pp. 11–24). San Francisco: Jossey-Bass.

SNYDER, P., & WAY, A. (January & February 1979). Alcoholism and the elderly. *Aging Magazine.*

SOCIAL SECURITY ADMINISTRATION. (1986). Increasing the Social Security retirement age: Older workers in physically demanding occupations or ill health. *Social Security Bulletin, 49*, 5–23.

SOCIETY FOR RESEARCH AND CHILD DEVELOPMENT. (1973). *Ethical standards for research with children.* Chicago: Society for Research and Child Development.

SOLIS, J. M., ET AL. (1990). Acculturation, access to care, and use of preventive services by Hispanics: Findings from HHANES 1982–1984. *American Journal of Public Health, 80* (Supplement), 11–19.

SONENSTEIN, F. L. (1987). Teenage childbearing . . . in all walks of life. *Brandeis Review, 7*(1), 25–28.

SORENSON, R. C. (1973). *Adolescent sexuality in contemporary America: Personal values and sexual behavior, ages 13–19.* New York: World.

SOURCE, J. F., & EMDE, R. N. (1981). Mother's presence is not enough: Effect of emotional availability on infant exploration. *Developmental Psychology, 17*, 737–745.

SPANIER, G. (1983). Married and unmarried cohabitation in the United States: 1980. *Journal of Marriage and the Family*, 277–288.

SPANIER, G., & FURSTENBERG, E. (1982). Remarriage after divorce: A longitudinal analysis of well-being. *Journal of Marriage and the Family*, 709–720.

SPEARMAN, C. (1904). "General intelligence" objectively determined and measured. *American Journal of Psychology, 14*, 201–293.

SPEECE, M. W., & BRENT, S. B. (1984). Children's understanding of death: A review of three components of a death concept. *Child Development, 55*, 1671–1686.

SPELKE, E. S. (1988). The origins of physical knowledge. In L. Weiskrantz (Ed.), *Thought without language* (pp. 168–184). Clarendon Press.

SPENCER, M. B. (1988). Self-concept development. In D. T. Slaughter (Ed.), *New Directions for Child Development, 42. Black children and poverty: A developmental perspective.* San Francisco: Jossey-Bass.

SPIRO, M. E. (1954). Is the family universal? The Israeli case. *American Anthropologist, 56*, 839–846.

SPIRO, M. E., & SPIRO, A. G. (1972). *Children of the kibbutz.* New York: Schocken Books.

SPITZE, G., & LOGAN, J. (1989). Gender differences in family support: Is there a payoff? *The Gerontologist, 29*, 108–113.

SPITZE, G., & LOGAN, J. (1990). Sons, daughters, and intergenerational social support. *Journal of Marriage and the Family, 52*, 420–430.

SPITZER, M. (1988) Taste acuity in institutionalized and noninstitutionalized elderly men. *Journal of Gerontology, 43*, P71–P74.

SPORE, D. L., MOR, V., PARRAT, P., HAWES, C., & HIRIS, J. (1997). Inappropriate drug prescriptions for elderly residents of board and care facilities. *American Journal of Public Health, 87*, 404–409.

SPURLOCK, J. (1984). Black women in the middle years. In G. Bauch & J. Brooks-Gunn (Eds.). *Women in midlife* (pp. 245–260). New York: Plenum.

SROUFE, L. A. (1977). Wariness of strangers and the study of infant development. *Child Development, 48*, 731–746.

SROUFE, L. A. (1978). Attachment and the roots of competence. *Human Nature, 1*, 50–57.

SROUFE, L. A. (1985). Attachment classification from the perspective of infant–caregiver relationships and infant temperament. *Child Development, 56*, 1–14.

SROUFE, L. A., & FLEESON, J. (1986). Attachment and the construction of relationships. In W. W. Hartup & Z. Rubin (Eds.), *Relationships and development* (pp. 51–72). Hillsdale, NJ: Erlbaum.

SROUFE, L. A., FOX, N. E., & PANEAKE, V. R. (1983). Attachment and dependency in a developmental perspective. *Child Development, 54*, 1615–1627.

STAGNER, R. (1985). Aging in industry. In J. Birren & K. Schaie (Eds.) *Handbook of the psychology of aging* (2nd ed., pp. 789–817). New York: Van Nostrand Reinhold.

STAINES, G., POTTICK, K., & FUDGE, D. (1986). Wives' employment and husbands' attitudes toward work and life. *Journal of Applied Psychology, 71*, 118–128.

STAMPFER, M. J., ET AL. (September 12, 1991). Postmenopausal estrogen therapy and cardiovascular disease: Ten-year follow-up from the nurses' health study. *New England Journal of Medicine*, p. 756.

STANGOR, C., & RUBLE, D. N. (1987). Development of gender role knowledge and gender consistency. *New Directions for Child Development, 38*, 5–22.

STANTON, H. E. (1981). A therapeutic approach to help children overcome learning difficulties. *Journal of Learning Disabilities, 14*, 220.

STARFIELD, B. (1992). Child and adolescent health status measures. In R. E. Behrman, (Ed.), *The Future of Children* (25–39). Los Angeles, CA: Center for the Future of Children of the David and Lucile Packard Foundation.

STAUB, E. (1971). The use of role playing and induction in children's learning of helping and sharing behavior. *Child Development, 42*, 805–816.

STECHLER, G., & SHELTON, A. (1982). Prenatal influences on human development. In B. Wolman (Ed.), *Handbook of developmental psychology.* Englewood Cliffs, NJ: Prentice Hall.

STEIN, A. H., & FRIEDRICH, L. K. (1975). Impact of television on children and youth. In E. M. Hetherington (Ed.), *Review of child development* (Vol. 5). Chicago: University of Chicago Press.

STEIN, P. J. (1976). *Single.* Englewood Cliffs, NJ: Prentice Hall.

STEIN, Z. A., & SUSSER, M. W. (1976). Prenatal nutrition and mental competence. In Lloyd, Still, J. D. (Ed.), *Malnutrition and intellectual development.* Littleton, MA: Publishing Sciences Group.

STEINBERG, L. (1980). *Understanding families with young adolescents.* Carrboro, NC: Center for Early Adolescents.

STEINBERG, L. (1981). Transformations in family relations at puberty. *Developmental Psychology, 17*, 833–840.

STEINBERG, L. (1986). Latchkey children and susceptibility to peer pressure: An ecological analysis. *Developmental Psychology, 22*, 433–439.

STEINBERG, L. (1987a). Recent research on the family at adolescence: The extent and nature of sex differences. *Journal of Youth and Adolescence, 16*, 191–198.

STEINBERG, L. (1987b). Single parents, stepparents, and the susceptibility of adolescents to antisocial peer pressure. *Child Development, 58*, 269–275.

STEINBERG, L. (1988). Reciprocal relation between parent–child distance and pubertal maturation. *Developmental Psychology, 24*, 122–128.

STEPHENS, W. N. (1963). *The family in cross-cultural perspective.* New York: Holt, Rinehart & Winston.

STERNBERG, R. (1986). A triangular theory of love. *Psychological Review, 93*, 119–135.

STERNBERG, R. J. (1984). Mechanisms of cognitive development: A componential approach. In R. J. Sternberg (Ed.), *Mechanisms of cognitive development.* New York: Freeman.

STERNBERG, R. J. (1985). *Beyond IQ: A triarchic theory of human intelligence.* Cambridge, UK: Cambridge University Press.

STERNBERG, R. J. (1988a). Lessons from the life span: What theorists of intellectual development among children learn from their counterparts studying adults. In E. M. Hetherington, R. N. Lerner, & M. Perlmutter (Eds.), *Child development* (pp. 259–276). Hillsdale, NJ: Erlbaum.

STERNBERG, R. J. (1988b). Intellectual development: Psychometric and information processing approaches. In M. H. Bornstein & M. E. Lamb, (Eds.), *Developmental psychol-*

ogy: An advanced textbook (2nd ed.). Hillsdale, NJ: Erlbaum.

STERNBERG, R. J. (Ed.) (1990). Wisdom: Its nature, origins, and development. New York: Cambridge University Press.

STERNBERG, R. J. (Ed.). (1982). Advances in the psychology of human intelligence. Hillsdale, NJ: Erlbaum.

STERNGLASS, E. J. (1963). Cancer: Relation of prenatal radiation to development of the disease in childhood. Science, 140, 1102–1104.

STEUVE, A., & O'DONNELL, L. (1984). The daughter of aging parents. In G. Baruch & J. Brooks-Gunn (Eds.), Women in midlife (pp. 203–226). New York: Plenum.

STEVENS, N. (1995). Gender and adaptation to widowhood in later life. Ageing and Society, 15, 37–58.

STEVENS-LONG, J., & COMMONS, M. L. (1992). Adult life: Developmental processes (4th ed., p. 106). Mountain View, CA: Mayfield.

STEVENSON, H. W. (December 1992). Learning from Asian schools. Scientific American, pp. 70–76.

STEVENSON, H., AZUMA, H., & HAKUTA, K. (Eds.). (1986). Child development and education in Japan. New York: Freeman.

STEVENSON, H. W., CHEN C. & LEE S. (1993) Mathematics achievement of Chinese, Japanese, and American children: Ten years later. Science, 53–58.

STEWART, R. B., MOBLEY, L. A., VAN TUYL, S. S., & SALVADOR, M. A. (1987). The first-born's adjustment to the birth of a sibling: A longitudinal assessment. Child Development, 58, 341–355.

STEWART, W. (1977). A psychosocial study of the formation of the early adult life structure in women. Unpublished doctoral dissertation. Columbia University, New York.

STIFFER, C. A., COULEHAN, C. M., & FISH, M. (1993). Linking employment to attachment: The mediating effects of maternal separation anxiety and interactive behavior. Child Development, 64, 1451–1460.

STIGLER, J. W., LEE, S., & STEVENSON, H. W. (1987). Mathematics classrooms in Japan, Taiwan, and the United States. Child Development, 58, 1272–1285.

STILLION, J. (1985). Death and the sexes: An examination of differential longevity, attitudes, behaviors, and coping styles. Washington, DC: Hemisphere.

STODDART, T., & NIEDERHAUSER, D. (1993). Technology and educational change, Computers in the Schools, 9(2–3), 5–14.

STOEL-GAMMON, C. (1989). Prespeech and early speech development of two late talkers. First Language, 9, 207–223.

STOLLER, E. P., & GIBSON, R. C. (1994). Worlds of differences: Inequality in the aging experience (pp. xvii–xxv). Thousand Oaks, CA: Pine Forge Press.

STOLLER, E. P., & GIBSON, R. C. (1994). Worlds of differences: Inequality in the aging experience, p. 3. Thousand Oaks, CA: Pine Forge Press.

STONE, L. J., SMITH, H. T., & MURPHY, L. B. (Eds.). (1973). The competent infant: Research and commentary. New York: Basic Books.

STONE, R., CAFFERATA, G., & SANGL, J. (1987). Care-givers of the frail elderly: A national profile. The Gerontologist, 27, 616–626.

STRASSBERG, Z., ET AL. (1994). Spanking in the home and children's subsequent aggression toward kindergarten peers. Development and Psychopathology, 6, 445–461.

STRAYER, F. F., & STRAYER, J. (1976). An ethnological analysis of social agonism and dominance relations among preschool children. Child Development, 47, 980–989.

STREISSGUTH, A. P. (1997). Fetal alcohol syndrome: A guide for families and communities. Paul H. Brookes Publishing Co.

STREISSGUTH, A. P., BARR, H., & MACDONALD, M. (1983). Maternal alcohol use and neonatal habituation assessed with the Brazelton scale. Child Development, 54, 1109–1118.

STREISSGUTH, A. P., MARTIN, D. C., BARR, H. M., SANDMAN, B. M., KIRCHNER, G. L., & DARBY, B. L. (1984). Intrauterine alcohol and nicotine exposure: Attention and reaction time in four-year-old children. Developmental Psychology, 20, 533–541.

STREISSGUTH, A. P., SAMPSON, P. D., BARR, H. M., DARBY, B. L., & MARTIN, D. C. (1989). I. Q. at age 4 in relation to maternal alcohol use and smoking during pregnancy. Developmental Psychology, 25(1), 3–11.

STROEVE, M., ET AL. (October 1992). Broken hearts or broken bonds: Love and death in historical perspective. American Psychologist, 47(10), 1205–1212.

STUBER, M. L. (August 1989). Coordination of care for pediatric AIDS. Journal of Developmental and Behavioral Pediatrics, 10(4), 201–204.

STULL, D. E., BOWMAN, K., & SMERGLIA, V. (July 1994). Women in the middle: A myth in the making? Family Relations, 43, 317–324.

STUNKARD, A. J. (1988). Some perspectives on human obesity: Its causes. Bulletin of the New York Academy of Medicine, 64, 902–923.

SUBBOTSKY, E. (1994). Early rationality and magical thinking in preschoolers. Space and time. British Journal of Developmental Psychology, 12, 97–108.

SUBSTANCE ABUSE AND MENTAL HEALTH SERVICES ADMINISTRATION (SAMSHA) (1997). Preliminary results from the 1996 National Household Survey on Drug Abuse. Washington, DC.

SUGARMAN, S. (December 1983). Why talk? Comment on Savage-Rumbaugh et al. Journal of Experimental Psychology, 112(4), 493–497.

SUPER, C. M., HERRERA, M. G., & MORA, J. O. (1990). Long-term effects of food supplementation and psychosocial intervention on the physical growth of Colombian infants at risk of malnutrition. Child Development, 61, 29–49.

SUPER, D. E. (1957). The psychology of careers. New York: Harper & Brothers.

SUPER, D. E. (1963). Career development: Self concept theory. New York: College Entrance Examination Board.

SUPER, D. E. (1974). Vocational maturity theory. In D. E. Super (Ed.), Measuring vocational maturity for counseling. Washington, DC: American Personnel and Guidance Association.

SUTHERLAND, G. R., & RICHARDS, R. I. (1994). Dynamic mutations. American Scientists, 82(2), 157–163.

SUTTON-SMITH, B., & ROSENBERG, B. G. (1970). The sibling. New York: Holt, Rinehart & Winston.

SWOBODA, M. J., & MILLAR, S. B. (1986). Networking—mentoring: Career strategy of women in academic administration. Journal of National Association of Women Deans, Administrators, and Counselors, 49, 8–13.

SZINOVACZ, M. E. (1998). Grandparents today: A demographic profile. The Gerontologist, 38, 37–52.

TAFT, L. I., & COHEN, H. J. (1967). Neonatal and infant reflexology. In J. Hellmuth (Ed.), The exceptional infant (Vol. 1). Seattle: Special Child Publications.

TANNER, J. M. (1978). Foetus into man: Physical growth from conception to maturity. Cambridge, MA: Harvard University Press.

TAVERIS, C. (1983). Anger: The misunderstood emotion. New York: Simon & Schuster.

TAYLOR, M., CARTWRIGHT, B. S., & CARLSON, S. M. (1993). A developmental investigation of children's imaginary companions. Developmental Psychology, 29(2), 276–285.

TEALE, W. & SULZBY, T. (1986). Emergent literacy: Writing and reading. Norwood, N.J.: Ablex.

TELLEGEN, A. D. T., LYKKEN, D. T., BOUCHARD, T. J., WILCOX, K., SEGAL, N. L., & RICH, S. (1988). Personality similarity in twins reared apart and together. Journal of Social and Personality Psychology, 59, 1031–1039.

TELLER, D., & BORNSTEIN, M. (1987). Infant color vision and color perception. In P. Salapatek & L. Cohen (Eds.), Handbook of infant perception (Vol. 1). New York: Academic Press.

TERMAN, L. M., & MERRILL, M. A. (1960). Revised Stanford-Binet Intelligence Scale (2nd ed.). Boston: Houghton Mifflin.

TETI, D. M., & ABLARD, K. A. (1989). Security of attachment and infant–sibling relationships: A laboratory study. Child Development, 60, 1519–1528.

TETI, D. M., GELFAND, D. M., MESSINGER, D. S., & ISABELLA, R. (1995). Maternal depression and the quality of early attachment: An examination of infants, preschoolers, and their mothers. Developmental Psychology, 31, 364–376.

THATCHER, R. W., WALKER, R. A., & GUIDICE, S. (1987). Human cerebral hemispheres develop at different rates and ages. Science, 236, 110–1113.

THEILGAARD, A. (1983). Aggression and the XYY personality. International Journal of Law and Psychiatry, 6, 413–421.

THELEN, E. (1987). The role of motor development in developmental psychology: A view of the past and an agenda for the future. In N. Eisenberg (Ed.), Contemporary topics in developmental psychology. New York: Wiley.

THELEN, E. (1989). The rediscovery of motor development: Learning new things from an old field. Developmental Psychology, 25(6), 946–949.

THELEN, E., & FOGEL, A. (1989). Toward an action-based theory of infant development. In J. J. Lockman & N. L. Kazen (Eds.), Action in social context: Perspectives on early development (pp. 23–64). New York: Plenum.

THOMAE, H. (1980). Personality and adjustment to aging. In J. E. Birren & R. B. Sloane (Eds.), *Handbook of mental health and aging*. Englewood Cliffs, NJ: Prentice Hall.

THOMAS, A., & CHESS, S. (1977). *Temperament and development*. New York: Brunner-Mazel.

THOMAS, L. E. (1979). Causes of mid-life change from high status careers. *Vocational Guidance Quarterly, 27*, 202–208.

THOMPSON, A. S. (1977). Notes on career development inventory—adult form. As quoted in R. P. Johnson & H. C. Riker (1981), Retirement maturity: A valuable concept for preretirement counselors. *Personnel and Guidance Journal, 59*, 291–295.

THOMPSON, L. (1991). Family work: Women's sense of fairness. *Journal of Family Issues, 12*(92), 181–196.

THOMPSON, L., & WALKER, A. J. (1989). Gender in families: Women and men in marriage, work and parenthood. *Journal of Marriage and the Family, 51*, 845–871.

THOMPSON, R. A. (1990). Vulnerability in research: A developmental perspective on research risk. *Child Development, 61*, 1–16.

THOMPSON, S. K. (1975). Gender labels and early sex role development. *Child Development, 46*, 339–347.

THORNDIKE, E. L. (1911). *Animal intelligence*. New York: Macmillan.

THORNTON, A. (1989). Changing attitudes toward family issues in the United States. *Journal of Marriage and the Family, 51*, 873–893.

THURSHER, M., SPENCE, D., & LOWENTHAL, M. (1974). Value confluence and behavioral conflict in intergenerational relations. *Journal of Marriage and the Family, 36*(2), 308–320.

THURSTONE, L. L. (1938). Primary mental abilities. *Psychometric Monographs*, No. 1.

TIEGER, T. (1980). On the biological basis of sex differences in aggression. *Child Development, 51*, 943–963.

TIKALSKY, F. D., & WALLACE, S. D. (1988). Culture and the structure of children's fears. *Journal of Cross-Cultural Psychology, 19*(4), 481–492.

TILGHER, A. (1962). Work through the ages. In S. Nosow & W. H. Form (Eds.), *Man, work, and society*. New York: Basic Books.

TIMIRAS, P. S. (1972). *Developmental physiology and aging*. New York: Macmillan.

TIMIRAS, P. S. (1978). Biological perspectives on aging. *American Scientist, 66*, 605–613.

TIMIRAS, P. S. (Ed.) (1994). *Physiological basis of aging and geriatrics*. Boca Raton, FL: CRC Press.

TIMNICK, L. (September 3, 1989). Children of violence. *Los Angeles Times Magazine*, 6–12, 14–15.

TJIAN, R. (1995). Molecular machines that control genes. *Scientific American, 272*(1), 54–61.

TOBIAS, S. (1989). Tracked to fail. *Psychology Today, 60* (9), 54–58.

TOBIN, S. S. (1988). *The unique psychology of the very old: Implications for practice. Issues in Aging* (Monograph No. 4). Chicago: Center for Applied Gerontology.

TOBIN, S., & LIEBERMAN, M. (1976). *Last home for the aged*. San Francisco: Jossey-Bass.

TOMASELLO, M., MANNLE, S., & KRUGER, A. C. (1986). Linguistic environment of one- to two-year-old twins. *Developmental Psychology, 22*, 169–176.

TONNA, E. A. (1977). Aging of skeletal and dental systems and supporting tissue. In C. E. Finch & L. Hayflick (Eds.), *Handbook of the biology of aging*. New York: Van Nostrand Reinhold.

TORREY, B. B. (1982). The lengthening of retirement. In M. W. Riley, R. P. Abeles, & M. Teitelbaum (Eds.), *Aging from birth to death* (Vol. 2, pp. 181–195). *Sociotemporal perspectives*. Boulder, CO: Westview.

TOUFEXIS, A. (1993). Sex has many accents. *Time*, May 24, 1993.

TROLL, L. E. (1980). Grandparenting. In L. W. Poon (Ed.), *Aging in the 1980s*. Washington, DC: American Psychological Association.

TROLL, L. E. (1985). *Early and middle adulthood: The best is yet to come—maybe* (2nd ed., p. 38). Monterey, CA: Brooks/Cole.

TROLL, L. E. (1989). Myths of midlife: Intergenerational relationships. In S. Hunter & M. Sundel (Eds.), *Midlife myths: Issues, findings and practice implications* (p. 213). Newbury Park, CA: Sage.

TROLL, L. E., MILLER, S., & ATCHLEY, R. C. (1979). *Families of later life*. Belmont, CA: Wadsworth.

TROLL, L. E., NEUGARTEN, B. L., & KRAINES, R. (1969). Similarities in values and other personality characteristics in college students and their parents. *Merrill-Palmer Quarterly, 15*, 323–336.

TRONICK, E. Z. (February 1989). Emotions and emotional communication. *American Psychologist, 44*(2), 112–119.

TSCHANN, J. M., JOHNSTON, J. R., & WALLERSTEIN, J. D. (November 1989). Resources, stressors, and attachment as predictors of adult adjustment after divorce: A longitudinal study. *Journal of Marriage and the Family, 51*, 1033–1046.

TURKINGTON, C. (1987). Special talents. *Psychology Today, 21*(9), 42–46.

TURNBULL, A. P., & TURNBULL, H. R., III. (1990). *Families, professionals and exceptionality: A special partnership* (2nd ed.). Columbus, OH: Merrill.

TURNBULL, C. M. (1972). *The mountain people*. New York: Simon & Schuster.

UDRY, J. R. (1988). Biological predispositions and social control in adolescent sexual behavior. *American Sociological Review, 52*, 841–855.

UHLENBERG, P., COONEG, T., & BOYD, R. (1990). Divorce for women after midlife. *Journal of Gerontology, 45*(1), 53–61.

UNITED NATIONS (1991). *Human development report, 1991*. New York: Oxford University Press.

UNIVERSITY OF MICHIGAN (1997). *The 1997 Monitoring the Future Study*. Ann Arbor, MI.

U.S. BUREAU OF THE CENSUS (1997). *Statistical abstract of the United States* (117th ed.). Washington, DC.

U.S. BUREAU OF THE CENSUS. (1988). *Statistical Analysis of the U.S.: 1988*. Washington, DC: Government Printing Office.

U.S. BUREAU OF THE CENSUS. (1990). *Current Population Reports*. Series P-25, Nos. 519, 917.

U.S. CENSUS BUREAU (1997). *Statistical abstract of the United States*. Washington, DC: U.S. Government Printing Office.

U.S. DEPARTMENT OF COMMERCE, ECONOMICS AND STATISTICS ADMINISTRATION, BUREAU OF THE CENSUS (September 1993). *We the American elderly*, p. 7.

U.S. DEPARTMENT OF COMMERCE, ECONOMICS AND STATISTICS ADMINISTRATION, BUREAU OF THE CENSUS (November 1993). *Racial and ethnic diversity of America's elderly population*, pp.1–8.

U.S. DEPARTMENT OF COMMERCE. (1987). *Statistical Abstract of the U.S.: 1987*. Washington, DC

U.S. DEPARTMENT OF COMMERCE. (1990). *Statistical Abstract of the U.S.: 1990*. Washington, DC

U.S. DEPARTMENT OF HEALTH AND HUMAN SERVICES. (1983). Regulations on the protection of human subjects. *45CFR, 46*, Subparts A & D.

USMIANI, S., & DANILUK, J. (1997). Mothers and their adolescent daughters: Relationship between self-esteem, gender role identity, and body image. *Journal of Youth and Adolescence, 26*, 45–62.

UZGIRIS, I. C. (1984). Imitation in infancy: Its interpersonal aspects. In M. Perlmutter (Ed.), *Minnesota Symposia on Child Psychology: Vol. 17. Parent–child interaction and parent–child relations*. Hillsdale, NJ: Erlbaum.

VACHON, M. (1986). A comparison of the impact of breast cancer and bereavement: Personality, social support, and adaptation. In S. Hobfoll (Ed.) *Stress, social support, and women*. Washington, DC: Hemisphere.

VAILLANT, G. (September 1977). The climb to maturity: How the best and brightest came of age. *Psychology Today*, p. 34ff.

VAN BAAL, J. (1966). *Dema: Description and analysis of Marind Anim culture, South New Guinea*. The Hague: Martinus Nijhoff.

VANDELL, D. L., & CORASANITI, M. A. (Fall 1990). Child care and the family: Complex contributions to child development. *New Directions for Child Development, 49*, 23–38.

VANDELL, D. L., & WILSON, C. S. (1987). Infants' interactions with mother, sibling and peer: Contrasts and relations between interaction systems. *Child Development, 58*, 176–186.

VASTA, R. (1982). Physical child abuse: A dual-component analysis. *Developmental Review, 2*, 125–149.

VERMA, I. M. (November 1990). Gene therapy. *Scientific American*, pp. 68–84.

VISHER, E., & VISHER, J. (1983). Stepparenting: Blending families. In H. McCubbin & C. Figley (Eds.), *Stress and the family* (Vol. 1). New York: Brunner/Mazel.

VITARO, F., TREMBLAY, R. E., KERR, M., PAGANI, L., & BUKOWSKI, W. M. (1997). Disruptiveness, friends' characteristics, and delinquency in early adolescence: A test of two competing models of development. *Child Development, 68*, 676–689.

VODA, A. (1982). Menopausal hot flash. In A. Voda, M. Dinnerstein, & S. O'Donnell (Eds.), *Changing perspectives on menopause.* Austin: University of Texas Press.

VOGEL, J. M. (1989). *Shifting perspectives on the role of reversal errors in reading disability.* Paper presented at the April meeting of the Society for Research in Child Development, Kansas City.

VON HOFSTEN, C. (1989). Motor development as the development of systems: comments on the special section. *Developmental Psychology, 25(6)*, 950–953.

VONDRA, J. I., BARNETT, D. & CICCHETTI, D. (1990). Self-concept, motivation, and competence among children from maltreating and comparison families. *Child Abuse and Neglect, 14*, 525–540.

VORHEES, C., & MOLLNOW, E. (1987). Behavioral teratogenesis. In J. Osofsky (Ed.), *Handbook of infant development* (2nd ed.). New York: Wiley.

VULLIAMY, D. G. (1973). *The newborn child* (3rd ed.). Edinburgh: Churchill Livingstone.

VYGOTSKY, L. S. (1956). *Selected psychological investigations.* Moscow: Izdstel'sto Akademii Pedagogicheskikh Nauk SSR.

VYGOTSKY, L. (1962). *Thought and language.* Cambridge, MA: MIT Press (Originally published 1934)

VYGOTSKY, L. S. (1978). Mind in society: The development of higher psychological processes. In M. Cole, V. John-Steiner, S. Scribner, & E. Souberman (Eds.). Cambridge, MA: Harvard University Press.

VYGOTSKY, L. S. (1987). Thinking and speech. In R. W. Rieber & A. S. Carton (Eds.) and N Minick (Trans.), *The collected works of L. S. Vygotsky, vol. 1: Problems of general psychology* (pp. 37–285). New York: Plenum. (Original work published in l934.)

WAGNER, R. C., & TORGERSON, J. K. (1987). The nature of phonological processing and its causal role in the acquisition of reading skills. *Psychological Bulletin, 101*, 192–212.

WAINRYB, C. (1995). Reasoning about social conflicts in different cultures: Druze and Jewish children in Israel. *Child Development, 66*, 390–401.

WALFORD, R. L. (1983). *Maximum lifespan.* New York: Norton.

WALKER, L., & WALLSTON, B. (1985). Social adaptation: A review of dual earner family literature. In L. L'Abate (Ed.), *The handbook of family psychology and therapy* (pp. 698–740). Homewood, IL: Dorsey.

WALLACE, P., & GOTLIB, I. (1990). Marital adjustment during the transition to parenthood: Stability and predictors of change. *Journal of Marriage and the Family, 52*, 21–29.

WALLERSTEIN, J., & BLAKESLEE, S. (1989). *Second chances: Men, women, and children a decade after divorce.* Ticknor & Fields.

WALLERSTEIN, J., CORBIN, S. B., & LEWIS, J. M. (1988). Children of divorce: A ten-year study. In E. M. Hetherington & J. Arasteh (Eds.), *Impact of divorce, single-parenting, and stepparenting on children.* Hillsdale, NJ: Erlbaum.

WALLIS, C. (September 10, 1984). The new origins of life. *Time,* pp. 46–50, 52–53.

WALLS, C. T. (Summer 1992). The role of the church and family support in the lives of older African Americans. *Generations*, 33–36.

WALSH, B. T. (1988). Antidepressants and bulimia: Where are we? *International Journal of Eating Disorders, 7*, 421–423.

WALSH, M. (1997). Women's place in the American labour force, 1870–1995. *The Historical Association 1997.* Malden, MA: Blackwell.

WARE, N., & STECKLER, N. (1983). Choosing a science major: The experience of women and men. *Women's Studies Quarterly, 11*, 12–15.

WARE, P. (1992). Anger and occupational well-being. *Psychology and Aging, 7(1)*, 37–45.

WASS, H., & CORR C. A. (1984). *Childhood and death.* Washington, DC: Hemisphere.

WATERLOW, J. C. (1994). Causes and mechanisms of linear growth retardation (stunting). *European Journal of Clinical Nutrition, 48* (Supplement 1), s1–4.

WATERMAN, A. S. (1985). Identity in the context of adolescent psychology. *New Directions for Child Development, 30*, 5–24.

WATERS, E. (1978). The reliability and stability of individual differences in infant–mother attachment. *Child Development, 49*, 483–494.

WATERS, E., WIPPMAN, J., & SROUFE, L. A. (1979). Attachment, positive affect and competence in the peer group: Two studies in construct validation. *Child Development, 50*, 821–829.

WATKINS, S. C. , MENKEN, J. A., & BONGAARTS, J. (1987). Demographic foundations of family change. *American Sociological Review, 52*, 346–358.

WATSON, A. J., & VALTIN, R. (1997). Secrecy in middle childhood. *International Journal of Behavioral Development, 21*, 431–452.

WATSON, G. (1957). Some personality differences in children related to strict or permissive parental discipline. *Journal of Psychology, 44*, 227–249.

WATSON, J. B. (1919). *Psychology from the standpoint of a behaviorist.* Philadephia: Lippincott.

WATSON, J. B. (1925). *Behaviorism.* New York: Norton.

WATSON, J. B., & RAYNER, R. (1920). Conditioned emotional reactions. *Journal of Experimental Psychology, 3*, 1–14.

WATSON, J. D., & CRICK, F. H. C. (1953). Molecular structure of nucleic acids. *Nature, 171*, 737–738.

WATSON, J. S. (1972). Smiling, cooing, and "the game." *Merrill-Palmer Quarterly, 18*, 323–339.

WATSON, J. S., & RAMEY, C. T. (1972). Reactions to response-contingent stimulation in early infancy. *Merrill-Palmer Quarterly, 18*, 219–227.

WATSON-GEGEO, K. A., & GEGEO, D. W. (1989) The role of sibling interaction in child socialization. In P. Zukow (Ed.), *Sibling interaction across cultures: Theoretical and methodological issues.* New York: Springer-Verlag.

WEBER, R. A., LEVITT, M. J., & CLARK, M. C. (1986). Individual variation in attachment security and strange situation behavior: The role of maternal and infant temperament. *Child Development, 37*, 56–65.

WECHSLER, D. (1974). *Wechsler Intelligence Scale for Children—Revised.* New York: Psychological Corporation.

WEG, R. (1983). Changing physiology of aging. In D. W. Woodruff & J. E. Bearon (Eds.), *Aging: Scientific perspectives and social issues.* Monterey, CA: Brooks/Cole.

WEG, R. B. (1989). Sensuality/sexuality of the middle years. In S. Hunter & M. Sundel. *Midlife myths: Issues, findings, and practice implications* (pp. 31–47). Newbury Park, CA: Sage.

WEGMAN, M. E. (1990). Annual summary of vital statistics—1989. *Pediatrics, 86(6)*, 835–847.

WEIKART, D. P., ET AL. (1984). *Changed lives: The effects of the Perry Preschool Program on youth through age 19.* Ypsilanti, MI: High/Scope Foundation.

WEIKART, D. P., ROGERS, L., & ADCOCK, C. (1971). *The cognitively oriented curriculum* (ERIC-NAEYC publication in early childhood education). Urbana: University of Illinois Press.

WEINBERG, R. A. (1989). Intelligence and IQ: Landmark issues and great debates. *American Psychologist, 44*, 98–104.

WEINRAUB, M., CLEMENS, L. P., SOCKLOFF, A., ETHRIDGE, T., GRACELY, E., & MYERS, B. (1984). The development of sex role stereotypes in the third year: Relationships to gender labeling, gender identity, sex-typed toy preference and family characteristics. *Child Development, 55*, 1493–1503.

WEINSTEIN, C. S. (1991). The classroom as a social context for learning. *Annual Review of Psychology, 42*, 493–525.

WEINSTEIN, G., & ALSCHULER, A. (1985). Educating and counseling for self-knowledge development. *Journal of Counseling and Development, 4*, 19–25.

WEISFELD, G. E., & BILLINGS, R. L. (1988). Observations on adolescence. In K. B. MacDonald (Ed.), *Sociobiological perspectives on human development.* New York: Springer-Verlag.

WEISMAN, A. D. (1972). *On dying and denying: A psychiatric study of terminality.* New York: Behavioral Publications.

WEISS, R. S. (1987). On the current state of the American family. *Journal of Family Issues, 8*, 464–467.

WEITH, M. E. (February 1994). Elder abuse: A national tragedy. *FBI Law Enforcement Bulletin,* pp 24–26.

WELLES-NYSTROM, B. (Summer 1988). Parenthood and infancy in Sweden. In R. A. LeVine, P. M. Miller, & M. M. West (Eds.), *New Directions for Child Development, 40. Parental behavior in diverse societies* (pp. 75–78).

WERNER, E. E. (1979). *Cross-cultural child development.* Monterey, CA: Brooks/Cole.

WERNER, E. E. (1989a). Children of the garden island. *Scientific American, 260(4)*, 106–111.

WERNER, E. E. (1989b). High-risk children in young adulthood: A longitudinal study from birth to 32 years. *American Journal of Orthopsychiatry, 59,* 72–81.

WERNER, E. E. (1995). Resilience in development. *Current Directions in Psychological Science, June,* 81–85.

WERSHOW, H. J. (Ed.). (1981). *Controversial issues in gerontology.* New York: Springer.

WESTINGHOUSE LEARNING CORPORATION. (1969). *The impact of Head Start: An evaluation of the effects of Head Start experience on children's cognitive and affective development.* Columbus: Westinghouse Learning Corporation, Ohio State University.

WHEELER, D. (1994). Preterm birth prevention. *Journal of Nurse-Midwifery, 39,* 2 (Supplement), 66s–80s.

WHITBOURNE, S. K. (1986a). *The me I know: A study of adult development.* New York: Springer-Verlag.

WHITBOURNE, S. K. (1986b). *Adult development* (2nd ed.). New York: Praeger.

WHITBOURNE, S. K. (1987). Personality development in adulthood and old age: Relationships among identity style, health, and well-being. In K. W. Schaie & C. Eisdorfer (Eds.), *Annual review of gerontology and geriatrics* (Vol. 7). New York: Springer.

WHITBOURNE, S. K. (February 20, 1991). *Adult development: Life span perspective.* Talk given at the Human Development Colloquium Series, University of Massachusetts, Amherst.

WHITE, B. L. (1971). *Human infants: Experience and psychological development.* Englewood Cliffs, NJ: Prentice Hall.

WHITE, B. L. (1975). *The first three years of life.* Englewood Cliffs, NJ: Prentice Hall.

WHITE, B. L. (1988). *Educating the infant and toddler.* Lexington, MA: Lexington Books.

WHITE, B. L., & HELD, R. (1966). Plasticity of sensorimotor development in the human infant. In J. F. Rosenblith & W. Allinsmith (Eds.), *Causes of behavior: Readings in child development and educational psychology.* Boston: Allyn & Bacon.

WHITE, B. L., & WATTS, J. (1973). *Experience and environment: Major influences on the development of the young child.* Englewood Cliffs, NJ: Prentice Hall.

WHITE, K. J., & KISTNER, J. (1992). The influence of teacher feedback on young children's peer preferences and perceptions. *Developmental Psychology, 28*(5), 933–940.

WHITE, R. W. (1959). Motivation reconsidered: The concept of competence. *Psychological Review, 66,* 297–333.

WHITEHURST, F. L., ET AL. (1988). Accelerating language development through picture book reading. *Developmental Psychology, 24,* 552–559.

WHITESIDE, M. F. (1989). Family rituals as a key to kinship connections in remarried families. *Family Relations, 38,* 34–39.

WHITING, B. B. (Ed.). (1963). *Six cultures: Studies of child rearing.* New York: Wiley.

WHITING, B. B., & EDWARDS, C. P. (1988). *Children of different worlds: The formation of social behavior.* Cambridge, MA: Harvard University Press.

WHITING, B. B., & WHITING, J. W. M. (1975). *Children of six cultures: A psychocultural analysis.* Cambridge, MA: Harvard University Press.

WILDHOLM, O. (1985). Epidemiology of premenstrual tension syndrome and primary dysmenorrhea. In M. Y. Dawood, J. L. McGuire, and L. M. Demers (Eds.). *Premenstrual syndrome and dysmenorrhea.* Baltimore, MD: Urban and Schwartzenberg.

WILKIE, J. R., RATCLIFF, K. S., & FERREE, M. M. (November 1992). Family division of labor and marital satisfaction among two-earner married couples. Paper presented at the annual conference of the National Council on Family Relations, Orlando, FL.

WILLHERT, J. (1993). Hello, I'm home alone. *Time,* 46–47.

WILLIAMS, D. R. (1992). Social structure and the health behavior of blacks. In K. W. Schaie, D. Blazer, & J. S. House (Eds.), *Aging, health behaviors, and health outcomes* (pp. 59–63). Hillsdale, NJ: Erlbaum.

WILLIAMS, F. (1970). Some preliminaries and prospects. In F. Williams (Ed.), *Language and poverty.* Chicago: Markham.

WILLIAMS, H. G. (1983). *Perceptual and motor development.* Englewood Cliffs, N.J.: Prentice Hall.

WILLIAMS, J. D., & JACOBY, A. P. (1989). The effects of premarital heterosexual and homosexual experience on dating and marriage desirability. *Journal of Marriage and the Family, 51,* 489–497.

WILLIAMS, J. E., BENNETT, S. M., & BEST, D. (1975). Awareness and expression of sex stereotypes in young children. *Developmental Psychology, 5*(2), 635–642.

WILLIS, S. (1985). Towards an educational psychology of the older adult learner: Intellectual and cognitive bases. In J. Birren & W. Schaie (Eds.), *Handbook of the psychology of aging* (2nd ed.). New York: Van Nostrand Reinhold.

WILLIS, S. (1990). Introduction to the special section on cognitive training in later adulthood. *Developmental Psychology, 26,* 875–878.

WILLIS, S. L. (1989). Adult intelligence. In S. Hunter & M. Sundel (Eds.), *Midlife myths: Issues, findings, and practice implications* (pp. 97–112). Newbury Park, CA: Sage.

WILLIS, S., & NESSELROADE, C. (1990). Long-term effects of fluid ability training in old-old age. *Developmental Psychology, 26,* 905–910.

WILLSON, J. R. (May 1990). Scientific advances, societal trends and the education and practice of obstetrician-gynecologists. *American Journal of Obstetrics and Gynecology, 162*(5).

WILSON, E. O. (1975). *Sociobiology, the new synthesis.* Cambridge, MA: Belknap Press of Harvard University Press.

WINCH, R. F. (1958). As quoted in B. I. Murstein (1980), Mate selection in the 1970s. *Journal of Marriage and the Family, 42,* 777–789.

WINICK, M., & BRASEL, J. A. (1977). Early manipulation and subsequent brain development. *Annals of the New York Academy of Sciences, 300,* 280–282.

WINN, M. (1983). *The plug-in drug* (2nd ed.). New York: Viking.

WINNER, E. (1986). Where pelicans kiss seeds. *Psychology Today, 8,* 25–35.

WINSBOROUGH, H. H. (1980). A demographic approach to the life-cycle. In K. W. Back (Ed.), *Life course: Integrative theories and exemplary populations* (pp. 250–282). Washington, DC: American Sociological Association.

WINSLER, A., DIAZ, R. M., & MONTERO, I. (1997). The role of private speech in the transition from collaborative to independent task performance in young children. *Early Childhood Research Quarterly, 12,* 59–79.

WITTERS, W., & VENTURELLI, P. (1988). *Drugs and society* (2nd ed.). Boston: Jones & Bartlett.

WOJAHN, E. (November 1983). A new wrinkle in retirement policies. *INC.,* 174–178. Boston: INC Publishing Company.

WOLFE, D. A., WOLFE, V. V., & BEST, C. L. (1988). Child victims of sexual abuse. In V. B. VanHasselt, R. L. Morrison, A. S. Bellack, & M. Herson (Eds.), *Handbook of family violence.* New York: Plenum.

WOLFENSTEIN, M. (1951). The emergence of fun morality. *Journal of Social Issues, 7*(4), 15–25.

WOLFENSTEIN, M. (1955). Fun morality: An analysis of recent American child-training literature. In M. Mead & M. Wolfenstein (Eds.), *Childhood in contemporary cultures* (pp. 168–178). Chicago: University of Chicago Press.

WOLFF, P. (1966). The causes, controls, and organization of behavior in the neonate. *Psychological Issues, 5*(No. 1, Monograph 17).

WOLFF, P. H. (1969). The natural history of crying and other vocalizations in early infancy. In B. M. Foss (Ed.), *Determinants of infant behavior* (Vol. 4). London: Methuen.

WOLPE, J., SALTER, A., & REYNA, L. J. (Eds.). (1964). *The conditioning therapies: The challenge in psychotherapy.* New York: Holt, Rinehart & Winston.

WOMEN'S REENTRY PROJECT. (1981). *Obtaining a degree: Alternative options for reentry women.* Washington, DC: Project on the Status and Education of Women.

WOODCOCK, L. P. (1941). *The life and ways of the two-year-old.* New York: Basic Books.

WORDEN, J. W. (1982). *Grief counseling and grief therapy: A handbook for the mental health practitioner.* New York: Springer.

WRIGHT, B. (1983). *Physical disability: A psychological approach* (2nd ed.). New York: Harper & Row.

WRIGHT, J., & HUSTON, A. (1983). A matter of form: Potentials of television for young viewers. *American Psychologist, 38,* 835–843.

WURTMAN, R. J. (1979). Symposium of choline and related substances in nerve and mental diseases, Tucson, AZ. (Reported by H. M. Schmeck in *New York Times,* January 9, 1979, p. C1ff.)

WYATT, P. R. (1985). Chorionic biopsy and increased anxiety. *The Lancet, 2,* 1312–1313.

WYDEN, B. (December 7, 1971). Growth: 45 crucial months. *Life,* p. 93ff.

YANKELOVICH, D. (1981). *New rules: Searching for self-fulfillment in a world turned upside-down.* New York: Random House.

YARROW, L. J., RUBENSTEIN, J. L., PEDERSEN, F. A., & JANKOWSKI, J. J. (1972). Dimensions of early stimulation and their differential effects on infant development. *Merrill-Palmer Quarterly, 18,* 205–218.

YONAS, A., & OWSLEY, C. (1987). Development of visual space perception. In P. Salapatek & L. Cohen (Eds.), *Handbook of infant perception* (Vol. 2, pp. 80–122). New York: Academic Press.

YOUCHA, G. (December 1982). Life before birth. *Science Digest, 90*(12), 46–53.

YOUNG, D. (1982). *Changing childbirth: Family birth in the hospital.* Rochester, NY: Childbirth Graphics.

YOUNG, E. W., JENSEN, L. C., OLSEN, J. A., & CUNDICK, B. P. (1991). The effects of family structure on the sexual behavior of adolescents. *Adolescence, 26*(104), 977–986.

YOUNG, K. T. (1990). American conceptions of infant development from 1955 to 1984: What the experts are telling parents. *Child Development, 61,* 17–28.

YOUNISS, J., & KETTERLINUS, R. D. (1987). Communication and connectedness in mother and father adolescent relationships. *Journal of Youth and Adolescence,* 265–280.

ZAHN-WAXLER, C., ET AL. (1992). Development of concern for others. *Developmental Psychology, 28*(1), 126–136.

ZAHN-WAXLER, C., & SMITH, K. D. (1992). The development of prosocial behavior. In V. B. Van Hasselt & M. Hersen (Eds.), *Handbook of social development: A lifespan perspective* (pp. 229–255). New York Plenum.

ZAJONC, R. B., & HALL, E. (February 1986). Mining new gold from old research. *Psychology Today,* pp. 46–51.

ZAJONC, R. B., & MARKUS, G. B. (1975). Birth order and intellectual development. *Psychological Review, 82,* 74–88.

ZAPOROZLETS, A. V., & ELKONIN, D. B. (Eds.). (1971). *The psychology of preschool children.* Cambridge, MA: MIT Press.

ZARIT, S. H., ORR, N. K., & ZARIT, J. N. (1985). *The hidden victims of Alzheimer's disease: Families under stress.* New York: New York University Press.

ZELNICK, M., & KANTNER, J. F. (1977). Sexual and contraceptive experience of young unmarried women in the United States,

1976 and 1971. *Family Planning Perspectives, 9,* 55–71.

ZESKIND, P. S., & RAMEY, C. T. (1978). Fetal malnutrition: An experimental study of its consequences on infant development in two caregiving environments. *Child Development, 49,* 1155–1162.

ZILL, N. (1991). U.S. children and their families: Current conditions and recent trends, 1989. *Newsletter of the Society for Research in Child Development,* pp. 1–3.

ZIMMERMAN, M. A., COPELAND, L. A., SHOPE, J. T., AND DIELMAN, T. E. (1997). A longitudinal study of self-esteem: Implications for adolescent development. *Journal of Youth and Adolescence, 26,* 117–140.

ZURAVIN, S. (1985). Housing and maltreatment: Is there a connection? *Children Today, 14*(6), 8–13.

Photo Credits

national LLC **459** B. Daemmrich/The Image Works **461** Ron Chapple/FPG International LLC **464** PhotoDisc, Inc. **468** Tom McCarthy/PhotoEdit **471** David Lissy/Picture Cube, Inc.

■ Chapter 14

480 D. Young-Wolff/PhotoEdit **482** Frank Siteman/PhotoEdit **484** Mike Mazzaschi/Stock Boston **487** David De Lossy/The Image Bank **488** Monkmeyer Press **491** Myrleen Ferguson/PhotoEdit **494** B. Daemmrich/The Image Works **496 (top)** Michael Weisbrot/Stock Boston **496 (bottom)** Jeffrey Myers/Stock Boston **501** The Photo Works/Photo Researchers, Inc. **502** Bob Daemmrich/Bob Daemmrich Photo, Inc. **503** Walter Hodges, Westlight **504** Rhoda Sidney/Stock Boston

■ Chapter 15

510 N. Frank/The Viesti Collection, Inc. **512** David Young-Wolff/PhotoEdit **513** D. Young-Wolff/PhotoEdit **514** Stacy Pick/Stock Bos-

ton **516** Steve Bourgeois/Unicorn Stock Photos **517** Dagmar Fabricius/Stock Boston **519** Michael Newman/PhotoEdit **522** D. Young-Wolff/PhotoEdit **526** Jeff Greenberg/PhotoEdit **530** Tommy Dodson/Unicorn Stock Photos **532** Joe Sohm/Unicorn Stock Photos **536** Wayne Floyd/Unicorn Stock Photos

■ Chapter 16

542 Bob Daemmrich/The Image Works **544** Keith Brofsky/PhotoDisc, Inc. **545** Michael Newman/PhotoEdit **547** Ken Lax/Photo Researchers, Inc. **549** Myrleen Ferguson/PhotoEdit **550** Bill Bachmann/Stock Boston **555** Marshall Prescott/Unicorn Stock Photos **556** D. Young-Wolff/PhotoEdit **559** Myrleen Ferguson/PhotoEdit **564** Frank Siteman/Stock Boston **566** Ami Katz/Unicorn Stock Photos **569** D. Young-Wolff/PhotoEdit **571** Joseph Sohm/Stock Boston **572** Chromosohm/Sohm MCMXCII/Photo Researchers, Inc.

■ Chapter 17

576 Myrleen Ferguson/PhotoEdit **578** Tom McCarthy/PhotoEdit **580** Frank Siteman/Picture Cube, Inc. **583** Edward Lettau/Photo Researchers, Inc. **586** Gamma-Liaison, Inc. **589** David Weintraub/Stock Boston **590** Ken Fisher/Tony Stone Images **593** Ron Chapple/FPG International LLC **597** Andy Levin/Photo Researchers, Inc. **599** Jim Harrison/Stock Boston **600** Owen Franken/Stock Boston

■ Chapter 18

604 Myrleen Ferguson/PhotoEdit **606** Jane Lewis/Tony Stone Images **609** D. Young-Wolff/PhotoEdit **613** David Weintraub/Science Source/Photo Researchers, Inc. **615** A. Rodham/Unicorn Stock Photos **616** Richard Sheinwald/AP/Wide World Photos **621** Mary Kate Denny/PhotoEdit **623** Tony Freeman/PhotoEdit

Index